INDEX ISLAMICUS

FOURTH SUPPLEMENT 1971–1975

INDEX ISLAMICUS

FOURTH SUPPLEMENT
1971–1975

A catalogue of articles on Islamic subjects in periodicals and other collective publications

Compiled by
J. D. Pearson

Mansell

Mansell Information/Publishing Limited
3 Bloomsbury Place,
London
WC1A 2QA

ISBN 0 7201 0639 7
ISSN 0306–9524

Printed and bound in Great Britain at
The Scolar Press Limited, Ilkley, Yorkshire.

British Library Cataloguing in Publication Data
Pearson, James Douglas
Index Islamicus.
4th supplement: 1971-1975.
1. Islam - Bibliography
I. Title
016.297 *Z7835.M6*
ISBN 0–7201–0639–7

Contents

Preface

This supplement combines all the titles included in the five annual parts published for the years 1971–5 as well as a good number of additions discovered after the parts were issued. In all, a total of some 10,000 essays on Islamic subjects is included, excerpted from innumerable parts and volumes of some 835 periodicals and a large number of Festschriften, Conference proceedings and volumes of papers by different hands. Starting in 1977 the *Index* is being published quarterly and will include books as well as articles: specimens of the former or notices of publication, prospectuses, etc. will be gratefully received.

The compilers acknowledge again help received from many quarters, especially from those who have presented volumes and offprints. Invaluable assistance has been provided by the *Turkologischer Anzeiger*, edited by Professor Andreas Tietze and György Hazai and published in the *Wiener Zeitschrift für die Kunde des Morgenlandes*.

J. D. Pearson

27 July 1976

List of sources

Periodicals

Those indexed for the first time in this Supplement are marked with an asterisk.

*AARP: art and archaeology research papers 1(1972)–8(1975)
Abbia. Revue culturelle camerounaise 25(1971)—27–8(1974).
al-Abhath. Quarterly journal of the American University of Beirut 22i–ii(1969), 24(1971), 25(1972).
Abr-Nahrain 11(1971)–15(1974–5).
Académie de droit international. Recueil des cours 131(1970, III)—143(1974, III).
Académie royale de Belgique. Bulletin de la Classe des lettres 1970x–xii—61i–xi(1975).
Acta Asiatica. Bulletin of the Institute of Eastern Culture 20(1971)–28(1975).
Acta ethnographica Academiae scientiarum Hungaricae 20(1971)—24i–ii(1975).
Acta geographica. Comptes rendus de la Société de géographie 3.ser., 5(1971)–21, 24(1975).
Acta linguistica (Academia scientiarum Hungarica) 20iii–iv(1970)–25(1975).
Acta linguistica Hafniensia; international journal of structural linguistics 13ii(1971)–15(1974).
*Acta numismatica 1(1971)–3(1973).
Acta Orientalia 33(1971)–36(1974).
Acta Orientalia (Academia scientiarum Hungarica) 24(1971)–29(1975).
Adab. Bimonthly Persian magazine of the Faculty of Letters, University of Kabul 17vi(1969-70) –23(1975) [*Wants* 19iii–iv, 20iii–iv].
*Ādāb. Journal of the Faculty of Arts, University of Khartoum 1(1972)—2–3(1975).
*Adab al-rafidain. College of Arts, Mosul University 1(1971)–5(1974).
Aegyptus 49(1969)–54(1974).
Aevum 45(1971)–49(1975).
Afghanistan 23(1970)–28iii(1975) [*Wants* 26iv]
Africa (London) 41(1971)–45(1975)
Africa (Rome) 26(1971)–30(1974) [*Wants* 29ii, iv]
Africa (Tunis) 3–4(1969–70).
Africa quarterly 10iv(1970)–15(1975–6).
The African historian 4i(1971), 6i(1973).
African language studies 12(1971)–16(1975).
African music 5i–iii(1971–4).
*African social research (Form. Human problems in Central Africa) 1(1966)–20(1975).
African studies 30(1971)–34(1975).
*African studies review 1(1972), 2(1973).
Africana bulletin 13(1970)–22(1975).
*Africana Marburgensia 1(1968)–8i(1975).
*Afrika Spectrum 1968–75.
Afrika und Übersee 54(1971)–58(1975).
*Afrika zamani 3(1974).
L'Afrique et l'Asie modernes 91–2(1970)–106(1975).
Afro-Asia 8–9(1969)—10–11(1970)
*Afroasiatic linguistics 1(1974)–2ix(1975).
*Das Altertum 16(1970)–21(1975).
Ambix 18(1971)–22(1975).
American anthropologist 75(1973)–77(1975).
American archivist 34(1971)–38(1975)
*American ethnologist 1(1974).
American historical review 76(1971)–80(1975)
*American journal of Arabic studies 1(1973)–3(1975).
American journal of archaeology 75(1971)–79(1975)
American journal of economics and sociology 30(1971)–34(1975).
American journal of philology 92(1971)–96(1975).
American journal of physical anthropology 34(1971)–43iii(1975)
American Neptune 31(1971)–35(1975)
American Numismatic Society Museum notes 12(1966)–20(1975).
Anadolu (Anatolia) 12(1968)–17(1973).

*Anadolu sanati araştīrmalarī 1(1968), 2(1970).
Anatolian studies 21(1971)–25(1975).
Anatolica 4(1971–2).
al-Andalus 33(1968)–40(1975).
*Ankara Üniversitesi Dil ve Tarih-Čografya Fakültesi dergisi 28i–ii(1970).
*Ankara Universitesi Siyasal bilgiler Fakültesi dergisi 25–26(1970–1)–28(1973) [*Wants* 28i–ii],
Annales africaines 1970–4.
Annales algériennes de geographie 6(1968), 8, 9 (1969–70), num. spec 1972.
Annales archéologiques arabes syriennes 20(1970)–24(1974).
Annales. Economies, sociétés, civilisations 26(1971)–30(1975).
*Annales d'Ethiopie 1(1955)–9(1972).
Annales de la Faculté de Droit d'Istanbul 18(no.29, 1968)–22(no. 38, 1972).
Annales de géographie 437(1971)–466(1975)..
Annales Islamologiques 5(1963), 9(1972)–12(1974).
*Annales marocaines de sociologie 1968–70.
Annales de l'Université d'Ankara 11(1965)–13(1974).
*Annali della Facoltà di lingue e letterature straniere di Ca' Foscari (serie orientale) 1(1970)–5(1974) [*Wants* 4].
Annali. Istituto italiano di numismatica 16–17(1969–70)—18–19(1971–2).
Annali. Istituto orientale di Napoli 21(1971)–25(1975).
Annali Lateranensi 33(1969)–37(1973).
Annals of the Association of American Geographers 60(1970)–65iii(1975).
Annals of the Bhandarkar Oriental Research Institute 51(1970)–55(1974).
*Annals of the Faculty of Arts, Ain Shams University (form. Annales de la Faculté des Lettres, Université Ibrahim Pacha) 1(1951)–10(1967) [*Wants* 2].
Annals of Oriental Research, University of Madras 23(1970–1)–25(silver jubilee no., 1975).
Année politique et économique 43(no. 218, 1970)–47(1974–5).
Annuaire de l'Afrique du Nord 7(1968)–12(1973).
Annuaire de l'Institut de philologie et d'Histoire orientales et slaves 20(1968–72).
Annual of the British School at Athens 1971–4.
Annual of the Department of Antiquities of Jordan 15(1970)–19(1974).
Annual of Leeds University Oriental Society 7(1969–73).
*Annual report. Society for Libyan studies 1(1969–70)–6(1974–5).
*Annual of the Swedish Theological Institute 1(1962)–8(1970–1).
Annuals of Faculty of Dar al-Ulum 1972–3.
Anthropological linguistics 13(1971)–17(1975).
*Anthropological quarterly 47(1974)–48(1975).
L'Anthropologie 75(1971)–79(1975).
Anthropos 66(1971)–70(1975).
Antiquaries journal 50ii(1970)–55i(1975)
Antiquity 45(1971)–49(1975).
*Antropoloji 1(1963)–7(1972–3).
*Anuario de estudios medievales 5(1968)–7(1970–1).
*Anzeiger der Philologisch-historischen Klasse der Österreichen Akademie der Wissenschaften 105(1968)–111(1974).
Apollo 93(1971)–101(1975).
*Arabian studies 1(1974)–2(1975).
Arabica 18(1971)–22(1975).
Archaeologica 103(1971), 104(1973)
Archaeological journal 127(1970)–131(1974).
Archäologische Mitteilungen aus Iran 4(1971)–7(1974)
Archaeology 24(1971)–28(1975).
Archiv fur Begriffsgeschichte 14ii(1970)–16(1972).
Archiv fur Diplomatik, Schriftgeschichte, Siegel- und Wappenkunde 16(1970)–19(1973).
Archiv für Kulturgeschichte 53(1971)–56(1974).
Archiv orientalni 39(1971)–43(1975).
Archiv für Papyrusforschung und verwandte Gebiete 21(1971)—22–3(1974).
Archiv für Völkerkunde 24(1969)–28(1975).
*Archive for history of exact sciences 6(1969–70)–14(1974–5).
Archives 10(1971)–12(1975).
Archives européennes de sociologie 12(1971)–16(1975).
Archives d'histoire doctrinale et littéraire du Moyen-Age 38 (1971)–41(1974).

Archives internationales d'histoire des sciences 88–9(1969)–96(1975).
Archives de philosophie 34(1971)–38(1975).
Archives de sociologie des religions 31(1971)–38(1974).
Archivio storico italiano 128(1971)–131(1975).
Archivo español de arqueologia 43(1970)—45–7(1972–4).
Archive español de arte 43(1971)–47(1974).
Archivum 17(1967)–21(1971).
Archivum linguisticum N.S.2(1971)–6(1975).
*Archivum Ottomanicum 1(1969)–4(1972).
*Ars decorativa (*form.* Az Iparmüvészeti Múzeum Évkönyvei, q.v.) 2(1974), 3(1975) [*Wants* 1].
Ars Orientalis 8(1970)–10(1975).
Årsbok. (Seminarierna i slaviska sprak . . . vid Lunds Universitet) 1969–70.
Art in America 59(1971)–62(1974).
Art bulletin 53(1971)–56(1974).
Art journal 30iii–iv(1971)–35ii(1975).
Art quarterly 34(1971)–37(1974).
*Arte orientale in Italia 1(1966)–4(1973).
Artibus Asiae 32iv(1970)–37iii(1975).
*Arts of Asia 1(1971)–5(1975).
Arts asiatiques 22(1970)–31(1975).
*Asia: annuario de estudios orientales 2(1970), 3(1971).
Asia Major 16(1971)–19(1974).
Asia quarterly (*form.* Revue du sud-est asiatique) 1971–5.
Asian affairs 58(1971)–N.S.6(1975).
Asian and African studies (Bratislava) 5(1969)–11(1975).
Asian and African studies (Jerusalem) 7(1971)–10(1974)
Asian studies 8iii(1970)–11ii(1973).
Asiatische Studien 25(1971)–29i(1975).
*Asien, Afrika, Latein-Amerika (*form.* Mitteilungen des Instituts für Orientforschung) 1(1973) –3(1975).
Atti della Accademia dei Lincei. Rendiconti, Classe di scienze morali, storiche e filologiche 25iii–vi(1970)–29vi(1975).
*Azania 1–9(1974).

Baessler Archiv 18ii(1970)–23i(1975).
*Balcanica 1(1970)–4(1973).
*Balkan studies 13(1972)–15(1974).
*Bastan chenassi va honar-e Iran (Revue d'archéologie et d'art iraniens) 6(1971).
Bedi Kartlisa 28(1971)–33(1975).
Beitrage zur Namenforschung 6(1971)–10(1975).
Belleten (Turk Tarih Kurumu) 35(1971)–39(1975).
Bengal past and present 90(1971)–94(1975).
Berliner Museen 21(1971)–23(1973).
Berytus 19(1970)–23(1974).
Bibliotheca Orientalis 28(1971)–32(1975)
Bibliothèque d'humanisme et renaissance 33(1971)–37(1975).
Bijdragen tot de taal-, land- en volkenkunde 127(1971)–131(1975).
Bodleian Library record 8v–vi(1971–2)—9i–iii(1973–4).
*Boğazici üniversitesi dergisi 1(1973), 2(1974).
*Boğazīcī üniversitesi halkbilimi yīllīği 1974.
Boletín de la Asociación española de orientalistas 6(1970)–11(1975).
Boletín de la Real academia de la historia 167ii(1970)–173(1975).
Bollettino d'arte del Ministero della pubblica istruzione 53(1968)–59(1974).
Bonner Jahrbücher 171(1971)–175(1975).
Boston Museum bulletin 353(1970)–368(1974) [*Wants* 351–2].
*British journal of the history of science 5(1971)–8(1975).
*British Library journal 1i–ii(1975).
British Museum quarterly 35(1971)–37(1973) *Cont. as:* British Library journal, *q.v.*
*British Society for Middle Eastern Studies bulletin 1(1974–5), 2(1975).
The Broolkyn Museum annual 11(1969–70) *Cont. as* Brooklyn Museum annual report.
*Bulletin of Arab research and studies 5(1974).
Bulletin archéologique du Comité des travaux historiques et scientifiques N.S.6(1970)–8(1972).

*Bulletin of the Asia Institute, Pahlavi University 1(1969)–3(1973), N.S.1,2(1975).
Bulletin de l'Association des géographes français 424–5—429–30(1975) [*Wants* 384–423].
Bulletin of the City Art Museum of St. Louis 6v(1971) [*Wants* 4iv–6iv].
Bulletin of the Cleveland Museum of Art 58(1971)–62(1975).
Bulletin of the Deccan College Research Institute 29(1968–9)–35ii(1975).
Bulletin de l'École française d'Extrême-Orient 58(1971)–62(1975).
Bulletin économique et sociale du Maroc 31(no.115, 1969)—128–9(1975).
Bulletin d'études orientales 21(1968)–26(1973).
*Bulletin of the Faculty of Arts, University of Libya 1(1958)–6(1974) [*Wants* 5].
Bulletin of the Faculty of Arts, University of Riyad 2(1971–2), 3(1973–4).
Bulletin of the Government Oriental Manuscripts Library, Madras 19ii(1972), 20(1972).
Bulletin hispanique 72iii–iv(1970)—77i–ii(1975).
Bulletin of the history of medicine 45(1971)–49(1975).
Bulletin de l'Institut égyptien 51(1969–70), 52(1970–1).
Bulletin de l'Institut fondamental d'Afrique noire 32iv(1970)–37ii(1975).
Bulletin de l'Institut français d'archéologie orientale 68(1969)–75(1975).
*Bulletin de l'Institut international d'administration publique 13(1970)–36(1975).
Bulletin of the Institute of Archaeology 10(1971)–12(1975).
Bulletin of the Institute of Historical Reaserch 44(1971)–48(1975).
Bulletin of the International committee on urgent anthropological and ethnological research 12(1970)–16(1974).
*Bulletin of the Iranian Culture Foundation 1i,ii(1969–73).
Bulletin of the John Rylands University Library 53ii(1971)–58i(1975).
Bulletin of the Medical Library Association 59(1971)–63(1975).
Bulletin of the Metropolitan Museum of Art 29v–x(1971)–33(1975) [*Wants* 30iv].
Bulletin du Musée de Beyrouth 22(1969)–26(1973).
Bulletin of the Museum of Far Eastern Antiquities 43(1971)–47(1975).
Bulletin of the Metropoliyan Museum of Art 29v–x(1971)–33(1975) [*Wants* 30iv].
Bulletin du Musée de Beyrouth 22(1969)–26(1973).
Bulletin of the Museum of Far Eastern Antiquities 43(1971)–47(1975).
Bulletin, Museum and Picture Gallery, Baroda 22(1970)–24(1972–3).
Bulletin de philosophie médiévale 10–12(1968–70)—16–17(1974–5).
Bulletin of the Prince of Wales Museum of Western India 11(1971)–12(1973).
Bulletin of the Rhode Island School of Design 58v–vi(1972)–61v(1975) [*Wants* 57–58iii, 59iii,v, 60i–iii, v–vi; 61i–iii, vi].
Bulletin of the School of Oriental and African Studies 34(1971)–38(1975).
Bulletin de la Société d'archéologie copte 20(1969–70).
*Bulletin de la Société de géographie d'Egypte 41–2(1968–9).
*Bulletin de la Société d'histoire du Maroc 1(1968)–3(1970–1).
Bulletin de la Société de linguistique de Paris 65(1970)–70(1975).
Bulletins et mémoires de la Société d'anthropologie de Paris 12. sér., 6iv(1970)–13. sér., 2(1975).
Burlington magazine 113(1971)–117(1975).
Bustan 11iv, 12i(1970–1).
Byzantinische Zeitschrift 64(1971)–68(1975)
Byzantinoslavica 32(1971)–36(1975).
Byzantion 40ii(1970)–45i(1975).

Cahiers d'Alexandrie 4ii–iv(1966–7).
Cahiers archéologiques 21(1971)–23(1974).
*Cahiers des arts et traditions populaires 1(1968)–4(1971).
Cahiers de civilisation médiévale 14(1971)–18(1975).
Cahiers d'études africaines 11(1971)–15iii(1975).
Cahiers Ferdinand de Saussure 26(1969)–29(1974–5).
Cahiers d'histoire 16(1971)–20(1975).
Cahiers de lexicologie 18(1971)–27(1975).
*Cahiers de linguistique, d'orientalisme et de slavistique 1–2(1973), 3–4(1974).
*Cahiers de linguistique théorique et appliquée 5(1968)–10(1973).
Cahiers du monde russe et soviétique 11iv(1970)–15(1974).
Cahiers d'Outre-Mer 24(1971)–112(1975).
Cahiers de Tunisie 18(1970)–23(1975).
Centaurus 15iii(1970)–19(1975).
Central Asiatic journal 15(1971)–19(1975).

*Cercetari de lingvistica 13(1968)–19i(1974).
Civilisations 20iv(1970)–25(1975).
Collectanea. Studia orientalia christiana 13(1968–9), 14(1970–1).
Comparative literature 23(1971)–27iii(1975).
*Comparative politics 1(1968–9)–8i(1975).
Comparative studies in society and history 13(1971)–17(1975).
Comptes rendus du Groupe linguistique d'études chamito-sémitiques 14(1969–70).
Comptes rendus des séances. (Académie des inscriptions et belles lettres.) 1970–4.
*Conoscenza religiosa 1969–75.
*Contributions to Asian studies 1(1971)–8(1975).
*Contributions to Indian sociology N.S.1(1967)–9i(1975).
Correspondance d'Orient. Etudes 15–16(1969)—19–20(1971–2).
Cuadernos de la Biblioteca española de Tetuán 5(1972)—9–10(1974).
*Cultura Turcica 8–10(1971–3).
*Cultures 1(1973)–2(1974–5).
Current anthropology 12(1971)–16(1975).
*Cyrillomethodianum 1(1971), 2(1973–4).

Dacca University studies 19A(1971).
*Daedalus 100(1971)–104(1975).
Demográfia nepessegtudományi folyoirat 13iv(1970)–18i(1975).
Deutsche Zeitschrift für Philosophie 18xii(1970)–23(1975).
The Developing economies 8 (1970)–13iii(1975).
*Development dialogue 1974–5.
Diogenes 73(1971)–92(1975).
*Dirasat. A research journal published by the University of Jordan. Humanities 1i–ii(1974).
*Dīş politika./Foreign policy 1(1971)–5i(1975).
*Doğu dilleri./Oriental languages. Review of the Institute for Oriental studies 1(1964–70), 2i, ii(1971–5).
Dumbarton Oaks papers 25(1971)–28(1974).

East and West 20(1970)–25ii(1975).
*Eastern Africa economic review 1(1969)–6(1974).
Eastern anthropologist 24(1971)–28(1975).
Economic development and cultural change 19iii(1971)–24i(1975).
Economic geography 46iv(1970)–51(1975).
Economic history review 24(1971)–28(1975).
*Economic journal 80(1970)–85(1975).
*Economica 27(1970)–N.S.42(1975).
*Economy and society 1(1972)–4(1975).
*Ecumenical review 23(1971)–27(1975).
*Edebiyat Fakültesi araştīrma dergisi (Atatürk Üniversitesi) 4(1972)–6(1973).
l'Egypte contemporaine 62(1971)–66(no.359, 1975).
*Egyptian historical review 17–18(1970–1), 20(1973), 22(1975).
English historical review 86(1971)–90(1975).
Epigrafika Vostoka 20(1971), 21(1972).
Epigraphia Indica (Arabic and Persian supplement) 1968, 1969.
Eranos-Jahrbuch 39(1970), 40(1971).
Die Erde 102(1971)–106(1975).
Erdkunde 25(1971)–29(1975).
*Estudios de Asia y Africa 1(1966)–28(1975) [*Wants* 24–5].
Estudios politicos e sociais 7iv(1969).
Ethnographia 82(1971)–86(1975).
L'Ethnographie 64(1970)–70(1975).
Ethnographisch-archäologische Zeitschrift 12(1971)–16(1975).
*Ethnologica 1(1959)–7(1975) [*Wants* 6].
Ethnologische Zeitschrift Zürich 1970i, 1971i, 1972ii, 1973–5i.
Ethnology 11(1972)–14(1975).
Ethnomusicology 15(1971)–19(1975)
Ethnos 36(1971)–38(1973).
Etnologiska studier 31(1971)-33(1974).
*Etudes balcaniques 6(1970)–11(1975).

*Etudes d'histoire africaine 2(1971)–7(1975).
Etudes philosophiques 1970iv–1975.
*Etudes philosophiques et littéraires 1(1967)–6(1973).
*Etudes rurales 37(1970)–58(1975).
*Etudes de sociologie tunisienne 1(1968).

*Faculty of Arts Journal, University of Jordan 1(1969)–4(1973) *Cont. as*: Dirasat.
Faenza 58(1972)–61(1975) [*Wants* 57].
Folia linguistica 4iii–iv(1970)–8(1975).
Fola Orientalia 12(1970)–16(1975).
Folk, Dansk etnografisk tidsskrift 13(1971)—16–17(1974–5).
Folklore 82(1971)–86(1975).
*Folklore (Calcutta) 10(1970)–16(1975).
*Folklore Research Center studies 1(1970)–5(1975).
Foreign affairs 49iv(1971)–54i(1975).
Foundations of language 7(1971)–13(1975) [*Wants* 8ii].
Freiburger Zeitschrift für Philosophie und Theologie 17iii(1970)–22iii(1975).

Garcia de Orta 16iv(1968)–19(1971), núm. spec (1972); serie de antropologia 1i–ii(1973); serie de geografia 1(1973), 2i(1974).
Gazette des beaux-arts 77(1971)–86(1975).
General linguistics 12(1972)–15(1975) [*Wants* 11].
Genève-Afrique: Acta Africana 10(1971)–14i(1975).
Geografiska annaler 53A(1971), 54A(1972); 53B(1971)–55B(1973).
Geographical journal 137(1971)–141(1975).
Geographical review 61(1971)–65(1975).
Geographical review of India 32(1970)–36(1974).
Geography 56(1971)–60(1975).
Gesnerus 28(1971)–31(1974).
*Ghana bulletin of theology 2vi(1964)–4viii(1975) [*Wants* 2vii, 3i].
Giornale critico della filosofia italiana 50(1971)–ser. 4, 6ii(1975).
Gladius 9(1970)–12(1974).
Glossa 4ii(1970)–9(1975).
Glotta. 49(1971)–53ii(1975).
Gnomon 43(1971)–47(1975).
*Government and opposition 1(1965–6)–10(1975).
Graecolatina et Orientalia 2(1970)–6(1975).
*Güney-Doğu Avrupa araştĭrmalarĭ dergisi 1(1972)—2–3(1973–4).
Gutenberg-Jahrbuch 1971–5.

*Hannon. Revue libanaise de geographie 1(1966)–5(1970) [*Wants* 3, 4].
Harvard journal of Asiatic studies 31(1971)–34(1974).
Harvard theological review 64(1971)–68i(1975).
Hebrew Union College annual 42(1971)–45(1974).
Hesperis-Tamuda 11(1970)–13(1972).
Hispania 30(no. 115, 1970)–32(1972).
Hispanic review 39(1971)–43(1975).
Historia 29(1971)–24(1975).
Historical journal 14(1971)–18(1975).
*Historiographia linguistica 1(1974), 2(1975).
Historische Zeitschrift 212(1971)–221(1975).
Historisches Jahrbuch 91(1971)–94(1974).
Historisk tidsskrift (Copenhagen) 12r., 5(1971)–13r., 2(1975).
History 56(1971)–60(1975).
History of education quarterly 11(1971)–15(1975).
History of religions 10iii(1971)–15ii(1975).
History and theory 10(1971)–14(1975).
L'Homme 10iv(1970)–15(1975).
*Humaniora Islamica 1(1973), 2(1974).

IBLA 127(1971)–136(1975).
IRAL 9(1971)–13(1975).

Ilahiyat Fakültesi dergisi 17(1969)–20(1975).
Imago mundi 24(1970)–27(1975).
India quarterly 27(1971)–31(1975).
Indian archives 17(1967–8)–22(1973).
The Indian economic and social history review 7iv(1970)–12iii(1975) [*Wants* 11ii–iv].
Indian horizons (*form.* Indo-Asian culture) 20(1971)–24iii(1975).
*Indian journal of history of science 1(1966)–10(1975).
Indian linguistics 31(1970)–36(1975).
Indian numismatic chronicle 5ii(1968)–10(1972).
*Indian political science review 4(1969)–9(1975).
Indian studies past and present 11(1969–70)–15ii(1973–4).
Indian yearbook of international affairs 15–16(1966–7), 17(1974).
Indica 8(1971)–12i(1975).
Indogermanische Forschungen 75(1970)–79(1974).
Indo-Iranian journal 13(1971)–17(1975).
Indo-Iranica 23(1970)–26iii(1973).
International affairs 47(1971)–51(1975).
International and comparative law quarterly 20(1971)–24(1975).
International journal of African historical studies 4(1971)–8(1975).
International journal of comparative sociology 10(1969)–16(1975).
International journal of Middle East studies 2(1971)–6iii(1975).
*International journal for philosophy of religion 1(1970)–6ii(1975).
*International review of missions 60(1971)–64(1975).
International social science journal 23(1971)–27(1975).
International studies 11ii(1969)–14iii(1975).
Az Imparmüvészeti Múzeum Évkönyvei 12(1970), 13(1970) *Cont. as:* Ars decorativa, *q.v.*
Iqbal 18iii(1970), 19ii(1971).
Iqbal review 11iv(1971)–16ii(1975).
Iran 9(1971)–13(1975).
Iran-shinasi 2ii(1971).
Iranian studies 3iii–iv(1970)–8iii(1975) [*Wants* 5iv].
Iranica antiqua 9(1972), 10(1973).
*Iranistische Mitteilungen 1(1968)–9(1975).
Iraq 33(1971)–37(1975).
Iraqi geographical journal 7(1971), 8(1974).
Isis 62(1971)–66(1975).
der Islam 47(1971)–52(1975).
Islam and the modern age 2(1971)–6(1975).
*Islam tetkikleri Enstitusu dergisi 1(1953)–6(1975).
Islamic culture 45(1971)–49(1975).
Islamic quarterly 15(1971)–17(1975) [*Wants* 14iv].
Islamic studies 10(1971)–14(1975).
Israel exploration journal 20iii(1970)–25(1975).
*Israel Oriental studies 1(1971), 2(1972).
*Israel yearbook on human rights 1(1971)–5(1975).
Izvestiya na Blgerskiya arkheologicheski institut 33(1972).

Jahrbuch des Museums für Völkerkunde zu Leipzig 27(1970)–30(1975).
*Jahrbuch für musikalische Volks- und Völkerkunde 1(1963)–7(1973).
Jahrbuch für Numismatik und Geldgeschichte 21(1971)–24(1974).
Jahrbuch der österreichischen Byzantinistik 16(1967), 17(1968), 20(1971)–22(1973).
Janus 57ii(1970)–62(1975).
Japan Institute of International Affairs, Annual review 4(1965–8), 5 (169–70).
Jerusalem studies in geography 1–2(1970–1).
Jewish quarterly review 61iii–iv(1971)–66ii(1975).
Journal of aesthetics and art criticism 29iii–iv(1971)–34ii(1975).
Journal of African and Asian studies 1(1967–8)–4i(1973).
Journal of African history 12(1971)–19(1975).
Journal of African law 15(1971)–19(1975).
*Journal of the American Academy of Religion 39(1971)–43(1975).
Journal of American Folklore 83(no.330, 1970)–87(1974).
Journal of the American Oriental Society 91(1971)–95(1975).

*Journal of the American Research Center in Egypt 1(1962)–12(1975).
Journal of the Andhra Historical Research Society 31(1965–6), 32(1971–2).
Journal of anthropology 27(1971)–31i(1975).
Journal of Arabic literature 2(1971)–6(1975)
Journal of the Arabic and Persian Society of the Panjab University 15i, ii(1970).
Journal of Asian and African studies (Japan) 4(1971)–19(1975).
Journal of Asian and African studies (Toronto) 6(1971)–10(1975).
Journal of Asian history 5(1971)–9(1975).
Journal of the Asiatic Society of Bombay 43–44(1968–9), 45–6(1970–1).
Journal of the Asiatic Society, Calcutta 11(1969)–14i(1972).
Journal of the Asiatic Society of Pakistan 15ii(1970)–19i(1974), 14(1968).
Journal asiatique 258(1970)–263(1975)
Journal of the Bihar Research Society 54(1968)–58(1972).
Journal of Commonwealth and comparative politics 9(1971)–13(1975).
*Journal of comparative family studies 1(1970)–6(1975).
Journal of conflict resolution 14iv(1970)–19(1975).
*Journal of contemporary Asia 1(1970)–5(1975).
Journal of contemporary history 6(1971)–10(1975).
The Journal of developing areas 5ii–iv(1970)–9(1975).
*Journal of development economics 1(1974)–2(1975).
Journal of development studies 7ii–iv(1971)–12i(1975).
Journal de droit international 98(1971–100iii(1974).
*Journal of economic history 29(1969)–35(1975)
Journal of the economic and social history of the Orient 14(1971)–18(1975).
*Journal of ecumenical studies 8(1971)–12(1975).
Journal of Egyptian archaeology 57(1971)–61(1975).
Journal of Ethiopian studies 9(1971)–13ii(1975) [*Wants* 12ii, 13i].
Journal of the Faculty of Arts, Malta 4ii(1970)–6ii(1975).
Journal of the Folklore Institute 7ii–iii(1970)–11(1974–5).
Journal of the Ganganath Jha Research Institute 27(1971)–29(1973).
Journal of general education 18ii(1967)–27(1975)
Journal of glass studies 13(1971)–16(1974).
Journal of the Gypsy Lore Society 50(1971)–52(1973), 4th ser., 1i(1974).
Journal of the Historical Society of Nigeria 5iii(1970)–7iii(1974).
Journal for the history of astronomy 2(1971)–6(1975).
Journal of the history of biology 2(1969)–8(1975).
Journal of the history of ideas 32(1971)–36(1975).
Journal of the history of medicine and allied sciences 26(1971)–30(1975).
Journal of the history of philosophy 9(1971)–13(1975).
*Journal of the Indian Anthropological Society 1(1966)–10(1975).
Journal of the International Commission of Jurists 6(1971)-15(1975).
*Journal of international economics 1(1971)–5(1975).
*Journal of the International Phonetic Association (*form.* Le Maître phonétique) 1(1971)–5(1975).
Journal of Islamic and comparative law 1(1966)–5(1974).
Journal of Jewish studies 20(1971)–26(1975).
Journal of the K. R. Cama Oriental Institute 41(1967)–44(1973).
Journal of linguistics 7(1971)–11(1975).
*Journal of the Madhya Pradesh Itihasa Parishad, Bhopal 6(1968), 7(1969).
Journal of the Maharaja Sayajirao University of Baroda 19(1970)–22iii & 23iii(1973–4) [*Wants* 21iii–iv, 22i].
Journal of Maltese studies 6(1971)–10(1975).
Journal of modern African studies 9(1971)–13(1975).
Journal of modern history 43(1971)–47(1975).
Journal of Near Eastern studies 30(1971)–34(1975)
Journal of Northwest Semitic languages 1(1971)–3(1974).
Journal of the Numismatic Society of India 28(1966)–36(1974).
Journal of the Oriental Institute, Baroda 20ii(1970)–25i(1975).
*Journal of the Oriental Society of Australia 1(1960)–10(1975).
Journal of Oriental studies 9(1971)–13(1975).
Journal of the Pakistan Historical Society 19(1971)–23(1975).
*Journal of Palestine studies 1(1971)–4(1975).

*Journal of peasant studies 1(1973–4), 2(1975).
Journal of personality 39(1971)–43(1975).
*Journal of Phonetics 1(1973)–3(1975).
*Journal of political economy 78(1970)–83(1975).
*Journal of political & military sociology 1(1973)–3(1975).
Journal of politics 33(1971)–37(1975).
Journal of the Regional Cultural Institute 3iii–iv(1970)–7(1974).
Journal of religion in Africa 1(1967)–7i(1975) [*Wants* 1i].
Journal of research (Humanities) 5(1970), 6i(1971).
Journal of the Research Society of Pakistan 7i(1970).
Journal of the Royal Asiatic Society 1970ii–1975i.
Journal of Semitic studies 16(1971)–20(1975).
Journal of social research 13ii(1970)–15ii(1972) [*Wants* 14].
Journal de la Société des africanistes 40(1969)–44(1974).
Journal de la Société Finno-Ougrienne 71(1971)–73(1974).
*Journal of the Society of Archer-Antiquaries 1(1958)–17(1974).
Journal of Southeast Asian studies 2(1971)–6(1975).
Journal of tropical geography 32(1971)–41(1975).
Journal of the University of Bombay (arts) 40(1971)–42(1973.
Journal of the University College, Durban 2ii(1970)–3ii(1975).
Journal of the University of Peshawar 13(1970)–15(1973).
Journal of the Warburg and Courtauld Institutes 34(1971)–38(1975).
Journal of world history/Cahiers d'histoire mondiale 12iv(1970)–14(1972) *Cont. as:* Cultures, *q.v.*

Kairos 13(1971)–17(1975).
Kano studies 1(1965–8), N.S. 1i(1973).
Kratkie soobshcheniya (AN SSSR. Institut arkheologii.) 126(1971)–143(1975) [*Wants* 125, 130].
Kratylos 14(1969)–18(1973).
Kunst des Orients 7(1970–1)–9(1973–4).

LIAS 1(1974), 2(1975).
Lagos notes and records 3(1971–2)–5(1974).
Lalit Kala 15(1974?)–17(1975?).
*Land reform, land settlement and cooperatives 1971–1975i.
Language 47(1971)–51(1975).
Language and speech 14(1971)–18(1975)
*Language in society 1(1972)–4(1975).
Law quarterly review 87(1971)–91(1975).
Levant 3(1971)–7(1975).
Levante 18(1971)–22(1975).
Libri 20iv(1971)–25(1975).
*Libyca 14–15(1966)–20(1972).
Lingua 26(1970–1)–37(1975).
Lingua e stile 6(1971)–10(1975).
Lingua Posnanensis 15(1972)–18(1975).
*Linguistic inquiry 1(1970)–6(1975).
Linguistics 65(1971)–166(1975).
La Linguistique 7(1971–2)–11(1975).
*al-Lisāniyyāt 1(1971), 2i(1972).
Livrustkammaren 12v–13(1973–5).

*Maghreb-Machrek 55(1973)–70(1975).
Majallat al-Azhar 43(1971)–47vii(1975).
Man. N.S. 6(1971)–10(1975).
Marg 24(1971)–28(1974–5).
*Materialy po istorii i filologii Tzentral'noy Azii 5(1970).
Mediaeval studies 33(1971)–37(1975).
*Medieval India; a miscellany 1(1969)–3(1975).
Medievalia et humanistica N.S. 2(1971)–5(1974).
Medical history 15(1971)–19(1975).
*Medizinhistorisches Journal 4(1969)–10iii(1975).

Mélanges de la Casa de Velasquez 6(1970)–10(1974).
Mélanges de l'Institut dominicain du Caire 11(1972), 12(1974).
Mélanges de l'Université Saint Joseph 46(1970–1), 47(1972).
Melita historica 5iii(1970)–6(1975).
Memoirs of the Ressarch Department of the Toyo Bunko 28(1970)–32(1974).
Memorie della Classe di scienze morali, storichi e filologichi, Accademia dei Lincei 14iv–vi (1969)–18ii(1975).
*Mesopotamia 1(1966)—8–9(1973–4).
*Metropolitan Museum journal 1(1968)–9(1974).
Middle East Journal 25(1971)–29(1975).
Middle Eastern studies 7(1971)–11(1975).
Midland history (*form.* University of Birmingham historical journal) 1(1971–2).
Milla wa-milla 11(1971)–15(1975).
*Millennium, journal of international studies 1(1971–2)–4(1975). [*Wants* 1i].
Miscelanea de estudios árabes y hebraicos 16–17(1967–8)–24i(1975).
Mitteilungen der Anthropologischen Gesellschaft in Wien 101(1971)–105(1975).
*Mitteilungen: Dokumentationsdienst Moderner Orient 1ii(1972)–4i(1975) [*Wants* 1i].
Mitteilungen des Instituts fur Orientforschung 16iv(1970)–17(1972) *Cont. as:* Asien, Afrika Lateinamerika, *q.v.*
Mitteilungen des Instituts für österreichische Geschichtsforschung 79(1971)–83ii(1975).
Modern Asian studies 5(1971)–9(1975).
*Mondes en développement 1(1973)–12(1975).
Moyen âge 77(1971)–81(1975).
Münchener Studien zur Sprachwissenschaft 29(1971)–33(1975).
Münchener theologische Zietschrift 22(1971)–26(1975).
Le Muséon 84(1971)–88(1975).
*al-Mushir (The counsellor) 16vii–ix(1974), 17(1975).
Muslim world 6(1971)–65(1975).
al-Mustansiriya University review 2(1970–1)–4(1973–4).

*Names 19(1971)–23(1975).
Narody Azii i Afriki 1971–5.
*Nederlands theologisch tijdschrift 23(1968–9)–29(1975) [*Wants* 26].
Neophilologus 55(1971)–59(1975).
Neuphilologische Mitteilungen 72(1971)–76(1975).
New scholasticism 45(1971)–49(1975).
Nigerian geographical journal 13ii(1970)–17(1974).
*Nigerian journal of Islam 1(1970–1), 2(1972–4).
Nordisk Numismatisk årsskrift 1968–9—1973–4.
Nordisk Numismatisk Union. Medlemsblad 1971–5.
Norsk tidsskrift for sprogvidenskap/Norwegian journal of linguistics 24(1971)–29(1975).
*Nouvelle revué du Caire 1(1975).
Nova acta Leopoldina 193(1970)–222(1975) [*Wants* 211–217].
Numen 18(1971)–22(1975).
Numismatic chronicle 10(1970–15(1975).
Numismatický sbornik 11(1969–70)–13(1973–4).
Numismatische Zeitschrift 86(1971)–90(1975).
*Nusantara 1(1972), 2(1972).

Objets et mondes 10iii(1970)–15ii(1975).
Onoma 15ii–iii(1970)—19i–ii(1975).
Orbis 20(1971)–24i(1975).
Oriens 21–2(1968–9), 23–4(1974).
Oriens antiquus 9iii–iv(1970)—13i–iii(1974).
Oriens christianus 55(1971)–59(1975).
Orient 49–52(1969).
*Orient (Opladen) 16(1975).
*Orient (Tokyo) 2(1962)–11(1975) [*Wants* 1].
Oriental art 17(1971)–21(1975).
Orientalia 40(1971)–44iii(1975).
Orientalia christina periodica 37(1971)–41(1975).
*Orientalia Gandensia 1(1964)–6(1972).

Orientalia Lovaniensia 2(1971)—6–7(1975–6).
Orientalia Suecana 19–20(1970–1)–22(1973).
Orientalistische Literaturzeitung 66(1971)–70iv(1975).
Oriente moderno 50ix–xi (1970)–55viii(1975).
Orissa historical research journal 13(1965)–15(1967).
*Orita 8(1974), 9i(1975).
Ost-Europa 21(1971)–25(1975).
*Oxford economic papers 22(1970)–27(1975).
Oxford Slavonic papers 4(1971)–8(1975).

Pacific affairs 44(1971)–48(1975.
Paideuma 16(1970)–21(1975).
*Pakistan archaeology 1(1964)–9(1970–1).
*Pakistan economic and social review 11ii(1973)–12(1974).
Pakistan philosophical journal 9iv(1971)–12ii(1974).
Palestine exploration quarterly 1971–5.
Palestinskiy sbornik 23(86, 1971)–25(88, 1974).
*Panjab University research bulletin (arts) 1(1951)–77(1969); 1(1970)–3i(1972).
Past and present 50(1971)–69(1975).
Patna University journal 21(1966), 22(1967).
*Pensamiento 25(1969)–31(1975).
*Peshawar University review 1i(1973).
Persica 5(1970–1)–6(1972–4).
Petermanns geographische Mitteilungen 115(1971)–119(1975).
Philippine historical review 3(1970), 4(1971).
Philippine social sciences and humanities review 35i,ii(1970), 37(1972).
(*Wants* 33iii–iv, 35iii–iv, 36).
Philippine sociological review 17(1969)–21(1973).
Philippine studies 18iv(1970)–23(1975).
*Philobiblon 15(1971)–19(1975).
Philosophical quarterly 21(1971)–25(1975).
Philosophical review 80(1971)–84(1975).
Philosophisches Jahrbuch 79(1972)–82(1975) [*Wants* 78].
Philosophy East and West 21(1971)–25(1975).
Phonetica 23(1971)–32(1975).
*Physis 11(1969)–16(1974).
*Pis'mennye pamyati vostoka 1968–71.
Political quarterly 42(1971)–46(1975).
Political science quarterly 86(1971)–90(1975).
Politique étrangère 36(1971)–40(1975).
Population 26(1971)–30(1975).
Population studies 25(1971)–29(1975).
Présence africaine 65–8(1968), 77(1971)–96(1975) [*Wants* 89].
Prilozi orijentalnu filologiju 14(1964)—20–21(1970–1).
Proceedings of the American Academy for Jewish research 37(1969)–40(1972).
Proceedings of the American Philosophical Society 114(1970)–119(1975).
Proceedings of the British Academy 56(1970)–60(1974).
Proceedings of the Royal Society of Medicine 64(1971)–68(1975).
Proche-Orient chrétien 21(1971)–25(1975).
Proche-Orient; études économiques, juridiques 66(1970)–79(1973).
Projet, civilisation, travail, économie 1971–5.
*Proverbium 1(1965)–25(1975).
Przeglad orientalistyczny 77(1971)–95(1975).

Quaderni dell'Istituto di glottologia 8(1964) *Cont. as:* Lingua e stile, *q.v.*
Quarterly journal of economics 85(1971)–89(1975).
Quarterly journal of the Mythic Society 60(1969)–65(1974) [*Wants* 59].
The Quarterly review if historical studies 10ii(1970–1)–15ii(1975–6).

Race 12iv(1971)–15(1974) *Cont. as:* Race and class 16(1974–5)–17ii(1975).
Recherches de science religieuse 59(1971)–63(1975).
Recherches de théologie ancienne et médiévale 37(1970)–41(1974).

Recueil Penant 81(1971)–84(1975).
Recueils de la Société Jean Bodin 21–3(1968–9), 1965.
*Religion 1(1971)–5, special issue (1975) [*Wants* 3i].
Religion and society 18(1971)–22(1975).
Religious studies 7(1971)–11(1975).
*Rema 1(1955)–12(1967–8).
*Renovatio 8(1973)–10(1975).
Research bulletin, Centre of Arabic Documentation 6(1970)–8(1972).
Review of the Geographical Institute of the University of Istanbul 12(1968–9)–14(1972–3).
Review of metaphysics 25(1971)–29ii(1975).
*Review of Middle East studies 1(1975).
Revista de archivos, bibliotecas y museos 73ii(1966)–78i(1975).
Revista del Instituto de estudios islámicos 16(1971)–17(1972–3).
Revista de política internacional 113(1971)–142(1975).
Revue algérienne des sciences juridiques, politiques et économiques 8(1971)–12(1975).
Revue archéologique 1969ii, 1971–5.
Revue belge de numismatique 117(1971)–121(1975).
Revue belge de philologie et d'histoire 48iv(1970)–53(1975).
Revue du droit public et de la science politique en France et à l'étranger 87(1971)–91(1975).
Revue des études armeniennes 7(1970)–10(1973–4).
Revue des études byzantines 29(1971)–33(1975).
Revue des études islamiques 39(1971)–41(1973).
Revue des études juives 129ii–iv(1970)–133(1974).
Revue des études slaves 48(1969), 49(1973).
Revue des études sud-est européennes 9(1971)–13(1975).
Revue de la Faculté des sciences économiques de l'Université d'Istanbul 28–9(1969–70).
*Revue française d'études politiques africaines 49(1970)–120(1975) [*Wants* 106–7].
Revue française d'histoire d'Outre-Mer 57iii, iv(1970)–62(nos. 226–7, 1975).
Revue française de science politique 21(1971)–25(1975).
Revue française de sociologie 11iv(1970)–16(1975).
Revue de géographie du Maroc 18(1970)—23–24(1973) [*Wants* 19].
Revue d'histoire et de civilisation du Maghreb 9(1970)–12(1974).
Revue d'histoire diplomatique 85(1971)–89ii(1975).
Revue d'histoire économique et sociale 49(1971)–52(1974).
*Revue d'histoire maghrébine 1(1974)–4(1975).
Revue d'histoire moderne et contemporaine 18(1971)–22(1975).
Revue d'histoire et de philosophie religieuses 1969, 1970iv, 1972, 53(1973)–55(1975).
Revue de l'histoire des religions 179(1971)–188(1975).
Revue de l'histoire des sciences et de leurs applications 24(1971)–28(1975).
Revue d'histoire des textes 1(1971)–4(1974).
Revue historique 245(1971)–254(1975).
Revue historique de l'armée 27(1971)–29(1973) *Cont. as:* Revue historique des armées 1(1974) 2(1975).
Revue historique de droit français et étranger 1970iv, 1971–53(1975).
Revue de l'Institut Napoléon 121(1971)—128–9(1973).
Revue de l'Institut de sociologie 1968–74.
Revue internationale des droits de l'antiquité 18(1971)–21(1974).
Revue internationale d'onomastique 23(1971)–27ii(1975).
Revue internationale de philosophie 24(1970–2)–29(1975).
Revue juridique et politique, indépendance et coopération 24ii(1971)–29(1975).
Revue de litterature comparée 45(1971)–49(1975).
La Revue du Louvre 20(1970)–25(1975).
Revue de métaphysique et de morale 76(1971)–80(1975).
Revue du Moyen Âge latin 21iii–iv(1965), 22(1966).
Revue numismatique 12(1970)–16(1974).
Revue de l'Occident musulman et de la Méditerranée 6(1969)–18(1974).
Revue philosophique de Louvain 69(1971)–74(4. ser., 20, 1975).
Revue al-Qanoun wa'l-iqtisad 39(1969)–44i(1974).
*Revue roumaine d'histoire 9–10(1970–1)–14(1975).
Revue roumaine de linguistique 16(1971)–20(1975).
Revue des sciences humaines 1971–5.
Revue des sciences philosophiques et théologiques 55(1971)–59(1975).

Revue sénégalaise de droit 7(1970)–17(1975).
Revue de synthèse 91(no. 59)–96(no. 80, 1975).
Revue thomiste 71(1971)–75(1975).
Revue al-ulum al-qanuniya wal-iqtisadiya 12ii(1970)–14(1972).
Ricerche slavistiche 17–19(1970–2), 20–1(1973–4).
Rivista di filosofia neo-scolastica 62(1970)–67(1975).
Rivista geografica italiana 78(1971)–82(1975).
Rivista storica italiana 83(1971)–87(1975).
Rivista degli studi orientali 45(1970)–49ii(1975).
Rocznik orientalistyczny 34(1971)–37(1974–5).
Romania 92(1971)–96(1975).

Saeculum 22(1971)–26(1975).
Sanat tarihi yĭllĭgĭ 4(1970–1)–6(1974–5).
*Şarkiyat mecmuasĭ 1(1956)–7(1972).
*Savanna 1(1972)–3(1974).
Sbornik Muzeya antropologii i etnografii 27(1971)–31(1975).
Schweizerische Zeitschrift für Geschichte 21(1971)–25(1975).
Scottish geographical magazine 87(1971)–91iii(1975).
Scripta mathematica 29(1973).
Scriptorium 25(1971)–29(1975).
Sefarad 31(1971)–34(1974).
*Selçuklu arastĭrmalarĭ dergisi 1–2(1969–70)–4(1975).
*Selected reports in ethnomusicology 1(1966–70)–2ii(1974–5).
*Semiotica 1(1969)–13(1975).
Semitica 20(1970)–25(1975).
*Semitics 1(1970)–4(1974).
Slavic review 30(1971)–34(1975).
Slavonic and East European review 49(1971)–53(1975).
Social and economic studies 19ii(1970)–24(1975).
*Social sciences (USSR Academy of sciences) 4(1973)–6iii(1975).
Social science(s) information sur les sciences sociales 9vi(1970)–14(1975).
Sociological bulletin 29(1971)–24i(1975).
Sociological review 19(1971)–23(1975).
Sociologus 21(1971)–25(1975).
Soobshcheniya Gosudarstvennogo Ermitazha 32(1971)–39(1974).
Sosyologi dergisi 21–2(1967–8).
*South Africa international 1(1970–1)–6ii(1975).
Sovetskaya arkheologiya 1971–5.
Sovetskaya etnografiya 1971–5v.
Sovetskaya tyurkologiya 1970–5 [*Wants* 1975, 3].
Speculum 46(1971)–50(1975).
Die Sprache 17(1971)–21(1975).
Språkliga bidrag 26(1971)–28(1972).
Statistical methods in linguistics 7(1971)–1975.
Stratégie 24(1971)–44(1975).
Studi italiani di filologia classica 42(1970)–47ii(1975).
Studi Veneziani 12(1970)–16(1974).
Studia et acta Orientalia 8(1971).
*Studia Iranica 1(1972)–4i(1975).
Studia Islamica 32(1970)–42(1975).
Studia linguistica 25(1971)–29(1975).
Studia Orientalia 40, 41, 43(1974)–46(1975) [*Wants* 45].
*Studia phonologica 1(1961)–9(1975).
Studia Rosenthalia 5(1971)–9(1975).
Studies in comparative religion 5(1971)–9(1975).
Studies in history and philosophy of science 1iv(1970)–6iii(1975).
Studies in Islam 6ii(1969)–10ii(1973).
Studies in linguistics 23(1973)–25(1975).
Studii şi cercetari lingvistica 21v(1970)–26(1975).
Sudan law journal and reports 1969–71.
Sudan notes and records 51(1970)–54(1973).

Sudhoffs Archiv 55(1971)–59(1975).
Südost-Forschungen 29(1970)–33(1974).
Sumer 22(1966)–30(1974).
Suomalaisen Tiedeakatemian toimituksia/Annales Academiae scientiarum Fennicae 169ii–196(1975) [*Wants* 190].
Symbolon 7(1971).
Syria 48(1971)–51(1974).
Systematics 9(1971)–11(1973–4).

Tahqiqat è eqtesadi 8(no. 21, 1971)–10(no. 30, 1975).
Tarikh 1ii–iv(1966–7), 2iii–iv, 3i, 3iv(1971)–5i(1975).
*Te reo 1(1958)–16(1973).
Theologische Quartalschrift 150iv(1970)–155(1975).
*Theoretical linguistics 1(1974), 2(1975).
Tiers monde 12(1971)–16(1975).
*Toid orientalistika alalt 2i, ii(1973).
T'oung pao 57(1971)–61(1975).
Traditio 27(1971)–31(1975).
Transactions and proceedings of the American Philological Association 100(1969)–104(1974).
Transactions of the American Philosophical Society 61(1971)–65(1975).
Transaction of the Cambridge Bibliographical Society 5iii(1971)–6iii(1974).
Transactions of the Glasgow University Oriental Society 23(1972), 24(1971–2).
Transactions of the Historical Society of Ghana 9(1968)–14(1973).
*Transactions. Institute of British Geographers 47(1969)–66(1975).
Transactions of the Philological Society 1970–3.
Transactions of the Royal Historical Society 21(1971)–25(1975).
Transactions of the Westermarck Society 8(1970), 9(1973).
*Transafrican journal of history 1(1971)–4(1974).
Travaux et jours 38(1971)–57(1975).
Tribus 20(1971)–24(1975).
Tropical man 3(1970)–5(1972–3).
Turcica 2(1970)–7(1975).
Türk dili arastĭrmalarĭ yĭllĭgĭ belleten 1971—1973–4.
The Turkish yearbook of international relations 9(1968)–11(1971).

Uganda journal 34ii(1970)–37(1973).
Ural-altaische Jahrbücher 43(1971)–47(1975).

*Verfassung und Recht in Ubersee 7i(1974).
Vestnik Leningtadskogo Universiteta; seriya istorii, yazyka i literatury 1971–5.
*Vestnik Moskovskogo Universiteta; seriya XIV: Vostokovedenie 1975i, ii.
Vetus Testamentum 21(1971)–25(1975).
Victoria and Albert Museum yearbook 3(1972), 4(1974).
Vierteljahresberichte (Forschungsinstitut der Friedrich-Ebert-Stiftung) 43(1971)–62(1975).
Vierteljahrschrift für Sozial- und Wirtschaftsgeschichte 58(1971)–62(1975).
Visva-bharati quarterly 34(1968–9)–39(1973–4).
Vizantiyskiy vremennik 31(1970)–36(1974).
Voprosy istorii 1971–5.
Voprosy yazykoznaniya 1971–5.

Die Welt des Islams 13(1971)–16(1975).
Die Welt des Orients 6(1971)–8i(1975).
Wiener Beiträge zur Kulturgeschichte und Linguistik 18(1974).
Wiener ethnohistorische Blätter 2(1971)–10(1975).
Wiener völkerkundliche Mitteilungen 16–17(1969–70)—20–21(1973–4).
Wiener Zeitschrift für die Kunde des Morgenlandes 63–4(1972)–67(1975).
Word 25(1969)–26(1970).
World politics 23ii(1971)–28i(1975).

Yearbook of the International Folk Music Council 2(1970–6(1974).
Yearbook of world affairs 25(1971)–29(1975).
*York papers in linguistics 2(1972)–5(1975) [*Wants* 1].

Zeitschrift für die alttestamentliche Wissenschaft 83(1971)–87(1975).
*Zeitschrift für Balkanologie 7(1969–70)–11(1975).
Zeitschrift der Deutschen Morgenländischen Gesellschaft 120ii(1970)–125(1975).
Zeitschrift des Deutschen Palästina -Vereins 87(1971)–91(1975).
Zeitschrift für Ethnologie 95(1970)–99(1974).
Zeitschrift für die gesamte Staatswissenschaft 127(1971)–131(1975).
Zeitschrift für Geschichtswissenschaft 18x(1970)–23(1975).
Zeitschrift für Kirchengeschichte 82(1971)–86(1975).
Zeitschrift für Kunstgeschichte 33iv(1970)–38(1975).
*Zeitschrift für Missionswissenschaft und Religionswissenschaft 55(1971)–59(1975).
Zeitschrift für philosophische Forschung 25(1971)–29(1975).
Zeitschrift für Phonetik, Sprachwissenschaft und Kommunikationsforschung 23vi(1970)–28 (1975).
Zeitschrift für Religions- und Geistesgeschichte 23(1971)–27(1975).
Zeitschrift für romanische Philologie 87(1971)–91(1975).
Zeitschrift für slavische Philologie 35ii(1970)–38(1975).
Zeitschrift für vergleichende Rechtswissenschaft 72(1971)–75i(1975).
Zeitschrift für vergleichende Sprachforschung auf dem Gebiete der indogermanischen Sprachen 85(1971)–89i(1975).
Zentralasiatische Studien des Seminars für Sprach- und Kulturwissenschaft Zentralasiens der Universität Bonn 5(1971)–9(1975).
Zentralblatt für Bibliothekswesen 85(1971)–89(1975).

Festschriften

Near Eastern studies in honor of William Foxwell **Albright**, ed. by Hans Goedicke. Baltimore, London, 1971.

Studies in politics: national and international. Prepared in honour of Dr. A. **Appadorai**. Delhi, 1971.

Medieval and Middle Eastern studies in honor of A. S. **Atiya**. Ed. S. A. Hanna. Leiden, 1972.

Mélanges linguistiques offerts à Émile **Benveniste**. (Collection linguistique publiée par la Société de linguistique de Paris, LXX.) Paris, 1975.

Man and his salvation. Studies in memoty of S. G. F. **Brandon**. Edited by Eric J. Sharpe and John R. Hinnells. Manchester U.P. 1973.

Mélanges Marcel **Cohen**. Études de linguistique, ethnographie et sciences connexes offertes . . . à l'occasion de son 80ème anniversaire. The Hague, 1970.

Wort und Religion. Kalima na dini. Studien zur Afrikanistik, Missionswissenschaft, Religionswissenschaft, Ernst **Dammann** zum 65. Geburtstag Hrsg. von H. –J. Greschat und H. Jungraithmayr. Stuttgart, 1969.

Prof. Poure **Davoud** memorial volume, II. Bombay, 1951.

S. K. **De** memorial volume. Editors: R. C. Hazra and S. C. Banerji. Calcutta, 1972.

Papers in linguistics and phonetics to the memory of Pierre **Delattre**, ed. by A. Valderman. The Hague, 1972.

Studies in Indian history and culture. Volume presented to Dr. P. B. **Desai** . . . on the occasion of his completing sixty years. Dharwar, 1971.

Beiträge zur Kunstgeschichte Asians. In memoriam E. **Diez**. Istanbul, 1963

Gruzinskoe istochnikovedenie. III. [Festschrift for V. D. **Dondua**.] AN Gruz SSR, Institut istorii, arkheologii i etnografii im. I. A. Dzhavakhishvili. Tbilisi, 1971.

Studies in art and literature of the Near East in honor of Richard **Ettinghausen**; edited by P. J. Chelkowski. [Salt Lake City] 1974.

Essays in Sudan ethnography presented to Sir Edward **Evans-Pritchard**. Ed. I. Cunnison and W. James. London, 1972.

The **Gaster** Festschrift. (J. Anc—Near East Soc., Columbia Univ. 5, 1973).

The Muslim East. Studies in honour of Julius **Germanus**. Edited by Gy. Káldy-Nagy. Budapest, 1974.

Ghalib: the poet and his age. Ed. Ralph Russell. London, 1972.

Orient and Occident. Essays presented to Cyrus H. **Gordon** on the occasion of his sixty-fifth birthday. Edited by Harry A. Hoffner, Jr. (Alter Orient und Altes Testament, Band 22.) Neukirchen-Vluyn, 1973.

A festschrift for Morris **Halle**. Ed. by Stephen R. Anderson and Paul Kiparsky. New York etc., 1973.

Langues et techniques, nature et société. (Offert en hommage à A. G. **Haudricourt** à l'occasion de son soixantième anniversaire par ses amis, collegès et élèves.) 2 vol. Paris, 1972.

W. B. **Henning** memorial volume. Ed. M. Boyce. London, 1970.

Iqbal: poet-philosopher of Pakistan. Ed. Hafeez Malik. 1971.

Commentationes Fenno-Ugricae in honorem E. **Itkonen** (Mémoires de la Société Fenno-ougrienne, 150), 1973.

The Saviour God: comparative studies in the concept of salvation presented to E. O. **James**. Ed. S. G. F. Brandon. Manchester U.P., 1963.

[Saṃskṛita.] Dr. Adityanath **Jha** felicitation volume, 3 vols. Delhi, 1969.

Issues in linguistics: papers in honor of Henry and Renée **Kahane**. Ed. B. B. Kachru. Urbana, 1973.

Studies in Jewish bibliography, history and literature in honor of I. Edward **Kiev**. Ed. C Berlin. New York, 1971.

Islamkundliche Abhandlungen aus dem Institut für Geschichte und Kultur des Nahen Orients an der Universität München. Hans Joachim **Kissling** sum 60. Geburtstag gewidmet von seinen Schülern. (Beiträge zur Kenntnis Südosteuropas und des Nahen Orients, XVII. Band.) München, 1974.

Festschrift für Ernst **Klingmüller**. Hrsg. von Fritz Hauss und Reimer Schmidt. Karlsruhe, 1974.

Échanges et communications. Mélanges offerts à C. **Lévi-Strauss** à l'occasion de son 60ème anniversaire réunis par J. Ponillon et P. Maranda. 2 vols. The Hague, Paris, 1970.

Livingstone: man of Africa. Memorial essays 1873–1973. Ed. B. Pachai. Longmans, 1973.
Choice and change; essays in honour of Lucy **Mair**. Ed. by J. Davis (London School of Economics Monographs on Social Anthropology, 50.) London, 1974.
Mansel' e armağan. Mélanges Mansel. Türk Tarih yayinlari, dizi VII–sa. 60. Ankara, 1974.
Comparative librarianship. Essays in honour of Professor D. N. **Marshall**. Ed. by N. N. Gidwani, Delhi, etc., 1973.
Industrial organization and economic development. In honor of E. S. **Mason**. Ed. J. W. Markham and G. F. Papanek. Boston, 1970.
Louis **Massignon**. (Ce cahier a été dirigé par Jean François Six) Paris [1970?].
Islamwissenschaftliche Abhandlungen Fritz **Meier** zum sechzigsten Geburtstag. Herausgegeben von Richard Gramlich. Wiesbaden, 1974.
Tyurkologicheskiy sbornik 1972. (Pamyati Platona Mikhaylovicha **Melioranskogo** posvyashchaetysa.) AN SSSR, Institut vostokovedeniya. Moskva, 1973.
Mémorial Jean de **Menasce**. Édité par Ph. Gignoux et A. Tafazzoli. Louvain, 1974.
Near Eastern numismatics, iconography, epigraphy and history. Studies in honor of George C. **Miles**. Dickran K. Kouymijian, editor. American University of Beirut, 1974.
Iran and Islam, in memory of the late Vladimir **Minorsky**. Ed. C. E. Bosworth. Edinburgh U.P., 1971.
Yād-nāme-ye Irāni-ye **Minorsky**. Ed. Mojtaba Minovi and Iraj Afshar. Tehran, Tehran University Publication no. 1241, 1969.
Dr. Satkari **Mookerji** felicitation volume. (The Chowkhamba Sanskrit series, vol. LXIX.) Varanasi, 1969.
[Yādnāme-ye Molla Sadra.] **Mullâ Sadrâ** commemoration volume. Tehran, 1961.
Mélange d'iranologie en memoir [*sic*] de feu Said **Naficy**. Université de Téhéran, Faculté des lettres et des sciences humaines. pub. no. 16. Rassemblé par Madame Parimarz Naficy. (=M̲ajalla-ye Dāneshkada-ye Adabiyyat wa- 'olum-e Ensānī, 19.) Tehran, 1972.
K.A. **Nilakanta Sastri** felicitation volume. Madras, 1971.
Themes in culture (essays in honor of Morris E. **Opler**.) Ed. by M. D. Zamora. Quezon City, 1971.
Studia classica et orientalia Antonio **Pagliaro** oblata. II. Roma, 1969.
Orientalia Hispanica sive studia F. M. **Pareja** octogenario dicata. Edenda curavit J. M. Barral. Volume 1: Arabica-Islamica, pars prior. Lugd. Bat. 1974.
Festschrift zum 65. Geburtstag von Helmut **Petri**. Hrsg. von Kurt Tauchmann unter Mitarbeit von Brigitte Steinfort und Margret Stobberg. Köln, Wien, 1972.
Vostochnaya filologiya. Philologia Orientalis. II. (Posvyashchaetsya pamyati Vladimira Sardionovicha **Puturidze**, 1893–1966.) Tbilisi, 1972.
Tyurkologicheskiy sbornik 1971. (Pamyati V. V. **Radlova**.) Moskva, 1972.
Dr. V. **Raghaven** Shashtyabdapurti felicitation volume. Madras, 1971.
Studies in Indo-Asian art and culture. Commemoration volume on the 69th birthday of Acharya **Raghu Vira**. New Delhi, 1972.
Proceedings of the colloquium on **Rashīd al-Dīn Fadlallāh**, Tehran–Tabriz 11–16 Aban 1348 (2–7 November 1969). Tehran, 1971.
Yādnāme-ye Jan **Rypka**. Collection of articles on Persian and Tajik literature. Prague, 1967.
Itihāsa-Chayanikā (Dr. **Sampurnanand** Felicitation Volume). 2 parts. Lucknow, 1965. (=J.U.P. Hist, Soc, 11–13).
Issbdovaniya po vostochnoy filologii. K semidesyatiletiyu professora G. D. **Sanzheeva**. 1974.
Serta Slavica in memoriam Aloisii **Schmaus**. München, 1971.
Studies in mysticism and religion presented to Gershom G. **Scholem** on his seventieth birthday by pupils, colleagues and friends. Jerusalem, 1969.
De fructu oris sui,; in honour of Adrianus **van Selms**. Ed. by I. H. Eybers *et al.* Leiden, 1971. (Pretoria oriental series, IX).
Sufi studies East and West. A symposium in honour of Idries **Shah**'s services to Sufi studies. Ed. by L. F. Rushbrook Williams. New York, 1973.
Simpoziumi per **Skenderbeun**. Pishtine, 1969.
In memoriam S. M. **Stern** (Israel Or. studies II, 1972).
Economic structure and development. Essays in honour of Jan **Tinbergen**. Edited by H. C. Bos, H. Linnemann and P. de Wolff. Amsterdam, London, 1973.
Voprosy filologii stran Azii i Afriki. Vylp.1. Sbornik v chest' professora Isaaka Natanovicha **Vinnikova**. Leningrad, 1971.
India's contribution to world thought and culture. **Vivekananda** Commemoration Volume. Ed. Lokesh Chandra [*et al.*]. Madras, 1970.

Islam and its cultural divergence. Studies in honor of G. E. **Von Grunebaum**, Urbana, 1971.
Islamic philosophy and the classical tradition. Essays presented . . . to Richard **Walzer** on his seventieth birthday. Ed S. M. Stern. Oxford, 1972.
Ex orbe religionum. Studia Geo **Widengren** XXIV mense apr. MCMLXXII quo die lustra tredecim feliciter explevit oblata . . . 2 vols. Lugd. Bat. 1974. (Studies in the history of religions, xxi–xxii.)
Iran (sbornik statey). (Pamyati professora Borisa Nikolaevicha **Zakhodera**.) Moskva, 1971.

Congresses and other collective works

Acta Iranica. 1re série: Commémoration Cyrus. Hommage universal I, II, III. 1974. 2me série: Hommages et opera minora. Monumentum H. S. Nyberg I, II. 1975.
Acta Orientalia Neerlandica. Proceedings of the Congress of the Dutch Oriental Society, held in Leiden . . . 1970. Ed P. W. Pestman. Leiden, 1971.
Actas del II Coloquio hispano-tunecino de estudios históricos (Madrid/Barcelona, mayo de 1972). Instituto hispano-árabe de cultura, Madrid, 1973.
Actas. IV congresso de estudos árabes e islâmicos, Coimbra-Lisboa, 1 a 8 de setembro de 1968. Leiden, 1971.
Actas. Congresso internacional de história dos descobrimentos. Lisboa, 1961.
Actes du Colloque de géographie agraire, Madrid, 23–27 mars 1971. Les sociétés rurales méditerranéennes. Institut de géographie d'Aix-en-Provence, Centre géographique d'études et de recherches méditerranéennes. 1972.
Actes du premier congrès d'études des cultures méditerranéennes d'influence araboberbère, publiés par Micheline Galley, avec la collaboration de David R. Marshall. Alger, 1973.
Actes du premier congrès international de linguistique sémitique et chamito-sémitique, Paris 16–19 juillet 1969 réunis par André Caquot et David Cohen. (Janua linguarum, series practica, 159.) The Hague, Paris, 1974.
Actes du II. Congrès international d'études nord-africaines, 27–29 novembre 1968. (ROMM, numéro spécial, 1970.) Gap, 1970.
Actes du XII Congrès international de l'histoire des sciences, 1968. Vol. III A. Paris, 1971.
Actes du Symposium international sur la Nubie, 1965. (Mémoires de l'Institut d'Egypte 59, 1969.)
Advances in language planning. Ed. by Joshua A. Fishman. (Contributions to the sociology of language, 5.) The Hague, Paris, 1974.
Africa in Soviet studies. USSR Academy of Sciences, Africa Institute, Moscow, 1969.
African Studies/Afrika Studien, dedicated to the IIIrd International Congress of Africanists in Addis Ababa. Edited by Thea Büttner and Gerhard Brehme. Berlin, 1973.
L'ambivalence dans la culture arabe. Par Jacques Berque [*et. al.*] Paris, 1967.
America and the Middle East. Special editor: Parker T. Hart. (Annals of the American Academy of Political and Social Science, vol. 401, May 1972.)
American Oriental Society, Middle West Branch. Semi-centennial volume, a collection of original essays ed. by D. Sinor. Bloomington, London (1969).
American University of Beirut festival book. Ed. Faud Sarouf and Suha Tamim. Beirut, 1967.
The Arab Middle East and Muslim Africa. Ed. T. Kerekes. London, 1961.
Arabic poetry; theory and development. Ed. by G. E. von Grunebaum. (Third Giorgio levi Della Vida biennial conference.) Wiesbaden, 1973.
Arabo-persidskie istochniki o tyurkskikh narodahk. An Kirgizskoy SSR, Otdel vostokovedeniya. Frunze, 1973.
Arabs and Berbers. From tribe to nation in North Africa. Edited by Ernest Gellner and Charles Micaud. London, 1973.
Arabskie strany, Turtziya, Iran, Afganistan: Istoriya, Ekonomika; AN SSSR Institut vostokovedeniya Moskva 1973.
The art of Iran and Anatolia from the 11th to the 13th centuty A.D. Edited by William Watson. (Colloquies on art and archaeology in Asia, no. 4.) London [1974].
Asian and African languages in social context. Collected papers. (Dissertationes Orientales, vol. 34.) Prague, 1974.
Asien in Vergangenheit und Gegenwart. Beiträge der Asienwissenschaftler des DDR zum XXIX. International en Orientalistenkongress 1973 in Paris. Berlin, 1974.
Aspects of Indian art. Papers presentsd in a symposium at the Los Angeles County Museum of Art, October 1970. Ed. by Pratapaditya Pal. Leiden, 1972.
Atti dell' VIII congresso internazionele di storia delle religioni (Roma 17–23 aprile 1955) pubblicati col concorso della Giunta centrale per gli studi storici e dell' UNESCO. Firenze, 1956.
Atti del convegno internazionale sol tema: la poesia epica e la sua formazione. Roma, 1970.

Beirut, crossroads of cultures. Lectures delivered at the Beirut College for Women, 1969. Beirut, 1970.

Christian-Muslim dialogue. Papers presented at the Broumana Consultation, 12–18 July 1972. Ed by S. J. Samartha and J. B. Taylor. Geneva, 1973.

Chuvashskiy yazyk, literatura i fol'klor. Sbornik statey, vypusk I. (Nauchno-issledovatedl'skiy institut pri sovete ministrov Chuvashskoy ASSR.) Cheboksary, 1972.

La collection hippocratique et son rôle dans l'histoire de la médecine. Colloque de Strasbourg (23–27 octobre 1972) . . . (Univ. des sciences humaines de Strasbourg. Travaux du Centre de recherche sur le Proche-Orient et la Grèce antiques, 2.) Leiden, 1975.

Colloque international sur l'histoire du Caire, 27 mars–5 avril 1969. [Cairo:] Gräfenhainchen pr. [1972].

Colloque juridique international, 22–24 mai 1967, Paris. Les investissements et le développement économique des pays du Tiers-Monde. Paris, 1968.

La Communauté et le problème du développement, fasc. 2: La Communauté et les pays mediterranéens. (Institut d'études européennes, Université Libre de Bruxelles. Enseignement complémentaire, N.S. 4.) Éditions de l'Institut de Sociologie, 1970.

Ve Congrès International d'Arabisants et d'Islamisants. Actes. Bruxelles, 31 Août–Septembre 1970. = Correspondance d'Orient no. 11, [1970?].

Contemporary philosophy; a survey ed. by Raymond Klibansky./La philosophie contemporaine; chroniques par les soins de R. K. Firenze, 1971.

Continuing issues in international politics, edited by Yale H. Ferguson and Walter F. Weiker, Pacific Palisades, Calif., 1973.

Contractual remedies in Asian countries. Under the auspices of the Indian Law Institute. Edited by Joseph Minattur. Bombay, 1975.

Contributions to generative phonology. Ed. M. K. Brame. Austin, 1972.

Crescent and star. Arab and Israeli perspectives on the Middle East conflict. Ed. Yonah Alexander and Nicholas N. Kittrie. New York and Toronto, 1913.

Cuadernos de historia del Islam, serie miscelanea, Islamica occidentalia, no. 1. Madrid, 1971.

Cultural resources in Lebanon. Lectures delivered at Beirut College for Women. Beirut, 1969.

Drevrie tyurkskie dialekty . . . ; i ikh otrazhenie v sovremennykh yazykakh: glossarii, ukazatel', affiksor. Pod red. I.A. Batmanova. Frunze, 1971.

The East under Western impact. Proceeding of conferences held by the Czechoslovak Society for Eastern Studies, 1967. (Dissertationes Orientales, 17.) Prague, 1969.

Elites in South Asia. Ed. E. R. Leach and S. N. Mukherjee. London, 1970.

The elusive peace in the Middle East. Edited by Malcolm H. Kerr. Albany, 1975.

English and continental views of the Ottoman Empire, 1500–1800. Papers read at a Clark library seminar, January 24, 1970 by Ezel Kural Shaw and C. J. Heywood. Los Angeles, 1972.

Essays in comparative social stratification. L. Plotnicov and A. Tuden, editors. U. Pittsburgh Press (1970).

Essays on the modernization of underdeveloped societies Ed.. A. R. Desai. 2 vols. Bombay, 1971.

Études sociologiques sur le Maroc. (Publ. du Bull. écon. et social du Maroc, série Sociologie.) (Ce recueil d'articles à été conçu et préparé par Abdelkebir Khatibi.) [Rabat-Chellah, 1971.]

Famine: a symposium daling with nutrition and relief operations in times of disaster. Swedish Nutrition Foundation, 1971.

Festgabe deutscher Iranisten zur 2500 Jahrfeier Irans. Hrsg. von W. Eilers. Stuttgart, 1971.

Fontes orientales ad historian populorum Europae meridie-orientalis . . . curavit A. S. Tveritinova *See* Vostochnye istochniki . . .

Geographers abroad. Essays on the problems and prospects of research in foreign areas. Marvin W. Mikesell, editor. (University of Chicago Department of Geography Research Paper no. 152.) Chicago, 1973.

A geography of Africa. Regional essays on fundamental characteristics, issues and problems. Ed. by R. Mansell Prothero. London, 1969.

Ghalib: the poet and his age. Ed. Ralph Russell. Papers read at the centenary celebrations at the School of Oriental and African Studies. London, 1972.

Gos. Muzey iskusstva narodov Vostoka. K 2500—letiyu iranskogo gosudarstva. Iskusstvo i arkheologiya Irana. Vsesoyuznaya konferentziya (1969g.) Doklady. Moskva, 1971.

Hamito-Semitica. Proceedings of a colloquium held by the historical section of the Linguistics Association (Great Britain) at the School of Oriental and African Studies, University of London, on the 18th, 19th and 20th of March, 1970. Edited by James and Theodora Bynon. The Hague, Paris, 1975.
Historical study of African religion; with special reference to East and Central Africa. Ed. T. O. Ranger and I. N. Kimambo. London, 1972.

Ibn al-Haitham. Proceedings of the celebrations of the 1000th anniversary held under the auspices of the Hamdard National Foundation, Pakistan. Ed. by Hakim Mohammed Said [1969?].
India and contemporary Islam. Proceedings of a Seminar. Ed. by S. T. Lokhandwalla. Simla, 1971.
India and the Arab World. Proceedings of the Seminar on India and the Arab World. Ed. by S. Maqbul Ahmed. New Delhi, 1969.
Indian history congress. Proceedings of the thirty second session, Jabalpur, 1970.
Indologen-Tagung 1971. Verhandlungen der Idologischen Arbeitstagung im Museum für Indische Kunst Berlin 7.–9. Oktober 1971. Hrsg. von Herbert Härtel und Volker Moeller. Wiesbaden, 1973.
International co-operation in orientalist librarianship: papers presented at the Library seminars [of 28th International Congress of Orientalists, 1971]. Ed. E. Bishop and J. M. Waller. Canberra, 1972.
International Islamic conference, February, 1968. Vol. 1, English papers. Editor, Dr. M. A. Khan. Islamabad, 1970.
International population conference, London, 1969. 4 vols. Liège, 1971.
Internationales Kulturhistorisches Symposion Mogersdorf 1969. Österreich und die Türken. Eisenstadt, 1972.
An introduction to business law in the Middle East, ed. by Brian Russell. London, 1975.
Les investissements et le développement économique des pays du Tiers-Monde. Paris, 1968.
Iqbal: poet-philosopher of Pakistan. Collection of articles on Iqbal by several authors. Ed. Hafeez Malik. (Studies in Oriental culture, 7.) New York, 1971.
Iran: continuity and variety, ed. by Peter J. Chelkowoki. (Fourth annual New York University Near Eastern round table 1970–71.) New York, 1971.
Iran (sbornik statey). AN SSR, Institut vostokovedeniya. Moskva, 1971.
Iran (sbornik statey). AN SSR, Institut vostokovedeniya. Moskva, 1973.
Iran Society silver jubilee souvenir 1944–1969. Calcutta, 1970.
Iranian civilization and culture. Essays in honour of the 2,500th anniversary of the founding of the Persian Empire. Edited by Charles J. Adams. Montreal, 1972.
Iskusstvo i arkheologiya Irana. Vsesoyuznaya konferentsia, 1969 g. Dokladui. K 2500—letiyu iranskogo go sudarstva. Moskva, 1971.
Iskusstvo portreta, 20–22 sent, 1972 goda. (Kratkie tezisy dokl. k nauchnoy konf.)
Islam and cultural change in the Middle Ages. Edited by Speros Vryonis, Jr. (Fourth Giorgio Levi della Vida biennial conference, 1973.) Wiesbaden, 1975.
Islamic art in the Metropolitan Museum of Art. Ed. R. Ettinghausen. New York, 1972.
The Islamic city: a colloquium. Ed. A. H. Hourani and S. M. Stern, Oxford, 1970.
Islamic civilization, 950–1150. Ed. D. S. Richards. Oxford, 1973.
Islamic law in modern India. Under the auspices of the Indian Law Institute, New Delhi. Edited by Tahir Mahmood. Bombay, 1972.
Issledovaniya po uygurskomu yazyku, I, II. Moskva, 1965, 1970.
Issledovaniya po vostochnym yazykam. AN SSSR: Institut vostokovedeniya: Moskva, 1973.
Istoriya i ekonomika stran Arabskogo Vostoka. AN SSSR: Institut vostokovedeniya. Moskva, 1973.
Istoriya, kul'tura, yazyki narodov Vostoka. AN SSSR—Institut vostokovedeniya. Moskva, 1970.
Iz istorii iskusstva velikogo goroda. (K 2500—letiyu Samarkanda). 1972.

Khozyaystvo i material naya kultura naroda Kavkaza v XIX–XX vv, I. Ed. V. K. Gardanov. Moskva, 1971.

Language use and social change. Problems of multilingualism with special reference to Eastern Africa. Studies presented and discussed at the ninth International African Seminar at University College, Dar es Salaam, December 1968. Edited with an introduction by W. H. Whiteley. Oxford University Press, 1971.
Libya in history; historical conference 16–23 March 1969. Ed. Fawzi F. Gadallah. University of Libya, Faculty of Arts, [n.d.]

Logic in classical Islamic culture, ed. by G. E. von Grunebaum. (First Giorgio levi della Vida biennial conference, 1967.) Wiesbaden, 1970.

Main currents of contemporary thought in Pakistan. Ed. Mohammed Said, II. Karachi, 1973.

Manpower mobility across cultural boundaries; social, economic and legal aspects. The case of Turkey and West Germany. Edited by R. E. Krane. (Social, economic and political studies of the Middle East, XVI.) Leiden, 1975.

The memorial volume of the Vth International Congress of Iranian Art and Archaeology. Teheran-Isfahan-Shiraz. 11–18 April, 1968. Teheran, 1972.

Mensch und Weltgeschichte. Zur Geschichte der Universalgeschichtsschreibung. Hrsg. von A. Randa. (Internationales Forschungszentrum für Grundfragen der Wissenschaften, 7.) Salzburg, München, 1969.

Mezhdunarodnye otnosheniya na Blizhnem i Srednem Vostoke posle Vtoroy Mirovoy Voyny (40–50–e gody). AN SSSR, Institut Vostokovedeniya. Moskva, 1974.

The Middle East: quest for an American policy. Ed. W. A. Beling. Albany, 1973.

Mifologiya i verovaniya narodov Vostochnoy i Yuzhhoy Azii. AN SSR, Institut etnografii. Moskva, 1973.

Modern Near East: literatūre and society. Ed. C. Max Kortepeter, (2nd Annual New York University Near Eastern Round Table, 1968–9). New York, 1971.

Le monde iranien et l'Islam. Sociétés et cultures. Vols. 1, 2, (Hautes Études Islamiques et Orientales d'Histoire Comparée.) Genève, 1971, 1974.

Musikkulturen Asiens, Afrikas und Ozeaniens im 19. Jahrhundert. Hrsg. von Robert Günther. Regensburg, 1973.

Myth of the state. Ed. H. Biezais. Stockholm, 1972.

Near Eastern round table, 1967–68, ed. R. Bayly Winder. Published jointly by the Near East Center and the Center for International Studies, New York University.

Nomadismus als Entwicklungsproblem. Bochumer Symposion 14./15. Juli 1967. Mit einen Vorwort von Prof. Dr. Willy Kraus. (Bochumer Schriften zur Entwicklungsforschung und Entwicklungspolitik, 5.) Bielefeld, 1969.

Northern Africa: Islam and modernization. Papers on the theme of Islamization, modernization, nationalism and independence presented and discussed at the Symposium arranged by the African Studies Association of the United Kingdom on the occasion of its annual general meeting, 14 September 1971. Ed. . . . by M Brett. London, 1973.

The Ottoman state and its place in world history. Edited by Kemal H. Karpat. (Social, economic and political studies of the Middle East, XI.) Leiden, 1974.

Les Palestiniens et la crise israélo-arabe. Textes et documents du Groupe de recherches et d'action pour le règlement du problème palestinien. (G.R.A.P.P.) 1967–1973. Paris, 1974.

Papers of the 3rd annual conference of the Nigerian Society for International Law. 1971.

Papers from the 11th regional meeting, Chicago linguistic society. 1975.

People and politics in the Middle East. Proceedings of the annual conference of the American Association for Peace in the Middle East. New Brunswick, N.J., 1971.

La Persia nel medievo (Atti del convegno internazionale sul tema:). Problemi attuali di scienza e di cultura. Accad. Naz–dei lincei: Roma, 1971.

Perspectives nouvelles sur l'histoire africaine. Comptes rendus du Congrès International d'Historiens de l'Afrique, University College, Dar es Salaam, Octobre 1965. Presentés par . . . Engelbert Mveng. Paris, Présence Africaine, 1971.

The philosophical forum. Vol. IV, no. 1 (New Series), Fall 1972. [Special number on Islamic philosophy.]

Political dynamics in the Middle East, edited by P. Y. Hammond and S. S. Alexander. New York, 1972.

The politics of the coup d'état, edited by W. G. Andrews and U. Ra'anan. New York, etc., 1969.

Population growth and economic development in Africa. Ed. S. H. Ominde and C. N. Ejiogu. London, 1972.

Problems and methods of the history of religions. Proceedings of the study conference organized by the Italian Society for the History of Religions on the occasion of the tenth anniversary of the death of R. Pettazzoni, 6th to 8th December 1969. Papers and discussions, ed. by U. Bianchi [*et al.*] (Studies in the history of religions, Supplements to *Numen, XIX.*) Leiden, 1972.

Problemy literatur orientalnych. Materiały II Międzynarodowego Sympozjum, Warszawa-Kraków 22–26 maja 1972. Polska Akademia Nauk, Komitet Nauk Orientalistycznych. Warszawa, 1974.
Proceedings of the All-India Oriental Conference, 25th session, Jadavpur University, Calcutta, October, 1969. Poona, 1972.
Proceedings of the IInd annual symposium on archaeological research in Iran, 29th October–1st November 1973. Firouz Bagherzadeh, editor. Tehran, 1974.
Proceedings of the Third International Conference of Ethiopian Studies, Addis Ababa, 1966. I. Institute of Ethiopian Studies, Haile Sellassie I University, 1969.
Proceedings of the sixth Seminar for Arabian Studies . . . 1972 London, 1973.
Proceedings of the IXth International Congress for the History of Religions, Tokyo and Kyoto, 1958. Tokyo, 1960.
Proceedings of the XVth World congress of philosophy. 1973.
Proceedings of the twenty seventh International Congress of Orientalists, Ann Arbor, Michigan, 1967. Wiesbaden, 1971.

Recueil d'études sur les moriscos andalous en Tunisie, préparé par M. de Epalza et R. Petit. 1973.
Relations between East and West in the Middle Ages, ed. by Derek Baker. Edinburgh U.P., 1973.
Religiya i obshchestvennaya mysl'narodov vostoka. Moskva, 1971.
Religiya i obshchestvennaya mysl' stran Vostoka. AN SSSR, Institut vostokovedeniya. Moskva, 1974.
Renaissance du onde arabe. Colleque interarabe de Louvain sous la direction de MM. Anouar Abdel-Malek, Abdel-Aziz Belal et Hassan Hanafi. Gembloux, 1972.
Researches in Altaic languages. Papers read at the 14th meeting of the Permanent International Altaistic Conference held in Szeged, August 22–28, 1971. Edited by Louis Ligeti. (Bibliotheca Orientalis Hungarica, XX.) Budapest, 1975.
Revolution in the Middle East and other case studies, ed. by P. J. Vatikiotis. (Studies on modern Asia and Africa, 9.) London, 1972.
Right and left. Essays on dual symbolic classification. Edited and with an introduction by Rodney Needham. Univ. Chicago Press, 1973.
Romano-Arabica. Edited by M. Anghelescu. (Romanian Association for Oriental Studies, Studies and documents, I.) Bucharest, 1974.
Rural politics and social change in the Middle East, R. Antoun and I. Harik, editors. Indiana U.P. 1972.
Russia and Asia Ed. W. S. Vucinich. Stanford, 1972.

Social change and politics in Turkey; a structural-historical analysis, by Kemal H. Karpat and contributors. (Social, economic and political studies of the Middle East, 7.) Leiden, 1973.
South Asian archaeology. Papers from the First international conference of South Asian archaeologists held in the University of Cambridge. Edited by Norman Hammond. London, 1973.
The Soviet Union and the Middle East. The post-World War II era. Edited by Ivo J. Lederer and Wayne S. Vucinich. Hoover Institution. Stanford, 1974.
Sprache, Geschichte und Kultur der altaischen Völker: Protokollband der XII Tagung der Permanent International Altaistic Conference 1969 in Berlin; hrsg. von G. Hazai und P. Zieme. Berlin, Akademie, 1974. (Schriften zur Geschichte und Kultur des Alten Orients, 5.)
Srednyaya Aziya i Iran; sbornik statey. Ed. A. A. Ivanov and S. S. Sorokin. Leningrad, 1972.
Strany Blizhnego i Srednego Vostoka: istoriya, ekonomika. Ed. L. M. Kulagina *et. al.* Moskva, 1972.
Strany i narody Vostoka pod obshchey red. D. A. Ol'derogge X, 1971.
Struktura i istoriya tyurkskikh yazykov. Ed. E. V. Sevortyan and others. Moskva, 1971.
Studi magrebini II. (Centro di studi magrebini, 2.) Napoli, 1968.
Gli studi sul Vicino Oriente in Italia dal 1921 al 1970. Roma, 1971. I. L'Oriente preislamico. II. L'Oriente islamico. (Pubblicazioni dell'Istituto per l'Oriente, nr. 63.)
Studia Turcica, edidit L. Ligeti. Budapest, Akadémiai Kiadó, 1971.
Studien zum Minderheitproblem im Islam I. (Bonner orientalistische Studien, N. S. 27/1.) Bonn, 1973.
Studies in modern Arabic literature. Edited by R. C. Ostle. Warminster, 1975.

Studies on Islam. A symposium on Islamic studies organized in cooperation with the Accademia dei Lincei in Rome. Amsterdam, 19-19 October 1973. Koninklijke nederlandse akademie van wetenschappen. Amsterdam, London, 1974.
Sviluppi recenti e tendenze modernistiche nelle religioni asiatiche. Atti del Convegno organizzato dalla Società Italiana di Storia delle Religioni e dall' Istituto Universitario Orientale di Napoli (7–8 aprile 1973). Supplemento n. 2, agli *Annali:* vol. 35 (1975), fasc. 1. Napoli, 1975.
Syncretism. Based on papers read at the Symposium on Cultural Contact, Meeting of religions, Syncretism held at Åbo on the 8th–10th September, 1966. Edited by Sven S. Hartman. (Scripti Instituti Donneriani Aboensis, III.) Stockholm, (1969).

The Third conference of the Academy of Islamic Research. (Al. Azhar.) 1966.
The Transformation of Palestine: essays on the origin and development of the Arab-Israeli conflict; ed. by Ibrahim Abu-Lughod. Evanston, 1971.
Tropical development 1880–1913: studies in economic progress. Ed. by W. Arthur Lewis. London, 1970.
XI. Türk Dil Kurultayında okunan bilimsel bildiriler, 1966.
[Communications read at the eleventh Turkish Language Congress]. Ankara, 1968.
Turkey; geographic and social perspectives. Edited by P. Benedict, Erol Tümertekin, Fatma Mansur. (Social, economic and political studies of the Middle East, IX.) Leiden, 1974.
Tyurkskaya leksikologia i leksikografia. Ed. N. A. Baskakov *et al.* AN SSSR. Institut Yazuikoznaniya. Moskva, 1971.
The U.S.S.R. and the Middle East. Edited by Michael Confino and Shimon Shamir. Jerusalem, 1973.

Voprosy etnogeneza tyurkoyazychnykh narodov Srednego Povolzh'ya. AN SSSR. Kazansky Filial. Institut Yazyka, Literatury i Istorii. Kazan, 1971.
Voprosy filologii stran Azii i Afriki II. Leningrad, 1973.
Voprosy metodov izucheniya istorii tyurkskikh yazykov. 1961.
Voprosy tatarskogo yazykoznaniya. 1971.
Vostochnye istochniki po istorii narodov Yugo-Vostochnoy i Tzentral'noy *Europy*, *Pod red. A. S. Tueritinovoy. II.*/Fontes orientales ad historian populorum Europae meridie-orientalis atque centralis pertirentes. Curavit: A. S. Tveritinova. II. Moskva, 1969.
Vostochnye yazyki; sbornik statey. Moskva, 1971.
Vostokovedenie, yazykovedenie. Redkollegiya: N. A. Mukhamedova, A. N. Shamatov, U. Z. Kariev. (Tashkentskiy ordena trudovogo kravnogo znameni gosudarstvenny y universitet im. V. I. Lenina, Nauchnye trudy, vypusk 433.) Tashkent, 1973.

War, technology and society in the Middle East. Edited by V. J. Parry and M. E. Yapp. London, 1975.

XVIII. deutscher Orientalistentag vom 1. bis 5. Oktober 1972 in Lübeck. Vorträge. Hrsg. von W. Voigt. ZDMG, Supplement II. Wiesbaden, 1974.

List of Abbreviations

ABORI	*Annals of the Bhandarker Oriental Research Institute*
AIEA	*Archivos del Instituto de estudios africanos*
AIEO	*Annales de l'Institut des études orientales*
AION	*Annali Istituto Orientale di Napoli*
BAEO	*Boletin de la Asociation Española de Orientalistas*
BASOR	*Bulletin of the American Schools of Oriental Research*
BEFEO	*Bulletin de L'Ecole française d'Extrême-Orient*
BEO	*Bulletin d'études orientales*
BFA	*Bulletin of the Faculty of Arts, Cairo University*
BIE	*Bulletin de l'Institut Égyptien*
BIFAN	*Bulletin de l'Institut fondamental d'Afrique noire*
BIFAO	*Bulletin de l'Institut français d'archéologie orientale*
BIIAP	*Bulletin de l'Institut International d'Administration Publique*
BJRL	*Bulletin of the John Rylands Library*
BMFEA	*Bulletin of the Museum of Far Eastern Antiquities*
BMQ	*British Museum quarterly*
BPP	*Bengal past and present*
B(R)SGI	*Bolletino della Società geografica italiana*
BSLP	*Bulletin de la Société de Linguistique de Paris*
BSMES	*British Society for Middle Eastern Studies*
BSOAS	*Bulletin of the School of Oriental and African Studies*
BTLV	*Bijdragen tot de taal-, land- en volkenkunde*
CATP	*Cahiers des arts et traditions populaires*
CRAIBL	*Comptes rendus des séances (Académie des inscriptions et belles-lettres)*
CT	*Cahiers de Tunisie*
EAZ	*Ethnographisch-archäologische Zeitschrift*
EZZ	*Ethnologische Zeitschrift Zürich*
GR	*Geographical review*
HJAS	*Harvard journal of Asiatic studies*
HUCA	*Hebrew Union College annual*
IC	*Islamic culture*
IHQ	*Indian historical quarterly*
IHRC	*Proceedings of the Indian Historical Records Commission*
IJMES	*International journal of Middle East studies*
IQ	*Islamic quarterly*
IRHT	*Institut de recherche et d'histoire des textes*
IS	*Islamic Studies*
JA	*Journal asiatique*
JAOS	*Journal of the American Oriental Society*
JAS . . .	*Journal of the Asiatic Society . . .*
JBRS	*Journal of the Bihar Research Society*
JESHO	*Journal of the economic and social history of the Orient*
JIH	*Journal of Indian history*
JMH	*Journal of modern history*
JMSUB	*Journal of the Maharaja Sayajirao University of Baroda*
JNES	*Journal of Near Eastern studies*
JNSI	*Journal of the Numismatic Society of India*
JOS (Hong Kong)	*Journal of Oriental Studies*
JPUHS	*Journal of the Panjab University Historical Society*
JQR	*Jewish quarterly review*
JRAI	*Journal of the Royal Anthropological Institute*
JRAS	*Journal of the Royal Asiatic Society*
JSFO	*Journal de la Société Finno-Ougrienne*
JSS	*Journal of Semitic studies*
JUPHS	*Journal of the United Provinces Historical Society*

KSIIMK	*Kratkie soobshcheniya o dokladakh i polevuikh issledovaniyakh Instituta istorii material'noi kulturui*
KSINA	*Kratkie soobshcheniya Instituta narodov Azii*
KSIV	*Kratkie soobshcheniya Instituta vostokovedeniya*
ME	*Middle East(ern)*
MEA	*Middle Eastern affairs*
MEAH	*Miscelanea de estudios árabes y hebraicos*
MEJ	*Middle East journal*
MESA Bull.	*Middle East Studies Association Bulletin*
MIDEO	*Mélanges de l'Institut dominicain d'études orientales du Caire*
MUSJ	*Mélanges de l'Université St.-Joseph*
MW	*Muslim world*
NAA	*Narodui Azii Afriki*
NTS	*Norsk tidsskrift for sprogvidenskap*
OCP	*Orientalia Christiana periodica*
OLZ	*Orientalistische Literaturzeitung*
OM	*Oriente moderno*
PEQ	*Palestine exploration quarterly*
PGM	*Petermanns geographische Mitteilungun*
PSQ	*Political science quarterly*
QJMS	*Quarterly journal of the Mythic Society*
RABM	*Revista de archivos, bibliotecas y museos*
RCAJ	*Royal Central Asian journal*
REI	*Revue des études islamiques*
REJ	*Revue des études juives*
RESEE	*Revue des études sud-est européannes*
RFHOM	*Revue française de l'histoire d'outre mer*
RFSE	*Revue de la Faculté des sciences économiques*
RGM	*Revue de géographie du Maroc*
RHR	*Revue de l'histoire des religions*
RIEI Madrid	*Revista del Instituto de Estudios Islámicos en Madrid*
RJPOM	*Revue juridique et politique de l'Outre-Mer*
RMD	*Revue marocaine de droit*
RMES	*Review of Middle Eastern Studies*
RO	*Rocznik orientalistyczny*
ROMM	*Revue de l'Occident Musulman et de la Mediterranée*
RRH	*Revue roumaine d'histoire*
RSO	*Rivista degli studi orientali*
SGE	*Soobshcheniya Gosudarstvennogo Ermitazha*
SI	*Studia Islamica*
SMAE	*Sbornik Muzeya antipologii i etnografii*
SO	*Studia orientalia*
ST	*Sovetskaya tyurkologiya*
SWJA	*Southwestern journal of anthropology*
TTK	*Türk Tarih Kurumu*
UAJ	*Ural-Altaische Jahrbücher*
UZIV	*Uchenuie zapiski Instituta vostokovedeniya*
VLU	*Vestnik Leningradskogo universiteta seriya istorii, yazuika i literaturui*
WBKL	*Wiener Beitrage zur Kulturgeschichte und Linguistik*
WI	*Die Welt des Islams*
WO	*Die Welt des Orients*
WVM	*Wiener völkerkundliche Mitteillungen*
WZKM	*Wiener Zeitschrift für die Kunde des Morgenlandes*
ZDMG	*Zeitschrift der Deutschen morgenländischen Gelsellschaft*
ZDPV	*Zeitschrift des Deutschen Palästina-Vereins*

Arrangement of the material

XLI Turkish Literature

XLII Berber Language and Literature 394

XLIII Education

I GENERAL. ISLAMIC STUDIES. BIBLIOGRAPHY

a GENERAL

BAUSANI, A. Islam as an essential part of Western culture. *Studies on Islam,* 1974, pp. 19-36.

DENNY, F.M. Introductory courses in Middle Eastern religion; two model syllabi. *MESA Bull.* 9ii(1975), pp. 1-19.

ENDE, W. Das Projekt einer Arabischen Enzyklopädie. *Mitteilungen. Dokumentationsdienst Moderner Orient* 3ii(1974), pp. 28-30.

GABRIELI, Fr. Arabisme et islamisme. *Studies on Islam,* 1974, pp. 7-18.

LECERF, J. Ammayya, Ummayya, Ulissanayya: peuples, nations et langues (*Daniel,* chapitre 3, versets 4 et 5). *BEO* 25(1972), pp. 239-255.

b ISLAMIC STUDIES

i General

AFSHAR, Iraj. Iranian studies. *J.Reg. Cult.Inst.* 3(nos. 11-12, 1970), pp. 135-142.

ANGHELESCU, N. Discussions sur l'objet de l'orientalisme. *Studia et acta or.* 8(1971), pp. 221-228.

ARRIBAS PALAU, M. Los estudios árabes y los ordenadores. *And* 34(1969), pp. 431-440

BATUNSKIY, M.A. O nekotorykh tendentziyakh v sovremennom zapadnom islamovedenii. *Religiya i obshchestvennaya mysl' narodov vostoka,* 1971, pp. 207-240.

BATUNSKIY, M.A. Razvitie predstavleniy ob Islame v zapadnoevropeyskoy srednevekovoy obshchestvennoy mysli (XI-XIV vv.). (The development of notions of Islam in West European social thought in the Middle Ages, XI-XIV centuries). *NAA* 1971(4), pp. 107-118.

BAZIN, L. Les études turques. *JA* 261 (1973), pp. 137-143.

BIJLEFELD, W.A. Islamic studies within the perspective of the history of religions. *MW* 62(1972), pp. 1-11.

BRAGINSKY, I.S. Iz istorii Iranistiki. *Iran (Pamyati B.N. Zakhodera),* 1971, pp. 16-27.

CAHEN, C., PELLAT, C. Les études arabes et islamiques. *JA* 261(1973), pp. 89-107.

CAQUOT, A. Les études sémitiques. *JA* 261 (1973), pp. 57-68.

CHARNAY, J.-P. The Arab intellectual between power and culture. *Diogenes* 83(1973), pp. 40-63.

CHARNAY, J.P. Ouvertures sur l'islamologie. *Etudes philos. et litt. (Actes du Coll. de Mohammédia)* 5(1971), pp. 33-47.

ENAYAT, Hamid. The politics of Iranology. *Iranian stud.* 6(1973), pp. 2-20.

FÓRNEAS, J.M. El "Barnamaŷ" de Muḥammad ibn Ŷābir al-Wādī Āšī. Materiales para su estudio y edición crítica. *And.* 38(1973), pp. 1-67.

FOUCHÉCOUR, C.-H. de. L'Iran moderne. *JA* 261(1973), pp. 125-133.

FYZEE, A.A.A. Middle Eastern studies: a proposal. *Studs. in Islam* 8(1971), pp. 29-48.

GABRIELI, F. Casual remarks of an Arabist. *Diogenes* 83(1973), pp. 1-11.

GALAND, L., GALAND-PERNET, P., LACOSTE, C. Les études berbères. *JA* 261(1973), pp. 109-116.

GEORGIEV, V.I. Die Balkanistik, ihre Geschichte und ihre Aufgaben. *Etudes Balkaniques* 10(1974) (1), pp. 5-10.

JALILI, Abd Hassan L'orientalisme et l'esprit de notre temps. *Proc.27th Int. Cong.Or.1967* (1971), pp. 231-232.

I GENERAL

LAROUI, Abdallah. For a methodology of Islamic studies. Islam seen by G. Von Grunebaum. *Diogenes* 83(1973), pp. 12-39.

LEWIS, B. El estudio del Islam. *And.* 36(1971), pp. 1-28.

MILLWARD, W.G. The social psychology of anti-Iranology. *Iranian studies* 8i-ii (1975), pp. 48-69.

'OLABI, Ahmad. L'héritage culturel arabe et les chercheurs d'aujourd'hui. *Travaux et jours* 51(1974), pp. 5-41.

PRITCHARD, P. New trends in the use of the computer for the study of the Middle East. *MESA bull.* 9iii(1975), pp. 16-26.

VAJDA, G. Le *Cursus studiorum* d'un savant Ottoman du XVIIIe siècle. *Folia Or.* 12 (1970), pp. 297-301

WAARDENBURG, J. Changes of perspective in Islamic studies over the last decades. *Humaniora Islamica* 1(1973), pp. 247-260.

WAARDENBURG, J. Islam studied as a symbol and signification system. *Humaniora Islamica* 2(1974), pp. 267-285.

Directory of graduate and undergraduate programs and courses in Middle East studies in the United States, Canada and abroad. *MESA Bull.* 6(Special issue, 1972), pp. 66.

See also VIII. a. *Iran.* Ghirshman.

See also XXIX. g. Pippidi.

See also XXXIV. d. Jarring.

Early history

BATLLORI, M. Raimondo Lullo e Arnaldo da Villanova ed i loro rapporti con la filosofia e con le scienze orientali del secolo XIII. *Oriente e Occidente nel medioevo,* 1971, pp. 145-159.

CÂNDEA, V. La diffusion de l'oeuvre de Dimitrie Cantemir en Europe du Sud-Est et au Proche-Orient. *Rev. et. sud-est eur.* 10(1972), pp. 345-361.

CIORANESCO, G. La contribution de Démètre Cantemir aux études orientales. *Turcica* 7(1975), pp. 205-232.

MATEI, I. Le maître de langue turque de Dimitrie Cantemir: Es'ad Efendi. *Rev. et. sud-est eur.* 10(1972), pp. 281-288.

Europe

ATAÖV, Türkkaya. Some notes on Soviet orientology. *Ankara Univ. Siyasal Bilgiler Fak. Dergisi* 27iii(1972), pp. 477-539.

BAUSANI, A. Cinquant'anni di Islamistica. *Studi sul Vicino Oriente in Italia,* II, 1971, pp. 1-26.

BAZIN, L. Les activités turcologiques en France. *Turcica* 2(1970), pp. 159-164.

BEČKA, Jiři. Iran in old Czech literature and scholarship. *Commémoration Cyrus. Hommage universel,* I, 1974, pp. 379-383.

BEČKA, Jiři. L'Iranologie tchécoslovaque. *Commémoration Cyrus. Hommage universel,* I, 1974, pp. 384-389.

BOYLE, J.A. The expansion of Oriental studies in West Germany. *BSMES bull.* 1 (1974-5), pp. 5-6.

BRAUNER, S., SELTER, G., VOIGT, M. Die Sektion Afrika- und Nahostwissenschaften der Karl-Marx-Universität Leipzig im 25. Jahr der Deutschen Demokratischen Republik. *Asien, Afrika, Lateinamerika* 2(1974), pp. 755-766.

CARDONA, G.R. Studi di iranistica in Italia dal 1880 ad oggi. *Commémoration Cyrus. Hommage universel.* I, 1974, pp. 348-359.

CARDONA, G.R. Studi di iranistica in Italia dal 1880 ad oggi. *Veltro* 14i-ii(1970), pp. 99-107.

DAVIS, A.R. Some implications of the Hayter Report. *JOS Australia* 2i(1963), pp. 2-6.

DOBRACA, Kasim. Islamic studies and libraries in Yugoslavia. *Peshawar Univ.rev.* 1i(1973), pp. 44-50.

DUBIŃSKI, A. Orientalistyka w działalności Akademii Nauk ZSRR. *Przegl. or.* 2(94, 1975), pp. 115-125.

DUBIŃSKI, A. Z dziejów wschodnoznawstwa rosyjskiego (w 250 rocnicę Akademii Nauk). *Przegl.or.* 92(1974), pp. 291-298.

EFIMOV, G.V. U istokov russkogo vostokovedeniya. *VLU ist., yaz., lit.* 1973(4), pp. 72-79.

EISELT, J. Forschungsarbeit des Naturhistorischen Museums Wien im und für den Iran. *Commémoration Cyrus. Hommage universel,* I, 1974, pp. 335-347.

EPALZA, M. de. Arabic studies in Spain today. *MESA bull.* 8ii(1974), pp. 1-7.

FENECH, E. Malta's contribution towards Arabic studies. *Actes I. Cong. et. cult. mediterr. d'infl. arabo-berb.,* 1973, pp. 256-260.

FLEMMING, B. Neuere wissenschaftliche Arbeiten und Forschungsvorhaben zur Sprache, Geschichte und Kultur der vorosmanischen und osmanischen Türkei in der Bundesrepublik Deutschland seit 1968. *Turcica* 5 (1975), pp. 131-147.

FRYE, R.N. Oriental studies in Russia. *Russia and Asia,* ed. W.S. Vucinich, 1972, pp. 30-51.

I GENERAL

GABRIELI, F. Il contributo italiano agli studi arabo-spagnoli. *Orientalia Hispanica* I, 1974, pp. 290-296.

GABRIELI, Fr. Gli studi arabo-islamici nella Università di Roma. *OM* 55(1975), pp. 1-7.

GANKOVSKY, Yu.V. A study of Iranian history and the history of culture in the USSR: some results and prospects. *Memorial vol. Vth Internat. Cong. Iranian Art and Archaeology,* 1972, Vol. 2, pp. 313-321.

GARDONA, G.R. Studi di iranistica in Italia dal 1680 ad oggi. *Acta Iranica* 1(1974), pp. 348-359.

HAARMANN, U. Die islamische moderne bei den deutschen Orientalisten. *Z.f.Kulturaustausch* 24ii(1974), pp. 5-18.

ISMAIL, Ezz El-Din Die Orientalistik in Deutschland, Skizze und Betrachtung. *Ann.Fac.Arts Ain Shams* 7(1962), pp. 115-122.

KAKUK, Suzanne Cent ans d'enseignement de philologie turque à l'Université de Budapest. *Studia Turcica, ed. L. Ligeti,* 1971, pp. 7-27

KAKUK, Z. Tyurkologicheskie issledovaniya v Vengrii. *ST* 1974(1), pp. 79-92.

KONONOV, A.N. Nekotorye itogi razvitiya sovetskoy tyurkologii i zadachi Sovetskogo komiteta tyurkologov. *ST* 1974(2), pp. 3-12.

LENTZ, W. Die Iranforschung und das gegenwärtige Deutschland. *Commémoration Cyrus. Hommage universel,* I, 1974, pp. 324-327.

MAYRHOFER, M. Irans Kultur- und Sprachenwelt in der Arbeit der Österreichischen Akademie der Wissenschaften. *Commémoration Cyrus. Hommage universel,* I, 1974, pp. 328-334.

MIQUEL, A., ARKOUN, M. Pour un renouveau des études arabes en France. *Etudes philos. et litt. (Actes du Coll. de Mohammédia)* 5 (1971), pp. 55-71.

NÉMETH, J. Die Orientalistik in Ungarn 1938. *The Middle East; studies in honour of J. Germanus,* 1974, pp. 11-22.

POPOVIC, A. Étude de l'empire ottoman et l'orientalisme dans les pays balkaniques. (Essai d'un répertoire bio-bibliographique et analytique de l'orientalisme yougo-slave.) *Turcica* 5(1975), pp. 154-159.

REYCHMAN, J. Stulecie turkologii na Uniwersytecie w Budapeszcie. (Le centenaire de la turcologie à l'Université de Budapest). *Przeglad Or.* 4(84) (1972), pp. 361-363.

REYCHMAN, J. Z dziejów orientalistyki w Finlandii. (Sur l'histoire d'orientalistique en Finlande). *Przeglad or.* 1972(3, no. 83), pp. 263-268.

SANTUCCI, R. Middle East studies in France. *MESA bull.* 9iii(1975), pp. 7-16.

SCARCIA, G. Islamistica e persianologia in Italia. *Annali Fac. Ling. Lett. stran. di Ca' Foscari (serie orientale)* 3(1972), pp. 147-153.

SKILLITER, S. British centres of Turkish studies. *Turcica* 5(1975), pp. 148-153.

TRYJARSKI, E. Polskaya tyurkologiya za posledniye desyat let (1964-1973). *ST* 1974(4), pp. 97-106.

TSERETELI, K. Georgische Orientalistik. *Mitt. Inst. Orientforschung* 17(1972), pp. 672-677.

TYLOCH, W. Polsko-radziecka współpraca orientalistów w trzydziestoleciu PRL. *Przegl.or.* 91(1974), pp. 193-201.

VUCINICH, W.S. The structure of Soviet Orientology: fifty years of change and accomplishment. *Russia and Asia,* ed. W.S. Vucinich, 1972, pp. 52-134.

Middle Eastern studies in British universities. *BSMES bull.* 1(1974-5), pp. 7-16, 84-93; 2(1975), pp. 21-22.

Asia

ABDUS SUBHAN. Persian Studies in Bengal. *Abr Nahrain* 13(1972-73), pp. 52-65.

AFSHAR, I. The present state of Iranian studies in Iran. *Abr-nahrain* 12(1971-2), pp. 6-14

ALIEV, G.Z. Le développement de la turcologie en Azerbaïdjan soviétique. *Et balkaniques* 9(1973), pp. 121-215.

BAŞGÖZ, Ilhan. Research facilities in Turkey--addendum. *MESA bull.* 9iii(1975), p. 27.

BRINNER, W.M. Research facilities in Israel. *MESA Bull.* 7i(1973), pp. 42-48.

GOPAL, Surendra. Indian studies in Soviet Central Asia. *Indo-Asian culture* 20ii (1971), pp. 19-33.

HAMBIS, L. L'Asie centrale et les études mongoles. *JA* 261(1973), pp. 145-151.

HUMPHREYS, S. Opportunities and facilities for research in Syria. *MESA Bull.* 8i(1974), pp. 16-21.

KATRAK, Jamshid Cawasji. Gujarati literature on Iranology. *Acta Iranica* 1(1974), pp. 360-378.

TACHAU, F. Research facilities in Turkey. *MESA Bull.* 9ii(1975), pp. 20-29.

Research facilities in Iran - addendum. *M.E.S.A. Bull.* 7iii(1973), p. 55.

Research facilities in Turkey. Addendum. *MESA Bull.* 7ii(1973), p. 31.

I GENERAL

Africa

BECHTOLD, P.K. Research facilities in the Sudan. *MESA Bull.* 7ii(1973), pp. 23-31.

BROWN, K., ROLLMAN, W.J. and WATERBURY, J. Research facilities in Morocco. *MESA Bull.* 4iii(1970), pp. 55-67

GLÜCK, J.J. Arabic at the University of South Africa. *Semitics* 4(1974), pp. 47-51.

HALE, G.A. and HALE, S. Research facilities in the Sudan: addendum. *MESA Bull.* 9ii(1975), pp. 30-35.

HUDSON, M.C. Research facilities in Lebanon. *MESA Bull.* 6iii(1972), pp. 17-25.

MILLER, S.G. Research facilities in Morocco - addendum. *M.E.S.A. Bull.* 7iii(1973), pp. 47-52.

RACAGNI, M. Research facilities in Tunisia. *MESA Bull.* 6i(1972), pp. 30-36.

America

DEVALLE, S.B.C. Los estudios de Asia en Buenos Aires. *Estudios orientales* 23 (8iii, 1973), pp. 310-313.

JAZAYERY, M.A. A directory of teachers of Persian in the United States and Canada. *M.E.S.A. Bull.* 7iii(1973), pp. 81-84.

JAZAYERY, M.A. Persian language instruction. *MESA Bull.* 6i(1972), pp. 9-29.

SHAW, S.J. Ottoman and Turkish studies in the United States. Comment by R.L. Chambers. *The Ottoman State and its place in World History,* ed. by Kemal H. Karpat, 1974, pp. 118-129.

SULEIMAN, M.W. The Middle East in American high school curriculum: a Kansa case study. *MESA bull.* 8ii(1974), pp. 8-19.

URQUIDI, V.L., LAMA, G. de la. The development of Asian studies in Latin America. *J.Or.Res.Madras* 37(1971), pp. 24-32.

WAARDENBURG, J. L'organisation des études concernant l'Islam et le Moyen-Orient à l'Université de Californie. (Les études islamiques dans le monde, IX.) *REI* 41 (1973), pp. 297-305.

ii Congresses. Societies. Institutions.

General. International

AHMED, Munir D. XXIXth International Congress of Orientalists, Paris (July 16-22, 1973). An overview of the themes dealing with contemporary Middle East. *Mitt. Dokumentationsdienst moderner Orient* 2ii(1973), pp. 57-67.

CZEGLÉDY, K. The XXIXth International Congress of Orientalists. *Acta Or.Hung.* 28 (1974), pp. 288-290.

DANDAMAEV, Muhammad A. Congrès International des Iranistes à Shiraz. *Acta Iranica* 1 (1974), pp. 3-12.

DIGARD, J.P. Les études iraniennes au IXe Congrès international des sciences anthropologiques et ethnologiques. *Studia Iranica* 3(1974), pp. 123-125.

GAFUROV, B.G., MIROSHNIKOV, L.I. Sotrudnichestvo uchenykh mira v issledovanii problem Tzentral'noy Azii (K Ashkhabadskoy konferentzii Yunesko). (Cooperation among scholars of the world in the research and problems of Central Asia). *NAA* 1972(4), pp. 3-7.

MARCHAL, R. Ve congrès international d'arabisants et d'islamisants. *Correspondance d'Orient: Etudes* 15-16(1969), pp. 105-111.

MOUBARAC, Youakim. Le XXVIIIe Congrès des Orientalistes à Canberra, du 6 au 12 Janvier 1971. *REI* 40(1972), pp. 197-203.

SARKAR, Jagadish Narayan. A note on International Congress of Orientalists, Canberra. *Q'ly rev.hist.stud.* 10(1970-1), pp. 227-233.

SERRA, L. Primo congresso "D'études des cultures méditerranéennes d'influence arabo-berbère". Malta 3-6 aprile 1972. *OM* 53(1973), pp. 643-644.

SPIES, O. Activities of the Turkish delegation in the 26th Congress of Orientalists. *Islâm Tetkikleri Enstitüsü dergisi* 4(1964), pp. 119-127.

TLILI, Béchir. Historicité, patrimoine et émancipation: note sur le Ier Congrès international d'histoire (1393 H/ 1973). *CT* 20(nos.79-80, 1972), pp. 263-268.

VIETZE, H.P. Die Permanent International Altaistic Conference und die XIII. Tagung, Strasbourg 1970. *EAZ* 12(1971) pp. 154-157.

VIETZE, H.P. Die XVI. Tagung der Permanent International Altaistic Conference in Szeged 1971. *Mitt. Inst. Orientforschung* 17(1972), pp. 677-680.

Das internationale Iranistentreffen in Rom 31. März - 5. April 1970. *Iranistische Mitteilungen* 5(1971), pp. 79-116.

See also IX. n. Modugno.

See also XXXIV. d. Landa

Europe

BERZA, M. L'AISEE et la collaboration scientifique internationale dans l'étude du Sud-Est européen. *RESEE* 12(1974), pp. 5-16.

I GENERAL

CARUSO, F. L'Istituto Italiano di Cultura di Teheran. *Veltro* 14i-ii(1970), pp. 183-187.

CONDURACHI, E. Le Xe anniversaire de l'Association internationale d'études du Sud-Est européen. *RRH* 13(1974), pp. 5-25.

DULINA, N.A. *et al.* VII Tyurkologicheskaya konferentziya v Leningrade. *ST* 1975 (5), pp. 107-125.

EISELT, J. Forschungsarbeit des naturhistorichen Museums Wien im und für den Iran. *Acta Iranica* 1(1974), pp. 335-347.

FILLIOZAT, J. La Société asiatique: d'hier à demain. *JA* 261(1973), pp. 3-12.

FRANZ, E. Zur Tagung der Arbeitsgemeinschaft Afghanistan vom 18.-19. Oktober 1974 in Saarbrücken. *Mitteilungen. Dokumentationsdienst Moderner Orient* 3ii(1974), pp. 51-56.

GARGANO, A. L'Ismeo e i rapporti culturali italo-iraniani. *Veltro* 14i-ii(1970), pp. 189-195.

GUZEV, V.G., DULINA, N.A., and NASILOV, D.M. Tyurkologicheskaya konferentziya pamyati V.V. Radlova. *Tyurkolog. sbornik (Pamyati V.V. Radlova,* 1972), pp. 280-290.

HANDŽIC, A. Problematika sakupljanja i izdavanja turskih istorijskih izvora u radu Orijentalnog instituta. (Problems in procuring and editing Turkish sources in the work program of the Institut of Oriental Studies.) *POF* 20-21(1970-71), pp. 213-221.

HOURANI, A.H. and LATHAM, J.D. The British Society for Middle Eastern Studies. *BSMES bull.* 1(1974-5), pp. 3-4.

KAŁUŻYŃSKI, S. Pół wieku Polskiego Towarzystwa Orientalistycznego. (Cinquante ans d'activités de la Société Polonaise d'Études Orientales). *Przeglad or.* 1972(3, no. 83), pp. 211-220.

KANUS-CREDE, H. Bericht über den 17. deutschen Orientalistentag vom 21. bis 27. Juli 1968 in Würzburg. *Iranistische Mitt.* 3i(1969), pp. 43-53.

KANUS-CREDE, H. Das internationale Iranistentreffen in Rom 31.März-5.April 1970. *Iranistische Mitt.* 5(1971), pp. 79-115.

KONONOV, A.N. Tyurkskoe yazykoznanie v Akademii nauk SSSR. *ST* 1974(3), pp. 3-18.

MAJID, M.A. A brief resume of the activities of the Iran Society (1944-1969). *Indo-Iranica* 23i-ii(1970), pp. 41-50.

MAYRHOFER, M. Irans Kultur- und Sprachwelt in der Arbeit der österreichischen Akademie der Wissenschaften. *Acta Iranica* 1(1974), pp. 328-334.

MAYRHOFER, M. Irans Kultur- und Sprachenwelt in der Arbeit der Österreichischen Akademie der Wissenschaften. *Bustan* 11 iv-12i(1970-1), pp. 11-13.

REUT, M. Arbeitsgemeinschaft Afghanistan. Colloque de Sarrebruck, du 17-19 octobre 1974. *Studia Iranica* 4(1975), p. 131.

ROBINSON, B.W. The sesquicentenary of the Royal Asiatic Society. *BSOAS* 36(1973), pp. 117-118.

SERAJUL HAQUE. German contribution to Arabic and Islamic studies. *JAS Bangladesh* 19 (1974), pp. 33-48.

SOUMILLE, P. Recherches et travaux du Centre d'histoire militaire de Montpellier sur le Maghreb, l'Afrique et le monde arabe. *CT* 19, nos. 75-76(1971), pp. 249-251.

TALBI, Mohamed. L'histoire économique du Moyen Orient. [London conference of 1967.] *CT* 23(nos. 91-92, 1975), pp. 395-397.

TIKHONOV, D.I. Sokrovishcha Aziatskogo muzeya i ikh sobirateli. *SMAE* 29(1973), pp. 4-33.

TODOROV, N. Le dixième anniversaire de la formation de l'Institut d'études balkaniques. *Etudes Balkaniques* 10(1974) (2), pp. 221-224.

WESTPHAL-HELLBUSCH, Sigrid. Hundert Jahre Museum für Völkerkunde Berlin. Abteilung Westasien. *Baessler Archiv* N.F. 21(1973), pp. 291-307.

Centre de Recherches et d'Etudes sur les Sociétés Méditerranéennes (C.R.E.S.M.), Aix-en-Provence. *Mitt. Dokumentationsdienst moderner Orient* 2ii(1973), pp. 16-21.

Deutsche Tagung "Forschung und Dokumentation über den Vorderen Orient" 24.-25. Oktober 1972 in Berlin-Tegel. *Mitt. Dokumentationsdienst moderner Orient* 1iii (1972), pp. 53-55.

Deutsche Tagung "Forschung und Dokumentation über den modernen Orient" (18.bis 20.März 1974 in Berlin). *Mitteilungen. Dokumentationsdienst Moderner Orient* 3ii(1974), pp. 52-60.

The first congress on Mediterranean studies of Arabo-Berber influence. *J.Fac.Arts Malta* 7(1971), pp. i-ii.

Institute for relations between Italy and the countries of Africa, Latin America and the Middle East. *Mitteilungen. Dokumentationsdienst Moderner Orient* 3ii(1974), pp. 19-22.

Il nuovo statuto dell'Istituto universitario orientale di Napoli. *Boll. Assoc. Africanisti italiani* 6(1973), pp. 50-55.

Ob organatzii Sovetskogo komiteta tyurkologov. *ST* 1974(2), pp. 113-115.

See also II. a. 7. Epalza.

I GENERAL

Asia

ABDUL WAHED, Muhammad. The Sana'a Centre of Yemeni Studies. *Mitt. Dokumentationsdienst moderner Orient* 2ii(1973), pp. 12-15.

ABDUS SUBHAN. Contributions of the Asiatic Society, Calcutta, to Arabic and Persian studies. *Proc.All-India Or.Conf.* 1969, pp. 273-277.

ALWAYE, Mohiaddin. The seventh conference of the Islamic Research Academy. *Maj.al-Azhar* 44vii(1972), pp. 1-12.

BAHA, Lal. The birth of a great home of learning. *Asian aff.* N.S.4(1973), pp. 151-159.

DANDAMAEV, Muhammad A. Congrès international des iranistes à Shiraz. *Commémoration Cyrus. Hommage universel,* I, 1974, pp. 3-12.

GHAZNAVI, Masood. Recent Muslim historiography in South Asia: the problem of perspective. *Ind.econ.soc.hist.rev.* 11(1974), pp. 183-215.

ITAYEM, M.A. The Royal Scientific Society (Jordan) and its Library. *Mitt. Dokumentationsdienst moderner Orient* 1iii(1972), pp. 27-29.

JISR, Bassem el-. Le premier Congrès islamique libanais. *Travaux et jours* 53(1974), pp. 13-29.

MAUTNER, M. The Harry S. Truman Research Institute of the Hebrew University of Jerusalem. *Mitt. Dokumentationsdienst moderner Orient* 1iii(1972), pp. 31-32.

MOBERLY, J.C. The Middle East Centre for Arab Studies (MECAS). *BSMES bull.* 1(1974-75), pp. 59-83.

SEVIM, Ali. Das Jubiläum der Schlacht von Malazgird (1071). *Der Islam* 49(1972), pp. 292-293.

SLABY, H. Das Österreichische Kulturinstitut in Teheran. *Bustan* 11iv-12i (1970-1), pp. 5-10.

TALBI, Mohamed. La crise de l'évolution de la civilisation dans le monde arabe. *CT* 20(nos.79-80, 1972), pp. 309-312.

TLILI, Béchir. La civilisation arabe entre l'authenticité et le renouvellement. Note sur le Ier Congrès d'Histoire de Beyrouth (10-16 mars 1975). *CT* 23(nos. 91-92, 1975), pp. 399-406.

WILD, St. Das Orient-Institut der DMG in Beirut -- Experiment oder Modell? *XVIII. Deutscher Orientalistentag* 1972, pp. XVI-XXVII.

YUSUF, K.M. A brief history of the Iran Society. *Iran Society silver jubilee souvenir* 1944-1969, pp. xiii-xx.

Scientific and technical research institutions in Iran. *Mitt. Documentationsdienst moderner Orient* 2i(1973), pp. 35-43.

See also I. b. 3. Cannon.

Africa

ALWAYE, A.M. Mohiaddin The sixth conference of Islamic Research Academy of Al-Azhar [Cairo - 1971]. *Majallat al-Azhar* 43iii(1971), pp. 1-6.

[ALWAYE, A.M. Mohiaddin.] The second session of the sixth conference of the Islamic Research Academy (10-27th April 1971, Cairo). *Majallat al-Azhar* 43iv(1971), pp. 14-16.

CHIAUZZI, G. L'università libica e le sue pubblicazioni. *OM* 55(1975), pp. 264-269.

FAFUNWA, A. Babs. Conference of Muslim lecturers and administrative staff of Nigerian universities. Appeal for funds. *Nigerian J. Islam* 1ii(1971), pp. 43-44.

KARIM, G.M. Rejoinder [to *Arabic at the University of South Africa*] from a postgraduate student. *Semitics* 4(1974), pp. 52-54.

MASMOUDI, Mohamed. Le Centre des arts et traditions populaires. *CATP* 1(1968), pp. 7-9.

NEJJAR, S. Vue d'ensemble sur les activités de la Société depuis sa création. *Bull Soc. hist. Maroc* 1 (1968), pp. 3-4

L'état actuel des recherches linguistiques en Tunisie. Communication de la Section de linguistique de l'I.P.S.E.J.E.S. (Tunis). *Actes I Cong.int.ling.sém.et chamito-sém.*, 1969(1974), pp. 338-346.

L'Institut de linguistique et de phonétique de l'Université d'Alger. *Al-Lisaniyyat* 1i(1971), pp. 101-104.

See also I. b. 3. Vacca.

See also III. a. 9. Dionisi.

See also XXIX. c. Matuz.

See also XXXVII. b. Fontaine.

See also XXXVII. l. Fontaine.

America

HAZAI, G. 10 Jahre der "Uralic and Altaic Series" der Indiana University publications. *Asian and African stud.Bratislava* 9(1973), pp. 171-173.

KILLEAN, C.G. American Association of teachers of Arabic. *MESA Bull.* 5ii (1971), pp. 95-96.

I GENERAL

LAMA, G. de la. III reunión del Comité-coordinador inter-universitario de los estudios orientales en América Latina. *Estudios orientales* 23(8iii, 1973), pp. 312-321.

ZARTMAN, W. The Middle East Studies Association of North America (MESA). *BSMES bull.* 2(1975), pp. 3-5.

iii Individual scholars

MAJID, M.A. Remembering the great savants. *Indo-Iranica* 24i-ii(1971), pp. 43-47.

BOSWORTH, C.E. Mr. M.R. Abd El-Muttalib (1917-1975). *BSMES bull.* 2(1975), p. 119.

DESTRÉE, A. Armand Abel. *BAEO* 9(1973), pp. 6-7.

JANSSENS, E. Armand Abel 1903-1973. *Correspondance d'Orient: Etudes* 19-20 (1971-2), pp. 3-6.

LYONS, M.C. *In memoriam* A.J. Arberry. *BAEO* 6(1970), pp. 13-15.

VAḤID, S.A. A.J. Arberry, a great student of Iqbāl. *Iqbal rev.* 13i(1972), pp. 37-50.

WICKENS, G.M. Arthur John Arberry 1905-1969. *Proc. Brit. Acad.* 58(1972), pp. 355-366.

RIAZ, Muhammad. Professor Arthur John Arberry and his contribution to Islamic literature. *J.Pak.Hist.Soc.* 20(1972), pp. 74-86.

PEREIRA, J. Ignazio Arcamone (1615-1683); first Italian Orientalist? *East and West* N.S.24(1974), pp. 153-157.

Ashmarin. *See* XL. f. Shiraliev.

LAPESA, R. Don Miguel Asín, lingüista. *And* 34(1969), pp. 451-460

See also II. d. 1. Epalza

McMURRIN, S.M. Aziz S. Atiya. *Medieval and Middle Eastern studies ... A.S. Atiya* 1972, pp. 3-4.

WALKER, P.E. Aziz S. Atiya, a biography. *Medieval and Middle Eastern studies ... A. S. Atiya* 1972, pp. 5-8.

OLPIN, A.R. Dr. Aziz S. Atiya and Utah. *Medieval and Middle Eastern studies ... A. S. Atiya* 1972, pp. 16-19.

HUZAYYIN, S.A. Professor Muhammad Awad (1896-1972). *Bull.Soc.Geog.d'Egypte* 41-2 (1968-69), pp. 1-4.

GABAIN, A. von. Persönliche Erinnerungen an W. Bang-Kaup. *Sprache, Geschichte und Kultur der altaischen Völker*, hrsg. G. Hazai und P. Zieme, 1974, pp. 51-55.

A.E.H.P. and A.R. Appreciation: Nevill Barbour. Asian aff. N.S.4(1973), p. 86.

PAREJA, F.M. In memoriam: Nevill Barbour. *BAEO* 9(1973), pp. 5-6.

KONONOV, A.N. V.V. Bartol'd - vydayushchiysya vostokoved. (K 40-letiyu so dnya smerti). *ST* 1970(6), pp. 56-61.

LOUCA, Anouar. Du bastion de Soleure à la Chine musulmane. Le champ scientifique de Max van Berchem. *Musées de Genève* 156 (1975), pp. 10-12.

LOUCA, Anouar. La correspondance de Max van Berchem. *MIDEO* 12(1974), pp. 231-236.

LOUCA, Anouar. Lettres de Ferdinand de Saussure à Max van Berchem. *Cah.Ferdinand de Saussure* 29(1974-5), pp. 13-36.

COHEN, D. Régis Blachère (1900-1973). *JA* 262(1974), pp. 1-10.

COURCELLE, P. Allocution à l'occasion de la mort de M. Régis Blachère. *CRAIBL* 1973, pp. 413-415.

ELISSÉEFF, N. Régis Blachère (1900-1973). *Aribica* 22(1975), pp. 1-5.

YALAOUI, Mohamed. Régis Blachère (1900-1973). *CT* 20(nos.77-78, 1972), pp. 207-208.

MALLOWAN, M.E.L. Obituary. Sir Maurice Bowra. *Iran* 10(1972), pp. iii-v

INAYATULAH. Professor E.G. Browne - a friend of the Muslim East. *Hamdard* 14i (1971), pp. 19-22, 33. [CWHM 72, 197]

BOSWORTH, C.E. The tomb in Cairo of John Lewis Burckhardt. *JSS* 18(1973), pp. 259-266.

PAREJA, F.M. *In memoriam* Juan Busquets Mulet. *BAEO* 7(1971), pp. 6-7.

DOUGLAS, E.H. Edwin Elliott Calverley. October 26, 1882-April 21, 1971. *MW* 61(1971), pp. 155-160

INAYATULLAH, Shaikh. Baron Carra de Vaux: his life and works (1867-1953). *Islamic stud.* 10(1971), pp. 201-207.

MEYER, E. Werner Caskel (1896-1970), *ZDMG* 122(1972), pp. 1-5.

BASKAKOV, N.A., TRYYARSKIY, N.A. Pamyati Dzherarda Klousona [Clauson]. *NAA* 1975 (3), pp. 245-249.

BOSWORTH, C.E. Sir Gerard Clauson (1891-1973). *BSMES bull.* 1(1974-5), pp. 39-40.

KONONOV, A.N., KLYASHTORNYY, S.G. Sir Gerard Clauson, 1891-1974. *ST* 1974(5), pp. 115-116.

RÓNA-TAS, A. In memoriam Sir Gerard Clauson. *Acta Or. Hung.* 29(1975), p. 393.

I GENERAL

LÓPEZ GARCÍA, B. Cartas inéditas de Francisco Codera a Pascual de Gayangos (reinvidicación de una figura del arabismo). *MEAH* 24(1975), pp. 29-68.

STRELCYN, S. Marcel Cohen. *BSOAS* 38 (1975), pp. 615-622.

SLOMP, J. Meeting between church and mosque. Introducing the work of Dr. Kenneth Cragg. *Al-Mushir* 14i-ii(1972), pp. 1-3

SCANLON, G.T. Sir Archibald Cresswell (1879-1974). *BSMES bull.* 1(1974-5), pp. 110-111.

MIRAKHMEDOV, A. Mamed Arif Magerram Ogly Dadashzade. *ST* 1975(6), pp. 119-120.

ROUX, J.P. Jean David-Weill (1898-1972). *JA* 260(1972), pp. 215-216.

In memoriam Ebrahim Poure Davoud (1886-1968). *Iranistische Mitteilungen* 4(1970), pp. 3-33.

SRIVASTAVA, Satya Prakash. Obituary - Rai Bahadur Prayag Dayal. *JNSI* 32(1970), pp. 216-217.

ARAKIN, V.D. N.K. Dmitriev i ego vklad v otechestvennuyu tyurkologiyu. *ST* 1973(4) pp. 71-81.

GARIPOV, T.M. N.K. Dmitriev i izuchenie russko-bashkirskogo dvuyazychiya. *Struktura i istoriya tyurkskikh yazykov*, 1971, pp. 33-41.

MUKHAMEDOVA, E.B. N.K. Dmitriev i turkmenskaya filologiya. *Struktura i istoriya tyurkskikh yazykov*, 1971, pp. 30-32.

SEVORTYAN, E.V. Lingvisticheskoe nasledie N.K. Dmitrieva i sovremennaya sovetskaya tyurkologiya. *Struktura i istoriya tyurkskikh yazykov*, 1971, pp. 7-19.

SHIRALIEV, M.Sh. N.K. Dmitriev i azerbaydzhanskoe yazykoznanie. *Struktura i istoriya tyurkskikh yazykov*, 1971, pp. 20-29.

KULIKOVA, A.M. B.A. Dorn i universitetskoe vostokovedenie v Rossii. *NAA* 1975 (2), pp. 220-228.

Camille Dumont (1913 - 1975). *Arabica* 22 (1975), p. 113.

HAMARNEH, Saleh K. A.A. Dūrī - an outstanding contemporary Arab scholar. *Folia Or.* 15(1974), pp. 277-280.

DZHANASHIYA, N.N. Sergey Simonovich Dzhikiya. *ST* 1974(1), pp. 115-116.

Professor Tadeusz Dzierżykray-Rogalski. *Africana bull.* 19(1974), pp. 125-130.

ANDREEV, I.A. Vasiliy Georgevich Egorov. *ST* 1974(1), pp. 123-124.

PORTER, B. Trefor E. Evans (1913-1974). *BSMES bull.* 1(1974-5), p. 41.

SHAHI, Ahmed al-. Sir Edward Evans-Pritchard (1902-1973). *BSMES bull.* 1(1974-5), pp. 111-112.

TALBI, Mohamed. Allal el-Fassi (1910-1974). *CT* 23(nos.89-90,1975), pp. 301-304.

BAYERLE, G. Lajos Fekete 1891-1969. *Archivum Ottomanicum* 1(1969), pp. 303-316.

RIZZITANO, U. In memoriam Fouad Sayyed. *MIDEO* 11(1972), pp. 543-549.

LAROCHE, J. Albert Gabriel, "le plus turc des Français", 2 août 1883-23 décembre 1972. *Turcica* 4(1972), pp. 7-14.

SOURDEL-THOMINE, J. Albert-Louis Gabriel (1883-1972). *REI* 41(1973), pp. 3-5.

BORRUSO, A., RIZZITANO, U. Francesco Gabrieli e la letteratura araba del Novecento. *OM* 54(1974), pp. 147-163.

TERÉS, E. En la jubilación de Don Emilio García Gómez. *And.* 40(1975), pp. I-VII.

Don Emilio García Gómez doctor "honoris causa" por la Universidad de Granada. *MEAH* 24(1975), pp. 7-27.

KÁLDY-NAGY, Gy. Julius Germanus. *The Middle East; studies in honour of J. Germanus*, 1974, pp. 7-10.

GABRIELI, F. In memoria di Sir Hamilton Gibb. *OM* 51(1971), p. 833.

HOURANI, A. Sir Hamilton Gibb 1895-1971. *Proc. Brit. Acad.* 58(1972), pp. 493-523.

LAMBTON, A.K.S. Sir Hamilton Alexander Roskeen Gibb. *BSOAS* 35(1972), pp. 338-345.

MAKDISI, G. Sir Hamilton Alexander Roskeen Gibb, January 2, 1895 - October 22, 1971. *JAOS* 93(1973), pp. 429-431.

POLK, W.R. Sir Hamilton Gibb between orientalism and history. *IJMES* 6(1975), pp. 131-139.

In memoriam Rodolfo Gil-Torres Benumeya (1901-1975). *Rev.de política int.* 138(1975), pp. 5-7.

Docteur Ernest-Gustave Gobert (1879-1973). *ROMM* 17(1974), pp. 7-17.

PAVÓN, B. *In memoriam* Manuel Gómez Moreno. *BAEO* 6(1970), pp. 5-7.

BASKAKOV, N.A. A.N. Samoylovich v pis'makh k V.A. Gordlevskomu. *ST* 1973(5), pp. 84-92.

BAUDE, D. In memoriam: Dr. Hilma Granqvist. *Ann. Dept. Antiq. Jordan* 17(1972), pp. 97-98.

WEIR, S. Obituary: Hilma Granqvist. *PEQ* 104(1972), pp. 169-170.

WEIR, S. Hilma Granqvist and her contribution to Palestine studies. *BSMES bull.* 2 (1975), pp. 6-13.

I GENERAL

GABRIELI, F. Casa Guidi. *Levante* 20ii (1973), pp. 17-19.

KONONOV, A.N. Pamyati Gylyba Gylybova (1892-1972). *NAA* 1974(1), pp. 247-248.

GLIDDEN, H.W. Harvey Porter Hall, 1909-1975. *MEJ* 29(1975), p. 433.

SCHIMMEL, A. Ein unbekanntes Werk Joseph von Hammer-Purgstalls. *WI* 15(1974), pp. 129-145.

KANUS-CREDE, H. In memoriam Olaf Hansen (1902-1969). *Iranistische Mitt.* 4(1970), pp. 34-40.

In memoriam Olaf Hansen (1902-1969). *Iranistische Mitteilungen* 4(1970), pp. 34-40.

KANUS-CREDE, H. In memoriam Walter Bruno Henning (1908-1967). *Iranistische Mitt.* 1(1969), pp. 4-18.

In memoriam Walter Bruno Henning (1908-1967). *Iranistische Mitteilungen* 1ii(1967), pp. 4-18; 2i(1968), pp. 86-92.

GAULMIER, J. A la decouverte du Proche-Orient: Barthelémy d'Herbelot et sa *Bibliothèque orientale. Bull.Fac.Lettres Strasbourg* 48(1969), pp. 1-6.

GRANJA, F. de la. Don Félix Hernández Giménez (1889-1975). *And.* 40(1975), pp. 225-231.

PAVON MALDONADO, B. Félix Hernandez Giménez. *Bol. Asoc. Esp. Orientalistas* 11(1975), pp. 3-5.

CHALMETA, P. Ambrosio Huici Miranda (1880-1973). *Bol. Asoc. esp. orientalistas* 10(1974), pp. 7-8.

BEGMATOV, E. Sabirdzhan Ibragimov. *ST* 1975(2), pp. 122-124.

SULTANOV, T.I. S.K. Ibragimov i ego istoriko-vostokovedcheskie issledovaniya. *Strany i narody Vostoka pod obshchey red. D.A. Ol'derogge*, X, 1971, pp. 241-248.

MOLLAEV, A. N.I. Il'minskiy o turkmenskom yazyke i etnografii. *ST* 1973(4), pp. 82-86.

HASAN, Syed. Dr. Muhammad Ishaque as I knew him. *Indo-Iranica* 23i-ii(1970), pp. 113-115.

NAIYER, S.A. Haider. Dr. M. Ishaque: a devotee of the temple of learning. *Indo-Iranica* 23i-ii(1970), pp. 116-118.

YUSUF, K.M. My impressions of Dr. Muhammad Ishaque. *Indo-Iranica* 23i-ii (1970), pp. 106-112.

First death anniversary of the Founder. Dr. M. Ishaque. *Indo-Iranica* 23iii (1970), pp. 39-43.

FYZEE, A.A.A. W. Ivanow (1886-1970). *Indo-Iranica* 23iii(1970), pp. 22-27.

FYZEE, A.A.A. Wladimar Ivanow (1886-1970). *JAS Bombay* 45-46(1970-71), pp. 92-97.

CANNON, G. Sir William Jones, language, and the Asiatic Society. *Indian horizons* 22ii(1973), pp. 5-21; 29iii-iv (1973), pp. 27-45.

CANNON, G. Sir William Jones, language, and the Asiatic Society. *Indian horizons* 22 iii-iv(1973), pp. 27-45.

CANNON, G. Sir William Jones, Sir Joseph Banks, and the Royal Society. *Notes and records, Roy. Soc., London* 29(1975), pp. 205-230.

MOJUMDER, Md. Abu Taher. Sir William Jones and the literature of the East. *JAS Bangladesh* 18(1973), pp. 221-229.

KANUS-CREDE, H. In memoriam Heinrich F.J. Junker (d. 3 April 1970). *Iranistische Mitt.* 4(1970), pp. 60-61.

ASLANOV, V.I. M.A. Kazem-Bek - yazykoved. *ST* 1970(6), pp. 62-69.

VAL'SKAYA, B.A. Yakov Vladimirovich Khanykov (1818-1862). *Strany i narody Vostoka pod obshchey red. D.A. Ol'derogge*, X, 1971, pp. 218-240.

BALEGH, Hédi. Tahar Khemiri. *CT* 20(nos. 77-78, 1972), pp. 211-212.

FILYUSHINA, V.N. Mamed Nazarovich Khydyrov. *ST* 1975(4), pp. 118-119.

MARTIN, E.B. James Kirkman, pioneer in East African coastal archaeology. *Kenya past and present* 2i(1973), pp. 40-41.

CZEGLEDY, K. Andrei Nikolaievich Kononov élu membre honoraire de l'Académie des Sciences de Hongrie. *Acta Or.Hung.* 28 (1974), pp. 287.

ISAEV, S.M. Toleubay Rakhimzhanovich Kordabaev. *ST* 1975(4), pp. 119-120.

KRACHKOVSKAYA, V.A. Puteshestvie I. Yu. Krachkovskogo na Blizhniy Vostok (1908-1910 gg.) *Palestinskiy sbornik* 25(88, 1974), pp. 10-19.

GRUNIN, T.I. Agafangel Efimovich Krymskiy (k 100-letiyu so dnya rozhdeniya). *ST* 1971 (1), pp. 70-75.

KOCHIBEY, Yu.N. A.E. Krymskiy v zarubezhnom vostokovedenii. *NAA* 1975(1), pp. 186-192.

SMILYANSKAYA, I.M. Agafangel Efimovich Kruimskiy (k stoletiyu so dnya rozhdeniya). *NAA* 1971 (4), pp. 208-216.

KHAKOV, V. Mukhutdin Khafizetdinovich Kurbangaliev. *ST* 1974(1), pp. 117-118.

GHIRSHMAN, R. Roger Lescot (1917-1975). *Studia Iranica* 9(1975), p. 241.

ADAM, A. Roger Le Tourneau 1907-1971. *L'Afrique et l'Asie modernes* 93-4(1971), pp. 3-7.

I GENERAL

ADAM, A. Roger Le Tourneau. *ROMM* 9(1971), pp. 9-14.

ADAM, A. Roger Le Tourneau (1907-1971). *ROMM* 13-14(1973), pp. 9-13.

ADAM, A. Roger Le Tourneau et le Maroc. *L'Afrique et l'Asie modernes* 93-4(1971), pp. 8-16.

BURKE, E. Roger Le Tourneau, 1907-1971. *IJMES* 3(1972), pp. 361-3.

GOLVIN, L. Roger Le Tourneau, l'homme, le savant. Travaux de Roger Le Tourneau. *ROMM* 10(1971), pp. 9-18.

MANTRAN, R. Roger Le Tourneau. (1907-1971). *Ann.Afr.Nord* 9(1970), pp. ix-xii

RONDOT, P. Roger Le Tourneau et l'Orient. *L'Afrique et l'Asie modernes* 93-4(1971), pp. 17-19.

Roger Le Tourneau (1907-1971). *Cah.de ling. d'orientalisme et de slavistique* 1-2(1973), pp. 1-5.

LEVSHIN
See also XL. n. Emel'chenko.

MANSFIELD, P. Mr. T. Little (1911-1975). *BSMES bull.* 2(1975), pp. 119-120.

UBRYATOVA, E.I. S.E. Malov i ego trudy. *ST* 1975(5), pp. 44-52.

See also XL. a. Fazylov.

See also XL. m. Baskakov.

ELISEEVA, N.V. Arkhiv iranista Yu. N. Marra (1893-1935). *Istoriya, kul'tura, yazuiki narodov Vostoka,* 1970, pp. 59-66

BERNUS, M. *In memoriam* Henri Massé. *BAEO* 6(1970), pp. 12-13.

WIET, M.G. Notice sur la vie et les travaux de M. Henri Massé. *CRAIBL* 1970, pp. 208-221.

MASSÉ, H. L. Massignon et L'Iran. *Louis Massignon* (1970), pp. 97-100

MONTEIL, V., MOUBARAC, Y. Hommage à Louis Massignon. *Etudes philos. et litt. (Actes du Coll. de Mohammédia)* 5(1971), pp. 9-30.

WAARDENBURG, J. L. Massignon's study of religion and Islam: an essay à propos of his Opera Minora. *Oriens* 21-22(1968-69), pp. 136-158.

BLAGOVA, G.F. P.M. Melioranskiy i izuchenie tyurkskoy toponimii. *Tyurkologicheskiy sbornik* 1972 *(Pamyati P.M. Melioranskogo),* pp. 51-61.

KONONOV, A.N. P.M. Melioranskiy i otechestvennaya tyurkologiya. *Sov. Tyurkologiya* 1970(1), pp. 16-23.

KONONOV, A.N. P.M. Melioranskiy i otechestvennaya tyurkologiya. *Tyurkologichesiy sbornik* 1972 *(Pamyati P.M. Melioranskogo),* pp. 7-17.

POPOV, A.I. P.M. Melioranskiy i izuchenie tyurkizmov v russkom yazyke. *Tyurkologicheskiy sbornik* 1972 *(Pamyati P.M. Melioranskogo),* pp. 36-50.

SHCHERBAK, A.M. P.M. Melioranskiy i izuchenie pamyatnikov tyurkskoy pis'mennosti. *Tyurkologicheskiy sbornik* 1972 *(Pamyati P.M. Melioranskogo),* pp. 24-35.

TENISHEV, E.R. P.M. Melioranskiy -- yazykoved. *Tyurkologicheskiy sbornik* 1972 *(Pamyati P.M. Melioranskogo),* pp. 18-23.

GIGNOUX, Ph. Jean de Menasce (1902-1973). *Studia Iranica* 2(1973), pp. 133.

LAZARD, G. Jean de Menasce (1902-1973). *JA* 262(1974), pp. 265-270.

NASTER, P. George C. Miles. *Rev. belge num.* 121(1975), pp. 196.

BURGOS, F.C. José Maria Millás Vallicrosa. In memoriam. *Bol.de la Real Academia de la Historia* 916(1970), pp. 217-221

VERNET, J. *In memoriam* José M. Millás Vallicrosa. *BAEO* 7(1971), pp. 5-6.

A.F. Miller, 1901-1973. *Etudes Balkaniques* 10(1974) (1), p. 147.

Anatoliy Filipovich Miller (1901-1973). *NAA* 1974(1), pp. 245-247.

Anatoliy Filippovich Miller. *Vopr.ist.* 1973(11), pp. 220-221.

LANG, D.M. Vladimir Fedorovich Minorsky. *Yād-nāme-ye Irāni-ye Minorsky,* 1969, pp. xiv.

ADAMOCIĆ, M. Giovanni Molino und seine türkische Grammatik. *Acta ling. Hung.* 24(1974), pp. 37-67.

BEŠEVLIEV, V. Gyula Moravcsik, 1892-1972. *Etudes Balkaniques* 9(1973) (2), pp. 147-148.

GODARD, Y.A. Quand? Hier.....un jour..... non autrefois... [Recollections of Said Naficy.] *Mélange d'iranologie en mémoir de feu Said Naficy,* 1972, pp. 93-95.

GUYOUNACHVILI, L. Saīd Naficy et la littérature russe. *Mélange d'iranologie en mémoir de feu Said Naficy,* 1972, pp. 105-109.

MILLOT, J.A. Souvenir de Said Naficy. *Mélange d'iranologie en mémoir de feu Said Naficy,* 1972, pp. 96-99.

BAUSANI, A. Nallino e l'Islam. *Levante* 20i(1973), pp. 24-32.

BORRUSO, A. C.A. Nallino: attualità del suo insegnamento. *Levante* 20i(1973), pp. 73-77.

CASTRO, F. Carlo Alfonso Nallino e i diritti orientali. *Levante* 20i(1973), pp. 67-72.

I GENERAL

CERQUA, C.S. Carlo Alfonso Nallino e il dialetto egiziano. *Levante* 20i(1973), pp. 54-59.

CERULLI, E. Ricordo di Carlo Alfonso Nallino. *Levante* 20i(1973), pp. 7-10.

GABRIELI, F. Nallino e la letteratura araba. *Levante* 20i(1973), pp. 42-46.

MINGANTI, P. Carlo Alfonso Nallino e le scienze presso gli arabi. *Levante* 20i (1973), pp. 47-53.

NALLINO, M. Momenti essenziali nella vita e nella carriera scientifica di mio padre. *Levante* 20i(1973), pp. 11-23.

RIZZITANO, U. C.A. Nallino e i musulmani di Sicilia. *Levante* 20i(1973), pp. 78-84.

RUBINACCI, R. Carlo Alfonso Nallino e l'Islam scismatico. *Levante* 20i(1973), pp. 33-41.

VACCA, V. Nallino e l'Istituto per l'Oriente. *Levante* 20i(1973), pp. 60-66.

CASTRO, F. Ricordo di Maria Nallino. *Ann. Fac.Ling.Lett.stran.Ca' Foscari* 5(1974), pp. 241-245.

GABRIELI, Fr. In memoria di Maria Nallino. *Levante* 22i(1975), pp. 7-9.

MINGANTI, P. Maria Nallino (1908-1974). 54(1974), pp. 560-563.

PAREJA, F.M. Maria Nallino. *Bol. Asoc. Esp. Orientalistas* 11(1975), pp. 5-6.

LIGETI, L. Julius Németh zum gruss. *Acta ling. Acad. Sci. Hung.* 20(1970), pp. 241-244.

ULLENDORFF, E. A letter from Th. Nöldeke to E. Mittwoch. *BSOAS* 34(1971), pp. 5-8

DUCHESNE-GUILLEMIN, J. Nécrologie. Henrik S. Nyberg. *JA* 263(1975), pp. 1-2.

KANUS-CREDE, H. In memoriam Henrik Samuel Nyberg (1889-1974). *Iranistische Mitt.* 9(1975), pp. 3-16.

RINGGREN, H. Henrik Samuel Nyberg. *Bol. Asoc. esp. orientalistas* 10(1974), p. 3.

RUNDGREN, Fr. Henrik Samuel Nyberg. *Acta Iranica,* 2. sér. *Monumentum H.S. Nyberg,* I (1975), pp. 7-14.

UTAS, B. Henrik Samuel Nyberg. *Acta Iranica,* 2. sér. *Monumentum H.S. Nyberg,* I (1975), pp. 1-5.

UTAS, B. Henrik Samuel Nyberg 28. XII. 1889-9. II. 1974. *Acta Or.* 36(1974), pp. 5-9.

WIDENGREN, G. Henrik Samuel Nyberg and Iranian studies, in the light of personal reminiscences. *Acta Iranica,* 2. sér. *Monumentum H.S. Nyberg,* II (1975), pp. 419-456.

MONROE, E. Arabia. St. John Philby's contribution to pre-Islamic studies. *Proc. 6th Seminar for Arabian studies,* 1972, pp. 29-35.

GUSEYNOV, R.A. N.V. Pigulevskaya i tyurkologiya. *ST* 1974(1), pp. 52-57.

HAUSSIG, H.W. Nina Viktorowna Pigulevskaja (1894-1970). *ZDMG* 121(1971), pp. 1-6

SELLHEIM, R. Martin Plessner. (Ein Nachruf). *Der Islam* 52(1975), pp. 1-5.

SEBAG, P. In memoriam. Louis Poinssot (1879-1967). *CT* 19, nos. 75-76(1971), p. 241-244.

KANUS-CREDE, H. In memoriam Arthur Upham Pope (1881-1969). *Iranistische Mitt.* 4 (1970), pp. 41-47.

SECRET, Fr. Notes sur G. Postel. *Bibliothèque d'humanisme et de renaissance* 35(1973), pp. 85-101; 37(1975), pp. 101-119.

KURBANOV, A.A., KUZMIN, O.D. Aleksandr Petrovich Potzeluevskiy. *Sov. Tyurkologiya* 1972(2), pp. 88-94.

KANUS-CREDE, H. In memoriam Ebrahim Poure Davoud (1886-1968). *Iranistische Mitt.* 4(1970), pp. 3-33.

DZHIKIYA, S.S. Ob uchenykh trudakh iranista [V.S. Puturidze]. *Vostochnaya filologiya. Philologia Orientalis.* II (Pamyati V.S. Puturidze), 1972, pp. 10-16.

DZHIKIYA, S.S. Ob uchenykh trudakh iranista. (V.S. Puturidze.) *Philologia orientalis* II, 1972, pp. 10-16.

SHANIDZE, A.G. Zametka o nauchnoy deyatel'nosti Vladimira Sardionovicha Puturidze. *Vostochnaya filologiya. Philologia Orientalis.* II(Pamyati V.S. Puturidze, 1972, pp. 7-9.

BLAGOVA, G.F. V.V. Radlov i izuchenie tyurkskoy toponimi v aspekte sovremennykh toponimicheskikh problem. *Tyurkolog. sbornik (Pamyati V.V. Radlova,* 1972), pp. 102-131.

KONONOV, A.N. V.V. Radlov i otechestvennaya tyurkologiya. *Tyurkolog. sbornik (Pamyati V.V. Radlova,* 1972), pp. 7-15.

NASILOV, D.M. V.V. Radlov i izuchenie drevneuygurskikh pamyatnikov. *Tyurkolog. sbornik (Pamyati V.V. Radlova,* 1972), pp. 64-101.

SHCHBERBAK, A.M. V.V. Radlov i izuchenie pamyatnikov runicheskoy pis'mennosti. *Tyurkolog. sbornik (Pamyati V.V. Radlova,* 1972), pp. 54-63.

SIL'CHENKO, M.S. V.V. Radlov i izuchenie tyurkskogo fol'klora. *Tyurkolog. sbornik (Pamyati V.V. Radlova,* 1972), pp. 16-19.

I GENERAL

TENISHEV, E.R. V.V. Radlov - fonetist i grammatist. *Tyurkolog. sbornik (Pamyati V.V. Radlova,* 1972), pp. 32-41.

TUGUSHEVA, L.Yu. V.V.Radlov - leksikograf i leksikolog. *Tyurkolog. sbornik (Pamyati V.V. Radlova,* 1972), pp. 42-53.

VAYNSHTEYN, S.I., KLYASHTORNYY, S.G. V.V. Radlov i istoriko-etnograficheskoe izuchenie tyurkskikh narodov. *Tyurkolog. sbornik (Pamyati V.V. Radlova,* 1972), pp. 20-31.

LATHAM, J.D. The Raja of Mahmudabad (1914-1973). *BSMES bull.* 1(1974-5), pp. 41-43.

LIGETI, L. Le professeur L. Rasonyi. *Acta Or.Hung.* 28(1974), pp. 147-150

STROHMAIER, G. Johann Jacob Reiske - der Märtyrer der arabischen Literatur. *Das Altertum* 20(1974), pp. 166-179.

KANUS-CREDĚ, H. In memoriam Christian H. Rempis (1901-1972) mit Schriftenverzeichnis. *Iranistische Mitt.* 7(1973), pp. 1-10.

DUBIŃSKI, A. Jan Reychman -- uczony, pedagog, popularyzator nauki. *Przegl. Or.* 1(93, 1975), pp. 5-11.

MEIER, F. Hellmut Ritter. *Der Islam* 48 (1971-2), pp. 193-205

PLESSNER, M. Hellmut Ritter (1892-1971). *ZDMG* 122(1972), pp. 6-18.

WALZER, R. Hellmut Ritter 27.2.1892 - 19.5. 1971. *Oriens* 23-24(1974), pp. 1-6.

ŠAKI, Manṣūr. In memoriam Jan Rypka (1886-1968). *Iranistische Mitteilungen* 3ii(1969), pp. i-iv.

Publications and articles about Jan Rypka. *Yádnáme-ye Jan Rypka* 1967, pp. 16-17.

SUĆESKA, A. In memoriam Dr. Hazim Šabanović. *Prilozi za or. filol.* 18-19(1968-9), pp. 5-7.

AZIMOV, P., CHARYYAROV, B. A.N. Samoylovich i turkmenskoe yazykoznanie. *ST* 1973(5), pp. 71-75.

FAZYLOV, E.I. A.N. Samoylovich - issledovatel' tyurkskikh pamyatnikov srednevekov'ya. *ST* 1973(5), pp. 58-65.

KONONOV, A.N. A.N. Samoylovich - grammatist. *ST* 1973(5), pp. 37-48.

MUSAEV, K.M. A.N. Samoylovich i sravnitel'naya leksikologiya tyurkskikh yazykov. *ST* 1973(5), pp. 49-57.

NASILOV, D.M. A.N. Samoylovich o klassifikatzii tyurkskikh yazykov. *ST* 1973(5), pp. 76-83.

NURALIEV, D. A.N. Samoylovich - issledovatel' turkmenskoy literatury i folklora. *ST* 1973(5), pp. 66-70.

CHOWDHURI, Jogindranath. Acharya Jadunath Sarkar (1870-1958) and a sketch of his works. *BPP* 94(1975), pp. 57-64.

DATTA, Kali Kinkar Acharya Jadunath Sarkar and the Indian Historical Records Commission. *Indo-Iranica* 24i-ii(1971), pp. 16-19.

RAY, Atul Chandra. Sir Jadunath Sarkar: as a man and a historian. *Indo-Iranica* 24i-ii(1971), pp. 20-28.

SARKAR, Jagadish Narayan. Thoughts on Acharya Jadunath Sarkar. *Indo-Iranica* 24i-ii(1971), pp. 1-15.

Sir Jadunath Sarkar: a biographical sketch. *Indo-Iranica* 24i-ii(1971), pp. 48-49.

GABRIELI, F. In Memoria di Tommaso Sarnelli. *OM* 53(1973), p. 182.

PAREJA, F.M. *In memoriam* Joseph Schacht. *BAEO* 6(1970), pp. 9-10.

GRAY, B. Obituary. Eric Schroeder. *Iran* 10(1972), pp. vi-vii

BOSCH VILA, J. Luis Seco de Lucena Paredes. *Bol. Assoc. esp. orientalistas* 10(1974), pp. 4-7.

ASLANOV, V.I., ALEKPEROV, A.K. Ervand Vladimirovich Sevortyan (k 70-letiyu so dnya rozhdeniya). *ST* 1971(5), pp. 139-141.

HAMĪDULLAH, M. Muhammad Shafī. (6/8/1883-14/3/1963). *Islâm Tetkikleri Enstitüsü dergisi* 4(1964), pp. 81-83.

LÓPEZ GARCÍA, B. F.J. Simonet ante el colonialismo (1859-1863): unos artículos en *La América*. *Cuadernos de historia del Islam, ser. misc.: Islamica occidentalia* 1(1971), pp. 159-178.

ISAACS, H. Sir Harry Sinderson Pasha (1891-1974). *BSMES bull.* 2(1975), pp. 55-56.

GHIRSHMAN, R. Maxime Siroux (1907-1975). *Studia Iranica* 4(1975), pp. 239-240.

V.D. Smirnov *See* XXIX. c. Tveritinova.

V.D. Smirnov *See also* XLI. a. Mashtakova.

PRUETT, G.E. History, transcendence, and world community in the work of Wilfred Cantwell Smith. *J.Amer.Acad.Religion* 41 (1973), pp. 573-590.

ZAIDI, M.H. Aloys Sprengers Beitrag zum Urdu-Studium. *XVIII. Deutscher Orientalistentag 1972: Vorträge,* pp. 259-265.

LATHAM, J.D. *In memoriam* S.M. Stern. *BAEO* 6(1970), pp. 11-12.

WALZER, R. Samuel M. Stern. In memoriam. *In memoriam S.M. Stern* (Israel Or. studies, II, 1972), pp. 1-14.

CHENNOUFI, Ali. Le Cheikh Tahar Ben Achour (1879-1973). *CT* 20(nos.77-78, 1972), pp. 205-206.

I GENERAL

VESELÝ, R. Prof. Dr. Felix Tauer zum 80. Lebensjubiläum. *Archiv or.* 41(1973), pp. 305-307.

GOLVIN, L. Henri Terrasse (1895-1971). Publications d'Henri Terrasse. *ROMM* 12(1972), pp. 7-21.

HUBERT, J. M. Henri Terrasse. *CRAIBL* (1971), pp. 592-596.

LAOUST, H. Henri Terrasse (1895-1971). *REI* 40(1972), pp. 3-6.

BECKINGHAM, C.F. Arthur Stanley Tritton. *BSOAS* 37(1974), pp. 446-447.

GROZDANOVA, E. A.S. Tveritinova, 1910-1973. *Etudes Balkaniques* 10(1974) (2), pp. 246-247.

Anna Stepanovna Tveritinova (1910-1973). *NAA* 1974(2), pp. 248-249.

Anna Stepanovna Tveritinova (1910-1973). *Pis'mennye pamyatniki Vostoka* 1970, pp. 465-466.

(Anon) Isaak Natanovich Vinnikov. Voprosy filologii stran Azii i Afriki, 1. *Sbornik I.N. Vinnikova,* 1971, pp. 3-14

ZLATKIN, I. Ya. Akademnik B. Ya. Vladimirtzov--istorik-vostokoved. *NAA* 1975(6), pp. 201-217.

ABEL, A. In memoriam. G.-E. von Grünebaum (1909-1972). *Corresp. d'Orient. Etudes* 17-18(1970), pp. 3-5.

BANANI, Amin. G.E. Von Grunebaum: toward relating Islamic studies to universal cultural history. *IJMES* 6(1975), pp. 140-147.

BANANI, Amin. In memoriam: Gustav Edmund von Grunebaum, *Iranian stud.* 4(1971), p. 103.

CAHEN, C. Notice nécrologique. Gustave E. von Grunebaum. *JESHO* 15(1972), pp. 1-2.

GABRIELI, F. Gustave E. von Grunebaum. *J. Or. Inst. Baroda.* 21(1972), pp. 87-88.

ROSENTHAL, F. In memoriam: Gustave E. von Grunebaum, 1909-1972. *IJMES* 4(1973), pp. 355-358.

SPULER, B. Gustav Edmund von Grunebaum (1909-1972). *Der Islam* 49(1972), p.248.

K., E. Professor G.E. von Grunebaum. *M.E.Stud.* 8(1972), pp. 439-440.

Gustave von Grunebaum. *MEJ* 26(1972), p.161.

See also I. b. 1. Laroui.

CAHEN, C. Notice nécrologique: Gaston Wiet. *JESHO* 14(1971), pp. 223-226

DUVAL, P.M. Notice sur la vie et les travaux de M. Gaston Wiet. *CRAIBL* 1974, pp. 477-485.

ÉLISSÉEFF, N. Gaston Wiet (1887-1971). *JA* 259(1971), pp. 1-9

HUBERT, J. M. Gaston Wiet. *CRAIBL* (1971), pp. 253-256.

LAOUST, H. Gaston Wiet (1887-1971). *REI* 39(1971), pp. 205-207.

ROSEN-AYALON, M. Gaston Wiet, 1887-1971. *Kunst des Orients* 8(1972), pp. 154-159.

PISCATORI, J. Quincy Wright's contribution to Middle Eastern studies. *MEJ* 29(1975), pp. 33-46.

BIYALIEV, A., ORUSBAEV, A. Konstantin Kuzmich Yudakhin, 1890-1975. *NAA* 1975 (4), pp. 246-248.

LAMBTON, A.K.S. Robert Charles Zaehner. *BSOAS* 38(1975), pp. 623-624.

SHARIF, Ahmed. Obituary: Mr. Mohammad Zahurul Islam. *JAS Pak.* 15(1970), pp. 166-168.

CLAUSON, G. Obituary. Professor Dr. Ananiasz Zajączkowski. *JRAS* 1970, p. 230

TRYJARSKI, E. *In memoriam* Ananiasz Zajaczkowski. *BAEO* 7(1971), pp. 7-9.

KUZNETZOVA, N.A. B.N. Zakhoder i ego trudui po istoriografii i istochnikovedeniyu. *Iran (Pamyati B.N. Zakhodera),* 1971, pp. 4-15

KONONOV, A.N. Viktor Maksimovich Zhirmunskiy kak tyurkolog. *ST* 1971(2), pp. 102-107.

Akademnik V.M. Zhirmunskiy kak yazykoved. *Vopr. yaz.* 4(1971), pp. 3-14.

c BIBLIOGRAPHY

i General. Bibliographies of bibliographies

ANGHELESCU, M. et BADICUT, I.T. Romano-Arabica (bibliographie sélective). *Romano-Arabica,* ed. M. Anghelescu, 1974, pp. 115-132.

BIJLEFELD, W.A. Introducing Islam: a bibliographical essay. *MW* 63(1973), pp. 171-184, 269-279.

BROUWERS, P. The Arabic language and books today. *Abr-nahrain* 12(1971-2), pp. 27-39

BROUWERS, P. Le livre arabe dans le monde. *Travaux et jours* 40(1971), pp. 39-56.

EICKELMAN, C. Directory of films on the Middle East. *MESA Bull.* 9ii(1975), pp. 45-57.

FAHD, Toufic. L'Islam, chronique bibliographique. *Rev.d'hist.et de philos.rel.* 5 (1971), pp. 175-190

I GENERAL

LANDAU, J.M. Some Soviet bibliographies on the Middle East. *ME stud.* 9(1973), pp. 227-230.

LANDAU, J.M. Some Soviet works on Islam. *Middle Eastern stud.* 9(1973), pp. 358-362.

LANDAU, J.M. Some Soviet Works on Modern Arabic Literature. *ME stud.* 7(1971), pp. 363-365.

MUDARRÈS, Jinan. Récentes études en arabe sur l'histoire et l'archéologie du Moyen-Orient ancien. *Berytus* 19(1970), pp. 151-158.

NURUDINOVIĆ, B. Bibliografija jugoslavenske orijentalistike 1961-1962. godine. (Bibliography of Yugoslav Oriental studies, 1961-1962.) *POF* 20-21(1970-71), pp. 441-523.

PEARSON, J.D. Notes on Islamic bibliography. *Comparative librarianship: essays in honour of D.N. Marshall,* 1973, pp. 199-207.

PEARSON, J.D. Towards total bibliographical control of Islamic studies. *BSMES bull.* 2(1975), pp. 112-116.

RIIS, P.J. Litteratur om klassisk og naerorientalsk arkaeologi i Danmark 1968-1972. *Historisk tidsskrift* Copenhagen 75(1975), pp. 77-105.

SCHEIBER, A. Ein mittelalterliches hebräisch-arabisches Bücherverzeichnis aus der Genisa. *Acta Or. Hung.* 29(1975), pp. 247-263.

SELLHEIM, R. Das Todesdatum des Ibn an-Nadim. *In memoriam S.M. Stern* (Israel Or. studies, II, 1972), pp. 428-432.

SHUISKI, S. Annual bibliography of works on Arabic literature published in the Soviet Union (1973). *J. Arabic lit.* 6 (1975), pp. 146-150.

VUCINICH, W.S. Soviet studies on the Middle East. *The Soviet Union and the Middle East,* ed. I.J. Lederer and W.S. Vucinich, 1974, pp. 177-229.

Book development in Arab countries: A Unesco report. *Cah. d'hist. mondiale* 14(1972), pp. 922-939.

Esquisse d'une bibliographie des traductions d'oeuvres philosophiques de langue arabe en langues européenes. *Études philos. et litt.* 3(1968), pp. 25-33

Ideologiya i taktika sovremennogo Islama za rubezhom. Ukazatel' rabot sovetskikh avtorov za 1952-1972 gg. *Religiya i obshchestvennaya mysl' stran Vostoka,* 1974, pp. 320-335.

Published books and Ph.D. dissertations in the field of Asian and African studies in the years 1971-1975 by faculty members of Israeli universities (Jewish studies excluded). *Asian and African studies* [Jerusalem] 10(1975), pp. 330-334.

Work in progress in British universities. *BSMES bull.* 1(1974-5), pp. 94-102; 2(1975), pp. 23-39, 100-104.

See also II. a. 1. Bijlefeld.

See also II. a. 2. *Europe.* Popovic.

See also II. a. 4. Sokolović.

See also II. a. 5. Bijlefeld.

See also II. c. 2. Brenner.

See also II. c. 2. Caspar.

See also II. d. 2. Nader

See also II. d. 2. Niewöhner

See also IX. a. Gabrieli.

See also IX. n. Gibbons.

See also XXXVI. h. Ghali.

See also XXXVII. i. Brockway.

See also XXXVII. l. Khoury.

ii Periodicals and their indexes

FONTAINE, J. Mouvement des revues tunisiennes en 1970. *IBLA* 127 (1971), pp. 183-184.

FONTAINE, J. Mouvement des revues tunisiennes en 1971. *IBLA* 35(no.129, 1972), pp. 175-176.

FONTAINE, J. Mouvement des revues tunisiennes en 1973. *IBLA* 37(no.133, 1974), pp. 190-192.

FONTAINE, J. Bilan des revues tunisiennes en 1974. *IBLA* 38,no.135(1975), pp. 169-173.

KECSKEMÉTI, I. Inhalt der Studia Orientalia I-XXXIX. *SO* 40(1971): iv, pp. 13.

LANDAU, J.M. Russian journals dealing with the Middle East. *ME studies* 7(1971), pp. 237-239

MASCERANHAS, L. Islamic reviews in Pakistan in English and Urdu. *Al-Mushir* 13vii-viii(1971), pp. 1-14

PELLAT, Ch. Les *Studia Islamica* ont vingt ans. *Arabica* 21(1974), pp. 1-10.

Alfavitnyy ukazatel statey, pomeshchennykh v "Epigrafike Vostoka" (XI-XX). *Ep.Vost.* 20(1971), pp. 117-121.

Bibliography of Urdu periodicals. Compiled by staff of Indian Institute of Islamic Studies. *Studies in Islam* 9(1972), pp. 167-259.

List of contents Nos. 1-20. *Tahqiqat-e eqtesadi* 8(no.21, 1971), pp. 137-145.

I GENERAL

Index to Asian and African studies, vol. i-x, 1965-1975. *Asian and African studies* [Jerusalem] 10(1975), pp. 335-338.

Tables décennales des Cahiers de Tunisie (1963-1972). *CT* 21(nos. 83-84, 1973), pp. 1-99.

See also III. a. 1. Mahmassani.

See also XXXI. k. Haghighi.

See also XL. a. Shiraliev

iii Publications of congresses, societies, institutions

CHIAUZZI, G. Attività editoriale del Ministero delle Informazioni di Libia. *OM* 54 (1974), pp. 475-478.

See also I. c. 7. Ende.

iv Individual countries and areas

Afghanistan

AKRAM, M. Bibliographie de l'Afghanistan. *Afghanistan* 27iii(1974), pp. 83-95; 27iv (1975), pp. 95-101.

MILLER, S.G. Research facilities in Afghanistan. *MESA Bull.* 9i(1975), pp. 31-41.

NILSON, D.L.F., NUR, Fazel, and KAMAL, Sajida A partially annotated bibliography of Afghan linguistics. *Afghanistan* 23i(1970), pp. 43-56; 23iii, pp. 65-72; 23iv, pp. 57-67.

Central Asia

HUSSEYNOV, R. Publications relatives aux études azerbaïdjanaises et de l'Albanie caucasienne. *Bedi Kartlisa* 33(1975), pp. 345-349.

MANZI, E. Recenti studi geografici sulla Siberia e l'Estremo Oriente Sovietico. *Riv. geog. ital.* 79(1972), pp. 412-417.

REYCHMAN, J. Ostatnie prace o polskim wkladzie w badania ludów Azji Pólnocno Wschodniej. (Les derniers travaux concernant l'apport polonais aux recherches sur les peuples de l'Asie Nord-Orientale.) *Przeglad or.* 1(81, 1972), pp. 63-66

See also XXXIV. d. Bennigsen

Egypt

ANAWATI, G.C. Textes arabes anciens édités en Egypte au cours des annees 1969 à 1971. *MIDEO* 11(1972), pp. 275-289.

ANAWATI, G.C. Textes arabes anciens édités en Egypte au cours des années 1969 à 1973. *MIDEO* 12(1974), pp. 91-186.

Iran. Iranian studies

AHMED, Munir D. Iranbibliographien; eine Übersicht. *Iranist.Mitt.* 7(1973), pp. 2-21.

BORSHCHEVSKY, Yu. E. and BREGEL, Yu. E. The preparation of a Bio-bibliographical survey of Persian literature. *IJMES* 3(1972), pp. 169-186

FOUCHÉCOUR, C.H. de. Les Iranica dans la deuxième édition de l'encyclopédie de l'Islam. *Stud. iranica* 1(1972), pp. 313-333.

KATRAK, Jamshid Cawasji. Gujarati literature on Iranology. *Commémoration Cyprus. Hommage universel,* I, 1974, pp. 360-378.

KRÍKAVOVÁ, A. Kurdische bibliographien. *Arch. or.* 41(1973), pp. 71-73.

MACHALSKI, Fr. La littérature de l'Iran en Pologne (aperçu bio-bibliographique). *Acta Iranica,* sér. 1, III, 1974, pp. 397-410.

See also XXXVIII. d. *Ossetic* Richter

See also XXXIX. a. Wilber

Middle East

AKBARABADI, Sa'id Ahmed Contribution of India to Arabic language and literature since independence. *India and the Arab World, ed. by S. Maqbul Ahmed,* 1969, pp. 24-28.

LANDAU, J.M. Soviet books on Israel. *ME stud.* 10(1974), pp. 348-350.

LANDAU, J.M. Soviet books on the Yemen. *ME stud.* 10(1974), pp. 234-237.

SOURDEL, D. Récentes éditions de textes arabes. *REI* 41(1973), pp. 159-164.

THODEN, R. Irakische Bibliographien und Bibliothekskataloge. *Dokumentationsdienst Moderner Orient, Mitt.* 4i(1975), pp. 54-59.

VOGEL, E.K. Bibliography of Holy Land sites. *HUCA* 42(1971), pp. 1-96.

Selected bibliography. *Crescent and star,* ed. by Y. Alexander and N.N. Kittrie, 1973, pp. 469-486.

See also XXII. c. Green, Stookey.

See also XXXVI. 1. Mangion

See also XXXVII.1. Alwan

North Africa

AMAN, Mohammed M. Bibliographical activities of the Arab countries of North Africa. *Int. libr. R.* 2(1970), pp. 263-273.

BAZAMA, M.M. Biblio - Libica 1841 - 1968. *J. Fac. Arts. R. Univ. Malta* 5(1973), pp. 253-260.

BROWN, W.A. The Bakka'iyya books of Timbuktu. *Res. Bull. CAD Ibadan* 3i(1967), pp. 40-44.

BURKE, E., III Recent books on colonial Algerian history. *ME studies* 7(1971), pp. 241-250.

FONTAINE, J. Bibliographie littéraire tunisienne 1972-1973. *J. Arabic lit.* 6(1975), pp. 151-153.

HARIKI, G. Bibliographie historique (1968-1969) Maroc-Espagne musulmane. *Bull.Soc. hist. Maroc* 2(1969), pp. 61-70.

MÖLLER, T., WICHMANN, U. Ausgewählte neuere Literatur zur Strategie und Politik im Maghreb. *Afrika Spectrum* 3/70, pp. 58-65.

PETIT, R. Bibliographie générale. *Recueil d'études sur les moriscos andalous en Tunisie,* préparé par M. de Epalza et R. Petit, 1973, pp. 9-15.

VALETTE, J. Le Maghreb. (Chronique de l'histoire d'Outre-Mer.) *Rev. franç. d'hist. d'outre-mer* 60(1973), pp. 616-643.

See also II. a. 2. *Africa.* Nimtz.

See also IX. f. Ende.

See also XLII. Galand.

Turkey. Turkish studies

Cyprus

LANDAU, J.M. Some Soviet works on Cyprus. *M.E.stud.* 11(1975), pp. 302-305.

MUMCU, Ahmet. Fragen der osmanischen Bibliographie. *Der Islam* 52(1975), pp. 119-124.

RICHTER, Erich. Die aserbaidschanische Bibliographie. Ein kurzer Überblick über die von der Bücherkammer der Aserbaidschanischen SSR in Baku herausgegebene laufende Bibliographie. *Biblos* 22(1973), pp. 329-342.

TIETZE, A. Turkologischer Anzeiger (*TA* 1). *WZKM* 67(1975), pp. 339-488.

Bibliographie de travaux turcologues français. *Turcica* 7(1975), pp. 264-303.

See also VIII. d. *Turkey* Du Quesne-Bird

See also XVI. c. Henry, Taleb-Bendiab.

See also XX. b. Taha.

See also XXVIII. v. Mastepanov

See also XXIX. c. Kappert
Kellner
Wurm

See also XXXIX. a. Wilber.

See also XL. a. Hattori

See also XL. f. Richter

See also XL. t. Asylgaraeva.

See also XL. z. Richter

See also XLI. a. Popovic.

See also XLI. a. Walsh.

v Individual scholars

WALKER, P.E. A bibliography of the books and articles of Professor Aziz Suryal Atiya. *Medieval and Middle Eastern studies ... A. S. Atiya* 1972, pp. 9-15.

DOERFER, G. Zum Schrifttum des kazantatarischen Gelehrten Üzbäk Bajčura. *UAJ* 46 (1974), pp. 149-157.

Spisok rabot chlena-korrespondenta AN TadzhSSR, Doktora filologicheskikh nauk professora I.S. Braginskogo, opublikovannykh v 1965-1975 gg. *NAA* 1975(3), pp. 220-223.

LEFORT, M. Index de l'oeuvre historique de Marius Canard. *Arabica* 22(1975), pp. 180-211.

See also I. b. 3. Carra de Vaux.

SLOMP, J. Bibliography of works published by Kenneth Cragg. *Al-Mushir* 14i-ii(1972), pp. 1-3.

Bibliographie des Schrifttums von Ernst Diez. *Beiträge zur Kunstgeschichte Asiens. In memoriam E. Diez,* 1963, pp. xiii-xv

Herbert W. Duda. *WZKM* 67(1975), pp. vii-viii.

NURJDINOVIĆ, Bisera. Bibliografija radova Glišе Elezovića. *Prilozi Or.Fil.Ist.* 14-15(1964-5), pp. 425-441

TABOROFF, J.H. Bibliography of the writings of Richard Ettinghausen. *Studies in art and literature of the Near East in honor of R. Ettinghausen,* 1974, pp. 5-25.

DÁVID, G. A bibliography of the works of Prof. Julius Germanus. *The Middle East; studies in honour of J. Germanus,* 1974, pp. 253-264.

BENZING, W. Bibliography of W.B. Henning. Addenda. *Iranistische Mitt.* 2(1968), pp. 86-92.

Henning. *See also* I. b. 3.

DAFTRY, Farhad Bibliography of the publications of the late W. Ivanov. *IC* 45(1971), pp. 55-67

Schriftenverzeichnis Gotthard Jäschke. *WI* 15(1974), pp. 5-25.

SCHIEMANN, L. Schriftenverzeichnis Hans Joachim Kissling. *Islamkundliche Abhandlungen H.J. Kissling,* 1974, pp. 9-16.

Le Tourneau *See* I. b. 3.

DULINA, N.A. Spisok trudov P.M. Melioranskogo i literatury o nem. *Tyurkologicheskiy sbornik* 1972 *(Pamyati P.M. Melioranskogo)*, pp. 396-400.

BACHARACH, J., KOUYMJIAN, D. A bibliography of the works of George C. Miles. *Near Eastern numismatics ... Studies in honor of G.C. Miles*, 1974, pp. xvii-xxv.

List of publications by V. Minorsky. *Yād-nāme-ye Irāni-ye Minorsky*, 1969, pp. xv-xxxi.

GYOUNACHVILI, Djamchide. Etude et propagation de l'oeuvre scientifique et littéraire de Said Naficy en URSS. *Mélange d'iranologie en mémoir de feu Said Naficy*, 1972, pp. 100-104.

Bibliografia degli scritti di C.A. Nallino. *Levante* 20i(1973), pp. 88-99.

Bibliografia degli scritti di Maria Nallino. *OM* 54(1974), pp. 564-565.

TOLL, Chr. Bibliographie H.S. Nyberg. *Acta Iranica*, 2. sér. *Monumentum H.S. Nyberg*, I (1975), pp. IX-XXXI.

Nachträge zur Bibliographie von H.S. Nyberg. *Iranistische Mitt.* 9(1975), pp. 17.

Spisok opublikovannykh i neopublikovannykh rabot V.S. Puturidze. *Vostochnaya filologiya. Philologia Orientalis.* II (Pamyati V.S. Puturidze), 1972, pp. 27-34.

DULINA, N.A. Khronologicheskiy perechen' trudov V.V. Radlova i literatury o nem. *Tyurkolog. sbornik (Pamyati V.V. Radlova*, 1972), pp. 261-279.

Bibliography [of the works by Jan Rypka]. *Yádnáme-ye Jan Rypka* 1967, pp. 10-15.

KUZNETZOVA, N.A. Obzor arkhiva akademika AN Tadzhikskoy SSR A.A. Semenova. *Iran* (Pamyati B.N. Zakhodera), 1971, pp. 28-40

PARROT, A. et al. Hommage à Ivan Stchoukine. *Syria* 49(1972), pp. 247-251.

Profesor von Grunebaum-Bibliografia. *Estudios or.* 7(1972), pp. 176-192.

KLEINKNECHT, A. List of the published works of Richard Walzer. *Islamic philosophy and the classical tradition:* essays presented to R. Walzer, 1972, pp. 5-16.

Zakhoder. *See also* I. b. 3.

vi Individual works and writers

BERNARDINI-MAZZINI, A. Abû l-Qâsim al-Šâbbî: bibliographie et oeuvres. *IBLA* (no.131, 1973), pp. 97-117.

KANAZI, G. The works of Abū Hilāl al-'Askarī. *Arabica* 22(1975), pp. 61-70.

KUDSI-ZADEH, A.A. Sayyid Jamāl al-Dīn al-Afghānī: a supplementary bibliography. *MW* 65(1975), pp. 279-291.

POLOSIN, V.V. Ob odnom pis'mennom istochnike "Fikhrista" Ibn an-Nadīma. *Pis'mennye pamyatniki Vostoka* 1971, pp. 86-108.

RAFEQ, Abdul-Karim. Ibn Abi'l-Surūr and his works. *BSOAS* 38(1975), pp. 24-31.

SALEH, Moustapha Abū'l-ʿAlā' al-Maʿarrī (363-449/973-1057). Bibliographie critique. Deuxième partie. *BEO* 23(1970), pp. 197-309

Bibliography of Ṭāhā Ḥusayn. *J. Arabic lit.* 6(1975), pp. 141-145.

See also II. d. 2. Bergé.

vii Typography

DIEHL, K.S. Lucknow printers 1820-1850. *Comparative librarianship: essays in honour of D.N. Marshall*, 1973, pp. 115-128.

ENDE, W. Bibliographie zur Geschichte des Druckwesens und der Presse in Saudi-Arabien. *Dokumentationsdienst Moderner Orient, Mitt.* 4i(1975), pp. 29-37.

KÁLDY-NAGY, Gy. Beginnings of the Arabic-letter printing in the Muslim world. *The Middle East; studies in honour of J. Germanus*, 1974, pp. 201-211.

KURDGELASHVILI, Sh. N. Rol' Rumninii v razvitii knigopechatiya v Gruzii i na arabskom Vostoke. *Actes I. Cong. int. ét. balkan. et Sud-est europ.* III (1969), pp. 821-828.

MARDERSTEIG, G. La singolare cronaca della nascita di un incunabolo. Il commento di Gentile da Foligno all'Avicenna stampato da Pietro Maufer nel 1477. *Italia medioev. umanist.* 8(1965), pp. 249-267. [CWHM 69, 114]

TRACY, W. Advances in Arabic printing. *BSMES bull.* 2(1975), pp. 87-93.

See also XXXVII. i. Brockway

d CATALOGUES

i Manuscripts: general

ALIEV, R. Volya issledovatelya i problema metoda sostavleniya kriticheskogo teksta. *Pis'mennye pamyatniki Vostoka* 1968, pp. 7-16.

ANSARI, Muhammad Azhar. Gopa Mau collection of Persian, Arabic and Urdu manuscripts. *Proc.32 Ind.hist.cong.* 1970, vol. 1, pp. 430-434.

ARUNOVA, M. Some Persian sources on the history of Turkey (On the work by Soviet Orientalists). *Belleten (TTK)* 36(No. 144, 1972), pp. 527-534.

I GENERAL

ARUNOVA, M.R. Soviet Scholars' study of oriental manuscripts on Afghanistan's history and culture. *Afghanistan* 24iv(1972), pp. 41-53

BAYERLE, G. Ottoman records in the Hungarian archives. *Archiv Ott.* 4(1972), pp. 5-22.

BOSWORTH, C.E. A catalogue of accessions to the Arabic manuscripts in the John Rylands University Library of Manchester. *BJRL* 56(1973-74), pp. 34-73, 256-296.

BOSWORTH, C.E. Manuscripts of Tha'ālibī's *Yatīmat ad-dahr* in the Süleymaniye Library, Istanbul. *JSS* 16(1971), pp. 41-49.

BOYER, P. Bref aperçu sur les Archives Sahariennes du Dépôt des Archives d'Outre-Mer d'Aix en Provence. *ROMM* 11(1972), pp. 181-185.

BREGEL', Yu.Z. Vostochnye rukopisi v Kazani. *Pismennye pamyatniki vostoka*, 1969, pp. 356-375.

BULATOV, M.S., DOLINSKAYA, V.G. Proportzii rukopisnykh knig Srednego Vostoka XV-XVI vv. *Iz istorii iskusstva veligogo goroda. (K 2500-letiyu Samarkanda.)*, 1972, pp. 170-184.

CROWE, Y. The archives of Max van Berchem: a note. *AARP* 2(1972), p. 115.

DECEI, A. Les manuscrits arabes dans les Archives d'état de Craiova. *Romano-Arabica*, ed. M. Anghelescu, 1974, pp. 77-80.

DMITRIEVA, L.V., MURATOV, S.N. Katalogi, spiski i obzory tyurkskikh rukopisey XVIII-XX vv. *Pismennye pamyatniki vostoka*, 1969, pp. 145-177.

DMITRIEVA, L.V. Obzor rukopisey tyurkskikh sbornikov v sobranii Instituta vostokovedeniya AN SSSR. *Pis'mennye pamyatniki Vostoka* 1968, pp. 98-102.

DMITRIEVA, L.V. Tyurkskie rukopisi kollektzii "novaya seriya" sobraniya Gosudarstvennoy Publichnoy biblioteki im M.E. Saltykova-Shchedrina. *Vost. sbornik 3*, 1972, pp. 76-85.

FAUBLÉE, J. Les manuscrits arabico-malgaches du Sud-Est. leur importance historique. *RFHO-M* 51(1970), pp. 268-287

FIEY, J.M. Les études syriaques et les manuscrits arabes chrétiens de Paris. *MIDEO* 12(1974), pp. 211-216.

FOUCHÉCOUR, C.H. de. Inventaire de manuscrits persans et arabes ayant appartenu à Cl. Huart. *Studia Iranica* 4(1975), pp. 93-116.

FRYE, R.N. Islamic book forgeries from Iran. *Islamwissenschaftliche Abhandlungen F. Meier*, 1974, pp. 106-109.

FYZEE, Asaf A.A. A collection of Fatimid manuscripts. *Comparative librarianship: essays in honour of D.N. Marshall*, 1973, pp. 209 220.

GIL, R. Iniciativa de la Dirección de cultura marroquí. Índice de manuscritos existentes en las bibliotecas de Marruecos. *BAEO* 9(1973), pp. 217-219.

HASAN, S.M. Jadunath Sarkar's collection of Persian manuscripts. *BPP* 90i(1971), pp. 118-121.

HASANDEDIĆ, Hivzija. Nekoliko zapisa iz orijentalnih rukopisa Arhiva Hercegovine u Mostaru. *Prilozi Or.Fil.Ist.* 16-17 (1966-7), pp. 117-124

HUNWICK, J.O.; GWARZO, H.I. Another look at the De Gironcourt papers. *Res. Bull. CAD Ibadan* 3i(1967), pp. 74-99.

IVANOV, V.A. Spiski rukopisey Bukharskoy kollektzii. *Pis'mennye pamyatniki Vostoka* 1970, pp. 407-436.

KÖBERT, R. Arabische Handschriften (in der Bibliothek des Bibelinstitutes). *Orientalia* NS 42(1973), pp. 387-392.

KONINGSVELD, P.Sj.van. The Arabic manuscripts collection of René Basset (1855-1924). *Bibl.Or.* 30(1973), pp. 370-385.

KONINGSVELD, P.Sj.van. Ten Arabic volumes of historical contents acquired by the Leyden University Library after 1957. *Studies on Islam*, 1974, pp. 92-110.

KORKUT, Besim. Još o arapskim dokumentima u Državnom arhivu u Dubrovniku. *Prilozi Or.Fil.Ist.* 14-15(1964-5), pp. 397-424

KOSTYGOVA, G.I. Persidskie i tadzhikskie rukopisi "novoy serii" v Gosudarstvennoy Publichnoy biblioteke im. M.E. Saltykova-Shchedrina. *Vost. sbornik 3*, 1972, pp. 61-75.

MACOMBER, W.F. Two new projects for microfilming Oriental manuscripts. *XVIII. Deutscher Orientalistentag 1972: Vortrage*, pp. 82-86.

MIKHAYLOVA, A.A. Obzor arabskikh rukopisey "novoy serii" Gosudarstvennoy Publichnoy biblioteki im M.E. Saltykova-Shchedrina. *Vost. sbornik 3*, 1972, pp. 43-60.

PEARSON, J.D. The bibliography of Persian manuscripts. *Memorial vol. Vth Internat. Cong. Iranian Art and Archaeology*, 1972, Vol. 2, pp. 155-160.

ROCHER, R. Nathaniel Brassey Halhed's collection of Oriental manuscripts. *Ann. Or.Research Madras*, Silver jubilee vol. (1975), pp. 1-10.

RODRIGUES, M.A. Thèmes arabes et islamiques de la collection de "mélanges" de la Bibliothèque Générale de l'Université de Coimbra. *Ve Congrès International d'Arabisants et d'Islamisants. Actes.*, [1970?], pp. 389-398.

SELLHEIM, R. The cataloguing of Arabic manuscripts as a literary problem. *Oriens* 23-24(1974), pp. 306-311.

I GENERAL

SHAW, S.J. Ottoman archival materials for the nineteenth and early twentieth centuries: the archives of Istanbul. *IJMES* 6(1975), pp. 94-114.

SMIRNOVA, O.I. Nekotorye voprosy kritiki teksta. ("Sbornik letopisey" Rashid ad-Dina, "Shakh-name" Firdousi i "Istoriya Bukhary" Narshakhi). *Pis'mennye pamyatniki Vostoka* 1968, pp. 155-165.

TAYLOR, F. The oriental manuscript collections in the John Rylands Library. *Bull. John Rylands Lib.* 54(1971-72), pp. 449-478

TERÉS SÁDABA. Los códices árabes de la "Colección Gayangos". *And.* 40(1975), pp. 1-52.

TOPUZOĞLU, Tevfik Rüştü. Istanbul manuscripts of works (other than *Yatīmat al-dahr*) by Thaʻālibī. *IQ* 17(1973), pp. 64-74.

TRAINI, R. I fondi di manoscritti arabi in Italia. *Studi sul Vicino Oriente in Italia,* II, 1971, pp. 221-276.

TRAINI, R. Les manuscrits yéménites dans les bibliothèques d'Istanbul. *Rev. d'hist. des textes* 3(1973), pp. 203-230.

TUSON, P. Forthcoming India Office Records publications relating to the Middle East. *BSMES bull.* 2(1975), pp. 46-50.

UDINA MARTORELL, F. Les documents arabes aux archives de la couronne d'Aragon à Barcelone, et l'influence culturelle arabe sur l'Espagne catalane. *Actes I. Cong. et. cult. mediterr. d'infl. arabo-berb.,* 1973, pp. 50-57.

UTAS, Bo. Notes on some public and semi-public libraries in the Near and Middle East containing Persian and other Moslem manuscripts (situation as of summer 1965). *Acta Or.* 33(1971), pp. 169-192.

UTAS, B. Ṭariq ul-taḥqiq. A. Manuscripts. *Afghanistan* 28i(1975), pp. 55-84.

ZHUKOVSKIY, V.A. Opisanie rukopisey Uchebnogo otdeleniya vostochnykh yazykov pri Aziatskom departamente Ministerstva inostrannykh del. *Pis'mennye pamyatniki Vostoka* 1971, pp. 431-518.

Manuscripts found in Yemen. *Research bull. CAD Ibadan* 8(1972), pp. 26-29.

See also II. a. 6. Dietrich.

See also IV. c. 2. Busard

See also IV. c. 5. Samsó.

See also IV. c. 6. Samsó.

See also IV. c. 8. Vázquez de Benito.

See also V. m. l. D'yakonova.

See also VI. d. Mackay.

See also XIX. j. Eisendle

See also XXIX. c. Tveritinova
XXXIX. b. Vorosheykina

See also XXIX. i. Shaw.

See also XXXVI. l. Belyaev.

See also XXXVIII. d. *Pashto.* Lebedeva.

See also XXXIX. b. Mirzoev.

See also XLII. Galand-Pernet.

ii Manuscripts: one or two items

DIGBY, S. A Qur'an from the East African coast. *AARP* 7(1975), pp. 49-55.

EBIED, R.Y. and YOUNG, M.J.L. An early eighteenth-century *ijāzah* issued in Damietta. *Muséon* 87(1974), pp. 445-465.

ETEMADI, Sarwar Goya. A rare manuscript of Nizami's Khamsa at Kabul. *Afghanistan* 25ii(1972), pp. 22-28.

FRASER, J. G. Marginalia of the Bibliothèque Nationale Ms. Samaritan 2. *Abr-Nahrain* 11(1971), pp. 105-109.

GIUNASVILI, Dž. A further note on the *Ta'rīkh-i Sīstān* manuscripts. *East and West* 21(1971), pp. 345-346.

KONINGSVELD, P.Sj. van. Psalm 150 of the Translation by Hafṣ ibn Albar al-Qūṭī (fl. 889 A.D.[?]) in the Glossarium Latino-Arabicum of the Leyden University Library. *Bibliotheca or.* 29(1972), pp. 277-280.

KONINGSVELD, P.S. van. Das von J.H. Hottinger (1620-1667) benutzte Exemplar des *Kitāb al-Fihrist* = Cod. Or. 1221 der Universitätsbibliothek zu Leiden. *Der Islam* 49(1972), pp. 294-295.

MACKAY, P.A. Certificates of transmission on a manuscript of the Maqāmāt of Harīrī (MS. Cairo, adab 105). *Trans. Amer. Philos. Soc.* 61iv(1971), 81pp.

ROSENTHAL, F. ms. Chester Beatty 3027 of al-Mubashshir. (From Arabic books and manuscripts, XIV.) *JAOS* 95(1975), pp. 211-213.

RUBINACCI, R. Il codice leningradense della Geografia di al-Idrīsī. *AION* 33 (N.S.23,1973), pp. 551-560.

TITLEY, N. A fourteenth-century Khamseh of Niẓāmī. *BM Qly* 36(1971), pp. 8-11.

TOGAN, A.Z.V. A new Persian manuscript. *Memorial vol. Vth Internat. Cong. Iranian Art and Archaeology,* 1972, Vol. 2, pp. 209-210.

TOPUZOĞLU, Tevfik Rüştü. Further Istanbul manuscripts of Thaʻālibī's *Yatīmat al-Dahr.* *IQ* 15(1971), pp. 62-65.

VAJDA, G. Une anthologie sur l'amitié attribuée à al-Ṯaʻālibī. *Arabica* 18 (1971), pp. 211-213.

VAJDA, G. La transmission de la mašyaha *(Asnāl-maqāṣid wa- a'dab al-mawārid)* d'Ibn al-Buḫārī d'après le manuscrit Reisülküttab 262 de la Bibliothèque Süleymaniye d'Istanbul. *RSO* 48(1973-4), pp. 55-74.

See also II. c. 2. Khan.

See also II. c. 3. Jong

See also II. c. 8. Khakee.

See also II. d. 2. Makdisi.

See also II. d. 2. Platti.

See also V. m. 1. James.

See also V. m. 1. Robinson

See also V. m. 1. Welch

See also VI. d. Bonebakker.

See also IX. e. Redjala.

See also XIII. d. Udina

See also XXXIX. b. Bayburdi.

See also XXIX. f. Johnston

See also XXXII. j. Tirmizi.

See also XL. x. Tugusheva.

See also XLI. a. Mamedov

See also XLI. a. Mashtakova.

See also XLII. Galand-Pernet.

iii Printed books

CONWAY, W.E. Checklist of Turcica in the Clark Library. *English and continental views of the Ottoman Empire, 1500-1800*, 1972, pp. 60-66.

KAYSER, W. Die Hamburger Turcica des 16. Jahrhunderts. Ein bibliographischer Versuch. Mit einer Einführung von Heidrun Wurm. *Philobiblon* 19(1975), pp. 4-53.

THODEN, R. Der "Union Catalogue of Asian Publications" [UCAP]. Quantitative und qualitative Untersuchungen an einem gedruckten alphabetischen Katalog. *Mitteilungen. Dokumentationsdienst Moderner Orient* 3i (1974), pp. 31-51; 3ii(1974), pp. 31-46.

See also XXIX. d. *General* Mihaljčić, Perić.

iv Photographic collections. Microfilms. Films

BJORKMAN, W. Mikrofilmsammlung in Uppsala. *Der Islam* 47(1971), p. 298.

MOUTSATSOS, B. Directory of films on the Middle East. *MESA Bull.* 5i(1971), pp. 39-55.

Accessions to the microfilm collection: analytical list. *Research bull. CAD Ibadan* 8(1972), pp. 35-51.

Directory of films on the Middle East. *MESA BULL.* 6ii(1972), pp. 44-45

e LIBRARIES. BOOK COLLECTING. LIBRARY PROBLEMS

AFSHAR, Iraj. Book publication and the creation of libraries in Iran. *J. Reg. Cult. Inst.* 1 iv(1968), pp. 16-23.

AFSHAR, Iraj. General information on the book industry in Iran. *Mitteilungen. Dokumentationsdienst Moderner Orient* 3ii(1974), pp. 5-11.

AFSHAR, Iraj. The need for Persian and Islamic subject headings in basic subject heading lists. *Internat. co-op. in Orientalist librarianship*, 1972, pp. 210-212.

BEHN, W., GREIG, P. Islamic filing. *The Indexer* 9i(1974), pp. 13-15.

BEHN, W. Persian library resources in Germany and their acquisition and bibliographical control. *BSMES bull.* 2(1975), pp. 108-112.

BENZAGHOU, Djemal. La bibliothèque nationale d'Algérie. *Mitt. Dokumentationsdienst MO* 1973(1), pp. 27-34.

CLAUSEN, U. Die Beschaffung von Grauer Literatur in Marokko, Algerien und Tunesien. *Mitteilungen. Dokumentationsdienst Moderner Orient* 3ii(1974), pp. 47-50.

COURY, M. Further notes on research facilities in the U.A.R. *MESA Bull.* 5ii(1971), pp. 92-94.

FREYTAG, E.-M. Das Bibliothekswesen in Iran. *Zentralblatt f.Bibliothekswesen* 86 (1972), pp. 15-26

GLAGOW, R., KOSZINOWSKI, T. Die Beschaffung von "Grauer Literatur" im Orient. *Mitt. Dokumentationsdienst moderner Orient* 2i(1973), pp. 50-70.

GOZALBES BUSTO, G. El libro y las bibliotecas en la España musulmana. *Cuadernos Bibl. Española de Tetuán* 5(1972), pp. 17-46.

GRISWOLD, W.J. The National Archives in Turkey. *MW* 64(1974), pp. 40-44.

HAIDER, Syed Jalaluddin. University libraries in Iran. *Libri* 24(1974), pp. 102-113.

HAIR, P.E.H., STEVENSON, R.C. Unpublished literary and linguistic material in Khartoum University Library. *African lang. R.* 9(1970-71), pp. 110-114.

HAIRI, Abdul-Hadi. Research facilities in Qum, Iran. [Library of Āyatullāh Mar'ashī-i Najafī.] *IJMES* 4(1973), pp. 366-367.

I GENERAL

HAMPSON, G. The Parkes Library, in the Library of the University of Southampton, England. *Mitt. Dokumentationsdienst moderner Orient* 2i(1973), pp. 44-49.

HANSEN, G. Das Katalogsystem der Dokumentations-Leitstelle Moderner Orient. *Mitt. Dokumentationsdienst moderner Orient* 1iii(1972), pp. 41-51.

HANSEN, G. Statistische Auswertung des Verzeichnisses "Deutsche Hochschulschriften über den modernen islamischen Orient" von Detlev Finke, Gerda Hansen und Rolf-Dieter Preisberg. *Mitt. Dokumentationsdienst moderner Orient* 2ii(1973), pp. 46-56.

HAUZIŃSKI, J. The legend of the destruction of the Alexandrinian Library by the Arabs in the 7th century. [Polish with Russian and English abstract.] *Kwart.hist.nauki techn.* 17(1972), pp. 639-654. [CWHM 77, 755]

HOPWOOD, D. Book acquisition from the Middle East. *Mitt. Dokumentationsdienst moderner Orient* 2ii(1973), pp. 22-28.

JONES, A. The computer and material in Middle Eastern languages. *BSMES bull.* 2 (1975), pp. 14-16.

KABESH, A. Overcoming some basic barriers to information dissemination in less industrialized countries. *Mitt. Dokumentationsdienst moderner Orient* 1ii(1972), pp. 9-19.

KHOURY, Yusuf K. Bibliographical activities of UNESCO in the Arab World. *Internat. co-op. in Orientalist librarianship,* 1972, pp. 213-229.

KREHL, L. Über die Sage von der Verbrennung der Aleksandrischen Bibliothek durch die Araber. *Vakıflar dergisi* 9(1971), pp. 434-446.

LAROUE-BENJELLOUN, Latifa. La Bibliothèque Générale et Archives du Maroc. *Mitteilungen. Dokumentationsdienst Moderner Orient* 3ii (1974), pp. 9-21.

LEVI, A. Natzional'naya bibliografiya Turtzii. *NAA* 1973(1), pp. 222-224.

MAHMUD, Khalil. The influence of the Holy Qur'an on the development of libraries. *Nigerian J. Islam* 1ii(1971), pp. 11-22.

MAMOUN, Izz Eldin. Libraries and documentation services in the Democratic Republic of the Sudan. *Mitt. Documentationsdienst moderner Orient* 2i(1973), pp. 5-26.

MOSCHONAS, Th.D. Sur la fin probable de la bibliothèque d'Alexandrie. *Cahiers d'Alexandrie* 4iv(1967), pp. 37-40.

NIAZI, Shaheer. The destruction of the Alexandrian Library. *J. Pakistan Hist. Soc.* 16(1968), pp. 163-174.

PARTINGTON, D.H. Arabic library collections: a study of the P.L.480 program by the Committee on the Middle East. *MESA Bull.* 9i(1975), pp. 12-30.

SHAFA, Shojaeddin. Nouveaux aspects de la grande bibliothèque Pahlavi. *Dokumentationsdienst Moderner Orient, Mitt.* 4i (1975), pp- 17-28.

SHENITI, Mahmud. Problems of standardisation in descriptive cataloguing of Arabic materials. *Internat. co-op. in Orientalist librarianship,* 1972, pp. 49-57.

STEWART, C.C. A new source on the book market in Morocco in 1830 and islamic scholarship in West Africa. *Hespéris Tamuda* 11 (1970), pp. 209-246

THODEN, R. Die Literatur zum Buch-, Bibliotheks-und Documentationswesen des Vorderen Orients 1970 bis Herbst 1973: Nachweis und Befund. *Mitt. Dokumentationsdient moderner Orient* 2ii(1973), pp. 29-45.

THODEN, R. Die Pflege der orientalischen und der orientbezogenen Literatur an der Staats- und Universitätsbibliothek Hamburg. *Mitt. Dokumentationsdienst moderner Orient* 1iii(1972), pp. 33-40.

THURMANN, E. Bibliophilie im islamischen Spanien. *Philobiblon* 18(1974), pp. 195-203.

YAMAN, Yakut. The Turkish National Library. *Mitt. Dokumentationsdienst moderner Orient* 2ii(1973), pp. 5-11.

La Bibliothèque Nationale d'Algérie. *Mitt. Dokumentationsdienst moderner Orient* 2i(1973), pp. 27-34.

La Bibliothèque Nationale de Tunisie. *Mitteilungen. Dokumentationsdienst Moderner Orient* 3ii(1974), pp. 12-18.

Bookstores specializing in second hand books on the Middle East. *MESA Bull.* 5iii(1971), pp. 45-47.

Le Centre National de Documentation du Royaume du Maroc. *Mitteilungen. Dokumentationsdienst Moderner Orient* 3ii(1974), pp. 22-27.

Directory of Library collections on the Middle East. *MESA Bull.* 8i(1974), pp. 22-44.

Dokumentations-Leitstelle Moderner Orient. Jahresbericht 1972. *Mitt. Dokumentationsdienst moderner Orient* 2i(1973), pp. 71-86.

Informationen aus der Dokumentations-Leitstelle Moderner Orient. *Mitt. Dokumentationsdienst moderner Orient* 1ii (1972), pp. 5-7.

La législation archivistique: Afrique. [Includes: Maroc, République arabe unie, Soudan, Tunisie.] *Archivum* 20(1970), pp. 1-156.

I GENERAL

La législation archivistique: Asie. [Includes: Afghanistan, Arabie séoudite, Irak, Iran, Israel, Liban, Syrie.] *Archivum* 20(1970), pp. 157-242.

Scientific and technical research institutions in Iran. *Mitt. Dokumentationsdienst MO* 1973(1), pp. 35-43.

A selective list of scientific and technical libraries in Egypt. *Mitt. Dokumentationsdienst moderner Orient* 1ii(1972), pp. 21-26.

See also I. b. 1. Dobraca.

See also I. b. 2. *Asia*. Itayem.

II RELIGION. THEOLOGY

a RELIGION: GENERAL

i General

ABBAS, Mohamad Galal. Islam - the religion of mankind. *Majallat al-Azhar* 45ii(1973), pp. 14-16.

ABEL, A. Influences du légendaire bouddhique dans le légendaire islamique. *Rend. Accad. Lincei* 26(1971), pp. 53-61.

ADAMS, C.J. The history of religions and the study of Islam. *ACLS newsl.* 25iii-iv, 1974, pp. 1-10.

ADAMS, C. Islamic religion. *MESA Bull.* 4iii(1970), pp. 1-15; 5i(1971), pp. 9-25.

AHMED, Ziauddin. Socio economic values of Islam, and their significance and relevance to the present day world. *Islamic stud.* 10(1971), pp. 343-355.

ALAIE, M. The apperception of Islamic culture. *Ann.Fac.Arts Ain Shams* 7(1962), pp. 85-113.

ALWAYE, Mohiaddin. The conception of life in Islam. *Majallat al-Azhar* 45ii(1973), pp. 1-5.

ALWAYE, A.M. Mohiaddin. Faith and moral qualities. *Majallat al-Azhar* 43iv (1971), pp. 1-5.

ALWAYE, Mohiaddin. Features of Islamic civilization. *Majallat al-Azhar* 45(no.6, 1973), pp. 1-5.

ALWAYE, Mohiaddin. Islam - a complete way of life. *Maj.al-Azhar* 46v(1974), pp. 1-5.

ALWAYE, Mohiaddin. Islam - the religion of knowledge and wisdom. *Majallat al-Azhar* 43vi(1971), pp. 1-6.

ALWAYE, Mohiaddin, Islam and human civilization. *Majallat al-Azhar* 43ix (1971), pp. 1-3.

ALWAYE, Mohiaddin. The principles of equality in Islam. *Majallat al-Azhar* 44ii(1972), pp. 1-6; 44iii(1972), pp. 1-6; 44iv(1972), pp. 1-4.

ALWAYE, A.M. Mohiaddin. Religion and the moral development of man. *Majallat al-Azhar* 43v(1971), pp. 1-7.

ALWAYE, Mohiaddin. The struggle in self-defence and for self preservation. *Majallat al-Azhar* 45x(1974), pp. 1-4.

ALWAYE, Mohiaddin. Towards an ideal society. *Maj.al-Azhar* 45viii(1973), pp. 1-5.

ALWAYE, Mohiaddin. The universal character of 'Islam'. *Majallat al-Azhar* 45(no.5, 1973), pp. 1-6.

ALWAYE, Mohiaddin. What does 'Islam' mean? - Absolute submission to the 'Will of God'. *Maj.al-Azhar* 44vi(1972), pp. 1-4.

ALWAYE, Mohiaddin. Who is the most honourable in the sight of God. *Majallat al-Azhar* 43viii(1971), pp. 1-4

AMORETTI, B.S. Sur le fanatisme dans l'Islam primitif. *AION* 34(n.s.24, 1974), pp. 90-102.

AREÁN, C. Sentimiento del mundo y concepción islámica del espacio. *RIEI Madrid* 16(1971), pp. 31-59.

ASHRAF, Ali. Sir Syed Ahmed Khan and the tradition of rationalism in Islam. *Islam and the modern age* 3iii(1972), pp. 12-21.

ASKARI, Hasan. Religion, morality and law. *Islam and the modern age* 5ii(1974), pp. 41-70.

BANETH, D.Z.H. What did Muhammad mean when he called his religion "Islam"? The original meaning of Aslama and its derivitives. *Israel Oriental studies* 1(1971), pp. 183-190.

BASSIM, Tamara Omar. L'Islam vu par Victor Hugo. *Ann.Fac.Arts Ain Shams* 7 (1962), pp. 127-131.

BAUSANI, A. Islam in the history of religions. *Problems and methods of the history of religions*, 1972, pp. 55-66.

BIJLEFELD, W.A. Introducing Islam: a bibliographical essay. *MW* 63(1973), pp. 171-184, 269-279.

BONO, S. Dibattiti in Algeria sulla storia e l'avvenire dell'Islam. *Levante* 21i-ii (1974), pp. 24-31.

II RELIGION

BOWMAN, J. Word and worship in Middle Eastern religions. *The Gaster Festschrift (J. Anc. Near East Soc. Columbia Univ.* 5, 1973), pp. 35-44.

CAGATAY, Neset. The concept of equality and brotherhood in Islam. *Internat. Islamic Conf.*, 1968, pp. 113-116.

CHARNAY, J.P. Ambivalence et devenir musulman. *L'ambivalence dans la culture arabe*, 1967, pp. 431-451.

CHARNAY, J.-P. Jeux de miroirs et crises de civilisations. Réorientations du rapport Islam/islamologie. *Arch. de sociol. des relig.* 33(1972), pp. 135-174.

CHARNAY, J.P. Préalables épistémologiques à une sociologie religieuse de l'Islam. *Arch.sc.soc.des rel.* 37(1974), pp. 79-86.

CRECELIUS, D. The emergence of the Shaykh al-Azhar as the pre-eminent religious leader in Egypt. *Colloque international sur l'histoire du Caire*, 1969, pp. 109-123.

DEMOZ, Abraham. Moslems and Islam in Ethiopic literature. *J. Ethiopian Studs.* 10(1972), pp.1-11.

DESSOUKI, Ali Towards a comparative study of experiences. Christian and Islamic experiences. *Islam and the modern age* 2ii(1971), pp. 49-56.

DJAIT, Hichem. Continuité et mutation: pour une dialectique du futur. *Etudes philos. et litt.* 5(1971), pp. 153-161.

DRUMMOND, R.H. Toward theological understanding of Islam. *J.ecumenical stud.* 9(1972), pp. 777-801.

EHRENFELS, U.R. Weibliche Elemente in der Symbolik des Islam. *Z. f. Missionswis. u. Religionswis.* 59(1975), pp. 44-51.

FĀRŪQI, Isma'īl R. al-. The essence of religious experience in Islam. *Numen* 20 (1973), pp. 186-201.

FĀRŪQI, Ismā'īl R. al-. Islām and art. *SI* 37(1973), pp. 81-109.

GELLNER, E. Post-traditional forms in Islam: the turf and trade, and votes and peanuts. *Daedalus* 102i(1973), pp. 191-206.

GEYOUSHI, Muhammad el-. Islam - a general review. *Maj.al-Azhar* 44v(1972), pp. 12-16.

GIBB, H.A.R. The heritage of Islam in the modern world (III). *IJMES* 2(1971), pp. 129-147.

HAMIDULLAH, Muhammad. Muslim contributions to the sciences and arts. *Majallat al-Azhar* 45(no.4, 1973), pp. 12-16; 45(no.5, 1973), pp. 7-16; 45(no.6, 1973), pp. 8-10.

HAMIDULLAH, Muhammed. The system of morality. *Majallat al-Azhar* 43v(1971), pp. 8-16; 43vi(1971), pp. 7-16.

HASAN, Abdul Hamid. Patronage of Islam to human values and ideals. *Majallat al-Azhar* 43iii(1971), pp. 7-15.

HASAN, Ahmad. A comparative study of Ijmā': Sangha, Sanhedrin and Church. *Islamic Stud.* 11(1972), pp. 251-279.

HASAN, Ahmad. Social justice in Islam. *Islamic stud.* 10(1971), pp. 209-219.

HASSAN, Abdel Hamid. Features of the ideal society in Islam. *Maj.al-Azhar* 44vii(1972), pp. 17-18; 44viii(1972), pp. 5-10.

HOBALLAH, M. The contribution of the religion of Islam to mutual understanding. *Proc.9th Int.Cong.Hist.Rel.*, 1958, pp. 736-739.

HUBBALLAH, Mahmoud. Islam: the religion of unity and universal brotherhood. *Majallat al-Azhar* 43i(1971), pp. 12-16.

HOFMAN, G. Yavlyaetsya li Islam gorodskoy religiey. *Istoriya i ekonomika stran Arabskogo Vostoka*, 1973, pp. 288-303.

HUSSAIN, S.S. The concept of equality and brotherhood in Islam II. *Internat. Islamic Conf.*, 1968, pp. 117-119.

INAYATULLAH, Shaikh. The ideals of Islam. *Iqbal R.* 14iii(1973), pp. 16-26.

JAFRI, Hussain M. Religion and the modern age. An examination of religious educational system and methodology. *Islam and the modern age* 5i(1974), pp. 39-48.

KAZIMI, M.A.K. The melting of dogmas. *Islam and the modern age* 5iii(1974), pp. 17-42.

KHADER, Bichara. L'Islam, soubassement idéologique de la Renaissance arabe. *Maghreb-Machrek* 66(1974), pp. 45-64.

KHĀN, Nazīr Ahmed. A commonwealth of Muslim nations. *Iqbal rev.* 13i(1972), pp. 71-79.

KHUNDMIRI, S. Alam. Contemporary religious situation. An existential analysis. *Islam and the modern age* 1 ii (1970), pp. 34-49.

KHUNDMIRI, S. Alam. Religion and its application to modern life. *IMA* 1iii(1970), pp. 1-8.

KHUNDUMIRI, Syed Alam. Religion and its application to modern life. *Maj. al-Azhar* 47iii(1975), pp. 10-16.

KHUNDMIRI, S. Alam. The tension between morality and law in Islam. *Islam and the modern age* 5ii(1974), pp. 71-80.

LECOMTE, G. Du profane et du sacré dans les "sciences arabes". *L'ambivalence dans la culture arabe*, 1967, pp. 419-428.

MAHMUD, Abdul Haleem. Three appeals issued by the Islamic Research Academy of al-Azhar. I. The Islamic unity; II. Arabic language; III. Muslim minorities. *Majallat al-Azhar* 45(no.7, 1973), pp. 4-13.

II RELIGION

MOHAMED, Ahmad Ragab. Islam calls for human brotherhood. *Maj.al-Azhar* 45i(1973), pp. 15-17.

MUSHIR UL-HAQQ. Religion, secularism and secular state: the Muslim case. *Religion and society* 18iii(1971), pp. 36-47.

NASR, Seyyed Hossein. Religion and Arab culture. *Cah. d'hist. mondiale* 14(1972), pp. 702-713.

NETTLER, R.L. Islam as a religion. *Humaniora Islamica* 2(1974), pp. 209-214.

NWYIA, P. Mutabilités et immutabilité en Islam. *Rech. sci. rel.* 63(1975), pp. 197-214.

PELLAT, Ch. Islam and history. *Islam and the modern age* 2iii(1971), pp. 1-16.

QURESHI, Anwar Iqbal. Islam's concept of life regarding economic matters. *Islamic Stud.* 11(1972), pp. 297-308.

REAT, N.R. The tree symbol in Islam. *Studies in comparative religion* 9(1975), pp. 164-182.

SAIYIDAIN, K.G. Islam's quest for religious unity. *Islam and the modern age* 3 iv (1972), pp. 1-21.

SCHALL, A. Der Islam als Weltreligion. *Die neue Ordnung* 21(1967), pp. 432-441.

SCHUON, Fr. On relics. *Studies in comparative religion* 9(1975), pp. 130-134.

SIDDIQUI, M.K.A. Knowledge about Muslims. *Islam and the modern age* 5iii(1974), pp. 99-105.

SMITH, J.I. Continuity and change in the understanding of "Islam". *Islam and the modern age* 4ii(1973), pp. 42-66 and *IQ* 16 (1973), pp. 121-139.

SPULER, B. Islam as a moral basis in history. *Islam and the modern age* 5ii(1974), pp. 5-13

USMANI, Nassem ul-Islam. Letter to Muslim 'Ulamas'. *Majallat al-Azhar* 43x(1971), pp. 14-16; 44i(1972), pp. 8-14

VAHIDUDDIN, S. The crisis of religious consciousness with special reference to Islam. *Islam and the modern age* 1 ii (1970), pp. 24-33.

VAN NIEUWEHUIJZE, C.A.O. Islam as a determinant of Middle East civilization. *Islam and the modern age* 1 i (1970), pp. 10-28.

VON GRUNEBAUM, G. Islam - Religión e ideología. *Estudios or.* 7(1972), pp. 161-175.

WAHEEDUZZAFER. Muslim socio-religious movements. *India and contemporary Islam*, ed. S.T. Lokhandwalla, 1971, pp. 132-142.

WALKER, D. Islam and the Arab West's commitment to Africanism. *Milla wa-Milla* 12(1972), pp. 36-48.

WATT, W. Montgomery. Ethical standards in world religions: IV. The teaching and practice of Islam. *Expository times* 85 (1973-4), pp. 132-135.

WATT, W. Montgomery. Learning from other faiths: IV. Islam. *Expository times* 83 (1971-2), pp. 260-263.

ZUBAIDA, Sami. Economic and political activism in Islam. *Economy and society* 1(1972), pp. 308-338.

See also I. b. 3. Waardenburg.

See also III. a. 1. Cragg.

ii Islam: local forms

General

AGWANI, M.S. Religion and politics in Islamic theory and practice. *Islam and the modern age* 2i(1971), pp. 45-62.

Africa

AHMED, Jamal M. Islam in the context of contemporary socio-religious thought of Africa. *Al-Abhath* 20ii(1967), pp. 1-36.

ALPERS, E.A. Towards a history of the expansion of Islam in East Africa: the matrilineal peoples of the southern interior. *Historical study of African religion*, 1972, pp. 172-201.

AMIJI, Hatim M. Some notes on religious dissent in nineteenth-century East Africa. *Afr.hist.stud.* 4(1971), pp. 603-616

BALOGUN, I.A.B. The influence of Islam among the Etsako of the Mid-Western State of Nigeria. *Adab (J.Fac.Arts. Khartoum)* 1 (1972), pp. 47-59.

BELTRAN, L. O Islã, a cultura e a língua árabes na África negra. *Afro-Ásia* 8-9 (1969), pp. 41-49.

BRENNER, L. Current trends in the study of African Islam. Review of a conference held at Boston University, April 27-28, 1973. "The maintenance and transmission of Islamic culture in tropical Africa." *African religious res.* 3ii(1973), pp. 4-12.

DAWODU, S.A. Youth and Islam in Nigeria. *Nigerian J. Islam* 1ii(1971), pp. 29-32.

DELVAL, R. Les Musulmans au Togo. *L'Afrique et l'Asie modernes* 100(1974), pp. 4-21.

DOI, A. Rahman I. Islam in Iboland. *Nigerian J.Islam* 2ii(1972-74), pp. 41-54.

DOI, A.R.I. Islam in Nigeria: changes since independence. *Islam and the modern age* 6iii(1975), pp. 30-56: 6iv(1975), pp. 5-21.

GBADAMOSI, G.O. The Imamate question among Yoruba Muslims. *J. Hist. Soc. Nigeria* 6 (1971-72), pp. 229-237.

II RELIGION

KABA, Lansiné. Islam, society and politics in pre-colonial Baté, Guinea. *Bull. IFAN* 35(1973), pp. 323-344.

KNAPPERT, J. The function of Arabic in the Islamic ritual on the East African Coast. *Ve Congrès International d'Arabisants et d'Islamisants. Actes.*, [1970?], pp. 285-296.

KNAPPERT, J. Islam in Mombasa. *Acta Orientalia Neerlandica* ed. P.W. Pestman, 1971, pp. 75-81.

M'BAYE, El-Hadji Ravane. Un aperçu de l'Islam Songhay ou Réponses d'Al-Magîlî aux questions posées par Askia El-Hadj Muḥammad, Empereur de Gao. *BIFAN* 34(1972), pp. 237-267.

MOREIRA, P. Gomes. A ciência do Corão entre os muçulmanos de Moçambique. *Actas IV congresso de estudos árabes e islâmicos* 1968(1971), pp. 445-477.

NIMTZ, A.H. Islam in Tanzania: an annotated bibliography. *Tanzania notes and records* 72(1973), pp. 51-74.

QUÉCHON, M. Réflexions sur certains aspects du syncrétisme dans l'islam ouest-africain. *Cah.ét.afr.* 11(no. 42, 1971), pp. 206-230.

QUIMBY, L. The dimensions of faith. Review of literature on West African Muslims. *African religious res.* 3ii(1973), pp. 13-26.

REECK, D.L. Islam in a West African chiefdom: an interpretation. *MW* 62(1972), pp. 183-194.

REICHERT, R. Denominações para os muçulmanos no Sudão ocidental e no Brasil. *Afro-Asia* 10-11 (1970), pp. 109-120.

RICARD, A. Islam et littérature en Afrique de l'Ouest. *Rev. franç. d'ét. pol. afr.* 113(1975), pp. 79-87.

RIZZITANO, U. L'Islam maghrébin d'aujourd'hui. *Studies on Islam,* 1974, pp. 75-91.

SALEH, Ali. Le début de l'Islam à la Grande Comore. *Afrika Zamani* 3(1974), pp. 23-29.

SANNEH, Lamin. The origins of clericalism in West African Islam. *J.African hist.* 17 (1976), pp. 49-72.

SHARIPOVA, R.M. Rol' rukovodstva "al-Azkhara" v sovremennoy modernatzii Islama. *Religiya i obshchestvennaya mysl' stran Vostoka,* 1974, pp. 159-182.

SHEIKH-DILTHEY, H. Die Ausbreitung des Islam im Kenyanischen Hinterland. *Der Islam* 52 (1975), pp. 95-108.

STONE, R.A. Religious ethic and the spirit of capitalism in Tunisia. *IJMES* 5(1974), pp. 260-273.

VOLL, J. Islam: its future in the Sudan. *MW* 63(1973), pp. 280-296.

VORONCHANINA, N. O prepodavanii Islama v Tunise. *Strany Blizhnego i Srednego Vostoka: istoriya, ekonomika,* 1972, pp. 27-40.

VORONCHANINA, N.I. Sekulyaristskie tendentzii v sovremennom Tunise. *Religiya i obshchestvennaya mysl' stran Vostoka,* 1974, pp. 124-158.

WAGNER, E. Arabische Heiligenlieder aus Harar. *ZDMG* 125(1975), pp. 28-65.

See also II. d. 4. Doi

See also XX. d. Arens.

See also XII. d. Hagopian.

See also XII. h. Ottenberg

See also XVIII. d. Fahim.

See also XX. c. Voll.

See also XXXVI. a. Mazrui

Near and Middle East. Egypt. North Africa

ABADAN-UNAT, Nermin, YÜCEKÖK, Ahmet N. Religious pluralism in Turkey. *Turkish yb. int.relations* 10(1969-70), pp. 24-49.

GASANOVA, E.Yu. Islam i printzip laytzisma v sovremennoy Turtzii. *Religiya i obshchestvennaya mysl' stran Vostoka,* 1974, pp. 94-114.

HAMADÉ, Marwan. L'Islam libanais, du nassérisme à la participation. *Travaux et jours* 53(1974), pp. 5-12.

JÄSCHKE, G. Vom Islam in der heutigen Türkei. *WI N.S.* 13(1971), pp. 145-162.

MASALA, A. La fede religiosa in Anatolia al giorno d'oggi. *Actas IV congresso de estudos árabes e islâmicos* 1968(1971), pp. 65-70.

NAGGAR, Y. el-. The religious phenomenon in modern Egypt. *IQ* 15(1971), pp. 133-142.

PARET, Rudi. Islam in new Turkey. *IMA* 1iii(1970), pp. 9-12.

SCARCIA AMORETTI, B. Ricognizioni islamiche 1973 nell'Iran meridionale. *AION* 35(N.S.25,1975), pp. 347-347.

SCHIMMEL, A. The ornament of the saints: the religious situation in Iran in pre-Safavid times. *Iranian stud.* 7iii-iv(1974), pp. 88-111.

SCHIMMEL, A. Zur gegenwartigen religiosen Lage in der Türkei. *Atti dell'VIII Cong. int. stor. rel.* (1955), pp. 446-447.

SCOTT, R.B. Qur'ān courses in Turkey. *MW* 61(1971), pp. 239-255.

SKLADANKOWA, M. Perska myśl filozoficzno-religijna. *Przegl.or.* 4(80), 1971, pp. 380-384.

SVETOZAROV, V.B. O modernatzii Islama v sovremennom Afganistane. (Po materialam ofitzial'noy pechati.) *Religiya i obshchestvennaya mysl' stran Vostoka,* 1974, pp. 115-123.

India. Pakistan. Ceylon

ABDUL RAHIM, M. Islam in Negapatam. *Bull. Inst. Trad. Cultures, Madras* 1974 July-Dec., pp. 85-99.

AHMAD, Aziz. Islam and democracy in Pakistan. *Contributions to Asian studies* 2 (1971), pp. 22-35.

AKBARADI, Maulana Said Ahmad. Islam in India today. *India and contemporary Islam,* ed. S.T. Lokhandwalla, 1971, pp. 335-339.

ASHRAF, S.A. Origin and culture of Bengali Muslims. *J. Reg. Cult. Inst.* 2 iv(1969), pp. 233-244.

ASKARI, Hasan. Technological revolution and Indian Muslims. *India and contemporary Islam,* ed. S.T. Lokhandwalla, 1971, pp. 316-321.

BALJON, J.M.S. Characteristics of Islam on the Indo-Pakistan subcontinent. *Studies on Islam,* 1974, pp. 51-62.

BAQIR, M. Islamic thought and practice in Pakistan. *Abr-Nahrain* 14(1973-4), pp. 40-52.

BEDAR, Abid Raza. Post-independence Indian Islam. *India and contemporary Islam,* ed. S.T. Lokhandwalla, 1971, pp. 44-52.

FAZLUR RAHMAN. Islam and the new Constitution of Pakistan. *J. Asian and African studies* [York Univ.] 8(1973), pp. 190-204.

HANSEN, H.H. A fragment of Indian street-Islam. *Folk* 16-17(1974-5), pp. 313-328.

KHALID, M.B. The caravan of Islam in the Indo-Pakistan sub-continent. *J. Reg. Cult. Inst.* 5(1972), pp. 95-109.

LEVIN, S.F. Islamskaya kritika monopoliy v Pakistane. *Religiya i obshchestvennaya mysl' stran Vostoka,* 1974, pp. 35-59.

MALIK, Hafeez. The spirit of capitalism and Pakistani Islam. *Contributions to Asian studies* 2(1971), pp. 59-78.

MISRA, S.C. Indigenisation and Islamization in Muslim society in India. *India and contemporary Islam,* ed. S.T. Lokhandwalla, 1971, pp. 366-371.

MOAZZAM, Anwar. The Indian Muslim: a dilemma of the dual personality. *India and contemporary Islam,* ed. S.T. Lokhandwalla, 1971, pp. 194-201.

NIZAMI, K.A. Socio-religious movements in Indian Islam (1763-1898). *India and contemporary Islam,* ed. S.T. Lokhandwalla, 1971, pp. 98-115.

POLONSKAYA, L.R. Novye tendentzii modernatzii Islama (na primere Pakistana). *Religiya i obshchestvennaya mysl' stran Vostoka,* 1974, pp. 7-34.

QURESHI, Saleem M.M. Religion and party politics in Pakistan. *Contributions to Asian studies* 2(1971), pp. 36-58.

SIDDIQI, Iqtidar Husain. Modern writings on Islam and Muslims in India. *Studs. in Islam* 8(1971), pp. 49-80.

YANUCK, Matrin. The Indian Muslim self-image: nine historians in search of a past. *Islam and the modern age* 4iv(1973), pp. 78-94.

See also II. a. 8. Bashiruddin.

See also II. c. 2. Eaton.

See also XXXII. q. Rahman.

South-East Asia. Far East

ALI, Abdul Mukti. Some consideration of spread of Islam in Indonesia. *Proc.9th Int.Cong.Hist.Rel.,* 1958, pp. 209-217.

BAKKER, D. The struggle for the future: some significant aspects of contemporary Islam in Indonesia. *MW* 62(1972), pp. 126-136.

BOLAND, B.J. Discussion on Islam in Indonesia today. *Studies on Islam,* 1974, pp. 37-50.

BURR, A. Religious institutional diversity - social structural and conceptual unity: Islam and Buddhism in a Southern Thai coastal fishing village. *J.Siam Soc.* 60ii(1972) pp. 183-215.

CHANDRA, Dilip Islam in modern Indonesia. A historical survey of its social and political role in Indonesia. *Islam and the modern age* 2iv(1971), pp. 96-108.

EFIMOVA, L.M. Musul'manskie partii i vybory 1971 g. v Indonezii. *Religiya i obshchestvennaya mysl' stran Vostoka,* 1974, pp. 79-93.

EFIMOVA, L.M. Osnovnye etapy bor'by musul'manskikh partiy i organizatziy za islamizatziyu indoneziyskogo gosudarstva. *Religiya i obshchestvennaya mysl' narodov vostoka,* 1971, pp. 153-174.

FORD, J.F. Some Chinese Muslims of the seventeenth and eighteenth centuries. *Asian affairs* 61(N.S.5, 1974), pp. 144-156.

HOOKER, M.B. Adat and Islam in Malaya. *BTLV* 130(1974), pp. 69-90.

IONOVA, A.I. Nekotorye voprosy sotzial'no-ekonomicheskoy teorii v sovremennoy Idonezii. (Traktovka islamskogo predpisaniya o zakate.) *Religiya i obshchestvennaya mysl' stran Vostoka,* 1974, pp. 60-78.

IONOVA, A.I. Problema ssudnogo protzenta v vystupleniyakh musul'manskikh ideologov sovremennoy Indonezii. *Religiya i obshchestvennaya mysl' narodov vostoka,* 1971, pp. 140-152.

MAJUL, Cesar Adib. The Muslims in the Philippines. A historical perspective. *Majallat al-Azhar* 42viii(1970), pp. 12-16

MEANS, G.P. The role of Islam in the political development of Malaysia. *Contemporary politics* 1(1968-69), pp. 264-284.

NAGUIB AL-ATTAS, Syed Muhammad. L'Islam et la culture malaise. *Archipel* 4(1972), pp. 132-150.

O'SHAUGHNESSY, T.J. How many Muslims has the Philippines? *Philippine stud.* 23 (1975), pp. 375-382.

O'SHAUGHNESSY, T. Islam in South-East Asia. *Studia missionalia* 16(1967), pp. 55-74. [Offprint in SOAS]

SCHUMANN, O. Islam in Indonesia. *Int.R. mission* 63(1974), pp. 429-438.

See also III. a. 1. Ahmed Ibrahim.

Europe

BENNIGSEN, A. The Muslims of European Russia and the Caucasus. *Russia and Asia,* ed. W.S. Vucinich, 1972, pp. 135-166.

MAMEDE, Suleiman Valy. O Islão em Portugal na actualidade. *Actas IV congresso de estudos árabes e islâmicos* 1968(1971), pp. 479-483.

POPOVIC, A. Les musulmans du sud-est européen dans la période post-ottomane. Problèmes d'approche. *JA* 263(1975), pp. 317-360.

POPOVIC, A. Problèmes d'approche de l'Islam yougoslave. *Ve Congrès International d'Arabisants et d'Islamisants. Actes.,* [1970?], pp. 367-376.

SCARCIA AMORETTI, B. A proposito di un recente "catechismo" islamico-bosniaco. *OM* 54(1974), pp. 1-5.

America

LOVELL, E.K. A survey of the Arab-Muslims in the United States and Canada. *MW* 63(1973), pp. 139-154.

See also II. a. 2. Reichert.

See also VI. d. Guevara Bazán

iii Pre-Islamic basis of Islam

ABDUL, Musa. The role of Abraham in the formation of Islam. *Orita* 8i(1974), pp. 58-70.

WATT, W. Montgomery. Belief in a "High God" in pre-Islamic Mecca. *JSS* 16(1971), pp. 35-40.

WATT, W.M. The 'High God' in pre-Islamic Mecca. *Ve Congrès International d'Arabisants et d'Islamisants. Actes.,* [1970?], pp. 499-505.

VADET, J.C. Les *Hanīfs*: "La plus grande Loi de Moïse", Les Saintes Myriades et la naissance de l'exégèse islamique. *Rev. des ét. juives* 130(1971), pp. 165-182.

iv Muhammad, the Prophet

ABDUL RAUF, Muhammad. A Muslim response to "The pre-Islamic period of Sīrat al-Nabī". *MW* 62(1972), pp. 42-48.

AFFIFY, Hussain el-Tiby. Glimpses of the life of Prophet Muhammad. *Maj.al-Azhar* 44iv(1972), pp. 5-8.

ALI, Maulana Muhammad. The world Prophet and the world religion. *Maj. al-Azhar* 47iv(1975), pp. 6-12.

ALTMANN, A. "The ladder of ascension". *Studies in mysticism and religion presented to G.G. Scholem,* 1967, pp. 1-32.

ALWAYE, Mohiaddin. The life of the Prophet is the exemplary pattern of conduct. *Maj. al-Azhar* 47iii(1975), pp. 1-5.

ALWAYE, Mohiaddin. The miraculous journey of the Prophet from Mecca to Jerusalem. *Maj. al-Azhar* 47v(1975), pp. 1-5.

ALWAYE, Mohiaddin. Al-Mi'raj - the ascent of the Prophet. *Maj.al-Azhar* 44v(1972), pp. 1-7.

ALWAYE, Mohiaddin. Spotlight on the life of the Prophet. *Majallat al-Azhar* 45iii(1973), pp. 1-11; 45iv(1973), pp. 1-5.

AUSTIN, R.W. "I seek God's pardon ... " [On Abū Madyan]. *Stud. in comp. relig.* 7(1973), pp. 92-94.

BASETTI-SANI, G. Muhammad è un vero profeta? *Renovatio* 10(1975), pp. 412-435.

BASETTI-SANI, G. Su alcune interpretazioni cattoliche di Muhammad. *Renovatio* 8(1973), pp. 606-624.

BOUSQUET, G.-H. Mahomet et l'Islâm, selon un passage peu connu de la Légende Dorée. *Ann. Inst. Phil. Hist. Or.* 20(1968-72), pp. 137-144.

BRAVMANN, M.M. The origin of the principle of 'ismah: Muḥammad's "immunity from sin". *Muséon* 88(1975), pp. 221-225.

EPALZA, M. de. Los nombres del Profeta en la teologia musulmana. *Miscelanea Comillas* 32(1975), pp. 149-203.

GOLDBERG, A. Die Vorstellung von der Schekhina bei Muhammad. *Kairos,* pp. 188-199.

KISTER, M.J. On the papyrus of Wahb b. Munabbih. *BSOAS* 37(1974), pp. 547-571.

MOINUL.HAQ, S. Prophet Muhammad: the advent of a new religio-social order. *J. Pakistan Hist. Soc.* 20(1972), pp. 1-33.

MORABIA, A. Surnaturel, prodiges prophétiques et incubation dans la ville de l'Envoyé d'Allâh. *SI* 42(1975), pp. 93-114.

NEWBY, G.D. An example of Coptic literary influence on Ibn Isḥāq's *Sīrah.* *JNES* 31 (1972), pp. 22-28

PORTER, J.R. Muhammad's journey to heaven. *Numen* 21(1974), pp. 64-80.

ROYSTER, J.E. The study of Muhammad: a survey of approaches from the perspective of the history and phenomenology of religion. *MW* 62(1972), pp. 49-70.

SCHIMMEL, A. The veneration of the Prophet Muḥammad, as reflected in Sindhi poetry. *The Saviour God: comparative studies in the concept of salvation presented to E.O. James,* 1963, pp. 129-143

SHAMIR, Yehuda. Allusions to Muhammad in Maimonides' theory of prophecy in his *Guide of the perplexed.* *JQR* 64(1973-74), pp. 212-224.

SOKOLOVIĆ, Sinanuddin. Prilog bibliografiji radova o Muhamedu a.s. objavljenih u nas. *Glasnik vrhovnog islamskog starjesinstva* 35(1972), pp. 42-51, 271-282, 382-387 [offprint in SOAS].

TAWFIQ, Muhammad Amin. Poetry in the Sira (biographical work on the Prophet). *Maj. al-Azhar* 47vii(1975), pp. 11-16.

TYABJI, Badr-ud-Din. The relationship between God and His messenger. *Islam and the modern age* 6ii(1975), pp. 73-86.

WENDELL, C. The pre-Islamic period of Sīrat al-Nabī. *MW* 62(1972), pp. 12-41.

WESSELS, A. Modern biographies of the life of the Prophet Muhammad in Arabic. *IC* 49(1975), pp. 99-105.

Perfection of religion and completion of prophethood. *Maj.al-Azhar* 46iii(1974), pp. 7-8.

The sermon of the Prophet on the Mount Arafat. *Maj. al-Azhar* 47iii(1975), pp. 6-9.

See also IX. b. Hamidullah

v The Koran

ABDUL, Musa O.A. The *Majma al-Bayān* of Ṭabarsī. *IQ* 15(1971), pp. 106-120.

ABDUL, Musa O.A. The unnoticed Mufassir Shaykh Ṭabarsī.. *IQ* 15(1971), pp. 96-105.

AFFIFI, Hussain el-Tiby. The attributes of 'Allah' - in the verses of the Quran. *Majallat al-Azhar* 44ii(1972), pp. 7-16

AFFIFY, Hussain el-Tiby. The attributes of Allah in the verses of the Quran. *Maj.al-Azhar* 44iii(1972), pp. 7-16; 44iv(1972), pp. 9-12.

AFFIFY, Hussain el-Tiby. The remembrance of Allah in the verses of the Holy Quran. *Maj.al-Azhar* 44v(1972), pp. 8-11.

AḤMED, Manzooruddīn. Key political concepts in the Qur'ān. *Islamic stud.* 10(1971), pp. 77-102.

ALI, Hashim Amir. The Qur'an in secular India. *Islam and the modern age* 6iii (1975), pp. 78-89.

ALLAM, M. Mahdi. The theory of forgiveness as expressed in the Quran. *3rd Conf.Acad. Isl.Research,* 1966, pp. 511-527

ALLARD, M. Quelques aspects de l'anthropologie coranique. *Ve Congrès International d'Arabisants et d'Islamisants. Actes.,* [1970?], pp. 21-30.

ALWAYE, Mohiaddin. The authenticity of the Holy Quran. *Maj.al-Azhar* 46ii(1974), pp. 1-7.

ALWAYE, Mohiaddin. The duties of believers towards God - in verses from the Quran. *Majallat al-Azhar* 43viii(1971), pp. 5-8

ALWAYE, A.M. Mohiaddin The effect of Quranic moral qualities on the life of man. *Majallat al-Azhar* 42viii(1970), pp. 1-5.

ALWAYE, Mohiaddin. The elements of universality and permanency in the teachings of the Quran. *Maj. al-Azhar* 45ix(1974), pp. 1-4.

ALWAYE, A.M. Mohiaddin. The Holy Quran describes qualities of true believers. *Majallat al-Azhar* 43ii(1971), pp. 1-4.

ALWAYE, Mohiaddin. The message of the Quran. *Maj.al-Azhar* 44viii(1972), pp. 1-4.

ALWAYE, Mohiaddin. Moderation of the Islamic regulations. *Maj.al-Azhar* 46iv(1974), pp. 1-5.

ALWAYE, Mohiaddin. The unique character of the Holy Quran. *Maj. al-Azhar* 45viii (1974), pp. 1-6.

ARNALDEZ, R. Le Moi divin et le Moi humain d'après le commentaire coranique de Faḫr Al-Dīn Al-Râzî. *SI* 36(1972), pp. 71-97.

ARNALDEZ, R. Trouvailles philosophiques dans le commentaire coranique de Fakhr Al-Din Al-Razi. *Etudes philos. et litt.* 3(1968), pp. 11-24.

AUDEBERT, C. Notes sur les recherches autour de l'*i'ǧāz* en Égypte au cours des vingt dernières années. *Cah.de ling.d'orientalisme et de slavistique* 1-2(1973), pp. 29-37.

AZAD, Moulana Abul Kalam. Divine justice in the concept of the Quran. *Majallat al-Azhar* 45(no.7, 1973), pp. 14-16.

II RELIGION

AZAD, Moulana Abul Kalam. Importance of Surat-ul-Fatiha. *Majallat al-Azhar* 43ii(1971), pp. 14-16.

BACHMANN, P. Das Skandalon des Propheten Yūnus und eine neue arabische Jona-Geschichte: *Yūnus fī batn al-hūt*, von 'Abd al-Ghaffār Mikkāsī. *Orientalia Hispanica* I, 1974, pp. 54-76.

BASETTI-SANI, G. Gesù Cristo nel Corano. *Renovatio* 4(1969), pp. 440-453.

BASETTI-SANI, G. Per una riflessione cristiana del Corano. *Renovatio* 6(1971), pp.

BAYERO, Alhaji Ado. The Qur'ān--revelation, collection and divine nature. *Nigerian J. Islam* 1i(1970), pp. 7-10.

BEESTON, A.F.L. Ships in a Quranic simile. *J. Arab. lit.* 4(1973), pp. 94-96.

BELGUEDJ, S. La collection hippocratique et l'embryologie coranique. *La collection hippocratique et son rôle dans l'histoire de la médecine,* 1975, pp. 321-333.

BELLAMY, J.A. The mysterious letters of the Koran: old abbreviations of the *Basmalah*. *JAOS* 93(1973), pp. 267-285.

BELTZ, W. Marginalia zu Sura 59, 24. *Z. f. Religions- u. Geistesgesch.* 27 (1975), pp. 81-82.

BELTZ, W. Über den Ur-Qur'ān. *Z. f. Religions- u. Geistesgesch.* 27(1975), pp. 169-171.

BIJLEFELD, W.A. Some recent contributions to Qur'anic studies: selected publications in English, French, and German, 1964-1973. *MW* 64(1974), pp. 79-102, 172-179, 259-274.

BISHAI, W.B. A possible Coptic source for a Qur'ānic text. *JAOS* 91(1971), pp. 125-128.

BOSWORTH, C.E. The Qur'anic prophet Shu'aib and Ibn Taimiyya's epistle concerning him. *Muséon* 87(1974), pp. 425-440.

BOULLATA, Issa J. Modern Qur'an exegesis. A study of Bint al-Shāṭi's method. *MW* 64 (1974), pp. 103-114.

BOWMAN, J. The Qur'an and Biblical history. *Ex orbe religionum. Studia Geo Widenaren oblata,* II, 1972, pp. 111-119.

BRAVMANN, M.M. The phrase *in kuntum fa'ilīna* in *Sūrat Yūsuf,* v.10. *Islam* 48(1971), pp. 122-125.

BROCKWAY, D. The second edition of volume 1 of Marracci's *Alcorani textus universus*. *MW* 64(1974), pp. 141-144.

BURTON, J. The collection of the Qur'ān. *Glasgow Or. Soc. Trans.* 23(1969-70), pp. 42-60.

BUSQUETS MULET, J. La *fātiḥa* en los cuentos populares baleáricos. *Orientalia Hispanica* I, 1974, pp. 155-157.

CALASSO, G. Note su *waswasa* 'sussurrare', nel Corano e nei *ḥadīṯ*. *AION* 33(NS.23,1973) pp. 233-246.

CANTEINS, J. Sigle e tematiche coraniche. *Conoscenza religiosa* 1974, pp. 221-249.

CRAGG, K. The Qur'an and the contemporary Middle East. *J.ecumenical stud.* 11(1974), pp. 1-12.

DENNY, F.M. The meaning of *ummah* in the Qur'ān. *History of religions* 15(1975), pp. 34-70.

DORRA-HADDAD, J. Coran, prédication nazaréenne. *Proche-Orient chrétien* 23(1973), pp. 148-155.

FIGUEROA, M.R. Algunas reflexiones sobre el Dios del Corán. *Estudios or.* 7(1972), pp. 193-210.

GALWASH, A. Muslim ethics and moralities. *Majallat al-Azhar* 45(no.6, 1973), pp. 11-16.

GIFFEN, L.A. In the artist's mind(?): some prevalent ideas about animals from the Qur'an and tradition literature. *Studies in art and literature of the Near East in honor of R. Ettinghausen,* 1974, pp. 105-131.

GISR, Shaikh Nadim al-. The Quran in Islamic education. *3rd Conf.Acad.Isl.Research,* 1966, pp. 133-184

HADDAD, Y.Y. The conception of the term *dīn* in the Qur'ān. *MW* 64(1974), pp. 114-123.

HAHN, E. Sir Sayyid Aḥmad Khān's *The controversy over abrogation (in the Qur'ān):* an annotated translation. *MW* 64(1974), pp. 124-133.

HALEPOTA, A.J. Islamic social order. A study based mainly on Sūra al-Nahl. *Islamic studies* 14(1975), pp. 115-122.

HOLWAY, J.D. The Qur'an in Swahili. Three translations. *MW* 61(1971), pp. 102-110.

HUSAINI, Ishak M. Christ in the Quran and in modern Arabic literature. *Proc.9th Int.Cong.Hist.Rel.,* 1958, pp. 642-648.

IDRIS, H.R. De la notion arabo-musulmane de voie salvatrice. *Orientalis Hispanica* I, 1974, pp. 398-410.

JARRY, J. La sourate IV et les soi-disant origines julianistes de l'Islam. *Ann. Islamologiques* 9(1970), pp. 1-7.

JOMIER, J. Un regard moderne sur le Coran avec le Dr. Kamel Hussein. *MIDEO* 12(1974), pp. 49-64.

JUYNBOLL, G.H.A. Fighting angels. *Ohio J. religious stud.* 2(1974), pp. 85-87.

JUYNBOLL, G.H.A. The position of Qur'an recitation in early Islam. *JSS* 19(1974), pp. 240-251.

II RELIGION

KANOUN, Abdullah. "Hadith", its scientific and religious value. *3rd Conf.Acad.Isl. Research,* 1966, pp. 65-89

KHAFEEF, Shaikh Aly al-. Sunna's role in expanding Islamic rules, and the refutation of suspicions cast at their authenticity or transmission. *3rd Conf.Acad.Isl.Research,* 1966, pp. 29-63

KHAN, Muin-ud-Din Ahmed. Reflection on the Quranic concept of the creation of universe and mankind. *Internat. Islamic Conf.,* 1968, pp. 32-35.

ḪAṬĪB, ʿAbd.al-Karīm al-. Christ in Qurʾan, the Taurāt, and the Injīl Translated and annotated by Kenneth E. Nolin. *MW* 61(1971), pp. 90-101.

KHOURY, A.Th. Le Dieu du Coran et le Dieu d'Abraham d'après les polémistes byzantins. *ZMR* 55(1971), pp. 266-270.

KÖBERT, R. Ein koranisches Agraphon. *Orientalia* 44(1975), pp. 198-199.

KÖBERT, R. Zur Bedeutung von *sibga* in Koran 2, 138. *Orientalia* 42(1973), pp. 518-519.

KÖBERT, R. Zur Bedeutung von Sure 2, 138. *Orientalia* 44(1975), pp. 106-107.

KOHLBERG, E. Some notes on the Imamate attitude to the Qur'an. *Islamic philosophy and the classical tradition:* essays presented to R. Walzer, 1972, pp. 209-224.

KYRRIS, Costas P. The admission of the souls of immoral but humane people into the *Limbus Puerorum,* according to the Cypriote Abbot Kaïoumos (VIIth century A.D.) compared to the Quran's *Al ʾArāf* (Suras 7^{44-46}, 57^{13f}). *Rev.ét.sud-est eur.* 9(1971), pp. 461-477.

LABBAN, Ibrahim Abdul-Maguid al-. The Quran in Islamic education. *3rd Conf.Acad.Isl. Research,* 1966, pp. 185-198

LAPIS, B. Die Anschauungen über die Arbeit im Koran. *Z. f. Religions- u. Geistesgesch.* 25(1973), pp. 97-111.

LICHTENSTADTER, I. Quran and Quran exegesis. *Humaniora Islamica* 2(1974), pp. 3-28.

MCDONOUGH, S. Imān and Islām in the Qurā'n. *Iqbal rev.* 12i(1971), pp. 81-88.

MADELUNG, W. The origins of the controversy concerning the creation of the Koran. *Orientalia Hispanica* I, 1974, pp. 504-525.

MAHMUD, Khalil. The influence of the Holy Qur'ān on the development of libraries. *Nigerian J. Islam* 1ii(1971), pp. 11-22.

MAKDISI, G. Quatre opuscules d'Ibn ʿAqīl sur le Coran. *BEO* 24(1971), pp. 55-66.

MAʿSUMI, M.S.H. Al-Biruni's devotion to the Qurʾān. *Islamic stud.* 13i(1974), pp. 45-57.

MURTUZA SIDDIQI, M. The message of the Quran as interpreted by Maulāna Abū'l Kalām Āzād. *India and contemporary Islam,* ed. S.T. Lokhandwalla, 1971, pp. 291-295.

MUSA ABDUL. The role of Abraham in the formation of Islam. *Orita* 8(1974), pp. 58-70.

NASR, Seyyed Hossein. Revelation, intellect and reason in the Quran. *Internat. Islamic Conf.,* 1968, pp. 59-62.

NASR, Seyyed Hossein. Revelation, intellect and reason in the Quran. *J. Reg. Cult. Inst.* 1 iii(1968), pp. 60-64.

NAUDÉ, J.A. Isaac typology in the Koran. *De fructu oris sui: essays in honour of Adrianus van Selms,* ed. by I.H. Eybers *et al.,* 1971, pp. 121-129.

NEWBY, G.D. Abraha and Sennacherib: a Talmudic parallel to the *tafsīr* on *sūrat al-fīl.* *JAOS* 94(1974), pp. 431-437.

NEWBY, G.D. Sūrat al-'Ikhlās. *Orient and Occident. Essays presented to C.H. Gordon,* 1973, pp. 127-130.

O'SHAUGHNESSY, T. Creation from nothing and the teaching of the Qur'an. *ZDMG* 120(1970), pp. 274-280.

O'SHAUGHNESSY, T.J. Creation with wisdom and with the world in the Qur'an. *JAOS* 91(1971), pp. 208-221.

O'SHAUGHNESSY, T.J. God's purpose in creating according to the Qur'an. *JSS* 20 (1975), pp. 193-209.

O'SHAUGHNESSY, T.J. God's throne and the biblical symbolism of the Qurʾān. *Numen* 20(1973), pp. 202-221.

O'SHAUGHNESSY, Th. Man's creation from clay and from seed in the Qurʾān. *BAEO* 7(1971), pp. 131-149.

PARET, Rudi. Textkritisch verwertbare Koranvarianten. *Islamwissenschaftliche Abhandlungen F. Meier,* 1974, pp. 198-204.

PHILONENKO, M. Une règle essénienne dans le Coran. *Semitica* 22(1972), pp. 49-52.

POPOVIC, A. Sur une "nouvelle" traduction du Coran en Serbo-Croate. *Arabica,* 20 (1973), pp. 82-84.

ROBSON, J. Aspects of the Qur'anic doctrine of salvation. *Man and his salvation; studies in memory of S.G.F. Brandon,* 1973, pp. 205-219.

ROMAN, A. Note sur le pronom *hum* des versets coraniques de la nomination divine. *Arabica* 19(1972), pp. 301-315.

RONCAGLIA, P. Éléments Ébionites et Elkésaïtes dans le Coran. Notes et hypothèses. *Proche-Orient chrétien* 21(1971), pp. 101-126.

II RELIGION

RYAN, P.J. The descending scroll: a study of the notion of revelation as apocalypse in the Bible and in the Qur'ān. *Ghana bull.theol.* 4viii(1975), pp. 24-39.

SAID, Subhi. On the misattribution of the work *al-Ḥujja* to Abū 'Abd Allāh al-Ḥusayn b. Khālawayh. *IQ* 17(1973), pp. 125-139.

SAIYIDAIN, K.G. The concept of a true Muslim according to the Holy Qur'ān. *Islam and the modern age* 1 i (1970), pp. 70-81.

SAIYIDAIN, K.G. Qurān's invitation to think. *Islam and the modern age* 4ii(1973), pp. 5-27.

SAYED, Abdel Sattar el. The miraculous character of the Quran. *Maj.al-Azhar* 44ix(1972), pp. 5-11; 44x(1972), pp. 6-13; 45ii(1973), pp. 6-13; 45iii(1973), pp. 12-17.

SCARCIA AMORETTI, B. Nota a *Corano* XVIII, 94. *Annali Fac.Ling.Lett.stran.di Ca' Foscari (serie orientale)* 1(1970), pp. 13-21.

SCHALL, A. Die Sichtung des Christlichen im Koran. *Mitt.und Forschungsbeiträge der Cusanus-Ges.* 9(1971), pp. 76-91.

SCHIMMEL, A. Die neue tschechische Koranübersetzung (mit einem Überblick über die neuesten tschechischen orientalistischen Arbeiten). *WO* 7(1973), pp. 154-162.

SCHUMANN, H.J. von, SCHUMANN, M. von. Der Koran wird nicht mehr wörtlich genommen. Sozialmedizinischer Umbruch in Tunesien. *Deutsch.Artzebl.-ärztl.Mitt.* 69(1972), pp. 2642-2645. [CWHM 77, 712]

SCHÜTZINGER, H. Die arabische Jeremia-Erzählung und ihre Beziehungen zur jüdischen religiösen Überlieferung. *Z.f. Religions- und Geistesgesch.* 25(1973), pp. 1-19.

SERAJUL HAQUE. The Holy Quran and rational thinking. *Internat. Islamic Conf.*, 1968, pp. 63-67.

SHERWANI, H.K. The socio-religious thought of Syed Aḥmad Khān (with special reference to the Quran). *India and contemporary Islam*, ed. S.T. Lokhandwalla, 1971, pp. 53-59.

SIDDIQI, Mazheruddin. Economic teachings of the Quran in application to modern times. *Internat. Islamic Conf.*, 1968, pp. 91-95.

SMITH, G.R. Oaths in the Qur'ân. *Semitics* 1(1970), pp. 126-156.

SMITH, J.I. and HADDAD, Y.Y. Women in the afterlife: the Islamic view as seen from the Qur'an and tradition. *J.Amer.Acad. Religion* 43(1975), pp. 39-50.

SPIES, Otto. Islam und Syntage. *Oriens Christianus* 57(1973), pp. 1-30.

TOGAN, Zeki Velidi. Quran and the Turks. *Internat. Islamic Conf.*, 1968, pp. 36-39.

TRITTON, A.S. The speech of God. *SI* 36(1972), pp. 5-22.

VALIU'D-DIN, Mir. The character that the Qur'an builds. *IC* 45(1971), pp. 1-23.

VALIUDDIN, Mir. The Quran and philosophy. *IMA* 1iii(1970), pp. 49-68.

VALIUDDIN, Mir. Successful living: the Qur'ānic approach. *Stud. in Islam* 6(1969), pp. 65-97.

VALIUDDIN, Mir. The way to control anger - the Qur'anic approach. *IC* 46(1972), pp. 63-73

WAARDENBURG, J. Un débat coranique contre les polythéistes. *Ex orbe religionum. Studia Geo Widengren oblata*, II, 1972, pp. 143-154.

WATT, W. Montgomery. The camel and the needle's eye. *Ex orbe religionum. Studia Geo Widengren oblata*, II, 1972, pp. 155-158.

WATT, W.M. The men of the Ukhdud (sura 85). *The Middle East; studies in honour of J. Germanus*, 1974, pp. 31-34.

WEINSTEIN, M.M. A Hebrew Qur'ān manuscript. *Studies in Bibliography and Booklore* 10 (1971-72), pp. 19-52.

WEISS, B. *Al-muṣḥaf al-murattal:* a modern phonographic "collection" *(jam')* of the Qur'ân. *MW* 64(1974), pp. 134-140.

WENDELL, C. The denizens of Paradise. *Humaniora Islamica* 2(1974), pp. 29-59.

WOODBERRY, J.D. Sin in the Quran and the Bible. *Al-Mushir* 13iii-iv(1971), pp. 1-5

ZAIN-UL-ABEDEEN. Man's nature and destiny - the Qur'anic view. *Religion and society* 20iii(1973), pp. 18-25, 26-34

ZAIN-UL-ABEDEEN. Man's nature and destiny - what do the Mufassirin say? *Religion and society* 20iii(1973), pp. 26-34.

The call to spend in the way of God - in verses from the Holy Quran. *Majallat al-Azhar* 46i(1974), pp. 5-6.

Conception of God - in verses from the Holy Quran. *Maj.al-Azhar* 44vi(1972), pp. 12-16.

The duties of believers towards God in verses from the Quran. II. *Majallat al-Azhar* 43ix(1971), pp. 4-6.

Prayers from the Quran. *Majallat al-Azhar* 45(no.4, 1973), pp. 7-11

The Prophet Muhammad - in verses from the Quran. *Maj.al-Azhar* 45i(1973), pp. 5-6.

The virtues of the true servants of God - in verses from the Quran. *Majallat al-Azhar* 45(no.6, 1973), pp. 6-7.

What kind of nation Muslims must be? - in verses from the Quran. *Majallat al-Azhar* 44i(1972), pp. 5-7.

See also I. d. 2. Digby.

See also I. e. 1. Mahmud.

See also II. a. 2. *Africa.* Moreira.

See also II. a. 7. Vernet.

See also II. a. 8. Butler.

See also III. a. 1. Arnaldez.

See also III. a. 1. Hidayatullah.

See also IV. a. Ben Milad.

See also IV. b. *Ghazzālī.* Kleinknecht.

See also IV. b. *Iqbal.* Azad.

See also V. u. 1. Hoerburger.

See also V. u. 1. Pacholczyk.

See also V. u. 1. Touma.

See also X. c. Kister

See also XXXVI. h. Miquel

See also XXXVI. h. Piemontese.

See also XXXVI. h. Ritchie.

See also XXXVI. h. Vitestam.

See also XL. e. Eckmann

See also XL. e. Togan.

vi Hadith

ALWAYE, Mohiaddin. The significance of Sunna or Hadith of the Prophet. *Maj.al-Azhar* 46iii(1974), pp. 1-6.

ATALLAH, W. De quelques prétendues idoles, *bağğa, sağğa,* etc. *Arabica* 20(1973), pp. 160-167.

BIANQUIS, T. La transmission du hadith en Syrie à l'époque fatimide: cinq notices tirées de l'*Histoire de la ville de Damas* d'Ibn ʿAsākir. *BEO* 25(1972), pp. 85-95.

DIETRICH, A. Zur überlieferung einiger *ḥadīt*-Handschriften der Zāhiriyya in Damascus. *Orientalia Hispanica* I, 1974, pp. 226-244.

JUYNBOLL, G.H.A. Aḥmad Muḥammad Shākir (1892-1958) and his edition of Ibn Ḥanbal's Musnad. *Der Islam* 49(1972), pp. 221-247.

JUYNBOLL, G.H.A. The ḥadīṯ in the discussion on birth-control. *Actas IV congresso de estudos árabes e islâmicos* 1968(1971), pp. 373-379.

KHACHAB, Y. El- Some aspects of "values" in the Islamic heritage: Traditions, Imama, and Consensus. *Proc.27th Int.Cong. Or.1967* (1971), p. 178.

KHOURY, R.G. L'importance d'Ibn Lahīʿa et de son papyrus conservé à Heidelberg dans la tradition musulmane du deuxième de l'hégire. *Arabica* 22(1975), pp. 6-14.

KISTER, M.J. Ḥaddithū 'an bani isrā'īla wa-lā ḥaraja: a study of an early tradition. *In memoriam S.M. Stern* (Israel Or. studies, II, 1972), pp. 215-239.

LECOMTE, G.. A propos de la resurgence des ouvrages d'Ibn Qutayba sur le ḥadīṯ aux VIe/XIIe et VIIe/XIIIe siecles. Les certificats de lecture du K. Ġarīb al-Ḥadīṯ et du K. Islāḥ al-ġalaṭ fī ġarīb al-ḥadīṯ Li-Abī ʿUbayd al-Qāsim B. Sallām. *BEO* 21(1968), pp. 347-409.

MEIER, Fritz. Ein profetenwort gegen die totenbeweinung. *Der Islam* 50(1973), pp. 207-229.

SCHUON, F. Remarks on the Sunnah. *Stud. comp. relig.* 6(1972), pp. 194-199.

SIDDIQI, M.Z. Aṭrāf al-ḥadīth. *Studs. in Islam* 8(1971), pp. 17-28.

SMITH, J.I. The meaning of 'Islām' in ḥadīth literature. *IC* 48(1974), pp. 139-148.

SPEIGHT, R. Marston. The will of Saʿd b. a. Waqqāṣ: the growth of a tradition. *Der Islam* 50(1973), pp. 249-267.

TRITTON, A. S. The camel and the needle's eye. *BSOAS* 34(1971), p.139.

VAJDA, G. La Mašyaha d Ibn al-Ḥaṭṭab al-Rāzī. Contribution à l'histoire du sunnisme en Egypte fāṭimide. *BEO* 23 (1970), pp. 21-29.

VITESTAM, G. Qatāda B. Diʿāma as-Sadūsī et la science du Ḥadīṯ. *Ve Congrès International d'Arabisants et d'Islamisants. Actes.,* [1970?], pp. 489-498.

See also II. a. 5. Giffen.

See also II. a. 5. Smith, Haddad

See also IX. c. Raḥmānī.

See also XIX. g. Rahmani

vii Polemics. Apologetics. Missions. Relations with other religions

ABEL, A. La "Réfutation d'un agarène" de Barthélémy d'Édesse. *SI* 37(1973), pp. 5-26.

ANAWATI, G.C. La personne du Christ d'apres deux livres recents d'auteurs musulmans. *Atti dell'VIII Cong. int. stor. rel.* (1955), pp. 443-446.

ANSARI, Zafar Ishaq. Truth, revelation and obedience. *Christian-Muslim dialogue,* ed. S.J. Samartha and J.B. Taylor, 1972, pp. 80-86.

ARGYRIOU, A. Pachomios Roussanos et l'Islam. *Rev.d'hist.et de philos.rel.* 51(1971), pp. 143-164

ARNALDEZ, R. Controverse d'Ibn Hazm contre Ibn Nagrila le juif. *ROMM* 13-14(1973), pp. 41-48.

ASAD, Muhammad. My pilgrimage to Islam. *Maj.al-Azhar* 46iv(1974), pp. 14-16.

II RELIGION

ASHRAF, Ali. Secularism in India: the key issues. *Islam and the modern age* 6iv (1975), pp. 22-39.

ASKARI, Hasan. The dialogical relationship between Christianity and Islam. *J. ecumenical stud.* 9(1972), pp. 477-488.

ASKARI, Hasan. Unity and alienation in Islam. *Edumenical R.* 25(1973), pp. 191-201.

ASKARI, Hasan. Worship and prayer. *Christian-Muslim dialogue,* ed. S.J. Samartha and J.B. Taylor, 1972, pp. 120-136.

AYYŪB, Mahmūd. Islam and Christianity. A study of Muhammad Abduh's view of the two religions. *Humaniora Islamica* 2 (1974), pp. 121-137.

BAARDA, T. Het ontstaan van de vier evangeliën volgens 'Abd al-Djabbar. *Ned. theol.tijds.* 28(1974), pp. 215-238.

BASETTI-SANI, G. Francesco d'Assisi e l'Islam. *Renovatio* 8(1973), pp. 47-72, 233-240.

BAUSANI, A. Modernismo e "eresie" nell'Islam contemporaneo. *Sviluppi recenti e tendenze modernistiche nelle religioni asiatiche,* 1975, pp. 9-23.

BHATTACHARYA, Aparna. Worship of Satyapir, an example of Hindu Muslim rapprochement in Bengal. *Proc.32 Ind.hist.cong.* 1970, vol. 2, pp. 204-207.

BIJLEFELD, W.A. God, the 'ultimate reality', and the 'real issues' of today: searching for some of the proper questions for a Muslim-Christian dialogue in our time. *Christian-Muslim dialogue,* ed. S.J. Samartha and J.B. Taylor, 1972, pp. 49-57.

BISHOP, E.F.F. The precincts and the shrine. *MW* 64(1974), pp. 165-171.

BLUE, L. Practical ecumenism: Jews, Christians and Moslems in Europe. *J. ecumenical stud.* 10(1973), pp. 17-29.

BOLAND, B.J. Missiologia in loco. Christendom en Islam en Indonesië. *Ned.theol. tijds.* 23(1968-9), pp. 46-65.

BUHAIRI, Marwan. Tocqueville on Islam. *al-Abhath* 24(1971), pp. 103-109.

BURNS, R.I. Christian-Islamic confrontation in the West: the thirteenth-century dream of conversion. *Amer.hist.R.* 76 (1971), pp. 1386-1412, 1432-1434.

CARDAILLAC, L. Morisques et Protestants. *And.* 36(1971), pp. 29-61.

CRAGG, K. "In the name of God ...." *Islam and the modern age* 4 i (1973), pp. 1-10.

CRAGG, K. 'In the name of God...' *Christian-Muslim dialogue,* ed. S.J. Samartha and J.B. Taylor, 1972, pp. 137-144.

CROSSLEY, J. The Islam in Africa project. *Int.R.mission* 61(1972), pp. 150-160.

DAN, Dafna. Education in hatred. *Crescent and star,* ed. by Y. Alexander and N.N. Kittrie, 1973, pp. 118-124.

DAN, Dafna. Jews in Arab countries. *Crescent and star,* ed. by Y. Alexander and N.N. Kittrie, 1973, pp. 187-196.

DANIEL, N. Le P. Moubarac et le dialogue islamo-chrêtien. *MIDEO* 12(1974), pp. 203-210.

DARROUZES, J. Tomos inédit de 1180 contre Mahomet. *Rev. ét. byzantines* 30(1972), pp. 187-197.

DAWODU, S.A. Youth and Islam in Nigeria. *Nigerian J. Islam* 1ii(1971), pp. 29-32.

DE SOUZA, A. Dialogue between religions in India: nature, purpose and problems. *Islam and the modern age* 3iii(1972), pp. 77-91.

DESSOUKI, Ali E. Hillal. Reflections on community relationship between Christians and Muslims in the Middle East. *Christian-Muslim dialogue,* ed. S.J. Samartha and J.B. Taylor, 1972, pp. 99-107.

DODGE, B. Mani and the Manichaeans. *Medieval and Middle Eastern studies ... A.S. Atiya* 1972, pp. 86-105.

DODGE, Bayard. The Ṣābians of Ḥarrān. *American University of Beirut Festival book,* 1967, pp. 59-85.

DOI, A.R.I. The Arab concept of Ifriqiya and the planting of Islam in Africa. *Africa qly* 12(1972-73), pp. 202-214.

ENVER, I.H. Contemporary Islam versus Hinduism. *India and contemporary Islam,* ed. S.T. Lokhandwalla, 1971, pp. 357-365.

EPALZA, M. de. Cordoba islamo-chrêtienne: un congrès et une prière commune. *Travaux et jours* 53(1974), pp. 105-117.

EPALZA, M. de. Cordova welcomes its Muslim friends. Some notes on a Muslim-Christian congress and on the prayers in Cordova's mosque-cathedral. *MW* 65 (1975), pp. 132-136.

EPALZA, M. de. Notes pour une histoire de polémiques anti-chrétiennes dans l'Occident Musulman. *Arabica* 18(1971), pp. 99-106.

EPALZA, M. de. La Tuḥfa, autobiografia y polémica islámica contra el Christianismo de 'Abdallah al-Tarȳumān (fray Anselmo Turmeda). *Memorie, Cl. sci. mor., stor e filol., ANL* 15(1971), pp. 522.

FRIEDMANN, Yohanan. Medieval Muslim views of Indian religions. *JAOS* 95(1975), pp. 214-221.

II RELIGION

FRIEDMANN, Y. The temple of Multan: a note on early Muslim attitudes to idolatry. *In memoriam S.M. Stern* (Israel Or. studies, II, 1972), pp. 176-182.

GABRIELI, F. Islam e Cristianesimo a confronto. *Levante* 19i-ii(1972), pp. 5-8.

GIMARET, D. Traces et parallèles du *Kitāb Bilawhar wa Būdāsf* dans la tradition arabe. *BEO* 24(1971), pp. 97-133.

GÓMEZ NOGALES, S. Santo Tomás y los árabes. Bibliografía. *Miscelanea Comillas* 32 (1975), pp. 205-250.

HAINES, B.L. South East Asian Muslims and Christians in consultation. *al-Mushir* 17 (1975), pp. 61-69.

HARTMAN, S.S. Les identifications de Gayōmart a l'époque islamique. *Syncretism*, 1969, pp. 263-294.

HARTMAN, S.S. Secrets for Muslims in Parsi scriptures. *Islam and its cultural divergence. Studies in honor of Gustave E. von Grunebaum*, 1971, pp. 63-75

HAUZIŃSKI, Jerzy. On alleged attempts at converting the Assasins to Christianity in the light of William of Tyre's account. *Folia Or.* 15(1974), pp. 229-246.

HAYIT, Baymirza. Der Islam und die anti-islamische Bewegung in der Sowjetunion. *Osteuropa* 22(1972), pp. 114-118

HELLER, L.M. Anti-Islamic polemic in Pascal's *Pensées* with particular reference to Grotius' *De Veritate Religionis Christianae*. *Neophilologus* 55(1971), pp. 246-260

HOFFMANN, H. Manichaeism and Islam in the Buddhist Kâlacakra system. *Proc. 9th Int.Cong.Hist.Rel.*, 1958, pp. 96-99.

HUSAIN, S. Abid. Report on the seminar on inter-religious understanding. *Islam and the modern age* 3i(1972), pp. 1-16

HUSAIN, S. Abid. Towards peace on the spiritual plane (Christian-Muslim dialogue, Broumana July 11-18, 1972). *Islam and the modern age* 3 iv (1972), pp. 89-95.

KAMALI, S.A. Islamic views of other religious communities. *Ghana bull.theol.* 2viii (1965), pp. 17-27.

KENNY, J.P. Towards better understanding of Muslims and Christians. *Nigerian J. Islam* 2i(1971-2), pp. 51-53.

KHAN, Abdul Majid. Islam and other religions and cultures. *India and contemporary Islam*, ed. S.T. Lokhandwalla, 1971, pp. 88-97.

KISHTAINY, Khalid. The anti-semitism blackmail. *Crescent and star*, ed. by Y. Alexander and N.N. Kittrie, 1973, pp. 101-108.

LAWAL, O.A. Islam and the youth. *Nigerian J. Islam* 1i(1970), pp. 48-50.

LAWRENCE, B.B. Shahrastānī on Indian idol worship. *SI* 38(1973), pp. 61-74.

LÖFFLER, P. Religion, nation and the search for a world community. Some comments from a Christian theological perspective. *Christian-Muslim dialogue*, ed. S.J. Samartha and J.B. Taylor, 1972, pp. 24-31.

LUTUIHAMALLO, P.D. Revelation, truth and obedience. *Christian-Muslim dialogue*, ed. S.J. Samartha and J.B. Taylor, 1972, pp. 73-79.

MAGNIN, J.G. Rencontre islamo-chrétienne. Conscience chrétienne et conscience musulmane aux prises avec les défis du développement. Tunis, 11-17 Novembre 1974. *IBLA* 37(no.134, 1974), pp. 329-343.

MALIK, A.J. Sermons in the mosque. *Al-Mushir* 13v-vi(1971), pp. 1-12

MATKOVSKI, A. L'Islam aux yeux des non-musulmans des Balkans. *Balcanica* 4(1973), pp. 203-211.

MELIKIAN-CHIRVANI, A.S. L'évocation littéraire du bouddhisme dans l'Iran musulman. *Le monde iranien et l'Islam* II, 1974, pp. 1-72.

MERAD, Ali. Revelation, truth and obedience. *Christian-Muslim dialogue*, ed. S.J. Samartha and J.B. Taylor, 1972, pp. 58-72.

MERIGOUX, J.-M. Un précurseur du dialogue islamo-chretien, Frère Ricoldo (1243-1320). *Rev. thomiste* 73(1973), pp. 609-621.

MILDENBERGER, M. The impact of Asian religions on Germany. *Int. rev. missions* 62 (no.245, 1973), pp. 34-42.

MONNOT, G. Les écrits musulmans sur les religions non-bibliques. *MIDEO* 11(1972), pp. 5-49.

MONNOT, G. L'histoire des religions en Islam, Ibn al-Kalbi et Rāzī. *RHR* 188 (1975), pp. 23-34.

MONNOT, G. Quelques textes de ʿAbd al-Jabbār sur le manichéisme. *RHR* 183(1973), pp. 3-9.

MONNOT, G. Sabéens et idolâtres selon ʿAbd al-Jabbār. *MIDEO* 12(1974), pp. 13-48.

MUFTIC, Mahmud. Psychological crusades of the modern time. *Nigerian J. Islam* 1ii (1971), pp. 23-28.

MUKTI ALI, H.A. Religions, nations and the search for a world community. *Christian-Muslim dialogue*, ed. S.J. Samartha and J.B. Taylor, 1972, pp. 18-23.

MUSHIR-UL-HAQ. Inter-religious understanding. A step toward the realization of the ideal of the world community. *Christian-Muslim dialogue*, ed. S.J. Samartha and J.B. Taylor, pp. 32-39.

II RELIGION

MUSHIRUL HAQ. Muslim understanding of Hindu religion. *Islam and the modern age* 4iv (1973), pp. 71-77.

NAGEL, T. Das Problem der Orthodoxie im frühen Islam. *Studien zum Minderheitenproblem im Islam* I, 1973, pp. 7-44.

NARAIN, Harsh. Feasibility of a dialogue between Hinduism and Islam. *Islam and the modern age* 6iv(1975), pp. 57-85.

OSORIO, E.L. Christian-Muslim integration. *Silliman J.* 20(1973), pp. 258-270.

PANDEY, B.M. Indian religions and the West: historical perspectives. *India's contribution to world thought ...,* 1970, pp. 615-622.

PERLMANN, M. Shaykh al-Damanhūrī against the churches of Cairo (1739). *Actas IV congresso de estudos árabes e islâmicos* 1968(1971), pp. 27-32.

PHILLIPS, D.H. The American missionary in Morocco. *MW* 65(1975), pp. 1-20.

PINES, S. "Israel, my firstborn" and the sonship of Jesus: a theme of Moslem anti-Christian polemics. *Studies in mysticism and religion presented to G.G. Scholem,* 1967, pp. 177-190.

QAMARUDDIN. Kabir as depicted in the Persian sufistic and historical works. *Islam and the modern age* 3i(1972), pp. 57-75

SADRE, Imam Musa al-. Truth, revelation and obedience. *Christian-Muslim dialogue,* ed. S.J. Samartha and J.B. Taylor 1972, pp. 42-48.

SALIBA, Issa A. The Bible in Arabic: the 19th-century Protestant translation. *MW* 65(1975), pp. 254-263.

SAMARTHA, S.J. Christian-Muslim dialogue in the perspective of recent history. *Christian-Muslim dialogue,* ed. S.J. Samartha and J.B. Taylor, 1972, pp. 10-15.

SAMARTHA, S.J. Looking beyond Broumana - 1972. *Christian-Muslim dialogue,* ed. S.J. Samartha and J.B. Taylor, 1972, pp. 145-155.

SAMARTHA, S.J. The Welcome Address - Christian-Muslim dialogue in the perspective of recent history. *Islam and the modern age* 3 iv (1972), pp. 43-48.

SAMB, Amar. L'Islam et le Christianisme, par Cheikh Moussa Kamara. Traduction et annotations. *Bull. IFAN* 35(1973), pp. 269-322.

SANGAR, S.P. Conversions of Hindus to Islam during Aurangzeb's reign. *Panjab Univ.res.bull.* (arts) 2ii(1971), pp. 61-68

SANNEH, Lamin. Amulets and Muslim orthodoxy. One Christian's venture into primal religious spirituality. *Int.R. mission* 63(1974), pp. 515-529.

SANNEH, Lamin O. Prayer and worship (Muslim and Christian): challenges and opportunities. *Christian-Muslim dialogue,* ed. S.J. Samartha and J.B. Taylor, 1972, pp. 110-119.

SANTOS, R.J. de los. How Christian-Muslim relations affect acculturation and development. *Silliman J.* 20(1973), pp. 252-257.

SCHOEN, U. Orientations pour un dialogue entre Chrétiens et Musulmans. *Rev. hist. philos. rel.* 55(1975), pp. 303-305.

SHARMA, S.L. and SRIVASTAVA, R.N. Institutional resistance to induced Islamization in a convert community - an empiric study in sociology of religion. *Sociol. bull.* 16i (1967), pp. 69-80.

SLOMP, J. Vergelijking van Islam en Christendom. *Gereformeerd theol. tijdschrift* 27(1972), pp. 216-230.

SMET, R.V. de. Advances in Muslim-Christian dialogue. *Islam and the modern age* 3i (1972), pp. 47-56

SOZE, A.A.A.K. Background & nature of Guru Nanak's mission: an Islamic viewpoint. *Islam and the modern age* 4 i (1973), pp. 51-65.

SPEIGHT, R.M. Attitudes toward Christians as revealed in the *Musnad* of al-Ṭayālisī. *MW* 63(1973), pp. 249-268.

SRISANTO, S. Church growth and the cultivation of positive Christian/Muslim relations. *Int.R.mission* 63(1974), pp. 355-361.

STEPANYANTZ, M.T. O religiozno-filosofskikh vzglyadakh Mukhammadaabdo. *Religiya i obshchestvennaya mysl' stran Vostoka,* 1974, pp. 287-298.

STILLMAN, N.A. The story of Cain and Abel in the Qur'an and the Muslim commentators-some observations. *JSS* 19(1974), pp. 231-239.

TALIB, Gurbachan Singh. Inter-religious harmony. *Islam and the modern age* 3 iv (1972), pp. 22-40.

TAYLOR, J.B. Community relationship between Christians and Muslims. *Christian-Muslim dialogue,* ed. S.J. Samartha and J.B. Taylor, 1972, pp. 90-98.

TRAPP, E. Die Dialexis des Mönchs Euthymios mit einem Sarazenen. *Jhb.der Österr.Byzantinistik* 20(1971), pp. 111-131

TRAPP, E. Die Stellung der beiden Apologien des Vat. gr. 1107 in der byzantinischen Islampolemik. *Jhb.Österr.Byz.Ges.*16(1967), pp. 199-202.

TURNER, C.J.G. A Slavonic version of John Cantacuzenus's *Against Islam.* *Slav. East Eur. R.* 51(1973), pp. 113-123.

UKPABI, S.C. Christianity and Islam and change in African society and religion. *Africa qly.* 11(1971), pp. 126-135.

VAN DER MERWE, W.J. Impact of Christianity and Islam upon Africa. *S.Afr.J.Afr.aff.* 4i(1974), pp. 17-32.

VERCELLIN, G. Azrachiti e Rauscianiti nell' Islam afghano. *Veltro* 16v-vi(1972), pp. 599-608.

VERNET, J. Le Tafsir au service de la polémique antimusulmane. *SI* 32(1970), pp. 305-309.

VOLL, J. Muḥammad Ḥayyā al-Sindī and Muḥammad ibn 'Abd al-Wahhāb: an analysis of an intellectual group in eighteenth-century Madīna. *BSOAS* 38(1975), pp. 32-39.

WALTZ, J. Historical perspectives on "early missions" to Muslims. A response to Allan Cutler. *MW* 61(1971), pp. 170-186.

WEISHER, B.M. Islamic influence in Christian mysticism. Comparative studies on the *Book of lover and beloved* of Raymundus Lullus. *al-Mushir* 17(1975), pp. 79-90.

WILD, S. Gott und Mensch im Libanon. Die Affäre Ṣādiq al-ʿAẓm. *Der Islam* 48(1971-2), pp. 206-253

WISMER, D. Jesus as word: Islam. *Milla wa-milla* 15(1975), pp. 15-26.

ZAEHNER, R.C. Why not Islam? *Religious studies* 11(1975), pp. 167-179.

In search of understanding and cooperation. Christian and Muslim consultation. Broumana, Lebanon, July 1972. *Int.R.mission* 61(1972), pp. 409-416.

Memorandum. In search of understanding and cooperation. Christian and Muslim contributions. *Christian-Muslim dialogue*, ed. S.J. Samartha and J.B. Taylor, 1972, pp. 156-163.

Ministry of Foreign Affairs, Jerusalem. On Arab anti-semitism. *Crescent and star*, ed. by Y. Alexander and N.N. Kittrie, 1973, pp. 125-130.

Muslims and Christians in society: towards good-will consultations and working together in South East Asia. *al-Mushir* 17 (1975), pp. 70-78.

Rencontre islamo-chrétienne à Rome. *Proche Orient chrétien* 21(1971), pp. 56-61.

See also I. b. 3. Rubinacci.

See also II. a. 4. Shamir.

See also II. a. 5. Jarry

See also II. b. 2. Sanneh.

See also XIII. a. Marston Speight.

See also XV. c. Ladjili.

See also XV. c. Soumille.

See also XVI. c. Cerbella.

See also XXXII. q. Saiyidain.

See also XXXIV. g. Jones.

See also XXXV. a. Granja

See also XXXVII. h. Granja

viii Modernism. Reform movements

AHMAD, N.D. Syed Ahmad Brelvi, his mission, life and teachings. *J.Research Soc.Pakistan* 7i(1970), pp. 78-89.

ALI, S.M. Saiyed Jamal-al Din Afghani: his visits to India. *JAS Bangladesh* 18(1973), pp. 207-219.

ANSARI, M. Abdul Haq. Necessity of religion in the modern age. *Islam and the modern age* 1 ii (1970), pp. 50-58.

ANWARUL HAG, M. The *Dīnī Da'wat* (Religious call) of Mawlānā Ilyās. *Proc.27th Int. Cong.Or.1967* (1971), pp. 397-398.

ARKOUN, Mohammed. Islam facing development. *Diogenes* 77(1972), pp. 71-91.

ASKARI, Hasan. Islam and modernity. *India and contemporary Islam*, ed. S.T. Lokhandwalla, 1971, pp. 217-228.

ASKARI, Hasan Modernity and faith. *IMA* liii(1970), pp. 39-48.

ASOPA, Sheel K. Religious revivalism in modern Turkey. *India and contemporary Islam*, ed. S.T. Lokhandwalla, 1971, pp. 37-43.

BALOGUN, I.A.B. Features of the *Ihyā' al-Sunna wa-Ikhmād al-Bidʿa* of Uthman b. Fodiye. *Res. Bull. CAD Ibadan* 6(1970), pp. 13-41.

BASHIRUDDIN, S. Modernity and traditionalism in Islam with special reference to contemporary India. *India and contemporary Islam*, ed. S.T. Lokhandwalla, 1971, pp. 229-251.

BATRĀN, 'Abd-al-'Aziz 'Abd-Allah. A contribution to the biography of Shaikh Muhammad ibn 'Abd-al-Karim ibn Muhammad ('Umar-A'mar) al-Maghīlī, al-Tilimsānī. *J. Afr. hist.* 14(1973), pp. 381-394.

BUSSE, H. Tradition und Akkulturation im islamischen Modernismus (19./20. Jahrhundert). *Saeculum* 26(1975), pp. 157-165.

BUTLER, R.A. Ghulam Ahmad Parvez: ideological revolution through the Qur'an. *al-Mushir* 17(1975), pp. 1-59.

BUTLER, R.A. Secularizing trends in West Pakistan. *Al-Mushir* 13i-ii(1971), pp. 1-25

CHARTIER, M. Khâlid Muḥammad Khâlid, héraut de la liberté perdue. *IBLA* (no.131, 1973), pp. 1-24.

II RELIGION

DELANOUE, G. Endoctrinement religieux et idéologie ottomane: l'addresse de Muh'ammad 'Abduh au Cheikh al-Islam, Beyrouth, 1887. *ROMM* 13-14(1973), pp. 293-312.

DE SOUZA, A. Changing conceptions of morality and law in modern society. *Islam and the modern age* 5i(1974), pp. 49-70.

DESSOUKI, Alli E. Hillal. The views of Salama Musa on religion and secularism. *Islam and the modern age* 4iii(1973), pp. 23-34.

FARUQI, Ziya-ul Hasan. The Tablīghī Jamā'at. *India and contemporary Islam*, ed. S.T. Lokhandwalla, 1971, pp. 60-69.

GIBB, H.A.R. Islam in the modern world. *The Arab Middle East and Muslim Africa*, ed. by T. Kerekes, 1961, pp. 9-25.

GÖKBILGIN, M. Tayyib. Kâtip Çelebi, interprète et rénovateur des traditions religieuses au XVIIIe siècle. *Turcica* 3 (1971), pp. 71-79.

HĀ'IRĪ, Abdul-Hādī. Afghani on the decline of Islam. *WI* 13(1971), pp. 121-125; N.S.14(1973), pp. 116-128.

HANNA, Sami, GARDNER, G. Khayr ad-Dīn (1822-1890) and Muḥammad 'Abduh (1849-1905): did they or didn't they? *AJAS* 2(1974), pp. 22-52.

HANNA, Sami A. The roots of Islam in modern Tunisia. *IC* 46(1972), pp. 93-100.

HAQ, Mushir U. Indian Muslims and personal law. *Islam and the modern age* 2i(1971), pp. 75-93.

HOPWOOD, D. A pattern of revival movements in Islam? *IQ* 15(1971), pp. 149-158.

HUSAINI, I.M. Islam and modern problems. *Maj.al-Azhar* 45i(1973), pp. 7-14.

ISHAQUE, Khalid. Iqbal and the modern man. *Iqbal rev.* 15iii(1974), pp. 12-21.

JAMAL KHWAJA, A. Modernism and traditionalism in Islam. *India and contemporary Islam*, ed. S.T. Lokhandwalla, 1971, pp. 252-269.

JANSEN, J.J.G. "I suspect that my friend Abdu (...) was in reality an agnostic". *Acta Orientalia Neerlandica* ed. P.W. Pestman, 1971, pp. 71-74.

JAWED, Nasim Ahmad. Religion and modernity: some nineteenth- and twentieth-century Indo-Pakistani ideas. *MW* 61(1971), pp. 73-89.

JOMIER, J. Quelques livres égyptiens modernes sur le problème religieux. *MIDEO* 11(1972), pp. 251-274.

KEDDIE, N.R. Islamic philosophy and Islamic modernism: the case of Sayyid Jamāl ad-Dīn al-Afghānī. *Proc.27th Int. Cong.Or.1967* (1971), p. 190.

KHAKIMOV, I.M. Prebyvanie musul'manskogo reformatora i politicheskogo deyatel'ya Vostoka Dzhamal' ad-dina Afgani v Rossii (1887-1889 gg). *Strany Blizhnego i Srednego Vostoka: istoriya, ekonomica,* 197? pp. 186-193.

KHAKIMOV, I.M. Sovremennaya istoriografiya OAR o Dzhamal' ad-Dine Afgani. *Religiya i obshchestvennaya mysl' narodov vostoka,* 1971, pp. 253-263.

KHALID, Detlev. Muslims and the purport of secularism. *Islam and the modern age* 5ii (1974), pp. 28-40.

KHAN, M.A. Saleem Religion and politics in Turkey. Survey of contemporary developments in the Muslim world. *Islam and the modern age* 2i(1971), pp. 94-108.

KHUNDMIRI, S. Alam. A critical examination of Islamic traditionalism. *Islam and the modern age* 2ii(1971), pp. 1-18.

KHUNDMIRI, S. Alam. A critical examination of Islamic traditionalism with reference to the demands of modernization. *India and contemporary Islam*, ed. S.T. Lokhandwalla, 1971, pp. 270-284.

KRAIEM, M. Au sujet des incidences des deux séjours de Moḥammed 'Abduh en Tunisie. *Rev.d'hist.maghrebine* 3(1975), pp. 91-94.

KUDSI-ZADEH, A.A. Afg͟hānī on Afghanistan. *IJMES* 4(1973), pp. 367-368.

KUDSI-ZADEH, A.A. Afghānī and Freemasonry in Egypt. *JAOS* 92(1972), pp. 25-35

KUDSI-ZADEH, A.A. Islamic reform in Egypt: some observations on the role of Afghani. *MW* 61(1971), pp. 1-12.

KUDSI-ZADEH, A.A. Jamāl al-Dīn al-Afghānī and the national awakening of Egypt: a reassessment of his role. *Ve Congrès International d'Arabisants et d'Islamisants. Actes.*, [1970?], pp. 297-305.

LAZARUS-YAFEH, Hava. Contemporary religious thought among the ʿUlamāʾ of al-Azhar. *Asian & Afr.Studs.* 7(1971), pp. 211-236.

LELONG, M. Unanimité et pluralisme dans la pensée islamique d'aujourd'hui. *ROMM* 15-16 (1973), pp. 127-138.

LEVIN, S.F. O tolkovaniyakh zapreshcheniya ssudnogo protzenta u Musul'man Pakistana v svyazi s burzhuaznoy reformatziey Islama. *Religiya i obshchestvennaya mysl' narodov vostoka,* 1971, pp. 117-139.

MAHMUD-UL-HAQ, Islamic modernism. A response to the challenge of modern age. *Islam and the modern age* 2ii(1971), pp. 80-86.

MARTINS DE CARVALHO, H. L'Islam actuel et les grands problèmes mondiaux. *Ve Congrès International d'Arabisants et d'Islamisants. Actes.*, [1970?], pp. 339-343.

MUJEEB, M. The status of the individual conscience in Islam. *Studies in Islam* 7(1970), pp. 125-149.

NOWAIHI, Mohamed al-. Problems of modernization in Islam. *MW* 65(1975), pp. 174-186.

NWYIA, P. L'Islam face à la crise du language moderne. *Travaux et jours* 38(1971), pp. 81-101.

PHILIPP, Mangol Bayat. The concepts of religion and government in the thought of Mîrzâ Āqâ Khân Kirmânî, a nineteenth-century Persian revolutionary. *IJMES* 5(1974), pp. 381-400.

QAMARUDDIN. Sayyid Muhammad Jaunpuri, a spiritual reformer. *IMA* 1iii(1970), pp. 91-109.

QAMAR UDDIN. Saiyid Muḥammad Jaunpurī and the Mahdawī movement in India. *Studs. in Islam* 8(1971), pp. 165-187.

ROSENTHAL, E.I.J. Religion and politics in Islam. *Islam and the modern age* 1 i (1970), pp. 50-64.

SAAB, H. Modèles islamiques de modernisation au Moyen-Orient. *Renaissance du monde arabe. Colloque interarabe de Louvain*, 1972, pp. 277-291.

SHEPARD, W.E. A modernist view of Islam and other religions. *MW* 65(1975), pp. 79-92.

SMITH, A.D. Nationalism and religion. The role of religious reform in the genesis of Arab and Jewish nationalism. *Arch.sc.soc. des rel.* 35(1973), pp. 23-43.

TURAN, Osman. The need of Islamic renaissance. *Internat. Islamic Conf.*, 1968, pp. 24-31.

WHEELER, G. Modernization in the Muslim East: the role of script and language reform. *Asian affairs* 61(N.S.5, 1974), pp. 157-164.

WILD, S. Ṣādiq al-ʿAẓm's book "Critique of religious thought". *Ve Congrès International d'Arabisants et d'Islamisants. Actes.*, [1970?], pp. 507-513.

See also II. a. 5. Sherwani.

See also II. c. 8. Millward.

See also IV. a. Muñoz Jiménez

See also V. a. *Representation*. Paret

See also IX. c. Umar.

See also IX. g. Malik

See also IX. k. Smith.

See also XVI. e. Doi

See also XXIX. j. Khalid.

See also XXXIII. c. Gul'dzhanov.

See also XXXVII. 1. Badawi

See also XLIII. a. Plancke.

b DOGMATICS. RELIGIOUS OBSERVANCE

ABDUL, Musa. The Ramadan fasts. *Nigerian J.Islam* 2ii(1972-74), pp. 33-39.

ABEL, A. La djizya: tribut ou rançon? *SI* 32(1970), pp. 5-19.

AHMED, Gulzar. Concept of war in Islam. *Internat. Islamic Conf.*, 1968, pp. 48-56.

AHMED, Ziauddin. The concept of jizya in early Islam. *Islamic studies* 14(1975), pp. 293-305.

ALAWI, Anwar Ahmad. The *Jizyah* or the Capitation Tax. *J. Pakistan Hist. Soc.* 16(1968), pp. 182-189.

ALI, Maulana Muhammed. Jihad--its meaning and significance. *Maj.al-Azhar* 45viii(1974), pp. 7-12; 45ix(1974), pp. 9-16; 45x(1975), pp. 9-16; 47i(1975), pp. 4-10; 47ii(1975), pp. 9-16.

ALWAYE, Mohiaddin. Fasting - an institution for moral elevation and spiritual development. *Majallat al-Azhar* 45(no.7, 1973), pp. 1-3.

ALWAYE, Mohiaddin. Fasting in Islam. *Majallat al-Azhar* 43vii(1971), pp. 1-6

ALWAYE, Mohiaddin. Hijra: the migration of the vanguard of Islam. *Majallat al-Azhar* 47i(1975), pp. 1-3.

ALWAYE, Mohiaddin. The institution of zakāt in Islam. *Maj. al-Azhar* 46vi (1974), pp. 1-7.

ALWAYE, Mohiaddin. Islam prohibits intoxicants and eating of pork. *Maj. al-Azhar* 47ii(1975), pp. 1-8.

ALWAYE, Mohiaddin. The pilgrimage in Islam. *Maj.al-Azhar* 44x(1972), pp. 1-3.

ALWAYE, Mohiaddin. The role of 'Hijrah' in the spread of Islam. *Majallat al-Azhar* 44i(1972), pp. 1-4.

ALWAYE, Mohiaddin. The significance of Ka'ba in Mecca. *Maj.al-Azhar* 44ix(1972), pp. 1-4.

ALWAYE, A.M. Mohiaddin. The significance of 'Hijrah'. *Majallat al-Azhar* 43i(1971), pp. 1-4.

ALWAYE, Mohiaddin. Social and physical values of fasting in Ramadan. *Maj.al-Azhar* 47vii(1975), pp. 1-5.

ALWAYE, Mohiaddin. The spiritual experience and the levelling influence of "hajj". *Maj. al-Azhar* 45x(1975), pp. 1-8.

ALWAYE, Mohiaddin Why Makka is chosen for Hajj. *Majallat al-Azhar* 43x(1971), pp. 1-4.

II RELIGION

'ANKAWI, Abdullah. The pilgrimage to Mecca in Mamluk times. *Arabian studs.* 1(1974), pp. 146-170.

ANSARI, Ali Ahmad. Direction of the Qibla. *Stud. in Islam* 6(1969), pp. 218-227.

ASKARI, Hasan. Worship and prayer. *Islam and the modern age* 4 i (1973), pp. 20-37.

FALLERS, L.A. and FALLERS, M.C. Notes on an Advent Ramadan. *J.Amer.Acad.Religion* 42(1974), pp. 35-52.

FISHER, H.J. Prayer and military activity in the history of Muslim Africa south of the Sahara. *J. Afr. hist.* 12(1971), pp. 391-406.

GEYOUSHI, Muhammad Ibrahim el- The pilgrimage (Hajj) and its significance. *Majallat al-Azhar* 43x(1971), pp. 5-8.

HAARMANN, U. Die Pflichten des Muslims -- Dogma und geschichtliche Wirklichkeit. *Saeculum* 26(1975), pp. 95-110.

HAMIDULLAH, Muhammad. Daily life of a Muslim. *Maj. al-Azhar* 46vi(1974), pp. 8-16; 45vii, pp. 7-16.

HAMIDULLAH, Muhammad. Devotional life and religious practices of Islam. *Majallat al-Azhar* 42viii(1970), pp. 6-11; 43i (1971), pp. 5-11

HAMIDULLAH, M. The service of worship: why in Arabic alone? *Majallat al-Azhar* 45x (1974), pp. 10-14.

JOMIER, J. Un aspect de l'activité d'al-Azhar du XVIIe aux débuts du XIXe siècle: les 'ɛqa'id ou professions de foi. *Colloque international sur l'histoire du Caire,* 1969, pp. 243-252.

KHALID, Sheikh Hassan. The doctrine of martyrdom in Islam. *Majallat al-Azhar* 46i (1974), pp. 7-16; 46ii(1974), pp. 8-16; 46 iii(1974), pp. 9-16.

KING, Russel. The pilgrimage to Mecca: some geographical and historical aspects. *Erdkunde* 26(1972), pp. 61-73

LAMBTON, A.K.S. A nineteenth century view of Jihād. *SI* 32(1970), pp. 181-192.

LAVERS, J.E. The adventures of a Kano pilgrim 1892-1893. *Kano studies* 4(1968), pp. 69-75.

MASRI, F.H. el-. The role of imams in the new Nigeria. *Nigerian J. Islam* 1i(1970), pp. 21-24.

NAQVI, Ali Raza. Laws of war in Islam. *Islamic stud.* 13i(1974), pp. 25-43.

NEUBAUER, E. Von. Muharram-Bräuche im heutigen Persien. *Der Islam* 49(1972), pp. 249-272.

POPOVIC, A. Sur les récits de Pèlerinage à la Mecque des musulmans yougoslaves (1949-1972). *SI* 39(1974), pp. 129-144.

RĀGIB, Yūsuf. Essai d'inventaire chronologique des guides à l'usage des pèlerins du Caire. *REI* 41(1973), pp. 259-280.

SANNEH, L.O. Prayer and worship (Muslim and Christian). *Islam and the modern age* 3 iv (1972), pp. 79-88.

SCHIMMEL, A. The meaning of prayer in Mowlana Jalaloddin Balkhi's work. *Afghanistan* 27iii(1974), pp. 33-45.

STRIKA, V. Un'interpretazione "psicologica" del *mihrāb*. *Annali Fac.Ling.Lett. stran.di Ca' Foscari (serie orientale)* 2 (1971), pp. 27-37.

STRIKA, V. Intorno a un "mihrāb" di Mossul. *AION* 35(N.S.25, 1975), pp. 201-214.

VALIUDDIN, Mir The secrets of Hajj (Pilgrimage to K'aba): the Sufi approach. *Islam and the modern age* 2iv(1971), pp. 42-70.

The farewell pilgrimage of the Prophet. *Maj. al-Azhar* 44x(1972), pp. 3-5.

Hajj (pilgrimage - in verses from the Quran). *Majallat al-Azhar* 45x(1974), pp. 15-16.

See also IV. c. 4. Rohr.

See also VI. d. Lavers.

See also VIII. c. *Arabia.* Tamari.

See also XIX. g. 'Ankawi.

See also XXXV. a. Urvoy.

c ASCETICISM. MYSTICISM. SECTS

i Asceticism. Monachism

FAKHRY, Majid. Three varieties of mysticism in Islam. *Religion* 2(1971), pp. 193-207.

KÖBERT, R. Zur Ansicht des frühen Islam über das Mönchtum (*rahbānīya*). *Orientalia* 42(1974), pp. 520-524.

MARQUET, Y. A propos des origines de la hierarchie mystique en Islam. *Ann.Fac.Lett. et Sci.Hum., Univ.Dakar* 3(1973), pp. 119-125.

NASR, Seyyed Hossein. Elements of continuity in the life of mysticism and philosophy in Iran. *Commémoration Cyrus. Hommage universel,* I, 1974, pp. 261-267.

ii Sufism

ABDUR RABB. Subhâni, a daring utterance of Abû Yazîd Al-Bistâmi. *J.Reg.Cult.Inst.* 5i (1972), pp. 19-36

'ABDUR RABB, Muhammad. Abū Yazīd al-Bisṭāmī's contribution to the development of Ṣūfīsm. *Iqbal rev.* 12iii(1971), pp. 49-73

ABEL, A. Réflexions sur le conditionnement collectif de l'Islam sous l'influence des écoles mystiques (IXe-XIIe s.). *Ve Congrès International d'Arabisants et d'Islamisants. Actes.*, [1970?], pp. 1-19.

ABU SAYEED NUR-UD-DIN. Attitude toward Sufism. *Iqbal: poet-philosopher of Pakistan*, ed. Hafeez Malik, 1971, pp. 287-300.

AHMAD, Nazir. The oldest Persian translation of the 'Awárifu'l-Ma'árif. *Indo-Iranica* 25iii-iv(1972), pp. 20-50.

AKHTAR, Waheed. Sufi approach to the problem of alienation. *Islam and the modern age* 6i(1975), pp. 65-87.

ALI, Hafiz Mohammad Tahir. Shaikh Muhibb-ullah of Allahabad - life and times. *IC* 47 (1973), pp. 241-256.

ARASTEH, A. Reza. Psychology of the Sufi way to individuation. *Sufi Studies: East and West,* 1973, pp. 89-113.

ARDALAN, Nader. La creazione nuova. *Conoscenza religiosa* 1975(3), pp. 323-330.

ARNALDEZ, R. Dynamique et polarité des états mystiques. *L'ambivalence dans la culture arabe,* 1967, pp. 143-152.

AUSTIN, R.W. Some observations on the study of Sufi origins. *Actas IV congresso de estudos árabes e islâmicos* 1968(1971), pp. 101-107.

AZMA, Nazeer el-. Some notes on the impact of the story of the Miʿrāj on Sufi literature. *MW* 63(1973), pp. 93-104.

BAIG, M. Safdar Ali. The concept of love in Sufism. *IC* 45(1971), pp. 267-273

BAIG, M. Safdar Ali. Sufism in Persian poetry. *Indo-Iranica* 23iv(1970), pp. 15-24.

BAKHTIAR, Laleh. La parte del principio femminile nella reintegrazione spirituale. *Conoscenza religiosa* 1975(3), pp. 309-322.

BANNERTH, E. Dhikr et khalwa d'après Ibn ʿAṭā' Allāh. *MIDEO* 12(1974), pp. 65-90.

BASRI, Mir S. Idries Shah: bridge between East and West - humour, philosophy and orientation. *Sufi Studies: East and West,* 1973, pp. 28-32.

BEHARI, Bankey. The way to ecstasy. *Sufi Studies: East and West,* 1973, pp. 183-205.

BEN AMEUR, Taoufik. À propos des "états" et des "demeures" dans la mystique musulmane. *IBLA* 38,no.135(1975), pp. 33-37.

BRAGINSKY, V.Y. Some remarks on the structure of the "Sya'ir Perahu" by Hamzah Fansuri. *BTLV* 131(1975), pp. 407-426.

BRENNER, L. Separate realities: a review of literature on sufism. *Int.J.Afr.hist.stud.* 5(1972), pp. 637-658.

CASPAR, R. Mystique musulmane. Bilan d'une décennie (1963-1973). *IBLA* 37(no. 133, 1974), pp. 69-101; 38(no.135, 1975), pp. 39-111.

CHEN, J.H.M. Literary comparisons and effects. *Sufi Studies: East and West,* 1973, pp. 33-45.

CHITTICK, W.C. Il sufismo operativo in Rūmī. *Conoscenza religiosa* 1975(3), pp. 272-288.

CORBIN, H. Le theme de la resurrection chez Molla Sadra Shirazi (1050/1640), commentateur de Sohrawardi (587/1191). *Studies in mysticism and religion presented to G.G. Scholem,* 1967, pp. 71-115

DANNER, V. The necessity for the rise of the term Ṣūfī. *Stud. comp. relig.* 6(1972), pp. 71-77.

DAVAR, Firoze C. The golden link of mysticism. *Iran Society silver jubilee souvenir* 1944-1969, pp. 49-55.

DIGBY, S. 'Abd al-Quddus Gangohi (1456-1537 A.D.): the personality and attitudes of a medieval Indian sufi. *Medieval India* 3(1975), pp. 1-66.

DOUGLAS, E.H. Prayers of al-Shādhili. *Medieval and Middle Eastern studies ... A.S. Atiya* 1972, pp. 106-121.

EATON, R.M. Sufi folk literature and the expansion of Indian Islam. *History of religions* 14(1974), pp. 117-127.

EBEID, Hilmi Makram. Possibilities of Eastern moral influence on modern civilization. *Sufi Studies: East and West,* 1973, pp. 209-220.

EL'CHIBEKOV, Kudratbek. Obshchie religiozno-filosofskie i fol'klorno-obosnovaniya ierarkhii dukhovenstva v sufizme i ismailizme. *Religiya i obshchestvennaya mysl' stran Vostoka,* 1974, pp. 299-319.

FAHD, Toufy. De Petrus Alfonsi à Idris Shah. *REI* 41(1973), pp. 165-179.

FARAH, C.E. Rules governing the šayh-muršid's conduct. *Numen* 21(1974), pp. 81-96.

FAREED, Sir Razik. Filling a gap in knowledge. *Sufi Studies: East and West,* 1973, pp. 206-208.

FATEMI, Nasrollah S. A message and method of love, harmony and brotherhood. *Sufi Studies: East and West,* 1973, pp. 46-73.

GARCÍA DOMINGUES, J.D. Os mestres luso-árabes de Ibn 'Arabī. *Orientalia Hispanica* I, 1974, pp. 297-304.

GERMANUS, A.K.J. Travel, teaching and living in the East. *Sufi Studies: East and West,* 1973, pp. 74-81.

GLUBB, Sir John. Idries Shah and the Sufis. *Sufi Studies: East and West,* 1973, pp. 139-145.

GRANJA, F. de la. El "Kitāb tuḥfat al-mugtarib bi-bilād al-Magrib". *RIEEI* 17 (1972-3), pp. 123-130; Arabic section pp. 1-245.

GÜVEN, Rasih. Origin of Islamic mysticism. *J. Reg. Cult. Inst.* 6i-ii(1973), pp. 79-98.

HALFF, B. Le *Maḥāsin al-maǧālis* d'Ibn al-ʿArīf et l'oeuvre du soufi hanbalite al-Anṣārī. *REI* 39(1971), pp. 321-325.

HAMARNEH, Saleh. Historico-literary aspects of the work of Idries Shah. *Sufi Studies: East and West,* 1973, pp. 82-88.

HAMIDULLAH, Muhammad. The cultivation of spiritual life. *Majallat al-Azhar* 43ii(1971), pp. 5-13.

HASCHMI, Mohammed Yahia. Spirituality, science and psychology in the Sufi way. *Sufi Studies: East and West,* 1973, pp. 114-132.

HIDAYATULLAH, The Hon. Mr. Justice M. Scope and effect of Sufi writings by Idries Shah. *Sufi Studies: East and West,* 1973, pp. xxxi-xxxvi.

HORTEN, M. Mystics in Islam. Trans. V.J. Hager. *Islamic stud.* 13(1974), pp. 67-93.

IZUTSU, Toshihiko. Creation and the timeless order of things: a study in the mystical philosophy of 'Ayn al-Quḍāt. *Philosophical forum* 4i(1972), pp. 124-140.

KASSIM, Mahmoud. La problème de la prédestination et du libre arbitre chez Leibniz et Ibn 'Arabi. *Annuals of Faculty of Dar al-Ulūm* 1972-3, pp. 1-26.

KEKLIK, Nihat The *Bulgha Fi'l-Ḥikma* of Ibn 'Arabī. *Proc.27th Int.Cong.Or.1967* (1971), p. 254.

KENNEDY, J.G., FAHIM, Hussein. Nubian dhikr rituals and cultural change. *MW* 64(1974), pp. 205-219.

KHALID, M.B. Thoughts on Sufism. *J. Reg. Cult. Inst.* 6i-ii(1973), pp. 65-78.

KHAN, Sahibzada Shaukat Ali. A rare manuscript of Jāmī. *IC* 47(1973), pp. 327-333.

KRITZECK, J. Dervish tales. *Sufi Studies: East and West,* 1973, pp. 153-157.

LANDAU, R. Experience, behaviour, and doctrine in the quest of man. *Sufi Studies: East and West,* 1973, pp. 133-138.

LANDOLT, H. Der Briefwechsel zwischen Kāšānī und Simnānī über Waḥdat al-Wuǧūd. *Der Islam* 50(1973), pp. 29-81.

LANDOLT, H. Mystique iranienne: Suhrawardī *Shaykh al-ishrāq* (549/1155-587/1191) et 'Ayn al-Quzāt-i Hamadānī (492/1098-525/1131). *Iranian Civilization and culture,* ed. C.J. Adams, 1972, pp. 23-37.

LAUGIER de BEAURECUEIL, S. de La pauvreté, attitude essentielle de l'homme en face de dieu, d'après ʿAbdallâh Anṣârî de Hérat (Ve/XIe siècle). *Atti dell'VIII Cong.int.stor.rel.* (1955), pp. 441-443

LAUGIER DE BEAURECUEIL, S. de. La structure du *Livre des étapes* de Khwaja Abdallah Anṣārī, *MIDEO* 11 (1972), pp. 77-125

LAUGIER DE BEAURECUEIL, S.de. La structure du *Livre des étapes* de Khwaja Abdallah Ansari. *Afghanistan* 26iii (1973), pp. 35-83.

MAHASSINI, Zeki El-. Idries Shah: philosopher, writer, poet - and the traditional teachers. *Sufi Studies: East and West,* 1973, pp. 146-152.

MAKDISI, G. Ibn Taimīya: a Ṣūfi of the Qādiriya order. *AJAS* 1(1973), pp. 118-129.

MAKDISI, G. L'Isnad initiatique soufī de Muwaffaq ad-Din Ibn Qudama. *Louis Massignon* (1970), pp. 88-96

MARDAM BEY, Adnan. Idries Shah: the man, the Sufi, and the guiding teacher. *Sufi Studies: East and West,* 1973, pp. 158-164.

MEIER, F. Ḫurāsān und das Ende der klassischen Ṣūfik. *La Persia nel medievo,* 1971, pp. 545-572

MOINUL HAQ, S. Early Sufi shaykhs of the subcontinent. *J.Pak.Hist.Soc.* 22(1974), pp. 1-18.

MOINUL HAQ, S. The origin and growth of Sufism (a brief survey). *J. Pak. Hist. Soc.* 21(1973), pp. 79-108.

MOINUL HAQ, S. Risālah Ḥaqqiyah of Shaykh Niẓām al-Dīn Balkhi. *J.Pakistan Hist.Soc.* 19(1971), pp. 223-264

MOSTOFI, Khosrow. Idries Shah, a latter-day Sufi. *Studies in art and literature of the Near East in honor of R. Ettinghausen,* 1974, pp. 209-228.

MUJEEB, M. Sufis and Sufism. *Dr. Adilya Nath Jha felicitation volume,* III, 1969, pp. 281-307.

NABI, Mohammad Noor. Bābā Farīd Ganj-i-Shakar and his mystical philosophy. *IC* 48 (1974), pp. 237-246.

NAKAMURA, Kōjirō. A structural analysis of *Dhikr* and *Nembutsu*. *Orient [Japan]* 7(1971), pp. 75-96.

NASR, Seyyed Hossein. The influence of Sufism on traditional Persian music. *Stud. comp. relig.* 6(1972), pp. 225-234.

NASR, Seyyed Hossein. Mysticism and traditional philosophy in Persia, Pre-Islamic and Islamic. *Studs.in compar.relig.* 5 (1971), pp. 235-240

NASR, Seyyed Hossein. The Persian works of Shaykh al-ishrâq Shihâb al-Din Suhrawardî. *Proc.27th Int.Cong.Or.1967* (1971), p. 170.

NASR, Seyyed Hossein. The spread of the illuminationist school of Suhrawardi. *Iranshināsi* 2ii(serial no.3, 1971), pp. 84-102.

NASR, Seyyed Hossein. The spread of the illuminationist school of Suhrawardi. *La Persia nel medievo,* 1971, pp. 255-265

NASR, Seyyed Hossein. Sufism and the integration of man. *J. Reg. Cult. Inst.* 1 ii(1967), pp. 35-43.

NASR, Seyyed Hossein. Il sufismo e la perennità della ricerca mistica. *Conoscenza religiosa* 1971, pp. 117-130.

NASR, Seyyed Hossein. Il sufismo e le esigenze spirituali dell'uomo contemporaneo. *Conoscenza religiosa* 1975(3), pp. 238-258.

NASR, Seyyed Hossein. Suhrawardi: The master of illumination, gnostic and martyr. *J. Reg. Cult. Inst.* 2 iv(1969), pp. 209-225.

NIZAMI, Azra. Socio-religious outlook of Abul Fazl. *Medieval India* 2(1972), pp. 99-151.

NWYIA, P. La catéchèse soufie au IVe siècle de l'Hégire. *Ve Congrès International d'Arabisants et d'Islamisants. Actes.,* [1970?], pp. 345-354.

NWYIA, P. Ḥallāǵ, *Kitāb al-Tawāsīn.* *MUSJ* 47(1972), pp. 186-238.

NWYIA, P. Niffari et l'Amour-Nazar. *Islamwissenschaftliche Abhandlungen F. Meier,* 1974, pp. 191-197.

PAUL, H.C. *Bāul*-poets on *Chāri-Chandra* (or four states of the mind). *JAS Bangladesh* 18(1973), pp. 1-53.

QURESHI, Ishtiaq Husain. Projecting Sufi thought in an appropriate context. *Sufi Studies: East and West,* 1973, pp. 25-27.

RAHMAN, M. The language of the Sufis. *Indo Iranica* 26ii-iii(1973), pp. 72-92.

SAIDI, Aga Ahmad. Idries Shah - background and work. *Sufi Studies: East and West,* 1973, pp. 1-12.

SCHIMMEL, A. Maulānā Jalāluddīn Rūmī's story on prayer (Mathnawi III 189). *Yádnáme-ye Jan Rypka* 1967, pp. 125-131.

SCHIMMEL, A. Mīr Dards Gedanken über das Verhältnis von Mystik und Wort. *Festgabe deutscher Iranisten zur 2500 Jahrfeier Irans,* 1971, pp. 117-132.

SCHIMMEL, A. Mystic impact of Hallaj. *Iqbal: poet-philosopher of Pakistan,* ed. Hafeez Malik, 1971, pp. 310-324.

SCHIMMEL, A. Šāh 'Abdul Latīfs Beschreibung des wahren Sufi. *Islamwissenschaftliche Abhandlungen F. Meier,* 1974, pp. 263-284.

SCHIMMEL, A. A 'sincere Muhammadan's' way to salvation. *Man and his salvation; studies in memory of S.G.F. Brandon,* 1973, pp. 221-242.

SCHIMMEL, A. The Sufi ideas of Shaykh Ahmad Sirhindi. *WI* N.S.14(1973), pp. 199-203.

SHAWARBI, Mohammed Yusuf. Shah: knowledge, technique, and influence. *Sufi Studies: East and West,* 1973, pp. 226-245.

SPENCER, S. The Sufi attitude. *Sufi Studies: East and West,* 1973, pp. 165-170.

STEPANYANTS, M.T. The demise of fatalism. *Iqbal: poet-philosopher of Pakistan,* ed. Hafeez Malik, 1971, pp. 301-309.

SULAMI, Abu Mahfuzul Karim. Mas'alat-o-sifatiz zakerin wal mutafakkerin. *Iran Society silver jubilee souvenir* 1944-1969, pp. 343-363.

TAMER, Aref. Sufism in the art of Idries Shah. *Sufi Studies: East and West,* 1973, pp. 171-182.

UTAS, B. Tariq ut-tahqiq. *Afghanistan* 28iii(1975), pp. 25-56.

VACCA, V. Dalla vita di un antico sufi egiziano, frammenti. 'Abd al-Wahhāb ash-Sha'rānī. *Bol. Asoc. esp. orientalistas* 10(1974), pp. 145-150.

VALIUDDIN, Mir. Cleansing of the heart: the Sufi approach. *Studies in Islam* 7(1970), pp. 29-61.

VALIUDDIN, Mir. The problem of the one and the many: the Sufi approach. *Islam and the modern age* 5iv(1974), pp. 11-23.

VALIUDDIN, Mir. Righteousness (a Ṣufi approach). *IC* 45(1971), pp. 157-170.

VALIUDDIN, Mir. Virtue is knowledge - the Sufi approach. *Islam and the modern age* 3iii(1972), pp. 65-76.

WANE, Yaya. *Ceerno* Muhamadu Sayid Baa ou Le soufisme intégral de Madiina Gunaas (Sénégal). *Cah. ét. afr.* 14(1974), pp. 671-698.

WEISCHER, B.M. Mysticism in the East and West. *Iqbal R.* 14i(1973), pp. 24-32.

WILLIAMS, L.F. Rushbrook. Shah in his Eastern context. *Sufi Studies: East and West,* 1973, pp. 13-24.

WINTER, M. Sha'rani and Egyptian society in the sixteenth century. *Asian and African studies* [Jerusalem] 9(1973), pp. 313-338.

YALMAN, Ahmed Emin. Islam, Sufism and tolerance. *Sufi Studies: East and West,* 1973, pp. 221-225.

ZARRINKOOB, A.H. Persian Sufism in its historical perspective. *Iranian studs.* 3(1970), pp. 139-220.

ZIAKAS, Gr.D. Η ἔννοια τῆς ἐλευθηρίας τῆς βουλήσεως καὶ τοῦ κακοῦ εἰς τὸν μεταγενέστερον ἰσλαμικον μυστικισμόν, Ἐν Ἐπιστημονικὴ Ἐπετηρὶς Θεολογικῆς Σχολῆς, Θεσσαλονικη, 1973, Τόμος ιε, σελ. 445-516.

ZOLLA, E. L'alchemista di Isfahan. *Conoscenza religiosa* 1975(3), pp. 264-268.

Bibi Hayati. Divano. Versione di C.C. *Conoscenza religiosa* 1975(3), pp. 269-271.

Simone di Taibūtheh. *Conoscenza religiosa* 1975(3), pp. 227-238.

See also II. b. 2. Valiuddin

See also II. c. 8. Pourjavady.

See also III. a. 3. Makdisi.

See also V. m. 1. Galerkina

See also V. u. 1. Nasr

See also XXXII. g. Nizami

See also XXXVI. f. Theodoridis.

See also XXXVIII. b. Achena.

See also XXXIX. b. Herman

See also XXXIX. c. Nasr.

See also XLI. a. Duchemin

iii Sufi orders

'ABDUL-'AZIZ 'ABDULLA BATRAN. The Qadiryya-Mukhtaryya brotherhood in West Africa: the concept of tasawwuf in the writings of Sidi al-Mukhtar al Kunti (1729-1811). *Transafr.J.hist.* 4(1974), pp. 41-70.

ALGAR, Hamid. Some Notes on the Naqshbandī ṭarīqat in Bosnia. *WI N.S.* 13(1971), pp. 168-203.

ALGAR, Hamid. Some notes on the Naqshbandi Tarīqat in Bosnia. *Studies comp. rel.* 9(1975), pp. 69-96.

AUSTIN, R.W.J. Counsels of a Sufi Master. *Studs.in compar.relig.* 5(1971), pp. 207-214

AUSTIN, R.W. A letter to disciples in prison. *Studies in comparative religion* 8(1974), pp. 39-41.

BANNERTH, E. Aspects humains de la Shādhiliyya en Egypte. *MIDEO* 11(1972), pp. 237-250.

BARNES, J.R. A short note on the dissolution of the dervish orders in Turkey. *MW* 64(1974), pp. 33-39.

BASETTI-SANI, G. Hosayn Ibn Mansour al-Hallaj, martire mistico del Islam. *Renovatio* 7(1972), pp. 217-238.

HAQ, M.M. The Shuttari order of Ṣufīsm in India and its exponents in Bihar and Bengal. *JAS Pakistan* 16(1971), pp. 167-175.

HOURANI, A. Shaikh Khalid and the Naqshbandi order. *Islamic philosophy and the classical tradition:* essays presented to R. Walzer, 1972, pp. 89-103.

JONG, P. de. Two anonymous manuscripts relative to the Ṣûfî orders in Egypt. *Bibl.Or.* 32(1975), pp. 186-190.

KISSLING, H.J. Eine Mevlevî-Version des Motivs vom Greis von Kreta. Πεπραγ. του Γ΄ Διεθνους Κρητολογικου Συνεδριος 1971, pp. 138-142.

KRÜGER, E. Vom Leumund der Derwische. *Islamkundliche Abhandlungen H.J. Kissling,* 1974, pp. 104-115.

LIMAM, H.M. Tidjaniya, Sanusiya and Mahdiya as studied in English works. *Rev. hist. maghreb.* 4(1975), pp. 163-173.

MACKEEN, A.M. Mohamed. The early history of Sufism in the Maghrib prior to Al-Shādhilī (D.656/1256). *JAOS* 91(1971), pp. 398-408.

MEHINAGIĆ, I. Četiri neobjavnjena izvora o hamzevijama iz sredine XVI vijeka. *Prilozi za or. filol.* 18-19(1968-9), pp. 217-266.

MOINUL HAQ, S. Rise and expansion of the Chishtis in the subcontinent. *J.Pak.Hist. Soc.* 22(1974), pp. 207-248.

POURJAVADY, Nasrollah, WILSON, P.L. The descendants of Shāh Niʿmatullāh Walī. *IC* 48(1974), pp. 49-57.

SEYDOU, C. Trois poèmes mystiques peuls du Foûta-Djalon. *REI* 40(1972), pp. 141-185.

SIDDIQI, M. Zameeruddin. The resurgence of the Chishti silsilah in the Punjab during the eighteenth century. *Proc.32 Ind.hist.cong.* 1970, vol. 1, pp. 408-412.

SOLIMAN, A.S. Le Mevlèviisme. Esquisse des rites tirée principalement de Methnewi et de ses commentaires. *Abr-Nahrain* 14(1973-4), pp. 122-137.

STADTMULLER, G. Der Derwischorden der Bektaschi in Albanien. *Serta Slavica in memoriam A. Schmaus,* 1971, pp. 683-688.

VAN ESS, J. Libanesische Miszellen. 6: Die Yašruṭiya. *WI* N.S.16(1975), pp. 1-103.

YOLA, Şenay. Zur Ornithophanie im Vilâyet nâme des Hâggî Bektaš. *Islamkundliche Abhandlungen H.J. Kissling,* 1974, pp. 178-189.

ZOLLA, E. Le confraternite sufi. *Conoscenza religiosa* 1975(3), pp. 259-264.

See also XV. e. Lourido Díaz.

See also XX. c. Warburg.

See also XXVIII. b. Lewis.

See also XXIX. h. Sadat.

iv Saints

'ABDUR RABB, Muhammad. The problem of possible Indian influence on Abū Yazīd al-Bisṭāmī. *J. Pakistan Hist. Soc.* 20(1972), pp. 34-58.

AHMAD, Nazir. An Old Persian treatise of the Bahmani period. *IC* 46(1972), pp. 209-226.

ALI, Sayyid Rizwan. Two great contemporaries of thirteenth century A.D.: Sultān al-'Ulama al-'Izz Ibn al-Salām and Ibn 'Arabi. *IC* 45(1971), pp. 192-201.

ANDRZEJEWSKI, B.W. A genealogical note relevant to the dating of Sheikh Hussein of Bale. *BSOAS* 38(1975), pp. 139-140.

ANDRZEJEWSKI, B.W. Sheikh Hussēn of Bāli in Galla oral traditions. *IV Cong.int.di studi etiopici* 1972(1974), pp. 463-480.

ANDRZEJEWSKI, B.W. The veneration of Sufi saints and its impact on the oral literature of the Somali people and on their literature in Arabic. *Afr.lang.stud.* 15(1974), pp. 15-53.

ANSARI, Nagmuddin. Some notes on the life, works and thoughts of Shaykh Saduddin Ahmad Ansari. *Afghanistan* 25 iv(1973), pp. 32-45.

BALJON, J.M.S. Psychology as apprehended and applied by Shâh Walî Allâh Dihlawî. *Acta Orientalia Neerlandica* ed. P.W. Pestman, 1971, pp. 53-60.

BIANQUIS, T. Ibn al-Nābulusī, un martyr sunnite au IVe siècle de l'hégire. *Ann. islamologiques* 12(1974), pp. 45-66

BOULOUKBACHI, Ali. La ceremonie du Qali Shuyan. *Objets et mondes* 11 (1971), pp. 133-140.

DAS, R.N. Shaikh Nizām-ud-Dīn Auliyā (an appraisal with special reference to his relations with the contemporary Sultans of Delhi). *IC* 48(1974), pp. 93-104.

ENAMUL HAQ, Muhammad. Pānch Pīr. *JAS Pak.* 15(1970), pp. 109-128.

GELLNER, E. Comment devenir marabout (étude anthropolog que). *Bull.économ.soc. Maroc* 128-9(1975?), pp. 3-43.

GEYOUSHI, Muhammad Ibraheem. Al-Tirmidhī's theory of saints and sainthood. *IQ* 15 (1971), pp. 17-61.

GOLOMBEK, L. The cult of saints and shrine architecture in the fourteenth century. *Near Eastern numismatics ... Studies in honor of G.C. Miles*, 1974, pp. 419-430.

KISTER, M.J. The "Kitab al-Miḥan", a book on Muslim martyrology. [illegible] 20([illegible]), pp. 210-218.

LEWIS, I.M. Sharif Yusuf Barkhadle: the blessed saint of Somaliland. *Proc. 3rd Int. Conf. Ethiopian stud.*, 1966, pp. 75-81.

MACKEEN, A.M. Mohamed. The rise of al-Shādhilī (d.656/1256). *JAOS* 91(1971), pp. 477-486.

MALIK, Hafeez. Shāh Walī Allāh's last testament: *al-Maqāla al-Waḍiyya fī al-Naṣīḥa wa al-Waṣiyya.* *MW* 63(1973), pp. 105-118.

NASR, Seyyed Hossein. In the name of God most merciful and compassionate; the life of Sadr al-Muti'allihîn Shîrâzî and a discussion of motion in the category of substance by His Holiness Ḥajj Sayyid 'Abu'l-Ḥasan Ḥusainî Qazwînî. Translated by Seyyed Hossein Nasr. *Mullâ Sadrâ commem. vol.*, 1961. pp. 7-21.

NWIYA, P. Makzūn al-Sinjārī, poète mystique alaouite. *SI* 40(1974), pp. 87-113.

QURAISHI, M.A. Maulana Muhammad B. Tahir Pattani. *J. Or. Inst. Baroda.* 21(1972), pp. 217-223.

RIAZ, Muhammad. Mir Sayyid Ali Hamadāni, a great reformer and writer. *J.Regional Cult.Inst.* 7(1974), pp. 127-137.

RIAZ, Muhammad. Mir Sayyid Muhammad Nur Bakhsh. *J. Pakistan Hist. Soc.* 17(1969), pp. 177-190.

ROEMER, H.R. Scheich Ṣafī von Ardabīl. Die Abstammung eines Ṣūfī-Meisters der Zeit zwischen Sa'di und Ḥāfiẓ. *Festgabe deutscher Iranisten zur 2500 Jahrfeier Irans*, 1971, pp. 106-116.

SALIM, Muhammad. A reappraisal of the sources on Shaykh Mu'in al-Din Ajmeri. *J. Pakistan Hist. Soc.* 16(1968), pp. 145-152.

SALIM, Muhammad. Shaykh Baha al-Din Zakariyya. *J. Pakistan Hist. Soc.* 17(1969), pp. 1-24.

SINGER, A. The dervishes of Kurdistan. *Asian affairs* 61(N.S.5, 1974), pp. 179-182.

VALSAN, M. Notes on the Shaikh al-'Alawī (1869-1934). *Studs.in compar.relig.* 5 (1971), pp. 145-150

WAGNER, E. Eine Liste der Heiligen von Harar. *ZDMG* 123(1973), pp. 269-292.

See also XII. f. Ferchiou.

See also XX. c. O'Fahey.

See also XXVIII. u. Cordun.

v Religious communities

JEMMA, D. Les confréries noires et le rituel de la derdeba à Marrakech. *Libyca* 19(1971), pp. 243-250.

MOINUL HAQ, S. Rise and expansion of the Chishtis in the subcontinent. *J.Pak.Hist. Soc.* 22(1974), pp. 157-181.

MOINUL HAQ, S. The Suhrawardis. *J.Pak. Hist.Soc.* 23(1975), pp. 71-103.

MORONY, M.G. Religious communities in late Sasanian and early Muslim Iraq. *JESHO* 17 (1974), pp. 113-135.

PROVANSAL, D. Le phénomène maraboutique au Maghreb. *Genève-Afrique* 14(1975), pp. 59-77.

vi Convents

AGAEVA, E.R. Anti-khalif Katari ibn al-Fudzha'a. *Strany Blizhnego i Srednego Vostoka: istoriya, ekonomica,* 1972, pp. 3-9.

FERCHIOU, S. Survivances mystiques et culte de possession dans le maraboutisme tunisien. *L'homme* 12(1972), pp. 47-69.

HANDŽIĆ, A. Jedan savremeni dokumenat o Šejhu Hamzi iz Orlovića. *Prilozi za or. filol.* 18-19(1968-9), pp. 205-215.

vii Sects. Heresy: general. Kharijites. Ibadites

ANAWATI, G.C. Un aspect de la lutte contre l'hérésie au XVème siècle d'après un inédit, attributé à Maqrizi (le Kitāb al-bayān al-mufīd fi'l-farq bayn al-tawḥīd wal-talhīd). *Colloque international sur l'histoire du Caire,* 1969, pp. 23-36.

CAHEN, Cl. Simples interrogations hérésiographes. (Yezidis, Nusayris, Shamsiyya, etc.) *Islamwissenschaftliche Abhandlungen F. Meier,* 1974, pp. 29-32.

KAZI, A.K. and FLYNN, J.G. Shahrastānī Kitāb al-milal wa'l-nihal. Translated. VI. The Shi'ites. *Abr-Nahrain* 15(1974-1975), pp. 50-98.

LEWICKI, T. Une croyance des Ibāḍites nord-africains sur la fin du monde: le pays de Ğugrāf. *Ve Congrès International d'Arabisants et d'Islamisants. Actes.,* [1970?], pp. 317-327.

LEWICKI, T. The Ibadites in Arabia and Africa. *J. world hist.* 13(1971), pp. 51-130.

PELLAT, C. Djāḥiz et les Khāridjites. *Folia Or.* 12(1970), pp. 195-209

RUBINACCI, R. L'*Adān* presso gl'Ibāditi. *Folia Or.* 12(1970), pp. 279-290

SOURDEL, D. Les conceptions Imāmites au début du XIe siècle d'après le Shaykh al-Mufīd. *Islamic civilization,* 1973, pp. 187-200.

TALBI, M. Chronique d'Ibn Saghir sur les imams rostemides de Tahert. *CT* 23(nos. 91-92, 1975), pp. 315-368.

VAN ESS, J. A new source of Muslim heresiography. *Proc.27th Int.Cong.Or. 1967* (1971), pp. 269-270.

WATT, W. Montgomery. The significance of the sects in Islamic theology. *Actas IV congresso de estudos árabes e islâmicos* 1968(1971), pp. 169-173.

WATT, W.M. The Study of the development of the Islamic sects. *Acta Orientalia Neerlandica* ed. P.W. Pestman, 1971, pp. 82-91.

See also II. c. 2. El'chibekov.

See also XII. b. Talbi.

See also XVI. c. Cuperly.

See also XX. d. Pouwels.

See also XXXI. j. Doroshenko.

viii Shiites

ADATIA, A.K. and KING, N.Q. Some East African *Firmans* of H.H. Aga Khan III. *J. rel. Africa* 2(1969), pp. 179-191.

AMIJI, Hatim. The Bohras of East Africa. *J.religion in Africa* 7(1975), pp. 27-61.

AUCAGNE, J. L'Imam Moussa Sadr et la communauté chiite. *Travaux et jours* 53(1974), pp. 31-51.

BRYER, D. The origins of the Druze religion. *Der Islam* 52(1975), pp. 47-84, 239-262.

CALMARD, J. Le chiisme imamite en Iran à l'époque seldjoukide, d'après le *Kitāb al-Naqḍ. Le monde iranien et l'Islam,* 1971, pp. 43-67.

CORBIN, H. L'initiation ismaélienne ou l'ésotérisme et le verbe. *Eranos* 1970 (1973), pp. 41-142.

CORBIN, H. Juvenilité et chevalerie en Islam iranien. *Eranos* 1971(1973), pp. 311-356.

CORBIN, H. Un roman initiatique ismaélien du Xe siècle. *Cahiers de civ. méd.* 15 (1972), pp. 121-142.

CORBIN, H. Lo shī'ismo duodecimano. *Conoscenza religiosa* 1972, pp. 255-260.

ELIASH, J. On the genesis and development of the Twelver-Shī'ī three-tenet Shahādah. *Der Islam* 47(1971), pp. 265-272.

ENDE, W. Schiitische Tendenzen bei sunnitischen Sayyids aus Ḥaḍramaut: Muḥammad b. ʿAqil al-ʿAlawī (1863-1931). *Der Islam* 50(1973), pp. 82-97.

FYZEE, A.A.A. The religion of the Ismailis. *India and contemporary Islam,* ed. S.T. Lokhandwalla, 1971, pp. 70-87.

HALM, H. Die Sieben und die Zwölf: die ismā'īlitische Kosmogonie und das Mazdak-Fragment des Šahrastānī. *XVIII. Deutscher Orientalistentag 1972: Vorträge,* pp. 170-177.

HAMDANI, Abbas. "The Yamanī Ismā'īlī Dā'ī Ḥātim b. Ibrāhīm al-Ḥamidī (d.596 H./1199 A.D.) and his book *Tuḥfat al-Qulūb*". *Proc.27th Int.Cong.Or.1967* (1971), pp. 270-272.

KHAKEE, Gulshan. Note on the Imām Shāhī Ms. at the Deccan College, Poona. *JAS Bombay* 45-46(1970-71), pp. 143-155.

KHAN, Ansar Zahid. Isma'ilism in Multan and Sind. *J. Pak. Hist. Soc.* 23(1975), pp. 36-57.

KHAN, M.S. The early history of Zaydī Shī'ism in Daylamān and Gīlān. *ZDMG* 125 (1975), pp. 301-314.

KOHLBERG, E. Some imāmī-shī'ī views on *taqiyya*. *JAOS* 95(1975), pp. 395-402.

LEWIS, B. Assassins of Syria and Isma'ilis of Persia. *La Persia nel medievo,* 1971, pp. 573-584

MAKAREM, Sami N. Al-Hākim bi-Amrillāh's appointment of his successors. *Al-Abhath* 23(1970), pp. 319-325.

MAKAREM, S.M. The hidden Imāms of the Ismā'-īlīs. *Al-Abhath* 22i-ii(1969), pp. 23-37.

MARQUET, Y. Les cycles de la souveraineté selon les épîtres des Iḫwān Al-Safā. *SI* 36(1972), pp. 47-69.

MARQUET, Y. Le šī'isme au IXe siècle à travers l'histoire de Ya'qūbī (1ère partie). *Arabica* 19(1972), pp. 1-45

MAZZAOUI, M. Shī'ism in the medieval, Ṣafavid, and Qājār periods: A study in Ithnā-'asharī continuity. *Iran: continuity and variety.* Ed. P.J. Chelkowski, New York, 1971. pp. 39-57.

MILLWARD, G.W. Aspects of modernism in Shī'a Islam. *SI* 37(1973), pp. 111-128.

MOHAGHEGH, Mehdi. Nāṣir-i Khusraw and his spiritual *Nisbah. Yād-nāme-ye Irāni-ye Minorsky,* 1969, pp. 143-148.

MOHEBBI, M. Khodayar. Les principes essentiels de la théologie chiite. *Ex orbe religionum. Studia Geo Widengren oblata,* II, 1972, pp. 126-133.

NAGEL, T. Die "Urǧūza al-Muḫtāra" des Qāḍī an-Nu'mān. *WI* 15(1974), pp. 96-128.

NANJI, Azim. Modernization and change in the Nizari Ismaili community in East Africa--a perspective. *J. religion in Africa* 6(1974), pp. 123-139.

NETTLER, R.L. A controversy on the problem of perception: two religious outlooks in Islām. *Humaniora Islamica* 1(1973), pp. 133-156.

POURJAVADY, N. and WILSON, P.L. Ismā'īlīs and Ni'matullāhīs. *SI* 41(1975), pp. 113-135.

PROZOROV, S.M. Evolyutziya doktrin "kraynikh" shiitov - gulat v Islame. *NAA* 1974(3), pp. 146-153.

PROZOROV, S.M. Ucheniya shiitov ob imamate v trude Al-Khasana al-Naubakhti (konetz IX v.). *Pis'mennye pamyatniki Vostoka* 1970, pp. 83-107.

RIAZ, Muhammad. Studies in the history of the Sabaeans. *J.Pak.Hist.Soc.* 21(1973), pp. 233-240.

RIZVI, Seyyid Saeed Akhtar, KING, N.Q. The Khoja Shia Ithna-asheriya community in East Africa (1840-1967). *MW* 64(1974), pp. 194-204.

RIZVI, Seyyid Saeed Akhtar, KING, N.Q. Some East African Ithna-asheri *jamaats* (1840-1967). *J. religion in Africa* 5(1973), pp. 12-22.

SCARCIA, G. Kūh-e Khwāgè: forme attuali del Mahdismo iranico. *OM* 53(1973), pp. 755-764.

SCARCIA AMORETTI, B. Nascita di un emāmzāde (1973). *OM* 54(1974), pp. 309-311.

SCARCIA AMORETTI, B. La *Risālat-al-imāma* di Naṣir al-Din Ṭūsī. *RSO* 47(1972), pp. 247-276.

SOURDEL, D. L'Imamisme vu par le Cheikh al-Mufīd. *REI* 40(1972), pp. 217-296.

STERN, S. Cairo as the centre of the Isma'ili movement. *Colloque international sur l'histoire du Caire,* 1969, pp. 437-450.

STROEVA, L.V. Provozglashenie "dnya voskreseseniya". (Iz istorii gosudarstva ismailitov v Irane XI-XIII vv.). *Iran: sbornik statey,* 1973, pp. 133-165.

TUCKER, W.F. Bayān b. Sam'ān and the Bayāniyya: Shī'ite extremists of Umayyad Iraq. *MW* 65(1975), pp. 241-253.

VAHDATI, Ataollah. Académies shiites. *Objets et mondes* 11 (1971), pp. 171-180.

VAN ESS, J. Libanesische Miszellen 5: Drusen und Black Muslims. *WI* N.S.14 (1973), pp. 203-213.

VERMEULEN, U. The rescript against the Shī'ites and the Rāfiḍites of Beirut, Ṣaida and district (746 A.H./1363 A.D.). *Orientalia Lovaniensia periodica* 4(1973), pp. 169-175.

WALKER, P. An Ismā'īli answer to the problem of worshipping the unknowable, neoplatonic God. *AJAS* 2(1974), pp. 7-21.

WALKER, P.E. The Ismaili vocabulary of creation. *SI* 40(1974), pp. 75-85.

WATT, W. Montgomery. The Muslim yearning for a saviour: aspects of early ʿAbbāsid Shīʿism. *The Saviour God: comparative studies in the concept of salvation presented to E.O. James*, 1963, pp. 191-204

ZENNER, W.P. and RICHTER, M.N. The Druzes as a divided minority group. *J. Asian and African studies* [York Univ.] 7(1972), pp. 193-203.

See also I. c. 4. Kudsi-Zadeh

See also II. a. 5. Kohlberg.

See also II. a. 7. Bryer.

See also II. c. 7. Kazi.

See also IX. e. Millward

See also X. e. Tucker.

See also XXIII. b. Ben-Dor.

See also XXXI. f. Scarcia

ix Other sects

ABU HAKIMA, Ahmad. Wahhabi religio-political movement of Arabia and its impact on India in the nineteenth century. *Fac. Arts J., Univ. Jordan* li(1969), pp. 25-32.

AHMED, Munir D. Ausschluss der Ahmadiyya aus dem Islam. Eine umstrittene Entscheidung des pakistanischen Parlaments. *Orient* [Hamburg] 16i(1975), pp. 112-143.

ANTONOVA, K.A. Ob uchenii i legendakh musulmanskoy sekty Akhmadiya. *Religiya i obshchestvennaya mysl' narodov vostoka*, 1971, pp. 103-116.

BAUSANI, A. Sviluppi istituzionali della religione Baha'i. *Atti dell' VIII Cong. int. stor. rel.* (1955), pp. 447-450.

COHEN, E. The Bahâ'ī community of Acre. *Folklore Research Center studies* 3(1972), pp. 119-141.

DELANOUE, G. Une épître de Ḥasan Al-Bannā aux Frères Musulmans. Translation de la *Risālat at-taʿalīm. Cah.de ling.d'orientalisme et de slavistique* 1-2(1973), pp. 55-83.

EBIED, R.Y. and YOUNG, M.J.L. An account of the history and rituals of the Yazīdīs of Mosul. *Muséon* 85(1972), pp. 481-522.

FARUQI, Ziya-ul-Hasan. A note on the Wahabiyah. *Islam and the modern age* 4 i (1973), pp. 38-50.

GASPARRO, G.S. I miti cosmogonici degli Yezidi. *Numen* 21(1974), pp. 197-227.

GASPARRO, G.S. I miti cosmogonici degli Yezidi. *Numen* 22(1975), pp. 24-41.

KAZEMI, Farhad. Some preliminary observations on the early development of Babism. *MW* 63(1973), pp. 119-131.

KHAN, Abdul Majid. The Ahmadīya movement. *India and contemporary Islam*, ed. S.T. Lokhandwalla, 1971, pp. 340-347.

KHAN, Muin-ud-Din Ahmad. Chronology of the Farā'iḍī movement. *J. Pak. Hist. Soc.* 13(1965), pp. 314-321.

LAVAN, S. Polemics and conflict in Ahmadiyya history: the '*Ulamā*', the missionaries, and the British (1898). *MW* 62(1972), pp. 283-303.

MATHUR, Y.B. The Mujāhidīn movement in modern India. *Stud. in Islam* 6(1969), pp. 193-217.

NAQAVI, Sayyid Ali Raza. Bābism and Bahā'ism--a study of their history and doctrines. *Islamic studies* 14(1975), pp. 185-217.

NIJENHUIS, J. Baha'i: world faith for modern man? *J.ecumenical stud.* 10(1973) pp. 532-551.

PUIN, G.R. Aspekte der wahhabitischen Reform, auf der Grundlage von Ibn Gannāms "Rauḍat al-afkār". *Studien zum Minderheitenproblem im Islam* I, 1973, pp. 45-99.

QAMAR UDDIN. The Dhikris of Makran. *Stud. in Islam* 6(1969), pp. 105-117.

TIRMIZI, A.I. The Mahdawī movement in Gujarat. *India and contemporary Islam*, ed. S.T. Lokhandwalla, 1971, pp. 116-124.

See also XXIX. d. *Yugoslavia* Handžić, Hadžijahić.

See also XXXVIII. d. *Kurdish.* Mokri.

d THEOLOGY

i General. Devotional literature

(see also II.a.1)

AHMED, Ziauddin. A survey of the development of theology in Islam. *Islamic Stud.* 11(1972), pp. 93-111.

BIANCHI, U. Alcuni aspetti abnormi del dualismo persiano. *La Persia nel medievo.* 1971, pp. 149-164

EPALZA, M. de. Algunos juicios teológicos de Asín Palacios sobre el Islam. *Pensamiento* 25(1969), pp. 145-182.

HALEPOTA, Aboul Wahid J. Psychology of Islamic belief in God. *Proc.9th Int. Cong.Hist.Rel.*, 1958, pp. 284-295.

HANAFI, H. Théologie ou anthropologie? *Renaissance du monde arabe. Colloque interarabe de Louvain*, 1972, pp. 233-264.

KNAPPERT, J. A Swahili Islamic prayer from Zaire. *Orientalia Lovaniensia periodica* 4(1973), pp. 197-201.

MARSHALL, D.R. Some early Islamic sermons. *J. Fac. Arts Royal Univ. Malta* 5(1972), pp. 91-110.

PINES, S. A note on an early meaning of the term *mutakallim*. *Israel Oriental studies* 1(1971), pp. 224-240.

VAHIDUDDIN, Syed. Professor Kenneth Cragg's approach to the Qur'anic consciousness of man. *Studies in Islam* 7(1970), pp. 19-28.

VAN ESS, J. The logical structure of Islamic theology. *Logic in classical Islamic culture*, ed. by G.E. von Grunebaum, 1970, pp. 21-50.

See also II. a. 5. Bosworth.

See also XXXVII. i. Pauliny.

ii Theologians and their writings

ALLARD, M. Un pamphlet contre al-Aš'arī. *BEO* 23(1970), pp. 129-165.

AWANG, Omar. The Umm al-Barāhīn of al-Sanūsī. *Nusantara* 2(1972), pp. 157-168.

BERGÉ, M. Continuité et progression des études tawḥīdiennes modernes de 1883 à 1965. *Arabica* 22(1975), pp. 267-279.

BRUNSCHVIG, R. Pour ou contre la logique grecque chez les théologiens-juristes de l'Islam: Ibn Hazm, al-Ghazālī, Ibn Taimiya. *Oriente e Occidente nel medioevo*, 1971, pp. 185-227.

BÜRGEL, J.C. Dogmatismus und Autonomie im wissenschaftlichen Denken des islamischen Mittelalters. *Saeculum* 23(1972), pp. 30-46.

COURTENAY, W.J. The critique on natural causality in the mutakallimun and nominalism. *Harvard theol. R.* 66(1973), pp. 77-94.

DAIBER, H. Zur Erstausgabe von al-Māturīdī, Kitāb at-Tauḥīd. *Islam* 52 (1975), pp. 299-313.

FRANK, R.M. Abu Hashim's theory of "states"; its structure and function. *Actas IV congresso de estudos árabes e islâmicos* 1968(1971), pp. 85-100.

GARDET, L. De quelques questions posées par l'étude du 'Ilm Al-Kalâm. *SI* 32(1970), pp. 129-142.

HORTEN, M. Theologians in Islam. *Islamic stud.* 12(1973), pp. 81-101.

LITTLE, D.P. Did Ibn Taymiyya have a screw loose? *SI* 41(1975), pp. 93-111.

MADELUNG, W. Early Sunnī doctrine concerning faith as reflected in the Kitāb al-Imān of Abū 'Ubayd al-Qāsim b. Sallām (d.224/839). *SI* 32(1970), pp. 233-254.

MAKDISI, G. Two more manuscripts of the *Book of penitents*. *Orientalia Hispanica* I, 1974, pp. 526-530.

MOIN, Mumtaz. Imam Abu Hanifah (life and personality). *J. Pakistan Hist. Soc.* 16 (1968), pp. 153-162.

NADER, A. Bibliographie d'ouvrages en langues européennes concernant le Kalam. *Bull.philos.méd.* 15(1973), pp. 191-209.

NIEWÖHNER, F. Verbesserungen zu den Titeln Nr.1-Nr.294 der Bibliographie von Albert Nader. Ergänzungen zu Albert Nader's Bibliographie d'ouvrages en langues européennes concernant le Kalam. *Bull.philos. med.* 16-17(1974-5), pp. 189-195.

PAULINY, Ján. Kisā'īs Werk *Kitāb qiṣaṣ al-anbiyā*. *Zborník Filos. Fak Univ. Komenského: Graecolatina et orientalia* 2(1970), pp. 191-282.

PESSAGNO, J.M. The Marji'a, Īmān and Abū 'Ubayd. *JAOS* 95(1975), pp. 382-394.

PLATTI, E. Deux manuscrits théologiques de Yaḥyā b. 'Adī. *MIDEO* 12(1974), pp. 217-229.

SCHUON, F. Dilemmas of theological speculation with special reference to Moslem scholasticism. *IQ* 17(1973), pp. 36-63.

SWARTZ, M. A seventh-century(A.H.) creed: the 'aqīda Wāsiṭīya of Ibn Taymīya. *Humaniora Islamica* 1(1973), pp. 91-131.

VACCA, V. Frammenti di al-Ša'rānī. *Bol. Asoc. Esp. Orientalistas* 11(1975), pp. 123-125.

VADET, J.C. La création et l'investiture de l'homme dans le sunnisme ou la légende d'Adam chez al-Kisā'ī. *SI* 42(1975), pp. 5-37.

VAJDA, G. La démonstration de l'unité divine d'après Yusuf al-Baṣīr. *Studies in mysticism and religion presented to G.G. Scholem*, 1967, pp. 285-315.

VAJDA, G. Le livre arbitre de l'homme et la justification de son assujetissement à la loi divine. Traduction et commentaire des chapitres XVII à XXXII du *Kitāb al-Muḥtawī* de Yūsuf al-Baṣīr. *JA* 262(1974), pp. 305-367; 263(1975), pp. 51-92.

VAJDA, G. La parole créée de Dieu d'après le théologien karaïte Yūsuf al-Baṣīr. *SI* 39(1974), pp. 59-76.

VAN ESS, J. Das Kitāb al-irǧā' des Ḥasan b. Muḥammad b. al-Ḥanafiyya. *Arabica* 21 (1974), pp. 20-52.

VAN ESS, J. Nachträge und Verbesserungen zu meinem Aufsatz in *Arabica* XXI(1974), Seite 20 ff. *Arabica* 22(1975), pp. 48-51.

VAN ESS, J. Ma'bad al-Ǧuhanī. *Islamwissenschaftliche Abhandlungen F. Meier*, 1974, pp. 49-77.

WATT, W.M. Was Wāṣil a Khārijite? *Islamwissenschaftliche Abhandlungen F. Meier*, 1974, pp. 306-311.

See also II. a. 7. Monnot.

iii Dogmatic schools and sects. Mu'tazilites

AHMED, Ziauddin. Some aspects of the political theology of Aḥmad b. Ḥanbal. *Islamic stud.* 12(1973), pp. 53-66.

BELGUEDJ, M.S. Ben Badis et le mu'tazilisme. *ROMM* 13-14(1973), pp. 75-86.

BEN-SHAMMAI, H. A note on some Karaite copies of Mu'tazilite writings. *BSOAS* 37(1974), pp. 295-304.

BERNARD, M. La notion de ʿIlm chez les premiers Muʿtazilites. *SI* 36(1972), pp. 23-45; 37(1973), pp. 27-56.

BRUNSCHVIG, R. Muʿtazilisme et Optimum (al-aṣlaḥ). *SI* 39(1974), pp. 5-23.

BRUNSCHVIG, R. Rationalité et tradition dans l'analogie juridico-religieuse chez le muʿtazilite ʿAbd al-Ǧabbār. *Arabica* 19(1972), pp. 213-221.

FRANK, R.M. Several fundamental assumptions of the Baṣra School of the Muʿtazila. *SI* 33(1971), pp. 5-18.

GALADANCI, Shehu A.S. The origin and doctrines of Mu'tazilah. *Kano studies* 1(1965), pp. 9-12.

GIMARET, D. La notion d' "impulsion irrésistible" (ilǧâ') dans l'éthique muʿtazilite. *JA* 259(1971), pp. 25-62

HOURANI, G.F. Juwaynī's criticisms of Mu'tazilite ethics. *MW* 65(1975), pp. 161-173.

HOURANI, G.F. The rationalist ethics of ʿAbd al-Jabbār. *Islamic philosophy and the classical tradition:* essays presented to R. Walzer, 1972, pp. 105-115.

MADELUNG, W. The spread of Māturīdism and the Turks. *Actas IV congresso de estudos árabes e islâmicos* 1968(1971), pp. 109-168.

NASR, S.H. *Al-ḥikmat al-ilāhiyyah* and *kalām*. *SI* 34(1971), pp. 139-149

SCHWARZ, M. Some notes on the notion of *iljā'* (constraint) in Mu'tazilite kalām. *In memoriam S.M. Stern* (Israel Or. studies, II, 1972), pp. 413-427.

VAJDA, G. Le "kalām" dans la pensée religieuse juive du Moyen Age. *RHR* 183(1973), pp. 143-160.

VAN ESS, J. Umar II and his epistle against the Qadarīya. *Abr-nahrain* 12 (1971-2), pp. 19-26

iv Theological and religious concepts

ABDUL KHALIQ. Sayyid Ahmad Khan on prophetic revelation. *Pakistan philos. J.* 11i(1972), pp. 61-71.

ABEL, A. Le dieu qui intercède auprès de lui-même. *Ann. Inst. Phil. Hist. Or.* 20 (1968-72), pp. 17-30.

AFFIFY, Hussain el-Tiby. The attributes of 'Allah'. *Majallat al-Azhar* 44i(1972), pp. 15-16.

ALWAYE, Mohiaddin. Life after death--in the conception of Islam. *Maj. al-Azhar* 45vii(1974), pp. 1-6.

BALJON, J.M.S. Two lists of prophets. A comparison between Ibn al-'Arabi's al-hikam and Shah Wali Allah al-Dihlawi's Ta'wil al-ahadith. *Ned.theol.tijds.* 22 (1967-8), pp. 81-89.

BELKHODJA, Habib. Le point de vue de l'Islam sur le travail. *CT* 20(nos.77-78, 1972), pp. 135-149.

BRAIMAH, B.A.R. The concept of sin in Islam. *Ghana bull. theol.* 4i(1971), pp. 31-40.

BRAIMAH, B.A.R. Morality in Islam. *Ghana bull. theol.* 4iii(1972), pp. 45-53.

BRAVMANN, M.M. Allāh's liberty to punish or to forgive. *Der Islam* 47(1971), pp. 236-237.

BRAVMANN, M. Meīr. The 'Completion' or 'Improvement' of a Laudable Deed: an ancient Arab ethnic motif. *Der Islam* 49(1972), pp. 273-276.

CALASSO, G. Intervento di Iblīs nella creazione dell'uomo. L'ambivalente figura del "nemico" nelle tradizioni islamiche. *RSO* 45(1970), pp. 71-90.

DOI, A.R.I. The Yoruba Mahdī. *J.religion in Africa* 4(1971), pp. 119-136

EBIED, R.Y., YOUNG, M.J.L. An exposition of the Islamic doctrine of Christ's second coming, as presented by a Bosnian Muslim scholar. *Orientalia Lovaniensia periodica* 5(1974), pp. 127-137.

GARDET, L. Quelques réflexions sur un problème de théologie et philosophie musulmanes: tout-puissance divine et liberté humaine. *ROMM* 13-14(1973), pp. 381-394.

GARDET, L. La révélation comme guide pour l'agir humain et la politique. *Proc. 27th Int.Cong.Or.1967* (1971), pp. 175-176.

GIMARET, D. Un problème de théologie musulmane: Dieu veut-il les actes mauvais? Thèses et arguments. *SI* 40(1974), pp. 5-73.

GIMARET, D. Un problème de théologie musulmane: Dieu veut-il les actes mauvais? Thèses et arguments. *SI* 41 (1975), pp. 63-92.

GIMARET, D. La théorie des *aḥwâl* d'Abû Hâšim al-Ǧubbâ'î d'après des sources aš'arites. *JA* 258(1970), pp. 47-76.

HAJJ, M.A. al-. The thirteenth century in Muslim eschatology: Mahdist expectations in the Sokoto Caliphate. *Res. Bull. CAD Ibadan* 3i(1967), pp. 100-115.

II RELIGION

HASAN, Ahmad. The concept of infallibility in Islam. *Islamic stud.* 11(1972), pp. 1-11.

JADAANE, F. La place des anges dans la théologie cosmique musulmane. *SI* 41 (1975), pp. 23-61.

JUYNBOLL, G.H.A. Fighting angels. *Ohio J. relig. stud.* 2i(1974), pp. 85-87.

KERR, M.H. Moral and legal judgment independent of revelation. *Proc.27th Int.Cong.Or.1967* (1971), pp. 176-178.

KHALID, Detlev H. Theocracy and the location of sovereignty. *Islamic stud.* 11(1972), pp. 187-209.

KHURI, Fuad I. Work in Islamic thought. *Al-Abhath* 21ii-iv(1968), pp. 3-13.

KISTER, M.J. "Rajab is the month of God ... A study in the persistence of an early tradition. *Israel Oriental studies* 1(1971), pp. 191-223.

LINGS, M. The seven deadly sins. *Stud. comp. religion* 5(1971), pp. 26-33.

MAʿSUMI, M.S.H. Islamic concept of human rights. *Islamic stud.* 11(1972), pp. 211-221.

MEIER, F. The ultimate origin and the hereafter in Islam. *Islam and its cultural divergence. Studies in honor of Gustave E. von Grunebaum,* 1971, pp. 96-112

MERAD, Ali, LATUIHAMALLO, P.D. and ANSARI, Zafar Ishaq. Truth, revelation and obedience. *Islam and the modern age* 3 iv (1972), pp. 79-88.

NARAIN, Harsh. The concept of revelation in Hinduism and Islam. *Islam and the modern age* 6i(1975), pp. 32-64.

RAYYAH HASHIM, M.A. al-. Free will and predestination in Islamic and Christian thought. *Kano studies* 3(1967), pp. 27-34.

SCHWARZ, M. "Acquisition" (*kasb*) in early *kalam. Islamic philosophy and the classical tradition,* 1972, pp. 355-387.

TRITTON, A.S. Man, *nafs, ruh, 'aql. BSOAS* 34(1971), pp. 491-495.

VAJDA, G. Le problème de la vision de Dieu d'après Yūsuf al-Baṣīr. *Islamic philosophy and the classical tradition,* 1972, pp. 473-489.

WAUGH, E. Jealous angels: aspects of Muslim religious language. *Ohio J. relig. stud.* 1ii(1973), pp. 56-72.

WOLFSON, H.A. The *Hatirani* in the Kalam and Ghazālī as inner motive powers of human actions. *Studies in mysticism and religion presented to G.G. Scholem,* 1967, pp. 363-379.

See also II. a. 5. Idris.

See also II. c. 2. Corbin
IV. b. *Ghazzali* Goodman

See also II. d. 2. Madelung.

See also IV. c. 7. Mahdihassan

See also IX. e. Cruz Hernández

III LAW

a THE SHARIʿAH. FIQH

i General. Sources

ABEL, A. Rôle de la structure juridique dans le developpement et le déclin de l'état musulman arabe. *Recueils Soc.Jean Bodin* 31(1973), pp. 533-554.

AHMED IBRAHIM. Law and religion - the Malaysian experience. *Islam and the modern age* 5iii(1974), pp. 5-16.

AKBARABADI, Sayeed Ahmed. How to effect changes in Islamic law. *Islamic law in modern India,* ed. Tahir Mahmood, 1972, pp. 114-122.

AKHTAR, Shameem An inquiry into the nature, origin and source of Islamic Law of Nations. *Islamic stud.* 10(1971), pp. 23-37.

ANDERSON, J.N.D. Modern trends in Islam: legal reform and modernisation in the Middle East. *Int. comp. law Q.* 20 (1971), pp. 1-21.

ANDERSON, J.N.D., COULSON, N.J. Modernization: Islamic law. *Northern Africa: Islam and modernization,* ed. M. Brett, 1973, pp. 73-83.

ANDERSON, J.N.D. Muslim personal law in India. *Islamic law in modern India,* ed. Tahir Mahmood, 1972, pp. 34-49.

ARNALDEZ, R. La place du Coran dans les Uṣūl Al-Fiqh, d'après le Muḥallā d'Ibn Ḥazm. *SI* 32(1970), pp. 21-30.

BRUNSCHVIG, R. De la fiction légale dans l'Islam médiéval. *SI* 32(1970), pp. 41-51.

BRUNSCHVIG, R. Logic and law in classical Islam. *Logic in classical Islamic culture,* ed. by G.E. von Grunebaum, 1970, pp. 9-20.

III LAW

BRUNSCHVIG, R. La théorie du *qiyās* juridique chez le ḥanafite al-Dabūsī (Ve/XIe siècle). *Orientalia Hispanica* I, 1974, pp. 150-154.

CASTRO, Fr. Gli studi di diritto islamico. *Studi sul Vicino Oriente in Italia,* II, 1971, pp. 409-436.

CHARNAY, P. Pluralisme normatif et ambiguïté dans le *fiqh. L'ambivalence dans la culture arabe,* 1967, pp. 382-396.

CRAGG, K. "An imperative path". Law and religion in relation. *Islam and the modern age* 5i(1974), pp. 29-38.

FANGARY, Mohamed Shawky el-. Problème de la décadence musulmane. *Rev. "Al Qanoun wal Iqtisad"* 39(1969), pp. 1-46.

FARIDI, F.R. Islamic personal law: scope and methodology of reform in India. *Islamic law in modern India,* ed. Tahir Mahmood, 1972, pp. 123-127.

FÜCK, J.W. Review article Schacht. *Origins of Mohammadan jurisprudence.* Oxford 1953 *J. Pakistan Hist. Soc.* 17(1969), pp. 291-299.

GHOUSE, Mohammad. Personal laws and the constitution in India. *Islamic law in modern India,* ed. Tahir Mahmood, 1972, pp. 50-58.

GRÄF, E. Recht und Sprache im Islam. *Z. vergl. Rechtswis.* 74(1974), pp. 66-123.

GRÄF, E. Vom Geist islamischen Rechts. *Festschrift E. Klingmüller,* 1974, pp. 115-144.

HAARMANN, U. Religiöses Recht und Grammatik im klassischen Islam. *XVIII. Deutscher Orientalistentag 1972: Vorträge,* pp. 149-169.

HAMIDULLAH, Muhammed. Judicial system of Islam. *Majallat al-Azhar* 43viii(1971), pp. 9-16; 43ix(1971), pp. 7-10.

HAMIDULLAH, M. La philosophie juridique chez les musulmans. *Ann.Fac.Droit Istanbul* 18 (1968), pp. 137-152.

HASAN, Ahmad. The classical definition of ijmā': the nature of consensus. *Islamic studies* 14(1975), pp. 261-270.

HASAN, Ahmad. Rationality of Islamic legal injunctions. *Islamic stud.* 13(1974), pp. 95-109.

HIDAYATULLAH, M. The role of the Qur'an in the development of the Shari'a. *Islam and the modern age* 6iii(1975), pp. 57-77.

ISHAQUE, Khalid M. Human rights in Islamic law. *Rev. Int. Comm. Juristes* 12(1974), pp. 30-39.

KALHUD, Shaikh Abdel Rahman al. Sacrificial offerings (hady) and the means of supplying the poor with their flesh. *3rd Conf.Acad. Isl.Research,* 1966, pp. 123-130

KHALID MAS'UD, M. Recent studies of Shāṭibī's al-Muwāfaqāt. *Islamic studies* 14(1975), pp. 65-75.

KOURIDES, P.N. The influence of Islamic law on contemporary Middle Eastern legal systems: the function and binding force of contracts. *Columbia J.transnat.law* 9 (1970), pp. 384-435.

KOURIDES, P.N. Traditionalism and modernism in Islamic law: a review. *Columbia J. transnat.law* 10(1971), pp. 493-506.

KRISHNA IYER, V.R. Reform of the Muslim personal law. *Islamic law in modern India,* ed. Tahir Mahmood, 1972, pp. 17-33.

KRSTIĆ, N. Muṣṭafa ibn Muḥammad al-Aqḥisari (Prušćak): Rasprava o kafi, duhanu i pićima. (Muṣtafa b. Muḥammad al-Aqhisari: Risāla fi ḥukm al-qahwa wa'd-duhan wa'l-ašriba. *POF* 20-21(1970-71), pp. 71-107.

LATIFI, Danial. Change and the Muslim law. *Islamic law in modern India,* ed. Tahir Mahmood, 1972, pp. 99-113.

LATIFI, D. Rationalism and Muslim law. *Islam and the modern age* 4iv(1973), pp. 43-70.

LIEBESNY, J. Comparative legal history: its role in the analysis of Islamic and modern Near East legal institutions. *Amer. J.comp.law* 20(1972), pp. 38-52.

LINANT DE BELLEFONDS, Y. Volonté interne et volonté déclarée en droit musulman. *Rev.int.droit comparé* 1958(3), pp. 1-12. [Offprint in SOAS]

MAHMASSANI, Maher. Tables septennales 1964-1970 des revues Études de droit libanais et Proche-Orient, études juridiques. *Proche-Orient; études juridiques (Ann. Fac. Droit Beyrouth* 75), 66(1970), pp. 1-156.

MAHMOOD, Tahir. Progressive codification of Muslim personal law. *Islamic law in modern India,* ed. Tahir Mahmood, 1972, pp. 80-98.

MURSHED, Syed Mahbub. Ethical basis of Islamic law: rights and obligations. *Internat. Islamic Conf.,* 1968, pp. 3-11.

MUSLEHUDDIN, Mohammad. Islamic jurisprudence and the rule of necessity and need. *Islamic stud.* 12(1973), pp. 37-52.

NAWAZ, M.K. Some reflections on modernization of Islamic law. *Islamic law in modern India,* ed. Tahir Mahmood, 1972, pp. 59-68.

NIXON, H.L. The development of Judaic and Islamic law - a comparison. *Islam and the modern age* 5ii(1974), pp. 14-27.

NOOR EL-HASSAN, Shaikh Mohammad. Sacrifices slaughtered during the time of pilgrimage and how to devise profiting by them in public projects. *3rd Conf.Acad.Isl.Research,* 1966, pp. 115-121

III LAW

NOTH, A. Zum Verhältnis von Recht und Geschichte im Islam. *Saeculum* 26(1975), pp. 341-346.

NOUR, A.M. Qias as a source of Islamic law. *J. Islamic and comparative law* 5 (1974), pp. 18-50.

SAMPATH, B.N. Conversion and inter-personal conflict of laws. *Islamic law in modern India*, ed. Tahir Mahmood, 1972, pp. 128-132.

SCARCIA AMORETTI, B. A proposito di una possibile versione del "Trattato dei dieci principi" di Nağm al-Dīn al-Kubrà. *RSO* 48(1973-4), pp. 98-108.

SIVARAMAYYA, B. Equality of sexes as a human and constitutional right and the Muslim law. *Islamic law in modern India*, ed. Tahir Mahmood, 1972, pp. 69-79.

UDOVITCH, A.L. Theory and practice of Islamic law: some evidence from the Geniza. *SI* 32(1970), pp. 289-303.

WATT, W. Montgomery. The closing of the door of iğtihād. *Orientalia Hispanica* I, 1974, pp. 675-678.

See also I. b. 3. Castro.

See also II. a. 6. Khachab.

See also III. b. Awa.

See also IX. n. Udovitch.

See also XX. c. Mokhlesur Rahman.

See also XXXVI. d. Haarmann.

ii Jurists and law books

ADAMS, C.J. The role of Shaykh al-Ṭūsī in the evolution of a formal science of jurisprudence among the Shī'ah. *Islamic stud.* 10(1971), pp. 173-180.

AHMED, Ziauddin. Aḥmad B. Ḥanbal and the problems of 'Īmān. *Islamic stud.* 12(1973), pp. 261-270.

AHMED, Ziauddin. Some aspects of the political theology of Ahmad B. Hanbal. *Islamic stud.* 12(1973), pp. 53-66.

ANSARI, Zafar Ishaq. Islamic juristic terminology before Šāfi'ī: a semantic analysis with special reference to Kūfa. *Arabica* 19(1972), pp. 255-300.

BERQUE, J. En lisant les *Nawâzil Mazouna* *SI* 32(1970), pp. 31-39.

BOGOLYUBOV, A.S. Rukopis' "Ar-rukn ar-rābi' fī-l-kiyās" v sobranii LO IVAN. *Pis'mennye pamyatniki Vostoka* 1970, pp. 45-51.

BRUNSCHVIG, R. Valeur et fondement du raisonnement juridique par analogie d'après al-Ġazālī. *SI* 34(1971), pp. 57-88

FARŪKI, Kemāl A. Al-Shāfi'ī's agreements and disagreements with the Mālikī and the Ḥanafī Schools. *Islamic stud.* 10(1971), pp. 129-136.

GURAYA, Muhammad Yusuf. Judicial principles as enunciated by Caliph 'Umar I. *Islamic stud.* 11(1972), pp. 159-185.

IDRIS, H.R. L'aube du mālikisme ifrīqiyen. *SI* 33(1971), pp. 19-40.

KHALID MAS'UD, M. Abū Isḥāq Shāṭibī: his his life and works. *Islàmic stùdies* 14 (1975), pp. 145-161.

LITTLE, D.P. A new look at *al-Aḥkām al-sulṭāniyya*. *MW* 64(1974), pp. 1-18.

MASUMI, M. Saghir Hasan. Burhān al-Sharī'-ah's "al-Muḥīṭ al-Burhānī". *Islam Tetkikleri Enst. dergisi* 5(1973), pp. 67-73.

MUSLEHUDDIN, Mohammad. Islamic jurisprudence and the rule of necessity and need. *Islamic stud.* 12(1973), pp. 37-52, 103-120.

NDIAYE, Moustapha. Analyse du livre de droit musulman de Cheikh Moussa Kamara. *Bull.IFAN* 37B(1975), pp. 449-456.

RANCILLAC, P. La *Risāla* d'al-Shāfi'ī (2e partie). *MIDEO* 11(1972), pp. 127-236.

TOLEDANO, H. Sijilmâsi's manual of Maghribî *'Amal, al-'amal al-muṭlaq*; a preliminary examination. *IJMES* 5(1974), pp. 484-496.

TURKI, Abdel Magid. La vénération pour Mālik et la physionomie du mālikisme andalou. *SI* 33(1971), pp. 41-65.

See also II. c. 4. Ali

See also III. a. 4. Toledano

See also XXIX. i. Steppat.

iii Legal rites and their variations

BERNAND, M. Nouvelles remarques sur l'*iğmā'* chez le Qāḍī 'Abd al-Ğabbār. *Arabica* 19 (1972), pp. 78-85

BERQUE, J. L'ambiguité dans le *fiqh*. *L'ambivalence dans la culture arabe*, 1967, pp. 232-252.

CHARNAY, J.P. Fonction de l'*ikhtilâf* en méthodologie juridique arabe. *L'ambivalence dans la culture arabe*, 1967, pp. 191-231.

CHEHATA, Chafik. L'*ikhtilâf* et la conception musulmane du droit. *L'ambivalence dans la culture arabe*, 1967, pp. 258-266.

HABIB, Kamal Mohammad: The concept of the Magian soul in Oswald Spengler's *Decline of the West*: an evaluation. *Iqbal rev.* 12i(1971), pp. 69-80.

HASAN, Ahmad. The argument for the authority of Ijmā'. *Islamic stud.* 10(1971), pp. 39-52.

HASAN, Ahmad. Modern trends in ijmā'. *Islamic stud.* 12(1973), pp. 121-153.

LINANT DE BELLEFONDS, Y. Les prétendues ambivalences du *fiqh*. *L'ambivalence dans la culture arabe*, 1967, pp. 253-257.

MAKDISI, G. The Hanbali school and Sufism. *Actas IV congresso de estudos árabes e islâmicos* 1968(1971), pp. 71-84.

MAKDISI, G. The Hanbali school and Sufism. *Humaniora Islamica* 2(1974), pp. 61-72

POONAWALA, Ismail K. A reconsideration of al-Qāḍī al-Nu'mān's *madhhab*. *BSOAS* 37(1974), pp. 572-579

SOURDEL, D. Deux documents relatifs à la communauté hanbalite de Damas. *BEO* 25 (1972), pp. 141-152.

VOLL, J. The madhhab of Ibn Kannān, the Damascene historian. *al-Abhath* 24(1971), pp. 83-86.

VOLL, J. The Non-Wahhābī Ḥanbalīs of Eighteenth Century Syria. *Der Islam* 49(1972), pp. 277-291.

See also XIX. f. Lapidus.

iv Justice and its operation

ABDUL, M.O.A. The problems of justice in man's relation to God. *Nigerian J. Islam* 1i(1970), pp. 41-48.

BERQUE, J. Cadis de Kairouan d'après un manuscrit tunisien. *ROMM* 13-14(1973), pp. 97-108.

CHALMETA, P. La ḥisba en Ifrīqiya et al-Andalus: étude comparative. *CT* 18 (nos. 69-70, 1970), pp. 87-105.

CHALMETA GENDRÓN, P. El "Kitab fi adab al-hisba" (Libro del buen gobierno del zoco) de al Saqatī. *And.* 33(1968), pp. 143-195, 367-434.

FLOOR, W.M. The Marketpolice in Qājār Persia. The office of Dārūgha-yi Bāzār and Muhtasib. *WI N.S.* 13(1971), pp. 212-229.

HEYD, U. The Ottoman Fetvā. *Proc. 27th Int.Cong.Or.1967* (1971), pp. 217-218.

JENNINGS, R.C. The office of vekil (wakil) in 17th century Ottoman Sharia courts. *SI* 42(1975), pp. 147-169.

LAYISH, Aharon *Qāḍīs* and *Sharī'a* in Israel. *Asian & Afr.Studs.* 7(1971), pp. 237-272.

TOLEDANO, H. Sijilmâsî's manual of Maghribî *'amal, Al-'amal al-muṭlaq*: a preliminary examination. *IJMES* 5(1974), pp. 484-496.

TURKI, Abdel Magid. Argument d'autorité, preuve rationnelle et absence de preuves dans la méthodologie juridique musulmane. *SI* 42(1975), pp. 59-91.

YADUVANSH, Uma. The decline of the role of the Qāḍīs in India - 1793 - 1876. *Stud. in Islam* 6(1969), pp. 155-171.

See also III. a. 9. Idris.

See also III. a. 9. Jennings.

See also XIX. h. Mīlād.

See XXIX. g. Jennings.

v Dhimmis. Status of foreigners

HAMIDULLAH, Muhammad. Status of non-Muslims in Islam. *Maj.al-Azhar* 45viii (1973), pp. 6-13; 45ix(1973), pp. 12-16.

VERMEULEN, U. Een bevelschrift betreffende de Dimmī's van Ḥiṣn al'Akrād (765/1364). *Orientalia Gandensia* 4(1967), pp. 69-76.

See also IX. m. Bishai.

vi International law

ABU ZAHRA, Muhammad. Rules of international relations in Islam. *Maj. al-Azhar* 47v(1975), pp. 6-12; 47vi(1975), pp. 5-10; 47vii(1975), pp. 6-10.

AGBEDE, I.O. Conflict between customary and non-customary systems of law: preliminary observations. *J. Islam. comp. law* 4 (1972), pp. 48-58.

BOORMAN, J.A. Economic coercion in international law: the Arab oil weapon and the ensuing juridical issues. *J. internat. law and economics* 9(1974), pp. 205-231.

CHARNAY, J.P. Dialectique entre droit musulman et juridisme industriel. *SI* 32(1970), pp. 77-87.

MUSTAFA, Zaki. The substantive law applied by Muslim courts in Ethiopia. Possible justifications for the continued application of the Sharia. *J. Ethiop. law* 9(1973), pp. 138-148.

MUSTAPHA, Mohamed Youssef. La théorie de "rebus sic stantibus" et son application aux contrats pétroliers. *Dirasat* 1(1974), pp. 7-27.

PEARL, D. Bangladesh: Islamic laws in a secular state. *South Asian R.* 8(1974), pp. 33-41.

ROSENNE, Shabtai. The Red Cross, Red Crescent, Red Lion and Sun and the Red Shield of David. *Israel yb.on human rights* 5(1975), pp. 9-54.

WADE, J.A. Capacity to marry: choice of law rules and polygamous marriages. (Based on *Radwan v. Radwan (No.2)*. *Int. comp.law Q.* 22(1973), pp. 571-575.

WEIS, P. The right to leave and to return in the Middle East. *Israel yb.on human rights* 5(1975), pp. 322-365.

See also IX. j. Abdallah.

See also XXIII. d. Armanazi.

See also XXIII. d. Iskandar.

See also XXIII. d. Jiryis.

See also XXIII. d. Mallison, Mallison.

vii Criminal law

BIJON, S. Sur le droit pénal des pays arabes. *Cauris* 5(1973), pp. 264-266.

MOUSTAPHA, Mahmoud Mahmoud. L'indemnisation de la victime de l'infraction pénale dans les législations des pays arabes. *Proche-Orient; études juridiques (Ann. Fac. Droit Beyrouth* 75*)*, pp. 233-234.

viii Sectarian law

ELIASH, J. The Ithnaʻasharī-Shīʻī juristic theory of political and legal authority. *Proc.27th Int.Cong.Or.1967* (1971), pp. 250-252.

LOKHANDWALLA, S.T. Islamic law and Ismāʻīlī communities (Khojas and Bohras). *India and contemporary Islam*, ed. S.T. Lokhandwalla, 1971, pp. 379-397.

WAKIN, J. Written documents in Islamic law. *Actas IV congresso de estudos árabes e islâmicos* 1968(1971), pp. 347-354.

See also II. c. 8. Kohlberg.

ix Marriage. Divorce. Status of women

AFZAL, Mohammad, BEAN, Lee L., HUSAIN, Imtiazuddin. Muslim marriages: age, mehr, and social status. *Pakistan development R.* 12 (1973), pp. 48-61.

AHMAD, Bashir. Status of women and settlement of family disputes under Islamic law. *Islamic law in modern India*, ed. Tahir Mahmood, 1972, pp. 186-191.

AKEL, Abderrazak el-. Derecho conyugal o derechos de la mujer en el Islam. (Resumen de la Tesis Doctoral.) *Cuadernos de la Bibl.Esp.de Tetuan* 8(1973), pp. 87-103.

ALWAYE, Mohiaddin. The status of woman in Islam. *Maj. al-Azhar* 47iv(1975), pp. 1-5.

CHEHATA, Chafik. Le droit de répudiation (*Talaq*) dans le droit positif des pays arabes. *Proc.27th Int.Cong.Or.1967* (1971), pp. 249-250.

CHEHATA, Chafic. La famille en Islam: problèmes d'actualité. *RJPIC* 28(1974), pp. 663-72.

CHIPP, S. Tradition vs. change. The All Pakistan Women's Association. *IMA* liii(1970), pp. 69-90.

CHMIELOWSKA, D. Emancypacja kobiety tureckiej. *Przegl. Or.* 1(93, 1975), pp. 25-30.

DEPREZ, J. Mariage mixte, Islam et nation (à propos d'une récente campagne contre le mariage mixte des Marocains). *Rev. alg.* 12(1975), pp. 97-142.

DILGER, K. Rechtsfortbildung durch "siyāsa" dargestellt am Beispiel des ṭalaq in Iran. *Islamkundliche Abhandlungen H.J. Kissling*, 1974, pp. 49-62.

DIONISI, B. A proposito del 3o congresso dell'*Union nationale des femmes algériennes. OM* 55(1975), pp. 62-66.

ESPOSITO, J.L. Women's rights in Islam. *Islamic studies* 14(1975), pp. 99-114.

FARUQI, Lamia L. al-. Women's rights and the Muslim Women. *Islam and the modern age* 3ii(1972), pp. 76-99.

HINCHCLIFFE, D. Polygamy in traditional and contemporary Islamic law. *IMA* liii(1970), pp. 13-38.

HINCHCLIFFE, D. The widow's dower-debt in India. *Islam and the modern age* 4iii(1973), pp. 5-22.

HOWARD, I.K.A. *Mut'a* marriage reconsidered in the context of the formal procedures for Islamic marriage. *J. Semitic stud.* 20(1975), pp. 82-92.

IDRIS, H.R. Le mariage en Occident musulman. *SI* 32(1970), pp. 157-167.

IDRIS, Hady Roger. Le marriage en Occident musulman, Analyse de fatwās médiévales extraites du "*Miʻyār*" d'Al-Wancharīchī. *ROMM* 12(1972), pp. 45-62; 17(1974), pp. 71-105.

JAFFER HUSSAIN, S. Judicial interpretation of Islamic matrimonial law in India. *Islamic law in modern India*, ed. Tahir Mahmood, 1972, pp. 175-185.

JENNINGS, R.C. Women in early 17th century Ottoman judicial records -- the Sharia court of Anatolian Kayseri. *JESHO* 18(1975), pp. 53-114.

KAROUI CHABBI, Belgacem. Réflexion sur la condition juridique de la femme arabo-musulmane, matriarcat et concubinage. *RJPIC* 28(1974), pp. 558-569.

KOURA, Salah-Eddine. Le divorce et la répudiation en Droit Musulman (charia) et le Droit Positif Algérien. *Rev.alger.des sci. jur.econ.pol.* 11iii(1974), pp. 111-112.

LATHAM, J.D. Ibn ʻAbd al-Raʼūf on the law of marriage: a matter of interpretation. *IQ* 15(1971), pp. 3-16.

LAYISH, Aharon. Woman and succession in the Muslim family in Israel. *Asian and African studies* [Jerusalem] 9(1973), pp. 23-62.

MANNAN, M.A. The development of the Islamic law of divorce in Pakistan. *J. Islamic and comparative law* 5(1974), pp. 89-98.

MINATTUR, J. On the magic of monogamy and similar illusions. *Islamic law in modern India*, ed. Tahir Mahmood, 1972, pp. 157-166.

NEJATULLAH SIDDIQI, M. Restraints on polygamy and Muslim personal law. *Islamic law in modern India*, ed. Tahir Mahmood, 1972, pp. 147-156.

PRUVOST, L. Condition juridique, politique et social de la femme: Le 9e Congrès de l'I.D.E.F. *IBLA* 37(no.134, 1974), pp. 349-364.

RASHIDUZ ZAFER, Mohammad. Islamic law: some conflicts and rationales. *J. Islam. comp. law* 4(1972), pp. 17-29.

SAFWAD, Osman. Contradiction entre situation de fait et situation de droit concernant la femme dans les pays arabes. *Rev.alg.* 11(1974), pp. 113-117.

SAMMARI, Mohamed Salah Rached. Réflexion sur la condition de la femme en droit musulman. *RJPIC* 28(1974), pp. 548-557.

SUKHDEV SINGH. Development of the concept of divorce in Muslim law. *Allahabad law R.* 5(1973), pp. 117-127.

TYABJI, Kamila. Polygamy, unilateral divorce and mahr in Muslim law as interpreted in India. *Islamic law in modern India*, ed. Tahir Mahmood, 1972, pp. 141-146.

ZAFER, M.R. Unilateral divorce in Muslim personal law. *Islamic law in modern India*, ed. Tahir Mahmood, 1972, pp. 167-174.

La femme et la législation des pays arabes à la lumière des accords internationaux. Recommandations du Séminaire de Beyrouth (27-31 mai 1974). *Travaux et jours* 52(1974), pp. 71-76.

See also II. a. 1. Ehrenfels.

See also II. a. 6. Juynboll.

See also III. c. *Algeria*. Borrmans.

See also VII. a. Keyser.

See also XII. a. Douedar.

See also XII. d. Maher.

See also XII. e. Ougouag-Kezzal.

See also XXXII. b. Aschenbrenner.

See also XXXVI. h. Burton.

See also XLI. a. Sönmez.

x Paternity, maintenance and guardianship

BORRMANS, M. Statut personnel et droit familial en pays musulmans. *Proche-Orient chrêtien* 23(1973), pp. 133-147

CASTRO, F. Illiceità della fecondazione artificiale in diritto musulmano secondo una recente pubblicazione dello *shaykh* Muḥammad Ǧawād Mughniyyah. *OM* 54(1974), pp. 222-225.

HASAN, S.M. Muslim law of legitimacy and section 112 of the Indian evidence act. *Islamic law in modern India*, ed. Tahir Mahmood, 1972, pp. 192-201.

KARMI, H.S. The family as a developing social group in Islam. *Asian affairs* 62 (N.S.6, 1975), pp. 61-68.

KHAN, M.E. Is Islam against family planning? *Islam and the modern age* 6ii (1975), pp. 61-72.

LATIFI, Daniyal. Adoption and the Muslim law. *J. Indian Law Inst.* 16(1974), pp. 118-122.

NAQVI, Syed Ali Raza. Modern reforms in Muslim family laws -- a general study. *Islamic studies* 13(1974), pp. 235-252.

SPIES, O. Arabische Quellenbeiträge zum Rechtsinstitut der Delegation (Ḥawāla). *Z. vergl. Rechtswis.* 73(1972), pp. 17-47.

ZAYID, Mahmud. The radicals and the fundamentalists and Muslim personal law. *Islam and the modern age* 5iii(1974), pp. 74-80.

xi Property. Contracts and dispositions

ADESANYA, S.A. Capacity of a Muslim-native of Nigeria to dispose of property in accordance with the English wills act. *J. Islam. comp. law* 4(1972), pp. 30-47.

ANDERSON, J.N.D. and COULSON, N.J. The Moslem ruler and contractual obligations. *New York Univ.Law Rev.* 33(1957), pp. 917-933. [Offprint in SOAS]

ÇAĞATAY, N. Ribā and interest concept and banking in the Ottoman Empire. *SI* 32(1970), pp. 53-68.

CHEHATA, Ch. Les concepts de Qabḍ Ḍamân et de Qabḍ Amâna en droit musulman Hanéfite. *SI* 32(1970), pp. 89-99.

HAMID, M.E. Does the Islamic law of contract recognise a doctrine of mistake? *J. Islam. comp. law* 4(1972), pp. 1-16.

HAMID, Mohamed Fatih el-. Duress and its effect on contract in Islamic law. *Sudan law J.and reports* 1971, pp. 334-344.

HASANUZZAMAN, S.M. The liability of partners in an Islamic Shirkah. *Islamic stud.* 10(1971), pp. 319-341.

KOHLI, Baldev. Right of pre-emption in modern social conditons. *Islamic law in modern India,* ed. Tahir Mahmood, 1972, pp. 219-227.

MAHMOOD, Tahir. Judicial reform of the law of pre-emption in India: impact on Muslim personal law. *Islamic law in modern India,* ed. Tahir Mahmood, 1972, pp. 213-218.

SCARCIA AMORETTI, B. Some observations on the evolution of the concept of private property in the Muslim world: methodological notes. *AION* 34(N.S.24, 1974), pp. 429-436.

SIDDIQUI, M. Najatullah. Moral bases of Islamic personal law. *Islam and the modern age* 5iv(1974), pp. 81-95.

See also III. a. 9. Layish.

See also XXXI. a. Nadvi

xii Testamentary bequests

ANDERSON, J.N.D. Islamic law of testate and intestate succession and the administration of deceased persons' assets. *Islamic law in modern India,* ed. Tahir Mahmood, 1972, pp. 202-206.

COULSON, N.J. Representational succession in contemporary Islamic law. *SI* 32(1970), pp. 101-108.

GARTHWAITE, G.R. Two Persian wills of Ḥājj ʿAlī Qulī Khān Sardār Asʿad. *JAOS* 95(1975), pp. 645-650.

KAUFHOLD, H. Islamisches Erbrecht in christichsyrischer Überlieferung. *Oriens Christ.* 59(1975), pp. 19-35.

MOSUGU, S.E. Moslem wills and the courts in Nigeria. *Nigerian J. contemp. law* 3 (1972), pp. 105-138.

RADDATZ, H.P. Frühislamisches Erbrecht, nach dem Kitāb al-farāʾiḍ des Sufyān at-Taurī. Edition und Kommentar. *WI* 13(1971), pp. 26-78.

SKAIST, A. Inheritance laws and their social background. *JAOS* 95(1975), pp. 242-247.

xiii Waqf

BEG, M.H. Gifts, family waqfs and pre-emption under Islamic law: some observations. *Islamic law in modern India,* ed. Tahir Mahmood, 1972, pp. 209-212.

BOL'SHAKOV, O.G. Dva vakfa Ibrakhima Tamgach-Khana v Samarkande. *Strany i narody Vostoka pod obshchey red. D.A. Ol'derogge,* X, 1971, pp. 170-178.

FAROQUI, Suraiya. *Vakif* administration in sixteenth century Konya. The *Zaviye* of Sadreddin-i Konevi. *JESHO* 17(1974), pp. 145-172.

KHALID RASHID, S. Administration of waqfs in India: some suggestions. *Islamic law in modern India,* ed. Tahir Mahmood, 1972, pp. 231-238.

LATIFI, Danial. Law of family waqfs: need for a reconsideration. *Islamic law in modern India,* ed. Tahir Mahmood, 1972, pp. 228-230.

MUHAMMAD AMIN, Muh. Un acte de fondation de waqf par une chrétienne (Xe siècle h., xvie s. chr.). Introduction et édition. *JESHO* 18(1975), pp. 43-52.

RABIE, Hassanein. Some financial aspects of the waqf system in medieval Egypt. *Eg. hist. rev.* 18(1971), pp. 1-24.

RIFAAT, Hassan-Tabet. Le Wakf, en droit Libanais, fraude à la loi successorale ou résurgence de la liberté? *Rev. jur. et pol.* 26(1972), pp. 1027-1038.

RIFAAT, Hassan-Tabet. Le wakf, fraude à la loi successorale ou résurgence de la liberté. *Proche-Orient; études juridiques (Ann. Fac. Droit Beyrouth 75),* pp. 235-246.

SOURDEL-THOMINE, J. et SOURDEL, D. Biens fonciers constitués *waqf* en Syrie fatimide pour une famille de Šarīfs damascains. *JESHO* 15(1972), pp. 269-296.

TAWFIQ, Muhammad Amin. Development of awqāf system in Egypt. *Maj. al-Azhar* 47vi(1975), pp. 11-16.

See also XIX. a. Crecelius

See also XIX. h. Veselý.

See also XXIX. d. *Czechoslovakia.* Blaškovič.

See also XXIX. d. *Yugoslavia* Behija.

See also XXIX. f. Mutafčieva.

See also XXIX. f. Pevzner.

See also XXIX. f. Tveritinova.

See also XLIII. a. Makdisi.

xiv Slaves

ABBAS, Mohammed Galal. Slavery between Islam and western civilization - a comparative study of attitudes. *Majallat al-Azhar* 43ix(1971), pp. 11-16; 43x(1971), pp. 9-13

FORAND, P.G. The relation of the slave and client to the master or patron in medieval Islam. *IJMES* 2(1971), pp. 59-66.

See also X. b. Petrushevskiy.

See also X. f. Beg.

b CUSTOMARY LAW

AWA, Mohames El-. The place of custom *('urf)* in Islamic legal theory. *IQ* 17 (1973), pp. 177-182.

BOUSQUET, G.H. Note sur un livre de droit coutumier bédouin. *Rev. hist. droit franç. et étranger* 50(1972), pp. 257-262.

CAMAJ, M. Der Niederschlag des Kanuns von Leke Dukagjini in der albanischen Volksepik. *Serta Slavica in memoriam A. Schmaus*, 1971, pp. 104-111.

CHELHOD, J. La société yéménite et le droit. *L'Homme* 15ii(1975), pp. 67-86.

GRÄF, E. Brauch/'urf und Sitte/'ada in der islamischen Jurisprudenz. *Fest.H.Petri*, 1973, pp. 122-144.

HOOKER, M.B. The challenge of Malay adat law in the realm of comparative law. *Int. comp. law Q.* 22(1973), pp. 492-514.

KANE, Maïmouna. Condition de la femme sénégalaise mariée selon la coutume ouoloff islamisée. *RJPIC* 28(1974), pp. 779-789.

SCHINKEL, H.-G. Bemerkungen zum Tränk- und Weiderecht der Nomaden Ost- und Nordostafrikas. *Jhb. Mus. Völkerk. Leipzig* 27(1970), pp. 241-265.

c STATUTE LAW

General. Codification of Muslim law

ANDERSON, J.N.D. The role of personal statutes in social development in Islamic countries. *Comp. stud. soc. hist.* 13 (1971), pp. 16-31.

FALAHI, Sami d. El-. The legal environment for negotiating commercial agreements in the Middle East. *An introduction to business law in the Middle East*, ed. B. Russell, 1975, pp. 73-87.

MOUSTAPHA, Mahmoud Mahmoud. Les techniques de l'individualisation judiciaire dans les législations des pays arabes. *Ann.de la Fac.de Droit de Beyrouth* 70(1971), pp. 745-763

NAQVI, S. Ali Raza. Problems of the codification of Islamic law. *Internat. Islamic Conf.*, 1968, pp. 40-47.

SAKSENA, Kashi Prasad. Need for a code of Muslim law. *Islamic law in modern India*, ed. Tahir Mahmood, 1972, pp. 133-137.

See also III. c. *India*. Lokhandwala.

Afghanistan

SINGH UBEROI, J.P. Men, women and property in Northern Afghanistan. *India and contemporary Islam*, ed. S.T. Lokhandwalla, 1971, pp. 398-416.

Africa south of the Sahara

CHAPAL, P. Le rôle de l'organisation de l'Unité Africaine dans le règlement des litiges entre Etats Africains. *Rev.alger. des sci.jur.econ.et pol.* 8(1971), pp. 875-911.

MATHURIN, M. Abdoulaye Diop. La dévolution successorale Musulmane: détermination des héritiers dans le code Sénégalais de la famille. *Rev. jur. et pol.* 26(1972), pp. 799-810.

SEID, Joseph Brahim. Coutumes successorales traditionnelles au Tchad islamisé. *Rev. jur. et pol.* 26(1972), pp. 811-818.

The flag law in Afghanistan. *Afghanistan* 27i(1974), pp. 1-8.

The law of state emblem. *Afghanistan* 27i (1974), pp. 9-11.

Algeria

ALLAG, Mme. La famille et le Droit en Algérie dans le contexte maghrébin. *Rev.alger.des sci.jur.econ.pol.* 11iii(1974), pp. 157-160.

BAZI, Safia. Pour une définition de la distinction Droit Public - Droit Privé (A propos des élections des Algériens aux I.R.P.). *Rev.algér.des sci.jur., econ.et pol.* 8(1971), pp. 633-638.

BELKACEM, Khadija. Le code des investissements privés en Algérie. *Rev. jur. et pol. indep. et coop.* 26(1972), pp. 299-332.

BENDEDDOUCHE, J. Note sur la réglementation algérienne du passage et du séjour des navires de guerre étrangers dans les eaux territoriales et intérieures de l'Algérie. (Décret du 5 octobre 1972). *Rev.alg.* 11(1974), pp. 461-474.

BENMELHA, Ghaoti. L'Etat Algérien devant la justice. *Rev.algérienne des sci.jur., econ.et pol.* 8(1971), pp. 331-362.

BERCHICHE, A.H. La notion d'infraction économique en droit positif algérien. *Rev. algér. des sci. jur., écon. et pol.* 9(1972), pp. 695-718.

BONTEMS, Cl. Les origines de la justice administrative en Algérie. *Rev. alg.* 12(1975), pp. 277-295.

BORRMANS, M. À propos d'une récente fatwâ relative au statut familial des émigrés algériens. *ROMM* 13-14(1973), pp. 131-140.

BORRMANS, M. Perspectives Algériennes en matière de droit familial. *SI* 37(1973), pp. 129-153.

DAVID, C. La liberté du commerce en Algérie. *Rev. algér. des sci. jur., écon. et pol.* 9(1972), pp. 633-652.

DOUEDAR, M. La libération du mariage. *Rev. alg.* 11(1974), pp. 133-147.

EDELMAN, B. Note sur le conctionnement de l'idéologie institutions représentatives du personnel). *Rev.algér.des sci.jur., econ.et pol.* 8(1971), pp. 639-668.

FENAUX, H. Á propos de "L'Etat Algérien devant la justice". *Rev.algérienne des sci.jur., econ.et pol.* 8(1971), pp. 363-366.

FENAUX, H. Éléments de droit judiciaire Algérien. *Rev.alg.sci.jur.econ.pol.* 9 (1972), pp. 95-127, 409-429; 10(1973), pp. 253-409.

GAILLARD, Cl. Le droit d'auteur en Algérie. *Rev.alg.* 12(1975), pp. 737-764.

HAMADI, Ghouti. La législation foncière en Algérie avant l'indépendance. *Rev. algér.des sci.jur., econ. et pol.* 8(1971), pp. 723-734.

HAZARD, J.N. The residue of Marxist influence in Algeria. *Columbia J.transnat. law* 9(1970), pp. 194-225.

ISSAD, Mohand. L'exécution des décisions judiciaires étrangères en droit algérien. *Penant* 84(no.743, 1974), pp. 6-14.

LOURDJANE, Ahmed. Le code pénal algérien. *Rev.jur.et pol.* 26(1972), pp. 77-96

MAHIOU, Ahmed. Le contentieux administratif en Algérie. *Rev. algér. des sci. jur., écon. et pol.* 9(1972), pp. 571-632.

MATHÉTÉS, O. La réforme judiciaire algérienne. *Ann. de L'Afr. du Nord* 5(1966), pp. 111-119.

POMEL, B. Contribution a l'étude du domaine de l'Etat et de son régime juridique L'exemple des ex-biens vacants. *Rev. algér. des sci. jur., écon. et pol.* 9(1972), pp. 719-760.

RAHAL, Mohamed. De la procédure d'injonction de payer. *Rev.algérienne des sci.jur., econ.et pol.* 8(1971), pp. 367-374.

SALAH-BEY, Mohamed-Chérif. Droit de la famille et problèmes idéologiques. *Rev. alger.des sci.jur.econ.pol.* 11iii(1974), pp. 97-110.

SALAH-BEY, Mohamed-Chérif. La filiation naturelle dans le projet de Code de la famille algérien. *Rev.alger.des sci.jur. econ.pol.* 11iii(1974), pp. 85-95.

SATOR, Kaddour. La competence des tribunaux et des cours, en matière de biens vacants. *Rev.algérienne des sci.jur., econ.et pol.* 8(1971), pp. 379-383.

SPITERI, J. La responsabilité pénale dans l'optique algérienne. *Rev. alg. des sci. jur., econ. et pol.* 10(1973), pp. 489-495.

VLACHOS, G. Le droit public du développment: le modèle Algérien. *Rev.jur.et pol. indep.et coop.* 27(1973), pp. 61-90; 255-294.

VLACHOS, G. Le régime juridique des hydrocarbures en Algérie. *Rev. jur. pol.* 28 (1974), pp. 103-128.

See also III. a. 9. Koura.

See also XII. e. *Algeria*. Sainte-Marie.

See also XVI. c. Abdi.

See also XVI. c. Collot.

See also XVI. c. Sur.

See also XVI. c. Terki.

See also XVI. cc. Sari.

See also XVI. d. Lourdjane.

Arabia

DILGER, K. Das Recht unter dem Einfluss des Sozialismus in der Volksrepublik Jemen. *Z. vergl. Rechtwis.* 75(1975), pp. 1-44 (resumes in English and Spanish).

SOLAIM, Soliman A. Saudi Arabia's judicial system. *MEJ* 25(1971), pp. 403-407.

See also V. c. *Arabia*. Strika.

Egypt., U.A.R.

ABDEL HAMID, Mohamed Sami and OMAR, Mohamed Abdel-Khalek. Egypt. *Contractual remedies in Asian countries*, ed. J. Minattur, 1962, pp. 1-13.

ALWAN, Abdul Sahib. Land tenure legislation for desert development in the A.R.E.. *Eg. contemp.* 64(no.351, 1973), pp. 97-109.

ANDERSON, J.N.D. Law reform in Egypt, 1850-1950. *Revolution in the Middle East*, ed. P.J. Vatikiotis, 1972, pp. 146-172.

HAROUN, Chehata. Réflexions très générales à propos d'un projet de révision de la loi sur les brevets d'invention en Egypte. *Égypte contemp.* 62, no. 346(1971), pp. 85-99

ISSA, Hossam M. Le critère de nationalité de sociétés d'après la Jurisprudence Mixte d'Egypte. *Rev.al-ulum al-qanuniya wal-iqtisadiya* 13i(1971), pp. 1-27

LEBOULANGER, Ph. La nouvelle législation égyptienne sur les investissements arabes et étrangers et les zones franches. *Maghreb Machrek* 68(1975), pp. 59-61.

MALACHE, M. Kamel A. Comparative study of marine insurance in Egyptian, French and English laws. *Eg. contemp.* 63(No. 349, 1972) pp. 229-252.

III LAW

India.

ALI, S.A. Impact of technology and Western values on Islamic law in India 1947-1965. *India and contemporary Islam*, ed. S.T. Lokhandwalla, 1971, pp.

BANERJEE, Phanindra Nath. Indian law officers in the early British Judiciary in Bengal. *Q'ly rev.hist.stud.* 10 (1970-1), pp. 209-212.

FYZEE, A.A.A. Mohammedan law in India. *India and the Arab World, ed. by S. Maqbul Ahmed*, 1969, pp. 86-94.

LOKHANDWALA, S.T. Some problems of Muslim law in India and the Arab world. *India and the Arab World, ed. by S. Maqbul Ahmed*, 1969, pp. 103-107.

Iran

AFCHAR, Hassan. Iran. *Contractual remedies in Asian countries*, ed. J. Minattur, 1962, pp. 91-105.

ANDERSON, J.N.D. Reforms in Islāmic law in Irān. *Iqbal rev.* 12iii(1971), pp. 16-27

BAGLEY, F.R.C. The Iranian Family Protection Law of 1967. A milestone in the advance of women's rights. *Iran and Islam, in memory of V. Minorsky*, 1971, pp. 47-64

LÖSCHNER, H. Der Erwerb der iranischen Staatsangehörigkeit. *Z. vergl. Rechtwiss.* 72(1971), pp. 78-121.

Jordan

ERBEL, B. Einige Anmerkungen zum jordanischen Personenstandsgesetz des Jahres 1966. *Islamkundliche Abhandlungen H.J. Kissling*, 1974, pp. 63-69.

Lebanon

BACCACHE, Elie. La faute dans la détermination du gardien en jurisprudence libanaise. *Ann.de la Fac.de Droit de Beyrouth* 70(1971), pp. 765-775

CHAMAS, Samy. La formule d'acte de cautionnement bancaire. Ses précarités. *Proche-Orient; études juridiques (Ann. Fac. Droit Beyrouth 75)*, pp. 217-232.

DOUENCE, J.C. L'article 58 de la Constitution libanaise et la jurisprudence administrative. *Ann. de la Fac. de Droit de Beyrouth* 72(1972), pp. 9-57.

DOUENCE, J.C. Les tendances actuelles des services publics industriels et commerciaux au Liban. *Annales de la Faculte de droit de Beyrouth* 67 (1971), pp. 523-542.

DURUPTY, M. Transposition et mutations du modèle administratif français (les cas libanais et tunisien). *Proche-Orient; études juridiques* 79(1973), pp. 143-198.

FABIA, C. Les transformations de sociétés en droit libanais. *Ann.de la Fac.de Droit de Beyrouth* 70(1971), pp. 681-720

FARAH, Naoum. Le Barreau face à ses problèmes. *Travaux et jours* 42(1972), pp. 5-19

GANNAGÉ, Pierre. Bref aperçu sur l'évolution du droit successoral au Liban. *Rev. jur. et pol.* 26(1972), pp. 1021-1026.

GANNAGÉ, P. Bref aperçu sur le statut de la femme en droit privé libanais. *RJPIC* 28(1974), pp. 979-985.

GANNAGÉ, P. L'influence de la nationalité de la mère en droit libanais. *Proche-Orient; études juridiques (Ann. Fac. Droit Beyrouth 75)*, pp. 249-256.

GANNAGÉ, P. La nationalité et les statuts communautaires au Liban. *Rev. jur.et pol.indép.et coop.* 25(1971), pp. 659-668.

GEMAYEL, Sleiman M. L'autonomie financière des établissements publics industriels et commerciaux, illusion ou réalité. *Annales de la Faculté de droit de Beyrouth* 67(1971), pp. 503-521.

JOREIGE, Ramzi. Le statut des agents des offices autonomes. *Annales de la Faculté de droit de Beyrouth* 67(1971), pp. 475-486.

LARROUMET, C. Droits et obligations de l'expéditeur et du destinataire envers le transporteur dans le contrat de transport de marchandises. *Ann. de la Fac. de Droit de Beyrouth* 72(1972), pp. 65-109.

MERLE, P. L'ordre du jour dans les assemblées générales d'actionnaires. *Proche-Orient; études juridiques* 79(1973), pp. 199-217.

MOARBES, A. Les contrats passés par les établissements publics industriels et commerciaux. *Annales de la Faculté de droit de Beyrouth* 67(1971), pp. 493-501.

NSOULI, Zakaria. La nature juridique et l'organisation des offices autonomes. *Annales de la Faculté de droit de Beyrouth* 67(1971), pp. 457-486.

RIFAAT, Hassan Tabet. L'influence des circonstances exceptionnelles sur la responsabilité des forces de sécurité au Liban. *Rev. jur. pol.* 27(1973), pp. 979-1006.

RIFAAT, Hassān-Tabet. La libanaise à l'assaut de ses droits politiques. *RJPIC* 28(1974), pp. 986-1000.

RIFAAT, Hassan-Tabet Perte de la nationalité libanaise par manque de loyalisme. *Rev.jur.et pol.indép.et coop.* 25(1971), pp. 669-684.

RIFAAT, Hassān-Tabet. La prostitution en droit public libanais. *RJPIC* 28(1974), pp. 1001-1010.

III LAW

SOUMRANI, M. La conception matérielle de la notion de cessation des paiements dans la loi libanaise No.2/67du 16 Janvier 1967 (loi Intra). *Ann. de la Fac. de droit Beyrouth* 76(1973), pp. 57-67.

TABBARAH, Bahige. La compétence en matière de responsabilité extra-contractuelle des établissements publics industriels et commerciaux. *Annales de la Faculté de droit de Beyrouth* 67(1971), pp. 487-491.

See also III. a. 13. Rifaat.

Libya

MINGANTI, P. Ricezione di pene *ḥadd* nella legislazione della Repubblica di Libia. *OM* 54(1974), pp. 265-274.

NAWAZ, M.K. Nationalization of foreign oil companies -- Libyan decree of 1 September 1973. *Indian J. internat. law* 14(1974), pp. 70-80.

Morocco.

BORRMANS, M. La famille et le droit positif maghrébin. *Rev.alg.* 11(1974), pp. 29-56.

BOUDERBALA, Negib et PASCON, P. Le droit et le fait dans la société composite. Essai d'introduction au système juridique marocain. *Bull.econ.et soc.Maroc* 32(117, 1970), pp. 1-17

GUIBAL, M. A propos de l'article 102 de la constitution marocaine (Constitution du 10 mars 1972). *RJPIC* 27(1975), pp. 318-335.

LABOUZ, M.F. Questions maghrébines du droit de la mer. *Maghreb-Machrek* 64(1974), pp. 47-54.

LAMODIÈRE, J. Les dahirs marocains du 2 mars 1973 portant reprise des terres et marocanisation de certaines activités économiques et le droit international. *J.droit int.* 101(1974), pp. 323-340.

ROUSSET, M. La réforme de la justice marocaine et ses incidences sur le contentieux administratif. *RJPIC* 27(1975), pp. 145-162.

See also XII. d. Etienne.

See also XVI. b. Francisi.

Pakistan

KAZI, A.K. Islamic law in Pakistan. *Abr-Nahrain* 11(1971), pp. 56-68.

Palestine

SCHWARZENBERGER, G. Privileged belligerency in guerrilla warfare: an implied test of legitimacy? *Rev.droits de l'homme* 4 (1971), pp. 535-553 [Offprint in SOAS]

South-East Asia

IBRAHIM, Ahmad. The administration of Muslim law in South-East Asia. *IC* 46(1972), pp. 245-263, 337-352; 47(1973), pp. 37-55

Sudan

AKOLAWIN, Natale Olwak. Personal law in the Sudan - trends and developments. *J.Afr.law* 17(1973), pp. 149-195.

DILGER, K. Das sudanesische Zivilgesetzbuch von 1971 und sein Verhältnis zu den anderen arabischen Zivilgesetzbüchern. *Z. vergl. Rechtswis.* 74(1974), pp. 39-65.

MEDANI, Amin M. Some aspects of the Sudan law of homicide. *J. Afr. law* 18(1974), pp. 92-103.

MUSTAFA, Zaki. Opting out of the common law: recent developments in the legal system of the Sudan. *J.Afr.law* 17(1973), pp. 133-148.

Syria

ARIOLI, A. Osservazioni in merito alla legge del 1968 sull'organizzazione dei sindacati siriani. *OM* 54(1974), pp. 168-179.

CHEBAT, Fouad. Aspects de sécularisation dans le droit syrien. *Ann.de la Fac.de Droit de Beyrouth* 70(1971), pp. 721-743

RIHAWI, Mustafa Sedki. L'accession de la femme à la fonction publique en droit syrien. *RJPIC* 28(1974), pp. 1011-1018.

RIHAWI, Sedki. Liquidation et partage des successions en droit Syrien. *Rev. jur. et pol.* 26(1972), pp. 1039-1058.

RIHAWI, Mustapha Sedki. Les perspectives offertes par le nouveau code de la nationalité syrienne. *Rev.jur.et pol. indép.et coop.* 25(1971), pp. 685-696.

RIHAWI, M. Sedki. La responsabilité du commettant du fait de son préposé en droit syrien. *Rev. jur. pol.* 27(1973), pp. 703-708.

Tunisia

AL-ANNÂBÎ, Aḥmad. Le rôle de la magistrature dans la réforme de la famille (en Tunisie). Présentation, traduction et notes par Maurice Borrmans. *OM* 51(1971), pp. 631-649

CHARFI, Mohamed. Le droit tunisien entre l'Islam et la modernité. *Rev.algér.des sci. jur.econ.pol.* 11iii(1974), pp. 11-27.

CHARFI, Mohamed. L'égalité entre l'homme et la femme dans le droit de la nationalité tunisienne. *RJPIC* 28(1974), pp. 579-592.

HACHAICHI, Fatma. La femme mère, problème démographique et juridique. *RJPIC* 28(1974), pp. 570-578.

HAMZAOUI, Mohamed Moncef El-. De la responsabilité des commettants du fait de leurs préposés en droit tunisien, particulièrement en droit civil. *Rev. jur. pol.* 27 (1973), pp. 601-610.

LADHARI, Mohamed. Le tribunal administratif de la Tunisie. *Bull. Inst. int. adm. publ.* 35(1975), pp. 163-200.

MABROUK, Mohieddine. La femme en droit public tunisien. *RJPIC* 28(1974), pp. 541-547.

NACHI, Mohamed. La nationalité tunisienne, attribution, acquisition et perte. *Rev. jur.et pol.indép.et coop.* 25(1971), pp. 587-602.

SEDRINE, Ahmed Ben. Les testaments et la protection de la famille légitime, contre les libéralités du défunt, en droit Tunisien. *Rev. jur. et pol.* 26(1972), pp. 827-832.

See also III. c. *Lebanon*. Durupty.

See also XII. f. Marchal.

Turkey

BELDICEANU, N. À propos d'un livre sur les lois pénales ottomanes. (U. Heyd, *Studies in old Ottoman criminal law.*) *JESHO* 17 (1974), pp. 206-214.

BERKIN, N.M. Darlegungen über Anwalts- und Prozessführungsrecht in Zivilsachen in der Türkei. *Ann.Fac.Droit Istanbul* 22(no.38, 1972), pp. 109-120.

BERKIN, Necmeddin. Parteivernehmung und Parteivorweisungspflicht im modernen Türkischen Zivilprossesrecht. *Ann.Fac.Droit Istanbul* 19(1969), pp. 69-80.

BERKIN, Necmeddin M. Das Wesen, die Tragweite und die Stellung der Sachverständigen in der Zivilrechtspflege und der türkischen Gerichtspraxis. *Ann.Fac.Droit Istanbul* 20 (no.36, 1970), pp. 249-258.

ÇELİK, Edip. La formation des traités en droit international et en droit turc. *Ann. Fac.Droit Istanbul* 20(no.36, 1970), pp. 1-50.

ELBİR, H.K. La participation des travailleurs aux de l'entreprise en droit turc. *Ann.Fac.Droit Istanbul* 22(no.38, 1972), pp. 121-139.

EREM, Faruk. Responsabilité pénale du banquier. *Banka ve ticaret hukuku dergisi* 7(1973), pp. 259-267.

ERMAN, S. Le norme penali e processuali penali contenute nella nuova Costituzione turca. *Ann.Fac.Droit Istanbul* 22(no.38, 1972), pp. 99-108.

ERMAN, Sahir, BAYRAKTAR, Köksal. La notion de "guerre" et de "combattant" dans le droit turc. *Ann.Fac.Droit Istanbul* 20(no.36, 1970), pp. 207-235.

FISEK, Sadan. Un aperçu de la situation juridique et sociale de la femme en Turquie. *RJPIC* 28(1974), pp. 1306-1314.

HEYD, Uriel *Kānūn* and *Sharī'a* in old Ottoman criminal justice. *Proc.Israel Acad.* 3(1969), pp. 1-18.

İMRE, Zahit. La responsabilité civile provenant des choses dangereuses en droit privé turc. *Ann.Fac.Droit Istanbul* 18(1968), pp. 1-64.

İMRE, Z. Le rôle du juge en présence des problèmes économiques en droit civil turc. *Ann.Fac.Droit Istanbul* 22(no.38, 1972), pp. 73-97.

KELEŞ, Ruşen. Some legal aspects of air pollution control in Turkey. *Ankara Univ. Siyasal Bilgiler Fak. Dergisi* 27iii(1972), pp. 443-455.

MAGNARELLA, P.J. The reception of Swiss family law in Turkey. *Anthrop. Q.* 46(1973) pp. 100-116.

OĞUZMAN, K. The collective bargaining agreement, strike lock-out and arbitration system in Turkey. *Ann.Fac.Droit Istanbul* 22(no.38, 1972), pp. 147-169.

OĞUZMAN, K. Le fondement juridique de la responsabilité de l'employeur en raison des accidents du travail. *Ann.Fac.Droit Istanbul* 21(no.37, 1971), pp. 129-150.

OKAY, S. La livraison des marchandises par mer en droit turc. *Ann.Fac.Droit Istanbul* 21(no.37, 1971), pp. 3-28.

ONDER, A. Der Einfluss des deutschen Rechts auf das türkische Strafprozessrecht. *Ann. Fac.Droit Istanbul* 22(no.38, 1972), pp. 366-378.

POSTACIOĞLU, İlhan E. Le rôle du juge en présence des problèmes économiques. *Ann.Fac. Droit Istanbul* 20(no.36, 1970), pp. 197-205.

SEVIG, Vedat R. Les effets possibles, en droit international privé turc, du projet de Convention sur la reconnaissance et l'execution des jugements étrangers en matière civile et commerciale. *Ann.Fac.Droit Istanbul* 18(1968), pp. 188-223.

TANDOĞAN, Halûk. La responsabilité civile du banquier en droit turc. *Banka ve ticaret hukuku dergisi* 7(1973), pp. 235-257.

TEKİNAY, S.S. La réparation du tort moral en matière de responsabilité causale. *Ann. Fac.Droit Istanbul* 22(no.38, 1972), pp. 141-145.

III LAW

TEKNALP, U. Der Genossenschaftsbegriff des Türkischen Genossenschaftsgesetzes und die Grossgenossenschaften, dargelegt unter besonderer Berücksichtigung des Nichmitgliedergeschäfts. *Ann.Fac.Droit Istanbul* 22(no.38, 1972), pp. 379-391.

TUNÇOMAĞ, K. Les modifications actuelles en droit du travail turc. *Ann.Fac.Droit Istanbul* 21(no.37, 1971), pp. 59-71.

ULUÇ, Mehmet R. The commercial arbitration of the International Chamber of Commerce and enforcement of its awards in Turkey and U.S. *Ann.Fac.Droit Istanbul* 18(1968), pp. 106-136.

YARSUVAT, D. Urbanization and administration of justice in Turkey. *Ann.Fac.Droit Istanbul* 22(no.38, 1972), pp. 393-414.

Military justice in Turkey. *Rev. Int. Commission. Jur.* 9(1972), pp. 16-17.

See also XXIX. f. Inalcik.

IV PHILOSOPHY. SCIENCE

a PHILOSOPHY

ANAWATI, G.C. Bibliographie de la philosophie médiévale en terre d'Islam pour les années 1959-1969. *Bull.philos.méd.* 10-12 (1968-70), pp. 316-369.

ANAWATI, G.C. Dix ans de recherches dans le domaine de la philosophie Musulmane: bilan des travaux des années 1960-1970. *Abr-nahrain* 12(1971-2), pp. 44-46

ANSARI, M. Abdul Haq. Liberation and Islam. *Ind. philos. annual* 5(1969), pp. 56-62.

ANSARI, M. Abdul Haq. Liberation and Islam. *Islam and the modern age* 1 i (1970), pp. 82-89.

BAKKALCIOĞLU, Ayfer. Of surrealism in Turkey. *Boğazici Univ. J.* 2(1974), pp. 1-12.

BELLMANN, D. Das arabische Kulturerbe im Blick idealistischer arabischer Kulturtheoretiker. *Asien in Vergangenheit und Gegenwart,* 1974, pp. 279-292.

BEN MILAD, Mahjoub. Ambiguïté et *mathānī* coraniques. *L'ambivalence dans la culture arabe,* 1967, pp. 366-381.

BERQUE, J. The algebraic and the experienced. *Diogenes* 86(1974), pp. 1-16.

BLACHÈRE, R. Origine de la théorie des *ad'dād. L'ambivalence dans la culture arabe,* 1967, pp. 397-403.

BOUHDIBA, A. Place et fonction de l'imaginaire dans la civilisation musulmane d'Occident. *Actas II Col. hisp.-tunec. estud. hist.,* 1973, pp. 209-214.

BRUNSCHVIG, R. Los teólogos-juristas del Islam en pro o en contra de la lógica griega: Ibn Ḥazm, al-Gazālī, Ibn Taymiyya. *And.* 35(1970), pp. 143-177.

CARRÉ, O. Bulletin d'islamologie. Quelques ouvrages récents sur la pensée et la philosophie arabo-musulmanes. *Rev. des sci. philos. et théol.* 57(1973), pp. 657-674.

CHARTIER, M. La rencontre Orient-Occident dans la pensée de trois philosophes égytiens contemporains: Ḥasan Ḥanafī, Fu'ād Zakariyya, Zakī Nağīb Maḥmūd. *OM* 53(1973), pp. 605-642.

CORBIN, H. Che cosa significa "tradizione"? Attualità della filosofia tradizionale in Iran. *Conoscenza religiosa* 1969, pp. 225-241.

CORBIN, H. For the concept of Irano-Islamic philosophy. *Philosophical forum* 4i(1972), pp. 114-123.

CORBIN, H. L'idée du Paraclet en philosophie iranienne. *La Persia nel medievo,* 1971, pp. 37-68

CORBIN, H. Para el concepto de una filosofía irano islámica. *And.*34(1969), pp. 395-407

CORBIN, H. Per il concetto di filosofia irano-islamica. *Conoscenza religiosa* 1973, pp. 424-431.

CORBIN, H. Pour le concept de philosophie irano-islamique. *Commémoration Cyrus. Hommage universel,* I, 1974, pp. 251-260.

DOI, A. Rahman I. Islamic thought and culture--their impact on Africa (with special reference to Nigeria). *Nigerian J. Islam* 1i(1970), pp. 25-33.

DOI, A.R. The Islamic view of freedom. *Islam and the modern age* 6ii(1975), pp. 41-60.

FERRARI, J. Notes sur quelques références à la pensée arabo-musulmane dans l'oeuvre de Kant. *Études philos. et litt.* 2(1968), pp. 37-41.

IV PHILOSOPHY. SCIENCE

GARDET, L. Les différents types de "dialectique". *L'ambivalence dans la culture arabe*, 1967, pp. 359-365.

GARDET, L. Signification du "renouveau mu'tazilite" dans la pensée musulmane contemporaine. *Islamic philosophy and the classical tradition:* essays presented to R. Walzer, 1972, pp. 63-75.

GARDET, L. La "théorie des oppositions" et la pensée musulmane. *Rev. thomiste* 75(1975), pp. 241-254.

GÄTJE, H. Zur Psychologie der Willenshandlungen in der islamischen Philosophie. *Saeculum* 26(1975), pp. 347-363.

GIWA, S.B. The role of reason in Islam I. *Internat. Islamic Conf.*, 1968, pp. 68-74.

GOLDMANN, L. Conditions de l'interprétation dialectique. *L'ambivalence dans la culture arabe*, 1967, pp. 356-358.

GOMEZ NOGALES, S. Influence du stoïcisme dans la philosophie musulmane. *Ve Congrès International d'Arabisants et d'Islamisants. Actes.*, [1970?], pp. 239-253.

GYEKYE, Kwame. The term *Istithnā'* in Arabic logic. *JAOS* 92(1972), pp. 88-92

GYEKYE, Kwame. The terms "Prima Intentio" and "Secunda Intentio" in Arabic logic. *Speculum* 46(1971), pp. 32-38

HAGER, J.V. Phases in the development of an Islamic world view. (From: *Die Philosophie des Islam.* by Max Horten.) *Islamic Stud.* 11(1972), pp. 231-249.

HALEPOTA, A.J. Affinity of Iqbal with Shah Waliyullah. *Iqbal rev.* 15i(1974), pp. 65-72.

HALEPOTA, A.J. Islamic conception of knowledge. *Islamic studies* 14(1975), pp. 1-8.

HALEPOTA, A.J. Shah Waliyullah and Iqbal, the philosophers of modern age. *Islamic studies* 13(1974), pp. 225-234.

HAWI, Sami S. Phenomenological radicalism in Muslim philosophy. *Pak.philos.J.* 12 (1974), pp. 58-86.

HIMMICH, Ben Salem. Idéologie et positivité (cas de l'Islam). *Études philos. et litt.* 6(1973), pp. 37-53.

HORTEN, M. Moral philosophers in Islam. [Trans. from German by V.J. Hager.] *Islamic stud.* 13i(1974), pp. 1-23.

HORTEN, M. The system of Islamic philosophy in general. [Trans. from German by V.J. Hager.] *Islamic stud.* 12(1973), pp. 1-36

JABRE, F. L'Être et l'Esprit dans la pensée arabe. *SI* 32(1970), pp. 169-180.

JADAANE, Fehmi. Les conditions socio-culturelles de la philosophie islamique. *SI* 38(1973), pp. 5-60.

JAMALPUR, B. The concept of Islamic philosophy in Iran. *Proc. XV world cong. philos.* 1973, vol.5(1975), pp. 715-718.

KAMALI, A.H. The heritage of Islamic thought. *Iqbal: poet-philosopher of Pakistan,* ed. Hafeez Malik, 1971, pp. 211-242.

KASSEM, H. The idea of justice in Islamic philosophy. *Diogenes* 79(1972), pp. 81-108.

KASSEM, Mahmoud. La teoría de la emanación en los filósofos musulmanes. *Pensamiento* 28(1972), pp. 131-144.

KHUNDMIRI, S.Alam. Man's nature and destiny - philosophic view in Islam. *Religion and society* 20iii(1973), pp. 35-42.

KIFTARO, Sheikh Ahmad. Role of reason in Islam III. *Internat. Islamic Conf.*, 1968, pp. 82-87.

LAHBABI, Mohamed-Aziz Pour un personnalisme africain. *Études philos. et litt.* 2(1968), pp. 33-36.

McDONOUGH, S. The social import of Parwez's religious thought. *Contributions to Asian studies* 2(1971), pp. 79-92.

MAHDI, Muhsin. Islamic philosophy in contemporary Islamic thought. *Al-Abhath* 20iv(1967), pp. 1-17.

MASUMI, M. Saghir Hasan. The role of reason in Islam II. *Internat. Islamic Conf.*, 1968, pp. 75-81.

MOHAGHAGH, Mehdi. The study of Islamic philosophy in contemporary Iran. *Contemporary philosophy,* ed. R. Klibansky, 1971, pp. 584-588.

MOREWEDGE, Parviz. A major contribution to the history of Islamic philosophy: a review article. *MW* 62(1972), pp.148-157.

MUÑOZ JIMÉNEZ, R. Modeles estructurales en la lógica arabe moderna: Muhammad 'Abduh. *Pensamiento* 28(1972), pp. 145-163.

NADER, A. Le logos dans la pensée musulmane. *Études philos. et litt.* 1 (1967), pp. 40-46.

NASR, Seyyed Hossein. Cosmografia e continuità culturale nell'Iran. *Conoscenza religiosa* 1974, pp. 252-267.

NASR, Seyyed Hossein. Elements of continuity in the life of mysticism and philosophy in Iran. *Acta Iranica* 1(1974), pp. 261-267.

NASR, Seyyed Hossein. The influence of traditional Islamic thought upon contemporary Muslim intellectual life. *Contemporary philosophy,* ed. R. Klibansky, 1971, pp. 578-583.

NASR, Sayyed Hossein. The life of mysticism and philosophy in Iran; Pre-Islamic and Islamic. *J.Reg.Cult.Inst.* 5i(1972), pp. 13-18

NASR, S.H. The meaning and role of philosophy in Islam. *J. Reg. Cult. Inst.* 6i-ii (1973), pp. 5-28; *ST* 37(1973), pp. 57-80.

NASR, Seyyed Hossein. Persia and the destiny of Islamic philosophy. *J. Reg. Cult. Inst.* 4(1971), pp. 67-80.

IV PHILOSOPHY. SCIENCE

NASR, Seyyed Hossein. Persia and the destiny of Islamic philosophy. *Stud comp. relig.* 6i (1972), pp. 31-42.

NASR, Seyyed Hossein. Philosophy East and West. Necessary conditions for meaningful comparative study. *J.Reg.Cult.Inst.* 7 (1974), pp. 157-169.

NASR, Seyyed Hossein. The significance of comparative philosophy for the study of Islamic philosophy. *Islam and the modern age* 4 i (1973), pp. 11-19.

NASR, Seyyed Hossein. The significance of comparative philosophy for the study of Islamic philosophy. *Studies comp. rel.* 7 (1973), pp. 212-218.

NASR, Seyyed Hossein. The tradition of Islāmic philosophy in Persia and its significance for the modern world. *Iqbal rev.* 12iii(1971), pp. 28-49

NASSAR, N. Remarques sur la renaissance de la philosophie dans la culture arabe moderne. *Renaissance du monde arabe. Colloque interarabe de Louvain,* 1972, pp. 331-341.

PEREZ FERNANDEZ, I. Verbización y nocionización de la metafísica en la tradición siro-árabe. *Pensamiento* 31(1975), pp. 245-271.

RAHMAN, Fazlur. Islamic thought in the Indo-Pakistan subcontinent and the Middle East. *JNES* 32(1973), pp. 194-200.

SAMIR, F. el. La pensée arabe face à la pensée occidentale. *Renaissance du monde arabe. Colloque interarabe de Louvain,* 1972, 295-308.

SANTO-TOMAS, J.J. de. Bulletins. Histoire de la pensée musulmane. *Rev.thomiste* 75 (1975), pp. 655-672.

SCHWARZ, M. Can we rely on later authorities for the views of earlier thinkers? A methodological note. *Israel Oriental studies* 1(1971), pp. 241-248.

SIDDIQUI, B.H. Concept of value in Islamic thought. *Pakistan philos. J.* 11i(1972), pp. 72-79.

SIMON, H. Elements of utopian thought in mediaeval Islamic philosophy. *Ve Congrès International d'Arabisants et d'Islamisants. Actes.,* [1970?], pp. 435-442.

VAHIDUDDIN, S. The basis of Islamic thought and the problem of its reconstruction. *India and contemporary Islam,* ed. S.T. Lokhandwalla, 1971, pp. 125-131.

VAN ESS, J. Skepticism in Islamic religious thought. *Al-Abhath* 21i(1968), pp. 1-18.

Esquisse d'une bibliographie des traductions d'oeuvres philosophiques de langue arabe (parfois persane) en langues européennes. *Et. philos. et litt.* [*Maroc*] 3(1968), pp. 25-33.

See also II. c. 1. Nasr.

See also II. c. 2. Nasr

See also II. d. 2. Bürgel.

See also II. d. 4. Gardet.

See also IV. b. *Ibn Rushd.* Ghannouchi.

See also IX. e. Pines

b INDIVIDUAL SCIENTISTS AND PHILOSOPHERS *in alphabetical order*

LEVEY, M., SOURYAL, Safwat S. Some fifteenth century Muslim scientists. *Studies in Islam* 7 (1970), pp. 1-8.

Bīrūnī

ALAVI, S.M. Ziauddin. Al-Bīrūnī's contribution to physical geography. *Ind.J.hist. sci.* 10(1975), pp. 230-234.

ANAS, Mohammad. Al-Beruni's mathematics and astronomy. *Afghanistan* 26i(1973), pp. 76-85.

ANSARI, S.M. Razaullah. On the physical researches of al-Bīrūnī. *Ind.J.hist.sci.* 10(1975), pp. 198-217.

ARZUMETOV, Yu.S. Al-Biruni in the history of medicine in Central Asia. *Sovetsk.Zdravookh.* 32(1973), (3), pp. 73-75. [CWHM 82,147]

ASIMOV, M.S. Al-Bīrūnī's astronomical treatise in the Dari language. *Ind.J.hist. sci.* 10(1975), pp. 254-256.

BAG, A.K. Al-Bīrūnī on Indian arithmetic. *Ind.J.hist.sci.* 10(1975), pp. 174-184.

BAUSANI, A. Al-Bīrūnī, un gran pensatore del medioevo islamico, nel millenario della nascita. *RSO* 48(1973-4), pp. 75-97.

BRADLEY, A.D. Al-Biruni's table of chords. *Maths.teacher* 63(1970), pp. 615-617.

CHATTERJEE, Bina. Al-Bīrūnī and Brahmagupta. *Ind.J.hist.sci.* 10(1975), pp. 161-165.

GHAYASUDDIN. Varāhamihira, the best Sanskrit source of al-Bīrūnī on Indian *jyotiṣa*. *Ind.J.hist.sci.* 10(1975), pp. 139-152.

HABIBI, Abdul Hayy. The 1000th birth anniversary of Allameh Abu Raihan Al-Beruni. *Afghanistan* 26i(1973), pp. 63-67.

HABIBI, Abdul Hayee. Where was al-Birun situated? *Ind.J.hist.sci.* 10(1975), pp. 257-258.

HUMBACH, H. Al-Biruni und die Sieben Strome des Awesta. *Bull.Iranian Culture Found.* 1ii(1973), pp. 47-52.

JALALI, G. An introduction to Beruni. *Afghanistan* 27i(1974), pp. 62-66.

JARZEBOWSKI, T. Astronomical works of Al-Beruni. *Afghanistan* 26ii(1973), pp. 6-14.

IV PHILOSOPHY. SCIENCE

KAZMI, Hasan Askari. Al-Birūni's longitudes and their conversion into modern values. *IC* 49(1975), pp. 165-176.

KENNEDY, E.S. Al-Bīrūnī's *Maqālīd 'ilm Al-Hay'a*. *JNES* 30(1971), pp. 308-314.

KENNEDY, E.S. Al-Bīrūnī's Masudic canon. *al-Abhath* 24(1971), pp. 59-81.

KHAN, M.S. A select bibliography of Soviet publications on al-Bîrûnî. *Janus* 62(1975), pp. 279-288.

LEWICKI, T. Abu 'r-Rajhan al-Biruni jako historyk kultury materialnej. *Przegl.or.* 90(1974), pp. 95-102.

MADKOUR, Ibrāhim. Al-Bīrūnī et Ibn Sīnā, representants d'une époque et d'une culture. *MIDEO* 12(1974), pp. 195-201.

MAINKAR, V.B. Metrology in al-Bīrūnī's *India*. *Ind.J.hist.sci.* 10(1975), pp. 224-229.

MANDEL'SHTAM, A.M. K dannym al-Biruni o Zakaspii. *Strany i narody Vostoka pod obshchey red. D.A. Ol'derogge*, X, 1971, pp. 163-169.

MAQBUL AHMAD, S. Al-Beruni and the decline of science and technology in medieval Islam, and his contributions to geography, with special reference to India. *Afghanistan* 26ii(1973), pp. 91-96.

MAQBUL AHMAD, S., BEHARI, Ram, and SUBBARAYAPPA, B.V. Al-Bīrunī - an introduction to his life and writings on the Indian sciences. *Ind.J.hist.sci.* 10 (1975), pp. 98-110.

MAQBUL AHMAD, S. Al-Bīrūnī as a synthesizer and transmitter of scientific knowledge. *Ind.J.hist.sci.* 10(1975), pp. 244-248.

MAQBUL AHMAD, S. Road-system of India as described by al-Biruni. *Medieval India* 2 (1972), pp. 1-2.

MEHDI GHARAVI, S. Two noteworthy manuscripts of al-Biruni's al-Tafhim. *IC* 49(1975), pp. 215-219.

MISHRA, S.J. New light on Albīrūni's stay and travel in India. *Central Asiatic J.* 15(1972), pp. 302-312

NADVI, Syed H.H. Al-Bīrūnī and his Kitāb al-jamāhir fī ma'rifat al-jawāhir: ethical reflections and moral philosophy. *Islamic studies* 13(1974), pp. 253-280.

NAYAR, Balkrishna Karunakar. Al-Bīrūnī and the arithmetical sequence of the Sanskrit *gaṇas*. *Ind.J.hist.sci.* 10(1975), pp. 259-270.

NAYAR, Balkrishna. Al-Bīrūnī and the authorities on Sanskrit prosody. *Ind.J.hist.sci.* 10(1975), pp. 153-158.

NAYAR, Balkrishna Karunakar. Al-Bīrūnī and science communication in Sanskrit. *Ind.J.hist.sci.* 10(1975), pp. 249-252.

NEWTON, R.R. The earth's acceleration as deduced from al-Biruni's solar data. *Memoirs R.Astron.Soc.* 76(1972), pp. 99-128.

NYLANDER, C. Al-Bērūnī and Persepolis. *Commēmoration Cyrus. Hommage universel*, I, 1974, pp. 137-150.

PANIKKAR, N.K. and SRINIVASAN, T.M. Al-Bīrūnī and the theory of tides. *Ind.J.hist.sci.* 10(1975), pp. 235-241.

RAI, R.N. Al-Bīrūnī and Indian eras. *Ind.J.hist.sci.* 10(1975), pp. 166-173.

RAMAKRISHNA BHAṬ, M. Al-Bīrūnī's treatment of the Laghujātaka and comets: a critique. *Ind.J.hist.sci.* 10(1975), pp. 271-276.

ROEMER, H.R. Al-Biruni in Deutschland. *The Middle East; studies in honour of J. Germanus*, 1974, pp. 23-29.

ROY, Sourin. Al-Bīrūnī and Hindu speculations on gravitation. *Ind.J.hist.sci.* 10 (1975), pp. 218-223.

SAMSÓ, J. En torno al Arquímedes árabe: el testimonio de al Bīrūnī. *And.* 36(1971), pp. 383-390.

SEN, S.N. Al-Bīrūnī on the determination of latitudes and longitudes in India. *Ind.J.hist.sci.* 10(1975), pp. 185-197.

SHAH, Mir Hussain. Beruni and his follower, Gardezi, on the festivals of the Hindus. *Afghanistan* 26iii(1973), pp. 90-94.

SHAMSI, F.A. Abu al-Rayhan al-Bayruni. *Islamic stud.* 13(1974), pp. 179-220.

SHASTRI, Ajay Mitra. Sanskrit literature known to al-Bīrūnī. *Ind.J.hist.sci.* 10 (1975), pp. 111-138.

SUBBARAYAPPA, B.V. Symposium on al-Bīrūnī and the Indian sciences. *Ind. J. hist. sci.* 7(1972), pp. 75-77.

WALZER, R. Al-Biruni and idolatry. *Acta Iranica*, sér. 1, III, 1974, pp. 317-323.

YASIN, Mohammad. Al-Biruni in India. *IC* 49(1975), pp. 207-213.

Al-Biruni: an introduction to his life and writings on the Indian sciences. Reproduced from the publication of the Indian National Science Academy. *Afghanistan* 24iv(1972), pp. 54-67

See also II. a. 5. Ma'sumi.

See also VI. d. Minorsky.

Fakhr al-din Razi

ARNALDEZ, R. Trouvailles philosophiques dans le commentaire coranique de Fakhr al-Dīn al-Rāzī. *Et. philos. et litt.* [*Maroc*] 3(1968), pp. 11-24.

FALATURI, A. Djavad. Fakhr al-Din al-Râzî's critical logic. *Yād-nāme-ye Irāni-ye Minorsky*, 1969, pp. 51-79.

IV PHILOSOPHY. SCIENCE

MONNOT, G. Les religions iraniennes chez Fakhr al-Din al-Razi. *Mémorial J. de Menasce*, 1974, pp. 81-85.

See also II. a. 5. Arnaldez.

Fārābī

ALONSO, M. Concordia entre el divino Platon y el sabio Aristoteles (by al-Farabi). Traducción, prólogo y notas probativas. *Pensamiento* 25(1969), pp. 21-70.

ARNALDEZ, R. Métaphysique et politique dans la pensée d'Al Farabi. *Ann.Fac. Arts Ain Shams* 1(1951), pp. 143-157.

BERTMAN, M.A. Al-Fārābī and Ibn Rushd on philosophy. *Iqbal rev.* 12i(1971), pp. 1-5.

BREWSTER, D.P. Al-Farábi's "Book of religion". *Abr-Nahrain* 14(1973-4), pp. 17-31.

GÄTJE, H. Die Gliederung der sprachlichen Zeichen nach al-Fārābī. *Der Islam* 47 (1971), pp. 1-24.

GRIGNASCHI, M. Les traductions latines des ouvrages de la logique arabe et l'abrégé d'Alfarabi. *Archives d'hist. doctr. et litt. du MA* 39(1972), pp. 41-107.

KOLMAN, E. L'anticipation de certaines idées de la logique mathématique chez al-Fārābī. *XIIe Cong.int.hist.sci.* 1968, *Actes*, IIIA (1971), pp. 97-101.

MAHDI, Muhsin. Alfarabi on philosophy and religion. *Philosophical forum* 4i(1972), pp. 5-25.

MAHDI, Muhsin. The Arabic text of Alfarabi's Against John the Grammarian. *Medieval and Middle Eastern studies ... A.S. Atiya* 1972, pp. 268-284.

PITSKHELAURI, G.Z. Medico-philosophical and natural scientific concepts of Al-Farabi. [Russian text.] *Sovetsk. Zdravookh.* 30viii (1971), pp. 75-77. [CWHM 76(1972), 33]

PLESSNER, M. Al-Fārābī's introduction to the study of medicine. *Islamic philosophy and the classical tradition*, 1972, pp. 307-314.

RAMÓN GUERRERO, R. La concepción del hombre en al-Fārābī. *MEAH* 23(1974), pp. 63-83.

SAJJĀDI, Ja'far. Abu Nasr Fārābī, the second teacher, a universal genius. *J. Regional Cult.Inst.* 7(1974), pp. 73-85.

VAJDA, G. Langage, philosophie, politique et religion, d'après un traité d'al-Fārābī. *JA* 258(1970), pp. 247-260.

ZIMMERMANN, F.W. Some observations on al-Farabi and logical tradition. *Islamic philosophy and the classical tradition*, 1972, pp. 517-546.

See also V. u. 1. Neubauer.

See also IX. g. Sankari.

See also XXXVI. a. Haddad.

Ghazzālī

ABUL QUASEM, Muhammad. Al-Gāzālī's conception of happiness. *Arabica* 22(1975), pp. 153-161.

ABUL QUASEM, Muhammad. Al-Ghazali's rejection of philosophic ethics. *Islamic stud.* 13(1974), pp.

ABŪ SHANAB, R.E. The philosophical significance of al-Ghazzālī. *Iqbal rev.* 13i(1972), pp. 51-70.

CANTARINO, V. Theory of light in al-Ghazzali's *Mishkāt al-Anwār*. *Amer. Or. Soc., Middle West Branch. Semi-centennial volume*, ed. by D. Sinor, 1969, pp. 27-40.

CHARNAY, J.P. Psychologie religieuse et réformisme social chez Ghazâlî. *L'ambivalence dans la culture arabe*, 1967, pp. 153-163.

GÄTJE, H. Logisch-semasiologische Theorien bei al-Ġazzālī. *Arabica* 21(1974), pp. 151-182.

GOODMAN, L.E. Ghazâlî's argument from creation. *IJMES* 2(1971), pp. 67-85, 168-188.

GWARZO, Hassan Ibrahim. The life and teachings of al-Ghazali. *Kano studies* 1(1965), pp. 13-17.

HANA, G.G. Zur Logik al-Gazālīs. *XVIII. Deutscher Orientalistentag 1972: Vorträge*, pp. 178-185.

KASSIM, Husain. Existentialist tendencies in Ghazālī and Kierkegaard. *Islamic stud.* 10(1971), pp. 103-128.

LAOUST, H. Ġazālī politique et juriste. *MUSJ* 46(1970-1), pp. 427-449

LAOUST, H. La survie de Ġazālī d'après Subkī. *BEO* 25(1972), pp. 153-172.

LAZARUS-YAFEH, H. Some notes on the term "taqlid" in the writings of al-Ghazzali. *Israel Oriental studies* 1(1971), pp. 249-256.

KLEINKNECHT, A. Al-Qisṭās al-mustaqīm; eine Ableitung der Logik aus dem Koran. *Islamic philosophy and the classical tradition: essays presented to R. Walzer*, 1972, pp. 159-187.

MADELUNG, W. Ar-Rāgib al-Isfāhanī und die Ethik al-Gazālīs. *Islàmwissenschaftliche Abhandlungen F. Meier*, 1974, pp. 152-163.

MOULDER, D.C. The first crisis in the life of Alghazālī. *Islamic Stud.* 11(1972), pp. 113-123.

NAUMKIN, V.V. Ideya "vysshego sostoyaniya" u al-Gazali. *NAA* 1973(5), pp. 112-121.

SHAMIM, Arifa. Ethics of al-Ghazali: introduction. *Iqbal rev.* 15iii(1974), pp. 30-43.

SHARMA, Arvind. The spiritual biography of Al-Ghazālī. *Stud. in Islam* 9(1972), pp. 65-85.

SHEIKH, M. Saeed. Al-Ghazali's influence on the West. *Pak.philos.J.* 11(1973), pp. 53-67.

VAJDA, G. Le ma'āriǧ al-quds fī madāriǧ ma'rifat al-nafs attribué à Gazālī et les écrits d'Ibn Sīnā. *In memoriam S.M. Stern* (Israel Or. studies, II, 1972), pp. 470-473.

WATSON, J.H. The religious beliefs of al-Ghazali. *Expository times* 86(1974-5), pp. 200-203.

Hunain b. Ishāq

ANAWATI, G.C. Les médicaments de l'oeil chez Ḥunayn Ibn Isḥāq. *Arabica* 21(1974), pp. 232-244.

CELENTANO, G. Le petit traité de Ḥunayn Ibn Isḥāq sur la prophylaxie et la thérapie des dents. *Arabica* 21(1974), pp. 245-251.

CELENTANO, G. Il trattatello di Ḥunain Ibn Ishāq sulla profilassi e terapia dei denti. [With translation and text.] *AION* 35(NS 25, 1975), pp. 45-80.

HADDAD, Rachid. Ḥunayn Ibn Isḥāq: apologiste chrétien. *Arabica* 21(1974), pp. 292-302.

KÖBERT, R. Zur Ḥunain-Biographie des Ibn abī Uṣaibi'a. *Orientalia* 43(1974), pp. 414-416.

NWYIA, P. Actualité du concept de religion chez Ḥunayn Ibn Isḥāq. *Arabica* 21(1974), pp. 313-317.

STROHMAIER, G. Ḥunayn Ibn Isḥāq et le serment hippocratique. *Arabica* 21(1974), pp. 318-323.

See also IV. c. 2. Fahd.Grignaschi.

Ibn al-Ḥaitham

PITSKHELAURI, G.Z. Ibn al-Haytam (965-1039). *Sovetsk.Zdravookh.* 32(1973), (5), pp. 84-87. [CWHM 82,714]

RASHED, Roshdi. Optique géometrique et doctrine optique chez Ibn Al Haytham. *Archive for history of exact sciences* 6 (1969-70), pp. 271-298.

SABRA, A.I. The astronomical origin of Ibn al-Haytham's concept of experiment. *XIIe Cong.int.hist.sci.* 1968, *Actes,* IIIA (1971), pp. 133-136.

STIEGLER, K. Ibn al Haythams Entdeckung der sphärischen Aberration. *Physis* 13 (1971), pp. 5-12.

VERMA, R.L. Al-Hazen. Father of modern optics. *al-'Arab* 8viii(1969), pp. 12-13

Many articles on Ibn al-Haitham are contained in Ibn al-Haitham. Proceedings of the celebrations of the 1000th anniversary held under the auspices of the Hamdard National Foundation, Pakistan. Ed. by Hakim Mohammed Said.

Ibn Rushd

BERQUE, J. Averroès et les contraires. *L'ambivalence dans la culture arabe,* 1967, pp. 133-141.

BERTMAN, M.A. Philosophical elitism: the example of Averroes. *Philos.J.*[Glasgow] 8(1971), pp. 115-121.

CANTARINO, V. Averroes on poetry. *Islam and its cultural divergence. Studies in honor of Gustave E. von Grunebaum,* 1971, pp. 6-10

CRUZ HERNANDEZ, M. El averroismo en el Occidente medieval. *Oriente e Occidente nel medioevo,* 1971, pp. 17-64.

CUNNINGHAM, F.A. Averroes *vs.* Avicenna on being. *New scholasticism* 48(1974), pp. 185-218.

DAMAS SEBASTIAN, J.M. de. Averroes, el Reino de Granada y Alhamar de Arjona. *Medicamenta* (Madrid) 27(1969), pp. 45-51. [CWHM 69, 112]

DOIG, J.C. Toward understanding Aquinas' *Com. in De anima.* A comparative study of Aquinas and Averroes on the definition of soul (*De anima* B, 1-2). *Riv. di filos. neo-scol.* 66(1974), pp. 436-474.

FLYNN, J.G. St. Thomas and Averroes on the nature and attributes of God. *Abr-Nahrain* 15(1974-1975), pp. 39-49.

GHANNOUCHI, Abdelmajid el. Les dimensions de notre liberté chez Ibn Rušd et ses prédecesseurs. *Actas II Col. hisp.-tunec. estud. hist.,* 1973, pp. 131-141.

GÓMEZ NOGALES, S. Ultimas investigaciones sobre el Tahafut de Averroes. *Actas IV congresso de estudos árabes e islâmicos* 1968(1971), pp. 311-324.

GONZALO MAESO, D. Averroes (1126-1198) y Maimonides (1135-1204), dos glorias de Cordoba. (Paralelo). *MEAH* 16-17ii (1967-8), pp. 139-164.

GUENNOUN, Abdellah. Averroes, el jurista. *Pensamiento* 25(1969), pp. 195-205.

HANA, G.G. L'unité de l'intellect: nécessité immanente au système d'Averroès? *Ve Congrès International d'Arabisants et d'Islamisants. Actes.,* [1970?], pp. 267-273.

HÖDL, L. Über die averroistische Wende der lateinischen Philosophie des Mittelalters im 13. Jahrhundert. *Recherches de théol.* 39(1972), pp. 171-204.

IVRY, A.L. Towards a unified view of Averroes' philosophy. *Philosophical forum* 4i(1972), pp. 87-113.

KOELBING, H.M. Averroes' concepts of ocular function. *J. hist. med. applied sci.* 27 (1972), pp.

MAZZARELLA, P. La critica di San Tommaso all' "averroismo gnoseologico". *Riv. di filos. neo-scol.* 66(1974), pp. 246-283.

NÉDONCELLE, M. Remarques sur la réfutation des averroïstes par Saint Thomas. *Riv. di filos. neo-scol.* 66(1974), pp. 284-292.

VANNI ROVIGHI, S. Gli averroisti bolognesi. *Oriente e Occidente nel medioevo,* 1971, pp. 161-183.

Ibn Sīnā

ABDUL HAMEED, Hakim. Gerard's latin translation of Ibn Sīnā's *Al-Qānūn*. *Studs. in Islam* 8(1971), pp. 1-7.

ABU SHANAB, R.E. Avicenna and Ockham on the problem of universals. *Pak.philos.J.* 11 (1973), pp. 1-14.

ALVERNY, M.T.d' Avicenna latinus (XI). *Archives d'hist. doctr. et litt. du MA* 39 (1972), pp. 321-341.

ALVERNY, M.Th. d'. Avicennisme en Italie. *Oriente e Occidente nel medioevo,* 1971, pp. 117-144.

ALVERNY, M.T.d' Les traductions d'Avicenne. Quelques résultats d'une enquête. *Ve Congrès International d'Arabisants et d'Islamisants. Actes.,* [1970?], pp. 151-158.

ANAWATI, G.C. Avicenne et l'alchimie. *Oriente e Occidente nel medioevo,* 1971, pp. 285-346.

ARNALDEZ, R. Un précédent avicennien du cogito cartésien? *Annales islamol.*11(1972), pp. 341-349.

BERTOLA, E. La noetica di Avicenna. *Riv. di filos. neo-scol.* 64(1972), pp. 169-212.

BROWN, H.V.B. Avicenna and the Christian philosophers in Baghdad. *Islamic philosophy and the classical tradition:* essays presented to R. Walzer, 1972, pp. 35-48.

CHARNAY, J.P. Nature et principe des contraires dans la médecine d'Avicenne. *L'ambivalence dans la culture arabe,* 1967, pp. 98-110.

FLYNN, J.G. St. Thomas and Avicenna on the nature of God. *Abr-Nahrain* 14(1973-4), pp. 53-65.

GARDET, L. The religious and philosophical attitude of Ibn-i-Sīnā (and its Hellenic sources). *J.Pak.Hist.Soc.* 21(1973), pp. 149-163.

GILSON, E. Avicenne en Occident au Moyen Age. *Oriente e Occidente nel medioevo,* 1971, pp. 65-95.

HOURANI, G.F. Ibn Sīnā on necessary and possible existence. *Philosophical forum* 4i(1972), pp. 74-86.

LUCCHETTA, F. La cosidetta "teoria della doppia verita" nella *Risāla aḍḥawiyya* di Avicenna e la sua trasmissione all'Occidente. *Oriente e Occidente nel medioevo,* 1971, pp. 97-116.

MOREWEDGE, P. Ibn Sīnā's concept of the self. *Philosophical forum* 4i(1972), pp. 49-73.

MOREWEDGE, Parviz. The logic of emanationism and Ṣūfism in the philosophy of Ibn Sīnā (Avicenna). *JAOS* 91(1971), pp. 467-476; 92(1972), pp. 1-18

MOREWEDGE, Parviz. Philosophical analysis and Ibn Sīnā's "Essence-Existence" distinction. *JAOS* 92(1972), pp. 425-435.

RIET, S. van. De Latijnse vertaling van Avicenna's *Kitab al-Nafs*. Inleidende studie. *Orientalia Gandensia* 1(1964), pp. 203-216.

RIET, S. van. Trois traductions latines d'un texte d'Avicenne: "al-Adwiya al-qalbiyya". *Actas IV congresso de estudos árabes e islâmicos* 1968(1971), pp. 339-344.

SCHIPPERGES, H. Zur Typologie eines 'Avicenna Hispanus'. *Sudhoffs Archiv* 57(1973), pp. 99-101.

TAMANI, G. Il commento di Yeda'yah Bederši al *Canone* di Avicenna. *Ann.Fac.Ling.Lett. stran.Ca' Foscari* 5(1974), pp. 1-17.

VAJDA, G. Un commentaire inconnu (?) sur le *Kitāb al-Išārāt wal-tanbīhāt* d'Ibn Sīnā. *JA* 258(1970), pp. 43-45.

VERBEKE, G. L'immortalité de l'âme dans le "de anima" d'Avicenne. Une synthèse de l'aristotélisme et du neoplatonisme. *Pensamiento* 25(1969), pp. 271-290.

YUSUF, K.M. Avicenna: his life and works. *Indo-Iranica* 25iii-iv(1972), pp. 158-170.

See also IV. b. *Bīrūnī*. Madkour.

See also IV. b. *Ghazzali*. Vajda.

See also IV. b. *Ibn Rushd*. Cunningham.

See also IV. c. 10. Charnay.

Ibn Ṭufail

HAWI, Sami S. Beyond naturalism: a brief study of Ibn Ṭufayl's *Ḥayy b. Yaqẓān*. *J. Pak.Hist.Soc.* 22(1974), pp. 249-267.

HAWI, Sami S. Ibn Ṭufayl: his motives for the use of narrative form and his method of concealment in *Ḥayy bin Yaqẓān*. *MW* 64 (1974), pp. 322-337.

HAWI, Sami S. Ibn Ṭufayl: on the existence of God and his attributes. *JAOS* 95 (1975), pp. 58-67.

IV PHILOSOPHY. SCIENCE

HAWI, Sami S. Ibn Tufayl's appraisal of his predecessors and the influence of these on his thoughts. *Islamic stud.* 13(1974), pp. 135-177.

HAWI, Sami S. Ibn Ṭufail's Hayy bin Yaqzān: its structure, literary aspects and method. *IC* 47(1973), pp. 191-211.

HAWI, Sami S. An Islamic naturalistic conception of abiogenesis -- the views of Ibn Ṭufayl. *IC* 49(1975), pp. 23-41.

HAWI, Sami S. *Philosophus Autodidactus:* lineage and perspective. *IC* 48(1974), pp. 201-220.

HAWI, Sami S. A twelfth-century philosophy of science. *Pak.philos.J.* 11(1973), pp. 15-36.

See also IV. a. Hawi.

Ibn Wahshīyya

FAHD, Toufic. Retour à Ibn Waḥshiyya. *Proc.27th Int.Cong.Or.1967* (1971), pp. 171-172.

SALINGER, G.C. Neoplatonic passages in the "Nabataean Agriculture", work of the tenth century ascribed to B. Wahshīya. *Proc.27th Int.Cong.Or.1967* (1971), pp. 233-234.

Ikhwan al-Safā

ABEL, A. De historische betekenis van de Loutere Broeders van Basra (Bassorah), een wijsgerig gezelschap in de Islam van de Xe eeuw. *Orientalia Gandensia* 1(1964), pp. 157-170.

BAUWENS, J. Zeventiende zendbrief van de "Rasā'īl Ikhwān aṣ Ṣafā'". Over de fysische lichamen. *Orientalia Gandensia* 1(1964), pp. 171-185.

BLUMENTHAL, D.R. A comparative table of the Bombay, Cairo and Beirut editions of the *Rasā'il Ikhwān al-Ṣafā'*. *Arabica* 21(1974), pp. 186-203.

MICHOT, J. L'épitre de la resurrection des Ikhwan as-Safa'. *Bull.philos.méd.* 16-17 (1974-5), pp. 114-148.

PLESSNER, M.M. Beiträge zur islamischen Literaturgeschichte IV: Samuel Miklos Stern, die Ikhwān aṣ-Ṣafā und die Encyclopedia of Islam. *In memoriam S.M. Stern* (Israel Or. studies, II, 1972), pp. 353-361.

DIWALD, S. Die Seele und ihre geistigen Kräfte: Darstellung und philosophiegeschichtlicher Hintergrund im K. Ikhwān aṣ-Ṣafā. *Islamic philosophy and the classical tradition:* essays presented to R. Walzer, 1972, pp. 49-61.

WIDENGREN, G. The gnostic technical language in the Rasā'il Ikhwān al-ṣafā'. *Actas IV congresso de estudos árabes e islâmicos* 1968(1971), pp. 181-203.

Iqbal

ABBOTT, F. View of democracy and the West. *Iqbal: poet-philosopher of Pakistan,* ed. Hafeez Malik, 1971, pp. 174-183.

ABDUL HAKIM, Khalifa. Iqbal's attempts at creative synthesis. *Iqbal rev.* 13iii(1972), pp. 17-23.

AḤMAD, Manzoor. Metaphysics of Persia and Iqbāl. *Iqbal rev.* 12iii(1971), pp. 101-117

AHSAN, Shakoor. Iqbal and nature. *Iqbal rev.* 13iii(1972), pp. 24-32.

ALLANA, G. Iqbal as a political philosopher. *Iqbal R.* 14iii(1973), pp. 61-68.

ANIKEYEV, N.P. The doctrine of personality. *Iqbal: poet-philosopher of Pakistan,* ed. Hafeez Malik, 1971, pp. 264-284.

AZAD, Jagan Nath. Iqbal, Schopenhauer and the Qur'an. *Islam and the modern age* 5iv (1974), pp. 58-64.

BURKI, Riffat. The concept of time in Iqbal's thought. *J.Reg.Cult.Inst.* 6(1973), pp. 103-128.

BURKI, Riffat Jahan Dawar. Iqbal and Bergson: *concept of time.* *Iqbal rev.* 12i(1971), pp. 6-11.

BURKI, Riffat. Iqbal and Tauhid. *Iqbal R.* 14iii(1973), pp. 9-15.

BURKI, Riffat. Iqbal's concept of Mard-e-Momin and Rumi's influence. *J. Reg. Cult. Inst.* 5(1972), pp. 61-83.

BURKI, Riffat Jehan Dawar. Iqbāl's concept of the *Mard-i Mu'min* and Rūmī's influence. *Iqbal rev.* 13i(1972), pp. 1-17.

BURKI, Riffat. Reason and intuition in Iqbal's philosophy. *J.Reg.Cult.Inst.* 7 (1974), pp. 171-210.

DAR, B.A. Inspiration from the West. *Iqbal: poet-philosopher of Pakistan,* ed. Hafeez Malik, 1971, pp. 187-210.

FAROOQI, Abbadullah. The impact of Khawaja Hafiz on Iqbal's thought. *Iqbal R.* 14i (1973), pp. 33-60.

FAROOQI, Abbadullah. The problem of good and evil as viewed by Iqbal. *Iqbal rev.* 13iii (1972), pp. 33-43.

FAROOQI, Hafiz Abbadullah. Iqbal's philosophy of life. *Iqbal R.* 14iii(1973), pp. 27-44.

FAROOQI, Hafiz Abbadullah. Iqbal's theory of knowledge. *Iqbal R.* 16i(1975), pp. 21-31.

FAROOQI, Abadullah. Islamic socialism and Iqbal. *Iqbal rev.* 15i(1974), pp. 1-7.

HASSAN, Riffat. The development of political philosophy. *Iqbal: poet-philosopher of Pakistan,* ed. Hafeez Malik, 1971, pp. 136-158.

HAWI, Sami S. Empiricism and beyond. *Iqbal rev.* 15i(1974), pp. 21-42.

IQBAL, Javid. Iqbal: my father. *Iqbal: poet-philosopher of Pakistan,* ed. Hafeez Malik, 1971, pp. 56-65.

ISRAILI, Shamoon. Iqbal: a progressive. *Indo Iranica* 26ii-iii(1973), pp. 127-142.

KHASHSHAB, Yahya al-. Iqbal. *Iqbal R.* 16i(1975), pp. 66-70.

KHATTAK, Yousuf. Iqbal's journey to Pakistan. *Iqbal rev.* 15i(1974), pp. 13-20.

KHUNDMIRI, S. Alam. Conception of time. *Iqbal: poet-philosopher of Pakistan,* ed. Hafeez Malik, 1971, pp. 243-263.

MAHMOOD, Abdul Kader. The freedom of will in the philosophy of Iqbal (1876-1938). *Maj.al-Azhar* 44vi(1972), pp. 5-11.

MALIK, Hafeez, MALIK, L.P. The life of the poet-philosopher. *Iqbal: poet-philosopher of Pakistan,* ed. Hafeez Malik, 1971, pp. 3-35.

MALIK, Hafeez. The man of thought and the man of action. *Iqbal: poet-philosopher of Pakistan,* ed. Hafeez Malik, 1971, pp. 69-107.

MAREK, J. Perceptions of international politics. *Iqbal: poet-philosopher of Pakistan,* ed. Hafeez Malik, 1971, pp. 159-173.

MAY, L.S. Iqbal's doctrine of Khudi. *Iqbal* 18iii(1971), pp. 55-64

MOIZUDDIN, M. Iqbal, Muslim unity and Islamic summit. *Iqbal R.* 16i(1975), pp. 1-5.

NICHOLSON, R.A. Iqbal's "Message of the East" (*Payam-i-Mashriq*). *Iqbal rev.* 13iii (1972), pp. 6-16.

NIAZI, Shaheer. Diotima, Tahira and Iqbal. *Iqbal rev.* 15iii(1974), pp. 22-29.

RAHBAR, Muhammad Daud. Glimpses of the man. *Iqbal: poet-philosopher of Pakistan,* ed. Hafeez Malik, 1971, pp. 36-55.

RASHEED, Ghulam Dastagir. Iqbal and the concept of perfect man. *Indo Iranica* 26ii-iii (1973), pp. 124-126.

REYAZUR RAHMAN. Iqbal's concept of power. *Iqbal rev.* 15iii(1974), pp. 44-56.

SCHIMMEL, A. The Western influence on Sir Muhammad Iqbal's thought. *Proc.9th Int.Cong.Hist.Rel.* 1958, pp. 705-708.

STEPANYANTS, M.T. Problems of ethics in Mohammad Iqbal's philosophy. *Iqbal R.* 14i (1973), pp. 1-8.

VAHID, S.A. The greatness of Iqbal. *Iqbal rev.* 15i(1974), pp. 8-12.

See also II. a. 8. Ishaque.

See also IV. a. Halepota.

See also XXXII. q. Burki.

See also XXXIX. a. Naimuddin.

Kindī

ALLARD, M. Comment al-Kindī a-t-il lu les philosophes grecs? *MUSJ* 46(1970-1), pp. 451-465

ALLARD, M. L'épître de Kindī sur les définitions. *BEO* 25(1972), pp. 47-83.

ALVERNY, M. Th. d'., HUDRY, F. Al-Kindi de radiis. *Archives d'hist. doctr. du Moyen-Age* 1974, pp. 139-260.

CORTABARRIA-BEITIA, A. La classification des sciences chez al-Kindi. *MIDEO* 11(1972), pp. 49-76.

IVRY, A.L. Al-Kindi as philosopher: the Aristotelian and Neoplatonic dimensions. *Islamic philosophy and the classical tradition:* essays presented to R. Walzer, 1972, pp. 117-139.

KLEIN-FRANKE, F. Die Ursachen der Krisen bei akuten Krankheiten. Eine wiederentdeckte Schrift al-Kindī's. *Israel Oriental stud.* 5(1975), pp. 161-188.

CORTABARRÍA, A. El metodo de al-Kindī visto a traves de sus *Risālas*. *Orientalia Hispanica* I, 1974, pp. 209-225.

CORTABARRIA BEITIA, A. Un traité philosophique d'al-Kindī. *MIDEO* 12(1974), pp. 5-12.

LINDBERG, D.C. Alkindi's critique of Euclid's theory of vision. *Isis* 62(1971), pp. 469-489

NUCHO, Fuad. The one and the many in Al-Kindī's metaphysics. *MW* 61 (1971), pp. 161-169.

RIAD, E. A propos d'une définition de la colère chez al-Kindī. *Orientalia suecana* 22(1973), pp. 62-65.

SHAMSI, F.A. Al-Kindi's epistle on what cannot be infinite and of what infinity may be attributed. *Islamic studies* 14 (1975), pp. 123-144.

VECCIA VAGLIERI, L., CELENTANO, G. Trois épîtres d'al-Kindī. *AION* 34(N.S.24, 1974), pp. 523-562.

See also IV. c. 6. Lindberg

See also V. u. 2. Shiloah.

See also XXXVII. f. Dagorn

Mullā Ṣadrā

ʿABDUL-HAQ, Muhammad. Metaphysics of Mullā Ṣadrā II. *Islamic stud.* 10(1971), pp. 291-317.

ʿABDUL HAQ, Muhammad. Mullā Ṣadrā's concept of substantial motion. *Islamic Stud.* 11(1972), pp. 79-91, 281-296

IV PHILOSOPHY. SCIENCE

FAZLUR RAHMAN. Mullā Ṣadrā's theory of knowledge. *Philosophical forum* 4i(1972), pp. 141-152.

NASR, Seyyed Hossein. Mullā Ṣadrā and the doctrine of the unity of being. *Philosophical forum* 4i(1972), pp. 153-161.

Nāsir al-dīn Tūsī

HARTNER, W. Naṣīr al-Dīn al-Ṭūsī's lunar theory. *Physis* 11(1969), pp. 287-304.

KREN, C. The rolling device of Naṣīr al-Dīn al-Ṭūsī in the *De sphera* of Nicole Oresme? *Isis* 62(1971), pp. 490-498

LIVINGSTON, J.W. Naṣīr al-Dīn al-Ṭūsī's al-Tadhkirah: a category of Islamic astronomical literature. *Centaurus* 17 (1972-3), pp. 260-275.

VESELOVSKY, N. Copernicus and Nasir al-Din al-Tusi. *J. hist. astron.* 4 (1973), pp. 99-130.

MOAYYAD, Heshmat. Some remarks on the Nasirean ethics by Naṣīr al-Dīn Ṭūsī. *JNES* 31(1972), pp. 179-186.

ROSIŃSKA, Gr. Naṣīr al-Dīn al-Ṭūsī and Ibn al-Shāṭir in Cracow? *Isis* 65(1974), pp. 239-243.

SALIK, Muhammad Tufail. Ethics of Nasir al-Din Tusi. *Iqbal* 18iii(1971), pp. 65-82

See also IV. c. 5. Kren

See also XXXIX. b. Moayyad.

Rāzī

AMMAR, S. Rhazes (850-923 J.C.) - a medical psychology, psychosomatic medicine and deontology. *Tunis.méd.* 47(1969), pp. 5-13. [CWHM 69, 1334]

AZEEZ PASHA, M. Al-Hawi (liber continens) of ar-Razi, Abu Bakr Muhammed bin Zakariya. *Bull. Ind. Inst. Hist. Med.* 4(1974), pp. 86-92, 158-162.

GOODMAN, L.E. The epicurean ethic of Muḥammad ibn Zakariyâ' Ar-Râzî. *SI* 34 (1971), pp. 5-26

GOODMAN, L.E. Rāzī's psychology. *Philosophical forum* 4i(1972), pp. 26-48.

LEVEY, M. A note on embalming procedures of al-Razi. *Pharm.in hist.* 12(1970), p. 169. [CWHM, 69, 1335]

MOHAGHEGH, Mehdi. Rāzi's *Kitab al-Ilm al-Ilāhi* and the Five Eternals. *Abr Nahrain* 13(1972-73), pp. 16-23.

MOHAGHEGH, Mahdi The *Shukūk* of Rāzī against Galen and the problem of the eternity of the world. *Proc.27th Int. Cong.Or.1967* (1971), pp. 240-242.

Sijistānī

JADAANE, Fehmi. La philosophie de Sijistānī. *SI* 33(1971), pp. 67-95.

KRAEMER, J.L. Three unpublished philosophical treatises of Abû Sulaymân as-Sijistânî. *Proc.27th Int.Cong.Or.1967* (1971), pp. 238-240.

KUGEL-TURKER, M. Le traité inédit de Sigistani sur la perfection humaine. *Pensamiento* 25(1969), pp. 207-224.

TROUPEAU, G. Un traité sur les principes des êtres attribué à Abū Sulaymān al-Sigistānī. *Pensamiento* 25(1969), pp. 259-270.

Tawhīdī

BERGÉ, M. Épitre sur les Sciences (*Risāla fī l-'Ulūm*) d'Abū Hayyān al-Tawhīdī (310/922(?) - 414/1023): glossaire et index analytique. *BEO* 21(1968), pp. 313-346.

Others

ALLARD, M. Ibn Bāǧǧa et la politique. *Orientalia Hispanica* I, 1974, pp. 11-19.

ALLARD, M. Un philosophe théologien: Muḥammad b. Yūsuf al-'Āmirī. *Rev. hist. rel.* 187(1975), pp. 59-69.

ARKOUN, Mohammed. Logocentrisme et vérité religieuse dans la pensée islamique d'après al-I'lām bi-manāqib al-Islām d'al-'Āmirī, *SI* 35(1972), pp. 5-51.

ARKOUN, Mohammed. Textes inédits de Miskawayh (M.421). *Annales Islamologiques* 5(1963), pp. 181-190.

BACHMANN, P. Quelques remarques sur le commentaire du premier livre des "Épidémies" par Ibn an-Nafīs. *Actas IV congresso de estudos árabes e islâmicos* 1968(1971), pp. 301-309.

BALJON, J.M.S. Psychology as apprehended and applied by Shâh Walî Allâh Dihlâwi. *Acta Orientalia Neerlandica,* 1971, pp. 53-60.

BERNAND, M. Le Savoir entre la volonté et la spontanéité selon an-Nazzām et al-Gāḥiẓ. *SI* 39(1974), pp. 25-57.

BUSARD, H.L.L., KONINGSVELD, P.S. van. Der *Liber de arcubus similibus* des Ahmed ibn Jusuf. *Annals of science* 30(1973), pp. 381-406.

BUTLER, R.A. Penseurs musulmans contemporains (3). Influences non-arabes et purification de l'Islam selon le Pakistanais Ghulâm Aḥmad Parwêz. *IBLA* 38(no.136, 1975), pp. 219-259.

CHARTIER, M. La pensée religieuse de Kâmil Ḥusayn. *IBLA* 37(no.133, 1974), pp. 1-44.

IV PHILOSOPHY. SCIENCE

CHERIF-CHERGUI, Abderrahmán. El principio de armonia en Sayyid Quṭb. *Orientalia Hispanica* I, 1974, pp. 195-208.

CURIESES DEL AGUA, A. Contestación al doctor Paul Ghalioungui, de Kuwait, sobre Ibn al Nafis y Miguel Servet. *Gac.méd.esp.* 43 (1969), pp. 3-5. [CWHM 69, 1412]

DEGEN, R., ULLMANN, M. Zum Dispensatorium des Sābūr ibn Sahl. *WO* 7(1974), pp. 241-258.

DOLS, M. Ibn al-Wardī's *Risālah al-naba' 'an al-waba'*, a translation of a major source for the history of the Black Death in the Middle East. *Near Eastern numismatics ... Studies in honor of G.C. Miles*, 1974, pp. 443-455.

DUNLOP, D.M. The *Mudhākarāt fī ʿIlm an-Nujūm* (Dialogues on Astrology) attributed to Abū Ma'shar al-Balkhī (Albumasar). *Iran and Islam, in memory of V. Minorsky*, 1971, pp. 229-246

ELKHADEM, H. Tacuini sanitatis, a little known edition of 1531. *Lias* 1(1974), pp. 119-128.

FAKHRY, M. The Platonism of Miskawayh and its implications for his ethics. *SI* 42 (1975), pp. 39-57.

FÓRNEAS, J.M. Un texto de Ibn Hišām al-Lajmī sobre las maquinas hidraulicas y su terminología técnica. *MEAH* 23(1974), pp. 53-62.

GEYOUSHI, Muhammad Ibraheem al-. Al-Tirmidhī's conception of the areas of interiority. *IQ* 16(1973), pp. 168-188.

GEYOUSHI, Muhammad Ibraheem al- Al-Tirmidhī's theory of gnosis. *IQ* 15(1971), pp. 164-188.

GHALI, Ibrahim Amin. Trois penseurs égyptiens. *Nouvelle Rev. du Caire* 1 (1975), pp. 219-239.

GHALIOUNGUI, P. An Arab precursor of Ibn-an-Nafis. *J.Kuwait Med.Ass.* 3(1969), pp. 87-98. [CWHM 64]

GHALIOUNGUI, P. Miguel Servet, Ibn al Nafis. *Gac.med.esp.* 43(1969), pp. 1-3. [CWHM 69, 1414]

GHANNOUCHI, Abdelmajid el-. "Des propositions modales": epître d'Ibn Malīḥ al-Raqqād. *Arabica* 18(1971), pp. 202-210.

HAMARNEH, Sami. Contributions of ʿAli Al-Ṭabarī to ninth-century Arabic culture. *Folia Or.* 12(1970), pp. 91-101

HARTNER, W. Ptolemy, Azarquiel, Ibn al-Shatir and Copernicus on Mercury. A study of parameters. *Arch. int. hist. sci.* 24(1974), pp. 5-25.

HILDER, G. Abu Ma'shars "Introductorium in astronomiam" und der altfranzösische "Roman de la rose". Ein Beitrag zur Tradition arabischer Astrologie und ihrer christlichen Deutung im 12. und 13. Jahrhundert. *Z. f. roman. Philol.* 88 (1972), pp. 13-33.

IBISH, Yussuf. La teoria del viaggiare di Ibn ʿArabī. *Conoscenza religiosa* 1973, pp. 418-423.

JAOUICHE, Khalil. Le livre du qarasṭūn de Ṯabit ibn Qurra. Étude sur l'origine de la notion de travail et du calcul du moment statique d'une barre homogène. *Archive for exact sciences* 13(1974), pp. 325-394.

JENSEN, Claus. Abū Nasr Mansūr's approach to spherical astronomy as developed in his treatise "The Table of Minutes". *Centaurus* 16(1971), pp. 1-19.

JENSEN, Cl. The lunar theories of Al-Baghdādī. *Archive for history of exact sciences* 8(1971-2), pp. 321-328.

KARPOVA, L. and ROSENFELD, B.A. The treatise of Thābit ibn Qurra on sections of a cylinder, and on its surface. *Arch. int. hist. sci.* 24(1974), pp. 66-72.

KARY-NIYAZOV, T.N. Exposé sur la langue de la version initiale du "Zidj d'Oulougbek". *XIIe Cong.int.hist.sci.* 1968, *Actes*, IIIA (1971), pp. 95-96.

KASSEM, Mahmoud. El problema de la predestinación y del libre albedrio en Leibnitz y en Ibn 'Arabī. *Pensamiento* 30 (1974), pp. 149-172.

KENNEDY, E.S. The equatorium of Abu al-Salt. *Physis* 12(1970), pp. 73-81.

KING, D.A. An analog computer for solving problems of spherical astronomy: the *shakkaziya* quadrant of Jamal al-Din al-Maridini. *Arch. int. hist. sci.* 24 (1974), pp. 219-242.

KING, D.A. A double-argument table for the lunar equation attributed to Ibn Yūnus. *Centaurus* 18(1973-4), pp. 129-146.

KING, D.A. Ibn Yunus' very useful tables for reckoning time by the sun. *Archive for exact sciences* 10(1973), pp. 342-394.

KING, D.A. Al-Khalili's auxiliary tables for solving problems of spherical astronomy. *J. hist. astron.* 4(1973), pp. 99-110.

KING, D.A. Al-Khalīlī's *qibla* table. *JNES* 34(1975), pp. 81-122.

KLEIN-FRANKE, F. 'Ubaidullāh b. Ǧibrīl b. Baḫtīšūʿ's These zur Therapie seelischer und körperlicher Krankheiten (MS Leiden 1332). *XVIII. Deutscher Orientalistentag* 1972, pp. 192-197.

KUHNE BRABANT, R. Avenzoar y la cosmética. *Orientalia Hispanica* I, 1974, pp. 428-437.

IV PHILOSOPHY. SCIENCE

KUNITZSCH, P. New light on al-Battānī's Zīj. *Centaurus* 18(1973-4), pp. 270-274.

KÜYEL, Mubahat Türker. Ibn uṣ-Ṣalâh comme exemple à la rencontre des cultures. *Araştırma* 9(1971), pp. 1-7.

LEVEY, M. The pharmacological table of Ibn Biklārish. *J. hist. med. applied sci.* 26 (1971), pp. 413-421.

LEVEY, M. Transmission of indeterminate equations as seen in an Istanbul manuscript of Abu Kamil. *Japanese stud.hist. sci.* 9(1970), pp. 17-25.

LORCH, R.P. The astronomy of Jabir ibn Aflah. *Centaurus* 19(1975), pp. 85-107.

MAHASSINI, Zeki el-. Idries Shah: the philosopher, writer and poet ... Illustrious Afghan of the 20th century. *Asda* (July 1971) [Unpaged offprint seen.]

MAKDISI, G. The Tanbīh of Ibn Taimīya on dialectic: the pseudo-'Aqīlian Kitāb al-farq. *Medieval and Middle Eastern studies ... A.S. Atiya* 1972, pp. 285-294.

MARTIN, J.D. The religious beliefs of Abu'l-ʿAtāhiya according to the Zuhdīyāt. *Glasgow Or. Soc. Trans.* 23(1969-70), pp. 11-28.

MILLAS VENDRELL, E. El comentario de Ibn-al-Mutannā a las tablas astronómicas de al-Jwārizmī. *Oriente e Occidente nel medioevo,* 1971, pp. 759-773.

MOESGAARD, K.P. Thābit ibn Qurra between Ptolemy and Copernicus: an analysis of Thābit's solar theory. *Archive for exact sciences* 12(1974), pp. 199-216.

MOOSA, Matti A new source on Aḥmad ibn al-Ṭayyib al-Sarakhsī: Florentine MS 299. *JAOS* 92(1972), pp. 19-24

MUḤAQQIQ, M. Sabzawārī, a nineteenth century Persian philosopher. *Iqbal rev.* 12 iii(1971), pp. 74-78

NASR, Seyyed Hossein. The spread of the illuminationist school of Suhrawardi. *Stud. comp. relig.* 6(1972), pp. 141-152.

NASR, Seyyed Hossein. Sadr al-Dīn Muhammad Ibn'Ibrâhîm Shîrâzî, the renewer of Islamic philosophy in the 11th/17th century by Sayyid Muḥammad Ḥusain Ṭabâṭabâ'î. Translated by Seyyed Hossein Nasr. *Mullâ Sadrâ commem. vol., 1961.* pp. 22-34.

NASRALLAH, J. Naẓīf Ibn Yumn: médecin, traducteur et théologien melchite du Xe siècle. *Arabica* 21(1974), pp. 303-312.

PHILIPP, Mangol Bayat. The concepts of religion and government in the thought of Mîrzâ Âqâ Khân Kirmânî, a nineteenth-century Persian revolutionary. *IJMES* 5 (1974), pp. 381-400.

PINES, S. Ahmad Miskawayh and Paul the Persian. *Iran-shināsi* 2ii(serial no.3, 1971), pp. 121-129.

PLESSNER, M. A medieval definition of a scientific experiment in the Hebrew *Picatrix. J. Warburg and Courtauld Insts.* 36(1973), pp. 358-359.

RASHED, Roshdi. L'induction mathématique: al-Karajī, as-Samaw'al. *Archive for history of exact sciences* 9(1972-3), pp. 1-21.

RASHED, Roshdi. Résolution des equations numériques et algèbre. Šaraf-al-Dīn al-Ṭūsī, Viète. *Archive for exact sciences* 12(1974), pp. 244-290.

RIAD, E. Miskawayh sur la colère. *Orientalia Suecana* 21(1972), pp. 34-52.

SAIDAN, A.S. The arithmetic of Abū'l-Wafā'. *Isis* 65(1974), pp. 367-375.

SAMIR, K. Le *Tahdīb al-aḫlāq* de Yaḥyā B. ʿAdī (m.974) attribué à Ǧāḥiẓ et à Ibn al-ʿArabī. *Arabica* 21(1974), pp. 111-138.

SANSO MOYA, J. Contribución à un analisis de la terminologia matemático-astronómica de Abū Naṣr Manṣūr b. 'Alī b. 'Irāq. *Pensamiento* 25(1969), pp. 235-248.

SCHIPPERGES, H. Die Kunst zu leben - ein Kodex in Granada. *Propharmacon* 1974, pp. 10-13. [CWHM 82,713]

SCHMITZ, R. und MOATTAR, Fariborz. Zur Biobibliographie Isma'il Ǧorǧanis (1040-1136). Der 'Schatz des Königs von Ḫwārazm'. *Sudhoffs Archiv* 57(1973), pp. 337-360.

SCHÖNFELD, J. Die Zahnheilkunde im "Kitāb al-musāfir" des al-Ǧazzār. *Sudhoffs Archiv* 58(1974), pp. 380-403.

SCHUB, M.B. Avenzohar. *S. Afr. med. J.* 46 (1972), pp. 665-666. [CWHM 76(1972),100]

SHILOAH, A. Ibn Hindū, le médecin et la musique. *In memoriam S.M. Stern* (Israel Or. studies, II, 1972), pp. 447-462.

SHLOMING, R. Thâbit ibn Qurra and the Pythagorean theorem. *Maths.teacher* 63 (1970), pp. 519-528.

SIDDIQUI, B.H. Miskawayh: life and works. *J.Regional Cult.Inst.* 7(1974), pp. 87-111.

SIDDIQUI, B.H. Miskawayh's theory of spiritual therapy. *J. Reg. Cult. Inst.* 1 iii(1968), pp. 22-36.

SOUÏSSI, M. Un mathématicien tuniso-andalou: al-Qalaṣādī. *Actas II Coloquio hispano-tunecino,* 1972, pp. 147-169.

SPIES, O., THIES, H.J. Die Propädeutik der arabischen Chirurgie nach Ibn al-Quff. *Südhoffs Archiv* 55(1971), pp. 373-393.

STERN, S.M. Ibn Masarra, follower of pseudo-Empedocles -- an illusion. *Actas IV congresso de estudos árabes e islâmicos* 1968(1971), pp. 325-337.

SWERDLOW, N. Al-Battānī's determination of the solar distance. *Centaurus* 17 (1972-3), pp. 97-105.

TERZİOĞLU, Arslan. Eine bisher unbekannte türkische Abhandlung über die Zahnheilkunde des Moses Hamon aus dem Anfang des 16. Jahrhunderts. *Sudhoffs Archiv* 58 (1974), pp. 276-282.

TROUPEAU, G. Le traité sur les hypostases et la substance de 'Abd Allāh Ibn al-Ṭayyib. *Orientalia Hispanica* I, 1974, pp. 640-644.

ULLMANN, M. Beitäge zum Text des Kitāb al-Ǧauharatain von al-Hāmdanī. *Islam* 48 (1971), pp. 90-99.

ULLMANN, M. Yūḥannā ibn Sarābiyūn. Untersuchungen zur Überlieferungsgeschichte seiner Werke. *Medizinhist.J.* 6(1971), pp. 278-296.

VADET, J.C. Les aphorismes latins d'Almansor, essai d'interprétation. *Annales Islamologiques* 5(1963), pp. 31-130.

VADET, J.C. Une défense de l'astrologie dans le madḫal d'Abū Ma'šar al Balḫī. *Annales Islamologiques* 5(1963), pp. 131-180.

VERMA, R.L. Pioneer in modern system of medicine (Ibn-an Nafīs). *al-'Arab* 8vi (1969), pp. 16-20

VERNET, J. Los médicos andaluces en el libro de "Las generaciones de médicos" de Ibn Ŷulŷul. *Anuario estud.med.* 5(1968), pp. 445-462.

WINDFUHR, G.L. Common sense and the Robai. Part 4. *Irān-shināsi* 2ii(serial no.3, 1971), pp. 130-131.

See also IV. a. Halepota.

See also IV. b. *al-Nazzām.* Bernand.

See also IV. c. 8. Serjeant.

See also IV. c. 10. Tritton.

c SCIENCE

i General

FĀRŪQĪ, Isma'īl R. al-. Science and traditional values in Islamic society. *Zygon* 2(1967), pp. 231-246.

HOURANI, G.F. The early growth of the secular sciences in Andalusia. *SI* 32(1970), pp. 143-156.

HUMMEL, K. Die Entwicklung der neuzeitlichen Naturwissenschaft in Iran. *WO* 6(1971), pp. 240-254.

KENNEDY, E.S. The Arabic heritage in the exact sciences. *Al-Abhath* 23(1970), pp. 327-344.

KHAN, M.S. A chapter on ancient Chaldean sciences in an eleventh-century Hispano-Arabic work. *IQ* 16(1972), pp. 12-35.

KHAN, M.S. A chapter on ancient Persia in an eleventh century Hispano-Arabic work. *Iran Society silver jubilee souvenir* 1944-1969, pp. 213-230.

LIVINGSTON, J.W. Ibn Qayyim al-Jawziyyah: a fourteenth century defense against astrological divination and alchemical transmutation. *JAOS* 91(1971), pp. 96-103.

MAQBUL AHMAD, S. Islam and science in history. *India and contemporary Islam,* ed. S.T. Lokhandwalla, 1971, pp. 311-315.

NAQVI, S.H.Z. Islam and the development of science. *Nigerian J. Islam* 2i(1971-2), pp. 11-20.

PLESSNER, M. Essay review. The history of Arabic literature. (On Sezgin, *Geschichte des arabischen Schrifttums, Bde. III-IV.) Ambix* 19(1972), pp. 209-215.

QADIRI, M.A.H. A review of history of biological and related sciences in the Middle East during the 9th to 13th century A.C. *Islamic stud.* 10(1971), pp. 137-143.

RAHMAN, A. Science, society and culture. *India and the Arab World, ed. by S. Maqbul Ahmed,* 1969, pp. 75-79.

ROMERO, H. Ciencia arabe en perspectiva. *An.chil.hist.med.* 1967-68, pp. 9-10, 17-53. [CWHM 64]

SOUISSI, Mohamed. En parcourant les préfaces des ouvrages scientifiques en langue arabe. *CT* 22(85-86, 1974), pp. 147-162.

VERNET, J. La introducción de la ciencia occidental en el mundo árabe. *Orientalia Hispanica* I, 1974, pp. 645-646.

ZIMMERMANN, Friedrich W., BROWN, H. Vivian B. Neue arabische Übersetzungstexte aus dem Bereich der spätantiken griechischen Philosophie. *Der Islam* 50(1973), pp. 313-324.

See also I. b. 3. Minganti.

ii Transmission of Greek science to the Arabs

AINTABI, Mohamed Fouad. Arab scientific progress and Menelaus of Alexandria. *XIIe Cong.int.hist.sci.* 1968, *Actes,* IIIA (1971), pp. 7-12.

ATALLAH, Wahib. L'intérêt des traductions arabes dans l'édition des textes hippocratiques. *La collection hippocratique et son rôle dans l'histoire de la médecine,* 1975, pp. 19-33.

BIELAWSKI, J. *Phédon* en version arabe et le Risālat al-tuffāḥa. *Orientalia Hispanica* I, 1974, pp. 120-134.

BURGEL, J.Ch. A new Arabic quotation from Plato's Phaido and its relation to a Persian version of the Phaido. *Actas IV congresso de estudos árabes e islâmicos* 1968(1971), pp. 281-290.

IV PHILOSOPHY. SCIENCE

BUSARD, H.L.L. Der *Codex orientalis* 162 der Leidener Universitätsbibliothek. *XIIe Cong.int.hist.sci.* 1968, *Actes*, IIIA (1971), pp. 25-31.

DAIBER, H. Ein bisher unbekannter pseudo-platonischer Text über die Tugenden der Seele in arabischer Überlieferung. *Der Islam* 47(1971), pp. 25-42; Nachtrag, 49 (1972), pp. 122-123.

DIETRICH, A. Quelques observations sur la matière médiévale de Dioscoride parmi les Arabes. *Oriente e Occidente nel medioevo*, 1971, pp. 375-394.

DUNLOP, D.M. The manuscript Taimur Pasha 290 Aḫlāq and the Summa Alexandrinorum. *Arabica* 21(1974), pp. 252-263.

ENDRESS, G. Some remarks on early Greek-Arabic translations and the development of Arabic philosophical terminology. *Proc.27th Int.Cong.Or.1967* (1971), pp. 170-171.

FAHD, Toufic. Ḥunayn Ibn Isḥāq est-il le traducteur des *Oneirocritica* d'Artémidore d'Éphèse? *Arabica* 21(1974), pp. 270-284.

GHORAB, A.A. The Greek commentators on Aristotle quoted in al- Āmirī's *"as-Sa'āda wa'l -is'ād."* *Islamic philosophy and the classical tradition:* essays presented to R. Walzer, 1972, pp. 77-88.

GRIGNASCHI, M. La "Physiognomonie" traduite par Ḥunayn Ibn Isḥāq. *Arabica* 21(1974), pp. 285-291.

KLEIN-FRANKE, F. Die Überlieferung der ältesten arabischen Handschrift von Pseudo-Aristoteles "De mundo". *Muséon* 87(1974). pp. 59-65.

KUNITZSCH, P. Über das Frühstadium der arabischen Aneignung antiken Gutes. *Saeculum* 26(1975), pp. 268-282.

MANZALAOUI, Mahmoud. The Pseudo-Aristotelian *Kitāb sirr al-asrār;* facts and problems. *Oriens* 23-24(1974), pp. 147-257.

MATTOCK, J.N. A translation of the Arabic epitome of Galen's book Περὶ ἠθῶν. *Islamic philosophy and the classical tradition*, 1972, pp. 235-260.

PINES, S. An Arabic summary of a lost work of John Philoponus. *In memoriam S.M. Stern* (Israel Or. studies, II, 1972), pp. 320-352.

PINGREE, D. The Greek influence on early Islamic mathematical astronomy. *JAOS* 93 (1973), pp. 32-43.

ROSENTHAL, F. The Arabic translation of a Pythagorean letter. (From Arabic books and manuscripts, XIII.) *JAOS* 95(1975), pp. 209-211.

ROSENTHAL, F. A commentator of Aristotle. *Islamic philosophy and the classical tradition*, 1972, pp. 337-349.

SERRA, G. Note sulla traduzione arabo-latina del *De generatione et corruptione* di Aristotele. *Giornale crit. della filos. ital.* 4a ser.,vol.4, anno 52(54, 1974), pp. 383-427.

STROHMAIER, G. Die arabische Sokrateslegende und ihre Ursprünge. *Studia Coptica*, 1974, pp. 121-136.

STROHMAIER, G. Diogenesanekdoten auf Papyrus und in arabischen Gnomologien. *Archiv f. Papyrusforschung* 22(1973), pp. 285-288.

STROHMAIER, G. Ethical sentences and anecdotes of Greek philosophers in Arabic tradition. *Ve Congrès International d'Arabisants et d'Islamisants. Actes.*, [1970?], pp. 463-471.

TEKELI, Sevim. "The duplication of the cube". Zail-i Tahrir al Uqlidas, Majmu'a and Sidra al-Muntaha. *XIIe Cong.int.hist. sci.* 1968, *Actes*, IIIA (1971), pp. 137-140.

ULLMANN, M. Die arabische Überlieferung der hippokratischen Schrift "De superfetatione". *Sudhoffs Archiv* 58(1974), pp. 254-275.

ULLMANN, M. Der literarische Hintergrund des Steinbuches des Aristoteles. *Actas IV congresso de estudos árabes e islâmicos* 1968(1971), pp. 291-299.

WIKANDER, St. De l'Inde à l'Espagne: l'origine de la "Poridat de las Poridades". *Actas IV congresso de estudos árabes e islâmicos* 1968(1971), pp. 267-269.

See also IV. b. *Ibn Ṭufail.* Hawi.

iii Transmission of Arabic science to the West

BUSARD, H.L.L. The translation of the *Elements* of Euclid from the Arabic into Latin by Hermann of Corinthia(?), books VII, VIII and IX. *Janus* 59(1972), pp. 125-187.

DUNLOP, D.M. Observations on the medieval Arabic version of Aristotle's *Nicomachean ethics*. *Oriente e Occidente nel medioevo*, 1971, pp. 229-250.

HAMARNEH, S. Arabic medicine and impact on teaching and practice of the healing arts in the West. *Convegno Internazionale ... 1969. Accademia Nazionale dei Lincei*, 1971, pp. 395-425. [CWHM 73(1972),50]

HOURANI, G.F. The medieval translations from Arabic to Latin made in Spain. *MW* 62(1972), pp. 97-114.

McVAUGH, M., BEHRENDS, F. Fulbert of Chartres' notes on Arabic astronomy. *Manuscripta* 15(1971), pp. 172-177.

NEBBIA, G. La trasmissione delle conoscenze sulle falsificazioni e frodi delle merci dall'antichità al medioevo islamico e occidentale. *Oriente e Occidente nel medioevo*, 1971, pp. 501-521.

REYCHMAN, J. Orientalistyka w dziejach nauki polskiej. (L'orientalistique dans l'histoire de la science polonaise). *Przegląd Or.* 4(84) (1972), pp. 359-361.

RODINSON, M. Les influences de la civilisation musulmane sur la civilisation européenne médiévale dans les domaines de la consommation et de la distraction: l'alimentation. *Oriente e Occidente nel medioevo,* 1971, pp. 479-499.

ROMANO, D. Le opere scientifiche di Alfonso X e l'intervento degli ebrei. *Oriente e Occidente nel medioevo,* 1971, pp. 677-711.

SILVERSTEIN, T. How Arabic science reached the west in the earlier twelfth century. *Rend. Accad. Lincei* 27(1972), pp. 283-294.

ÜLKEN, Hilmi Ziya. The influence of Islamic thought on Western philosophy. *Şarkiyat mecmuası* 4(1961), pp. 1-21.

VERNET, J. Les traductions scientifiques dans l'Espagne du Xe siècle. *CT* 18 (nos. 69-70, 1970), pp. 47-59.

VERNET-GINES, J. Tradición e innovación en la ciencia medieval. *Oriente e Occidente nel medioevo,* 1971, pp. 741-758.

WATT, W.M. L'influence de l'Islam sur l'Europe médiévale. *REI* 40(1972), pp. 297-327.

See also II. a. 1. Hamidullah.

See also IV. b. *Ibn Sīnā.* Alverny.

See also IV. b. *Ibn Sina* Lucchetta

See also IV. c. 2. Wikander.

See also IV. c. 7. Abel

See also IV. c. 10. Bietti

See also IV. c. 10. Levey

iv Mathematics

CHAUHAN, D.V. Al-Djummal and decimal notation in Indo-Muslim epigraphy. *Proc.32 Ind.hist.cong.* 1970, vol. 1, pp. 376-386.

FRAJESE, A. L'algebra dagli arabi all' Occidente. *Oriente e Occidente nel medioevo,* 1971, pp. 713-729.

KÖBERT, R. Zum Prinzip der *ġurāb*-Zahlen und damit unseres Zahlensystems. *Orientalia* 44(1975), pp. 108-112.

RASHED, Roshdi. Algèbre et linguistique: l'analyse combinatoire dans la science arabe. *Boston stud.philos.sci.* 11(1974), pp. 383-399.

SALIBA, G.A. The meaning of al-jabr wa'l-muqābalah. *Centaurus* 17(1972-3), pp. 189-204.

SCHUSTER, H.-S. Magische Quadrate im islamischen Bereich. Ihre Entlehnung ins Abendland im Mittelalter sowie ihre Vorstufen. *Der Islam* 49(1972), pp. 1-84.

VERNET, J. y CATALÁ, A. Arquímedes árabe: el tratado de los círculos tangentes. *And.* 33 (1968), pp. 53-93.

v Astronomy. Astrology. Almanachs

CIMINO, M. L'astronomia araba e la sua diffusione. *Oriente e Occidente nel medioevo,* 1971, pp. 647-676.

FEHÉRVÁRI, G. An eighth/fourteenth-century quadrant of the astrolabist al-Mizzī. *BSOAS* 36(1973), pp. 115-117.

GRANGE, H.G. Les traités arabes de navigation. De certaines difficultés particulières à leur étude. *Arabica* 19(1972), pp. 240-254.

HADDAD, Fuad I., KENNEDY, E.S. Geographical tables of medieval Islam. *al-Abhath* 24 (1971), pp. 87-102.

HALM, H. Zur Datierung des ismā'īlitischen "Buches der Zwischenzeiten und der zehn Konjunktionen" (Kitāb al-fatarāt wal-qirānāt al-ašara), HS Tübingen Ma VI 297. *WO* 8(1975), pp. 91-107.

HARPER, R.I. Prophatius Judaeus and the medieval astronomical tables. *Isis* 62 (1971), pp. 61-68.

HARTNER, W. The Islamic astronomical background to Nicholas Copernicus. *Colloquia Copernicana* III, 1975, pp. 7-16.

HARTNER, W. Trepidation and planetary theories. Common features in late Islamic and early Renaissance astronomy. *Oriente e Occidente nel medioevo,* 1971, pp. 609-632.

KENNEDY, E.S., KRIKORIAN-PREISLER, Haiganoush. The astrological doctrine of projecting the rays. *Al-Abhath* 25(1972), pp. 3-15.

KENNEDY, E.S. Planetary theory in the medieval Near East and its transmission to Europe. *Oriente e Occidente nel medioevo,* 1971, pp. 595-607.

KHOURY, R.G. Un fragment astrologique inédit attribué à Wahb b. Munabbih (m. 110 ou 114/728 ou 732). *Arabica* 19(1972), pp. 139-144.

KING, D.A. On the astronomical tables of the Islamic middle ages. *Colloquia Copernicana* III, 1975, pp. 37-56.

KONINGSVELD, P.Sj. van. ʿUmar ibn al-Muẓaffar ibn Rūzbahān Šams al-Dīn Abū l-Mafāḫir = ʿUmar ibn al-Muẓaffar ibn Rūzbahān ibn Ṭāhir (Fl. 615 H.) *Arabica* 20(1973), p. 81.

IV PHILOSOPHY. SCIENCE

KONINGSVELD, P.S. van ʿUmar ibn al-Muẓaffar ibn Rūzbahān ibn Ṭāhir Šams ad-Dīn Abu 'l-Mafākhir (fl. 615 H) and his study of *Kitāb al-Miğisṭī*. *Der Islam* 50(1973), pp. 168-169.

KUNITZSCH, P. Die arabische Herkunft von zwei Sternverzeichnissen in cod. Vat. gr. 1056. *ZDMG* 120ii (1970), pp. 281-287

KUNITZSCH, P. Die arabischen Sternbilder des Südhimmels. *Islam* 51(1974), pp. 37-54; 52(1975), pp. 263-277.

KUNITZSCH, P. Zur Tradition der "Unwetter-sterne". *ZDMG* 122(1972), pp. 108-117.

LAZARD, G. A quelle époque a vécu l'astronome Mohammad b. Ayyub Tabari. *Yād-nāme-ye Irāni-ye Minorsky*, 1969, pp. 96-103.

NEBEZ, J. und SCHLOSSER, W. Ein kurdisches Mond-Observatorium aus neuerer Zeit. *ZDMG* 122(1972), pp. 140-144.

PELLAT, C. L'astrolabe sphérique d'al-Rūdānī. *BEO* 26(1973), pp. 7-83.

PETRI, W. Tradition und Fortscritt in der Astronomie des Mittelalters. *Oriente e Occidente nel medioevo*, 1971, pp. 633-645.

PETRI, W. Uigur and Tibetan lists of the Indian lunar mansions. *Ind. J. hist. sci.* 1(1966), pp. 83-90.

PORTER, N.A. The nova of A.D. 1006 in European and Arab records. *J. hist. astron.* 5(1974), pp. 99-104.

RYBKA, E. Mouvement des planètes dans l'astronomie des peuples de l'Islam. *Oriente e Occidente nel medioevo*, 1971, pp. 579-594.

ṢALEḤ, Jamil 'Ali as-. Solar and lunar distances and apparent velocities in the astronomical tables of Ḥabash al-Ḥāsib. *Al-Abhath* 23(1970), pp. 129-177.

SALIBA, G.A. Easter computation in medieval astronomical handbooks. *Al-Abhath* 23(1970), pp. 179-212.

SAMSÓ, J. À propos de quelques manuscrits astronomiques des bibliothèques de Tunis: contribution à une étude de l'astrolabe dans l'Espagne musulmane. *Actas II Coloquio hispano-tunecino*, 1972, pp. 171-190.

SAMSÓ, J. Dos notas sobre astrología medieval. *And.* 36(1971), pp, 215-222.

SAMSÓ, J. Una hipótesis sobre cálculo por aproximación con el cuadrante šakkāzī. *And.* 36(1971), pp. 117-126.

SAMSÓ, J. Sobre la astronomía de al-Biṭrūŷī. *And.* 36(1971), pp. 461-465.

STROHMAIER, G. The stature of the supra-lunar world from Anaxagoras to Ibn al-Haitham. *Colloquia Copernicana* III, 1975, pp. 17-20.

TIBBETTS, G.R. Comparisons between Arab and Chinese navigational techniques. *BSOAS* 36(1973), pp. 97-108.

VERNET, J. Copernico y los arabes. *Actas II Col. hisp.-tunec. estud. hist.*, 1973, pp. 191-208.

See also IV. b. *Ibn Shatir*. Hartner.

See also IV. c. 2. Pingree.

See also IV. c. 4. Kennedy

See also V. g. Hartner.

See also XIX. e. Kunitzsch.

vi Physics. Scientific instruments

GINGERICH, O., KING, D. and SALIBA, G. The 'Abd al-a'imma astrolabe forgeries. *J. hist. astron.* 3(1972), pp. 188-198.

JACKSON, D.E.P. The Arabic translation of a Greek manual of mechanics. *IQ* 16(1972), pp. 96-103.

JANIN, L. Le cadran solaire de la Mosquée Umayyade à Damas. *Centaurus* 16(1972), pp. 285-298.

JAOUICHE, Khalil. La statique chez les Arabes. *Oriente e Occidente nel medioevo*, 1971, pp. 731-740.

KHAWAM, R.R. Les statues animées dans les Mille et Une Nuits. *Annales ESC* 30(1975), pp. 1084-1104.

LIVINGSTON, J. The Mukhula, an Islamic conical sundial. *Centaurus* 16(1972), pp. 299-308.

ROHR, R.R.J. et JANIN, L. Deux astrolabes -quadrants turcs. *Centaurus* 19(1975), pp. 108-124.

ROHR, R.R.J. Sonnenuhr und Astrolabium im Dienste der Moschee. *Centaurus* 18(1973-4), pp. 44-56.

SAMSÓ, J. À propos de quelques manuscrits astronomiques des bibliothèques de Tunis: contribution à une étude de l'astrolabe dans l'Espagne musulmane. *Actas II Col. hisp.-tunec. estud. hist.*, 1973, pp. 171-190.

VERNET, J. y CATALÁ, A. Un ingeniero árabe del siglo XI: al-Karaŷī. *And.* 35(1970), pp. 69-91.

vii Alchemy. Chemistry

ABEL, A. De l'alchimie arabe à l'alchimie occidentale. *Oriente e Occidente nel medioevo*, 1971, pp. 251-283.

BERQUE, J. Hellénisme et alchimistes arabes. *L'ambivalence dans la culture arabe*, 1967, pp. 111-115.

MAHDIHASSAN, S. Imitation of creation by alchemy and its corresponding symbolism. *Abr-nahrain* 12(1971-2), pp. 99-117

ULLMANN, M. Kleopatra in einer arabischen alchemistischen Disputation. *WZKM* 63-64(1972), pp. 158-175.

See also IV. b. *Ibn Sina* Anawati

viii Biology. Agriculture. Irrigation

ATTIÉ ATTIÉ, Bachir. L'origine d'al-falāḥa ar-rūmīya et du pseudo-Qusṭūs. *Hesp. Tamuda* 13(1972), pp. 139-181.

BESANÇON, J. Un séminaire de la FAO consacré au proche orient. *Hannon* 2(1967), pp. 139-143.

BINSWANGER, K. Einiges über Brutanstalten in Nordafrika. *Islamkundliche Abhandlungen H.J. Kissling,* 1974, pp. 36-48.

BOLENS, L. De l'idéologie aristotélicienne à l'empirisme médiéval: les sols dans l'agronomie hispano-arabe. *Annales ESC* 30 (1975), pp. 1062-1083.

BOLENS, L. Empirisme médiéval et progrès scientifique: la classification botanique en Andalousie (XIe-XIIe siècles). *Schweiz. Z. f. Gesch.* 25(1975), pp. 257-268.

BOLENS, L. Engrais et protection de la fertilité dans l'agronomie hispano-arabe XIe-XIIe siècles. *Etudes rurales* 46(1972), pp. 34-60.

CAHEN, C. Notes pour une histoire de l'agriculture dans les pays musulmanes médiévaux. *JESHO* 14(1971), pp. 63-68.

FAHD, Toufic. Le calendrier des travaux agricoles d'après *al-filāḥa al-nabaṭiyya. Orientalia Hispanica* I, 1974, pp. 245-272.

FAHD, T. Conduite d'une exploitation agricole d'après "L'Agriculture Nabatéenne". *SI* 32 (1970), pp. 109-128.

FAHD, Toufy. Genèse et cause des saveurs d'après l'agriculture nabat'éenne. *ROMM* 13-14(1973), pp. 319-329.

FAHD, T. Genése et causes des couleurs d'après l'agriculture nabatéenne. *Islamwissenschaftliche Abhandlungen F. Meier,* 1974, pp. 78-95.

FAHD, Toufic. Un traité des eaux dans *al-Filāḥa an-Nabaṭiyya* (hydrogéologie, hydraulique agricole, hydrologie). *La Persia nel medievo,* 1971, pp. 277-326

GIFFEN, L.A. The lion and the panther, the ibex and the beaver: remarks on the durability of some zoological "knowledge". *Studies in art and literature of the Near East in honor of R. Ettinghausen,* 1974, pp. 229-238.

GRANDGUILLAUME, G. Régime économique et structure du pouvoir: le système des foggara du Touat. *ROMM* 13-14(1973), pp. 437-457.

HARVEY, J.H. Gardening books and plant lists of Moorish Spain. *Garden hist.* 3ii(1975), pp. 10-21.

HUMPHREYS, P.N. Ornithological notes (The Society's Anatolian tour, 1971). *Asian aff.* 58(N.S.2, 1971), pp. 315-316.

SANGAR, S.P. Fruits in Mughal India. *J.Or. Inst.Baroda* 20(1970-71), pp. 172-180

SERJEANT, R.B. Agriculture and horticulture: some cultural interchanges of the medieval Arabs and Europe. *Oriente e Occidente nel medioevo,* 1971, pp. 535-548.

SERJEANT, R.B. The cultivation of cereals in mediaeval Yemen. A translation of the *Bughyat al-Fallāḥīn* of the Rasūlid Sultan, al-Malik al-Afḍal al-'Abbās b. 'Alī, composed circa 1370 A.D. *Arabian studies* 1 (1974), pp. 25-74.

SERJEANT, R.B. Porcupines in the Yemen. *Arabian studies* 1(1974), p. 180.

SOLIGNAC, M. Mohamed Al-Karagi, ingénieur hydrologue (m.410/1019). *IBLA* 37(no.134, 1974), pp. 315-328.

THEODORIDES, J. Orient et Occident au Moyen Age: l'oeuvre zoologique de Frédéric II de Hohenstaufen. *Oriente e Occidente nel medioevo,* 1971, pp. 549-569.

TUMA, E.H. Agriculture and economic development in the Middle East. *MESA Bull.* 5iii(1971), pp. 1-19.

VÁZQUEZ DE BENITO, M. de la C. El manuscrito n.XXX de la collección Gayangos. *BAEO* 9(1973), pp. 73-124; 10(1974), pp. 215-308.

See also VII. d. Fahd.

See also IX. e. Falina.

See also XIX. e. Cahen.

See also XXII. a. Serjeant.

See also XXXII. c. Ohri.

ix Mineralogy

WEIL, J.W. Einige Edelmetalle und Edelsteine als Rätsel-Namen in der Gedichtsammlung *Alf ǧariya wa-ǧariya.* *WZKM* 65/66(1973-74), pp. 151-154.

x Medicine. Pharmacology. Dentistry

AZEEZ PASHA, M. Brief biographies of eminent Unani hekeems of India, based on Nuz-Hatul-Khwatir (pleasure of hearts), by Allama-Abdul-Hayyi. *Bull. Inst. Hist. Med.* 3 (1973), pp. 24-34; 4 (1974), pp. 27-31, 163-170.

AZEEZ PASHA, M. Establishment of Unani hospitals in Islamic countries. *Bull. Inst. Hist. Med.* 3(1973), pp. 68-70.

AZEEZ PASHA, M. Al-Hawi (Liber continens) of Ar-Razi, Abu Bakr Muhammed Bin Zakariya. *Bull.Ind.Inst.Hist.Medicine* 4(1974), pp. 86-92.

IV PHILOSOPHY. SCIENCE

AZEEZ PASHA, M. Muheet-a-Azam (a great Unani pharmacopeia). A short note on the author and the book. *Bull. Ind. Inst. Hist. Med.* 4(1974), pp. 19-26.

BACHMANN, P. Arzt und Krankheit in einigen Gedichten des arabischen Lyrikers al-Mutanabbi. *Medizinhist.J.* 4(1969), pp. 99-120.

BELGUEDJ, M. La médecine arabe; vue generale et problèmes. *Bull.Fac.Lettres Strasbourg* 48(1969), pp. 7-18.

BEN MILED, A. L'Imam al-Mazri, juriste et médecin. *Pag. Storia Med.* 17i(1973), pp. 5-15. [CWHM 79(1973), 800]

BIETTI, G. Le influenze dell'oftalmologia araba sulla oftalmologia medioevale europea. *Oriente e Occidente nel medioevo*, 1971, pp. 445-452.

BODROLIGETI, A. The medical terminology in the Kitāb bayṭarat al-vaziḥ, a fourteenth century Mamluk-Kipchak treatise on veterinary medicine. *Istanbul Üniv. Edebiyat Fak. Türk dili ve edebiyati dergisi* 21(1973), pp. 115-125.

BRANDENBURG, D. Medizinisches im iranischen Nationalepos (Shâh-Nâma) des Firdausî. *Med.Mschr.* 25(1971), pp. 274-279. [CWHM 72, 510]

BRANDENBURG, D. Das Werkzeug des Schriftkünstlers. Zur medizinischen Handschriftenkunde des alten Islams. *Med. Mschr.* 25 (1971), pp. 463-467. [CWHM 73(1972),49]

BRECHNA, Abdul Ghafour. The "Ayars", the surgeons and the orthopedic surgeons of Khorasan at the end of the ninth century of Hejira. *Afghanistan* 26i(1973), pp. 34-37.

BÜRGEL, J. Ch. Psychosomatic methods of cures in the Islamic Middle Ages. *Humaniora Islamica* 1(1973), pp. 157-172.

DERAKHSHANI, M. The National Institute of Psychology of Iran. *Mitteilungen. Dokumentationsdienst Moderner Orient* 3ii(1974), pp. 5-8.

DIETRICH, A. Une pharmacopée arabe inconnue. *Actas IV congresso de estudos árabes e islâmicos* 1968(1971), pp. 273-280.

DIETRICH, A. Quelques observations sur la matière médicale de Dioscoride parmi les Arabes. *Convegno Internazionale ... 1969 Accademia Nazionale dei Lincei*, 1971, pp. 375-390. [CWHM 73(1972),3]

DOLS, M.W. Plague in early Islamic history. *JAOS* 94(1974), pp. 371-383.

EBIED, R.Y., YOUNG, M.J.L. A manuscript of Ḥunayn's *Masā'il fī ʿilm al-ṭibb* in the Leeds University collection. *Arabica* 21 (1974), pp. 264-269.

FURLEY, D.J., WILKIE, J.S. An Arabic translation solves some problems in Galen. ["An in arteriis natura sanguis contineatur".] *Class rev.* 86(1972), pp. 164-167. [CWHM 79 (1973), 472]

GARCÍA BALLESTER, L.; GARCÍA BALLESTER, Samsó. Tradición y novedad en el Galenismo árabe de los siglos IX y SI: la doctrina del pulso, el pronóstico y un caso de aplicación de "masaje cardíaco". *And.* 37(1972), pp. 337-351.

GURAYA, M.Y. The importance of health in Islam and in Islamic countries. *Hamdard* 14iii-iv(1971), pp. 103-122. [CWHM 74,no.756]

GHALIOUNGUI, P. Ancient Egyptian remedies and mediaeval Arabic writers. *BIFAO* 68 (1969), pp. 41-46.

HAMARNEH, Sami. Arabic medicine and its impact on teaching and practice of the healing arts in the West. *Oriente e Occidente nel medioevo*, 1971, pp. 395-429.

HAMARNEH, Sami. Development of Arabic medical therapy in the tenth century. *J.hist. med.* 27(1972), pp. 65-79

HAMARNEH, Sami. Ecology and therapeutics in medieval Arabic medicine. *Sudhoffs Archiv* 58(1974), pp. 165-185.

HAMARNEH, Sami. A history of Arabic pharmacy. *Physis* 14(1972), pp. 5-54.

HAMARNEH, Sami. Origins of Arabic drug and diet therapy. *Physis* 11(1969), pp. 267-286.

HAMARNEH, Sami. Pharmacy in medieval Islam and the history of drug addiction. *Medical history* 16(1972), pp. 226-237.

HARFOUCHE, Jamal K., ATALLAH, Bassil, HADDAD, Nadra E. Childhood accidents: an emerging health problem in developing countries. *American University of Beirut Festival book*, 1967, pp. 87-102.

HASCHMI, M.Y. Medizinische Betrachtungen bei al-Maʿarri. *Pag. storia med.* 16(1972), pp. 5-15. [CWHM 74, no. 895]

ISKANDAR, A.Z. A study of al-Samarqandī's medical writings. *Muséon* 85(1972), pp. 451-479.

JOHNSTONE, P. Tradition in Arabic medicine. *PEQ* 107(1975), pp. 23-37.

KAHHAK, Abdelkader. Un diplôme de médecin à Fès en 1832. *Bull.de la Soc.d'hist.du Maroc* 3(1970-1), pp. 23-28

KLEIN-FRANKE, F. Paracelsus Arabus. Eine Studie zur "alchemistischen Medizin" im Orient. *Medizinhist.J.* 10(1975), pp. 50-54.

KÖKMEN, E. A fantastic craniotomy - excerpt from the 17th century Turkish travelogue of Evliyâ Çelebi. Case report. *J. Neurosurg.* 37(July,1972), pp. 103-104. [CWHM 76 (1972),236]

IV PHILOSOPHY. SCIENCE

KUHNKE, L. The "doctoress" on a donkey: women health officers in nineteenth century Egypt. *Clio méd.* 9(1974), pp. 193-205. [CWHM 83,264]

KUHNKE, L. Early nineteenth century ophthalmological clinics in Egypt. *Clio med.* 7 (1972), pp. 209-214. [CWHM 77, 199]

LEVEY, M. and SOURYAL, Safwat S. Galen's "on the secrets of women" and "on the secrets of men" from the unique arabic text. *Stud. in Islam* 9(1972), pp. 1-37.

LEVEY, M. Influence of Arabic pharmacology on medieval Europe. *Oriente e Occidente nel medioevo,* 1971, pp. 431-444.

LEVEY, M. The pharmacology of Ibn Biklārish in the introduction to his Kitāb al-Mustaʿīnī. *Stud. in Islam* 6(1969), pp. 98-104.

LEVEY, M. Preventive medicine in ninth century Persia. *Studs. in Islam* 8(1971), pp. 8-16.

LEVEY, M. Theory of medicine in the eleventh century in the 'Book of adjustment of Al-Nasawī'. *Studies in Islam* 7(1970), pp. 189-204.

McVAUGH, M. The 'Humidum radicale' in thirteenth-century medicine. *Traditio* 30(1974), pp. 259-283.

McVAUGH, M. Theriac at Montpellier 1285-1325 (with an edition of the *'Questiones de tyriaca'* of William of Brescia. *Sudhoffs Archiv* 56(1972), pp. 113-144.

MALONE, Joseph J. Surgeon Colvill's fight against plague and cholera in Iraq 1868-1878. *American University of Beirut Festival book,* 1967, pp. 163-183.

MESSIHA, Khalil. Reconsiderations and origin of an Arabic medical prescription. *Ann.Islamologiques* 9(1970), pp. 123-126.

MONTAGUE, J. Blind welfare in Tunisia. *J. Blind welfare* 52(no.612, 1968), pp. 94-97.

MONTAGUE, J. Disease and public health in Tunisia: 1882-1970. *Current bibliog. African aff.* 4(1971), pp. 250-260.

MONTAGUE, J. L'organisation de la pharmacie en Tunisie au XIXe siècle. *Rev. d'hist. de la pharmacie* 21(no.219, 1973), pp. 615-621.

MONTAGUE, J. Psychiatry and mental health in Tunisia: a review of modern research. *Transcultural psychiatric research rev.* 9 (1972), pp. 42-46.

MONTAGUE, J. Notes on medical organization in nineteenth century Tunisia. *Medical history* 17i(1973), pp. 75-82.

MONTAGUE, J. The Tunisian Orthotics and Prosthetics Center. *Internat. rehabilitation rev.* 20iii(1969), pp. 9-10.

PASHA, M. Azeez. Muheet-a-azam (a great Unani pharmacopeia). A short note on the author and the book. *Bull.Ind.Inst.Hist. Medicine* 4(1974), pp. 19-25.

PERLMANN, M. Notes on the position of Jewish physicians in medieval Muslim countries. *In memoriam S.M. Stern* (Israel Or. studies, II, 1972), pp. 315-319.

RADBILL, S.X. The first treatise of pediatrics. *Amer. J. dis. child.* 122(1971), pp. 369-376. [CWHM 74,no.1350]

RONCHI, V. L'influenza dell'ottica araba sulla cultura dell'occidente nel medioevo. *Oriente e Occidente nel medioevo,* 1971, pp. 453-475.

SAMSÓ, J. En torno al "Collar de la paloma" y la medicina. *And.* 40(1975), pp. 213-219.

SCHIPPERGES, H. Zum Bildungsweg eines arabischen Arztes. *Orvostört.Közl.* 60-61 (1971), pp. 13-31. [CWHM 72, 85]

SCHMUCKER, W. Ein Beitrag zur Indo-Arabischen Arzneimittelkunde und Geistesgeschichte. *ZDMG* 125(1975), pp. 66-98.

SIDDIQI, M.Z. Arabian medicine in India. *J. Ganganatha Jha Kendriya Sanskrit Vidyapeetha* 27(1971), pp. 151-166.

SUBBA REDDY, D.V. The origins and growth of indigenous Unani medical literature in medieval India. *Indian J.hist.med.* 16(1969), pp. 20-25. [CWHM 64]

SUBLET, J. La peste prise aux rêts de la jurisprudence: le traité d'Ibn Ḥağar al-ʿAsqalānī sur la peste. *SI* 33(1971), pp. 141-149.

TERZIOĞLU, Arslan. Mittelalterliche islamische Krankenhäuser. Unter Berücksichtigung der psychiatrischen Krankenpflege sowie ihre Einflüsse auf die abendländischen Hospitäler. *Annales Univ. Ankara* 13(1974), pp. 47-76.

TRITTON, A.S. The healing art and the limits of change in nature according to Ibn Hazm. *BSOAS* 35(1972), pp. 128-133

ULLMANN, M. Ein Fragment des *Kitāb al-Malakī* von al-Mağūsī. *Der Islam* 52(1975), pp. 109-111.

ULLMANN, Manfred. Die Schrift des Badīġūras über die Ersatzdrogen. *Der Islam* 50(1973), pp. 230-248.

VAJDA, G. Quelques mots sur la version arabe d'un ouvrage médical turc-ottoman du XVIIe siècle. *Acta Or. Acad. Sci. Hung.* 27(1973), pp. 345-349.

VERMA, R.L. The growth of Greco-Arabian medicine in medieval India. *Ind. J. hist. sci.* 5(1970), pp. 347-363.

VERMA, R.L., KESWANI, N.H. The physiological concepts of *ūnānī* medicine. *The science of medicine and physiological concepts in Ancient and Medieval India,* ed. N.H. Keswani, 1974, pp. 145-163.

IV PHILOSOPHY. SCIENCE

VERMA, R.L., KESWANI, N.H. *Unānī* medicine in medieval India - its teachers and texts. *The science of medicine and physiological concepts in Ancient and Medieval India*, ed. N.H. Keswani, 1974, pp. 127-142.

ZIMMERMANN, F.W. The chronology of Isḥāq Ibn Ḥunayn's *Ta'rīḫ al-aṭibba'*. *Arabica* 21 (1974), pp. 324-330.

Un Diplôme de Médecin Marocain à Fès en 1832. *ROMM* 7(1970), pp. 195-210.

See also II. a. 5. Belguedj

See also VI. a. McLaren.

See also IV. c. 3. Hamarneh.

See also VI. d. Livingston.

See also IX. e. Falina.

See also IX. m. Spiridonov.

See also XV. c. Huard, Sonolet.

See also XXIX. f. Kreiser.

See also XXXI. e. Salim.

See also XXXI. h. Barbarossa, Bartolomei.

See also XXXII. n. Acharya.

See also XXXV. a. Schipperges.

V ART

a FINE ART: GENERAL

BALIC, Smail. Österreich und das islamische Kulturerbe. *Österreichische Osthefte* 15(1973), pp. 275-282.

BERNUS, Mlle. Arts de l'Islam - arts figuratifs. *Archeologia* (Paris) 41(1971), pp. 24-30.

BOUROUIBA, R. Les représentations figurées dans l'art h'ammadide. *RHCM* 12 (1974), pp. 7-23.

BURCKHARDT, T. Arab or Islamic art? *Stud. comp. religion* 5(1971), pp. 16-25.

BURCKHARDT, T. Caractères pérennes de l'art Arabe. *Cah. d'hist. mondiale* 14(1972), pp. 899-912.

BURCKHARDT, T. Perennial values in Islamic art. *Al-Abhath* 20i(1967), pp. 1-11.

FARUQI, Isma'il R. al-. Misconceptions of the nature of Islamic art. *Islam and the modern age* 1 i (1970), pp. 29-49.

FARUQI, Isma'il R. al-. On the nature of the work of art in Islam. *Islam and the modern age* 1 ii (1970), pp. 68-81.

FERNÁNDEZ PUERTAS, A. El lazo de ocho occidental o Andaluz. Su trazado, canon proporcional, series y petrones. *And.* 40 (1975), pp. 199-203.

GRABAR, O. Histoire de l'art et archéologie islamiques. État de la question. *Maghreb Machrek* 67(1975), pp. 68-80.

GRABAR, O. New methods and approaches in Islamic art and archaeology. *Proc.27th Int.Cong.Or.1967* (1971), p. 277.

JONES, D.; MICHELL, G. Squinches and pendentives: problems and definitions. *AARP* 1(1972), pp. 9-25.

MADDEN, E.H. Some characteristics of Islamic art. *J.aesthetics art criticism* 33 (1974-5), pp. 423-430.

MARCHAL, H. Arts de l'Islam. *Rev. Louvre Musées France* 21 (1971), pp. 219-224.

MARCHAL, H. Introduction aux arts de l'Islam. *Archeologia* (Paris) 41(1971), pp. 16-23.

MASON, J.P. Structural congruities in the Arab genealogical form and the arabesque motif. *MW* 65(1975), pp. 21-38.

NASR, Seyyed Hossein. The significance of the void in the art and architecture of Islam. *IQ* 16(1973), pp. 115-120.

PAPADOPOULO, A. Pour une esthétique de l'art musulman. *AARP* 5(1974), pp. 50-59.

PARET, Rudi. Das islamische Bilderverbot und die Schia (Nachtrag). *ZDMG* 120 (1970), pp. 271-273.

PUGACHENKOVA, G.A. K izucheniyu istorii iskusstva narodov, stran i istoriko-kul'turnykh regionov Blizhnego i Srednego Vostoka. (The study of the history of arts of the peoples, countries, and historico-cultural regions of the Near and Middle East.) *NAA* 1973(1), pp. 122-127.

QURESHI, I.H. Muslim art. *Al-Abhath* 20iii(1967), pp. 17-28.

ROSEN-AYALON, M. Further considerations pertaining to Umayyad art. *Israel exploration J.* 23(1973), pp. 92-100.

ROUX, J.P. Le taureau sauvage maîtrisé. Recherches sur l'iconographie médiévale du Proche-Orient. *Syria* 48 (1971), pp. 187-201.

SALMAN, Isa. Islam and figurative art. *Sumer* 25(1969), pp. 59-96.

VLAS BORRELLI, L. Proposte per un'attività di restauro nello Yemen. *Bollettine d'arte*, ser.V, 59(1974), pp. 186-196.

Islamic pattern. *AARP* 1(1972), pp. 1-8.

See also II. a. 1. Fārūqī.

See also VII. a. Mason.

Influences and parallels

BERNARD, C. Some aspects of Delacroix's orientalism. *Bull.Cleveland Mus.Art* 58 (1971), pp. 123-127

BERNASCONI, D. Mythologie d'Abd el-Kader dans l'iconographie française au XIXe siècle. *Gaz. beaux-arts* 77 (1971), pp. 51-62.

BOULLATA, Kamal. Classical Arab art and modern European painting: a study in affinities. *MW* 63(1973), pp. 1-14.

BOUROUIBA, Rachid. L'influence de l'art sanhadjien du Maghrib sur l'art des Normands de Sicile. *Actes I. Cong. et. cult. mediterr. d'infl. arabo-berb.*, 1973, pp. 182-198.

CARSWELL, J. East and West: a study in aesthetic contrasts (part II). The illustrations to Sir Thomas Herbert's travel writings. *AARP* 3(1973), pp. 82-96.

CARSWELL, J. Eastern and western influence on art of the seventeenth century in Iran. *Memorial vol. Vth Internat. Cong. Iranian Art and Archaeology*, 1972, Vol. 2, pp. 277-281.

CERULLI, E. Art et technique de la Perse en Afrique orientale. *Acta Iranica* 1(1974), pp. 203-216.

ETTINGHAUSEN, R. Chinese representations of Central Asian Turks. *Beiträge zur Kunstgeschichte Asiens. In memoriam E. Diez*, 1963, pp. 208-222

FORSTNER, M. Zur Madonna mit der Šahāda. *ZDMG* 122(1972), pp. 102-107.

GARÍN Y ORTIZ DE TARANCO, F.M. Prefiguración oriental del gotico abovedado hispano-levantino. *BAEO* 9(1973), pp. 173-179.

GARTON, T. Islamic elements in early Romanesque sculpture in Apulia. *AARP* 4(1973), pp. 100-116.

GRABAR, O. Survivances classiques dans l'art de l'Islam. *Ann.arch.arabes syriennes* 21(1971), pp. 371-380.

GUILMAIN, J. A note on the "arabesques" in the Diatessaron, Florence, Bibl. Laur., Orient 81. *Art bull.* 55(1973), pp. 38-39.

HOMAYOUN, Gholamali. Ein Überblick über die Einflüsse der iranischen Architektur auf die europäische. *Memorial vol. Vth Internat. Cong. Iranian Art and Archaeology*, 1972, Vol. 2, pp. 325-352.

INGRAMS, R.A. Reubens and Persia. *Burlington mag.* 116(no.853, 1974), pp. 190-197.

KIEL, M. Armenian and Ottoman influences on a group of village churches in North-Eastern Macedonia. *Rev. ét. arm.* N.S.8(1971), pp. 267-282.

LASSUS, J. Éléments greco-romains et byzantins dans l'art islamique. *Ann.arch. arabes syriennes* 21(1971), pp. 387-398.

LORANDI, M. I modelli orientali dei castelli federiciani: i Qasr omayyadi e la loro influenza nella genesi dell'architettura sveva. *Bollettino d'arte* 58(1973), pp. 9-26.

NADERZAD, B. Louis XIV, La Boulaye et l'exotisme persan. *Gaz.beaux arts* 79 (1972), pp. 29-38

ORGEL, S. Inigo Jones' Persian entertainment. *AARP* 2(1972), pp. 59-69.

OTT, C. Influência arábica na arte baiana. *Afro-Asia* 10-11 (1970), pp. 35-42.

OTTO-DORN, K. Darstellungen des turco-chinesischen Tierzyklus in der islamischen Kunst. *Beiträge zur Kunstgeschichte Asiens. In memoriam E. Diez*, 1963, pp. 131-165

PAVÓN MALDONADO, B. Influjos occidentales en el Arte del Califato de Córdoba. *And.* 33 (1968), pp. 205-220.

POPE, A.U. Possible Iranian contributions to the beginning of Gothic architecture. *Beiträge zur Kunstgeschichte Asiens. In memoriam E. Diez*, 1963, pp. 1-29

RICE, D.T. Decorations in the Seljukid style in the Church of Saint Sophia of Trebizond. *Beiträge zur Kunstgeschichte Asiens. In memoriam E. Diez*, 1963, pp. 87-120

RICE, D.T. Iranian elements in English art of the eleventh and twelfth centuries. *Bull. Asia Inst., Pahlavi Univ.*, 1 (1969), pp. 27-35.

WATSON, K. French romanesque and Islam. Influences from al-Andalus on architectural decoration. *AARP* 2(1972), pp. 1-27.

See also V. c. *North Africa.*

See also V. c. *Syria* Rogers

See also VIII. a. *Iran* Lomtatidze et al.

Museums

ATIL, Esin. Ottoman art at the Freer Gallery. *Sanat tarihi yıllığı* 4(1970-1), pp. 185-207

V ART

BRISCH, K. Recent acquisitions of the Museum of Islamic art. *Apollo* 101(1975), pp. 422-423.

COSTA, P. Il Museo Archeologico Nazionale dello Yemen. *Levante* 18iv(1971), pp. 5-35

DENNY, W.B. Some Islamic objects in the Gardner Museum. *Fenway court* (Isabella Stewart Gardner Museum), *Annual report* 1971, pp. 3-13.

DESTREE, A. L'art islamique de Perse dans les collections belges. Note à propos d'une récente exposition aux Musées Royaux d'Art et d'Histoire. *Corresp. d'Orient. Etudes* 17-18(1970), pp. 105-114.

ETTINGHAUSEN, R. Almost one hundred years ago. *Islamic art in the Metropolitan Museum of Art*, ed. R. Ettinghausen, 1972, pp. 1-8.

HARDIE, P. Oriental art for occidental eyes. *Apollo* 99(no.147, 1974), pp. 362-367.

KOŞAY, Hâmit Zübeyir. Die türkischen Museen in der republikanischen Ära. *Cultura Turcica* 8-10(1971-73), pp. 86-109.

MEKHITARIAN, Arpag. L'art musulman aux Musées Royaux d'Art et d'Histoire, Bruxelles. *Proc.27th Int.Cong.Or.1967* (1971), pp. 260-261.

MOTAMEDI, H. The Museum of Islamic art in Ghazni. *Afghanistan* 24iv(1972), pp. 11-13

PAL, Prataditya. The Palevsky-Heeramaneck collection of Islamic art. *Apollo* 101 (1975), pp. 104-107.

SCANLON, G.T. Islamic art at the Orangerie. *Oriental Art* 18(1) 1972, pp. 94-96

SOURDEL-THOMINE, J. A propos de quelques catalogues de musées et expositions. *REI* 40(1972), pp. 393-397.

SHAMSUDDIN. The Salar Jung museum. *Indo-Asian culture* 20iii(1971), pp. 49-50

YOUNG, M.S. Half the world is Isfahan. *Apollo* 98(no.141, 1973), pp. 396-398.

Islamic art. *Met. Mus. Art Bull.* 31i (1975), pp. 1-53.

Islamic art at the Los Angeles County Museum of Art. *Arts of Asia* 4ii(1974), pp. 35-41.

Qatar gets a new museum. *Apollo* 101(1975), p. 298.

Nuove acquisizioni del Museo Nazionale d'Arte Orientale. Arte islamica. *Bollettino d'arte* 57(1972), pp. 249-253; 58(1973), pp. 244-247.

The year in review for 1971 [catalogue]. *Bull.Cleveland Mus.Art* 59i(1972), pp. 3-47

Exhibitions

LATHAM, J.D. The World of Islam Festival programme. *BSMES bull.* 2(1975), pp. 94-99.

MARCHAL, H. Orangerie des Tuileries. Arts de l'Islam. *Rev. du Louvre* 21(1971), pp. 219-224.

PARROT, A. Une exposition des arts de l'Islam à Paris. *Archeologia* (Paris) 41 (1971), pp. 6-7.

ROUX, J.P. Les arts de l'Islam et l'exposition de l'Orangerie. *Archeologia* (Paris) 41(1971), pp. 8-15.

SUTTON, D. Pattern and profundity: the Islamic exhibition at the Orangerie. *Apollo* 94(n.s. 116, 1971), pp. 270-276.

See also V. o. Gallotti Minola.

b FINE ART: LOCAL FORMS

Afghanistan

BRESHNA, A.G. A glance at the history of fine arts in Afghanistan. *Afghanistan* 25 iii (1972), pp. 11-21.

FRIEDMAN, A.L. The Handicrafts of Afghanistan. *Afghanistan* 25ii(1972), pp. 11-21.

SENGUPTA, S. India helps Afghanistan in preserving her heritage. *Afghanistan* 26iii(1973), pp. 23-33.

SHAHRANI, Enayatullah. The history of fine arts in Afghanistan. *Afghanistan* 26iii(1973), pp. 17-22.

See V. b. *Central Asia.* Rowland.

See VIII. a. *Afghanistan.* Taddei.

Central Asia. Caucasus

BRENTJES, B. Zur frühen Kunst der Nomadenvölker Zentralasiens. Überlegungen und Hypothesen. *Asien, Afrika, Lateinamerika* 2 (1974), pp. 614-624.

GRUBE, E.J. The decorative arts of Central Asia in the Timurid period. *Afghanistan* 24ii-iii(1971), pp. 60-75

LELEKOV, L.A. O nekotorykh iranskikh elementakh v iskusstve drevney Rusi. *Iskusstvo i arkheologiya Irana*, 1971, pp. 183-189

MESHKERIS, V.A. Nekotorye obshchie cherty v rannesrednevekovom iskusstve Sredney Azii i sopredel'nykh stran. *Iskusstvo i arkheologiya Irana*, 1971, pp. 216-226

REMPEL', L.I. Iskusstvo Rusi i Vostok kak istoriko-kul'turnaya i khudozhestvennaya problema. *Iskusstvo i arkheologiya Irana*, 1971, pp. 285-295

ROWLAND, B. Iranian elements in the art of Afghanistan and central Asia: The formation of a central Asian style. *Memorial vol. Vth Internat. Cong. Iranian Art and Archaeology*, 1972, Vol. 2, pp. 379-382.

V ART

Egypt

GRABAR, O. Imperial and urban art in Islam: the subject matter of Fatimid art. *Colloque international sur l'histoire du Caire,* 1969, pp. 173-189.

India

BANERJI, Adris. Art of the eighteenth century Bengal. *Q.rev.hist.stud.* 14 (1974-5), pp. 96-105.

MATE, M.S. History of art. *Bull.Deccan Coll. Res.Inst.* 33(1973), pp. 117-152.

MORLEY, G. On applied arts of India in Bharat Kala Bhavan. *Chhavi: golden jubilee vol.,* 1971, pp. 107-129.

NEOG, Maheswar. The so-called Mughal head-gear in art and in use in Assam. *J.Univ. Gauhati: arts* 20i(1969), pp. 17-24.

SILVA, M.M. de C. Obras de arte indo-portuguesa de carácter mongólico. *Garcia de Orta,* núm. especial 1972, pp. 527-533.

SKELTON, R. A decorative motif in Mughal art. *Aspects of Indian art,* ed. Pratapaditya Pal, 1972, pp. 147-152.

YOUNG, M.Y. A flower from every meadow. *Apollo* 97(no.134,1973), pp. 429-431.

Mughal painting. *Marg* 25iv(1972), pp. 61-63.

Iran

ASADULLAEVA, S.Kh. Proizvedeniya iranskikh masterov v Sobranii Gosudarstvennogo Muzeya Iskusstv im. R. Mustafaeva. *Iskusstvo i arkheologiya Irana,* 1971, pp. 41-49

BAER, E. Notes on the formation of Iranian imagery in the thirteenth century. *Art of Iran and Anatolia ...* ed. W. Watson, 1974, pp. 96-109.

COOPER, L.H. Genius and invention - artists and artisans of Iran. *Apollo* 97(no. 133, 1973), pp. 296-303.

ETTINGHAUSEN, R. Stylistic tendencies at the time of Shah ʿAbbas. *Iranian stud.* 7iii-iv (1974), pp. 593-628.

GRABAR, O. Sasanian and Islamic art through the ages. *Apollo* 93(no.110, 1971), pp. 255-263.

HOFFMANN, D. Iran, hommes du vent, gens de terre. *Rev. Louvre Musées France* 21(1971), pp. 225-226.

MELIKIAN-CHIRVANI, A.S. The westward progress of Khorasanian culture under the Seljuks. *Art of Iran and Anatolia ...* ed. W. Watson, 1974, pp. 110-126.

NASR, Seyyed Hossein. The significance of the void in the art and architecture of Islamic Persia. *J. Reg. Cult. Inst.* 5(1972), pp. 121-128.

NASR, Seyyed Hossein. Sacred art in Persian culture. *Studies in art and literature of the Near East in honor of R. Ettinghausen,* 1974, pp. 161-179.

POPE, A.U. Art as an essential of Iranian history. *Acta Iranica* 1(1974), pp. 153-162.

SHAYEGAN, Darius. Culture and art in Iran: from the past into the future. *Cultures* 1iv(1974), pp. 53-74.

ZOKA, Yahya. Iranian crafts and life. *J. Reg. Cult. Inst.* 4(1971), pp. 35-47.

See also V. b. *North Africa.* Cerulli.

See V. b. *Turkey.* Yetkin.

See also XXIX. a. Schnyder.

See also XXXI. a. Pope.

See also XXXIX. b. Melikian-Chirvani.

Iraq

HAMEED, Abdul Aziz. The origin and characteristics of Samarra's bevelled style. *Sumer* 22 (1966), pp. 83-99.

North Africa

BENCHEIKH, Naceur. Mythes, réalités et significations de l'activité picturale en Tunisie. *Ann.Afr.nord* 12(1973), pp. 151-168.

BOUHDIBA, A. Contemporary Tunisian crafts. *Cultures* 2iii(1975), pp. 119-135.

CERULLI, E. Art et technique de la Perse en Afrique orientale. *Commémoration Cyrus. Hommage universel,* I, 1974, pp. 203-216.

GUÉRARD, M. L'art du Maghreb à l'exposition de l'Orangerie des Tuileries. *Archeologia* (Paris) 41(1971), pp. 31-37.

Spain

PAVÓN, B. Arte mozárabe y arte mudéjar en Toledo: paralelismos. *BAEO* 6(1970), pp. 117-152.

PAVÓN MALDONADO, B. La formación del arte hispanomusulmán. Hacia un corpus de la ornamentación del Califato de Córdoba. *And.* 38(1973), pp. 195-242.

TERRASSE, H. Formación y fuentes del arte mudéjar toledano. *Arch.esp.art.* 43(1970), pp. 385-393.

TERRASSE, H. Influences hispaniques sur l'art hafside. *And* 34(1969), pp. 175-182.

Tunisia

See XII. f. Sugier.

Turkey

BURRILL, K.R.F. From *Gazi* state to republic: a changing scene for Turkish artists and men of letters. *Studies in art and literature of the Near East in honor of R. Ettinghausen,* 1974, pp. 239-289.

CHOEEKCHAN, Kh.A. Zametki o sovremennom iskusstve Turtzii (zhivopis', grafika, karikatura, skulptura, keramika). *NAA* 1974(5), pp. 163-168.

ESIN, E. The cosmic mountain, the tree and the auspicious bestiary in Turkish iconography. *AARP* 8(1975), pp. 34-42.

ESIN, E. The cosmic symbolism of the dracontine arch and apotropaic mask in Turkish symbolism. *AARP* 4(1973), pp. 32-51.

ETTINGHAUSEN, R. The flowering of Seljuq art. *Metrop. Mus. J.* 3(1970), pp. 113-131.

FEHERVARI, G. Some problems of Seljuq art. *Art of Iran and Anatolia* ... ed. W. Watson, 1974, pp. 1-12.

HILLENBRAND, R. Reflections on O. Aslanapa's *Turkish art and architecture. IQ* 17(1973), pp. 75-91.

KUBAN, Doǧan. Claude Cahen's "Pre-Ottoman Turkey" and some observations on Turkish city, Turkish art and architecture in Anatolia. *Anadolu sanatı araştırmaları* 2 (1970), pp. 19-30.

MAJDA, T. IV Międzynarodowy Kongres sztuki Tureckiej. (Le IVe Congrès International de l'Art Turque). *Przegląd Or.* 4(84) (1972), p. 367.

ÖNEY, Gönül. Anatolian Seljuk influence on Byzantine figural art. *Selçuklu araştırmaları dergisi* 3(1971), pp. 105-118.

ÖNEY, Gönül. Elements from ancient civilizations in Anatolian Seljuk art. *Anadolu (Anatolia)* 12 (1968), pp. 27-38.

ROUX, J.P. Turquie d'hier et d'aujourd'hui. *Objets et mondes* 13(1973), pp. 107-116.

THIERRY, S. Présence de la Turquie. Arts et traditions populaires d'Anatolie. *Objets et mondes* 13(1973), pp. 117-124.

ÜNVER, Gülbün. Flower bouquets with and without vases in the Ottoman art. *Vakıflar dergisi* 9(1971), pp. 324-326.

YETKIN, Suut K. Interaction of Turkish and Persian art. *Memorial vol. Vth Internat. Cong. Iranian Art and Archaeology,* 1972, Vol. 2, pp. 398-400.

c ARCHITECTURE

General

ANAND, Mulk Raj. Colour, form and design in Islamic architecture. *Marg* 24i(1970), pp. 13-16

ANAND, Mulk Raj. Space, time and deity: the background of Islamic architecture. *Marg* 24i(1970), pp. 5-12

BAER, E. Early Muslim architecture. *OLZ* 68(1973), pp. 117-126.

BOUROUIBA, R. Note sur les plans des mosquées. *RHCM* 10(1973), pp. 41-55.

BRETANITZKIY, L.S. O statuse i professional'nykh znaniyakh zodchikh Perednego Vostoka XI-XVI vv. (*mukhandis* - znachenie i soderzhanie termina). *NAA* 1973(6), pp. 84-96.

BRETANITZKIY, L.V. Problemy izucheniya arkhitekturnogo naslediya Perednego Vostoka epokhi feodalizma. *Iskusstvo i arkheologiya Irana,* 1971, pp. 76-85

BULATOV, M.S. U istokov arkhitekturnoy nauki srednego vostoka. (Sources of architectural science in the Middle East.) *NAA* 1973(1), pp. 92-101.

DIEM, W. Untersuchungen zu Technik und Terminologie der arabischislamischen Türschlösser. *Der Islam* 50(1973), pp. 98-156.

FINSTER, B. Zu der Neuauflage von K.A.C. Creswells "Early Muslim Architecture". *Kunst des Orients* 9(1973-4), pp. 89-98.

KEALL, E.J. Some thoughts on the early *eyvan. Near Eastern numismatics ... Studies in honor of G.C. Miles,* 1974, pp. 123-130.

MEINECKE, M. Zur Entwicklung des islamischen Architekturdekors im Mittelalter. *Der Islam* 47(1971), pp. 200-235.

RĀĜIB, Yūsuf. Les premiers monuments funéraires de l'Islam. *Ann.Islamologiques* 9 (1970), pp. 21-36.

ROGERS, J.M. The 11th century - a turning point in the architecture of the *Mashriq*? *Islamic civilization,* 1973, pp. 211-249.

Afghanistan

ANAND, Mulk Raj. The development of Islamic architecture in Afghanistan. *Marg* 24i (1970), pp. 17-46

BEHRENS, H., KLINKOTT, M. Das Ivan-Hofhaus in Afghanisch-Sistan dargestellt und beschrieben an ausgewählten Bauaufnahmen. *Archäol.Mitt.aus Iran* N.F.6(1973), pp. 231-252.

CAROE, O. The Gauhar Shah musalla (mosque) in Herat. *Asian affairs* 60(N.S.4, 1973), pp. 295-298.

V ART

CASIMIR, M., GLATZER, B. Kurzmitteilung über eine bisher unbekannte ghoridische Moschee in Badghis, Afghanistan. *Zentralasiat.Studien* 5(1971), pp. 191-197

CASIMIR, M.J. and GLATZER, B. Šāh-i Mašhad, a recently discovered madrasah of the Ghurid period in Garǧistān (Afghanistan). *East and West* 21(1971), pp. 53-68.

FISCHER, Kl. Architecture au Seistan islamique. *Afghanistan* 27i(1974), pp. 12-34.

FISCHER, K. Interrelations of Islamic architecture in Afghanistan. The remains of Afghan Seistan. Notes on the evolution of Islamic architecture in Turan, Iran and India. *Marg* 24i(1970), pp. 47-56

FISCHER, K. Types of architectural remains in the Northern parts of Afghan Seistan. *Bull. Asia Inst. Pahlavi Univ.* 2(1971), pp. 40-72.

GLATZER, B. The Madrasah of Shah-i-Mashhad in Badgis. *Afghanistan* 25 iv(1973), pp. 46-68.

HOAG, J. The tomb of Ulugh Beg and Abdu Rassaqat Ghazni, a prototype for the Taj Mahal. *Memorial vol. Vth Internat. Cong. Iranian Art and Archaeology,* 1972, Vol. 2, pp. 102-107.

KLEISS, W. Ein islamischer Vierpfeilerbau in Abaglu bei Takestan. *Archäol.Mitt.aus Iran* N.F.6(1973), pp. 273-279.

MELIKIAN-CHIRVANI, Assadullah Souren. Baba Hatem. Un chef d'oeuvre inconu d'epoque ghaznévide en Afghanistan. *Memorial vol. Vth Internat. Cong. Iranian Art and Archaeology,* 1972, Vol. 2, pp. 108-124.

MOLINE, J. The Minaret of Ǧām. *Kunst des Orients* 9(1973-4), pp. 131-148.

PARPAGLIOLO, M.T.Sh. The Bagh-i Babur. *Afghanistan* 28iii(1975), pp. 57-93.

PARPAGLIOLO SHEPHARD, M.T. Il Bagh-i Babur. Un progetto di restauro. *Veltro* 16v-vi (1972), pp. 579-597.

POUGATCHENKOVA, G.A. A l'étude des monuments Timurides d'Afghanistan. *Afghanistan* 23iii(1970), pp. 24-49.

PUGACHENKOVA, G.A., KHAKIMOV, Z.A. *Khanaka* Sheykha Sadreddina-maloizvestnyy pamyatnik timuridskogo vremeni v Afganistane. (Khanaka Sheikh Sadreddin, a little-known memorial of the Timuride Epoch in Afghanistan.) *NAA* 1972(2), pp. 140-144

REUTHER, H. Die Lehmziegelwölbungen von Gol-i Safed. Versuch einer Typologie. *Archäol.Mitt.aus Iran* N.F.6(1973), pp. 253-263.

SOURDEL-THOMINE, J. Le mausolée dit de Baba Hatim en Afghanistan. *REI* 39(1971), pp. 293-320.

ZANDER, G. L'IsMEO e i restauri di monumenti. *Veltro* 16v-vi(1972), pp. 563-578.

Africa (excluding Egypt)

BORRÁS GUALIS, G. Iglesias mudéjares de Herrera de los Navarros y El Villar de los Navarros (Zaragoza). *And.* 33 (1968), pp. 445-457.

BOUROUIBA, Rachid. Mihrabs Hammadides. *REI* 40(1972), pp. 329-342.

CHITTICK, N. The mosque at Mbuamaji and the Nabahani. *Azania* 4(1969), pp. 159-160.

DEVERDUN, G. Une étude inédite (1882) sur la grande mosquée de Kairouan. *ROMM* 7(1970), pp. 47-48.

GHARIB, R. Borj Ghazi Mustafa. *Rev. hist. maghreb.* 4(1975), pp. 221-223.

GOLVIN, L. Contribution à l'étude de l'architecture religieuse en Ifrîqiya aux XIe et XIIe siècles. *Ve Congrès International d'Arabisants et d'Islamisants. Actes.,* [1970?], pp. 225-238.

GOLVIN, L. Note sur le mot *ribât'* (terme d'architecture) et son interprétation en Occident musulman. *ROMM* 6(1969), pp. 95-101.

GOLVIN, L. Les plafonds à muqarnas de la Qal'a des Banū Hammād et leur influence possible sur l'art de la Sicile à la période normande. *ROMM* 17(1974), pp. 63-69.

LATHAM, J.D. Towns and cities of Barbary: the Andalusian influence. *IQ* 16(1973), pp. 189-204.

LÉZINE, A. Note sur la Grande Mosquée de Tunis. *CT* 18(nos. 71-72, 1970), pp. 187-191.

LÉZINE, A. Sur deux châteaux musulmans d'Ifrîqiya. *REI* 39(1971), pp. 87-103.

MARÇAIS, G. Testour et sa grande mosquée. Contribution à l'étude des andalous en Tunisie. *Recueil d'études sur les moriscos andalous en Tunisie,* préparé par M. de Epalza et R. Petit, 1973, pp. 271-284.

MOUGHTIN, J.C. The Friday mosque, Zaria City. *Savanna* 1(1972), pp. 143-163.

POINSSOT, L. Quelques édifices tunisiens du Moyen Âge et des temps modernes. *CT* 19, nos. 75-76(1971), pp. 211-222.

REVAULT, J. Aspects de l'élément andalous dans les palais et demeures de Tunis. *Recueil d'études sur les moriscos andalous en Tunisie,* préparé par M. de Epalza et R. Petit, 1973, pp. 291-303.

REVAULT, J. Dar Ben Abd Allah. *CATP* 1(1968), pp. 113-137.

REVAULT, J. Deux mîd'âs tunisoises (XVe et XVIIe siècles). *ROMM* 15-16(1973), pp. 275-290.

REVAULT, J. Une résidence Ḥafṣide: l'ʿAbdalliya à la Marsa. *CT* 19i-ii(1971), pp. 53-65.

SEBAG, P. Grands travaux à Tunis à la fin du XVIIIe siècle. *ROMM* 15-16(1973), pp. 313-321.

SMITH, G.R. A recessed *minbar* in the mosque of Simambaya. *Azania* 8(1973), pp. 154-156.

THEBERT, Y. L'utilisation de l'eau dans la Maison de la Peche à Bulla Regia. *CT* 19i-ii(1971), pp. 11-17.

ZBISS, Slimane-Mustafa. Présence espagnole à Tunis. *Recueil d'études sur les moriscos andalous en Tunisie,* préparé par M. de Epalza et R. Petit, 1973, pp. 267-270.

Arabia

COSTA, P. La Moschea Grande di Ṣan'ā'. *AION* 34(N.S.24, 1974), pp. 487-506.

DOE, B. and SERJEANT, R.B. A fortified tower-house in Wādī Jirdān (Wāḥidī sultanate). *BSOAS* 38(1975), pp. 1-23, 276-295.

GALDIERI, E. A masterpiece of Omani 17th century architecture. The palace of Imam Bilarab bin Sultan al-Yaaraba at Jabrin. *J.Oman stud.* 1(1975), pp. 167-179.

LEWCOCK, R.B., SMITH, G.R. Three medieval mosques in the Yemen. *Oriental art* 20 (1974), pp. 75-86, 192-203.

LEWCOCK, R., SMITH, G.R. Two early mosques in the Yemen: a preliminary report. *AARP* 4(1973), pp. 117-130.

STRIKA, V. Studi saudiani. (I. Le moschee di Gedda. II. Aspetti giuridici delle attività archeologiche.) *AION* 35(N.S.25, 1975), pp. 555-585.

See also XXII. b. Fayein.

Central Asia. Caucasus

ASANOV, A.A. Mechet' Bibi-Khanym. (Kratkaya kharakteristika konstruktziy i perspektivy ikh ukrepleniya.) *Iz istorii iskusstva velikogo goroda. (K 2500-letiyu Samarkanda.),* 1972, pp. 119-160.

BARTOL'D, V.V. "V.V. Bartol'd's article *O Pogrebenii Timura* ("The burial of Tīmūr"), translated by J.M. Rogers." *Iran* 12(1974), pp. 65-87.

BASITKHAROVA, Z.B. Sposoby postroeniya nekotorykh girikhov v pamyatnikakh XIV-XVII vv. *Iz istorii iskusstva veligogo goroda. (K 2500-letiyu Samarkanda.),* 1972, pp. 161-169.

BORODINA, I.F. Mavzoley Astana-Baba. *Arkhitekturnoe nasledstvo* 20(1972), pp. 162-168.

BRENTJES, B. Bemerkungen zur historischen Stellung der seldschukischen Architektur in Mittelasien. *Asien in Vergangenheit und Gegenwart,* 1974, pp. 347-354.

BRETANITSKY, L.S. The Shirvanshah palace in Baku, Azerbaijan. *Archaeology* 26 (1973), pp. 163-169.

BULATOV, M.S. Arochno-svodchatye formy v zodchestve srednevekovogo Samarkanda. *Iz istorii iskusstva velikogo goroda. (K 2500-letiyu Samarkanda.),* 1972, pp. 53-93.

KHAN-MAGOMEDOV, S.O. Vorota Derbenta. *Arkhitekturnoe nasledstvo* 20(1972), pp. 126-141.

MAN'KOVSKAYA, L.Yu. Novoe v izuchenii Mecheti Bibi-Khanym (po rabotam 1967 g.). *Iz istorii iskusstva velikogo goroda. (K 2500-letiyu Samarkanda.),* 1972, pp. 94-118.

PALIMPSESTOVA, T.B., RUNICH, A.P. O essentukiyskikh mavzoleyakh i stavke Uzbek-Khana. (Sur les mausolées d'Essentouki et le quartier général d'Ouzbek-Khan.) *Sov. arkh.* 1974(2), pp. 229-239.

REMPEL', L.I. Ob otrazhenii obrazov sogdiyskogo iskusstva v Islame. (K voprosu o kul'takh Shakhi-Zinda, Khazret-Khyzra i Khodzha-Daniyara v Samarkande.) *Iz istorii iskusstva velikogo goroda. (K 2500-letiyu Samarkanda.),* 1972, pp. 36-52.

SCARCIA, G. Neoclassicismo azerbaigiano: 'San Taddeo' e 'Isḥāq-Paša'. *Annali Fac. Ling. Lett. stran. di Ca' Foscari (serie orientale)* 3(1972), pp. 167-172.

TZKITISHVILI, O.V. Voprosu o kharaktere vvutrenney zastroyki nekotorykh shakhristanov Sredney Azii i Madiny al-Mansura. *Gruzinskoe istochnikovedenie* III, 1971, pp. 52-58.

Egypt

ABD AR-RAZIQ, Ahmed. Trois fondations féminines dans l'Égypte mamlouke. *REI* 41(1973), pp. 95-126.

FATHY, Hassan. The *Qa'a* of the Cairene Arab house, its development and some new usages for its design concepts. *Colloque international sur l'histoire du Caire,* 1969, pp. 135-152.

GARCIN, J.C. Remarques sur un plan topographique de la Grande Mosquée de Qûs. *Ann.Islamologiques* 9(1970), pp. 97-108.

HUMPHREYS, R.S. The expressive intent of the Mamluk architecture of Cairo: a preliminary essay. *SI* 35(1972), pp. 69-119.

IBRAHIM, Laila A. Four Cairene Miḥrābs and their dating. *Kunst des Orients* 7i (1970-1), pp. 30-39.

KESSLER, Chr. Funerary architecture within the city. *Colloque international sur l'histoire du Caire,* 1969, pp. 257-267.

KUBIAK, W., SCANLON, G.T. Fustat: re-dating Bahgat's houses and the aqueduct. *AARP* 4(1973), pp. 138-148.

LÉZINE, A., ABDUL TAWAB, A.R. Introduction à l'étude des maisons anciennes de Rosette. *Ann. Islamologiques* 10(1972), pp. 149-205.

LÉZINE, A. Persistance de traditions pré-islamiques dans l'architecture domestique de l'Égypte musulmane. *Annales islamol.* 11(1972), pp. 1-22.

LÉZINE, A. La protection contre la chaleur dans l'architecture musulmane d'Égypte. *BEO* 24(1971), pp. 7-17.

LÉZINE, A. Les salles nobles des palais mamelouks. *Ann. Islamologiques* 10(1972), pp. 63-148.

MISIOROWSKI, A., SIARKEWICZ. The constructional and conservation problems of the Ameer Qurqumas complex, Cairo. *Ochrona zabytków* 2(105) XXVII(1974), pp. 103-115.

MISIOROWSKI, A. Polish restoration work on the al-Amir al-Kabir complex in Cairo. *Africana bull.* 19(1974), pp. 9-30.

MUHAMMAD, Ghazi Rajab. The minaret of Ibn Tulun: its construction and description. *Sumer* 23 (1967), pp. 83-96.

RĀGIB, Yūsuf. Le mausolée de Yūnus al-Sa'dī est-il celui de Badr al-Ǧamālī? *Arabica* 20(1973), pp. 305-307.

RĀGIB, Yūsuf. Sur deux monuments funéraires du cimetière d'al-Qarāfa al-Kubrā au Caire. *Ann. islamologiques* 12(1974), pp. 67-84.

RĀGIB, Yūsuf. Sur un groupe de mausolées du cimetière du Caire. *REI* 40(1972), pp. 189-195.

RAYMOND, A. Les constructions de l'émir 'Abd al-Raḥmān Kathudā au Caire. *Annales islamol.* 11(1972), pp. 235-251.

ROGERS, J.M. Seljuk influence on the monuments of Cairo. *Kunst des Orients* 7i(1970-1), pp. 40-68.

WILLIAMS, J.A. The monuments of Ottoman Cairo. *Colloque international sur l'histoire du Caire,* 1969, pp. 453-463.

Europe

BEĆIRBEGOVIĆ, M. Prosvjetni objekti islamske arhitekture u Bosni i Hercegovini. (Edifices d'instruction de l'architecture islamique en Bosnie-Herzegovine.) *POF* 20-21(1970-71), pp. 223-364.

BOŠKOVIĆ, Dj. Quelques observations sur l'architecture musulmane en Yougoslavie. *Mélanges Mansel,* 1974, pp. 691-694.

ČELIĆ, Džemal, JADRIĆ, R. i REDŽIĆ, Husref. Restauracija i revitalizacija središnjeg dijela Sarajevske čaršije. (Restauration et revivification de la partie centrale du vieux bazar de Sarajevo.) *Nase starine* 13(1972), pp. 135-148.

DURIĆ-ZAMALO, Divna. Prilog poznavanju beogradskih džamija. (Beilage zur Kenntnis von Belgrader Moscheen.) *Prilozi Or.Fil. Ist.* 14-15(1964-5), pp. 123-139

FRYZEŁ, T. Relikty muzułmańskiej przeszłości Konstancy. (Les restes du passé musulman à Constanze.) *Przeglad or.* 1(81, 1972), pp. 66-68

GERŐ, Gy. The question of school and master in the study of the history of Muslim architecture in Hungary. *The Middle East; studies in honour of J. Germanus,* 1974, pp. 189-199.

KIEL, M. Some early Ottoman monuments in Bulgarian Thrace. *Belleten TTK* 38(no.152, 1974), pp. 635-654.

KORNRUMPF, H.J. Zum Alter des Demirbaba-Tekke bei Isperich (Bulgarien). *Südostforschungen* 31(1972), pp. 337-339.

MUJEZINOVIĆ, Mehmed, TIHIĆ, Smail. Ferhadija džamija u Sarajevu. (Die Ferhad-Bey-Moschee in Sarajevo.) *Nase starine* 11(1967), pp. 59-66.

STANIĆ, R., SANDŽAKTAR, M. Konservacija Karađoz-Begwe medrese u Mostaru. (Die Wiederherstellungensarbeiten an der Medresse der Karadjoz-Beg in Mostar.) *Naše starine* 11(1967), pp. 87-100.

TIHIĆ, Smail. Hadžimuratovića daira i Gazihusrevbegov hamam u Sarajevu u novoj funkciji. (La "daira" Hadži-Muratovic et le hammam Gazi-Husrevbey à Sarajevo en fonction nouvelle.) *Naše starine* 11 (1967), pp. 169-174.

See also VI. c. Terzioğlu.

India. Pakistan

ASHFAQUE, S.M. The grand mosque of Banbhore. *Pak.archaeology* 6(1969), pp. 182-209.

BANERJI, Adris. Monuments of Murshidabad District. *Yisva-bharati Q.* 38(1972-3), pp. 13-24.

BURTON-PAGE, J. Indo-islamic architecture: a commentary on some false assumptions. *AARP* 6(1974), pp. 14-21.

CHAGHATAI, M. Abdullah. A fugitive architect. *Afghanistan* 23i(1970), pp. 28-28.

DAVAR, Satish. Imperial workshops at Fatehpur Sikri: the royal kitchen. *AARP* 5(1974), pp. 28-41.

DESAI, Z.A. The Indo-Islamic architecture of Bihar. *IC* 46(1972), pp. 17-38

DESAI, Z.A. The Indo-Islamic architecture of Bihar. *Indo-Iranica* 25iii-iv(1972), pp. 118-143.

DHAKY, M.A. The minarets of the Hilāl Khān Qāẓi Mosque, Dholka. *JAS, Calcutta* 14 (1972), pp. 18-24.

V ART

DIGBY, S. The tomb of Buhlūl Lōdī. *BSOAS* 38(1975), pp. 550-561.

HAMID ALI, M., KHAN, Ahmad Nabi. The necropolis of the Beglars at Miyan Wahyun, Hyderabad (Sind). *Pak.archaeology* 7(1970-71), pp. 135-149.

HASAN, S.M. The impact of Iran on the architecture of India and Pakistan. *J. Reg. Cult. Inst.* 4(1971), pp. 113-129.

HUSAIN, A.B.M. The date of the Stonecutters' Masjid at Fathpur - Sikri. *JAS Pakistan* 15(1970), pp. 185-190.

HUSAIN, A.B.M. The twin minaret of the Mosques in the sub-continent. *Rajshahi Univ. stud.* 5(1973), pp. 1-4.

JOSHI, M.C. Some Nagari inscriptions on the Qutb Minar. *Medieval India* 2(1972), pp. 3-7.

KANWAR, H.I.S. Geography of the Taj. *Indo Asian culture* 20i(1971), pp. 36-46.

KANWAR, H.I.S. Harmonious proportions of the Taj Mahal. *IC* 49(1975), pp. 1-21.

KANWAR, H.I.S. Origin and evolution of the design of the Charbagh garden. *IC* 48(1974), pp. 105-117.

KANWAR, H.I.S. The site of the Taj Mahal, Agra. *IC* 49(1975), pp. 195-205.

KANWAR, H.I.S. Subterranean chambers of the Taj Mahal. *IC* 48(1974), pp. 159-175.

KANWAR, H.I.S. Ustad Ahmad Lahori. *IC* 48 (1974), pp. 11-32.

KHAN, Ahmad Nabi. Conservation of the Hiran Minar and Baradari at Sheikhpura. *Pak. archaeology* 6(1969), pp. 236-250.

KHAN, Ahmad Nabi. The mausoleum of Šaih 'Alā' al-Dīn at Pākpatan (Punjāb). A significant example of the Tugluq style of architecture. *East and West* N.S.24 (1974), pp. 311-326.

KHAN, Muhammad Wali Ullah. Khan-e-Daurans and Bahadar Khans and their tombs. *J. res.(humanities)* 6i(1971), pp. 79-92.

MEISTER, M.W. The "Two-and-a-half-day" mosque. *Oriental Art* 18(1) 1972, pp. 57-63

NATH, R. Bagh-i-Gul-Afshan of Babur at Agra. *Indo-Iranica* 23iii(1970), pp. 14-21.

NATH, R. Chauburj: the tomb of Babur at Agra. *IC* 48(1974), pp. 149-158.

NATH, R. Concept of the Qutb Minar. *IC* 49(1975), pp. 43-62.

NATH, Ram. Curved-roof and bent-cornice style of the Mughals. *Medieval India* 3 (1975), pp. 198-208.

NATH, R. Depiction of animate motifs at the tomb of I'timad-ud-Daulah at Agra. *IC* 47 (1974), pp. 289-300.

NATH, R. The Diwan-i-Khas of Fatehpur Sikri: a symbol of Akbar's belief in Surya-purusa. *Q.rev.hist.stud.* 12(1972-73), pp. 197-211.

NATH, R. [Gardens of the Mughals]. *Marg* 26i(1972), pp. 9-48.

NATH, R. Invasion of the Taj-Mahal. *Q. rev.hist.stud.* 14(1974-5), pp. 83-96.

NATH, R. Mausoleum of Mariam Samani at Sikandara (Agra). *Quart. rev. hist. studs.* 10 (1970-71), pp. 73-79.

NATH, R. The Motī-Masjid of the Red Fort. *Indica* 8i(1971), pp. 19-26

NATH, R. Mysteries of Phansighar at Agra Fort. *J.Ind.hist.* 48(1970), pp. 673-690.

NATH, R. On the identification of the tomb of Muḥammad Bin Tughlaq. *Indo Iranica* 26 ii-iii(1973), pp. 93-96.

NATH, R. The stone-cutters' mosque at Fatehpur Sikri. *Lalit Kala* 16(1974), pp. 48-49.

QANUNGO, Sudhindra Nath. Significance of the fish in Lucknow architecture. *Indo-Asian culture* 20iii(1971), pp. 46-48

RIZVI, S.A.A. Mughal town planning. Fathpūr-Sikrī: a case study. *Abr-Nahrain* 15(1974-1975), pp. 99-112.

SANYAL, Hitearanjan. Regional religious architecture in Bengal. A study in the sources of origin and character. *Marg* 27 ii(1974), pp. 31-43.

SANYAL, Hitesranjan. Religious architecture in Bengal (15th-17th century): a study of the major trends. *Proc.32 Ind.hist.cong.* 1970, vol. 1, pp. 413-422.

SANYAL, Hitesranjan. Religious architecture in Bengal (15th-17th century): a study of the major trends. *J. Ind. Anthrop. Soc.* 5(1970), pp. 187-203.

SARKAR, Jagadish Narayan. Some aspects of Mughal architectural decorations. *Quart. rev. hist. stud.* 11(1971-2), pp. 211-216.

SMART, E.S. Graphic evidence for Mughal architectural plans. *AARP* 6(1974), pp. 22-23.

TAPLOO, R. The origin and development of Islamic tombs in India. *Q.rev.hist.stud.* 14(1974-5), pp. 173-182; 15i(1975-6), pp. 20-30.

Haryana heritage: medieval. *Marg* 27iv(1974), pp. 22-42.

Islamic architecture. *Marg* 25iv(1972), pp. 25-29.

Islamic architecture. *Marg* 27ii(1974), pp. 14-30.

See also XXXII. c. Troll.

V ART

Iran

ADLE, Chahryar. Le minaret du Masjed-e jâme' de Semnâ, *circa* 421-25/1030-34. *Studia Iranica* 4(1975), pp. 177-186.

ADLE, Chahryar et MELIKIAN-CHIRVANI, Assadullah Suren. Les monuments du XIe siècle du Dâmqân. *Stud. iranica* 1(1972), pp. 229-297.

ADLE, Chahryâr, Note sur le "Qabr-i Šāhruh" de Damghan. *Le monde iranien et l'Islam* II, 1974, pp. 173-186.

ARDALAN, Nader. Color in Safavid architecture: the poetic diffusion of light. *Iranian stud.* 7iii-iv(1974), pp. 164-178.

ARDALAN, Nader. Il colore nell'architettura safavidica: la diffusione metaforica della luce. *Conoscenza religiosa* 1975(3), pp. 300-308.

ASLANAPA, Oktay. Excavation for the Qeyqubadiye villas at Kayseri (1964). *J. Reg. Cult. Inst.* 1 ii(1967), pp. 7-23.

BAKHTIYAR, Ali. The Masjid Ali of Isfahan. *Bull. Asia Inst., Pahlavi Univ.* 1 (1969), pp. 1-2.

BAKHTIAR, A.A. Newly reported Buyid-Seljuk monuments in Khuzestan and Isfahan. *Memorial vol. Vth Internat. Cong. Iranian Art and Archaeology*, 1972, Vol. 2, pp. 2-14.

BAKHTIAR, Ali. The Royal Bazaar of Isfahan. *Iranian stud.* 7iii-iv(1974), pp. 320-347.

BAKHTIAR, Ali Asghar, Some unrecorded Sassanian monuments. *Proc. 27th Int. Cong. Or. 1967* (1971), pp. 259-260.

BIVAR, A.D.H. The Tomb at Resget: its architecture and inscriptions. *Memorial vol. Vth Internat. Cong. Iranian Art and Archaeology*, 1972, Vol. 2, pp. 15-23.

BORODINA, I.F. Cherty obshchnosti i razlichiya khudochestvennogo oblika inter'erov tzentricheskikh zdaniy Khorasana i Maverannakhara XIV-XV vv. *Iskusstvo i arkheologiya Irana*, 1971, pp. 65-75

BURKETT, M.E. The tower at Karat Khorassan. *Oriental art* N.S. 19(1973), pp. 43-49.

FEHÉRVÁRI, Géza. Two early mihrabs outside Shiraz. *Bull. Asia Inst., Pahlavi Univ.* 1 (1969), pp. 3-11.

GALDIERI, E. Découvertes à Masjed-e Jāme. *Proc. II. Annual Symposium on arch. res. in Iran*, 1973, pp. 267-271.

GALDIERI, E. The Masgid-i Guma Isfahan: an architectural facade of the 3rd century H. *AARP* 6(1974), pp. 24-34.

GALDIERI, E. Les palais d'Isfahan. *Iranian stud.* 7iii-iv(1974), pp. 380-405.

GALDIERI, Eugenio. Two building phases of the time of Šāh ʿAbbas I in the Maydān-i Šāh of Isfahan - Preliminary note. *East and West* 20(1970), pp. 60-69.

GOLOMBEK, L.V. Anatomy of a mosque -- the *Masjid -i Shāh* of Isfahān. *Iranian civilization and culture*, ed. C.J. Adams, 1972, pp. 5-14.

GOLOMBEK, L. The chronology of Turbat-i Shaikh Jām. *Iran* 9 (1971), pp. 27-44.

GOLOMBEK, L. A thirteenth century funerary mosque at Turbat-i Shaykh Jam. *Bull. Asia Inst., Pahlavi Univ.* 1 (1969), pp. 13-26.

GULICK, J. Private life and public face: cultural continuities in the domestic architecture of Isfahan. *Iranian stud.* 7iii-iv (1974), pp. 629-651.

HAMBLY, G. A note on Sulṭānīyeh/Sulṭānābād in the early 19th century. *AARP* 2(1972), pp. 89-98.

HILLENBRAND, R. The development of Saljuq mausolea in Iran. *Art of Iran and Anatolia* ... ed. W. Watson, 1974, pp. 40-59.

HILLENRAND, R. Saljūq monuments in Iran. *Oriental Art* 18(1) 1972, pp. 64-77

HILLENBRAND, R. Saljūq monuments in Iran: II - The "Pīr" Mausoleum at Tākistān. *Iran* 10(1972), pp. 45-55

HOMAYOUN, Gholamali. Die Felsarchitektur in Maimand. *Archäol. Mitt. aus Iran* N.F.6(1973), pp. 281-295.

HOUSEGO, J. The Southern route to Mashhad: carananserais between Yazd and Torbat Haidariyeh. *AARP* 6(1974), pp. 41-55.

HUTT, A. Three minarets in the Kirmān region. *JRAS* 1970, pp. 172-180

HUTT, A. An unusual domed octagonal building in Southern Iran. *AARP* 1(1972), pp. 26-33.

KIANI, M.Y. Robat Sepanj. *Archäologische Mitteilungen aus Iran* N.F.7(1974), pp. 227-230.

KLEISS, W. Beobachtungen in Kharraqan. *Archäologische Mitteilungen aus Iran* N.F.7(1974), pp. 223-225.

KLEISS, W. Die Festung Qaleh Seidj Dukkan Bei Sarpol-i Zohab in West -Iran. *Archäologische Mitteilungen aus Iran* N.F.7(1974), pp. 215-221.

KLEISS, W. Strassenstationen und Karawanserails in West-Iran. *Archäologische Mitteilungen aus Iran* N.F.7(1974), pp. 231-250.

LUSCHEY-SCHMEISSER, I. Ein neuer Raum in Nayin. *Archäol. Mitt. aus Iran* N.F.5(1972), pp. 309-314.

MORTON, A.H. The Ardabīl shrine in the reign of Shāh Ṭahmāsp I. *Iran* 12(1974), pp. 31-64; 13(1975), pp. 39-58.

NASR, Seyyed Hossein. Il significato del vuoto nell'arte e nell'architettura dell'Islam. *Conoscenza religiosa* 1974, pp. 152-157.

PICCONI, R. Progetti italiani per l'illuminazione artistica di monumenti. *Veltro* 14i-ii(1970), pp. 163-167.

PIEMONTESE, A.M. The photograph album of the Italian diplomatic mission to Persia (Summer 1862). *East and West* 22(1972), pp. 249-311.

POUGACHENKOVA, G.A. Découvertes et études des monuments architecturaux de Mawara'Al-Nahr et de Khurasan (1957-1967). *Memorial vol. Vth Internat. Cong. Iranian Art and Archaeology*, 1972, Vol. 2, pp. 368-378.

SCARCIA, G. Sulla distrutta moschea di Damāvand. *Annali Fac. Ling. Lett. stran. di Ca' Foscari (serie orientale)* 2(1971), pp. 135-137.

SCARCIA, G. The "Vihār" of Qonqor-olong. Preliminary report. *East and West* N.S. 25(1975), pp. 99-104.

SIROUX, M. Caravansérials seldjoucides iraniens. *Art of Iran and Anatolia ...* ed. W. Watson, 1974, pp. 134-149.

SIROUX, M. L'évolution des antiques mosquées rurales de la région d'Ispahan. *Arts asiatiques* 26(1973), pp. 65-112.

SIROUX, M.F. Le palais de Sarvistân et ses voûtes. *Studia Iranica* 2(1973), pp. 49-65.

SOURDEL-THOMINE, J. Renouvellement et tradition dans l'architecture Saljūqide. *Islamic civilization*, 1973, pp. 251-263.

STERN, S.M., BEAZLEY, E. and DOBSON, A. The fortress of Khān Lanjān. *Iran* 9 (1971), pp. 45-57.

STRIKA, V. La grande moschea di Damasco e l'ideologia Ommiade. *Annali Fac. Ling. Lett. stran. di Ca' Foscari (serie orientale)* 3(1972), pp. 55-74

TAJVIDI, Akbar. La contribution des architectes iraniens au développement de l'architecture Islamique. *Memorial vol. Vth Internat. Cong. Iranian Art and Archaeology*, 1972, Vol. 2, pp. 205-208.

VORONINA, V.L. Konstruktziya i obraz v arkhitekture srednevekogo Irana. *Iskusstvo i arkheologiya Irana*, 1971, pp. 95-102

WATSON, O. The Masjid-i ʿAlī, Quhrūd: an architectural and epigraphic survey. *Iran* 13(1975), pp. 59-74.

WHITEHOUSE, D. The houses of Siraf, Iran. *Archaeology* 24 (1971), pp. 255-262.

WHITEHOUSE, D. Staircase minarets on the Persian Gulf. *Iran* 10(1972), pp. 155-158

WIET, G. Les travaux d'utilite publique sous le Gouvernement des Buyides. *Memorial vol. Vth Internat. Cong. Iranian Art and Archaeology*, 1972, Vol. 2, pp. 228-241.

WILBER, D.N. Le Masǧid-i ǧāmi' de Qazwin. *REI* 41(1973), pp. 199-229.

ZANDER, G. L'Ismeo e i lavori di restauro di monumenti in Iran. *Veltro* 14i-ii(1970), pp. 141-161.

ZANDER, G. Observations sur l'architecture civile d'Ispahan. *Iranian stud.* 7iii-iv (1974), pp. 294-319.

ZANDER, G. La restauration de quelques monuments historiques d'Ispahan: une nouvelle lumière sur les problèmes d'histoire de l'architecture s'y rattachant. *Memorial vol. Vth Internat. Cong. Iranian Art and Archaeology*, 1972, Vol. 2, pp. 246-259.

ZIPOLI, R. L'iscrizione del Qal'e-ye Rudxān presso Fuman. *RSO* 49(1975), pp. 63-66.

ZIPOLI, R. La *mosallā* di Yazd: un equivoco sul termine *ma'bad*. *Ann.Fac.Ling.Lett.stran. Ca' Foscari* 5(1974), pp. 205-208.

Survey of excavations in Iran during 1970-71. *Iran* 10(1972), pp. 165-186

See also II. c. 4. Golombek.

See also V. c. *India*. Hasan.

See also VIII. c. *Iran*. Holod.

Iraq

ABBŪ, 'Adil Najim. Qubbat al Sulaibiya. *Sumer* 29(1973), pp. 111-116.

BRUNO, A. Stabilization project of the al-Hadba minaret in Mossul, Iraq. *Mesopotamia* 2(1967), pp. 119-226.

COSTA, P. Islamic shrines on the Šaṭṭ al-Nīl. *AION N.S.* 21 (1971), pp. 199-214.

HAMEED, Abdul Aziz. New lights on the Ashiq palace of Samarra. *Sumer* 30 (1974), pp. 183-194.

STRIKA, V., KHALĪL, Jābir. Preliminary report of the survey of Islamic monuments in Baghdād. *Mesopotamia* 7-8(1973-4), pp. 261-292.

STRIKA, V. Il santuario di al-Kāẓimayni a Baghdād. *OM* 54(1974), pp. 6-22.

STRIKA, V. Il *Survey* dei monementi islamici di Baghdad. *Annali Fac. Ling. Lett. stran. di Ca' Foscari (serie orientale)* 3(1972), pp. 163-165.

See also II. b. Strika.

V ART

Jordan

GAUBE, H. An examination of the ruins of Qasr Burqu'. *Ann. Dept. Antiquities, Jordan* 19(1974), pp. 93-100.

Lebanon

GHOSN, R.S. Beirut architecture. *Beirut, crossroads of cultures,* 1970, pp. 185-202.

KALAYAN, Haroutune. The sea castle of Sidon. *Bull. du Musée de Beyrouth* 24 (1973), pp. 81-90.

Palestine

BURGOYNE, M.H. The continued survey of the Ribāṭ Kurd/Madrasa Jawhariyya Complex in Ṭarīq Bāb al-Ḥadīd. *Levant* 6(1974), pp. 51-64.

BURGOYNE, M.H. Some Mameluke doorways in the old city of Jerusalem. *Levant* 3 (1971), pp. 1-30.

BURGOYNE, M. Ṭarīq Bāb al-Ḥadīd - A Mamlūk street in the old city of Jerusalem. *Levant* 5(1973), pp. 12-35.

ÉCOCHARD, M. A propos du Dôme du Rocher et d'un article de M. Oleg Grabar. *BEO* 25 (1972), pp. 37-45.

WALLS, A.G. The mausoleum of the Amir Kīlānī. *Levant* 7(1975), pp. 39-76.

WALLS, A.G. The Turbat Barakat Khān or Khalidi Library. *Levant* 6(1974), pp. 25-50.

South East Asia

A travers le vieux Djakarta, I. La mosquée des Balinais. *Archipel* 3(1972), pp. 97-101.

Spain. Sicily

CABANELAS, D. La antigua policromía del techo de Comares de la Alhambra. *And.* 35(1970), pp. 423-451.

EWERT, C. El miḥrāb de la mezquita mayor de Almería. *And.* 36(1971), pp. 391-460.

GARCÍA, C. Una mezquita? *MEAH* 18-19i(1969-70), pp. 117-124.

GARIN, F.M. Antecedentes orientales del primer gótico levantino. *BAEO* 7(1971), pp. 151-157.

HARVEY, J.H. Spanish gardens in their historical background. *Garden hist.* 3i(1974), pp. 7-14.

JONES, D. The Cappella Palatina in Palermo: problems of attribution. *AARP* 2(1972), pp. 41-57.

KING, G. The mosque Bāb Mardūm in Toledo and the influences acting upon it. *AARP* 2(1972), pp. 29-40.

LOSA, A. Influência andaluza na arquitectura portuguesa dos séculos XIX e XX. *Actas IV congresso de estudos árabes e islâmicos* 1968(1971), pp. 539-564.

MARTÍNEZ CAVIRÓ, B. El arte mudéjar en el Convento toledano de Santa Isabel. *And.* 36(1971), pp. 177-195.

MARTÍNEZ CAVIRÓ, B. El arte mudéjar en el Monasterio de Santa Clara la Real de Toledo. *Archivo español de arte* 46 (1973), pp. 369-390.

MONTOYA INVARATO, R. Sobre los ábsides mudéjares toledanos y su sistema de trazado. *And.* 38(1973), pp. 455-481.

PAVON MALDONADO, B. Arte mudéjar en Castilla la Vieja y León. Exhumación y reivindicaciones artisticas. *Bol. Asoc. Esp. Orientalistas* 11(1975), pp. 149-192.

PAVÓN MALDONADO, B. El castillo de Dos Barrios (Toledo). Contribución al estudio del arabismo de los castillos de la Península Ibérica. *And.* 37(1972), pp. 445-452.

PAVÓN MALDONADO, B. El castillo de Oreja (Toledo). Contribución al estudio del arabismo de los castillos de la Península Ibérica. *And.* 40(1975), pp. 181-189.

PAVÓN MALDONADO, B. Consideraciones sobre las mezquitas aljamas de Córdoba y Madinat al-Zahra. *Bol. Asoc. esp. orientalistas* 10(1974), pp. 323-330.

PAVÓN MALDONADO, B. Escudos y reyes en el Cuarto de los Leones de la Alhambra. *And.* 35(1970), pp. 179-197.

PAVÓN MALDONADO, B. Las gárgolas de la Alhambra. *And* 34(1969), pp. 189-199.

PAVÓN MALDONADO, B. Sobre el origen sirio de las almenas decorativas hispano-musulmanas. *And* 34(1969), pp. 201-204.

PAVÓN MALDONADO, B. Sobre el romanismo de los aleros califales. *And.* 36(1971), pp. 197-201.

RUBIERA MATA, M.J. Los poemas epigráficos de Ibn al-Ŷayyāb en la Alhambra. *And.* 35(1970), pp. 453-473.

STRIKA, V. Intorno all'ipotesi "ommiade" dei castelli di Federico II. *AION* 33(N.S.23, 1973), pp. 594-602.

TERRASSE, H. Dispositions générales de mosquées espagnoles. *And* 34(1969), pp. 183-187.

TERRASSE, H. Une "qubba" funéraire d'époque almohade au Portugal. *And* 34(1969), p. 421.

See also IX. m. Shepard.

See also IV. c. 8. Harvey.

Syria

HAMILTON, R.W. Pastimes of a Caliph: another glimpse. *Levant* 4(1972), pp. 155-156.

ORY, S. La mosquée de 'Umar à Buṣrā. *Actas IV congresso de estudos árabes e islâmicos* 1968(1971), pp. 577-580.

ROGERS, J.M. A renaissance of classical antiquity in North Syria. *Ann.arch.arabes syriennes* 21(1971), pp. 347-356.

TCHALENKO, G. Traits originaux du peuplement de la Haute-Syrie du 1er au 7e siècle, tels que les révèle l'architecture. *Ann.arch.arabes syriennes* 21(1971), pp. 289-292.

See also V. c. *Spain* Pavón Maldonado

Turkey

BATES, Ülkü Ülküsal. An introduction to the study of the Anatolian Türbe and its inscriptions as historical documents. *Sanat tarihi yıllığı* 4(1970-1), pp. 73-84

BATUR, Afife. On the alternatively constructed wall in Ottoman mosques. *Anadolu sanatı araştırmaları* 2(1970), pp. 217-227.

BATUR, Selçuk. On the problem of the late prayer hall and Sultan's lodge in nineteenth century imperial mosques. *Anadolu sanatı araştırmaları* 2(1970), pp. 105-112.

CROWE, Y. Divrigi; problems of geography, history and geometry. *Art of Iran and Anatolia* ... ed. W. Watson, 1974, pp. 28-39.

CROWE, Y. The East window of the Great Mosque in Divriği. *AARP* 2(1972), pp. 105-113.

ESIN, Emel. The genesis of the Turkish Mosque and Madrasa complex. *Proc.27th Int.Cong.Or.1967* (1971), pp. 616-617.

ESIN, Emel. The genesis of the Turkish mosque and madrasa complex. *AION* 32(N.S. 22, 1972), pp. 151-185.

EYICE, Semavi. La mosquée - Zaviyah de Seyyid Mehmed Dede à Yenişehir. Recherches sur l'architecture turque du XIVe siècle. *Beiträge zur Kunstgeschichte Asiens. In memoriam E. Diez,* 1963, pp. 49-68

HALFORD-MACLEOD, A.S. Hittite and Seljuk (The Society's Anatolian tour, 1971). *Asian aff.* 58(N.S.2, 1971), pp. 309-314

İLTER, Fügen. An East Anatolian building from the age of Timur: Yelmaniye Medrese. *Anadolu* 17(1973), pp. 109-122.

İLTER, Fügen The Squat Minaret Mosque in Birgi. *Anadolu* (Anatolia) 13(1969), pp. 83-88.

JOJA, C. Contributions to the study of the domestic stone architecture of Istanbul. *Rev. ét. sud-est europ.* 11(1973), pp. 57-79.

KRAMER, J. Architekturteile des Seyitgazi -Tekke (Vilâyet Eskişehir) und die Michaelskirche von Nakoleia. *Jhb. d. österr. Byzantinistik* 22(1973), pp. 241-250.

KUBAN, Doğan. The mosque and hospital at *Divriği* and the origin of Anatolian-Turkish architecture. *Proc.27th Int.Cong. Or.1967* (1971), pp. 255-256.

KUBAN, Doğan. Les mosquées à coupole à base hexagonale. *Beiträge zur Kunstgeschichte Asiens. In memoriam E. Diez,* 1963, pp. 35-47

KUBAN, Doğan. On the interpretation of Islamic art. Islamic architecture and Ottoman architecture: hints for a re-evaluation. *Anadolu sanatı araştırmaları* 1(1968), pp. 28-47.

KURAN, Aptullah. Early works of the architect Sinan. *Belleten T T K* 37(1973), pp. 545-556.

KURAN, Aptullah. Thirteenth and fourteenth century mosques in Turkey. *Archaeology* 24 (1971), pp. 234-254.

MEINECKE-BERG, V. Marmofliesen. Zum Verhältnis von Fliesendekoration und Architektur in der osmanischen Baukunst. *Kunst des Orients* 8(1972), pp. 35-59.

MELIKIAN-CHIRVANI, A.S. Recherches sur les sources de l'art ottoman, Les stèles funéraires d'Ayasoluk I. *Turcica* 4(1972), pp. 103-133.

ÖNEY, Gönül. The influence of early Islamic stucco work in Iran on Anatolian Seljuk art. *Belleten T.T.K.* 37(no.147,1973), pp. 267-277.

ÖNEY, Gönül. Lion figures in Anatolian Seljuk architecture. *Anadolu* (Anatolia) 13(1969), pp. 43-67

ROGERS, J.M. The date of the Çifte Minare Medrese at Erzurum. *Kunst des Orients* 8(1972), pp. 77-119.

ROGERS, J.M. Seljuk architectural decoration at Sivas. *Art of Iran and Anatolia* ... ed. W. Watson, 1974, pp. 13-27.

STEWART, R. Turkey's largest Mosque goes up in Ankara. *J.Reg.Cult.Inst.* 7i(1974), pp. 59-62.

TAESCHNER, F. Die Türbe der Isfendiyar Oğlu in Sinop. *Beiträge zur Kunstgeschichte Asiens. In memoriam E. Diez,* 1963, pp. 31-33

ÜNAL, Rahmi Hüseyin. Deux monuments inédits d'époque pré-ottomane à Arapkir(Malatya). *Edebiyat Fak. araştirma dergisi* 4(1972), pp. 63-69.

ÜNAL, Rahmi Hüseyin. Deux caravansérails peu connus de l'époque pré-ottomane au sud de Karaman (Konya). *AARP* 3(1973), pp. 59-69.

ÜNAL, Rahmi Hüseyin. Monuments islamiques pré-ottomans de la ville de Bayburt et de ses environs. *REI* 40(1972), pp. 99-127.

YETKIN, Sherare. Some influences of great Seljuks on Anatolian seljuk architectural decoration. *J. Reg. Cult. Inst.* 2 iv(1969), pp. 193-208.

YETKIN, Şerare. The Turkish monuments in Sillyon (Yanköykisari). *Mélanges Mansel,* 1974, pp. 861-872.

See also V. b. *Turkey.* Hillenbrand.

See also V. c. *Iran.* Sourdel-Thomine.

See also V. v. 3. Oney.

d SCULPTURE

ALLEN, J. de V. Swahili ornament: a study of the decoration of the 18th century plasterwork and carved doors in the Lamu region. *AARP* 3(1973), pp. 1-13.

ALLEN, J. de V. A further note on Swahili ornament. *AARP* 4(1973), pp. 87-92.

BAER, E. The "pila" of Játiva. A document of secular urban art in Western Islam. *Kunst des Orients* 7(1970-1), pp. 142-166.

DOE, B. Ancient capitals from Aden. *Arabian studies* 1(1974), pp. 176-179.

ERDMANN, K. Die beiden türkischen Grabsteine im Türk ve Islâm Eserleri Müzesi in Istanbul. *Beiträge zur Kunstgeschichte Asiens. In memoriam E. Diez,* 1963, pp. 121-130

FEHÉRVÁRI, G. Tombstone or Miḥrāb? A speculation. *Islamic art in the Metropolitan Museum of Art,* ed. R. Ettinghausen, 1972, pp. 241-254.

FRANZ, H.G. Wesenszüge Omayyadischer Schmuckkunst. *Beiträge zur Kunstgeschichte Asiens. In memoriam E. Diez,* 1963, pp. 69-86

İNAL, Güner. The place of the dragon relief at Susuz Han in the Asian Cultural Circle. *Sanat tarihi yıllığı* 4(1970-1), pp. 183-184

KESSLER, C. Reflections on the development of Cairene dome decoration. *Proc. 27th Int.Cong.Or.1967* (1971), pp. 257-259.

KISHORE, Brij. Swastika in the medieval monuments of Agra. *Itihāsa-Chayanikā (Dr. Sampurnanand Felicitation vol.* = JUPHS 11-13), Part II (1965), pp. 15-20

MELIKIAN-CHIRVANI, Assadullah Souren. Recherches sur les sources de l'art ottoman. Les stèles funéraires d'Ayasoluk II. *Turcica* 7(1975), pp. 105-121.

NATH, R. Depiction of fabulous animals (Gaj-Vyala) at the Delhi gate of Agra Fort. *Medieval India* 2(1972), pp. 45-52.

ÖGEL, Semra. Einige Bemerkungen zum Sternsystem in der Steinornamentik der Anatolischen Seldschuken. *Beiträge zur Kunstgeschichte Asiens. In memoriam E. Diez,* 1963, pp. 166-172

ROUX, J.P. Essai d'interpretation d'un relief figuratif seldjoukide. *Arts asiatiques* 23 (1971), pp. 41-49.

TERRASSE, H. La sculpture monumentale à Cordoue au IXe siècle. *And* 34(1969), pp. 409-417

TUSHINGHAM, A.D. The Takht-i marmar (marble throne) in Teheran. *Iranian civilization and culture,* ed. C.J. Adams, 1972, pp. 121-127.

e GLASS. ROCK CRYSTAL. JADE

ABDUL-KHALIQ, Hana'. Glass objects newly obtained by the Iraq Museum. *Sumer* 28 (1972), pp. 47-52.

BRILL, R.H. A laboratory study of a fragment of painted glass from Begram. *Afghanistan* 25ii(1972), pp. 75-81.

BRILL, R.H. Report on chemical analyses of some glasses from Afghanistan. *Afghanistan* 26iii(1973), pp. 84-89.

CHARLESTON, R. Glass in Persia in the Safavid period and later. *AARP* 5(1974), pp. 12-27.

CLAIRMONT, C. Some Islamic glass in the Metropolitan Museum. *Islamic art in the Metropolitan Museum of Art,* ed. R. Ettinghausen, 1972, pp. 141-152.

CUTLER, A. The mythological bowl in the treasury of San Marco at Venice. *Near Eastern numismatics ... Studies in honor of G.C. Miles,* 1974, pp. 235-254.

DIGBY, S. A corpus of 'Mughal' glass. *BSOAS* 36(1973), pp. 80-96.

GRAY, B. Thoughts on the origin of "Hedwig" glasses. *Colloque international sur l'histoire du Caire,* 1969, pp. 191-194.

MILLER, Yu. Nefrit v prikladnom iskusstve Turtzii XVII veka. *Soobshch.Gos.Ermitazha* 35(1972), pp. 66-69.

PINDER-WILSON, R.H. and SCANLON, G.T. Glass finds from Fustat: 1964-71. *J. glass studies* 15(1973), pp. 12-30.

PONZI, M.N. Glassware from Abu Skhair (Central Iraq). *Mesopotamia* 7(1972), pp. 215-237.

PONZI, M.N. Islamic glassware from Seleucia. *Mesopotamia* 3-4(1968-69), pp. 67-104.

REUT, M. Le verre soufflé de Hérat. *Studia Iranica* 2(1973), pp. 97-111.

'USH, Muḥammad Abū-l-Faraj al. Incised Islamic glass. *Archaeology* 24 (1971), pp. 200-203.

See also XII. f. Masmoudi.

f IVORY

GOLVIN, L. Note sur quelques objets en ivoire d'origine musulmane. *ROMM* 13-14 (1973), pp. 413-436.

PINDER-WILSON, R.H. and BROOKE, C.N.L. The reliquary of St. Petroc and the ivories of Norman Sicily. *Archaeologica* 104(1973), pp. 261-305.

UKHANOVA, I. Yakuyskaya reznaya kost' v sobranii Ermitazha. *Soobshch.Gos.Ermitazha* 35(1972), pp. 41-44.

g METAL WORK. JEWELLERY

ABDULLAEV, T.A. Khudozhestvennye metallicheskie izdeliya Samarkanda. *Iz istorii iskusstva velikogo goroda. (K 2500-letiyu Samarkanda.),* 1972, pp. 252-268.

ABRAHAMOWICZ, Z. Ein Spiegelbild der Türkei im achtzehnten Jahrhundert. *Der Islam* 52 (1975), pp. 132-140.

ASLANAPA, Oktay. A metal object bearing the inscription of the Safavid Shah Suleyman. *J.Reg.Cult.Inst.* 6(1973), pp. 143-144.

ATIL, Esin. Two Il-hanid candlesticks at the University of Michigan. *Kunst des Orients* 8(1972), pp. 3-33.

BAER, E. An Islamic inkwell in the Metropolitan Museum of Art. *Islamic art in the Metropolitan Museum of Art,* ed. R. Ettinghausen, 1972, pp. 199-211.

BAER, E. The Nisan Tasi: a study in Persian-Mongol metal ware. *Kunst des Orients* 9(1973-4), pp. 1-46.

BATTESTI, T. Montagne de turquoises. *Objets et mondes* 15(1975), pp. 25-38.

CAMPBELL, S. The perfume merchant's bowl in the Royal Ontario Museum (970.268.5). *Oriental art* 19(1973), pp. 275-291.

DIGBY, S. A medieval Kashmiri bronze vase. *AARP* 2(1972), pp. 99-103.

DIGBY, Simon. More historic Kashmir metalwork? *Iran* 12(1974), pp. 181-185.

DODD, E.C. On a bronze rabbit from Fatimid Egypt. *Kunst des Orients* 8(1972), pp. 60-76, 160.

FERNÁNDEZ PUERTAS, A. Candiles epigrafiados de finales del siglo XI o comienzos del XII. *MEAH* 24(1975), pp. 109-114.

GOLVIN, L. Note sur l'industrie du cuivre en Occident musulman au Moyen Age. *Cah.de ling.d'orientalisme et de slavistique* 1-2 (1973), pp. 117-126.

GROHMANN, A. Die Bronzeschale M. 31-1954 im Victoria and Albert Museum. *Beiträge zur Kunstgeschichte Asiens. In memoriam E. Diez,* 1963, pp. 283-287

GYUZALYAN, L.T. Persidskoe stikhotvorenie na medrom tazike iz byvshey kollektzii D.S. Raysa. *Ep. Vost.* 21(1972), pp. 40-41.

HARPER, P.O. An eighth century silver plate from Iran with a mythological scene. *Islamic art in the Metropolitan Museum of Art,* ed. R. Ettinghausen, 1972, pp. 153-168.

HARTNER, W. The Vaso Vescovali in the British Museum: a study on Islamic astrological iconography. *Kunst des Orients* 9(1973-4), pp. 99-130.

IVANOV, A. Kol'tzp Shakh-Dzalhana. (The ring of Shah-Jahan.) *Soobsch. Gos.Ermitazha* 34(1972), pp. 25-29.

IVANOV, A.A. Bronzovyy tazik serediny XIV v. (Bronze mid-fourteenth century basin.) *Srednyaya Aziya i Iran: sbornik statey,* 1972, pp. 114-134.

IVANOV, A.A. Tri predmeta so stikhami Dzhami. *Ep.Vost.* 20(1971), pp. 97-103.

'IZZI, Wafiyya. Objects bearing the name of al-Nasir Muhammad and his successors. *Colloque international sur l'histoire du Caire,* 1969, pp. 235-241.

KLYASHTORNYY, S., LUBO-LESNICHENKO, E. Bronzovoe zerkalo iz Vostochnogo Turkestana s runicheskoy nadpis'yu. *Soobshch. Gos. Ermitazha* 39(1974), pp. 45-48.

KRAMAROVSKIY, M. Zolotoy kovsh mongol'skogo vremeni iz Predkavkaz'ya. *Soob. Gos. Ermitazha* 36(1973), pp. 65-70.

MARCHAL, R. L'art du bronze islamique d'Afghanistan dans les collections du Louvre. *Rev. du Louvre* 24(1974), pp. 7-18.

MARSHAK, B.I. Bronzovyy kurshin iz Samarkanda. (Bronze ewer from Samarkand.) *Srednyaya Aziya i Iran: sbornik statey,* 1972, pp. 61-90.

MELIKIAN, Souren. Le bassin du Sultan Kara Arslan Ibn il-Qazi. *Proc. 27th Int. Cong. Or. 1967* (1971), pp. 256-257

MELIKIAN-CHIRVANI, Assadullah Souren. Les bronzes du Khorâssân. *Studia Iranica* 3(1974), pp. 29-50.

MELIKIAN-CHIRVANI, Assaduliah Souren. Les bronzes du Khorâssân - II. Une école inconnue du XIIe siècle. *Studia Iranica* 4 (1975), pp. 51-71.

V ART

MELIKIAN-CHIRVANI, Assadullah Souren. Les bronzes du Khorâssân 3. Bronzes inédits du Xe et du XIe siècles. *Studia Iranica* 4(1975), pp. 187-205.

MELIKIAN-CHIRVANI, Assadullah Souren. Recherches sur l'école du bronze ottoman au XVIe siècle. *Turcica* 6(1975), pp. 146-167.

MELIKIAN-SHIRVANI, A.S. Safavid metalwork: a study in continuity. *Iranian stud.* 7iii-iv(1974), pp. 543-585.

MELIKIAN-CHIRVANI, Asadullah Souren. The white bronzes of early Islamic Iran. *Metropolitan Mus. J.* 9(1974), pp. 123-150.

MIKHALEVICH, G.P. Soobshchenie Nasir ad-Dina Tusi o reznom izumrude Khorezmshakh Tekesha. (Account by Nasir al-Din of an engraved emerald owned by the Khwarezm Shah Tekesh.) *Srednyaya Aziya i Iran: sbornik statey*, 1972, pp. 107-113.

NICKEL, H. A Mamluk axe. *Islamic art in the Metropolitan Museum of Art*, ed. R. Ettinghausen, 1972, pp. 213-225.

ROSEN-AYALON, M. Four Iranian bracelets seen in the light of early Islamic art. *Islamic art in the Metropolitan Museum of Art*, ed. R. Ettinghausen, 1972, pp. 169-186.

SCACE, J.M. and ELWELL-SUTTON, L.P. A problem piece of Kashmiri metalwork. *Iran* 9 (1971), pp. 71-85.

SCERRATO, U. Coppia di candelabri di Isfahan di epoca Qāǧār. *Arte orientale in Italia*, II, 1971, pp. 27-48.

SCERRATO, U. Oggetti metallici di età islamica in Afghanistan. III - Staffe ghaznavidi. *AION* 31(N.S. 21, 1971), pp. 455-466

SCERRATO, U. Oggetti metallici di età islamica in Afghanistan. IV-Su un tipo di amuleto del XII secolo. *AION* 32(n.s. 22, 1972), pp. 287-310.

SCERRATO, U. Su un problematico vaso ad alette nel museo di Mazār-i Sharīf (Afghanistan). *AION* 31(N.S. 21, 1971), pp. 543-547

SCERRATO, U. Un tipo di spruzzaprofumi in bronzo di epoca selgiuchide. *AION* 32(N.S. 22, 1972), pp. 25-33

SETHOM, Samira. Note sur une paire de fibules marocaines. *Cah. des arts et traditions populaires* 4(1971), pp. 97-101.

SOURDEL-THOMINE, J. Clefs et serrures de la Kaʿba. Notes d'épigraphie arabe. *REI* 39(1971), pp. 29-42.

'USH, M. Abu-l-Faraj al-. A bronze ewer with a high spout in the Metropolitan Museum of Art and analogous pieces. *Islamic art in the Metropolitan Museum of Art*, ed. R. Ettinghausen, 1972, pp. 187-198.

See also V. m. i. Welch.

See also VIII. d. *North Africa*. Bourouiba.

See also XII. e. Ougouag-Kezzal.

See also XII. e. Savary.

See also XII. f. Ayachi.

See also XII. f. Sugier.

See also XVIII. d. Schienerl.

See also XXVIII. d. Daunidova.

h ARMS AND ARMOUR

ELWELL-SUTTON, L.P. Persian armorial inscriptions. *Actas IV congresso de estudos árabes e islâmicos* 1968(1971), pp. 573-576.

ESIN, E. L'arme zoomorphe du guerrier turc. (Etude iconographique.) *Sprache, Geschichte und Kultur der altaischen Völker*, hrsg. G. Hazai und P. Zieme, 1974, pp. 193-217.

FINÓ, J.F. Machines de jet médiévales. *Gladius* 10(1972), pp. 25-43.

KALUS, L. Boucliers circulaires de l'Orient musulman (évolution et utilisation). *Gladius* 12(1974), pp. 59-133.

MILLER, Yu. Vostochnoe oruzhie. *Soobshch. Gos. Ermitazha* 39(1974), pp. 75-76.

PANT, G.N. A study of Indian swords. *Itihāsa-Chayanikā (Dr. Sampurnanand Felicitation vol.* = JUPHS 11-13), Part II (1965), pp. 75-86

i ENAMEL. LACQUER

ADAMOVA, A. O syuzhete odnoy persidskoy miniatyury na lartze. (On the subject of a Persian miniature in the Hermitage collection.) *SGE* 34(1972), pp. 29-32.

CAMPS-FABRER, H. Problèmes posés par l'origine de l'orfèvrerie émaillée en Afrique du Nord. *II.Cong.int.ét.nord-afr.* 1970, pp. 95-110.

CIG, Kemal M. The Iranian Lacquer Technique works in the Topkapi Saray Museum. *Memorial vol. Vth Internat. Cong. Iranian Art and Archaeology*, 1972, Vol. 2, pp. 24-33.

GRUBE, E.J. A lacquered panel painting from the collection of Lester Wolfe in the Museum of the University of Nôtre-Dame. *Orientalia Hispanica* I, 1974, pp. 376-397.

ROBINSON, B.W. A Royal Qājār enamel. *Iran* 10(1972), pp. 25-30

TUSHINGHAM, A.D. Persian Enamels. *Memorial vol. Vth Internat. Cong. Iranian Art and Archaeology*, 1972, Vol. 2, pp. 211-222.

V ART

j WOODCARVING

BRENTJES, B. Zu einigen samanidischen und nachsamanidischen Holzbildwerken des Seravschantales im Westen Tadshikistans. *Central Asiatic J.* 15(1972), pp. 295-297

CARSWELL, J. A carpentry note. *AARP* 7(1975), p. 48.

DUPAIGNE, B. Chique et tabatières de courges gravées en Afganistan. *Objets et mondes* 15(1975), pp. 57-68.

JENKINS, M. An eleventh-century woodcarving from a Cairo nunnery. *Islamic art in the Metropolitan Museum of Art,* ed. R. Ettinghausen, 1972, pp. 227-240.

KURZ, O. Folding chairs and Koran stands. *Islamic art in the Metropolitan Museum of Art,* ed. R. Ettinghausen, 1972, pp. 299-314.

PAVÓN MALDONADO, B. Alero mudéjar toledano del Museo Arqueológico de la Alhambra. *And.* 34(1969), pp. 423-430

PAVÓN MALDONADO, B. Las maderas mudejares pintadas del Monasterio de Santa Clara de Astudillo. Los últimos restos de una primicia artística irredenta. *And.* 40 (1975), pp. 191-197.

PAVÓN MALDONADO, B. Una silla de taracea del reinado de Muḥammad VII de Granada. *Bol. Asoc. esp. orientalistas* 10(1974), pp. 330-333.

POYTO, R. La porte ornée de Tamezguida en Grande-Kabylie. *Libyca* 16(1968), pp. 217-219.

SCERRATO, U. Vassoio damaschinato indo-musulmano da Siālkot in una collezione privata a Roma. *Arte orientale in Italia,* II, 1971, pp. 13-25.

TERRASSE, H. Un bois sculpté du XIIe siècle trouvé à Marrakech. *And* 34(1969), pp. 419-420

See also V. d. Allen.

k BOOKBINDING. LEATHER

LOUIS, A. Les industries du cuir à Tunis hier et aujourd'hui, éléments bibliographiques. *ROMM* 15-16(1973), pp. 145-151.

MA'IL HERAVY, G.R. Mir. Book-making in Afghanistan during the last century. *Afghanistan* 25 iii (1972), pp. 68-77.

SHORE, A.F. Fragment of a decorated leather binding from Egypt. *BM Qly* 36(1971), pp. 19-23.

l CALLIGRAPHY

ALPARSLAN, Ali. Ecoles calligraphiques turques. *Islam Tetkikleri Enst. dergisi* 5(1973), pp. 265-278.

BHATTY, W.K. Sadequain: the stylish contemporary of Pakistan. *Arts of Asia* 3ii(1973), pp. 54-58.

GHULAM, Yousif. Examples of calligraphy in the arts of Islamic Iran. *Bull. Asia Inst. Pahlavi Univ.* 2(1971), pp. 1-10.

MAKAR, Farida. Le coufique carré. *Nouvelle Rev. du Caire* 1(1975), pp. 181-201.

NEYSARI, Salim. The development of Persian letter shapes with special reference to the teaching of handwriting to beginners. *J. Reg. Cult. Inst.* 4(1971), pp. 139-163.

RIZVI, S.A. Yaseen. The art of calligraphy. *J. Reg. Cult. Inst.* 5(1972), pp. 89-94.

See also V. k. Ma'il Heravy.

m PAINTING

i Miniature painting

ADAMOVA, A. Dva portreta Fatkh-Ali Shakha iz sobraniya Ermitazha i kadzharskiy ofitzial'nyy stil'. (Two portraits by Mihr-'Ali.) *Soobshch. Gos. Ermitazha.* 33(1971), pp. 85-88.

ADAMOVA, A. O syuzhete odnoy persidskoy miniatyury na lartze. (On the subject of a Persian miniature in the Hermitage collection.) *Soobsch. Gos Ermitazha* 34(1972), pp. 29-32.

AHMAD, Tasneem. Nādiru'l-'Aṣr Manṣūr. *Indo-Iranica* 25(1972), pp. 51-55.

AKIMUSHKIN, O.F. Eshche raz o khudozhnike Siyavush-Beke. *Vostochnaya filologiya. Philologia Orientalis.* II(Pamyati V.S. Puturidze), 1972, pp. 193-198.

AKIMUSHKIN, O.F. Portret Navoi. *Iskusstvo i arkheologiya Irana,* 1971, pp. 20-25

ANAND, Mulk Raj. The Turkish heritage in painting. *Marg* 26iv(1973), pp. 2-16.

ARCHER, W.G. The world of the Punjab Hills. Pahari miniatures in the British Museum. *Apollo* 101(1975), pp. 392-393.

ASHRAFI, M.M. K voprosu periodizatzii i evolyutzii zhivopisnykh shkol Irana v XVI v. *Strany Blizhnego i Srednego Vostoka: istoriya, ekonomica,* 1972, pp. 462-467.

ASHRAFI, M.M. O tvorchestve bukharskogo khudozhnika XVI v. Makhmuda Mazakhkhiba. *NAA* 1975(4), pp. 143-148.

ATASOY, Nurhan. The documentary value of Ottoman miniatures. *Mélanges Mansel,* 1974, pp. 749-755.

ATASOY, Nurhan. Four Istanbul albums and some fragments from fourteenth century Shah-Namehs. *Ars Orientalis* 8(1970), pp. 19-48

V ART

ATASOY, Nurhan. Illustrations prepared for display during Shahname recitations. *Memorial vol. Vth Internat. Cong. Iranian Art and Archaeology*, 1972, Vol. 2, pp. 262-272.

ATIL, Esin. Ottoman miniature painting under Sultan Mehmed II. *Ars Orientalis* 9 (1973), pp. 103-120.

AYNI, L.S. Miniatyury rukopisi "Shakhname" 1333 g. iz Leningrada i nekotorye voprosy zarozhdeniya persidskoy miniatury. *Iskusstvo i arkheologiya Irana*, 1971, pp. 9-19

AYNI, Lyutfiya. "Timuridskaya" miniatyura i ee spetzifika. (Some features of the Timurid miniatures.) *NAA* 1971(3), pp. 141-143.

BEACH, M.C. The context of Rajput painting. *Ars Orientalis* 10(1975), pp. 11-17.

BHATTY, W.K. Miniature paintings. *Arts of Asia* 2iv 1972, pp. 38-43.

BINNEY, E. Later Mughal painting. *Aspects of Indian art*, ed. Pratapaditya Pal, 1972, pp. 118-123.

BOWMAN, J. Muslim pictorial art. *Milla wa-milla* 15(1975), pp. 3-15.

CAGMAN, Filiz. Ottoman Turkish miniatures. *Marg* 26iv(1973), pp. 29-52.

CHAGHATAI, M. Abdulla. Muhammadi: an artist of the Safavid period. *J. Reg. Cult. Inst.* 4(1971), pp. 91-105.

DAS, Asok Kumar. Ustād Manṣūr. *Lalit Kalā* 17(1975?), pp. 32-39.

DAVID-WEILL, J. Sur quelques illustrations de Kalila et Dimna. *Beiträge zur Kunstgeschichte Asiens. In memoriam E. Diez*, 1963, pp. 256-263

DENNY, W.B. A sixteenth-century architectural plan of Istanbul. *Ars Orientalis* 8 (1970), pp. 49-63

DUDA, D. Die Buchmalerei der Ğalā'iriden. *Der Islam* 48 (1971), pp. 28-76; 49 (1972), pp. 153-220.

D'YAKONOVA, N.V. Bukharskiy spisok "Gulistana" Sa'di iz sobraniya Gosudarstvennoy Publichnoy biblioteki im. M.E. Saltykova-Shchedrina. (A manuscript of the *Golistan* by Sa'di.) *Srednyaya Aziya i Iran: sbornik statey*, 1972, pp. 136-148.

D'YAKONOVA, N.V. Portret i kontzeptziya lichnosti v zhivopisi Vostochnogo Turkestana (V-XI vv.). *Iskusstvo portreta, 20-22 sent. 1972 goda. (Kratkie tezisy dokl.k nauchnoy konf.)*, pp. 7-9.

ESİN, Emel. An angel figure in the Miscellany Album H.2152 of Topkapı. *Beiträge zur Kunstgeschichte Asiens. In memoriam E. Diez*, 1963, pp. 264-282

ESIN, Emel. Le développement hétérodoxe de la peinture figurative religieuse turque-islamique. *Ve Congrès International d'Arabisants et d'Islamisants. Actes.*, [1970?], pp. 197-208.

ESIN, Emel. Four Turkish Bakhshi active in Iranian Lands. *Memorial vol. Vth Internat. Cong. Iranian Art and Archaeology*, 1972, Vol. 2, pp. 53-73.

FAROOQUI, Anis. A critical study of Indo-Persian style of painting. *IC* 48(1974), pp. 247-252.

FAROOQI, Anis. Painters of Akbar's court. *IC* 48(1974), pp. 119-126.

FEHÉR, G., Jun. Hungarian historical scenes recorded in Turkish chronicle illustrations. *Acta Or. Hung.* 25(1972), pp. 475-490.

FEHÉR, G. Hungarian history in Islamic miniature-painting. *The Middle East; studies in honour of J. Germanus*, 1974, pp. 175-187.

FEHÉR, Géza, Jun. Miniatures turques du XVIe siècle relative à l'histoire de Hongrie. *Iparmüvészeti Múz.Evkönyvei* 12 (1969), pp. 227-236

FRAAD, I.L., ETTINGHAUSEN, R. Sultanate painting in Persian style, primarily from the first half of the fifteenth century. *Chhavi: golden jubilee vol.*, 1971, pp. 48-66.

GALERKINA, O. On some miniatures attributed to Bihzād from Leningrad collections. *Ars Orientalis* 8(1970), pp. 121-138

GALERKINA, O. Some characteristics of Persian miniature painting in the latter part of the 16th century. *Oriental art* N.S.21(1975), pp. 231-241.

GALERKINA, O.I. Sufiyskie motivy v iranskoy miniatyure vtoroy poloviny XVI v. *Iskusstvo i arkheologiya Irana*, 1971, pp. 102-110

GHOSH, D.P. Eastern school of mediaeval Indian painting (thirteenth-eighteenth century A.D.). *Chhavi: golden jubilee vol.*, 1971, pp. 91-103.

GODARD, Yedda A. A propos de quelques miniatures. *Memorial vol. Vth Internat. Cong. Iranian Art and Archaeology*, 1972, Vol. 2, pp. 90-98.

GOLOMBEK, L. Toward a classification of Islamic painting. *Islamic art in the Metropolitan Museum of Art*, ed. R. Ettinghausen, 1972, pp. 23-34.

GORELIK, M.V. Portrety Bekhzada (k voprosu o tvorcheskom metode). *Iskusstvo i arkheologiya Irana*, 1971, pp. 111-120

GOSWAMY, B.N. and JHAMB, H. Leaves from an illustrated manuscript on falconry. *Oriental art* N.S. 19(1973), pp. 61-67.

GRABAR, O. The illustrated Maqāmāt of the thirteenth century: the bourgeoisie and the arts. *The Islamic city*, 1970, pp. 207-222.

V ART

GRABAR, O. Pictures or commentaries: the illustrations of the *Maqāmāt* of al-Ḥarīrī. *Studies in art and literature of the Near East in honor of R. Ettinghausen,* 1974, pp. 85-104.

GRAY, B. Chinese style in some drawings in the Topkapi. *Memorial vol. Vth Internat. Cong. Iranian Art and Archaeology,* 1972, Vol. 2, pp. 99-101.

GRAY, B. A Timurid copy of a Chinese Buddhist picture. *Islamic art in the Metropolitan Museum of Art,* ed. R. Ettinghausen, 1972, pp. 35-38.

GREK, T. Portret Akbara raboty Manokhara. (A miniature portrait of Akbar by Manohar.) *Soobsch. Gos Ermitazha* 34(1972), pp. 21-23.

GRIGOLIYA, A.M. Tvorchestvo miniatyuristov iz roda Afshar po materialam Gosudarstvennogo Muzeya Iskusstv Gruzinskoy SSR. *Iskusstvo i arkheologiya Irana,* 1971, pp. 121-133

GRUBE, E.J. The earliest known paintings from Islamic Cairo. *Colloque international sur l'histoire du Caire,* 1969, pp. 195-198.

GRUBE, E.J. Four pages from a Turkish 16th century Shahnamah in the collection of the Metropolitan Museum of Art in New York. *Beiträge zur Kunstgeschichte Asiens. In memoriam E. Diez,* 1963, pp. 237-255

GUILLAUME, G. Soliman-le-Magnifique, l'apogée de la peinture turque et Ivan Stchoukine. *Arts asiatiques* 26(1973), pp. 271-290.

GÜRSOY, Emine. Anachronism in contemporary popular religious painting in Iran. *Boğazici Univ. J.* 2(1974), pp. 19-23.

GYUZAL'YAN, L.T. Vostochnaya miniatyura, izobrazhayushchaya zapadnyy peyzazh. (An Oriental miniature with a European landscape.) *Srednyaya Aziya i Iran: sbornik statey,* 1972, pp. 163-169.

HAMID, Isa Salman al-. The characteristics of the miniatures of the Mesopotamian School. *Sumer* 23 (1967), pp. 125-132.

HOUSEGO, J. "Honour is according to habit": Persian dress in the sixteenth and seventeenth centuries. *Apollo* 93,no.109 (1971), pp. 204-209.

İNAL, Güner. A manuscript of the Shāhnāmeh from the period of Shāh Ismā'īl and its influences on the later Shāhnāmeh illustrations. *Sanat Tarihi Yıllığı* 5(1972-3), pp. 530-545.

IVANOV, A. Kalamdan s portretom yunoshi v latakh. *Soobshch. Gos. Ermitazha* 39 (1974), pp. 56-59.

JAMES, D. Mamluke painting at the time of the 'Lusignan Crusade', 1365-70. A study of the Chester Beatty Nihāyat al-su'l wa'l-umniya ... etc. MS of 1365. *Humaniora Islamica* 2(1974), pp. 73-87.

JAMES, D. Space-forms in the works of the Baghdād *Maqāmat* illustrators, 1225-58. *BSOAS* 37(1974), pp. 305-320.

JOHNSON, B.B. A preliminary study of the technique of Indian miniature painting. *Aspects of Indian art,* ed. Pratapaditya Pal, 1972, pp. 139-146.

KAGANE, L.L. Portrety Khayr-ed-dina Barbarossy. *Iskusstvo portreta, 20-22 sent. 1972 goda. (Kratkie tezisy dokl.k nauchnoy konf.),* pp. 12-13.

KALANTARI, Manutcher. Le Livre des Rois et les peintures des maisons de thé. *Objets et mondes* 11 (1971), pp. 141-158.

KARPOVA, N.K. Miniatyury iz rukopisi "Khamse" Nizami 1491 g. v sobranii Gosudarstvennogo muzeya iskusstva narodov Vostoka. *Iskusstvo i arkheologiya Irana,* 1971, pp. 341-347

KERIMOV, K.D. Rol' tabrizskoy shkoly v razvitii miniatyurnoy zhivopisi v Kazvine. *Iskusstvo i arkheologiya Irana,* 1971, pp. 163-171

KRISHNA, Anand. A study of the Akbari artist: Farrukh Chela. *Chhavi: golden jubilee vol.,* 1971, pp. 353-373.

KRISHNA, Kalyan. Problems of a portrait of Jahangir in the Musée Guimet, Paris. *Chhavi: golden jubilee vol.,* 1971, pp. 392-394.

LEE, S.E. and SIMSAR, Mehmed A. "Tuti-nama", tales of a parrot. *Art in America* 54(1966), pp. 49-56.

LEVINE, D. Great events and shining actions. (Miniatures in an Akbarname.) *Bull.Cleveland Mus.Art* 63(1976), pp. 89-95.

MAGUIRE, M.E. The *Shāhnāmah* and the Persian miniaturist. *Studies in art and literature of the Near East in honor of R. Ettinghausen,* 1974, pp. 133-136.

MARCHAND, E. An imprint of Central Asian painting on some Moslem miniatures. *East and West* N.S.24(1974), pp. 147-151.

MEINARDUS, Otto. The equestrian deliverer in eastern iconography. *Oriens Christianus* 57(1973), pp. 142-155.

MEREDITH-OWENS, G.M. A genealogical roll in the Metropolitan Museum. *Islamic art in the Metropolitan Museum of Art,* ed. R. Ettinghausen, 1972, pp. 87-90.

MEREDITH-OWENS, G.M. Islamic illustrated chronicles. *J. Asian history* 5 (1971), pp. 20-34.

MEREDITH-OWENS, G.M. Persian manuscripts illumination and painting. *Iranian civilization and culture,* ed. C.J. Adams, 1972, pp. 47-58.

MEREDITH-OWENS, G.M. A rare illustrated Persian manuscript. *Memorial vol. Vth Internat. Cong. Iranian Art and Archaeology,* 1972, Vol. 2, pp. 125-131.

V ART

MEREDITH-OWENS, G.M. Some remarks on the miniatures in the Society's *Jāmi' al-tawārīkh*. *JRAS* 1970, pp. 195-199

MILLER, Yu.A. Tipologiya indiyskogo srednevekogo portreta (po dannym miniatyury). *Iskusstvo portreta, 20-22 sent. 1972 goda. (Kratkie tezisy dokl.k nauchnoy konf.)*, pp. 10-12.

MINAI, A. Ustad Kamal'-al' Mol'k - osnovopolozhnik iranskoy zhivopisi. *Iskusstvo i arkheologiya Irana*, 1971, pp. 227-236

MOSTAFA, Mohamed. An illustrated manuscript on chivalry from the late Circassian Mamluk period. (A preliminary report.) *BIE* 51 (1969-70), pp. 1-13.

MOSTAFA, Mohamed. Miniature paintings in some Mamluk manuscripts. *BIE* 52(1970-71), pp. 5-15.

NASR, Seyyed Hossein. "Il mondo dell'immaginazione" ed il concetto di spazio nella miniatura persiana. *Conoscenza religiosa* 1970, pp. 11-16.

NASR, Seyyed Hossein. "The World of Imagination" and the concept of space in Persian miniatures. *Memorial vol. Vth Internat. Cong. Iranian Art and Archaeology*, 1972, Vol. 2, pp. 132-136.

NIZAMUDDIN, M. More light on the description of a rare illustrated XVIth century manuscript of the Gulistan of Sa'di' in Hyderabad Deccan. *Memorial vol. Vth Internat. Cong. Iranian Art and Archaeology*, 1972, Vol. 2, pp. 137-151.

OHRI, Vishwa Chandra. Kangra painting of pre-Sansār Chand period. *Lalit Kalā* 17 (1975?), p. 43.

PAL, Pratapaditya. The enduring charm of Indian paintings. *Allen Memorial Art Mus. bull.* 28(1971), pp. 61-65.

PAL, Pratapaditya. Indian art from the Paul Walter collection. February 6 - March 12, 1971. Catalogue. *Allen Memorial Art Mus. bull.* 28(1971), pp. 67-103.

PAPADOPOULO, A. Esthétique de l'art musulman. La peinture. *Annales ESC* 28(1973), pp. 681-710.

PARIMOO, Ratan. A new set of early Rajasthani paintings. *Lalit Kalā* 17(1975?), pp. 9-13.

PINDER-WILSON, R.H. Paintings of the Jala'irid period - a reconsideration. *Memorial vol. Vth Internat. Cong. Iranian Art and Archaeology*, 1972, Vol. 2, pp. 161-166.

REIFF, R. Rajput miniatures in the Paul Walter collection. *Art J.* 31(1971-2), pp. 181-185.

REINDL, H. Zu einigen Miniaturen und Karten aus Handscriften Matraqči Naṣuḥ. *Islamkundliche Abhandlungen H.J. Kissling*, 1974, pp. 146-171.

RENDA, Günsel. The miniatures of Silsilename, No. 1321 in the Topkapı Saray Museum Library. *Sanat Tarihi Yıllığı* 5(1972-3), pp. 481-495.

ROBINSON, B.W. R.A.S. MS 178: an unrecorded Persian painter. *JRAS* 1970, pp. 203-209

ROBINSON, B.W. Shāh 'Abbās and the Mughal Ambassador Khān 'Alām: The pictorial record. *Burlington mag.* 114(no. 827, 1972), pp. 58-63

ROBINSON, B.W. The Shāhnāmeh manuscript Cochran 4 in the Metropolitan Museum of Art. *Islamic art in the Metropolitan Museum of Art*, ed. R. Ettinghausen, 1972, pp. 73-86.

ROBINSON, B.W. Two Persian manuscripts in the Library of the Marquess of Bute. Part I. Two Mathnawi poems, c.1410 (Bute MS 351). *Oriental art* 15(1971), pp. 333-336.

ROBINSON, B.W. Two Persian manuscripts in the Library of the Marquess of Bute (part II). *Oriental Art* 18(1) 1972, pp. 50-56

ROBINSON, B.W. An unpublished manuscript of the Gulistan of Sa'di. *Beiträge zur Kunstgeschichte Asiens. In memoriam E. Diez*, 1963, pp. 223-236

ROGERS, M.J. The genesis of Safavid religious painting. *Memorial vol. Vth Internat Cong. Iranian Art and Archaeology*, 1972, Vol. 2. pp. 167-188.

RÜHRDANZ, K. Islamische Miniaturhandschriften aus den Beständen der DDR. *Wiss. Z. Univ. Halle* 22(1973), vi, pp. 123-125.

SAHAY, C.M.N. Indian miniature painting, with illustrations from the collection of the National Museum in New Delhi. *Arts of Asia* 4iv(1974), pp. 25-41.

SHAH, Husain. A master piece of Timurid art. *Afghanistan* 25 iv(1973), pp. 22-28.

SIMS, E.G. Prince Baysunghur's Chahar maqaleh. *Sanat tarihi yilliği* 6(1974-5), pp. 375-409.

SIMS, E.G. The Timurid imperial style: its origins and diffusion. *AARP* 6(1974), pp. 56-67.

SINGH, Chandramani. European themes in early Mughal miniatures. *Chhavi: golden jubilee vol.*, 1971, pp. 401-410.

SKELTON, R. Early Golconda painting. *Indologen-Tagung 1971*, hrsg. H. Härtel und V. Moeller, pp. 182-195.

SKELTON, R. An illustrated manuscript from Bakharz. *Memorial vol. Vth Internat. Cong. Iranian Art and Archaeology*, 1972, Vol. 2, pp. 198-204.

SMART, E. Four illustrated Mughal Baburnama manuscripts. *AARP* 3(1973), pp. 54-58.

SOUCEK, P. Comments on Persian painting. *Iranian stud.* 7iii-iv(1974), pp. 72-87.

SOUCEK, P.P. Niẓāmī on painters and painting. *Islamic art in the Metropolitan Museum of Art*, ed. R. Ettinghausen, 1972, pp. 9-21.

SÖYLEMEZOĞLU, Nerkis. An illustrated copy of Hamdī's *Yūsuf we Züleykhā* dated A.H. 921/1515 A.D. in the Bayerische Staatsbibliothek in Munich. *Near Eastern numismatics ... Studies in honor of G.C. Miles*, 1974, pp. 469-478.

STCHOUKINE, I. La *Khamseh* de Niẓāmī, H. 753, du Topkapi Sarayi Müzesi d'Istanbul. *Syria* 49(1972), pp. 239-246.

STCHOUKINE, Ivan. Un manuscrit illustré de la bibliothèque de Bāyazid II. *Arts asiatiques* 24(1971), pp. 9-22

STCHOUKINE, I. Maulānā Shaykh Mohammad, un maître de l'école de Messhed du XVIe siècle. *Arts asiatiques* 30(1974), pp. 7-11.

STCHOUKINE, I. Notes sur des images de l'École d'Iṣfahān de la fin du XVIe et du XVIIe siècle. *Syria* 48 (1971), pp. 203-212.

STCHOUKINE, I. La peinture à Baghdad sous Sulṭān Pīr Budāq Qāra-Qoyūnlū. *Arts asiatiques* 25(1972), pp. 3-18.

STCHOUKINE, I. Qāsim ibn 'Alī et ses peintures dans les Aḥsan al-Kibār. *Arts asiatiques* 28(1973), pp. 45-54.

STRIKA, V. Note introduttive a un'estetica islamica: la miniatura persiana. *Rend. Accad.Lincei* 28(1973), pp. 699-727.

STRIKA, V. La prospettiva "spianata" nella miniatura persiana. *Mesopotamia* 7(1972), pp. 239-258.

SWIETOCHOWSKI, M. The development of traditions of book illustration in pre-Safavid Iran. *Iranian stud.* 7iii-iv(1974), pp. 49-71.

SWIETOCHOWSKI, M.L. The historical background and illustrative character of the Metropolitan Museum's Mantiq al-Tayr of 1483. *Islamic art in the Metropolitan Museum of Art*, ed. R. Ettinghausen, 1972, pp. 39-72.

TITLEY, N. Development of fourteenth-fifteenth century painting in Khorasan, Iran and Turkey. *Marg* 26iv(1973), pp. 17-28.

TITLEY, N. Miniature paintings illustrating the works of Amir Khusrau: 15th, 16th, 17th centuries. *Marg* 28iii(1974-5), pp. 19-52.

TITLEY, N. Persian miniatures of the 14th, 15th, 16th centuries and its influence on Indian painting. *Marg* 28iii(1974-5), pp. 13-15.

TITLEY, N.M. Shiraz and Isfahan Persian miniatures of the 1470's. Some unpublished manuscripts. *Oriental art* 20(1974), pp. 52-60.

TITLEY, N.M. A 14th-century Niẓāmī manuscript in Tehran. *Kunst des Orients* 8 (1972), pp. 120-125.

TITLEY, N. A 15th century Khamseh of Niẓāmī. *Oriental art* 17(1971), pp. 239-244.

UNGER, E. de. A recently discovered Persian manuscript from the 14th century. *Iparmüvészeti Múz.Evkönyvei* 12(1970), pp. 211-220.

VERMA, S.P. Mughal painter's aesthetic. (A study based on the sixteenth century miniatures.) *Q.R.hist.stud.* 15(1975-6), pp. 98-101.

VEYMARI, B.V. Shirazskaya shkola miniatury XIV-XVI vv. *Iskusstvo i arkheologiya Irana*, 1971, pp. 86-94

WALEY, P. and **TITLEY**, N.M. An illustrated Persian text of Kalila wa Dimna dated 707/1307-8. *British Library J.* 1(1975), pp. 42-61.

WELCH, S.C. Two drawings, a tile, a dish, and a pair of scissors. *Islamic art in the Metropolitan Museum of Art*, ed. R. Ettinghausen, 1972, pp. 291-298.

WELCH, S.C. 78 pictures from a world of Kings, Heroes and Demons. The Houghton Shah-nameh. *Bull. Met. Mus. Art* 29 (1971), pp. 341-357.

WELLESZ, E.F. The Baysonghor manuscript in the Vienna National Library. *Memorial vol. Vth Internat. Cong. Iranian Art and Archaeology*, 1972, Vol. 2, pp. 223-227.

See also I. d. 2. Titley.

See also V. a. *Influences and parallels.* Ingrams.

See also V. m. 2. Esin

See also V. u. 1. Campbell.

See also VII. a. Gorelik

See also XXXI. g. Robinson.

See also XXXI. g. Welch.

See also XXXII. i. Ahmad.

ii Painting on walls, ceilings, etc.

ADAMOVA, A.T. Dve kartiny rannekadzhar skogo perioda. (Two pictures of the early Qajar period.) *Srednyaya Aziya i Iran: sbornik statey*, 1972, pp. 170-177.

BELENITSKI, A.M. et **MARSHAK**, B.I. L'art de Piandjikent à la lumière des dernières fouilles (1958-1968). *Arts asiatiques* 23 (1971), pp. 3-39.

BENCHEIKH, N. Mythes, réalités et significations de l'activité picturale en Tunisie. *Annuaire Afrique du Nord* 12 (1973).

ESIN, Emel. Oldruğ-Turuğ, the hierarchy of sedent postures in Turkish iconography. *Kunst des Orients* 7i(1970-1), pp. 1-29.

ESIN, Emel. The Turk al-'ağam of Sāmarrā and the paintings attributable to them in the Ğawsaq al-Ḫāqānī. *Kunst des Orients* 9(1973-4), pp. 47-88.

GRUBE, E. Wall paintings in the seventeenth century monuments of Isfahan. *Iranian stud.* 7iii-iv(1974), pp. 511-542.

JAYASWAL, Prashant Kumar. The so called bazar Mughal School paintings. *Lalit Kala* 15(1974?), p. 56.

JONES, D. Notes on a tattooed musician: a drawing of the Fatimid period. *AARP* 7(1975), pp. 1-14.

KHAN, Ahmad Nabi. Restoration of the fresco decoration at the Mosque of Maryam Zamani at Lahore. *Pak.archaeology* 7(1970-71), pp. 121-134.

ROBINSON, B.W. The Amery collection of Persian oil paintings. *Stud. iranica* 1(1972), pp. 43-53.

SANTIAGO SIMÓN, E.de. Restos de un zócalo morisco en una casa del Albaicin. *MEAH* 23(1974), pp. 121-122.

SOKOLOVSKIY, V. O zhivopisi "Malogo" zala dvortzovogo kompleksa gorodishcha kalai Kakhkakh I (Shakhristan, Tadzhikskaya SSR). *Soobshch. Gos. Ermitazha* 39(1974), pp. 48-52.

TAHA, Munir Yousif. A mural painting from Kufa. *Sumer* 27(1971), pp. 77-79.

ZAČINOVIĆ, Jusuf. Zidne dekoracije Ferhadije džamije u Sarajevu. (Wall decorations of Ferhadija mosque at Sarajevo.) *Naše starine* 13(1972), pp. 221-232.

See also V. m. l. Chaghatai.

n MOSAICS

FINSTER, B. Die Mosaiken der Umayyaden-moschee von Damaskus. *Kunst des Orients* 7(1970-1), pp. 83-141.

GAUTIER VAN BERCHEM, M. Anciens décors de mosaïques dans la salle de prière dans la mosquée des Omayyades à Damas. *MUSJ* 46 (1970-1), pp. 285-304.

NATH, R. Glass-mosaic decoration and the Shish-Mahal of Agra Fort. *IC* 45 (1971), pp. 25-34.

STERN, H. Notes sur les mosaiques du Dome du Rocher et de la mosquée de Damas, à propos d'un livre de Mme Marguerite Gautier van Berchem. *Cah. archeol.* 22 (1972), pp. 201-225.

See also V. m. l. Titley

o CERAMICS

'ABD AR-RĀZIQ, Aḥmad. Notes on Islamic graffito ware of the Near East. *Ann.Islamologiques* 9(1970), pp. 179-186.

ABDERRAHIM-REICHLEN, A.M. Les poteries d'El Aouna: approche d'un décor curviligne et floral. *Libyca* 19(1971), pp. 251-261.

ADAMS, R. McC. Tell Abu Sarifa. a Sassanian-Islamic ceramic sequence from South Central Iraq. *Ars Orientalis* 8(1970), pp. 87-119.

ADLE, Chahryar. Un disque de fondation en céramique (Kâšân, 711/1312). *JA* 260(1972), pp. 277-297.

ALLAN, J.W. Abū l-Qāsim's treatise on ceramics. *Iran* 11(1973), pp. 111-120.

ALLAN, J.W. Some observations on the origins of the medieval Persian faience body. *Art of Iran and Anatolia ...* ed. W. Watson, 1974, pp. 60-67.

ARAPOVA, T.B., RAPOPORT, I.V. K istorii kul'turnykh svyazey Irana i Kitaya v XVI - nachale XVIII vv. (po materialam keramicheskogo proizvodstva). *Iskusstvo i arkheologiya Irana,* 1971, pp. 26-41

ASLANAPA, Oktay. Turkish ceramic art. *Archaeology* 24 (1971), pp. 209-219.

BAKIRER, Ömür. The excavations at Korucutepe, Turkey, 1968-70: the medieval glazed pottery. *JNES* 33(1974), pp. 96-108.

BALASHOVA, G. Dva kuvshina so shtampovannym ornamentom iz Munchak-Tepe (Uzbekskaya SSR). *Soobshch. Gos. Ermitazha* 39(1974), pp. 52-56.

BALASHOVA, G.N. Glinyanyy kurshin XII-XIII vv. s epicheskimi stzenami. (A twelfth-thirteenth century pottery jug decorated with epic subjects.) *Srednyaya Aziya i Iran: sbornik statey,* 1972, pp. 91-106.

BERNUS, M. Acquisitions de céramiques iraniennes. *Rev. du Louvre* 22(1972), pp. 193-204.

BERNUS, M. Céramiques du Proche-Orient arabe. *Rev.du Louvre* 23(1973), pp. 40-44.

BOEHMER, R.M. Keramik aus der Umgebung von Batas. *Sumer* 30(1974), pp. 101-108.

BULATOV, N.M. Kobal't v keramike Zolotoy Ordy. (Cobalt en céramique de la Horde d'Or.) *Sov. arkh.* 1974(4), pp. 135-141.

CARSWELL, John. A fourteenth century Chinese porcelain dish from Damascus. *American University of Beirut Festival book,* 1967, pp. 39-58.

CARSWELL, J. Six tiles. *Islamic art in the Metropolitan Museum of Art,* ed. R. Ettinghausen, 1972, pp. 99-124.

V ART

CARSWELL, J. Some fifteenth-century hexagonal titles from the Near East. *Victoria and Albert Mus. yb.* 3(1972), pp. 59-75.

CHAMPAULT, D. Notes sur certains aspects de la céramique au Nord Yémen. *Objets et mondes* 14(1974), pp. 107-116.

DENNY, W.B. Blue-and-white Islamic pottery on Chinese themes. *Boston Mus.bull.* 72, no.368(1974), pp. 76-99.

ETTINGHAUSEN, R. Comments on later Iranian ceramics. A review article based on Arthur Lane, *Later Islamic pottery ... Artibus Asiae* 35(1973), pp. 165-169.

FEHÉRVÁRI, G. An early eighteenth-century Persian blue and white. *JRAS* 1970, pp. 137-141

FEHÉRVÁRI, Géza. Islamic pottery from Iran. *Apollo* 93,no.108 (1971), pp. 106-112.

FRIERMAN, J.D. and GIAUQUE, R.D. Saljūq faīence and Tīmūrid earthenware from Tammīsha: some preliminary technological notes. *Iran* 11(1973), pp. 180-184.

GALLOTTI MINOLA, M. Mostra "occident-orient" a Strasburgo. *Faenza* 58(1972), pp. 93-94.

GRABAR, O. Notes on the decorative composition of a bowl from Northeastern Iran. *Islamic art in the Metropolitan Museum of Art*, ed. R. Ettinghausen, 1972, pp. 91-98.

GRAZHDANKINA, N.S., RTVELADZE, E.V. Vliyanie Khorezma na keramicheskoe proizvodstvo zolotoordininskogo goroda Madzhara (L'influence du Kharezm sur l'industrie céramique de la ville de Modjar (La Horde d'Or). *Sov. Arkh.* 1971(1), pp. 127-139

HADIDI, Adnan. The pottery from Tell Siran. *Fac. Arts J., Univ. Jordan* 4 (1973), pp. 23-38.

KALB, Ph. Rote Glättstreifen-Keramik in Afghanistan. *Archäol.Mitt.aus Iran* N.F.6 (1973), pp. 265-271.

KUBIAK, W.B. Crusaders' pottery of Al-Mīnā found at Fusṭāṭ. *Folia Or.* 12(1970), pp. 113-123

KUBIAK, W.B. Medieval ceramic oil lamps from Fusṭāṭ. *Ars Orientalis* 8(1970), pp. 1-18

KURDIAN, H. A note on Persian blue and white wares with Armenian monograms in the Victoria and Albert Museum, London. *JRAS* 1975, pp. 54-56.

KURZ, O. The strange history of an Alhambra vase. *And.* 40(1975), pp. 205-212.

KVIRKVELIA, G.G. Iranskaya lyustrovaya keramika XVIII-XIX vv. (po materialam Gosudarstvennogo muzeya Gruzii). *Iskusstvo i arkheologiya Irana,* 1971, pp. 154-162

McMEEKIN, I. An introduction to Oriental ceramics. *JOS Australia* 1961 (no. 2), pp. 3-6.

MASLENITZYNA, S.P. K atributzii dvukh chash "Minai" iz kollektzii GMINV. *Iskusstvo i arkheologiya Irana,* 1971, pp. 199-206

MEDLEY, M. Islam, Chinese porcelain and Ardabīl. *Iran* 13(1975), pp. 31-37.

MIKAMI, Tsugio. The relation between Persian pottery and Chinese ceramics in medieval Iran. *Memorial vol. Vth Internat. Cong. Iranian Art and Archaeology,* 1972, Vol. 2, pp. 360-361.

MIKHAL'CHENKO, S.E. Sistematizatziya massovoy nepolivnoy keramiki zolotoordynskikh gorodov Povolzh'ya. (Systematisation de la poterie non glaçurée provenant des villes de Horde d'Or du bassin de Volga.) *Sov. arkheologiya* 1973(3), pp. 118-132.

NATH, R. Glazed-tile decoration and Chini-ka-rauza. *Medieval India* 1(1969), pp. 260-262.

NAUMANN, R. Eine keramische Werkstatt des 13. Jahrhunderts auf dem Takht-i Suleiman. *Beiträge zur Kunstgeschichte Asiens. In memoriam E. Diez,* 1963, pp. 301-307

ONEY, Gönül. Kubadabad ceramics. *Art of Iran and Anatolia* ... ed. W. Watson, 1974, pp. 68-84.

PAVÓN MALDONADO, B. La loza doméstica de Madīnat al-Zahrā'. *And.* 37(1972), pp. 191-227.

PIRVERDYAN, N.A. Iranskie tkani sefevidskogo vremeni s syuzhetnymi izobrazheniyami (voprosy atributzii). *Iskusstvo i arkheologiya Irana,* 1971, pp. 241-252

POPE, J.A. Chinese influences on Iznik pottery: a re-examination of an old problem. *Islamic art in the Metropolitan Museum of Art,* ed. R. Ettinghausen, 1972, pp. 125-139.

POSAC MON, C. Loza dorada nazarí hallada en Ceuta. *Actas IV congresso de estudos árabes e islâmicos* 1968(1971), pp. 565-571.

PUGACHENKOVA, G.A., REMPEL', L.I. Samarkandskie ochazhki. *Iz istorii iskusstva velikogo goroda. (K 2500-letiyu Samarkanda.),* 1972, pp. 206-234.

RAPOPORT, I. K voprosu o kitayskikh vliyaniyakh v keramike Irana "iranskie seladony". (On the problem of Chinese influence on Iranian ceramics (Iranian celadon wares). *SGE* 34(1972), pp. 23-29.

RAPOPORT, I. K voprosu o kitayskikh uliyaniyakh v keramike Irana "iranskie seladony". (On the problems of Chinese influence on Iranian ceramics (Iranian celadon wares).) *Soobsch. Gos. Ermitazha* 35(1972), pp. 23-25.

RAPOPORT, I.V. Monokhromnaya keramika Irana XVI-XVII vv. s rel'efnymi izobrazheniyami. O sryazi keramiki s miniatyurnoy zhivopis'yu. (Iranian sixteenth-seventeenth century ceramics in monochrome with relief designs.) *Srednyaya Aziya i Iran: sbornik statey,* 1972, pp. 149-156.

ROSEN-AYALON, M. Islamic pottery from Susa. *Archaeology* 24 (1971), pp. 204-208.

SAUER, J.A. A ceramic note on the Arabic "Ostracon" from Tell Siran. *Ann. Dept. Antiquities, Jordan* 18(1973), pp. 15-16.

SCERRATO, U. Ceramiche di tradizione islamica a Napoli. *Studi magrebini II,* 1968, pp. 191-199.

SCHNYDER, R. Mediaeval incised and carved wares from North West Iran. *Art of Iran and Anatolia* ... ed. W. Watson, 1974, pp. 85-95.

SCHNYDER, R. Saljuq pottery in Iran. *Memorial vol. Vth Internat. Cong. Iranian Art and Archaeology,* 1972, Vol. 2, pp. 189-197.

TASHKHODZHAEV, Sh.S. Voprosy istoricheskoy klassifikatzii polivnoy keramiki Afrasiaba. *Iz istorii iskusstva veligogo goroda. (K 2500-letiyu Samarkanda.),* 1972, pp. 185-205.

TOUEIR, Kassem. Céramiques mameloukes à Damas. *BEO* 26(1973), pp. 209-217.

WILKINSON, C.K. Ceramic relationships between Nishapur, Merv and Samarkand. *Memorial vol. Vth Internat. Cong. Iranian Art and Archaeology,* 1972, Vol. 2, pp. 242-245.

ZOZAYA, J. Cerámicas islámicas del Museo de Soria. *Bol. Asoc. Esp. Orientalistas* 11(1975), pp. 135-148.

See also V. m. i. Welch.

See also V. v. 3. 'Abd Ar-Râziq

See also V. v. 3. Oney.

See also VII. a. Matson.

See also VIII. a. *Iran.* Whitehouse.

See also VIII. d. *Egypt.* Bianquis, Scanlon, Watson.

See also XII. e. Brini.

See also XII. e. Lefebvre.

p TEXTILES

BRETT, M.K. Indian painted and dyed cottons for the European market. *Aspects of Indian art,* ed. Pratapaditya Pal, 1972, pp. 167-171.

DENNY, W.B. Ottoman Turkish textiles. *Textile Museum J.* 3(1972), pp. 55-66.

DUPAIGNE, B. Un artisan d'Afghanistan. Sa vie, ses problèmes, ses espoirs. *Objets et mondes* 14(1974), pp. 143-170.

EGYED, Edit. On a textile from the Safavid period. *Iparművészeti Múz. Evkönyvei* 12(1970), pp. 21-34.

FEDOROVICH, E.F. Issledovaniya srednevekovykh tkaney Samarkanda. *Iz istorii iskusstva veligogo goroda. (K 2500-letiuu Samarkanda.),* 1972, pp. 235-242.

HABIB, Mustapha el. Notes sur un tiraz au nom de Abi l-Mansur al'Aziz bi l-lah, le Fatimide (365-386H./975-996 ap. J.-C.) *Rev.du Louvre* 23(1973), pp. 299-302.

KAHLENBERG, M. A Mughal personage velvet. *Burlington mag.* 115(no.828, 1973), pp. 723-725.

KAHLENBERG, M.H. Textiles from the Islamic world. *Apollo* 101(1975), pp. 108-109.

KLEIN, A. Tesig-Bandweberei mit Gold- und Silberfaden in San'a. *Baessler-Archiv* 22 (1974), pp. 225-246.

NEMTZEVA, N.B. K istorii tkaney i odezhdy naseleniya Sredney Azii XV v. *Iz istorii iskusstva velikogo goroda. (K 2500-letiyu Samarkanda.),* 1972, pp. 243-251.

PIRVERDYAN, N.A. K voprosu o persidskikh syuzhetnykh tkanyakh XVI-XVII vv. (Some Persian sixteenth and seventeenth century fabrics with figural subjects.) *Srednyaya Aziya i Iran: sbornik statey,* 1972, pp. 157-162.

SUGIER, C. Survivances d'une civilisation de la laine chez les Jebalia du sud tunisien. *Cah.des arts et traditions populaires* 4 (1971), pp. 35-48.

SCHMIDT, H. Morgenländische und abendländische Seidenmuster in Mittelalter. *Beiträge zur Kunstgeschichte Asiens. In memoriam E. Diez,* 1963, pp. 193-207

See also V. g. 'Izzi.

See also XII. f. Annabi

See also XII. f. Skhiri.

q COSTUME

BEN TANFOUS, Aziz. Les ceintures de femmes en Tunisie. *Cah. des arts et traditions populaires* 4(1971), pp. 103-122.

KAHLENBERG, M.H. A study of the development and use of the Mughal patkā (sash) with reference to the Los Angeles County Museum of Art collection. *Aspects of Indian art,* ed. Pratapaditya Pal, 1972, pp. 153-166.

SCARCE, J. A Persian brassière. *AARP* 7 (1975), pp. 15-21.

SKHIRI, Fathia. Les châles des matmata. *Cah. des arts et traditions populaires* 4 (1971), pp. 49-53.

See also V. a. *Influences and parallels.* Ingrams.

See also V. m. 1. Housego.

See also XII. e. Ougouag-Kezzal.

See also XII. f. Mahjoub.

See also XII. f. Sethom.

See also XII. f. Sugier.

See also XII. f. Zouari.

See also XXX. c. Rondot.

See also XXXII. k. Sharma.

See also XXIII. b. Weir, Kawar.

r EMBROIDERY

JOMIER, J. Le maḥmal du Sultan Qānṣūh al-Ghūrī (début XVIe siècle). *Annales islamol.* 11(1972), pp. 183-188.

M'HARI, L. Gold- und Silberfadenstickerei in Constantine/Algerien. *Abh. Ber. Staatl. Mus. Völkerk., Dresden* 34(1975), pp. 165-169.

See also XII. e. Ougouag-Kezzal.

s CARPETS

ASLANAPA, Oktay. Ein anatolischer Tierteppich vom Ende des 15. Jahrhunderts. *Beiträge zur Kunstgeschichte Asiens. In memoriam E. Diez,* 1963, pp. 173-181

CAMMANN, S. van R. Cosmic symbolism on carpets from the Sanguszko group. *Studies in art and literature of the Near East in honor of R. Ettinghausen,* 1974, pp. 181-208.

CAMMANN, S. The systematic study of Oriental rugs: techniques and patterns. *JAOS* 95(1975), pp. 248-260.

DENNY, W.B. Anatolian rugs: an essay on method. *Textile Museum J.* 3iv(1973), pp. 7-25.

DICKIE, J. Iconography of the prayer rug. *Oriental Art* 18(1) 1972, pp. 41-49

DIMAND, M.S. The Isfahan School of Rug Weaving in the time of Shah Abbas the Great. *Memorial vol. Vth Internat. Cong. Iranian Art and Archaeology,* 1972, Vol. 2, pp. 34-35.

DIMAND, M.S. Persian hunting carpets of the sixteenth century. *Boston Mus.Bull.* 69(nos. 355-6, 1971), pp. 15-20

DIMAND, M.S. The seventeenth-century Isfahan school of rug weaving. *Islamic art in the Metropolitan Museum of Art,* ed. R. Ettinghausen, 1972, pp. 255-266.

EILAND, M.L. Comments on the origins of Safavid carpets. *Memorial vol. Vth Internat. Cong. Iranian Art and Archaeology,* 1972, Vol. 2, pp. 36-52.

ELLIS, C.G. The Portuguese carpets of Gujarat. *Islamic art in the Metropolitan Museum of Art,* ed. R. Ettinghausen, 1972, pp. 267-289.

ETTINGHAUSEN, R. The Boston Hunting Carpet in historical perspective. *Boston Mus. Bull.* 69(nos. 355-6, 1971), pp. 70-81

GOMBOS, K. An interesting Tekke-Turkoman carpet. *Ars decorativa* 2(1974), pp. 129-141.

HEINZ, D. Die persischen Teppiche im Österreichischen Museum für angewandte Kunst. *Bustan* 11iv-12i(1970-1), pp. 23-29.

HEINZ, D. Die persischen Teppiche im Österreichischen Museum für angewandte Kunst. *Commémoration Cyrus. Hommage universel,* II, 1974, pp. 401-413.

HOUSEGO, J. The 19th century Persian carpet boom. *Oriental art* 19(1973), pp. 169-171.

ONDER, Mehmet. Sur un tapis iranien aux distiques. *Memorial vol. Vth Internat. Cong. Iranian Art and Archaeology,* 1972, Vol. 2, pp. 152-154.

REINHARD, U., REINHARD, V. Notizen über türkische Webteppiche, insebesondere bei süd- und südwest-türkischen Nomaden. *Baessler-Archiv* 22(1974), pp. 165-223.

ROLL, C. Prayer rugs of the East. *Arts of Asia* 4iv(1974), pp. 47-57.

SALMON, L. Description of the Boston Carpet. *Boston Mus.Bull.* 69(nos. 355-6, 1971), pp. 82-87

UNGER, E. de. A notable carpet collection: the McMullan collection at the Hayward Gallery. *Oriental art* 19(1973), pp. 172-179.

WELCH, S.C. Two Shahs, some miniatures, and the Boston carpet. *Boston Mus.Bull.* 69(nos. 355-6, 1971), pp. 6-14

YETKIN, Şerare. Zwei Türkische Kilims. *Beiträge zur Kunstgeschichte Asiens. In memoriam E. Diez,* 1963, pp. 182-192

t OTHER FINE ARTS

ANDREWS, P.A. The white house of Khurasan: the felt tents of the Iranian Yomut and Gökleñ. *Iran* 11(1973), pp. 93-110.

DUMMETT, M. A note on some fragments [of playing cards] in the Benaki Museum. *AARP* 4(1973), pp. 93-99.

DUMMETT, M. and ABU-DEEB, Kamal. Some remarks on Mamluk playing-cards. *J. Warburg and Courtauld Insts.* 36(1973), pp. 106-128.

GIBERT, S. Sobre Otto Kurz: "Libri cum characteribus ex nulla materia compositis". *And.* 38(1973), pp. 243-247.

HOLTER, K. Ein mamlukisches Kartenspiel. *WZKM* 67(1975), pp. 165-167.

KURZ, O. Libri cum characteribus ex nulla materia compositis. *In memoriam S.M. Stern* (Israel Or. studies, II, 1972), pp. 240-247.

ROSENFELD, H. Zur Datierbarkeit früher Spielkarten in Europa und im Nahen Orient. *Gutenberg Jhb.* 1975, pp. 353-371.

ÜLKÜTAŞIR, M. Şakir. Gartenkunst und türkische Gärten bei den alten Türken. *Cultura Turcica* 8-10(1971-73), pp. 174-184.

See XXX. b. Semsar.

u MUSIC. THEATRE

i Music

ASKARI, S.H. Amir Khusraw and music. *Dr. Satkari Mookerji felicitation volume,* 1969, pp. 19-33.

AUGIER, P. Ethnomusicologie saharienne. Les documents sonores recueillis récemment en Ahaggar et au Gourara. *Libyca* 20(1972), pp. 291-311.

AUGIER, P. La musique populaire au Sahara algérien. *Annuaire Afrique du Nord* 12(1973), pp. 169-179.

AUGIER, P. La polyrythmie dans les musiques du Sahara. *Libyca* 19(1971), pp. 217-233.

AUGIER, P. Répertoire des musiques sahariennes. Bilan de travaux. *ROMM* 11(1972), pp. 171-179.

BARKESHLI, M. Recherche des degrés de la gamme iranienne à partir de la sensation subjective de consonance. *Acta Iranica,* sér. 1, III, 1974, pp. 339-360.

BAUD-BOVY, S. Chansons d'Epire du Nord et du Pont. *Yearbook Int. Folk Music Council* 3(1971), pp. 120-127.

BENCHEIKH, J.E. Les musiciens et la poèsie. Les écoles d'Iṣḥāq al-Mawsilī (m.225 H.) et d'Ibrāhīm al-Mahdī (m. 224 H.). *Arabica* 22(1975), pp. 114-152.

BLUM, S. Persian folksong in Meshhed (Iran), 1969. *Yb. Int. Folk Music Council* 6(1974), pp. 86-114.

BOSE, Fr. Arabische Elemente in der südspanischen Volksmusik. *Baessler-Archiv* N.S.23(48,1975), pp. 231-238.

BRAHASPATI, K.C.D. Muslim influence on Venkatamakhī. *Dr. Adilya Nath Jha felicitation volume,* III, 1969, pp. 514-538.

CACHIA, P. A 19th century Arab's observations on European music. *Ethnomusicology* 17(1973), pp. 41-51.

CAMILLERI, Ch. The growing awareness by Mediterranean countries of their musical homogeneity due to Arabo-Berber culture. *Actes I. Cong. ét. cult. méditerr. d'infl. arabo-berb.,* 1973, pp. 58-62.

CARON, N. La création d'un centre de musique traditionnelle iranienne. *Studia Iranica* 2(1973), pp. 257-266.

CATON, M. The vocal ornament Takīyah in Persian music. *Sel.rep.ethnomusicology* 2i(1974), pp. 43-53.

CHABRIER, J.C. Music in the Fertile Crescent: Lebanon, Syria, Iraq. *Cultures* 1iii(1974), pp. 36-58.

CHRISTENSEN, D. Ein Tanzlied der Hakkari-Kurden und seine Varianten. *Baessler-Archiv* N.S.23(48,1975), pp. 195-215.

CHRISTENSEN, D. Tanzlieder der Hakkari-Kurden. Eine materialkritische Studie. *Jhb.musikal.Volks- u.Völkerk.* 1(1963), pp. 11-47.

ELSNER, J. Zu Prinzipien arabischer Musizierpraxis. *Jhb.musikal.Volks- u. Völkerk.* 3(1967), pp. 90-95.

ERLMANN, V. Some sources of music in Western Sudan from 1300-1700. *African music* 5iii (1973-74), pp. 34-39.

FARMER, H.G. Corrigenda to the 'Siyāḥat nāma' of Evliyā Chelebi. *Oriens* 21-22 (1968-69), pp. 233-234.

FARUQI, L.I.al. Muwashshaḥ: a vocal form in Islamic culture. *Ethnomusicology* 19(1975), pp. 1-29.

FÖDERMAYR, Fr. Die Musik der Tuareg. *Jhb. musikal.Volks- u.Völkerk.* 5(1970), pp. 55-72.

GHĀNIM, Muḥammad 'Abdū. Verse used in Ṣan'ānī songs. *Al-Abhath* 25(1972), pp. 17-326.

GUIGNARD, M. Mauritanie. Les Maures et leur musique au XIXème siècle. *Musikkulturen Asiens, Afrikas und Ozeaniens im 19. Jhdt,* hrsg. R. Günther, 1973, pp. 241-265.

HOERBURGER, F. Gebetsruf und Qor'ān-Rezitation in Kathmandu(Nepal). *Baessler-Archiv* N.F.23(48,1975), pp. 121-137.

HOERBURGER, F. Orientalische Elemente in Volkstanz und Volkstanzmusik Nordgriechenlands. *Jhb.musikal.Volks- u.Völkerk.* 3 (1967), pp. 96-104.

KHAN, Abdul Halim Jaffer. Hazrat Amir Khusro. *J. Ind. Musicol. Soc.* 4ii(1973), pp. 1-20.

KRISHNASWAMI, S. Musical changes in Uzbekhistan. *J.Ind.Musicol.Soc.* 5ii(1974), pp. 13-17.

KUBICA, V. Klassische Tradition und Volkstradition der arabischen Musik im Irak. *Abh. Ber. Staatl. Mus. Völkerk., Dresden* 34(1975), pp. 467-472.

KUCKERTZ, J. und MASSOUDIEH, Mohammad Taghi. Volksgesänge aus Iran. *Baessler-Archiv* N.S.23(48,1975), pp. 217-229.

MAINGUY, M.H. "Liban-musique". *Travaux et jours* 39 (1971), pp. 49-56.

MANIK, L. Zwei Fassungen einer von Safī al-Dīn notierten Melodie. *Baessler-Archiv* N.F.23(48,1975), pp. 145-151.

MASSOUDIEH, Taghi. Hochzeitslieder aus Balucestan. *Jhb.musikal.Volks- u.Völkerk.* 7(1973), pp. 58-69.

MASSOUDIEH, Mohammad T. Tradition und Wandel in der persischen Musik des 19. Jahrhunderts. *Musikkulturen Asiens, Afrikas und Ozeaniens im 19. Jhdt,* hrsg. R. Günther, 1973, pp. 73-94.

NASR, S.H. The influence of Sufism on traditional Persian music. *J.Reg.Cult. Inst.* 3(nos. 11-12, 1970), pp. 79-88.

NAṢR, Seyyed Ḥosein. The influence of Sufism on traditional Persian music. *IC* 45(1971), pp. 171-179.

NETTL, B. Persian popular music in 1969. *Ethnomusicology* 16(1972), pp. 218-239.

NETTL, B., RIDDLE, R. Taqsim Nahawand: a study of sixteen performances by Jihad Racy. *Yb.Int.Folk Music Council* 5(1973), pp. 11-50.

NEUBAUER, E. Neuere Bücher zur arabischen Musik. *Der Islam* 48 (1971), pp. 1-27.

NEUBAUER, E. Die Theorie vom Īqā'. I. Übersetzung des Kitāb al-Īqā'āt von Abū Naṣr al-Fārābī. *Oriens* 21-22(1968-69), pp. 196-232.

PACHOLCZYK, J.M. Vibrato as a function of modal practice in the Qur'ān chant of Shaikh 'Abdu'L-Bāsiṭ 'Abdu'ṣ-Ṣamad. *Sel. rep.ethnomusicology* 2i(1974), pp. 33-41.

QURESHI, Regula. Ethnomusicological research among Canadian communities of Arab and East Indian origin. *Ethnomusicology* 16(1972), pp. 381-396.

RADZHABOV, I.R. O muzyke Samarkanda. *Iz istorii iskusstva velikogo goroda. (K 2500-letiyu Samarkanda.),* 1972, pp. 298-313.

REICHE, J.P. Stilelemente süd-türkischer Davul-Zurna-Stücke. *Jhb.musikal.Volks- u.Völkerk.* 5(1970), pp. 9-54.

REINHARD, K. Musik am Schwarzen Meer. Erste Ergebnisse einer Forschungsreise in die Nordost-Türkei. *Jhb.musikal. Volks- u.Völkerk.* 2(1966), pp. 9-58.

REINHARD, K. Die Türkei im 19. Jahrhundert. *Musikkulturen Asiens, Afrikas und Ozeaniens im 19. Jhdt,* hrsg. R. Günther, 1973, pp. 21-48.

SÂ, R. de. Musique egyptienne. *MIDEO* 12 (1974), pp. 187-194.

SCHNEIDER, M. Nochmals asiatische Parallelen zur Berbermusik. *Ethnologica* N.F.2(1960), pp. 433-438.

SCHNEIDER, M. Zur Metrisierung einer arabischen Melodie. *Baessler-Archiv* N.F.23(48,1975), pp. 153-157.

SHILOAH, Amnon. A group of Arabic wedding songs from the village of Deyr al-Asad. *Folklore Res. Center studies* 4(1974), pp. 267-296.

SHILOAH, Amnon. Le poète-musicien et la création poético-musicale au Moyen Orient. *Yb. Int. Folk Music Council* 6 (1974), pp. 52-63.

SHILOAH, A. Les sept traites de musique dans le manuscrit 1705 de Manisa. *Israel Oriental studies* 1(1971), pp. 303-315.

SIGNELL, K. Comments on Wouter Swet's review of "Music of the Mevlevî". *Yearbook Int. Folk Music Council* 3(1971), pp. 140-141.

SIMON, A. Dahab--ein blinder Sänger Nubiens. Musik und Gesellschaft im Nordsudan. *Baessler-Archiv* N.F.23(48, 1975), pp. 159-194.

SLOBIN, M. Rhythmic aspects of the Tajik *Maqam.* *Ethnomusicology* 15(1971), pp. 100-104

STEINLE, P. Sitar player, Ustad Vilayat Khan. *Arts of Asia* 3iii(1973), pp. 27-29.

TOUMA, Habib Hasan. Die Koranrezitation: eine Form der religiösen Musik der Araber. *Baessler-Archiv* N.F.23(48,1975), pp. 87-120.

TOUMA, Habib Hassan. Die Musik der Araber im 19. Jahrhundert. *Musikkulturen Asiens, Afrikas und Ozeaniens im 19. Jhdt,* hrsg. R. Günther, 1973, pp. 49-71.

WADE, B. Chīz in khyāl: the traditional composition in the improvised performance. *Ethnomusicology* 17(1973), pp. 443-459.

WRIGHT, O. *Elmuahym* and *Elmuarifa.* *BSOAS* 37(1974), pp. 655-659.

ŻERAŃSKA, S. Arabska średniowieczna kultura muzyczna. (L'art musical arabe au Moyen Age). *Przegląd or.* 1972(3, no. 83), pp. 268-272.

Chants de la naissance à Sfax. *Cah.des arts et traditions populaires* 4(1971), pp. 29-33.

See also II. c. 2. Nasr.

See also IV. b. *Ibn Hindu.* Shiloah.

See also XII. b. Harries.

See also XII. c. Augier.

See also XXVIII. b. Franz.

See also XXVIII. ll. Gulisashvili.

See also XXVIII. u. Sulițeanu.

See also XLIII. h. Klitz and Cherlin.

ii Musical instruments

CAMPBELL, R.G. Instrumentenkundliche Notizen zu sechs türkischen Miniaturen. *Baessler-Archiv* N.F.23(48,1975), pp. 31-37.

DELABY, L. Tambours silencieux en Sibérie méridionale. *Objets et mondes* 15(1975), pp. 69-76.

ENAYETULLAH, Anwar. Musical instruments of Pakistan. *J.Reg.Cult.Inst.* 3(nos. 11-12, 1970), pp. 89-96.

KHATSCHI, K. Das Intervallbildungsprinzip des persischen Dāstgāh Shūr. *Jhb.musikal. Volks- u.Völkerk.* 3(1967), pp. 70-84.

NETTL, B. Aspects of form in the instrumental performance of the Persian *āvāz*. *Ethnomusicology* 18(1974), pp. 405-414.

PICKEN, L.E.R. Stripped-bark whistles: rites and roles. *Baessler-Archiv* N.F.23 (48,1975), pp. 61-86.

REINHARD, K. Die türkische Doppelklarinette çifte. *Baessler-Archiv* 22(1974), pp. 139-163.

SHILOAH, Amnon. Un ancien traité sur le 'ūd d'Abū Yūsuf al Kindī. Traduction et commentaire. *Israel or.stud.* 4(1974), pp. 179-205.

TRAERUP, B. Sharki--eine Langhalslaute in Kosovo (Jugoslavien). *Baessler-Archiv* N.F.23(48,1975), pp. 39-59.

VYZGO, T.S. Afrasiabskaya lyutnya. *Iz istorii iskusstva velikogo goroda. (K 2500-letiyu Samarkanda.)*, 1972, pp. 269-297.

WOODSON, C. The effect of a snare on the tone of a single-headed frame drum, the Moroccan Bendīr. *Sel.rep.ethnomusicology* 2i(1974), pp. 103-117.

iii Theatre. Cinema. Broadcasting

ABUL NAGA, Attia. Le théâtre Arabe et ses origines. *Cah. d'hist. mondiale* 14(1972), pp. 880-898.

AND, Metin. Origins and early development of the Turkish theater. *Rev.nat.lit.* 4i (1973), pp. 53-64.

AZIZA, Mohamed. Molière et le théâtre arabe. *Etudes philos. et litt. (Actes du Coll. de Mohammédia)* 5(1971), pp. 129-132.

BARTINA, S. Posible origen anatólico de la sardana. *BAEO* 6(1970), pp. 83-107.

BENCHENEB, Rachid. Les dramaturges arabes et le récit-cadre des Mille et une Nuits. *ROMM* 18(1974), pp. 7-18.

BENCHENEB, Rachid. Les grands thèmes du théâtre arabe contemporain. *ROMM* 7(1970), pp. 9-14.

BENCHENEB, Rachid. Les mémoires de Mahieddine Bachtarzi ou vingt ans de théâtre algérien. *ROMM* 9(1971), pp. 15-20.

BENCHENEB, Rachid. Les Mille et une Nuits et les origines du théâtre arabe. *SI* 40 (1974), pp. 133-160.

BENCHENEB, Rachid. Regards sur le théâtre algérien. *ROMM* 6(1969), pp. 24-27.

BENCHENEB, Rachid. Les sources françaises du théâtre égyptien. *ROMM* 8(1970), pp. 9-23.

CALMARD, J. Le mécénat des représentations de *ta'ziye*. I. Les précurseurs de Nâseroddin Chấh. *Le monde iranien et l'Islam* II, 1974, pp. 73-126.

CHARFEDDINE, Moncef. Où en est le théâtre tunisien? *IBLA* 38(no.136, 1975), pp. 323-325.

CHERIAA, Tahar. L'adaptation au cinéma des oeuvres littéraires dans les pays de culture arabe. *IBLA* 37(no.133, 1974), pp. 103-137.

FADEEVA, I.E. Pervyy turetzkii professional'-nyy teatr. (The first Turkish professional theatre). *NAA* 1972(3), pp. 139-145.

FOROUGH, Mehdi. The literary and artistic value of the "Ta'zia" (religious play). *Memorial vol. Vth Internat. Cong. Iranian Art and Archaeology*, 1972, Vol. 2, pp. 83-89.

HAGGAGI, Ahmad al-. European theatrical companies and the origin of the Egyptian theater (1870-1923). *AJAS* 3(1975), pp. 83- 91.

HAMARNEH, S.K. An outline of the contemporary Arab theatre. *Problemy literatur orientalnych*, 1974, pp. 81-85.

HENNEBELLE, M., HENNEBELLE, G. Cinéma et société au Maghreb. *Ann.Afr.nord* 12(1973), pp. 131-150.

LELONG, M. Un nouveau film tunisien: Et demain ... de Brahim Babaï. *IBLA* 35(no.129, 1972), pp. 173-174.

LELONG, M. Les Vèmes Journées cinématographiques de Carthage. *IBLA* 37(no.134, 1974), pp. 365-370.

MERKEL, U. Deutsches Theater im Maghreb - Voraussetzungen, Schwierigkeiten, Möglichkeiten des deutsch-arabischen Dialogs. *Z.f.Kulturaustausch* 24ii(1974), pp. 62-71.

METTROP, A. Six mois de thèatre à Tunis, septembre 1970-février 1971. *IBLA* 127 (1971), pp. 172-176.

MOOSA, Matti. Naqqāsh and the rise of the native Arab theatre in Syria. *J. Arabic lit.* 3(1972), pp. 106-117.

MOOSA, M. Ya'qūb Ṣanū' and the rise of Arab drama in Egypt. *IJMES* 5(1974), pp. 401-433.

PERONCEL-HUGOZ, J.P. Une interview exclusive de Youssef Chahine. *Nouvelle Rev. du Caire* 1(1975), pp. 203-211.

RAKHMANOV, M.R. Iz istorii drevnego teatra Samarkanda. *Iz istorii iskusstva velikogo goroda. (K 2500-letiyu Samarkanda.)*, 1972, pp. 314-331.

ROTH-LALY, A. Emprunt et spontanéité dans le théâtre algérien de langue dialectale. *Actes I. Cong. ét. cult. méditerr. d'infl. arabo-berb.*, 1973, pp. 305-311.

SAYADI, Salem. Le cinéma tunisien, ses moyens, ses problèmes. *IBLA* 35(no.129, 1972), pp. 141-148.

TIMOFEEV, I. Egipetskiy teatr teney "Khayal az-zill". *Voprosy vostochnogo literaturovedeniya i tekstologii*, 1975, pp. 32-38.

TURGAY-AHMAD, Bedia. Modern Turkish theater. *Rev.nat.lit.* 4i(1973), pp. 65-81.

YAR-SHATER, Ehsan. Developments of Persian drama in the context of cultural confrontation. *Iran: continuity and variety, ed. by P.J. Chelkowski*, 1971, pp. 21-38

ZAKHOS-PAPAZAHARIOU, E. Les origines et survivances ottomanes au sein du théâtre d'ombres grec. *Turcica* 5(1975), pp. 32-39.

See also XII. e. Hammeri.

See also XVI. a. Hennebelle.

See also XXXVII. l. 'Awad.Ra'i.Stetkevych

See also XXXVII. l. Hanna, Salti.

See also XXXVII. l. Moosa

See also XXXIX. a. Chelkowski.

See also XLI. a. Brands.

v APPLIED ARTS

i General. Manual crafts. Paper making. Postage stamps

BROMBERGER, C. Habitations du Gilân. *Objets et mondes* 14(1974), pp. 3-56.

CHAUDHURY, Mamata. The technique of preparing writing materials in early India with special reference to al-Biruni's observations. *IC* 48(1974), pp. 33-38.

ṬĀHIR, Muṣṭaphā Anwar. Traité de la fortification des demeures contre l'horreur des séismes (Taḥṣīn al-manāzil min hawl al-zalāzil) d' Abū l-Ḥasan 'Alī ibn al-Ǧazzar, écrit à l'occasion du tremblement de terre de 984 H./1576. *Ann. islamologiques* 12(1974), pp. 131-159.

Iqbal's poetry on Pakistani stamps. *J. Reg. Cult. Inst.* 1 ii(1967), pp. 25-28.

ii Cookery

CARSWELL, J. Fit for the Sultan. *AARP* 5 (1974), pp. 1-4.

See also V. c. *India*.

See XII. f. Skhiri.

See also XXXII. j. Khan

iii Archery. Horsemanship. Falconry. Military art and science. Sports and games

'ABD AR-RĀZIQ, Aḥmad. La chasse au faucon d'après des céramiques du Musée du Caire. *Ann.Islamologiques* 9(1970), pp. 109-121.

ABD AR-RAZIQ, Ahmad. La chasse au guépard d'après les sources arabes et les oeuvres d'art musulman. *Arabica* 20(1973), pp. 11-24.

'ABD AR-RĀZIQ, Aḥmad. Deux jeux sportifs en Égypte au temps des Mamlūks. *Ann. islamologiques* 12(1974), pp. 95-130.

ALLEN, M.J.S. and SMITH, G.R. Some notes on hunting techniques and practices in the Arabian Peninsula. *Arabian studies* 2(1975), pp. 108-147.

AMAVI, Mohammad Ahmad Hussain el-. Old Arabian rounds. *J. Soc. Archer Antiquaries* 12 (1969), pp. 11-13.

GAUNT, G.D., GAUNT, A.M. Mongol archers of the thirteenth century. *J. Soc. archer-antiquaries* 16(1973), pp. 18-22.

GROSSET-GRANGE, H. Comment naviguent aujourd'hui les arabes de l'Océan indien: addenda et corrigenda. *Arabica* 22(1975), pp. 51-60.

HANAWAY, W.L., Jr. The concept of the hunt in Persian literature. *Boston Mus.Bull.* 69(nos. 355-6, 1971), pp. 21-69

HUDA, M.Z. Faras Nāmah-i-Hāshimī and Shālihotra. *J. Asiatic Soc. Pakistan* 14(1969), pp. 143-165.

ISLES, F. Turkish flight arrows. *J. Soc. Archer Antiquaries* 4(1961), pp. 25-28.

LATHAM, J.D. A propos of archery in the Maghrib: the oriental background. *II. Cong.int.ét.nord-afr.* 1970, pp. 123-130.

V ART

McEWEN, E. Inscriptions on Islamic composite bows. *J. Soc. Archer Antiquaries* 13(1970), pp. 17-18.

McEWEN, E.; ELMY, D. Whistling arrows. *J. Soc. Archer Antiquaries* 13(1970), pp. 23-26.

ONEY, Gonul. Mounted hunting scenes of Anatolian Seljuks in comparison with Iranian Seljuks. *Memorial vol. Vth Internat. Cong. Iranian Art and Archaeology,* 1972, Vol. 2, pp. 362-367.

PATERSON, W.F. Archery in Moghul India. An illustrated manual of instruction in the collection of the Marquess of Bute. *IQ* 16(1972), pp. 81-95.

P[ATERSON], W.F. The Fustat ring. *J. Soc. Archer Antiquaries* 10(1967), p. 40.

PATERSON, W.F. Musée de l'Homme. *J. Soc. Archer Antiquaries* 10(1967), pp. 18-20.

PATERSON, W.F. Persian archery of the 14th century. *J. Soc. Archer Antiquaries* 5 (1962), pp. 20-22.

PATERSON, W.F. The Sassanids. *J. Soc. Archer Antiquaries* 12(1969), pp. 29-32.

PATERSON, W.F. Shooting under a shield. *J. Soc. Archer Antiquaries* 12(1969), pp. 27-28.

PATERSON, W.F. The skein bow. *J. Soc. Archer Antiquaries* 7(1964), pp. 24-27.

PATERSON, W.F. Thumb guards. *J. Soc. Archer Antiquaries* 6(1963), pp. 14-15.

PUJO, J. Les boutres à Djibouti: une survivance de l'âge de la voile. *Pount* 2(1967), pp. 9-15.

SARKAR, Jagadish Narayan. Some aspects of military thinking and practice in medieval India. *Q. rev.hist.stud.* 11(1971-2), pp. 9-18

SOUCEK, Sv. Certain types of ships in Ottoman-Turkish terminology. *Turcica* 7 (1975), pp. 233-249.

STOLZ, K. Von der Falkenjagd am Khalifenhofe zu Cordoba. [Unknown journal] pp. 18-19.

VIRÉ, F. À propos de *La chasse au guépard d'après les sources arabes et les oeuvres d'art musulman* par Abd ar-Raziq. *Arabica* 21(1974), pp. 84-88.

VIRÉ, F. À propos des chiens de chasse *salūqī* et *zaġārī*. *REI* 41(1973), pp. 231-240.

VIRÉ, F. La chasse à la glu (*tadbīq*) en Orient médiéval. *Arabica* 20(1973), pp. 1-10.

See also II. b. 2. Fisher.

See also V. m. 1. Goswamy and Jhamb.

See also V. m. 1. Mostafa.

See also XIX. j. Farhi.

See also XXII. a. Clouet.

See also XXXII. c. Yusuf

See also XXXIX. c. Sarkar.

VI GEOGRAPHY: GENERAL

a GEOGRAPHY

ENGLISH, P.W. Geographical perspectives on the Middle East: the passing of the ecological trilogy. *Geographers abroad,* M.W. Mikesell editor, 1973, pp. 134-164.

HIRSCHBERG, H.Z. The Jewish quarter in the Muslim town. *Proc.27th Int.Cong.Or. 1967* (1971), pp. 224-227.

KEDDIE, N.R. Is there a Middle East? *IJMES* 4(1973), pp. 255-271.

KOBORI, Iwao. Some notes on diffusion of qanat. *Orient* [Japan] 9(1973), pp. 43-66.

LANDAY, S. The ecology of Islamic cities: the case for the ethnocity. *Econ.geog.* 47 (1971), pp. 303-313.

McLAREN, Donald S. Population, food and disease in the Near East. *American University of Beirut Festival book,* 1967, pp. 185-219.

MANTRAN, R. Droits d'entrée sur les navires à Istanbul au milieu du XVIIe siècle (Rüsumat-i ihtisabiye). *Turcica* 5(1975), pp. 94-107.

MIQUEL, A. Comment lire la littérature géographique arabe du moyen age? *Cahiers de civ. méd.* 15(1972), pp. 97-104.

ROWTON, M.B. Urban autonomy in a nomadic enrironment. *JNES* 32(1973), pp. 201-215.

SCHLIEPHAKE, K. Terminologie du paysage culturel arabo-islamique. *CT* 22(85-86, 1974), pp. 209-213.

SOMOGYI, J. De. Economic geography of Islamic countries. *IC* 45 (1971), pp. 35-54.

VI GEOGRAPHY

TERÉS, E. "Al-Walaŷa", topónimo árabe. *And.* 33 (1968), pp. 291-309.

VIGUERA, M.J. El *nasnās:* un motivo de *'aǧa'ib. Orientalia Hispanica* I, 1974, pp. 647-674.

WIRTH, E. Recent structural changes of the traditional Near-Eastern city from a point of view of geography. *Proc.27th Int.Cong.Or.1967* (1971), pp. 185-186.

See also XXII. a. Tibbetts.

See also XXXV. a. Castrillo Márquez

b MAPS

AYOUBI, Mohamed Z. Les toponymes libanais. *Hannon* 2(1967), pp. 133-138.

GOLDENBERG, L.A. The atlases of Siberia by S.U. Remezov as a source for old Russian urban history. *Imago mundi* 25 (1971), pp. 39-46.

HADJ-SADOK, Maḥammad. Kitāb al-Dja'rāfiyya. Mappemonde du calife al-Ma'mūn reproduite par Fazārī (IIIe/IXe s.) rééditée et commentée par Zuhrī (VIe/XIIe s.). Texte arabe établi avec introduction en français (résumé en arabe). *BEO* 21 (1968), pp. 7-310.

KUMEKOV, B.E. Strana kimakov po karte al-Idrisī. *Strany i narody Vostoka pod obshchey red. D.A. Ol'derogge,* X, 1971, pp. 194-198.

MADAN, P.L. Cartographic records in the National Archives of India. *Imago mundi* 25(1971), pp. 79-80.

SOUCEK, S. The 'Ali Macar Reis atlas' and the Deniz kitabi: their place in the genre of portolan charts and atlases. *Imago mundi* 25(1971), pp. 17-27.

TAKÁCS, J. Arabic geographic names in cartography. *Onoma* 17(1972-3), pp. 216-223.

See also V. m. l. Reindl.

See also XXVI. a. Besançon.

See also XXIX. f. Abrahamowicz

c MUSLIM GEOGRAPHERS

ALIEV, S.M. O datirovke nabega rusov, upomyanutykh Ibn Isfandiyarom i Amoli. (On the dating of the raids of the Rus mentioned in the works of Ibn Isfandiar and Amoly.) *Fontes orientales... curavit A.S. Tveritinova* II, 1969, pp. 316-321.

BECKINGHAM, C.F. Ibn Ḥauqal's map of Italy. *Iran and Islam, in memory of V. Minorsky,* 1971, pp. 73-78

BEYLIS, V.M. Narody vostochnoy Evropy v kratkom opisanii Mutakhkhara al-Makdisi (X v.) (La population de l'Europe orientale dans l'écrit de Mutahhar al-Maqdisi.). *Fontes orientales...curavit A.S. Tveritinova* II, 1969, pp. 304-311.

BORSHCHEVSKIY, Yu.E. "Musul'manskiy geograf Mukhammad b. Yakhyā iz Indii", "Geografiya" Khāfiz-i Abrū, "Dzhakhān-nāme" i Mukhammad b. Bakhr ar-Rukhnī. *Pis'mennye pamyatniki Vostoka* 1970, pp. 52-66.

BUSSE, Heribert. Kermān im 19. Jahrhundert nach der Geographie des Wazīrī. *Der Islam* 50(1973), pp. 284-312.

GRAF, H. -J. Die Stadt der Waräger. *Beiträge Z.Namenforschung* 7(1972), p. 291.

GRAF, H.-J. Zur Bezeichnung der Waräger im Orient; eine Berichtigung (zu R. Hennig, Die Namengebung nordeuropäscher Länder bei den mittelalterlichen Arabern, ZNF 15, 1939). *Beitr. z. Namenforschung* 6(1971), p. 336

HAMARNEH, Saleh K. Are there one or two authors of the work Ar-Rawḍ al-mi'ṭār by Al-Ḥimyarī? *Folia Or.* 12(1970), pp. 79-90

KARAEV, O. Izvlecheniya svedeniy iz geografii al-Idrisi "Kitab nuzkhat al-mushtak fi-khtirak al-afak (Razvlechenie istomlennogo v stranstvii po oblastyam) o nekotorykh tyurkskikh plemenakh. *Arabo-persidskie istochniki o tyurkskikh narodakh,* 1973, pp. 49-59.

KARAEV, O. Zemli Toguzguzov, Karlukov, Khazlazhiya, Khilkhiya, Kimakov i Kirgizov po karte al-Idrisi. *Arabo-persidskie istochniki o tyurkskikh narodakh,* 1973, pp. 3-48.

KARAHAN, Abdulkadir. The region of Sind in the Mir'āt al-mamālik of Captain Seydi Ali. *J.Reg.Cult.Inst.* 7(1974), pp. 211-216.

KHALIDI, Tarif. Mas'ūdī's lost works: a reconstruction of their content. *JAOS* 94 (1974), pp. 35-41.

KMIETOWICZ, F. Artāniya-Artā. *Folia or.* 14(1972-73), pp. 231-260.

LEBON, J.H.G. The Islamic city from the 7th to 12th centuries A.H. in the light of cartographical evidence. *Proc. 27th Int.Cong.Or.1967* (1971), p. 179.

LEWICKI, T. Paesi cristiani d'Occidente nel Kitāb ṣūrat al-arḍ di Ibn Hawqal. *Oriente e Occidente nel medioevo,* 1971, pp. 523-533.

LEWICKI, T. "Türkische" Stadt Dānā nach einem Bericht des arabischen Geographen Ibn al-Faqīh. *Folia Or* 13(1971), pp. 161-170.

MAQBUL AHMAD, S. Multan (as described by Arab writers). *J.Ind.hist.,* Golden jubilee vol. 1973, pp. 361-367.

MIQUEL, A. La description du Maghreb dans la géographie d'al-Iṣṭ'akhri. *ROMM* 15-16 (1973), pp. 231-239.

MIQUEL, A. La pensée antonymique à travers un texte de la géographie arabe. *L'ambivalence dans la culture arabe,* 1967, pp. 164-171.

OMAN, G. A propos du second ouvrage géographique attribué au géographe arabe Al-Idrīsī: Le "Rawḍ al-uns wa nuzhat al-Nafs". *Folia Or.* 12(1970), pp. 187-193

PRITSAK, O. An arabic text on the trade route of the corporation of Ar-Rūs in the second half of the ninth century. *Folia Or.* 12(1970), pp. 241-259

RUBINACCI, R. La data della Geografia di al-Idrīsī. *Actas IV congresso de estudos árabes e islâmicos* 1968(1971), pp. 531-535.

RUBINACCI, R. La ville du Caire dans la géographie d'al-Idrīsī. *Colloque international sur l'histoire du Caire,* 1969, pp. 405-414.

SAIDI, Omar. Kitab al uyun wa-l-hadaiq fi ahbar al-haqaiq. Tome IV: Extraits relatifs à L'Occident Musulman et en particulier à l'Ifriqyya (256-350 A.H.). *CT* 21(nos. 81-82, 1973), pp. 73-122.

SEMENOVA, L.A. Iz izvestiy Masʿudi o Kavkaze. (Quelques nouvelles d'el-Macoudi sur le Caucase.) *Fontes orientales...curavit A.S. Tveritinova* II, 1969, pp. 312-315.

SIMONE, A de, Palermo nei geografi e viaggiatori arabi del medioevo. *Studi magrebini II,* 1968, pp. 129-189.

SOUCEK, Sv. À propos du livre d'instructions nautiques de Pīrī Re'īs. *REI* 41 (1973), pp. 241-255.

TALBI, M. Réimpression. Description de l'Ifriqiya et d'Andalus au milieu du VIIIe/XIVe siècle. Extrait des Masālik al-Abṣār fī mamālik al-Amṣār d'Ibn Fadl Allah al-'Umari (700-749/1301-1349). *CT* 21 (nos. 81-82, 1973), pp. 225-259.

TEPLY, K. Evliyā Çelebī in Wien. *Der Islam* 52(1975), pp. 125-131.

TERZIOĞLU, Arslan. Evliya Çelebi's Beschreibung der südosteuropäischen Hospitäler und heilbäder des 17. Jahrhunderts und ihre kulturgeschichtliche Bedeutung. *Rev. ét. sud-est eur.* 13(1975), pp. 429-442.

TORRES PALOMO, M.P. Sierra Nevada en los escritores árabes. *MEAH* 16-17 (1967-8), pp. 57-88.

TROUPEAU, G. Observations sur la traduction latine de la description de la France dans l'abrégé de la géographie d'Edrisi. *ROMM* 15-16(1973), pp. 359-366.

ZABORSKI, A. Some Eritrean Place-names in Arabic medieval sources. *Folia Or.* 12 (1970), pp. 327-337

See also I. d. 2. Rubinacci.

See also XII. b. Jongeling.

See also XII. b. Lewicki

See also XIX. e. Miquel.

See also XXII. b. In Der Smitten.

See also XXXV. g. Redjala.

d TRAVEL

ABDUL KARIM. Chittagong coast as described by Sidī Alī Chelebī, a sixteenth century Turkish navigator. *JAS Bangladesh* 16(1971), pp. 233-241.

ABDUR RAHIM, Six hundred years after - in the foot-steps of Ibn Battuta in Andalusia. *Peshawar Univ.rev.* 1i(1973), pp. 1-21.

AḤMAD BIN MĀǦID La Ḥāwiya: abrégé versifié des principes de nautique (Ḥāwiyat al-'Ihtiṣār fī 'Uṣūl 'Ilm al-Biḥār). Texte arabe établi avec introduction et analyse en français par Ibrahim Khoury. *BEO* 24(1971), pp. 249-386.

BECKINGHAM, C.F. The travels of Pero da Covilhã and their significance. *Cong.int. hist.descobrimentos. Actas* III, 1961, pp. 1-14

BEN-ARIEH, Yehoshua. The geographical exploration of the Holy Land. *PEQ* 104(1972), pp. 81-92.

BENVENISTE, E. Un village, près de Persépolis. *Yād-nāme-ye Irāni-ye Minorsky,* 1969, pp. 7-16.

BEVIS, R. Spiritual geology: C.M. Doughty and the land of the Arnos. *Vict.stud.* 16 (1972), pp. 163-181. [CWHM 77, 501]

BONEBAKKER, S.A. Three manuscripts of Ibn Jubayr's *Riḥla.* *RSO* 47(1972), pp. 235-245.

BOSWORTH, C.E. Some correspondence in the John Rylands University Library of Manchester concerning John Lewis Burckhardt and Lady Hester Stanhope's physician. *Bull. John Rylands Univ. Lib.* 55(1972), pp. 33-59.

CAHEN, Cl. Ibn Jubayr et les maghrébins de Syrie. *ROMM* 13-14(1973), pp. 207-209.

CARSWELL, J. East and West: a study in aesthetic contrasts: Sir Thomas Herbert and his travel writings. *AARP* 2(1972), pp. 71-87.

CHIU Ling-Yeong Chinese maritime expansion, 1368-1644. *JOS Australia* 3i(1965), pp. 27-47.

CHUMOVSKI, T. Uma enciclopédia maritima árabe do século XV. *Cong.int.hist.descobrimentos. Actas* III, 1961, pp. 43-55

COSTA, P. Pietro della Valle. *Levante* 18, pp. 30-46.

VI GEOGRAPHY

DEV, Arjun. India in the eyes of early Muslim scholars. *India's contribution to world thought ...*, 1970, pp. 589-596.

DUPUIS, J. La diffusion médiévale du maïs dans l'ancien monde et l'hypothèse de voyages arabes en Amérique précolumbienne. *CR trim.Acad.sci.Outre-Mer* 34(1974), pp. 381-406.

GARROD, O. Reconnaissance in Turkey (The Society's Anatolian tour, 1971). *Asian aff.* 58(N.S.2, 1971), pp. 305-309.

GAULMIER, J. Note sur le voyage de Renan en Syrie (1865). *BEO* 25(1972), pp. 229-237.

GIANNOPOULOS, I.G. Ὁ Ἐβλιὰ Τσελεμπῆ εἰς τὴν Λευκάδα. Ἐπετηρὶς τῆς Ἑταιρείας Λευκαδικῶν Μελετῶν 2(1972) pp. 377-393

GIANNOPOULOS, I.G. Ἡ περιήγησις τοῦ Ἐβλιὰ Τσελεμπῆ ἀνὰ τὴν Στερεὰν Ἑλλάδα. Ἐπετηρὶς Ἑταιρείας Στερεοελλαδικῶν Μελετῶν 2(1969) pp 139-198

GODARD, A. D'Alep à Baghdad en caravane, 1908. *Persica* 5(1970-1), pp. 47-68.

GROSSET-GRANGE, H. Comment naviguent aujourd'hui les Arabes de l'Océan Indien? Suivi d'un glossaire de la navigation arabe dans l'Océan Indien. *Arabica* 19(1972), pp. 46-77

GUEVARA BAZÁN, R.A. Some notes for a history of the relations between Latin America, the Arabs and Islam. *MW* 61 (1971), pp. 284-292.

GUIRAL, P. Un architecte français en Afrique du Nord dans la première moitié du XIXe siècle. *ROMM* 6(1969), pp. 103-111.

HAJJ, Muhammad, A. al and LAVERS, J.E. The travel notes of al-Sharif Hasan b. al-Husain. *Kano studies* N.S.1i(1973), pp. 3-24.

IBRAGIMOV, N. "Puteshestvie" Ibn Battuty (perevody i publikatzii). *Voprosy vostochnogo literaturovedeniya i tekstologii*, 1975, pp. 70-84.

KHOURY, R. Sur une observation entomologique de Pierre Belon du Mans. À propos d'une édition récente de son *Voyage en Égypte* (1547). *BIFAO* 72(1972), pp. 237-244.

KISSLING, H.J. Zur Beschreibung des Rhône-Deltas in der Bahrîye des Pîrî-Re'îs. *Islam Tetkikleri Enst. dergisi* 5(1973), pp. 279-287.

KOHLI, Surinder Singh. Guru Nanak's travels in the Middle East. *India's contribution to world thought ...*, 1970, pp. 597-600.

KOWALSKA, M. Ibn Fadlān's account of his journey to the state of the Bulgārs. *Folia or.* 14(1972-73), pp. 219-230.

KREUTEL, R.F. Neues zur Evliyā-Celebī-Forschung. *Der Islam* 48(1971-2), pp. 269-279

LAVERS, J.E. The adventures of a Kano pilgrim 1891-1893. *Kano studies* 1iv(1968), pp. 69-81.

LEWIS, A. Maritime skills in the Indian Ocean, 1368-1500. *JESHO* 16(1973), pp. 238-264.

LHOTE, H. Recherches sur Takedda, ville décrite par le voyageur arabe Ibn Battouta et située en Aïr. *Bull. IFAN* 34(1972), pp. 429-470.

LIVINGSTON, J.W. Evliya Çelebi on surgical operations in Vienna. *Al-Abhath* 23(1970), pp. 223-245.

LOCKHART, D.M. The Palmella manuscript of Dom Joao de Castro's Roteiro de Goa a Suez. *Proc. 3rd Int. Conf. Ethiopian stud.*, 1966, pp. 117-121.

MACKAY, P.A. The first modern visitor to Alahan. *Anat.stud.* 21(1971), pp. 173-174.

MACKAY, P.A. The manuscripts of the *Seyahatname* of Evliya Çelebi. *Islam* 52 (1975), pp. 278-298.

MANTRAN, R. La description des côtes de l'Algérie dans le Kitab-i Bahriye de Pirî Reis. *ROMM* 15-16(1973), pp. 159-168.

MARCUS, H.G., PAGE, M.E. John Studdy Leigh: first footsteps in East Africa? *Int.J.Afr. hist.stud.* 5(1972), pp. 470-478.

MARINHO, J.A. Vias de comunicacão entre a Índia e a Europa dos séc. XV a XIX. *Bol. Inst. Angola* 47(1973), pp. 5-23.

MAUNY, R. Les navigations médiévales sur les côtes sahariennes antérieures à la découverte portugaise (1434). *Cong.int.hist. descobrimentos. Actas* III, 1961, pp. 421-432

MEILLASSOUX, C. L'Itinéraire d'Ibn Battuta de Walata à Malli. *J.Afr. hist.* 13(1972), pp. 389-395.

MINORSKY, V. On some of Biruni's informants. *Afghanistan* 25 i(1972), pp. 23-27.

NADEL, I.B. G.W. Cooke and Laurence Oliphant: Victorian travellers to the Orient. *JAOS* 94(1974), pp. 120-122.

NYLANDER, C. Al-Bērūnī and Persepolis. *Acta Iranica* 1(1974), pp. 137-150.

ORHONLU, Cengiz. Seydi Ali Reis. *J. Reg. Cult. Inst.* 1 ii(1967), pp. 44-57.

PIEMONTESE, A.M. Descrizioni d'Italia in viaggiatori persiani del XIX secolo. *Annali Fac. Ling. Lett. stran. di Ca' Foscari (serie orientale)* 1(1970), pp. 63-106.

VI GEOGRAPHY

PREMARE, A.L. de. Les notes de voyage d'Abu Ishaq Brahim Ibn Al-Hajj Al-Numayri Al-Andalusi en l'année 745 h. 1344 J.C. *Rev. d'hist. et de civ. du Maghreb* 9(1970), pp. 31-37.

RASHID, Abdur. India and Pakistan in the fourteenth century as described by Arab travellers. *Cong.int.hist.descobrimentos. Actas* III, 1961, pp. 479-498

RIZZITANO, U. Ibn Giubair dal tempio della Mecca alla Chiesa della Martorana. *Levante* 19i-ii(1972), pp. 37-50.

RODRIGUES, M.A. Aspectos da presença árabe no "Itinerário de Terra Santa" de Fr. Pantaleão de Aveiro. *Actas IV congresso de estudos árabes e islâmicos* 1968(1971), pp. 397-443.

RUIZ DE CUEVAS, T. Una excursion al Yebel Alam. *Cuadernos de la Bibl.Esp.de Tetuan* 7 (1973), pp. 57-65.

SHAYYAL, Gamal Eldin el- The cultural relations between Alexandria and the Islamic West in Al-Andalus and Morocco. *RIEI Madrid* 16(1971), pp. 61-69.

TOYNBEE, A. Impressions of an English traveller in Libya. *Bull. Fac. Arts Univ. Libya* 3(1969), pp. 9-14.

TURBET-DELOF, G. Une "description" des ports marocains imprimée en fraude à Paris en 1682. *ROMM* 9(1971), pp. 185-199.

TURBET-DELOF, G. Sébastien Bremond et la Tunisie. *CT* 18(nos. 71-72, 1970), pp. 193-195.

TVERITINOVA, A.S. Izvlecheniya iz opisaniya posol'stva v Rossiyu Shekhdi Osmana v 1758 g. (Extraits de "la Description de la mission en Russie en 1758" par Chehdi Osman.) *Fontes orientales...curavit A.S. Tveritinova* II, 1969, pp. 296-303.

WIDERA, B. Reisebericht des Abu Hamid zur Geschichte Ost- und Mitteleuropas im 12. Jahrhundert. *Z.f.G.* 20(1972), pp. 75-79

WILD, S. Al-'Utaifī's journey to Lebanon in 1043/1634. *Al-Abhath* 23(1970), pp. 213-222.

ZIROJEVIĆ, O. Putopisi u ogledalu deftera. (Travelogues as reflected in defters.) *Prilozi Or.Fil.Ist.* 16-17 (1966-7), pp. 125-134

ZOLONDEK, L. Nineteenth-century Arab travellers to Europe: some observations on their writings. *MW* 61 (1971), pp. 28-34.

See also V. c. *Iran*. Hambly.

See also V. u. 1. Farmer.

See also VI. c. Simone.

See also XXII. a. Tibbetts.

See also XXV. b. Charles.

See also XXXV. a. Fernández-Capel Baños.

See also XXXIX. b. Grigor'ev.

See also XLI. a. Mashtakova.

VII ETHNOLOGY. ANTHROPOLOGY. SOCIOLOGY. DEMOGRAPHY. FOLKLORE

a ETHNOLOGY. ANTHROPOLOGY. SOCIOLOGY. DEMOGRAPHY

ABDAL-ATI, Hammudah. Modern problems, classical solutions. An Islamic perspective on the family. *J.compar.family stud.* 5(1974), pp. 37-54.

ABEL, A. Esquisse d'une problématique de la sociologie du monde musulman. *Actas IV congresso de estudos árabes e islâmicos* 1968(1971), pp. 357-366.

ABU ZAHRA, Shaikh Mohammad. Human society under the aegis of Islam. *3rd Conf.Acad. Isl.Research,* 1966, pp. 369-496

ADAM, A. Quelques réflexions sur la sociologie musulmane. *ROMM* 13-14(1973), pp. 14-21.

ALWAYE, Mohiaddin. Towards an ideal society. *Maj. al-Azhar* 45viii(1973), pp. 1-5.

ANTOUN, R.T. Three approaches to the cultural anthropology of the Middle East. Syllabus. *MESA Bull.* 5ii(1971), pp. 24-53.

ASWAD, B.C. Arab- American studies.*MESA bull.* 8iii(1974), pp. 13-26.

ATALLAH, Wahib. Aymu'l-Lāh. Vestige d'un culte chtonien. *Arabica* 22(1975), pp. 162-169.

ATALLAH, W. Le droit d'asile chez les Arabes. *Arabica* 18(1971), pp. 262-278.

ATALLAH, W. Un ritual de serment chez les Arabes: *al-yamīn al-ġamūs*. *Arabica* 20 (1973), pp. 63-73.

VII ETHNOLOGY

AUDROING, J.F. *et al.*, Recherche des corrélations entre les variables démographiques, sociologiques et économiques dans les pays arabes. *Population* Paris 30(1975), pp. 61-80.

BARCLAY, H.B. Is there a theme of equality in the Arab rural community? *Themes in culture; essays in honor of M.E. Opler*, 1971, pp. 285-306.

BEESTON, A.F.L. The game of *maysir* and some modern parallels. *Arabian studies* 2(1975), pp. 1-6.

BILL, J.A. Class analysis and the dialectics of modernization in the Middle East. *IJMES* 3(1972), pp. 417-434.

CHARNAY, J.P. La musulmane dans la ville moderne. *Politique étrangère* 36(1971), pp. 141-145.

CHASTELAND, J.C. Problems of demographic data collecting in Arab countries of the Middle East. *Int.population conf.* London, 1969, I, p. 370.

CHELHOD, J. A contribution to the problem of the pre-eminence of the right, based on Arabic evidence. *Right & left*, ed. R. Needham, 1973, pp. 239-262.

COHEN, A. The politics of marriage in changing Middle Eastern stratification systems. *Essays in comparative social stratification. L.Plotnicov and A.Tuden, editors*, 1970, pp. 195-209.

COHEN, E. Arab boys and tourist girls in a mixed Jewish-Arab community. *Int.J. compar.sociol.* 12(1971), pp. 217-233.

COHN, Haim H. Discrimination of Jewish minorities in Arab countries. *Israel yrbk. on human rights* 1(1971), pp. 127-133.

COURBAGE, Y., FARGUES, Ph. La population des pays arabes d'Orient. *Population* [Paris] 30(1975), pp. 1111-1141.

DESTRÉE, A. Le développement des Etats du Moyen-Orient et la crise du nomadisme. *Rev. Inst.Sociol.* 42(1969), pp. 263-281

DODD, P.C. The effect of religious affiliation on woman's role in Middle Eastern Arab society. *J.compar.family stud.* 5 (1974), pp. 117-129.

DODD, P.C. Family honor and the forces of change in Arab society. *IJMES* 4(1973), pp. 40-54.

FELLMAN, J. The Middle East as a cultural-linguistic continent. *Anthropos* 70(1975), pp. 930-932.

FERNEA, R.A. Gaps in the ethnographic literature on the Middle Eastern village: a classificatory exploration. *Rural politics and social change in the Middle East*, ed. by R. Antoun and I. Harik, 1972, pp. 75-102.

FOSSIER, R. Les mouvements populaires en occident au XIe siècle. *CRAIBL* (1971), pp. 257-269.

GELLNER, E. A pendulum swing theory of Islam. *Annales maroc. sociol.* 1968, pp. 5-14.

GORELIK, M.V. Blizhnevostochnaya miniatyura XII-XIII vv. kak etnografichesky istochnik. [Opuit izucheniya muzhskogo kostyuma]. (The Near East miniature of the XII-XIII centuries as an ethnographic source (men's dress.) *Sov.etn.* 172ii pp. 37-50

HAMDANI, Muwaffak al- and ABU-LABAN, Baha. Game involvement and sex-role socialization in Arab children. *Int. J. comp. sociol.* 12(1971), pp. 182-191.

HARDING, G. L. The Safaitic tribes. *Al-Abhath* 22iii-iv (1969), pp. 3-25.

HARIK, Iliya F. The ethnic revolution and political integration in the Middle East. *IJMES* 3(1972), pp. 303-323.

HARIK, I.F. The impact of the domestic market on rural-urban relations in the Middle East. *Rural politics and social change in the Middle East*, ed. by R. Antoun and I. Harik, 1972, pp. 337-363.

HASSAN, Abdel-Hamid. The spirit of Islam is the chief factor in reforming contemporary society. *3rd Conf.Acad.Isl.Research*, 1966, pp. 497-510

HILAL, Jamil. The management of male dominance in "traditional" Arab culture: a tentative model. *Civilisations* 21 (1971), pp. 85-95.

HUSSAIN, S.M. The Muslim population in Africa. *Nigerian J. Islam* 1ii(1971), pp. 33-36.

JAMOUS, R. Réflexions sur la segmentarité et le mariage arabe. *Annales maroc. sociol.* 1969, pp. 21-26.

KEYSER, J.M.B. The Middle Eastern case: is there a marriage rule? *Ethnology* 13 (1974), pp. 293-309.

KHATIBI, Abdelkébir. Sociologie du monde arabe -- positions. *Bull. écon. soc. Maroc* 126(1975), pp. 1-9.

KROPÁCEK, L. Seeking an explanatory scheme for the sociology of the Middle East. *Ar. Or.* 43(1975), pp. 359-363.

KRUPP, A. Neue Wege zur Erforschung des Volksislam. *Islamkundliche Abhandlungen H.J. Kissling*, 1974, pp. 116-126.

LAPIDUS, I.M. The evolution of Muslim urban society. *Comp. stud. soc. hist.* 15(1973), pp. 21-50.

LEWIS, B. Raza y color en el Islam. *And.* 33 (1968), pp. 1-51.

LONGRIGG, S.H. Sixty years of Arab social evolution. *Asian aff.* N.S.4(1973), pp. 17-26.

VII ETHNOLOGY

McCORD, W. and LUTFIYYA, Abdulla. Urbanization and world view in the Middle East. *Essays on modernization of underdeveloped societies*, Vol. 2. Ed. A.R. Desai, Bombay, 1971. pp. 557-579.

MARKOV, G.E. Die Dynamik der gesellschaftlichen Organisation bei den Nomaden Asiens. *Jhb. Mus. Völkerk. Leipzig* 28(1972), pp. 176-180.

MASON, J.P. Structural congruities in the Arab genealogical form and the arabesque motif. *MW* 65(1975), pp. 21-38.

MATSON, F.R. The archaeological present: Near Eastern village potters at work. *Amer. J. archaeol.* 78(1974), pp. 345-347.

NELSON, C. Public and private politics: women in the Middle Eastern world. *Amer. ethnol.* 1(1974), pp. 551-563.

OTHMAN, Ibrahim. Assimilation with special reference to the Arabs in the United States of America. *Fac. Arts J. Univ. Jordan* 3ii (1972), pp. 62-74.

OWEN, W.F. Two rural sectors: their characteristics and roles in the development process. *Rural politics and social change in the Middle East*, ed. by R. Antoun and I. Harik, 1972, pp. 403-431.

PATAI, R. Jus primae noctis. *Folklore Res. Center studies* 4(1974), pp. 177-180.

PELLAT, C. Peut-on connaître le taux de natalité au temps du Prophète? *JESHO* 14(1971), pp. 107-135.

PETRAKIS, N.L. and others. Evidence for a genetic cline in earwax types in the Middle East and Southeast Asia. *Amer. J. phys. anthrop.* 35(1971), pp. 141-144.

PITT-RIVERS, J. Women and sanctuary in the Mediterranean. *Échanges et communications. Mélanges C. Lévi-Strauss* II. 1970, pp. 862-875.

REINTJENS, H. Die bint al 'amm-Institution im Vorderen Orient. *Fest.H.Petri*, 1973, pp. 407-413.

RIPINSKY, M.M. Cultural idiom as an ecologic factor: two studies. [Walibiri of Central Australia and pastoral nomads of Southwest Asia]. *Anthropos* 70(1975), pp. 449-460.

ROSENFELD, H. Non-hierarchical, hierarchical and masked reciprocity in the Arab village. *Folklore Res. Center studies* 4(1974), pp. 199-222.

ROSENFELD, H. An overview and critique of the literature on rural politics and social change. *Rural politics and social change in the Middle East*, ed. by R. Antoun and I. Harik, 1972, pp. 45-74.

ROWTON, M. Enclosed nomadism. *JESHO* 17 (1974), pp. 1-30.

SADAN, J. À propos de martaba: remarques sur l'étiquette dans le monde musulman médiéval. *REI* 41(1973), pp. 51-69.

SALZMAN, P.C. Tribal chiefs as middlemen: the politics of encapsulation in the Middle East. *Anthrop.Q.* 47(1974), pp. 203-210.

SCHNEIDER, J. Of vigilance and virgins: honor, shame and access to resources in Mediterranean societies. *Ethnology* 10 (1971), pp. 1-24

SEIWERT, W.-D. Ökonomische und soziale Bedingungen für die wirtschaftliche Integration der Hirtennomaden in den arabischen Ländern. *Jhb. Mus. Völkerkunde Leipzig* 29(1973), pp. 83-135.

SÉRAYDARIAN, L. Exode des compétences des pays arabes. *Ann. de la Fac. de droit de Beyrouth* 73(1972), pp. 225-239.

SI HAMZA BOUBAKEUR, S.E. Position de l'Islam à l'égard de la contraception. *Rev. Hist.Méd.hébr.* 24(1971), p. 117. [CWHM 72, 768]

SPOONER, B. The status of nomadism as a cultural phenomenon in the Middle East. *J. Asian and African studies* [York Univ.] 7(1972), pp. 122-131.

TOMEH, Aida K. Birth order and familial influences in the Middle East. *J.compar. family stud.* 2(1971), pp. 88-106.

VALLIN, J. Séminaire sur la fécondité dans les pays Arabes. *Population (Paris)* 26 (1971), pp. 385-388.

WIRTH, E. Der Nomadismus in der modernen Welt des Orients - Wege und Möglichkeiten einer wirtschaftlichen Integration. *Nomadismus als Entwicklungsproblem* 1969, pp. 93-104.

WIRTH, Eugen. Zum Problem des Bazars (sûq, çarşi). Versuch einer Begriffsbestimmung und Theorie des traditionellen Wirtschaftszentrums der orientalisch-islamischen Stadt. *Orient* [Germany] 15(1974), pp. 16-17.

WIRTH, E. Zum Problem des Bazars (Sūq, çarşi). Versuch einer Begriffsbestimmung und Theorie des traditionellen Wirtschaftszentrums der orientalisch-islamischen Stadt. III. Das Problem der Entstehung des Bazars. *Der Islam* 52(1975), pp. 6-46.

WULFF, H.E. The islamic craft guilds and their socio-religious background. *JOS Australia* 3ii(1965), pp. 66-74.

ZAIM, Issam el- L'industrialisation et les sociétés arabes. *Eg. contemp.* 63(no.347, 1972), pp. 49-61.

L'activité féminine dans la population non agricole en Amérique latine et dans quelques pays musulmans. *Population* [Paris] 28 (1973), pp. 952-954.

See also II. a. 5. Allard.

See also III. a. 9. Pruvost.

See also V. a. Mason.

See also IX. a. Lapidus.

See also IX. g. Bailey.

See also IX. n. Bourgey.

See also XII. a. Planhol.

See also XII. a. Shafei.

See also XXXVII. l. Loya.

See also XLIII. a. Zahlan.

b FUTUWWA. AKHIS. FURUSIYYA

RIAZ, Muhammad. Chivalry in Islamic history. *J.Reg.Cult.Inst.* 6(1973), pp. 145-158.

See XXXVII. l. Vatikiotis.

c FOLKLORE

CEJPEK, J. The father-son combat as seen by an Iranist. *Yádnáme-ye Jan Rypka* 1967, pp. 247-254.

CERBELLA, G. Le tradizioni, motivo di dialogo fra Occidente e Oriente. *Levante* 19i-ii(1972), pp. 51-58.

CHAND, Tara and ABIDI, S.A.H. *Darya-i-asmar:* a unique and hitherto unknown Persian translation of the *Kathasaritsagara* and an important link in the cultural relations between Iran and India. *IC* 46(1972), pp. 235-244.

DORRI, Dzh. Iz istorii narodnoy "smekhovoy kul'tury" v Irane. (From the history of folk comedy culture in Iran.) *NAA* 1971(6), pp. 66-75.

ELWELL-SUTTON, L.P. The unfortunate heroine in Persian folk-literature. *Yād-nāme-ye Irāni-ye Minorsky*, 1969, pp. 37-50.

FODOR, A. The role of *Fir'awn* in popular Islam. *J.Egypt.archaeol.* 61(1975), pp. 238-240.

GRAND'HENRY, J. Berceuses, énigmes et chansons arabes de Cherchell (Algérie). *Folia Or.* 16(1975).

KHROMOV, A. The problem of the Yaghnobi folklore. *Yádnáme-ye Jan Rypka* 1967, pp. 255-260.

LA GRANJA, F. de. Cuentos árabes en la "Florests Española" de Melchor de Santa Cruz. *And.* 35(1970), pp. 381-400.

LA GRANJA, F. de. Nuevas notas a un episodio del "Lazarillo de Tormes". *And.* 36(1971), pp. 223-237.

PAULINY, J. Zur Rolle der Quṣṣāṣ bei der Entstehung und Überlieferung der populären Prophetenlegenden. *Asian and African studies* [Bratislava] 10(1974), pp. 125-141.

SCOBIE, A. The battle of the pygmies and the cranes in Chinese, Arab, and North American Indian sources. *Folklore* 86 (1975), pp. 122-132.

SOLIMAN, Ahmad El-Said. Quelques survivances paiennes dans la littérature populaire des Turks Musulmans. *BFA Cairo Univ.* (1972), pp. 1-16.

SPIES, O. Arabische Stoffe in der Disciplina Clericalis. *Rhein. Jhb. Volkskunde* 21 (1973?), pp. 170-199.

UYSAL, Ahmet E., WALKER, W.S. Saintly fools and the Moslem establishment. *J. Amer. folklore* 87(1974), pp. 357-361.

See also II. c. 2. Chen.

See also II. c. 2. Kritzeck.

See also XXVIII. b. Başgöz.

d PROVERBS

AQUILINA, J. Comparative Maltese and Arabic proverbs. *Proc.27th Int.Cong.Or. 1967* (1971), pp. 209-210.

BADRI, Malik B. Recall of proverbs as an indicator of culture orientations: a cross-cultural study. *American University of Beirut Festival book*, 1967, pp. 1-18.

BAŞGOZ, Mehmet Ilhan. Riddle-proverbs and the related forms in Turkish folklore. *Proverbium* 18(1972), pp. 655-668.

DHUBAIB, A.M.al-. Ancient Arabic proverbs: some critical and comparative observations. *Ann. Leeds Univ. Or. Soc.* 7(1969-73), pp. 32-49.

ELÇIN, Sükrü. Proverbs in the Turkish language (word, concept, examples). *Proverbium* 15(1970), pp. 28-34.

FAHD, T. Psychologie animale et comportement humain dans les Proverbes arabes. *Bull.Fac.Lettres Strasbourg* 48(1969), pp. 19-45.

FAHD, T. Psychologie animale et comportement humain dans les proverbes arabes. *Rev.synt.* 92(1971), pp. 5-43; 93(1972), pp. 43-63; 95(1974), pp. 233-256.

GARCÍA GÓMEZ, E. Hacia un "refranero" arabigoandaluz, V: Versión del libro sobre refranes de "al-'Iqd al-farīd" (siglo X). A. Preliminares y refranero de Akṯam y Buzurŷmihr. *And.* 37(1972), pp. 249-323.

GARCÍA GÓMEZ, E. Los proverbios rimados de Ben Luyūn de Almería (1282-1349). Selección. *And.* 37(1972), pp. 1-75.

KALONTAROV, Ya.I. Kurdskie poslovitzy i pogovorki. *Proverbium* 21(1973), pp. 808-811.

KARAMSHOEV, D. O yazykovoy osnove pamirskikh poslovitz v sravnenii s tadzhikskimi. *Proverbium* 13(1969), pp. 349-359.

LEVIN, I. Parömiologische Erstlinge vom Pamir für Archer Taylor. *Proverbium* 15 (1970), pp. 61-65.

MASTEPANOV, S.D. O sobiranii i publikatzii osetinskikh poslovitz i pogorok. Bibliograficheskiy obzor. *Proverbium* 22(1973), pp. 835-844.

REZVANIAN, M.H. L'humour dans les proverbes persans. *Proverbium* 14(1969), pp. 399-407.

ŞENALTAN, Semahat. Türkische Entsprechungen zu germanisch-romantischen Sprichwörtern bei Düringsfeld. *Proverbium* 13 (1969), pp. 337-348.

THEODORIDIS, D. Zum türkischen Sprichwörtergedicht des Levni. *Proverbium* 25 (1975), pp. 983-984.

TILAVOV, B. Novye paremiologicheskie issledovaniya v Tadzhikistane. *Proverbium* 21(1973), pp. 802-805.

TILAVOV, B. O roli literatury v razvitii tadzhikskikh poslovitz i pogovorok. *Proverbium* 16(1971), pp. 557-562.

TILAVOV, B. Parallelizm v tadzhikskikh narodnykh poslovitzakh. *Proverbium* 9 (1967), pp. 197-200.

TILAVOV, B. Statisticheskiy analiz khudozhestvennoy formy tadzhikskikh narodnykh poslovitz. *Proverbium* 21 (1973), pp. 769-775.

ZENNER, W.P. Ethnic stereotyping in Arabic proverbs. *J.Amer.folklore* 83(no. 330, 1970), pp. 417-429

See also XXVII. b. Khayyat.

See also XXXVI. 1. Talaat

See also XXX. e. Tilavov.

e MAGIC

ANAWATI, G.C. Trois talismans musulmans en arabe provenant du Mali (marché de Mopti). *Annales islamol.* 11(1972), pp. 287-339.

ATSIZ, Buğra. Mülhimenâme. *Islamkundliche Abhandlungen H.J. Kissling,* 1974, pp. 29-35.

EBIED, R.Y. and YOUNG, M.J.L. A fragment of a magic alphabet from the Cairo Genizah. *Sudhoffs Archiv* 58(1974), pp. 404-408.

ELWELL-SUTTON, L.P. Magic and the supernatural in Persian folk-literature. *Ve Congrès International d'Arabisants et d'Islamisants. Actes.,* [1970?], pp. 189-196.

FAHD, Toufic. L'oniromancie orientale et ses répercussions sur l'oniromancie de l'Occident médiéval. *Oriente e Occidente nel medioevo,* 1971, pp. 347-374.

FODOR, A. Malhamat Daniyal. *The Middle East; studies in honour of J. Germanus,* 1974, pp. 85-133.

FODOR, A. Notes on an Arabic amulet scroll. *Acta Or. Acad. Sci. Hung.* 27(1973), pp. 268-269.

GRAND'HENRY, J. Divination et poésie populaire arabe en Algérie: à propos de quelques *Būqāla* inédites. *Arabica* 20(1973), pp. 53-62.

KLEIN-FRANKE, F. The geomancy of Aḥmad b. ʿAli Zunbul: a study of the Ambic Corpus hermeticum. *Ambix* 20(1973), pp. 26-35.

MAHDI HASSAN, S. A prognostic system of divination of Chinese origin. *IC* 49 (1975), pp. 221-222.

PRINS, A.H.J. Islamic maritime magic: a ship's charm from Lamu. *Wort und Religion, Kalima na dini, E. Dammann zum 65. Geburtstag,* 1969, pp. 294-304.

ULLMANN, M. War Ḥunain der Übersetzer von Artemidors Traumbuch? *WI N.S.* 13(1971), pp. 204-211.

VERNET, J. Kepler y los horóscopos de Mahoma y Lutero. *And.* 37(1972), pp. 453-462.

See also XXXVII. h. Continente Ferrer.

See also XXXIX. h. Boskov.

VIII HISTORY: AUXILIARY SCIENCES

a ARCHAEOLOGY

General

GRABAR, O. Islamic archaeology: an introduction. *Archaeology* 24 (1971), pp. 197-199.

SAUNERON, S. Les travaux de l'Institut français d'Archéologie orientale en 1969-1970 (avec 19 planches). *BIFAO* 69 (1971), pp. 283-304.

See also V. a. *General.* Grabar.

See X. b. Scanlon.

Afghanistan

AMIRI, Ghulam Rahman. Share Ghulghula (the city of screams) of Tar-o-Sar. *Afghanistan* 26ii(1973), pp. 79-90.

BERNARD, P. La campagne de fouilles de 1970 à Aï Khanoum (Afghanistan). *CRAIBL* (1971), pp. 385-452.

FISCHER, K. Archäologische Landesaufnahme im Afghanischen Sistan. *Indologen-Tagung 1971*, hrsg. H. Härtel und V. Moeller. pp. 204-209.

FISCHER, Kl. Archaeological field surveys in Afghan Seistan 1960-1970. *South Asian archaeology*, ed. N. Hammond, 1973, pp. 131-155.

FISCHER, K. Archaeological reconnaissance in Afghan Seistan, with special reference to Saljuq art. *Art of Iran and Anatolia* ... ed. W. Watson, 1974, pp. 150-155.

FISCHER, Kl. Nimruz and the archaeology of Afghanistan. *Afghanistan* 26iii(1973), pp. 1-16.

TADDEI, M. Problemi di storia dell'arte e ricerca archeologica. *Veltro* 16v-vi(1972), pp. 549-561.

See also VIII. a. *Iran.* Fischer.

Africa (excluding Egypt)

BERTHIER, P. Campagnes de fouilles à Chichaoua d'avril-mai 1965 à octobre-novembre 1967. *Bull. Soc. hist. Maroc* 1 (1968), pp. 23-28.

BERTHIER, P. Campagnes de fouilles à Chichaoua (avril-mai 1965 à avril-mai 1968) - 2e partie. *Bull. Soc. hist. Maroc* 2 (1969), pp. 7-26.

BERTHIER, P. Recherches archéologiques à la Zaouïa Bel Moqaddem (Chichaoua - Haouz de Marrakech). *Hespéris Tamuda* 11(1970), pp. 141-169

CAMPS, G. Une "Société archéologique" à Fez au XVIe siècle: les Canésin de Jean-Léon l'Africain. *ROMM* 13-14(1973), pp. 211-216.

CHITTICK, N. An archaeological reconnaissance of the Southern Somali coast. *Azania* 4(1969), pp. 115-130.

CHITTICK, N. Discoveries in the Lamu Archipelago. *Azania* 2(1967), pp. 37-67.

CHITTICK, N. Kilwa: a preliminary report. *Azania* 1(1966), pp. 1-36.

CHITTICK, N. Unguja Ukuu: the earliest imported pottery, and an Abbasid dinar. *Azania* 1(1966), pp. 161-163.

DAOULATLI, Abdelaziz. Recherches archéologiques à la Kasbah de Tunis. *Africa* (Tunis) 3-4(1969-70), pp. 253-296.

EUZENNAT, M. Sur la frontière romaine en Tunisie méridionale. *CRAIBL* (1972), pp. 7-27.

LÉZINE, A. Tripoli. Notes archéologiques. *Libyca antiqua* 5(1968), pp. 55-67.

LHOTE, H. Dalle gravée de la Chaîne des Ergab (Algérie). *Objets et mondes* 13(1973), pp. 99-106.

MASCARELLO, A. Note archéologique sur Dellys. *Rev. d'hist. et de civ. du Maghreb* 9(1970), pp. 13-17.

OMAN, G. La necropoli islamica di Dahlak Kebir nel Mar Rosso. *Africa*[*Rome*] 29(1974), pp. 43-54.

RACHEWILTZ, B. de Missione etno-archeologica nel Sahara Maghrebino. Rapporti: preliminari. *Africa* [*Rome*] 27(1972), pp. 519-568.

REBUFFAT, R. Nouvelles recherches dans le sud de la Tripolitaine. *CRAIBL* 19(1972), pp. 319-339.

RILEY, J.A. Sidi Khrebish excavations, Benghazi, 1972-73. *Ann. rep. Soc. Libyan Stud.* 4(1972-3), pp. 11-20.

ROBERT, S., ROBERT, D. Douze années de recherches archéologiques en République islamique de Mauritanie. *Ann. Fac. Lettres Dakar* 2(1973), pp. 195-233.

ROBERT, S. Fouilles archéologiques sur le site presumé d'Aaoudaghost (1961-1968). *Folia Or.* 12(1970), pp. 261-278

ROSENBERGER, B. Tāmdult, cité minière et caravanière présaharienne (IXe-XIVe S.) *Hespéris Tamuda* 11(1970), pp. 103-139

WHITEHOUSE, D. Excavations at Ajdabiyah: an interim report. *Ann. Rep. Soc. Libyan Studies* 3(1971-72), pp. 12-21.

WHITEHOUSE, D. Excavations at Ajdabiyah: second interim report. *Ann. rep. Soc. Libyan Stud.* 4(1972-3), pp. 20-27.

British archaeology in Libya, 1943-70. *Ann. Rep. Soc. Libyan Studies* 1(1969-70), pp. 6-11.

See also VIII. a. *Egypt* Dąbrowska-Smektała

Arabia

CARTER, T.H. The Arab-Iranian Gulf, the cultural crossroad of the Ancient Near East. *Archaeology* 26(1973), pp. 16-23.

DE CARDI, B., VITA-FINZI, Cl., and COLES, A. Archaeological survey in Northern Oman, 1972. *East and West* N.S.25(1975), pp. 9-75.

DE CARDI, B. Archaeological survey in the Northern Trucial States. *East and West* 21(1971), pp. 225-289.

DE CARDI, B. The British archaeological expedition to Qatar 1973-1974. *Antiquity* 48, no. 191(1974), pp. 196-200.

DOE, B. Ancient capitals from Aden. *Arabian studs.* 1(1974), pp. 176-179.

GARBINI, G. Nuovi dati sull'antico Yemen da recenti scoperte. *Ve Congrès International d'Arabisants et d'Islamisants. Actes.*, [1970?], pp. 219-224.

OMAN, G. The Islamic necropolis of Dahlak Kebīr in the Red Sea. Report on a preliminary survey carried out in April 1972. *East and West* N.S.24(1974), pp. 249-295.

PARR, P.J., HARDING, G.L. and DAYTON, J.E. Preliminary survey in N.W. Arabia, 1968. *Bull. Inst. Archaeology* 10(1971), pp. 23-61.

TOSI, M. Dilmun. [A review article. An account of the archaeological research in the Arab states on the Peersian Gulf of the Danish expedition led by P.V. Glob and G. Bibby.] *Antiquity* 45 (no. 177, 1971), pp. 21-25.

WHITCOMB, D.S. The archaeology of Oman: a preliminary discussion of the Islamic periods. *J.Oman stud.* 1(1975), pp. 123-157.

WILKINSON, T.J. Sohar ancient fields project. Interim report no. 1. *J.Oman stud.* 1(1975), pp. 159-166.

WINNETT, F.V. and REED, W.L. An archaeological-epigraphical survey of the Hā'il area of Northern Sa'udi Arabia. *Berytus* 22(1973), pp. 53-100.

Some results of the third International Conference on Asian Archaeology in Bahrain, March 1970: new discoveries in the Persian/Arabian Gulf States and relations with artifacts from countries of the Ancient Near East. *Artibus Asiae* 33(1971), pp. 291-338.

See also V. c. *Arabia.* Strika.

Caucasus

KERVRAN, M. Une forteresse d'Azerbaidjan: Samīrān. *REI* 41(1973), pp. 71-93.

Central Asia

ATAGARRYEV, E. and BERDYEV, O. The archaeological exploration of Turkmenistan in the years of Soviet power. *East and West* 20(1970), pp. 285-306.

ERDÉLYI, I.F. Fouilles archéologiques en Bachkirie et la préhistoire hongroise. *Acta Or. Hung.* 25(1972), pp. 301-312.

FAKHRUTDINOV, R.G. Zadachi arkheologicheskogo izucheniya kazanskogo khanstva. (Objectifs de l'exploration archéologique du Khanat de Kazan.) *Sov. arkheologiya* 1973(4), pp. 113-122.

GUSEVA, T.V. Remeslennye masterskie v vostochnom prigorode Novogo Saraya. (Ateliers artisanaux dans la banlieue orientale de Nouveau Sarai.) *Sov. arkh.* 1974(3), pp. 125-141.

KOUZMINA, Héléna. Nouvelles découvertes archéologiques en Asie centrale. *Rev. hist.* 497 (1971), pp. 5-18

POLESSKIKH, M.R. Issledovanie pamyatnikov tipa Zolotarevskogo gorodishcha. *Voprosui etnogeneza tyurkoyazuichnuikh narodov Srednego Povolzh'ya* 1971, pp. 202-216.

Egypt

AHMED, Abbas Sid. The antiquities of Mograt island. *SNR* 52(1971), pp. 1-22.

DĄBROWSKA-SMEKTAŁA, E. Polish excavations in Egypt and the Sudan in the season 1969-1970. *Africana bull.* 14(1971), pp. 166-170

KUBIAK, W., SCANLON, G.T. Fusṭāṭ expedition: preliminary report, 1966. *J.American Res. Cent.Egypt* 10(1973), pp. 11-25.

VIII HISTORY

PROMIŃSKA, E. Paleopathology according to age at the Moslem Necropoles at Kom el-Dikka, Alexandria (Egypt). *Africana bull.* 14(1971), pp. 171-173

SAUNERON, S. Les travaux de l'Institut Français d'Archéologie Orientale en 1972-1973. *BIFAO* 73(1973), pp. 217-263.

SCANLON, G.T. Ancilliary dating materials from Fustat. *Proc. 27th Int. Cong. Or. 1967* (1971), p. 187.

SCANLON, G.T. Fāṭimid filters: archaeology and Olmer's typology. *Ann. Islamologiques* 9(1970), pp. 37-64.

SCANLON, G.T. Fustat: archaeological reconsiderations. *Colloque international sur l'histoire du Caire,* 1969, pp. 415-428.

SCANLON, G.T. Fusṭāṭ expedition: preliminary report 1968. *J. Amer. Res. Center Egypt* 11(1974), pp. 81-91.

SCANLON, G.T. The Fustat mounds. *Archaeology* 24 (1971), pp. 220-233.

WILD, H. Note concernant des antiquités trouvées, non à Deir Dronka, mais dans la nécropole d'Assiout. *BIFAO* 69 (1971), pp. 307-309.

Europe

WARREN, P. and MILES, G.C. An Arab building at Knossos. *Annual Brit. School Athens* 67(1972), pp. 285-296.

India. Pakistan

Lahore Fort excavations 1958. *Pak. archaeology* 5(1968), pp. 156-160.

Iran

BARNETT, R.D. Sir Robert Ker Porter - Regency artist and traveller. *Iran* 10 (1972), pp. 19-24

BIVAR, A.D.H. and FEHÉRVÁRI, G. Excavations at Ghubayrā, 1971: first interim report. *JRAS* 1974, pp. 20-141.

DAVARY, Djelani. Die Ruinenstadt Bost am Helmand. *Acta Iranica,* 2. sér. *Monumentum H.S. Nyberg,* I (1975), pp. 201-208.

DESHAYES, J. Rapport préliminaire sur les septième et huitième campagnes de fouille à Tureng Tepe (1967 et 1969). *Bull. Asia Inst., Pahlavi U.* 3(1973), pp. 81-97.

DESHAYES, J. Rapport preliminaire sur la neuvième campagne de fouille à Tureng Tepe (1971). *Iran* 11(1973), pp. 141-152.

DOLLFUS, G. Djaffarabad 1969-1970. Rapport préliminaire sur les deux premières campagnes de fouilles. *Syria* 48 (1971), pp. 61-84.

FEHERVARI, G. Archaeological Reconnaisance in Kirman province in the autumn of 1966. *Memorial vol. Vth Internat. Cong. Iranian Art and Archaeology,* 1972, Vol. 2, pp. 74-82.

FEHERVARI, G. An octagonal shrine excavated at Ghubayra. *AARP* 6(1974), pp. 35-40.

FISCHER, K. Historical, geographical and philological studies on Seistan by Bosworth, Daffinà and Gnoli in the light of recent archeological field surveys. *East and West* 21(1971), pp. 45-51.

GALDIERI, E. Relazione sulle attività dell'Is.M.E.O. in Iran: restauri a Persepoli e Isfahan. *La Persia nel medievo,* 1971, pp. 389-403

GHIRSHMAN, R. Activité des missions archéologiques françaises en Iran depuis la première guerre mondiale. *Commémoration Cyrus. Hommage universel,* I, 1974, pp. 319-323.

GHIRSHMAN, R. Les sanctuaires de Masjid-i Solaiman (Iran). *CRAIBL* (1972), pp. 30-40.

GHIRSHMAN, M.R. La terrasse sacrée de Masjid-i-Solaiman (Iran), campagne de 1970. *CRAIBL* 1970, pp. 653-666.

HANSMAN, J. and STRONACH, D. Excavations at Shahr-i Qūmis, 1971. *JRAS* 1974, pp. 8-19.

HUFF, D. Sasanidisch-frühislamische Ruinenplatze im Belqis-Massiv in Azerbeidjan. *Archäologische Mitteilungen aus Iran* N.F.7(1974), pp. 203-213.

KIANI, M.Y. Recent excavations in Jurjan; a summary. *Art of Iran and Anatolia* ... ed. W. Watson, 1974, pp. 126-133.

KLEISS, W. Bericht über Erkundungsfahrten in Iran im Jahre 1970. *Archäol. Mitt. aus Iran* N.F.4(1971), pp. 51-111.

KLEISS, W. Bericht über Erkundungsfahrten in Iran im Jahre 1971. *Archäol. Mitt. aus Iran* N.F.5(1972), pp. 135-242.

LOMTATIDZE, G.A., MAMAYASHVILI, N.F., CHKHATARASHVILI, M.N. K voprosu o kul'turnykh svyazyakh srednevekovoy Gruzii s Iranom (po arkheologicheskim materialam). *Iskusstvo i arkheologiya Irana,* 1971, pp. 190-198

NISSEN, H.J., REDMAN, C.L. Preliminary notes on an archeological surface survey in the Plain of Behbehan and the lower Zuhreh Valley. *Bastan Chenassi va Honar-e Iran* 6(1971), pp. 48-50.

PERROT, J., LE BRUN, A. et LABROUSSE, A. Recherches archéologiques à Susiane en 1969 et en 1970. *Syria* 48 (1971), pp. 21-51.

SABATHÉ, G. Principes généraux du règime juridique des fouilles archéologiques. *Proc. II. Annual Symposium on arch. res. in Iran,* 1973, pp. 287-306.

SALJOQUI, Fikri. The gravestone of Gawhar Shad. *Afghanistan* 25 iv(1973), pp. 29-31.

SCERRATO, U. La missione archeologica italiana nel Sistan persiano. *Veltro* 14i-ii (1970), pp. 123-140.

SCHIPPMANN, K. Forschungs- und Ausgrabungsergebnisse in Irān seit 1965. *Mitt. D. Or. Ges.* 104(1972), pp. 45-79.

TOSI, M. Shahr-i Sokhta: un insediamento protourbano nel Sistan iraniano. *La Persia nel medievo,* 1971, pp. 405-417

WHITEHOUSE, D. Chinese stoneware from Siraf: the earliest finds. *South Asian archaeology,* ed. N. Hammond, 1973, pp. 241-255.

WHITEHOUSE, D. Excavations at Sīrāf. Fourth interim report. *Iran* 9 (1971), pp. 1-17.

WHITEHOUSE, D. Excavations at Sīraf: fifth interim report. *Iran* 10(1972), pp. 63-87

WHITEHOUSE, D. Excavations at Sīrāf: Sixth Interim Report. *Iran* 12(1974), pp. 1-30.

WHITEHOUSE, D. Recent discoveries at Siraf. *Proc. II. Annual Symposium on arch. res. in Iran,* 1973, pp. 272-275.

WIJNEN, M. Excavations in Iran, 1967-1972. *Persica* 6(1972-74), pp. 51-93.

See also V. c. *Iran.* Adle and Melikian-Chirvani.

Iraq

YAWER, T.R. The fortress of Bash Tabiya. *Adab al-Rafidain* 4(1972), pp. 32-48.

See also XXVII. b. Nissen.

Jordan

'AMR, A. Jalil. Excavation at Meqablein. *Ann. Dept. Antiquities, Jordan* 18(1973), pp. 73-74.

HORN, S.H. The 1971 season of excavations at Tell Hesban. *Ann. Dept. Antiq. Jordan* 17(1972), pp. 15-22.

HORN, S.H. The 1973 season of excavations at Tell Hesbân. *Ann. Dept. Antiquities, Jordan* 19(1974), pp. 151-156.

THOMPSON, H.O. Excavating in Jordan. *Fac. Arts J. Univ. Jordan* 3i(1972), pp. 32-45.

THOMPSON, H.O. The excavation of Tell Siran (1972). *Ann. Dept. Antiquities, Jordan* 18(1973), pp. 5-14.

THOMPSON, H.O. Excavations on campus. *Fac. Arts J. Univ. Jordan* 3ii(1972), pp. 43-52.

THOMPSON, H.O. A tomb at Khirbet Yajuz. *Ann. Dept. Antiq. Jordan* 17(1972), pp. 37-45.

THOMPSON, H.O., DE VRIES, B. A water tunnel at Muqibleh. *Ann. Dept. Antiq. Jordan* 17 (1972), pp. 89-90.

ZAYADINE, Fawzi. Recent excavations on the Citadel of Amman. *Ann. Dept. Antiquities, Jordan* 18(1973), pp. 17-35.

Lebanon

SALAMÉ-SARKIS, Hassān. Chronique archéologique du Liban-Nord, II: 1973-1974. *Bull. du Musée de Beyrouth* 24 (1973), pp. 91-102.

Palestine

LIPIŃSKI, E. Archaeology of Palestine. *Folia Or.* 16(1975), pp. 267-287.

TOOMBS, L.E. Tell el-Ḥesi, 1970-71. *PEQ* 106i(1974), pp. 19-31.

Spain

CASTEJÓN, R. Las excavaciones en Medina Azahara de 1970 a 1973. *Bol. Asoc. esp. orientalistas* 10(1974), pp. 312-317; 11(1975), pp. 219-221.

PAVÓN MALDONADO, B. Estudio arqueológico de nuevos capiteles califales y dos lápidas granadinas descubiertas en Torrijos. *And.* 33 (1968), pp. 435-444.

ROSSELLÓ BORDOY, G. La arqueologia musulmana en Mallorca: estado de la cuestión. *BAEO* 6(1970), pp. 153-164.

SECO DE LUCENA PAREDES, L. Acerca de la qawraŷa de la Alcazaba Vieja de Granada. *And.* 3 (1968), pp. 197-203.

Syria.

GRABAR, O. Preliminary report on the third season of excavations at Qasr al-Hayr Sharqi. *Ann.arch.Syrie* 20(1970), pp. 45-54

GRABAR, O. Three seasons of excavations at Qaṣr al-Ḥayr Sharqi. *Ars Orientalis* 8 (1970), pp. 65-85

HARPER, R.P. Excavations at Dibsi Faraj, Northern Syria, 1972. *Ann.arch.arabes syriennes* 24(1974), pp. 25-37.

SALAMÉ-SARKIS, Hassan. Chronique archéologique du Liban-Nord. *Bull. Mus. Beyrouth* 24(1971), pp. 91-102.

VOÛTE, P.H.E. Chronique des fouilles et prospections en Syrie de 1965 à 1970. *Anatolica* 4(1971-72), pp. 83-132.

Turkey

ASLANAPA, Oktay Pottery and kilns from the Iznik excavations between 1963 and 1966. *Proc.27th Int.Cong.Or.1967* (1971), pp. 188-189

BELDICEANU-STEINHERR, I. et BELDICEANU, N. Deux villes d'Anatolie préottomane: Develi et Qarahisār d'après des documents inédits. *REI* 39(1971), pp. 337-386.

FRENCH, D. *and others*. Aşvan 1968-1972. An interim report. *Anatolian stud.* 23(1973), pp. 69-307.

The excavations at Korucutepe, Turkey, 1968-70: preliminary report. I: Architecture and general finds, by M. van Loon. II: The fortification wall, by C.M. Bier. III: Statistical description of significant groups of pottery, by M. Kelly-Bucellati. *JNES* 32(1973), pp. 357-444.

Recent archaeological research in Turkey. *Anat.stud.* 21(1971), pp. 5-58.

Recent archaeological research in Turkey. *Anatol. stud.* 22(1972), pp. 11-61.

Recent archaeological research in Turkey. *Anatolian stud.* 23(1973), pp. 13-68.

Recent archaeological research in Turkey. *Anatolian stud.* 24(1974), pp. 17-59.

See also V. c. *Turkey* Bates

b PALAEOGRAPHY

HABIBUR RAHMAN. Arabic script - its origin and development. *Pak.archaeology* 6(1969), pp. 264-273.

SCHNEIDER, M. Deux actes de donation en arabe. *Annales d'Ethiopie* 8(1970), pp. 79-85.

TROUPEAU, G. À propos des chiffres utilisés pour le foliotage des manuscrits arabes. *Arabica* 21(1974), p. 84.

c EPIGRAPHY

General

ETTINGHAUSEN, R. Arabic epigraphy: communication or symbolic affirmation. *Near Eastern numismatics ... Studies in honor of G.C. Miles,* 1974, pp. 297-317.

HEIN, W. Arabische und persische Mobiliaraufschriften II. *WZKM* 63-64(1972), pp. 151-157.

SOURDEL-THOMINE, J. Perspectives nouvelles dans le domaine de l'épigraphie arabe. *Actas IV congresso de estudos árabes e islâmicos* 1968(1971), pp. 527-529.

See also I. d. 1. Crowe.

Afghanistan

BIVAR, A.D.H. Seljuqid Ziyarats of Sar-i Pul (Afghanistan). *Afghanistan* 27iii(1974), pp. 46-64.

CRANE, H. and TROUSDALE, W. Helmand-Sistan project. Carved decorative and inscribed bricks from Bust. *Afghanistan* 28ii(1975), pp. 25-48.

CRANE, H., TROUSDALE, W. Helmand-Sistan project. Carved decorative and inscribed bricks from Bust. *East and West* 22(1972), pp. 215-226.

FISCHER, K. Archäologische Landesaufnahme im Norden von Afghanisch-Sistan 1968-1972. *Archäol.Mitt.aus Iran* N.F.6(1973), pp. 213-230.

MUKHTAROV, A. Inscriptions with Babur's name in the upper reaches of the Zarafshan. *Afghanistan* 25ii(1972), pp. 49-56.

Africa (excluding Egypt)

BARAMKI, Dimitri C. Rupestrian art of Libya. *American University of Beirut Festival book,* 1967, pp. 19-38.

DAGORN, R. Quelques réflexions sur les inscriptions arabes des nécropoles kairouanaises. *ROMM* 13-14(1973), pp. 239-258.

DAOULATI, Abdelaziz. Inscription à la mosquée andalouse d'el-'Aliya. *Recueil d'études sur les moriscos andalous en Tunisie,* préparé par M. de Epalza et R. Petit, 1973, pp. 285-290.

FREEMAN-GRENVILLE, G.S.P., MARTIN, B.G. A preliminary list of the Arabic inscriptions of the Eastern African coast. *JRAS* 1973, pp. 98-122.

JOMIER, J. Deux nouveaux fragments de stèles prismatiques conservés a Montpellier. *Arabica* 19(1972), pp. 316-317.

OMAN, G. La Necropoli islamica di Dahlak Kebir (Mar Rosso). *AION* 33(N.S.23, 1973), pp. 561-569.

SCHNEIDER, M. Notes au sujet de l'epitaphe du premier Sultan de Dahlak. *J.Ethiopian stud.* 11ii(1973), pp. 167-168.

SCHNEIDER, M. Stèles funéraires arabes de Quiha. *Ann. d'Ethiopie* 7 (1967), pp. 107-118.

SCHNEIDER, M. Stèles funéraires musulmanes de la province du Choa. *Annales d'Ethiopie* 8(1970), pp. 73-78

TEDESCHI, S. Il capostipite della dinastia dei sultani di Dahlak. *Africa* [Rome] 28 (1973), pp. 65-72.

Arabia

CASKEL, W. Der Sinn der Inschrift in Ḥiṣn Al-Ġurāb. *Folia Or.* 12(1970), pp. 51-60

KRACHKOVSKAYA, V.A. O nekotoruikh arabskikh graffiti iz Tzentral'noy Aravii. *Voprosui filologii stran Azii i Afriki, 1. Sbornik I.N. Vinnikova* 1971, pp. 160-166.

VIII HISTORY

OMAN, G. La necropoli islamica di Dahlak Kebir (Mar Rosso). II. *AION* N.S.24(34, 1974), pp. 209-215.

STEINDLER, G. Moscati. Su un graffito di Ḥirran (Yemen). *AION* 32(N.S. 22, 1972), pp. 519-520.

TAMARI, Sh. An inscription of Qānṣūh al-Ġūrī from ʿAqabat al-ʿUrqūb. *Rend. Accad. Lincei* 26(1971), pp. 173-187.

See also X. c. Kister

Central Asia. Caucasus

BRENTJES, B. Drei figurative verzierte Kenotaphe aus Aserbaidshan. *Bibl.Or.* 30(1973), pp. 389-390.

KRACHKOVSKAYA, V.A. O kuficheskoy nadpisi na bashne vneshney steny goroda Ari. *Folia Or.* 12(1970), pp. 103-111

YUSUPOV, G.V. Itogi polevykh epigraficheskikh issledovaniy 1961-1963 gg. v Tatarskoy ASSR. *Ep. Vost.* 21(1972), pp. 48-55.

Egypt

GRABAR, O. The inscriptions of the Madrasah-mausoleum of Qaytbay. *Near Eastern numismatics ... Studies in honor of G.C. Miles*, 1974, pp. 465-468.

MILES, G.C. An Egyptian tombstone of 515H./A.D. 1121 in the National Museum, Athens. *J. Amer. Res. Center Egypt* 11 (1974), pp. 77-79.

ORY, S. Six stèles d'Asyūṭ. *Annales islamol.* 11(1972), pp. 37-47.

PINDER-WILSON, R.H. An inscription of Badr al-Jamālī. *BM Qly* 36(1971), pp. 51-53.

SOURDEL-THOMINE, J. Quelques réflexions sur l'écriture des premiers stèles arabes du Caire. *Annales islamol.* 11(1972), pp. 23-35.

STEIN, L. Eine Inschriftentafel aus der Oase Dāḫla (Arabische Republik Ägypten). *Abh. Ber. Staatl. Mus. Völkerk., Dresden* 34(1975), pp. 267-269.

Europe

MARGOS, A. Armyansko-turetzkie nadpisi XVIII-XIX vv. v Bolgarii. *Ep. Vost.* 21 (1972), pp. 56-59.

MUJEZINOVIĆ, M. Kronogram na novopazarskoj banji. (The chronogram on the Hammam in Novi Pazar.) *POF* 20-21(1970-71), pp. 437-440.

MUJEZINOVIĆ, Mehmed. Turski natpisi u Travniku i njegogoj okolini. (Turkish inscriptions in the region of Travnik.) *Prilozi Or.Fil.Ist.* 14-15(1964-5), pp. 141-187; 16-17(1966-7), pp. 213-306.

India. Pakistan

ABDUL KARIM. A fresh study of the Biral inscription of Saif al-Dīn Fīrūz Shāh. *JAS Bangladesh* 17(1972), pp. 1-10.

ABDUL KARIM. Notes on the Navagram inscription of Nuṣrat Shāh. *JAS Bangladesh* 17ii(1972), pp. 1-8.

AHMED, Qeyamud-Din. Some inscriptions of Jahāngīr in Bihar. *Epigraphia Indica (Arab. and Pers. sup.)* 1969(1973), pp. 1-14.

CHAUHAN, D.V. Al-Djummal and decimal notation in Indo-Muslim epigraphy. *ABORI* 52(1971), pp. 87-96.

DIGBY, S. The fate of Dāniyāl, Prince of Bengal, in the light of an unpublished inscription. *BSOAS* 36(1973), pp. 588-602.

KADIRI, A.A. Mughal inscriptions from Mahārāshtra. *Epigraphia Indica (Arab. and Pers. sup.)* 1969(1973), pp. 29-48.

KHAN, Ahmad Nabi. A Persian inscription of the Mughul period at Margala pass near Rawalpindi. *Pak.archaeology* 6(1969), pp. 274-284.

KHAN, M.F. Inscriptions of Shāh Jahān from Madhya Pradesh. *Epigraphia Indica (Arab. and Pers. sup.)* 1969(1973), pp. 15-28.

RAHIM, S.A. Nine inscriptions of Akbar from Rājasthān. *Epigraphia Indica (Arab. and Pers. sup.)* 1969(1973), pp. 49-60.

SIDDIQI, W.H. and DESAI, Z.A. Inscriptions of Emperor Akbar from Uttar Pradesh. *Epigraphia Indica (Arab. and Pers. sup.)* 1969(1973), pp. 61-86.

Epigraphy in Pakistan. Islamic period. *Pak. archaeology* 5(1968), pp. 281-283.

See also IV. c. 4. Chauhan.

See also XXXII. c. Ahluwalla.

See also XXXII. j. Nath.

Iran

AFSHAR, Iraj. The grave-stone of Bondar-Abad. *Bull. Asia Inst. Pahlavi Univ.* 2 (1971), p. facing p. 1.

AFSHAR, Iraj. Two 12th century grave-stones of Yazd in Mashad and Washington. *Studia Iranica* 2(1973), pp. 203-211.

DONOHUE, J.J. Three Buwayhid inscriptions. *Arabica* 20(1973), pp. 74-80.

HOLOD, R. The monument of Duvāzdah Imām in Yazd and its inscription of foundation. *Near Eastern numismatics ... Studies in honor of G.C. Miles*, 1974, pp. 285-288.

MILES, George C. The inscriptions of the Masjid-i Jāmiʿ at Ashtarjān. *Iran* 12(1974), pp. 89-98.

SOTOODEH, Manoochehr. Drei alte kufische Inschriften aus Iran. *ZDMG* 125(1975), pp. 315-316.

See also V. c. *Iran*. Bivar.

See also V. c. *Iran*. Galdieri.

See also V. c. *Iran*. Watson.

See also V. g. Aslanapa.

Libya

LOWICK, N.M. The Arabic inscriptions on the Mosque of Abū Ma^{c}rūf at Sharwas. *Soc. Libyan Stud. Ann. report* 5(1973-4), pp. 14-19.

Palestine. Jordan

OXTOBY, W.G. Kilroy in the desert. *Ann. Dept.Antiq.Jordan* 15(1970), pp. 21-23.

SHARON, M. Arabic inscriptions from the excavations at the Western Wall. *Israel expl.J.* 23(1973), pp. 214-220.

Spain

DÍAZ-ESTEBAN. Dos lápidas musulmanas en Torrijos (Toledo). *BAEO* 7(1971), pp. 159-170.

FERNÁNDEZ PUERTAS, A. Dos lápidas hispano-musulmanas: la del castillo de Trujillo y una guardada en el museo de Evòra. *MEAH* 22 (1973), pp. 145-152.

FERNÁNDEZ PUERTAS, A. Tablas epigrafiadas de época almoravid y almohade. *MEAH* 23 (1974), pp. 113-119.

OSABA Y RUIZ DE ERENCHUN, B. Estela mozárabe inédita y el monasterio burgalés de Valeranicas. *RABM* 78(1975), pp. 519-526.

PAVÓN MALDONADO, B. Dos epitafios islámicos de Cáceres. *And.* 35(1970), pp. 199-201.

Syria. Lebanon

BOUNNI, Adnan. Antiquités palmyréniennes dans un texte arabe du Moyen Age. *MUSJ* 46(1970-1), pp. 329-339

JAMME, A. The Safaitic collection of the Art Museum of Princeton University. *JAOS* 91(1971), pp. 136-141.

JARRY, J. Inscriptions de Syrie du nord relevées en 1969. *Ann.Islamologiques* 9 (1970), pp. 215-221.

JARRY, J. Inscriptions Arabes, Syriaques et Grecques du Massif du Bélus en Syrie du nord. *Ann.Islamologiques* 9(1970), pp. 187-214.

ORY, Solange. Les différents types d'écriture de la Buṣrā būrīde. *MUSJ* 46(1970-1), pp. 305-327

SALAMÉ-SARKIS, Hassan. Inscriptions coufiques du Château de Tripoli. *Bull. Mus. Beyrouth* 24(1971), pp. 61-82.

Turkey. Cyprus

JARRY, J. Inscriptions syriaques et arabes inédites du Ṭūr ʿAbdīn. *Ann. Islamologiques* 10(1972), pp. 207-250.

MANTRAN, R. Bilan et perspectives de l'épigraphie turque pour les périodes pré-ottomane et ottomane. *Rev. hist. maghreb.* 4(1975), pp. 217-220.

MASSON, M.E. Fragmenty nadpisi karakhanidskogo mavzoleya s gorodishcha Afrasiab. *Ep.Vost.* 20(1971), pp. 77-84.

VEKILOV, A.P. Ob odnom pamyatnike turetzkoy epigrafiki v Leningrade. *Voprosui filologii stran Azii i Afriki, 1. Sbornik I.N. Vinnikova* 1971, pp. 166-170.

d NUMISMATICS

General

BACHARACH, J.L. The Dinar versus the Ducat. *IJMES* 4(1973), pp. 77-96.

BACHARACH, J.E.; AWAD, H.A. The problem of the obverse and reverse in Islamic numismatics. *Num. chron.* 13(1973), pp. 183-191.

BARRON, C.S. Some preliminary remarks concerning countermarked Islamic coins of the 9th century A.D./15th century A.D. *Numism.circular* 83(1975), p. 480.

CAHEN, C. Tari, mancus et amiral. *JESHO* 14(1971), pp. 310-311

GARBARINO, Taddeo. Monete cufiche nell' Italia meridionale. *Levante* 18iii (1971), pp. 25-34.

GRIERSON, P. Muslim coins in thriteenth-century England. *Near Eastern numismatics ... Studies in honor of G.C. Miles*, 1974, pp. 387-391.

HENNEQUIN, G. De la monnaie antique à la monnaie musulmane. *Annales ESC* 30(1975), pp. 890-899.

KMIETOWICZ, A. A hoard of dirhems from Szczecin-Niemierzyn. *Folia Or* 13(1971), pp. 143-160.

LAERE, R. van. De larijnen: een handelsmunt in het Nabije en Midden Oosten (16e - 19e eeuw). *Rev. belge num.* 121(1975), pp. 157-163.

MILES, G.C. Additions to Zambaur's *Munzprägungen des Islams*. *Amer.Num.Soc.Museum notes* 12(1971), pp. 229-233.

MILES, G.C. A necklace of coins in the Brooklyn Museum. *Berytus* 22(1973), pp. 25-30.

MUNZEL, K. Beiträge zur islamischen Numismatik. *Jhb. f. Numismatik u. Geldgesch.* 22(1972), pp. 103-108; 24 (1974), pp. 195-202.

NOONAN, T.S. Medieval Islamic copper coins from European Russia and surrounding regions: the use of the *fals* in early Islamic trade with Eastern Europe. *JAOS* 94(1974), pp. 448-453.

SALMAN, Isa. Coins presented to the Gulbenkian Museum. *Sumer* 29(1973), pp. 101-110.

TOLL, C. Minting technique according to Arabic literary sources. *Orientalia Suecana* 19-20(1970-71), pp. 125-139

'USH, Muḥammad Abū-l-Faraj al-. Rare Islamic coins: additions. *Near Eastern numismatics ... Studies in honor of G.C. Miles,* 1974, pp. 193-201.

USH, M. Abu-l-Faraj al-. Traces du classicisme dans la numismatique arabe-islamique. *Ann.arch.arabes syriennes* 21(1971), pp. 303-327.

See also I. c. 4. Bacharach, Kouymjian.

Afghanistan

ALBUM, S. An Umayyad hoard from Afghanistan. *Amer.Num.Soc.Museum notes* 12(1971), pp. 241-246.

BIVAR, A.D.H. Fresh evidence on the 'Sijistan Barbarous' series of Arab Sasanian dirhams. *JNSI* 30(1968), pp. 152-157.

BIVAR, A.D.H. A Mongol invasion hoard from Eastern Afghanistan. *Afghanistan* 28i(1975), pp. 16-28.

BIVAR, A.D.H. A Mongol invasion hoard from Eastern Afghanistan. *Near Eastern numismatics ... Studies in honor of G.C. Miles,* 1974, pp. 369-381.

HENNEQUIN, G. Grandes monnaies Sāmānides et Ghaznavides de l'Hindu Kush, 331-421 A.H. Étude numismatique et historique. *Ann.Islamologiques* 9(1970), pp. 127-177.

MACDOWALL, D.W. The Shahis of Kabul and Gandahara. *Afghanistan* 23iv(1971), pp. 68-87.

Africa (excluding Egypt)

ARROYO, H. Un trésor de dirhams de la fin de l'empire mérinide. *Rev.num.* 6.sér., 16(1974), pp. 115-122.

BOUROUIBA, Rachid Monnaies et bijoux trouvés à la Qal'a des Bani Hammâd. *II. Cong.int.ét.nord-afr.* 1970, pp. 67-77.

CHITTICK, N. A coin hoard from near Kilwa. *Azania* 2(1967), pp. 194-198.

CHITTICK, H.N. On the chronology of the Sultans of Kilwa. *Num. chron.* 13(1973), pp. 192-200.

CHITTICK, N. Six early coins from near Tanga. *Azania* 1(1966), pp. 156-157.

EUSTACHE, D. Les ateliers monétaires du Maroc. *Hespéris Tamuda* 11(1970), pp. 95-102

EUSTACHE, D. Le Corpus des dirhams idrîsites, présentation et conclusions sur la numismatique et l'histoire des Idrîsides. *Bull. Soc. hist. Maroc* 2 (1969), pp. 27-36.

MITCHELL, H.W. Fakhr al-Dunya and Nasir al-Dunya. Notes on two East African topics. *Num.chron.* 10(1970), pp. 253-257

Arabia

BATES, M.L. Notes on some Ismā'īlī coins from Yemen. *Amer. num. soc. Mus. notes* 18(1972), pp. 149-162.

BATES, M.L. Unpublished Wajīhid and Būyid coins from 'Uman in the American Numismatic Society. *Arabian studs.* 1(1974), pp. 171-175.

BIRKHAZI, Ramzi J. Coins of al-Yaman 132-569 A.H. *Al-Abhath* 23(1970), pp. 3-127.

HUSSAIN, M.K. Copper taweelah of Haṣa. *Ind numismatic chron.* 8(1970), pp. 41-44.

LOWICK, N.M. Trade patterns on the Persian Gulf in the light of recent coin evidence. *Near Eastern numismatics ... Studies in honor of G.C. Miles,* 1974, pp. 319-333.

SHAMMA, Samir. A hoard of fourth century dinars from Yemen. *Amer.Num.Soc.Museum notes* 12(1971), pp. 235-239.

The Caliphs

AWAD, Henri Amin. Seventh century Arab imitations of Alexandrian dodecanummia. *Amer. num. soc. Mus. notes* 18(1972), pp. 113-117.

GORDUS, A.A. Non-destructive analysis of Parthian, Sasanian, and Umayyad silver coins. *Near Eastern numismatics ... Studies in honor of G.C. Miles,* 1974, pp. 141-162.

MILES, G.C. A unique Umayyad dinar of 91 H./A.D. 709-10. *Rev. num.* 6 ser.,14 (1972), pp. 264-268.

ROTTER, G. The Umayyad fulūs of Mosul. *Amer. num. soc. Mus. notes* 19(1974), pp. 165-198.

Central Asia. Caucasus

ALBUM, St. Notes on the coinage of Muhammad ibn al-Husayn al-Rawwadi. *Rev. num.* 6 ser.,14(1972), pp. 99-104.

VIII HISTORY

BURNASHEVA, R. Monety bukharskogo khanstva pri Mangytakh (seredina XVIII-nachalo XX v.). *Ep. Vost.* 21(1972), pp. 67-80.

BYKOV, A.A. Kuficheskie monety iz klada, naydennogo v Sarkele. (Kufic coins from the hoard fround in Sarkel.) *Palestinskiy sbornik* 25(88, 1974), pp. 136-143.

BYKOV, A.A. Three notes on Islamic coins from hoards in the Soviet Union. *Near Eastern numismatics ... Studies in honor of G.C. Miles,* 1974, pp. 203-210.

DAVIDOVICH, E.A. Klad saganianskikh monet vtoroy chetverti XI v. kak istoricheskiy istochnik. *Pis'mennye pamyatniki Vostoka* 1968, pp. 73-97.

DAVIDOVICH, E.A. Monety Fergany kak istochnik dlya kharakteristiki instituta feodal'nykh pozhalovaniy za sluzhbu v Sredney Azii X v. *Pismennye pamyatniki vostoka,* 1969, pp. 110-141.

DU QUESNE-BIRD, N. The shortage of coinage in post-Timurid Georgia. *Numismatic Circular* 76(1968), pp. 375-376.

FEDOROV, M.N. Afrasiabskiy klad zolotykh monet vtoroy poloviny XII v. *Ep.Vost.* 21 (1972), pp. 32-34.

FEDOROV, M.N. Iz istorii denezhnogo obrashcheniya v Sredney Azii kontza VIII--pervoy poloviny XII v. (K probleme "chernykh dirkhemov.") (A propos de l'histoire de la circulation monétaire en Asie Centrale de VIII - première moitié de XII s.s. (Le problème des dirhams noirs.)) *Sov. arkheologiya* 1973(2), pp. 75-82.

FEDOROV, M.N.; RTVELADZE, E.V. Numizmaticheskie nakhodki v Uzbekistane v 1966-1968 *gg. Ep. Vost.* 21(1972), pp. 82-83.

FEDOROV, M.N. O pokupatel'noy sposobnosti dirkhema i dinara v Sredney Azii i sopredel'nykh s neyu stranakh v IX-XII vv. (Sur le pouvoir d'achat du dirhem et du dinar en Asie Centrale et aux pays limitrophes.) *Sov.Arkh.* 1972(2), pp. 73-80

GRYAZNEVICH, P. Tabaristanskie poludrakhmy iz kollektzii Aziatskogo Muzeya v sobranii Ermitazha. (Tabaristan coins from the collection of the Asiatic Museum.) *Soobshch. Gos. Ermitazha* 33(1971), pp. 94-100.

KHODZHANIYAZOV, T. Khronika numizmaticheskikh i epigraficheskikh nakhodok na territorii Turkmenskoy SSR v 1966-1968 gg. *Ep. Vost.* 21(1972), pp. 81-82.

KHODZHANIYAZOV, T. Klad zolotykh monet XII v. iz Kunya-Urgenchkogo rayona Turkmenskoy SSR. *Ep.Vost.* 20(1971), pp. 91-94.

KMIETOWICZ, A. Two Sāmānid dirhams from al-Ṭayaqān. *Near Eastern numismatics ... Studies in honor of G.C. Miles,* 1974, pp. 211-217.

KOUYMJIAN, D.K. A unique coin of the Shirvānshāh Minūchihr II dated A.H. 555/1160 A.D. *Near Eastern numismatics ... Studies in honor of G.C. Miles,* 1974, pp. 339-346.

LEWICKI, T. Le commerce des Sāmānides avec l'Europe orientale et centrale à la lumière des trésors de monnaies coufiques. *Near Eastern numismatics ... Studies in honor of G.C. Miles,* 1974, pp. 219-233.

MUKHAMADIEV, A.G. Den'gi, denezhnaya terminologiya i denezhnyy schet Bulgara v predmongol'sky period. (Les monnaies, la terminologie s'y rapportant et le système monétaire de l'état des Bulgares sur la Volga à l'époque antérieure à l'invasion des Mongols. *Sov.Arkh.* 1972(2), pp. 63-72

RTVELADZE, E.V. O mednykh imennykh monetakh Tokhtamysha i podrazhaniyakh im. *Ep. Vost.* 21(1972), pp. 42-47.

RTVELADZE, E.V., TASHKHODZHAEV, Sh.S. Ob odnoy tyurko-sogdiyskoy monete s khristianskimi simbolami. *Viz. vrem.* 35(1973), pp. 232-234.

RTVELADZE, E.V.; RTVELADZE, L.L. Pervyy fel's Yakhyi ibn Asada. *Ep. Vost.* 21(1972), pp. 30-31.

SEYFEDDINI, M.A. Nekotorye svedeniya ob azerbaydzhanskom gosudarstve Aḳsunḳuridov. *Ep. Vost.* 21(1972), pp. 35-39.

See also XXXIV. d. Fedorov.

See also XL. c. Klyashtornyy.

Crusaders

METCALF, D.M. Some provenanced finds of Crusader bezants. *Num.chron.,* 7th ser., 15(1975), pp. 198-199.

PORTEOUS, J. The early coinage of the Counts of Edessa. *Num.chron.,* 7th ser., 15(1975), pp. 169-182.

Egypt

BACHARACH, J.L., AWAD, Henri Amin. The early Islamic bronze coinage of Egypt: additions. *Near Eastern numismatics ... Studies in honor of G.C. Miles,* 1974, pp. 185-192.

BACHARACH, J.L. Al-Ikhshīd, the Ḥamdānids and the Caliphate: the numismatic evidence. *JAOS* 94(1974), pp. 360-370.

BATES, M.L. Thirteenth century Crusader imitations of Ayyūbid silver coinage: a preliminary survey. *Near Eastern numismatics ... Studies in honor of G.C. Miles,* 1974, pp.

BERMAN, Ariel. The beginning of Ottoman coinage in Egypt. *Numism.circular* 83 (1975), pp. 150-152.

BERMAN, Ariel. Uniform buttons as surrogate money during the Egyptian campaign. *Numism.circular* 83(1975), p. 385.

VIII HISTORY

BIANQUIS, Th., SCANLON, G.T., WATSON, A. Numismatics and the dating of early Islamic pottery in Egypt. *Near Eastern numismatics ... Studies in honor of G.C. Miles,* 1974, pp. 163-173.

CAHEN, Cl. La frappe des monnaies en Égypte au VIe/XIIe siècle d'après le *Minhāj* d'al-Makhzūmī. *Near Eastern numismatics ... Studies in honor of G.C. Miles,* 1974, pp. 335-338.

COOPER, R.S. A note on the *dīnār jayshī*. *JESHO* 16(1973), pp. 317-318.

LACHMAN, S. The coins struck by Ali Bey in Egypt. *Numism.circular* 83(1975), pp. 198-201, 336-338.

LACHMAN, S.A. A hoard of silver coins of Barsbāy. *Amer. num. soc. Mus. notes* 18 (1972), pp. 163-166.

LACHMAN, S. The Kurush struck by Ali Bey in Egypt. *Num.chron.* 11(1971), pp. 327-328

LAUNOIS, A. Catalogue des monnaies fatimites entrées au Cabinet des Médailles depuis 1896. *BEO* 24(1971), pp. 19-53.

MANTRAN, R. Inscriptions turques de l'époque turque du Caire. *Annales islamol.* 11(1972), pp. 211-233.

PIGELER, H. Un fals inconnu du sultan mamelouk al-Nāṣir Aḥmad. *Rev.num.* 6.sér., 16(1974), pp. 167-171.

See also VIII. d. *Africa* Mitchell

See also VIII. f. Allan

Europe

GORINI, G. Moneta araba del X secolo rinvenuta a Roncajette (Padova). *Studi Veneziani* 12(1970), pp. 59-62

MILES, G.C. An eighth century Arab coin found in Herakleion. *Textile Museum J.* 3 (1972), pp. 225-227.

India. Pakistan

ABDUL GHAFUR, Muhammad. Fourteen Kufic inscriptions of Banbhore, the site of Daybul. *Pak.archaeology* 5(1968), pp. 65-90.

ABDUL KARIM. Significance of the words "Al-Ḥusain Shāhī" in the coins of Sulṭān Al-Din Fatḥ Shāh. *J. Asiatic Soc. Pakistan* 14(1969), pp. 129-141.

AGRAWAL, Jagannath. Silver coins of Qutbuddin Aibak. *JNSI* 35(1973), pp. 213-214.

AHMED, Nisar. Empress Nūr Jahān and her coins. *Itihāsa-Chayanikā (Dr. Sampurnanand Felicitation vol.* = JUPHS 11-13), Part II (1965), pp. 27-39

ALI, M. Amjad. A copper coin of Nasīr-ud-din Abu'l Fat'h Isma'il Shaḥ. *JNSI* 28(1966), pp. 219-220.

ALI, M. Amjad. The mint Machlipatan Bandar. *JNSI* 30(1968), pp. 162-166.

ALI, M.Amjad. A new coin type of Ahmad Shah Bahmani. *JNSI* 30(1968), p. 225.

ANSARI, Hasan Nishat. Coins of Sultans Alauddin Masud Shah and Nasiruddin Mahmud Shah from North Bihar. *Ind. numismatic chron.* 5(1966), pp. 72-80.

ANSARI, Hasan Nishat. A date on the coins of Saifuddin Hamza Shah of Bengal - A rejoinder. *Ind. numismatic chron.* 7(1969), pp. 87-90.

ANSARI, Hasan Nishat. A hoard of Turko-Muslim billon coins from North Bihar. *JNSI* 29i(1967), pp. 33-37.

BAJPAI, K.D. Indian numismatics today. *J. Madhya Pradesh Itihasa Parishad* 7(1969), pp. 47-49.

BHATT, S.K. Mint records of Malharnagar (Indore 1866 A.D.). *JNSI* 36(1974), pp. 92-96.

BHATT, S.K. A silver double tanka of Baz Bahadur. *JNSI* 36(1974), pp. 134-136.

BHATTA, S.K. A silver half tanka of Baz Bahadur, 969 H. *JNSI* 34(1972), pp. 87-89.

BIDDULPH, C.H. The coinage of Chamba State. *JNSI* 28(1966), pp. 177-181.

BIDDULPH, C.H. Copper coins of the East India Company of Chinapatam (Madras) Mint issued in the name of Aurangzeb Alamgir. *JNSI* 28(1966), pp. 223-225.

CHOUDHURY, Vasant and ROY, Parimal. Hitherto unknown lion-type coins of Nasiru-d-din Mahmud Shah I of Bengal. *JNSI* 36(1974), pp. 83-87.

DEYELL, J.S. A token in the style of East India Company coins. *JNSI* 36(1974), pp. 154-155.

DIGBY, S. The coinage and genealogy of the later Jāms of Sind. *JRAS* (1972), pp. 125-134.

GUPTA, Parmeshwari Lal. A date on the coins of Saifuddin Hamza Shah of Bengal. *Ind. numismatic chron.* 6(1967), pp. 40-41.

GUPTA, P.L. A gold coin of Ahmad Shah Bahadur. *JNSI* 31(1969), pp. 79-80.

GUPTA, P.L. Jodhpur coins in the name of Edward VIII. *JNSI* 29i(1967), pp. 58-59.

GUPTA, Parmeshwari Lal. Nāgarī legend on horseman ṭaṅkah of Muhammad bin Sām. *JNSI* 35(1973), pp. 209-212.

GUPTA, Parmeshwari Lal. The silver coins of Akbar. *Ind. numismatic chron.* 6(1967), pp. 72-104.

VIII HISTORY

GUPTA, Parmeshwari Lal. Two hoards of silver Mughal coins from Bihar. *Ind. numismatic chron.* 6(1967), pp. 18-31.

HANDA, Devendra. Jaler, Jalesar or Jagner? *JNSI* 33ii(1971), p. 122.

HANDA, Devendra. A new copper coin of Muhammad Ibrāhīm Ali Khān of Tonk. *JNSI* 32 (1970), pp. 213-214.

HANDA, Devendra. A rare coin of Shamsu-d-Din Mahmud Shah. *JNSI* 34(1972), pp. 85-86.

HANDA, Devendra. The smallest copper coin of Alau-d-din Khilji. *JNSI* 36 (1974), pp. 129.

HANDA, Devendra. Some new coins of Nasiru-d-din Khusru. *JNSI* 36(1974), pp. 127-128.

HANDA, Devendra. A unique coin of Shāh Ālam II. *JNSI* 31(1969), pp. 188-189.

HUSAIN, M.K. Dapoli hoard of silver larins. *JNSI* 30(1968), pp. 158-161.

HUSSAIN, M.K. Gold coin of Ahmad Shah Bahadur. *JNSI* 30(1968), pp. 232-233.

HUSAIN, M.K. The silver lārins. *JNSI* 29ii(1967), pp. 54-72.

KADIRI, A.A. Karnatak-Bijapur. A new mint of Aurangzeb. *JNSI* 34(1972), pp. 60-64.

KADIRI, A.A. The Mughal mint Nasīrābād. *JNSI* 33ii(1971), pp. 88-92.

KADIRI, A.A. A unique copper coin of Akbar from Orissa. *JNSI* 31(1969), pp. 57-62.

KUKURANOV, L.N. Two rare Mughal half-rupee coins. *JNSI* 35(1973), pp. 246-249.

LOWICK, N.M. The horseman type of Bengal and the question of commemorative issues. *JNSI* 35(1973), pp. 196-208.

LOWICK, N.M. More on Sulaimān Mīzā and his contemporaries. *Num. chron.* 12(1972), pp. 282-287.

MANKAD, B.L. Some interesting coins in Baroda Museum. *JNSI* 30(1968), pp. 222-224.

MISHRA, Kamala Prasad. The currency system of eighteenth century Upper India: a case study of the Banaras Region. *JNSI* 33ii (1971), pp. 78-87.

MISRA, S.C. The Sikka and the Khutba: a Sher Shahi experiment. *Medieval India* 1(1969), pp. 39-47.

NASIR, Pervin T. Coins of the early Muslim period from Banbhore. *Pak.archaeology* 6 (1969), pp. 117-181.

NIYOGI, Roma. A half rupee of Shah Shuja. *JNSI* 34(1972), pp. 230-233.

NIYOGI, Roma. Two new coins of Bengal sultans. *JNSI* 36(1974), pp. 88-91.

OMAN, G. On eight coins of Akbar found in a rock-shelter near Ghālīgai, Swāt. *East and West* 20(1970), pp. 105-108.

PRASAD, H.K. Coin hoards from Bihar. *Ind. numismatic chron.* 8(1970), pp. 45-109.

PRASAD, H.K. Coin hoards from Orissa. *Ind. numismatic chron.* 6(1967), pp. 63-71; 7 (1969), pp. 78-82.

PRASAD, Ram Janma. Coins of Babur and Humayun in Patna Museum. *Ind. numismatic chron.* 5(1966), pp. 81-97.

PRASAD, Ram Janam. Silver coins of Akbar in Patna Museum. *Ind. numismatic chron.* 6 (1967), pp. 105-112.

RAO, U.S. A new couplet rupee of Jahangir. *JNSI* 29ii(1967), pp. 83-85.

RTVELADZE, E.T. Dva dinara deliyskikh sultanov s gorodishcha Madzhar. *Sov.Arkh.* 1972(1), pp. 269-271

SELLE, J. Coinage feud between Aurangzeb and E.I.Co. *JNSI* 31(1969), pp. 63-68.

SELLE, J. A silver tankah of Nusrat Shah. *JNSI* 31(1969), pp. 76-78.

SETHI, R.K. Counter-struck Vithoba coin of Aurangzeb. *JNSI* 30(1968), pp. 226-229.

SETHI, R.K. Counter-struck Vithoba coin of Aurangzeb - an explanation. *JNSI* 33i(1971), pp. 137-138.

SETHI, R.K. Earliest known coin of Shahjahan minted during the reign of Jahangir. *Ind. numismatic chron.* 7(1969), pp. 73-77.

SETHI, R.K. A unique coin of Aurangzeb minted after his death. *JNSI* 30(1968), pp. 229-231.

SETHI, R.K. A unique coin (?) of Shah Alam II - a reconsideration. *JNSI* 33i(1971), pp. 138-139.

SIDDIQUI, A.H. A copper coin Murtaza Nizam Shah II of Punanagar mint. *JNSI* 36(1974), pp. 140-141.

SIDDIQUI, A.H. The copper coins of Imad Shahi dynasty of Barar. *JNSI* 36(1974), pp. 142-143.

SIDDIQUI, A.H. A new legend on a copper coin of Ibrahim Barid. *JNSI* 28(1966), pp. 82-83.

SIDDIQUI, A.H. A new type copper coin of Mahmud Shah Bahmani. *JNSI* 28(1966), pp. 220-223.

SIDDIQUI, A.H. A new type copper coin of Muhammad bin Tughluq. *JNSI* 28 (1966), pp. 217-218.

SIDDIQUI, A.H. A note on copper coins of Feroz Shah Bahmani. *JNSI* 28(1966), pp. 79-82.

SIDDIQUI, A.H. A note on the copper coins of Murtaza Nizam Shah II. *JNSI* 28(1966), pp. 84-86.

SIDDIQUI, A.H. On copper coins of Shah Alam I of Parenda Mint. *JNSI* 28(1966), pp. 218-219.

SIDDIQUI, A.H. On the coins of Jahangir and Shah Jahan of Ahmadnagar Mint. *JNSI* 28(1966), pp. 87-89.

SIDDIQUI, A.H. Some Barid Shahi coins. *JNSI* 36(1974), pp. 137-139.

SINGHAL, C.R. Akbari tankas of Udaipur Mint. *JNSI* 28(1966), pp. 76-78.

SINGHAL, C.R. The Rohtās Mint. *JNSI* 28(1966), pp. 74-76.

SIRCAR, D.C. A silver coin of Rama-Tanka type. *JNSI* 28(1966), pp. 90-94.

SRIVASTAVA, A.K. Coin collection in the State Museum, Lucknow. *JNSI* 35(1973), pp. 225-232.

THAKOR, Mahendrasinhji. Gold coins of the Sultans of Gujarat discovered from village Kothiakhad, district Kaira. *J. Or. Inst. Baroda* 22(1972), p. 156.

WAKANKAR, V.S. Coins from Kayatha. *Ind. numismatic chron.* 7(1969), pp. 83-86.

WIGGINS, K. Copper coinage of Kishangarh. *JNSI* 34(1972), pp. 234-237.

Iran

ALBUM, St. Power and legitimacy. The coinage of Mubāriz al-Dīn Muḥammad ibn al-Muẓaffar at Yazd and Kirmān. *Le monde iranien et l'Islam* II, 1974, pp. 157-171.

BEHBIN, Said. Current Iranian coins. *J. Reg. Cult. Inst.* 1 iv(1968), pp. 35-36.

BYKOV, A.A. Dva novykh dirkhema Daysama ibn Ibrakhima al-Kurdi. *Ep.Vost.* 20 (1971), pp. 74-76.

BYKOV, A.A. Redkiy samanidskiy fel's. *Ep.Vost.* 20(1971), pp. 72-73.

HINZ, W. Die Spätmittelalterlichen Währungen im Bereich des Persischen Golfes. *Iran and Islam, in memory of V. Minorsky,* 1971, pp. 303-314

HINZ, W. The value of the toman in the middle ages. *Yād-nāme-ye Irāni-ye Minorsky,* 1969, pp. 90-95.

LOWICK, N.M. An early tenth century hoard from Isfahan. *Num.chron.,* 7th ser., 15 (1975), pp. 110-154.

LOWICK, N.M. Seljuq coins. *Num.chron.* 10(1970), pp. 241-251

MILES, G.C. Another Kākwayhid note. *Amer. num. soc. Mus. notes* 18(1972), pp. 139-148.

MILES, G.C. The coinage of the Bāwandids of Ṭabaristān. *Iran and Islam, in memory of V. Minorsky,* 1971, pp. 443-460

MILES, G.C. Coinage of the Ziyārid dynasty of Ṭabaristān and Gurgān. *Amer. num. soc. Mus. notes* 18(1972), pp. 119-137.

MILES, G.C. Coins of the Assassins of Alamūt. *Or. Lovaniensia per.* 3(1972), pp. 155-162.

MORTON, A.H. An Iranian hoard of forged dirhams. *Num.chron.,* 7th ser., 15(1975), pp. 155-168.

MORTON, A.H. Trois dinars de l'Ustundār Naṣr. *Rev.num.* 6.sér., 16(1974), pp. 100-114.

'USH, Muhammad Abū-l-Faraj al-. Dirhams Abū Dāwūdides (Banū Bānījūrī). *Rev. num.* 6 ser.,15(1973), pp. 169-176.

See also VIII. d. *India* Husain, M.K.

See also XXXI. g. Rakhmani.

Iraq

BIKHAZI, Ramzi Jibran. Ḥamdānid coins of Madīnat al-Salām A.H. 330-331. *Near Eastern numismatics ... Studies in honor of G.C. Miles,* 1974, pp. 255-277.

DESHAZO, A.S., BATES, M.L. The Umayyad Governors of al-ʿIrāq and the changing annulet patterns on their dirhams. *Num.chron.* 14 (1974), pp. 110-118.

Jordan

HADIDI, Adnan. Some bronze coins from Amman. *Ann. Dept. Antiquities, Jordan* 18(1973), pp. 51-53.

Morocco. Tangier

CAGNE, J. Du nouveau dans les études de numismatique et d'histoire monétaire du Maroc. *Bull. écon. soc. Maroc* 126 (1975), pp. 111-115.

Palestine.

SHAMMA, Samir. The coinage of the Ṭūlūnids in Filasṭīn; a short historical note. *al-Abhath* 24(1971), pp. 43-49.

SHAMMA, Samir. The Ikhshidid coins of Filasṭīn. *Al-Abhath* 22iii-iv (1969), pp. 27-46.

Spain. Sicily

GRANBERG, B. Fyra nya spanska omajjaddirhemer från Gotland. (Four new Spanish Omayyad dirhems from Gotland.) *Nordisk numismatisk arsskrift* 1971, pp. 5-19.

VIII HISTORY

GRIERSON, P., ODDY, W.A. Le titre du tari sicilien du milieu du XIe siècle à 1278. *Rev.num.* 6.sér., 16(1974), pp. 123-134.

RODRÍGUEZ LORENTE, J.J. El dinar almorávide de "Tadla". Una ceca inédita del emir Yusuf ibn-Tashfin (A.H.480-500 A.D. 1087-1106). *Acta numismatica* 2(1972), pp. 165-166.

Syria

AWAD, Henri Amin. A hoard of Ikhshīdid dirhams. *al-Abhath* 24(1971), pp. 51-58.

BALOG, P. Un fals d'al-Kāmil Shams al-dīn Sunqur, sultan mamelouk rebelle de Damas. *Rev. num.* 6 ser.,15(1973), pp. 177-179.

BROWN, H.M. Some reflections on the figured coinage of the Artuqids and Zengids. *Near Eastern numismatics ... Studies in honor of G.C. Miles*, 1974, pp. 353-358.

See also VIII. d. *Egypt.*

Turkey. Turkish peoples

ARTUK, Ibrahim. Early Ottoman coins of Orhan Ghazi as confirmation on his sovereignty. *Near Eastern numismatics ... Studies in honor of G.C. Miles*, 1974, pp. 457-464.

CANIVET, P., ZAQZOUQ. The Ottoman gold hoard discovered in Nikertay, kept now in the Hama Museum. *Annales arch.arabes syr.* 23(1973), pp. 201-224.

DU QUESNE-BIRD, N. Turkish numismatics - a survey of the recent literature. *Numism. circular* 83(1975), pp. 10, 19.

FEDOROV, M.N. Ob odnoy gruppe karakhanidskikh monet 380-404 gg. kh. *Ep.Vost.* 20 (1971), pp. 85-89.

KISSLING, H.J. Über eine Goldmünze Sultan Muṣṭafā's I. *WI* N.S.14(1973), pp. 163-170.

LACHMAN, S. The initial letters on Ottoman coins of the eighteenth century. *Amer. num. soc. Mus. notes* 19(1974), pp. 199-224.

LACHMAN, S. The standard of the silver coinage of the Ottoman Sultan Selim III. *Numismatic Circular* 77(1969), p. 167.

LACHMAN, S. An unlisted coin of Sultan Murad V. *Numism.circular* 83(1975), p. 382.

LINDNER, R.P. The challenge of Qilich Arslan IV. *Near Eastern numismatics ... Studies in honor of G.C. Miles*, 1974, pp.

LOWICK, N.M. Les premières monnaies artuqides: une exhumation tardive. *Rev. num.* 6.sér., 16(1974), pp. 95-99.

MACKENZIE, K. An eighteenth century coin die. *Numism.circular* 83(1975), p. 196.

MACKENZIE, K.M. A remarkable altun of Mustafa II. *Numism.circular* 83(1975), p. 15.

PERE, Nuri. Turkish current coins. *J.Reg. Cult.Inst.* 5i(1972), pp. 51-55

SASS, B. The silver and bullion coins minted at Constantinople under Sultan Maḥmūd II (1223-1255 H.) *Amer. num. soc. Mus. notes* 18(1972), pp. 167-175.

WELLER, H. Turkic countermarks. *Numism. circular* 83(1975), pp. 475-477.

ZAQZOUQ, A. The Ottoman gold hoard discovered in Nikertay, kept now in the Ḥamā Museum. *Rev. belge num.* 119(1973), pp. 145-160.

See also XXIX. a. Bulliet.

Seals

BHATT, S.K. Seals of Akbar's reign. *J. Madhya Pradesh Itihasa Parishad* 7(1969), pp. 59-61.

HAZARD, H.W. The sigillography of Crusader Caesarea. *Near Eastern numismatics ... Studies in honor of G.C. Miles*, 1974, pp. 359-368.

IVANOV, A.A. Pechat' Gaukhar-Shad. *Strany i narody Vostoka pod obshchey red. D.A. Ol'derogge*, X, 1971, pp. 199-201.

KAUS, Hurmuz. A few seals of Indian Muslim women. *Numismatic Circular* 76 (1968), pp. 5-6.

Glass weights

BALOG, P. The Fāṭimid glass jeton. *Annali Ist. ital. numismatica* 18-19 (1971-2), pp. 175-264.

BALOG, P. Sasanian and early Islamic ornamental glass vessel-stamps. *Near Eastern numismatics ... Studies in honor of G.C. Miles*, 1974, pp. 131-140.

MILES, G.C. Umayyad and ʿAbbāsid glass weights and measure stamps in the Corning Museum. *J.glass studies* 13(1971), pp. 64-76

Metrology

SMITH, J.M., BENIN, St. In a Persian market with Mongol money. *Near Eastern numismatics ... Studies in honor of G.C. Miles*, 1974, pp. 431-442.

SPERBER, D. Islamic metrology from Jewish sources II. *Num. chron.* 12(1972), pp. 275-282.

Medals

Médailles iraniennes pour notre Musée. *Objets et mondes* 12(1972), pp. 67.

e PAPYROLOGY

DAVID-WEILL, J., ADDA, M., CAHEN, C. Lettres à un marchand égyptien du III/IXe siècle. *JESHO* 16(1973), pp. 1-14.

DAVID-WEILL, J. Papyrus arabes du Louvre II. *JESHO* 14(1971), pp. 1-24.

FAHMY, Aly Mohamed. The value of papyri in the study of the history of Egypt under Arab rule. *Abr-nahrain* 12(1971-2), pp. 85-93

ISSERLIN, B.S.J. The Nessana papyri. The Greek transcriptions of Arabic. *Ann. Leeds Univ. Or. Soc.* 7(1969-73), pp. 17-31.

KRACHKOVSKAYA, V.A. Arabskie papirusy iz Khirbat al-Mird na poberezh'e Mertvogo Morya. *Ep.Vost.* 20(1971), pp. 65-71.

See also II. a. 4. Kister.

See also XIX. b. Plumley.

f HERALDRY

ALLAN, J.W. Mamlūk sultanic heraldry and the numismatic evidence: a reinterpretation. *JRAS* 1970, pp. 99-112

MEINECKE, M. Die Bedeutung der mamlukischen Heraldik für die Kunstgeschichte. *XVIII. Deutscher Orientalistentag 1972: Vorträge*, pp. 212-240.

PAVÓN MALDONADO, B. Notas sobre el escudo de la orden de la banda en los palacios de Don Pedro y de Muhammad V. *And.* 37(1972), pp. 229-232.

IX HISTORY: GENERAL

a GENERAL. MORE THAN ONE COUNTRY

ABDEL-MALEK, A. Renaissance et révolution: le problème critique. *Renaissance du monde arabe. Colloque interarabe de Louvain*, 1972, pp. 347-365.

ABEL, A. Introduction critique à une étude sur la renaissance du monde arabe. *Correspondance d'Orient: Etudes* 15-16(1969), pp. 3-43.

ABEL, A. L'Introduction d'éléments iraniens dans le monde Syro-Egyptien du Xe au XIIIe siècle. *La Persia nel medievo*, 1971, pp. 165-177

AGWANI, M.S. Aspects of political change in the Arab East. *India and the Arab World, ed. by S. Maqbul Ahmed*, 1969, pp. 47-50.

AHWANI, Abdul Aziz al- . Evolution of social pattern in the Arab world. *India and the Arab World, ed. by S. Maqbul Ahmed*, 1969, pp. 95-102.

ANABTAWI, Samir N. The Third World and the Middle East since the Six-Day War. *The Middle East.* Ed. W.A. Beling, 1973, pp. 237-259.

ARNALDEZ, R. Tradition et changement dans le monde islamique. *Etudes philos. et litt.* 5(1971), pp. 135-151.

ASAD, Talal. Two European images of non-European rule. *Economy and society* 2(1973), pp. 263-277.

ASHTOR, E. Nouvelles refléxions sur la thèse de Pirenne (à propos d'une réimpression de "Mahomet et Charlemagne"). *Schweiz.Zeits.für Geschichte* 20(1970), pp. 601-607

ASHTOR, Eliyahu. Républiques urbaines dans le Proche-Orient à l'époque des Croisades? *Cah. civ. méd.* 18(1975), pp. 117-131.

AWAD, L. Contemporary Arab culture: motivations and ends. *Cah. d'hist. mondiale* 14(1972), pp. 756-770.

BADAWI, Abdel Rahman. Sciences humaines et vie culturelle dans le monde Arabe. *Cah. d'hist. mondiale* 14(1972), pp. 771-799.

BAHA EL-DIN, Ahmed. The Arab cultural image in world context. *Cah. d'hist. mondiale* 14(1972), pp. 814-830.

BARBOUR, N. Arabs and Norsemen: the expansion and settlement of the Arabs between 632 and 1100 and of the Scandinavians between 789 and 1250. *Asian aff.* 58(N.S.2, 1971), pp. 159-165.

BATUNSKIY, M.A. Razvitie predstavleniy ob Islame v zapadnoevropeyskoy srednevekovoy obshchestvennoy muisli (XI-XIV vv.). *NAA* 1971(4), pp. 107-118.

BECKINGHAM, C.F. Islam: a political history [review article]. *Asian aff.* 58(N.S.2, 1971), pp. 321-324.

BELAL, A.A. Quelques aspects fondamentaux de l'approche socio-économique du problème de la renaissance et de l'unité du monde arabe. *Renaissance du monde arabe. Colloque interarabe de Louvain*, 1972, pp. 17-37.

IX HISTORY

BELLMANN, D. Bemerkungen zum Bild des "revolutionären Helden" in der Gegenwartsliteratur der arabischen Länder. *Asien, Afrika, Lateinamerika* 2(1974), pp. 569-579.

BENIGNI, R. Österreichische Botschaftsberichte über arabische Länder. Register zu den im Haus-, Hof- und Staatsarchiv in Wien befindlichen Akten der Kaiserlichen Internuntiatur, der späteren Botschaft, in Konstantinopel von 1750 bis 1918. *Biblos* 22(1973), pp. 52-83, 190-233, 307-328, 415-441.

BENNOUNA, Mohammed. La presse française et la crise du Moyen-Orient, mai-juin 1967: Analyse du contenu de cinq grands quotidiens français. *Rev.alger.des sci.jur.econ.et pol.* 8(1971), pp. 937-1000.

BERQUE, J. Vers une culture Arabe contemporaine. *Cah. d'hist. mondiale* 14(1972), pp. 729-755.

BHATTACHARYYA, N.N. India's contribution to Islamic thought and culture. *India's contribution to world thought ...,* 1970, pp. 573-577.

BILL, J.A. The military and modernization in the Middle East. *Contemporary politics* 2(1969-70), pp. 41-62.

BOSWORTH, C.E. Recruitment, muster, and review in medieval Islamic armies. *War, technology and society in the Middle East,* ed. V.J. Parry and M.E. Yapp, 1975, pp. 59-77.

BROWN, P. Mohammed and Charlemagne, by Henri Pirenne. *Daedalus* 103i(1974), pp. 25-33.

BRYSON, T.A. A note on Near East relief: Walter George Smith, Cardinal Gibbons and the question of discrimination against Catholics. *MW* 61 (1971), pp. 202-209.

BURROWES, R., MUZZIO, D. and SPECTOR, B. Sources of Middle East international event data. *MESA Bull.* 5ii (1971), pp. 54-71.

CAHEN, Cl. Les changements techniques militaires dans le Proche Orient médiéval et leur importance historique. *War, technology and society in the Middle East,* ed. V.J. Parry and M.E. Yapp, 1975, pp. 113-124.

CAHEN, C. Reflexions sur la connaissance du monde Musulman par les Historiens. *Folia Or.* 12(1970), pp. 41-49

CARLETON, A. 'Near East' versus 'Middle East'. *IJMES* 6(1975), pp. 237-238.

CARTER, M. The Kātib in fact and fiction. *Abr-Nahrain* 11(1971), pp. 42-55.

CHERKASSKIY, L. Ya. Leninizm i nekotorye problemy sotrudnichestva s razvivayushchimisya stranami. *Strany Blizhnego i Srednego Vostoka: istoriya, ekonomica,* 1972, pp. 487-502.

COURY, R. Why can't they be like us? *RMES* 1(1975), pp. 113-133.

DANTZIG, B.M. K voprosu o kapitulyatziyakh na Blizhnem Vostoke. (On the question of capitulation on the Near East.) *NAA* 1971(3), pp. 134-140.

DJAIT, H. L'Islam ancien récupéré à l'histoire. *Annales ESC* 30(1975), pp. 900-914.

DJOUNDI, M. Fonds et aspects de la lutte arabe. *Renaissance du monde arabe. Colloque interarabe de Louvain,* 1972, pp. 47-108.

DONOHUE, J.J. Culture arabe et monde moderne. *Travaux et jours* 55(1975), pp. 55-67.

EBIED, R.Y.; YOUNG, M.J.L. Extracts in Arabic from a chronicle erroneously attributed to Jacob of Edessa. *Orientalia Lovaniensia periodica* 4(1973), pp. 177-196.

FLORE, V.D. La trasformazione degli scali italiani dagli inizi del secolo XVI all'apertura del Canale di Suez. *Recueils Soc.Jean Bodin* 33(1972), pp. 245-256.

GABRIELI, Fr. Recenti studi di storia musulmana in Italia. *Bull. Fac. Arts, Univ. Libya* 2(1968), pp. 71-83.

GARCIA DOMINGUES, J.D. A concepção do mundo árabe-islâmico n'*Os Lusíadas*. *Garcia de Orta,* núm. especial 1972, pp. 201-226.

GIL B. GRIMAU, R. Ojeada al horizonte de los acontecimientos en Oriente Medio. *Revista polít. int.* 140(1975), pp. 139-144.

GIL BENUMEYA, R. El Cercano Oriente ante los acontecimientos de Egipto. *Rev. de polítca int.* 116(1971), pp. 75-84.

GIL BENUMEYA, R. Los nuevos rumbos arabes segun la "Carta de Tripoli". *Rev. de politica int.* 113(1971), pp. 115-123.

GLASNECK, J. Imperialistische Historiographie und nationale Befreiungsbewegung. Haupttendenzen in der bürgerlichen amerikanischen und britischen Literatur über die Entwicklung des Nahen Ostens seit 1945. *Zeits. f. Geschichtswissenschaft* 21(1973), pp. 656-670.

GOITEIN, S.D. Formal friendship in the medieval Near East. *Proc. Amer. Philos. Soc.* 115(1971), pp. 484-489.

GOITEIN, S.D. Islam and world history. *Proc.27th Int.Cong.Or.1967* (1971), p. 236.

GOLDBERG, A.J. United Nations Security Council resolution 242 and the prospects for peace in the Middle East. *Columbia J. transnat.law* 12(1973), pp. 187-195.

GOTTSCHALK, H.L. Das Abendland und das muslimische Morgenland heute. (Fortsetzung zu: WZKM 62, S. 133-145) III. Der Rückhalt im Eigenen. *WZKM* 63-64(1972), pp. 128-150.

GRAMLICH, R. Vom islamischen Glauben au die "gute alte Zeit". *Islamwissenschaftliche Abhandlungen F. Meier,* 1974, pp. 110-117.

IX HISTORY

GRAN, P. The Middle East in the historiography of advanced capitalism. *RMES* 1 (1975), pp. 135-154.

HABACHI, R. Pour un dialogue des cultures. *Renaissance du monde arabe. Colloque interarabe de Louvain,* 1972, pp. 323-330.

HAMMOND, P.Y. An introductory perspective on the Middle East. *Political dynamics in the Middle East,* ed. P.Y. Hammond and S.S. Alexander, 1972, pp. 5-29.

HARRELL, R.H. Conditions of conflict between nations: an overview of Middle Eastern and North African nations. *The Middle East.* Ed. W.A. Beling, 1973, pp. 126-145.

HASSAN, Riaz. The nature of Islamic urbanization - a historical perspective. *J. Pakistan Hist. Soc.* 17(1969), pp. 77-83.

HOFFMAN, G. Zum Problem der Klassenstruktur in der feudalen arabisch-islamischen Stadt und seiner Relevanz für die vergleichende Forschung. *Asien, Afrika, Latein-Amerika* 2(1974), pp. 276-286.

HÖPP, G. Zu den Anfängen sozialistischen Denkens in arabischen Ländern (bis 1919). *Asien, Afrika, Latein-Amerika* 1(2, 1973), pp. 53-70.

HORNUS, J.-M. L'Europe et les destinées du Proche-Orient (1815-1848). [Review article.] *Rev. d'hist. et de philos. rel.* 54(1974), pp. 535-544.

HOURANI, A.H. Introduction: The Islamic city in the light of recent research. *The Islamic city,* 1970, pp. 9-24.

HOURANI, A. Revolution in the Arab Middle East. *Revolution in the Middle East,* ed. P.J. Vatikiotis, 1972, pp. 65-72.

HOURANI, G.F. A decade of revolution: social and political changes, 1949-1959. *The Arab Middle East and Muslim Africa,* ed. by T. Kerekes, 1961, pp. 27-45.

HOVANNISIAN, R.G. The ebb and flow of the Armenian minority in the Arab Middle East. *MEJ* 28(1974), pp. 19-32.

HUREWITZ, J.C. Changing military perspectives in the Middle East. *Political dynamics in the Middle East,* ed. P.Y. Hammond and S.S. Alexander, 1972, pp. 69-113.

HUREWITZ, J.C. Soldiers and social change in plural societies: the contemporary Middle East. *War, technology and society in the Middle East,* ed. V.J. Parry and M.E. Yapp, 1975, pp. 400-411.

HUSSEIN-TAHA, Moënis. L'Unesco et l'étude de la culture Arabe contemporaine. *Cah. d'hist. mondiale* 14(1972), pp. 915-921.

INALCIK, Hilal. The socio-political effects of the diffusion of fire-arms in the Middle East. *War, technology and society in the Middle East,* ed. V.J. Parry and M.E. Yapp, 1975, pp. 195-217.

ISHAQUE, Khalid M. Role of history in the growth of national consciousness. *J. Pakistan Hist. Soc.* 17(1969), pp. 25-39.

JANOWITZ, J. Some observations on the comparative analysis of Middle Eastern military institutions. *War, technology and society in the Middle East,* ed. V.J. Parry and M.E. Yapp, 1975, pp. 412-440.

KALEDIN, V.V. Blizhniy Vostok vo vneshney politiki Frantzii 60-kh godov. *Arabskie strany, Turtziya, Iran, Afganistan,* 1973, pp. 79-88.

KATTAN, Naim. Diversité et facteurs d'unité dans la culture Arabe. *Cah. d'hist. mondiale* 14(1972), pp. 714-726.

KEDDIE, Nikki R. Intellectuals in the modern Middle East: a brief historical consideration. *Daedalus* 101iii(1972), pp. 39-57.

KELLY, J.B. Recollections and reflections of a British diplomat. [Review of *Middle East in revolution,* H. Trevelyan.] *Middle Eastern stud.* 9(1973), pp. 363-370.

KHAN, Yusuf Husain. Islamic polity. *Studies in Islam* 7 (1970), pp. 65-110.

KHRUSTALEV, M.A. Kolonial'naya politika imperializma v arabskikh stranakh v pervoy polovine XX veka. *Vopr. ist.* 1973(7), pp. 88-100.

KISSLING, H.J. Venedig und der islamische Orient bis 1500. *Venezia e il Levante fino al sec.XV,* 1973, pp. 361-387.

KÜRKÇÜOĞLU, Ömer E. The Middle East - on the fifth anniversary of the June War. *Dış politika* 2iii(1972), pp. 67-73.

LACOUTURE, J. The changing balance of forces in the Middle East. *J. Palestine studies* 2iv(1973), pp. 25-32.

LANDEN, R.G. History of the medieval Middle East: A.D. 622-1799. Syllabus. *MESA Bull.* 4iii(1970), pp. 16-54

LAPIDUS, I.M. Notes and comments [on the preceding papers in this journal on history and anthropology in the study of Islam]. *Humaniora Islamica* 2(1974), pp. 287-299.

LAPIDUS, I.M. Relations between town and countryside in the medieval Muslim world. *Proc.27th Int.Cong.Or.1967* (1971), pp. 223-224.

LAZAREV, M.S. Vtoraya mirovaya voyna i strany Blizhnego i Srednego Vostoka. Politicheskoe polozhenie v Turtzii, Irane, Afganistane i arabskikh stranakh. *Mezhdunarodnye otnosheniya na Blizhnem i Srednem Vostoke,* 1974, pp. 3-43.

LENCZOWSKI, G. The Arab cold war. *The Middle East.* Ed. W.A. Beling, 1973, pp. 55-72.

LEWIS, B. Islamic concepts of revolution. *Revolution in the Middle East,* ed. P.J. Vatikiotis, 1972, pp. 30-40.

IX HISTORY

LIESER, P. Zur Genesis der Energiekrisis, der vierte Nahostkrieg, Erdölpolitik und internationale Beziehungen. *Orient* [Hamburg] 16ii(1975), pp. 21-56.

LOBYNTZEVA, M.A. K voprosu o sozdanii Aziatskogo departamenta Ministerstva inostrannuikh del Rossii. *Iran (Pamyati B.N. Zakhodera)*, 1971, pp. 84-91.

McCLELLAND, C.A.; GILBAR, A.A. An interaction survey of the Middle East. *The Middle East.* Ed. W.A. Beling, 1973, pp. 149-168.

MAHDI, Muhsin. The book and the master as poles of cultural change in Islam. *Islam and cultural change in the Middle Ages,* ed. Sp. Vryonis, Jr., 1975, pp. 3-15.

MANTRAN, R. Evolución politica y económica de los paises árabes contemporáneos. *Estudios orientales* 3(1968), no. 8, pp. 224-254.

MAZOYER, H. Considérations et réflexions sur le Proche-Orient. *CR trim. des séances Acad. sci. Outre-mer* 33(1973), pp. 551-565.

MEDZINI, M. China and the Arab-Israel conflict. *International problems* 13(1974), pp. 323-334.

MILSON, M. Medieval and modern intellectual traditions in the Arab world. *Daedalus* 101iii(1972), pp. 17-37.

MINGANTI, P. Gli studi sulle vicende politiche del mondo arabo nel XX secolo. *Studi sul Vicino Oriente in Italia,* II, 1971, pp. 99-108.

MOURSI, F. Quelques problèmes de la période de transition. *Renaissance du monde arabe. Colloque interarabe de Louvain,* 1972, pp. 111-121.

MUSTAPHA, Ahmed Abdel-Rahim. History, change, and Arab culture. *Cah. d'hist. mondiale* 14(1972), pp. 691-701.

O'KANE, J.P. Trois manifestations islamiques. *Travaux et jours* 47(1973), pp. 113-129.

OWEN, R. The Middle East in the eighteenth century - an 'Islamic society in decline? A critique of Gibb and Bowen's *Islamic society and the West.* *RMES* 1(1975), pp. 101-112.

PENZINA, O. U istokov blizhnevostochnogo krizisa. *Strany Blizhnego i Srednego Vostoka: istoriya, ekonomica,* 1972, pp. 134-144.

PETIT, O. Langue, culture et participation du monde arabe contemporain. *IBLA* 34 (no. 128, 1971), pp. 259-294.

POLK, W.R. Generations, classes and politics, 1952-1959. *The Arab Middle East and Muslim Africa,* ed. by T. Kerekes, 1961, pp. 105-119.

PONK, V. Great Britain and the Near East - after World War I: *Islam and the modern age* 4 i (1973), pp. 66-87.

POTZKHVERIYA, B.M. Politika Turtzii v arabskikh stranakh. *Mezhdunarodnye otnosheniya na Blizhnem i Srednem Vostoke,* 1974, pp. 44-73.

QAZZAZ, Ayad-ul. Army officers and land reforms in Egypt, Iraq and Syria. *Sociological bull.* 20(1971), pp. 159-177.

RICHARD, B. L'Islam et les musulmans chez les chroniqueurs castillans du milieu du Moyen Age. *Hespéris-Tamuda* 12(1971), pp. 107-132.

RIZZITANO, U. Gli studi di storia araba. *Studi sul Vicino Oriente in Italia,* II, 1971, pp. 27-67.

RODINSON, M. Dynamique de l'évolution interne et des influences externes dans l'histoire culturelle de la Méditerranée. *Actes I. Cong. et. cult. mediterr. d'infl. arabo-berb.,* 1973, pp. 21-30.

ROSENTHAL, E.I.J. The role of the state in Islam: theory and the medieval practice. *Der Islam* 50(1973), pp. 1-28.

ROSTOW, E.V. The Middle East crisis in the perspective of world politics. *Intern. aff.* 47(1971), pp. 275-288.

RUNCIMAN, Sir St. Muslim influences on the development of European civilization. *Şarkiyat mecmuası* 3(1959), pp. 13-24.

RUSTOW, D.A. Political ends and military means in the late Ottoman and post-Ottoman Middle East. *War, technology and society in the Middle East,* ed. V.J. Parry and M.E. Yapp, 1975, pp. 386-399.

SAFRAN, Nadav. Engagement in the Middle East. *Foreign affairs* 53(1974-75), pp. 45-63.

SHARABI, Hishami. Political and intellectual attitudes of the young Arab generation. *The Arab Middle East and Muslim Africa,* ed. by T. Kerekes, 1961, pp. 47-61.

SHAWI, Hamid al-. L'intervention des militaires dans la vie politique de la Syrie, de l'Irak et de la Jordanie - Un essai d'interprétation socio-politique. *Politique étrangère* 39(1974), pp. 343-374.

SIDDIQI, W.H. India's contribution to Arab civilization. *India's contribution to world thought ...,* 1970, pp. 579-588.

SINGH, K.R. Implications of the new US-Soviet equation for West Asia. *Int. studies* 13(1974), pp. 695-718.

STERN, S.M. The Constitution of the Islamic city. *The Islamic city,* 1970, pp. 25-50.

TAMIR, Zvi N. Hostilities during cease-fire in the Middle East. *International problems* 13(1974), pp. 311-322.

TIBAWI, A.L. The Cambridge History of Islam: a critical review. *IQ* 17(1973), pp. 92-100.

TSKITISHVILI, Otar. Two questions connected with the topography of the oriental city in the early middle ages. *JESHO* 14(1971), pp. 311-320

TUENI, Ghassan. After October: military conflict and political change in the Middle East. *J.Palestine studies* 3iv(1974), pp. 114-130.

ÜÇOK, Bahriye. Les souverains-femmes dans l'histoire de l'Islam. *Doğu dilleri* 1iii(1969), pp. 1-13.

ULLMAN, R.H. After Rabat: Middle East risks and American roles. *Foreign affairs* 53 (1975), pp. 284-296.

VANDERMEERSCH, L. Les relations sino-arabes au XVe et au XVIe siècle. *Cah.de ling. d'orientalisme et de slavistique* 1-2(1973), pp. 271-278.

VERNANT, J. Situation et perspectives en Méditeranée orientale. *Politique étrangère* 39(1974), pp. 629-639.

WAHBA, Magdi. Cultural planning in the Arab world. *Cah. d'hist. mondiale* 14(1972), pp. 800-813.

WATT, W.M. L'influence de l'Islam sur l'-Europe médiévale. *REI* 41(1973), pp. 127-156.

YAMUNI, V. Los países árabes en su lucha por la independencia. *Asia. Anuario de estudios orientales* 3(1970), pp. 156-188.

YAPP, M.E. The modernization of Middle Eastern armies in the nineteenth century: a comparative view. *War, technology and society in the Middle East*, ed. V.J. Parry and M.E. Yapp, 1975, pp. 330-366.

YIZHAR, M. The United States Middle East resolution as viewed by foreign powers. *Int. problems* 12i-ii(1973), pp. 59-81.

ZNIBER, M. Conceptions traditionnelles et conceptions nouvelles dans l'histoire culturelle des Arabes. *Bull. Soc. hist. Maroc* 1 (1968), pp. 31-32.

ZNIBER, Mohammed. Considérations historiques sur la problématique arabe actuelle. *Annales maroc.de sociol.* 1970, pp. 11-33.

A call from the Azhar's Rector and its Ulemas, to the Muslim world: peoples and governments. *Majallat al-Azhar* 45x(1974), pp. 5-6.

Formazione della Federazione delle Repubbliche Arabe fra Egitto, Libia e Siria. *OM* 51(1971), pp. 313-316

A statement addressed by the Academy of Islamic Research to the Arab and Muslim nation and the advocates of peace in the world. *Majallat al-Azhar* 45x(1974), pp. 7-9.

United Nations: Report of the Secretary-General on the activities of the Special Representative to the Middle East. *MEJ* 26(1972), pp. 69-77

See also I. b. 2. Tlili.

See also IV. c. 3. Rodinson

See also V. m. 1. Meredith-Owens.

See also IX. e. Schowingen

See also IX. g. Husseynov

b CHRONOLOGY

AHMAD, Qeyamuddin. A note on the art of composing chronograms. *IC* 46(1972), pp. 163-169.

BEESTON, A.F.L. New light on the Himyaritic calendar. *Arabian studies* 1(1974), pp. 1-6.

GWARZO, Hassan Ibrahim. The theory of chronograms as expounded by the 18th century Katsina astronomer-mathematician Muḥammad b. Muḥammad. *Res. Bull. CAD Ibadan* 3i (1967), pp. 116-123.

HAMIDULLAH, M. The concordance of the Hijrah and Christian eras for the lifetime of the Prophet. *J. Pakistan Hist. Soc.* 16(1968), pp. 213-219.

HAMIDULLAH, Muhammad The Nasi', the Hijra Calendar and the need of a new concordance for the Hijra and Gregorian eras. *Proc. 27th Int.Cong.Or.1967* (1971), pp. 267-268.

HAMIDULLAH, M. The *Nasi'*, the *Hijrah* calendar and the need of preparing a new Concordance for the *Hijrah* and Gregorian eras. *J. Pakistan Hist. Soc.* 16(1968), pp. 1-18.

SAYESS, Shaikh Mohammad Aly al. The determination of the beginning of lunar months. *3rd Conf.Acad.Isl.Research,* 1966, pp. 93-114

SOUISSI, Mohamed. Le calendrier hégirien: ses origines, ses modifications, modèles proposés ou pratiques. *CT* 22(nos.87-88, 1974), pp. 7-34.

STERN, S.M. Abū ʿĪsā ibn al-Munajjim's chronography. *Islamic philosophy and the classical tradition,* 1972, pp. 437-466.

See also XXVII. c. Ende.

c BIOGRAPHY

AHMAD, Nazir. Muḥammad Ṣādiq Iṣfahānī, an offical of Bengal of *Shāh* Jahān's time. *Indo-Iranica* 24iii-iv (1971), pp. 102-124.

ALI, S.M. Syed Amir Ali. *J. Asiatic Soc. Pakistan* 14(1969), pp. 305-324.

DIXON, A.A. A malcontent from the Umayyad period. *IC* 47(1973), pp. 31-36.

HUMBERT-FOURCADE, G. Table ronde de l'Onomasticon arabicum (Gand, 6-9 octobre 1973). *Rev. d'hist. des textes* 4(1974), pp. 431-435.

KEDOURI, Elie. Afghani in Paris: a note. *ME stud.* 8(1972), pp. 103-105

KEDOURIE, Elie. The death of Adib Ishaq. *ME stud.* 9(1973), pp. 95-109.

KHALIDI, Tarif. Islamic biographical dictionaries: a preliminary assessment. *MW* 63(1973), pp. 53-65.

KHALIDOV, A.B. Biograficheskiy slovar' al-Andarasbani. *Pis'mennye pamyatniki Vostoka* 1971, pp. 143-161.

KHALIDOV, A.W. Neizvestnyy biograficheskiy slovar XII v. iz Khorezma. *Folia Or* 13(1971), pp. 67-75.

MARTÍNEZ MONTÁVEZ, P. ʿAbdel-Nāser - en su muerte - y los poetas. *RIEI Madrid* 16(1971), pp. 7-29.

MUSTAFIZUR RAHMAN, M. Imām Abū Mansūr al Māturidī (333/944). *JAS Pakistan* 16(1971), pp. 197-208.

RAHMANI, Aftab Ahmad. The life and works of Ibn Hajar Al-ʿAsqalani. *IC* 45(1971), pp. 275-293; 47(1973), pp. 57-74, 159-174, 257-273.

SHACKEL, C. English translation of Sir Sayyid Aḥmad Khan's "Sīrat-e-Farīdīya". *IC* 46(1972), pp. 307-336.

UMAR, Muhammad Mirzā Mazhar Jānjānān. A religious and social reformer of the eighteenth century. *Stud in Islam* 6(1969), pp. 118-119.

VAJDA, G. La mašyaḫa de 'Abd al-Qādir al-Yūnīnī. *JA* 259(1971), pp. 223-246.

ZAKKAR, Suhayl. Biographie de Niẓām al-Mulk de Kamāl al-Dīn ibn al-ʿAdīm. *BEO* 24(1971), pp. 227-248.

See also XXXVII. h. Terés

d HISTORIOGRAPHY: GENERAL

ADAMIYAT, Fereydoun. Problems of Iranian historiography. *Iranian stud.* 4(1971), pp. 132-156.

CAHEN, Cl. Al-Makīn ibn al-'Amīd et l'historiographie musulmane: un cas d'interpénétration confessionnelle. *Orientalia Hispanica* I, 1974, pp. 158-167.

FARUQI, Nisar Ahmed. Some methodological aspects of the early Muslim historiography. *Islam and the modern age* 6i(1975), pp. 88-98.

HAMIDULLAH, Muhammad. Contribution des musulmans méditerranéens à la science historique. *ROMM* 15-16(1973), pp. 35-42.

JAHN, K. China in der islamischen Geschichtsschreibung. *Anzeiger Österr.Akad. Wis.,Phil.-hist.Kl.* 108(1971), pp. 63-73.

JAHN, K. Die 'Geschichte der Kinder Israels' in der islamischen Historiographie. *Anzeiger Österr.Akad.Wis.,Phil.-hist.Kl.* 109(1972), pp. 67-76.

KAMIAN, B. Est-il possible d'enrichir l'historiographie africaine en puisant dans le passé traditionnel et islamique? *Perspectives nouvelles sur l'histoire africaine,* présentés par E. Mveng, 1971, pp. 102-110

KOUYMJIAN, D.K. Problems of medieval Armenian and Muslim historiography: the Mxit'ar of Ani fragment. *IJMES* 4(1973), pp. 465-475.

LEVTZION, N. Considérations sur l'historiographie musulmane en Afrique. *Perspectives nouvelles sur l'histoire africaine,* présentés par E. Mveng, 1971, pp. 31-35

MOHIBBUL HASAN. Some aspects of Persian historiography in Medieval India. *Mitt. Inst.Orientforschung* 16(1970), pp. 578-586.

MURTAZA, Hamida. The origin of the Muslim historiography. *J. Pakistan Hist. Soc.* 16(1968), pp. 198-201.

OSMAN SID AHMED ISMAIL. La tradition historiographique de l'Islam africain. *Perspectives nouvelles sur l'histoire africaine,* présentés par E. Mveng, 1971, pp. 36-42.

SALJŪQ, ʿAffān. Some notes on the early historiography of the Saljūqid period in Irān. *Iqbal rev.* 12iii(1971), pp. 91-99

TOGAN, Zeki Velidi. The concept of critical historiography in the Islamic world of the Middle Ages. *Islamic studies* 14(1975), pp. 175-184.

YOUNG, M.J.L. Unexploited sources for the history of the people of the Maghrib. *Rev. d'hist.maghrebine* 3(1975), pp. 107-110.

See also XIX. g. Haarmann

See also XIX. g. Little.

See also XXXV. a. Chalmeta Gendrón.

e MUSLIM HISTORIANS

AHMAD, Anis. Educational thought of Ibn Khaldun. *J. Pakistan Hist. Soc.* 16(1968), pp. 175-181.

BACHARACH, J.L. Circassian Mamluk historians and their quantitative economic data. *J.American Res.Center in Egypt* 12 (1975), pp. 75-87.

BATSEVA, S.M. The social foundations of Ibn Khaldūn's historico-philosophical doctrine. *IQ* 15(1971), pp. 121-132.

BATSIEVA, S. Les idées économiques d'Ibn Haldūn. *Orientalia Hispanica* II, 1974, pp. 96-104.

BELKHAYAT-CLEMENT, Fouzia. La notion du contrôle social chez Ibn Khaldûn. *IBLA* (no.131, 1973), pp. 25-52.

IX HISTORY

BLACHÈRE, Régis. Quelques réflexions sur les formes de l'encyclopédisme en Égypte et en Syrie du VIIIe/XIVe siècle à la fin du IXe/XVe siècle. *BEO* 23 (1970), pp. 7-19.

BOYLE, J.A. Rashīd al-Dīn: the first world historian. *Iran* 9 (1971), pp. 19-26.

BOYLE, J.A. Rashid al-Din: the first world historian. *J. Pakistan Hist. Soc.* 17(1969), pp. 215-227.

BOYLE, J.A. The significance of the Jāmiʿ al-Tawārīkh as a source on Mongol history. *Proceedings of the colloquium on Rashīd al-Dīn Faḍlallāh.* 1971, pp. 1-8.

CARRÉ, O. A propos de la sociologie politique d'Ibn Khaldûn. [Review article.] *Rev. franç. sociol.* 14(1973), pp. 115-124.

CAHEN, C. ʿAbdallaṭīf al-Baghdādī, portraitiste et historien de son temps. Extraits inédits de ses mémoires. *BEO* 23 (1970), pp. 101-128.

CHARNAY, J.-P. Modèle théorique de l'histoire socio-culturelle musulmane: les dialectiques maghrebines d'Ibn Khaldûn. *Actes I. Cong. et. cult. mediterr. d'infl. arabo-berb.*, 1973, pp. 234-250.

CRUZ HERNÁNDEZ, M. La concepción del profetismo de Ibn Jaldūn y la comprensión del Islam. *Pensamiento* 25(1969), pp. 93-101.

DECEI, A. et CIOCILTAN, V. La mention des roumains (Walaḥ) chez al-Maqdisi. *Romano-Arabica,* ed. M. Anghelescu, 1974, pp. 49-54.

DIETRICH, A. A propos d'un précis d'histoire gréco-romaine dans la chronique universelle arabe de Müneccimbaşi. *Ve Congrès International d'Arabisants et d'Islamisants. Actes.*, [1970?], pp. 175-188.

DJEGHLOUL, A. Ibn-Khaldoun et la science sociale. *Rev. alg.* 12(1975), pp. 463-528.

FALINA, A.I. Rashid ad-Din -- vrach i estestvoispytatel'. (Po materialam "Perepiski" Rashid ad-Dina). *Pis'mennye pamyatniki Vostoka* 1971, pp. 127-142.

FALINA, A.I. Termin "akche" u Rashid ad-Dina. *Pis'mennye pamyatniki Vostoka* 1970, pp. 193-203.

FISCHER, W. Die Prosa des Abū Mihnaf. *Islamwissenschaftliche Abhandlungen F. Meier,* 1974, pp. 96-105.

FISCHEL, W.J. Pre-Islamic civilization of Iran as seen by Ibn Khaldun. *Bull. Iranian Culture Found.* 1ii (1973), pp. 25-39.

FORAND, P.G. Abû Zakarîyâ' Yazid b. Muḥammad al-Azdî's *Ta'rîkh al-Mawṣil* as a source for Ibn al-Athîr's *Al-Kâmil fi'l-Ta'rîkh.* *Proc.27th Int.Cong.Or.1967* (1971), p. 278.

GÓMEZ NOGALES, S. Teoria y método de la ciencia en Ibn Haldūn. *Orientalia Hispanica* I, 1974, pp. 351-375.

GOODMAN, L.E. Ibn Khaldun and Thucydides. *JAOS* 92(1972), pp. 250-270.

GRIGNASCHI, M. La *Nihāyatu-l-ʿArab fī aḫbāri-l-Furs wa-l-ʿArab* et les *Siyaru mulūki-l-ʿAǧam* du PS. Ibn-al-Muqaffa . *BEO* 26(1973), pp. 83-184.

HAMARNEH, Saleh K. The ancient monuments of Alexandria according to accounts by medieval arab authors (IX-XV century). *Folia Or* 13(1971), pp. 77-110.

HASHMI, Yusuf Abbas. The lacuna in Bayhaqi. *J. Pakistan Hist. Soc.* 16 (1968), pp. 136-144.

JAHN, K. Die Erweiterung unseres Geschichtsbildes durch Rašīd al-Dīn. *Anzeiger Österr.Akad.Wis.,Phil.-hist.Kl.* 107(1970), pp. 139-149.

JAHN, K. Rashīd al-Dīn as world historian. *Yádnáme-ye Jan Rypka* 1967, pp. 79-87.

JAHN, K. Rashīd al-Dīn's knowledge of Europe. *Proceedings of the colloquium on Rashīd al-Dīn Faḍlallāh.* 1971, pp. 9-25.

JAHN, K. Universalgeschichte im islamischen Raum. *Mensch und Weltgeschichte,* hrsg. A. Randa, 1969, pp. 145-170.

KHAN, Amanullah. Al-Waqidi - an assessment of his position as an historian. *J.res.(humanities)* 5ii(1970), pp. 81-92.

KLYASHTORNYY, S.G. Drevneyshee upominanie slavyan v nizhnem Povolzh'e. (La mention la plus ancienne des Slaves de basse Volga.) *Fontes orientales* ... curavit A.S. Tveritinova, I, 1964, pp. 16-18.

LEWICKI, T. Iz nauchnykh issledovaniy arabskikh istochnikov. Neizvestny arabskie dokumenty o slavyanakh 720 g. (Un témoignage arabe inconnu (A.D.720) sur les Slaves.) *Fontes orientales* ... curavit A.S. Tveritinova, I, 1964, pp. 6-15.

LEWICZKI, T. Die Namen der slawischen Völker in den Werken der frühmittelalterlichen arabischen Schriftsteller. *The Middle East; studies in honour of J. Germanus,* 1974, pp. 39-51.

LEWICKI, T. Sources arabes extérieures pour l'histoire de l'Afrique au sud du Sahara. *Perspectives nouvelles sur l'histoire africaine,* présentés par E. Mveng, 1971, pp. 23-30.

LUTHER, K.A. The Saljūqnāmah and the Jāmiʿ al-Tawārīkh. *Proceedings of the colloquium on Rashīd al-Dīn Faḍlallāh.* 1971, pp. 26-35.

MÉNAGE, V.L. Three Ottoman treatises on Europe. *Iran and Islam, in memory of V. Minorsky,* 1971, pp. 421-433

MENGES, K.H. Rašīdu'-d-Dīn on China. *JAOS* 95(1975), pp. 95-98.

IX HISTORY

MENGES, K.H. Über einige Namen in Rašīdu-'d-Dīns Geschichte Chinas. *Islam* 52 (1975), pp. 314-319.

MILLWARD, W.G. Al-Ya'qūbī's sources and the question of Shī'a partiality. *Abr-nahrain* 12(1971-2), pp. 47-74

NIZAMI, K.A. Rashīd al-Dīn Fazl Allah and India. *Proceedings of the colloquium on Rashīd al-Dīn Faḍlallāh.* 1971, pp. 36-53.

OUMLIL, Ali. Ibn Khaldoun ou une expérience à la base d'une théorie. *Bull.de la Soc. d'hist.du Maroc* 3(1970-1), pp. 15-18

PANTŮČKOVÁ, E. Zur analyse eines der historischen Bestandteile von Aḥmedīs Iskendernāme. *Arch. or.* 41(1973), pp. 28-41.

PINES, S. Ibn Khaldūn and Maimonides. A comparison between two texts. *SI* 32(1970), pp. 265-274.

PINES, S. The societies providing for the bare necessities of life according to Ibn Khaldūn and to the philosophers. *SI* 34 (1971), pp. 125-138

POLYAK, A.N. Novuie arabskie materialy pozd-nego srednevekov'ya o vostochnoy i tzentral'noy Evrope. (New Arabic and other material from the late middle ages on East and Central Europe.) *Fontes orientales ...* curavit A.S. Tveritinova, I, 1964, pp. 29-66.

QAZI, Nabibakhsh. A rare manuscript of *Daqā'iq at-Tarīq* - a Persian *Mathnavi* by Aḥmad-e Rūmī. *Proc.27th Int.Cong.Or.1967* (1971), p. 279

RAḤMĀNI, Aftab Ahmad. The life and works of Ibn Ḥajar al-'Asqalānī. *IC* 46(1972), pp. 171-178; 265-272, 353-362.

REDJALA, Mbarek. Une copie de la Muqaddima de l'exemplaire du Kitāb al-'ibar offert par Ibn Ḫaldūn à l'Université al-Qarawiyīn de Fès. *Rev. d'hist. des textes* 3(1973), pp. 193-201.

REDJALA, M'barek. Un texte inédit de la *Muqaddima*. *Arabica* 22(1975), pp. 320-323.

ROTTER, G. Abū Zur'a ad-Dimašqī (st. 281/894) und das Problem der frühen arabischen Geschichtsschreibung in Syrien. *WO* 6(1971), pp. 80-104.

ROTTER, G. Zur Überlieferung einiger historischer Werke Madā'inīs in Ṭabarīs Annalen. *Oriens* 23-24(1974), pp. 103-133.

SANKHDHER, B.M. Mirza Abu Talib Khan: an economic thinker and historian. *Q'ly rev.hist.stud.* 10(1970-1), pp. 213-216.

SCHOWINGEN, K.F. von. Der bleibende Sinngehalt von Nizamulmulk's Siyasetnama: Gedanken zur historischen Kontinuität. *Hist.Jhb.* 91(1971), pp. 292-308.

SCHÜTZINGER, H. Ibn Abī Šaiba und sein Ta'rīx. Eine Untersuchung an Hand des MS. Berlin 9409. *Oriens* 23-24(1974), pp. 134-146.

SELJUQ, Affan. Ibn Khaldūn's study of physical environment. *J.Pak.Hist.Soc.* 21 (1973), pp. 219-226.

SEMENOVA, L.A. Eshche odna versiya traktata Akhū Mukhsina. *Pis'mennye pamyatniki Vostoka* 1970, pp. 150-164.

SHATZMILLER, M. Les circonstances de la composition du *Musnad* d'Ibn Marzūq. *Arabica* 22(1975), pp. 292-299.

SIDDIQUI, B.H. Miskawayh on the purposes of historiography. *MW* 61 (1971), pp. 21-27.

SOURDEL, D. Une profession de foi de l'historien al-Ṭabarī. *Actas IV congresso de estudos árabes e islâmicos* 1968(1971), pp. 497-498.

SPULER, B. Rachīd ad-Dīn: homme d'Etat et son époque. *Proceedings of the colloquium on Rashīd al-Dīn Faḍlallāh.* 1971, pp. 54-67.

SUŠIĆ, H. Metodološke pretpostavke historije u djelu Ibn Haldūn-a. *Prilozi za or. filol.* 18-19(1968-9), pp. 47-58.

TALBI, Mohamed A propos d'Ibn al-Raqīq. *Arabica* 19(1972), pp. 86-96

TURAN, Osman. Raṣhīd üd-dīn et l'Histoire des Turcs. *Proceedings of the colloquium on Rashīd al-Dīn Faḍlallāh.* 1971, pp. 68-80.

VERNET, J. La fecha de composición de la Zā'irayāt al-'alam. *And* 34(1969), pp. 245-246.

YOUNG, W.L. From history to political sociology: Ibn Khaldun, Islam and the Islamic state. *Q.rev.hist.stud.* 13(1973-74), pp. 201-204.

ZAIDI, M.H. Khwurshāh bin Qubād al-Husainī and his Tārikh-i-Qutbī. *Proc. 27th Int.Cong.Or.1967* (1971), pp. 280-282.

See also II. c. 8. Marquet.

See also IX. n. Boulakia.

See also XII. b. Lewicki.

See also XV. a. Hess.

See also XXVIII. n. Tumanovich.

See also XXXII. c. Siddiqi and Ahmad

See also XXXV. g. Redjala.

See also XXXIX. d. Krüger.

f THE PRESS. RADIO

AHANG, Mohammad Kazem. The background and beginning of the Afghan press system. *Afghanistan* 23ii(1970), pp. 53-58; 24i (1971), pp. 11-17; 24ii-iii(1971), pp. 48-51; 25iii(1972), pp. 53-55.

ENDE, W. Bibliographie zur Geschichte der Presse im Irak. *Mitteilungen. Dokumentationsdienst Moderner Orient* 3ii(1974), pp. 23-30.

HADDAD, W.W. The Christian Arab press and the Palestine question: a case study of Michel Chiha of Bayrūt's *Le jour*. *MW* 65 (1975).

KANUS-CREDÉ, H. Die persische Presse der Ära Mossadegh. *Iranistische Mitteilungen* 2i(1968), pp. 2-85.

KILPATRICK, H. BBC broadcasting to the Middle East. *BSMES bull.* 2(1975), pp. 17-18.

MANSFIELD, P. The British media and the Middle East. *BSMES bull.* 1(1974-5), pp. 54-58.

SCHINASI, M. *Sirâdj al-akhbâr.* L'opinion afghane et la Russie. *Cah.monde russe et sov.* 12(1971), pp. 467-479

SOURIAU, Chr. La presse maghrébine: situation actuelle et développement. *Rev.alg.* 11(1974), pp. 379-409.

See also XVI. d. Martel.

See also XIX. a. Marsot

See also XIX. j. Verdery.

See also XXIX. d. *Yugoslavia* Eren

See also XXIX. h. Clogg.

See also XXIX. i. Zheltyakov

See also XXXI. j. Kanus-Crede.

See also XXXIII. c. Ahang.

See also XLIII. b. Turin.

g POLITICAL SCIENCE. POLITICAL PARTIES

ABDEL MALEK, Anouar. Naciones y revoluciones. Planteamiento del problema. *Estudios orientales* 23(8iii, 1973), pp. 229-252.

ABEL, A. Gouvernès et gouvernants en terre d'Islam. *Recueils Soc. Jean Bodin* 22(1969), pp. 355-389.

ADEGBITE, Lateef. The Islamic way of nation-building. *Orita* 8(1974), pp. 106-113.

AHMAD, Aziz. An eighteenth century theory of Caliphate. *Proc.27th Int.Cong.Or. 1967* (1971), pp. 221-222.

AHMAD, Muhammad Aziz. The concept of mulk in the political theory of Islam. *Univ. studies* [Karachi] 5i(1968), pp. 1-31.

AHMAD, Mohammad Khalafallah. Two political documents from early Islamic literature. *3rd Conf.Acad.Isl.Research*, 1966, pp. 529-535

AHMED, Manzooruddin. *Umma:* the idea of a universal community. *Islamic studies* 14(1975), pp. 27-54.

BAILEY, F.G. Conceptual systems in the study of politics. *Rural politics and social change in the Middle East*, ed. by R. Antoun and I. Harik, 1972, pp. 21-44.

BAUMANN, H. und SCHÖNFELDER, I. Probleme der sozialen Vertiefung der nationalen Befreiungsbewegung in Nordafrika und Nahost. Bericht über eine wissenschaftliche Arbeitstagung der Sektion Afrika- und Nahostwissenschaften der Karl-Marx-Universität Leipzig vom 26. bis 29. November 1974 in Leipzig. *Asien. Afrika. Latein-Amerika* 3(1975), pp. 337-347.

BEHZADI, Hamid. The principles of legitimacy and its influence upon the Muslim political theory. *Islamic stud.* 10(1971), pp. 277-290.

BEN-DOR, G. The politics of threat: military intervention in the Middle East. *J. pol. mil. soc.* 1(1973), pp. 57-69.

BINDER, L. Political development in the Middle East. *Essays on modernization of underdeveloped societies*, Vol. 2. Ed. A.R. Desai, Bombay, 1971. pp. 458-473.

BRUNSCHVIG, R. La prosternation devant le souverain et la doctrine de l'Islam. *Atti dell'VIII Cong. int. stor. rel.* (1955), pp. 437-439.

BUTTERWORTH, C.E. Rhetoric and Islamic political philosophy. *IJMES* 3(1972), pp. 187-198

CARRÉ, O. Évolution de la pensée politique arabe au Proche-Orient depuis juin 1967. *Rev. française de sci. pol.* 23(1973), pp. 1046-1079.

CHARNAY, J.P. Action et politique en Islam. *L'ambivalence dans la culture arabe*, 1967, pp. 407-418.

DAWISHA, A.I. The transnational party in regional politics: the Arab Ba'th party. *Asian affairs* 61(N.S.5, 1974), pp. 22-31.

ERAN, Oded. Soviet perception of Arab communism and its political role. *The U.S.S.R. and the Middle East*, ed. by M. Confino and Sh. Shamir, 1973, pp. 109-119.

HAMIDULLAH, Muhammed. The political system of Islam. *Majallat al-Azhar* 43vii(1971), pp. 7-16

HOROWITZ, I.L. Political systems of the Middle East. *People and politics in the Middle East*, ed. M. Curtis, 1971, pp. 217-219.

IX HISTORY

HOTTINGER, A. The depth of Arab radicalism. *Foreign aff.* 51(1972-1973), pp. 491-504.

HUSSEYNOV, Rauf A. Le sultan et le calife (de l'histoire de la suzeraineté et de la vassalité en Asie Occidentale aux XIe et XIIe siècles). *Bedi Kartlisa* 28 (1971), pp. 199-207.

JAWED, Nasim A. Islamic socialism: an ideological trend in Pakistan in the 1960s. *MW* 65(1975), pp. 196-215.

KAMEL, M. Le role politique et idéologique de la petite bourgeoisie dans le monde arabe. *Renaissance du monde arabe. Colloque interarabe de Louvain,* 1972, pp. 366-426.

KERR, M.H. Regional Arab politics and the conflict with Israel. *Political dynamics in the Middle East,* ed. P.Y. Hammond and S.S. Alexander, 1972, pp. 31-68.

KERR, M.H. Socialisme révolutionnaire et tradition islamique. *Renaissance du monde arabe. Colloque interarabe de Louvain,* 1972, pp. 427-434.

KESSLER, C. The politics of Islamic egalitarianism. *Humaniora Islamica* 2(1974), pp. 237-252.

LAMBTON, A.K.S. Islamic mirrors for princes. *La Persia nel medievo,* 1971, pp. 419-442

LAMBTON, A.K.S. Some new trends in Islamic political thought in late 18th and early 19th century Persia. *SI* 39(1974), pp. 95-128.

LEWIS, B. On some modern Arabic political terms. *Orientalia Hispanica* I, 1974, pp. 465-471.

MALIK, Hafeez. Islamic political parties and mass politicization. *Islam and the modern age* 3ii(1972), pp. 26-64.

MARKS, J.H. On 'citizenship' in the Near East. *Humaniora Islamica* 2(1974), pp. 197-206.

MOORE, C.H. On theory and practice among Arabs. [Review article] *World politics* 24(1971), pp. 106-126.

MOORE, C.H. Raisons de la faillite du parti unique dans les pays arabes. *ROMM* 15-16 (1973), pp. 241-252.

MZĀLI, Muhammad. Authenticité et ouverture. Présentation et traduction par M. Borrmans. *OM* 55(1975), pp. 29-48.

NIZAMUDDIN, M. *Sulūk al-Mulūk* of Faḍl Allah ibn Rūzbihān. *J. Pak. Hist. Soc.* 13(1965), pp. 310-313.

PETRACEK, K. The category of the past in the reaction of modern Arab political thought to impulses from Europe. *The East under Western impact* (Dissertationes Orientales 17, 1969), pp. 30-40.

POLIVKOVA, Z. The internal continuity of Islamic institutions in the constitutional system of the Arab countries. *The East under Western impact* (Dissertationes Orientales 17, 1969), pp. 48-56.

REID, D.M. The Syrian Christians and early socialism in the Arab world. *IJMES* 5 (1974), pp. 177-193.

RINGGREN, H. On the Islamic theory of the state. *Myth of the state,* ed. H. Biezais, 1972, pp. 103-108.

ROSENTHAL, E.I.J. Politisches Denken im Islam. Die Entwicklung von Averroes bis Ibn Khaldun. *Saeculum* 23(1972), pp. 295-318.

ROSENTHAL, E.I.J. Politisches Denken im Islam. Kalifatstheorie und Politische Philosophie. *Saeculum* 23(1972), pp. 148-171.

SAID, Abdul Aziz. Clashing horizons: Arabs and revolution. *People and politics in the Middle East,* ed. M. Curtis, 1971, pp. 278-292.

SANKARI, Farouk A. Plato and al-Fārābī: a comparison of some aspects of their political philosophy. *Studies in Islam* 7 (1970), pp. 9-18.

SCHMUCKER, W. Studien zur Baath-Ideologie. *WI* N.S.14(1973), pp. 47-80.

THOMPSON, W.R. Toward explaining Arab military coups. *J. polit. and milit. sociol.* 2(1974), pp. 237-250.

TIMM, Kl. Zur Strategie der Sozialistischen Internationale gegenüber den Parteien der nationalen Befreiungsbewegung in arabischen Staaten. *Asien. Afrika. Latein-Amerika* 3(1975), pp. 911-914.

TYAN, E. Gouvernés et gouvernants en Islam sunnite. *Receuils Soc. Jean Bodin* 22(1969), pp. 390-402.

TYAN, E. Le système monocratique dans l'Islam sunnite. *Recueils Soc. Jean Bodin* 20(1970), pp. 503-514.

VATIKIOTIS, P.J. The politics of the Fertile Crescent. *Political dynamics in the Middle East,* ed. P.Y. Hammond and S.S. Alexander, 1972, pp. 225-263.

WATT, W.M. God's Caliph. Qur'ānic interpretations and Umayyad claims. *Iran and Islam, in memory of V. Minorsky,* 1971, pp. 565-574

ZARTMAN, I.W., PAUL, J.A. and ENTELIS, J.P. An economic indicator of socio-political unrest. *IJMES* 2(1971), pp. 293-310.

See also IX. a. Höpp.

See also IX. e. Young

See also X. d. Hinds.

h EMBLEMS

KRUSE, H. Rāya and Liwā' in Islamic tradition. *Proc.27th Int.Cong.Or.1967* (1971), pp. 283-284.

See also XXXI. g. Echraqi.

i PAN-ISLAMIC MOVEMENTS. PAN-AFRICANISM

AGUDA, Oluwadare. Arabism and pan-Arabism in Sudanese politics. *Mawazo* 4i(1973), pp. 7-26.

AGUDA, Oluwadare. Arabism and pan-Arabism in Sudanese politics. *J.mod.Afr.stud.* 11 (1973), pp. 177-200.

AGUDA, Oluwadare. Pan-Arabism versus Pan-Africanism: a dilemma for African unity. *Q.J. admin.* [Ife] 7(1973), pp. 357-371.

ALKHATEEB, Fouad. Islamic unity. *Nigerian J. Islam* 1i(1970), pp. 11-14.

AUDA, Abdel Malik Pan-Africanism in Egyptian national culture. *Eg. contemp.* 62 (no. 343, 1971), pp. 17-40

BELING, W.A. Arabism: an ecological variable in the politics of the Middle East. *The Middle East.* Ed. W.A. Beling, 1973, pp. 32-54.

BRETON, H. Le pétrole libyen au service de l'unité arabe? *Rev. fr. de sci. pol.* 22(1972), pp. 1256-1274.

CARRÉ, O. Les conditions de la cohésion arabe. *Projet* 84(1974), pp. 436-444.

DAWN, C.E. Pan-Arabism and the failure of Israeli-Jordanian peace negotiations, 1950. *Islam and its cultural divergence. Studies in honor of Gustave E. von Grunebaum,* 1971, pp. 27-51

DJAÏT, H. Problématique et critique de l'idée d'unité arabe. *Renaissance du monde arabe. Colloque interarabe de Louvain,* 1972, pp. 488-498.

ELEWAINY, Mohamed Aly. Africa and the fourth Arab Israeli war. *Bull.Arab res.and stud.* 5(1974), pp. 65-81.

FRYZEŁ, T. Historycnne etapy rozwoju jedności arabskiej po II wojnie światowej. *Przegl. Or.* 1(93, 1975), pp. 13-24.

HAJJAJ, Aref S. Der Panarabismus Gamal Abdel-Nassers. *WI* 15(1974), pp. 247-251.

HASAN, S.A. Islamic unity and world co-operation. *Internat. Islamic Conf.,* 1968, pp. 12-23.

HUSRY, Khaldun S. King Faysal and Arab unity, 1930-33. *J. contemp. hist.* 10 (1975), pp. 323-340.

JOARDER, Safiuddin. The question of Arab unity; an Arab plan considered. *JAS Bangladesh* 18(1973), pp. 129-146.

KRAŠA, M. The idea of Pan-Asianism and the nationalist movement in India. *Arch. or.* 40(1972), pp. 238-260.

KYUKK, G. Nekotorye problemy idei arabskogo edinstva. *Istoriya i ekonomika stran Arabskogo Vostoka,* 1973, pp. 151-164.

MAQDICI, A. Culture et unité nationale dans la renaissance arabe. *Renaissance du monde arabe. Colloque interarabe de Louvain,* 1972, pp. 499-529.

NWIYA, P. Note sur le bureau permanent pour la coordination de l'arabisation dans le Monde arabe. *Maghreb-Machrek* 57(1973), pp. 39-40.

NYANG, Sulayman Sheih. Islam and Panafricanism. *Afrique et Asie modernes* 104 (1975), pp. 42-50.

REYAZUL HASAN. The Islamic summit conference. *Iqbal rev.* 15i(1974), pp. 43-64.

RUBIO GARCÍA, L. Ideologia y realidades en la dinámica de la OUA (II); Nueve años de reuniones del consejo y de la conferencia. *Rev. de política int.* 124(1972), pp. 57-89.

SAMRA, Mahmud. Pan-Islamism and Arab nationalism. (A study of the ideas of Syrian Muslim writers, 1860-1918). *Fac. Arts J. Univ. Jordan* 3ii(1972), pp. 5-32.

WALKER, D. Islam and the Arab West's commitment to Africanism. *Nigerian J.Islam* 2ii (1972-74), pp. 19-31.

See also XVI. b. Burke

See also XXVI. c. Minganti.

j THE ARAB LEAGUE

ABDALLAH, Ezzedine. La convention de la Ligue arabe sur l'exécution des jugements. Étude comparative du droit conventionnel comparé avec le droit interne. *Acad. de droit int., Recueil de cours* 138(1973 I), pp. 503-627.

BECHTOLD, P.K. New attempts at Arab cooperation: the Federation of Arab Republics, 1971? *MEJ* 27(1973), pp. 152-172.

BOUTROS-GHALI, B. La Ligue des états arabes. *Acad. de droit int., Recueil de cours* 137(1972 III), pp. 1-82.

BOUTROS-GHALI, B. La réforme de la Ligue arabe. *Renaissance du monde arabe. Colloque interarabe de Louvain,* 1972, pp. 479-487.

CARRÉ, O. La Ligue des États arabes. *Rev. fr. de sci. pol.* 21(1971), pp. 362-381.

GIL BENUMEYA, R. Los treinta anos de la Liga Árabe. *Revista pol. int.* 139 (1975), pp. 159-167.

RASHED, Abdel Hamid. Wie gesamtarabisch ist die Arabische Liga? *Z.f.Kulturaustausch* 24ii(1974), pp. 19-22.

WISSA-WASSEF, C. La Ligue des Etats arabes face aux conflits inter-arabes. *Politique étrangère* 38(1973), pp. 51-83.

See also IX. n. Kück.

See also XX. c. *Aguda*

k NATIONALISM

AGWANI, M.S. Islam and Arab nationalism. *India and contemporary Islam,* ed. S.T. Lokhandwalla, 1971, pp. 145-149.

CEMAM. Unité nationale et liberté d'expression. *Travaux et jours* 48(1973), pp. 119-137.

GORDON-POLONSKAYA, L.R. Ideology of Muslim nationalism. *Iqbal: poet-philosopher of Pakistan,* ed. Hafeez Malik, 1971, pp. 108-135.

HADDAD, George M. Muṣṭafā Kāmil: a self-image from his correspondence with Juliette Adam. *MW* 63(1973), pp. 132-138.

HAGOPIAN, E.C. Arab nationalism, the Arab-Israeli crisis, and the African response. *Pan-African J.* 3ii(1970), pp. 78-92.

JARGY, S. Les origines culturelles du nationalisme arabe: réflexions autour de la *nahḍa* en Syrie, dans la deuxième moitié du XIXe s. *Orientalis Hispanica* I, 1974, pp. 411-427.

KEDOURIE, E. Revolutionary nationalism in Asia and Africa. *Government and opposition* 3(1968), pp. 453-464.

KHAN, Yusuf Husain. Indian Muslims and the Caliphate. *India and contemporary Islam,* ed. S.T. Lokhandwalla, 1971, pp. 168-174.

KRITZECK, J. Islam y nacionalismo árabe. *Estudios orientales* 4(1969), no. 9, pp. 1-15.

KRUSE, H. Traditional Islam and political development. *India and contemporary Islam,* ed. S.T. Lokhandwalla, 1971, pp. 175-193.

LEWIS, W.H. Islam and nationalism in Africa. *The Arab Middle East and Muslim Africa,* ed. by T.Kerekes, 1961, pp. 63-83.

MAHMUDUL HAQ. 'Alī 'Abdu'r-Rāziq on Islam and state. *India and contemporary Islam,* ed. S.T. Lokhandwalla, 1971, pp. 150-157.

MUZIKÁŘ, J. Arab nationalism and Islam. (Djamāl 'Abd-an Nāṣir and his attitude to Islam.) *Ar. Or.* 43(1975), pp. 193-209, 302-323.

PFAFF, R.H. The function of Arab nationalism. *Contemporary politics* 2(1969-70), pp. 147-167.

SHAWI, Hamid al-. Essai d'analyse spectrale du nationalisme arabe depuis la seconde guerre mondiale. *Politique étrangère* 38(1973), pp. 569-584.

SILBERMANN, G. National identity in Nasserist ideology. *Asian and Afr. stud.* 8(1972), pp. 49-85.

SMITH, A.D. Nationalism and religion. The role of religious reform in the genesis of Arab and Jewish nationalism. *Arch.sc.soc. des rel.* 35(1973), pp. 23-43.

See also II. a. 8. Smith.

See also VII. a. Harik.

See also IX. j. Samra.

See also XVI. a. Barbour

See also XVI. c. Walker.

l COMMUNISM AND ISLAM

BALLUZ, Nayef. Nichtkapitalististische Entwicklung und Islam. *Mitt Inst.Orientforschung* 16(1970), pp. 521-540.

FANGARY, Mohamed Shawky el-. Problème de la décadence du monde musulman. *Rev. al Qanoun wal Iqtisad* 40(1970), pp. 141-179; 41(1971), pp. 1-35.

FANGARY, Mohamed Shawky el- Rôle de l'intelligence musulmane dans l'évolution des conceptions marxistes. *Eg. contemp.* 62 (no. 343, 1971), pp. 83-91.

FRYŹEL, T. Socjalizm a Islam. *Przeglad Or.* 1973(1, no.85), pp. 9-17.

HÖPP, K. Bemerkungen zur Periodisierung der Geschichte des sozialistischen Denkens in den arabischen Ländern bis zur Mitte der dreissiger Jahre des 20. Jahrhunderts. *Asien in Vergangenheit und Gegenwart,* 1974, pp. 25-38.

KHËPP, G. K voprosu ob istorii sotzialisticheskoy mysli v arabskikh stranakh (do 1917 g.). *Istoriya i ekonomika stran Arabskogo Vostoka,* 1973, pp. 275-287.

RO'I, Yaacov. The role of Islam and the Soviet muslims in Soviet Arab policy. *Asian and African stud.* (Israel Or.Soc.) 10(1974-5), pp. 157-189.

See also XXVII. c. Dann.

m EAST-WEST RELATIONS

ADOMEIT, H. Soviet policy in the Middle East: problems of analysis. *Soviet stud.* 27(1972), pp. 288-305.

IX HISTORY

AGWANI, M.S. India and the Arab world 1947-1964. *Indian horizons* 22ii(1973), pp. 46-63.

ALKAZAZ, Aziz. Der arabisch-europäische Dialog. Ziele, Möglichkeiten und Voraussetzungen im wirtschaftlichen Bereich. *Orient* [Hamburg] 16i(1975), pp. 23-40.

AZAR, E.E. Conflict escalation and conflict reduction in an international crisis: Suez, 1956. *J. conflict resolution* 16(1972), pp. 183-201.

BARBOUR, N. The Emperor Frederick II, King of Jerusalem and Sicily, and his relations with the Muslims. *Orientalia Hispanica* I, 1974, pp. 77-95.

BELDICEANU, N. En marge d'un livre sur la mer Noire. *REI* 39(1971), pp. 389-393.

BELYAEV, I. The Middle East in contemporary world affairs. *J. Palestine studies* 2iv (1973), pp. 13-24.

BENCHENAB, Saadeddine. Algeria and India. *India and the Arab World, ed. by S. Maqbul Ahmed,* 1969, pp. 143-146.

BERINDRANATH, Dewan. Islam as a factor in Indo-Pak relations. *India and contemporary Islam,* ed. S.T. Lokhandwalla, 1971, pp. 348-356.

BIERBACH, M., LUGENHEIM, K.-H. Feste Freundschaft und Zusammenarbeit zwischen der DDR und den afro-asiatischen Staaten. Zur Reise des Vorsitzenden des Ministerrates der DDR, Horst Sindermann, in arabische und südasiatische Staaten vom 18. November bis 2. Dezember 1974. *Asien. Afrika, Latein-Amerika* 3(1975), pp. 209-214

BISHAI, W.B. Negotiations and peace agreements between Muslims and non-Muslims in Islamic history. *Medieval and Middle Eastern studies ... A.S. Atiya* 1972, pp. 50-61.

BOUTEFLIKA, Abdelaziz. L'Algérie et l'Europe: perspective de coopération. *Rev. alg. des sci. jur., econ. et pol.* 10(1973), pp. 527-538.

BRAUN, U. Der Irak und die Staaten der Arabischen Halbinsel in der sowjetischen Aussenpolitik. *Ost-Europa* 23(1973), pp. 376-384.

BÜREN, R. Bemerkungen zum Stellenwert der arabischen Staaten in der aussenpolitischen Konzeption der Bundesrepublik Deutschland. *Z.f.Kulturaustausch* 24ii(1974), pp. 41-50.

CAHEN, C. Saint Louis et l'Islam. *JA* 258(1970), pp. 3-12.

CALVOCORESSI, P. Britain and the Middle East. *Political dynamics in the Middle East,* ed. P.Y. Hammond and S.S. Alexander, 1972, pp. 425-444.

CAMPBELL, J.C. The continuing crisis. *The Soviet Union and the Middle East,* ed. I.J. Lederer and W.S. Vucinich, 1974, pp. 11-24.

CAMPBELL, J.C. The Soviet Union and the United States in the Middle East. *America and the Middle East,* ed. P.T. Hart, 1972, pp. 126-135.

CAMPBELL, J.C. The Soviet Union and the United States in the Middle East. *Continuing issues in international politics,* ed. Y.H. Ferguson and W.F. Weiker, 1973, pp. 70-81.

CANTORI, L.J. The international relations of the Middle East. Syllabus. *MESA Bull.* 5iii(1971), pp. 20-44.

CHHABRA, Hari Sharan. The competition of Israel and the Arab states for friendship with the African states. *India Q.* 31(1975), pp. 362-370.

COHEN, S.A. Britain's policy towards Mesopotamia before 1914: the case for a revision. *Asian and African stud.* (Israel Or.Soc.) 10(1974-5), pp. 79-88.

COOKE, J.J. and HEGGOY, A.A. The American periodical press and Ahmed Ben Bella. *MW* 61(1971), pp. 293-302.

DADANT, P.M. American and Soviet defense systems vis-à-vis the Middle East. *The Middle East.* Ed. W.A. Beling, 1973, pp. 169-200.

DE ARAÚJO OLIVEIRA, H. A posição e o valor estratégicos dos países árabes e islâmicos na actualidade. *Soc. Geog. Lisboa. Boletim* 91(1973), pp. 91-114.

DEM'YANENKO, A.P. Iz istorii politiki Germanii na Blizhnem Vostoke nakanune vtoroy mirovoy voyny. (Concerning the history of policy in the Near East on the eve of World War I.) *NAA* 1973(1), pp. 138-144.

DESAI, Z.A. Relations of India with Middle-Eastern countries during the 16th-17th centuries. *J.Or.Inst.Baroda* 23(1973), pp. 75-106.

DJAIT, Hichem. Europe and Islam: historic dynamics. *Diogenes* 91(1975), pp. 1-15.

DODGE, B. American educational and missionary efforts in the nineteenth and early twentieth centuries. *America and the Middle East,* ed. P.T. Hart, 1972, pp. 15-22.

DOMENACH, J.L. La politique japonaise au Moyen-Orient avant et après la guerre d'octobre. *Maghreb Machrek* 67(1975), pp. 61-68.

DUNLOP, D.M. Arab relations with Tibet in the 8th and early 9th centuries A.D. *Islam Tetkikleri Enst. dergisi* 5(1973), pp 301-318.

EKEMODE, G.O. Arab influence in 19th century Usambara. *African historian* 2iv(1968), pp. 14-20.

ETR, Riad el-. Value of cultural relations. *India and the Arab World, ed. by S. Maqbul Ahmed,* 1969, pp. 141-142.

IX HISTORY

FARSOUN, K., *et al.* Mid-East perspectives from the American left. *J.Palestine stud.* 4i(1974), pp. 94-119.

FIELD, J.A. Trade, skills and sympathy: the first century and a half of commerce with the Near East. *America and the Middle East*, ed. P.T. Hart, 1972, pp. 1-14.

GHUL, Mahmud. Divergence and convergence in Mediterranean cultures. (A study in the bases of identification and conflict.) *Islam and the modern age* 5iv(1974), pp. 5-10.

GIL BENUMAYA, R. Los Estados árabes ante Europa Occidental. *Rev. de política int.* 124(1972), pp. 145-154.

GLUNK, R. Zwischen Kultur und Aussenpolitik - zu einer arabischen Kritik an Kulturinstituten. *Z.f.Kulturaustausch* 24ii(1974) pp. 108-114.

GOMANE, J.P. L'action japonaise au Moyen-Orient. *L'Afrique et l'Asie modernes* 102 (1974), pp. 40-52.

GRIMAUD, N. Le conflit pétrolier franco-algérien. *Rev. fr. de sci. pol.* 22(1972), pp. 1276-1307.

HAMBIS, L. Saint Louis et les Mongols. *JA* 258(1970), pp. 25-33.

HARE, R.A. The great divide: World War II. *American and the Middle East*, ed. P.T. Hart, 1972, pp. 23-30.

HART, P.T. Where we stand. *America and the Middle East*, ed. P.T. Hart, 1972, pp. 136-142.

HINSLEY, F.H. The Middle East and the great powers. *People and politics in the Middle East*, ed. M. Curtis, 1971, pp. 250-257.

HOLLENBACH, J.W. The image of the Arab in nineteenth century English and American literature. I. *MW* 62(1972), pp. 195-208.

HORELICK, A.L. and BECKER, A.S. Soviet policy in the Middle East. *Political dynamics in the Middle East*, ed. P.Y. Hammond and S.S. Alexander, 1972, pp. 553-636.

HOWARD, H.N. The regional pacts and the Eisenhower doctrine. *America and the Middle East*, ed. P.T. Hart, 1972, pp. 85-94.

HUDSON, M.C. The Arab states' policies toward Israel. *Transformation of Palestine*, ed. I. Abu-Lughod, 1971, pp. 309-336.

HUDSON, M.C. Politique intérieure et politique extérieure américaine dans ses rapports avec le conflit israélo-arabe. *Politique étrangère* 39(1974), pp. 641-658.

IBRAHIM, Ibrahim A. Isma'il Maẓhar and Husayn Fawzi: Two Muslim "radical" westernizers. *ME stud.* 9(1973), pp. 35-41.

INGRAM, E. A preview of the great game in Asia - IV: British agents in the Near East in the war of the Second Coalition, 1798-1801. *Middle East Stud.* 10(1974), pp. 15-35.

ISNARD, H. Le monde méditerranéen, périphérie de l'Europe. *ROMM* 15-16(1973), pp. 89-97.

KAMEL, Ayhan. Turkey's relations with the Arab world. *Diş politika* 4iv 1974, pp. 91-107.

KARAHAN, Abdulkadir. An outline of the cultural relations existing between Turkey, Iran and Pakistan. *Iqbal R.* 16i(1975), pp. 32-42.

KENT, G. Congress and American Middle East policy. *The Middle East.* Ed. W.A. Beling, 1973, pp. 286-305.

KERR, M.H. Nixon's second term: policy prospects in the Middle East. *J. Palestine stud.* 2(1973), pp. 14-29.

KHALFIN, N.A., VOLODARSKIY, M.I. Sovremennaya burzhuaznaya istoriografiya o nekotorykh voprosakh mezhdunarodnykh otnosheniy na Srednem Vostoke v pervoy treti XIX veka. (Certain aspects of international relations in the Middle East in the first three decades of the 19th century as reflected in contemporary bourgeois historiography.) *Vopr. ist.* 1971(7), pp. 192-199.

KHALID, Detlev. Aḥmad Amīn and Muḥammad Iqbāl. *Iqbal rev.* 12i(1971), pp. 39-68.

KHEYFETZ, A.N. Sovetskie respubliki i narody Vostoka (1918-1922). *Vopr. ist.* 1972(11), pp. 18-32.

KIMCHE, J. What is a pro-Arab policy? *Asian aff.* 58(N.S.2, 1971), pp. 140-146.

KOLKOWICZ, R. The Soviet policy in the Middle East. *The U.S.S.R. and the Middle East*, ed. by M. Confino and Sh. Shamir, 1973, pp. 77-87.

KRASSOWSKI, A. The Middle East Development division. *J.admin.o'seas* 14(1975), pp 4-16.

LAQUEUR, W.Z. Soviet dilemmas in the Middle East. *The U.S.S.R. and the Middle East*, ed. by M. Confino and Sh. Shamir, 1973, pp. 89-108.

LEDERER, I.J. Historical introduction. *The Soviet Union and the Middle East*, ed. I.J. Lederer and W.S. Vucinich, 1974, pp. 1-10.

LYAUTEY, P. Les secrets du Nouvel-Orient, en conflit avec l'Occident. Quel devrait être le rôle de la France? *CR trim.Acad. sci.Outre-Mer* 34(1974), pp. 337-345.

MALLOUHI, Abdul-Moen. Influence of Indian culture. *India and the Arab World, ed. by S. Maqbul Ahmed*, 1969, pp. 147-148.

MANERA REGUEYRA, E. El Mediterráneo actual y sus problemas. *Rev. de polít. int.* 123(1972), pp. 91-115.

IX HISTORY

MAQBUL AHMED, S. Indo-Arab relations - problems and prospects. *India and the Arab World, ed. by S. Maqbul Ahmed,* 1969, pp. 136-140.

MASQUET, B. La coopération culturelle franco-marocaine. *Maghreb-Machrek* 60(1973), pp. 21-26

MAZRUI, Ali A. Black Africa and the Arabs. *Foreign affairs* 53(1975), pp. 725-742.

MEJCHER, H. British Middle East policy, 1917-21: the interdepartmental level. *J. contemp. hist.* 8(1973), pp. 81-101.

MELKA, R.L. Max Freiherr von Oppenheim: Sixty years of scholarship and political intrigue in the Middle East. *ME stud.* 9(1973), pp. 81-93.

MORGENTHAU, H. The ideological and political dynamics of the Middle Eastern policy of the Soviet Union. *The U.S.S.R. and the Middle East,* ed. by M. Confino and Sh. Shamir, 1973, pp. 71-76.

NASR, Seyyed Hossein. The Western world and its challenges to Islam. *IQ* 17(1973), pp. 3-25.

ODEN, D.H. The Great Powers, Israel and the United Nations, 1948-1967. *International problems* 13(1974), pp. 291-310.

OFER, Gur. The economic burden of Soviet involvement in the Middle East. *The U.S.S.R. and the Middle East,* ed. by M. Confino and Sh. Shamir, 1973, pp. 215-246.

ORR, J.B. Theological perspectives on the Arab-Israeli conflict. *The Middle East.* Ed. W.A. Beling, 1973, pp. 335-347.

PADMANBAHAN, L.K. India, Israel and the Arab world. *International problems* 14 (1975), pp. 11-14.

PAPADAKIS, A. Gennadius II and Mehmet the Conqueror. *Byzantion* 42(1972), pp. 88-106.

PAVLOV, M.A. Sotzialisticheskiy internatzional i Blizhniy Vostok. *NAA* 1973(5), pp. 23-34.

PERLMUTTER, Amos. The fiasco of Anglo-American Middle East policy. *People and politics in the Middle East,* ed. M. Curtis, 1971, pp. 220-249.

PINCHUK, Ben-Cion. Soviet penetration into the Middle East in historical perspective. *The U.S.S.R. and the Middle East,* ed. by M. Confino and Sh. Shamir, 1973, pp. 61-69.

QUANDT, W.B. Domestic influences on U.S. foreign policy in the Middle East: the view from Washington. *The Middle East.* Ed. W.A. Beling, 1973, pp. 263-285.

QUANDT, W.B. Les États-Unis et le monde arabe. *Maghreb Machrek* 68(1975), pp. 42-48.

QUANDT, W.B. United States policy in the Middle East: constraints and choices. *Political dynamics in the Middle East,* ed. P.Y. Hammond and S.S. Alexander, 1972, pp. 489-551.

RA'ANAN, Uri. The USSR and the Middle East: some reflections on the Soviet decision-making process. *Orbis* [Tufts] 17(1973), pp. 946-977.

RO'I, Yaacov. The role of Islam and the Soviet Muslims in Soviet Arab policy. Part two. *Asian and African studies* [Jerusalem] 10(1975), pp. 259-280.

RO'I, Yaacov. Soviet policy in the Middle East: the case of Palestine during World War II. *Cah. monde russe soviétique* 15(1974), pp. 373-408.

RONDOT, P. Etats arabes: prémices d'une coopération avec l'Afrique. *Rev.franç.ét. pol.afr.* 9, no. 104(1974), pp. 15-18.

RONDOT, P. Western Europe and the Middle East. *Political dynamics in the Middle East,* ed. P.Y. Hammond and S.S. Alexander, 1972, pp. 445-488.

RUBIN, B. America's Mid-East policy: a marxist perspective. *J.Palestine stud.* 2(1973), pp. 51-67.

SAID, E. US policy and the conflict of powers in the Middle East. *J. Palestine stud.* 2(1973), pp. 30-50.

SAMARRAI, A. Some geographical and political information on Western Europe in the medieval Arabic sources. *MW* 62(1972), pp. 304-322.

SAOUMA, G. Le Japon et les pays arabes. *L'Afrique et l'Asie* 106(1975), pp. 41-48.

SAUNDERS, J.J. The relations between European and Muslim history. *Proc.27th Int.Cong.Or.1967* (1971), pp. 236-237.

SCHILLING, W. Sowjetpolitik im Nahen Osten. *Ost-Europa* 22(1972), pp. 391-402.

SCHULDINER, Z. Las relaciones egipto-URSS. *Estudios orientales* 7(1972), pp. 294-334.

SHAFA, Shoja eddin. L'Iran et l'Italie de l'empire romaine à nos jours. *Acta Iranica* 1(1974), pp. 307-315.

SHEPARD, S. Islamic monuments in christian hands. *IC* 46(1972), pp. 293-295.

SHEYBANI, Nezamoddin Mojir. The influence of Iranian civilization on the West. *J. Reg. Cult. Inst.* 4(1971), pp. 107-112.

SIVERSON, R.M. The evaluation of self, allies, and enemies in the 1956 Suez crisis. *J. conflict resolution* 16(1972), pp. 203-210.

SPIRIDONOV, Ĭ. Bulgarian-Turkish medical relations. [Russian with English abstract.] *Asklepiy* (Sofia) 2(1972), pp. 97-100. [CWHM 77, 1495]

STEINBACH, U. Neuere Entwicklungen in den politischen Beziehungen zwischen der Sowjetunion und der Türkei, Griechenland und Zypern. *Ost-Europa* 23(1973), pp. 531-539.

STEINBACH, U. Sowjetische Nahostpolitik am Scheideweg. *Ost-Europa* 23(1973), pp. 385-395.

STEPHENS, R. The great powers and the Middle East. *J. Palestine studies* 2iv (1973), pp. 3-12.

STÖBER, H. Afrika und der Nahe Osten. Traditionen und neue Tendenzen in den afro-arabischen Beziehungen. *Asien. Afrika. Latein-Amerika* 3(1975), pp. 669-678.

SZÉKELY, Gy. Les contacts entre hongrois et musulmans aux IXe - XIIe siècles. *The Middle East; studies in honour of J. Germanus,* 1974, pp. 53-74.

TECHNAU, G. Bilharzlosebekämpfung in Fayoum - ein deutsch-ägyptisches Gemeinschafts-projekt. *Z.f.Kulturaustausch* 24ii(1974), pp. 72-73.

TERRY, J. Israel's policy toward the Arab states. *Transformation of Palestine,* ed. I. Abu-Lughod, 1971, pp. 337-354.

TERRY, J., MENDENHALL, G. 1973 US press coverage on the Middle East. *J.Palestine stud.* 4i(1974), pp. 120-133.

THORPE, J.A. The United States and the 1940-1941 Anglo-Iraqi crisis: American policy in transition. *MEJ* 25 (1971), pp. 79-89.

TLILI, Béchir. Les rapports arabo-turcs à la veille de la Grande Guerre (1907-1913). *CT* 23(nos.89-90,1975), pp. 33-140.

VOIGT, V. Hungarian sources in early Mediterranean contacts. *Actes I. Cong. et. cult. mediterr. d'infl. arabo-berb.,* 1973, pp. 213-216.

WAGNER, C.H. Elite American newspaper opinion and the Middle East: commitment vs. isolation. *The Middle East.* Ed. W.A. Beling, 1973, pp. 306-334.

WATT, W.M. L'influence de l'Islam sur l' Europe médiévale. *REI* 40(1972), pp. 7-41.

YIZHAR, M. Origins of the American involvement in the Middle East. *International problems* 13(1974), pp. 335-346.

YODFAT, Argeh Y. The Soviet Union and Israel. *International problems* 13(1974), pp. 347-362.

YOUNG, L. American blacks and the Arab-Israeli conflict. *J. Palestine studies* 2i (1972), pp. 70-85.

ZOPPO, C. The American-Soviet Mediterranean confrontation and the Middle East. *The Middle East.* Ed. W.A. Beling, 1973, pp. 201-236.

Borse di cooperazione tecnica assegnate a cittadini dei paesi arabi. *Levante* 21iv (1974), pp. 40-46.

La Fiera del Levante e il Mondo arabo. *Levante* 21iii(1974), pp. 19-24.

Institute for relations between Italy and the countries of Africa, Latin America and the Middle East. *Mitteilungen. Dokumentationsdienst Moderner Orient* 3ii(1974), pp. 19-22.

See also II. c. 2. Basri.

See also II. c. 2. Ebied.

See also VI. d. Guevara Bazán

See also IX. a. Bennouna

See also IX. a. Kelly.

See also IX. a. Kissling.

See also IX. n. Akins.

See also IX. n. Berry.

See also IX. n. Bockmeyer.

See also IX. n. Cattan.

See also IX. n. Costa.

See also IX. n. Duclos.

See also IX. n. Ehrenkreutz.

See also IX. n. Mabro

See also IX. n. Rifaï.

See also IX. n. Spillmann

See also IX. n. Due grandi realizzazzioni

See also XVI. a. Fuglestad-Aumeunier.

See also XVI. a. Ruf.

See also XVI. a. Talha.

See also XVI. aa. Mellah.

See also XVI. b. Dero-Jacob

See also XVI. bb. Lourido Diaz.

See also XVI. c. Danziger.

See also XVII. c. Cortese

See also XIX. g. Hours.

See also XIX. i. Ingram.

See also XIX. m. Bonn.

See also XIX. m. Terry

See also XXII. c. Yodfat.

See also XXIII. d. Dessouki.

See also XXIII. d. Dimant.

See also XXIII. d. Ibrahim.

See also XXIII. d. Sheffer

See also XXVI. c. Crawford.

See also XXVII. c. Cerbella.

See also XXIX. i. Issawi.

See also XXIX. i. Thobie.

See also XXIX. j. Kürkçüoğlu.

See also XXIX. j. Spector.

See also XXXI. g. Brulez.

See also XXXI. i. Destrée.

See also XXXIII. c. Ingram.

n ECONOMIC HISTORY. ECONOMICS

ABDEL MALEK, Ménès. Réflexions sur l'intégration économique des pays du Pacte de Tripoli. *Annales de la Faculté de Droit de Beyrouth* 68 (1971), pp. 109-125.

ABDESSALEM, Belaïd. Les problèmes pétroliers. *Rev. alg.* 10(1973), pp. 709-715.

'ABDUL JABBĀR BEG, Muḥammad. Workers in the Ḥammāmāt in the Arab Orient in the early Middle Ages. *RSO* 47(1972), pp. 77-80.

AHMED, Ziauddin. Dr. Najjar's *Al-Madkhal ila'l-nazariyyat al-iqtiṣādiyyah fi'l-manhaj al-islāmī* (an introduction to the economic theory of Islam). *Islamic studies* 13(1974), pp. 269-280.

AKINS, J.E. The oil crisis: this time the wolf is here. *Foreign aff.* 51(1972-1973), pp. 462-490.

ALKAZAZ, Aziz. Die importierte Inflation in den Ländern des Vorderen Orients und in den OPEC-Staaten. Ergebnisse einer japanischen Untersuchung. *Orient* [Hamburg] 16iii(1975), pp. 68-78.

AMID-HOZOUR, Esmail. The crude oil supply: the Middle East, Irān, and the Shell Oil Company. *Tahqīqāt e eqtesādi* 9(25-26, 1972), pp. 31-46.

AMIN, Galal A. Arab economic growth and imbalances, 1945-1970. *Eg. contemp.* 63(no.350, 1972), pp. 257-295.

AMIN, Galal A. Income distribution and economic development in the Arab world, 1950-1970. *Eg. contemp.* 64(352, 1973), pp. 115-145.

AMIN, Galal. The oil crisis -- an Arab point of view. *Eg. contemp.* 65(1974), pp. 291-299.

AMUZEGAR, Jahangir. Ideology and economic growth in the Middle East. *MEJ* 28(1974), pp. 1-9.

AMUZEGAR, Jajangir The oil story: facts, fiction and fair play. *Foreign affairs* 51(1972-73), pp. 676-689.

ANDREASYAN, R. Oil and the anti-imperialist struggle. *Social sciences* [Moscow] 6i(1975), pp. 90-100.

ARABI, M. Abdullah âl-. The Islamic economy and contemporary economy. *3rd Conf. Acad.Isl.Research*, 1966, pp. 201-366

ASHTOR, E. Banking instruments between the Muslim East and the Christian West. *J.Europ. econ.hist.* 1(1972), pp. 553-573.

ASHTOR, E. La découverte de la voie maritime aux Indes et les prix des épices. *Hist. econ. du monde mediterraneen 1450-1650. Mel. F. Braudel*, pp. 31-47.

ASHTOR, E. Profits from trade with the Levant in the fifteenth century. *BSOAS* 38(1975), pp. 250-275.

ASHTOR, Salaires dans l'orient médiéval à la basse-époque. *REI* 39(1971), pp. 103-117.

ASKEROVA, G. O regĭonal'nom ekonomicheskom sotrudnichestve arabskikh stran. *Arabskie strany, Turtziya, Iran, Afganistan*, 1973, pp. 187-195.

BAALI, F. Agrarian reform policies and development in the Arab World. *Amer.J. econ.sociol.* 33(1974), pp. 161-173.

BALASANOV, Yu. G. Mirnoe ispol'zovanie atomnoy energii v razvivayushchikhsya stranakh. *Strany Blizhnego i Srednego Vostoka: istoriya, ekonomica*, 1972, pp. 245-259.

BARGER, T.C. Middlé Eastern oil since the Second World War. *America and the Middle East*, ed. P.T. Hart, 1972, pp. 31-44

BARKAN, Ömer Lutfi. The price revolution of the sixteenth century: a turning point in the economic history of the Near East. *IJMES* 6(1975), pp. 3-28.

BARTHEL, G. Die arabischen Ölmilliarden und das "recycling" - Ursachen und Wirkungen. *Asien. Afrika. Latein-Amerika* 3(1975), pp. 429-438.

BARTHEL, G. Der Kampf um das arabische Erdöl -- Stand und Perspektive. *Asien in Vergangenheit und Gegenwart*, 1974, pp. 181-201.

BASILE, A. Coopération économique régionale et objectifs d'industrialisation. *Ann. Fac. Droit Beyrouth* 74(1972), pp. 503-531.

BASILE, A. Le marché commun arabe. *Annales de la Faculté de Droit de Beyrouth* 68 (1971), pp. 67-76.

BASILE, A. Les mouvements de capitaux et les investissements arabes au Moyen-Orient. *Ann.de la Fac.de droit de Beyrouth* 69 (1971), pp. 269-291.

IX HISTORY

BASILE, A. La vocation régionale de la place financière de Beyrouth. *Ann. Fac. Droit Beyrouth* 77-8 (1973), pp. 143-155.

BERREBY, J.J. Fondements historiques et politiques des conflits pétroliers contemporains. *Rev. fr. de sci. pol.* 22(1972), pp. 1191-1204.

BERRY, J.A. Oil and Soviet policy in the Middle East. *MEJ* 26(1972), pp. 149-160.

BLITZER, Ch., MEERAUS, A., STOUTJESDIJK, A. A dynamic model of OPEC trade and production. *J. development econ.* 2 (1975), pp. 319-335

BOCKMEYER, M. Die Wirtschaftsbeziehungen zwischen der Bundesrepublik Deutschland und der Arabischen Welt. *Z.f.Kulturaustausch* 24ii(1974), pp. 35-40.

BOULAKIA, J.D.C. Ibn Khaldûn: a fourteenth century economist. *J. political economy* 79(1971), pp. 1105-1118.

BOURGEY, A. Pétrole et croissance urbaine dans le Moyen-Orient arabe. *Mondes en développement* 8(1974), pp. 123-141.

BROWN, V. The role of government in Middle East trade. *An introduction to business law in the Middle East*, ed. B. Russell, 1975, pp. 89-101.

CAHEN, C. Les finances urbaines dans le moyen âge musulman. *Ve Congrès International d'Arabisants et d'Islamisants. Actes.*, [1970?], pp. 145-150.

CAHEN, C. Quelques questions sur les Radanites. *Der Islam* 48(1971-2), pp. 333-334

CAHEN, C. De la suprématie économique musulmane à la suprématie économique européenne à la fin du Moyen Âge; principaux facteurs. *Proc.27th Int.Cong. Or.1967* (1971), p. 204.

CATTAN, G. La cooperazióne economica arabo-europea nel settore bancario e finanziario. *Levante* 21i-ii(1974), pp. 15-21

CHARNAY, J.P. Logique socio-économique au Prôche-Orient. *Politique étrangère* 38 (1973), pp. 533-568.

CHARNAY, J.P. Une trajectoire arabe du rejaillissement culturel à l'affirmation économique. *Renaissance du monde arabe. Colloque interarabe de Louvain*, 1972, pp. 38-46.

CHATELUS, M. Donnees et problèmes de l'industrialisation dans les États arabes du Moyen-Orient. *Annales de la Faculté de Droit de Beyrouth* 68 (1971), pp. 5-66.

CHATELUS, M. Pétrole et perspectives de développement: analyse de quelques états du Moyen-Orient. *Mondes en développement* 10(1975), pp. 221-241.

CHATELUS, M. Les politiques industrielles des états arabes du Moyen-Orient. *Ann.de la Fac.de Droit de Beyrouth* 71(1972), pp. 1-50

CHATELUS, M. Problèmes de formulation et d'exécution des objectifs du plan. *Ann. Fac. Droit Beyrouth* 74(1972), pp. 375-408

CONSTANTIN, Fr. et COULON, Chr. Islam, pétrole et dépendance: un nouvel enjeu africain. *Rev. franç. d'ét. pol. afr.* 113(1975), pp. 28-53.

COSTA, S. Prospettive di cooperazione economica fra le industrie italiane ed i Paesi arabi. *Levante* 21iii(1974), pp. 33-41.

DESOUTTER, B. Le transport terrestre du pétrole: élément de la crise du Proche-Orient. *Maghreb-Machrek* 64(1974), pp. 34-47.

DONINI, P.G. Distribuzione geografica dei concentramenti industriali nei paesi arabi. *OM* 53(1973), pp. 645-655.

DUCHÊNE, Fr. The arms trade and the Middle East. *Polit. Q.* 44(1973), pp. 453-465

DUCLOS, L.J. L'épisode de Téhéran. *Rev. fr. de sci. pol.* 22(1972), pp. 1236-1255.

DUCLOS, L.J. Les problèmes pétroliers au Moyen Orient. *Orient* 49-50(1969), pp. 9-24

DUCRUET, J. Le jeu mondial des pétroliers. *Travaux et jours* 50(1974), pp. 51-91.

DURI, 'Abdal 'Aziz. Notes on taxation in early Islam. *JESHO* 17(1974), pp. 136-144.

EHRENKREUTZ, A.S. Another Orientalist's remarks concerning the Pirenne thesis. *JESHO* 15(1972), pp. 94-104.

FARMANFARMAIAN, Khodadad [*and others*]. How can the world afford OPEC oil? *Foreign affairs* 53(1975), pp. 201-222.

FARRUKH, Omar. Banking and insurance in relation to the Islamic concept of *riba*. *Internat. Islamic Conf.*, 1968, pp. 123-129.

FISCHER, D., GATELY, D., and KYLE, J.F. The prospects for OPEC: a critical survey of models of the world oil market. *J. development econ.* 2(1975), pp. 363-386.

GANNAGÉ, E. Communauté Européenne et espace Méditerranéen. *Ann. Fac. Droit Beyrouth* 74(1972), pp. 469-502.

GANNAGÉ, E. Coopération financière arabe et institutions régionales. *Ann. Fac. Droit Beyrouth* 77-8 (1973), pp. 91-141.

GEAHCHAN, M.L. Balance des paiements et région arabe. *Ann. Fac. Droit Beyrouth* 77-8 (1973), pp. 11-52.

IX HISTORY

GIBBONS, V. A bibliography of Middle Eastern statistical documents. *MESA bull.* 8ii (1974), pp. 20-34.

GIL, Moshe. The Rādhānite merchants and the land of Rādhān. *JESHO* 17(1974), pp. 299-328.

GOETZ, H. The Islâmic Orient, North Western India and the Silk Route to China in the Parzival of Wolfram von Eschenbach and other epics of the time. *Proc.27th Int.Cong.Or.1967* (1971), pp. 288-289.

GOITEIN, Shelomo D. El comercio mediterráneo anterior a las cruzadas: algunos hechos y problemas. *Estudios orientales* 3(1968), no. 8, pp. 207-223.

GOITEIN, S.D. Geniza documents on the transfer and inspection of houses. *ROMM* 13-14 (1973), pp. 401-412.

GOTTHEIL, F.M. An economic assessment of the military burden in the Middle East. *J. conflict resolution* 18(1974), pp. 502-513.

HAFFAR, Ahmad R. Economic development in Islam in Western scholarship. *Islam and the modern age* 6ii(1975), pp. 5-22; 6iii (1975), pp. 5-29.

HENKER, F. Arbeitnehmer aus arabischen Ländern in der Bundesrepublik Deutschland. *Z.f.Kulturaustausch* 24ii(1974), pp. 74-76.

HENKER, F. Gewerkschaften in arabischen Ländern. *Z.f.Kulturaustausch* 24ii(1974), pp. 29-35.

HENNEQUIN, G.P. Problèmes théoriques et pratiques de la monnaie antique et médiévale. *Ann.Islamologiques* 10(1972), pp. 1-51.

IBRAHIM, Saad E.M. Over-urbanization and under-urbanism: the case of the Arab world. *IJMES* 6(1975), pp. 29-45.

IDRIS, H.R. Contribution à l'étude de la vie économique en Occident musulman médiéval: glanes de données chiffrées. *ROMM* 15-16 (1973), pp. 75-87.

ISAEV, V.A. O znachenii vneshney torgovli dlya ekonomicheskogo razvitiya arabskikh stran. *NAA* 1975(6), pp. 121-129.

ISMAILOV, D. Sozdanie regional'nogo soyuza razvitiya i ego deyatel'nost'. *Strany Blizhnego i Srednego Vostoka: istoriya, ekonomica,* 1972, pp. 304-313.

ISSAWI, C. Economic history and the Middle East. *MESA Bull.* 8i(1974), pp. 1-8.

ISSAWI, C. Growth and structural change in the Middle East. *MEJ* 25(1971), pp. 309-324.

IVANOVA, I.P. K voprosu ob osnovnoy disproportzii v otraslevoy strukture ekonomiki na primere arabskikh stran. *Istoriya i ekonomika stran Arabskogo Vostoka,* 1973, pp. 124-139.

JACOBI, J. Antwort auf einige Fragen über die Rādānīya. *Islam* 52(1975), pp. 226-238.

JACOBI, J. Die Rādānīya. *Der Islam* 47 (1971), pp. 252-264.

JEFFREYS, M.D.W. Arab-introduced exotics in East Africa. *Afr.Stud.* 33(1974), pp. 55-57.

KALDY-NAGY, Gy. Dannye k istorii levantinskoy torgovli v nachale XVII stoletiya. (Beiträge zur Geschichte des Handels in der Levante zu Beginn des XVII Jahrhunderts.) *Fontes orientales... curavit A.S. Tveritinova* II, 1969, pp. 322-337.

KALYMON, B.A. Economic incentives in OPEC oil pricing policy. *J. development econ.* 2(1975), pp. 337-362.

KARAÇAM, Selçuk. A report on RCD-regional cooperation for development. *Dış politika* 1i(1971), pp. 156-162.

KARAUSH, A.A. Rol' sovremennov biologicheskoy nauki i meditziny v razreshenii nekotorykh sotzialno-ekonomicheskikh problem razvivayushchikhsya stran. *Strany Blizhnego i Srednego Vostoka: istoriya, ekonomica,* 1972, pp. 86-97.

KLYUCHNIKOV, K.F. Ekonomicheskie problemy obrazovaniya i podgotovki kadrov v stranakh Arabskogo Vostoka. *Istoriya i ekonomika stran Arabskogo Vostoka,* 1973, pp. 140-150.

KONDRAT'EVA, N.P. Rezul'taty i opyt deyatel'nosti mezhdunarodnykh kredito-finansovykh organizatziy v razvivayushchikhsya stranakh Azii. *Strany Blizhnego i Srednego Vostoka: istoriya, ekonomica,* 1972, pp. 320-334.

KRASSOWSKI, A. The Middle East Development Division. *J. admin. overseas* 14 (1975), pp. 4-16.

KÜCK, G. Genesis und Wesen arabischer Einheitsbestrebungen aus ökonomischer Sicht. *Mitt. Inst. Orientforschung* 17(1972), pp. 560-577.

LABIB, Subhi Y. Capitalism in medieval Islam. *J.econ.hist.* 29(1969), pp. 79-96.

LABROUSSE, H. L'ocean Indien sans le canal de Suez. *Point* 11(1972), pp. 3-13.

LANDAY, S. The ecology of Islamic cities: the case for the ethnocity. *Econ. geog.* 47 ii (supplement, 1971), pp. 303-313.

LEE, J.F.K. Tax considerations. *An introduction to business law in the Middle East,* ed. B. Russell, 1975, pp. 37-54.

LEVI, M. La C.E.E. et les pays de la Méditeranée. *Politique étrangère* 37(1972), pp. 801-820.

LEVY, W.J. Oil power. *Foreign aff.* 49(1971), pp. 652-668.

IX HISTORY

LEVY, W.J. Oil power. *Continuing issues in international politics*, ed. Y.H. Ferguson and W.F. Weiker, 1973, pp. 369-383.

LOI, S. Paesi arabi alla fiera di Bologna e prospettive di collaborazione per l'editoria italiana. *Levante* 22ii (1975), pp. 29-33.

MABRO, R., MONROE, E. Arab wealth from oil: problems of its investment. *Int. aff.* 50 (1974), pp. 15-27.

MABRO, R. OPEC after the oil revolution. *Millennium* 4(1975-6), pp. 191-199

MAHMUD AHMAD, Sh. Banking in Islam. *Internat. Islamic Conf.*, 1968, pp. 130-141.

MALLAKH, Ragaei El. Industrialization in the Middle East: obstacles and potential. *M.E.S.A. Bull.* 7iii(1973), pp. 28-46.

MANN, G. Die OPEC und die Auseinandersetzung mit dem Imperialismus. *Asien. Afrika. Latein-Amerika* 3(1975), pp. 603-620.

MANSOUR, Fawzi. Die Erdölpreise und die Krise des kapitalistischen Weltsystems. *Asien. Afrika. Latein-Amerika* 3(1975), pp. 421-428.

MASUD, M. Some reflection on the economic system of Islam. *Internat. Islamic Conf.*, 1968, pp. 96-105.

MATYUKHIN, I.S. Torgovo-ekonomicheskoe sotrudnichestvo Sovetskogo Soyuza s arabskimi stranami i ego rol' v razvitii ikh natzional'noy ekonomiki. *Istoriya i ekonomika stran Arabskogo Vostoka*, 1973, pp. 190-199.

MEJCHER, H. Die britische Erdölpolitik im Nahen Osten 1914-1956. *VSWG* 59(1972), pp. 350-377.

MEYER, A.J. Patterns of recent economic development in the Arab states. *The Arab Middle East and Muslim Africa*, ed. by T. Kerekes, 1961, pp. 95-103.

MODUGNO, G. La conferenza mondiale delle Nazioni Unite sulla alimentazione (Roma, 5-16 novembre 1974). *OM* 55(1975), pp. 54-61.

NAFFI, Hadi el-. Échanges commerciaux et région arabe. *Ann. Fac. Droit Beyrouth* 77-8 (1973), pp. 53-89.

NAFICY, Fatullāh. Developments in the oil industry in the year 1970. *Tahqiqāt e eqtesādi* 8(Nos. 23-4, 1971), pp. 53-69.

NASIR, Jamal. Practical, financial and legal considerations for companies doing business in Arab countries. *An introduction to business law in the Middle East*, ed. B. Russell, 1975, pp. 25-36.

NIEUWENHUIJZE, C.A.O. van. The importance of economic action in Islamic civilization. *Proc. 27th Int.Cong.Or.1967* (1971), p. 203.

NOURAIE, Fereshteh M. An analysis of Malkam Xān's economic ideas. *Tahqiqāt e eqtesādi* 8(no.22, 1971), pp. 114-122.

OWEN, E.R.J. The economic aspects of revolution in the Middle East. *Revolution in the Middle East*, ed. P.J. Vatikiotis, 1972, pp. 43-64.

PENROSE, E. The multinational oil corporations in the Middle East and the "oil crisis". *Mondes en développement* 5(1974), pp. 77-100.

PURINI, G.P. Petrodollari per l'Africa. *Levante* 22ii(1975), pp. 5-15.

RICHES, D. Some British connexions with the Levant. *Asian affairs* 61(N.S.5, 1974), pp. 165-175.

RIFAI, Taki. La crise pétrolière internationale (1970-1971): essai d'interpretation. *Rev. fr. de sci. pol.* 22(1972), pp. 1205-1236.

ROMAGNOLI, A. New construction technologies for Arab countries. *Levante* 22iii-iv(1975), pp. 56-70.

ROTHER, K. Ergebnisse und Probleme von Agrarreformen im Mittelmeerraum. *Erdkunde* 25(1971), pp. 292-298.

SANGAR, S.P. Export of Indian cloth to Africa and Middle East in the seventeenth century. *Proc.32 Ind.hist.cong.* 1970, vol. 2, pp. 126-130.

SAYIGH, Yusif A. Arab oil policies: self-interest versus international responsibility. *J. Palestine stud.* 4iii(1975), pp. 59-73.

SHINDY, Wagih. Arab oil, surplus funds and the international financial system: an Arab point of view. *Egypte contemp.* 66,no.359(1975), pp. 5-27.

SMART, Ian. Die Supermächte und der Nahe Osten. *Europa-Archiv* 29i(1974), pp. 9-21.

SMILYANSKAYA, I.M. Sistemy zemel'noy sobstvennosti i sotzial'naya stratifikatziya na Blizhnem Vostoke (pozdnee srednevekov'e). (Systems of land ownership and social stratification in the Near East, late medieval period.) *NAA* 1971(1), pp. 63-77.

SPILLMANN, G. En marge de la crise du pétrole. *L'Afrique et l'Asie modernes* 105(1975), pp. 36-55.

SPINKS, N. The practical aspects of doing business in the Middle East. *An introduction to business law in the Middle East*, ed. B. Russell, 1975, pp. 55-72.

TANAMLY, Abdel Moneim el. Merchant banking in the Middle East. *Eg. contemp.* 65(1974), pp. 439-452.

TAŞHAN, Seyfi. Oil. needs, crises, policies. *Dış politika* 3ii(1973), pp. 59-80.

TUMA, E.H. Population, food and agriculture in the Arab countries. *MEJ* 28(1974), pp. 381-395.

UDOVITCH, A.L. The "law merchant" in the medieval Islamic world. *Logic and classical Islamic culture*, ed. by G.E. von Grunebaum, 1970, pp. 117-130.

UDOVITCH, A.L. Reflections on the institutions of credits and banking in the medieval Islamic Near East. *SI* 41(1975), pp. 5-41.

ULE, W. Islam und Wirtschaft. *Der Islam* 47(1971), pp. 136-167.

VERNIÈRES, M. Disponibilités en main-d'oeuvre qualifiée et objectifs de développement. *Ann. de la Fac. de droit de Beyrouth* 73(1972), pp. 139-154.

VERNIÈRES, M. Emploi, main-d'oeuvre et objectifs d'industrialisation. *Ann. Fac. Droit Beyrouth* 74(1972), pp. 447-466.

WATSON, A.M. The Arab agricultural revolution and its diffusion, 700-1000. *J. econ.hist.* 34(1974), pp. 8-35.

WIRTH, E. Die orientalische Stadt. Ein Überblick aufgrund jüngerer Forschungen zur materiellen Kultur. *Saeculum* 26 (1975), pp. 45-94.

WIRTH, E. Zum Problem des Bazars (sūq, çarşı). Versuch einer Begriffsbestimmung und Theorie des traditionellen Wirtschaftszentrums der orientalisch-islamischen Stadt. *Islam* 51(1974), pp. 203-260.

YEGĀNEH, Mohammād, The Tehrān oil negotiations. *Tahqiqāt e eqtesādi* 8(Nos. 23-4, 1971), pp. 33-52.

YOUSSEF, Nadia H. Differential labor force participation of women in Latin American and Middle Eastern countries: the influence of family characteristics. *Social forces* 51(1972), pp. 135-153.

ZAIM, Issam el. Du dernier recours par les arabes à leur arme pétrolière. *Rev. alg.* 10(1973), pp. 781-794.

ZAIM, I. el-. L'hégemonie pétrolière étrangère et l'industrialisation pétrolière arabe. *Renaissance du monde arabe. Colloque interarabe de Louvain,* 1972, pp. 167-227.

ZAIM, Issam al-. Les implications industrielles et économiques des régimes pétroliers d'exploitation indirecte dans les Pays Arabes. *Rev. algêr. des sci. jur., econ. et pol.* 9(1972), pp. 431-470.

ZAIM, Issam el- Les implications industrielles et économiques des régimes pétroliers d'exploitation indirecte dans les pays Arabes (La souveraineté pétrolière et les contrats de concession, d'association et d'entreprise). *Eg. contemp.* 63(No. 349, 1972), pp. 133-180.

ZIAUL HAQ. Economic problems of the Muslim society of today. *Internat. Islamic Conf.*, 1968, pp. 106-110.

ZIAUL HAQUE. Metayage and tax-farming in the medieval Muslim society. *Islamic studies* 14(1975), pp. 219-237.

Agricultural co-operative development in the Middle East. *Year-book of agricultural co-operation* 1972, pp. 1-12.

La croissance économique et le niveau de qualification de la population active dans divers pays du Moyen-Orient. *Ann. de la Fac. de droit de Beyrouth* 73(1972), pp. 155-200.

Due grandi realizzazzioni della cooperazione economica italo-arabe. *Levante* 21i-ii (1974), pp. 22-23.

A look through industrial information, with special reference to food industries. Prepared by the Sudan Industrial Research and Consultancy Institute, Department of Documentation and Industrial Information, Khartoum. *Dokumentationsdienst Moderner Orient, Mitt.* 4i(1975), pp. 5-16.

Tavola rotonda italō-araba sui problemi dell'industrializzazione edilizia. *Levante* 22iii-iv(1975), pp. 5-12.

La XXX fiera del Mediterraneo ed il mondo arabo. *Levante* 22ii(1975), pp. 34-37.

See also I. b. 2. Talbi.

See also II. a. 1. Qureshi.

See also VII. a. Audroing.

See also VII. a. Seraydarian.

See also VIII. d. *General.* Noonan.

See also IX. a. Mantran.

See also IX. e. Bacharach.

See also IX. g. Zartman

See also IX. j. Breton.

See also IX. m. Grimaud.

See also X. a. Nadiradze.

See also X. b. Ehrenkreutz.

See also X. f. Spuler.

See also XXVIII. n. Mokrynin.

X EARLY HISTORY OF ISLAM. THE CALIPHATE

a PRE-ISLAMIC BACKGROUND

GARBINI, G. Les débuts de l'histoire dans la Péninsule arabe. *Actas IV congresso de estudos árabes e islâmicos* 1968(1971), pp. 499-504.

KHAN, Ahmad. The tanning cottage industry in Pre-Islamic Arabia. *J. Pakistan Hist. Soc.* 19(1971), pp. 85-100.

KISTER, M.J. Some reports concerning Mecca from Jāhiliyya to Islam. *JESHO* 15(1972), pp. 61-93.

KÖBERT, R. Ein Gassanidenschloss namens *al-barīṣ* im vorislamischen Damascus? *Orientalia* 43(1974), pp. 165-170.

RYCKMANS, J. Les inscriptions sud-arabes anciennes et les études arabes. *AION* 35 (N.S.25,1975), pp. 443-463.

SCHMUCKER, W. Die christliche Minderheit von Nağrān und die Problematik ihrer Beziehungen zum frühen Islam. *Studien zum Minderheitenproblem im Islam* I, 1973, pp. 183-281.

b GENERAL

ABEL, A. Roi des rois ou Khalife (du Prophète) de Dieu? *Atti dell'VIII Cong. int. stor. rel.* (1955), pp. 434-437.

BARBOUR, N. The expansion and settlement of the Arabs between 632 and 1100 and of the Scandinavians between 789 and 1250. *Ve Congrès International d'Arabisants et d'Islamisants. Actes.*, [1970?], pp. 89-96.

CAHEN, C. Y a-t-il eu des corporations professionnelles dans le monde musulman classique? *The Islamic city,* 1970, pp. 51-63.

CHEIRA, M.A. Le statut des pays de ʿAhd aux VIIe et VIIIe S. *Ann.Fac.Arts Ain Shams* 1(1951), pp. 43-53.

CONSTANTELOS, D.J. The Moslem conquests of the Near East as revealed in the Greek sources of the seventh and the eighth centuries. *Byzantion* 42(1972), pp. 325-357.

DŪRĪ, ʿAbdul ʿAzīz al-. The origins of iqṭāʿ in Islam. *Al-Abhath* 22i-ii(1969), pp. 3-22.

EHRENKREUTZ, A.S. Economic factors and the Caliphate to the tenth century. *Proc.27th Int.Cong.Or.1967* (1971), p. 204.

FORAND, P.G. The status of the land and inhabitants of the Sawād during the first two centuries of Islām. *JESHO* 14(1971), pp. 25-37.

HAMIDULLAH, Muhammad. Le chef de l'état musulman à l'époque du Prophète et des Caliphes. *Recueils Soc. Jean Bodin* 20 (1970), pp. 481-514.

HAMIDULLAH, Muhammad. General history of Islam. *Maj.al-Azhar* 46iv(1974), pp. 6-13.

IWASIÓW-PARDUS, B. Problem wladzy w okresie narodzin Islamu. *Przegl.or.* 90(1974), pp. 151-160.

KHOURY, R.G. Die Bedeutung der Handschrift Bad' al-halq wa-qiṣaṣ al-anbiya des Abū Rifā'a 'Umāra b. Watīma b. Mūsā b. al-Furāt al-Fārisī (gest. 289 H./902) für die Erforschung des Frühislams. *XVIII. Deutscher Orientalistentag 1972: Vorträge,* pp. 186-191.

KLEIN-FRANKE, F. Die Geschichte des frühen Islam in einer Schrift des Georgios Gemistos Pletho. *Byz. Z.* 65 (1972), pp. 1-8.

LEWIS, B. On the revolutions in early Islam. *SI* 32(1970), pp. 215-231.

NADIRADZE, L.I. Problemy instituta ikta v arabskom khalifate v sovetskoy istoriografii. *Istoriya i ekonomika stran Arabskogo Vostoka,* 1973, pp. 199-232.

PETRUSHEVSKIY, I.P. K istorii rabstva v khalifate VII-X vekov. (On the history of slavery in the Khalifate.) *NAA* 1971(3), pp. 60-71.

PIGULEVSKAYA, N.V. Vizantiya i Vostok. (Byzance et l'Orient.) *Pal.Sb.* 23(86, 1971), pp. 3-16.

PROZOROV, S.M. Iz istorii religiozno-politicheskoy ideologii v rannem khalifate. *Istoriya, kul'tura, yazyki narodov Vostoka* 1970, pp. 76-79.

RINGGREN, H. Some religious aspects of the Caliphate. *Atti dell'VIII Cong. int. stor. rel.* (1955), pp. 433-434.

SCANLON, G.T. Housing and sanitation: some aspects of medieval public service. *The Islamic city,* 1970, pp. 179-194.

See also III. a. 14 Forand.

See also V. m. l. Grabar.

X EARLY HISTORY

c MUHAMMAD AND HIS TIME

ABU-JABER, Faiz. The status of women in early Arab history. *Islam and the modern age* 4ii(1973), pp. 67-76.

AHMAD, Ziauddin. Financial policies of the Holy Prophet -- a case study of the distribution of ghanima in early Islam. *Islamic studies* 14(1975), pp. 9-25.

ALWAYE, Mohiaddin. The importance of the 'Hijrah'. *Maj.al-Azhar* 45i(1973), pp. 1-4.

ALWAYE, Mohiaddin. The truce of Hudeybiya and the conquest of Mecca. *Majallat al-Azhar* 45ix(1973), pp. 1-6.

ASWAR, A. Mohammad al-. Umar ibn el-Khattab. *Majallat al-Azhar* 47i(1975), pp. 11-16.

DARGAHI, Gholam Husain The shaping of Ḥizbullah or "Muḥammad's virtuous polity", A.D. 624-632. *IC* 45(1971), pp. 145-156.

GURAYA, Muhammad Yousuf. The concept of Sunnah: a historical study. *Islamic stud.* 11(1972), pp. 13-44.

HAMIDULLAH, Muhammad. Le chef de l'état musulman à l'époque du Prophète et des califes. *Recueils Soc. Jean Bodin* 20 (1970), pp. 481-502.

HAMIDULLAH, Muhammad. Le premier empire musulman du temps du Prophète et de ses trois successeurs. *Recueils Soc.Jean Bodin* 31(1973), pp. 509-532.

HILL, D.R. The role of the camel and the horse in the early Arab conquests. *War, technology and society in the Middle East*, ed. V.J. Parry and M.E. Yapp, 1975, pp. 32-43.

JUYNBOLL, G.H.A. The Qur'ān reciter on the battlefield and concomitant issues. *ZDMG* 125(1975), pp. 11-27.

KISTER, M.J. Maqām Ibrāhīm. A stone with an inscription. *Muséon* 84(1971), pp. 477-491.

MALLAH, Hashim al-. The constitution of al-Madina. *Adab al rāfidayn* 5(1974), pp. 3-11.

NOTH, A. Die literarisch überlieferten Verträge der Eroberungszeit als historische Quellen für die Behandlung der Unterworfenen Nicht-Muslims durch ihre neuen muslimischen Oberherren. *Studien zum Minderheitenproblem im Islam* I, 1973, pp. 282-314.

ROMANIDES, J.S. Islamic Universalism and the Constitution of Medina. Ποίημα Εὐγνώμον, τιμητικὸς τόμος ἐπὶ τῇ 40ετηρίδι συγγραφικῆς δράσεως καὶ τῇ 35ετηρίδι καθηγεσίας τοῦ Βασιλείου Μ. Βέλλα, Ἀθῆναι, 1969, σελ. 614-618

SIMON, R. Sur l'institution de la mu'ākhāh; entre le tribalisme et l'*umma*. *Acta Or. Acad. Sci. Hung.* 27(1973), pp. 333-343.

See also XXXVII. e. Paret

d ORTHODOX CALIPHS

ASWAR, A. Muhammad al-. Abu Bakr el-Siddiq. (Personages of Islam, 1.) *Maj. al-Azhar* 45ix(1974), pp. 5-8.

ASWAR, A. Muhammad al-. Aly ibn Abi Taleb. (Personages of Islam, 4.) *Maj. al-Azhar* 47v(1975), pp. 13-16.

ASWAR, Ahmed Muhammad. Uthman ibn Affan. (Personages of Islam, 3.) *Maj. al-Azhar* 47iv(1975), pp. 13-16.

DAMME, M. van. Het Kalifaat van ʿAlī volgens Dīnawarī. *Orientalia Gandensia* 1(1964), pp. 187-202.

FORAND, P. Early Muslim relations with Nubia. *Der Islam* 48 (1971), pp. 111-121.

HAMIDULLAH, Muhammad. Administration of justice under the early Caliphate: (Instructions of Caliph ʿUmar to Abū Mūsā al-Ashʿarī) (17 H). *J. Pakistan Hist. Soc.* 19(1971), pp. 1-50.

HAMIDULLAH, Muhammad. Constitutional problems in early Islam. *Islam Tetkikleri Enst. dergisi* 5(1973), pp. 15-35.

HINDS, M. The banners and battle cries of the Arabs at Siffin (657 AD). *al-Abhath* 24(1971), pp. 3-42.

HINDS, M. The murder of the Caliph ʿUthmân. *IJMES* 3(1972), pp. 450-469.

HINDS, M. The Siffīn arbitration agreement. *J. Semitic stud.* 17(1972), pp. 93-129.

HUSSAIN, M. Hadi. Umar b. Abdul Aziz: his place in muslim history. *Iqbal rev.* 15iii (1974), pp. 1-11.

JARRY, J. La conquete du Fayoum par les musulmans d'après le Futūḥ al-Bahnasā. *Ann.Islamologiques* 9(1970), pp. 9-19.

JUYNBOLL, G.H.A. The date of the great *fitna*. *Arabica* 20(1973), pp. 142-159.

NOTH, A. Der Charâkter der ersten grossen Sammlungen von Nachrichten zur frühen Kalifenzeit. *Der Islam* 47(1971), pp. 168-199.

See also X. c. Hamidullah.

e UMAYYADS

ʿABDUL BARI. Economic aspects of the Muslim state during Caliph Hishām (A.H. 105-125-A.D. 724-743). *IC* 46(1972), pp. 297-305.

X EARLY HISTORY

BARTHOLD, W.W. Caliph 'Umar II and the conflicting reports on his personality. *IQ* 15(1971), pp. 69-95.

BIRÓ, M.B. Marwān ibn Muhammad's Georgian campaign. *Acta Or. Hung.* 29(1975), pp. 289-299.

BOSWORTH, C.E. Raja Ibn Ḥaywa al-Kindī and the Umayyad Caliphs. *IQ* 16(1972), pp. 36-80.

BOSWORTH, Clifford Edmund. 'Ubaidallāh b. Abī Bakra and the "Army of Destruction" in Zābulistān (79/698). *Der Islam* 50(1973), pp. 268-283.

GABRIELI, F. Considerazioni sul califfato omayyade. *AION* 34(N.S.24, 1974), pp. 507-521.

GABRIELI, F. Considerationes sobre el Califato Omeya de Oriente. *al-Andalus* 39(1974), pp. 407-430.

NOTH, A. Zur Verhältnis von kalifaler Zentralgewalt und Provinzen in umayyadischer Zeit: die "Sulḥ" - "'Anwa" Trasitionen für Ägypten und den Iraq. *WI* N.S.14(1973), pp. 150-162.

TUCKER, W.F. Rebels and gnostics: al-Mugīra ibn Sa'īd and the Mugīriyya. *Arabica* 22(1975), pp. 33-47.

See also X. d. Juynboll.

See also XXVII. c. Hinds

f ABBASIDS

'ABDEL TAWAB, 'Abdel Rahman. Deux investitures du calife abbasside, al-Mustanǧid Billâh Abûl Muzaffar Yûsuf. *Annales islamol.* 11(1972), pp. 154-162.

'ABDUL JABBAR BEG, Muhammad. A contribution to the economic history of the Caliphate: a study of the cost of living and the economic status of artisans in Abbasid Iraq. *IQ* 16(1973), pp.140-167.

'ABDUL JABBAR BEG, Muhammad. The Mukārī: a group of transport workers in 'Abbasid Middle East. *J.Pak.Hist.Soc.* 23(1975), pp. 143-151.

'ABDUL JABBAR BEG, Muhammad. The 'serfs' of Islamic society under the 'Abbāsid regime. *IC* 49(1975), pp. 107-118.

ALĪ, Ṣāleḥ Aḥmad el-. A new version of Ibn al-Muṭarrif's list of revenues in the early times of Hārūn al-Rashīd. *JESHO* 14(1971), pp. 303-310

ARIOLI, A. La rivolta di Abū Sarāya: appunti per una tipologia del leader islamico. *Ann. Fac.Ling.Lett.stran.Ca' Foscari* 5(1974), pp. 189-197.

ARIOLI, A. La rivolta di Abū Sarāya: appunti per una tipologia del leader islamico. *Ann. Fac.Ling.Lett.stran.Ca' Foscari* 5(1974), pp. 189-197.

BARNARD, L.W. Byzantium and Islam. The interaction of two worlds in the iconoclastic era. *Byzantinoslavica* 26(1975), pp. 25-37.

BENCHEIKH, J.E. Un outrageur politique au IIIe/IXe siècle. Ibn Bassām al-'Abartā'ī (m. vers 302 h.). *Arabica* 20(1973), pp. 261-291.

BOSWORTH, C.E. Barbarian invasions: the coming of the Turks into the Islamic world. *Islamic civilization,* 1973, pp. 1-16.

BOSWORTH, C.E. Sanawbarī's elegy on the pilgrims slain in the Carmathian attack on Mecca (317/930): a literary-historical study. *Arabica* 19(1972), pp. 222-239.

CAHEN, C. Nomades et sédentaires dans le monde musulman du milieu du Moyen Age. *Islamic civilization,* 1973, pp. 93-104.

CHABBI, J. 'Abd al- Ḳādir al-Djīlānī, personnage historique. *SI* 38(1973), pp. 75-106.

DUNLOP, D.M. A diplomatic exchange between al-Ma'mūn and an Indian king. *Medieval and Middle Eastern studies ... A.S. Atiya* 1972, pp. 133-143.

ELISSÉEFF, N. Un document contemporain de Nūr ad-Dīn: sa notice biographique par Ibn 'Asākir. *BEO* 25(1972), pp. 106-140.

FORSTNER, M. Sīstān während des Kalifats des Abbasiden al-Musta'īn (248/862-252/866) nach dem *Tārīḫ-i Sīstān.* *Der Islam* 48 (1971), pp. 77-89.

GOITEIN, S.D. Changes in the Middle East 950-1150 as illustrated by the Documents of the Cairo Geniza. *Islamic civilization,* 1973, pp. 17-32.

HAIRI, Abdulhadi. Naṣīr al-Dīn Ṭusī. His alleged role in the fall of Baghdad. *Ve Congrès International d'Arabisants et d'Islamisants. Actes.,* [1970?], pp. 255-266.

HARTMANN, A. La conception gouvernementale du calife an-Nāṣir li-Dīn Allāh. *Orientalia suecana* 22(1973), pp. 52-61.

HARTMANN, A. Türken in Bagdad zur Zeit der späten 'Abbāsiden am Beispiel der Herrschaft an-Nāṣir li-Dīn Allāhs (1180-1225). *Islam* 51(1974), pp. 282-297.

IDRIS, H.R. L'Occident musulman à l'avènement des 'Abbāsides, d'après le chroniqueur zīrīde al-Raqīq. *REI* 39(1971), pp. 209-291.

KAABI, Mongi. Les origines Tāhirides dans la da'wa 'abbāside. *Arabica* 19(1972), pp. 145-164.

LAOUST, H. Les agitations religieuses à Baghdād aux IVe et Ve siècles de l'Hégire. *Islamic civilization,* 1973, pp. 169-185.

MAKDISI, G. The Sunnī revival. *Islamic civilization,* 1973, pp. 155-168.

OMAR, Farouk. The nature of the Iranian revolts in the early 'Abbāsid period. *IC* 48 (1974), pp. 1-9.

over

X EARLY HISTORY

OMAR, Farouk. Some aspects of the 'Abbāsid-Ḥusaynid relations during the early 'Abbāsid period 132-193 A.H./750-809 A.D. *Arabica* 22(1975), pp. 170-179.

OMAR, Farouk. Some observations on the reign of the 'Abbāsid Caliph al-Mahdī 158/775-169/785. *Arabica* 21(1974), pp. 139-150.

OMAR, Farouk. Some observations on the reign of the Abbasid Caliph al-Mahdi 158/775-169/785. *Sumer* 30(1974), pp. 195-203.

POPOVIC, A. Encore quelques détails autour du problème des Zanj. *Actas IV congresso de estudos árabes e islâmicos* 1968(1971), pp. 367-371

SKALANEK, B. Est-ce que le calif Harun ar-Rashid avait écrit à Hamza al-Kharidji de Sistan? *Yād-nāme-ye Irāni-ye Minorsky*, 1969, pp. 190-196.

SPULER, B. Trade in Eastern Islamic countries (early period). *Actas IV congresso de estudos árabes e islâmicos* 1968(1971), pp. 487-496.

STRIKA, V. Il califfato 'abbaside nel *Dīwān* di Ibn al-Mu'tazz. *Ann.Fac.Ling.Lett.stran. Ca' Foscari* 5(1974), pp. 19-34.

STROHMAIER, G. Abu l-'Abbās - der Elefant Karls des Grossen. *Mitt.Inst.Orientforschung* 17(1971-72), pp. 365-368.

TRITTON, A.S. Sketches of life under the Caliphs (III). *MW* 62(1972), pp. 137-147.

See also V. m. 2. Esin.

XI NORTH AFRICA: GEOGRAPHY

a GENERAL

BEAUDET, G., LE COZ, J. Aspects de la recherche géographique en Afrique du Nord. *Annuaire Afrique du Nord* 12(1973), pp. 1013-1030.

CASTEVERT, Marie-Claire, CASTEVERT, Claude. Premier bilan des recherches géographiques au Magreb. *Annales Algériennes de Geographie* 6(1968), pp. 44-49.

CERBELLA, G. La primavera e le cicogne nel Nordafrica e nel Levante. *Levante* 18, pp. 47-52.

GIESSNER, K., STUCKMANN, G. Das Afrika-Kartenwerk: die Serie "Östlicher Maghreb". *Afrika Spectrum* 3/70, pp. 52-57.

GROVE, A.T. Climatic changes in Africa in the last 20,000 years. *Ann. Algér. de géog.* Num.spec., 1972, pp. 73-91.

HÖLLER, E. Der Seeweg Nordwestafrika: eine laderaummeteorologische Gefahrenzone *Afrika Spectrum* 1973, (2), pp. 227-234.

LAWLESS, R.I. The concept of *tell* and *sahara* in the Maghreb: a reappraisal. *Inst. Brit. Geographers. Trans.* 57(1972), pp. 125-137

PLANHOL, X. de. Pour une géographie viticole du monde musulman. *Actes Colloque géog. agraire,* 1971, pp. 147-151.

PONCET, J. Les problèmes de l'environnement méditerranéen. *ROMM* 15-16(1973), pp. 257-267.

SCHEMAINDA, R. Über einige Besonderheiten im ozeanologischen Gepräge der nordwestafrikanischen Auftriebswasserregion. *PGM* 118 (1974), pp. 95-103.

VANACKER, Cl. Géographie économique de l'Afrique du Nord selon les auteurs arabes, du IXe siècle au milieu du XIIe siècle. *Annales ESC* 28(1973), pp. 659-680.

VYCICHL, W. Augila: Studien zur nordafrikanischen Toponymie. *Muséon,* 86(1973), pp. 175-178.

ZAGÓRSKI, B.R. La toponymie du nord-ouest de l'Afrique à l'époque pré-coloniale. *Africana bull.* 20(1974), pp. 109-119.

b MOROCCO

ADAM, A. Les Berbères à Casablanca. *ROMM* 12(1972), pp. 23-44.

ANDRE, A. et GHARBAOUI, A. el. Aspects de la morphologie littorale de la Péninsule de Tanger. *Rev. géog. Maroc* 23-24(1973), pp. 125-149.

BARATHON, J.J. Sédimentation néogène, néotectonique et évolution récente du bassin de Kebdani et de ses bordures. *RGM* 22(1972), pp. 61-74.

BEAUDET, G. Le Quaternaire marocain: état des études. *RGM* 20(1971), pp. 3-56

BLAIKIE, P.M. The spatial structure of information networks and innovative behaviour in the Ziz valley, Southern Morocco. *Geografiska annaler* 55B(1973), pp. 83-105.

XI NORTH AFRICA: GEOGRAPHY

BLEUCHOT, H. Une ville minière marocaine: Khouribga. *ROMM* 6(1969), pp. 29-51.

BOUQUEREL, J. Le chemin de fer au Maroc et son rôle dans le développement économique du pays. *Cahiers d'Outre-Mer* 28(no.111,1975), pp. 218-251.

BOUQUEREL, J. Les investissements industriels au Maroc: aspects géographiques. *RGM* 20(1971), pp. 57-68

CALVET, Cl. Le climat solaire de Casablanca. *Rev. géog. Maroc* 23-24 (1973), pp. 87-94.

CALVET, C. Variation séculaire et distribution des précipitations au Maroc. *RGM* 21(1972), pp. 79-84.

CHARVET, J.-P. La plaine des Triffa: étude d'une région en développement (1). *RGM* 21(1972), pp. 3-29

COUVREUR-LARAÏCHI, F. Les précipitations dans quelques stations du littoral de la mer d'Alboran. *RGM* 21(1972), pp. 85-103.

DELANNOY, H. Aspects du climat de la région de Marrakech. *RGM* 20(1971), pp. 69-106

DUCHAC, R. Propositions pour une recherche sur le développement de Khouribga. *ROMM* 7(1970), pp. 49-69.

EHRIG, F.R. Die Arganie. Charakter, Ökologie und wirtschaftliche Bedeutung eines Tertiärreliktes in Marokko. *PGM* 118(1974), pp. 117-125.

FAY, G. Problèmes d'aménagement à Kénitra. *RGM* 18(1970), pp. 47-58.

FLOURIOT, J. Le périmètre agricole du Loukkos. *RGM* 21(1972), pp. 31-41.

FOSSET, R. Les caractères démographiques et géographiques de la population du Maroc en 1971. *Maghreb-Machrek* 57(1973), pp. 30-38.

FOSSET, R. L'évolution de la propriété en Chapuia de 1962 à 1969. *Actes Colloque géog. agraire*, 1971, pp. 23-26.

HAMMOUDI, A. L'évolution de l'habitat dans la vallée du Draa. *RGM* 18(1970), pp. 33-45.

LAGDIM, M.B. La tannerie traditionnelle à Marrakech. *RGM* 18(1970), pp. 20-32.

LAOUINA, A.E. Observations géomorphologiques dans la région du Moyen Sebou, en amont de Fès. *Rev. géog. Maroc* 23-24 (1973), pp. 95-123.

LAWLESS, R.I. L'évolution de peuplement, de l'habitat et des paysages agraires du Maghreb. *Ann. de geog.* 81(no.446, 1972), pp. 451-464.

LECOMPTE, M. Aperçu sur la végétation d'altitude dans le Rif occidental calcaire (massif de Talassemtane). *Rev. géog. Maroc* 23-24(1973), pp. 79-86.

MANDLEUR, A. Croissance et urbanisation de Marrakech. *RGM* 22(1972), pp. 31-60.

MITCHELL, C.W. and WILLIMOTT, S.G. Dayas of the Moroccan Sahara and other arid regions. *Geog. J.* 140(1974), pp. 441-453.

OLIVA, P. Aspects et problèmes géomorphologiques de l'Anti-Atlas occidental. *RGM* 21(1972), pp. 43-78.

PASCON, P. Théorie générale de la distribution des eaux et de l'occupation des terres dans le Haouz de Marrakech. *RGM* 18(1970). pp. 3-19.

RISER, J. Le barrage Mansour Eddahbi et les aménagements agricoles de la vallée du Dra Moyen. *Rev. géog. Maroc* 23-24 (1973), pp. 167-177.

ROCHE, J. La grotte de Taforalt. *Bull. de la Soc. d'hist.du Maroc* 3(1970-1), pp. 7-14

ROSENBERGER, B. Les anciennes exploitations minières et les anciens centres métallurgiques du Maroc. *RGM* 18(1970), pp. 59-102.

SCHMITZ, H. Bildung und Wandel zentralörtlicher Systeme in Nord-Marokko. *Erdkunde* 27(1973), pp. 120-131.

SEBILLOTTE, M. Les cultures de céréales en sec dans le Maroc oriental. *Rev. géog. Maroc* 23-24(1973), pp. 51-77.

WEISROCK, A. Introduction à l'étude du Pléistocène dans la région du Moyen Tensift (SW du Maroc). *Rev. géog. Maroc* 23-24(1973), pp. 151-166.

c ALGERIA

ACHENBACH, H. Römische und gegenwärtige Formen der Wassernutzung im Sahara-Vorland des Aurès (Algerien). *Die Erde* 104(1973), pp. 157-175.

AINAD-TABET. Mise au point sur ... les activités portuaires d'Alger et d'Oran comparées. *Annales Algériennes de Geographie* 6(1968), pp. 31-35.

ARNOLD, A. Das algerische Eisenbahnnetz. *Die Erde* 104(1973), pp. 66-74.

BARDINET, B. Cartographie statistique et organisation de l'espace en Algérie. *Tiers-monde* 12(1971), pp. 369-373.

BAYLE-OTTENHEIM, J. Les ressources non énergétiques du sous-sol maghrébin. *Maghreb-Machrek* 56(1973), pp. 22-29.

BOUMAZA, Nadir. Un domaine autogéré dans le Sersou: "Chebbah Mohamed" (Daïra de Tissemsilt). *Ann.algériennes de géog.* 4(no. 8, 1969), pp. 123-128.

BRULE, J.C. Une coopérative d'anciens moudjahidine dans le bassin de Djidjelli: "Khelalef Mohamed Tahar". *Ann.algériennes de géog.* 4(no. 8, 1969), pp. 43-49.

XI NORTH AFRICA: GEOGRAPHY

BRULE, J.C., COTE, M. et NESSON, C. Les palmeraies de l'Oued Righ. *Ann.algériennes de geog.* 5(no. 9, 1970), pp. 93-106.

BRUN, Fr. La sociéte rurale "pied-noir" en Algérie et dans le Midi Méditerranéen. *Actes Colloque géog. agraire,* 1971, pp. 49-52.

CASABO-BERNA, Suzel, Un groupe de domaines socialistes maraîchers: les domaines d'Aïn Taya. *Ann.algériennes de géog.* 4(no. 8, 1969), pp. 89-105.

CASTEVERT, C. et COTE, M. Hassi-Messaoud. *Ann.algériennes de geog.* 5(no. 9, 1970), pp. 107-116.

CASTEVERT, C. Un domaine autogéré de la région d'Annaba: le domaine "Boucetta Ali". *Ann.algériennes de géog.* 4(no. 8, 1969), pp. 21-41.

COTE, M. Un bel exemple de reconversion du vignoble: le domaine "Bouglouf Braiek" (Bassin de Skikda). *Ann.algériennes de géog.* 4(no. 8, 1969), pp. 73-88.

COTE, M. Un domaine céréalier de 3000 hectares dans le Sétifois: "Rouba Tayeb". *Ann.algériennes de géog.* 4(no. 8, 1969), pp. 129-147.

GRANGAUD, Mme. Les activités portuaires comparées de Skikda et d'Annaba. *Annales Algériennes de Geographie* 6(1968), pp. 36-39.

ISNARD, Hildebert. Reflexions sur une carte. *Annales Algériennes de Geographie* 6(1968), pp. 40-43.

ISNARD, H. Les structures de l'agriculture privée en Algérie. *Actes Colloque géog. agraire,* 1971, pp. 61-73.

JOSSE, R. Problèmes sahariens: recherches géographiques dans la Saoura. *Ann.algériennes de geog.* 5(no. 9, 1970), pp. 45-92.

LENORMAND, P. Un domaine viticole de l'Oranie: le domaine "Si Brahim". *Ann. algériennes de géog.* 4(no. 8, 1969), pp. 51-71.

MUTIN, G. Un domaine intensif de la Mitidja: le domaine 113 à Oued el Alleug. *Ann.algériennes de géog.* 4(no. 8, 1969), pp. 7-19.

MUTIN, G. Le morcellement foncier en terre socialiste: quelques exemples en Mitidja. *Ann.algériennes de géog.* 4 (no. 8, 1969), pp. 165-168.

NESSON, C. Un domaine autogéré au Sahara: le domaine "Hamlaoui Brahim" à Ourir. *Ann.algériennes de géog.* 4(no. 8, 1969), pp. 149-163.

PÉCHOUX, P.Y. Mostaganem, ou la mutation d'une région coloniale en Algérie. *Ann. géog.* 84,no.466(1975), pp. 699-713.

SARI, Djilali. Un domaine de la vallée du Chélif: le domaine "Sidi Oqba" (El Asnam). *Ann.algériennes de géog.* 4(no. 8, 1969), pp. 107-121.

SARI, D.J. Université d'Alger - La récupération et la valorisation des hydrocarbures par l'Etat Algérien. *Ann. Algér. de géog.* Num.spec., 1972, pp. 209-237.

TAIEB, Messaoud. La structure urbaine d'Alger. *Ann. de géogr.* 80 (1971), pp. 33-44.

TEULIÈRES, R. Le versant occidental du massif de la Bouzaréa-Baïnem. Les sols rouges sur micaschistes et gneiss. *Ann. algériennes de geog.* 5(no. 9, 1970), pp. 5-43.

TOMAS, F. Les débuts d'un périmètre irrigué: le domaine Maïz Bachir (plaine d'Annaba). *Ann.algériennes de géog.* 4(no. 8, 1969), pp. 169-172.

WAGNER, H.G. Siedlungsgefüge im südlichen Ostalgerien (Nememcha). *Erdkunde* 25(1971), pp. 118-135.

Essai de synthèse sur les exploitations agricoles socialistes. *Ann.algériennes de géog.* 4(no. 8, 1969), pp. 173-179.

d TUNISIA

AOUANI, Muhammed el. A la recherche des influences andalouses dans les campagnes tunisiennes: essai de mise au point. *Recueil d'études sur les moriscos andalous en Tunisie,* préparé par M. de Epalza et R. Petit, 1973, pp. 374-377.

BONNENFANT, P.; LANDY R. Gammouda: essor d'un centre urbain dans la steppe tunisienne. *IBLA* 35(no.130, 1972), pp. 305-344.

DOUIB, Abdelmajid. La région de Zarzis - II. Contact européen et exploitation du sol de 1881 à 1959. *CT* 20(nos.79-80, 1972), pp. 171-178.

DUBOIS, R.E. Un problème de développement urbain: le Kef (Tunisie). *Cah. d'Outre-Mer* 26(1973), pp. 129-149.

KASSAB, Ahmed. L'evolution d'un village "andalous": Testour. *Recueil d'études sur les moriscos andalous en Tunisie,* préparé par M. de Epalza et R. Petit, 1973, pp. 359-368.

MIOSSEC, A. Les pluies exceptionelles de mars 1973 en Tunisie. *Bull.Assoc.Géog. Franç.* 427-8(1975), pp. 279-288.

MONCHICOURT, Ch. La région de Tunis. Réimpression. *CT* 22(nos.87-88(1974), pp. 199-230.

PONCET, J. Les structures agraires tunisiennes après l'expérience des "unités coopératives de production". *Actes Colloque géog. agraire,* 1971, pp. 167-169.

SALVATORI, S. La felice ossessione delle oasi tunisine. *Levante* 19iv(1972), pp. 26-37.

XI NORTH AFRICA: GEOGRAPHY

SETHOM, Hafedh. L'apport andalous à la civilisation rurale de la presqu'île du Cap Bon. *Recueil d'études sur les moriscos andalous en Tunisie*, préparé par M. de Epalza et R. Petit, 1973, pp. 369-373.

STEPHENSON, D.E. Specialized labor migration in Tunisia: preliminary conclusions. *Ann. Algér. de géog.* Num.spec., 1972, pp. 59-72.

e LIBYA

ALLAN, J.A. British economic, geographical, sociological and related studies in Libya 1943-1971. *Ann. Rep. Soc. Libyan Studies* 2(1970-71), pp. 12-18.

ALLAN, J.A. The end of the first phase at Kufrah: expectations and achievements. *Soc. Libyan Stud. Ann. report* 6(1974-5), pp. 33-36.

BARTH, H.K. Bericht über die First Geographical Conference of Libya "The geography of Libya", University of Libya, Benghazi. *Erdkunde* 29(1975), pp. 150-151.

BLAKE, G.H. The form and function of Misratah's commercial centre. *Bull. Fac. Arts, Univ. Libya* 2(1968), pp. 9-40.

BROGAN, O. Round and about Misurata. *Soc. Libyan Stud. Ann. report* 6(1974-5), pp. 49-58.

BURU, Mukhtar. Soil analysis and its relation to land use in El-Marj plain, Cyrenaica. *Bull. Fac. Arts, Univ. Libya* 2(1968), pp. 41-70.

JOHNSON, D.L. Ecological and historical factors in the pastoral nomadism of Eastern Cyrenaïca. *Ann. Algér. de géog.* Num.spec., 1972, pp. 130-140.

McLACHLAN, K.S. Aspects of agriculture and agricultural settlement in Western Tripolitania (Libya). *Ann. Algér. de géog.* Num. spec., 1972, pp. 141-155.

McLACHLAN, K. Landed property and economic change in Tripolitania. *Bull. Fac. Arts, Univ. Libya* 2(1968), pp. 85-100.

PLANHOL, X. de. Elements ottomans dans la physionomie géographique de la Cyrénaique. *Bull.Assoc.Géog.Franç.* 429-30(1975), pp. 353-363.

SPEETZEN, H. Notes on the Tauorga project. *Soc. Libyan Stud. Ann. report* 5(1973-4), pp. 12-14.

f SAHARA

ATTIA, H.; ROUISSI, M. Structures agraires et développement dans le Sud Tunisien. *Ann. Algér. de géog.* Num.spec., 1972, pp. 15-34.

BERNUS, E. Les palmeraies de l'Aïr. *ROMM* 11(1972), pp. 37-50.

BERNUS, S. Recherches sur les centres urbains d'Agadez et d'In Gall. *ROMM* 11(1972), pp. 51-56.

BLAKE, G.H. International tourism in the northern Sahara: present state and future prospects. *Ann. Algér. de géog.* Num.spec., 1972, pp. 104-112

BLAKE, G.H. Libya and the Arab world; a geographical view. *Bull.Fac.Arts Libya* 4 (1972), pp. 9-22

CHAVENTRÉ, A. Méthode graphique de représentation des généalogies. *ROMM* 11(1972), pp. 59-65.

CORDERO TORRES, J.M. Marruecos y el Sahara español. *Rev. de polit. int.* 122(1972), pp. 233-234.

DRESCH, J. "Déserts" comparés: Sahara-Australie. *Bull.Assoc.Géog.Franç.* 424-5 (1975), pp. 129-133.

ESTORGES, P.; MAHROÛR, M.; DAGORNE, A.; AUMASSIP, G. Remarques morphologiques sur les sebkhas de la région de Ouargla. *Ann. Algér. de géog.* Num.spec., 1972, pp. 204-208.

MAHROUR, M. Présentation générale du Sahara algérien: l'occupation du sol - la répartition de la population. *Ann. Algér. de géog.* Num.spec., 1972, pp. 6-14.

MAINGUET, M. Étude comparée des ergs, à l'échelle continentale (Sahara et déserts d'Australie). *Bull.Assoc.Géog.Franç.* 424-5(1975), pp. 135-140.

MITCHELL, C.W. Applications of the land system method to natural resource surveys in the Moroccan Sahara. *Ann. Algér. de géog.* Num.spec., 1972, pp. 113-129.

MONÈS, Hussain. Las rutas de comercio en el Sahara africano segun los escritores árabes. *Actas IV congresso de estudos árabes e islâmicos* 1968(1971). pp. 505-522.

NESSON, Claude. Densité des puits et niveaux piézométriques dans les palmeraies de l'Oued Righ. *Ann. Algér. de géog.* Num.spec., 1972, pp. 181-203.

ROUVILLOIS-BRICOL, M. Les transformations de l'oasis de Ouargla: aspects et problèmes. *Ann. Algér. de géog.* Num.spec., 1972, pp. 45-58.

TAIEB, M. Le périmètre d'irrigation de Sidi Okba: problèmes et perspectives d'aménagement. *Ann. Algér. de géog.* Num.spec., 1972, pp. 35-44.

THORP, M.B. Some aspects of the geomorphology of the Air Mountains, Southern Sahara. *Trans. Inst. Brit. Geographers* 47 (1969), pp. 25-46.

WILLIMOTT, S.G. The Hassan Addakhil barrage project: its impact on the irrigation system of the Ziz valley in the Moroccan Sahara. *Ann. Algér. de géog.* Num.spec., 1972, pp. 92-103.

XII NORTH AFRICA: ETHNOLOGY, SOCIOLOGY

a GENERAL

ALLMEN-JORAY, M. et F. von. Attitudes concernant la taille de la famille et la régulation des naissances. *Population (Paris)* 26, num. spéc. (mars 1971), pp. 47-78.

ATTAL, R. Index aux "Proverbes arabes de l'Algérie et du Maghreb" de M. Ben Cheneb. *Folklore Research Center studies* 3(1972), pp. 9-65.

BAUMER, M.C., REY, P.A. Pastorialisme, aménagement, cartographie de la végétation et développement intégral harmonisé dans les régions circum-sahariennes. *Genève-Afrique* 13(1974), pp. 22-40

BENNOUNE, Mahfoud. The Maghribin migrant workers in France. *Race & class* 17i(1975), pp. 39-56.

BRAHIMI, D. Les voyageurs naturalistes du XVIIIe siècle aux origines de l'ethnographie maghrebine. *CT* 19i-ii(1971), pp. 67-86.

BRANDL, L. Early Christianity in Africa: North Africa, the Sahara, the Sudan, Central and East Africa. A contribution to ethnohistory. *Présence africaine* 96 (1975), pp. 467-495.

BRETEAU, C.H., GALLEY, M. Littérature populaire et société. *Ann.Afr.nord* 12(1973), pp. 265-271.

CAMPS, G. Recherches sur les origines des cultivateurs noirs du Sahara. *ROMM* 7(1970), pp. 35-45.

CHARNAY, J-P. De la grande maison au couple moderne: Interférences entre Droit, Psychologie et Economie dans l'évolution de la famille maghrébine. *Rev.alger.des sci.jur. econ.pol.* 11iii(1974), pp. 57-83.

CHELHOD, J. La civilisation des Bédouins. *Pount* 1971, 11, pp. 15-20.

COATALEN, P. Réflexions sur la société chleuh. *Annales maroc.de sociol.* 1969, pp. 27-31.

CORCOS, D. Réflexions sur l'onomastique judéo-nord-africaine. *Folklore Research Center stud.* 1(1970), pp. 1-27.

DOUEDAR, Maryse. Libération du mariage. *Rev.alger.des sci.jur.econ.pol.* 11iii(1974), pp. 133-147.

GAST, M. Persistance protohistorique dans l'alimentation des populations du Sahara central. *ROMM* 6(1969), pp. 89-93.

GELLNER, E. Système tribal et changement social en Afrique du Nord. *Annales maroc. sociol.* 1969, pp. 3-19.

GOLDBERG, H.E. The social context of North African Jewish patronyms. *Folklore Research Center studies* 3(1972), pp. 245-257.

GRIMAUD, N. Les juifs d'Afrique du Nord, leur situation et leurs problèmes en 1968. *II.Cong.int.ét.nord-afr.* 1970, pp. 273-296.

IDRIS, H.R. Des prémices de la symbiose arabo-berbère. *Actes I. Cong. et. cult. mediterr. d'infl. arabo-berb.*, 1973, pp. 382-393.

KHATIBI, A. Documents sur le colloque de sociologie maghrebine (Rabat, Juin 1967). *Annales maroc. sociol.* 1969, pp. 147-178.

LEFEVRE-WITIER, P. Quelques aspects de l'anthropobiologie au Sahara. *ROMM* 12(1972), pp. 63-68.

LE HOUEROU, H.N. La désertisation du Sahara septentrional et des steppes limitrophes (Libye, Tunisie, Algérie). *Annales Algériennes de Geographie* 6(1968), pp. 5-30.

LE TOURNEAU, R. Position sociale et culturelle de l'élite dirigeante d'Afrique du Nord. *Cah.de ling.d'orientalisme et de slavistique* 1-2(1973), pp. 7-27.

MARTHELOT, P. Agression démographique et développement urbain. Variantes sur le thème: villeneuves et médinas. *II.Cong. int.ét.nord-afr.* 1970, pp. 297-309.

PERINBAM, B.M. Trade and society in the western Sahara and the western Sudan: an overview. *Bull. IFAN* 34(1972), pp. 778-801.

PILLEBOUE, M. Les agriculteurs rapatriés d'Afrique du Nord. L'exemple de l'Indre. *Etudes rurales* 47(1972), pp. 73-97.

PLANHOL, X. de. Regional diversification and social structure in North Africa and the Islamic Middle East: a geographic approach. *Rural politics and social change in the Middle East,* ed. by R. Antoun and I. Harik, 1972, pp. 103-117.

XII NORTH AFRICA: ETHNOLOGY

SAADA, L. Un problème de socio-sémiotique: les intersections culturelles. *Actes I. Cong. et. cult. mediterr. d'infl. arabo-berb.*, 1973, pp. 453-464.

SAFWAD, Osman. Contradiction entre situation de fait et situation de Droit concernant la femme dans les pays arabes. *Rev.alger.des sci.jur.econ.pol.* 11iii(1974), pp. 113-117.

SHAFEI, A.M.N. El-. Administrative and other problems of data collection in North African and West Asian Arabic-speaking countries. *Int.population conf.* London, 1969, I, pp. 286-293.

SIMON, G. and NOIN, D. La migration maghrébine vers l'Europe. *Cah. d'outre mer* 25(no. 99, 1972), pp. 241-276.

TIBI, Bassam. Armeé und sozialer Wandel in Nordafrika. *Afrika Spectrum* 1971(no. 1), pp. 34-55.

VATIN, J.C. Questions culturelles et questions à la culture. *Ann.Afr.nord* 12(1973), pp. 3-16.

See also XIII. a. Lacoste.

See also XVI. a. Adam.

See also XXXVII. 1. Yetiv.

b BERBERS

ADAM, A. Berber migrants in Casablanca. *Arabs and Berbers*, ed. E. Gellner and C. Micaud, 1973, pp. 325-343.

ADAM, A. Quelques constantes dans les processus d'acculturation chez les Berbères du Maghreb. *Actes I. Cong. et. cult. mediterr. d'infl. arabo-berb.*, 1973, pp. 439-444.

ALPORT, E.A. The Mzab. *Arabs and Berbers*, ed. E. Gellner and C. Micaud, 1973, pp. 141-152.

ARNAUD, J. Le mythe tribal chez Kateb Yacine. *Actes I. Cong. et. cult. mediterr. d'infl. arabo-berb.*, 1973, pp. 285-292.

BARBOUR, N. The Berbers in al-Andalus. *Actes I. Cong. et. cult. mediterr. d'infl. arabo-berb.*, 1973, pp. 170-174.

BERNATZIK, E. Siedeln und Wohnen bei den Berbern im Hohen Atlas (Marokko). *Wiener ethnohist. Blätter* 8(1974), pp. 59-99.

BOURDIEU, P. La Maison kabyle ou le monde renversé. *Échanges et communications. Mélanges C. Lévi-Strauss* II, 1970, pp. 739-758.

BURKE III, E. The image of the Moroccan state in French ethnological literature: a new look at the origin of Lyautey's Berber policy. *Arabs and Berbers*, ed. E. Gellner and C. Micaud, 1973, pp. 175-199.

CAMPS, G. Pour une encyclopédie berbère. *Actes I. Cong. et. cult. mediterr. d'infl. arabo-berb.*, 1973, pp. 475-477.

CAMPS-FABRER, H. L origine des fibules berbères d'Afrique du Nord. *ROMM* 13-14 (1973), pp. 217-230.

COATALEN, P. Ethnologie barbare *Annales maroc.de sociol.* 1970, pp. 3-10.

CORAM, A. Note on the role of the Berbers in the early days of Moroccan independence. *Arabs and Berbers*, ed. E. Gellner and C. Micaud, 1973, pp. 269-276.

DUCLOS, L.J. The Berbers and the rise of Moroccan nationalism. *Arabs and Berbers*, ed. E. Gellner and C. Micaud, 1973, pp. 217-229.

DUNN, R.E. Berber imperialism: the Ait Atta expansion in South-east Morocco. *Arabs and Berbers*, ed. E. Gellner and C. Micaud, 1973, pp. 85-107.

FAVRET, J. Traditionalism through ultra-modernism. *Arabs and Berbers*, ed. E Gellner and C. Micaud, 1973, pp. 307-324.

FERCHIOU, S. Les semi-nomades du Nefzaoua. *ROMM* 11(1972), pp. 127-136.

GALAND-PERNET, P. Poésies berbères. *Ann. Afr.nord* 12(1973), pp. 259-264.

GAST, M. Le don des sandales dans la cérémonie du mariage chez les Kel Ahaggar (Algérie). *Actes I. Cong. et. cult. mediterr. d'infl. arabo-berb.*, 1973, pp. 522-527

GELLNER, E. Political and religious organization of the Berbers of the Central High Atlas. *Arabs and Berbers*, ed. E. Gellner and C. Micaud, 1973, pp. 59-66.

HARRIES, J. and RAAMOUCH, Mohamed Berber popular songs of the Middle Atlas. *Afr. lang. stud.* 12 (1971), pp. 52-70.

HART, D.M. Conflicting models of a berber tribal structure in the Moroccan Rif: the segmentary and alliance systems of the Aith Waryachar. *ROMM* 7(1970), pp. 93-99.

JEDREJ, M.C. Ingessana throwing knives. *Anthropos* 70(1975), pp. 42-48.

JONGELING, G. Materials furnished by Arab geographers for the history of some Berber tribes in the 'Provincia Barca'. *Actes I. Cong. et. cult. mediterr. d'infl. arabo-berb.*, 1973, pp. 209-212.

LACOSTE-DUJARDIN, C. Littérature orale populaire maghrebine: le conte en berbère: l'exemple du conte kabyle. *Ann.Afr.nord* 12 (1973), pp. 249-257.

LAPHAM, R.J. Population policies in the Maghrib. *MEJ* 26(1972), pp. 1-10

LAWLESS, R.I. The lost Berber villages of Eastern Morocco and Western Algeria. *Man* N.S. 7(1972), pp. 114-122

XII NORTH AFRICA: ETHNOLOGY

LEWICKI, T. Du nouveau sur la liste des tribus berberes d'Ibn Hawkal. *Folia Or.* 13(1971), pp. 171-200.

LEWICKI, T. Le monde berbère vu par les écrivains arabes. *Actes I. Cong. et. cult. mediterr. d'infl. arabo-berb.*, 1973, pp. 31-42.

LEWICKI, T. Les origines de l'Islam dans les tribus berbères du Sahara occidental: Mūsā ibn Nuṣayr et ʿUbayd Allāh ibn al-Habhāb. *SI* 32(1970), pp. 203-214.

LOUIS, A., SIRONVAL, M.M. Le mariage traditionnel en milieu berbère dans le Sud de la Tunisie. *ROMM* 12(1972), pp. 93-121

LOUIS, A. Les prestations réciproques en milieu berbère du Sud tunisien. *Anthropos* 68(1973), pp. 456-472.

LOUIS, R.P.A. Le monde "berbère" de l'extrême sud tunisien. *ROMM* 11(1972), pp. 107-125

LUTZKAYA, N.S. K voprosu o marokkanskikh berberakh. *Istoriya i ekonomika stran Arabskogo Vostoka*, 1973, pp. 165-173.

MARAIS, O. The political evolution of the Berbers in independent Morocco. *Arabs and Berbers*, ed. E. Gellner and C. Micaud, 1973, pp. 277-283.

MARTHELOT, P. Ethnie et région: le "phénomène" berbère au Maghreb. *Actes I. Cong. et. cult. mediterr. d'infl. arabo-berb.*, 1973, pp. 465-474.

MARTHELOT, P. La "maintenance" des groupes berbérophones au Maghreb: un problème de géographie régionale? *ROMM* 15-16(1973), pp. 189-195.

MYLIUS, N. und MYLIUS, N.G. Bei den Ait Hadiddou. Bericht über eine Informationsreise zu den Berbern. *WVK* 18(N.F. 13, 1971), pp. 69-78.

QUANDT, W.B. The Berbers in the Algerian political elite. *Arabs and Berbers*, ed. E. Gellner and C. Micaud, 1973, pp. 285-303.

SOULIÉ, G.J.L. La Berbérie oubliée. *Afr.et l'Asie* 91-2(1970), pp. 3-12.

SPAAK, J.D. Y a-t-il équilibre socio-économique dans le Haut-Atlas occidental? *L'Afrique et l'Asie modernes* 100(1974), pp. 22-51.

TALBI, Mohamed. Hérésie, acculturation et nationalisme des Berbères bargawâta. *Actes I. Cong. et cult. mediterr. d'infl. arabo-berb.*, 1973, pp. 217-233.

TILLION, G. Les deux versants de la parenté berbère. *Actes I. Cong. et. cult. mediterr. d'infl. arabo-berb.*, 1973, pp. 43-49.

VINOGRADOV, A.R. The socio-political organization of a Berber 'taraf' tribe: pre-Protectorate Morocco. *Arabs and Berbers*, ed. E. Gellner and C. Micaud, 1973, pp. 67-83.

WATERBURY, J. Tribalism, trade and politics: the transformation of the Swasa of Morocco. *Arabs and Berbers*, ed. E. Gellner and C. Micaud, 1973, pp. 231-257.

See also V. a. *Influences*. Bourouiba.

See also XIII. a. La Veronne.

See also XVI. b. Ben Kaddour.

See also XVI. b. Coram.

See also XVI. b. Marais.

See also XVI. c. Kaddache.

See also XLII. Galand-Pernet.

c TUAREGS

AUGIER, P. Quelques observations sur les échelles musicales des Touaregs de l'Ahaggar. *Libyca* 16(1968), pp. 163-170.

BERNUS, E. Les composantes géographiques et sociales des types d'élevage en milieu Touareg. *Notes et docs. voltaïques* 6iii (1973), pp. 12-22.

BERNUS, E. Espace géographique et champs sociaux chez les Touareg Illabakan (République du Niger). *Etudes rurales* 37-39 (1970), pp. 46-64.

BERNUS, E. Incongruités et mauvaises paroles touarègues (Touaregs Iullemmeden Kel Dinnik). *J. Soc. africanistes* 42(1972), pp. 89-94.

BOURGEOT, A. Le contenu sociologique de l'appelation twareg (Kel Ahaggar): Histoire d'un nom. *ROMM* 11(1972), pp. 71-79.

BOURGEOT, A. Le costume masculin des Kel Ahaggar. *Libyca* 17(1969), pp. 355-376.

BOURGEOT, A. Idéologie et appellations ethniques: l'exemple twareg. Analyse des catégories sociales. *Cah. et. afr.* 12(1972), pp. 533-554.

BOURGEOT, A. Nomadisme et sédentarisation. Le processus d'intégration chez les Kel Ahaggar. *ROMM* 11(1972), pp. 85-92.

CHAVENTRÉ, A. [and others]. Un "isolat" du Sud Sahara: les Kel Kummer. *Population* [Paris] 27(1972), pp. 769-800.

CHAVENTRE, A. et DEGOS, L. Rôle et importance du système HL-A en anthropologie. Applications aux Kel Kummer. *Bulletins et memoires de la Soc. d'anthrop. de Paris* 13.ser.,2(1975), pp. 99-106.

DEGOS, L. [and others]. Un "isolat" du Sud Sahara: les Kel Kummer. Description des divers systèmes sanguins. *Population* [Paris] 28(1973), pp. 1109-1124.

DIETERLEN, G., LIGERS, Z. Contribution à l'étude des bijoux touareg. *J. Soc. africanistes* 42(1972), pp. 29-53.

FUGLESTAD, F. Les révoltes des Touareg du Niger (1916-17). *Cah. ét. afr.* 13(1973), pp. 82-120.

GAST, M. Témoignages nouveaux sur Tine Hinane, ancêtre légendaire des Touareg Ahaggar. *ROMM* 13-14(1973), pp. 395-400.

GAST, M. Usages des encens et parfums en Ahaggar. *Libyca* 16(1968), pp. 171-174.

JACQUARD, A. Un "isolat" du sud Sahara. Les Kel Kummer. V,VI. *Population* [Paris] 29(1974), pp. 517-534.

JEMMA, D. Les artisans de l'Ahaggar. *Libyca* 20(1972), pp. 269-290.

KEENAN, J.H. Social change among the Tuareg of Ahaggar(Algeria). *Arabs and Berbers*, ed. E. Gellner and C. Micaud, 1973, pp. 345-360.

KEENAN, J.H. "The Tuareg veil". (Le voile chez les Touareg). *ROMM* 17(1974), pp. 107-118.

LEFEVRE-WITIER, P., RUFFIÉ, J. Notes sur l'hétérogénéité biologique des touaregs. *ROMM* 11(1972), pp. 99-105.

MAKULSKI, J.K. Évolution du modèle de la personnalité des Touareg Kel Ahaggar. *Africana bull.* 15(1971), pp. 55-82.

MUSEUR, M. Quelques aspects récents de l'économie sociale du Hoggar. *Rev. Inst. Sociol.* 1974, pp. 299-315.

SALMON, P. Les Touareg de l'Ahaggar et du Tassili-n-Ajjer. Essai de synthèse historique. *Correspondance d'Orient: Etudes* 19-20(1971-2), pp. 47-65.

SWIFT, J. Le nomadisme pastoral entant que forme d'utilisation des terres: les Touareg de l'Adrar des Iforas. *Etudes maliennes* 5[1973?], pp. 35-44.

NICOLAISEN, J. The structural study of kinship behaviour with particular reference to Tuareg concept. *Folk* 13(1971), pp. 167-194

See also V. u. l. Födermayr

d MOROCCO

ADAM, A. Les classes sociales urbaines au Maroc. *II.Cong.int.ét.nord-afr.* 1970, pp. 223-238.

ADAM, A. La politique culturelle au Maroc. *Ann.Afr.nord* 12(1973), pp. 107-128.

AMIN, Amhed al- . L'évolution de la femme et le problème du mariage au Maroc. *Présence africaine* 68(1968), pp. 32-51

ASSERMOUH, Ahmed. Marrakech et ses douars spontanés. *Bull. econ. et soc. du Maroc* 118-9(1972), pp. 81-97.

ATTIA, H. et BENHALIMA, H. L'homme et l'environnement chez les Béni Mguild. *Rev. géog. Maroc* 23-24(1973), pp. 179-182.

BARON, P. et HAMMOUDI, A. Alimentation et nutrition dans les Chiadmas. *Bull.écon. soc.Maroc* 128-9(1975?), pp. 99-116.

BELGHITI, Malika. Les relations féminines et le statut de la femme dans la famille rurale - dans trois villages de la Tessaout. *Etudes sociologiques sur le Maroc* (1971), pp. 289-361

BELGHITI, Malika; CHRAIBI, Najat et ADIB, Tamou. La ségrégation des garçons et des filles a la campagne. *Bull. econ. soc. Maroc.* 33(nos, 120-1, 1971), pp. 81-144.

BEN-AMI, Issachar. Le mariage traditionnel chez les juifs marocains. *Folklore Res. Center studies* 4(1974), pp. 9-103.

BONNET, J. et BOSSARD, R. Aspects géographiques de l'émigration marocaine vers l'Europe. *Rev. géog. Maroc* 23-24(1973), pp. 5-50.

BROWN, K. Histoire culturelle de Salé: profil d'un 'alim du 19e siècle. *Bull. écon.soc.Maroc* 32(no.116,[1970?]), pp. 49-62.

CHARNAY, J.P. Les cadres moyens dans les pays musulmans: esquisse d'une problématique. *Annales maroc. sociol.* 1968, pp. 31-57.

COATALEN, P. Réflexions sur la société chleuh (Région de Tafraoute). *Annales maroc. sociol.* 1969, pp. 27-31.

CORCOS, D. Quelques aspects de la société juive dans le vieux Maroc. Les prénoms des Juifs marocains. *Folklore Research Center studies* 3(1972), pp. 143-229.

DETHIER, J. 60 ans d'urbanisme au Maroc. L'évolution des idées et des réalisations. *Bull. econ. et soc. du Maroc* 118-9(1972), pp. 5-56.

DUCHAC, R., BENTAHAR, Mekki. Fonction des villes moyennes. Contribution à une sociologie des migrations au Maroc. *Bull. écon. soc. Maroc* 33(no. 122, 1973), pp. 83-97.

DU PUIGAUDEAU, O. Arts et coûtumes des Maures. *Hesp.Tamuda* 13(1972), pp. 183-224.

EICKELMAN, D.F. Is there an Islamic city? The making of a quarter in a Moroccan town. *IJMES* 5(1974), pp. 274-294.

ETIENNE, B. De la nouvelle fonction normative du droit public dans la société maghrébine. *II.Cong.int.ét.nord-afr.* 1970, pp. 239-262.

GHARBAOUI, Ahmed El. L'homme et le maïder. *Bull.écon.soc.Maroc* 128-9(1975?), pp. 93-97.

GHARBAOUI, Ahmed. Le proletariat maghrebin immigre dans la banlieue nord-ouest de Paris. *Bull.écon.soc.Maroc* 31(no. 115, 1969), pp. 25-49

HAGOPIAN, E.C. The status and role of the Marabout in pre-protectorate Morocco. *Ethnology* [Pittsburg] 3(1964), pp. 42-52.

HART, D.M. The Ait Ba 'Amran of Ifni: an ethnographic survey. *ROMM* 15-16(1973), pp. 61-74.

HART, D.M. The tribe in modern Morocco: two case studies. *Arabs and Berbers*, ed. E. Gellner and C. Micaud, 1973, pp. 25-58.

HENSENS, J. Enquête nationale sur l'habitat rural traditionnel au Maroc - été 1970. *Bull. econ. et soc. du Maroc* 118-9(1972), pp. 99-115.

HENSENS, J. La "villa" comme habitat urbain. *Bull. écon. soc. Maroc* 33(no.122, 1973), pp. 123-131.

IKIN, E.W. *et al.* The blood groups and haemoglobin of the Jews of the Tafilalet Oases of Morocco. *Man* 7(1972), pp. 595-600.

JACQUES-MEUNIE, D. Notes sur l'histoire des populations du sud marocain. *ROMM* 11(1972), pp. 137-150.

JOLÉ, M., KHATIBI, Abdelkabir, MARTENSSON, M. Urbanisme, idéologie et ségrégation: exemple de Rabat. *Annales maroc.de sociol.* 1970, pp. 35-54.

KHATIBI, Abdelkabir. Etat et classes sociales. *Etudes sociologiques sur le Maroc* (1971), pp. 3-15

KROTKI, K.J. et BEAUJOT, R. La population marocaine: reconstitution de l'évolution de 1950 à 1971. *Population* [Paris] 30 (1975), pp. 335-367.

LA BASTIDE, H. de. Une grande famille du Sud-marocain: les Ma el-Aïnin. *Maghreb-Machrek* 56(1973), pp. 37-39.

LAHLIMI, Ahmed. Les collectivités rurales traditionnelles et leur évolution. *Etudes sociologiques sur le Maroc* (1971), pp. 17-41

LAHLOU, Abbes. Etûde sur la famille traditionnelle de Fès. *Rev.Inst.Sociol.* 41 (1968), pp. 407-441

LAPHAM, R. Modernisation et contraception au Maroc Central. *Population (Paris)* 26, num. spéc. (mars 1971), pp. 79-104.

LAZAREV, Grigori. Changement social et développement dans les campagnes marocaines. *Etudes sociologiques sur le Maroc* (1971), pp. 129-143

LAZAREV, G. Les concessions foncières au Maroc. Contribution à l'étude de la formation des domaines personnels dans les campagnes marocaines. *Annales maroc. sociol.* 1968, pp. 99-135.

LAZAREV, Grigori. Les concessions foncières au Maroc. Contribution à l'étude de la formation des domaines personnels dans les campagnes marocaines. *Etudes sociologiques sur le Maroc* (1971), pp. 43-79

MAHER, V. Divorce ánd property in the Middle Atlas of Morocco. *Man* 9(1974), pp. 103-122.

MARTINEZ, N. Significati mistici delle stoviglie nel Marocco. *Conoscenza religiosa* 1971, pp. 87-93.

MINER, H.M. Traditional mobility among the weavers of Fez. *Proc. Amer. Philos. Soc.* 117(1973), pp. 17-36.

MORSY, Zaghloul. Profils culturels et conscience critique au Maroc. *J. world hist.* 12(1970), pp. 588-602.

PASCON, P. et BENTAHAR, M. Ce que disent 296 Jeunes ruraux. *Etudes sociologiques sur le Maroc* (1971), pp. 145-287

PASCON, P. La formation de la société marocaine. *Bull. econ. soc. Maroc* 33(Nos. 120-1, 1971). pp. 1-25.

PASCON, P. La main-d'oeuvre et l'emploi dans le secteur traditionnel. *Etudes sociologiques sur le Maroc* (1971), pp. 81-127

PASCON, P. Méthode d'étude des structures agraires au niveau villageois. *Bull.écon. soc.Maroc* 128-9(1975?), pp. 117-134.

PETONNET, C. Espacé, distance et dimension dans une société musulmane, à propos du bidonville marocain de Douar Doum à Rabat. *L'Homme* 12(1972), pp. 47-84.

PLETSCH, A. Wandluñgen der Bevölkerungs-struktur und Bevölkerungsbewegungen im Südmarokkanischen Oasengebiet. *Erdkunde* 26(1972), pp. 130-138.

PUIGAUDEAU, O. du. Arts et coutumes des Maures (III). *Hespéris Tamuda* 11(1970), pp. 5-82

RABATÉ, M.R. Les jeux de l'Achoura dans la vallée du Dra (Sud Marocain). *Objets et mondes* 10 (1970), pp. 239-262.

RADI, Abdelwahad. Processus de socialisation de l'enfant marocain. *Annales maroc. sociol.* 1969, pp. 33-47; also published in *Etudes philos. et litt.* 4 (1969), pp. 37-51.

ROSEN, L. Muslim-Jéwish relations in a Moroccan city. *IJMES* 3(1972), pp. 435-449.

ROSEN, L. Rural political process and national political structure in Morocco. *Rural politics and social change in the Middle East*, ed. by R. Antoun and I. Harik, 1972, pp. 214-236.

ROSEN, L. The sociál and conceptual framework of Arab-Berber relations in Central Morocco. *Arabs and Berbers*, ed. E. Gellner and C. Micaud, 1973, pp. 155-173.

XII NORTH AFRICA: ETHNOLOGY

SAYIGH, Yusif A. Problems and prospects of development in the Arabian Peninsula. *IJMES* 2 (1971), pp. 40-58.

SCHMITZ, H. Der marokkanische Souk. *Erde,* 104(1973), pp. 320-333.

SEDDON, D. Aspects of underdevelopment and development in north-east Morocco. *Choice and change; essays in honour of Lucy Mair,* 1974, pp. 134-160.

SEDDON, J.D. Social and economic change in Northeast Morocco. *Current anthropology* 12(1971), pp. 227-229.

SEDDON, J.D. Views and studies of Moroccan society from 1870 to 1970. [Bibliography.] *Annales maroc.de sociol.* 1970, pp. 77-96.

SEFRIOUI, A. L'artisanat marocain. *Annuaire Afrique du Nord* 12(1973), pp. 181-191.

STILLMAN, Y. The evil eye in Morocco. *Folklore Research Center stud.* 1(1970), pp. 81-94.

ZAFRANI, Haim. Etudes et recherches sur la littérature écrite et orale des juifs du Maroc des quatre derniers siècles. *ROMM* 18 (1974), pp. 159-167.

La plan familial au Maroc. *Population* [Paris] 27(1972), pp. 1145-1147.

See also XII. b. Âdam.

See also XVI. a. Eickelman.

e ALGERIA

BAHRI, A. et DELLOUCI, B. L'emploi en Algérie à travers le recensement de 1966. *Population (Paris)* 26, num. spéc. (mars 1971), pp. 13-23.

BAILLET, P. Une population urbanisée: les rapatriés d'Algérie. *Bull.Assoc.Géog. Franç.* 427-8(1975), pp. 269-278.

BARRÈRE, G. L'aghrem de Eherir au Tassili N'Ajjer. *Libyca* 17(1969), pp. 337-342.

BENABADJI, Mohammed et CHAMLA, M.-C. Les groupes sanguins ABO et RH des Algériens. *L'Anthropologie* 75(1971), pp. 427-442

BERQUE, J. Retour à Mazouna. *Annales ESC* 27(1972), pp. 150-157

BOUBEKEUR, Farida, *et al.* Les femmes des hautes plaines constantinoises vues par elles-mêmes. *Rev.alg.* 11(1974), pp. 161-164.

BOUISRI, A. et PRADEL DE LAMAZE, F. La population d'Algérie d'après le recensement de 1966. *Population (Paris)* 26, num. spéc. (mars, 1971), pp. 25-46.

BOURCIER DE CARBON, P. Projections de la population algérienne jusqu'en 2001. *Population* [Paris] 28(1973), pp. 291-334.

BRINI, M.L. Poterie de Guerrouma, Algérie. *Objets et mondes* 12(1972), pp. 45-52.

CHAMLA, M.-C. et DEMOULIN, Fr. Données démographiques sur une commune rurale de l'Aurès (Bouzina, Algérie). *L'Anthropologie* 79(1975), pp. 285-298.

CHAMPAULT, D. Notes sur quelques rites relatifs à l'enfance au Sahara nord-occidental. *L'Ethnographie* N.S.64(1970), pp. 87-98.

CHAMPAULT, D. Les pèlerins de l'eau. *Actes I. Cong. et. cult. mediterr. d'infl. arabo-berb.,* 1973, pp. 538-540.

CHARNAY, J.P. De la grande maison au couple moderne. Interférences entre droit, psychologie et économie dans l'évolution de la famille maghrébine. *Rev.alg.* 11 (1974), pp. 57-83.

CHAULET, Cl. Les fonctions de la famille patriarchale dans le "secteur traditionnel" et leurs modifications possibles dans le cadre de la révolution agraire. *Rev. alg.* 11(1974), pp. 119-126.

CHIRK BELHADJ, B. Répartition des hémoglobinoses en Algérie (1964-1970). *Libyca* 20 (1972), pp. 33-41.

CLAVIÈRES, M. Fabrication de la poterie au Chenoua. *Libyca* 16(1968), pp. 199-205.

COLONNA, F. Une fonction coloniale de l'ethnologie dans l'Algérie de l'entre-deux guerres: la programmation des élites moyennes. *Libyca* 20(1972), pp. 259-267.

COLONNA, F. Verdict scolaire et position de classe dans l'Algérie coloniale. *Rev. franç. sociol.* 14(1973), pp. 180-201.

DEJEUX, J. Principales manifestations culturelles en Algérie depuis 1962. *Ann.Afr. nord* 12(1973), pp. 77-96

DIONISI, B. A proposito del III Congresso dell'Union Nationale des Femmes Algériennes. *OM* 55(1975), pp. 62-66.

ETIENNE, B., LECA, J. La politique culturelle de l'Algérie. *Ann.Afr.nord* 12(1973), pp. 44-76.

FARRAG, A. Social Control amongst the Mzabite Women of Beni-Isguen. *ME stud.* 7 (1971), pp. 317-328.

FREUND, W.S. Le tourisme à Djerba, répercussions sociales. *II.Cong.int.ét. nord-afr.* 1970, pp. 263-272.

GALLAIS-HAMONO, G., NOIROT, D. et POUPAT, B. L'intégration des rapatriés d'Algérie en France. *Population* [Paris] 30(1975), pp. 303-334.

GALLISSOT, R. Precolonial Algeria. *Economy and society* 4(1975), pp. 418-445.

XII NORTH AFRICA: ETHNOLOGY

GRANDGUILLAUME, G. L'évolution des contacts culturels dans une médina de l'Ouest algérien (Nedroma). *Actes I. Cong. et. cult. mediterr. d'infl. arabo-berb.*, 1973, pp. 445-452.

GUILLON, M. Les rapatriés d'Algérie dans la region parisienne. *Annales de geog.* 83(no.460,1974), pp. 644-675.

HAMMERI, Hasseine. Folklore musical des Chaouia constantinois. *Actes I. Cong. et. cult. mediterr. d'infl. arabo-berb.*, 1973, pp. 335-340.

HEGGOY, A.A. Cultural disrespect: European and Algerian views on women in colonial and independent Algeria. *MW* 62(1972), pp. 323-334.

HEGGOY, A.A. On the evolution of Algerian women. *Afr.stud.rev.(Syracuse)* 17(1974), pp. 449-456.

HEGGOY, A.A. The two societies of French Algeria and the failure of coexistence. *Africa Q.* 13(1973), pp. 23-37.

JANON, M. Stèles funéraires en bois sculpté de Cherchel. *Libyca* 15(1967), pp. 343-355.

JOSSE, R. Problemës de mise en valeur du Hoggar et de croissance urbaine à Tamanrasset. *Cah. d'Outre-Mer* 24(no. 95, 1971), pp. 245-293.

KÖBERT, R. Samʿānī über ʿAlī ar-Riḍā. *Orientalia* 41(1972), pp. 387-389.

KOMOROWSKI, Z. Les descendants des soudanais en Algérie et leurs traditions. *Africana bull.* 15(1971), pp. 43-53.

LEFEBVRE, G. Les poteries du Chenoua - étude des formes. *Libyca* 15(1967), pp. 269-287.

LEFEBVRE, L. Enquete sur le portage de l'eau en Algérie - résultats obtenus en septembre 1966 - . *Libyca* 16(1968), pp. 175-189.

LEFEBVRE, L. Étude sur les villages de regroupement du Chenoua en 1966-1967. *Libyca* 15(1967), pp. 289-306.

LEFEBVRE, L. Seconde étude des villages de regroupment du Chenoua. Étude de quelques maisons isolées de la région (septembre 1967). *Libyca* 16(1968), pp. 207-215.

MAISON, D. La population de l'Algérie. *Population* [Paris] 28(1973), pp. 1079-1107.

MICHEL, A. Sur l'usage des méthodes contraceptives dans la population algérienne à Paris. *Population (Paris)* 26 (1971), pp. 149-151.

MIETTE, R. Les cooperatives pastorales en Algérie. *L'Afrique et l'Asie modernes* 101 (1974), pp. 35-40.

MIETTE, R. Les cooperatives polyvalentes en Algérie. *L'Afrique et l'Asie modernes* 102(1974), pp. 31-39.

MIETTE, R. Nomades et nomadisme de la pseudo-steppe algérienne. *L'Afrique et l'Asie modernes* 97-9(1972), pp. 4-16.

MIETTE, R. Le problème de la steppe en Algérie. *L'Afrique et l'Asie modernes* 100 (1974), pp. 52-61.

MUSSO, J. Masques de l'Achoura en Grande-Kabylie. *Libyca* 18(1970), pp. 269-274.

NÉGADI, Gourari et VALLIN, J. La fécondité des algériennes: niveau et tendances. *Population* [Paris] 29(1974), pp. 491-515.

NOUSCHI, A. Notes sur les migrations en Algérie dans la première moitié du XIXème siècle. *Actes I. Cong. et. cult. mediterr. d'infl. arabo-berb.*, 1973, pp. 269-275.

OUGOUAG-KEZZAL, Ch. Bref aperçu historique sur la broderie arabe; sur une vieille brodeuse au coeur d'Alger. *Libyca* 17(1969), pp. 343-349.

OUGOUAG-KEZZAL, Ch. Le costume et la parure de la mariée à Tlemcen. *Libyca* 18(1970), pp. 253-268

OUGOUAG-KEZZAL, Ch. Un exemple historique de la valeur morale des bijoux et leur symbolique chez les Arabes. La Taoussa. *Libyca* 17(1969), pp. 351-353.

OUGOUAG-KEZZAL, C. Le sadaq et le mariage suivant le "Urf" (rite) de Sidi Ma'ammar. *Libyca* 19(1971), pp. 235-241.

PEILLON, P. Rôle des forces externes dans la distribution de l'habitat rural: l'exemple de la Basse Kabylie. *Tiers monde* 13(no. 51, 1972), pp. 603-619.

PERETTI, J.M. La crise mondiale et le monde rural traditionnel. *Rev.alg.* 11(1974), pp. 53-68.

PIRSON, R. Pour une tentative d'approche de la problématique urbaine. L'exemple de la ville d'Alger. *Rev. Inst. Sociol.* 1972-4, pp. 721-731.

RACIM, Mohamed. Les arts citadins et les artisans algérois. *CATP* 2(1968), pp. 15-20.

SAINTE-MARIE, A. Législation foncière et société rurale. L'application de la loi du 26 juillet 1873 dans les douars de l'Algérois. *Etudes rurales* 57(1975), pp. 61-87.

SANSON, H. Approche sociodémographique de la société algérienne. *II.Cong.int. ét.nord-afr.* 1970, pp. 327-332.

SAVARY, J.P. Anneaux de cheville d'Algérie. *Libyca* 14(1966), pp. 381-414.

SAVARY, J.P. Anneaux de cheville d'Algérie. (Note complémentaire.) *Libyca* 16(1968), pp. 191-198.

SAVARY, J.P. Cimetières à stèles en bois taillé du Douar Sahel sud-ouest de Marengo. *Libyca* 15(1967), pp. 307-342.

TABAH, L. Une enquete sur la fécondité en Algérie. Applications de l'Analyse factorielle des correspondances. *Population* [Paris] 27(1972), pp. 729-768.

TABUTIN, D. Mortalite infantile et juvénile en Algérie du Nord. *Population* [Paris] 29(1974), pp. 41-59.

TABUTIN, D. La polygamie en Algérie. *Population* [Paris] 29(1974), pp. 313-325.

TOUAT, Larbi. Développement économique et nouvelles familles algériennes. *Rev.alg.* 11(1974), pp. 149-156.

VALLIN, J. Influence de divers facteurs économiques et sociaux sur la fécondité de l'Algérie. *Population* [Paris] 28(1973), pp. 817-842.

VALLIN, J. La mortalité en Algerie. *Population* [Paris] 30(1975), pp. 1023-1046.

YAKER-RAHMANI, L. À la rencontre du printemps. *Libyca* 17(1969), pp. 333-335.

YAKER-RAHMANI, L. Description d'une "zerda" en Petite Kabylie, dans la région du Cap-Aokas. *Libyca* 16(1968), pp. 221-222.

YAKER-RAHMANI, L. Présages de la région de Cap-Aokas (Petite Kabylie). *Libyca* 15 (1967), pp. 264-268.

Nouvelles données sur la population algérienne (Algérie du Nord). *Population* [Paris] 29(1974), pp. 1141-1148.

See also V. j. Poyto.

See also V. u. l. Augier.

See also XI. f. Aumassip.

See also XVI. c. Bormans.

See also XVI. c. Dobosiewicz.

See also XLIII. b. Lucas.

f TUNISIA

ABDUL-WAHAB, Hasan Husni. Coup d'oeil général sur les apports ethniques étrangers en Tunisie. *Recueil d'études sur les moriscos andalous en Tunisie,* préparé par M. de Epalza et R. Petit, 1973, pp. 16-20.

ABU-ZAHRA, Nadia. Inequality of descent and egalitarianism of the new national organizations in a Tunisian village. *Rural politics and social change in the Middle East,* ed. by R. Antoun and I. Harik, 1972, pp. 267-286.

ABU-ZAHRA, Nadia. Material power, honour, friendship and the etiquette of visiting. *Anthrop. q'ly* 47(1974), pp. 120-138.

ALOUANE, Youssef. Quelques données sociales sur la ville de Tunis. *Etudes de sociologie tunisienne* 1 (1968), pp. 261-299.

AMMAR, Mohamed Salah. La lecture-loisir en milieu familial tunisien. *IBLA* 38(no. 136, 1975), pp. 261-279.

ANNABI, Muhammad al-. La chéchia tunisienne. *Recueil d'études sur les moriscos andalous en Tunisie,* préparé par M. de Epalza et R. Petit, 1973, pp. 304-307.

ASHFORD, D.E. Succession and social change in Tunisia. *IJMES* 4(1973), pp. 23-39

AUMASSIP, G., *et al.* Aperçu sur l'évolution du paysage quaternaire et le peuplement de la région de Ouargla. *Libyca* 20(1972), pp. 205-257.

AYACHI, Tahar. L'artisanat du cuivre en Tunisie. *CATP* 1(1968), pp. 157-192.

BAYRAM, Alia. La naissance à Tunis dans les milieux de la bourgeoisie traditionnelle. *Cah.des arts et traditions populaires* 4 (1971), pp. 7-16.

BONNENFANT, P. L'évolution de la population d'une oasis tunisienne: El-Guettar. *IBLA* 35(no.129, 1972), pp. 97-140.

BOUHDIBA, Abdelwahab. Les conditions de vie des mineurs de la région de Gafsa. *Etudes de sociologie tunisienne* 1 (1968), pp. 165-233.

CAMILLERI, C. Une communauté maltaise en Tunisie entre les groupes arabo-berbère et français. *Actes I. Cong. et. cult. mediterr. d'infl. arabo-berb.,* 1973, pp. 406-423.

CHAMLA, M.C.; SAHLY, A. Les empreintes digitales et palmaires des Tunisiens. *Libyca* 20(1972), pp. 11-31.

CHAMLA, M.C. et SAHLY, A. Le pli palmaire transverse chez les Tunisiens. *Anthropologie* 77(1973), pp. 107-118.

COHEN-HADRIA, E. La politique démographique de la Tunisie. *Maghreb Machrek* 70 (1975), pp. 25-30.

DJEDIDI, Tahar Labib. Culture et société en Tunisie. *Ann.Afr.nord* 12(1973), pp. 19-27.

FERCHIOU, S. Les fêtes maraboutiques en Tunisie -- "Zarda". *Actes I. Cong. et. cult. mediterr. d'infl. arabo-berb.,* 1973, pp. 532-537.

FONTAINE, J., BRECHOUX, Th. Documents sur le problème de l'Arabisation. *IBLA* 38 (no.136, 1975), pp. 299-321.

HANNA, Sami A. Changing trends in Tunisian socialism. *MW* 62(1972), pp. 230-240.

JONGMANS, D.G. Mzia et Horma. Relations entre service, estime sociale et prospérité dans une société en transformation. *CATP* 3(1969), pp. 101-133.

JONKER, C. Exploration anthropologique pour une étude du ménage familial en Kroumirie. *Cah. des arts et traditions populaires* 4 (1971), pp. 55-84.

KACEM, Abdelaziz. La politique culturelle tunisienne. *Ann.Afr.nord* 12(1973), pp. 29-44.

LOUIS, A. Aux matmatas et dans les ksars du sud: l'olivier et les hommes. *CATP* 3 (1969), pp. 43-66.

LOUIS, A. Contacts entre culture "berbère" et culture arabe dans le Sud tunisien. *Actes I. Cong. et. cult. mediterr. d'infl. arabo-berb.*, 1973, pp. 394-405.

LOUIS, A. Habitat et habitations autour des ksars de montagne dans le Sud tunisien. *IBLA* 127 (1971), pp. 123-147.

LOUIS, A. L'habitation troglodyte dans un village des Matmata. *CATP* 2(1968), pp. 33-60.

LOUIS, A. Orientation bibliographique: ethnographie tunisienne. *CATP* 1(1968), pp. 193-206; 2(1969), pp. 117-168; 3(1969), pp. 135-171 &c.

LOUIS, A. Sédentarisation des semi-nomades du Sud-Tunisien et changements culturels. *Maghreb-Machrek* 65(1974), pp. 55-61.

LOUIS, A. Sellerie d'apparat et selliers de Tunis. *CATP* 1(1968), pp. 41-100.

MAHJOUB, Neziha. Un aspect particulier des réserves alimentaires dans la maison des Amdoun et de Balta. *Cah. des arts et traditions populaires* 4(1971), pp. 85-96.

MAHJOUB, Neziha. Le costume hanéfite des hommes de religion et de justice à Tunis. *CATP* 2(1968), pp. 79-92.

MARCHAL, R. Droit et coûtumes de Tunisie. *Ann. Inst. Phil. Hist. Or.* 20(1968-72), pp. 305-315.

MARCOUX, A. La croissance de la population de la Tunisie. *Population (Paris)* 26, num. spéc. (mars 1971), pp. 105-123.

MASMOUDI, Mohamed. Deux autres peintures sous verre à thème héroïque. *CATP* 3(1969), pp. 85-98.

MASMOUDI, Mohamed, JONGMANS, D.G. Enquête anthropologique en Khroumirie. *CATP* 2 (1968), pp. 93-113.

MASMOUDI, Mohamed. L'habitation traditionnelle dans la banlieue de Sfax. *CATP* 1(1968), pp. 11-39.

MASMOUDI, Mohamed. Une peinture sous verre à thème héroïque. *CATP* 2(1968), pp. 5-14.

PICOUET, M. Aperçu des migrations intérieures en Tunisie. *Population (Paris)* 26, num. spéc. (mars 1971), pp. 125-148.

PIRSON, R. Du nomadisme à la sédentarité dans le Sud-Tunisien comme exemple de désagrégation d'un ordre socio-démocratique. *Civilisations* 25i-ii(1975), pp. 124-143.

SACK, R. The impact of education on individual modernity in Tunisia. *Int. J. comp. sociol.* 14(1973), pp. 245-272.

SAMMUT, C. La minorité maltaise de Tunisie: ethnie arabe ou européenne? *Actes I. Cong. et. cult. mediterr. d'infl. arabo-berb.*, 1973, pp. 424-438.

SEKLANI, Mahmoud. L'émigration tunisienne en particulier pour le Sud tunisien. *Population* [Paris], num. spéc., mars 1974, pp. 107-120.

SETHOM, Samira. La confection du costume féminin d'Hammamet. *CATP* 1(1968), pp. 101-111.

SETHOM, Samira. La tunique de mariage en Tunisie. *CATP* 3(1969), pp. 5-20

SIMMONS, J. The political economy of land use: Tunisian private farms. *Rural politics and social change in the Middle East*, ed. by R. Antoun and I. Harik, 1972, pp. 432-452.

SKHIRI, Fathia. Deux couvertures de Testour. *CATP* 3(1969), pp. 21-39.

SKHIRI, Fathia. Deux couvertures de Testour. *Recueil d'études sur les moriscos andalous en Tunisie*, préparé par M. de Epalza et R. Petit, 1973, pp. 317-334.

SKHIRI, Fathia. Les traditions culinaires andalouses à Testour. *CATP* 2(1968), pp. 21-28.

SKHIRI, Fathia. Les traditions culinaires andalouses à Testour. *Recueil d'études sur les moriscos andalous en Tunisie*, préparé par M. de Epalza et R. Petit, 1973, pp. 349-358.

SKIK, Hichem. Les Maltais en Tunisie. *Actes I. Cong. et. cult. mediterr. d'infl. arabo-berb.*, 1973, pp. 83-90.

SRAIEB, Nourredine. Mutations socio-économiques de la famille en Tunisie. *Rev.alger. des sci.jur.econ.pol.* 11iii(1974), pp. 127-132.

SUGIER, C. Les bijoux de la mariée à Moknine. *CATP* 1(1968), pp. 139-156.

SUGIER, C. Les coiffes féminines de Tunisie. *CATP* 2(1968), pp. 61-78.

SUGIER, Cl. Les coiffes féminines de Tunisie. *Recueil d'études sur les moriscos andalous en Tunisie*, préparé par M. de Epalza et R. Petit, 1973, pp. 335-348.

SUGIER, C. Le thème du lion dans les arts populaires tunisiens. *CATP* 3(1969), pp. 67-84.

TEYSSIER, P. Le vocabulaire d'origine espagnole dans l'industrie tunisienne de la chéchia. *Recueil d'études sur les moriscos andalous en Tunisie,* préparé par M. de Epalza et R. Petit, 1973, pp. 308-316.

VALLIN, J. L'enquête nationale démographique tunisienne. *Population (Paris)* 26, num. spéc. (mars 1971), pp. 205-244.

VALLIN, J. Limitation des naissances en Tunisie. *Population (Paris)* 26, num. spéc. (mars 1971), pp. 181-204.

VORONCHANINA, N.I. Emantzipatziya musul'manskoy zhenshchiny v Tunise. *Istoriya i ekonomika stran Arabskogo Vostoka,* 1973, pp. 52-70.

ZARKA, Chr. Maison et société dans le monde arabe. *L'Homme* 15ii(1975), pp. 87-102.

ZOUARI, Ali. La naissance à Sfax dans la société traditionnelle. *Cah.des arts et traditions populaires* 4(1971), pp. 17-27.

ZOUARI, Ali. Sanaa et maalma dans la région de Sfax. *CATP* 2(1968), pp. 29-32.

See also III. c. *Tunisia* Al-Annâbî

See also IV. c. 10. Montague.

See also V. p. Sugier.

See also XI. d. Dubois.

See also XII. b. Ferchiou.

See also XII. b. Louis.

See also XVI. c. Perinbam.

See also XVI. dd. Chatti.

See also XVI. dd. Cornet.

See also XXXVI. l. Saada.

g LIBYA

BASAGNA, R., SAYAD, Ali. La pratique matrimoniale aux At-Yanni. *Libyca* 19(1971), pp. 199-216.

DALTON, W.G. Economic change and political continuity in a Saharan Oasis community. *Man* 8(1973), pp. 266-284.

FIKRY, M. La femme et les conflits de valeurs en Libye. *ROMM* 18(1974), pp. 93-110.

GOLDBERG, H. From shaikh to mazkir: structural continuity and organizational change in the leadership of a Tripolitanian Jewish community. *Folklore Research Center stud.* 1(1970), pp. 29-41.

KAMEL, K. *et al.* Anthropological studies among Libyans--Erythrocyte genetic factors, serum haptoglobin phenotypes and anthropometry. *Amer. J. phys. anthrop.* 43(1975), pp. 103-111.

NOURI, Qais N. Al-. Modern professionalism in Libya: attitudes of university students. *Int. soc. sci.* J.27(1975), pp. 691-702.

SOURIAU, C. La société féminine en Libye. *ROMM* 6(1969), pp. 127-155.

See also XVII. cc. Hartley.

h OTHER PARTS OF AFRICA. MALTA

BALOGUN, I.A.B. The influence of Islam among the Etsako of the Mid-Western State of Nigeria. *Adab* [Khartoum], pp. 47-59.

BARKOW, J.H. Muslims and Maguazawa in North Central State, Nigeria: an ethnographic comparison. *Canadian J.Afr.stud.* 7(1973), pp. 59-76.

BRENEZ, J. L'observation démographique des milieux nomades. L'enquête de Mauritanie. *Population* 26(1971), pp. 721-736.

CASSAR PULLICINO, J. Some considerations in determining the Semitic element in Maltese folklore. *Actes I. Cong. et. cult. mediterr. d'infl. arabo-berb.,* 1973, pp. 371-381.

GRINDAL, B.T. Islamic affiliations and urban adaptation: the Sisala migrant in Accra, Ghana. *Africa* 43(1973), pp. 333-346

HOROWITZ, M.M. Barbers and bearers; ecology and ethnicity in an Islamic society. *Africa* 44(1974), pp. 371-382.

MEYEROWITZ, E.L.R. The origins of the "Sudanic" civilization. *Anthropos* 67 (1972), pp. 161-175

NORRIS, H.T. Sahel nomads' attitudes to drought. *Savanna* 2(1973), pp. 143-144.

OTTENBERG, S. A Moslem Igbo village. *Cah.ét.afr.* 11(no. 42, 1971), pp. 231-260.

XIII NORTH AFRICA: HISTORY
General

a GENERAL

ADAMU, Muhammad Uba. Some notes on the influence of North African traders in Kano. *Kano studies* 4(1968), pp. 43-40

BERQUE, J. De nouveau sur les Ban Hilâl? *SI* 36(1972), pp. 99-111.

BERQUE, J. Tradition and innovation in the Maghrib. *Daedalus* 102i(1973), pp. 239-250.

BONO, S. Sources italiennes pour l'histoire du Maghreb. *Rev. hist. maghrêb.* 2(1974), pp. 192-194.

BONO, S. Storiografia e fonti occidentali sul Maghreb dal XVI al XIX secolo. *Africa* [Rome] 28(1973), pp. 237-255.

BONO, S. Gli studi sulla storia del Maghreb dal secolo XVI al 1830. *Studi sul Vicino Oriente in Italia,* II, 1971, pp. 69-98.

BRAHIMI, D. Eloge de l'Arabe. *RHCM* 10 (1973), pp. 89-95.

BRETT, M. Problems in the interpretation of the history of the Maghrib in the light of some recent publications. *J. Afr. hist.* 13 (1972), pp. 489-506.

BURKE, E., III. Towards a history of the Maghreb. *M.E.stud.* pp. 306-323.

CLAUSEN, U. Der Konflikt um die Spanische Sahara. *Orient* [Germany] 16iv(1975), pp. 21-38.

DEVISSE, J. Routes de commerce et échanges en Afrique Occidentale en relation avec la Méditerranée. Un essai sur le commerce africain médiéval du XIe au XVIe siècle. *Rev. d'hist. econ. et soc.* 50(1972), pp. 357-397.

DUFOURCQ, C.E. Les relations de la Péninsule Ibérique et de l'Afrique du Nord au XIVe siècle. *Anuario estud.med.* 7(1970-71), pp. 39-63.

EPALZA, M. de. Un important fonds européen: la section "Africa" de la Bibliotheque Nationale de Madrid. *Rev. hist. maghrêb.* 1(1974), pp. 81-82.

GELLNER, E. Cohesion and identity: the Maghreb from Ibn Khaldun to Emile Durkheim. *Government and opposition* 10(1975), pp. 203-218.

HERMASSI, Elbaki. Political traditions of the Maghrib. *Daedalus* 102i(1973), pp. 207-224.

JAMALI, M.F. The Arab Maghrib and the Bandung Conference. *Rev. hist. maghrêb.* 2(1974), pp. 177-180.

JOHANSEN, B. Tradition und Moderne in der Dualismus-Theorie. *Z. f. Kulturaustausch* 25iv(1975), pp. 21-28.

KHATIBI, Abdelkebir. Hiérarchies pré-coloniales - les théories - *Bull. econ. soc. Maroc* 33(Nos. 120-1, 1971), pp. 27-61.

LACOSTE, Y. General characteristics and fundamental structures of mediaeval North African society. *Economy and society* 3 (1974), pp. 1-17.

LA VERONNE, Ch. Distinction entre Arabes et Berbères dans les documents d'archives européenes des XVIème et XVIIème et XVIIème siècles, concernant le Maghreb. *Actes I. Cong. et. cult. mediterr. d'infl. arabo-berb.,* 1973, pp. 261-265.

LE TOURNEAU, R. Nouvelles orientations des Berbères d'Afrique du Nord 950-1150. *Islamic civilization,* 1973, pp. 127-153.

LE TOURNEAU, R., FLORY, M., DUCHAC, R. Revolution in the Maghreb. *Revolution in the Middle East,* ed. P.J. Vatikiotis, 1972, pp. 73-119.

LEWIS, W.H. North Africa: calculus of policy. *America and the Middle East,* ed. P.T. Hart, 1972, pp. 56-63.

MARSTON SPEIGHT, R. Témoignage des sources musulmanes sur la présence chrétienne au Maghreb de 26-747 à 184-800. *IBLA* 35(no. 129, 1972), pp. 73-96.

MIÈGE, J.L. Probleme kultureller Einflussnahme im Maghreb der vorkolonialen Zeit. *Z. f. Kulturaustausch* 25iv (1975), pp. 7-9.

ROUSSIER, J. Un bilan de l'influence française en Afrique du Nord. *Cong.int.hist. descobrimentos. Actas* VI, 1961, pp. 353-367

RÓWNY, K. Independence and international treaties valid under protectorate. [Includes North Africa.] *Africana bull.* 17(1972), pp. 43-74.

SAÏDI, Omar. Kitāb al 'uyūn wa-l-Ḥadā'iq fī Ahbār al Ḥaqā'iq tome IV: Extraits relatifs à l'Occident musulman et en particulier à l'Ifriqyya (256)350 A.H.). *CT* 20(nos.79-80, 1972), pp. 45-100.

SANDS, W. Prospects for a united Maghrib. *The Arab Middle East and Muslim Africa*, ed. by T. Kerekes, 1961, pp. 85-94.

TAVERDOVA, E.A. Razvitie kul'tury v arabskikh stranakh Afriki. *NAA* 1975(5), pp. 83-95.

TURBET-DELOF, G. Mélanges babbaresques. 1.- Cervantès et la question morisque (1615). 2.- Les Turqueries de Molière. 3.- Une "Relation" inconnue de la bataille de l'Uued Djidiouïa (1701). *RHCM* 10(1973), pp. 81-87.

URUM, V. Sur les relations de la Roumanie avec les pays arabes de l'Afrique du Nord. *Romano-Arabica*, ed. M. Anghelescu, 1974, pp. 37-48.

VALLVE, J. Al-Andalus et l'Ifriqiya au VIIIe siècle: histoire et légende. *CT* 18(nos. 69-70, 1970), pp. 21-30.

YACONO, X. L'histoire moderne et contemporaine du Maghreb dans les archives arabes et turques. *Rev. hist.* 250(1973), pp. 403-416.

Conclusion: Islam and the study of the region. *Northern Africa: Islam and modernization*, ed. M. Brett, 1973, pp. 147-159.

See also XVI. e. Adumu.

See also XIX. a.

See also XXXV. a. Petit.

b MOROCCO

BROWN, K. Histoire sociale de Salé, 1830-1930. *Bull.de la Soc.d'hist.du Maroc* 3 (1970-1), pp. 19-21

BROWN, K. An urban view of Moroccan history. Salé, 1000-1800. *Hespéris-Tamuda* 12(1971), pp. 5-106.

HAKIM, Mohammad Ibn Azzuz. Fuentes para la historia de Tetuan y notas sobre su fundacion. *Cuadernos de la Bibl.Esp.de Tetuan* 8(1973), pp. 7-48.

HOENERBACH, W. und KOLENDA, J. Šefšawen (Xauen). Geschichte und Topographie einer marokkanischen Stadt. *WI* N.S.14 (1973), pp. 1-46; N.S.16(1975), pp. 104-165

LATHAM, J.D. The rise of the 'Azafids of Ceuta. *In memoriam S.M. Stern* (Israel Or. studies, II, 1972), pp. 263-287.

LATHAM, D. The strategic position and defence of Ceuta in the later Muslim period. *IQ* 15(1971), pp. 189-204.

ZAFRANI, H. Les problèmes monétaires au Maroc dans la littérature juridique des rabbins marocains. *Rev. hist.* 252(1974), pp. 73-80.

ZAFRANI, H. La vie intellectuelle juive au Maroc de la fin du 15ème au début du 20ème siècle. *ROMM* 9(1971), pp. 201-211.

See also XXXV. a. Barbour.

c ALGERIA

AGERON, C.R. Si M'hammed Ben Rahal (1856?-1928) oder das Schicksal eines in zwei Kulturkreisen heimischen Algeriers. *Z. f. Kulturaustausch* 25iv (1975), pp. 9-19.

CHRAMIEC, A., WOLAK, Z. Développement historique de la ville d'Alger. (Remarques concernant le plan de l'aménagement urbain de l'agglomération algéroise. *Africana bull.* 17(1972), pp. 75-89.

GRANDGUILLAUME, G. Une médina de l'Ouest algérien: Nédroma. *ROMM* 10(1971), pp. 55-80.

MASSIERA, P. M'sila du Xè au XVè siècle. *CT* 22(85-86, 1974), pp. 177-207.

TEMIMI, A. Inventaire sommaire des registres arabes et turcs d'Alger. *Rev. hist. maghréb.* 1(1974), pp. 83-96.

d TUNISIA

BERQUE, J. Ulémas tunisois de jadis et de naguère. Notes de lecture sur les *Musāmarāt al-Ẓarīf*. *CT* 20(nos. 77-78, 1972), pp. 87-124.

BONNENFANT, P. Béja, de la conquête musulmane à 1881. *IBLA* 127 (1971), pp. 3-33.

BONO, S. Commerci e collaborazione tecnica fra Italia e Tunisia nei secoli scorsi. *Levante* 20iii-iv(1973), pp. 29-40.

TLILI, Béchir. La recherche historique en Tunisie: bilan et perspectives. *CT* 20 (nos.77-78, 1972), pp. 125-133

UDINA, F. Documents relatifs à la Tunisie dans les Archives de la Couronne d'Aragon. *CT* 18(nos. 69-70, 1970), pp. 107-116.

See also XXXV. a. Epalza

e LIBYA

BRETT, M. The Zughba at Tripoli, 429H. (1037-8 A.D.). *Soc. Libyan Stud. Ann. report* 6(1974-5), pp. 41-47.

VELLA, A.P. The relations between the Order of Malta and Tripoli. *Libya in history* 1968, pp. 349-379.

XIV NORTH AFRICA: HISTORY
From the Arab Conquest till the Ottoman period

a ARAB CONQUEST

DJAIT, H. L'Afrique arabe au VIIIe siècle (86-184H./705-800). *Annales ESC* 28(1973), pp.

IDRIS, H.R. L'Occident musulman (Ifriqiya et al-Andalus) à l'avènement des Abbasides d'après le chroniqueur ziride al-Raqiq. *Ve Congrès International d'Arabisants et d'Islamisants. Actes.*, [1970?], pp. 275-283.

TALBI, Mohamed. Un nouveau fragment de l' histoire de l'Occident musulman (62-196/682-812). L'épopée d'Al-Kahina. *CT* 19i-ii(1971), pp. 19-52.

See also XXXV. b. Vallvé.

d FATIMIDS

HAMDANI, Abbas. Some aspects of the history of Libya during the Fatimid period. *Libya in history* 1968, pp. 321-346.

NÈGRE, A. À propos d'une expédition fatimide à Wargilan (Ouargla) d'après Abu Zakariyya al-Wargilani. *RHCM* 10(1973), pp. 37-39.

YALAOUI, M. Les relations entre Fātimides d'Ifriqiya et Omeyyades d'Espagne à travers le Dīwān d'Ibn Hānī. *Actas II Col. hisp.-tunec. estud. hist.*, 1973, pp. 13-30.

YALAOUI, Mohamed. Sur une possible régence du prince fatimide 'Abdallah b. Mu'izz en Ifriqiya au IVè/Xè siècle. *CT* 22(85-86, 1974), pp. 7-22.

e ZIRIDS

BELFIORE, G. Ibn Rašīq: l'ambiente, il critico, l'uomo. *Ve Congrès International d'Arabisants et d'Islamisants. Actes.*, [1970?], pp. 107-130.

BRETT, M. The military interest of the battle of Ḥaydarān. *War, technology and society in the Middle East*, ed. V.J. Parry and M.E. Yapp, 1975, pp. 78-88.

STILLMAN, N.A. Un témoignage contemporain de l'histoire de la Tunisie ziride. *Hesp Tamuda* 13(1972), pp. 37-59.

g ALMORAVIDS

JESUS RUBIERA, M. Sur un possible auteur de la chronique intitulée al-Ḥulal al-mawšiyya fi ḏikr al-ajbār al-marrākušiyya. *Actas II Col. hisp.-tunec. estud. hist.*, 1973, pp. 143-146.

MESSIER, R.A. The Almoravids. West African gold and the Mediterranean basin. *JESHO* 17(1974), pp. 31-47.

NORRIS, H.T. New evidence on the life of 'Abdullah b. Yāsīn and the origins of the Almoravid movement. *J. Afr. hist.* 12(1971), pp. 255-268.

ZBISS, Slimane-Mostafa. Considérations sur la tentative de restauration du pouvoir almoravide, en Maghreb central et oriental. *Actas II Coloquio hispano-tunecino*, 1972, pp. 31-40.

See also XIV. h. Zbiss.

h ALMOHADES

BOUROUIBA, Rachid. La doctrine almohade. *ROMM* 13-14(1973), pp. 141-158.

BRUNSCHVIG, R. Encore sur la doctrine du Mahdi Ibn Tūmart. *Folia Or.* 12(1970), pp. 33-40

DAGORN, R. Le document almohade de Poblet. *CT* 23(nos. 91-92, 1975), pp. 69-90.

HABIB HILA, M.al-. Quelques lettres de la chancellerie de Ceuta au temps des 'Azafides. *Actas II Col. hisp.-tunec. estud. hist.*, 1973, pp. 41-47.

LE TOURNEAU, R. Sur la disparition de la doctrine almohade. *SI* 32(1970), pp. 193-201.

ZBISS, Slimane-Mostafa. Considérations sur la tentative de restauration du pouvoir almoravide, en Maghreb central et oriental. *Actas II Col. hisp.-tunec. estud.*, 1973, pp. 31-40.

See also XIV. g. Jesus Rubiera.

XIV NORTH AFRICA: HISTORY

i HAFSIDS

COLIN, G.S. À propos de *al-Fārisiyya fī-mabādi' al-dawla al-ḥafṣiyya* d'Ibn al-Qunfuḏ al-Qusanṭīnī (édition critique de Muḥammad al-Šādlī al-Nayfar et 'Abd al-Maǧīd Turki, Tunis 1968, 356 pp.: introduction, texte arabe, notes et index). *Arabica* 18 (1971), pp. 107-108.

DAOULATLI, 'Abd al-'Aziz. Les relations entre le sultan Qala'un et l'Ifriqiya. D'après deux documents égyptiens (680 Hg/1281 J.C. - 689 Hg/1290 J.C.). *ROMM* 17 (1974), pp. 43-62.

DHINA, Atallah. Actes de la "Chancellerie" Tlemcienne. *RHCM* 12(1974), pp. 25-33.

GUIRAL, J. Les relations commerciales du royaume de Valence avec la Berbérie au XVe siècle. *Mélanges de la Casa de Velazquez* 10(1974), pp. 99-131.

SEBAG, P. Une nouvelle de Bandello. *IBLA* 127 (1971), pp. 35-62.

TALBI, Mohamed. Les contacts culturels entre l'Ifrīqiya hafside (1230-1569) et le sultanat nasride d'Espagne (1232-1492). *Actas II Col. hisp.-tunec. estud. hist.*, 1973, pp. 63-90.

UDINA MARTORELL, F. Sur les rapports entre la Tunisie et l'Aragon entre 1360-1379. *Actas II Coloquio hispano-tunecino*, 1972, pp. 49-62.

j ZIYANIDS

See also XIV. g. Zbiss.

k MARINIDS

DHINA, Attallah. Etude comparative de deux "traités de Tlemcen": celui de 1286 entre le royaume abdalwâdide et la Couronne d'Aragon et celui de 1339 entre le roi Jacques III de Majorque et le sultan marînide Abu'l-Hasan. *Rev. hist. civ. Maghreb* 11(1974), pp. 29-42.

HILA, M. al-Habib. Quelques lettres de la chancellerie de Ceuta au temps des 'Azafides. *Actas II Coloquio hispano-tunecino*, 1972, pp. 41-47.

LATHAM, D. The later "Azafids". *ROMM* 15-16 (1973), pp. 109-125.

See also XIV. h. Habib Hila.

l PORTUGUESE IN AFRICA

BRÁSIO, A. A integração dos descobrimentos o expansão ultramarina do Infante D. Henrique na cruzada geral do papado. *Cong. int. hist. descobrimentos. Actas* VI, 1961, pp. 73-84

HALIM, A. Prince Henry the navigator and Morocco. *Cong. int. hist. descobrimentos. Actas* VI. 1961, pp. 105-114

SERRÃO, J.V. A conquista de Ceuta no Diário veneziano de Antônio Morosini. *Cong. int. hist. descobrimentos. Actas* III, 1961, pp. 543-550

XV NORTH AFRICA: HISTORY
Ottoman Period, Sharifian Morocco

a GENERAL

HESS, A.C. Firearms and the decline of Ibn Khaldun's military elite. *Archiv Ott.* 4 (1972), pp. 173-201.

LA VERONNE, Ch. et BALAGNA, J. M'hammed al-Watiq, prince zéianide ou aventurier (1613). *Rev. hist. maghréb.* 1(1974), pp. 67-76.

LEWIS, B. Corsairs in Iceland. *ROMM* 15-16 (1973), pp. 139-144.

SOUCEK, S. Remarks on some Western and Turkish sources dealing with the Barbarossa brothers. *Güney-Doğu Avrupa araştırmaları dergisi* 1(1972), pp. 63-76.

SOUCEK, S. The rise of the Barbarossas in North Africa. *Arch. ott.* 3(1971), pp. 238-250.

STAMBOULI, F., ZGHAL, A. La vie urbaine dans le Maghreb précolonial. *Ann. Afr. Nord* 11 (1972), pp. 191-213.

b ALGERIA

BOSSY, M. Lettres adressées d'Alger au Grand-Duché de Toscane. *RHCM* 10(1973), pp. 58-79.

BOYER, P. Alger en 1645 d'après les notes du R.P. Herault. (Introduction à la publication de ces dernières.) *ROMM* 17(1974), pp. 19-41.

BOYER, P. Espagne et Kouko. Les négociations de 1598 et 1610. *ROMM* 8(1970), pp. 25-40.

BOYER, P. La révolution dite "des aghas" dans la Régence d'Alger (1659-1671). *ROMM* 13-14(1973), pp. 159-170.

CIESLAK, E. Les pirates d'Alger et le commerce maritime de Gdansk au milieu du XVIIIe siècle. *Rev. d'hist. écon. et soc.* 50(1972), pp. 110-125.

DHINA, A. Lettres d'Abu Tashufin I et de Hilal-le-Catalan conservées aux Archives de la Couronne d'Aragon à Barcelone. *RHCM* 10(1973), pp. 108-117.

FILESI, T. Napoli e Algeri (1824-1834). *Africa*[*Rome*] 28(1973), pp. 545-574.

KRIEKEN, G.V. Une escale hollandaise à Stora. *Rev.d'hist.maghrebine* 3(1975), pp. 84-90.

PILLORGET, R. Un incident diplomatique franco-turc sous Louis XIII. Le massacre d'une ambassade de la Régence d'Alger (14 mars 1620). *Rev. hist. dipl.* 88 (1974), pp. 44-58.

YACONO, X. Notes sur les établissements turcs dans la plaine du Sig. *Rev. d'hist. et de civ. du Maghreb* 9(1970), pp. 53-56.

ZIMOVÁ, N. Turkish penetration in the Sahara. *Asian and African studies* [Bratislava] 10(1974), pp. 177-181.

See also XII. e. Nouschi.

c TUNISIA

ABDESSELEM, Ahmed. Contribution à l'étude de la politique et de l'administration d'Aḥmad Bey (1837-1855). La délégation de pouvoirs de 1846. *CT* 19i-ii(1971), pp. 109-118.

ABUN-NASR, Jamil M. The Beylicate in seventeenth-century Tunisia. *IJMES* 6(1975), pp. 70-93.

BACHROUCH, Taoufik. Sur la fiscalité muradite. Présentation d'une source et de premiers résultats d'une enquête en cours. *CT* 20(nos.79-80, 1972), pp. 125-146.

BEN SMAIL, Mohamed et VALENSI, L. Le règne de Hammouda Pacha dans la chronique d'Ibn Abī-ḍ-Ḍiyāf. *CT* 19i-ii(1971), pp. 87-108.

BRAHIMI, D. Quelques jugements sur les maures andalous dans les régences turques au XVIIe siècle. *Recueil d'études sur les moriscos andalous en Tunisie,* préparé par M. de Epalza et R. Petit, 1973, pp. 135-149.

BRAHIMI, D. Témoignages sur l'île de Tabarque au XVIIIe siècle. *ROMM* 7(1970), pp. 15-35.

BUONOCORE, F. Due tragici avvenimenti nella Reggenza di Tunisi all'inizio del XIX secolo: visiti attraverso il carteggio del Consolato delle Due Sicilie conservato nell' Archivio di Stato di Napoli. *Africa* [*Rome*] 23 (1968), pp. 165-195.

CARDAILLAC, L. Morisques en Provence. *Recueil d'études sur les moriscos andalous en Tunisie,* préparé par M. de Epalza et R. Petit, 1973, pp. 89-102.

CARDAILLAC, L. Procès pour abus contre les morisques en Languedoc. *Recueil d'études sur les moriscos andalous en Tunisie,* préparé par M. de Epalza et R. Petit, 1973, pp. 103-113.

CHERIF, Mohamed-Hédi. Témoignage du "mufti" Qasim 'Azzum sur les rapports entre Turcs et autochtones dans la Tunisie de la fin du XVIe s. *CT* 20(nos.77-78, 1972), pp. 39-50.

DEMEERSEMAN, A. Une mission tunisienne en France dans la première moitié du XIXe siècle. *IBLA* 127 (1971), pp. 63-92.

EPALZA, M. de. Moriscos et andalous en Tunisie au XVIIe siècle. *Recueil d'études sur les moriscos andalous en Tunisie,* préparé par M. de Epalza et R. Petit, 1973, pp. 150-186.

EPALZA, M. de. Moriscos y andalusíes en Túnez durante el siglo XVII. *And* 34(1969), pp. 247-327

GEHRING, G. Les relations entre la Tunisie et l'Allemagne avant le Protectorat français. *CT* 18(nos. 71-72, 1970), pp. 7-155.

HUARD, P., SONOLET, J. La derrière maladie et la mort de Sidi Mohamed Ben Kassem (1811-59), Bey de Tunis. *Ouest méd.* 25(1972), pp. pp. 479-484. [CWHM 77, 1346]

LADJILI, J. La Paroisse de Tunis au XVIIIème siècle d'après les registres de Catholicité. *IBLA* 37(no.134, 1974), pp. 227-277.

MABROUK, Mohieddine. Administration et personnel administratif de la Tunisie précoloniale. *Rev. jur. et pol. indep. et coop.* 26(1972), pp. 175-200.

PENELLA, J. Le transfert des moriscos espagnols en Afrique du Nord. *Recueil d'études sur les moriscos andalous en Tunisie,* préparé par M. de Epalza et R. Petit, 1973, pp. 77-88.

PIERI, H. L'accueil par des tunisiens aux morisques expulsés d'Espagne: un témoignage morisque. *Recueil d'études sur les moriscos andalous en Tunisie,* préparé par M. de Epalza et R. Petit, 1973, pp. 128-134.

SEBAG, P. Sur une chronique des beys mouradites. Une oeuvre posthume de Guilleragues? *IBLA* (no.131, 1973), pp. 53-78.

SOUMILLE, P. et PEYRAS, J. Un aspect des relations austro-tunisiennes au dix-huitième siècle. *IBLA* 35(no.129,1972), pp. 1-31.

SOUMILLE, P. Une correspondance inédite entre 'Aḥmed Bey et le Pape Pie IX (1849-1851). *Rev.d'hist.maghrebine* 3(1975), pp. 95-99.

TLILI, Béchir. Contribution à l'étude de la pensée sociale et politique de Bayram V (1840-1889). *ROMM* 15-16(1973), pp. 327-343.

TLILI, Béchir. L'idée d'un bon gouvernement ottoman dans la pensée de Bayram V (1840-1889). *CT* 20(nos.79-80, 1972), pp. 147-170.

TLILI, Béchir. La notion de ʿUmrân dans la pensée tunisienne précoloniale. *ROMM* 12 (1972), pp. 131-151.

TLILI, Mchir. Note sur la notion d'état dans la pensée de Ah'mad ibn Abî Ad'-d'Iyâf, réformateur tunisien du XIXème siècle (1804/5-1874). *ROMM* 8(1970), pp. 141-170.

TURKI, Abdelmajid. Documents sur le dernier exode des andalous vers la Tunisie. *Recueil d'études sur les moriscos andalous en Tunisie*, préparé par M. de Epalza et R. Petit, 1973, pp. 114-127.

See also XV. b. Krieken.

See also XXXV. a. Latham

See also XXXVI. a. Harvey

See also XXXVI. a. Oliver Asin

See also XXXVI. a. Penella

See also XXXVI. a. Sarnelli

d LIBYA

ENTELIS, J.P. Ideological change and an emerging counterculture in Tunisian politics. *J.mod.Afr.stud.* 12(1974), pp. 543-568.

FAROQHI, Suraiya. Der Aufstand des Yahya ibn Yahya as-Suwaydi. *Der Islam* 47 (1971), pp. 67-92.

FILESI, T. Un ambasciatore tripolino a Napoli e un console napoletano a Tripoli nel 1742 (dal carteggio dell' Archivio di Stato di Napoli). *Africa* [*Rome*] 26 (1971), pp. 157-186.

FOLAYAN, Kola Tripoli and the war with the U.S.A., 1801-5. *J.Afr.hist.* 13(1972), pp. 261-270

FOLAYAN, Kola. Umar al-Mukhtar of Libya: a preliminary note. *Ife African studies* 1i(1974), pp. 54-65.

TURBET-DELOF, G. Le père Mercédaire Antoine Quartier et sa chronique tripolitaine des années 1660-1668. *CT* 20(nos.77-78, 1972), pp. 51-58.

VELLA, A.P. The order of Malta and the defence of Tripoli 1530-1551. *Melita historica* 6(1975), pp. 362-381.

ZIMOVÁ, Nad'a. Quelques aspects de la deuxième période Ottomane dans la Tripolitaine. *Arch. or.* 41(1973), pp. 42-51.

e SHARIFS OF MOROCCO

ALLAIN, J.C. Les Belges au Maroc à la veille du protectorat français (1906-1912). *Rev. hist. dipl.* 87(1973), pp. 320-340.

ARRIBAS PALAU, M. La acogida dispensada a Jorge Juan por la ciudad de Tetuan en febrero de 1767. *Cuadernos de la Bibl.Esp.de Tetuan* 7(1973), pp. 7-25.

ARRIBAS PALAU, M. Cartas del sultán Mawlāy al-Yazīd a la Casa Comercial España de Casablanca. *RABM* 77(1974), pp. 423-434.

ARRIBAS PALAU, M. Una descripción de la batalla librada entre Mawlāy al-Yazīd y Mawlāy Hišām cerca de Marrākuš. *Orientalia Hispanica* I, 1974, pp. 45-53.

ARRIBAS PALAU, M. Dos condenados a muerte, indultados por intercesión del embajador marroquí Muḥammad b. 'Uṯmān. *MEAH* 24 (1975), pp. 69-98.

ARRIBAS PALAU, M. Embajadas marroquies a España proyectadas en 1792. *Ve Congrès International d'Arabisants et d'Islamisants. Actes.*, [1970?], pp. 41-61.

ARRIBAS PALAU, M. La expedición española de ayuda a Mawlāy Hišām (Diciembre 1791-Febrero 1792). *MEAH* 18-19i(1969-70), pp. 43-105.

ARRIBAS PALAU, M. La proclamación de Mawlay al-Yazid celebrada en Casablanca. *Cuadernos Bibl. Española de Tetuán* 5(1972), pp. 9-16.

ARRIBAS PALAU, M. La repatriación de los misioneros franciscanos y demás españoles de Marruecos en 1790. *RABM* 75(1968-72), pp. 19-89.

AYANDELE, E.A. Moulay Abdel Aziz, herald of French conquest of the Sherifian empire. *Tarikh* 1 ii(1966), pp. 26-38.

BALAGNA, J. Deux lettres inédites du Sultan saʿadien Mûlay ʿAbdallah ibn Muhammad al Chaykh (1023 H/1614). *ROMM* 10(1971), pp. 19-25.

CABANELAS, D. El duque de Medina Sidonia y las relaciones entre Marruecos y España en tiempos de Felipe II. *MEAH* 23(1974), pp. 7-27.

CABANELAS, D. Pedro Venegas de Córdoba, embajador de Felipe II en Marruecos. *MEAH* 22 (1973), pp. 129-144.

XV NORTH AFRICA: HISTORY

CAILLÉ, J. Ambassadeurs, chargés de missions et consuls hollandais au Maroc à l'époque des sultans saadiens. *Hespéris Tamuda* 11(1970), pp. 171-207.

CAILLÉ, J. La mission à Marrakech du hollandais Pieter Maertenz. Coy (1605-1609). *Rev. hist. dipl.* 87(1972), pp. 97-123.

DAGHFOUS, Radhi. De l'origine des Banu Hilal et des Banu Sulaym. *CT* 23(nos. 91-92, 1975), pp. 41-68.

DEMEERSEMEN, A. Responsabilité du Bâš-mamlûk Ḥusayn Hûǧa dans la crise économico-financière de la Tunisie. *IBLA* 35(no.130, 1972), pp. 219-260.

DEVERDUN, G. Dahir sa'dide de renouvellement (1632) (respect des coutumes et exonération d'impôt). *ROMM* 13-14(1973), pp. 313-317.

DZIUBINSKI, A. L'armée et la flotte de guerre marocaines à l'époque des sultans de la dynastie saadienne. *Hesp Tamuda* 13(1972), pp. 61-94.

GANDIN, J.M. La remise de Larache aux Espagnols en 1610. *ROMM* 7(1970), pp. 71-92.

HAKIM, Mohammad ibn Azzuz. La embajada de Pedro Venegas en Marruecos (1579-1581). *Cuadernos Bibl. Espan. Tetuan* 6(1972), pp. 1-46.

HARAKAT, Brahim. Le makhzen sa'adien. *ROMM* 15-16(1973), pp. 43-60.

LA VERONNE, C. de. Relations entre le Maroc et la Turquie dans la seconde moitié du XVIe siècle et le début du XVIIe siècle (1554-1616). *ROMM* 15-16 (1973), pp. 391-401.

LA VÊRONNE, C. de. Séjour en Andalousie de deux princes Sa'diens apres la bataille d'el Ksar El-Kebir (1589-1595). *MEAH* 16-17 (1967-8), pp. 47-55

LA VÉRONNE, C. de. Séjour en Andalousie de deux princes Sa'diens après la bataille d'El Qçar el-Kébir (1589-1595). *ROMM* 7 (1970), pp. 187-194.

LOURIDO DIAZ, R. Hacia la desaparicion de la esclavitud cristiano-musulmana entre Marruecos y Europa (siglo XVIII). *Cuadernos Bibl. Española de Tetuán* 5(1972), pp. 47-79.

LOURIDO DÍAZ, R. El morabitismo y la dinastia 'alawī en la segunda mitad del siglo XVIII. Politica religiosa del sultán Sīdī Muḥammad b. 'Abd Allāh. *Cuadernos de historia del Islam, ser. misc.: Islamica occidentalia* 1(1971), pp. 125-157.

LOURIDO, R. Sīdī Muḥammad b. 'Abd Allāh y sus intentos de creación de una marina de guerra al estilo europeo (1769-1777). *Hespêris-Tamuda* 12(1971), pp. 133-156.

MEUNIER, D. Une description du Maroc au début du XVIIIème siècle. *Rev. hist. maghreb.* 4(1975), pp. 215-216.

MOJUETAN, B.A. Myth and legend as functional instruments in politics: the establishment of the 'Alawī dynasty in Morocco. *J. Afr. hist.* 16(1975), pp. 17-27.

MOUGIN, L. Remarques sur les débuts du marabout Al-'Ayyâchî (1563-1641). *ROMM* 18 (1974), pp. 119-124.

PELLAT, C. Un document sur les rapports entre Chorfa et Berbères. *ROMM* 15-16(1973), pp. 253-256.

POSAC MON, Carlos. La rebellion de Tanger en 1643. *Cuadernos Bibl. Espan. Tetuan* 6(1972), pp. 79-112.

RICHARDS, D.S. A letter to Charles I of England from the Sultan al-Walīd of Morrocco. *IQ* 17(1973), pp. 26-35.

SALMI, J.-M. l'accès aux langues occidentales au Maroc à la veille du Protectorat français. *Actes I. Cong. et. cult. mediterr. d'infl. arabo-berb.*, 1973, pp. 266-268.

STILLMAN, N.A. A new source for eighteenth-century Moroccan history in the John Rylands University Library of Manchester: the Dombay papers. *Bull. J.R. Univ. Libr.* 57(1974-5), pp. 463-486.

ZAFRANI, Haim. Les problèmes monétaires au Maroc dans la littérature juridique *(taqqanot* et *responsa)* des rabbins marocains. *JA* 262(1974), pp. 37-46.

See also I. b. 3. López García.

See also XVII. b. Lourido Diaz.

See also XIX. h. Raymond.

XVI NORTH AFRICA: HISTORY
Modern Period

a GENERAL

ABUN-NASR, Jamil M. French colonial rule in the Maghrib. *Tarikh* 2iv(1969), pp. 32-58.

ABUN-NASR, J.M. Independence movements in the Maghrib. *Tarikh* 4i(1971), pp. 54-67.

ADAM, A. Urbanisation et changement culturel au Maghreb. *Ann.Afr.Nord* 11(1972), pp. 215-232.

AGÜERO, Celma El sentido social de un movimiento religioso: el mahdismo en Africa moderna. *Estudios orientales* 6ii (no. 16, 1971), pp. 152-162.

BARBOUR, N. North West Africa: independence and nationalism. *Northern Africa: Islam and modernization,* ed. M. Brett, 1973, pp. 85-95.

BONO, S. Le controversie di frontiera dell' Algeria con il Marocco e con la Tunisia (1956-1970). *OM* 50 (1970), pp. 602-633.

BOYER, P. L'odyssée d'une tribu saharienne: Les Djeramna (1881-1929). *ROMM* 10(1971), pp. 27-54.

BROWN, L. Carl. The many faces of colonial rule in French North Africa. *ROMM* 13-14 (1973), pp. 171-191.

CARLIER, J-L. La première Etoile Nord-Africaine (1926-1929). *Rev. alg. sci. jur. econ. et pol.* 9(1972), pp. 907-966.

CLAUSS, M.W. Der Maghreb im internationalen Feld. *Afrika Spectrum* 3/70, pp. 5-16.

COOKE, J.J. The army archives at Vincennes: archives for the study of North African history in the colonial period. *MW* 61 (1971), pp. 35-38.

DAOUD, Zakya. Kulturelle Beziehungen zwischen Frankreich, der Bundesrepublik Deutschland und dem Maghreb. Die Rolle der ausländischen Kulturzentren in den Maghrebländern. *Z. f. Kulturaustausch* 25iv(1975), pp. 125-128.

DEBBASCH, Ch. Les élites maghrébines devant la bureaucratie. *Annuaire Afr. Nord* 7(1968), pp. 11-12.

DUCHAC, R. Les urbanisations au Maghreb. Homologies et disparités. *Ann.Afr.Nord* 11 (1972), pp. 5-17.

EICKELMAN, D.F. Islam and the impact of the French colonial system in Morocco. A study in historical anthropology. *Humaniora Islamica* 2(1974), pp. 215-235.

ETIENNE, B. Succession d'état et conditions des habitants. *Ann. de L'Afr. du Nord* 5 (1966), pp. 25-50.

ETIENNE, B. L'unité maghrébine à l'épreuve des politiques étrangères nationales. *Ann. Afr.Nord* 9(1970), pp. 85-100

FLORY, M. Problématique institutionnelle de l'unité maghrébine. *Ann.Afr.Nord* 9 (1970), pp. 157-161

FLORY, M. La succession aux traités lors de la décolonisation de l'Afrique du Nord. *Ann. de L'Afr. du Nord* 5(1966), pp. 11-24.

FOUILLOUX, G. La succession des états de l'Afrique du Nord aux biens publics français. *Ann. de L'Afr. du Nord* 5(1966), pp. 51-79.

FRISCH, A. Frankreich und die Maghreb-staaten. *Afrika Spectrum* 3/70, pp. 42-51.

FUGLESTAD-AUMEUNIER, V. La coopération italo-maghrébine. *Maghreb-Machrek* 63(1974), pp. 20-32.

GALLAGHER, C.F. The Maghrib and the Middle East. *Political dynamics in the Middle East,* ed. P.Y. Hammond and S.S. Alexander, 1972, pp. 395-423.

GOUBERVILLE, Capitaine de. Le corps franc d'Afrique 1942-1943. *Rev.hist.armée* 4 (1971), pp. 50-58.

GUKASYAN, L.G. Mezhdunarodnye otnosheniya stran Magriba v 1945-1956 gg. *Mezhdunarodnye otnosheniya na Blizhnem i Srednem Vostoke,* 1974, pp. 106-128.

HENNEBELLE, M. et G. Cinéma et société au Maghreb. *Annuaire Afrique du Nord* 12 (1973), pp. 131-150.

HEPP, M.A. Le général Laperrine, organisateur de la pacification du Sahara. *Rev. hist.armée* 2(1971), pp. 142-167.

JACQUES, R. Opposition and control in Tunisia, Morocco and Algeria. *Government and opposition* 1(1965-6), pp. 389-404.

KRÄMER, M. Überlegungen zur strategischen Position des Maghreb. *Afrika Spectrum* 70, pp. 17-26.

KUM'A N'DUMBE III, Alexandre. L'Allemagne nazie et l'Afrique du Nord. *Cahiers d'histoire* 19(1974), pp. 353-373.

XVI NORTH AFRICA: HISTORY

LAHJOMRI, A., LA BASTIDE, H. de. Situation et avenir de la langue et de la culture françaises au Maghreb. *Etudes philos. et litt. (Actes du Coll. de Mohammédia)* 5(1971), pp. 73-103.

LA VERONNE, C. de. Quelques processions de captifs en France à leur retour du Maroc, d'Algérie ou de Tunis (XVIIe-XVIIIe siècles). *II.Cong.int.ét.nord-afr.* 1970, pp. 131-142.

LE TOURNEAU, R. Tendances unitaires du Maghreb jusqu'en 1962. Aperçu historique. *Ann.Afr.Nord* 9(1970), pp. 3-8

LIAUZU, C. Jalons pour une étude des Biribi. *CT* 19i-ii(1971), pp. 119-152.

LING, D.L. Planners of protectorates: Cambon in Tunisia and Lyautey in Morocco. *MW* 64(1974), pp. 220-227.

MAMMERI, Mouloud. Gelebte Kultur und legitime Kultur im Maghreb. *Z. f. Kulturaustausch* 25iv(1975), pp. 29-33.

MARCHAT, H. Les origines diplomatiques du "Maroc Espagnol" (1880-1912). *ROMM* 7(1970), pp. 101-170.

NOUSCHI, A. Histoire, politique et légitimité au Maghreb. *Ann Afr. Nord* 10(1971), pp. 11-23.

PHILLIPS, D.H. The American missionary in Morocco. *MW* 65(1975), pp. 1-20.

PUIGAUDEAU, O. du. Une nouvelle généalogie de Cheikh Mā-el-'Aīnin Ū. Māmīn. *Hespéris-Tamuda* 12(1971), pp. 157-193.

RASSAT, J. Die Integrationsbemühungen in Maghreb. *Afrika Spectrum* 2/68, pp. 81-86.

RONDOT, P. L'Islam dans la politique des Etats du Maghreb. *Politique étrangère* 38(1973), pp. 41-50.

RUF, W.K. La politique étrangère des Etats maghrébins. *Maghreb-Machrek* 59(1973), pp. 22-33.

SANTUCCI, J.C. Les garanties des biens privés et la succession aux engagements antérieurs souscrits envers les personnes privées. *Ann. de L'Afr. du Nord* 5(1966), pp. 81-98.

SANTUCCI, J.C. L'unification maghrébine: réalisations institutionelles et obstacles politiques. *Ann.Afr.Nord* 9(1970), pp. 129-156

SHINAR, Pessah. The historical approach of the reformist 'Ulamā' in the contemporary Maghrib. *Asian & Afr.Studs.* 7 (1971), pp. 181-210.

SRIEB, Noureddine. Politiques culturelles nationales et unité maghrébine. *Ann.Afr. Nord* 9(1970), pp. 101-127

SUTTON, K. Political association and Maghreb economic development. *J. mod. Afr. studs.* 10(1972), pp. 191-202.

SZYMANSKI, E. The policy of France in Northern Africa after the Second World War. *Dzieje najnowsze* 1(1969), pp. 23-36 [*Polish sci. per.* 10(70), 1969.]

TALHA, Larbi. L'évolution du mouvement migratoire entre le Maghreb et la France. *Maghreb-Machrek* 61(1974), pp. 17-34.

TURIN, Y. Culture et politique au XIXe siècle. (Reflexions sur l'impérialisme culturel, de type médical, en milieu colonial.) *Rev. hist. maghréb.* 1(1974), pp. 35-38.

VALETTE, J. Quelques aspects nouveaux de l'expédition Flatters. *ROMM* 15-16(1973), pp. 375-390.

VATIN, J.C. Questions culturelles et questions à la culture. *Annuaire Afrique du Nord* 12(1973), pp. 3-16.

WATERBURY, J. The Soviet Union and North Africa. *The Soviet Union and the Middle East*, ed. I.J. Lederer and W.S. Vucinich, 1974, pp. 78-120.

YACONO, X. L'histoire moderne et contemporaine du Maghreb dans les archives arabes et turques. *Rev.d'hist.maghrebine* 3(1975), pp. 65-74.

ZAMITI, Khalil. Ideologische Implikationen des Spezifizitätsbegriffs und Entkolonisierung der Gesellschaftswissenschaften. *Z. f. Kulturaustausch* 25iv(1975), pp. 33-37.

ZGHAL, A. La construction nationale au Maghreb. *Renaissance du monde arabe. Colloque interarabe de Louvain,* 1972, pp. 136-166.

ZGHAL, Abdelkader. Nation-building in the Maghreb. *Int. soc. sci. J.* 23 (1971), pp. 435-451.

Die Assoziierung der Maghrebstaaten im Lichte einer Mittelmeerpolitik der Europäischen Gemeinschaften. *Afrika Spectrum* 3/70, pp. 27-41.

aa ECONOMICS

AKSYUK, L.N. Cherbaya metallurgiya stran Severnoy Afriki (isklyuchaya Sudan) i perspektivy ee razvitiya. *Arabskie strany, Turtziya, Iran, Afganistan,* 1973, pp. 170-178.

BENACHENOU, Abdellatif. Forces sociales et accumulation du capital au Maghreb. *Annuaire Afrique du Nord* 12(1973), pp. 315-342.

BENBACHIR, Said. L'administration régionale dans les pays du Maghreb. *Cah. afr. admin. publ.* 9(1973), pp. 195-204. [English version: Regional government in the Maghreb countries, pp. 205-214].

BENYOUSSEF, Amor. Recherche des fondements économiques de l'integration au Maghreb. *Ann.Afr.Nord* 9(1970), pp. 9-84

CARRIÈRE, P. L'insertion dans le milieu rural languedocien des agriculteurs rapatriés d'Afrique du Nord. *Etudes rurales* 52(1973), pp. 57-79.

CASTELLO, J. Le développement de l'industrie sidérurgique en Afrique du Nord. *Maghreb-Machrek* 55(1973), pp. 15-20.

DEVISSE, J. Routes de commerce et échanges en Afrique occidentale en relation avec la Méditerranée. Un essai sur le commerce africain médiéval du XIe au XVIe siècle. *Rev. d'hist. écon. et soc.* 50(1972), pp. 42-73.

DOUGHERTY, J.J. Land-lease and the opening of French North and West Africa to private trade. *Cah.ét.afr.* 15(1975), pp. 481-500.

DUCHAC, R. Chronique de l'émigration. *Annuaire Afrique du Nord* 12(1973), pp. 1065-1069.

ETIENNE, B. Maghreb et C.E.E. *Annuaire Afr. Nord* 8(1969), pp. 169-201.

FLORY, M. Schéma pour une étude idéologique de la coopération. *ROMM* 13-14(1973), pp. 331-342.

GHEZALI, Mahfoud. Les relations Maghreb-CEE. *Rev.alg.* 12(1975), pp. 611-736.

MASLOV, V.A. Problemy transportirovki prirodnogo gaza iz arabskikh stran Severnoy Afriki z Zapadnuyu Evropu i SShA. *Istoriya i ekonomika stran Arabskogo Vostoka,* 1973, pp. 184-189.

MELLAH, Mohamed Farid. L'integration du Maghreb face à l'Association à la Communauté Economique Européenne. *Corresp. d'Orient. Etudes.* 17-18(1970), pp. 7-79.

OUALALOU, Fathallah. Überlegungen zu den neuen Formen der Kooperation zwischen dem Maghreb und Europa. *Z. f. Kulturaustausch* 25iv(1975), pp. 116-124.

SCHLIEPHAKE, K. Die ländliche Wasserversorgung in Nordafrika. Probleme und Zukunft der landwirtschaftlichen Bewässerung. *Afrika spectrum* 1972(2), pp. 52-74.

STEMER, E. Les pays du Maghreb producteurs d'engrais phosphatés. *Maghreb-Machrek* 59 (1973), pp. 34-37.

VIRABOV, A.G. Economic integration of the Maghrib: prospects and reality. *Africa in Soviet studies* 1969, pp. 56-65.

See also IV. c. 8. Binswanger.

b MOROCCO

ADAM, A. La politique culturelle au Maroc. *Annuaire Afrique du Nord* 12 (1973), pp. 107-128.

ADAM, A. Sur l'action du *Galilée* à Casablanca en 1907. *ROMM* 6(1969), pp. 9-21.

AGERON, C.R. La politique berbère du Protectorat Marocain de 1913 à 1934. *Rev. hist. mod. contemp.* 18 (1971), pp. 50-90.

ALLAIN, J.C. L'emprunt des bijoux de la couronne chérifienne (1907-1910). *Rev. hist.dipl.* 85(1971), pp. 152-169.

ARDANT, Ph. Bilanz der französisch-marokkanischen kulturellen Zusammenarbeit. *Z. f. Kulturaustausch* 25iv(1975), pp. 75-81.

ARRIBAS PALAU, M. La ayuda prestada a España por el canciller Mure de Pelane en 1791 y 1792. *II. Cong.int.ét.nord-afr.* 1970, pp. 31-44.

BEN KADDOUR, Abdaslam. The Neo-Makhzan and the Berbers. *Arabs and Berbers,* ed. E. Gellner and C. Micaud, 1973, pp. 259-267.

BROWN, K. The impact of the Dahir berbère in Salé. *Arabs and Berbers,* ed. E. Gellner and C. Micaud, 1973, pp. 201-215.

BURKE, E. A comparative view of French native policy in Morocco and Syria, 1912-1925. *ME stud.* 9(1973), pp. 175-186.

BURKE, E. (III). Pan-Islam and Moroccan resistance to French colonial penetration, 1900-1912. *J.Afr.hist.* 13(1972), pp. 97-118.

BURKE, E. Rural resistance and popular protest in Morocco: a study of the tribal rebellion of 1911. *ROMM* 13-14(1973), pp. 193-206.

CAGNE, J. Nation et nationalisme au Maroc. Les journées d'études des 12 et 13 mai 1967. *Bull. Soc. hist. Maroc* 1 (1968), pp. 5-7.

CAGNE, J. Les origines du mouvement Jeune Marocain. *Bull. Soc. hist. Maroc* 1 (1968), pp. 8-17.

CHAMBERGEAT, P. Observations sur le système électoral marocain. *Ann. de L'Afr. du Nord* 5(1966), pp. 99-109.

CLAUSEN, U. Zur innenpolitischen Entwicklung Marokkos von 1973 bis 1975. *Orient* [Hamburg] 16iii(1975), pp. 10-17.

COLSON, J.Ph. Aspects constitutionnels et politiques du Maroc indépendant. *Rev.du droit public* 91(1975), pp. 1281-1305.

COOKE, J.J. France and Morocco: the 1894 origins of the colonial protectorate. *Africa Q.* 15iii(1975-6), pp. 5-20.

CORAM, A. The Berbers and the coup. *Arabs and Berbers,* ed. E. Gellner and C. Micaud, 1973, pp. 425-430.

DAMIS, J. Early Moroccan reactions to the French protectorate: the cultural dimension. *Humaniora Islamica* 1(1973), pp. 15-31.

DAMIS, J. The Moroccan political scene. *MEJ* 26(1972) pp. 25-53

XVI NORTH AFRICA: HISTORY

DAVIS, R.H.C. William of Tyre. *Relations between East and West in the Middle Ages*, ed. D. Baker, 1973, pp. 64-76.

DELEAU, J. L'administration marocaine. *BIIAP* 27(1973), pp. 465-480.

DERO-JACOB, A.C. Modernisme et traditionalisme dans la politique marocaine de la France avant l'indépendance. *Corresp. d'Orient. Etudes.* 17-18 (1970), pp. 81-104.

DUPONT, J. Constitution et consultations populaires au Maroc. *Ann.Afr.Nord* 9(1970), pp. 163-194

ESCALLIER, R. La croissance urbaine au Maroc. *Ann.Afr.Nord* 11(1972), pp. 145-173.

FRANCISI, A. Marocco: il complotto di marzo e il processo di Qenitrah. *OM* 54(1974), pp. 240-258.

GELLNER, E. Patterns of rural rebellion in Morocco during the early years of independence. *Arabs and Berbers*, ed. E. Gellner and C. Micaud, 1973, pp. 367-374.

GELLNER, E. Patterns of tribal rebellion in Morocco. *Revolution in the Middle East*, ed. P.J. Vatikiotis, 1972, pp. 120-145.

GOURDON, J. Les élections communales marocaines du 3 octobre 1969. *Annuaire Afr. Nord* 8(1969), pp. 329-338.

GUILLEN, P. L'Allemagne et le Maroc de 1870 à 1905. *Bull. Soc. hist. Maroc* 1 (1968), pp. 20-22.

GUILLEN, P. La finance française et le Maroc de 1902 à 1904. *Bull. Soc. hist. Maroc* 2 (1969), pp. 37-42.

GUILLEN, P. La résistance du Maroc à l'emprise française au lendemain des accords franco-anglais d'avril 1904. *II. Cong.int.ét.nord-afr.* 1970, pp. 115-122.

HOISINGTON, W. Commerce and conflict: French businessmen in Morocco, 1952-55. *J. contemp. hist.* 9ii(1974), pp. 49-67.

JOHANSEN, B. Biographien als Beitrag zur Historiographie. Einige Bemerkungen zu: Attilio Gaudio, Allal El Fassi ou l'Histoire de l'Istiqlal (Paris 1972). *Islam* 51(1974), pp. 125-130.

JOUIN, Y. Le "camouflage" des goums marocains pendant la période d'armistice (1940-1942). *Rev.hist.armée* 2(1972), pp. 100-117.

LAROUI, Abdallah. Cultural problems and social structure: the campaign for Arabization in Morocco. *Humaniora Islamica* 1(1973), pp. 33-46.

LAROUI, A. Traduction et traditionalisation: le cas du Maroc. *Renaissance du monde arabe. Colloque interarabe de Louvain*, 1972, pp. 265-276.

LOURIDO DIÁZ, R. El sultán 'alawī Sīdī Muḥammad b. 'Abd Allāh (1757-1790) y sus sueños de hegemonía sobre el Islám occidental. *Orientalia Hispanica* I, 1974, pp. 472-489.

LUCCIONI, J. L'avènement de Sidi Mohammed Ben Youssef au trône du Maroc (1927). *ROMM* 12(1972), pp. 123-129.

LUCCIONI, J. L'éloignement de Sidi Mohammed ben Arafa du trône des Alaouites en septembre 1955. *ROMM* 8(1970), pp. 101-112.

MALKI, Habib el-. Le financement des plans marocains depuis 1960. *Bull.econ.et soc. Maroc* 32(117, 1970), pp. 19-39

MARAIS, O. Berbers and the Moroccan political system after the coup. *Arabs and Berbers*, ed. E. Gellner and C. Micaud, 1973, pp. 431-432.

MARAIS, O. Élites intermédiaires, pouvoir et légitimité dans le Maroc indépendant. *Ann. Afr. Nord* 10(1971), pp. 179-201.

MARAIS, O. Sociologie politique de Fès. *ROMM* 15-16(1973), pp. 169-174.

MARAIS, O., WATERBURY, J. Thèmes et vocabulaire de la propagande des élites politiques au Maroc. *Annuaire Afr. Nord* 7(1968), pp. 57-78.

MARCHAT, H. La France et l'Espagne au Maroc pendant la période du Protectorat (1912-1956). *ROMM* 10(1971), pp. 81-109.

MASSON, A. Urbanisation et habitat du grand nombre: l'approche marocaine. *Ann.Afr.Nord* 11(1972), pp. 105-143.

MIEGE, J.L. L'arrière plan diplomatique de la guerre du Rif. *ROMM* 15-16(1973), pp. 219-230.

OUALALOU, F. Réflexions sur les nouvelles formes de "coopération" entre le Maghreb et l'Europe. *Bull.écon.soc.Maroc* 128-9 (1975?), pp. 135-154.

PALAZZOLI, J. La mort lente du mouvement national au Maroc. *Ann.Afr.Nord* 11(1972), pp. 233-251.

PALAZZOLI, M. The evolution of the Moroccan national movement since independence. *Northern Africa: Islam and modernization*, ed. M. Brett, 1973, pp. 123-146.

PAVLUTZKAYA, E.V. Otrazhenie klassovykh protivorechiy marokkanskogo obshchestva v konstitutzionnom prave. *Arabskie strany, Turtziya, Iran, Afganistan*, 1973, pp. 122-129.

PERSELL, S.M. L'affaire de La Tourmaline (1897-1898). Les réactions françaises à la présence anglaise au Maroc. *Rev.hist. dipl.* 85(1971), pp. 142-151.

REGNIER, J.J. et SANTUCCI, J.C. Armée, pouvoir et légitimité au Maroc. *Ann Afr. Nord* 10(1971), pp. 137-178.

RIZZITANO, U. Le Maroc contemporain et ses problèmes culturels. *Actas IV congresso de estudos árabes e islâmicos* 1968(1971), pp. 385-394.

ROUDAN, M. Justice, pouvoir et politique au Maroc. *Ann.Afr.Nord* 11(1972), pp. 253-286.

ROUSSET, M. Administration et société au Maroc. *ROMM* 15-16(1973), pp. 301-311.

ROUSSET, M. Le pouvoir réglementaire au Maroc: dix années d'évolution. *Rev. jur. et pol. indep. et coop.* 26(1972), pp. 333-358.

ROUSSET, M. Le rôle du ministère de l'intérieur et sa place au sein de l'administration marocaine. *Annuaire Afr. Nord* 7(1968), pp. 91-106.

SAULAY, J. Le XVIIe tabor marocain en Indochine, 1951-1952. *Rev.hist.armée* 2(1974), pp. 63-94.

SEDDON, J.D. Local politics and state intervention: Northeast Morocco from 1870 to 1970. *Arabs and Berbers,* ed. E. Gellner and C. Micaud, 1973, pp. 109-139.

SINGH, K.R. European rivalries in Morocco before 1912. *Studies in politics: national and international,* 1971, pp. 397-409.

SINGH, K.R. Morocco: crisis of political leadership. *Africa qly.* 11(1971), pp. 175-202

SRAÏEB, Noureddine. Enseignement, élites et systèmes de valeur: le Collège Sadiki de Tunis. *Ann Afr. Nord* 10(1971), pp. 103-135.

SZYMANSKI, E. Les tribus de "Guich" et le Makhzen sous le règne de Sidi Mohammed ben Abd Allah. *II.Cong.int.ét.nord-afr.* 1970, pp. 195-202.

TIMM, Kl. Revolutionäre Alternative für Marokko. *OLZ* 69(1974), col. 5-15.

TURIN, Y. "Médecine de propagande" et colonisation, l'expérience de Bouffarick, en 1835. *II.Cong.int.ét.nord-afr.* 1970, pp. 185-194.

VINOGRADOV, Amal and WATERBURY, J. Situations of contested legitimacy in Morocco: an alternative framework. *Comp. stud. soc. hist.* 13(1971), pp. 32-59.

WATERBURY, J. The coup manqué. *Arabs and Berbers,* ed. E. Gellner and C. Micaud, 1973, pp. 397-423.

WATERBURY, J. Kingdom-building and the control of opposition in Morocco: the monarchical uses of justice. *Government and opposition* 5(1969-70), pp. 54-66.

WEISCHER, B.M. Die islamische Kultur zwischen Kontinuität und Wandel. *Z.f.Kulturaustausch* 24ii(1974), pp. 23-25.

WILSON, K. The Agadir crisis, the Mansion House speech, and the double-edgedness of agreements. *Hist. J.* 15(1972), pp. 513-532.

ZARTMAN, W. Political pluralism in Morocco. *Government and opposition* 2(1966-7), pp. 568-583.

See also XII. b. Burke.

See also XII. b. Coram.

See also XII. b. Duclos.

See also XII. b. Marais.

See also XII. d. Eickelman.

See also XVI. c. Burke.

See also XVII. a. Sahara espagnol: ...

bb ECONOMICS

AGOURRAM, Abdeljalil et BELAL, Abdel-Aziz Bilan de l'économie marocaine depuis l'indépendance. *Bull.écon.soc.Maroc* 32 (no. 116,[1970?]), pp. 1-27.

AGOURRAM, Abdeljalil. L'hydraulique agricole au Maroc. *Bull.écon.soc.Maroc* 31(no. 115, 1969), pp. 1-12

ALAMI M'CHICHE MUSTAPHA. Problèmes de l'ingénierie au Maroc. *Bull. écon. soc. Maroc* 127(1975), pp. 1-53.

ASSIME, Abdellah. Comment peut-on envisager une solution aux problèmes posés par l'utilisation des ressources humaines au Maroc. *Bull. écon. soc. Maroc* 126(1975), pp. 33-46.

BARON, P. Esquisse nutritionelle du Maroc rural. *Bull. écon. soc. Maroc* 126(1975), pp. 47-80.

BÉGUIN, H. La ville et l'industrie au Maroc. *Tiers-monde* 12(1971), pp. 145-166.

BELAL, Abdel Aziz, AGOURRAM, Abdeljalil L'économie marocaine depuis l'indépendance. *Annuaire Afr. Nord* 8(1969), pp. 145-168.

BELAL, Abdel-Aziz, AGOURRAM, Abdel-Jalil. Les problèmes posés par la politique agricole dans une économie "dualiste". Les leçons d'une expérience. Le cas marocain. *Bull. écon. soc. Maroc* 33(no.122, 1973), pp. 1-36.

BELAL, Abdelaziz. L'utilisation des ressources humaines au Maroc (1926-1970) de Abdallah Assime. *Bull. écon. soc. Maroc* 126(1975), pp. 107-110.

BONNET, J. Note sur l'économie marocaine en 1969. *RGM* 18(1970), pp. 119-128.

BOUDERBALA, N. Quelques données élémentaires sur l'évolution des structures agraires dans la plaine du Rharb. *RGM* 20 (1971), pp. 119-124

BOUDERBALA, N., CHRAÏBI, M., PASCON, P. La question agraire au Maroc. *Bull. écon. soc. Maroc* 123-125(1974), pp. 423.

CHERKAOUI, Souâd. La dette publique intérieure au Maroc. *Bull.écon.soc.Maroc* 31(no. 115, 1969), pp. 51-98

CHEVALIER, J.M. Problèmes économiques d'un pays importateur de pétrole: le cas du Maroc. *Mondes en développement* 5 (1974), pp. 125-156.

CHRAIEI, Mohamed. Techniques d'irrigation et structures agraires. *Bull. econ. soc. Maroc* 33(nos, 120-1, 1971), pp. 63-80.

DOMINGO, J. L'industrie marocaine de la conserve de poissons. *Cah. d'outre mer* 25(no.99, 1972), pp. 307-337.

DUNN, R.E. The trade of Tafilalt: commercial change in South-East Morocco on the eve of the protectorate. *Afr.hist. stud.* 4(1971), pp. 271-304.

FARID MELLAH, Mohamed. Le Maroc dans la politique méditerranéenne de la communauté économique européenne. *Bull. écon. soc. Maroc* 126(1975), pp. 81-106.

GERMOUNI, Mohammed. Une approche économique de l'engineering. *Bull. econ. soc. Maroc* 127(1975), pp. 55-64.

GRAR, Ahmed. Les structures agraires dans la Chaouia (Ouled Saïd). *Bull.econ.et soc. Maroc* 32(117, 1970), pp. 41-74

GUESSOUS, Bensalem. Les relations du Maghreb avec la Communauté économique européenne. *La Communauté et les pays méditerranéens* 1970, pp. 37-53.

HAMDOUCH, M. Bachir. Le cadre institutionnel des échanges extérieurs du Maroc avant l'indépendance du régime de la "Porte Ouverte" au "Protectionnisme de Zone". *Bull.écon.soc.Maroc* 128-9(1975?), pp. 45-91.

IMANI, A. The family planning programme in Morocco. *Population growth and economic development in Africa,* 1972, pp. 365-368.

KHATIBI, A. Note descriptive sur les élites administratives et économiques marocaines. *Annuaire Afr. Nord* 7 (1968), pp. 79-90.

KOHEN, Mhamed el. L'association du Maroc à la Communauté économique européenne. Une étape importante. *La Communauté et les pays méditerranéens* 1970, pp. 55-81.

LAMBERT, P. Le commerce extérieur du blé de 1945 à 1970. *Bull. écon. soc. Maroc* 33 (no.122, 1973), pp. 99-109.

LAMGHILI, Ahmed el-Kohen. La commercialisation intérieure des céréales au Maroc. *Maghreb-Machrek* 60(1973), pp. 34-39.

LOURIDO DIAZ, R. Los intercambios comerciales hispano-marroquies en el siglo XVIII. *Cuadernos de la Bibl.Esp.de Tetuan* 8(1973), pp. 49-86.

MALKI, Habib el-. Comment sortir du sous-développement? *Bull. écon. soc. Maroc* 33 (no.122, 1973), pp. 111-122.

MALKI, Habib El. Le surplus économique, instrument d'analyse de la théorie du développement. *Bull. écon. soc. Maroc* 126(1975), pp. 11-32.

MDAGHRI, Driss Alaoui. Maghrebische Zusammenarbeit und kulturelle Beziehungen zu Europa. *Z. f. Kulturaustausch* 25iv (1975), pp. 108-116.

MELLAH, Mohamed Farid. La négociation Maroc-CEE en vue de conclure un nouvel accord d'association sur des bases élargies. *Correspondance d'Orient: Etudes* 19-20(1971-2), pp. 7-45.

OUALALOU, Fathallah. L'apport étranger et l'agriculture marocaine. *Bull. écon. soc. Maroc* 33(no. 122, 1973), pp. 37-63.

OURABAH, Mahmoud Le processus de planification. *Rev.algér.des sci.jur., econ. et pol.* 8(1971), pp. 685-699.

TROIN, J.F. Essai méthodologique pour une étude des petites villes en milieu sous-développé: les structures commerciales urbaines du Nord marocain. *Ann. de géogr.* 80(no. 441, 1971), pp. 513-533.

PALAZZOLI, C. Le système fiscal marocain. *BIIAP* 20(1971), pp. 733-748.

PÉRÉ, M. Quelques aspects du tourisme au Maroc à travers l'exemple d'Agadir. *RGM* 22(1972), pp. 3-30.

PONASIK, D.S. Les fonctions modernes du souk marocain. *Bull.écon.soc.Maroc* 128-9 (1975?), pp. 155-177.

PONIKIEWSKI, A. Social and agrarian relations in Moroccan agriculture. *Africana bull.* 18(1973), pp. 127-141.

RAKI, Mohammed. Dualisme rural - cas du Gharb. *Bull. écon. soc. Maroc* 33(no. 122, 1973), pp. 65-82.

RISER, J. Le commerce extérieur du Maroc en 1969. *RGM* 18(1970), pp. 103-118.

ROUSSET, M. L'aménagement du territoire et la régionalisation au Maroc. *Bull. Inst. internat. d'admin. publ.* 31(1974), pp. 479-81.

SANTUCCI, J. Cl. Le plan quinquennal marocain 1973-1977. *Maghreb Machrek* 67(1975), pp. 52-61.

SARI, Djilali. Ghazaouët: débouché de l'Oriental marocain. *Maghreb-Machrek* 60(1973), pp. 27-33.

SEBBAR, Hassan. Tourisme et développement -- le cas du Maroc. *Bull. écon. soc. Maroc* 127(1975), pp. 65-84.

SEFRIOUI, A. L'artisanat marocain. *Ann.Afr. nord* 12(1973), pp. 181-191.

Analyse économique: Rabat-Salé. *Bull. econ. et soc. du Maroc* 118-9 (1972), pp. 57-80.

See also VIII. d. *Morocco.* Cagne.

See also XI. b. Bouquerel

See also XI. b. Charvet.

See also XII. b. Spaak.

c ALGERIA

ABDI, Nourredine. Perspectives d'évolution de la propriété privative des terres agricoles ou à vocation agricoles en Algérie dans le cadre de la Révolution Agraire. *Rev. alg. des sci. jur., econ. et pol.* 10 (1973), pp. 223-237.

AGERON, C.R. Une émeute anti-juive à Constantine (août 1934). *ROMM* 13-14(1973), pp. 23-40.

AGERON, Ch. R. Ferhat Abbas et l'évolution politique de l'Algérie musulmane pendant la deuxième guerre mondiale. *Rev. hist. maghreb.* 4(1975), pp. 125-144.

AINAD-TABET, Redouane. Le 8 Mai 1945: Jacquerie ou revendication agraire. *Rev. alg. sci. jur. econ. et pol.* 9(1972), pp. 1007-1016.

AKKACHA, Mahieddine. La participation des travailleurs algériens aux institutions représentatives dans les entreprises françaises. *Rev. alg. des sci. jur., econ. et pol.* 10(1973), pp. 497-509.

ALEXANDRE, Fr. Le P.C.A. de 1919 à 1939 - données en vue d'éclaircir son action et son rôle. *Rev.alg.* 11(1974), pp. 175-214.

AUTIN, J.L. Quelques aspects socio-politiques de la Révolution Agraire. *Rev. alg. des sci. jur., econ. et pol.* 10(1973), pp. 141-159.

BAUMANN, H. State of development and activities of the revolutionary democratic government in Algeria. *African studies - Afrika-Studien*, ed. Thea Büttner and G. Brehme, 1973, pp. 169-194.

BEGHOUL, Youcef. La libération nationale par la voie populaire: l'appel au pays réel. *Rev.alg.* 11(1974), pp. 214-271.

BELHAMISSI, Moulay. Les combats de Mazagran (février 1840) Légende et réalité. *RHCM* 12(1974), pp. 35-51.

BEN NAOUM, Ahmed. Les lois foncières coloniales et leurs effets en Algérie (1830-1930). *Rev. alg. des sci. jur., econ. et pol.* 10 (1973), pp.7-31.

BERNARD, Ch. La monnaie comme instrument de transition vers le mode de production capitaliste en Algérie (1851-1885). *Rev. alg.* 12(1975), pp. 297-323.

BLEUCHOT, H. Approches idéologiques de l'élaboration du statut de la fonction publique en Algérie. *ROMM* 15-16(1973), pp. 205-217.

BORRMANS, M. Le "Ministère de l'Enseignement Originel et des Affaires Religieusse", en Algérie, et son activité culturelle, *OM* 52(1972), pp. 467-481.

BOSC, R. Algérie: la voix d'une nation émergente parmi les nations prolétaires. *Projet* 90(1974), pp. 1121-1124.

BOUHOUCHE, Ammar. Conditions et attitudes des travailleurs algériens émigrés en France. *Rev. alg. des sci. jur., econ. et pol.* 10(1973), pp. 511-525.

BOYER, P. Le problème Kouloughli dans la régence d'Alger. *II.Cong.int.ét.nord-afr.* 1970, pp. 79-94.

BURKE, E. III. Parties and elites in North African politics: Algeria and Morocco. *Africa today* 18iv(1971), pp. 50-59.

BYE, M. Vers l'association à la production et au développement mondial. Un exemple: les accords franco-algériens. *Les investissements et le développement économique des pays du Tiers-Monde* 1968, pp. 348-386.

CAMELIN, A. Le service de santé en Algérie, de la conquête aux accords d'Evian. *Rev.hist.armée* 1(1972), pp. 46-63.

CERBELLA, G. L'azione dell'emiro Abd el-Qâder contro i Drusi, massacratori, nel 1860, dei Cristiani di Damasco. *Africa* [Rome] 28(1973), pp. 51-64.

CERBELLA, G. Cristianesimo ed Islamismo nel pensiero dell'Emiro Abd-el-Qâdir. *Africa [Rome]* 27(1972), pp. 179-192.

CHENNTOUF, Tayeb. Un document inédit sur le 8 mai 1945 dans le Constantinois: le rapport du Général Tubert. *Rev.alg.* 11 (1974), pp. 289-316.

CHENNTOUF, Tayeb. Question coloniale et questions ouvrières chez les travailleurs français de l'Ouest algérien: la Ligue des travailleurs français du département d'Oran (1892-1895). *Rev. d'hist. mod. contemp.* 22(1975), pp. 433-445.

CHEVALDONNE, Fr. Fonctionnement d'une institution idéologique coloniale: la diffusion de cinéma dans les zones rurales d'Algérie avant la deuxième Guerre Mondiale. *Rev. alg.* 12(1975), pp. 529-548.

COLLOT, Cl. Le Congrès Musulman Algérien (1937-1938). *Rev.alg.* 11(1974), pp. 71-161.

COLLOT, C. Le parti du peuple algérien. *Rev.algérienne des sci.jur., econ.et pol.* 8(1971), pp. 133-204.

COLLOT, Cl. Tradition et innovation dans l'administration française: l'experience algérienne de 1955 à 1962. *Rev. hist. de droit franç.* 4.ser.,52(1974), pp. 628-657.

XVI NORTH AFRICA: HISTORY

COLLOT, C. L'Union Populaire Algérienne (1937-1939). *Rev. alg. sci. jur. econ. et pol.* 9(1972), pp. 967-1005.

COLONNA, F. Cultural resistance and religious legitimacy in colonial Algeria. *Economy and society* 3(1974), pp. 233-252.

COOKE, J.J. Eugene Etienne and the failure of assimilation in Algeria. *Africa qly* 11 (1971-72), pp. 285-296.

COOKE, J.J. Eugène Etienne and the emergence of colon dominance in Algeria, 1884-1905. *MW* 65(1975), pp. 39-53.

CUBERTAFOND, B. Réflexions sur la politique algérienne. *Maghreb-machrek* 69 (1975), pp. 25-31.

CUPERLY, P. Muḥammad Aṭfayyaš et sa Risâla šafiya fî ba'ḍ tawârîḫ ahl wâdî Mizâb. *IBLA* 35(no.130, 1972), pp. 261-303.

DANZIGER, R. Abd al-Qadir's first overtures to the British and the American (1835-1836). *ROMM* 18(1974), pp. 45-63.

DEJEUX, J. Principales manifestations culturelles en Algérie depuis 1962. *Annuaire Afrique du Nord* 12(1973), pp. 77-96.

DEMIA, Sakina. Pour une analyse critique du nationalisme algérien. *Rev.alg.* 11 (1974), pp. 13-42.

DESTANNE DE BERNIS, G. Le plan quadriennal de l'Algérie (1970-1973). *Ann.Afr.Nord* 9(1970), pp. 195-230

DOBOSIEWICZ, Z. Siły społeczno-polityczne współczesnej Algerii. (Les forces sociaux-politiques de l'Algérie contemporaine.) *Przegląd or.* 82(1972), pp. 115-124.

DUCHAC, R. Révolution et socialisme en Tunisie et en Algérie. *Ann. de L'Afr. du Nord* 5(1966), pp. 133-151.

EMERIT, M. Alger en 1800, d'après les mémoires inédits de Le Maye. *Rev. hist. maghrêb.* 2(1974), pp. 171-176.

EMERIT, M. Description de l'Algérie en 1787 par l'officier russe Kokovtsov. *Rev. hist. maghreb.* 4(1975), pp. 209-213.

EMERIT, M. L'exploitation des os des musulmans pour le raffinage du sucre. *Rev. hist maghrêb.* 1(1974), pp. 11-13.

ÉMERIT, M. La question algérienne en 1871. *Rev. hist. mod. contemp.* 19(1972), pp. 256-264.

EMERIT, M. La thèse de Jacques Valette (consacrée à un journaliste sans génie, Jacques Duval). *Rev. hist. maghreb.* 4 (1975), pp. 195-196.

ETIENNE, Br. Bilanz der französisch-algerischen Kooperation. *Z. f. Kulturaustausch* 25iv(1975), pp. 86-97.

ETIENNE, B. Le flou urbain: l'affrontement des modèles. *Ann.Afr.Nord* 11(1972), pp. 29-38.

ETIENNE, Br. et LECA, J. La politique culturelle de l'Algérie. *Annuaire Afrique du Nord* 12(1973), pp. 45-76.

ETIENNE, B. Le vocabulaire politique de légitimité en Algérie. *Ann Afr. Nord* 10(1971), pp. 69-101.

FERRAND, B. Reforme territoriale des wilayate et formation de l'état algérien. *Rev. alg.* 12(1975), pp. 561-568.

FISCHER, G. Le non-alignment et la conférence d'Alger (septembre 1973). *Tiers-monde* 16(no.56, 1973), pp. 855-876.

FRANCHET, J. La formulation de l'espace algérien. *Ann.Afr.Nord* 11(1972), pp. 39-53.

GELLNER, E. The unknown Apollo of Biskra the social base of Algerian puritanism. *Government and opposition* 9(1974), pp. 277-310.

GHOZALI, Nasser Eddine. Opposition explicite et collaboration implicite: Le mouvement National Algérien (M.N.A.) de Messali Hadj. *Rev. alg. sci. jur. econ. et pol.* 9(1972), pp. 1017-1042.

GIL BENUMEYA, R. Argelia y sus significados veinte años despues. *Rev.polit.int.* 136 (1974), pp. 139-147.

GOURDON, H., HENRY, J.R., HENRY-LORCERIE, Fr. Roman colonial et idéologie coloniale en Algérie. *Rev.alg.* 11(1974), pp. 7-252.

GRIMAUD, N. Evolution du syndicalisme en Algérie. *Maghreb-Machrek* 57(1973), pp. 26-30.

GUIRAL, P. Observations et réflexions sur les sévices dans l'armée d'Afrique. *ROMM* 15-16(1973), pp. 15-20.

HEGGOY, A.A. Algerian women and the right to vote: some colonial anomalies. *MW* 64(1974), pp. 228-235.

HENRY, J.R. et TALEB-BENDIAB, Abderrahim. Contribution à la bibliographie du mouvement national algérien. *Rev.alg.* 11(1974), pp. 317-384.

HÖPP, G. Islam und nationale Emanzipation in Algerien - zur Entstehungsgeschichte der "Gesellschaft der algerischen 'ulama'". *Asien,Afrika,Lateinamerika* 3(1975), pp. 85-104.

JAŁOWIECKI, B. L'étude d'une ville post-coloniale -- le cas d'Alger. *Africana bull.* 20(1974), pp. 121-162.

KADDACHE, M. L'Emir Khaled, jeune étudiant et officier. *RHCM* 10(1973), pp. 101-107.

XVI NORTH AFRICA: HISTORY

KADDACHE, Mahfoud. L'utilisation du fait berbère comme facteur politique dans l'Algérie coloniale. *Actes I. Cong. et. cult. mediterr. d'infl. arabo-berb.*, 1973, pp. 276-284.

KENNETT, L. Jules Gérard: a forgotten figure in Algerian history. *MW* 64(1974), pp. 45-49.

KOERNER, Fr. L'extrême droite en Oranie (1936-1940). *Rev. hist. mod. contemp.* 20(1973), pp. 568-594.

KOERNER, Fr. Les répercussions de la guerre d'Espagne en Oranie (1936-1939). *Rev. d'hist. mod. contemp.* 22(1975), pp. 476-487.

KOERNER, F. Sources de l'histoire contemporaine de l'Algerie conservées à Oran (1830-1955). *Rev. d'hist. et de civ. du Maghreb* 9(1970), pp. 95-103.

LANDA, R.G. Izuchenie alzhirskoy revolyutzii v SShA. *NAA* 1975(4), pp. 175-187.

LECA, J. Administration locale et pouvoir politique en Algérie. *Ann. Afr. Nord* 10(1971), pp. 203-232.

LECA, J. Kulturelle Identität im Maghreb: der Fall Algerien. *Z. f. Kulturaustausch* 25iv(1975), pp. 45-55.

LECA, J. Parti et Etat en Algérie. *Annuaire Afr. Nord* 7(1968), pp. 13-42.

LEONE, E. de. La reggenza di Algeri alla vigilia dell'occupazione francese secondo le fonti italiane. *II.Cong.int.ét.nord-afr.* 1970, pp. 143-152.

LETOURNEAU, R. L'Algérie et les Chorfa d'Ouezzane à la fin du XIXe siècle. *II. Cong.int.ét.nord-afr.* 1970, pp. 153-161.

LINDNER, Jerzy. La voie non capitaliste du développement de l'Algérie. *Africana bull.* 13 (1970), pp. 57-74.

LUCAS, P. Déchiffrement dialectique de l' histoire et libération de la connaissance fanon et la lutte de libération Algérienne. *Rev. alg. sci. jur. econ. et pol.* 9(1972), pp. 1043-1053.

MAHIOU, Ahmed Les collectivités locales en Algérie. *Annuaire Afr. Nord* 8(1969), pp. 285-309.

MAHIOU, Ahmed. Les forces politiques en Algérie entre les deux guerres mondiales. *Rev.alg.* 11(1974), pp. 7-10.

MARCHAT, H. Fromentin en Afrique. *ROMM* 13-14(1974), pp. 119-137.

MARTHELOT, P. Réflexions sur certaines conséquences de la révolution agraire en Algérie. *Maghreb-Machrek* 65(1974), pp. 32-35.

MAZOUNI, Abdellah. Cultures et sociétés: le cas de l'Algérie de 1962 à 1973. *Rev. alg.* 12(1975), pp. 147-159.

MELKI, J.C. Réalisation et financement du plan quadriennal algérien de développement. *Maghreb-Machrek* 65(1974), pp. 16-32.

MERAD, Ali. L'émir Khaled (1875-1936) vu par Ibn Bâdîs (1889-1940). *ROMM* 9(1971), pp. 21-35.

MEYNIER, G. Aspects de l'économie de l'Est algérien pendant la guerre de 1914-1918. *Rev.hist.* 247(1972), pp. 81-116.

MEYNIER, G. Loyalisme et insécurité en Algérie pendant la guerre de 1914-1918. *CT* 19, nos. 75-76(1971), pp. 183-207.

MEYNIER, G. Le sud constantinois en 1912 d'après "Le cri de l'Algérie", journal anticolonialiste constantinois. *Hespéris-Tamuda* 12(1971), pp. 165-182.

MIAILLE, M. Le controle de l'état sur les associations en Algérie. *Rev. alg.* 12(1975), pp. 47-76.

MICHEL, H. La classe dirigeante algérienne, le parti et la fonction publique. *ROMM* 15-16(1973), pp. 197-203.

MIGNON, J.M. Le plan communal algérien: l'expérience des programmes spéciaux de Constantine et d'Annaba. *Tiers monde* 15(1974), pp. 389-396.

NADIR, A. Le mouvement réformiste algérien et la guerre de libération nationale. *Rev. hist. maghreb.* 4(1975), pp. 174-183.

NADIR, Ahmed. Les ordres religieux et la conquête française (1830-1851). *Rev. alg. sci. jur. econ. et pol.* 9(1972), pp. 819-868.

NIMSCHOWSKI, H. Die FLN-Partei Algeriens. Ihre Entwicklung und gegenwärtige Rolle. *Asien, Afrika, Lateinamerika* 2(1974), pp. 933-946.

NIMSCHOWSKI, H. The politico-ideological concept of the leading revolutionary democratic forces of Algeria regarding the socialistically orientated process of social transformation. *African studies - Afrika-Studien*, ed. Thea Büttner and G. Brehme, 1973, pp. 195-211.

PERINBAM, B.M. Fanon and the revolutionary peasantry - the Algerian case. *J.mod.Afr. stud.* 11(1973), pp. 427-445.

PERONCEL-HUGOZ, J.P. Le front de libération nationale: parti unique de l'Algérie. *Rev. fr. ét. pol. africaines* 66(1971), pp. 34-52.

PLUM, Werner. Wechsel der Führungskräfte in der Befreiungsfront Algeriens. *Orient* [Germany] 14(1973), pp. 156-161.

PRIEUR, M. L'institutionnalisation du parti socialiste Destourien. *Ann. de L'Afr. du Nord* 5(1966), pp. 121-132.

REKLAJTIS, E. Contribution à la recherche historique au sujet des relations algéro-polonaises. *RHCM* 10(1973), pp. 97-99.

XVI NORTH AFRICA: HISTORY

REMILI, A. Parti et Administration en Algérie. *Annuaire Afr. Nord* 7(1968), pp. 43-56.

REY-GOLDZEIGER, A. Les problèmes algériens du Second Empire vus par les historiens français. *Rev. hist. mod. contemp.* 21(1974), pp. 111-126.

RUF, W. and AMMANN, K. Die begriffe "Nation", "Revolution" und "Sozialismus" in den Reden der Präsidenten Boumedienne und Bourguiba. *Vierteljahresberichte (Fr. Ebert-Stiftung)* 44(1971), pp. 181-192.

SAADALLAH, Belkacem. The Algerian ulamas, 1919-1931. *Rev. hist. maghréb.* 2(1974), pp. 138-168.

SAINTE-MARIE, A. La commune d'Azeffoun à la fin du XIXème siècle. *Rev.alg.* 11 (1974), pp. 40-460

SAINTE-MARIE, A. La province d'Alger vers 1870: l'établissement du douar- commune et la fixation de la nature de la propriété en territoire militaire dans le cadre du Senatus-Consulte du 22 Avril 1863. *ROMM* 9 (1971), pp. 37-61.

SANSON, H. Prise de la ville, prise du pouvoir. *Ann.Afr.Nord* 11(1972), pp. 19-28.

SARI, Djilali. Problèmes démographiques algériens. *Maghreb-Machrek* 63(1974), pp. 32-42.

SARI, D. La restructuration des centres urbains en Algérie. *Ann.Afr.Nord* 11(1972), pp. 55-75.

SIVAN, Emanuel. Leftist outcasts in a colonial situation: Algerian communism, 1927-1935. *Asian and African studies* [Jerusalem] 10(1975), pp. 209-257.

SIVAN, Emanuel. 'Slave owner mentality' and Bolshevism: Algerian communism, 1920-1927. *Asian and African studies* [Jerusalem] 9(1973), pp. 154-195.

SMITH, Tony. Muslim impoverishment in colonial Algeria. *ROMM* 17(1974), pp. 139-162.

SPILLMANN, G. Algérie 1974. *L'Afrique et l'Asie modernes* 103(1974), pp. 3-18.

SPILLMANN, G. Controverse entre Napoléon III et Mac-Mahon au sujet du Royaume Arabe d'Algérie. *Comptes rend. trimest. Acad. des Sciences d'Outre-Mer.* 33(1973), pp. 157-167.

SUR, S. Aspects juridiques du différend pétrolier Franco-Algérien: la position algérienne. *Ann. Afr. Nord* 10(1971), pp. 233-265.

TALEB BENDIAB, Abderrahim. Précisions structurelles sur le Congrès Musulman Algérien. *Rev.alg.* 11(1974), pp. 163-174.

TEMIMI, Abdeljelil. Le drapeau constantinois à l'époque de Hadj Ahmed, dernier Bey de Constantine. *ROMM* 15-16(1973), pp. 323-326.

TERKI, Nourredine. La notion de possession dans l'article 78 de l'Ordonnance no. 71-73 du 8 novembre 1971. *Rev. alg. des sci. jur., econ. et pol.* 10(1973), pp. 213-221.

THOUMELIN, J.B., TURIN, Y. Peut-on parler d'une "Commune" de Blida? (d'apres *le Tell). Rev. hist. civ. Maghreb* 11(1974), pp. 19-27.

TIBI, Bassam. Zur gesellschaftlichen Realität des "islamischen Sozialismus" in Algerien unter dem Militärregime. *Vierteljahresberichte* 50(1972), pp. 333-352.

TLILI, Béchir. L'Algérie au lendemain de la Grande Guerre: revendications et réformisme. Un document inédit sur la situation politique et administrative des indigènes de l'Algérie (1920-1921). *CT* 22(nos.87-88,1974), pp. 93-153.

TURIN, Y. La culture dans "l'authenticité et l'ouverture" au Ministère de l'enseignement originel et des affaires religieuses. *Annuaire Afrique du Nord* 12(1973), pp. 97-105.

VATIN, J-C. Conditions et formes de la domination coloniale en Algérie (1919-1945). *Rev. alg. sci. jur. econ. et pol.* 9(1972), pp. 873-906.

VATIN, J.C. Histoire en soi et histoire pour soi: 1919-1945 et après. *Rev.alg.* 11 (1974), pp. 275-287.

VATIN, J.Cl. Nationalisme et socialisation politique. De quelques conditions du regroupement national entre 1919 et 1945. *Rev.alg.* 11(1974), pp. 43-52.

VON SIVERS, P. Insurrection and accommodation: indigenous leadership in Eastern Algeria, 1840-1900. *IJMES* 6 (1975), pp. 259-275.

VON SIVERS, P. The realm of justice: apocalyptic revolts in Algeria (1849-1879). *Humaniora Islamica* 1(1973), pp. 47-60.

WALKER, D. The origins of arab nationalism in Algeria. *IC* 46(1972), pp. 285-292.

YACONO, X. Un affranchissement d'esclaves à Alger en 1847. *Rev. hist. maghréb.* 1 (1974), pp. 75-81.

YACONO, X. Les premiers prisonniers algériens de l'Ile Sainte-Marguerite (1841-1843). *Rev. hist. maghréb.* 1 (1974), pp. 39-61.

YACONO, X. Les prisonniers de la smala d'Abd el-Kader. *ROMM* 15-16(1973), pp. 415-434.

YACONO, X. Quelques remarques sur la politique indigène du prince Napoléon en Algérie (24 juin 1858-7 mars 1959). *II. Cong.int.ét.nord-afr.* 1970, pp. 203-220.

ZARTMAN, I.W. Les élections départementales algériennes du 25 mai 1969. *Annuaire Afr. Nord* 8(1969), pp. 311-327.

See also I. c. 4. Burke.

See also IX. m. Cooke

See also XII. b. Quandt.

See also XVII. c. Destanne de Bernis.

cc ECONOMICS

ABDI, Nourredine. La réforme agraire en Algérie. *Maghreb-machrek* 69(1975), pp. 33-41.

ADAM, M. Localisation des industries nouvelles et population urbaine en Algérie. *Annuaire Afr. Nord* 8(1969), pp. 43-54.

AGERON, C.R. Fiscalite française et contribuables musulmans dans le Constantinois. *Rev. d'hist. et de civ. du Maghreb* 9(1970), pp. 79-94.

AIT AMARA, Hamid. Quelques aspects de la restructuration agraire. *Rev. alg. des sci. jur., econ. et pol.* 10(1973), pp. 161-176.

AKSYUK, L.N. O nekotorykh osobennostyakh osvoeniya krupnykh zhelezorudnykh mestorozhdeniy razvivayushchikhsya stran na primere Gara Dzhebilet (Alzhir) *Strany Blizhnego i Srednego Vostoka: istoriya, ekonomica,* 1972, pp. 226-234.

BARAK, M. Quelques remarques à propos d'une "contribution à une réflexion théorique sur l'entreprise socialiste en Algérie. *Rev.alg.* 11(1974), pp. 259-298.

BARDINET, C.; CABOT, J. Population active et critère d'urbanisation en Algérie à la veille du plan quadriennal (1970-1973). *Tiers-monde* 14(1973), pp. 615-630.

BARTHEL, G., GRIENIG, H., KÜCK, G. Tendenzen der wirtschaftlichen Entwicklung in Algerien, Ägypten und Syrien. *Asien, Afrika, Latein-Amerika* 1(1, 1973), pp. 101-116.

BECKER, G. Möglichkeiten und Ziele einer kulturellen Zusammenarbeit zwischen der Bundesrepublik Deutschland und Frankreich in Algerien. *Z. f. Kulturaustausch* 25iv (1975), pp. 133-140.

BENACHENOU, Abdellatif. Reflexions sur la politique des revenus en Algérie. *Rev. alg.* 12(1975), pp. 7-45.

BENAISSA, Saïd. La déconcentration financière. *Rev.alg.* 11(1974), pp. 337-378.

BENCHEIKH, Madjid. Le conseil national économique et social. *Rev. alg.* 12 (1975), pp. 77-95.

BENDEDDOUCHE, J. Remarques sur l'entreprise privée algérienne. *Rev. alg. des sci. jur., econ. et pol.* 10(1973), pp. 411-450.

BENISSAD, M.E. La formation économique de l'Algérie et le dualisme. *Mondes en développement* 10(1975), pp. 243-271.

CHENNTOUF, Tayeb. Où en est la discussion sur le mode de production de l'Algérie précoloniale? *Rev. alg. des sci. jur., econ. et pol.* 10(1973), pp. 465-485.

COUTSINAS, G. A propos des deux circuits de l'économie urbaine. Un exemple algérien. *Tiers Monde* 16(1975), pp. 773-781.

DAVID, C. Les coopératives agricoles et la Révolution Agraire. *Rev. alg. des sci. jur., econ. et pol.* 10(1973), pp. 177-212.

DAVID, M. La Banque Nationale d'Algérie. *Rev.alg.sci.jur.econ.pol.* 9(1972), pp. 7-54

DESTANNE de BERNIS, G. L'économie algérienne depuis d'indépendance. *Annuaire Afr. Nord* 8(1969), pp. 13-41

DESTANNE DE BERNIS, G. Les problèmes pétroliers algériens. *Rev. alg.* 10 (1975), pp. 717-758.

EIKENBERG, C. Berufsausbildung und Fachkräftebedarf in Algerien. *Afrika Spectrum* 1973, (1), pp. 29-41.

GRIMAUD, N. Les finances publiques de l'Algérie. *Maghreb-Machrek* 56(1973), pp. 30-37.

HELIE, D. L'autogestion industrielle en Algérie. *ROMM* 6(1969), pp. 113-126.

KHABITZOV, B. Nekotorye problemy neftyanoy promyshlennosti Alzhira (1958 - 1970 gg.) *Strany Blizhnego i Srednego Vostoka: istoriya, ekonomica,* 1972, pp. 442-453.

KULIEV, F.N. Bor'ba frantzuzkoy kommunisticheskoy partii protiv zagovorov ul'trakolonialistov v Alzhire v 1960-1962 gg. *Arabskie strany, Turtziya, Iran, Afganistan,* 1973, pp. 257-262.

LAULANIE, J.F. de. La croissance de l'économie algérienne (1963-1968). *Rev. algérienne des sci.jur., econ.et pol.* 8 (1971), pp. 83-120.

LE PAPE, M. Avant la révolution agraire algérienne. [Review article.] *Cah.ét.afr.* 14(1974), pp. 397-400.

LEQUY, R. L'agriculture algérienne de 1954 à 1962. *ROMM* 8(1970), pp. 41-99.

LERAT, S. Hassi Messaoud. *Cah. d'outre mer* 24(1971), pp. 16-31.

MARTENS, J.C. Le processus d'industrialisation en Algérie. *Correspondance d'Orient: Etudes* 15-16(1969), pp. 45-79.

MARTIN, M.C. Perspectives de développement en Saoura. *Maghreb-machrek* 69 (1975), pp. 51-59.

MIAILLE, M. Contribution à une reflexion théorique sur l'entreprise socialiste algérienne. *Rev. algér. des sci. jur., écon. et pol.* 9(1972), pp. 653-693.

MIAILLE, M. Réflexion sur une contribution théorique concernant l'entreprise socialiste algérienne. Réponse à quelques remarques. *Rev.alg.* 11(1974), pp. 299-335.

XVI NORTH AFRICA: HISTORY

MIETTE, R. L'agriculture dans le développement algérien. *Asie et Afrique modernes* 104(1975), pp. 22-41.

MIETTE, R. L'autogestion agricole en Algérie. *L'Afrique et l'Asie modernes* 103 (1974), pp. 19-31.

NOUSCHI, A. Note sur les investissements français en Algérie. Essai méthodologique. *CT* 23(nos.89-90,1975), pp. 19-31.

OLLIVIER, M. Révolution Agraire et mobilisation des masses. *Rev. alg. des sci. jur., econ. et pol.* 10(1973), pp. 33-140.

PASCALLON, P. et LAULANIE, J.F. de. L'expérience monétaire algérienne: du satellisme à l'indépendance monétaire (suite). *Rev.algérienne des sci.jur., econ.et pol.* 8(1971), pp. 7-82.

PICHOT, A. Le système algérien de comptabilité nationale. *Tiers Monde* 16 (1975), pp. 783-793.

SARI, Djilali. L'application de la première étape de la défense du patrimoine forestier de la Révolution Agraire. *Rev. alg. des sci. jur., econ. et pol.* 10(1973), pp. 239-245.

SARI, D. L'équilibre économique traditionnel de l'Ouarsenis. *Rev. d'hist. et de civ. du Maghreb* 9(1970), pp. 57-78.

SARI, Djalali. L'équilibre économique traditionnel des populations de l'Ouarsenis central. *ROMM* 9(1971), pp. 63-89.

SARI, Djilali. L'évolution de l'emploi en Algerie. *Maghreb-machrek* 69(1975), pp. 42-50.

SARI, D. La récupération et la valorisation des hydrocarbures par l'Etat Algérien. *Rev.algérienne des sci.jur., econ.et pol.* 8(1971), pp. 419-443.

SCHLIEPHAKE, K. Die algerische Agrarrevolution. *Afrika spectrum* 1972(no.1), pp. 44-59.

SCHLIEPHAKE, K. Die algerische Erdölwirtschaft: binnen-wirtschaftliche Probleme und energiepolitische Konsoquenzen. *Afrika Spectrum* 1974/3, pp. 139-151.

SCHLIEPHAKE, K. Arbeitskreis zur Terminologie der arabisch-islamischen Kulturlandschaft. *Afrika Spectrum* 1973, (1), pp. 106-107.

SCHLIEPHAKE, K. Changing the traditional sector of Algeria's agriculture. *Land reform* 1973(1), pp. 19-28.

SMIRNOV, G.V. Rol' gosudarstva v reshenii problemy nakopleniya v ANDR. *NAA* 1973(5) pp. 13-22.

SMITH, Tony. The political and economic ambitions of Algerian land reform. *MEJ* 29(1975), pp. 259-278.

SUTTON, K. Agrarian reform in Algeria - the conversion of projects into action. *Afrika spectrum* 1/1974, pp. 50-68.

TOUAT, Larbi. Développement économique et nouvelles familles algériennes. *Rev.alger. des sci.jur.econ.pol.* 11iii(1974), pp. 149-156.

VALBERG, P. Cinq ans après. Bilan des accords franco-algériens de coopération industrielle et pétrolière du 29 juillet 1965. *Annuaire Afr. Nord* 8(1969), pp. 55-91.

VAN MALDER, R. La révolution agraire en Algérie: tournant politique ou infléchissement technique? *Civilisations* 25 (1975), pp. 251-271.

VLACHOS, G.S. Le régime juridique des entreprises publiques en Algérie. *Rev. algér. des sci. jur., econ. et pol.* 9(1972), pp. 471-504.

WIELEZYNSKI, M. Produktion von Kompetenzen und Technologie-instituten in Algerien. *Z. f. Kulturaustausch* 25iv (1975), pp. 129-132.

Le gaz naturel algérien. *Maghreb-Machrek* 55(1973), pp. 21-34.

Planification et développement en Algérie. *Levante* 22i(1975), pp. 17-26.

See also III. c. *Algeria*. David.

See also III. c. *Algeria*. Vlachos.

See also IV. c. 8. Grandguillaume.

See also V. t. Louis.

See also XI. c. Arnold.

See also XI. c. Sari.

See also XVI. c. Smith.

d TUNISIA

ABDESSELEM, Ahmed. "Révolutions barbaresques" et poésie arabe: réflexions sur la vie et l'oeuvre d'un prince-poète tunisien du XVIIIe siècle. *CT* 22(nos.87-88,1974), pp. 35-40.

ARNOULET, Fr. Participation tunisienne à la guerre de Crimée (1854-1856). *CT* 20(nos. 79-80, 1972), pp. 269-284.

ASHFORD, D.E. Succession and social change in Tunisia. *ROMM* 13-14(1973), pp. 49-65.

BARDIN, P. Les débuts difficiles du protectorat tunisien (mai 1881-avril 1882). *Rev. hist. dipl.* 85 (1971), pp. 17-64.

BENHAMIDA, Khemaïs. Kulturelle Identität und Unterricht. Versuch einer Analyse der gegenwärtigen Situation in Tunesien. *Z. f. Kulturaustausch* 25iv(1975), pp. 56-61.

XVI NORTH AFRICA: HISTORY

BEN SALEM, L. Origines géographiques et sociales des cadres de l'administration économique, des offices et sociétés nationales en Tunisie. *Annuaire Afr. Nord* 7(1968), pp. 107-127.

BEN SALEM, Lilia. Versuch einer Inhaltsanalyse des Begriffs der kulturellen Identität im Tunesien der siebziger Jahre unseres Jahrhunderts. *Z. f. Kulturaustausch* 25iv(1975), pp. 61-65.

BERCHER, L. En marge du pacte "fondamental". Un document inédit. *CT* 20(nos.79-80, 1972), pp. 243-260.

BILINSKY, Y. Moderate realism in an extremist environment: Tunisia and the Palestine question (1965-1970). *ROMM* 13-14(1973), pp. 109-123.

BONNENFANT, P. Une ville moyenne de Tunisie: Beja. *CT* 19i-ii(1971), pp. 153-206.

BORRMANS, M. Authenticité et ouverture par Muḥammad Mzâlî. *OM* 55(1975), pp. 29-48.

BOUKRAA, R. Développement national et développement régional en Tunisie. *Renaissance du monde arabe. Colloque interarabe de Louvain*, 1972, pp. 122-135.

CAMAU, M. Le discours politique de légitimité des élites tunisiennes. *Ann Afr. Nord* 10(1971), pp. 25-68.

CANNON, B.D. Tunisian money adjustments and the Union Latine, 1872-1894. *Rev. hist. maghrêb.* 2(1974), pp. 107-115.

CLAUSEN, U. Der IX. Kongress der tunesischen sozialistischen Destur-Partei und die Präsidial- und Legislativwahlen vom November 1974. *Orient* [Hamburg] 16i (1975), pp. 15-22.

R.D. L'armature urbaine tunisienne et son devenir. *Ann.Afr.Nord* 11(1972), pp. 175-189.

DJEDIDI, Tahar Labib. Culture et société en Tunisie. *Annuaire Afrique du Nord* 12 (1973), pp. 19-27.

DURUPTY, M. Les élections présidentielles et législatives tunisiennes du 2 Novembre 1969. *Annuaire Afr. Nord* 8(1969), pp. 339-357.

FONDE, J.J. "L'escadron sacré" dans le Sud Tunisien. *Rev.hist.armée* (1943), pp. 99-118.

GALLAGHER, N.E. The Arab medical organization in nineteenth century Tunisia. *Rev. hist. maghreb.* 4(1975), pp. 145-149.

GARMADI, S. Les problèmes du plurilinguisme en Tunisie. *Renaissance du monde arabe. Colloque interarabe de Louvain*, 1972, pp. 309-322.

GERMANN, R.E. L'administration dans le système politique tunisien. *Annuaire Afr. Nord* 7(1968), pp. 139-156.

GIL BENUMEYA, R. La realidad tunecina en la evolución del Magreb. *Rev.polit.int.* 134 (1974), pp. 139-149.

GREEN, A.H. French Islamic policy in Tunisia, 1881-1918: a preliminary inquiry. *Rev.d'hist.maghrebine* 3(1975), pp. 5-17.

GREEN, A.H. The Tunisian ulama and the establishment of the French Protectorate 1881-1882. *Rev. hist maghrêb.* 1(1974), pp. 14-25.

HADI CHÉRIF, Mohamed Expansion européenne et difficultés tunisiennes de 1815 à 1830. *II.Cong.int.ét.nord-afr.* 1970, pp. 111-114.

HAHN, L. Tunisian political reform: procrastination and progress. *MEJ* 26(1972), pp. 405-414.

HARBER, C.C. Tunisian land tenure in the early French protectorate. *MW* 63(1973), pp. 307-315.

JULIEN, Ch. A. Une lettre de Habib Bourguiba à Andrée Viollis. *Rev. hist. maghrêb.* 2(1974), pp. 181-184.

KACEM, Abdelaziz. La politique culturelle tunisienne. *Annuaire Afrique du Nord* 12(1973), pp. 29-44.

KLIBI, Chedly. Allocution au I Colloque d'historiens tuniso-espagnol, à Hammamet. *Recueil d'études sur les moriscos andalous en Tunisie*, préparé par M. de Epalza et R. Petit, 1973, pp. 383-385.

KRAIEM, M. L'adhésion de l'U.G.T.T. à la Fédération syndicale mondiale. *Rev. hist maghrêb.* 1(1974), pp. 26-34.

KRAIEM, M. Autobiographie et relations avec la Résidence, de Tahar Khereddine Pacha, Ministre de la justice de la Régence. *Rev. hist. maghrêb.* 2(1974), pp. 185-191.

KRAIEM, M. Aux origines du Parti Communiste Tunisien 1919-1929. *Rev. hist. maghrêb.* 2(1974), pp. 116-137.

KRAIEM, M. Le parti reformiste tunisien (1920-1926). *Rev. hist. maghreb.* 4 (1975), pp. 150-162.

KRAIEM, M. La question du droit syndical en Tunisie (1881-1932). *Rev.d'hist.maghrebine* 3(1975), pp. 27-44.

LANDURÉ, J.L. La Tunisie en quête d'un équilibre politique. *RJPUF* 25(1971), pp. 377-400; 26(1972), pp. 3-46

LIAUZU, Cl. Des précurseurs du mouvement ouvrier: les libertaires en Tunisie à la fin du XIXe siècle. *CT* 21(nos. 81-82, 1973), pp. 153-182.

LIAUZU, Cl. Situation coloniale et opinion publique: petits blancs et socialistes pendant trente ans de luttes électorales. *CT* 22(nos.87-88,1974), pp. 41-91.

LIAUZU, Cl. Les traminots de Tunis du début du siècle à la deuxième guerre mondiale. *CT* 23(1975), pp. 141-190, 235-281.

LO JACONO, Cl. Sul projetto d'unione fra Tunisia e Libia. *OM* 54(1974), pp. 259-264.

LOURDJANE, Ahmed. La réforme pénitentaire en Algérie. *RJPIC* 28(1974), pp. 441-462.

MABROUK, M. L'organisation administrative tunisienne depuis l'indépendance. *Annuaire Afr. Nord* 7(1968), pp. 157-173.

MARSDEN, A. Britain and her conventional rights in Tunis, 1888-1892. *II.Cong.int. ét.nord-afr.* 1970, pp. 163-173.

MARTEL, A. Un témoin des débuts de l'indépendance tunisienne: l'Action. *ROMM* 15-16 (1973), pp. 175-187.

MARTEL, P.A. Tunisie, le temps des gestionnaires. *Maghreb Machrek* 67(1975), pp. 46-51.

MICAUD, C.A. Leadership and development. The case of Tunisia. *Contemporary politics* 1(1968-69), pp. 468-484.

MICAUD, C.A. Politics in North Africa: Tunisia. *Africa today* 18iv(1971), pp. 60-64.

MORRISSON, C. Le IVe Plan tunisien. *Maghreb-Machrek* 66(1974), pp. 35-41.

PASTOR, P. de. La révélation d'octobre: le VIIIe congrès du parti socialiste destourien. *Afrique et Asie* 95-96(1971), pp. 41-64.

RUF, W.K. The Bizerta crisis: a Bourguibist attempt to resolve Tunisia's border problems. *MEJ* 25 (1971), pp. 201-211.

RUF, W. Le Bourguibisme et la politique étrangère tunisienne. *Proc.27th Int. Cong.Or.1967* (1971), p. 164.

SALIVAROVÁ, M. L'analyse sociologique du socialisme tunisien. *Asian and African studies* [Bratislava] 5(1969), pp. 77-85.

SAMMOUD, Hamadi. Souci de spécificité chez un intellectuel tunisien, Tahar Haddad. *IBLA* 37(no.133, 1974), pp. 45-67.

SAMMUT, C. La genèse du nationalisme tunisien: le mouvement Jeunes-Tunisiens. *Rev. hist. maghrêb.* 2(1974), pp. 151-168.

SAMMUT, C. L'impérialisme capitaliste français et le nationalisme tunisien (1881-1914). *Rev. hist. maghrêb.* 1 (1974), pp. 62-66.

SAMMUT, C. L'installation du Protectorat français et la réforme du système monétaire tunisien (d'apres les Archives du Quai d'Orsay, Paris). *Rev. hist. maghreb.* 4(1975), pp. 184-194.

SERNA, A. de la. La Tunisie et l'Espagne à l'heure actuelle. *Recueil d'études sur les moriscos andalous en Tunisie*, préparé par M. de Epalza et R. Petit, 1973, pp. 378-382.

SOUMILLE, P. Le cimetière européen de Bab-el-Khadra à Tunis. Étude historique et sociale. *CT* 19, nos. 75-76(1971), pp. 129-182.

SOUMILLE, P. Les Européens de Tunisie et les questions religieuses de 1893 à 1901: études d'une opinion publique. *Rev.d'hist. maghrebine* 3(1975), pp. 56-64.

SRAIEB, Noureddine. Note sur les dirigeants politiques et syndicalistes tunisiens de 1905 à 1934. *ROMM* 9(1971), pp. 91-118.

TEMIMI, Abdeljélil. Considérations nouvelles sur la révolution d'Ali ben Gadehem. *ROMM* 7(1970), pp. 171-185.

TEMIMI, A. La thèse de M. Béchir Tlili ou la décadence du métier d'historien. (Les rapports culturels et idéologiques entre l'Orient et l'Occident, en Tunisie au XIXe siècle, 1830-1880.) *Rev. hist. maghreb.* 4(1975), pp. 205-208.

TLILI, Béchir. Á propos de la formation du fait national et de l'idéologie nationaliste en Tunisie: un colloque sur "L'identité culturelle et la conscience nationale" (Tunis, mars 1974). *CT* 22 (nos.87-88(1974), pp. 237-250.

TLILI, Béchir. Au seuil du nationalisme tunisien: documents inédits sur le pan-islamisme au Maghreb (1919-1923). *Africa* [Rome] 28(1973), pp. 211-236.

TLILI, Béchir. Contribution à l'élucidation de la pensée réformiste tunisienne moderne et contemporaine (1830-1930). *Africa* [Rome] 30(1975), pp. 317-345.

TLILI, Béchir. Un document inédit de al-Ṭâhir Ḥayr ad-Dîn, réformateur et ministre de la justice (1875-1937). *CT* 22(85-86, 1974), pp. 215-226.

TLILI, Bachir. Eléments pour une approche de la pensée socio-economique de Kheredine (1810-1889). *ROMM* 9(1971), pp. 119-152.

TLILI, Béchir. Problématique des processus de formation des faits nationaux et des idéologies nationalistes dans le monde islamo-méditerranéen de l'entre deux-guerres (1919-1930). L'exemple de la Tunisie. *CT* 21(nos. 81-82, 1973), pp. 183-221.

TLILI, Béchir. Socialistes et Jeunes-Tunisiens à la veille de la Grande Guerre (1911-1913). *CT* 22(85-86, 1974), pp. 49-134.

TLILI, Béchir. Syndicalisme révolutionnaire et questions tunisiennes à la veille de la Grande Guerre: le groupement de La Bataille (1911-1912). *CT* 23(nos. 91-92, 1975), pp. 133-233.

TOUMI, Mohsen. Le Néo-Destour dans le mouvement national tunisien. *Rev. fr. ét. pol. africaines*, 9(no.98,1974), pp. 26-53.

TOUMI, Mohsen. Le parti socialiste destourien. *Rev. franç. d'ét. pol. afr.* 111(1975), pp. 32-68.

TRIULZI, A. Una fonte ignorata per la storia della Tunisia: i dispacci dei consoli americani a Tunisi, 1797-1867. *OM* 51(1971), pp. 653-678.

TRIULZI, A. Italian-speaking communities in early nineteenth century Tunis. *ROMM* 9 (1971), pp. 153-184.

VORONCHANINA, N.I. Bor'ba za zhenskuyu emansipatziyu v Tunise v nachale XX v. *Arabskie strany, Turtziya, Iran, Afganistan,* 1973, pp. 3-14.

ZGHAL, Abdelkader, KAROUI, Hachmi. Decolonization and social science research: the case of Tunisia. *M.E.S.A. Bull.* 7iii (1973), pp. 11-27.

ZGHAL, Abdelkader. L'élite administrative et la paysannerie en Tunisie. *Annuaire Afr. Nord* 7(1968), pp. 129-137.

ZGHAL, Abdelkader. The reactivation of tradition in a post-traditional society. *Daedalus* 102i(1973), pp. 225-237.

ZUDINA, L.P. Evolyutziya agrarnoy politiki nezavisimogo Tunisa. *Istoriya i ekonomika stran Arabskogo Vostoka,* 1973, pp. 107-123.

See also II. a. 2. *Tunisia.* Stone.

See also XVI. c. Duchac.

See also XVI. c. Ruf and Ammann.

See also XXXVII. 1. Hanna

dd ECONOMICS

ALOUANE, Youssef. Attitudes et comportements des coopérateurs dans deux unités de production du Nord. *Etudes de sociologie tunisienne* 1 (1968), pp. 81-163.

ASSELAIN, J. C. La réforme des structures commerciales en Tunisie depuis 1962. *Annuaire Afr. Nord* 8(1969), pp. 115-143.

BAHROUN, Sadok. Annual planning in Tunisia. *J. development planning* 3(1971), pp. 60-98.

BASSO, J. Die französisch-tunesische Kooperation. *Z. f. Kulturaustausch* 25iv(1975), pp. 98-107.

BELGAID, Noureddine H. Motivation et aspiration ouvrières. *Etudes de sociologie tunisienne* 1 (1968), pp. 235-257.

BOUKRAA, Ridha. L'entreprise industrielle en milieu rural. *Etudes de sociologie tunisienne* 1 (1968), pp. 43-80.

BOUKRAA, Ridha. Quelques considérations générales sur la nouvelle organisation du système coopératif dans la région du Kef. *Etudes de sociologie tunisienne* 1 (1968), pp. 301-310.

CHATTI, Mustapha. Le Conseil économique et social de Tunisie. *Maghreb-Machrek* 66 (1974), pp. 41-44.

CHEREL, J. Les unités coopératives de production du nord Tunisien. *Tiers-monde* 12 (1971), pp. 303-350.

CORNET, H. Expériences et témoinages: l'économique et le social. Expériences Tunisiennes. *Afr.et l'Asie* 91-2(1970), pp. 35-39.

DUFOUR, J. The problem of collectively owned land in Tunisia. *Land reform* 1971, (1), pp. 38-51.

ELDBLOM, L. Structure foncière d'une communauté muselmane. Une étude des possibilités du dévelopement économique et social. (Le cas de l'oasis de Ghadamès, Libye.) *CT* 20(nos.79-80, 1972), pp. 179-205.

GILBERT, H. Le pétrole en Tunisie. *Maghreb-Machrek* 55(1973), pp. 37-41.

LAURENT, J. La Tunisie à l'heure multinationale. *Rev. afr. management* 1iii(1973), pp. 111-129.

LIAUZU, C. La pêche et les pêcheurs de thon en Tunisie dans les années 1930. *ROMM* 12 (1972), pp. 69-91.

LIAUZU, C. Les pêcheurs tunisiens à la veille de la deuxième guerre mondiale. *IBLA* 34(no. 128, 1971), pp. 295-332.

LIAUZU, C. Les syndicats en Tunisie au temps du Cinquantenaire. *Annuaire Afrique du Nord* 12(1973), pp. 1031-1044.

MARTENS, A., PINDYCK, R.S. An optimal control model for multi-sectoral investment planning in Tunisia. *J. development economics* 2(1975), pp. 99-119.

NOUSCHI, A. La crise de 1930 en Tunisie et les débuts du Néo-Destour. *ROMM* 8(1970), pp. 113-123.

PEYROL, M. L'expérience des coopératives en Tunisie. *Rev. fr. ét. pol. africaines* 61 (1971), pp. 33-48.

PONCET, J. L'économie tunisienne depuis l'indépendance. *Annuaire Afr. Nord* 8 (1969), pp. 93-114.

PONCET, J. La régionalisation en Tunisie. *Tiers-monde* 14(1973), pp. 597-614.

PONCET, J. La Tunisie se développe-t-elle? *II.Cong.int.ét.nord-afr.* 1970, pp. 311-325.

SFAR, Othman. Les carrières médicales en Tunisie. *IBLA* 127 (1971), pp. 167-171.

SIGNOLES, P. Migrations intérieures et villes en Tunisie. *CT* 20(nos.79-80, 1972), pp. 207-240.

SIMMONS, J.L. Agricultural cooperatives and Tunisian development. (Part II.). *MEJ* 25 (1971), pp. 45-57.

SIRONVAL, M.M. Animation rurale en Tunisie, dans le cadre du Ministère de l'Agriculture. *IBLA* 127 (1971), pp. 177-182.

TLILI, Béchir. En marge des lères journées de Hammamet: la recherche en sciences sociales en Tunisie. *CT* 21(nos. 81-82, 1973), pp. 265-271.

VOIZARD, P. Paul Bourde et l'olivier de Tunisie. *CR trim.séances Acad.Sci. Outre-mer* 34(1974), pp. 205-219.

ZAMITI, Melika. Kulturelle Bedürfnisse und Wünsche der tunesischen Arbeiter in Frankreich. *Z. f. Kulturaustausch* 25iv (1975), pp. 82-86.

ZOUARI, Taieb. La grève des carriers de Tunis. Juillet 1936. *Etudes de sociologie tunisienne* 1 (1968), pp. 311-315.

ZUDINA, L.P. Formy izdol'shchiny v "traditzionnom" sektore Tunisa v 50-e gody XX. v. *Strany Blizhnego i Srednego Vostoka: istoriya, ekonomica,* 1972, pp. 295-303.

See also II. a. 5. Schumann, Schumann.

See also XII. f. Sraieb.

e WEST AFRICA

ABDUL HAMID, Abdul Ali. The sources of Diyā' al-ta'wil. *Research bull. CAD Ibadan* 8(1972), pp. 1-25.

ABUBAKAR, Sa'ad. The Emirate-type of government in the Sokoto Caliphate. *J.Hist.Soc. Nigeria* 7(1974), pp. 211-229.

ADELEYẸ, R.A. Rābiḥ B. Faḍlallāh and the diplomacy of European imperial invasion in the Central Sudan, 1893-1903. *J. Hist. Soc. Nigeria* 5 (1970), pp. 399-418.

ADAMU, Muhammad Uba. Some notes on the influence of North African traders in Kano. *Kano studies* 1iv(1968), pp. 43-49.

BA, Oumar. "L'Anti-sultan ou Al Hâjj Omar Tâl du Foûta", de Fernand Dumont. *Présence afr.* 91(1974), pp. 65-72.

BALOGUN, Isma'il A.B. The life and work of the Mujaddid of West Africa, ʻUthmān B. Fūdī, popularly known as Usumanu Ḍan Fodio. *Islamic stud.* 12(1973), pp. 271-292.

BALOGUN, Ismail A.B. The penetration of Islam into Nigeria. *Nigerian J. Islam* 1i(1970), pp. 35-39; 1ii(1971), pp. 37-42.

BARKOW, J.H. Muslims and Maguzawa in North Central State, Nigeria: an ethnographic comparison. *Canadian J.Afr.stud.* 7(1973), pp. 59-76.

BATHILY, Abdoulaye. A discussion of the traditions of Wagadu with some reference to ancient Ghana, including a review of oral accounts, Arab sources and archaeological evidence. *Bull.IFAN* 37B(1975), pp. 1-94.

BATRAN, Abdal Aziz. An introductory note on the impact of Sidi al-Mukhtar al-Kunti (1729-1811) on West African Islam in the 18th and 19th centuries. *J.Hist.Soc.Nigeria* 6(1971-73), pp. 347-352.

BELL, N.M. The age of Mansa Musa of Mali: problems in succession and chronology. *Int. J.Afr.hist.stud.* 5(1972), pp. 221-234.

BOYD, J. Some government documents from Daura (1910-1918). *Res. bull. CAD Ibadan* 7(1971), pp. 22-26.

COLVIN, L.G. Islam and the state of Kajoor: a case of successful resistance to jihad. *J. Afr. hist.* 15(1974), pp. 587-606.

CURTIN, P.D. Jihad in West Africa: early phases and inter-relations in Mauritania and Senegal. *J. Afr. hist.* 12(1971), pp. 11-24.

DIAS FARINHA, A. Un exemple de la présence de la langue arabe dans la côte occidentale de l'Afrique: l'Histoire de ʻAbd Al-Qādir. *Ve Congrès International d'Arabisants et d'Islamisants. Actes.,* [1970?], pp. 171-174.

DOI, A.R.I. Shehu ʻUthmān dan Fodio, 1754-1817: The great African Mujāhid and Mujaddid. *Studies in Islam* 7 (1970), pp. 111-122.

DONALD, L. Arabic literacy among the Yalunka of Sierra Leone. *Africa* 44(1974), pp. 71-81.

EUBA, Titiliọla. Muḥammad Shitta Bey and the Lagos Muslim community (1850-1895). *Nigerian J. Islam* 2i(1971-2), pp. 21-30.

EUBA, Titilola. Shitta Bey and the Lagos Muslim community. *Nigerian J.Islam* 2ii (1972-74), pp. 7-18.

FISHER, H.J. Hassebu: Islamic healing in Black Africa. *Northern Africa: Islam and modernization,* ed. M. Brett, 1973, pp. 23-47.

FISHER, A.G.B., FISHER, H.J. Nachtigal's experience in Tibesti, 1869; African immigration restrictions in the mid-nineteenth century. *Adab* [Khartoum], pp. 24-46.

FISHER, H.J., ROWLAND, V. Firearms in the Central Sudan. *J. Afr. hist.* 12(1971), pp. 215-239.

FISHER, H.J. 'He swalloweth the ground with fierceness and rage': the horse in the Central Sudan. *J. Afr. hist.* 13(1972), pp. 369-88; 14(1973), pp. 355-379.

GARH, M.S. el-. Manhaj al-'ābidīn (the path of the servants), by 'Uthmān ibn Fūdī, translated. *Res. bull. CAD Ibadan* 7(1971), pp. 27-54.

GERRESCH, Cl. Jugements du *Moniteur du Sénégal* sur Al-hajj 'Umar, de 1857 à 1864. *Bull. IFAN* 35(1973), pp. 574-592.

HAJJ, Muhammad al-. A seventeenth century chronicle on the origins and missionary activities of the Wangarawa. *Kano studies* 1iv(1968), pp. 7-42.

XVI NORTH AFRICA: HISTORY

HISKETT, M. The development of Islam in Hausaland. *Northern Africa: Islam and modernization,* ed. M. Brett, 1973, pp. 57-64.

HUNWICK, J.O. The dynastic chronologies of the Central Sudan states in the sixteenth century: some reinterpretations. *Kano studies* N.S.1i(1973), pp. 35-55.

KLEIN, M.A. Social and economic factors in the Muslim revolution in Senegambia. *J. Afr. hist.* 13(1972), pp. 419-441.

LAVERS, J.E. Jibril Gaini: a preliminary account of the career of a Mahdist leader in North-Eastern Nigeria. *Res. Bull. CAD Ibadan* 3i(1967), pp. 16-39.

LEVTZION, Nehemia. Maḥmūd Ka'tī fut-il l'auteur du Ta'rīkh al-Fattāsh? *Bull. IFAN* 33(1971), pp. 665-674

LEVTZION, N. A seventeenth-century chronicle by Ibn al-Mukhtār: a critical study of *Ta'rīkh al-fattāsh. BSOAS* 34(1971), pp. 571-593.

LIMAGNE, J. La politique étrangère de la République Islamique de Mauritanie. *Rev. fr. ét. pol. africaines* 75(1972), pp. 34-46.

LOURIDO DÍAZ, R. La obra histórica de al-Zayyānī sobre los 'alawies y su influencia en la historiografia marroqui. *BAEO* 6(1970), pp. 165-193.

LOVEJOY, P.E. Long distance trade and Islam: the case of the nineteenth-century Hausa kola trade. *J.Hist.Soc.Nigeria* 5 (1970-1), pp. 537-547.

MASON, M. The fall of Etsu Abubakr: the account of Ubandawakin Bida. *Kano studies* N.S.1i(1973), pp. 57-82.

MEGAHED, Horeya T. The empires of Western Sudan: a political analysis. *Afr.stud.rev. (Cairo)* 1(1972), pp. 23-41.

MIKHAYLOVA, G.D. Sozdanie gornodobyvayushchey promyshlennosti Mavritanii. *Strany Blizhnego i Srednego Vostoka: istoriya, ekonomica,* 1972, pp. 359-369.

MISKE, A.B. La lutte des classes en Mauritanie. *Renaissance de monde arabe. Colloque interarabe de Louvain,* 1972, pp. 435-454.

NJEUMA, M.Z. Adamawa and Mahdism: the career of Hayatu Ibn Sa'id in Adamawa, 1878-1898. *J. Afr. hist.* 12(1971), pp. 61-77.

OLORUNTIMEHIN, B. Olatunji. The idea of Islamic revolution and Tukulor constitutional evolution. *Bull.IFAN* 33(1971), pp. 675-692

OSUNTOKUN, Jide. Nigeria's colonial government and the Islamic insurgency in French West Africa, 1914-1918. *Cah. ét. afr.* 15(no.57,1975), pp. 85-93.

OSUNTOKUN, J. The response of the British colonial government in Nigeria to the Islamic insurgency in the French Sudan and the Sahara during the First World War. *Bull. IFAN* 36(1974), pp. 14-24.

PITTE, J.-R. Les controverses autour de la découverte de Tombouctou au début du XIXe siècle. *Rev. hist.* 254(1975), pp. 81-104.

ROBINSON, D. Abdul Qadir and Shaykh Umar: a continuing tradition of Islamic leadership in Futa Toro. *Int.J.Afr.hist.stud.* 6(1973), pp. 286-303.

ROBINSON, D. The impact of Al-Hajj 'Umar on the historical traditions of the Fulbe. *J. Folklore Inst.* 8(1971), pp. 101-113.

ROBINSON, D. The Islamic revolution of Futa Toro. *Int.J.Afr.hist.stud.* 8(1975), pp. 185-221.

ROBINSON, D., CURTIN, P and JOHNSON, J. A tentative chronology of Futa Toro from the sixteenth through the nineteenth centuries. *Cah. et. afr.* 12(1972), pp. 555-592.

SAISON, B. La Mauritanie; aperçu général. *Annuaire Afrique du Nord* 12(1973), pp. 295-314.

SALIFOU, A. Malan Yaroh, un grand négociant du Soudan central à la fin du XIXe siècle. *J. Soc. africanistes* 42(1972), pp. 7-27.

SAMB, Amar. Essai sur la contribution du Sénégal à la littérature d'expression arabe. *Bull.IFAN* 33(1971), pp. 658-663

SAMB, Amar L'Islam et l'histoire du Sénégal. *Bull.IFAN* 33(1971), pp. 461-507

SARTAIN, E.M. Jalāl ad-Dīn as-Suyūṭī's relations with the people of Takrūr. *J.Semitic studs.* 16(1971), pp. 193-198.

SKINNER, D. The Arabic letter books as a source for Sierra Leone history. *Africana research bull.* 3iv(1973), pp. 41-50.

SMITH, R. Peace and palaver: international relations in pre-colonial West Africa. *J. Afr. hist.* 14(1973), pp. 599-621.

SÖLKEN, H. Zur Biographie des Imām 'Umaru von Kete-Kratyi. *Africana Marburgensia* 3ii (1970), pp. 24-30.

STĘPNIEWSKA, B. Portée sociale de l'Islam au Soudan Occidental, aux XIVe-XVIe s. *Africana bull.* 14(1971), pp. 35-58

STEVENS, P. The Kisra legend and the distortion of historical tradition. *J. Afr. hist.* 16(1975), pp. 185-200.

STEWART, C.C. Political authority and social stratification in Mauritania. *Arabs and Berbers,* ed. E. Gellner and C. Micaud, 1973, pp. 375-393.

STEWART, C.C. Southern Saharan scholarship and the *Bilad al-Sudan. J.African hist.* 17(1976), pp. 73-93.

TIMM, K. "Islam Noir", "Historische Ethnologie" und ein "Kulturwandel" in Westafrika. *EAZ* 14(1973), pp. 17-53.

XVI NORTH AFRICA: HISTORY

TRIAUD, J.L. La question musulmane en Côte d'Ivoire (1893-1939). *RHOM* 62 (1974), pp. 542-571.

VERMEL, P. L'influence du Madhisme au Nigéria. *L'Afrique et l'Asie modernes* 93-4(1971), pp. 47-60.

ZEBADIA, A. The career of 'Aḥmed Al-Bakkāy in the oral evidences and recorded documents. *Rev.d'hist.maghrebine* 3(1975), pp. 75-83.

Asma'a bint 'Uthman b. Fudi. *Research bull. CAD Ibadan* 8(1972), pp. 33-34.

See also II. c. 3. 'Abdul-'Aziz 'Abdulla Batran.

See also IX. e. Bell.

See also XVII. c. Gwarzo.

XVII NORTH AFRICA: HISTORY

Spanish in North Africa,
Italians in North Africa

a SPANISH IN NORTH AFRICA

ARRIBAS PALAU, M. Datos sobre el comercio entre España y Marruecos en tiempo de Mawlāy al-Yazīd. *Hesp.Tamuda* 13(1972), pp. 95-138.

ARRIBAS PALAU, M. Un mal confidente de Salmon en Marruecos: el genovés Gerónimo Tasistro. *MEAH* 23(1974), pp. 29-52.

AYACHE, G. Beliounech et le destin de Ceuta entre le Maroc et l'Espagne. *Hesp.Tamuda* 13(1972), pp. 5-36.

BARBIER, M. L'avenir du Sahara espagnol. *Politique étrangère* 40(1975), pp. 353-380.

CHANDLER, J.A. Spain and her Moroccan protectorate 1898-1927. *J. contemp. hist.* 10(1975), pp. 301-322.

COLA ALBERICH, J. El Sahara y la amistad hispano-arabe. *Rev.polit.int.* 136(1974), pp. 177-181.

DUFOURCQ, C.E. Un impérialisme médiéval face au Maghrib: la naissance et l'essor de l'empire catalan, d'après des travaux récents. *CT* 20(nos.79-80, 1972), pp. 101-124.

GOZALBES BUSTO, G. La republica andaluza de Rabat en el siglo XVII. *Cuad. Bibl. esp. Tetuan* 9-10(1974), pp. 11-464.

LATHAM, J.D. On the strategic position and defence of Ceuta in the later Muslim period. *Orientalia Hispanica* I, 1974, pp. 445-464.

LA VÉRONNE, Ch. de. Población del Presidio de Orán en 1527. *RABM* 76(1973), pp. 70-108.

MORENO, A. Sahara espanol: una descolonización contravertida. *Revista pol. int.* 139(1975), pp. 73-91.

PELISSIER, R. Sahara espagnol: l'escalade. *Rev.franç.ét.pol.afr.* 9(no. 105), pp. 15-18.

Sahara espagnol: l'impatience du Maroc. *Rev.franç.ét.pol.afr.* 9, no. 104(1974), pp. 11-14.

See also XVI. c. Koerner.

b TANGIER

FARINHA, A. Dias. Correspondência de D. Jorge Mascarenhas, governador de Tânger (1622-1624). *Actas IV congresso de estudos árabes e islâmicos* 1968(1971), pp. 209-223.

LOURIDO DIAZ, R. Relaciones políticas anglo-marroquíes en la segunda mitad del siglo XVIII. Bases militares españolas en Tanger durante el bloquero de Gibraltar por Carlos II. *Hispania* 31 (no.118, 1971), pp. 337-383.

c LIBYA

ALLAN, J.A. Agricultural development in Libya since independence. *Northern Africa: Islam and modernization,* ed. M. Brett, 1973, pp. 111-121.

ALLAN, J.A. Drought in Libya: some solutions available to an oil-rich government. *African aff.* 73(1974), pp. 152-158.

ATALLAH, B., FIKRY, M. Le phénomène urbain en Libye. Problèmes juridiques et sociaux. *Ann.Afr.Nord* 11(1972), pp. 79-103.

BALDISSERA, Eros. Sul recente progetto d'unione tra Egitto e Libia. *OM* 52(1972), pp. 485-490.

BALTA, P. L'Afrique et la guerre d'octobre. *Maghreb-Machrek* 64(1974), pp. 15-18.

BLEUCHOT, H. Les fondements de l'idéologie du colonel Mouammar El-Kadhafi. *Maghreb-Machrek* 62(1974), pp. 21-27.

BRETON, H. L'idéologie politique du régime républicain en Libye. *Ann.Afr.Nord* 9 (1970), pp. 231-241

BRETON, H. La Libye républicaine: essai d'analyse d'un changement politique. *Annuaire Afr. Nord* 8(1969), pp. 359-373.

XVII NORTH AFRICA: HISTORY

:ORTESE, G. L'esodo della collettività italiana della Libia e le provvidenze predisposte dal Governo italiano a favore dei rimpatriati. *Africa* [Rome] 26(1971), pp. 313-346.

:UMMING, D. Consultations on a constitution for Tripoli, between Jeremy Bentham and Hassuna D'Ghies, 1823. *Ann. Rep. Soc. Libyan Studies* 3(1971-72), pp. 21-35.

:UMMING, D. James Bruce in Libya, 1766. *Ann. Rep. Soc. Libyan Studies* 1(1969-70), pp. 12-18.

UMMING, Sir D. Libya in the First World War. *Libya in history* 1968, pp. 383-392.

)ESTANNE DE BERNIS, G. La Libye et l'Algérie: stratégies de développement comparées. *Ann. Afr. Nord* 10(1971), pp. 267-296.

'OLAYAN, Kola. Italian colonial rule in Libya. *Tarikh* 4iv(1974), pp. 1-10.

'OLAYAN, Kola. The resistance movement in Libya. *Tarikh* 4iii(1973), pp. 46-56.

'OLAYAN, Kola. The "Tripolitan War", a reconsideration of the causes. *Africa* [Rome] 27(1972), pp. 615-626

FOLAYAN, K. Umar al-Mukhtar of Libya: a preliminary note. *Ife Afr.studies* 1i(1974), pp. 54-65.

'OWLER, G.L. Decolonization of rural Libya. *Annals Assoc. Amer. Geographers* 63(1973), pp. 490-506.

'OWLER, G.L. Italian colonization of Tripolitania. *Annals Assoc. Amer. Geographers* 62(1972), pp. 627-640.

FUNK, H. Libyen nach der Revolution von 1969. *Mitt Inst.Orientforschung* 17 (1971), pp. 37-48.

;LAGOW, Rainer. Libyens Haltung zum Nahostproblem. *Orient* [Germany] 15(1974), pp. 19-24.

;OLDBERG, H. Ecologic and demographic aspects of rural Tripolitanian Jewry: 1853-1949. *IJMES* 2 (1971), pp. 245-265.

WARZO, Hassan Ibrahim. Seven letters from the Tripoli archives. *Kano studies* 1iv (1968), pp. 50-68.

'ASSAN, Mohamed Ibrahim. Kufra depression, a study in economic development. *Bull.Fac. Arts Libya* 4(1972), pp. 199-201.

IAYFORD, E.R. The Libyan revolution according to Meredith O. Ansell and Ibrahim Massaud al-Arif. *Humaniora Islamica* 1(1973), pp. 61-75.

'ROSHIN, N.I. Iz istorii natzional'no-osvoboditel'noy bor'by liviyskogo naroda pod rukovodstvom Omara al'-Mukhtara (1923-1931 gg.). *Istoriya i ekonomika stran Arabskogo Vostoka,* 1973, pp. 233-246.

:ATHMANN, L. Archive material on the modern history of Libya. *African studies - Afrika-Studien,* ed. Thea Büttner and G. Brehme, 1973, pp. 53-67.

RONDOT, P. Libye: une politique toujours controversée. *Rev.franç.ét.pol.afr.* 9, no. 103(1974), pp. 10-14.

SANGER, R.H. Libya: conclusions on an unfinished revolution. *MEJ* 29(1975), pp. 409-417.

SAVIANO, L. Il partito socialista italiano e la guerra di Libia (1911-1912). *Aevum* 48(1974), pp. 102-130.

SEGRÈ, C.G. Italo Balbo and the colonization of Libya. *J. contemp. hist.* 7(1972), pp. 141-155.

SERRA, L. La rivoluzione libica. *Ve Congrès International d'Arabisants et d'Islamisants. Actes.,* [1970?], pp. 419-433.

SURI, Salaheddin Hasan. The genesis of the political leadership of Libya, 1952-1969. *Rev. hist. maghreb.* 4(1975), pp. 197-204.

TALHA, L. Le pétrole et l'économie libyenne. *Ann. de L'Afr. du Nord* 5(1966), pp. 153-234.

ULE, W. The Libyan Arab Republic between tradition and modernity. *Orient* [Hamburg] 16iii(1975), pp. 18-26.

WISSA-WASSEF, C. Les structure agraires du Liban. Etude critique des sources d'information. *Maghreb-Machrek* 65(1974), pp. 36-45.

See also XVI. d. Lo Jacono.

See also XIX. m. Aznar Sánchez.

See also XXVI. d. Durupty.

cc ECONOMICS

ALLAN, J.A. Recent developments in agriculture in Libya, with special reference to areas close to Tripoli. *Bull. Fac. Arts Univ. Libya* 3(1969), pp. 37-77.

BUTANI, D.H. The political economy of Libya. *Mondes en développement* 9(1975), pp. 107-124.

CHIAUZZI, G. Materiali per lo studio dei riti agrari in Libia. *Africa [Rome]* 27(1972), pp. 193-230.

HAJJAJI, Salem A. Agricultural development and settlement in the Kufra region of Libya. *Land reform* 1974, pp. 68-88.

HARTLEY, R.G. Distribution and density of population. *Bull. Fac. Arts, Univ Libya* 3(1969), pp. 79-168.

TALHA, L. L'économie libyenne depuis les découvertes pétrolières. *Annuaire Afr. Nord* 8(1969), pp. 203-284.

See also XI. e. Allan.

See also XII. g. Dalton.

XVIII EGYPT: GEOGRAPHY. ETHNOLOGY. SOCIOLOGY

a GEOGRAPHY: GENERAL

AWAD, Hassân. L'Ouadi Ba'ba'a: un cas de l'inadaptation du réseau hydrographique à la structure au Sinaï. *Ann.Fac.Arts Ain Shams* 1(1951), pp. 113-123.

BANNA, Ali A. El-. An outline of the economic and human geography of the Wadi Tumilat region. *Ann.Fac.Arts Ain Shams* 10(1967), pp. 243-255.

DEWACHTER, M. Graffiti des voyageurs du XIXe siècle relevés dans le temple d'Amada en Basse-Nubie (avec 5 planches). *BIFAO* 69 (1971), pp. 131-169.

DEWACHTER, M. Le voyage nubien du comte Carlo Vidua (fin Février-fin Avril 1820). *BIFAO* 69 (1971), pp. 171-189.

DOV NIR. Marine terraces of Southern Sinai. *GR* 61 (1971), pp. 32-50.

EMBABI, Nabil Sayed. Desert varnish in the Kharga Oases depression and its palaeo-climatic significance. *Annals Fac.Arts Ain Shams Univ.* 12(1969), pp. 89-94.

EMBABI, Nabil el-Sayed. The semi-playa deposits of Kharga depression, the Western Desert, Egypt. *Bull.Soc.Geog.d'Egypte* 41-2(1968-69), pp. 73-88.

FANTOLI, A. Il viaggio d'una donna al Sinai sedici secoli or sono. *Levante* 19i-ii(1972), pp. 9-36.

GINDY, Amin R. Alpha radioactivity of the basement rocks in the area West and South-west of Qoseir, Red Sea Province, U.A.R. *BIE* 52(1970-71), pp. 157-197.

HAGEDORN, H. und MECKELEIN, W. The centenary of the Rohlfs expedition to Egypt. *Erde* 106(1975), pp. 308-312.

HASSAN, M. Youssef, SALAMA, Salwa A. Contribution to the coral fauna of the Maestrichtian-Palaeocene "paper shales" and "snow-white chalk" of the oases of the South Western Desert of Egypt. *BIE* 51(1969-70), pp. 73-98.

KASSAS, M., GIRGIS, W.A. Plant life in the Nubian Desert east of the Nile, Egypt. *BIE* 51(1969-70), pp. 47-71.

KASSAS, M., GIRGIS, W.A. Studies on the ecology of the Eastern Desert of Egypt. I. The region between latitude 27°30' and latitude 25°30'N. *Bull.Soc.Geog.d'Egypte* 41-2(1968-69), pp. 43-72.

NAGUIB, A.I., MOUCHACCA, J.S. The mycoflora of Egyptian desert soils. *BIE* 52(1970-71) pp. 37-60.

PHILIP, G., BASTA, E.Z., KHALIL, J.B. Petrological studies on some soil sediments from Faiyum area and the Nile valley - chemical and mechanical analyses. *BIE* 52(1970-71), pp. 99-118.

RIAD, Mohmed. Cultural regions in South-East Egypt. *Annals Fac.Arts Ain Shams Univ.* 12(1969), pp. 69-88.

SADEK, Daulat A. Geographical research for regional planning in Egypt. *Ann. Fac.Arts Ain Shams* 7(1962), pp. 39-45.

SADEK, Daulat A. The growth and character of Aswan. *Ann.Fac.Arts Ain Shams* 7 (1962), pp. 29-37.

TOSSON, S., SAAD, N.A. Origin of the iron ore of Umm Gerifat area, Egypt. *BIE* 52 (1970-71), pp. 17-35.

WARD, W.A. The Shasu "Bedouin": notes on a recent publication. *JESHO* 15(1972), pp. 35-60.

YOUSSEF, Mourad I., BASSIOUNI, Mohammed A., CHERIF, Omar H. Some stratigraphic and tectonic aspects of the miocene in the North-Eastern part of the Eastern Desert (Egypt). *BIE* 52(1970-71), pp. 119-154.

See also VI. c. Rubinacci.

See also XIX. n. Barbour.

b THE NILE

BARAKAT, M.G. and IMAM, M. Preliminary note on the occurrence of old indurated sand dunes in the district of Gomasa, Northern Nile delta. *African studies rev.* 2(1973), pp. 1-9.

BARBOUR, K.M. The Nile basin: social and economic revolution. *A geography of Africa: regional essays* ... ed. by R. Mansell Prothero, pp. 78-153.

DIXON, J.L. Survey: the Nile and its basin. *Uganda J.* 35(1971), pp. 123-138.

SATO, Tsugiataka. Irrigation in rural Egypt from the 12th to 14th centuries - especially in case of the irrigation in Fayyūm. *Orient* [Japan] 8(1972), pp. 81-92.

SOMOGYI, J.de. The Nile-Red Sea canal. *Actas IV congresso de estudos árabes e islâmicos* 1968(1971), pp. 523-526.

VANDERSLEYEN, C. Des obstacles que constituent les cataractes du Nil. *BIFAO* 69 (1971), pp. 253-266.

VERNER, M. Periodical water-volume fluctuations of the Nile. *Archiv or.* 40(1972), pp. 105-130.

c SUEZ CANAL

ADAMS, J. A statistical text of the impact of the Suez Canal on the growth of India's trade. *Ind.econ.soc.hist.rev.* 8(1971), pp. 229-240.

BASSIOUNI, C. Navigation rights in the Suez Canal. *Crescent and star,* ed. by Y. Alexander and N.N. Kittrie, 1973, pp. 309-314.

KÖHLER, W. Die Wiedereröffnung des Suezkanals. Politische, wirtschaftliche und strategische Aspekte. *Orient* [Hamburg] 16ii(1975), pp. 57-80.

LABROUSSE, H. L'Océan indien sans le Canal de Suez. *Pount* 1971, 11, pp. 3-13.

WISSA-WASSEF, C. Les projets d'aménagement de la zone du Canal de Suez. *Maghreb Machrek* 68(1975), pp. 48-58.

Ministry of Foreign Affairs, Jerusalem. Israel and the Suez Canal. *Crescent and star,* ed. by Y. Alexander and N.N. Kittrie, 1973, pp.

d ETHNOLOGY. SOCIOLOGY

ABDEL HAKIM, Mohamed Sobhi. The population of Egypt. A demogeographic study. *BFA Cairo Univ.* (1972), pp. 17-44.

ABDUL QAYYUN, Shah. Women in West Asia: a case study of Egypt. *Islam and the modern age* 4iii(1973), pp. 54-83.

ABU-LUGHOD, J. Rural migration and politics in Egypt. *Rural politics and social change in the Middle East,* ed. by R. Antoun and I. Harik, 1972, pp. 315-334.

AKHAVI, Shahrough. Egypt's socialism and Marxist thought: some preliminary observations on social theory and metaphysics. *Comp. stud. soc. hist.* 17(1975), pp. 190-211.

BAER, G. A note on the controversy over 'the dissolution of the Egyptian village community'. *IJMES* 6(1975), pp. 241-244.

BAILEY, C. Bedouin star-lore in Sinai and the Negev. *BSOAS* 37(1974), pp. 580-596.

BAILEY, C. Bedouin weddings in Sinai and the Negev. *Folklore Res. Center studies* 4(1974), pp. 105-132.

BOECKX, C. Réforme agraire et structures sociales en Egypte nassérienne. *Civilisations* 21(1971), pp. 373-393.

BONNÉ, B., GODBER, M., ASHBEL, S., MOURANT, A.E. and TILLS, D. South-Sinai Beduin. A preliminary report on their inherited blood factors. *Amer.J.phys.anthr.* N.S. 34(1971), pp. 397-408.

DĄBROWSKA-SMEKTAŁA, Elzbieta. Bezpłodność i magia. (Infertilité et magic en Égypte.) *Przeglad or.* 1(81, 1972), pp. 25-30

DE GRÉ, G. Realignments of class attitudes in the military and bourgeoisie in developing countries: Egypt, Peru and Cuba. *Int.J. compar.sociol.* 15(1974), pp. 35-46.

DUNHAM, H.W. and LULFIYYA, Abdulla Sociology in Egypt. *J.Asian and Afr. studs.* (Toronto) 6(1971), pp. 118-126.

DZIERŻYKRAY-ROGALSKI, T., PROMIŃSKA, E. Seasonal rhythms of mortality in Sanuris (Faiyum Oasis). *Africana bull.* 14(1971), pp. 59-68

FAHIM, Hussein M. Change in religion in a resettled Nubian community, Upper Egypt. *IJMES* 4(1973), pp. 163-177.

FAHIM, Hussein M. The ethnological survey of Egyptian Nubia; retrospect and prospect. *Bull. Int. Cttee Urgent Anthrop. Ethnol. Res.* 14(1972), pp. 65-80.

FARRAG, A.M. Remarriages, multiple marriages and polygamous nuptiality tables in the United Arab Republic - 1960. *Int.population conf.* London, 1969, III, pp. 2180-2181.

FERNEA, R.A. "Ethnographic survey of Nubia": statement of purpose and organization. *Actes du Symposium internat. sur la Nubie,* 1965 *(Mem. Inst. Egypte* 59, 1969), pp. 15-20.

FIEDLER, M., STROUHAL, E., PETRÁČEK, K. Contribution to the research on Egyptian Nubian descent groups. *Arch. Or.* 39 (1971), pp. 434-472.

FODOR, A. The evil eye in today's Egypt. *Folia Or* 13(1971), pp. 51-65.

GARZOUZI, E. The demographic aspects of women's employment in the United Arab Republic. *Int.population conf.* London, 1969, I, pp. 1614-1619.

HANSEN, H.H. Clitoridectomy: female circumcision in Egypt. *Folk* 14-15(1972-73), pp. 15-26.

HARIK, I.F. Mobilization policy and political change in rural Egypt. *Rural politics and social change in the Middle East,* ed. by R. Antoun and I. Harik, 1972, pp. 287-314.

KENNEDY, J.G. Aman Doger: Nubian monster of the Nile. *J.Amer.folklore* 83(no. 330, 1970), pp. 438-445

KHALIFA, Atef M. A proposed explanation of the fertility gap differentials by socio-economic status and modernity: the case of Egypt. *Population stud.* 27(1973), pp. 431-442.

MARTIN, M. Jeunesse d'Egypte. *Travaux et jours* 41(1971), pp. 5-27.

MOORE, C.H. Les syndicats professionnels dans l'Egypte contemporaine: l'encadrement de la nouvelle classe moyenne. *Maghreb-Machrek* 64(1974), pp. 24-34.

NELSON, C. Religious experience, sacred symbols, and social reality. An illustration from Egypt. *Humaniora Islamica* 2(1974), pp. 252-266.

RAYMOND, A. Les grandes épidémies de peste au Caire aux XVIIe et XVIIIe siècles. *BEO* 25(1972), pp. 203-210.

RIAD, Mohamed The Ababda of Sayala (Egyptian Nubia). *Ann.Fac.Arts Ain Shams* 8 (1963), pp. 113-152.

RIAD, Mohamed, and ABDEL RASOUL, Kawthar. Influence of space relations on the tribal groupings of Korosko (Egyptian Nubia). *Annals Fac.Arts Ain Shams Univ.* 12(1969), pp. 35-48.

SAMI KASSEM, M. Business executives in Egypt, India and the U.S. *Int. J. comp. sociol.* 12(1971), pp. 101-113.

SCHIENERL, P.W. Ein bisher unbeachtet gebliebenes tiergestaltiges Amulett aus Kairo. *Arch.f.Völkerkunde* 28(1975), pp. 143-145.

SCHIENERL, P.W. Silberanhänger aus der Oase Siwa. *Archiv f. Völkerkunde* 27 (1973), pp. 145-156.

STAFFA, S.J. The culture of medieval Cairo as reflected in folk literature. *ME stud.* 10(1974), pp. 333-347.

STEIN, L. Wandel traditioneller Machtorgane im arabischen Raum unter besonderer Berücksichtigung der Verhältnisse bei den Aulad Ali-Beduinen in der Arabischen Republik Ägypten. *Jhb. Mus. Völkerk. Leipzig* 28(1972), pp. 243-256.

STILLMAN, Yedida K. The wardrobe of a Jewish bride in medieval Egypt. *Folklore Res. Center studies* 4(1974), pp. 297-304.

TIMM, Kl. Traditionelle Ideologie und religiöse Autoritäten in Ägypten. *Jhb. Mus. Völkerk. Leipzig* 28(1972), pp. 257-306.

TOMICHE, Nada. La *mawwāl* égyptien. *Mélanges Marcel Cohen*, 1970, pp. 429-438.

La lactation chez les égyptiennes du Caire. *Population* [Paris] 28(1973), pp. 677-679.

See also XII. a. Tibi.

See also XIX. a. Reid.

See also XIX. n. Gołębiowski

XIX EGYPT: HISTORY

a GENERAL

AGWANI, M.S. Religion and politics in Egypt. *Internat.stud.* 13(1974), pp. 367-388.

ALEXANDER, S.S. The interaction of economic, political and social aspects of development in Egypt and the Fertile Crescent. *Industrial organization and economic development. In honor of E.S. Mason.* 1970, pp. 366-395.

ANAWATI, G.C. Factors and effects of arabization and islamization in medieval Egypt and Syria. *Islam and cultural change in the Middle Ages*, ed. Sp. Vryonis, Jr., 1975, pp. 17-41.

BRETT, M. The spread of Islam in Egypt and North Africa. *Northern Africa: Islam and modernization*, ed. M.Brett, 1973, pp. 1-12.

CHERNOVSKAYA, V.V. Ofitzerskiy korpus Egipta kak sotzial'naya gruppa (1850-1952). *NAA* 1975(3), pp. 67-78.

COOPER, R.S. Land classification terminology and the assessment of the *kharāj* tax in medieval Egypt. *JESHO* 17(1974), pp. 91-102.

CRECELIUS, D. The organization of *WAQF* documents in Cairo. *IJMES* 2 (1971), pp. 266-277.

DAVIS, E. Political development or political economy?: political theory and the study of social change in Egypt and the Third World. *RMES* 1(1975), pp. 41-61.

DESSOUKI, Ali. The mass political culture of Egypt. *MW* 61 (1971), pp. 13-20.

GARCIN, J.C. Jean-Léon l'Africain et 'Aydhab. *Annales islamol.* 11(1972), pp. 189-209.

GERMANUS, A.K.J. Cairo, the town of the Arabian Nights. *Colloque international sur l'histoire du Caire*, 1969, pp. 169-171.

GIL, Moshe. Maintenance, building operations, and repairs in the houses of the Qodesh in Fustat. *JESHO* 14(1971), pp. 136-195.

GIL, Moshe. Supplies of oil in medieval Egypt: a Geniza study. *JNES* 34(1975), pp. 63-73.

GIURESCU, C.C. Romanian trade relations with Egypt until 1914. *Romano-Arabica*, ed. M. Anghelescu, 1974, pp. 9-21.

XIX EGYPT: HISTORY

HENNEQUIN, G. Mamlouks et métaux précieux. A propos de la balance des paiements de l'état syro-égyptien à la fin du moyen âge. *Ann. islamologiques* 12(1974), pp. 37-44.

HENNEQUIN, G. Points de vue sur l'histoire monétaire de l'Egypte musulmane au moyen âge. *Ann. islamologiques* 12(1974), pp. 1-36.

KUBIAK, W.B. New materials for the history of Alexandrian commerce. *Proc.27th Int. Cong.Or.1967* (1971), pp. 289-291.

MARSOT, Afaf Lutfi al-Sayyid. The cartoon in Egypt. *Comp. stud. soc. hist.* 13 (1971), pp. 2-15.

MARSOT, Afaf Lutfi al-Sayyid. Egyptian historical research and writing on Egypt in the 20th century. *MESA Bull.* 7ii(1973), pp. 1-15.

MARTHELOT, P. Recherche d'identité et mutation urbaine: l'exemple du Caire. *ROMM* 18 (1974), pp. 111-118.

MORIMOTO, Kôsei. Land tenure in Egypt during the early Islamic period. *Orient* [Japan] 11(1975), pp. 109-153.

NEHER-BERNHEIM, R. Frontières du Sinaï - Un siècle de diplomatie au Moyen-Orient 1840-1948. *Politique étrangère* 36(1971), pp. 147-164.

O'BRIEN, P. Turning points in Egyptian economic history. *Proc.27th Int.Cong. Or.1967* (1971), pp. 207-208.

PEVZNER, S.B. Rasskaz Ibn 'Abd al-Khakama o drevney istorii Egipta. *Pis'mennye pamyatniki Vostoka* 1971, pp. 61-85.

REID, D.M. Egyptian history through stamps. *MW* 62(1972), pp. 209-229.

REID, D.M. The rise of professions and professional organizations in modern Egypt. *Comp. stud. soc. hist.* 16(1974), pp. 24-57.

RICHARDS, D.S. Arabic documents from the Karaite community in Cairo. *JESHO* 15(1972), pp. 105-162.

SHARIPOVA, R.M. Sovremennaya istoriografiya OAR o roli universiteta "al-Azkhar" v period burzhuaznoy reformatzii Islama v Egipte v kontze XIX - nachale XX v. (obzor rabot 1950-1960-kh godov). *Religiya i obshchestvennaya mysl' narodov vostoka,* 1971, pp. 241-252.

SOMOGYI, J. de. The Canal of the Commander of the Faithful, the Muslim prototype of the Suez Canal. *Proc.27th Int.Cong.Or. 1967* (1971), p. 289.

STONE, R. Egypt. *Tropical development 1880-1913*, ed. by W.A. Lewis, 1970, pp. 198-220.

VATIKIOTIS, P.J. The modern history of Egypt Alla Franca. A review article [of *Egypt, imperialism and revolution* by J. Berque]. *Middle East Stud.* 10(1974), pp. 80-92.

WAHBA, Magdi. Réflexions sur un dialogue possible. *Nouvelle Rev. du Caire* 1 (1975), pp. 213-217.

See also VIII. e. Fahmy

See also IX. n. Goitein.

b ARAB CONQUEST

LAPIDUS, I.M. The conversion of Egypt to Islam. *In memoriam S.M. Stern* (Israel Or. studies, II, 1972), pp. 248-262.

LUFT, U. Der Beginn der islamischen Eroberung Ägyptens im Jahre 639. Eine Betrachtung zur islamischen Geschichtsschreibung des 9. Jahrhunderts. *Forschungen und Berichte, Staatl. Mus. Berlin* 16(1974), pp. 123-128.

MUKHTĀR, 'Abd al-Mun'im. On the survival of the Byzantine administration in Egypt during the first century of the Arab rule. *Acta Or. Acad. Sci. Hung.* 27(1973), pp. 309-319.

PLUMLEY, J.M. An eighth-century Arabic letter to the king of Nubia. *J.Egypt. archaeol.* 61(1975), pp. 241-245.

BLACHÈRE, R. La fondation du Caire et la renaissance de l'humanisme arabo-islamique au IVème siècle. *Colloque international sur l'histoire du Caire,* 1969, pp. 95-96.

d IKSHIDIDS

BACHARACH, J.L. The career of Muḥammad ibn Ṭughj al-Ikhshīd, a tenth-century governor of Egypt. *Speculum* 50(1975), pp. 586-612.

BERGER, M. Cairo to the American traveller of the nineteenth century. *Colloque international sur l'histoire du Caire,* 1969, pp. 51-66.

BIANQUIS, T. L'acte de succession de Kāfūr d'après Maqrīzī. *Ann. Islamologiques* 12(1974), pp. 263-269.

BIANQUIS, Thierry. Les derniers gouverneurs Ikhchidides a Damas. *BEO* 23 (1970), pp. 167-196.

e FATIMIDS

BESHIR, Beshir Ibrahim. New light on Nubian Fāṭimid relations. *Arabica* 22 (1975), pp. 15-24.

BIANQUIS, T. La prise du pouvoir par les Fatimides en Égypte (357-363/968-974). *Annales islamol.* 11(1972), pp. 48-108.

CAHEN, C. L'administration financière de l'armée fatimide d'après al-Makhzūmī. *JESHO* 15(1972), pp. 163-182.

CAHEN, Cl. et ADDA, M. Les éditions de l'Itti'āz al-hunafā' (histoire fatimide) de Maqrīzī par Aḥmad Hilmy, Sadok Hunī (Khouni), Fātiḥa Dib et Peter Kessler. *Arabica* 22(1975), pp. 302-320.

CAHEN, C. Al-Makhzūmī et Ibn Mammātī sur l'agriculture égyptienne médiévale. *Annales islamol.* 11(1972), pp. 141-151.

CAHEN, Cl. Les marchands étrangers au Caire sous les Fatimides et les Ayyubides. *Colloque international sur l'histoire du Caire,* 1969, pp. 97-101.

CRESSWELL, K.A.C. The founding of Cairo. *Colloque international sur l'histoire du Caire,* 1969, pp. 125-130.

GABRIELI, F. Le Caire de Nasir-i Khusrev. *ROMM* 13-14(1973), pp. 357-360.

GABRIELI, Fr. Le Caire de Nāṣir-i Khusrev. *Colloque international sur l'histoire du Caire,* 1969, pp. 155-157.

IMAMUDDIN, S.M. Administration under the Fatimids. *J. Asiatic Soc. Pakistan* 14(1969), pp. 253-269.

KUNITZSCH, P. Zur Namengebung Kairos (al-Qāhir - Mars?). *Islam* 52(1975), pp. 209-225.

LEWIS, B. An interpretation of Fatimid history. *Colloque international sur l'histoire du Caire,* 1969, pp. 287-295.

MAGUED. La personnel de la cour Fatimide en Egypte. *Ann.Fac.Arts Ain Shams* 3 (1955), pp. 147-160.

MAKAREM, Sami N. Al-Ḥākim bi-Amrillāh, an essay in historical reinterpretation. *Proc.27th Int.Cong.Or.1967* (1971), pp. 229-230.

MIQUEL, A. L'Égypte vue par un géographe arabe du IVe/Xe siècle: al-Muqaddasī. *Annales islamol.* 11(1972), pp. 109-139.

MOTZKIN, Aryeh L. Elijah ben Zechariah. A member of Abraham Maimūnī's Court. *REJ* 128 (1969), pp. 339-348.

SCANLON, G.T. A note on Fatimid-Saljūq trade. *Islamic civilization,* 1973, pp. 265-274.

STILLMAN, N.A. A case of labor problems in medieval Egypt. *IJMES* 5(1974), pp. 194-201.

STILLMAN, N.A. The eleventh century merchant house of Ibn 'Awkal (a Geniza study). *JESHO* 16(1973), pp. 15-88.

VON GRUNEBAUM, G.E. The nature of the Fatimid achievement. *Colloque international sur l'histoire du Caire,* 1969, pp. 199-215.

WALKER, P.E. A Byzantine victory over the Fatimids at Alexandretta (971), *Byzantion* 42(1972), pp. 431-440.

WIET, G. Un proconsul fatimide de Syrie: Anushtakin Dizbiri (*mort en 433/1042*). *MUSJ* 46(1970-1), pp. 383-407

See also II. a. 6. Vajda.

See also II. c. 8. Nagel.

See also VIII. e. David-Weill *et al.*

See also XXII. c. Hamdani.

f AYYUBIDS

BEHEIRY, Salah El-. Le décret de nomination de l'historien Ibn Wāṣil au poste de professeur de la Mosquée al-Aqmar. *Ann. islamologiques* 12(1974), pp. 85-94.

BRINNER, W.M. Some Ayyūbid and Mamlūk documents from non-archival sources. *In memoriam S.M. Stern* (Israel Or. studies, II, 1972), pp. 117-143.

CAHEN, C. Addenda sur Al-Djazarī. *In memoriam S.M. Stern* (Israel Or. studies, II, 1972), pp. 144-147.

CHAPOUTOT-REMADI, Mounira. Une institution mal connue: le khalifat abbaside du Caire. *CT* 20(nos.77-78, 1972), pp. 11-23.

EHRENKREUTZ, A.S. Saladin's coup d'état in Egypt. *Medieval and Middle Eastern studies ... A.S. Atiya* 1972, pp. 144-157.

ELBEHEIRY, Salah ad-din. Les lettres d' *Al-Nāsir Dāwūd. Proc.27th Int.Cong.Or. 1967* (1971), pp. 173-174.

LAPIDUS, I.M. Ayyubid religious policy and the development of schools of law in Cairo. *Colloque international sur l'histoire du Caire,* 1969, pp. 279-286.

RICHARDS, D.S. The early history of Saladin. *IQ* 17(1973), pp. 140-159.

SOURDEL, D., SOURDEL-THOMINE, J. Un texte d'invocations en faveur de deux princes ayyūbides. *Near Eastern numismatics ... Studies in honor of G.C. Miles,* 1974, pp. 347-352.

WADDY, C. An historian looks at the Middle East: based on the life of Ibn Wasil, contemporary historian of the Ayyubid dynasty. *Milla wa-milla* 11(1972), pp. 13-19.

See also XIX. e. Cahen.

g MAMLUKS

'ANKAWI, 'Abdullah. The pilgrimage to Mecca in Mamlūk times. *Arabian studies* 1(1974), pp. 146-170.

ASHTOR, E. Etude sur quelques chroniques mamloukes. *Israel Oriental studies* 1(1971), pp. 272-297.

AYALON, D. Discharges from service, banishments and imprisonments in Mamluk society. *In memoriam S.M. Stern* (Israel Or. studies, II, 1972), pp. 25-50.

XIX EGYPT: HISTORY

AYALON, D. The Mamluks and naval power. A phase of the struggle between Islam and Christian Europe. *Proc.Israel Acad.* 1 (1967), No. 8.

AYALON, D. The Muslim city and the Mamluk military aristocracy. *Proc.Israel Acad.* 2(1968), pp. 311-329.

AYALON, D. On one of the works of Jean Sauvaget (La poste aux chevaux dans l'Empire des Mamlouks). *Israel Oriental studies* 1 (1971), pp. 298-302.

AYALON, D. Preliminary remarks on the *Mamluk* military institution in Islam. *War, technology and society in the Middle East,* ed. V.J. Parry and M.E. Yapp, 1975, pp. 44-58.

BOSWORTH, C.E. Christian and Jewish religious dignitaries in Mamluk Egypt and Syria: Qalqashandī's information on their hierarchy, titulature, and appointment (I). *IJMES* 3(1972), pp. 59-74, 119-216.

CHAPOUTOT-REMADI, Mounira. L'agriculture dans l'Empire Mamluk au moyen âge d'après al-Nuwayrī. *CT* 22(85-86, 1974), pp. 23-45.

DARRAĞ, Aḥmad. La vie d'Abū'l-Maḥāsin Ibn Tagrī Birdī et son oeuvre. *Annales islamol.* 11(1972), pp. 163-181.

EVRARD, J.B. Die Statthalter Syriens im letzten halben Jahrhundert der Mamlukenherrschaft: Safad. *Islamkundliche Abhandlungen H.J. Kissling,* 1974, pp. 70-83.

GARCIN, J.C. La "méditerranéisation" de l'empire mamelouk sous les sultans Bahrides. *RSO* 48(1973-4), pp. 109-116.

GOTTSCHALK, H.L. Beiträge zur Mamluken-Geschichte. *WI* N.S.14(1973), pp. 192-199.

HAARMANN, U. Auflösung und Bewahrung der klassischen Formen arabischer Geschichtsschreibung in der Zeit der Mamluken. *ZDMG* 121(1971), pp. 46-60

HABASHI, Hassan. The Egyptian expeditions against Castelrosso and Rhodes. *Ann.Fac. Arts Ain Shams* 6(1961), pp. 51-69.

HABASHI, Hassan. A fifteenth century crusade attempt against Egypt. *Ann.Fac.Arts Ain Shams* 5(1959), pp. 1-18.

HOLT, P.M. The position and power of the Mamlūk sultan. *BSOAS* 38(1975), pp. 237-249.

HOLT, P.M. The Sultanate of al-Manṣūr Lāchīn (696-8/1296-9). *BSOAS* 36(1973), pp. 521-532.

HOURS, F. Fraude commerciale et politique internationale: les relations entre l'Égypte et Venise d'après une lettre de Qayt Bay (1472-1473). *BEO* 25(1972), pp. 173-183.

KHASANOV, A.A. Formirovanie cherkesskoy gruppirovki mamlyukov v Egipte. *Arabskie strany, Turtziya, Iran, Afganistan,* 1973, pp. 158-165.

LITTLE, D.P. An analysis of the relationship between four Mamluk chronicles for 737-45. *JSS* 19(1974), pp. 252-268.

LITTLE, D.P. The historical and historiographical significance of the detention of Ibn Taymiyya. *IJMES* 4(1973), pp. 311-327.

LITTLE, D.P. The recovery of a lost source for Bāḥrī Mamlūk history: al-Yūsufī's Nuzhat al-nāẓir fī sīrat al-malik alnāṣir. *JAOS* 94(1974), pp. 42-54.

MILLER, T.S. A new chronology of Patriarch Lazarus' persecution by the Mamluks (1349-1367). *OCP* 41(1975), pp. 474-478.

MUNAJJID, Salah al-Din al-. Une inscription inédite de l'époque mamelouk à Damas. *MUSJ* 46(1970-1), pp. 419-425

PLANTE, J.G. The Ethiopian embassy to Cairo of 1443. A Trier manuscript of Gandulph's report, with an English translation. *J.Ethiop.stud.* 13ii(1975), pp. 133-140.

RABIE, Hassanein. The training of the Mamlūk fāris. *War, technology and society in the Middle East,* ed. V.J. Parry and M.E. Yapp, 1975, pp. 153-163.

RAHMANI, Aftab Ahmad. The life and works of Ibn Ḥajar al-ʿAsqalānī. *IC* 45(1971), pp. 203-212.

RICHARDS, D. The Coptic bureaucracy under the Mamluks. *Colloque international sur l'histoire du Caire,* 1969, pp. 373-381.

ROGERS, J.M. Evidence for Mamluk-Mongol relations, 1260-1360. *Colloque international sur l'histoire du Caire,* 1969, pp. 385-403.

SADEQUE, Syedah Fatima. The court and household of the Mamlūks of Egypt. (13th-15th centuries). *J. Asiatic Soc. Pakistan* 14(1969), pp. 271-288.

SADEQUE, Syedah Fatima. Development of al-Barid or mail-post during the reign of Baybars I of Egypt (1260-1276 A.D.). *J. Asiatic Soc. Pakistan* 14(1969), pp. 167-183.

SOUKA, Fatma. Au temps des Mameluks. *Ann.Fac.Arts Ain Shams* 8(1963), pp. 205-208.

SUBLET, J. L'historiographie mamelouke en question. *Arabica* 22(1975), pp. 71-77.

VERMEULEN, U. Tolkenwezen of vertaaldienst in de Mamluken-Kanselarij te Kaīro. *Orientalia Gandensia* 3(1966), pp. 147-157.

WANSBROUGH, J. The safe-conduct in Muslim chancery practice. *BSOAS* 34 (1971), pp. 20-35.

See also VIII. f. Allan

See also VIII. f. Meinecke.

See also XIV. i. Daoulatli.

See also XIX. f. Brinner.

See also XIX. f. Cahen.

See also XXXIV. h. Ayalon.

See also XXXIV. h. Haarmann.

h OTTOMANS

ABD AL RAHEIM, Abd al Raheim A. *Hazzal-quhūf:* a new source for the study of the *fallāhīn* of Egypt in the XVIIth and XVIIIth centuries. *JESHO* 18(1975), pp. 245-270.

ASRAR, N. Ahmet. The myth about the transfer of the Caliphate to the Ottomans. *J. Reg. Cult. Inst.* 5(1972), pp. 111-120.

GARCIA, S. Tres españoles en la corte del último sultān de Egipto. *BAEO* 7 (1971), pp. 121-130.

GARCIN, J.C. Émirs Hawwāras et Beys de Ǧirga aux XVIe et XVIIe siècles. *Ann. islamologiques* 12(1974), pp. 245-255.

GARCIN, J.Cl. L'insertion sociale de Sha'rānī dans le milieu cairote. (D'après l'analyse des Ṭabaqāt de cet auteur.) *Colloque international sur l'histoire du Caire,* 1969, pp. 159-168.

HESS, A.C. The Ottoman conquest of Egypt (1517) and the beginning of the sixteenth-century world war. *IJMES* 4(1973), pp. 55-76.

HOURANI, A. The Syrians in Egypt in the eighteenth and nineteenth centuries. *Colloque international sur l'histoire du Caire,* 1969, pp. 221-233.

KHADEM, Saad el. Quelques reçus de commerçants et d'artisans du Caire des XVIIème et XVIIIème siècles. *Colloque international sur l'histoire du Caire,* 1969, pp. 269-275.

KUHNKE, L. Early nineteenth century ophthalmological clinics in Egypt. *Clio medica* 7(1972), pp. 209-214.

LIVINGSTON, J.W. ʿAlī Bey al-Kabīr and the Jews. *ME studies* 7 (1971), pp. 221-228.

MANTRAN, R. Les relations entre le Caire et Istanbul durant la période ottomane. *Colloque international sur l'histoire du Caire,* 1969, pp. 301-311.

MARSOT, Afaf Lutfi al-Sayyid Marsot Comments on the economic situation of the *ʿulamā'* in 18th century Egypt. *Proc. 27th Int.Cong.Or.1967* (1971), pp. 263-264.

MARSOT, Afaf Lutfi al-Sayyid. The political and economic functions of the 'ulamā' in the 18th century. *JESHO* 16(1973), pp. 130-154.

MARSOT, Afaf Lutfi al-Sayyid. A socio-economic sketch of the 'ulama in the eighteenth century. *Colloque international sur l'histoire du Caire,* 1969, pp. 313-322.

MĪLĀD, Salwā 'Alī Ibrāhīm. Registres judiciaires du tribunal de la Ṣāliḥiyya Naǧmiyya. *Ann. islamologiques* 12(1974), pp. 161-243.

MOUELHY, Ibrahim el-. Nouveaux documents sur le fallah et le régime des terres sous les Ottomans. *Annales islamol.* 11(1972), pp. 253-261.

NALLINO, M. L'Egypte dans les *Diari* de Marin Sanudo. *Colloque international sur l'histoire du Caire,* 1969, pp. 335-336.

RAYMOND, A. Deux familles de commerçants *fâsî* au Caire à la fin du XVIIIe siècle. *ROMM* 15-16(1973), pp. 269-273.

RAYMOND, A. Problèmes urbains et urbanisme au Caire aux XVIIème et XVIIIème siècles. *Colloque international sur l'histoire du Caire,* 1969, pp. 353-372.

RUIZ BRAVO-VILLASANTE, C. La sociedad egipcia de fines del siglo XIX vista por un diplomático español. *Orientalia Hispanica* I, 1974, pp. 574-600.

SARNELLI CERQUA, Cl. Un voyageur arabo-andalou au Caire au XVIIème siècle: al-Shih'ab Aḥmad al-Ḥadjarī. *Colloque international sur l'histoire du Caire,* 1969, pp. 103-106.

VESELÝ, R. Trois certificats délivrés pour les fondations pieuses en Égypte au XVIe siècle. Troisième contribution à la question des fondations pieuses ottomanes d'Égypte et de la diplomatique judiciaire. *Oriens* 21-22(1968-69), pp. 248-299.

See also II. c. 2. Winter.

See also VIII. d. *Egypt.* Mantran.

i NAPOLEON. FRENCH OCCUPATION

ANIS, M. The development of British interest in Egypt in the 18th century, 1775-1798. *Ann.Fac.Arts Ain Shams* 3 (1955), pp. 161-196.

GUELLOUZ, Ezzedine. Analyse idéologique d'un projet d'expédition d'Egypte: le projet de Venture de Paradis, orientaliste philosophe (1780). *CT* 21(nos. 81-82, 1973), pp. 123-151.

INGRAM, E. A preview of the great game in Asia - III: the origins of the British expedition to Egypt in 1801. *Middle Eastern stud.* 9(1973), pp. 296-314.

LABROUSSE, H. La mer rouge et l'expédition de Bonaparte en Egypte. *Pount* 2(1967), pp. 3-8.

NOVIČEV, A.D. Der Einfall der Franzosen in Ägypten und der französisch-türkische Krieg 1798-1802. *Z.f.G.* 9(1971), pp. 1139-1153.

RAYMOND, A. Deux commerçants de Byblos et de Saïda au Caire, à la fin du XVIIIe siècle. *MUSJ* 46(1970-1), pp. 409-418

RAYMOND, A. Deux leaders populaires au Caire à la fin du XVIIIe et au début du XIXe siècle. *Nouvelle Rev. du Caire* 1 (1975), pp. 281-298.

SILVERA, A. Bonaparte and Talleyrand. The origins of the French Expedition to Egypt in 1798. *AJAS* 3(1975), pp. 1-13.

SOROUGY, M.M. el-. Egyptian historiography of Napoleon Bonaparte in the twentieth century. *Eg. hist. rev.* 20(1973), pp. 3-27.

See also IV. c. 10. Kuhnke.

j MUHAMMAD ALI AND THE KHEDIVES, 1805–1879

ALLEN, R. Writings of members of "the Nazli Circle". *J.Amer. Research Cent. in Egypt* 8(1969-70), pp. 79-84.

BERQUE, J. et SHAKAA, Mustafa al-. La Gamâliya depuis un siècle. *Colloque international sur l'histoire du Caire*, 1969, pp. 67-93.

BOSWORTH, C.E. Henry Salt, consul in Egypt 1816-1827 and pioneer Egyptologist. *Bull. J.R. Univ. Libr.* 57(1974-5), pp. 69-91.

EISENDLE, E. MS.1729 - Panegyrisches Porträt eines österrischen Arztes [Prof. A. Reyer in Egypt, 1850-60]. *Biblos* 23 (1974), pp. 310-314.

ESHETE, Aleme. Une ambassade du Ras Ali en Egypte: 1852. *J. Ethiopian studies* 9 (1971), pp. 1-8.

FARHI, D. Niẓām-i Cedid - military reform in Egypt under Meḥmed ʿAlī. *Asian and African Stud.* 8(1972), pp. 151-183.

HANNA, Sami A. The Saint-Simonians and their application of state-socialism in Egypt. *Medieval and Middle Eastern studies ... A.S. Atiya* 1972, pp. 199-210.

HENNE, H. Zur Arbeit von Hans-Theodor Kosh "Dr. Wilhelm Reil-Bey (1820-1880). Ein abtrünniger Homöopath als Balneologe in Ägypten" in Medizinhistorisches Journal, 1968, Bd.3, Heft 2, S.101-113, 168-70. Erwiderung, *Medizinhist.J.* 4(1969), pp. 171-175.

KROPÁČEK, L. The confrontation of Darfur with the Turco-Egyptians under the viceroyships of Muḥammad'Alī, 'Abbās I and Muḥammad Sa'īd. *Asian and African studies* [Bratislava] 6(1970), pp. 73-86.

LOUCA, A. Colonisation et révolution nationale au XIXe siècle. La correspondance d'un suisse en Egypte: John Ninet. *Schweiz. Z. Gesch.* 22(1972), pp. 237-281.

MARTIN, M. Deux notes sur les travaux en Égypte en 1817-19. *Ann. islamologiques* 12(1974), pp. 257-261.

MUSTAFA, Ahmed Abdel-Rahim. The breakdown of the monopoly system in Egypt after 1840. *Ann.Fac.Arts Ain Shams* 10(1967), pp. 203-222.

MUSTAFA, Ahmed Abdel-Rahim. The Hekekyan papers. *Ann.Fac.Arts Ain Shams* 10(1967), pp. 169-178.

MUSTAFA, Ahmed Abdel-Rahim. Some aspects of Egypt's foreign relations under Abbas I with special reference to the Tanzîmât dispute. *Ann.Fac.Arts Ain Shams* 8 (1963), pp. 63-82.

NOVICHEV, A.D. Predposylki konflikta mezhdu Sultanom Makhmudom II i Mukhammedom Ali v 1839-1841 gg. (iz istorii bor'by Egipta za nezavisimost'). (The reasons for the conflicts between Sultan Mahmud II and Mohammed Ali in 1839-1841. *VLU* 1971 (4), pp. 59-68.

RATMAN, L. Problemy vosstaniya Orabi 1879-1882 gg. v Egipte. *Istoriya i ekonomika stran Arabskogo Vostoka*, 1973, pp. 247-274.

SCHÖLCH, A. Constitutional developments in nineteenth century Egypt - a reconsideration. *Middle East Stud.* 10(1974), pp. 3-14.

SCHÖLCH, A. Die Rolle der 'Ulamā' in der ägyptischen Krise der Jahre 1879 bis 1882. *XVIII. Deutscher Orientalistentag 1972: Vorträge*, pp. 250-258.

SHAKED, Haim. The biographies of ʿUlamāʾ in Mubārak's *Khiṭaṭ* as a source for the history of the ʿUlamāʾ in 19th century Egypt. *Asian & Afr.Studs.* 7(1971), pp. 41-76.

SHARIPOVA, R.M. Izmeneniya v deyatel'nosti universiteta al'-Azhar (60-e gody XX v.) *Strany Blizhnego i Srednego Vostoka: istoriya, ekonomica*, 1972, pp. 193-204.

SILVERA, A. Edme-Francois Jomard and Egyptian Reforms in 1839. *ME stud.* 7(1971), pp. 301-316.

SISLIAN, J.H. Religiöse Toleranz und das Problem der Bekehrung zur Zeit Mehmed Alis. *Saeculum* 22(1971), pp. 377-386

SPILLMANN, G. L'influence française en Égypte de 1800 à 1850. *Rev.hist.armée* 3(1973), pp. 7-20.

STAJUDA, T. Pierwsza nowoczesna partia polityczna w Egipcie (al-ḥizb al-waṭanī). *Przegl. or.* 2(94, 1975), pp. 147-154.

TABOULET, G. Ferdinand de Lesseps et l'Egypte avant le canal (1803-1854). *RFHOM* 60(no.219, 1973), pp. 143-171.

TABOULET, G. Ferdinand de Lesseps et l'Egypte avant le canal (1803-1854). *Rev. franç. d'hist. d'outre-mer* 60 (1973), pp. 364-407.

TIGNOR, R.T. Muhammad Ali, moderniser of Egypt. *Tarikh* 1 iv(1967), pp. 4-14.

TIGNOR, R.L. New directions in Egyptian modernisation: Ismail, Khedive of Egypt, 1836-1879. *Tarikh* 2iii(1968), pp. 64-71.

VERDERY, R.N. The publications of the Būlāq Press under Muḥammad ʻAlī of Egypt. *JAOS* 91(1971), pp. 129-132.

VOLKOFF, O.V. Le mystère du Mamelouk de la Citadelle. *Cahiers d'Alexandrie* 4iv (1967), pp. 13-29.

WALZ, T. Notes on the organization of the African trade in Cairo, 1800-1850. *Annales islamol.* 11(1972), pp. 263-286.

See also II. a. 8. KUDSI-ZADEH, A.A.

See also XIX. h. Hourani.

See also XXXVII. l. Khouri

k MODERN EGYPT, 1882-1922

ABBAS, Raouf. Labor movement in Egypt: 1899-1952. *Dev.economies* 11(1973), pp. 62-75.

BOTORAN, C. Sur l'histoire des relations roumano-égyptiennes entre les deux guerres mondiales (1919-1939). *Romano-Arabica,* ed. M. Anghelescu, 1974, pp. 21-35.

CANNON, B.D. Nubar Pasha, Evelyn Baring and a suppressed article in the Drummond-Wolff Convention. *IJMES* 5(1974), pp. 468-483.

CANNON, B.D. A reassessment of judicial reform in Egypt, 1876-1891. *Int.J.Afr.hist. stud.* 5(1972), pp. 51-74.

ESEDEBE, P. Olisanwuche. The independence movement in Egypt, 1880-1922. *Tarikh* 3iv(1971), pp. 1-11.

GAMAL, Shawky el. An unpublished document in the history of the Anglo-French competition for the domination in Upper Nile. *African studies R.* [Cairo] 1(1972), pp. 9-20.

HUNTER, F.R. The Cairo archives for the study of élites in modern Egypt. *IJMES* 4 (1973), pp. 476-488.

ISHIDA, Susumu. Delta barrages and Egyptian economy in the nineteenth century. *Developing economies* 10(1972), pp. 166-184.

JOMIER, J. L'iman Mohammad ʻAbdoh et la Caisse d'Epargne (1903-1904). *ROMM* 15-16 (1973), pp. 99-107.

KAZZIHA, Walid Wassel. The political and social bases for the development of self-governing institutions in Egypt, 1883-1914. *Egypte contemp.* 354(64, 1973), pp. 479-491.

LOUCA, Anouar. A la recherche de John Ninet. *Ann.Fac.Arts Ain Shams* 8(1963), pp. 209-216.

MARSOT, Afaf Lutfi Al-Sayyid. The Porte and Ismail Pasha's quest for autonomy. *J. American Res.Center in Egypt* 12(1975), pp. 89-96.

MOWAT, R.C. From liberalism to imperialism: the case of Egypt, 1875-1887. *Hist. J.* 16(1973), pp. 109-124.

OWEN, R. The Cairo building industry and the building boom of 1897 to 1907. *Colloque international sur l'histoire du Caire,* 1969, pp. 337-350.

OYEDEJI, E.B.L. Cromer in Egypt--an assessment. *African historian* 2iv(1968), pp. 21-24.

RATHMANN, L. Ägypten in Exil (1914-1918) -- Patrioten oder Kollaborateure des deutschen Imperialismus? *Asien in Vergangenheit und Gegenwart,* 1974, pp. 1-23.

SEYMOUR, C.L. The bombardment of Alexandria: a note. *Engl. hist. R.* 87(1972), pp. 790-794.

VOIGT, M. Some aspects of the economic development of Egypt 1918-1945. *African studies - Afrika-Studien,* ed. Thea Büttner and G. Brehme, 1973, pp. 37-52.

See also XIX. j. Louca.

See also XIX. j. Ratman.

See also XIX. j. Schölch.

See also XIX. n. Abbas.

See also XXIX. i. Hirszowicz.

l MODERN EGYPT, 1922-1957

ATTAR, Mohamed El-. Shifts in industrial structure and change in job pattern in the United Arab Republic 1937-1960. *Eg. contemp.* 62 (no. 344, 1971), pp. 155-167.

CONTU, G. Le donne comuniste e il movimento democratico femminile in Egitto fino al 1965. *OM* 55(1975), pp. 237-247.

FOKEEV, G.V. Bor'ba za likvidatziyu posledstviy agressii protiv Egipta v 1956-1957 godakh. (The struggle to eliminate the consequences of the 1956-1957 aggression against Egypt). *Vopr. Ist.* 1972(8), pp. 64-78.

FRIDMAN, L.A. Dynamics of agricultural output in Egypt (1913-1966). *Africa in Soviet studies* 1969, pp. 33-55.

GHAZALI, Abd-el-Hamid el-. Pre-planning economic structure. A comparative quantitive study of the Indian and Egyptian economies during 1945-1950. *Rev. al Qanoun wal Iqtisad* 40(1970), pp. 181-249.

GLAVANIS, P. Historical interpretation or political apologia? P.J. Vatikiotis and modern Egypt. *RMES* 1(1975), pp. 63-77.

IBRAHIM, Ibrahim I. The intellectual roots of "populistic democracy" in Egypt. *Al-Abhath* 21ii-iv(1968), pp. 31-43.

KRÁSA, M. Relations between the Indian National Congress and the Wafd party of Egypt in the thirties. *Arch. or.* 41(1973), pp. 212-233.

MAKEEV, D.A. Iz istorii razvitiya sovetsko-egipetskikh ekonomicheskikh svyazey (1922-1939 gg.). *NAA* 1974(3), pp. 51-63.

MANOR, Yohanan. Origines et causes de l'orientation pro-soviétique de l'Egypte 1952-1955. *Int. problems* 12i-ii(1973), pp. 44-58.

MELIGI, Abdel-Moneim el-. Recent developments in human sciences in Egypt (U.A.R.) (1952-1958). *Ann.Fac.Arts Ain Shams* 6 (1961), pp. 1-33.

MILOSLAVSKIY, G. Assotziatziya brat'ev-musulman v Egipte. *Strany Blizhnego i Srednego Vostoka: istoriya, ekonomica,* 1972, pp. 97-110.

REID, D.M. The national Bar Association and Egyptian politics, 1912-1954. *The International Journal of African Historical Studies* 7:4(1974), pp. 608-646.

SBACCHI, A. Anglo-Italian negotiations for the recognition of the Italian empire. And Haile Selassie vs. the National Bank of Egypt and the Cable and Wireless Co. 1937-1938. *Africa*[Rome] 30(1975), pp. 555-574.

SMITH, C.D. The 'crisis of orientation': the shift of Egyptian intellectuals to Islamic subjects in the 1930's. *IJMES* 4 (1973), pp. 382-410.

WARBURG, G. Lampson's ultimatum to Faruq, 4 February, 1942. *M.E. stud.* 11(1975), pp. 24-32.

WISSA-WASSEF, C. Les relations entre l'Egypte et les deux Etats allemands depuis la seconde guerre mondiale. *Politique étrangère* 37(1972), pp. 609-638.

YOUNG, W.L. Human resources and economic development: manpower, education, and the "Lewis model" in Egypt, 1952-1967. *Genève-Afrique* 14(1975).

ZAYID, Mahmud. New light on the Anglo-Egyptian negotiations for conclusion of the 1936 Treaty. *Al-Abhath* 22iii-iv (1969), pp. 59-102.

See also IX. m. Ibrahim.

See also XIX. k. Botoran.

See also XIX. k. Mowat.

See also XIX. k. Voigt.

See also XIX. n. Abbas.

m THE UNITED ARAB REPUBLIC

ABDUL ALIM, A.K.M. A study of the break-up of the United Arab Republic in September, 1961. *Dacca Univ. studies* 19A(1971), pp. 89-99.

ABU JABER, Faiz S. The development of Indo-Egyptian relations. *Ind. polit. sci. R.* 4(1970), pp. 157-170.

AWAD, Fouad H. Investments and economic development in the U.A.R. - 1959/60-1967/68. A study of methodology and application. *Eg. contemp.* 62 (no. 344, 1971), pp. 189-211.

AZNAR SÁNCHEZ, J. La union de Egipto y Libia y el nacimiento de un nuevo estado. *Rev. de polit. int.* 125(1973), pp. 67-89.

BARCIA TRELLES, C. El conflicto del Oriente Medio y sus repercusiones ecumenicas. Glosas de un espectador. *Revista de polít. int.* 131(1974), pp. 7-36.

BELYAEV, I.P. Gamal' Abdel' Naser (nekotorye cherty ideynoy evolyutzii). Gamal Abdel Nasser: Landmarks in ideological evolution. *NAA* 1972(2), pp. 73-89.

BINDER, L. Transformation in the Middle Eastern subordinate system after 1967. *The U.S.S.R. and the Middle East,* ed. by M. Confino and Sh. Shamir, 1973, pp. 251-271.

BONN, G. Anwar el Sadat - Ägypten und die Deutschen. *Z.f.Kulturaustausch* 24ii(1974), pp. 51-56.

BRETON, J.M. Le contrôle supérieur de l'État en République arabe d'Égypte. *BIIAP* 26(1973), pp. 53-94.

De JONG, F. Sociology in a developing country, the United Arab Republic: orientations and characteristics. *Sociol. Rev.* 19 (1971), pp. 241-252.

DESHPANDE, G.P. Strategy of the united front against imperialism: a study of Sino-UAR relations, 1956-1959. *Int.stud.* 14(1975), pp. 357-374.

EFIMOV, E.S. Nekotorye itogi realizatzii pervogo pyatiletnego plana sotzial'nogo i ekonomicheskogo razvitiya Egipta (1959/60 - 1964/65 gg.) i ego vliyanie na razvitie ekonomiki strany. *Strany Blizhnego i Srednego Vostoka: istoriya, ekonomica,* 1972, pp. 259-275.

ELSHAHAT, M.A. and NASSAR, S.Z. Onion situation: production and prices (Egypt, 1960-1970). *Eg. contemp.* 63(no.347, 1972), pp. 25-31.

FARAG, Adel Botros. Le Conseil d'Etat egyptien après 25 ans de sa création. *Eg. contemp.* 63(no. 348, 1972), pp. 105-127.

FUNK, H. and GRZESKOWIAK, M. Das "Programm der nationalen Aktion" in Ägypten. *Mitt. Inst. Orientforschung* 17(1972), pp. 511-559.

GIL BENUMAYA, R. Actualidad de Egipto ante los veinte años de su revolucion. *Rev. de polit. int.* 122(1972), pp. 235-243.

GIL BENUMEYA, R. La nación egipcia y la obra de Anuar Sadat. *Rev.polit.int.* 133(1974), pp. 149-158.

GLAGOW, Rainer. Ägypten und Libyen - Einheit in Etappen. *Orient* [Germany] 14(1973), pp. 178-181.

GLAGOW, R. Die ägyptische Arabische Sozialistische Union im Wandel. *Orient* [Germany] 16iv(1975), pp. 39-67.

GLAGOW, R. Einige Aspekte der gegenwärtigen politisch-ideologischen Diskussion in Ägypten. *Orient* [Hamburg] 16i(1975), pp. 41-66.

GLAGOW, R. Neue Perspektiven in der ägyptischen Innen- und Wirtschaftspolitik. *Orient* [Hamburg] 16ii(1975), pp. 81-106.

GOŁĘBIOWSKI, Ryszard. Social and economic changes in a Delta Village in the period 1952-1966. *Africana bull.* 14(1971), pp. 69-93

GRYADUNOV, Yu.S. Dvadtzat' let yul'skoy revolyutzii v Egipte. *NAA* 1972(5), pp. 17-28.

HANAFY, Abdallah Abdel Kader. Egyptian marketing system; changes and development 1952-1967. *Eg.contemp.* 355(65, 1974), pp. 33-60.

HARIK, I. The single party as a subordinate movement: the case of Egypt. *World politics* 26(1973), pp. 80-105.

HOLBIK, K. and DRACHMAN, E. Egypt as recipient of Soviet aid, 1955-1970. *Z.f.d. gesamte Staatswissens.* 127 (1971), pp. 137-165.

HÜBNER, G. Entwicklungen und Perspektiven der Wirtschafts- und Aussenhandelspolitik der Arabischen Republik Ägypten. *Asien, Afrika, Latein-Amerika* 2(1974), pp. 365-376.

KAMEL, M. Dialogue entre l'héritage culturel et le modernisme dans la pensée égyptienne contemporaine. *Travaux et jours* 46 (1973), pp. 53-71.

KEDOURIE, E. Anti-Marxism in Egypt. *The U.S.S.R. and the Middle East*, ed. by M. Confino and Sh. Shamir, 1973, pp. 321-334.

KERR, M.H. The United Arab Republic: the domestic, political, and economic background of foreign policy. *Political dynamics in the Middle East*, ed. P.Y. Hammond and S.S. Alexander, 1972, pp. 195-224.

KÜCK, G. Zur Rolle des privaten Sektors in der Industrie Ägyptens 1961 bis 1971. *Asien in Vergangenheit und Gegenwart*, 1974, pp. 165-179.

LEYMARIE, Ph. Egypte: Nixon au Caire. *Rev. franç.ét.pol.afr.* 9, no. 103(1974), pp. 15-17.

MANSOUR, Fawzy. Development of the Egyptian financial system up to June 1967. (A study in the relation between finance and socio-economic development.) *Rev. al-Ulum al-Qanuniya wal-Iqtisadiya* 13ii(1971), pp. 1-114.

MARTIN, Th. La réouverture du canal de Suez: quelques conséquences entre Méditerranée et Océan indien. *Stratégie* 38 (1974), pp. 49-76.

MINGANTI, P. Islam e proprietà agraria in una recente *fetwà*. *OM* 55(1975), pp. 273-281.

MINGANTI, P. Morte di Giamāl ʻAbd en Nāser. *OM* 50 (1970), pp. 597-602.

MOORE, C.H. Authoritarian politics in uncorporated society. The case of Nasser's Egypt. *Comparative politics* 6(1974), pp. 193-218.

MOORE, C.H. Professional syndicates in contemporary Egypt. The "containment" of the new middle class. *AJAS* 3(1975), pp. 60-82.

NAGI, Mostafa H. Internal migration and structural changes in Egypt. *MEJ* 28(1974), pp. 261-282.

O'KANE, J.P. Islam in the new Egyptian constitution: some discussions in *al-Ahrām*. *MEJ* 26(1972), pp. 137-148.

PAŁYGA, E.J. Stosunki dyplomatyczne i konsularne polsko-egipskie. *Przegl.or.* 91 (1974), pp. 209-218.

ROBBE, M., FUNK, H. Sozialistisches Denken in Ägypten. *Asien in Vergangenheit und Gegenwart*, 1974, pp. 39-52.

RONDOT, P. Egypte: atténuer les "contradictions" arabes. *Rev.franç.ét.pol.afr.* 9 (no. 105), pp. 19-23.

RONDOT, P. Gamal Abdel Nasser. *Afr.et l'Asie* 91-2(1970), pp. 26-34.

SAATY, Hassan El-. Social dynamics in industry, a monographic study of an Egyptian enterprise. *Ann.Fac.Arts Ain Shams* 4(1957), pp. 1-46.

SAATY, Hassan El-. Some aspects of the social implications of technological change in Egypt. *Ann.Fac.Arts Ain Shams* 6(1961), pp. 35-49.

SADAT, Anwar el-. Where Egypt stands. *Foreign aff.* 51(1972), pp. 114-123.

SHAHAAT, M.A. El; NASSAR, S.Z. An economic analysis of state farm credit in Egypt, 1960-1970. *Egypte contemp.* 64(no.353, 1973), pp. 93-106(301-314)

SHAMIR, Shimon. The Marxists in Egypt: the "licensed infiltration" doctrine in practice. *The U.S.S.R. and the Middle East*, ed. by M. Confino and Sh. Shamir, 1973, pp. 293-319.

SLAIEH, Ezzat N. The Egyptian-Soviet friendship treaty of 1971: some cautious interpretations. *Ind.pol.sci.rev.* 8(1974), pp. 7-26.

TERRY, J.I. Official British reaction to Egyptian nationalism after World War I. *Al-Abhath* 21ii-iv(1968), pp. 15-29.

TIXIER, G. L'Union des Républiques Arabes et la constitution égyptienne du 11 septembre 1971. *Rev. droit public* 88(1972), pp. 1129-1173.

TRISHINA, I. Torgovyy balans Egipta (1959-1970 gg.). *Arabskie strany, Turtziya, Iran, Afganistan,* 1973, pp. 227-234.

VATIKIOTIS, P.J. Notes for an assessment of the Soviet impact on Egypt. *The U.S.S.R. and the Middle East,* ed. by M. Confino and Sh. Shamir, 1973, pp. 273-289.

VATIKIOTIS, P.J. The Soviet Union and Egypt: the Nasser years. *The Soviet Union and the Middle East,* ed. I.J. Lederer and W.S. Vucinich, 1974, pp. 121-34.

Constitution of the Arab Republic of Egypt. *MEJ* 26(1972), pp. 55-68

Ministry of Foreign Affairs, Jerusalem. Egypt's unlawful blockade of the Gulf of Aqaba. *Crescent and star,* ed. by Y. Alexander and N.N. Kittrie, 1973, pp. 303-308.

Le mouvement étudiant en Égypte (décembre 1972-février 1973). *Travaux et jours* 47 (1973), pp. 131-142.

See also II. a. 2. *Egypt.* Naggar.

See also IX. k. Muzikář.

See also IX. k. Silbermann.

See also XVII. c. Baldissera.

See also XIX. l. Contu.

See also XIX. l. Young.

See also XXIII. d. Khalidi.

See also XXXIII. d. Duclos

n ECONOMICS

ABDEL-FADIL, Mahmoud. Economic development in Egypt in the new High Dam era. *Eg. contemp.* 65(no.356, 1974), pp. 247-273.

ABED, G. Labour absorption in industry: an analysis with reference to Egypt. *Oxford econ. papers* 27(1975), pp. 400-425.

ADAMOWICZ, Mieczyslaw. Transformation of agricultural structure in the United Arab Republic: aims of agricultural policy and methods of its implementation. *Africana bull.* 13 (1970), pp. 75-88.

AFIFI, Hani. The Egyptian experience of agrarian reform. *East Afr. J. rural development* 5i-ii(1972), pp. 193-200.

AWAD, Fouad H. Industrial policies in the A.R.E.. *Eg. contemp.* 64(no.351, 1973), pp. 5-54.

BARBOUR, K.M. The distribution of industry in Egypt: a new source considered. *Trans. Inst. Brit. Geographers* 50(1970), pp. 155-176.

BLAKE, G.H. Oil in Egypt. *Geography* 59 (1974), pp. 49-51.

CHAPMAN, D. Economic aspects of a nuclear desalination agro-industrial project in the United Arab Republic. *Amer. J. agric. econ.* 55(1973), pp. 433-440.

ELSHAHAT, M.A.,, YASSEN, S.S. A statistical analysis of the relationship of cooperative marketing and of cotton production in Egypt. *Égypte contemp.* 62, no. 346(1971), pp. 41-54

FEEL, Ahmed M.T. El-, *et al.* The application of benefit cost analysis for economic evaluation of the High Dam project in Egypt. *Eg.contemp.* 65(no.356, 1974), pp. 275-290.

FIXLER, L.D., FERRAR, R.L., SULLIVAN, E. The economic and political consequences of a convertible Egyptian pound. *Egypte contemp.* 66,no.359(1975), pp. 29-54.

FIXLER, L.D., FERRAR, R.L., SULLIVAN, E. The economic and political consequences of a convertible Egyptian pound. *MEJ* 29 (1975), pp. 451-460.

GAMEH, Gameh M. Determination of agricultural productivity in Egypt: multiple regression analysis. *Égypte contemp.* 62, no. 346(1971), pp. 55-73

GASHEV, B.N., SMIRNOVA, G.I. Razvitie neftyanoy promyshlennosti v Egipte. *Istoriya i ekonomika stran Arabskogo Vostoka,* 1973, pp. 71-87.

IBRAHIM, Abdul Rahman Zaki. Price incentives in the development of Egyptian agriculture. *Eg.contemp.* 355(65, 1974), pp. 75-84.

ISMAIL, Mohamad Mahrous. The economics of the iron and steel industry in Egypt. *Egypte contemp.* 64(no.353, 1973), pp. 5-42 (213-250)

JASIŃSKI, B. The policy of the government of the Arab Republic of Egypt towards the private industrial sector. *Africana bull.* 18(1973), pp. 89-100.

JASIŃSKI, W. Some important aspects of the utilization of manpower in the Arab Republic of Egypt. *Studies on the developing countries* 4(1974), pp. 46-67.

KANDEEL, Abdel-Fattah. "Planned surplus" for economic development: a note on the price policy for electric power from the Aswan High Dam. *Eg. contemp.* 63(no.350, 1972), pp. 297-309.

KHEIR-EL-DINE, Hanaa A. Some aspects of regional differences in the U.A.R. *Eg. contemp.* 62 (no. 343, 1971), pp. 61-82.

KHOLIE, Osman A. el-. Disparities of Egyptian personal income distribution as reflected by family budget data. *Egypte contemp.* 354 (64, 1973), pp. 33-372.

KHOLEI, Osman A. Evaluation of soil conserving policies by comparing land productivity classifications. *Egypte contemp.* 64(no.353, 1973), pp. 75-92(283-300)

KÜCK, G. Zur Einbeziehung ausländischen Kapitals in die wirtschaftliche Entwicklung von Ländern auf nichtkapitalistischem Weg. Erfahrungen und Probleme Ägyptens. *Asien, Afrika, Latein-Amerika* 1(2, 1973), pp. 71-90.

KUŹNIAR, A. Irrigation problems in the development of agriculture in Lower Egypt. *Africana bull.* 17(1972), pp. 91-113.

LUSHNIKOVA, L.I. Rol' gosudarstva v formirovanii fonda vnutrennikh denezhnykh nakopleniy v arabskoy respublike Egipet. *Istoriya i ekonomika stran Arabskogo Vostoka,* 1973, pp. 174-183.

LUTZKEVICH, V.A., KLEKOVSKIY, R.V. Tendentzii ekonomicheskogo razvitiya Arabskoy Respubliki Egipet. *NAA* 1973(5), pp. 139-147.

MABRO, R. Migrations internes et sous-emploi urbain: le cas de l'Égypte. *Travaux et jours* 45(1972), pp. 65-76.

MANSOUR, Mahmoud E.I. Main obstacles to a faster agricultural economic development in the A.R.E. *Eg. contemp.* 64(352, 1973), pp. 176-187.

MANSOUR, Mahmoud E.I. Some possible models for the reshuffling of the main agricultural resources in Northern Egypt. *Egypte contemp.* 354(64, 1973), pp. 373-400.

METWALLY, M.M. A note on sources of output growth in Egypt. *Eg. contemp.* 65 (1974), pp. 467-473.

MONTASSER, Essam. Egypt's pattern of trade and development: a model of import substitution growth. *Eg.contemp.* 65(no.356, 1974), pp. 141-245.

MOUSSA, Ahmad Rashad. The expansion of Egypt's exports of cotton textiles and stability of export proceeds and sales of cotton. *Rev. al Qanoun wal Iqtisad* 40(1970), pp. 121-140.

MUTALOV, V.M. Khlopkovodstvo sovremennogo Egipta i ego perspektivy. *Arabskie strany, Turtziya, Iran, Afganistan,* 1973, pp. 211-218.

NASSAR, Saad Zaki. Regulation and control of the agricultural prices in the developing countries, with special reference to Egypt. *Égypte contemp.* 62, no. 346(1971), pp. 23-39

PANFILENKO, E.N. Elektrifikatziya Egipta. *Arabskie strany, Turtziya, Iran, Afganistan,* 1973, pp. 219-226.

PANPHILENKO, E. Neft' Egipta i blizhnevostochnyy kri:is. *Strany Blizhnego i Srednego Vostoka: istoriya, ekonomica,* 1972, pp. 369-379.

RACHID, A.R.H. The establishment of heavy industry in a developing country. A case study. *Eg. contemp.* 62 (no. 344, 1971), pp. 143-154.

RADMAN, Wolf. The Suez Maritime Canal Universal Company: a precedent? From Lesseps to SUMED, the Egyptian oil pipeline. *Orient* [Germany] 15(1974), pp. 3-8.

RADWAN, Samir. Towards a political economy of Egypt: a critical note on writings on the Egyptian economy. *RMES* 1(1975), pp. 93-100.

RIZK, Mohamed M., AFR, Mohamed A. Economic efficiency in Egyptian agriculture. *Egypte contemp.* 354(64, 1973), pp. 401-426.

SHAHAT, M.A. el-, NASSAR, S.Z. Estimates of labour surplus in agriculture in Egypt. *Eg. contemp.* 355(65, 1974), pp. 85-93.

SMIRNOVA, G.I. Perspektivy razvitiya neftyanoy promyshlennosti Egipta. *Strany Blizhnego i Srednego Vostoka: istoriya, ekonomica,* 1972, pp. 408-416.

TOUKHY, Abdel Naby el. The quality of labour and its incidence on the socio-economic development in the A.R. Egypt. *Egypte contemp.* 354(64, 1973), pp. 427-434.

WISSA-WASSEF, C. Le développement économique de l'Egypte, objectif essentiel de la politique du président Sadate. *Maghreb-Machrek* 66(1974), pp. 25-34.

WISSA WASSEF, C. D'où vient la crise du coton en Égypte? *Tiers-monde* 14(1973), pp. 417-424.

WISSA WASSEF, C. Le prolétariat et le sous-prolétariat industriel et agricole en République arabe unie. *Orient* 51-2(1969), pp. 87-112

Agricultural co-operation in Egypt. *Yearbook of agricultural co-operation* 1972, pp. 13-22.

See also XVI. cc. Barthel, Grienig, Kück.

See also XIX. a. Giurescu.

See also XIX. a. Morimoto.

See also XIX. m. Minganti.

See also XXIX. c. Veselý.

XX THE SUDAN. OTHER PARTS OF EAST AFRICA

a GEOGRAPHY

ABDEL HAFEEZ, A.T. and SAEED, A.M. Quality of White, Blue and main Nile waters for irrigation purposes in Khartoum district. *SNR* 52(1971), pp. 110-115.

AHMAD, Hassan Aziz. The Zeidab Estate, 1903-1924. *Adab: J. Fac. Arts, Khartoum* 2-3(1975), pp. 83-97.

BOUSHI, Ismail Mudathir El-. The shallow ground water of the Gezira Formation at Khartoum and the N. Gezira. *SNR* 53(1972), pp. 154-163.

BUSHRA, El-Sayed el-. The distribution of land use within major Sudanese towns. *Adab (J.Fac.Arts, Khartoum)* 1(1972), pp. 60-72.

GELLERT, J.F. Die Rolle des Klimas und der natürlichen Vegetation bei der Entwicklung der Weidewirtschaft in den semiariden Tropen Afrikas - dargestellt am Beispiel des Hochlandes von Südwestafrika (Namibia) und der Provinzen Kordofan und Darfur der DR Sudan. (The importance of climate and natural vegetation for the development of pasture farming in the semi-arid tropics of Africa, represented at the example of the Highlands of South-West-Africa (Namibia) and the Provinces of Kordofan and Darfur of the DR of Sudan.) *PGM* 115(1971), pp. 274-282

GRAHAM, A.M.S. Adapting to water shortage in a year of poor rains: a case study from the Sudan. *Savanna* 2(1973), pp. 121-125.

HAMMER, R.M. Rainfall patterns in the Sudan. *J. trop. geog.* 35(1972), pp. 40-50.

MULA, Hafiz G. A geophysical survey of J. Aulia region. *SNR* 53(1972), pp. 164-168.

QUEZEL, P. A preliminary description of the vegetation in the Sahel region of north Darfur. *SNR* 51(1970), pp. 119-125.

RODEN, D. Regional inequality and rebellion in the Sudan. *Geog. R.* 64(1974), pp. 498-516.

SAYED EL-BUSHRA, El-. The definition of a town in the Sudan. *Sudan notes and records* 54(1973), pp. 66-72.

SHAABAN, Soad. Bedscha-Hadandowa. Eine wissenschaftliche Forschungsreise in das Gebiet der Bedscha. *African studies R.* 1(1972), pp. 43-62.

TAHA, Taha el Jack. The development of the Managil South-Western extension to the Gezira scheme, Sudan. *Land reform* 1975, no. 1, pp. 25-37.

THORNTON, D.S. Agricultural development in the Gezira Scheme. *SNR* 53(1972), pp. 100-115.

TOM, Mahdi Amin el-. A harmonic analysis of the rainfall over the Sudan. *J.trop.geog.* 37(1973), pp. 9-15.

TOM, Mahdi Amin El-. Toward a rational estimation of average rainfall in the Sudan. *SNR* 53(1972), pp. 125-153.

TOM, Mahdi Amin el-. The variability of the pentade rainfall in the Sudan. *East Afr. geog. R.* 11(1973), pp. 82-87.

VAIL, J.R. Jebel Umm Marafieb: an extinct volcano near Berber. *Sudan notes and records* 54(1973), pp. 188-192.

WHITEMAN, A.J. Comments on the classification of the basement complex of the Red Sea hills. *SNR* 51(1970), pp. 126-130.

WILLIAMS, M.A.J., ADAMSON, D.A. The physiography of the Central Sudan. *Geog. J.* 139 (1973), pp. 498-508.

See also XVIII. a. Dewachter

b ETHNOLOGY

ABDEL GHAFFAR M. AHMED. Nomadic competition in the Funj area. *Sudan notes and records* 54(1973), pp. 43-56.

AHMED, Abdel Ghaffar Mohammed. The Rufa'a al-Hoj economy. *Essays in Sudan ethnography*, 1972, pp. 173-188.

ARIFI, Salih A. el-. Pastoral nomadism in the Sudan. *East African geog. R.* 13 (1975), pp. 89-103.

ASAD, Talal. Political inequality in a Kababish tribe. *Essays in Sudan ethnography*, 1972, pp. 126-148.

BUSHRA, El-Sayed El-. Population growth and economic development in the Sudan. *Bull. Arab res.and stud.* 5(1974), pp. 3-12.

CUNNISON, I. Blood money, vengeance and joint responsibility: the Baggara case. *Essays in Sudan ethnography*, 1972, pp. 105-125.

DAWI, Taj al-Anbia Ali al-. Social characteristics of big merchants and businessmen in El Obeid. *Essays in Sudan ethnography*, 1972, pp. 201-216.

DELMET, Chr. Notes sur les populations du Djebel Guli (Southern Dar Fung, Soudan). *L'Homme* 14(1974), pp. 119-134.

DENG, F.M. Dynamics of identification. A basis for national integration in the Sudan. *Africa today* 20iii(1973), pp. 19-28.

ECSEDY, Cs. Aspects of hunting among the Maiak of the Hill Burun Sudan. *Acta ethn. Acad. Sci. Hung.* 22(1973), pp. 293-318.

EVANS-PRITCHARD, E.E. Notes on Zande proper names. *SNR* 53(1972), pp. 187-191.

EVANS-PRITCHARD, E.E. Sources, with particular reference to the Southern Sudan. *Cah. ét. afr.* 11 (1971), pp. 129-179.

GRANDIN, N. Sud-Soudan: une élite dans l'impasse. *Cah. ét. afr.* 13(1973), pp. 158-162.

HAALAND, G. Nomadisation as an economic career among the sedentaries in the Sudan savannah belt. *Essays in Sudan ethnography*, 1972, pp. 149-172.

HALE, S. Nubians in the urban milieu: Greater Khartoum. *Sudan notes and records* 54(1973), pp. 57-65.

HARRIES-JONES, P. The Jamuʿiya development scheme: an essay on the utility of 'instant anthropology'. *Essays in Sudan ethnography*, 1972, pp. 217-247.

HASAN, Hasan Iman and O'FAHEY, R.S. Notes on the Mileri of Jabal Mun. *SNR* 51(1970), pp. 152-161.

HENIN, Roushdi A. Collection of demographic data on nomadic populations. (The Sudan: a case study). *Int.population conf.* London, 1969, I, pp. 306-324.

HENIN, R.A. The level and trend of fertility in the Sudan. *Population growth and economic development in Africa*, 1972, pp. 77-83.

HILL, L.G. On camel brands. *SNR* 53(1972), pp. 1-17.

HILL, R.L. River and marine harbour craft - II. *SNR* 53(1972), pp. 204-214.

HOFMANN, I. Heiratsbräuche im Gebiet von Alt-Dongola (Sudan). *Anthropos* 67(1972), pp. 152-160

HOLÝ, L. Residence among the Berti. *Essays in Sudan ethnography*, 1972, pp. 58-70.

JAHN, Samia al Azharia. Der deutsche Afrikaforscher Leo Frobenius als erster Sammler sudan-arabischer Volkserzählungen. *Paideuma* 21(1975), pp. 30-46.

KHATTAB, A.G.H. and HADARI, A.M. El-. Nutritional evaluation of diets in the Nuba Mountains. *SNR* 53(1972), pp. 192-195.

MIELKE, J.H., ARMELAGOS, G.J. and VAN GERVEN, D.P. Trabecular involution in femoral heads of a prehistoric (X-group) population from Sudanese Nubia. *Amer.J.phys.anthr.* 36 (1972), pp. 39-44

MINKOVSKAYA, E. Otrazhenie drevnikh religioznykh predstavleniy v sovremennom fol'klore narodov Sudana. *Voprosy vostochnogo literaturovedeniya i tekstologii*, 1975, pp. 61-69.

MÜHLBACHER-HANSEN, I. Die Erforschung der Ethnien des oberen Nilgebietes 1769-1861. *Wiener ethnohist. Blätter* 9 (1974), pp. 17-72.

REHFISCH, F. A rotating credit association in the Three Towns. *Essays in Sudan ethnography*, 1972, pp. 189-200.

RODEN, D. Down-migration in the Moro hills of S. Kordofan. *SNR* 53(1972), pp. 79-99.

SANTANDREA, P.S. I Kresh (Bahr el Ghazâl, Sudan). *Annali Lateranensi* 33 (1969), pp. 125-210.

SHAABAN, Soad. Bedscha - Hadendowa. Eine wissenschaftliche Forschungsreise in das Gebiet der Bedscha. *African studies R.* [Cairo] 1(1972), pp. 43-62.

SHAHI, Ahmed S. al-. Proverbs and social values in a Northern Sudanese village. *Essays in Sudan ethnography*, 1972, pp. 87-104.

STEIN, L. "Kulturelles Erbe im Westsudan." *Mitt. aus dem Mus. f. Völkerk. Leipzig* 39(1974), pp. 17-22.

TAHA, Abdel-Rahman E. Ali. The political role of the labour movement in the Sudan 1946-1969. *Adab (J.Fac.Arts, Khartoum)* 1 (1972), pp. 13-23.

TAHA, El-Waleed Mohamed. Money and banking in the Sudan: an annotated bibliography. *SNR* 53(1972), pp. 196-201.

TUBIANA, M.J. Exogamie clanique et l'Islam: l'exemple kobé. Implications économiques et politiques du renoncement à l'exogamie en faveur du marriage avec la fille de l'oncle paternel. *L'homme* 15 iii-iv(1975), pp. 67-81.

TUBIANA, M.J., TUBIANA, J. Un peuple noir aux confins du Tchad et du Soudan: les Beri aujourd'hui. *Cah. d'Outre-Mer* 26 (1973), pp. 250-261.

TUBIANA, M.J. Système pastoral et obligation de transhumer chez les Zaghawa (Soudan-Chad). *Etudes rurales* 42(1971), pp. 120-171.

See also III. b. Schinkel.

See also XII. e. Komorowski.

c HISTORY

ABBAS, P. Growth of black political consciousness in Northern Sudan. *Africa today* 20iii(1973), pp. 29-43.

XX THE SUDAN

ABBAS IBRAHIM MUHAMMAD ALI. The British military officers and the Sudan, 1886-1896. *Sudan notes and records* 54(1973), pp. 17-31.

ABDALLA, Isma'il Hussein. The choice of Khashm al-Girba area for the resettlement of the Halfawis. *SNR* 51(1970), pp. 56-74.

ABDALLA, I.H. The 1959 Nile Waters Agreement in Sudanese-Egyptian Relations. *ME stud.* 7(1971), pp. 329-342.

ABDEL A'AL ABDALLA OSMAN. Milestones in the history of surgical practice in the Sudan. *Sudan notes and records* 54(1973), pp. 139-152.

AGUDA, Oluwandare. Arabism and Pan-Arabism in Sudanese politics. *Mawazo* 4i(1973), pp. 7-26.

AGUDA, Oluwadare. The state and the economy in the Sudan: from a political scientist's point of view. *J. devel. areas* 7(1973), pp. 431-448.

AHMAD, Abdel Ghaffar Muhammad. The role of the sedentary population in Rufa'a al-Hoj politics. *SNR* 52(1971), pp. 33-45.

ALI, Abbas Ibrahim Muhammad. British attitudes towards the Mahdist revolution, 1881-1885. *Eg. hist. rev.* 17(1970), pp. 3-21.

ALI, Abbas Ibrahim Muhammad. The British debate on the containment of the Sudanese Mahsist revolution, November 1883-February 1885. *Adab: J. Fac. Arts, Khartoum* 2-3(1975), pp. 1-43.

ALI, Abbas Ibrahim Muhammad. Contemporary British views on the Khalifa's rule. *SNR* 51(1970), pp. 31-46.

ALI TAHA, Abdel-Rahman. The political role of the labour movement in the Sudan 1946-1969. *Adab* [Khartoum], pp. 13-23.

ASKAROVA, D.A. Rabochee i profsoyuznoe dvizhenie Sudana (1956-1969). *NAA* 1975 (1), pp. 147-156.

AWAD, Mohammed Hashim. The evolution of landownership in the Sudan. *MEJ* 25 (1971), pp. 212-228.

BAYOUMI, A. Medical research in the Sudan since 1903. *Medical hist.* 19(1975), pp. 271-285.

BECHTOLD, P. Military rule in the Sudan: the first five years of Ja'far Numayri. *MEJ* 29 (1975), pp. 16-32.

BELL, J. Bowyer. The Sudan's African policy: problems and prospects. *Africa today* 20 iii(1973), pp. 3-12.

BROCKETT, A.M. Emir Suleyman ibn Inger Abdullah - a further episode. *SNR* 51 (1970), pp. 47-55.

BUSHRA, El-Sayed el-. Towns in the Sudan in the eighteenth and early nineteenth centuries. *SNR* 52(1971), pp. 63-70.

DEKMEJIAN, R.H. and WYSZOMIRSKI, M.J. Charismatic leadership in Islam: the Mahdi of the Sudan. *Comp.stud.soc.hist.* 14(1972), pp. 193-214

DENG, Francis Mading. The dynamics of identification. A basis for national integration in the Sudan. *Orient* [Germany] 14 (1973), pp. 161-164.

GAMAL, Shawky el-. An unpublished document in the history of the Anglo-French competition for the Upper Nile. *Afr.stud.rev. (Cairo)* 1(1972), pp. 9-22.

GRAY, R. Some aspects of Islam in the Southern Sudan during the Turkiya. *Northern Africa: Islam and modernization*, ed. M. Brett, 1973, pp. 65-72.

GRAY, R. The southern Sudan. *J. contemp. hist.* 6 (1971), pp. 108-120.

GRIBBIN, R.E. Two relief crises: Biafra and Sudan. *Africa today* 20iii(1973), pp. 47-59.

HADRA, Tawheeda Osman. The use of the Sudan in some English novels. *SNR* 53 (1972), pp. 67-78.

HAJJ, Muhammad A. Al-, LAVERS, J.E. The travel notes of Al-Sharif Hasa b. Al-Husayn. *Kano stud.* N.S. 1i(1973), pp. 3-24.

HASSAN AHMED IBRAHIM. The Sudan in the 1936 Anglo-Egyptian treaty. *Sudan notes and records* 54(1973), pp. 1-16.

HAYCOCK, B.G. The history department study tours in the area from Abidya to Mograt, 1969-1971. *Adab (J.Fac.Arts, Khartoum)* 1 (1972), pp. 1-12.

HAYCOCK, B.G. Mediaeval Nubia in the perspective of Sudanese history. *SNR* 53 (1972), pp. 18-35.

HERZOG, R. Unveröffentlichte Beobachtungen über die Bischarin. *Festschrift H. Petri*, 1973, pp. 167-184.

HILL, R. A register of named power-driven river and marine harbour craft commissioned in the Sudan 1856-1964. *SNR* 51 (1970), pp. 131-146.

HOLT, P.M. The Islamization of the Nilotic Sudan. *Northern Africa: Islam and modernization*, ed. M. Brett, 1973, pp. 13-22.

HOWELL, J. Local government reform in the Sudan. *J. admin. overseas* 12(1973), pp. 28-36.

HOWELL, J. Politics in the Southern Sudan. *African affairs* 72(1973), pp. 163-178.

HUNWICK, J.O. The dynastic chronologies of the Central Sudan States in the sixteenth century: some reinterpretations. *Kano stud.* N.S. 1i(1973), pp. 35-55.

LEVTZION, Nehemia. Was Maḥmūd Ka'tī the author of *Ta'rīkh al-fattāsh*? *Res. Bull. CAD Ibadan* 6(1970), pp. 1-12.

XX THE SUDAN

LEWICKI, T. Un état soudanais médiéval inconnu: le royaume de Zāfūn(u). *Cah. ét.afr.* 11(1971), pp. 501-525.

LIMAGNE, J. La guerre civile du Soudan. *Rev. fr. ét. pol. africaines* 73(1971), pp. 54-73.

LY, Madina. Quelques remarques sur le Tarikh el-Fettach. *Bull. IFAN* 34(1972), pp. 471-493.

McLOUGHLIN, P.F.M. Labour market conditions and wages in the three towns, 1900-1950. *SNR* 51(1970), pp. 105-118.

MERCER, P. Shilluk trade and politics from the mid-seventeenth century to 1861. *J. Afr. hist.* 12(1971), pp. 407-426.

MOKHLESUR RAHMAN, Md. British policy and the administration of Shari'a law in the Sudan, 1899-1916. *Islam and the modern age* 5iv (1974), pp. 46-57.

MOKHLESUR RAHMAN, Md. Northern Sudan and the British policy towards the Christian missions (1899-1912). *Rajshahi Univ.stud.* 5(1973), pp. 100-112.

MONOD, T. En marge de la conquête marocaine du Soudan: La lettre espagnole de 1648. *Mélanges Marcel Cohen,* 1970, pp. 459-461.

MUKHLESUR RAHMAN. Reginald Wingate and the question of loyalty of the Sudanese Muslims during the World War I. *Rajshahi univ. studies* 4(1972), pp. 89-100.

MUSA, Omar el-Hag. Reconciliation, rehabilitation and development efforts in Southern Sudan. *MEJ* 27(1973), pp. 1-6.

NASR, Ahmed Abdel Rahim. British policy towards Islam in the Nuba mountains, 1920-1940. *SNR* 52(1971), pp. 23-32.

O'FAHEY, R.S. The affair of Ahmad Agha. *SNR* 53(1972), pp. 202-203.

O'FAHEY, R.S. Arabic documents from Darfur. *Bull.Int.Cttee.on urgent anthrop. and ethnol.res.* 12(1970), pp. 117-118.

O'FAHEY, R.S. Al-Bulalawi or al-Hilali? *Sudan notes and records* 54(1973), p. 197.

O'FAHEY, R.S. Kordofan in the eighteenth century. *Sudan notes and records* 54 (1973), pp. 32-42.

O'FAHEY, R.S. and SPAULDING, J.L. Hāshim and the Musabba'āt. *BSOAS* 35(1972), pp. 316-333.

O'FAHEY, R.S. Saints and sulṭāns: the role of Muslim holy men in the Keira Sultanate of Dār Fūr. *Northern Africa: Islam and modernization,* ed. M. Brett, 1973, pp. 51-56.

O'FAHEY, R.S. Slavery and the slave trade in Dār Fūr. *J. Afr. hist.* 14(1973), pp. 29-43.

RING, B.M.M. Political relationships between Northern and Southern blacks in the Sudan. *Africa today* 20iii(1973), pp. 13-18.

RODEN, D. The twentieth century decline of Suakin. *SNR* 51(1970), pp. 1-22.

SANDERSON, L. Education and administrative control in colonial Sudan and Northern Nigeria. *African affairs* 74 (1975), pp. 427-441.

SANDERSON, G.N. Sudanese nationalism and the independence of the Sudan. *Northern Africa: Islam and modernization,* ed. M. Brett, 1973, pp. 97-109.

SANHORY, M.H.El. An approach to industrial planning in Sudan. *Orient* [Hamburg] 16i(1975), pp. 67-86; 16ii (1975), pp. 107-132.

SHAKED, Haim., SOUERY, Esther., and WARBURG, G. The Communist party in the Sudan, 1946-1971. *The U.S.S.R. and the Middle East,* ed. by M. Confino and Sh. Shamir, 1973, pp. 335-374.

SHAKED, Haim. The presentation of the Sudanese Mahdi in a unique Arabic manuscript biography. *Abr Nahrain* 13(1972-73) pp. 24-32.

SHAKED, Haim. The presentation of the Sudanese Mahdi in a unique Arabic manuscript biography. *Milla wa-milla* 11(1972), pp. 20-27.

SPAULDING, J. The Funj: a reconsideration. *J.Afr.hist.* 13(1972), pp. 39-53.

STOOKEY, R.W. Social structure and politics in the Yemen Arab Republic. *MEJ* 28(1974), pp. 248-260, 409-418.

TAHA, El Waleed Mohamed. From dependent currency to central banking in the Sudan: a survey. *SNR* 51(1970), pp. 95-104.

TERAIFI, Al-Agab A. Localisation policies and programmes in the Sudan, 1945/1970. *J. admin. overseas* 12(1973), pp. 125-135.

UKPABI, S.C. The independence movement in the Sudan. *Tarikh* 4i(1971), pp. 41-53.

VOLL, J.O. The British, the 'Ulamâ', and popular Islam in the early Anglo-Egyptian Sudan. *IJMES* 2 (1971), pp. 212-218.

VOLL, J. Effects of Islamic structures on modern Islamic expansion in the Eastern Sudan. *Int.J.Afr.hist.stud.* 7(1974), pp. 85-98.

VOLL, S. The introduction of native administration in the Anglo-Egyptian Sudan. *al-Abhath* 24(1971), pp. 111-123.

WARBURG, G.R. From Anṣar to Umma: sectarian politics in the Sudan, 1914-1945. *Asian and African studies* [Jerusalem] 9 (1973), pp. 101-153.

WARBURG, G. Religious policy in the Northern Sudan: 'Ulamā' and Ṣūfism 1899-1918. *Asian & Afr.Studs.* 7(1971), pp. 89-119.

La constituzione permanente della Repubblica Demotrica del Sudan. *OM* 53(1973), pp. 656-674.

XX THE SUDAN

Sudan, joy of peace, burden of pioneering. *Africa today* 20iii(1973), pp. 44-46.

See also II. a. 8. Balogun.

See also IX. j. Aguda.

See also XIX. j. Kropáček.

cc ECONOMICS

ABDEL BAGI ABDEL GHANI BABIKER. Die Landwirtschaft in der Demokratischen Republik Sudan. *PGM* 118(1974), pp. 181-188.

ALI, Mohamed Abdel Rahman. Determinants of local government expenditure and intergovernmental allocation of government expenditure in the Sudan. *East Afr. econ. R.* 5i(1973), pp. 39-54.

ALI ABDALLA ALI. The Sudan's invisible trade, 1956-1969: a brief survey. *Sudan notes and records* 54(1973), pp. 124-138.

BERTIN, F. Quelques signes de l'arabisation des noms portés par les Issa. *Pount* 3(1967), pp. 29-30.

BONTINCK, F. La double traversée de l'Afrique par trois "Arabes" de Zanzibar (1845-1860). *Et.hist.africaine* 6(1974), pp. 5-53.

BUSHRA, El-Sayed El-. The development of industry in Greater Khartoum, Sudan. *East Afr.geog.R.* 10(1972), pp. 27-50.

BUSHRA, El-Sayed el-. The distribution of land use within major Sudanese towns. *Adab* [Khartoum], pp. 60-72.

DELMET, Chr. Extraction d'huile comestible d'un insecte (Agonoscelis versicolor) au djebel Guli (Soudan). *Etudes rurales* 52(1973), pp. 138-140.

FARAH HASSAN ADAM and APAYA, W.A. Agricultural credit in the Gezira. *Sudan notes and records* 54(1973), pp. 104-115.

FILONIK, A.O. Kooperativnoe stroitel'stvo v Sudane. *Strany Blizhnego i Srednego Vostoka: istoriya, ekonomica,* 1972, pp. 433-441.

FILONIK, A.O. O nizshikh formakh kapitala v sudanskoy derevne. *Strany Blizhnego i Srednego Vostoka: istoriya, ekonomica,* 1972, pp. 478-487.

JACK TAHA, Taha el. The development of Managil South-Western extension to the Gezira scheme--a case study. *J. admin. overseas* 14(1975), pp. 240-250.

JEDREJ, M.C. and STREMELAAR, G. Guneid sugar scheme: a sociological consideration of some aspects of conflict between management and tenants. *SNR* 52(1971), pp. 71-78.

MARZOUK, M.S. An econometrical model of Sudan. Simulation experiment of growth prospects. *J. development economics* 1 (1974), pp. 337-358.

MEDANI, A.I. Consumption patterns of the Gezira-Managil tenants. *SNR* 52(1971), pp. 79-87.

MOHAMED ABDEL RAHMAN ALI. Calculating the contribution of a structural shift to economic growth in the Sudan: 1955-1967. *Sudan notes and records* 54(1973), pp. 116-123.

MOHAMMED HASHIM AWAD. Agricultural development in the Gezira scheme: a rejoinder. *Sudan notes and records* 54 (1973), pp. 193-196.

SAEED, Osman Hassan. Marketability of securities as an incentive for voluntary savings: a case study of the Sudan. *SNR* 52(1971), pp. 88-100.

SULIMAN, Ali Ahmed. The effect of labour turn-over and absenteeism on the cost of production in the Sudan textile industry. *Eastern Africa econ. R.* 3ii(1971), pp. 49-62.

Co-operation in Sudan 1969-70. *Year-book of agricultural co-operation* 1972, pp. 116-120.

See also XVI. aa. Aksyuk.

d OTHER PARTS OF EAST AFRICA

AKINỌLA, G.A. Slavery and slave revolts in the Sultanate of Zanzibar in the nineteenth century. *J. Hist. Soc. Nigeria* 6(1971-72), pp. 215-228.

ALI, Mohamed Abdel Rahman. The propensity to consume and economic development in a dual economy: Sudan 1955-1967. *SNR* 53 (1972), pp. 116-124.

ALPERS, E. A revised chronology of the sultans of Kilwa in the eighteenth and nineteenth centuries. *Azania* 2(1967), pp. 145-163.

ARENS, W. Islam and Christianity in subsaharan Africa: ethnographic reality or ideology. *Cah.ét.afr.* 15(1975), pp. 443-456.

AZIZ ESMAIL. Towards a history of Islam in East Africa. *Kenya hist. R.* 31(1975), pp. 147-158.

BERG, F.J.; WALTER, B.J. Mosques, population and urban development in Mombasa. *Hadith* 1(1968), pp. 47-100.

BROWN, B. Muslim influence on trade and politics in the Lake Tanganyika region. *Afr.hist.stud.* 4(1971), pp. 617-629

CAULK, R.A. Yohannes IV, the Mahdists, and the colonial partition of north-east Africa. *Transafr.J.hist.* 1ii(1971), pp. 23-42.

CHITTICK, N. The early history of Kilwa Kivinje. *Azania* 4(1969), pp. 153-158.

CHITTICK, N. Two traditions about the early history of Kilwa. *Azania* 3(1968), pp. 197-200.

XX THE SUDAN

COOKEY, S.J.S. Tippu Tib and the decline of the Congo Arabs. *Tarikh* 1 ii(1966), pp. 58-69.

ERLICH, Haggai. 1885 in Eritrea: 'the year in which the dervishes were cut down'. *Asian and African studies* [Jerusalem] 10 (1975), pp. 281-329.

FISHER, A.G.B., FISHER, H.J. Nachtigal's experience in Tibesti, 1869; African immigration restrictions in the mid-nineteenth century. *Adab (J.Fac.Arts, Khartoum)* 1 (1972), pp. 24-46.

GREGSON, R.E. Trade and politics in South-East Africa: the Moors, the Portuguese and the kingdom of Mwenemutapa. *African social research* 16(1973), pp. 413-446.

HOLWAY, J.D. C.M.S. contact with Islam in East Africa before 1914. *J. relig. Afr.* 4(1972), pp. 200-212.

KASOZI, A.B.K. The history of Islam in Uganda. *Uganda Clio* 1971(1), pp. 71-78.

LABROUSSE, H. Le "Mad Mullah" du Somaliland. *Pount* 8(1970), pp. 15-28.

MARTIN, B.G. Arab migrations to East Africa in medieval times. *Int. J. Afr. hist. stud.* 7(1974), pp. 367-390.

MARTIN, J. Une visite de la reine de Mohéli à Paris. *Pount* 8(1970), pp. 29-40.

NOUAILLE-DEGORGE, Br. Le facteur islamique dans le conflit érythréen. *Rev. franç. d'ét. pol. afr.* 113(1975), pp. 65-78.

ODED, Arye. The Arab and Islamic impact on Buganda during the reign of Kabaka Mutesa I. *Asian and African studies* [Jerusalem] 9(1973), pp. 196-237.

PAGE, M.E., BENNETT, P.R. The inscribed sandals of Tippu Tip. *J. Soc. africanistes* 42(1972), pp. 187-191.

PAGE, M.E. Livingstone, the Arabs and the slave trade. *Livingstone: man of Africa,* 1973, pp. 131-151.

PAGE, M.E. The Manyema hordes of Tippu Tip: a case study in the social stratification and the slave trade in Eastern Africa. *Int. J.Afr.hist.stud.* 7i(1974), pp. 69-84.

PAGE, M.E. Tippu Tip and the Arab "Defense" of the East African slave trade. *Etudes d'hist. afr.* 6(1974), pp. 105-117.

POUWELS, R.L. Tenth century settlement of the East African coast: the case for Qarmatian/Isma'ili connections. *Azania* 9 (1974), pp. 65-74.

RIZVI, S. Saeed Akhtar. "Zenj": its first known use in Arabic literature. *Azania* 2(1967), pp. 200-201.

ROBERTS, A. The history of Abdullah Ibn Suliman. *African social research* 4 (1967), pp. 241-270.

RONDOT, P. Quelques remarques sur le personnage et le rôle historique de Mohammed 'Abdillé Hassan. *Pount* 8(1970), pp. 7-14.

RZEWUSKI, E. *Asili ya Bangwana* - origine des Bangwana. Enregistrements de la tradition orale relative à l'histoire de la communauté musulmane de Kisingani. *Africana bull.* 21(1974), pp. 117-146.

TEDESCHI, S. Note storiche sulle isole Dahlak. *Proc. 3rd Int. Conf. Eth. Studies,* 1966, pp. 49-74.

TRIULZI, A. Trade, Islam, and the Mahdia in Northwestern Wallaggā, Ethiopia. *J. Afr. hist.* 16(1975), pp. 55-71.

WAGNER, E. Arabic documents on the history of Harar. *J.Ethiop.stud.* 12i(1974), pp. 213-224.

WAGNER, E. Genealogien aus Harar. *Islam* 51(1974), pp. 97-118.

WAGNER, E. Imamat und Sultanat in Harar. Ein Beitrag zur Auseinandersetzung zwischen religiösem und weltlichem Herrschaftsanspruch in islamischen Randgebieten. *Saeculum* 26(1975), pp. 283-292.

YOUNG, T. Cuyler. East Africa and classical Islam: some remaining research problems in relationships. *Transafr.J.hist.* 2ii(1972), pp. 3-10.

See also II. d. 4. Hajj.

See also IX. n. Jeffreys.

See also XXII. c. Chittick.

XXI THE CRUSADES AND LATIN KINGDOMS

a CRUSADES

ANDREA, A.J., MOTSIFF, I. Pope Innocent III and the diversion of the Fourth Crusade army to Zara. *Byzantinoslavica* 33(1972), pp. 6-25.

BEEBE, B. The English baronage and the Crusade of 1270. *Bull. Inst. Hist. Res.* 48(1975), pp. 127-148.

BLACK, R. La storia della Prima Crociata di Benedetto Accolti e la diplomazia fiorentina rispetto all'Oriente. *Archivio stor. ital.* 131(1973), pp. 3-25.

BRETON, R. Monographie du château de Markab, en Syrie. *MUSJ* 47(1972), pp. 253-274.

BRUNDAGE, J.A. The army of the First Crusade and the Crusade vow: some reflections on a recent book. *Mediaeval studies* 33(1971), pp. 334-343.

BURNS, R.I. Immigrants from Islam: the Crusaders' use of Muslims as settlers in thirteenth century Spain. *Am.Hist.R.* 80 (1975), pp. 21-42.

CAHEN, C. Une inscription mal comprise concernant le rapprochement entre Maronites et Croisés. *Medieval and Middle Eastern studies ... A.S. Atiya* 1972, pp. 62-63.

CARDINI, C. La storia e l'idea di Crociata negli studi odierni (1945-1967). *Anuario estud.med.* 5(1968), pp. 641-662.

DUPARC QUIOC, S. Recherches sur l'origine des poèmes épiques de croisade et sur leur utilisation éventuelle par les grandes familles féodales. *La poesia epica e la sua formazione,* 1970, pp. 771-796.

DUPONT, L. Humanisme et croisade: Torrentius et les Turcs. *Rev. belge philol.* 50(1972), pp. 447-458.

FRANCE, J. The crisis of the first Crusade: from the defeat of Kerbogah to the departure from Arqa. *Byzantion* 40(1970), pp. 276-308.

FRANCE, J. The departure of Tatikios from the Crusader Army. *Bull. Inst. Hist. Res.* 44(110, 1971), pp. 137-147.

FRANCE, J. An unknown account of the capture of Jerusalem. *Engl. hist. R.* 87(1972), pp. 771-783.

GOITEIN, S.D. Tyre--Tripoli--'Arqa. Geniza documents from the beginning of the Crusader period. *JQR* 66(1975), pp. 5-88.

HITTI, P.K. The impact of the Crusades on Eastern Christianity. *Medieval and Middle Eastern studies ... A.S. Atiya* 1972, pp. 211-217.

IGLESIAS, A.A. Notas sobre el ideal de cruzada en Don Enrique "El Naveganta". *Cong.int.hist.descobrimentos. Actas* IV, 1961, pp. 257-274

JACOBY, D. The encounter of two societies: Western conquerors and Byzantines in the Peloponnesus after the Fourth Crusade. *Amer. hist. R.* 78(1973), pp. 873-896.

KENNAN, E. Innocent III and the first political crusade: a comment on the limitations of papal power. *Traditio* 27(1971), pp. 231-249

LABIB, Subhi. Die Kreuzzugsbewegung aus arabisch-islamischer Sicht. Interaction oder Challenge. *Medieval and Middle Eastern studies ... A.S. Atiya* 1972, pp. 240-267.

LABROUSSE, H. Renaud de Châtillon, héros de légende et la conquête de la mer Rouge par les Croisés (1183). *Pount* 9(1971), pp. 31-45.

LEFEVRE, R. La Crociata del 1270 a Tunisi nella documentazione dell'Archivio di Stato di Napoli. *Africa* [*Rome*] 27(1972), pp. 439-462.

MAYO, P.C. The Crusaders under the palm. Allegorical plants and cosmic kingship in the *Liber floridus*. *Dumbarton Oaks papers* 27(1973), pp. 29-67.

MOLLAT, M. Le "Passage" de Saint Louis à Tunis. Sa place dans l'histoire des croisades. *Rev. d'hist. econ. et soc.* 50(1972), pp. 289-303.

NICOL, D.M. Introduction. *Relations between East and West in the Middle Ages,* ed. D. Baker, 1973, pp. 1-10.

PATERSON, W.F. The battle of Arsuf. *J. Soc. Archer Antiquaries* 8(1965), pp. 20-23.

PONTIERI, E. Alfonso I d'Aragona e la "crociata" di Callisto III. *RANL* 29 (1974), pp. 61-68.

PRAWER, J. A Crusader tomb of 1290 from Acre and the last archbishops of Nazareth. *Israel expl. J.* 24(1974), pp. 241-251.

QUELLER, D.E., COMPTON, T.K., CAMPBELL, D. A. The Fourth Crusade: the neglected minority. *Speculum* 49(1974), pp. 441-463.

XXI THE CRUSADES AND LATIN KINGDOMS

ROUSSET, P. Sainte Cathérine de Sienne et le problème de la croisade. *Schweiz.Z. Gesch.* 25(1975), pp. 499-513.

RUNCIMAN, S. The legacy of the crusades. *J. Pak. Hist. Soc.* 13(1965), pp. 293-305.

SCHWINGES, R.Ch. Kreuzzugsideologie und Toleranz im Denken Wilhelms von Tyrus. *Saeculum* 25(1974), pp. 367-385.

SIVAN, E. Modern Arab historiography of the crusades. *Asian and African Stud.* 8(1972), pp. 109-149.

WEITZMANN, K. Four icons on Mount Sinai: new aspects in Crusader art. *Jhb. d. österr. Byzantinistik* 21(1972), pp. 279-293.

WHITE, L. The Crusades and the technological thrust of the West. *War, technology and society in the Middle East,* ed. V.J. Parry and M.E. Yapp, 1975, pp. 97-112.

See also IV. c. 3. Watt.

See also IV. c. 3. Watt.

See also XXIX. f. Göllner.

b LATIN KINGDOMS

CAHEN, C. Un document concernant les Melkites et les Latins d'Antioche au temps des Croisades. *Rev.des études byzantines* 29 (1971), pp. 285-292

COWDREY, H.E.J. The Latin Kingdom of Jerusalem. *History* 57(1972), pp. 228-234.

DMITRIEV, G. Drevneyshee pravo v srednevekovoy Palestine i v Kilikiyskom armyanskom tzarstve. *Byzantinoslavica* 34(1973), pp. 19-27.

DOWSETT, C.J.F. A twelfth-century Armenian inscription at Edessa. *Iran and Islam, in memory of V. Minorsky,* 1971, pp. 197-227

EDBURY, P. The Ibelin counts of Jaffa: a previously unknown passage from the 'Lignages d'Outremer'. *Engl. hist. R.* 89(1974), pp. 604-610.

FERRARD, C.G. The amount of Constantinopolitan booty in 1204. *Studi veneziani* 13(1971), pp. 95-104.

FILHOL, R. Gouvernants et gouvernés dans les principautés franques d'Orient. *Recueils Soc.Jean Bodin* 24(1966), pp. 101-125.

HENDRICKX, B. Baudouin IX de Flandre et les empéreurs byzantins Isaac II l'Ange et Alexis IV. *Rev.belge philol.hist.* 49 (1971), pp. 482-489

HENDRICKX, B. The main problems of the history of the Latin Empire of Constantinople (1204-1261). *Rev. belge philol.* 52(1974), pp. 787-799.

KEDAR, B.Z. The general tax of 1183 in the crusading kingdom of Jerusalem: innovation or adaptation? *Engl. hist. R.* 89(1974), pp. 339-345.

KOLIAS, G. Les raisons et le motif de l'invasion de Robert Guiscard à Byzance. *Actes I. Cong. int. ét. balkan. et sud-est europ.* III (1969), pp. 357-361

MAYER, H.E. Studies in the history of Queen Melisende of Jerusalem. *Dumbarton Oaks papers* 26(1972), pp. 95-182.

NIERMAN, J.H. Levantine peace following the Third Crusade: a new dimension in Frankish-Muslim relations. *MW* 65(1975), pp. 107-118.

PRAWER, J. Estates, communities and the constitution of the Latin Kingdom. *Proc. Israel Acad.* 2(1968), pp. 101-142.

RIDER, R. Vie et survie de quelques familles illustrés du royaume de Jérusalem. *Le Moyen age* 4.sér.,28 (1973), pp. 251-267.

RILEY-SMITH, J. The *Assise sur la ligece* and the Commune of Acre. *Traditio* 27(1971), pp. 179-204

RILEY-SMITH, J. Government in Latin Syria and the commercial privileges of foreign merchants. *Relations between East and West in the Middle Ages,* ed. D. Baker, 1973, pp. 109-132.

RILEY-SMITH, J. A note on confraternities in the Latin kingdom of Jerusalem. *Bull. Inst. Hist. Res.* 44(No. 110, 1971), pp. 301-308.

RILEY-SMITH, J. Some lesser officials in Latin Syria. *Engl.hist.R.* 87(no. 342, 1972), pp. 1-26

VESEY, D.W.T.C. William of Tyre and the art of historiography. *Medieval stud.* 35 (1973), pp. 433-455.

VILLAIN-GANDOSSI, Chr. Les attributions du baile de Constantinople dans le fonctionnement des échelles du Levant au XVIe siecle (d'après le ms. 83 Fonds turc anc. de la Bibl. Nat. de Paris). *Recueils Soc. Jean Bodin* 33(1972), pp. 227-244.

WOODINGS, A.F. The medical resources and practice of the Crusader states in Syria and Palestine 1096-1193. *Medical History* 15 (1971), pp. 268-276.

XXII ARABIA

a GEOGRAPHY

ABDO, Asaad. The evolution of modern roads in Saudi Arabia. *Bull.Soc.Geog.d'Egypte* 41-2(1968-69), pp. 23-42.

ABUL-HAGGAG, Y. Remarks on the artesian water of Nejd, Saudi Arabia. *Ann.Fac. Arts Ain Shams* 8(1963), pp. 103-111.

BEVIS, R. Spiritual geology: C.M. Doughty and the land of the Arabs. *Victorian stud.* 16(1972), pp. 163-181.

CHELHOD, J. Le Yémen, cet inconnu. *Pount* 12 (1973), pp. 3-11.

CLOUET, A.-G. La navigation au long cours yéménite de nos jours vers l'Afrique orientale. *Pount* 12(1973), pp. 13-18.

CORNELIUS, P.F.S. *et al.* The Musandam expedition 1971-72; scientific results: part 1. *Geog. J.* 139(1973), pp. 400-425.

DOSTAL, W. The Shiḥūḥ of Northern Oman: a contribution to cultural ecology. *Geog. J.* 138(1972), pp. 1-7

FALCON, N.L. The Musandam (Northern Oman) expedition 1971/1972. *Geog. J.* 139(1973), pp. 1-19.

FISHER, W.B. and BOWEN-JONES, H. Development surveys in the Middle East. *Geog. J.* 140(1975), pp. 454-466.

HARRISON, D.L. The Oman flora and fauna survey, 1975. *J.Oman stud.* 1(1975), pp. 181-186.

KOPP, H. Die räumliche Differenzierung der Agrarlandschaft in der Arabischen Republik Jemen (Nordjemen). Bericht nach einer Studienreise. *Erdkunde* 29(1975), pp. 59-68.

LEATHERDALE, J. and KENNEDY, R. Mapping Arabia. *Geog. J.* 141(1975), pp. 240-251.

MANDAVILLE, J. Some experiments with solar ground stills in eastern Arabia. *Geog.J.* 138(1972), pp. 64-66

MASRY, Abdullah H. Factors of growth in the civilisation of S.W. Arabia: an ethno-ecological approach. *Bull.Fac.Arts U.Riyad* 3 (1973-74), pp. 41-65.

MIQUEL, A. La terre d'Arabie selon Hamdānī. *Nouvelle Rev. du Caire* 1(1975), pp. 241-263.

PURINI. G. Puri. I nuovi stati del golfo arabico. *Levante* 20iii-iv(1973), pp. 5-25.

ROBINSON, G.P.G. The Musandam expedition: scientific results. *Geog. J.* 140(1974), pp. 94-104.

SCHOLZ, F. Sesshaftwerdung von Beduinen in Kuwait. *Erdkunde* 29(1975), pp. 223-234.

SERJEANT, R.B. The cultivation of cereals in mediaeval Yemen. *Arabian studs.* 1(1974), pp. 25-74.

S[ERJEANT], R.B. Porcupines in the Yemen. *Arabian studs.* 1(1974), p. 180.

STEVENS, J.H. and CRESSWELL, E. The future of date cultivation in the Arabian Peninsula. *Asian aff.* 59(N.S. 3,1972), pp. 191-197.

STEVENS, J.H. Man and environment in Eastern Saudi Arabia. *Arabian studies* 1(1974), pp. 135-145.

STEVENS, J.H. Oasis agriculture in the Central and Eastern Arabian peninsula. *Geography* 57(1972), pp. 321-326.

STRIKA, V. Due capitali saudiane: Gedda e Riàd. *Levante* 21iii(1974), pp. 25-32.

TIBBETTS, G.R. Arabia in the fifteenth-century navigational texts. *Arabian studies* 1(1974), pp. 86-101.

WILKINSON, J.C. The Oman question: the background to the political geography of South-East Arabia. *GJ* 137(1971), pp. 361-371.

See also II. b. 2. King

See also VIII. c. *Arabia.* Tamari.

b ETHNOLOGY

ANSARI, Ghaus. Proposed ethnographic survey of traditional systems of medicine and treatment in Kuwait. *Bull. Int. Cttee Urgent Anthrop. Ethnol. Res.* 14(1972), pp. 81-82.

ATALLAH, Wahib. *Al-buss.* Vestige de cultes chtoniens en Arabie. *Arabica* 22 (1975), pp. 25-32.

CHELHOD, J. L'Arabie du Sud vue par Carsten Niebuhr. *ROMM* 18(1974), pp. 19-44.

CHELHOD, J. Les cérémonies du mariage au Yémen. *Objects et mondes* 13(1973), pp. 3-34.

CHELHOD, J. La civilisation des bédouins. *Pount* 11(1972), pp. 15-20.

CHELHOD, J. L'organisation sociale au Yémen. *L'Ethnographie* N.S.64(1970), pp. 61-86.

CHELHOD, J. La parenté et le mariage au Yémen. *L'Ethnographie* N.S.67(1973), pp. 47-90.

CHELHOD, J. La société yéménite et le kat. *Objets et mondes* 12(1972), pp. 3-22.

DEQUIN, H. A basis of operation for the nomads of the desert. Development aspects of settling nomads in Saudi Arabia and Ethiopia. *Orient* [Germany] 14(1973), pp. 177-178.

DOSTAL, W. Sozio-ökonomische Aspecte der Stammesdemokratie in Nordost-Yemen. *Sociologus* N.S.24(1974), pp. 1-15.

DOSTAL, W. Two South Arabian tribes: al-Qarā and al-Harāsīs. *Arabian studies* 2(1975), pp. 33-42.

FAYEIN, C. La vie pastorale au Dhofar. *Objets et mondes* 11(1971), pp. 321-332.

FAYEIN, C. Al Zohrah: village de la Tihâma. *Objets et mondes* 13(1973), pp. 161-172.

HEARD-BEY, Fr. Development anomalies in the Beduin oases of al-Liwa. *Asian affairs* 61(N.S.5, 1974), pp. 272-286.

HEARD-BEY, F. Social changes in the Gulf States and Oman. *Asian aff.* 3(1972), pp. 309-316.

HERZOG, R. Unveröffentlichte Beobachtungen über die Bischarin. *Fest.H.Petri,* 1973, pp. 167-184.

INAYAT-UR-RAHMAN. The ethnological wealth in Swat. *Pak.archaeology* 6(1969), pp. 285-300.

IN DER SMITTEN, W.Th. The Persian Gulf dhows: new notes on the classification of mid-Eastern sea-craft. *Persica* 6(1972-74), pp. 157-178.

JOHNSTONE, T.M. Folklore and folk literature in Oman and Socotra. *Arabian studies* 1 (1974), pp. 7-24.

JOHNSTONE, T.M. Oath-taking and vows in Oman. *Arabian studies* 2(1975), pp. 7-18.

KATAKURA, Motoko. Some social aspects of Bedouin settlements in Wādi Fātima, Saudi Arabia. *Orient* [Japan] 9(1973), pp. 67-108.

KHAN, M.A. Saleem. Saudi Arabia: Wahabism and oil. Survey of contemporary development in the Muslim world. *Islam and the modern age* 2ii(1971), pp. 87-101.

MAHGOUB, Mohamed A. Migration and structural change in Kuwaiti society. *Eastern anthropologist* 26(1973), pp. 197-199.

POURCELET, Fr. Expériences et témoignages. Évolution récente de deux villages du Koweit. *L'Afrique et l'Asie modernes* 93-4(1971), pp. 61-67.

RAYAH, Mubarak B. el-. The problems of Kerma culture of ancient Sudan re-considered in the light of ancient Sudan civilization as a continuous process. *EAZ* 15(1974), pp. 287-304.

RIPINSKY, M.M. The camel in ancient Arabia. *Antiquity* 49(1975), pp. 295-298.

RUGH, W. Emergence of a new middle class in Saudi Arabia. *MEJ* 27(1973), pp. 7-20.

SERJEANT, R.B. South Arabia and Ethiopia - African elements in the South Arabian population. *Proc. 3rd Int. Conf. Eth. Studies,* 1966, pp. 25-33.

SERJEANT, R.B. The "White Dune" at Abyan: an ancient place of pilgrimage in Southern Arabia. *JSS* 16 (1971), pp. 74-83.

VREEDE DE STUERS, C. Girl students in Kuwait. *BTLV* 130(1974), pp. 110-131.

WILKINSON, J.C. Bayāsirah and Bayādir. *Arabian studies* 1(1974), pp. 75-85.

WILSON, R. Hajjah market. *Arabian studies* 2(1975), pp. 204-210.

La population du Koweit. *Population* [Paris] 28(1973), pp. 156-158.

See also III. b. Chelhod.

See also V. o. Champault

See also XXII. a. Dostal

See also XXII. a. Stevens.

c HISTORY

ABIR, M. The 'Arab rebellion' of Amir Ghālib of Mecca (1788-1813). *ME studies* 7 (1971), pp. 185-200.

ALI, Hussein, WHITTINGHAM, K. Notes towards an understanding of the revolution in South Yemen. *Race* 16(1974), pp. 83-100.

ALKAZAZ, Aziz. Der Aufbau moderner Forschungsinstitutionen in Saudi-Arabien. Ein einführender Bericht. *Orient* [Hamburg] 16i(1975), pp. 99-111.

ANTHONY, J.D. The Union of Arab Emirates. *MEJ* 26(1972), pp. 271-287.

AZNAR SANCHEZ, J. Problemática en torno al golfo Pérsico. *Rev.de política int.* 119(1972), pp. 145-158

BALDRY, J. The powers and mineral concessions in the Idrīsī Imāmate of 'Asīr. *Arabian studies* 2(1975), pp. 76-107.

BARI, M.A. The early Wahhābīs, some contemporary assessments. *Proc.27th Int.Cong.Or.1967* (1971), pp. 264-266.

BECKER, A.S. Oil and the Persian Gulf in Soviet policy in the 1970s. *The U.S.S.R. and the Middle East,* ed. by M. Confino and Sh. Shamir, 1973, pp. 173-214.

XXII ARABIA

BENIGNI, Rudolf. Österreichische Botschaftsberichte über arabische Länder. Register zu den im Haus-, Hof- und Staatsarchiv in Wien befindlichen Akten der Kaiserlichen Internuntiatur, der späteren Botschaft, in Konstantinopel von 1750 bis 1918. *Biblos* 22(1973), pp. 52-83, 190-233, 307-328, 415-441.

BLAKE, G. and KING, R. The Hijaz railway and the pilgrimage to Mecca. *Asian aff.* 3(1972), pp. 317-325.

BONDAREVSKIY, G.L. Germaniskiy imperialism v bor'be za Krasnomorskiy basseyn (konetz XIX - nachalo XX veka). *Istoriya i ekonomika stran Arabskogo Vostoka,* 1973, pp. 3-42.

BONDAREVSKIY, G.L. Osvoboditel'naya bor'ba narodov Yemena v kontze XIX v. i pozitziya Velikobritannii. (The Yemeni peoples' liberation struggle at the close of the 19th century and British colonial policy.) *Vopr. ist.* 1971(6), pp. 100-115.

BÖRNER, A., RICHTER, S. Zu einigen Aspekten der politischen Konzeption der revolutionär-demokratischen Führungskrafte in der VDR Jemen. *Asien. Afrika. Latein-Amerika* 3(1975), pp. 817-820.

BOXHALL, P. The diary of a Mocha coffee agent. *Arabian studies* 1(1974), pp. 102-118.

BRIZARD, S. Actualités arabes. Les grands ulémas d'Arabie Saoudite en Europe. *L'Afrique et l'Asie modernes* 103(1974), pp. 45-48.

CARTER, J. Graves of three descendants of Badr Bū Ṭuwayriq in Zafar of Oman. *Arabian studies* 2(1975), p. 211.

CHITTICK, N. The east African coast and the Persian Gulf. *Memorial vol. Vth Internat. Cong. Iranian Art and Archaeology,* 1972, Vol. 2, pp. 292-295.

DALLAPORTA, Chr. Les transferts institutionnels et politiques dans l'émirat d'Abou D'habi. *Politique étrangère* 39 (1974), pp. 689-717.

DAWISHA, A.I. Intervention in the Yemen: an analysis of Egyptian perceptions and policies. *MEJ* 29(1975), pp. 47-63.

DE GAURY, G. Memories and impressions of the Arabia of Ibn Saud. *Arabian studies* 2(1975), pp. 19-32.

EDENS, D.G. The anatomy of the Saudi revolution. *IJMES* 5(1974), pp. 50-64.

FRADE, F. Faisal Ibn Saud, cumbre de una familia esforzada. *Rev.polit.int.* 133(1974), pp. 171-202.

FRADE, F. Una nueva vision de Lawrence de Arabia. *Rev. de política int.* 129(1973), pp. 143-174.

GANDY, C. The Yemen revisited. *Asian aff.* 58(N.S.2, 1971), pp. 295-304.

GIL BENUMEYA, R. Actualidad y continuidad en la Arabia del rey Faisal. *Rev.polit.int.* 132(1974), pp. 141-150.

GIL BENUMEYA, R. Una nueva problematica oriental en torno al Golfo Persico. *Rev. de politica int.* 114(1971), pp. 165-174.

GIL BENUMEYA, R. La otra actualidad "oriental" en torno al Mar Rojo. *Revista de polít. int.* 131(1974), pp. 137-144.

GOLUBOVSKAYA, E.K. Sotzial'no-klassovyy sostav sil, prishedshikh k vlasti v rezul'tate revolyutzii 26 sentyabrya 1962 g. v Yemene. *Istoriya i ekonomika stran Arabskogo Vostoka,* 1973, pp. 88-106.

GONCHAROV, V. Kuveyt. Vozmozhnosti rasshireniya sovetsko-kuveytskogo sotrudnichestva. *Arabskie strany, Turtziya, Iran, Afganistan,* 1973, pp. 25-31.

GREEN, A.H., STOOKEY, R.W. Research in Yemen: facilities, climate and current projects. *MESA bull.* 8iii(1974), pp. 27-46.

GROMADZKI, G. Polityka Wielkiej Brytanii w Zatoce Perskiej. *Przegląd or.* 3(79, 1971), pp. 225-233.

GROMADZKI, G. Powstanie Ludowej Republiki Południowego Jemenu. (Fondation de République Populaire du Yémen du Sud). *Przeglad or.* 1972(3, no. 83), pp. 221-230.

HAKIMA, Ahmed Mustafa. Wahhabi religio-political movement of Arabia and its impact on India in the nineteenth century. *India and the Arab World, ed. by S. Maqbul Ahmed,* 1969, pp. 17-23.

HAMDANI, Abbas. The dā'ī Ḥātim ibn Ibrāhīm al-Ḥāmidī (d. 596 H. / 1199 A.D.) and his book *Tuḥfat al-qulūb.* *Oriens* 23-24(1974), pp. 258-300.

HEARD-BEY, Frauke. The Gulf States and Oman in transition. *Asian aff.* 59(N.S.3, 1972), pp. 14-22.

HIYARI, M.A. The origins and development of the amīrate of the Arabs during the seventh/thirteenth and eighth/fourteenth centuries. *BSOAS* 38(1975), pp. 509-524.

HOLDEN, D. The Persian Gulf: after the British Raj. *Foreign aff.* 49(1971), pp. 721-735.

HUREWITZ, J.C. The Persian Gulf: British withdrawal and Western security. *America and the Middle East,* ed. P.T. Hart, 1972, pp. 106-115.

INGRAM, E. A preview of the great game in Asia-I: The British occupation of Perim and Aden in 1799. *ME stud.* 9(1973), pp. 3-18.

KENNEDY, E.M. The Persian Gulf: arms race or arms control? *Foreign affairs* 54(1975), pp. 14-35.

XXII ARABIA

KHANOV, A.A. Arabskie knyazhestva persidskogo zaliva v mezhdunarodnykh otnosheniyakh 1945-1953 gg. *Mezhdunarodnye otnosheniya na Blizhnem i Srednem Vostoke*, 1974, pp. 147-167.

KHRUSTALEV, M.A. Sotzial'naya struktura sovremennogo sauduyskogo obshchestva. *NAA* 1973(4), pp. 27-35.

KIRKMAN, J. and DOE, B. The first days of British Aden: the diary of John Studdy Leigh. *Arabian studies* 2(1975), pp. 179-203.

KOSZINOWSKI, Th. Die Bedeutung des Nahostkonflikts für die Aussenpolitik Saudi-Arabiens. *Orient* [Hamburg] 16i (1975), pp. 87-98.

KOSZINOWSKI, Thomas. Schwerpunkte der Aussenpolitik Saudi-Arabiens. *Orient* [Germany] 14(1973), pp. 181-185.

KRUSE, H., AZZAZI, Mohamed el-. Verwaltungshilfe für die Arabische Republik Jemen. *Z. f.Kulturaustausch* 24ii(1974), pp. 86-97.

LABAUNE, P. et BRIZARD, S. Les problèmes politico-religieux dans la République arabe du Yémen (1962-1972). *L'Afrique et l'Asie modernes* 101(1974), pp. 41-47.

LABROUSSE, H. L'épopée portugaise en mer Rouge (1507-1560). *Pount* 10(1972), pp. 3-12.

LABROUSSE, H. Les négociants marseillais à Cheikh-Said à la fin du XIXe siècle. *Pount* 3(1967), pp. 3-6.

LACKNER, H. Revolution in the Gulf. *Race* 15(1974), pp. 515-527.

LAGADEC, J. La fin du conflit yéménite. *Rev.franç.sci.pol.* 24(1974), pp. 344-355.

LANDAU, J.M. Ottoman propaganda in the Ḥidjāz before the First World War - some new manuscript evidence. *Proc.27th Int. Cong.Or.1967* (1971), p. 292.

LIENHARDT, P. The authority of shaykhs in the Gulf: an essay in nineteenth-century history. *Arabian studies* 2 (1975), pp. 61-75.

MADELUNG, W. The identity of two Yemenite historical manuscripts. *JNES* 32(1973), pp. 175-180.

MARTIN, J. Socotra: l'île des Chelonophages. *Rev. fr. ét. pol. africaines* 50(1970), pp. 52-59.

MARTIN DE LA ESCALERA, C. Irán y el predominio en el golfo Pérsico. *Rev.de política int.* 119(1972), pp. 159-173

MAZRUI, Ali A. Afro-Arab relations and the role of the Gulf States of Eastern Arabia. *Pan Africanist* 6(1975), pp. 30-32.

MONROE, E. Arabia--from incense to oil. *Asian affairs* 62(N.S.6,1975), pp. 253-263.

MORSY ABDULLAH, M. Changes in the economy and political attitudes, and the development of culture on the coast of Oman between 1900 and 1940. *Arabian studies* 2 (1975), pp. 167-178.

NARAYAN, R. U S postures in West Asia: defence arrangements with Saudi Arabia - a case study. *Studies in politics: national and international*, 1971, pp. 298-323.

NOSENKO, V.I. Krizis angliyskogo gospodstva b knyazhestyakh zony Persidskogo zaliva i pozitziya Saudovskoy Aravii (1965-1968 gg.) *Strany Blizhnego i Srednego Vostoka: istoriya, ekonomica*, 1972, pp. 110-125.

OCHSENWALD, W.L. The financing of the Hijaz railroad. *WI* N.S.14(1973), pp. 129-149.

OCHSENWALD, W.L. Ottoman subsidies to the Hijaz, 1877-1886. *IJMES* 6(1975), pp. 300-307.

ÖZBARAN, Salih. The Ottoman Turks and the Portuguese in the Persian Gulf, 1534-1581. *J. Asian hist.* 6(1972), pp. 45-87.

PANKHURST, R. Indian trade with Ethiopia, the Gulf of Aden and the Horn of Africa in the nineteenth and early twentieth centuries. *Cah. ét. afr.* 14(1974), pp. 453-497.

PERRY, J.R. Mīr Muhannā and the Dutch: patterns of piracy in the Persian Gulf. *Studia Iranica* 2(1973), pp. 79-95.

PFETSCH, F.R. Die demokratische Volksrepublik Jemen - ihre Entwicklung seit der Unabhängigkeit 1967. *Vierteljahresberichte (Fr. Ebert-Stiftung)* 43(1971), pp. 51-65.

PORATH, Yehoshua. The Palestinians and the negotiations for the British-Hijazi Treaty, 1920-1925. *Asian and Afr. stud.* 8(1972), pp. 20-48.

RONDOT, Ph. Le sultanat d'Oman devant la rébellion du Dhofar. *Maghreb Machrek* 70 (1975), pp. 38-46.

RUDENKO, A.N. Problemy sotzialno-ekonomicheskogo razvitiya Yemena posle likvidatzii monarkhii. *Strany Blizhnego i Srednego Vostoka: istoriya, ekonomica*, 1972, pp. 145-155.

SAID, R.J. The 1938 reform movement in Dubai. *Al-Abhath* 23(1970), pp. 247-318.

SAID EL ATTAR, Mohamed. Réflexions sur la situation en Arabie. *Politique étrangère* 37(1972), pp. 333-350.

SALEEM KHAN, M.A. 'Oman: an Ibadhi-tribal-monarchic syndrome. *Islam and the modern age* 5i(1974), pp. 71-90; 5ii(1974), pp. 52-70.

SERJEANT, R.B. The two Yemens: historical perspectives and present attitudes. *ASIAN AFF.* N.S.4(1973), pp. 3-16.

SHAAFY, M.S.M.el. The military organisation of the first Sa'udi state. *Ann. Leeds Univ. Or. Soc.* 7(1969-73), pp. 61-74.

SHERALIEVA, D.M. Angliyskaya politika v otnoshenii Tzentral'noy Aravii v nachale XX v. *Strany Blizhnego i Srednego Vostoka: istoriya, ekonomica,* 1972, pp. 204-216.

SMITH, G.R. The Yemenite settlement of Tha'bāt. Historical, numismatic and epigraphic notes. *Arabian studies* 1(1974), pp. 119-134.

SYLVESTER, A. The tragedy and hope of Southern Sudan. *Civilisations* 22(1972), pp. 79-91.

TIXIER, G. Évolution politique et constitutionnelle du Koweit. *Rev. jur. pol.* 28 (1974), pp. 27-42.

TROELLER, G. Ibn Sa'ud and Sharif Husain: a comparison in importance in the early years of the first World War. *Hist.J.* 14 (1971), pp. 627-633

VAL'KOVA, L.V. Mezhdunarodnye otnosheniya Yemena v 1945-1962 gg. *Mezhdunarodnye otnosheniya na Blizhnem i Srednem Vostoke,* 1974, pp. 129-147.

VAL'KOVA, L.V. Saudovskaya Araviya: vnutrennee polozhenie i vneshnyaya politika. *NAA* 1975(6), pp. 40-49.

VIENNOT, P. Documents sur la révolution sud-yéménite et la guérilla du Dhofar, traduits de l'arabe. *Orient* 51-2(1969), pp. 113-154

WILKINSON, J.C. Arab-Persian relationships in late Sasanid Oman. *Proc.6th Seminar for Arabian studies,* 1972, pp. 40-51.

WILKINSON, J.C. The Julanda of Oman. *J. Oman stud.* 1(1975), pp. 97-108.

WILLIAMSON, A. Hurmuz and the trade of the Gulf in the 14th and 15th centuries A.D. *Proc.6th Seminar for Arabian studies,* 1972, pp. 52-68.

WISSA-WASSEF, C. L'Arabie Séoudite et le conflit israélo-arabe. *Politique étrangère* 39(1974), pp. 185-199.

WRIGHT, D. The changed balance of power in the Persian Gulf. *Asian affairs* 60(N.S.4, 1973), pp. 255-262.

YODFAT, Aryeh Y. The U.S.S.R. and the rebellion in Dhofar Province of Oman. *S. Africa Internat.* 6i(1975), pp. 21-27.

YUROV, Yu.G. Pozitziya Irana v voprose o statuse Bakhreynskikh ostrovov. *Vestn. Mosk. Univ. Vostokovedenie* 1973(1), pp. 10-20.

The permanent constitution of the Yemen Arab Republic. *MEJ* 25(1971), pp. 389-481.

See also VIII. d. *Arabia.*

See also IX. m. Braun.

See also XXI. a. Labrousse.

See also XXII. a. Wilkinson

See also XXIV. c. Ochsenwald.

See also XXIX. i. Abu-Manneh.

See also XXXI. j. Cottrell.

d ECONOMICS

ABDO, Ass'ad S. Road traffic in Saudi Arabia. *Bull. Fac. Arts, Univ. Riyad* 2(1971-2), pp. 77-95.

ALKAZAZ, Aziz. Der Aufbau moderner Forschungsinstitutionen in Saudi-Arabien. Ein einführender Bericht. *Dokumentationsdienst Moderner Orient, Mitt.* 4i(1975), pp. 38-53.

BOXHALL, P. The diary of a Mocha coffee agent. *Arabian studs.* 1(1974), pp. 102-118.

CHAPMAN, R.A. Administrative reform in Saudi Arabia. *J.admin.overseas* 13(1974), pp. 332-347.

CHELHOD, J. Le Bédouin et le droit. *ROMM* 11(1972), pp. 151-159.

KERGAN, J.L. Social and economic changes in the Gulf countries. *Asian affairs* 62 (N.S.6,1975), pp. 282-289.

KIMCHE, D. The opening of the Red Sea to European ships in the late eighteenth century. *ME stud.* 8(1972), pp. 63-71

KNAUERHASE, R. Saudi Arabia's economy at the beginning of the 1970s. *MEJ* 28 (1974), pp. 126-140.

MALLAKH, Ragaei El-. Economic requirements for development, Oman. *MEJ* 26(1972), pp. 415-427.

MARRIOTT, A.C. Co-operative activity in the Yemen Arab Republic. *Year-book of agricultural co-operation* 1972, pp. 145-154.

MELIKIAN, L.H. Actual and desired occupational status of acculturated Saudi youth. *al-Abhath* 24(1971), pp. 125-132.

NATH, V. Economic development and regional cooperation: Kuwait. Review article. *Econ.devel.and cultural change* 20(1972), pp. 342-349.

SABBAGH, Ghazi. Co-operative development in the Kingdom of Saudi Arabia. *Year-book of agricultural co-operation* 1972, pp. 109-115.

SALEEM KHAN, M.A. Oil politics in the Persian Gulf region. *India Q.* 30(1974), pp. 25-41.

SHA'AFY, M.S. al-. Notes on the economic history of Juddah in the first half of the nineteenth century. *Bull.Fac.Arts U.Riyad* 3(1973-74), pp. 23-39.

XXII ARABIA

SILGUY, Y.Th. de. Le fonds koweitien de développement économique arabe. Une forme particulière d'aide aux pays en voie de développement. *Maghreb Machrek* 70(1975), pp. 30-37.

STEVENS, J.H. Some effects of irrigated agriculture on soil characteristics in Ras al-Khaimah, Union of Arab Emirates. *Arabian studies* 2(1975), pp. 148-166.

ZAIM, Issam el-. La dépendance pétrolière du Golfe arabique. Rénovation et contradiction. *Rev. alg.* 12(1975), pp. 449-462.

ZAIM, Issam El-. Dependencia petrolera en el golfo: oportunidades y riesgos. *Estudios de Asia y Africa* 10i(1975), pp. 17-34.

See also XXII. a. Stevens and Cresswell.

See also XXII. b. Khan

See also XXXI. k. Shestopalov.

XXIII PALESTINE

a GEOGRAPHY

REICHMAN, Shalom. The evolution of land transportation in Palestine (1920-1947). *Jerusalem stud. in geog.* 2(1971), pp. 55-90.

See also VI. d. Ben-Arieh.

b ETHNOLOGY

ABU-LUGHOD, J.L. The demographic transformation of Palestine. *Transformation of Palestine,* ed. I. Abu-Lughod, 1971, pp. 139-163.

ASAD, Talal. Anthropological texts and ideological problems: an analysis of Cohen on Arab villages in Israel. *Economy and society* 4(1975), pp. 251-282.

ASAD, Talal. Anthropological texts and ideological problems: an analysis of Cohen on Arab villages in Israel. *RMES* 1(1975), pp. 1-40.

BARTH, M. On Palestinians in Israel: a report on a journey to Israel from May 23-June 9, 1972. *J.ecumenical stud.* 10 (1973), pp. 121-127.

BEN-DOR, Gabriel. The military in the politics of integration and innovation: the case of the Druze minority in Israel. *Asian and African studies* [Jerusalem] 9 (1973), pp. 339-369.

GLASSNER, M.I. The Bedouin of Southern Sinai under the Israeli administration. *Geog.R.* 64(1974), pp. 31-60.

HAGOPIAN, E., ZAHLAN, A.B. Palestine's Arab population: the demography of the Palestinians. *J.Palestine stud.* 3iv(1974), pp. 32-73.

HALPERN, B. Israel and Palestine: the political use of ethics. *People and politics in the Middle East,* ed. M. Curtis, 1971, pp. 9-15.

HOFMAN, J.E. Readiness for social relations between Arabs and Jews in Israel. *J. conflict resolution* 16(1972), pp. 241-251.

JABRA, Adib J.S. Palestine Arab refugee work. *Famine: a symposium.* 1971, pp. 156-164.

JIRYIS, Sabri. The Arabs in Israel. *Crescent and star,* ed. by Y. Alexander and N.N. Kittrie, 1973, pp. 134-150.

JIRYIS, Sabri. Recent Knesset legislation and the Arabs in Israel. *J.Palestine stud.* 1i(1971), pp. 53-67.

MARX, E. Circumcision feasts among the Negev Bedouins. *IJMES* 4(1973), pp. 411-427.

MAYER, E. Becoming modern in Bayt al-Shabab. *MEJ* 29(1975), pp. 279-293.

MERLIN, S. Demography and geography in Palestine. *People and politics in the Middle East,* ed. M. Curtis, 1971, pp. 182-204.

PERES, Yochanan. Ethnic relations in Israel. *People and politics in the Middle East,* ed. M. Curtis, 1971, pp. 31-68.

PERETZ, D. The Palestine Arabs: a national entity. *People and politics in the Middle East,* ed. M. Curtis, 1971, pp. 69-92.

ROSENFELD, H. Non-hierarchical, hierarchical and masked reciprocity in an Arab village. *Anthrop. q'ly* 47(1974), pp. 129-166.

SEBBAN-KAHN, A. La cuisine dans un village arabe de Jérusalem-Est (Sūr-Baher). *Folklore Research Center studies* 3(1972), pp. 259-265.

SEBBAN-KAHN, A. Le mariage arabo-musulman (Sūr-Baher, Jérusalem-Est). *Folklore Res. Center studies* 4(1974), pp. 141-166.

SIRHAN, Bassem. Palestinian refugee camp life in Lebanon. *J.Palestine stud.* 4ii(1975), pp. 91-107.

SMYTHE, H.H., WEINTRAUB, S. Intergroup relations in Israel. *People and politics in the Middle East*, ed. M. Curtis, 1971, pp. 16-30.

SYRKIN, M. Who are the Palestinians? *People and politics in the Middle East*, ed. M. Curtis, 1971, pp. 93-110.

TOLEDANO, S. Israel's Arabs - a unique national minority. *Int. problems* 12i-ii (1973), pp. 39-43.

WEIR, S., KAWAR, Widad. Costumes and wedding customs in Bayt Dajan. *PEQ* 107(1975), pp. 39-52.

ZENNER, W.P. Some aspects of ethnic stereotype content in the Galilee: a trial formulation. *M E Stud.* 8(1972), pp. 405-416.

ZURIEK, E.T. The Palestinians in the consciousness of Israeli youth. *J.Palestine stud.* 4ii(1975), pp. 52-75.

Ministry of Foreign Affairs, Jerusalem. The Arabs of Israel. *Crescent and star*, ed. by Y. Alexander and N.N. Kittrie, 1973, pp. 151-161.

See also I. b. 3. Weir.

See also III. a. 9. Layish.

See also V. u. 1. Shiloah.

See also XVIII. d. Bailey.

c HISTORY: GENERAL

AGWANI, M.S. The great powers and the partition of Palestine. *Studies in politics: national and international*, 1971, pp. 348-368.

BEN-ARIEH, Y. The growth of Jerusalem in the nineteenth century. *Annals Assoc. Amer. Geographers* 65(1975), pp. 252-269.

BOSWORTH, C.E. William Lithgow of Lanark's travels in Syria and Palestine, 1611-1612. *JSS* 20(1975), pp. 219-235.

DESAI, W.S. Israel in history. *Studies in politics: national and international*, 1971, pp. 369-396.

HADDAD, G.M. The chronicle of Abbud al-Sabbagh and the fall of Daher al-Umar of Acre. *Al-Abhath* 20ii(1967), pp. 37-44.

HOEXTER, Miriam. The role of the Qays and Yaman factions in local political divisions. Jabal Nāblus compared with the Judean hills in the first half of the nineteenth century. *Asian and African studies* [Jerusalem] 9(1973), pp. 249-311.

HOOLE, W.S. A visit to the Holy Land in 1837. *JAOS* 95(1975), pp. 633-644.

HOPKINS, I.W.J. The four quarters of Jerusalem. *PEQ* 103(Jul.-Dec. 1971), pp. 68-84.

MANDEL, N.J. Ottoman policy and restrictions on Jewish settlement in Palestine: 1881-1908. *ME stud.* 10(1974), pp. 312-332.

MOTZKIN, A.L. A thirteenth-century Jewish physician in Jerusalem. *MW* 60 (1970), pp. 344-349.

REIF, S.C. A mission to the Holy Land -- 1839. *Glasgow Univ. Or. Soc. Trans.* 24 (1974), pp. 1-13.

STEPPAT, F. Ein Contrat Social in einer palästinischen Stadt 1854. *WI* 15(1974), pp. 233-246.

TAHA, Ahmad. The Muslims and Jerusalem. *Maj.al-Azhar* 46v(1974), pp. 6-8.

TAYLOR, A.R. The isolation of Israel. *J. Palestine stud.* 4i(1974), pp. 82-93.

TIBAWI, A.L. The city of Jerusalem. *IQ* 16(1972), pp. 3-11.

ZENNER, W.P. Aqiili Agha: the strongman in the ethnic relations of the Ottoman Galilee. *Comp.stud.soc.hist.* 14(1972), pp. 169-188

GUTMANN, D. Comment: the uses of reminiscence. [On W.P. Zenner's article "Aqiili Agha".] *Comp.stud.soc.hist.* 14(1972), pp. 188-192

See also XXV. c. Hornus

d HISTORY: MODERN PALESTINE

ABID, Ibrahim al-. Israel and negotiations. *Crescent and star*, ed. by Y. Alexander and N.N. Kittrie, 1973, pp. 399-401.

ABID, Ibrahim al-. Palestine: questions and answers. *Crescent and star*, ed. by Y. Alexander and N.N. Kittrie, 1973, pp. 320-323.

ABU-GHAZALEH, Adnan. Arab cultural nationalism in Palestine during the British mandate. *J.Palestine stud.* 1iii(1972), pp. 37-63.

ABU LUGHOD, Ibrahim. Educating a community in exile: the Palestinian experience. *J. Palestine stud.* 2(1973), pp. 94-111.

ADAMS, M. The requirements for a settlement in the Middle East. *Asian affairs* 62(N.S.6, 1975), pp. 131-139.

AGHA, Hussein J., KHALIDI, Ahmed S. The Arab-Israeli conflict: an outline of alternatives, war and de facto peace. *J.Palestine stud.* 1iii(1972), pp. 95-107.

AGWANI, M.S. The Palestine conflict in Asian perspective. *Transformation of Palestine*, ed. I. Abu-Lughod, 1971, pp. 443-462.

AHMAD, Syed Barakat. India and Palestine: the genesis of a foreign policy. *India Q.* 29(1973), pp. 300-307.

AKSENTIJEVIĆ, M. Reflections on the Palestinian resistance. *J. Palestine studies* 2i(1972), pp. 111-119.

XXIII PALESTINE

ALLON, Yigal. The Soviet involvement in the Arab-Israel conflict. *The U.S.S.R. and the Middle East,* ed. by M. Confino and Sh. Shamir, 1973, pp. 147-154.

ALROY, G.C. Closing horizons: Israelis and nationalism. *People and politics in the Middle East,* ed. M. Curtis, 1971, pp. 303-305.

ANISIMOV, L.N. Missiya Yarringa na Blizhnem Vostoke i manervy izrailskoy diplomatii. *Vopr.ist.* 1975(2), pp. 58-73.

ANKORI, Zvi. The continuing Zionist revolution. *Crescent and star,* ed. by Y. Alexander and N.N. Kittrie, 1973, pp. 66-98.

ARMANAZI, Ghayth. The rights of the Palestinians; the international definition. *J. Palestine stud.* 3iii(1974), pp. 88-96.

ASHKAR, Riad. The Syrian and Egyptian campaigns. *J.Palestine stud.* 3ii(1973), pp. 15-33.

ASHMAWI, Mohie el-Din Ali. Civilian rights under belligerent occupation, with special study of Israeli violations of human rights in occupied Arab territories. *Eg. contemp.* 63(no.350, 1972), pp. 343-456.

AVINERI, Shlomo. The new left and Israel. *People and politics in the Middle East,* ed. M. Curtis, 1971, pp. 293-302.

AVNERY, Uri. Uma guerra fratricida entre semitas. *Afro-Asia* 8-9(1969), pp. 71-91.

AYOUTY, Yassin El-. O.A.U. mediation in the Arab-Israeli conflict. *Genève-Afrique* 14(1975), pp. 5-29.

BARAKAT, Halim and DODD, P. Palestinian refugees: two surveys of uprootedness. *Political dynamics in the Middle East,* ed. P.Y. Hammond and S.S. Alexander, 1972, pp. 325-354.

BARAKAT, Halim. Social factors influencing attitudes of university students in Lebanon towards the Palestinian resistance movement. *J.Palestine stud.* 1i(1971), pp. 87-112.

BEAUFRE, Général. La quatrième guerre israélo-arabe. *Stratégie* 36(1973), pp. 5-19.

BEAUFRE, Général. Le rapprochement URSS/Etats-Unis et la 4e guerre du Moyen-Orient: conséquences pour la stratégie et l'Europe. *Stratégie* 35(1973), pp. 5-16.

BEAUFRE, Général. Réflexions sur la crise du Moyen-Orient. *Stratégie* 24(1970), pp. 5-23.

BÉCHIR BEN YAHMED. Doomed to peace. *Foreign affairs* 54(1975), pp. 127-133.

BEIT-HALLAHMI, B. Some psychosocial and cultural factors in the Arab-Israel conflict: a review of the literature. *J. conflict resolution* 16(1972), pp. 269-280

BELENKOVA, T.P. S.S. Abamelek-Lazarev - russkiy issledovatel' vostochnoy Palestiny. *Strany Blizhnego i Srednego Vostoka: istoriya, ekonomica,* 1972, pp. 20-27.

BELFIGLIO, V.J. The United Nations and the question of Palestine. *International problems* 14(1975), pp. 45-54.

BELL, C. The October Middle East war. A case study in crisis management during detente. *Int. affairs* 50(1974), pp. 531-543.

BELL, J. Israel's nuclear option. *MEJ* 26(1972), pp. 379-388.

BEN-DAK, J.D. and AZAR, E.E. Research perspectives on the Arab-Israeli conflict: introduction to a symposium. *J. conflict resolution* 16(1972), pp. 131-134.

BEN-DAK, J.D. Some directions for research towards peaceful Arab-Israeli relations: analysis of past events and gaming simulation of the future. *J. conflict resolution* 16(1972), pp. 281-295.

BERQUE, J. Fait et droit en Palestine. *Les Palestiniens et la crise israélo-arabe,* 1974, pp. 98-106.

BERQUE, J. Les nations et le peuple arabe devant le Palestine. *Les Palestiniens et la crise israélo-arabe,* 1974, pp. 24-35.

BERTÒLA, M. Osservazioni sulla raccolta di documenti Palestinesi di Doreen Ingrams. *OM* 53(1973), pp. 282-294.

BHIM SINGH, HELOU, A. An examination of documents on which the state of Israel is based. *Crescent and star,* ed. by Y. Alexander and N.N. Kittrie, 1973, pp. 52-65.

BHUTANI, Surendra. Israel and the question of Arab-Israeli conflict resolution. *India Q.* 31(1975), pp. 198-208.

BIRAN. Yaïr. Le point actuel du conflit israélo-arabe. Nouvelle tentative de pondération des facteurs du conflit et des perspectives de son évolution. *International problems* 14(1975), pp. 15-31.

BITAR, Salah al-Din. The implications of the October War for the Arab world. *J. Palestine stud.* 3ii(1973), pp. 34-45.

BLECHMAN, B.M. The impact of Israel's reprisals on behaviour of the bordering Arab nations directed at Israel. *J. conflict resolution* 16(1972), pp. 155-181.

BLOCH, Ch. La guerre d'octobre et les nouvelles perspectives pour Israël et ses voisins. *Politique étrangère* 38(1973), pp. 585-596.

BOWDEN, T. The politics of the Arab rebellion in Palestine 1936-39. *M.E. stud.* 11(1975), pp. 145-174.

BROWNE, D.R. The voices of Palestine: a broadcasting house divided. *MEJ* 29 (1975), pp. 133-150.

XXIII PALESTINE

BRUZONSKY, M.A. The U.S. and Israel: proposals to avert another Middle East war. *International problems* 14(1975), pp. 30-44.

BURNS, E.L.M. Peace in the Middle East. *The elusive peace in the Middle East,* ed. M.H. Kerr, 1975, pp. 311-347.

BURROWES, R. and MUZZIO, D. The road to the Six Day War: aspects of an enumerative history of four Arab states and Israel, 1965-1967. *J. conflict resolution* 16(1972), pp. 211-226.

BUTTIN, M., CABRÉ, O. et RODINSON, Brève chronologie de la Palestine. *Les Palestiniens et la crise israëlo-arabe,* 1974, pp. 210-264.

CAMPBELL, J.C. American efforts for peace. *The elusive peace in the Middle East,* ed. M.H. Kerr, 1975, pp. 249-310.

CARRÈRE D'ENCAUSSE, H. L'URSS et la guerre d'octobre. *Rev.franç.sci.pol.* 24(1974), pp. 785-800.

CHAMUSSY, R. Un épisode du conflit arabo-israëlien: mai 1973 au Liban. *Travaux et jours* 49(1973), pp. 5-31.

CHAMUSSY, R. Les trois visages d'une même guerre. *Travaux et jours* 50(1974), pp. 5-33.

CHILDERS, E.B. The wordless wish: from citizens to refugees. *Transformation of Palestine,* ed. I. Abu-Lughod, 1971, pp. 165-206.

CHOMSKY, N. Reflections on the Arab-Israeli conflict. *J.contemp.Asia* 5(1975), pp. 337-344.

CHOURAQUI, A. L'actuelle destruction de Jérusalem. *OM* 53(1973), pp. 733-741.

COHEN, Aharon. Israel and Jewish-Arab peace. Governmental and nongovernmental approaches. *The elusive peace in the Middle East,* ed. M.H. Kerr, 1975, pp. 102-165.

COHEN, Amnon. The army in Palestine in the eighteenth century - sources of its weakness and strength. *BSOAS* 34 (1971), pp. 36-55.

COHEN, M.J. Appeasement in the Middle East: the British white paper on Palestine, May 1939. *Hist. J.* 16(1973), pp. 571-596.

COHEN, M.J. British strategy and the Palestine question, 1936-39. *J. contemp. hist.* 7(1972), pp. 157-183.

COHEN, M.J. Direction of policy in Palestine, 1936-45. *M.E.stud.* 11(1975), pp. 237-261.

COHEN, M.J. Sir Arthur Wauchope, the Army, and the Rebellion in Palestine, 1936. *ME stud.* 9(1973), pp. 19-34.

COLOMBE, M. Retour sur le passé: Le problème de la Palestine dans les souvenirs d'un ancien premier ministre du royaume d'Irak: Muhammad Fadil al-Djamali. *Orient* 49-50(1969), pp. 49-72; 51-2 (1969) pp. 67-83

COMAY, M. The Arab refugees. *Crescent and star,* ed. by Y. Alexander and N.N. Kittrie, 1973, pp. 205-216.

COTTAM, R. The United States and Palestine. *Transformation of Palestine,* ed. I. Abu-Lughod, 1971, pp. 387-412.

COULAND, J. Les positions actuelles des états et organisations directement intéressés et les chances d'une coexistence équitable. *Les Palestiniens et la crise israëlo-arabe,* 1974, pp. 36-68.

DADIANI, L.Ya. Sotzial-demokratiya, sionizm i blizhnevostochnyy vopros. *Vopr. ist.* 1975(7), pp. 78-94.

DAJANI, N.I. Economic impact of the Israeli aggression. *Crescent and star,* ed by Y. Alexander and N.N. Kittrie, 1973, pp. 334-336.

DAVIS, Uri. Palestine into Israel. *J.Palestine stud.* 3i(1973), pp. 88-105.

DERSHOWITZ, A. Preventive detention of citizens during a national emergency - a comparison between Israel and the United States. *Israel yrbk. on human rights* 1 (1971), pp. 295-321.

DESSOUKI, Ali E. Hillal. Arab intellectuals and al-nakba: the search for fundamentalism. *ME stud.* 9(1973), pp. 187-195.

DICKERSON, G. Education for the Palestine refugees: the UNRWA/UNESCO programme. *J. Palestine stud.* 3iii(1974), pp. 122-130.

DIMANT, I. David und Goliath im Nahen Osten. Die israelitischen und arabischen Streitkräfte in der Militärpresse der UdSSR. *Ost-Europa* 23(1973), pp. 807-813.

DINSTEIN, Yoram. Terrorism and wars of liberation applied to the Arab-Israeli conflict: an Israeli perspective. *Israel yb. on human rights* 3(1973), pp. 78-92.

DOWTY, A. The application of international guarantees to the Egypt-Israel conflict. *J. conflict resolution* 16(1972), pp. 253-267.

DUCLOS, L.J. La bataille d'octobre. *Rev. franç.sci.pol.* 24(1974), pp. 710-744.

DUCLOS, L.J. Description de l'occupation militaire israëlienne. *Les Palestiniens et la crise israëlo-arabe,* 1974, pp. 149-161.

DUCLOS, J.L. Description de l'occupation militaire israëlienne. *Politique étrangère* 37(1972), pp. 499-534.

DUCLOS, L.J. L'équilibre militaire israëlo-arabe. *Maghreb Machrek* 67(1975), pp. 41-46.

XXIII PALESTINE

DUCLOS, J.L. La lutte des Palestiniens contre Israël. *Afr.et l'Asie* 91-2(1970), pp. 13-23.

DUCLOS, L.J. Palestine: libération nationale ou guerre révolutionnaire? *Rev. fr. de sci. pol.* 21(1971), pp. 892-910.

EBAN, Abba. Economic effects. *Crescent and star*, ed. by Y. Alexander and N.N. Kittrie, 1973, pp. 337-338.

EBAN, Abba. Israel's action in Sinai and from a state of war to a state of peace. *Crescent and star*, ed. by Y. Alexander and N.N. Kittrie, 1973, pp. 324-327.

ELEWAINY, Mohammed Aly. The role of agricultural settlements in Israeli propaganda. *Eg. contemp.* 64(352, 1973), pp. 189-196.

ENTELIS, J.P. Palestinian revolutionism in Lebanese politics: the Christian response. *MW* 62(1972), pp. 335-351.

FIRESTONE, Ya'akov. Crop-sharing economics in mandatory Palestine. *M.E. stud.* 11(1975), pp. 3-23, 175-194.

FIRESTONE, Ya'akov. Production and trade in an Islamic context: sharika contracts in the traditional economy of Northern Samaria, 1853-1943 (II). *IJMES* 6(1975), pp. 308-325.

FODA, Ezzeldin. The legitimacy of resistance and human rights in the occupied territory. *Crescent and star*, ed. by Y. Alexander and N.N. Kittrie, 1973, pp. 343-354.

FRIEDLANDER, S. Policy choices before Israel. *Political dynamics in the Middle East*, ed. P.Y. Hammond and S.S. Alexander, 1972, pp. 115-154.

GALTUNG, J. Conflict theory and the Palestine problem. *J. Palestine studies* 2i (1972), pp. 34-63.

GAZIT, Shlomo. Policy in the administered territories. *Israel yrbk. on human rights* 1(1971), pp. 278-282.

GENDZIER, I.L. Palestine and Israel: the bi-national idea. *J.Palestine stud.* 4ii(1975), pp. 12-35.

GENET, J. The Palestinians. *J.Palestine stud.* 3i(1973), pp. 3-34.

GENNAOUI, J. Les organisations palestiniennes. *Projet* 95(1975), pp. 599-604.

GENNAOUI, J. La résistance palestinienne: interview d'un leader de la SAIKA. *Projet* 88(1974), pp. 894-899.

GHAREEB, E. The US arms supply to Israel during the War. *J.Palestine stud.* 3ii(1973), pp. 114-121.

GIEBELS, L.A.M. De Nederlandse consulaire vertegenwoordiging in Palestina van 1918 tot 1940. / The Dutch consular representation in Palestine from 1918 until 1940. *Studia Rosenthaliana* 5 (1971), pp. 71-102.

GIEBELS, L.A.M. Een nieuwe joodse toekomst: congres demonstratie, Balfour-declaratie, Palestina. *Studia Rosenthaliana* 8(1974), pp. 214-238.

GIL BENUMEYA, R. Actualidad de los sectores judios opuestos al sionismo. *Rev. de política int.* 126(1973), pp. 179-187.

GIL BENUMEYA, R. Destrucción y renovación en lo actual de Palestina. *Rev.de política int.* 118(1971), pp. 185-194.

GIL BENUMEYA, R. Palestina e Israel, en la transición próximo-oriental. *Rev. de polít. int.* 123(1972), pp. 131-141.

GIL BENUMEYA, R. Programas y destinos de las fronteras de Israel. *Rev. de política int.* 129(1973), pp. 95-104.

GOLDMANN, Nahum. The psychology of Middle East peace. *Foreign affairs* 54 (1975), pp. 113-126.

GORDON, Avishag H. The Middle East October 1973 war as reported by the American networks. *International problems* 14(1975), pp. 76-85.

GOTTHEIL, F.M. Arab immigration into pre-state Israel: 1922-1931. *Middle Eastern stud.* 9(1973), pp. 315-324.

GRIFFITH, W.E. Le Moyen-Orient avant la prochaine guerre. *Politique etrangere* 40 (1975), pp. 117-140.

GRIFFITH, W.E. La quatrième guerre du Proche-Orient, la crise de l'énergie et la politique américaine. *Politique étrangère* 39(1974), pp. 5-37.

HADAMARD, J. Plaintes de la Ligue israélienne des droits de l'homme 8 juin 1970. *Les Palestiniens et la crise israélo-arabe*, 1974, pp. 115-129.

HADAMARD, J. Quelques aspects des finances israéliennes. *Les Palestiniens et la crise israélo-arabe*, 1974, pp. 144-148.

HADAMARD, J. Ségrégation croissante à l'université. Témoignages directs d'Israël. *Les Palestiniens et la crise israélo-arabe*, 1974, pp. 109-114.

HADAR, Zvi. Administrative detentions employed by Israel. *Israel yrbk. on human rights* 1(1971), pp. 283-289.

HADAWI, Sami. The Arab refugees. *Crescent and star*, ed. by Y. Alexander and N.N. Kittrie, 1973, pp. 199-204.

HADAWI, Sami. Israeli expansionism. *Crescent and star*, ed. by Y. Alexander and N.N. Kittrie, 1973, pp. 219-227.

HADDAD, G.M. Arab peace efforts and the solution of the Arab-Israeli problem. *The elusive peace in the Middle East*, ed. M.H. Kerr, 1975, pp. 166-248.

XXIII PALESTINE

HADDAD, H.S. The Biblical bases of Zionist colonialism. *J.Palestine stud.* 3iv(1974), pp. 97-113.

HAMADÉ, Marwan. Un front diplomatique en pleine mouvance. Du kilomètre 101 au "désengagement" via Alger et Genève. *Travaux et jours* 50(1974), pp. 35-49.

HAMID, Rashid. What is the PLO? *J. Palestine stud.* 4iv(1975), pp. 90-109.

HARBOTTLE, M. The October Middle East war. Lessons for UN peacekeeping. *Int. affairs* 50(1974), pp. 544-553.

HARKABI, Y. The Arab slogan of a democratic state. *Crescent and star*, ed. by Y. Alexander and N.N. Kittrie, 1973, pp. 28-51.

HARKABI, Yehoshafat. Ending the Arab-Israeli conflict. *People and politics in the Middle East*, ed. M. Curtis, 1971, pp. 258-277.

HASBY, Aziz. La qualification de l'agression dans la guerre de Palestine. *Rev. alg.* 12(1975), pp. 337-447.

HECHICHE, Abdelwahab. Renaissance et déclin de la résistance palestinienne. *Politique étrangère* 38(1973), pp. 597-620.

HERADSTVEIT, D. Israeli elite perceptions of the Arab-Israel conflict. *J. Palestine stud.* 2(1973), pp. 68-93.

HEYKAL, Mohammed Hassanein. War and peace in the Middle East. *J.Palestine stud.* 1i (1971), pp. 3-20.

HIRST, D. Rush to annexation: Israel in Jerusalem. *J.Palestine studies* 3iv(1974), pp. 3-31.

HOFFMANN, S. A new policy for Israel. *Foreign aff.* 53(1974-75), pp. 405-431.

HOOFIEN, S. A case of high treason. *Studia Rosenthaliana* 8(1974), pp. 205-213.

HOOFIËN, S.E. De Nederlandse consulaire vertegenwoordiger in Palestina van 1918 tot 1940. *Studia Ros.* 7(1973), pp. 75-89.

HOROWITZ, D. and LISSAK, M. Authority without sovereignty. The case of the National Centre of the Jewish community in Palestine. *Government and opposition* 8(1973), pp. 48-71.

HOUGUENAGUE, G. A propos de la réédition de "L'Itinéraire de Paris à Jérusalem". *CT* 19, nos. 75-76(1971), pp. 231-237.

HUDSON, M. The Palestinian resistance movement since 1967. *The Middle East.* Ed. W.A. Beling, 1973, pp. 101-125.

HUDSON, M.C. Developments and setbacks in the Palestine resistance movement 1967-1971. *J.Palestine stud.* 1iii(1972), pp. 64-84.

HUREWITZ, J.C. Superpower rivalry and the Arab-Israel dispute: involvement or commitment? *The U.S.S.R. and the Middle East*, ed. by M. Confino and Sh. Shamir, 1973, pp. 155-169.

HUSAINI, Ishaq Musa al-. Israel is based on racialism. *Majallat al-Azhar* 43iv (1971), pp. 6-13, 16.

IBRAHIM, Saad. American domestic forces and the October war. *J.Palestine stud.* 4i(1974), pp. 55-81.

IBRAHIM, Saad E.M. Arab images of the United States and the Soviet Union before and after the June War of 1967. *J. conflict resolution* 16(1972), pp. 227-240.

ISKANDAR, Marwan. The Arab boycott in international law. *Crescent and star*, ed. by Y. Alexander and N.N. Kittrie, 1973, pp. 330-333.

ITAYIM, Fuad. Arab oil - the political dimension. *J.Palestine stud.* 3ii(1973), pp. 84-97.

JAAFARI, Lafi Ibrahim. The brain drain to the United States: the migration of Jordanian and Palestinian professionals and students. *J.Palestine stud.* 3i(1973), pp. 119-131.

JABBER, Fuad. The Arab regimes and the Palestinian revolution, 1967-71. *J.Palestine stud.* 2ii(1973), pp. 79-101.

JABBER, Fuad A. Israel's nuclear options. *J.Palestine stud.* 1i(1971), pp. 21-38.

JABBER, Fuad. Not by war alone: curbing the Arab-Israeli arms race. *MEJ* 28(1974), pp. 233-247.

JACOB, Abel. Trends in Israeli public opinion on issues related to the Arab-Israeli conflict, 1967-1972. *Jewish J.sociol.* 16(1974), pp. 187-208.

JANKOWSKI, J.P. The Palestinian Arab revolt of 1936-1939. *MW* 63(1973), pp. 220-233.

JEANNIÈRE, A. Impasse au Prôche-Orient. *Projet* 91(1975), pp. 3-9.

JIRYIS, Sabri. The legal structure for the expropriation and absorption of Arab lands in Israel. *J. Palestine studies* 2iv(1973), pp. 82-104.

KALKAS, B. The revolt of 1936: a chronicle of events. *Transformation of Palestine*, ed. I. Abu-Lughod, 1971, pp. 237-274.

KANAFANI, Ghassan. Document. L'épopée du loup et de l'agneau. *Travaux et jours* 45(1972), pp. 77-81.

KANOVSKY, Eliyahu. Economic aspects of the Arab-Israeli conflict. *People and politics in the Middle East*, ed. M. Curtis, 1971, pp. 123-131.

XXIII PALESTINE

KATOND, Diur. Los Estados africanos y el conflicto del Oriente medio: el caso de la República de Zaire. *Rev.polit.int.* 137 (1975), pp. 47-57.

KERR, M.H. The Arabs and Israelis: perceptual dimensions to their dilemma. *The Middle East.* Ed. W.A. Beling, 1973, pp. 3-31.

KERR, M.H. The changing political status of Jerusalem. *Transformation of Palestine,* ed. I. Abu-Lughod, 1971, pp. 355-377.

KHALIDI, Ahmed S. The War of Attrition. *J. Palestine stud.* 3i(1973), pp. 60-87.

KHALIDI, Walid. Nasser's memoirs of the first Palestine war. Translated and annotated. *J.Palestine stud.* 2ii(1973), pp. 3-32.

KHATIB, Rouhi al-. The judaization of Jerusalem. *Crescent and star,* ed. by Y. Alexander and N.N. Kittrie, 1973, pp. 238-258.

KHOURI, F.J. Arab refugees and the Arab-Israeli dilemma. *People and politics in the Middle East,* ed. M. Curtis, 1971, pp. 144-168.

KIMCHE, J. The second Arab awakening. *People and politics in the Middle East,* ed. M. Curtis, 1971, pp. 169-181.

KHOURI, F.J. United Nations peace efforts. *The elusive peace in the Middle East,* ed. M.H. Kerr, 1975, pp. 19-101.

KOLVENBACH, P.H. Octobre en titres. *Travaux et jours* 50(1974), pp. 93-103.

KRAMMER, A. Soviet motives in the partition of Palestine, 1947-48. *J.Palestine stud.* 2ii(1973), pp. 102-119.

KURODA, Yasumasa. Young Palestinian commandos in political socialization perspective. *MEJ* 26(1972), pp. 253-270.

LA SERRE, F. de. L'Europe des neuf et le conflit israélo-arabe. *Rev.franç.sci.pol.* 24(1974), pp. 801-811.

LAZARUS-YAFEH, Hava. An enquiry into Arab textbooks. *Asian and Afr. stud.* 8(1972), pp. 1-19.

LECA, J. Crises et conflits au Proche-Orient. *Rev.franç.sci.pol.* 24(1974), pp. 698-709.

LEHN, W. The Jewish National Fund. *J.Palestine stud.* 3iv(1974), pp. 74-96.

LEVEAU, R., RIFAÏ, Taki. L'arme du pétrole. *Rev.franç.sci.pol.* 24(1974), pp. 745-769.

LEYMARIE, Ph. Les Palestiniens: un "oui, mais ..." à Genève. *Rev.franç.ét.pol.afr.* 9, no. 103(1974), pp. 7-9.

LOSMAN, D.L. The arab boycott of Israel. *IJMES* 3(1972), pp. 99-122

MACINTYRE, R.R. The Palestine Liberation Organization. Tactics, strategies and options towards the Geneva Peace Conference. *J. Palestine stud.* 4iv(1975), pp. 65-89.

MAJDALANY, Jibran. On the necessity for an anti-racialist solution to the Palestine conflict. *Crescent and star,* ed. by Y. Alexander and N.N. Kittrie, 1973, pp. 109-117.

MALAWER, S. Israeli foreign policy and international legal issues, 1948-1971. *International problems* 13(1974), pp. 269-282.

MALLISON, W.T. The Balfour Declaration: an appraisal in international law. *Transformation of Palestine,* ed. I. Abu-Lughod, 1971, pp. 61-111.

MALLISON, W.T., MALLISON, S.V. The juridical characteristics of the Palestinian resistance: an appraisal in international law. *J.Palestine stud.* 2ii(1973), pp.

MALLISON, W.T., MALLISON, S.V. The role of international law in achieving justice and peace in Palestine-Israel. *J.Palestine stud.* 3iii(1974), pp. 77-87.

MANDEL, N.J. Ottoman practice as regards Jewish settlement in Palestine: 1881-1908. *M.E. stud.* 11(1975), pp. 33-46.

MARMORSTEIN, E. European Jews in Muslim Palestine. *M.E. stud.* 11(1975), pp. 74-87.

MAZRUI, Ali A. Zionism and race in Afro-Semitic relations. *Transformation of Palestine,* ed. I. Abu-Lughod, 1971, pp. 463-486.

MEIR, G. Israel in search of lasting peace. *Foreign aff.* 51(1972-1973), pp. 447-461.

MISRA, K.P. India and the status of Aqaba and Tiran. *International problems* 13(1974), pp. 283-290.

MUSHKAT, Marion. El territorio y el conflicto del Medio Oriente. *Revista polít. int.* 140(1975), pp. 51-79.

NACHMIAS, D. Status inconsistency and political opposition: a case study of an Israeli minority group. *MEJ* 27(1973), pp. 456-470.

NAHAS, Dunia. L'évolution des organisations palestiniennes. *Travaux et jours* 52(1974), pp. 77-99.

NAHAS, Dunia. La résistance palestinienne dans les territoires occupés. *Travaux et jours* 55(1975), pp. 35-53.

NAKHLEH, E.A. The anatomy of violence: theoretical reflections on Palestinian resistance. *MEJ* 25 (1971), pp. 180-200.

NAZZAL, Nafez Abdullah. The Zionist occupation of Western Galilee, 1948. *J.Palestine stud.* 3iii(1974), pp. 58-76.

NICLAUSE, M. Le Sinaï: enjeu de la paix. (Le conflit israélo-égyptien de juillet 1967 à octobre 1971.) *L'Afrique et l'Asie modernes* 97-9(1972), pp. 17-74.

XXIII PALESTINE

NIKITINA, G.S. Palestina posle vtoroy mirovoy voyny. Obrazovaniye gosudarstva Izrail' i ego vneshnyaya politika v 1948-1951 gg. *Mezhdunarodnye otnosheniya na Blizhnem i Srednem Vostoke*, 1974, pp. 168-199.

NOROUZI, Davoud. Der Kampf Ägyptens um die Überwindung der Folgen der israelischen Aggression. *Mitt.Inst.Orientforschung* 17 (1971-72), pp. 163-179.

ODEN, D.H. Israeli press views of the United Nations. (Part II: the Arab-Israeli conflict 1957-1967). *International problems* 14(1975), pp. 49-56.

PENROSE, F.E. Le conflit du Moyen-Orient et la crise de l'énergie. Leurs effets sur les relations internationales. *Maghreb Machrek* 70(1975), pp. 47-55.

PERETZ, D. The Palestine Arab refugee problem. *Political dynamics in the Middle East*, ed. P.Y. Hammond and S.S. Alexander, 1972, pp. 269-324.

PERETZ, D. Israeli diversity: the problems of internal opposition. *The Middle East*. Ed. W.A. Beling, 1973, pp. 73-100.

PERETZ, D. The United States, the Arabs, and Israel: peace efforts of Kennedy, Johnson, and Nixon. *America and the Middle East*, ed. P.T. Hart, 1972, pp. 116-125.

PERLMUTTER, A. A.D. Gordon: a transcendental Zionist. *ME studies* 7 (1971), pp. 81-87.

PIERSON-MATHY, P. La deuxième conférence internationale d'appui aux peuples arabes. Une manifestation de solidarité internationale en faveur du peuple palestinien. *Rev.Inst.Sociol.* 42(1969), pp. 283-303

PORATH, Yehoshua. Al-Ḥājj Amīn al-Ḥusaynī, Mufti of Jerusalem - his rise to power and the consolidation of his position. *Asian & Afr.Studs.* 7(1971), pp. 121-156.

POUPARD, O. La révolution palestinienne et l'Etat palestinien. *Politique étrangère* 40(1975), pp. 475-491.

QAWUQJI, Fauzi al-. Memoirs, 1948. Part II. *J. Palestine studies* 2i(1972), pp. 3-33.

QUANDT, W.B. The Middle East conflict in US strategy, 1970-71. *J.Palestine stud.* 1i (1971), pp. 39-52.

RAPHAELI, Nimrod. The absorption of Orientals into Israeli bureaucracy. *ME stud.* 8(1972), pp. 85-91

RICHARDSON, J.P. Arab civilians and the October War. *J.Palestine stud.* 3ii(1973), pp. 122-129.

ROBBE, M. Politischer Zionismus: Mythos contra Fortschritt. *Asien, Afrika, Latein-Amerika* 2(1974), pp. 89-102.

ROBBE, M., HAIKAL, Moustapha, NOROUZI, Davoud. Der vierte Nahost-Krieg: Ausgangspunkt zum Frieden? *Asien, Afrika, Latein-Amerika* 2 (1974), pp. 353-364, 554-568

RODINSON, M. Plan Hussein ... et terrorisme international. Qu'en penser? *Les Palestiniens et la crise israélo-arabe*, 1974, pp. 83-97.

RODINSON, M. Possibilités de la coexistence. *Les Palestiniens et la crise israélo-arabe*, 1974, pp. 69-82.

RODOLFO, C. Le conflit israélo-arabe durant le premier semestre 1969: La République arabe unie entre la guerre et la paix. *Orient* 49-50(1969), pp. 125-203

RÖHNER, E. Zum Palästina-Problem. *Asien, Afrika, Latein-Amerika* 3(1975), pp. 287-294.

RONDOT, Ph. Le l'Organisation de Libération de la Palestine à un gouvernement provisoire palestinien. *L'Afrique et l'Asie* 106(1975), pp. 3-28.

RONDOT, P. Révolution palestinienne, conférence de Genève et "refus arabe". *Politique étrangère* 39(1974), pp. 331-342.

ROSE, N.A. The Arab rulers and Palestine, 1936: the British reaction. *J. mod. hist.* 44(1972), pp. 213-231.

ROSE, N. The debate on partition, 1937-38: the Anglo-Zionist aspect. II. The withdrawal. *ME studies* 7 (1971), pp. 3-24.

ROSSI, M. L'O.N.U. et la crise du Proche-Orient de 1967. *Politique étrangère* 40 (1975), pp. 525-555.

RUBIN, B. US policy, January-October 1973. *J.Palestine stud.* 3ii(1973), pp. 98-113.

RUBIN, B. Waiting for Geneva. *J.Palestine stud.* 4i(1974), pp. 31-42.

RUEDY, J. Dynamics of land alienation. *Transformation of Palestine*, ed. I. Abu-Lughod, 1971, pp. 119-138.

RUGH, W.A. Arab media and politics during the October War. *MEJ* 29(1975), pp. 310-328.

RYAN, J.L. Refugees within Israel: the case of the villagers of Kafr Bir'im and Iqrit. *J. Palestine studies* 2iv(1973), pp. 55-81.

SAFRAN, Nadav. Israel's internal politics and foreign policy. *Political dynamics in the Middle East*, ed. P.Y. Hammond and S.S. Alexander, 1972, pp. 155-194.

SAFRAN, Nadav. The war and the future of the Arab Israeli conflict. *Foreign aff.* 52 (1973-4), pp. 215-236.

SAID, E.W. Arabs and Jews. *J.Palestine stud.* 3ii(1973), pp. 3-14.

SAID, E.W. Chomsky and the question of Palestine. *J. Palestine stud.* 4iii (1975), pp. 91-104.

XXIII PALESTINE

SCHLEIFER, S. Abdullah. The fall of Jerusalem, 1967. *J.Palestine stud.* 1i(1971), pp. 68-86.

SHAMGAR, Meir. The observance of international law in the administered territories. *Israel yrbk.on human rights* 1(1971), pp. 262-277.

SHARABI, Hisham. Liberation or settlement: the dialectics of Palestinian struggle. *J. Palestine stud.* 2ii(1973), pp. 33-48.

SHEFFER, G. Intentions and results of British policy in Palestine: Passfield's White Paper. *ME stud.* 9(1973), pp. 43-60.

SHEFFER, G. The involvement of Arab states in the Palestine conflict and British-Arab relationship before world war II. *Asian and African stud.*(Israel Or.Soc.), 10(1974-5), pp. 59-78.

SHEFI, Dov. Taxation in the administered territories. *Israel yrbk. on human rights* 1(1971), pp. 290-294.

SHIHATA, Ibrahim F.I. The territorial question and the October war. *J.Palestine stud.* 4i(1974), pp. 43-54.

SHOUFANI, Elias. Israeli reactions to the War. *J.Palestine stud.* 3ii(1973), pp. 46-64.

SHOUFANI, Elias. The Sinai wedge. *J.Palestine stud.* 1iii(1972), pp. 85-94.

SLAIEH, Ezzat N. Conflicting irredentisms in Palestine: a case-study of struggle for domination. *India Q.* 29(1973), pp. 199-210.

SMOUTS, M.C. L'ONU et la guerre d'octobre. *Rev.franç.sci.pol.* 24(1974), pp. 812-827.

SOEN, D. Les groupes ethniques orientaux en Israël. Leur place dans la stratification sociale. *Revue française de Sociologie.* 12(1971), pp. 218-227.

SPECTOR, I. The Soviet Union and the Palestine conflict. *Transformation of Palestine*, ed. I. Abu-Lughod, 1971, pp. 413-442.

STENDEL, Ori. The rights of the Arab minority in Israel. *Israel yrbk. on human rights* 1(1971), pp. 262-277.

STEVENS, R.P. Smuts and Weizmann. *J.Palestine stud.* 3i(1973), pp. 35-59.

STEVENS, R.P. Zionism as a phase of Western imperialism. *Transformation of Palestine*, ed. I. Abu-Lughod, 1971, pp. 27-59.

STEWART, D. Herzl's journeys in Palestine and Egypt. *J.Palestine stud.* 3iii(1974), pp. 18-38.

STORK, J. The American new left and Palestine. *J. Palestine studies* 2i(1972), pp. 64-69.

STORK, J., ROSE, S. Zionism and American Jewry. *J.Palestine stud.* 3iii(1974), pp. 39-57.

SULEIMAN, M.W. Attitudes of the Arab elite toward Palestine and Israel. *Amer. polit. sci. rev.* 67(1973), pp. 482-489.

SULEIMAN, Michael. National stereotypes as weapons in the Arab-Israeli conflict. *J. Palestine stud.* 3iii(1974), pp. 109-121.

SUS, Ibrahim. Western Europe and the October War. *J.Palestine stud.* 3ii(1973), pp. 65-84.

TAHA, Ahmed. The tragedy of al-Aqsa mosque. *Maj. al-Azhar* 45viii(1974), pp. 13-16.

TAMKOÇ, Metin. Conventional thinking and the Palestine conflict. *Diş politika* 4iv(1974), pp. 108-125.

TAYLOR, A.R. Vision and intent in Zionist thought. *Transformation of Palestine*, ed. I. Abu-Lughod, 1971, pp. 9-26.

TEKOAH, Yosef. Barbed wire shall not return to Jerusalem. *Crescent and star*, ed. by Y. Alexander and N.N. Kittrie, 1973, pp. 259-277.

TOINET, M.F. Les États-Unis, le Proche-Orient et la situation intérieure américaine. *Rev.franç.sci.pol.* 24(1974), pp. 770-783.

TOMEH, G.J. When the UN dropped the Palestinian question. *J.Palestine stud.* 4i(1974), pp. 15-30.

TOUMA, E. Autres textes palestiniens. Position du Rakah: "A propos de l'idée d'un état palestinien. *Les Palestiniens et la crise israélo-arabe*, 1974, pp. 181-196.

TREVISAN SEMI, E. Conflitti culturali in Israele. *OM* 50 (1970), pp. 735-743.

TREVISAN SEMI, E. La questione palestinese e le origini del sionismo in un saggio di 'Aḥad Ha-'Am. *OM* 55(1975), pp. 228-236.

TUENI, Ghassan. After October: military conflict and political change in the Middle East. *J.Palestine stud.* 3iv(1974), pp. 114-130.

TURKI, Fawaz. To be a Palestinian. *J.Palestine stud.* 3iii(1974), pp. 3-17.

USSISHKIN, A. The Jewish Colonisation Association and a Rothschild in Palestine. *Middle Eastern stud.* 9(1973), pp. 347-357.

VERDERY, R.N. Arab "disturbances" and the Commissions of Inquiry. *Transformation of Palestine*, ed. I. Abu-Lughod, 1971, pp. 275-303.

VERETÉ, Mayir. Kitchener, Grey and the question of Palestine in 1915-1916: a note. *ME stud.* 9(1973), pp. 223-226.

WAINES, D. The failure of the nationalist resistance. *Transformation of Palestine*, ed. I. Abu-Lughod, 1971, pp. 207-235.

XXIII PALESTINE

WARD, R.J. Economics of an internationalized Jerusalem. *IJMES* 2(1971), pp. 311-317.

WEINSTOCK, N. The impact of Zionist colonization on Palestinian Arab society before 1948. *J.Palestine stud.* 2ii(1973), pp. 49-63.

WEINSTOCK, N. The impact of Zionist colonization on Palestinian Arab society. *Essays on modernization of underdeveloped societies*, Vol. 2. Ed. A.R. Desai, Bombay, 1971. pp. 524-539.

WILKENFELD, J., LUSSIER, V.L. and TAHTINEN, D. Conflict interactions in the Middle East, 1949-1967. *J. conflict resolution* 16(1972), pp. 135-154.

WILSON, E.M. The American interest in the Palestine question and the establishment of Israel. *America and the Middle East*, ed. P.T. Hart, 1972, pp. 64-73.

WILSON, E.M. The Palestine papers, 1943-1947. *J. Palestine studies* 2iv(1973), pp. 33-54.

YAHIA, F. The Palestine people and international law. *Crescent and star*, ed. by Y. Alexander and N.N. Kittrie, 1973, pp. 6-27.

YISRAELI, D. The Third Reich and Palestine. *ME stud.* 7(1971), pp. 343-354.

YIZHAR, M. The United States Middle East resolution as viewed by the Arabs and the Moslem states of the Northern tier. *International problems* 14(1975), pp. 55-67.

ZAHLAN, A.B. The science and technology gap in the Arab-Israeli conflict. *J.Palestine stud.* 1iii(1972), pp. 17-36.

ZAVALA, J. de. El conflicto de Oriente Medio: nuevas consideraciones sobre una guerra inacabada. *Revista de polít. int.* 131(1974) pp. 37-60.

ZUREIK, Elia T. Arab youth in Israel: their situation and status perceptions. *J.Palestine stud.* 3iii(1974), pp. 97-108.

The Arab League. The Jarring mission. *Crescent and star*, ed. by Y. Alexander and N.N. Kittrie, 1973, pp. 374-390.

Arnold Toynbee on the Arab-Israeli conflict. *J. Palestine stud.* 2(1973), pp. 1-13.

Association for Peace. Solutions to the Palestinian problem. *Crescent and star*, ed. by Y. Alexander and N.N. Kittrie, 1973, pp. 402-405.

Institute for Palestine Studies. The gulf of Aqaba and the straits of Tiran. *Crescent and star*, ed. by Y. Alexander and N.N. Kittrie, 1973, pp. 294-302.

Intervista di Nāyef Ḥawāṭmah. *OM* 53(1973), pp. 118-120.

The military balance of power in the Middle East. *J.Palestine stud.* 1iii(1972), pp. 3-16.

Ministry of Foreign Affairs, Jerusalem. Arab boycott. *Crescent and star*, ed. by Y. Alexander and N.N. Kittrie, 1973, pp. 339-340.

Ministry of Foreign Affairs, Jerusalem. International guarantees and international police forces. *Crescent and star*, ed. by Y. Alexander and N.N. Kittrie, 1973, pp. 391-397.

Ministry of Foreign Affairs, Jerusalem. Israel in the administered areas. *Crescent and star*, ed. by Y. Alexander and N.N. Kittrie, 1973, pp. 174-186.

Ministry of Foreign Affairs, Jerusalem. The provisional nature of the 1949 armistice lines. *Crescent and star*, ed. by Y. Alexander and N.N. Kittrie, 1973, pp. 228-235.

Ministry of Foreign Affairs, Jerusalem. War by terror. *Crescent and star*, ed. by Y. Alexander and N.N. Kittrie, 1973, pp. 355-371.

Palestine emigration and Israeli land expropriation in the occupied territories. *J.Palestine stud.* 3i(1973), pp. 106-118.

Palestine Research Center. Reign of terror. *Crescent and star*, ed. by Y. Alexander and N.N. Kittrie, 1973, pp. 162-173.

Les prisonniers arabes en Israel: rapport d'Amnesty international (juin 1970). *Les Palestiniens et la crise israélo-arabe*, 1974, pp. 130-143.

Programma politico della Rivoluzione palestinese. *OM* 53(1973), pp. 112-118.

Projet fédéral palestinien (recommendation de la minorité de la Commission spéciale des Nations Unies, septembre 1947). *Les Palestiniens et la crise israélo-arabe*, 1974, pp. 197-209.

Textes fondamentaux des organisations de résistance (1968-1971). *Les Palestiniens et la crise israélo-arabe*, 1974, pp. 165-180.

See also I. c. 3. Selected bibliography.

See also IX. f. Haddad.

See also IX. g. Kerr.

See also IX. i. Dawn

See also IX. ii. Elewainy.

See also IX. j. Beling.

See also IX. k. Hagopian.

See also IX. m. Farsoun.

See also IX. m. Oden.

See also IX. m. Terry, Mendenhall.

XXIII PALESTINE

See also IX. m. Yodfat.

See also XVI. d. Bilinsky.

See also XVIII. c. Ministry of Foreign Affairs, Jerusalem.

See also XIX. m. Ministry of Foreign Affairs, Jerusalem.

See also XXII. c. Porath.

See also XXIII. b. Hofman.

See also XXIII. b. Merlin.

See also XXIV. c. Slaieh.

See also XXV. c. Ma'oz.

See also XXVI. c. Stemer-Picard.

See also XXXVII. b. Sivan.

See also XXVII. c. Dalle.

See also XXXVII. l. Canova

e ECONOMICS

DANIEL, A. Arab co-operation in Israel. *Year-book of agricultural co-operation* 1972, pp. 81-93.

FIRESTONE, Ya'akov. Production and trade in an Islamic context: sharika contracts in the transitional economy of Northern Samaria, 1853-1943. *IJMES* 6(1975), pp. 185-209.

REKHESS, Elie. The employment in Israel of Arab labourers from the administered areas. *Israel yb.on human rights* 5(1975), pp. 389-412.

SUSSMAN, Zvi. The determination of wages for unskilled labor in the advanced sector of the dual economy of Mandatory Palestine. *Econ. devel. and cult. change* 22(1973), pp. 95-113.

XXIV JORDAN

a GEOGRAPHY

BASTA, E.Z., SUNNA, B.F. Mineralogy and mode of occurrence of copper ores in Wadi Araba, Jordan. *BIE* 52(1970-71), pp. 199-224.

BEHEIRY, Salah A. Desert landscapes in Southern Jordan. *Fac. Arts J. Univ. Jordan* 3i(1972), pp. 5-31.

BEHEIRY, Salah A. Geomorphology of Central East Jordan. *Bull.Soc.Geog.d'Egypte* 41-2 (1968-69), pp. 5-22.

SAHAWNEH, Fouzi. Rainfall patterns and forecasting in Jordan. *Fac. Arts J. Univ. Jordan* 3ii(1972), pp. 83-92.

SALEH, Hassan A.K. An estimation of the water balance in Jordan. *Fac. Arts J. Univ. Jordan* 3ii(1972), pp. 33-42.

SALEH, Hassan A.K. Problems of water erosion in the East Jordan valley. *Fac. Arts J., Univ. Jordan* 2(1971), pp. 5-16.

SALEH, Hassan A.K. Wind erosion in the East bank of Jordan. *Dirasat* 1(1974), pp. 119-138.

b ETHNOLOGY

ANTOUN, R.T. Social organization and the life cycle in an Arab village. *Ethnology* [Pittsburgh], pp. 294-308.

CUNNINGHAM, R.B. Dimensions of family loyalty in the Arab Middle East; the case of Jordan. *J. devel. areas* 8(1973), pp. 55-63.

NASIR, Sari J. Working women in the changing society of Jordan. *Fac. Arts J., Univ. Jordan* 1ii(1969), pp. 7-41.

c HISTORY

COHEN, Amnon. The Jordanian Communist party in the West bank, 1950-1960. *The U.S.S.R. and the Middle East,* ed. by M. Confino and Sh. Shamir, 1973, pp. 419-437.

DANN, Uriel. T.E. Lawrence in Amman, 1921. *Abr Nahrain* 13(1972-73), pp. 33-41.

GARIN, M. La Jordanie un an après la guerre civile. *L'Afrique et l'Asie modernes* 93-4(1971), pp. 68-73.

GHOBASHY, Omar Z. The development of the Jordan river. *Crescent and star,* ed. by Y. Alexander and N.N. Kittrie, 1973, pp. 279-285.

KOSZINOWSKI, Th. Zur jüngsten Entwicklung der Aussenpolitik Jordaniens. *Orient* [Hamburg] 16iii(1975), pp. 79-90.

LO JACONO, Cl. I governi transgiordanici dal 1921 al 1948. *OM* 55(1975), pp. 67-78.

NUSEIBEH, Hazem Zeki. The foreign policy of Jordan. *Dis politika* 1iii(1971), pp. 128-139.

XXIV JORDAN

OCHSENWALD, W.L. Opposition to political centralization in South Jordan and the Hijaz, 1900-1914. *MW* 63(1973), pp. 297-306.

RONDOT, P. Une nouvelle étape de la politique jordanienne: le Plan Hussein. *L'Afrique et l'Asie modernes* 93-4(1971), pp. 74-79.

SLAIEH, Ezzat N. The Jordanian-Palestinian civil war of 1970: a quest for justice and peace. *India Q.* 30(1974), pp. 52-59.

SUTCLIFFE, C.R. The East Ghor Canal project: a case study of refugee resettlement, 1961-1966. *MEJ* 27(1973), pp. 471-482.

Ministry of Foreign Affairs, Jerusalem. The Arab plan to divert the headwaters of the river Jordan. *Crescent and star*, ed. by Y. Alexander and N.N. Kittrie, 1973, pp. 286-291.

See also IX. i. Dawn

See also XXIII. c. Bosworth

See also XXVI. c. Howard.

See also XXVII. c. Simon.

d ECONOMICS

PURINI, G.P. Il nuovo piano di sviluppo triennale della Giordania. *Levante* 19iv (1972), pp. 5-10.

TAYEH, A.K. Twenty years of co-operation in Jordan. *Year-book of agricultural co-operation* 1972, pp. 94-102.

XXV SYRIA

a GEOGRAPHY

DETTMANN, K. A geographical appraisal of Islamic and western elements in Damascus. *Proc. 27th Int. Cong. Or. 1967* (1971), pp. 181-182.

PIGNON, J. Une géographie de l'Espagne morisque. *Recueil d'études sur les moriscos andalous en Tunisie*, préparé par M. de Epalza et R. Petit, 1973, pp. 64-76.

PROST-TOURNIER, J.M. La population de Damas. *Hannon. Rev. Libanaise de géog.* 5(1970), pp. 129-145.

ZUCKERMANN, B. Die Euphrat projekt in der Syrischen Arabischen Republik und sein Einfluss auf die Territorialstruktur der syrischen Volkswirtschaft. (The Euphrates project in the Syrian Arab Republic and its influence on the territorial structure of Syrian political economy.) *PGM* 115(1971), pp. 98-101

See also XIX. a. Anawati.

See also XIX. a. Anawati.

See also XXVI. a. Blanchet.

b ETHNOLOGY

BARBOT, M. Cris de la rue à Damas. *BEO* 25 (1972), pp. 291-318.

CHARLES, H. L'organisation de la vie maritime à l'Ile d'Arwâd (Syrie). *ROMM* 13-14 (1973), pp. 231-238.

NAFFAKH, Rabah La conception du monde chez les Beggāra. *REI* 39(1971), pp. 119-143.

TAMZOK, Omar-Farouk. Das System der sozialen Sicherheit in Syrien. *Orient* [Germany] 14 (1973), pp. 170-176.

c HISTORY

ALI, Saleh Ahmad al-. Al-Madā'in and its surrounding area in Arabic literary sources. *Mesopotamia* 3-4(1968-69), pp. 417-439.

BALDISSERA, E. La composizione dei governi siriani dal 1918 al 1965. (Note e materiali.) *OM* 52(1972), pp. 617-630.

BALDISSERA, E. Note di storia siriana: gli ultimi giorni del regno siriano di Faiṣal ibn Ḥusein. *OM* 52(1972), pp. 341-356.

BAUMGART, W. Politik und Religion in Syrien im. 19. Jahrhundert. Zu einigen neuen Büchern. *ZMR* 55(1971), pp. 104-108.

BIANQUIS, T. Notables ou malandrins d'origine rurale à Damas à l'époque Fatimide. (Textes traduits de l'arabe.) *BEO* 26(1973), pp. 185-201.

BRANDT, Yu. K voprosu o nekotorykh osnovnykh tendentziyakh siriysko-livanskogo osvoboditel'nogo dvizheniya pered pervoy mirovoy voynoy. *Istoriya i ekonomika stran Arabskogo Vostoka*, 1973, pp. 43-51.

CAHEN, Cl. Aperçu sur les impôts du sol en Syrie au Moyen Âge. *JESHO* 18(1975), pp. 233-244.

DONOHUE, J.J. La nouvelle constitution syrienne et ses détracteurs. *Travaux et jours* 47(1973), pp. 93-111.

XXV SYRIA

EBIED, R.Y., YOUNG, M.J.L. A list of Ottoman governors of Aleppo, A.H. 1002-1168. *AION* 34(n.s.24, 1974), pp. 103-108.

ELISSÉEFF, N. Damas à la lumière des théories de Jean Sauvaget. *The Islamic city,* 1970, pp. 157-177.

FARAG, Nadia. The Lewis affair and the fortunes of Al-Muqtataf. *ME stud.* 8(1972), pp. 73-83

GIL BENUMEYA, R. Permanencia y mutación en la realidad de Siria. *Rev.polit.int.* 137 (1975), pp. 173-183.

GORBUNOVA, N.M. Kommunisticheskaya partiya Sirii v bor'be za ukreplenie nezavimosti i demokraticheskoe razvitie strany (1954-1958 gg.) *Strany Blizhnego i Srednego Vostoka: istoriya, ekonomika,* 1972, pp. 40-49.

GRABAR, O. Notes on the population of the Jazīrah in early Islamic times. *Amer. Or. Soc., Middle West Branch. Semi-centennial volume,* ed. by D. Sinor, 1969, pp. 89-98.

HORNUS, J.M. Les Russes dans la Syrie et la Palestine ottomanes. [Review article on D. Hopwood, *The Russian presence in Syria and Palestine, 1843-1914,* Clarendon Press, 1969.] *Rev.hist.et philos.rel.* 52(1972), pp. 105-109

JOARDER, Safiuddin. Syria under the French mandate: an over-view. *J. Asiatic Soc. Pakistan* 14 (1969), pp. 91-104.

KAYLANI, Nabil M. The rise of the Syrian Ba'th, 1940-1958: political success, party failure. *IJMES* 3(1972), pp. 3-23.

KELIDAR, A.R. Religion and state in Syria. *Asian affairs* 61(N.S.5, 1974), pp. 16-22.

KHADER, Bichara. Structures et réformes agraires en Syrie. *Maghreb-Machrek* 65 (1974), pp. 45-55.

KHAYAT, H.M. The Šī'ite rebellions in Aleppo in the 6th A.H./12th A.D. century. *RSO* 46 (1971), pp. 167-195.

KOSZINOWSKI, Thomas. Syrien und der vierte arabisch-israelische Krieg. *Orient* [Germany] 15(1974), pp. 24-28.

LAPIDUS, I.M. Muslim urban society in Mamlūk Syria. *The Islamic city,* 1970, pp. 195-205

LEVY, Avigdor. The Syrian Communists and the Ba'th power struggle, 1966-1970. *The U.S.S.R. and the Middle East,* ed. by M. Confino and Sh. Shamir, 1973, pp. 395-417.

MA'OZ, Moshe. Attempts at creating a political community in modern Syria. *MEJ* 26(1972), pp. 389-404.

MA'OZ, Moshe. The Jews in mid-nineteenth century Syria and Palestine: a community in transition. *Proc.27th Int.Cong.Or. 1967* (1971), pp. 262-263.

MA'OZ, Moshe. The 'Ulamā' and the process of modernization in Syria during the mid-nineteenth century. *Asian & Afr. Studs.* 7(1971), pp. 77-88.

NOVIKOV, N.V. Ustanovlenie diplomaticheskikh otnosheniy SSSR s Siriey i Livanom. *Vopr. ist.* 1973(10), pp. 128-143.

RAFEQ, Abdul Karim. The local forces in Syria in the seventeenth and eighteenth centuries. *War, technology and society in the Middle East,* ed. V.J. Parry and M.E. Yapp, 1975, pp. 277-307.

RAFEQ, Abdul Karim. Les registres des tribunaux de Damas comme source pour l'histoire de la Syrie. *BEO* 26(1973), pp. 219-226.

RAFEQ, Abdul-Karim. Syrian historical studies on Syria. *MESA bull.* 9iii(1975), pp. 1-6.

SCHMUCKER, W. Studien zur Baathideologie. II. Der Neobaath. *WI* 15(1974), pp. 146-182.

SHAMIR, Shimon. The effects of the *Hacc* on the socio-economic and political structure of Syria in the 18th century. *Proc.27th Int.Cong.Or.1967* (1971), pp. 216-217.

SHAMIR, S. Midhat Pasha and the anti-Turkish agitation in Syria. *ME stud.* 10(1974), pp. 115-141.

SKURATOWICZ, J. International relations of the Arab Republic of Syria. *Sprawy międzynarodowe* 27(6), 1974, pp. 127-138.

VAN DUSEN, M.H. Political integration and regionalism in Syria. *MEJ* 26(1972), pp. 123-136.

VOLL, J. Old 'ulama' families and Ottoman influence in eighteenth century Damascus. *AJAS* 3(1975), pp. 48-59.

See also II. a. 7. Dodge.

See also III. a. 3. Sourdel.

See also III. a. 13 Sourdel-Thomine et Sourdel.

See also IX. c. Zakkar.

See also IX. g. Dawisha.

See also IX. k. Jargy.

See also XIV. h. Bourouiba.

See also XVI. b. Burke.

See also XVI. c. Cerbella.

See also XXVI. c. Howard.

See also XXIX. i. Farah.

XXV SYRIA

d ECONOMICS

FRYZEL, T. Wojna 1967 roku na Bliskim Wschodzie a jedność arabska. (The War of 1967 in Near East and the Arab unity.) *Universitas Iagellonica acta scientarum litterarumque, Schedae politicae* 7(1974), pp. 31-53.

GIL BENUMEYA, R. Encrucijadas actuales del pueblo palestino. *Rev.polit.int.* 135(1974), pp. 163-173.

HAIM, S.G. The Ba'ath in Syria. *People and politics in the Middle East,* ed. M. Curtis, 1971, pp. 132-143.

IMAM, Ahmed Zaki el-. The co-operative movement in the Syrian Arab Republic. *Yearbook of agricultural co-operation* 1972, pp. 121-130.

KEILANY, Ziad. Socialism and economic change in Syria. *ME stud.* 9(1973), pp. 61-72.

KELLY, J.B. 'TLS' in the Desert. *J.Imperial and commonwealth hist.* 1(1973), pp. 358-379.

KHADER, Bichara. Propriété agricole et réforme agraire en Syrie. *Civilisations* 25i-ii(1975), pp. 62-83.

MAKDISI, Samir A. Syria: rate of economic growth and fixed capital formation 1936-1968. *MEJ* 25 (1971), pp. 157-179.

ROULEAU, E. The Palestinian quest. *Foreign affairs* 53(1975), pp. 264-283.

SANTUCCI, R. La Syrie ba'thiste (1963-1973): un effort de construction compromis par la guerre? *L'Afrique et l'Asie modernes* 97-9(1972), pp. 75-94.

Discours de Yasser Arafat devant l'Assemblée générale des Nations Unies (13 nov. 1974). *Travaux et jours* 53(1974), pp. 79-104.

See also XVI. cc. Barthel, Grienig, Kück.

See also XIX. g. Hennequin.

XXVI LEBANON

a GEOGRAPHY

ARNAUD, R. Étude morphologique du Jabal Aarbé et de ses abords. *Hannon* 2(1967), pp. 91-116.

BESANÇON, J. Les cartes du Liban. *Hannon* 1(1966), pp. 105-142.

BESANÇON, J., HOURS, F. Une coupe dans le Quaternaire récent: Saaïdé-I (Béqaa central -Liban). *Hannon. Rev. Libanaise de géog.* 5(1970), pp. 29-63.

BESANÇON, J. Les formations plio-quaternaires du Ouâdi Yahfoûfa. *Hannon* 2(1967), pp. 61-82.

BESANÇON, J. Les plateaux du Sud-Ouest. *Hannon* 1(1966), pp. 83-104.

BESANÇON, J., HOURS, F. Préhistoire et géomorphologie: les formes du relief et les dépôts quaternaires dans la région de Joub Jannine (Béqaa méridionale - Liban). *Hannon. Rev. Libanaise de géog.* 5(1970), pp. 63-95.

BLANCHET, G. Nouveaux aperçus sur le climat du Liban. *Hannon* 1(1966), pp. 1-19.

BLANCHET, G. Les régimes thermiques de Beyrouth et de Damas: étude comparée. *Hannon* 2(1967), pp. 117-126.

BOURGEY, A. Problèmes de géographie urbaine au Liban. *Hannon. Rev. Libanaise de géog.* 5(1970), pp. 97-128.

DUBERTRET, L. Géologie et peuplement au Liban. *Hannon. Rev. Libanaise de géog.* 5 (1970), pp. 11-20.

GUERRE, A. Les glissements de terrain de Beskinta. *Hannon* 2(1967), pp. 127-131.

GUERRE, A., SANLAVILLE, P. Sur les hauts niveaux marins quaternaires du Liban. *Hannon. Rev. Libanaise de géog.* 5(1970), pp. 21-28.

KALO, M. Les transports en commun à Saida. *Hannon* 1(1966), pp. 29-36.

KAREH, R. Les sources sous-marines de Chekka. *Hannon* 2(1967), pp. 35-59.

KARKABI, S. Aperçu général sur la grotte de Jiïta. *Hannon* 2(1967), pp. 83-89.

KARKABI, S. La spéléologie et le Spéléo-Club du Liban. *Hannon. Rev. Libanaise de géog.* 5(1970), pp. 1-10.

LAMOUROUX, M. Altération des roches dures carbonatées sous les climats humide et subhumide du Liban. *Hannon* 2(1967), pp. 25-34.

MURR, M. Reflexions sur la géographie du Liban. *Hannon* 1(1966), pp. 21-28.

RUPPERT, H. Recent dislocations and structural changes of Beirut's commercial quarters. *Proc.27th Int.Cong.Or.1967* (1971), pp. 183-184.

SALAAM, Assem. City planning in Beirut and its outskirts. *Beirut, crossroads of cultures,* 1970, pp. 167-184.

SANLAVILLE, P. Le calcaire dans la morphologie littorale du Liban. *Hannon* 2(1967), pp. 17-24.

SANLAVILLE, P. L'évolution de la plaine du Aakkar. *Hannon* 1(1966), pp. 71-82.

ZEIN, Ghada el-. Le Koura et son oliveraie. *Hannon* 1(1966), pp. 37-70.

b ETHNOLOGY

ABOU, Salim. La composition ethnique de Beyrouth. *Beirut, crossroads of cultures,* 1970, pp. 92-112.

ACCAD-SURSOCK, R. La femme libanaise: de la tradition à la modernité. *Travaux et jours* 52(1974), pp. 17-38.

ALLARD, M. Les Libanais en Argentine de l'émigration à l'intégration. *Travaux et jours* 48(1973), pp. 5-15.

ALOUCHE, R. La femme libanaise et le travail. *Travaux et jours* 52(1974), pp. 61-70.

BAGROS, S. Les cheminements du désir. *Travaux et jours* 48(1973), pp. 71-75.

BAGROS, S. Lorsqu'une française épouse un libanais. Étude de cas. *Travaux et jours* 52(1974), pp. 39-60.

BARAKAT, Halim. Social and political integration in Lebanon: a case of social mosaic. *MEJ* 27(1973), pp. 301-318.

BASTIDE, R. Immigrés dans l'Autre Amérique ou l'anti-Proust. *Travaux et jours* 48 (1973), pp. 85-91.

CHAMOUN, Mounir. Les aléas d'une double appartenance. *Travaux et jours* 48(1973), pp. 65-70.

CHAMOUN, Mounir. Couples. *Travaux et jours* 52(1974), pp. 3-14.

CRESSWELL, R. Parenté et propriété foncière dans la montagne libanaise. *Etudes rurales* 40(1970), pp. 7-79.

DUBAR, Cl. Structure confessionnelle et classes sociales au Liban. *Rev. franç. de sociologie* 15(1974), pp. 301-328.

FARSOUN, Samih K., FARSOUN, K. Class and patterns of association among kinsmen in contemporary Lebanon. *Anthrop. q'ly* 47 (1974), pp. 93-111.

GEAHCHAN, M.L. L'emigration des cerveaux et le système éducatif au Liban. *Ann. de la Fac. de droit de Beyrouth* 73(1972), pp. 241-258.

GHAZALY, L.G. La femme et la terre. *Travaux et jours* 56-7(1975), pp. 75-93.

HAMALIAN, Arpi. The Shirkets: visiting pattern of Armenians in Lebanon. *Anthrop. q'ly* 47(1974), pp. 71-92.

HANF, T. Le comportement politique des étudiants libanais. *Travaux et jours* 46 (1973), pp. 5-52.

KANIKI, M.H.Y. Attitudes and reactions towards the Lebanese in Sierra Leone during the colonial period. *Canadian J.Afr.stud.* 7(1973), pp. 97-113.

KASPARIAN, R. L'enquête sur la population active au Liban. *Ann. Fac. Droit Beyrouth* 68 (1971), pp. 87-107.

KHALAF, Samir. Family associations in Lebanon. *J.compar.family stud.* 2(1971), pp. 235-250.

KHURI, Fuad I. Sectarian loyalty among rural migrants in two Lebanese suburbs: a stage between family and national allegiance. *Rural politics and social change in the Middle East,* ed. by R. Antoun and I. Harik, 1972, pp. 198-213.

MÉTRAL, J. Pour une anthropologie spontanée. *Travaux et jours* 48(1973), pp. 77-84.

NAFFAH, J. Dermatoglyphics and flexion creases in the Lebanese population. *Amer. J. phys. anthrop.* N.S.41(1974), pp. 391-409.

NASR, Nafhat and PALMER, M. Family, peers, social control, and political activism among Lebanese college students. *J. developing areas* 9(1974), pp. 377-394.

REINICH, R. Le processus de changement dans un village sunnite de Chouf. *Travaux et jours* 54(1975), pp. 115-123.

RODIONOV, M.A. Iz istorii formirovaniya etnokonfessional'noy struktury naseleniya Livana. (Structure ethno-confessionnelle de la société libanaise.) *Sov. etn.* 1973 (4), pp. 25-38.

SICKING, T. Dépérissement d'un village libanais. *Travaux et jours* 47(1973), pp. 1-21.

SWEET, L.E. Visiting patterns and social dynamics in a Lebanese Druze village. *Anthrop. q'ly* 47(1974), pp. 112-119.

ZAAROUR, J. L'autre Liban. *Travaux et jours* 48(1973), pp. 55-63.

La population du Liban. *Population* [Paris] 29(1974), pp. 1148-1151.

c HISTORY

AJAY, N.Z. Political intrigue and suppression in Lebanon during World War I. *IJMES* 5(1974), pp. 140-160.

AUCAGNE, J. La crise libanaise et les prises de position religieuses. *Travaux et jours* 56-7(1975), pp. 69-73.

XXVI LEBANON

AUCAGNE, J. Marxisme inévitable? *Travaux et jours* 43(1972), pp. 57-66.

CHAMUSSY, R. La crise de nouveau. *Travaux et jours* 55(1975), pp. 23-34.

CHAMUSSY, R. Une difficile année sociale. *Travaux et jours* 53(1974), pp. 53-77.

CHAMUSSY, R. Incertitudes libanaises. *Travaux et jours* 56-7(1975), pp. 55-67.

CHEVALLIER, D. Signes de Beyrouth en 1834. *BEO* 25(1972), pp. 211-228.

COULAND, J. Le parti communiste libanais cinquante ans après. *Maghreb Machrek* 68 (1975), pp. 61-75.

CRAWFORD, A. Foreign communities in Beirut. *Beirut, crossroads of cultures,* 1970, pp. 113-132.

DALLE, I. Le Liban, la résistance palestinienne et Israël. *L'Afrique et l'Asie modernes* 97-9(1972), pp. 175-182.

DONINI, Pier Giovanni. Le elezioni presidenziali del 1970 nel Libano. *OM* 50(1970), pp. 745-769.

ENTELIS, J.P. Belief-system and ideology formation in the Lebanese Katâ'ib party. *IJMES* 4(1973), pp. 148-162.

ENTELIS, J.P. Party transformation in Lebanon: Al-Kata'ib as a case study. *Middle Eastern stud.* 9(1973), pp. 325-340.

ENTELIS, J.P. Structural change and organizational development in the Lebanese Kata'ib party. *MEJ* 27(1973), pp. 21-35.

FARAH, Naoum. 1970: une année politique charnière pour le Liban. *Travaux et jours* 38 (1971), pp. 115-120.

FRYZEL, T. Problemy wewnetrznej polityki Libanu. *Przegl.or.* 90(1974), pp. 103-111.

GIL BENUMEYA, R. El Líbano y su otra cuestión del Próximo Oriente. *Rev. de política int.* 120(1972), pp. 87-95.

GOITEIN, S.D. An eleventh century letter from Tyre in the John Rylands Library. *Bull.J.R. Lib.* 54(1971), pp. 94-102.

GORBUNOVA, N.M. Livan. Problemy formirovaniya natzional'nogo fronta progressivnykh sil (1965-1970 gg.). *Arabskie strany, Turtziya, Iran, Afganistan,* 1973, pp. 32-42.

GUBSER, P. The *Zu'amā'* of Zahlah: the current situation in a Lebanese town. *MEJ* 27(1973), pp. 173-189.

HOURS, F. Beyrouth au Moyen Age. *Beirut, crossroads of cultures,* 1970, pp. 43-64.

HOWARD, H.N. The Soviet Union in Lebanon, Syria and Jordan. *The Soviet Union and the Middle East,* ed. I.J. Lederer and W.S. Vucinich, 1974, pp. 134-156.

HUDSON, M.C. Democracy and social mobilization in Lebanese politics. *Contemporary politics* 1(1968-69), pp. 245-263.

ISSAWI, Ch. Lebanese agriculture in the 1850s: a British consular report. *AJAS* 1(1973), pp. 66-80.

JALABERT, H. Beyrouth sous les Ottomans: 1516-1918. *Beirut, crossroads of cultures,* 1970, pp. 65-91.

JOHNSON, M. Confessionalism and individualism in Lebanon: a critique of Leonard Binder (ed.), *Politics in Lebanon:* New York, 1966. *RMES* 1(1975), pp. 79-91.

KÖHLER, W. Die Staatskrise des Libanon. *Orient* [Germany] 16iv(1975), pp. 68-104.

MALIK, C.H. Beirut - crossroads of cultures. *Beirut, crossroads of cultures,* 1970, pp. 203-220.

MINGANTI, P. Unità araba e socialismo nell'ideologia del *ba'th* siriano. *OM* 55 (1975), pp. 208-227.

NANTET, J. Le Liban: un modèle pour le monde arabe? *Genève-Afrique* 13(1974), pp. 72-84.

SAIDAH, R. The prehistory of Beirut. *Beirut, crossroads of cultures,* 1970, pp. 1-13.

SALEM, E. Forces et agents du modernisme et du changement social au Liban. *Renaissance du monde arabe. Colloque interarabe de Louvain,* 1972, pp. 457-475.

SALIBI, K.S. The Lebanese Emirate, 1667-1841. *Al-Abhath* 20iii(1967), pp. 1-16.

SALIBI, Kamal S. The Lebanese identity. *J. contemp. hist.* 6 (1971), pp. 76-86.

SALIBI, Kamal S. The Sayfās and the *Eyalet* of Tripoli 1579-1640. *Arabica* 20(1973), pp. 25-52.

SALIBI, Kamal S. The secret of the house of Ma'n. *IJMES* 4(1973), pp. 272-287.

SPAGNOLO, J.P. Constitutional change in Mount Lebanon: 1861-1864. *ME studies* 7 (1971), pp. 25-48.

SPAGNOLO, J.P. Mount Lebanon, France and Dâûd Pasha. *IJMES* 2 (1971), pp. 148-167.

STEMER-PICARD, E. Le Liban et la résistance palestinienne. *Rev. franç. sci. pol.* 25(1975), pp. 5-22.

STOAKES, F. The supervigilantes: the Lebanese Kataeb party as a builder, surrogate and defender of the state. *M.E.stud.* 11 (1975), pp. 215-236.

SULEIMAN, M.W. Crisis and revolution in Lebanon. *MEJ* 26(1972), pp. 11-24

WARD, W.A. Ancient Beirut. *Beirut, crossroads of cultures,* 1970, pp. 14-42.

Communiqué du parti communiste libanais. *Travaux et jours* 49(1973), pp. 35-49.

Le difficile printemps libanais. *Travaux et jours* 55(1975), pp. 5-22.

Point de vue du Parti des phalanges libanaises. *Travaux et jours* 49(1973), pp. 51-64.

See also XXIII. d. Entelis.

See also XXV. c. Brandt.

See also XLIII. e. Iskandar.

d ECONOMICS

ACHKAR, Adel. Statistiques syndicales 1966 - 1971. *Travaux et jours* 45(1972), pp. 5-23.

ALY, Hamdi F. and ABDUN-NUR, Nabil. An appraisal of the six year plan of Lebanon (1972-1977). *MEJ* 29(1975), pp. 151-164.

AYOUB, G. et SAAD, Zeina el-. Deux responsables syndicaux parlent. *Travaux et jours* 45(1972), pp. 43-64.

CAMPBELL, R. Le problème du chômage du vendredi au Liban. *Travaux et jours* 49 (1973), pp. 65-81.

CHAKHTOURA, M. La convention collective des employés de banque. *Travaux et jours* 44(1972), pp. 75-86.

CHAMUSSY, R. Le décret 1943 et le patronat libanais. *Travaux et jours* 41 (1971), pp. 49-64.

CHEBAT, Anis. Les ingénieurs au Liban. *Travaux et jours* 43(1972), pp. 25-28.

CRUISE O'BRIEN, R. Lebanese entrepreneurs in Senegal: economic integration and the politics of protection. *Cah. ét. afr.* 15(no.57,1975), pp. 95-115.

DEBBANÉ, J. Projet de budget 1971 au Liban. *Ann. Fac. Droit Beyrouth* 68 (1971), pp. 77-85.

DE WULF, L. First-order effect of the tax payments by income class. The case of Lebanon 1968. *Ann. Fac. Droit Beyrouth* 74 (1972), pp. 533-553.

DUBAR, Claude. L'affiliation syndicale des typographes au Liban. Une enquête sur les ouvriers du "Nahar". *Travaux et jours* 45(1972), pp. 25-42.

DURAND, H. Étude d'un modèle de développement pour le Liban et projections préliminaires au programme quinquennal 1970-1974. *Ann.de la Fac.de Droit de Beyrouth* 71(1972), pp. 51-92

DURUPTY, M. Transposition et mutations du modèle administratif français (les cas libanais et tunisien). *Bull. Inst. int. adm. publ.* 33(1975), pp. 79-120.

EDDÉ, J. Ingénieurs et architectes Libanais. *Travaux et jours* 43(1972), pp. 29-36.

GANNAGÉ, E. Le crédit agricole au Liban. *Ann.de la Fac.de droit de Beyrouth* 69 (1971), pp. 237-268.

GEMAYEL, Sleiman M. Liban. L'autonomie financière des établissements publics industriels et commerciaux, illusion ou réalité? *Rev. du droit public et de la sci. pol.* 87(1971), pp. 451-467.

GHATTAS, E. Lebanon's financial crisis in 1966: a systemic approach. *MEJ* 25 (1971), pp. 31-44.

GHOSN, C. et KHABBAZ, Gaby. Formation syndicale au Liban. *Travaux et jours* 44(1972), pp. 9-30.

GORBUNOVA, N.M. Osobennosti sotzial'no-ekonomicheskoy i politicheskoy struktury Livana. *NAA* 1973(6), pp. 27-34.

GRAINDORGE, P., WAISFISZ, B. The co-operative movement in Lebanon. *Year-book of agricultural co-operation* 1972, pp. 103-108.

GREENE, B.A. Rural urban migration and the role of rural development in industrial development: the case of Lebanon. *Ann. Fac. Droit Beyrouth* 74(1972), pp. 411-425.

GUBSER, P. The politics of economic interest groups in a Lebanese town. *M.E.stud.* 11(1975), pp. 262-283.

HUDSON, J. The Līṭānī River of Lebanon: an example of Middle Eastern water development. *MEJ* 25 (1971), pp. 1-14.

JAHEL, G. Les établissements financiers au Liban. *Ann. de la Fac. de droit de Beyrouth* 73(1972), pp. 259-266.

KASPARIAN, R. Qualification de la main-d'oeuvre et structure économique au Liban. *Ann. de la Fac. de droit de Beyrouth* 73(1972), pp. 201-223.

KAYAYAN, A.K. and FRANCIS, D.G. Mechanization and the division of labor: a study of farm families in the Beka'a plain of,Lebanon. *J. Asian and African studies* [York Univ.] 8(1973), pp. 17-26.

KOLVENBACH, P.H. Analyse d'une rubrique cinématographique. *Travaux et jours* 47 (1973), pp. 23-47.

KUBURSI, Atif A. The import structure of Lebanon: a quantitive analysis. *J. developing areas* 9(1974), pp. 87-98.

LELART, M. Introduction à l'étude de mécanismes monétaires libanais. *Ann.de la Fac.de droit de Beyrouth* 69(1971), pp. 209-235.

MEL'NIKOV, E.N. Osobennosti razvitiya sovremennogo Livana. (Some features of the development of contemporary Lebanon.) *NAA* 1971(3), pp. 51-59.

NÉÉMA, P. L'architecte Libanais dans un monde en changement. *Travaux et jours* 43(1972), pp. 37-48.

NIGHTINGALE, R.W. Food processing in Lebanon's industrial development. *Ann. Fac. Droit Beyrouth* 74(1972), pp. 433-445.

XXVI LEBANON

PAIX, C. La portée spatiale des activités tertiaires de commandement économique au Liban. *Tiers monde* 16(1975), pp. 135-182.

RIZKALLAH-BOULAD, Magda. La régie des tabacs et son syndicat. *Travaux et jours* 44(1972), pp. 47-73.

SAADE, Riad Fouad. Réalités de l'agriculture libanaise. *Tiers-monde* 14(1973), pp. 425-436.

SADR, Kazem. Land tenure and agricultural development in Lebanon. *Land reform* 1973 (2), pp. 24-30.

STEPHAN, M. Une revue syndicale: al-Awâssef. *Travaux et jours* 44(1972). pp. 31-45.

See also III. c. *Lebanon*. Douence

See also IX. n. Basile.

XXVII IRAQ

a GEOGRAPHY

MIEGEL, A. Territoriale Entwicklungstendenzen der Industrie im Irak. (Territorial tendencies of development of the industry of Iraq.) *PGM* 115(1971), pp. 191-197

b ETHNOLOGY

ASHTOR, E. Un mouvement migratoire au haut Moyen Age: migrations de l'Irak vers les pays méditerranéens. *Annales ESC* 27(1972), pp. 185-214

CERBELLA, G. Bagdad, città di mille ricordi. *Levante* 22i(1975), pp. 10-16.

GHANIMA, G. Proverbes baghdadiens. *Orient* 51-2(1969), pp. 43-61

KHAYYAT, Latif. Judeo-Iraqi proverbs on man and wife. *Proverbium* 24(1974), pp. 943-947.

NISSEN, H.J. Survey of an abandoned modern village in Southern Iraq. *Sumer* 24 (1968), pp. 107-114.

PETERS, E.L. Shifts in power in a Lebanese village. *Rural politics and social change in the Middle East,* ed. by R. Antoun and I. Harik, 1972, pp. 165-197.

QAZZAZ, Ayad Al-. Impressions of sociology in Iraq. *Int. soc. sci. J.*27(1975), pp. 781-786.

QAZZAZ, Ayad al-. Sociology in underdeveloped countries - A case study of Iraq. *Sociol.R.* 20(1972), pp. 93-103

VINOGRADOV, A. Ethnicity, cultural discontinuity and power brokers in northern Iraq: the case of the Shabak. *Amer.ethnologist* 1(1974), pp. 207-218.

See also XXVII. c. Wendell.

c HISTORY

ALI, Saleh Ahmad el-. The foundation of Baghdad. *The Islamic city,* 1970, pp. 87-101.

BADEAU, J.S. They lived once thus in Baghdad. *Medieval and Middle Eastern studies ... A.S. Atiya* 1972, pp. 38-49.

CERBELLA, G. Italia e ʿIrāq. *Levante* 20ii (1973), pp. 5-16.

COHEN, S.A. Sir Arthur Nicolson and Russia: the case of the Baghdad railway. *Hist.J.* 18(1975), pp. 863-872.

DANN, Uriel. The Communist movement in Iraq since 1963. *The U.S.S.R. and the Middle East,* ed. by M. Confino and Sh. Shamir, 1973, pp. 377-394.

DANN, U. The crisis of summer 1959 in the relations between the Iraqi Communist Party and the Qassem regime. *Proc.27th Int.Cong.Or.1967* (1971), pp. 162-163.

DANN, U. A historical miscellany: communist life in Baghdad in the summer of 1959. *Asian and Afr. stud.* 8(1972), pp. 86-91.

EDMONDS, C.J. The Iraqi-Persian frontier: 1639-1938. *Asian affairs* 62(N.S.6, 1975), pp. 147-154.

EDMONDS, C.J. The Kurdish national struggle in Iraq [review article] *Asian aff.* 58(N.S.2, 1971), pp. 147-158.

ENDE, W. Neue arabische Memoirenliteratur zur Geschichte des modernen Irak. *Der Islam* 49(1972), pp. 100-109.

FRANCIS, R.M. The British withdrawal from the Bagdad Railway project in April 1903. *Hist. J.* 16(1973), pp. 168-178.

HINDS, M. Kûfan political alignments and their background in the mid-seventh century A.D. *IJMES* 2(1971), pp. 346-367.

XXVII IRAQ

HUSRY, Khaldūn S. The Assyrian affair of 1933. *IJMES* 5(1974), pp. 161-176, 344-360.

JAMSHEER, Hassan A. Geneza powstania narodowego w Iraku (30. VI.1920-3.II.1921). *Przegl. or.* 4(88,1973), pp. 281-291.

JOSEPH, J. The Assyrian affair: a historical perspective. *IJMES* 6(1975), pp. 115-117.

KEDOURIE, E. Continuity and change in modern Iraqi history. *Asian affairs* 62 (N.S.6, 1975), pp. 140-146.

KEDOURIE, E. The Jews of Baghdad in 1910. *ME stud.* 7(1971), pp. 355-362.

KHADDURI, Majid. Iraq, 1958 and 1963. *The politics of the coup d'etat,* ed. W.G. Andrews and U. Ra'anan, 1969, pp. 65-88.

KHAN, M.A. Saleem. Iraq: a sectarian polity. *Islam and the modern age* 3i(1972), pp. 76-99

KHAN, Muhammad Golam Idris. British policy in Iraq, 1828-43. *JAS Bangladesh* 18(1973), pp. 173-194.

KUDSI-ZADEH, A.A. A diary on Mesopotamia in 1906. *WI* 13 (1971), pp. 125-128.

LASSNER, J. The Caliph's personal domain: the city plan of Baghdad re-examined. *The Islamic city,* 1970, pp. 103-118.

MACKAY, P.A. Patronage and power in 6th/12th century Baghdad. The life of the vizier ʿAḍud al-Dīn ibn al-Muẓaffar. *SI* 34(1971), pp. 27-56

MEJCHER, H. Oil and British policy towards Mesopotamia, 1914-18. *M.E.Stud.* 8(1972), pp. 377-391.

NECHKIN, G.N. Sotzional'no-ekonomicheskie preobrazovaniya v Irake. (Social-economic and political transformations in Iraq.) *NAA* 1973(1), pp. 12-23.

QAZZAZ, Ayad al- Power elite in Iraq, 1920-1958. *MW* 61(1971), pp. 267-283.

ROGERS, J.M. Sāmarrā: a study in medieval town-planning. *The Islamic city,* 1970, pp. 119-155.

SAMBELYAN, K.Kh. Profsoyuznoe dvizhenie v Irake v 1945-1958 gg. *Strany Blizhnegc i Srednego Vostoka: istoriya, ekonomica,* 1972, pp. 156-163.

SHAWI, Hamid al-. L'Irak et le dernier conflit israélo-arabe. *Maghreb-Machrek* 64 (1974), pp. 19-23.

SIMON, R.S. The Hashemite 'conspiracy': Hashemite unity attempts, 1921-1958. *IJMES* 5(1974), pp. 314-327.

STRIKA, V. Baghdad: vicende di una capitale dalle origini ai nostri giorni. *Levante* 22ii(1975), pp. 16-28.

VAN DAMME, M. Les sources écrites concernant l'oeuvre du secrétaire buyide Abû Ishâq as-Sâbî. *Actes I. Cong. et. cult. mediterr. d'infl. arabo-berb.,* 1973, pp. 175-181.

VINOGRADOV, Amal. The 1920 revolt in Iraq reconsidered: the role of tribes in national politics. *IJMES* 3(1972), pp. 123-139

WENDELL, C. Baghdâd: *Imago Mundi,* and other foundation-lore. *IJMES* 2 (1971), pp. 99-128.

YOUNG, H.E. Wilkie. Mosul in 1909. *ME studies* 7 (1971), pp. 229-235.

See also II. c. 5. Morony.

See also III. c. Santucci.

See also IX.i Husry.

See also IX. m. Braun.

See also X. b. Forand.

See also XIX. a. Alexander.

See also XXX. c. Bois.

See also XXX. c. Kamal'.

See also XXX. c. Labh.

See also XXXI. j. Djalili.

d ECONOMICS

ADAMS, M.E. Lessons from agrarian reform in Iraq. *Land reform* 1972(1), pp. 56-64.

AHMED, Mohammed M.A., EZZY, J.M. al-. The role of supervised credit in land settlement: case studies of Mikdadiya and Kanaan, Iraq. *Land reform* 1971, (2), pp. 21-28.

ALNASRAWI, Abbas. The changing pattern of Iraq's foreign trade. *MEJ* 25(1971), pp. 481-490

FUAD ZEVAR AGA. Nekotorye itogi agrarnykh preobrazovaniy v Irake. *Arabskie strany, Turtziya, Iran, Afganistan,* 1973, pp. 245-251.

JABBAR, Muḥammad ʿAbdul. Agricultural and irrigation labourers in social and economic life of ʿIrāq during the Umayyad and ʿAbbāsid Caliphates. [An examination of contracts (ʿuqud)]. *IC* 47(1973), pp. 15-30.

KHVESH, Issam Rashid. Novyy zakon ob agrarnoy reforme v Irake. *Arabskie strany, Turtziya, Iran, Afganistan,* 1973, pp. 252-256.

LAMBTON, A.K.S. Co-operative societies in Iraq. *Year-book of agricultural co-operation* 1972, pp. 37-57.

NAJJAR, Mahdi al-; SWARUP, R. Role of agricultural planning in the development of Iraq. *Adab al-rafidain* 2(1971), pp. 55-64.

XXVII IRAQ

PALMER, M. Some political determinants of economic reform: agrarian reform in Iraq. *J. Asian and African studies* [York Univ.] 6(1971), pp. 169-178.

POUROS, T.L. Agricultural co-operation and training in Iraq. *Year-book of agricultural co-operation* 1972, pp. 58-67.

SALMAN, A. Rasul. Le commerce extérieur et développement économique de l'Irak. *Bull. Arab research and studies* 5(1974), pp. 13-23.

XXVIII TURKEY. TURKISH PEOPLES

a GEOGRAPHY OF ASIA MINOR

ABADAN-UNAT, Nermin. Turkish external migration and social mobility. *Turkey; geographic and social perspectives,* ed. by P. Benedict [et al.], 1974, pp. 362-402.

AKÇURA, Tuğrul. Urbanization in Turkey and some examples. *Turkey; geographic and social perspectives,* ed. by P. Benedict [et al.], 1974, pp. 295-326.

ARDEL, Ahmet et KURTER, Ajun. La topographie sous-marine de la Mer de Marmara. *Rev. Geog.Inst., Univ.Istanbul* 13(1970-71), pp. 41-53

ARDOS, Mehmet. Observations sur la structure et la géomorphologie de la Montagne de Hacibaba à l'ouest de Karaman (Anatolie Centrale). *Rev. Geog. Inst., Univ. Istanbul* 14(1972-3), pp. 119-130.

BATES, D. Shepherd becomes farmer. A study of sedentarization and social change in southeastern Turkey. *Turkey; geographic and social perspectives,* ed. by P. Benedict [et al.], 1974, pp. 92-133.

BENEDICT, P. The changing role of provincial towns. A case study from southwestern Turkey. *Turkey; geographic and social perspectives,* ed. by P. Benedict [et al.], 1974, pp. 240-280.

BİLGİN, Turgut Formes volcaniques a l'est de Ceyhan et "Leçe" de Hassa. *Rev.Geog. Inst., Univ.Istanbul* 13(1970-71), pp. 97-111

DÖNMEZ, Yusuf. The position of the Kütahya plain and its surroundings - from the point of climatology. *Rev. Geog. Inst., Univ. Istanbul* 14(1972-3), pp. 131-154.

ELBRUZ, Leyla Sayar. The changing order of socio-economic life--State-induced change. *Turkey; geographic and social perspectives,* ed. by P. Benedict [et al.], 1974, pp. 139-155.

ERİNÇ, Sirri. The Gediz earthquake of 1970. *Rev.Geog.Inst., Univ.Istanbul* 13(1970-71), pp. 67-83

ERINÇ, Sirri. Turkey: outlines of a cultural geography. *Rev. Geog. Inst., Univ. Istanbul* 14(1972-3), pp. 1-23.

GÜRİZ, Adnan. Land ownership in rural settlements. *Turkey; geographic and social perspectives,* ed. by P. Benedict [et al.], 1974, pp. 71-91.

HÜTTEROTH, W.D. The influence of social structure on land division and settlement in inner Anatolia. *Turkey; geographic and social perspectives,* ed. by P. Benedict [et al.], 1974, pp. 19-47.

KIRAY, Mübeccel B. Social change in Çukurova. A comparison of four villages. *Turkey; geographic and social perspectives,* ed. by P. Benedict [et al.], 1974, pp. 179-203.

KOLARS, J. Systems of change in Turkish village agriculture. *Turkey; geographic and social perspectives,* ed. by P. Benedict [et al.], 1974, pp. 204-233.

LOUIS, H. Zur geomorphologie der Umgebung von Ankara. *Ankara Üniversitesi. Dil ve Tarih-Coğrafya Fakültesi Dergisi* 28i-ii (1970), pp. 1-30.

MATER, Barıs. Morphological characteristics and genesis of chromic luvisol in the Elbistan Basin. *Rev. Geog. Inst., Univ. Istanbul* 14(1972-3), pp. 107-118.

NIŞANCI, A. Klimagebiete der Türkei und ihre Niederschlagsverhältnisse. *Atatürk Üniv.Edeb.Fak.araştırma dergisi* 7(1976), pp. 281-292.

SARAN, Nephan. Squatter settlement (gecekondu) problems in Istanbul. *Turkey; geographic and social perspectives,* ed. by P. Benedict [et al.], 1974, pp. 327-361.

SHORTER, F.C. and TEKÇE, Belgin. The demographic determinants of urbanization in Turkey, 1935-1970. *Turkey; geographic and social perspectives,* ed. by P. Benedict [et al.], 1974, pp. 281-294.

SÖZER, A. Necdet. Types d'habitat et repartition géographiques des villages dans le Plaine d'Erzurum. (Anatolie Orientale). *Rev.Geog.Inst., Univ.Istanbul* 13(1970-71), pp. 113-118

SPÄTH, H.-J. Bodenerosion und Bodenfeuchtebilanz in Zentralanatolien--ein Beispiel für bewirtschaftete winterkalte Trockensteppen. *Erdkunde* 29(1975), pp. 81-92.

STEWIG, R. Vergleichende Untersuchung der Einzelhandelsstrukturen der Städte Bursa, Kiel und London/Ontario. *Erdkunde* 28(1974), pp. 18-30.

TOLUN, B. Beitrag zur Stadtbevölkerung von Tekirdağ. *Rev. Geog. Inst. Univ. Istanbul* 14(1972-3), pp. 177-93.

TUGAÇ, Ahmet. Indices of modernization. Erenköy, a case of local initiative. *Turkey; geographic and social perspectives,* ed. by P. Benedict [et al.], 1974, pp. 156-178.

TÜMERTEKİN, Erol. The development of human geography in Turkey. *Turkey; geographic and social perspectives,* ed. by P. Benedict [et al.], 1974, pp. 5-18.

TÜMERTEKİN, Erol. Effects of urban centers on rural settlements. *Rev. Geog. Inst., Univ. Istanbul* 14(1972-3), pp. 97-106.

TÜMERTEKİN, Erol. The growth and changes in the central business districts of Istanbul. *Rev.Geog.Inst.Univ.Istanbul* 12(1968-9), pp. 27-37

TÜMERTEKİN, Erol. A note on the geographic origins of individuals engaged in selected occupation in Istanbul. *Rev. Geog. Inst. Univ. Istanbul* 14(1972-3), pp. 195-202.

TUNÇDİLEK, Necdet. Types of rural settlement and their characteristics. *Turkey; geographic and social perspectives,* ed. by P. Benedict [et al.], 1974, pp. 48-70.

YALÇINLAR, İsmail. La Massif d'Anamur et ses caractères géomorphologiques (Turquie). *Rev.Geog.Inst.Univ.Istanbul* 12(1968-9), pp. 3-16

YALÇINLAR, İsmail Observations geologiques dans l'Antolie Centrale. *Rev.Geog.Inst., Univ.Istanbul* 13(1970-71), pp. 141-156

YALÇINLAR, İsmail. Observations sur les structures et les formes du relief de l'Anatolie Occidentale. *Rev.Geog.Inst. Univ.Istanbul* 12(1968-9), pp. 39-55

YALÇINLAR, İsmail. Structures géologiques de la Chaine du Taurus dans la région de Feke-Saimbeyli. *Rev.Geog.Inst., Univ. Istanbul* 13(1970-71), pp. 55-66

YALÇINLAR, İsmail. Structures géologiques fondamentales de l'Anatolie Orientale. *Rev. Geog. Inst., Univ. Istanbul* 14(1972-3), pp. 25-41.

YALÇINLAR, İsmail. Volcan éteint de Nemrut et sa caldeira (Anatolie de l'Est). *Rev. Geog. Inst. Univ. Istanbul* 14(1972-3), pp. 203-216.

See also XXIX. f. Hütteroth.

b TURKISH PEOPLES: GENERAL. ETHNOLOGY AND HISTORY. OTTOMANS

ALANGU, Tahir. Continuous folkloric relations and mutual elements between Turkey and the Balkan nations: some problems of emigrant folklore. *Boğazici Univ. halkbilimi yilliği* 1974, pp. 9-17.

ANSAY, Tuğrul. Die Eheschliessung der Türken in der Bundesrepublik Deutschland. *WI* 15 (1974), pp. 26-38.

ASWAD, B.C. Visiting patterns among women of the elite in a small Turkish city. *Anthrop. q'ly* 47(1974), pp. 9-27.

BADINY, F.J. Altaic peoples' theocracy. *Proc.27th Int.Cong.Or.1967* (1971), p. 612.

BAŞGÖZ, Ilhan. Earlier references to kukla and karagöz. *Turcica* 3(1971), pp. 9-21.

BAŞGÖZ, İlhan. Folklore studies and nationalism in Turkey. *J. Folklore Inst.* 9(1972), pp. 162-176.

BATES, D.G. Differential access to pasture in a nomadic society: the Yörük of Southeastern Turkey. *J. Asian and African studies* [York Univ.] 7(1972), pp. 48-59.

BATES, D.G. Normative and alternative systems of marriage among the Yörük of Southeastern Turkey. *Anthrop.Q.* 47(1974), pp. 270-287.

BENEDICT, P. The Kabul Günü: structured visiting in an Anatolian provincial town. *Anthrop. q'ly* 47(1974), pp. 28-47.

BLAGOVA, G.F. Iz istorii razvitiya tyurkskikh etnonimov v russkom yazyke. *Vopr. yaz.* 1974(1), pp. 91-107.

BORATAV, Pertev Naili. La littérature populaire turque contemporaine. *Turcica* 5(1975), pp. 47-67.

BORATAV, Pertev Naili. Saya, une fête pastorale des Turcs d'Anatolie et d'Azerbaïdjan. *Turcica* 3(1971), pp. 22-30.

BUSCH, R.C. Over the bounding domains--the limits of kinship and kinship terms in Turkish. *Anthrop. linguistics* 16 (1974), pp. 415-419.

CASSON, R.W. Paired polarity relations in the formal analysis of a Turkish kinship terminology. *Ethnology* 12(1973), pp. 275-297.

CREMERS, W. Schamanistische Überbleibsel in der heutigen anatolischen Folklore. *Turcica* 3(1971), pp. 49-58.

CUISENIER, J. Parenté et organisation sociale dans le domaine turc. *Annales ESC* 27(1972), pp. 923-948.

DAHER, Y. Agricultura Anatolica. Die volkstümlichen landwirtschaftlichen Geräte. Eine wort- und kulturgeschichtliche Untersuchung mit besonderer Berücksichtigung der Türkvölker. *SO* 42 (1970), pp. 162; 43ii, pp. 12.

DANKOFF, R. Kāšjarī on the tribal and kinship organisation of the Turks. *Archiv Ott.* 4(1972), pp. 23-43.

DANKOFF, R. Kāšgarī on the beliefs and superstitions of the Turks. *JAOS* 95 (1975), pp. 68-80.

DÖNMEZER, S. Criminality in a small community of rapid urbanization and industrialization. *Ann.Fac.Droit Istanbul* 22(no.38, 1972), pp. 55-71.

ERDENTUĞ, Nermin. Age groups. *Antropoloji* 2(1964), pp. 1-7.

ERDENTUĞ, Nermin. A comparative ethnological study of the rural societies of Turkey, Iran and Pakistan. *Antropoloji* 3(1965), pp. 7-10.

ERDENTUĞ, Nermin. Cultural change in the Turkish traditional societies. *Antropoloji* 4(1967-8), pp. 81-88.

ERDENTUĞ, Nermin. An ethnological comparison of rural communities in Turkey, Iran and Pakistan. *J. Reg. Cult. Inst.* 5(1972) pp. 85-87.

ERDENTUĞ, Nermin. A few studies of the Chair of Etnology in the Faculty of Letters (Dil ve Tarih-Coğrafya Fakültesi) University of Ankara. *Antropoloji* 2 (1964), pp. 100-104.

ERDENTUĞ, Nermin. The necessity of application of social anthropology on the works of community development in Turkey. *Antropoloji* 3(1965), pp. 11-12.

ERDENTUĞ, Nermin. Some similarities between the Turkish and Japanese cultures. *Antropoloji* 4(1967-8), pp. 65-70.

ERGIL, D. Class relations and the Turkish transformation in historical perspective. *SI* 39(1974), pp. 77-94.

ESIN, Emel. *Tös* and *Moncuk*. Notes on Turkish flag-pole finials. *Central Asiatic J.* 16(1972), pp. 14-36.

FAROOQ, Ghazi M. and TUNCER, Baran. Fertility and economic and social development in Turkey: a cross-sectional and time series study. *Population studies* 28(1974), pp. 263-276.

FIŞEK, Nusret H. The population policy of Turkey. *Int.population conf.* London, 1969, pp. 1394-1406.

FRANZ, E. Beispiele türkischer Volksliedkunst. Drei ausgewählte Liedtexte aus İcadiye. *Der Islam* 52(1975), pp. 85-94.

GEISER, P. and SEVER, Sezer. Social transformation in Turkey: an example of a relation between social interaction and social space. *J. Asian and African studies* [York Univ.] 7(1972), pp. 176-192.

GILLOV, Haluk. Demographic factors on the economic development of Turkey. *Int. population conf.* London, 1969, I, pp. 427-428.

GİRİTLİ, İsmet. Currents in youth movements of Turkey. *Ann.Fac.Droit Istanbul* 20(no.36, 1970), pp. 259-265.

GÖKALP, Altan. *Böle*, "la soeur aînée", les filles de l'exil en Anatolie. *Turcica* 7(1975), pp. 65-72.

GOKALP, C. L'émigration turque en Europe et particulièrement en France. *Population* [Paris] 28(1973), pp. 335-360.

GÖNEY, Süha. Ländliche Dorfhäuser im Mengen-Becken (NW. Anatolien). *Rev. Geog. Inst., Univ. Istanbul* 14(1972-3), pp. 155-176.

GRÖNHAUG, Reidar. Changing community structures and inter-community relationships in Southern Turkey. *Folk* 13(1971), pp. 149-166

GÜRELLİ, N. Urbanization and crime (in Turkey). *Ann.Fac.Droit Istanbul* 22(no.38, 1972), pp. 357-364.

JAGCHID, S. Trade, peace and war between the nomadic Altaics and the agricultural Chinese. *Proc.27th Int.Cong.Or.1967* (1971), pp. 593-594.

JASON, H. and SCHNITZLER, O. The Eberhard-Boratav index of Turkish folk tales in the light of the new revision of Aarne-Thompson's *Types of the folktale. Folklore Research Center stud.* 1(1970), pp. 43-80.

JOHANSON, U. Die guten Sitten beim Essen und Trinken: Bericht von einem Feldforschungspraktikum uber Gastfreundschaft, Konsumptionsnormen und Wirtschaftsdenken im Wandel bei türkischen Gastarbeitern. *Sociologus* 23(1973), pp. 41-70.

KANDIYOTI, D. Social change and social stratification in a Turkish village. *J.peasant stud.* 2(1975), pp. 206-219.

KONONOV, A.N. Istoriya priobreteniya, perevodov, izdaniy i izucheniya sochineniya Abu-l-Gazi "Rodoslovnaya tyurok". *ST* 1971 (1), pp. 3-12.

KOSSWIG, L. Eigentumszeichen (Damga) in Anatolien. *Oriens* 23-24(1974), pp. 333-405

KUDAT, Ayse. Institutional rigidity and individual initiative in marriages of Turkish peasants. *Anthrop.Q.* 47(1974), pp. 288-303.

LEVINE, N. Old culture - new culture: a study of migrants in Ankara, Turkey. *Social forces* 51(1972), pp. 355-368.

XXVIII TURKEY. TURKISH PEOPLES

LEWIS, G. The Saint and the Major General. *Anatol. stud.* 22(1972), pp. 250-253.

LOUIS, H. Die Bevölkerungsverteilung in der Türkei 1965 und ihre Entwicklung seit 1935. *Erdkunde* 26(1972), pp. 161-177.

MAGNARELLA, P.J.; TÜRKDOĞAN, Orhan. Descent affinity and ritual relations in Eastern Turkey. *Amer. Anth.* 75(1973), pp. 1626-1633.

MAGNARELLA, P.J. Turkish townsmen view Apollo. *MEJ* 26(1972) pp. 181-183.

MEEKER, M.E. The great family aghas of Turkey: a study of a changing political culture. *Rural politics and social change in the Middle East,* ed. by R. Antoun and I. Harik, 1972, pp. 237-266.

MITCHELL, W.A. Turkish villages in interior Anatolia and von Thunen's "Isolated State": a comparative analysis. *MEJ* 25(1971), pp. 355-387

MUKHAMED'YAROV, Sh.F. Drevneyshie etnicheskie svyazi narodov Povolzh'ya s Zapadnoy Sibir'yu. *Sprache, Geschichte und Kultur der altaischen Völker,* hrsg. G. Hazai und P. Zieme (XII. PIAC, 1974), pp. 427-438.

NÉMETH, J. Noms ethniques turcs d'origine totémistique. *Studia Turcica, ed. L. Ligeti,* 1971, pp. 349-359

NICOLAS, M. La pêche à Bodrum. *Turcica* 3(1971), pp. 160-180.

NICOLAS, M. Porte-bonheur et devises du chauffeur turc. *Turcica* 5(1975), pp. 40-46.

NIKONOV, V.A. Obychay svyazannykh imen u tyurkoyazychnykh narodov. (Une coutume des populations turkophones: des noms connexes.) *Sov. etn.* 1973(6), pp. 82-89.

NUTKU, Özdemir. The "Nahil": a symbol of fertility in Ottoman festivities. *Ann. Univ. Ankara* 12(1966 - Publ. 1972), pp. 63-71.

OZANKAYA, Özer. Social life in four Anatolian villages. *Ankara Univ. Siyasal Bilgiler Fak. Dergisi* 27iii(1972), pp. 613-633.

POMERANTZEVA, E.V. Yarilki. *Sov. etn.* 1975(3), pp. 127-130.

RITTER, G. Landflucht und Städtewachstum in der Türkei. *Erdkunde* 26(1972), pp. 177-196.

RÓNA-TAS, A. Dream, magic power and divination in the Altaic world. *Acta Or. Hung.* 25(1972), pp. 227-236.

ROUX, J.P. Le lièvre dans la tradition turque. *Turcica* 3(1971), pp. 40-48.

ROUX, J.P. Quelques objets numineux des Turcs et des Mongols. I. Le bonnet et la ceinture. *Turcica* 7(1975), pp. 50-64.

SAATCIOĞLU, Armağan. A biometrical investigation on the three anthropometric characters and their changes according to the socio-economic groups in Turkey. *Antropoloji* 7(1972-3), pp. 175-199.

SCHMITT, G. Wo siedelten nachweislich türkische Stämme im ersten Jahrhundert vor bzw. nach der Zeitenwende? *Acta or. Hung.* 24(1971), pp. 337-358.

SHASTINA, N.P. Mongol and Turkic ethnonyms in the Secret History of the Mongols. *Researches in Altaic languages,* ed. L. Ligeti, 1975, pp. 231-244.

SOLIMAN, Ahmad el-Said. Quelques survivances païennes dans la littérature populaire des Turcs musulmans. *Abr Nahrain* 13(1972-73) pp. 1-15.

SRIKANTAN, K.S. Regional and rural-urban socio-demographic differences in Turkey. *MEJ* 27(1973), pp. 275-300.

STEWIG, R. Versuch einer Auswertung der Reisebeschreibung von Ibn Baṭṭūṭa (nach der englischen Übersetzung von H.A.R. Gibb) zur Bedeutungsdifferenzierung westanatolischer Siedlungen. *Der Islam* 47 (1971), pp. 43-58.

STIRLING, P. Cause, knowledge and change: Turkish village revisited. *Choice and change; essays in honour of Lucy Mair,* 1974, pp. 191-229.

SUZUKI, P. Black American servicemen and Turkish workers in West Germany: two cultural responses to prejudice and discrimination. *Sociologus* 23(1973), pp. 89-94.

TATARZYŃSKA, I. Mesir -- tureckie święto wiosny. *Przegl. or.* 1(93, 1975), pp. 75-77.

TÜMERTEKİN, Erol. Gradual internal migration in Turkey: a test of Ravenstein's hypothesis. *Rev. Geog. Inst., Univ. Istanbul* 13 (1970-71), pp. 157-169

ÜLKEN, Hilmi Ziya. Les origines de la culture nationale en Turquie. *Ann. Univ. Ankara* 12(1966 - Publ. 1972), pp. 47-57.

WALKER, W.S.; UYSAL, Ahmet E. An ancient god in modern Turkey: some aspects of the cult of Hızır. *J. Amer. folklore* 86(1973), pp. 286-289.

WEIKER, W.F. Social sciences in contemporary Turkey. *MESA Bull.* 5ii(1971), pp. 72-82.

YASA, Ibrahim. The "Gecekondu" family. *Ankara Univ. Siyasal Bilgiler Fak. Dergisi* 27iii(1972), pp. 575-584.

YÜCE, Nuri. Eine Variante der Tepegöz-Erzählung aus dem Taurus-Gebirge vom Keşli-Stamm. *Turcica* 3(1971), pp. 31-39.

See also V. m. 2. Esin

See also V. u. 1. Reiche

See also VI. c. Karaev.

See also VII. d. Başgoz.

See also XXIX. jj. Yasa.

See also XXX. b. Korogly

See also XL. a. Blagova.

See also XL. a. Dul'zon.

See also XL. a. Pais

See also XL. aa. Busch.

See also XLI. a. Elçin.

c EARLY TURKS

AALTO, P. Iranian contacts of the Turks in Pre-Islamic times. *Studia Turcica, ed. L. Ligeti,* 1971, pp. 29-37

AALTO, P. Nomen Romanum. *UAJ* 47(1975), pp. 1-9.

ABRAMZON, S.M. Formy sem'i u dotyurkskikh i tyurkskikh plemen Yuzhnoy Sibiri, Semirech'ya i Tyan'-Shanya v drevnosti i srednevekov'e. *Tyurkologicheskiy sbornik* 1972 *(Pamyati P.M. Melioranskogo),* pp. 287-305.

BAZIN, L. Turcs et sogdiens: les enseignements de l'inscription de Bugut (Mongolie). *Mél. ling. É. Benveniste,* 1975, pp. 37-45.

BEŠEVLIEV, V. Aus der Geschichte der Protobulgaren. *Études balkaniques* 6ii (1970), pp. 39-56.

BOMBACI, A. The husbands of Princess Hsien-li Bilgä. *Studia Turcica, ed. L. Ligeti,* 1971, pp. 103-123

BRENTJES, B. Romulus und Remus mit der Wölfin aus Nordtadshikistan. Ein Beitrag zu den byzantinischen-türkischen Beziehungen im 6. Jahrhundert. *Cent.Asiatic J.* 15(1971), pp. 183-185.

CANKOVA-PETKOVA G. A propos de l'histoire de la fortresse bulgare Moundraga. *UAJ* 47(1975), pp. 35-40.

CHARPENTIER, C.J. Three commercial sectors: some structural observations in the Bazaar of Istanbul. *Zeits.f.Ethn.* 99(1974), pp. 224-253.

CHATTERJI, S.K. Hindus and Turks from prehistoric times: India-Central Asia contacts and links: the first phase. *S.K. De memorial vol.,* 1972, pp. 11-29.

CZEGLÉDY, K. On the numerical composition of the ancient Turkish tribal confederations. *Acta Or. Hung.* 25(1972), pp. 275-281.

DIYARBEKIRLI, Nejat. Vestiges de croyances altaïques dans l'art seldjoukide. *Turcica* 3(1971), pp. 59-70.

ECSEDY, H. Tribe and tribal society in the 6th century Turk Empire. *Acta Or. Hung.* 25(1972), pp. 245-262.

GABAIN, A. v. Frühe Zeugen der Scherengitter-Jurte. *Studia Turcica, ed. L. Ligeti,* 1971, pp. 169-173

GRACH, A.D. Voprosy datirovki i semantiki drevnetyrukskikh tamgoobraznykh izobrazheniy Gornogo Kozla. *Tyurkologicheskiy sbornik* 1972 *(Pamyati P.M. Melioranskogo),* pp. 316-333.

HARMATTA, J. Irano-Turcica. *Acta Or. Hung.* 25(1972), pp. 263-273.

KHALIKOV, A. Kh. K voprosu o nachalě tyurkizatzii naseleniya Povolzh'ya i Priural'ya. (Contribution au problème des débuts de la turkisation des régions de Volga et d'Oural.) *Sov.etn.* 1972(1), pp. 100-109.

KÖHALMI, Käthe U. Drei alte innerasiatische Benennungen des Waffengürtels. *Studia Turcica, ed. L. Ligeti,* 1971, pp. 267-279

LIU, Mau-Tsai. Chinas Beziehungen zu den Ost-Türken (T'u-chüeh) im Spiegel kaiserlicher Schreiben. *Oriens Extremus* 21(1974), pp. 1-15.

POTAPOV, L.P. Umay -- bozhestvo drevnikh tyurkov v svete etnograficheskikh dannykh. *Tyurkologicheskiy sbornik* 1972 *(Pamyati P.M. Melioranskogo),* pp. 265-286.

PRAKASH, Buddha. The Turks in ancient Indian history. *Studies in Indo-Asian art and culture,* 1972, pp. 27-38.

SAVINOV, D.G. Etnokul'turnye svyazi naseleniya Sayano-Altaya v drevnetyurkskoe vremya. *Tyurkologicheskiy sbornik* 1972 *(Pamyati P.M. Melioranskogo),* pp. 339-350.

SMIRNOV, A.P. O stolitze gosudarstva volzhskikh bulgar. (A propos de la capitale de l'état des Bulgares sur la Volga.) *Sov. Arkh.* 1972(1), pp. 98-102

TRIFONOV, Yu.I. Ob etnicheskoy prinadlezhnosti pogrebeniy s konem drevnetyurkskogo vremeni (v svyazi s voprosom o strukture pogrebal'nogo abryada tyurkov-tugyu.) *Tyurkologicheskiy sbornik* 1972 *(Pamyati P.M. Melioranskogo),* pp. 351-374.

VÁSÁRY, I. Runiform signs on objects of the Avar period (6th - 8th cc. A.D.). *Acta Or. Hung.* 25(1972), pp. 335-347.

VRYONIS, Speros. Evidence of human sacrifice among early Ottoman Turks. *J.Asian hist.* 5(1971), pp. 140-146.

ZIEME, P. Neue Funde zur Geschichte der Türken in der Mongolei. *Das Altertum* 18(1972), pp. 255-258.

See also XL. c. Stebleva.

d HUNS

DAUNIDOVA, A.V. K voprosu o khunnskikh khudozhestvennuikh bronzakh. (A propos de bronzes artistiques de la culture des Huns.) *Sov. Arkh.* 1971(1), pp. 93-104.

DOERFER, G. Zur Sprache der Hunnen. *Cent. Asiatic J.* 17(1973), pp. 1-50.

HAUSSIG, H.W. Über die Bedeutung der Namen Hunnen und Awaren. *UAJ* 47(1975), pp. 95 103.

LOT-FALCK, E. Le principe de l'*ilbis* et ses rapports avec la fureur meurtrière et le chamanisme. *Sprache, Geschichte und Kultur der altaischen Völker,* hrsg. G. Hazai und P. Zieme (XII. PIAC, 1974), pp. 363-374.

MAENCHEN-HELFEN, Otto J. Iranian names of Huns. *W.B. Henning memorial vol.,* 1970, pp. 272-275.

NEWMAN-PERPER, E. Ancient clues to the Hsiung-nu problem in the light of recently-examined Ch'u Tomb sites. *Proc.27th Int. Cong.Or.1967* (1971), p. 606.

SAMOLIN, W. The art of the European Huns: antecedents and successors. *Proc.27th Int.Cong.Or.1967* (1971), pp. 605-606.

SCHRAMM, G. Hunnen, Pannonier, Germanen. Sprachliche Spuren von Völkerbeziehungen im 5. Jh. n. Chr. *Z.Balkanologie* 11(1975), pp. 71-97.

SEYIDOV, M.A. Zametki o gunnskoy mifologii (po istochnikam VII v.) *Sov. Tyurkologiya* 1970(2), pp. 107-116.

e COMANS

GERAS'KOVA, L.S. Polovetzkaya statua iz s. Chernukhino. *Sov. arkh.* 1974(3), pp. 256-257.

PÁLÓCZI-HORVÁTH, A. L'immigration et l'établissement des Comans en Hongrie. *Acta Or. Hung.* 29(1975), pp. 313-333.

PLETNEVA, S.A. Zhenskaya polovetzkaya statua s rebenkom. *Sov. arkh.* 1974(3), pp. 258-262.

See also XL. t. Makhmutov.

f PECHENEGS

FAKHRUTDINOV, R.G. O stepeni zaselennosti bulgarami territorii sovremennoy Chuvashskoy ASSR. *Voprosy etnogeneza tyurkoyazychnykh narodov Srednego Povolzh'ya* 1971, pp. 175-201.

FARZALIEV, T.A., ABBASOV, I.I. O razvitii azerbaydzhanskoy sovetskoy fol'kloristiki. (On development of the Soviet Azerbaijanian folk-lore science.) *Sov. Tyurkologiya* 1972(5), pp. 115-122.

GYÖRFFY, G. Sur la question de l'établissement des Petchénègues en Europe. *Acta Or. Hung.* 25(1972), pp. 283-292.

KHALIKOVA, E.A. Pogrebel'nyy obryad tankeevskogo mogil'nika (K voprosu ob istokakh naseleniya Volzhskoy Bulgarii IX-X vv.). *Voprosy etnogeneza tyurkoyazychnykh narodov Srednego Povolzh'ya* 1971, pp. 64-93.

KHLEBNIKOVA, T.A. Alekseevskoe gorodishche (K voprosu o svoeobrazii ranne-bolgarskoy kul'tury rayona Nizhnego Prikam'ya). *Voprosy etnogeneza tyurkoyazychnykh narodov Srednego Povolzh'ya* 1971, pp. 156-174.

PETRENKO, A.G. Nekotoruie osobennosti razvitiya zhivotnovodstva I tuis. n.e. u prishlykh plemen Volzhsko-Kamskogo kraya. *Voprosy etnogeneza tyurkoyazychnykh narodov Srednego Povolzh'ya* 1971, pp. 55-63.

STAROSTIN, P.N. Etno-kul'turnye obshchnosti predbulgarskogo vremeni v nizhnem Prikam'e. *Voprosy etnogeneza tyurkoyazychnykh narodov Srednego Povolzh'ya* 1971, pp. 37-54.

TRYJARSKI, E. A Note on the relations between the Pechenegs and Poland. *Studia Turcica, ed. L. Ligeti,* 1971, pp. 461-468

g ALTAI TURKS

BASKAKOV, N.A. Dusha v drevnikh verovaniyakh tyurkov Altaya. (L'âme dans les anciennes croyances des Turks d'Altaï.) *Sov. etn.* 1973(5), pp. 108-113.

LÖRINCZ, L. Parallelen in der mongolischen und altaitürkischen Epik. *Studia Turcica, ed. L. Ligeti,* 1971, pp. 321-330

NOVGORODOVA, E.A. Ethnocultural relations of the tribes of the Mongol Altai (Mongol-Altaic *tergen*). *Researches in Altaic languages,* ed. L. Ligeti, 1975, pp. 195-200.

SAF'YANOVA, A.V. Izmenenie polozheniya zhenshchiny za gody sovetskoy vlasti (Modification de la position sociale de la femme à l'époque soviétique - d'après les données du territoire d'Altaï). *Sov. etn.* 1973(2).

h AZERBAIJANIS

TORCHINSKAYA, E.G. Muzhskaya odezhda azerbaydzhantzev XIX - nachala XX v. po sobraniyu Gosudarstvennogo Muzeye etnografii narodov SSR. *Khozyaystvo i material'naya kul'tura narodov Kavkaza v XIX-XX vv.,* ed. V.K. Gardanov, I, 1971, pp. 136-154.

TROFIMOVA, A.G. Obzor kollektziy odezhdy narodov Azerbaydzhana Gosudarstvennogo muzeya Gruzii im. akad. S.N. Dzhanashina. *Khozyaystvo i material'naya kul'tura narodov Kavkaza v XIX-XX vv.,* ed. V.K. Gardanov, I, 1971, pp. 155-208.

See also XXVIII. b. Boratav.

XXVIII TURKEY. TURKISH PEOPLES

i BASHKIRS

AKHMETSHIN, B.G. Otrazhenie usloviy truda i byta gornorabochikh Bashkirii v predaniyakh i drugikh ustnykh rasskazakh. *Sov. Etn.* 1974(1), pp. 119-124.

j CHUVASH

BUSYGIN, E.P., ZORIN, N.V. Dekorativnoe oformlenie russkogo sel'skogo zhilishcha v chuvashskoy i tatarskoy ASSR. *Sov.etn.* 1974(3), pp. 96-103.

DENISOV, P.V. Etnograficheskoe izuchenie chuvashkogo naroda za gody sovetskoy vlasty. (The ethnographic study of the Chuvashes during the Soviet period.) *Sov.etn.* 1971 vi, pp. 28-37

DZENISKEVICH, G.I. K voprosu o kul'te yerekha u chuvashey *SMAE* 28(1972), pp. 221-236.

EZENKIN, V.S. Ideyno-khudozhestvennye osobennosti tvorchestva M.N. Danilova Chalduna. *Chuvashskiy yazyk, literatura i fol'klor,* I, 1972, pp. 327-352.

IVANOV, I.S. O nekotorykh chertakh obshchnosti poetiki pesen mari i chuvashey. *Chuvashskiy yazyk, literatura i fol'klor,* I, 1972, pp. 414-417.

KRASNOV, Yu.A. Problema proiskhozhdeniya chuvashskogo naroda v svete arkheologicheskikh dannykh. (Problème de la provenance du peuple tchouvache et données archéologiques.) *Sov. arkh.* 1974(3), pp. 112-124.

MIKHAYLOV, M.M. O nekotorykh osobennostyakh chuvashsko-russkogo dvuyazychiya. *Chuvashskiy yazyk, literatura i fol'klor,* I, 1972, pp. 365-370.

SIDOROVA, E.S. Chuvashskiy fol'klor v tvorchestve K.V. Ivanova. *Chuvashskiy yazyk, literatura i fol'klor,* I, 1972, pp. 352-364.

SIDOROVA, E.S. Iz nablyudeniy nad sovremennymi chuvashskimi bytovymi skazkami. *Chuvashskiy yazyk, literatura i fol'klor,* I, 1972, pp. 418-424.

SIDOROVA, E.S. V.S. Razumov i fol'klornyy sbornik "Samana". *Chuvashskiy yazyk, literatura i fol'klor,* I, 1972, pp. 407-414.

k CRIMEAN TATARS

CONSTANTIN, Gh.I. Akhmet Akhaj, der Doppelgänger des Odschas Nasreddin bei den Krim-Tataren. *Turcica* 3(1971), pp. 80-99.

MUZAFAROV, R. Ob izuchenii fol'klora krymskikh tatar. *ST* 1970(6), pp. 110-113.

ROYZENZON, L.I., MEMETOVA, A.S. Sbornik krymskotatarskikh poslovitz i pogovorok. *Proverbium* 24(1974), pp. 953-955.

See also XXXIV. g. Collins.

l KARAKALPAKS.

KAMALOV, S. Osvoboditel'noe dvizhenie karakalpakov v sredine XIX veka. *CAJ* 18(1974), pp. 43-48.

ll KAZAKHS

ARGYNBAEV, Kh. Svad'ba i svadebnye obryady u kazakhov v proshlom i nastoyashchem. *Sov. etn.* 1974(6), pp. 69-77.

BASKAKOV, N.A. Zhilishcha priiliyskikh kazakhov. *Sov.Etn.* 1971(3), pp. 104-115.

BLOMKVIST, E.E. K voprosu o dvuyazychii i tyurkskikh zaimstvovaniyakh v govore "ural'tzev" Amudar'inskogo oazisa. *SMAE* 28(1972), pp. 265-271.

DAKHSHLEYGER, G.F. K istorii ob'edineniya kazakhskikh zemel' v Kazakhskoy SSR. *Sov. etn.* 1974(6), pp. 13-24.

GOLOBUTZKIY, V.A. Zaporozhskaya Sech'. (The Zaporozhe Cossacks.) *Vopr. ist.* 1971(1), pp. 108-121.

GULISASHVILI, B.A. Ladui kazakhskoi narodnoi dombrovoi muzuiki. (Modes in the Kazakh dombra folk music.) *Soobshcheniya AN Gruz.* SSR 61(1), 1971, pp. 249-252.

KÖNIG, W. Der traditionelle Machtapparat der Kasachen. Kolonialer Wandel -- sozialistische Umgestaltung. *Jhb. Mus. Völkerk. Leipzig* 28(1972), pp. 181-191.

KURYLEV, V.P. Materialy po zemledeliyu kazakhov Mangyshlaka v kontze XIX - nachale XX v. *Sov. etn.* 1975(3), pp. 98-107.

REYCHMAN, J. Nowe prace o zainteresowaniach polskich zesłańców folklorem Kazachskim w XIX wieku. *Przegl.or.* 4(80), 1971, pp. 392-396.

SAGUCHI, Toru. The ethnic groups of the Great Horde Kazakhs. *Proc.27th Int.Cong. Or.1967* (1971), p. 615.

TÜRKDOĞAN, Orhan. L'Installation des immigrants Kazaks dans un bourg turc. *UAJ* 43(1971), pp. 107-115.

VINOGRADOV, V.B., MAGOMADOVA, T.S. O meste pervonachal'nogo rasseleniya grebenskikh kazakov. (On the original idea of settlement of the Greben Cossacks). *Sov. etn.* 1972(3), pp. 31-42.

VOSTROV, V.V., DAKHSHLEYGER, G.F., KAUANOVA, Kh. Etnograficheskoe izuchenie kazakhskogo naroda. (The ethnographic study of the Kazakh people). *Sov. etn.* 1972(4), pp. 34-41.

See also XXIX. g. Granstrem.

n KIRGHIZES

ABRAMZON, S.M., SIMAKOV, G.N., FIRSHTEYN, L.A. Nov' kirgizskogo sela. *Sov.etn.* 1974(5), pp. 29-45.

MOKRYNIN, V.P. Torgovye svyazi Kirgizistana (VI-X vv.). *Arabo-persidskie istochniki o tyurkskikh narodakh*, 1973, pp. 99-122.

TUMANOVICH, N.N. Sochinenie Mirzy Mukhammed-Khaydera "Ta'rikh-i Rashidi" kak istochnik po istorii kirgizov i Kirgizii. *Arabo-persidskie istochniki o tyurkskikh narodakh*, 1973, pp. 60-98.

See also XXVIII. v. Kyzlasov.

o OGUZ

AGADZHANOV, S.G. Oguzskie plemena Sredney Azii IX-XIII vv. (istoriko-etnograficheskiy ocherk). *Strany i narody Vostoka pod obshchey red. D.A. Ol'derogge*, X, 1971, pp. 179-193.

GOLDEN, P.B. The migrations of the Oǧuz. *Archiv Ott.* 4(1972), pp. 45-84.

MUKHAMEDOVA, Z.B. Oguzsko-turkmenskie etnotoponimy. *Sprache, Geschichte und Kultur der altaischen Völker*, hrsg. G. Hazai und P. Zieme (XII. PIAC, 1974), pp. 439-446.

See also XL. bb. Korkmaz.

p TATARS

DROBIZHEVA, L.M. Sotzial'no-kul'turnye osobennosti lichnosti i natzional'nye ustanovki (po materialam issledovaniy v Tatarskoy ASSR). (Social-cultural personality traits and nationality attitudes: on data from the Tatar Autonomous Soviet Socialist Republic.) *Sov.Etn.* 1971(3), pp. 3-15.

KANAPACHI, M. 'Pommiki arabska-bielaruskaj piśmiennaści', *Niva*, 20, Bialystok, 1963, pp. 3, 5. [J.Byeloruss.stud. 2 (1970), p. 167, f.n. 39]

KAZAKOV, E.P. Pogrebal'nyy inventar' tankeevskogo mogil'nika. *Voprosy etnogeneza tyurkoyazychnykh narodov Srednego Povolzh'ya* 1971, pp. 94-155.

KHALIKOV, A.Kh. Istoki formirovaniya tyurkoyazychnykh narodov Povolzh'ya i Priural'ya. *Voprosy etnogeneza tyurkoyazychnykh narodov Srednego Povolzh'ya* 1971, pp. 7-36.

MEREDITH-OWENS, G.M. and NADSON, A. The Byelorussian Tartars and their writings. *J.Byelorussian studies* 2(1970), pp. 141-176. [Offprint in SOAS]

SERRUYS, H. Yellow Hairs and Red Hats in Mongolia. *Central Asiatic J.* 15 (1971), pp. 131-155.

TOMILOV, N.A. Sovremennye etnicheskie protzessy u tatar gorodov zapadnoy Sibiri. (Processus ethniqués modernes chez les Tartares des villes de la Sibérie Occidentale.) *Sov. etn.* 1972(6), pp. 87-97.

ZAJACZKOWSKI, A. 'Tak zwany chamaił tatarski ze zbioru rekopisów w Warszawie'. *Sprawozdania z czynności i posiedzeń Polskiej Akademii Umiejetności*, LII, 4, Cracow, 1952, pp. 302-313. [J. Byeloruss. stud. 2(1970), p. 167, f.n. 38]

See also XXVIII. j. Busygin, Zorin.

q TURCOMANS

ANNAKLYCHEV, Sh. K istorii formirovaniya rabochego klassa Turkmenistana. *Sov.etn.* 1974(5), pp. 17-28.

BRENTJES, B. Zur Herkunft der ersten Ackerbauervölker Turkmeniens. *Cent. Asiatic J.* 15(1971), pp. 186-191.

IRONS, W. Nomadism as a political adaptation: the case of Yomut Turkmen. *Amer.ethnol.* 1 (1974), pp. 635-658.

MARKOV, G.E. Die Turkmenen der Oase von Bacharden. *Jhb. Mus. Völkerkunde Leipzig* 29(1973), pp. 137-152.

ORAZOV, A. Skotovodcheskie obryady u turkmen dolin Sumbara i Chendyra. *Sov.etn.* 1974(2), pp. 100-105.

SMECHKO, T.N. Kharakter zhivotnovodcheskogo khozyaystva u Turkmen Khorezma. (Features of animal husbandry among the Khorezm Turkmens.) *Sov.etn.* 1971vi, pp. 45-53

VASIL'EVA, G.P. Sovremennoe sostoyanie narodnogo dekorativno-prikladnogo iskusstva turkmen. *Sov.etn.* 1974(5), pp. 60-73.

r UIGHURS

GABAIN, A. v. Die Qočo-Uiguren und die nationalen Minderheiten. *Sprache, Geschichte und Kultur der altaischen Völker*, hrsg. G. Hazai und P. Zieme, 1974, pp. 241-249.

ZIEME, P. Die Uiguren und ihre Beziehungen zu China. *Central Asiatic J.* 17(1973), pp. 282-293.

ZIEME, P. Zur buddhistischen Stabreimdichtung der alten Uiguren. *Acta Or. Hung.* 29(1975), pp. 187-211.

s UZBEKS

BASILOV, V.N. Tashmat-bola. *Sov. etn.* 1975(5), pp. 112-124.

BATTERSBY, H.R. A survey of Uzbek settlement, with regard to some economic and shelter changes, in the Khwarizm Khiva oasis, North to the delta of the Amu Darya, based on Russian ethnographic reports. *Tarih araştırmaları dergisi* 7(1969), pp. 17-32.

LAUDE-CIRTAUTAS, I. Uzbek female folk healers. *Researches in Altaic languages*, ed. L. Ligeti, 1975, pp. 91-98.

LOBACHEVA, N.P. O protzesse formirovaniya novoy semeynoy obryadnosti (po materialam Uzbekistana). (Du processus de formation des nouveaux rites familiaux (à l'exemple de l'Ouzbékistan).) *Sov.etn.* 1972(1), pp. 3-13.

SNESAREV, G.P. Tri khorezmskie legendy v svete demonologicheskikh predstavleniy. (Trois légendes khwarezmiennes à la lumière des notions démonologiques.) *Sov. etn.* 1973(1), pp. 48-59.

TASHBAEVA, T. Iz istorii arendy (izhora) i tovarishchestva (shirkat) v sel'skom khozyaystve dorevolyutzionnogo Uzbekistana. *Sov. etn.* 1975(3), pp. 109-114.

TOLSTOVA, L.S. Drevnye motivy v fol'klore uzbekov yuzhnogo Khorezma. (Les motifs anciens dans le folklore des Uzbek du Khwarism du Sud). *Sov. etn.* 1973(2), pp. 25-31.

USMANOV, Arif. Nekotorye svedeniya ob uzbekakh Afganistana. *CAJ* 19(1975), pp. 220-226.

VASIL'EVA, G.P. Turkmenskie zhenskie ukrasheniya. *Sov. etn.* 1973(3), pp. 90-98.

See also I. b. 3. Nuraliev.

See also XXX. e. Pestryakov.

See also XXXIII. b. Franz.

t YAKUTS

DOLGIKH, B.O. Proiskhozhdenie Dolgan. *Sibirskiy etnog.sbornik* 5(1963), pp. 92-141.

EREMEEV, V.P. I.A. Khudyakov i yakutskiy fol'klor. *ST* 1973(3), pp. 70-73.

IVANOV, E.F. "Opisanie Yakutov" Ya. I. Lindenau. *Sov.Etn.* 1971(3), pp. 89-95.

IVANOV, S.V. Starinnyy yakutskiy obryad, svyazannyy s rozhdeniem rebenka. *SMAE* 27 (1971), pp. 142-149

KUCHINSKIY, A. Opisanie Sibiri XVIII v. (Materialy L. Senitzkogo o sibirskikh aborigenakh i ikh kul'ture). (Description de la Sibérie au XVIIIe siècle (matériaux de L. Senicki concernant les aborigènes sibériens et leur culture).) *Sov.etn.* 1972(1), pp. 31-38.

LOT-FALCK, E. Psychopathes et chamans yakoutes. *Échanges et communications. Mélanges C. Lévi-Strauss* I, 1970, pp. 115-129.

LOT-FALCK, E. Ütügän chez les Jakut. *Researches in Altaic languages*, ed. L. Ligeti, 1975, pp. 127-135.

u EUROPEAN TURKS

AHMET-NAGI, Ali Geafer. Notes concernant le folklore de la population tatare de la République socialiste de Roumanie. *Studia et acta or.* 8(1971), pp. 145-173.

ALEKSEEV, V.P. Ocherk proiskhozhdeniya tyurkskikh narodov vostochnoy Evropui v svete dannykh kraniologii. *Voprosy etnogeneza tyurkoyazychnykh narodov Srednego Povolzh'ya* 1971, pp. 232-271.

CORDUN, V. Les saints thaumaturges d'Ada Kaleh. *Turcica* 3(1971), pp. 100-115.

DYKER, D.A. The ethnic Muslims of Bosnia - some basic socio-economic data. *Slav.& E. Eur.Rev.* 50(1972), pp. 238-256

FILIPOVIĆ, Milenko. Orijentalna komponenta u narodnoj kulturi Južnih Slovena. (Orientalische Komponente in der Volkskultur der Südslaven.) *Prilozi Or.Fil.Ist.* 16-17 (1966-7), pp. 101-116

KANAPACKI. Pomniki arabska-bielaruskaj piśmiennaści. *Niva* 20(1963), pp. 3, 5. [*J.Byeloruss.stud.* 2(1970), p. 167, f.n. 39.]

KOLEVA, E. Historisch-demographische Angaben über die Bevölkerung des Plovdiver Gebietes in der Zeit der Türkenherrschaft. *Jhb.Mus.Völkerk.Leipzig* 30(1975), pp. 51-60.

LOCKWOOD, W.G. Converts and consanguinity: the social organization of Moslem Slavs in Western Bosnia. *Ethnology* [*Pittsburg*] 11(1972), pp. 55-79.

MÁNDOKY, E. Chants *šïng* des Tatars de la Dobroudja recueillis en Bulgarie. *Studia Turcica, ed. L. Ligeti,* 1971, pp. 331-348

MARUNEVICH, M.V. Nekotorye osobennosti razvitiya narodnogo zhilishcha gagauzov v XIX i nachale XX veka. *Sov. etn.* 1975(5), pp. 82-95.

MEREDITH-OWENS, G.M. and NADSON. A. The Byelorussian Tartars and their writings. *J.Byelorussian studies* 2(1970), pp. 141-176. [Offprint in SOAS]

POKROVSKAYA, L.A. Musul'manskie elementy v sisteme khristianskoy religioznoy terminologii gagauzov. *Sov.etn.* 1974(1), pp. 139-144.

SEREBRYAKOVA, M.N. Formy sovremennoy sem'i v sel'skikh rayonakh Tzentral'noy Anatolii. *Sov.etn.* 1974(1), pp. 151-157.

SULIŢEANU, Gh. La musique des "Şiñ". *Studia et acta or.* 8(1971), pp. 175-198.

SULITEANU, G. Le *n'demez,* une ancienne coutume de travail collectif chez les Tatars de Dobroudja. *Turcica* 4(1972), pp. 78-102.

TRYJARSKI, E. The tamgas of the Turkic tribes from Bulgaria. *UAJ* 47(1975), pp. 189-200.

XXVIII TURKEY. TURKISH PEOPLES

ZAJACZKOWSKI, A. Tak zwany chamaił tatarski ze zbioru rękopisów w Warszawie. *Sprawozdania z czynności i posiedzeń Polskiej Akademii Umiejętności* LII, 1952, pp. 302-313. [*J.Byeloruss.stud.* 2(1970), p. 167, f.n. 38.]

ZAJĄCZKOWSKI, W. K etnogenezu gagauzov. *Folia Or.* 15(1974), pp. 77-86.

ZAJĄCZKOWSKI, W. Türkische Vierzeiler-*Māni* aus Bulgarien. *Folia or.* 14(1972-73), pp. 119-153.

See also XL. k. Guboglo.

v OTHERS

BORGOYAKOV, M.I. Skifsko-tyurkskie (khakasskie) etnograficheskie i fol'klornye paralleli. *NAA* 1975(6), pp. 111-120.

D'YAKONOVA, V.P. Tzam u tuvintzev. *SMAE* 27(1971), pp. 113-129

GUSEYNOV, R.A. Tyurkskie etnicheskie gruppy XI-XII vv. v Zakavkaz'e. *Tyurkologicheskiy sbornik* 1972 *(Pamyati P.M. Melioranskogo)*, pp. 375-381.

KYZLASOV, L.R. Eshche raz o terminakh "khakas" i "kyrgyz". (Once again about the terms "Khakass" and "Kirghiz".) *Sov.Etn.* 1971(3), pp. 59-67.

MASTEPANOV, S.D. O sobiranii i publikatzii polovitz i pogovorok Kabardino-Balkarii. Bibliograficheskiy obzor. *Proverbium* 12 (1971), pp. 312-328.

MEEKER, M.E. The Black Sea Turks: some aspects of their ethnic and cultural background. *IJMES* 2(1971), pp. 318-345.

POMISHIN, S.B. O transportnom ispol'zovanii olenya Tofalarami. (De l'emploi de la renne pour le transport des biens par les Tofalar.) *Sov.etn.* 5(1971), pp. 128-131.

SHAMANOV, I.M. Narodny kalendar' karachaevtzev. (Le calendrier populaire des Karatchaïs.) *Sov.Etn.* 1971(5), pp. 108-117.

TAUBE, E. Izuchenie fol'klora v tuvintzev Mongol'skoy Narodnoy Respubliki. *Sov. etn.* 1975(5), pp. 106-111.

TAUBE, E. Das Kastrierfest bei den Cengel-Tuwinern. *Asien in Vergangenheit und Gegenwart,* 1974, pp. 443-457.

See also XXX. d. Kaloev

See XL. c. Ungvitzkaya.

See also XL. d. Sikaliev

XXIX TURKEY: HISTORY. CYPRUS

a SELJUKS

BAŞTAV, Şerif. La bataille rangée de Malazgirt et Romain Diogène. *Cultura Turcica* 8-10(1971-73), pp. 132-152.

BEYLIS, V.M. Iz nablyudeniy nad tekstom i terminologiey sbornika rasskazov, stikhov i pisem Mas'uda ibn Namdara (ok.1111g.). *Pis'mennye pamyatniki Vostoka* 1968, pp. 17-31.

BEYLIS, V.M. Iz nablyudeniy nad tekstom Mas'ūda ibn Nāmdāra. II. *Pis'mennye pamyatniki Vostoka* 1970, pp. 5-44.

BULLIET, R.W. Numismatic evidence for the relationship between Ṭughril Beg and Chaghrī Beg. *Near Eastern numismatics ... Studies in honor of G.C. Miles,* 1974, pp. 289-296.

CAHEN, C. Questions d'histoire de la province de Kastamonu au XIIIe siècle. *Selçuklu araştırmaları dergisi* 3(1971), pp. 145-158.

GUSEYNOV, R.A. Iz istorii otnosheniy Vizantii s sel'dzhukami (po siriyskim istochnikam). (A propos des relations entre Byzance et Seldjouks (d'après les sources syriaques).) *Pal.Sb.* 23(86, 1971), pp. 156-167.

JANSSENS, E. La bataille de Mantzikert (1071) selon Michel Attaliate. *Ann. Inst. Phil. Hist. Or.* 20(1968-72), pp. 291-304.

KÖYMEN, M.A. The importance of Malazgirt victory with special reference to Iran and Turkey. *J.Reg.Cult.Inst.* 5i(1972), pp. 5-12

LAMBTON, A.K.S. Aspects of Saljūq-Ghuzz settlement in Persia. *Islamic civilization,* 1973, pp. 105-125.

LUTHER, K.A. Rāvandī's report on the administrative changes of Muḥammad Janān Pahlavān. *Iran and Islam, in memory of V. Minorsky,* 1971, pp. 393-406

MAKDISI, G. Les rapports entre Calife et Sultân ā l'époque Saljûqide. *IJMES* 6(1975), pp. 228-236.

MATUZ, J. Der Niedergang der anatolischen Seldschuken: die Entscheidungsschlacht am Kösedağ. *Central Asiatic J.* 17(1973), pp. 180-199.

MELIKOFF, I. Gazı Melik Danışmend et la conquête de Sivas. *Selçuklu araştırmaları dergisi* 4(1975), pp. 187-195.

NAGEL, T. Über die Ursprünge der Religionspolitik der ersten seldschukischen Sultane. *XVIII. Deutscher Orientalistentag 1972: Vorträge*, pp. 241-248.

SCHNYDER, R. Political centres and artistic powers in Saljūq Iran; problems of transition. *Islamic civilization*, ed. D.S. Richards, 1973, pp. 201-209.

SELJUQUE, Affan. Saljuqid history and the contemporary poets. *J.Pak.Hist.Soc.* 20 (1972), pp. 65-73.

TANKUT, Gönül. Exterior space concept in medieval Anatolian Seljuk town. *Proc. 27th Int.Cong.Or.1967* (1971), pp. 227-228

VISMARA, G. Le relazioni dell'Impero con gli emirati selgiuchici nel corso del secolo decimoquarto. *Byzantinische Forschungen* 3(1971), pp. 210-221.

ZAMIR, Monika Rowšan. Malekšāh, Al-Moqtadi and Nezām ol-Molk. *J.Regional Cult.Inst.* 7(1974), pp. 121-126.

See also V. b. *Turkey*. Kuban.

See also VIII. d. *Turkey*.

See also IX. a. Potzkhveriya.

See also XIX. c. Scanlon.

See also XXXIV. h. Guzman.

b EMIRATES

EGLAR, Z. and MAGNARELLA, P.J. A view of social classes in the eleventh century Karakhanid State. *Anthropos* 66(1971), pp. 232-238.

GRIGNASCHI, M. La monarchie karakhanide de Kachgar et les relations de dépendance personnelle dans le "Kutadğubilig (La science qui donne le bonheur) de Yūsuf Ḫass Hâcib. *Recueils Soc. Jean Bodin* 20(1970), pp. 515-626.

GUSEYNOV, R.A. Titulatura i tamga il'-degizidov (iz istorii feodal'noy simboliki i atributiki XII v.) *Sov.Tyurkologiya* 1970(4), pp. 87-93.

c OTTOMANS: GENERAL

AHMAD, Syed Riaz. Some reflections in the modernisation of civil bureaucracy in Turkey. *J.Univ.Peshawar* 15(1973), pp. 13-20.

AIRAS, P. Probleme des türkischen Kriegszwecks. Westeuropäische Auffassungen nach der grossen osmanischen Expansion. *Tarih araştırmaları dergisi* 7(1969), pp. 33-47.

ALEXANDRESCU-DERSCA BULGARU, M.M. Dimitrie Cantemir, istoric al Imperiului otoman. *Studii. Revistă de istorie* 26(1973), pp. 971-989.

ALTUĞ, Yılmaz. Legal rules concerning land tenure in the Ottoman Empire. *Ann.Fac.Droit Istanbul* 18(1968), pp. 153-169.

ARMBRUSTER, A. Jakob Unrests Ungarische Chronik. *RRH* 13(1974), pp. 473-508.

BAER, G. The structure of Turkish guilds and its significance for Ottoman social history. *Proc.Israel Acad.* 4(1969-70), pp. 176-196.

BALIĆ, Smail. Die Kultur der Osmanen. *Biblos* 20(1971), pp. 87-102.

BĀZARGĀN, F. The impact of the ancient culture of Turkey on her national culture. *J. Reg.Cult.Inst.* 7i(1974), pp. 53-57.

BELDICEANU-STEINHERR, I. A propos d'un ouvrage sur la polémique ottomane contre les Safawides. *REI* 39(1971), pp. 395-400.

BERLIN, C. A sixteenth-century Hebrew chronicle of the Ottoman Empire: the *Seder Eliyahu Zuta* of Elijah Capsali and its message. *Studies in Jewish bibliography, history and literature in honor of I. Edward Kiev*. Ed. C. Berlin. New York, Ktav Publishing House, 1971. pp. 21-44.

BEROV, L. Changes in price conditions in trade between Turkey and Europe in the 16th-19th century. *Etudes balkaniques* 10ii-iii (1974), pp. 168-178.

BREEBAART, D.A. Miscellanea: the Fütüvvetnāme-i kebīr. A manual on Turkish guilds. *JESHO* 15(1972), pp. 203-215.

BULLIET, R.W. The Shaikh Al-Islam and the evolution of Islamic society. *SI* 35(1972), pp. 53-67.

ERGIL, Doğu. The political forces behind secularism and Islamic conservatism in Turkey. *Islamic studies* 14(1975), pp. 55-64.

ERGIL, Doğu. Secularization as class conflict: the Turkish example. *Asian affairs* 62(N.S.6, 1973), pp. 69-80.

FISHER, A.W. Les rapports entre l'empire Ottoman et la Crimée. L'aspect financier. *Cah. du monde russe et sov.* 13(1972), pp. 368-381.

GABAIN, A.v. Sinologie im Interesse der türkischen Geschichtsforschung. *UAJ* 45 (1973), pp. 261-263.

GÖKBİLGİN, Tayyib. L'empire ottoman: formation, évolution, disparition. *Recueils Soc.Jean Bodin* 31(1973), pp. 555-564.

HADŽIBEGIĆ, Hamid. Turetzkie pravovye pamyatniki kak istoricheskiy istochnik. (Actes legislatifs turcs en tant que sources historiques.) *Fontes orientales* ... curavit A.S. Tveritinova, I, 1964, pp. 67-75.

HALE, W. Anglo-Turkish relations: a historical conspectus. *Dis politika* liii(1971), pp. 140-150.

HESS, A.C. The battle of Lepanto and its place in Mediterranean history. *Past and Present* 52(1972), pp. 53-73.

HOURANI, A. The Ottoman background of the modern Middle East. *The Ottoman State and its place in World History,* ed. by Kemal H. Karpat, 1974, pp. 61-78.

ILIESCU, O. Le montant du tribut payé par Byzance à l'Empire ottoman en 1379 et 1424. *Rev.ét.sud-est eur.* 9(1971), pp. 427-432.

INALCIK, Halil. Capital formation in the Ottoman Empire. *J.econ.hist.* 29(1969), pp. 97-140.

INALCIK, H. L'Empire ottoman. *Actes I. Cong. int. ét. balkan. et sud-est europ.* III (1969), pp. 75-104.

INALCIK, Halil. The periods of development of the idea of republic in Turkey. *Cultura Turcica* 8-10(1971-73), pp. 5-9.

ISSAWI, C. The Ottoman Empire in the European economy, 1600-1914. Some observations and many questions. *The Ottoman State and its place in World History,* ed. by Kemal H. Karpat, 1974, pp. 107-117.

IZEDDIN, M. Supplices et tragédies de palais sous les sultans ottomans. *Orient* 49-50 (1969), pp. 27-44

KABRDA, J. Turetzkie istochniki po istorii pravoslavnoy tzerkvi v osmanskoy imperii. (Les sources turques relatives a l'histoire de l'église orthodoxe dans l'Empire Ottoman.) *Fontes orientales... curavit A.S. Tveritinova* II, 1969, pp. 172-179.

KAFÉ, E. Le mythe turc et son declin dans les relations de voyage des européens de la Renaissance. *Oriens* 21-22(1968-69), pp. 159-195.

KAPPERT, P., KELLNER, B., und WURM, H. Dissertationen zu Geschichte und Kultur des Osmanischen Reiches, angenommen an deutschen, österreichischen und schweizerischen Universitäten seit 1945. *Der Islam* 49(1972), pp. 110-119.

KARPAT, Kemal H. The stages of Ottoman History: a structural comparative approach. Comment by C.A.O. van Nieuwenhuijze. *The Ottoman State and its place in World History,* ed. by Kemal H. Karpat, 1974, pp. 79-106.

KARPAT, Kemal H. The transformation of the Ottoman state, 1789-1908. *IJMES* 3(1972), pp. 243-281.

KISSLING, H.J. "Logistisches" zur frühosmanischen Heeresgeschichte. *WI* 15(1974), pp. 85-95.

KOPČAN, V. Bemerkungen zur Benutzung der europäischen Quellen in der osmanischen Geschichtsschreibung. *Asian and African studies* [Bratislava] 11(1975), pp. 147-160.

KORTEPETER, C.M. The Islamic-Ottoman social structure: the quest for a model of Ottoman history. *Near Eastern round table* 1967-68, ed. by R. Bayly Winder, pp. 1-40.

KORTEPETER, C.M. The structure of the Ottoman State as a model for the study of the history and politics of the Middle East. *Proc.27th Int.Cong.Or.1967* (1971), pp. 213-215.

KREISER, K. Zur inneren Gliederung der osmanischen Stadt. *XVIII. Deutscher Orientalistentag 1972: Vorträge,* pp. 198-212.

KREUTEL, R.F. Beiträge zur Textinterpretation der *Menâqyb-y Sulṭan Bâjezid Hân b. Meḥmed Hân.* *Der Islam* 47(1971), pp. 278-285.

MCNEILL, W.H. The Ottoman Empire in world history. Comment by A.C. Hess. *The Ottoman State and its place in World History,* ed. by Kemal H. Karpat, 1974, pp. 34-50.

MARDIN, Şerif. Center-periphery relations: a key to Turkish politics. *Daedalus* 102i (1973), pp. 169-190.

MATUZ, J. A propos d'une contribution bibliographique pour servir les études ottomanes historiques. (Hans Georg Majer, Osmanistische Nachträge zum INDEX ISLAMICUS (1906-1965), dans: Südostforschungen, XXVII (1968), pp. 242-291). *OLZ* 68(1973), cols. 449-451.

MATUZ, J. Fragen der osmanisch-türkischen Quellenkunde. *OLZ* 67(1972), pp. 229-237.

MATUZ, J. Zur osmanischen Diplomatik. *OLZ* 70(1975), pp. 118-130.

MEINARDUS, O.F.A. Testimonies to the economic vitality of Balat, the medieval Miletus. *Belleten T.T.K.* 37(no.147,1973), pp. 289-296.

MÉNAGE, V.L. Another text of Uruč's Ottoman chronicle. *Der Islam* 47(1971), pp. 273-277.

PARRY, V.J. La Manière de combattre. [In English.] *War, technology and society in the Middle East,* ed. V.J. Parry and M.E. Yapp, 1975, pp. 218-256.

PERTUSI, A. I primi studi in Occidente sull'origine e la potenza dei Turchi. *Studi Veneziani* 12(1970), pp. 465-552

SADIQ, Mohammad. Islam and the Turkish transformation. *India and contemporary Islam,* ed. S.T. Lokhandwalla, 1971, pp. 285-290.

ST. CLAIR, A.N. Türkengefahr. *Islamic art in the Metropolitan Museum of Art*, ed. R. Ettinghausen, 1972, pp. 315-334.

SCHAENDLINGER, A.C. Die Probleme der Redaktionen der Chronik des Ibrāhīm Pečevī (Pečuylu). *WZKM* 63-64(1972), pp. 176-186.

SHAW, Ezel Kural. The double veil: travelers' views of the Ottoman Empire, sixteenth through eighteenth centuries. *English and continental views of the Ottoman Empire, 1500-1800*, 1972, pp. 3-29.

STAJNOVA, M. Fonction et emploi de l' expression "Bir akçe ve bir habbe" (pas d'akçe, pas un seul grain) dans quelques formules finales des documents officiels osmano-turcs. *Études balkaniques* 1972(2), pp. 110-114.

SZYLIOWICZ, J.S. Students and politics in Turkey: a historical perspective. *Proc. 27th Int.Cong.Or.1967* (1971), pp. 293-294.

TAPPE, E.D. The Skene family in South-East Europe. *Rev. ét. sud-est eur.* 10(1972), pp. 581-584.

TEKELI, Ilhan. On institutionalized external relations of cities in the Ottoman Empire - a settlement models approach. *Études balkaniques* 1972(2), pp. 49-72.

TOYNBEE, A.J. The Ottoman Empire's place in world history. Comment by J.W. Barker. *The Ottoman State and its place in World History*, ed. by Kemal H. Karpat, 1974, pp. 15-33.

TÜNCEL, Bedreddin. L'influence des "Lumières" sur l'Empire Ottoman. *Turcica* 2(1970), pp. 165-177.

TÜRKKAN, Oğuz R. On the Turkish presence in the Americas before Columbus. *Cultura Turcica* 8-10(1971-73), pp. 157-173.

TVERITINOVA, A.S. Lexical material as a source of studying agricultural traditions of the Ottoman empire. *Research in Altaic languages*, ed. L. Ligeti, 1975, pp. 307-314.

TVERITINOVA, A.S. O turetzkikh dokumentalnuikh materialakh v rukopisnuikh kollektziyakh Leningrada. *Actes I. Cong. int. ét. balkan. et sud-est europ.* III (1969), pp. 431-436.

TVERITINOVA, A.S. V.D. Smirnov - istorik Turtzii. *ST* 1971(4), pp. 105-114.

ÜNVER, Süheyl. The history of tulips in Turkey. *Vakıflar dergisi* 9(1971), pp. 271-276.

VESELA, Z. The conditions for the emergence of capitalism in the central Osman Empire and the effect of European penetration. *The East under Western impact* (Dissertationes Orientales 17, 1969), pp. 57-65.

VESELÝ, R. Die Hauptprobleme der Diplomatik arabischer Privaturkunden aus dem spätmittelalterlichen Ägypten. *Arch. or.* 40(1972), pp. 312-343.

VRYONIS, Sp. Byzantine and Turkish societies and their sources of manpower. *War, technology and society in the Middle East*, ed. V.J. Parry and M.E. Yapp, 1975, pp. 125-152.

VRYONIS, Sp. Religious change and continuity in the Balkans and Anatolia from fourteenth through the sixteenth century. *Islam and cultural change in the Middle Ages*, ed. Sp. Vryonis, Jr., 1975, pp. 127-140.

YURDAYDIN, Hüseyin G. An Ottoman historian of the XVIth century: Naṣūḥ al-Maṭrākī and his *Beyān-i menāzil-i sefer-i 'irāḳayn* and its importance for some 'Irāqī cities. *Turcica* 7(1975), pp. 179-187.

See also XXVI. c. Jalabert.

See also XXXI. a. Perry.

See also XXXIV. g. Desaive.

d OTTOMAN EMPIRE IN EUROPE

General

ARATÓ, E. The effect of international politics and external forces on the national liberation movement of the Balkan peoples in the 19th century. *Actes I. Cong. int. ét. balkan. et sud-est europ.* IV (1969), pp. 737-748.

BEROV, L. Problèmes de la métrologie dans les territoires balkaniques à l'époque de la domonation ottomane (XVe-XIXe ss.) *Etudes balkaniques* 1975(2), pp. 22-39.

BEŠEVLIEV, B. Ein neuer Beitrag zur Kartographie der Balkanhalbinsel. *Etudes Balkaniques* 9(1973) (1), pp. 62-66.

CVETKOVA, B. Quelques problèmes du féodalisme ottoman à l'époque du XVIe s. au XVIIIe s. *Actes I. Cong. int. ét. balkan. et sud-est europ.* III (1969), pp. 709-720.

DARBINIAN, M.O. Simeon Lekhatzi o stranakh yugo-vostochnoy Evropy. (Le récit de Siméon Lehazi sur les pays de l'Europe du Sud-Est.) *Fontes orientales ...* curavit A.S. Tveritinova, I, 1964, pp. 253-275.

DONTAS, D. Russian policy and the Balkan Federation of 1867. *Actes I. Cong. int. ét. balkan. et sud-est europ.* IV (1969), p. 359.

DOSMYAN, I.S. Balkanskiy vopros v period venskogo kongressa 1814-1815 gg. *Études balkaniques* 7i(1971), pp. 57-75.

DUBOVATZ, I. Dimitriy Tutzovich i revolyutzionnaya perspektiva na Balkanakh. *Actes I. Cong. int. ét. balkan. et sud-est europ.* IV (1969), pp. 547-554.

DZHAIBAZOVSKI, K. Vliyanie avtonomii serbskogo knyazhestva na tranzitnuyu torgovlyu balkanskikh narodov na territorii knyazhestva v pervy polovine XIX veka. *Balcanica* 1(1970), pp. 107-117.

FISCHER-GALATI, S. Revolutionary activity in the Balkans in the eighteenth century. *Actes I. Cong. int. ét. balkan. et sud-est europ.* IV (1969), pp. 327-337.

GENOV, Tz. Dobrovol'cheskoe dvizhenie na Balkanakh vo vremya serbsko-turetzkoy voynui 1876 g. *Actes I. Cong. int. ét. balkan. et sud-est europ.* IV (1969), pp. 231-241.

GÖLLNER, C. Einige Betrachtungen zur türkischen Herrschaft in den Balkanländern. *Actes I. Cong. int. ét. balkan. et sud-est europ.* III (1969), pp. 491-494.

HERTZ, A.Z. Ada Kale: the key to the Danube (1688-1690). *Arch. ott.* 3(1971), pp. 170-184.

HERTZ, A.Z. Armament and supply inventory of Ottoman Ada Kale, 1753. *Archiv Ott.* 4(1972), pp. 95-171.

HRISTOV, H. The agrarian problem and the national liberation movements in the Balkans. *Actes I. Cong. int. ét. balkan. et sud-est europ.* IV (1969), pp. 65-70.

IMBER, C.H. The costs of naval warfare, the account of Hayreddin Barbarossa's Herceg Novi campaign in 1539. *Archiv Ott.* 4(1972), pp. 203-216.

INALCIK, Halil. The Turkish impact on the development of modern Europe. Comment by C.M. Kortepeter. *The Ottoman State and its place in World History*, ed. by Kemal H. Karpat, 1974, pp. 51-60.

IONESCU-NIŞCOV, T. La politique des alliances en tant qu'expression de la lutte des peuples balkaniques pour l'indépendance et la formation des états nationaux durant la septième décenne du XIXe siècle. *Actes I. Cong. int. ét. balkan. et sud-est europ.* IV (1969), pp. 423-432.

ISRAEL, S. Communautés et influences réciproques dans le domaine de la médecine des peuples balkaniques au cours de la période ottomane. *Actes I. Cong. int. ét. balkan. et sud-est europ.* III (1969), pp. 829-834.

ISUSOV, M. BRSDP (t.s.) i solidarnost' balkanskikh narodov nakanune balkanskikh voyn. *Actes I. Cong. int. ét. balkan. et sud-est europ.* IV (1969), pp. 543-546.

JELAVICH, B. Balkan nations under European protectorship. *Actes I. Cong. int. ét. balkan. et sud-est europ.* IV (1969), pp. 397-408.

KALIĆ, J. Les contacts commerciaux de pays balkaniques avec la Hongrie durant la seconde moitié du XVe s. *Actes I. Cong. int. ét. balkan. et sud-est europ.* III (1969), pp. 619-626.

KARASEV, V.G. i KONOBEEV, V.D. O svyazyakh russkikh, serbskikh i bolgarskikh revolyutzionerov v 60-70-kh godakh XIX veka. *Actes I. Cong. int. ét. balkan. et sud-est europ.* IV (1969), pp. 201-213.

KHUREZYANU, D. Nekotorye voprosy izucheniya mezhdunarodnykh sotzialisticheskikh svyazey na yugo-vostoke Evropy v kontze XIX-go veka *Actes I. Cong. int. ét. balkan. et sud-est europ.* IV (1969), pp. 541-542.

KOCHEV, N. Ideyno-teoreticheskie korni isikhazma. *Et. balkaniques*, 1973(1), pp. 48-61.

LAMPE, J.R. Varieties of unsuccessful industrialization in the Balkan states before 1914. *J.econ.hist.* 35(1975), pp. 56-85.

LEWIS, B. Ali Pasha on nationalism. *Midd East Stud.* 10(1974), pp. 77-79.

LIPSHITZ, E.E. Vizantiyskiy zemledel'cheskiy zakon i ego sud'by v srednevekovykh balkanskikh gosudartvakh. *Actes I. Cong. int. et. balkan. et sud-est europ.* III (1969), pp. 385-392

LISEV, S. Die Balkanstadt im Mittelalter. *Actes I. Cong. int. ét. balkan. et sud-est europ.* III (1969), pp. 249-252

MARTINOVIĆ, N. La société "Crnogorski borac" et l'Omladina balkanique. *Actes I. Cong. int. ét. balkan. et sud-est europ.* IV (1969), pp. 191-194.

MATKOVSKI, Aleksandar. Prilog pitanju devširme. (A contribution to the problem of devshirme.) *Prilozi Or.Fil.Ist.* 14-15 (1964-5), pp. 273-309

MIHALJČIĆ, R. i PERIĆ, V. Contribution à la bibliographie de nos villes sous la domination turque. *Balcanica* 3(1973), pp. 635-684.

NAROCHNITZKIY, A.L.N. Politika Rossii na Balkanakh v 1801-1812 gg. v svete novoy dokumental'noy publikatzii. *Actes I. Cong. int. ét. balkan. et sud-est europ.* IV (1969), pp. 161-168.

NAUMOV, E.P. Problemy ekonomicheskogo razvitiya balkanskikh stran v epokhu turetzkoy ekspansii (sel'skoe khozyaystvo Serbii, Zety i Severnoy Albanii vo vtoroy polovine XIV i pervoy polovine XV vv.). *Balcanica* 2(1971), pp. 117-132.

NIEDERHAUSER, E. Les intellectuels et la société balkanique au XIXe siècle. *Actes I. Cong. int. ét. balkan. et sud-est europ.* IV (1969), pp. 409-421.

NOVICHEV, A.D. Ekonomicheskie i sotzial'nye sdvigi v Maloy Azii i na Balkanakh v pervoy polovine XIX v. i nachale Tanzimata. *Actes I. Cong. int. ét. balkan. et sud-est europ.* IV (1969), pp. 13-22.

ORHONLU, Cengiz. The Institution of "Suyolcu" in the 16th century. *Actes I. Cong. int. ét. balkan. et sud-est europ.* III (1969), pp. 673-676.

PALOTASH, E. Avstro-Vengriya i Balkany v kontze XIX veka. *Actes I. Cong. int. ét. balkan. et sud-est europ.* IV (1969), pp. 719-728.

PAPADOPOULLOS, T. Acculturation problems in the Balkan peninsula. *Actes I. Cong. int. ét. balkan. et sud-est europ.* IV (1969), pp. 751-759.

PAPADRIANOS, J. Les informations apportées par Georges Sphrantzès sur le rôle du despote serbe, Djuradj Brankovic, dans les relations hongro-turques, durant les années 1451-1452. *Cyrillomethodianum* 2 (1973-4), pp. 165-169.

PASKALEVA, V. Die Entwicklung der städtischen Wirtschaft in den Balkanländern in der ersten Hälfte des XIX. Jahrhunderts. *Actes I. Cong. int. ét. balkan. et sud-est europ.* IV (1969), pp. 43-53.

POPOV, N., MIKHAYLOVA-MRYVKAROVA, M. Dokumenty o balkanskikh stranakh v arkhivnom sobranii Vostochnogo Otdela Narodnoy Biblioteki imeni Kirilla i Mefodiya. *Actes I. Cong. int. ét. balkan. et sud-est europ.* III (1969), pp. 421-430

PRIBIĆ, N. George Fisher - Šagić, an early nineteenth century immigrant from Serbia to the United States and a protagonist of Balkan solidarity. *Actes I. Cong. int. ét. balkan. et sud-est europ.* IV (1969), pp. 147-160.

PRIMOV, B. Manifestations et common features and unity of the Balkan Peoples in the Middle Ages until the 14th century. *Actes I. Cong. int. ét. balkan. et sud-est europ.* III (1969), pp. 263-264.

REYCHMAN, J. Les échos de la révolution polonaise de 1794 dans les pays Balkaniques. *Actes I. Cong. int. ét. balkan. et sud-est europ.* IV (1969), pp. 441-447.

RIZAJ, Skender. Counterfeit of money on the Balkan Peninsula from the XV to the XVII century. *Balcanica* 1(1970), pp. 71-79.

SKENDI, S. Crypto-Christianity among the Balkan Peoples under the Ottomans. *Actes I. Cong. int. ét. balkan. et sud-est europ.* III (1969), pp. 563-566.

SOKOLOSKI, M. Le développement de quelques villes dans le sud des Balkans au XVe et XVIe siècles. *Balcanica* 1(1970), pp. 81-106.

STANESCU, E. Les "Stratiotes". Diffusion et survivance d'une institution byzantine dans le Sud-est de l'Europe. *Actes I. Cong. int. ét. balkan. et sud-est europ.* III (1969), pp. 227-234.

SVANIDZE, M. Kh. O yurdlukakh i odzhaklykakh kak odnoy iz form zemlevladeniya v osmanskoy imperii (na primere childyrskoyo eyalata). *Actes I. Cong. int. ét. balkan. et sud-est europ.* III (1969), pp. 545-550.

TADIĆ, J. L'unité économique des Balkans et de la région méditerranéenne. *Actes I. Cong. int. ét. balkan. et sud-est europ.* III (1969), pp. 633-640.

TAPPE, E.D. Two English travellers in S.E. Europe: Jeremi [*sic*] Bentham and John Sibthorp. *Actes I. Cong. int. ét. balkan. et sud-est europ.* IV (1969), pp. 519-522.

THOMOV, T.S. Les appelations de "Bogomiles" et "Bulgares" et leurs variantes et équivalents en Orient et en Occident. *Et. balkaniques* 9(1973), pp. 77-99.

TODOROV, N. Balkanskiy gorod XV-XIX vv. v sostave osmanskoy imperii. *Études balkaniques* 7iv(1971), pp. 28-54.

TODOROV, N. Osmanskie dokumenty v sofiyskoy Narodnoy biblioteke kak istochnik svedeniy o sotzial'no-ekonomicheskom razvitii balkanskogo goroda. (Les documents Osmano-Turcs de la Bibliothèque Nationale de Sofia en tant que source du développement socio-économique de la ville Balkanique.) *Fontes orientales...curavit A.S. Tveritinova* II, 1969, pp. 194-211.

TRAJKOV, V. Le transfert par territoire roumain d'armes russes destinées à la Serbie (octobre-décembre 1862). Le rôle des Bulgares. *Études balkaniques* 6ii (1970), pp. 90-97.

TRAKO, S. Pretkosovski događaji u Hešt bihištu Idrisa Bitlisija. (The pre-Kosovo events from Hešt Bihišt by Idris Bitlisi.) *POF* 20-21(1970-71), pp. 159-204.

TRENKOV, H. Information bibliographique courante sur les études du sud-est européen. *Actes I. Cong. int. ét. balkan. et sud-est europ.* IV (1969), pp. 243-245.

TURCZYNSKI, E. Originäre und imperiale Impulse der Nationalbewegung in Südosteuropa. *Actes I. Cong. int. ét. balkan. et sud-est europ.* IV (1969), pp. 365-389.

ÜNVER, Suheyl. Les épidémies de choléra dans les terres balkaniques aux XVIIIe et XIXe siècles. *Etudes Balkaniques* 9(1973) (4), pp. 89-97.

VINOGRADOV, K.B. Osnovnye osobennosti politiki Avstro-Vengrii na Balkanakh v 1909-1913 gg. *Actes I. Cong. int. ét. balkan. et sud-est europ.* IV (1969), pp. 845-859.

WERNER, E. Yürüken und Wlachen. *Actes I. Cong. int. ét. balkan. et sud-est europ.* III (1969), pp. 605-608.

ZAKHOS-PAPAZAHARIOU, E. Babel balkanique. Histoire politique des alphabets utilisés dans les Balkans. *Cah. du monde russe et sov.* 13(1972), pp. 145-179.

See also XXIX. d. (Albania) Pulaha.

Albania

BUDA, A. Albanien und die Balkankrise der Jahre 1878-1881. *Actes I. Cong. int. ét. balkan. et sud-est europ.* IV (1969), pp. 121-130.

BUDA, A. La place des Albanais dans l'histoire européenne du VIIIe au XVIIIe ss. *Actes I. Cong. int. ét. balkan. et sud-est europ.* III (1969), pp. 57-74.

CHOCHIEV, V.G. K tolkovaniyu termina "Arnavut". (Po povodu odnoy oshibki Khammera). *Philologia orientalis* II, 1972, pp. 217-219.

FRASHËRI, K. Şemseddin Sami Frashëri. Idéologie du mouvement national albanais. *Actes I. Cong. int. ét. balkan. et sud-est europ.* IV (1969), pp. 817-830.

KISSLING, H.J. Scanderbeg, stratega e politico. *Shêjzat (le pleiadi)* 15 (1971), pp. 3-11. [Offprint in S.O.A.S.]

KISSLING, H.J. Gli stradioti albanesi in Italia nella prima epoca rinascimentale. *Shêjzat* 18(1974), pp. 1-13.

KORNRUMPF, H.J. Ahmed Cevdet Pasa über Albanien und Montenegro. Aus Tezkere Nr. 18. *Der Islam* 47(1971), pp. 93-135.

LEWIN, E. Die historischen Voraussetzungen der nationalen Unabhängigkeitsbewegung in Albanien. *Études balkaniques* 6ii(1970), pp. 24-38.

MILE, L. Sur le caractère du pouvoir d'Ali Pacha de Tépélène. *Actes I. Cong. int. ét. balkan. et sud-est europ.* IV (1969), pp. 97-109.

NAÇI, S. Le Pachalik de Scutari considéré dans son développement socio-politique au XVIIIe siècle. *Actes I. Cong. int. ét. balkan. et sud-est europ.* IV (1969), pp. 131-142.

PALL, F. Renseignements inédits sur la participation albanaise à la guerre de Naple (1459-1463). *Actes I. Cong. int. ét. balkan. et sud-est europ.* III (1969), pp. 469-476.

POLLO, S., PLASARI, N. Le rôle du peuple albanais dans l'histoire moderne et contemporaine. *Actes I. Cong. int. ét. balkan. et sud-est europ.* III (1969), pp. 157-168.

PULAHA, S. Les matériaux documentaires médiévaux osmano-turcs des Archives centrales d'histoire et de la Bibliothèque nationale de Tirana et leur importance pour l'histoire nationale. *Actes I. Cong. int. ét. balkan. et sud-est europ.* III (1969), pp. 845-856.

PUTO, A. Aspects de la lutte diplomatique à propos de l'indépendance albanaise en 1912-1913. *Actes I. Cong. int. ét. balkan. et sud-est europ.* IV (1969), pp. 831-843.

RAHIMI, Šukri. Albanci u borbi za nacionalnu emancipaciju posle mladoturske revolucije. (les Albanais dans la lutte pour l'émancipation nationale après la révolution jeune turque.) *Jugosl. istorijski časopis* 1970(1-2), pp. 71-87

SCHWANKE, R. Die historische Studie von Pisko über Skanderbeg, Wendepunkt in der skanderbeghistoriographie. *Simpoziumi per Skanderbeun*, Pishtine, 1969, pp. 443-453.

SENKEVICH, I.G. Iz istorii albanskogo osvoboditel'nogo dvizheniya v 1866-1869 gg. (po materialam sovetskikh arkhivov). *Actes I. Cong. int. ét. balkan. et sud-est europ.* IV (1969), pp. 111-119.

SHKODRA, Z. Le marché albanais au XVIIIe siècle. *Actes I. Cong. int. ét. balkan. et sud-est europ.* IV (1969), pp. 761-774.

SKIOTIS, D.N. From bandit to Pasha: first steps in the rise to power of Ali of Tepelen, 1750-1784. *IJMES* 2 (1971), pp. 219-244.

STOYKOV, R. Odin neizvestnyy istochnik albanskoy onomastiki serediny XV v. *Actes I. Cong. int. ét. balkan. et sud-est europ.* III (1969), pp. 551-556.

ZAMPUTI, I. Aspects du mouvement albanais de libération dans les premiers siècles de la domination ottomane notamment au cours de 1593-1620. *Actes I. Cong. int. ét. balkan. et sud-est europ.* III (1969), pp. 857-868.

Many articles on Skanderbeg and his times, written in the Albanian and Serbo-Croat languages, will be found in the volume Simpoziumi per Skanderbeun/Simpozijum o Skenderbegu (9-12 maj 1968), *published by the Instituti Albanogjik i Prishtines, 1969.*

See also XL. aa. Chochiev.

Bulgaria

ALEXIEVA, Afrodita. La littérature scolaire pendant la Renaissance bulgare et la littérature pédagogique grecque de la première moitié du XIXe s. (jusqu'à la guerre de Crimée). *Ét. balkaniques* 1972(3), pp. 32-49.

ANGELOV, D. Bulgarie. *Actes I. Cong. int. ét. balkan. et sud-est europ.* III (1969), pp. 27-36.

BEŠEVLIEV, V. Καμπαγάνος = Qap(a)γan. *Acta Or. (Hung.)* 29(1975), pp. 93-97.

CVETKOVA, B.A. Actes concernant la vie économique de villes et portes balkaniques aux XVe et XVI e siècles. *REI* 40(1972), pp. 345-390.

CVETKOVA, B.A. Turetzkie dokumenty po istorii bolgaro-russkikh otnosheniy v XIX v. (Documents turcs sur les relations Bulgaro-Russes du XIXe s.) *Fontes orientales...curavit A.S. Tveritinova* II, 1969, pp. 161-171.

CVETLER, J. Die Tätigkei der tschechischen Juristen in Ostrumelien 1880-1885 als ein Beitrag zum Aufbau des Bulgarischen Staates. *Actes I. Cong. int. ét. balkan. et sud-est europ.* IV (1969), pp. 665-676.

DAMJANOV, S. La France et la Bulgarie à l'époque des Guerres balkaniques (1912-1913). *Études balkaniques* 7ii(1971), pp. 18-46.

DIÓSZEGI, I. Österreich-Ungarns Aussenpolitik während der bulgarischen Krise 1885-87. *Actes I. Cong. int. ét. balkan. et sud-est europ.* IV (1969), pp. 709-718.

GĂLĂBOV, Gălăb D. Turetzkie dokumenty po istorii goroda Karlovo. (Documents officiels turcs concernant l'histoire de la ville de Karlovo (District de Plovdiv, Bulgarie.) *Fontes orientales ...* curavit A.S. Tveritinova, I, 1964, pp. 162-185.

GROZDANOVA, E. Les fondements économiques de la commune rurale dans les régions bulgares (VVe-XVIIIe siècles). *Etudes Balkaniques* 10(1974) (1), pp. 30-45.

KUZEV, A. Die Beziehungen des Königs von Vidin Ivan Sracimir zu den osmanischen Herrschern. *Études balkaniques* 7iii (1971), pp. 121-124.

MIJATEV, P. Turetzkie epigraficheskie pamyatniki kak istochniki po istorii kul'tury bolgarskikh zemel XIV-XIX vv. (Les monuments épigraphiques turcs - sources de l'histoire culturelle des terres bulgares au cours des XIVe - XIXe s.) *Fontes orientales...curavit A.S. Tveritinova* II, 1969, pp. 180-193.

MILKOVA, F.G. K kharakteristike kesimskoy formy ekspluatatzii krest'yan v bolgarskikh zemlyakh do osvobozhdeniya. *Actes I. Cong. int. ét. balkan. et sud-est europ.* IV (1969), pp. 71-76.

NIKITIN, S.A. Bolgarskiy gorod v 1879 g. po dannym russkoy perepisi. *Actes I. Cong. int. ét. balkan. et sud-est europ.* IV (1969), pp. 77-94.

OVNANYAN, S.V. Rol' armyanskikh knigopechatnikov Konstantinopolya v rasprostranenii prosveshcheniya v Bolgarii. *Actes I. Cong. int. ét. balkan. et sud-est europ.* IV (1969), pp. 529-538.

PINSON, M. Ottoman Bulgaria in the first Tanzimat period--the revolts in Nish (1841) and Vidin (1850). *M.E. stud.* 11 (1975), pp. 103-146.

POPOV, N.G. Novye materialy o proshlom Maleshevo. (Données sur le passe de Maléchevo.) *Fontes orientales ...* curavit A.S. Tveritinova, I, 1964, pp. 231-235.

ŠAROVA, K. L'insurrection d'avril (1876) et sa place dans l'histoire de la Bulgarie et des Balkans. *Actes I. Cong. int. ét. balkan. et sud-est europ.* IV (1969), p. 229.

STOIKOV, R. Bolgarskie derevni i ikh naselenie v kratkikh reestrakh, dzhiz'e XVII v. (Localités bulgares et leur population dans les registres - Djizie du XVIIe s.) *Fontes orientales... curavit A.S. Tveritinova* II, 1969, pp. 218-237.

TAMBORRA, A. La crise balkanique de 1885 et l'Italie. *Actes I. Cong. int. ét. balkan. et sud-est europ.* IV (1969), pp. 699-708.

TODOROV, N. Le peuple bulgare et ses rapports avec les peuples balkanniques. *Actes I. Cong. int. ét. balkan. et sud-est europ.* III (1969), pp. 145-156.

VAZVAZOVA-KARATÉODOROVA, K. Documents des archives des révolutionnaires bulgares datant de l'époque de la renaissance bulgare et reflétant l'idée de collaboration et d'unité d'action des peuples balkaniques. *Actes I. Cong. int. ét. balkan. et sud-est europ.* IV (1969), pp. 263-268.

VELEVA, M. Kul'turnye svyazi mezhdu Bolgariey i Serbiey v pervom desyatiletii XX veka. *Actes I. Cong. int. ét. balkan. et sud-est europ.* IV (1969), pp. 687-689

YONOV, M.P. Putevnie zapiski Zh.P. Forez'ena kak istochnik dlya istorii bolgarskikh zemel' (1582 g.) *Actes I. Cong. int. ét. balkan. et sud-est europ.* III (1969), pp. 477-488.

See also XXIX. d. (Greece) Chegarot.

See also XXIX. d. *Greece.* Danova.

Czechoslovakia (Bohemia)

BLAŠKOVIČ, J. Das Sultansdekret (Sünurname) über das Vakf im Bezirk Nové Zámky. *Ar. Or.* 42(1974), pp. 300-309.

HAVRÁNKOVÁ, R. Les relations entre les Tchèques et les peuples balkaniques aux XIXe et XXe ss. *Actes I. Cong. int. ét. balkan. et sud-est europ.* IV (1969), pp. 677-685.

RATKOŠ, P. Die Slowakei während der Osmanischen Expansion der Jahre 1526-1532. (Der erste osmanische Feldzug in die Slowakei vom Jahr 1530.) *Actes I. Cong. int. ét. balkan. et sud-est europ.* III (1969), pp. 738-752.

VESELÁ-PRENOSILOVÁ, Z. Le peuple de la Slovaquie du Sud dans ses rapports envers l'occupation ottomane. *Etudes balkaniques* 11(1975), pp. 107-113.

Greece. Crete

ANASTASSIADOU, I. Les Russo-Turcs à Zante en 1798. *Balkan studies* 14(1973), pp. 12-46.

ARNAKIS, G.G. The Cretan revolution of 1866 and the mission of Alexander Rangavis to the United States. *Actes I. Cong. int. ét. balkan. et sud-est europ.* IV (1969), pp. 391-395.

ARSH, G.L. Novye dannye ob otnoshenii tzarskogo pravitel'stva k "Filiki Eterii". *Actes I. Cong. int. ét. balkan. et sud-est europ.* IV (1969), pp. 449-458.

ASDRACHAS, S.I. Marchés et prix du blé en Grèce au XVIIIe siècle. *Südostforschungen* 31(1972), pp. 178-209.

XXIX TURKEY: HISTORY. CYPRUS

BEGOVIC, M. Sur l'application du droit pendant le règne turc dans nos pays. *Balcanica* 4(1973), pp. 361-367.

BELDICEANU, N. Margarid: un timar monastique. *Rev. ét. byzantines* 33 (1975), pp. 227-255.

BELDICEANU, N. et BELDICEANU-STEINHERR, I. Un paléologue inconnu de la région de Serres. *Byzantion* 41(1971), pp. 5-17

BELDICEANU-STEINHERR, I. La Vita de Seyyd 'Alī Sulṭān et la conquête de la Thrace par les Turcs. *Proc.27th Int. Cong.Or.1967* (1971), pp. 275-276.

CHEGAROV, I. Rayno Popovich - radetel' greko-bolgarskogo sotrudnichestva. *Actes I. Cong. int. ét. balkan. et sud-est europ.* IV (1969), pp. 481-485.

DANOVA, N. Le retentissement de l'insurrection crétoise de 1866-1869 au sein de l'opinion publique bulgare. *Études balkaniques* 1972(2), pp. 98-109.

DASCALAKIS, A. Le rôle de la civilisation grecque dans les Balkans. *Actes I. Cong. int. ét. balkan. et sud-est europ.* III (1969), pp. 105-116.

DUJČEV, I. Contribution à l'histoire de la conquête turque en Thrace aux dernières décades du XIVe siècle. *Et. balkaniques* 9(1973), pp. 80-92.

ENEPEKIDES, P.K. Archivforschungen in Wien, München und in Paris zur Geschichte des europäischen Philhellenismus. *Actes I. Cong. int. ét. balkan. et sud-est europ.* IV (1969), pp. 339-342.

ENEPEKIDES, P.K. Die neugefundenen Akten des Wiener Kriegsarchivs zur siebenjährigen Festungshaft Alexander Ypsilantis. *Actes I. Cong. int. ét. balkan. et sud-est europ.* IV (1969), pp. 461-474.

FANTUCCI ORLANDO, M.G. Su le chiese e i monasteri ortodossi sotto dominazione turca. Le notizie di Teodosio Zygomalas e di Pierre Belon. *Aevum* 46(1972), pp. 37-48.

GIANNOPOULOS, I.G. Συμβολὴ εἰς τὴν βιβλιογραφίαν τῆς Στερεᾶς Ἑλλάδος κατὰ τὴν Τουρκοκρατίαν. Ἐπετηρὶς Ἑταιρείας Στερεοελλαδικῶν Μελετῶν 1(1968). pp 385-436

ILIOU, P. Pour une étude quantitative du public des lecteurs grecs à l'époque des Lumière et de la Révolution (1749-1832). *Actes I. Cong. int. ét. balkan. et sud-est europ.* IV (1969), pp. 475-480.

KABRDA, J. Zakonopolozhenie ob Amfisse. (Le Kanun-name d'Amphissa.) *Fontes orientales* ... curavit A.S. Tveritinova, I, 1964, pp. 222-230.

PALOKRUŠEVA, G. Conséquences ethniques de l'Islamisation des Miacs en Macédoine. *Ethnologia slavica* 5(1973), pp. 37-47.

PAPACOSTEA-DANIELOPOLU, C. L'organisation de la Compagnie grecque de Brașov (1777-1850). *Balkan studies* 14(1973), pp. 313-323.

SKENDI, St. The songs of the klephts and the hayduks--history or oral literature? *Serta Slavica in memoriam A. Schmaus*, 1971, pp. 666-673.

SKIOTIS, D. Mountain warriors and the Greek Revolution. *War, technokogy and society in the Middle East*, ed. V.J. Parry and M.E. Yapp, 1975, pp. 308-329.

TODOROV, N., TRAJKOV, V. L'insurrection grecque de 1821-1829 et les Bulgares. *Études balkaniques* 7i(1971), pp. 5-26.

VACALOPOULOS, C.A. Probleme in Bezug auf das Leben und den Tod von Alexander Ypsilantis. *Balkan studies* 15(1974), pp. 61-79.

VACALOPOULCS, A. Quelques problèmes relatifs à la résistance de Manuel II Paléologue contre les turcs ottomans dans la Macédoine grecque (1383-1391). *Actes I. Cong. int. ét. balkan. et sud-est europ.* III (1969), pp. 351-355.

VINCENT, A. The two sultanas: the Cretan War (1645-1669) in South Slav heroic songs. *Univ.Birmingham Hist.J.* 12(1970), pp. 237-242.

ZACHARIADOU, E.A. The conquest of Adrianople by the Turks. *Studi Veneziani* 12(1970), pp. 211-217

ZACHARIADOU, E.A. Ottoman documents from Archives of Dionysiou (Mount Athos) 1495-1520. *Südostforschungen* 30(1971), pp. 1-36.

ZOÏDIS, G. L'écho de la révolution de Crète de 1866 en Roumanie. *Actes I. Cong. int. ét. balkan. et sud-est europ.* IV (1969), pp. 775-792.

See also XXIX. d. Alexieva.

Hungary

BAYERLE, G. The agricultural production and its distribution in the county of Novigrad. *Proc.27th Int.Cong.Or.1967* (1971), pp. 590-591.

BUR, M. Balkanskie kuptzy v Vengrii - XVIII vek. *Ét. balkaniques* 1972(3), pp. 50-70.

DAVID, G. Some aspects of 16th century depopulation in the Sanjāq of Simontorny *Acta Or.Hung.* 28(1974), pp. 63-74.

FEKETE, L. Das Heim des 'Ali Celebi, eines turkischen Defterbeamters in Buda. *Fontes orientales...curavit A.S. Tveritinova II*, 1969, pp. 29-75.

FEKETE, L. Torgovlya v Bude v period turetzkogo gospodstva vo vtoroy polovine XVI v. (Le commerce de la ville de Buda durant la seconde moitié du XVIe siècle, sous la domination turque.) *Fontes orientales ...* curavit A.S. Tveritinova, I, 1964, pp. 91-118.

HALASI-KUN, T. Unidentified medieval settlements in southern Hungary. Ottoman: *dolna-, sredna-* and *gorna-*. *Archivum Ottomanicum* 2(1970), pp. 154-190.

HALASI-KUN, T. Unidentified medieval settlements in Southern Hungary. Ottoman: *nam-i diğer*. *Studia Turcica, ed. L. Ligeti,* 1971, pp. 213-230

HALASI-KUN, T. Unidentified medieval settlements in Southern Hungary: addenda to "Ottoman: *nam-i diğer*". *Archiv Ott.* 4(1972), pp. 85-94.

HALASI-KUN, T. Unidentified medieval settlements in Southern Hungary, Ottoman: *nezd-i .... et socii*. *Archivum ottomanicum* 3 (1971), pp. 5-169.

HEGYI, K. Le condominium hungaro-ottoman dans les eyalets hongrois. *Actes I. Cong. int. ét. balkan. et sud-est europ.* III (1969), pp. 593-604.

HORVÁTH, Ann. The cattle trade of a Hungarian town (*Szolnok*) in the period of Turkish domination. *Studia Turcica, ed. L. Ligeti,* 1971, pp. 235-240

HORVÁTH, A. Le commerce dans l'eyalet de Buda durant la seconde moitié du XVI.-ème siècle. *Tarih araştırmaları dergisi* 7 (1969), pp. 57-63.

KÁLDY-NAGY, Gy. The effect of the *Tīmār*-system on agricultural production in Hungary. *Studia Turcica, ed. L. Ligeti,* 1971, pp. 241-248

KOPČAN, V. Ottoman narrative sources to the Uyvar expedition 1663. *Asian and African studies* [Bratislava] 7(1971), pp. 89-100.

MÉSZÁROS, L., HAUSFATTER, K. A hódoltsági mezővárosok népességszámának kérdéséhez (1546-1562). (To the question of the population number of Hungarian country-towns under Turkish rule.) *Demográfia* 17(1974), pp. 108-122, 213-235.

PERÉNYI, J. Trois villes hongroises sous la domination ottomane au XVIIe s. *Actes I. Cong. int. ét. balkan. et sud-est europ.* III (1969), pp. 581-592.

SCHEIBER, A. Jüdische Grabsteine in Ofen zur Türkenzeit. *Acta Or. Hung.* 25(1972), pp. 465-474.

TARDY, Lajos. Ungarns antiosmanische Bündnisse mit Staaten des Nahen Ostens und deren Vorgeschichte. *Anatolica* 4(1971-72), pp. 139-156.

TEPLY, K. Mehmed Çolak Beğ - Leopold Freiherr von Zungaberg. *Mitt.Inst.österr. Geschichtsforschung* 80(1972), pp. 113-155

TURKOVÁ, H. Über die Belagerung von Uyvār (Neuhäusel, Nové Zámky) im Jahre 1663 durch die Türken. *Archiv or.* 41(1973), pp. 325-339.

VASS, E. Éléments pour compléter l'histoire de l'administration des finances du vilayet de Buda au XVIe siècle. *Studia Turcica. ed. L. Ligeti,* 1971, pp. 483-490

VASS, E. Quatre documents ottomans concernant la contribution d'une puszta hongroise au XVIIe siècle. *Acta Or.Hung.* 28(1974), pp. 253-262.

VASS, E. Türkische Beiträge zur Handelgeschichte der Stadt Vác (Waitzen) aus dem 16. Jahrhundert. *Acta or. Hung.* 24 (1971), pp. 1-39.

VASS, E. Zwei türkische Fährenlisten von Ráckeve und Dunaföldvár aus den Jahren 1562-1564. *Acta Or. Hung.* 25(1972), pp. 451-463.

VESELÁ, Z. Contribution aux rapports de la Sublime Porte avec la Transylvanie pendant la deuxième moitié du XVIIe s. *Actes I. Cong. int. ét. balkan. et sud-est europ.* III (1969), pp. 753-760.

See also I. d. l. Bayerle.

See also V. m. l. Fehér.

Romania

ALEXANDRESCU-DERSCA BULGARU, M.M. Aspecte ale vieţii economice din oraşele şi tîrgurile Dobrogei sub stăpînerea otomană (sec. XV-XVII). *Studii. Revistă de istorie* 26 (1973), pp. 33-48.

BELDICEANU, N. et BELDICEANU-STEINHERR, I. Déportation et pêche à Kilia entre 1484 et 1508. *BSOAS* 38(1975), pp. 40-54.

BELDICEANU, N. La Moldavie ottomane à la fin du XVe siècle et au début du XVIe siècle. *Proc.27th Int.Cong.Or.1967* (1971), pp. 273-274.

BELDICEANU, N. Le vozarlīq: une institution ponto-danubienne. *Südostforschungen* 32(1973), pp. 73-90.

BERINDEI, D. Les Principautés Roumaines Unies et la lutte de libération nationale du sud-est de l'Europe. *Actes I. Cong. int. ét. balkan. et sud-est europ.* IV (1969), pp. 319-325.

BERINDEI, Mihnea. Le problème des "Cosaques" dans la seconde moitié du xvie siècle. A propos de la révolte de Ioan Voda, voiévode de Moldavie. *Cah. du monde russe et sov.* 13(1972), pp. 338-367.

BERZA, M. Roumanie. *Actes I. Cong. int. ét. balkan. et sud-est europ.* III (1969), pp. 51-56.

BERZA, M. Turcs, Empire ottoman et relations roumano-turques dans l'historiographie moldave des XVe-XVII e siècles. *Rev. ét. sud-est eur.* 10(1972), pp. 595-627.

XXIX TURKEY: HISTORY. CYPRUS

BINDER, P. Transylvanian Saxons as Turkish clerks. Marcus Scherer and Marcus Benkner. *Rev. ét. sud-est europ.* 12(1974), pp. 397-401.

BOROIANU, C. Les sources de l'Histoire de Del Chiaro. *Rev. et. sud-est eur.* 10(1972), pp. 323-334.

CAZACU, M. L'impact ottoman sur les pays roumains et ses incidences monétaires (1452-1504). *RRH* 12(1973), pp. 159-192.

CERNOVODEANU, P. Contributions to Lord Paget's journey in Wallachia and Transylvania (1702). *RESEE* 11(1973), pp. 275-284.

CERNOVODEANU, P. Les marchands balkaniques, intermédiaires du commerce entre l'Angleterre, La Valachie et la Transylvanie durant les années 1660-1714. *Actes I. Cong. int. ét. balkan. et sud-est europ.* III (1969), pp. 649-658.

CHERTAN, E.E. Rossiya i bor'ba Rumynii za nezavisimost' (1859-1875 gg.) *Actes I. Cong. int. ét. balkan. et sud-est europ.* IV (1969), pp. 803-816.

CIACHIR, N. Certains aspects de l'attitude de la Roumanie envers le mouvement révolutionnaire des Balkans 1875-Avril 1877. *Actes I. Cong. int. ét. balkan. et sud-est europ.* IV (1969), pp. 311-318.

CIOBANU, V. Les relations politiques de l'empire ottoman et de la Pologne au XVIIIe siècle et les principautés roumaines. *Rev. ét. sud-est eur.* 13 (1975), pp. 443-446.

CIUREA, D. Considérations sur la littérature historique et géographique des XVIIe-XVIIIe siècles (essai de classification). *Rev. roumaine d'hist.* 10(1970), pp. 823-834.

COLUMBEANU, S. Acţiuni navale în Marea Neagră în timpul lui Ştefan cel Mare. *Revista de istorie* 28(1975), pp. 73-89.

CONSTANTINU, Fl. et PAPACOSTEA, S. Les réformes des premiers Phanariots en Moldavie et en Valachie: essai d'interpretation. *Balkan studies* 13(1972), pp. 89-118.

CORFUS, I. Intervenţia polonă în Moldova şi consecinţele ei asupra războiului lui Mihai Viteazul cu Turcii. *Revista de istorie* 28(1975), pp. 527-540.

CORIVAN, N. La question de l'union dans les projets européens d'organisation des principautés roumaines (1855-1857). *Rev. roumaine d'hist.* 9(1970), pp. 963-974.

DAN, M., GOLDERBERG, S. Marchands balkaniques et levantins dans le commerce de la Transylvanie aux XVIe s., XVIIe ss. *Actes I. Cong. int. ét. balkan. et sud-est europ.* III (1969), pp. 641-648.

DECEI, A. Deux documents turcs concernant les expéditions des sultans Bayazid ler et Murad II dans les pays roumains. *Rev. roum.hist.* 1974(3), pp. 395-413.

DECEI, A. Izvoare turceşti despre Mihai Viteazul. *Revista arhivelor* 37(1975), pp. 157-169.

DECEI, A.; LĂZĂRESCU, D.A. Quelques problèmes de l'histoire des roumains dans les ouvrages historiques étrangers, jusqu'à la fin du XIXe siècle. *Rev. roumaine d'hist.* 9(1970), pp. 669-725.

DECEI, A. Les relations entre Michel le Brave et l'Empire ottoman. *Rev. roumaine d'hist.* 14(1975), pp. 457-482.

DICULESCU, V., IANCOVICI, S. Les relations commerciales de Valachie avec la péninsule balkanique. *Actes I. Cong. int. ét. balkan. et sud-est europ.* IV (1969), pp. 55-60.

DIMITROV, Str. At. Turetzkie dokumenty o sostoyanii Khotinskoy okrugi (nakhie) v pervoy polovine XVIII v. (Türkische Dokumente uber die Zustande in der Nachia Hotin wahrend der ersten Halfte des XVIII Jahrhunderts.) *Fontes orientales... curavit A.S. Tveritinova* II, 1969, pp. 140-161.

GEMIL, Tahsin. Les pays roumains dans la politique européenne de la Porte ottomane au XVIIe siècle. *Rev. ét. sud-est eur.* 13(1975), pp. 425-428.

GEORGESCO, V. L'application des Novelles byzantines περι προτιμήσεως dans les principautés roumaines à la fin du XVIIIe et début du XIXe siècle. *Actes I. Cong. int. ét. balkan. et sud-est europ.* IV (1969), pp. 281-288.

GIURESCU, C.C. Les relations des pays roumains avec Trébizonde aux XIVe-XIXe siècles. *RRH* 13(1974), pp. 239-246.

GÖKBILGIN, M. Tayyib. Ajalet Rumelija (preveo dr. H. Sabanović.) *Prilozi Or.Fil. Ist.* 16-17 (1966-7), pp. 307-342

GONŢA, A. Adunarea ţării din primăvara anului 1574 în Moldova. *Revista de istorie* 27(1974), pp. 887-896.

GRIGORAŞ, N. Politica internă a lui Ioan Vodă cel Viteaz. *Revista de istorie* 27 (1974), pp. 871-885.

GRIGORAŞ, N. Relaţiile Moldovei cu Imperiul Otoman pînă la domnia lui Ştefan cel Mare. *Revista de istorie* 28(1975), pp. 33-49.

GUBOGLU, M. Dva ukaza (1801 g.) i "svyashchennyy reskript" (1802 g.) svyazannye s turetzko-russko-rumyenskimi otnosheniyakh. (Deux firmans (1801) et le Hatt-i Cherif (1802) concernant les relations turco-russo-roumaines.) *Fontes orientales...curavit A.S. Tveritinova* II, 1969, pp. 238-273.

GUBOGLU, M. Mihai Viteazul in documente turceşti. *Revista arhivelor* 37(1975), pp. 143-144.

XXIX TURKEY: HISTORY. CYPRUS

GUBOGLU, M. Turetzkiy istochnik 1740 g. o Valakhii, Moldavii i Ukraine. (Une source historique turque de 1740 concernant la valachie. La Moldavie et l'Ukraine.) *Fontes orientales* ... curavit A.S. Tveritinova, I, 1964, pp. 131-161.

GUBOGLU, M. Une version turque du règlement organique. La première constitution roumaine (1831-1858). *Studia et acta or.* 8(1971), pp. 209-219.

HERLIHY, P. A report on the commerce of Moldavia and Wallachia in 1840. *RESEE* 12 (1974), pp. 121-137.

HOPE, T.I. Rapoartele lui sir William Sidney Smith asupra stării principatelor Moldova şi Ţara Românească în anul 1792. *Studii. Revistă de istorie* 26(1973), pp. 715-727.

HOPE, T.J. Sir Henry Bulwer and the Wallachian elections of 1857. *Balkan studies* 14(1973), pp. 324-330.

INALCIK, Halil. Eastern and Western cultures in Dimitrie Cantemir's work. *RRH* 13(1974), pp. 31-42.

IONESCU, M. Objectifs balkaniques de la diplomatie roumaine de 1867-1869. *Actes I. Cong. int. ét. balkan. et sud-est europ.* IV (1969), pp. 185-190.

JANCOVICI, S. Nouvelles données sur le Delibaşa Mihali - combattant de 1821. *Études balkaniques* 1972(2), pp. 45-48.

MACIU, V. Le peuple roumain à l'époque moderne et contemporaine. *Actes I. Cong. int. ét. balkan. et sud-est europ.* III (1969), pp. 131-144.

MACIU, V. Les relations roumano-turques pendant la révolution de 1848. *Rev. roumaine d'hist.* 10(1970), pp. 43-62.

MACUREK, J. Les pays au carrefour des influences culturelles du Sud-est européen et de l'Europe Centrale. *Actes I. Cong. int. ét. balkan. et sud-est europ.* III (1969), pp. 223-226.

MANOLESCU, R. Sur la participation des marchands de la péninsule balkanique au commerce avec la Valachie et la Transylvanie, dans la première moitié du XVIe siècle. *Rev. ét. sud-est eur.* 13(1975), pp. 403-405.

MATEESCU, T. Les diocèses orthodoxes de la Dobroudja sous la domination ottomane. *Balkan studies* 13(1972), pp. 279-300.

MATEI, I. Quelques problèmes concernant le régime de la domination ottomane dans les pays roumains (concernant particulièrement la Valachie). *Rev.ét.sud-est.eur.* 10(1972), pp. 65-81

MATEI, Ion. Quelques problèmes concernant le régime de la domination ottomane dans les pays Roumains. *Rev. ét. sud-est europ.* 11(1973), pp. 81-95.

MATEI, I. Sur les relations d'Ahmed Vefik Pacha avec les roumains. Notes en marge de certaines données de sa correspondance. *Studia et acta or.* 8(1971), pp. 71-102.

MAXIM, M. Considérations sur la circulation monétaire dans les pays roumains et l'empire ottoman dans la seconde moitié du XVIs siècle. *Rev. ét. sud-est eur.* 13(1975), pp. 407-415.

MIHORDEA, V. Les lignes du développement de la diplomatie roumaine au XVIIIe siècle. *Rev. roumaine d'hist.* 9(1970), pp. 43-62.

MUTAFCHIEVA, V. "Kyrdzhaliyskoe vremya". *Et.balkaniques* 9(1973), pp. 100-120.

NETEA, V. La philosophie des lumières, arme de combat pour l'émancipation du peuple roumain. *Actes I. Cong. int. ét. balkan. et sud-est europ.* IV (1969), pp. 293-299.

ORHUNLU, Cengiz. The geography of Walachia written by a Turkish politician. *Rev. ét. sud-est eur.* 13(1975), pp. 447-452.

PAPACOSTEA, Ş. La Moldavie état tributaire de l'Empire Ottoman au XVe siècle: le cadre international des rapports établis en 1455-1456. *RRH* 12(1973), pp. 445-461.

PAPACOSTEA, Ş. La Moldavie état tributaire de l'empire ottoman au XVe siècle: le cadre international des rapports établis en 1455-1456. *Rev.roum.hist.* 1974(3), pp. 445-461.

PIPPIDI, A. Aux origines du régime phanariote en Valachie et Moldavie. *RESEE* 11 (1973), pp. 353-355.

PLEŞIA, D., ANDREESCU, Ş. Un épisode inconnu des campagnes du voïévode Dan II prince de Valachie. *Rev. roum. hist.* 1974(3), pp. 545-557.

ROTMAN, Cr. Zur Frage osmanischer Teilnahme am dreissig-jährigen Krieg. (Vorabend des um 1620 osmanischen Feldzuges gegen die Moldau.) *Rev. ét. sud-est eur.* 13(1975).

SEMENOVA, L.E. Russko-valaskie politicheskie svyazi (1712-1713 gg.). *Actes I. Cong. int. ét. balkan. et sud-est europ.* III (1969), pp. 765-770.

SFUROERAS, B. Un "Canun-Name" sui diritti di famiglie fanariote nell'amministrazione dell'Impero ottomano. *Actes I. Cong. int. ét. balkan. et sud-est europ.* III (1969), p. 489.

SIMIONESCU, Şt Ţările Române şi începutul politicii răsăritane antiotomane a imperiului Habsburgic (1526-1594). *Revista de istorie* 28(1975), pp. 1197-1214.

ŞTEFĂNESCU, Şt. La pensée politique de Démètre Cantemir et les rapports de la Moldavie avec les états voisins au début du XVIIIe siècle. *RRH* 12(1973), pp. 859-873.

ŞTEFĂNESCU, L. Les rapports économiques de la ville de Bucarest avec le sud-est européen pendant la deuxième moitié du XVIIIe siècle. *Actes I. Cong. int. ét. balkan. et sud-est europ.* IV (1969), pp. 7-11.

STOICESCU, N. L'armée de la Valachie sous le règne de Michel le Brave (1593-1601). *Rev. ét. sud-est eur.* 13(1975), pp. 353-366.

VELICHI, C.N. Précisions et données inédites au sujet du capitaine Georges Mamartchov Buiukliu. *RESEE* 12(1974), pp. 103-120.

VELICHI, C. La Roumanie et les mouvements nationaux des Balkans (1840-1877). *Actes I. Cong. int. ét. balkan. et sud-est europ.* IV (1969), pp. 301-310.

VESELÁ-PŘENOSILOVÁ, Z. Quelques remarques sur l'évolution de l'organisation urbaine en Empire Ottoman. *Ar.Or.* 42(1974), pp. 200-224.

VINOGRADOV, V.N. Derzhavy i ob'edinenie dunayskikh knyazhestv. (K voprosu o pozitzii russkoy diplomatii.) *Actes I. Cong. int. ét. balkan. et sud-est europ.* IV (1969), pp. 793-802.

See also XXIX. d. (Greece) Zoidis.

See also XXIX. f. Gorovei.

See also XXIX. f. Mehmed.

Yugoslavia

ALIČIĆ, Ahmed. Čifluci Husein kapetana Gradaščevića. (Husein-captain Gradashcevich chiflics.) *Prilozi Or.Fil.Ist.* 14-15 (1964-5), pp. 312-328

ALIČIĆ, A.S., HASANDEDIĆ, H. Popis terzija, čurčija i ćebedžija u Mostaru iz 1755. godine. *Prilozi za or. filol.* 18-19(1968-9), pp. 315-371.

BEHIJA, Zl. Popis vakufa u Bosni iz prve polovice XVI stoljeća. (The register of the waqfs in Bosnia during the first half of the eighteenth century.) *POF* 20-21 (1970-71), pp. 109-158.

BELDICEANU, N. Les Valaques de Bosnie à la fin du XVe siècle et leurs institutions. *Turcica* 7(1975), pp. 122-134.

BOJANIĆ, Dusanka. Dve godine istorije Bosanskog krajišta (1479. i 1480) prema Ibn Kemalu. (Deux ans d'histoire de la Marche de Bosnie - selon Ibn Kemal.) *Prilozi Or. Fil.Ist.* 14-15(1964-5), pp. 33-50

BOJANIĆ-LUKAĆ, D. Deux ans d'histoire de la Marche de Bosnie selon Ibn Kemal. *Actes I. Cong. int. ét. balkan. et sud-est europ.* III (1969), pp. 731-737.

BYCHBAROV, M., PAVLOV, D. Filosofskie osnovy revolyutzionno-demokraticheskoy ideologii v yugoslavyanskikh stranakh. *Actes I. Cong. int. ét. balkan. et sud-est europ.* IV (1969), pp. 215-227.

DJORDJEVIC, D. Les Yougoslaves au XIX et au XXe s. *Actes I. Cong. int. ét. balkan. et sud-est europ.* III (1969), pp. 117-130.

DJURDJEV, B. Les changements historiques et ethniques chez les peuples slaves du Sud après la conquête turque. *Actes I. Cong. int. ét. balkan. et sud-est europ.* III (1969), pp. 575-578.

DJURDJEV, B. Drevneyshiy sokhranivshiysya turetzkiy defter (reesto) Sremskogo sandzhaka. (Le plus ancien registre cadastral turc conservé du Sandjak de la Syrmie.) *Fontes orientales* ... curavit A.S. Tveritinova, I, 1964, pp. 119-130.

EREN, Ismail. Turska štampa u Jugoslaviji (1866-1966). *Prilozi Or.Fil.Ist.* 14-15 (1964-5), pp. 359-395

FEHIM, S.Dž. Još nekoloko dokumenta o Užičkom Šejhu. *Prilozi za or. filol.* 18-19 (1968-9), pp. 267-284.

GORDON, L.M. A young Croat's encounter with an exotic Muslim culture: a Serbo-Croatian travel epic of the nineteenth century. *Humaniora Islamica* 1(1973), pp. 189-205.

GRAFENAUER, B. Die Völker Jugoslaviens. *Actes I. Cong. int. ét. balkan. et sud-est europ.* III (1969), pp. 37-50.

HANDŽIĆ, Adem. O Islamizaciji u sjeveroistočnoj Bosniu u XV i XVI vijeku. (On conversion into Islam in North-East Bosnia in 15th and 16th century. *Prilozi Or. Fil. Ist.* 16-17 (1966-7), pp. 5-48

HANDŽIĆ, A., HADŽIJAHIĆ, M. O progonu hamzevija u Bosni 1573 godine. (On persecution of Hamzawis in Bosnia in 1573.) *POF* 20-21(1970-71), pp. 51-70.

HEYER, F. Die Bedeutung der serbischen Orthodoxen Kirche für die "Serbische Revolution" nach der Darstellung des deutschen Historikers Leopold Ranke. *Actes I. Cong. int. ét. balkan. et sud-est europ.* IV (1969), pp. 507-518.

IDRIZOVIĆ, Muris. Mehmed Šakir Kurtćehajić. *Prilozi Or.Fil.Ist.* 14-15(1964-5), pp. 353-358

IGNYATOVICH, Dzh. Dogovor knyazya Mikhaila s "Dobrodetel'noy druzhinoy" o yugoslavskom tzarstve i nekotorye sobytiya v 1867-68 gg. *Actes I. Cong. int. ét. balkan. et sud-est europ.* IV (1969), pp. 169-183.

IVANOSKI, O. Yuzhnoslavyanskie sotzialisty otnositel'no osvoboditel'noy bor'bui makedonskogo naroda v kontze XIX v. *Actes I. Cong. int. ét. balkan. et sud-est europ.* IV (1969), pp. 573-581.

KOVAČEVIĆ, E. Hududname bosanskog vilajeta prema Austriji poslije Karlovačkog mira. (The Hududname concerning the borders of the Bosnian vilayet with Austria after the Peace of Karlovci.) *POF* 20-21(1970-71), pp. 365-436.

LACHMANN, R. Antitürkischer Traktat und
serbische Volkstradition. Ein Beitrag zur
Diskussion um die sogenannten "Pamiętniki
Janczara". *Serta Slavica in memoriam A.
Schmaus,* 1971, pp. 427-434.

McGOWAN, B. Food supply and taxation on
the Middle Danube (1568-1579). *Archivum
Ottomanicum* 1(1969), pp. 139-196.

MAJER, H.G. Ein Brief des Serdar Yeğen
Osman Pascha an den Kurfürsten Max
Emanuel von Bayern vom Jahre 1688 und
seine Übersetzungen. *Islamkundliche
Abhandlungen H.J. Kissling,* 1974, pp.
130-145.

MAJER, H.G. Ein Nišān des Osmanenprinzen
Ahmed, des Statthalters von Amasya, für
die Zâviye des Schejch Bahâ' ed-Din vom
Jahre 906/1501. *Südostforschungen* 31
(1972), pp. 319-331.

MAKEDONSKI, S. L'exarchat bulgare et
l'enseignement scolaire en Macédoine
(1870-1912). *Études balkaniques* 7ii
(1971), pp. 104-119.

MARINOVIĆ, A. Développement des registres
cadastraux-fonciers dans la république du
Dubrovnik médieval. *Actes I. Cong. int.
êt. balkan. et sud-est europ.* III (1969),
pp. 369-376.

MATKOVSKI, A. La résistance des paysans
macédoniens contre l'attachement à la glèbe
au temps de la domination ottomane. *Actes
I. Cong. int. êt. balkan. et sud-est europ.*
III (1969), pp. 703-708.

NAUMOV, E.P. K voprosu o sotzial'noy
strukture serbskom derevni v 30-kh -50-kh
gg. XIX v. *Études balkaniques* 6ii(1970),
pp. 124-133.

OIKONOMIDES, N. Le haradj dans l'Empire
byzantin du XVe s. *Actes I. Cong. int. êt.
balkan. et sud-est europ.* III (1969), pp.
681-688.

PETROVICH, N. Sto let so dnya pervogo sobraniya Ob'edinennoy Omladiny Serboskoy.
*Actes I. Cong. int. êt. balkan. et sud-est
europ.* IV (1969), pp. 199-200.

POPOVIĆ, Toma. Ejnehanova kriza. (Ejnehans'
crisis.) *Prilozi Or.Fil.Ist.* 14-15(1964-5),
pp. 51-71

POPOVIĆ, Toma. Spisak hercegovačkih names-
nika u XVI veku. (List of the Hercego-
vinian Sandjakbeys. *Prilozi Or.Fil.Ist.*
16-17 (1966-7), pp. 93-99

ŠABANOVIĆ, H. Bosanski divan. *Prilozi za
or. filol.* 18-19(1968-9), pp. 9-45.

ŠABANOVIĆ, Hazim. Ḥaşan Kafi Pruščak.
(Hasan Kâfî Aqhisârî.) *Prilozi Or.Fil.Ist.*
14-15(1964-5), pp. 5-31

ŠCRIVANIĆ, G. The most important stages
in the development of toponymy of Yugoslav
lands on old maps. *Actes I. Cong. int. êt.
balkan. et sud-est europ.* III (1969), pp.
275-276.

STOIANOVICH, T. Les structures milléna-
ristes sud-slaves aux XVII et XVIIIe ss.
*Actes I. Cong. int. êt. balkan. et sud-est
europ.* III (1969), pp. 809-820.

SUČESKA, Avdo. O položaju Poljica u Osman-
skoj državi. (On the position of Poljice
in the Ottoman state.) *Prilozi Or.Fil.Ist.*
16-17 (1966-7), pp. 77-91

SUČESKA, Avdo. Popis čifluka u rogatičkom
kadiluku iz 1835. godine. (List of chiflics in the cadiluk of Rogatica 1835).
Prilozi Or.Fil.Ist. 14-15(1964-5), pp. 189-
271

TARNANIDES, J. Le rappel de la prise de
Belgrade de 1521 par les turcs dans les
Βραχεὰ χρονικὰ. *Cyrillomethodianum* 2
(1973-4), pp. 160-164.

TRAKO, Salih. Bitka na Kosovu 1389. godine
u istoriji Idrisa Bitlisija. (The battle
of Bosovo 1389 in the history of Idris
Bitlisi.) *Prilozi Or.Fil.Ist.* 14-15(1964-
5), pp. 329-351

VOJE, I. La structure de la classe des
marchands en Bosnie et en Serbie pendant la
deuxième moitié du XVe s. *Actes I. Cong.
int. êt. balkan. et sud-est europ.* III
(1969), pp. 627-632.

See also XXIX. d. *Albania* Kornrumpf

See also XXIX. d. (Bulgaria) Veleva.

See also XXIX. d. *Greece.* Skendi.

See also XLI. a. Mušić

See also XLI. a. Popovic.

e-j OTTOMAN HISTORY BY PERIOD

e To 1402 A. D.

DUJČEV, Ivan. Die Krise der spätbyzantin-
ischer Gesellschaft und die türkische Eroberung des 14. Jahrhunderts. *Jb. f. Gesch.
Osteuropas* N.F. 21(1973), pp. 481-492.

GÜNDISCH, G. Siebenbürgen in der Türken-
abwehr, 1395-1526. *Rev.roum.hist.* 1974(3),
pp. 415-443.

HERNANDEZ, Fr. The Turks with the Grand
Catalan Company, 1305-1312. *Boğazici
Univ. J.* 2(1974), pp. 25-45.

İNALCIK, H. The conquest of Edirne (1361).
Arch. ott. 3(1971), pp. 185-210.

PETROVIĆ, Dj. Fire-arms in the Balkans on
the eve of and after the Ottoman conquests of the fourteenth and fifteenth
centuries. *War, technology and society
in the Middle East,* ed. V.J. Parry and
M.E. Yapp, 1975, pp. 164-194.

SHCHERBAK, A.M. Sal-name (po rukopisi B
721, khranyashcheysya v Rukopisnom otdele
LO IVAN SSSR). *Pis'mennye pamyatniki
Vostoka* 1971, pp. 171-189.

SPREMIĆ, M. I tributi veneziani nel Levante nel XV secolo. *Studi veneziani* 13(1971), pp. 221-251.

TINNEFELD, F. Pachymeres und Philes als Zeugen für ein frühes Unternehmen gegen die Osmanen. *Byz. Zeits.* 64 (1971), pp. 46-54.

f 1403-1566

ABRAHAMOWICZ, Z. Staraya turetzkaya karta Ukrainy s planom vzryba dneprovskikh porogov i ataki turetzkogo flota na Kiev. (Une ancienne carte turque de l'Ukraine avec le plan de l'explosion des rapides du Dnieper et de l'attaque de la flotte turque contre Kiev.) *Fontes orientales... curavit A.S. Tveritinova II,* 1969, pp. 76-97.

ALEXANDRESCU-DERSCA, M. Quelques données sur le ravitaillement de Constantinople au XVIe s. *Actes I. Cong. int. ét. balkan. et sud-est europ.* III (1969), pp. 661-672.

ALEXANDRESCU-DERSCA BULGARU, M.M. L'action diplomatique et militaire de Venise pour la défense de Constantinople (1452-1453). *Rev. roumaine d'hist.* 13(1974), pp. 247-267.

ATSIZ, Bedriye. Über eine Urkunde Sultan Süleyman's des Prächtigen. *Islamkundliche Abhandlungen H.J. Kissling,* 1974, pp. 17-28.

BACQUÉ-GRAMMONT, J.L. Une lettre du prince ottoman Bâyazîd b. Meḥmed sur les affaires d'Iran en 1480. *Studia Iranica* 2(1973), pp. 213-234.

BELDICEANU, N. Un acte sur le statut de la communauté juive de Trikala. *REI* 40(1972), pp. 129-138.

BELDICEANU-STEINHERR, I. Le règne de Selīm Ier: tournant dans la vie politique et religieuse de l'empire ottoman. *Turcica* 6 (1975), pp. 34-48.

BELDICEANU-STEINHERR, I. Un transfuge qaramanide auprès de la Porte ottomane. Reflexions sur quelques institutions. *JESHO* 16(1973), pp. 155-167.

BERINDEI, M. Contribution à l'étude du commerce ottoman des fourrures moscovites. La route moldavo-polonaise. 1453-1700. *Cah. monde russe et sov.* 12(1971), pp. 393-409

BINNER, R. Griechische Emigration und Türkenkrieg. Anmerkungen zu einer Denkschrift von Janus Laskaris aus dem Jahre 1531. *Südostforschungen* 30(1971), pp. 37-50.

BOUDARD, R. Le sultan Zizim vu à travers les témoignages de quelques écrivains et artistes italiens de la Renaissance. *Turcica* 7(1975), pp. 135-156.

BRON, M. Taktyka walki w polu Turków osmańskich w XVI wieku. *Przegl. Or.* 1 (93, 1975), pp. 65-72.

BURI-GÜTERMANN, J. Ein Türke in Italien aus einer unbekannten Handschrift der Nationalbibliothek Wien. *ZDMG* 124, pp. 59-72.

CARTER, F.W. The commerce of the Dubrovnik republic 1500-1700. *Econ. H.R.* 24 (1971), pp. 370-394.

ERDER, L. The measurement of preindustrial population changes: the Ottoman Empire from the 15th to the 17th century. *M.E. stud.* 11(1975), pp. 284-301.

FEHÉR, G. Jr. Recent Data of the Turkish Campaign of 1543. *Studia Turcica, ed. L. Ligeti,* 1971, pp. 161-167

FISHER, A.W. Muscovite-Ottoman relations in the sixteenth and seventeenth centuries. *Humaniora Islamica* 1(1973), pp. 207-217.

GÖKBİLGİN, M. Tayyib. Un registre de dépenses de Bâyazîd II durant la campagne de Lépante de 1499. *Turcica* 5(1975), pp. 80-93.

GÖLLNER, C. Zur Problematik der Kreuzzüge und der Türkenkriege im 16. Jahrhundert. *Rev. ét. sud-est europ.* 13 (1975), pp. 97-115.

GOROVEI, Ş.S. Autour de la paix moldo-turque de 1489. *Rev. roum. hist.* 1974(3), pp. 535-544.

GÖYÜNÇ, Nejat. *Ṭur 'Abdīn* im 16. Jahrhundert nach den osmanischen Katasterbüchern. *XVIII. Deutscher Orientalistentag* 1972, pp. 142-148.

GRISLIS, Egil. Luther and the Turks. *MW* 64(1974), pp. 180-193, 275-285.

HAN, V. 15th and 16th century trade in glass between Dubrovnik and Turkey. *Balcanica* 4(1973), pp. 163-178.

HÜTTEROTH, W.D. The pattern of rural settlement in 16th century Anatolia and its decline. *Proc. 27th Int. Cong. Or. 1967* (1971), pp. 182-183.

INALCIK, H. Suleiman the lawgiver and Ottoman law. *Archivum Ottomanicum* 1(1969), pp. 105-138.

IVONIN, Yu.E. Iz predystorii vostochnogo voprosa v pervoy polovine XVI veka. (Angliya i franko-turetzkiy soyuz.) *VLU* 1974, (2), pp. 62-66.

JOHNSTON, N.J. The urban world of the Matraki manuscript. *JNES* 30(1971), pp. 159-166.

KÁLDY-NAGY, Gy. Suleimans Angriff auf Europa. *Acta Or. Hung.* 28(1974), pp. 163-212.

KELLENBENZ, H. Handelsverbindungen zwischen Mitteleuropa und Istanbul über Venedig in der ersten Hälfte des 16. Jahrhunderts. *Actes I. Cong. int. ét. balkan. et sud-est europ.* III (1969), pp. 839-841.

KIEL, M. A note on the history of the frontiers of the Byzantine Empire in the 15th century. *Byzantinische Zeitschr.* 66(1974), pp. 351-353.

KISSLING, H.J. Fîrûz-Beg, Grenzstatthalter Sultan Bâyezîd's II. (1481-1512), und der Salinenkrieg von Cattaro. *Geschichte in der Gesellschaft, Fest.K.Bosl* 1973, pp. 292-311.

KISSLING, H.J. Kemāl Re'īs e il"duca di Catanzaro". [offprint in SOAS] *Almanacco calabrese* 1972-3, pp. 31-41.

KISSLING, H.J. Quelques problèmes concernant Iskender-Paša, Vizir de Bāyezîd II. *Turcica* 2(1970), pp. 130-137.

KREISER, Kl. Bešīr Čelebī -- Hofarzt Ibrâhîm Qaramans und Vertrauter Meḥmeds II. Fâtih. *Islamkundliche Abhandlungen H.J. Kissling,* 1974, pp. 92-103.

KUNISCH, J. Das Nürnberger Reichsregiment und die Türkengefahr. *Hist. Jhb.* 93(1973), pp. 57-72.

LAQUEUR, H.P. Einige Anmerkungen zur Weinbereitung im osmanischen Reich im 16. Jahrhundert. *Islamkundliche Abhandlungen H.J. Kissling,* 1974, pp. 127-129.

LEFEBVRE, M.M. Quinze firmans du Sulṭān Meḥmed le Conquérant. *REI* 39(1971), pp. 147-173.

MEHMED, Mustafa A. La crise ottomane dans la vision de Hasan Kiafi Akhisari (1544-1616). *Rev. ét. sud-est eur.* 13(1975), pp. 385-402.

MEHMED, Mustafa A. La politique ottomane à l'égard de la Moldavie et du khanat de Crimée vers la fin du règne du sultan Mehmed II "le conquérant". *Rev.roum.hist.* 1974(3), pp. 509-533.

MICHAILIDIS, D. Un lamento inedito sulla caduta di Costantinopoli (Cod. Alexandr., Bibl. patr. 30 [361], ff. 149v - 150 m). *Byz. Z.* 65(1972), pp. 303-326.

MILLER, Yu. Medal' l.Neyfarera s portretom Khayr-ed-Dina Barbarossy. *Soobshch. Gos. Ermitazha* 38(1974), pp. 61-65.

MOKRI, Mohammad. Un *farmân* de Sultân Bâyqâra recommandant la protection d'une ambassade ottomane en Khorâsân en 879/1474. *Turcica* 5(1975), pp. 68-79.

MUTAFČIEVA, V.; DIMITROV, S. Die Agrarverhältisse im Osmanischen Reiche im XV-XVI Jh. *Actes I. Cong. int. ét. balkan. et sud-est europ.* III (1969), pp. 689-702.

MUTAFČIEVA, V. *et al.* Die Wakfe in Karaman (XV.-XVI. Jahrhundert). *Etudes balkaniques* 1975(1), pp. 53-75.

NIEWÖHNER-EBERHARD, E. Machtpolitische Aspekte des osmanisch-safawidiischen Kampfes um Baghdad im 16/17. Jahrhundert. *Turcica* 6(1975), pp. 103-127.

PALL, Fr. Preteso scambio di lettere tra Giorgio Brankovich, principe di Serbia, e Iancu de Hunedoara (Hunyadi) a proposito del pericolo ottomano intorno al 1450. *RESEE* 12(1974), pp. 79-86.

PATRINELIS, C. The exact time of the first attempt of the Turks to seize the Churches and convert the Christian people of Constantinople to Islam. *Actes I. Cong. int. ét. balkan. et sud-est europ.* III (1969), pp. 567-572.

PEVZNER, S.B., TVERITINOVA, A.S. Vakufnaya gramota Khani-Khatun--vnuchki sultana Mekhmeda II. *Pis'mennye pamyatniki Vostoka* 1970, pp. 108-133.

TARDY, L. Rapports d'Antal Verancsics, ambassadeur du roi de Hongrie à Stambul, sur la Géorgie (1553-1557, 1567-1568). *Bedi Kartlisa* 28 (1971), pp. 208-230.

TVERITINOVA, A.S. Dva spiska kanun-name sultana Selima I iz sovetskikh rukopisnykh kollektziy. *Sprache, Geschichte und Kultur der altaischen Völker,* hrsg. G. Hazai und P. Zieme (XII. PIAC, 1974), pp. 631-636.

TVERITINOVA, A.S. Nekotorye zamechaniya o znachenii vakufnogo zemlevladeniya v istorii osmanskoy imperii v svyazi s publikatziey vakufnoy gramoty Khani-Khatun. *Pis'mennye pamyatniki Vostoka* 1970, pp. 134-149.

VILLAIN-GANDOSSI, C. Contribution à l'étude des relations diplomatiques et commerciales entre Venise et la Porte ottomane au XVIe siècle. *Südost-Forsch.* 29(1970), pp. 290-298

See also III. a. 13. Faroqui.

See also V. m. 1. Denny

See also XV. e. Veronne.

See also XXII. c. Özbaran.

See also XXIX. e. Gündisch.

See also XXIX. e. Petrović.

See also XXIX. e. Shcherbak.

See also XXXI. g. Bacqué-Grammont

See also XL. aa. Guzev.

g 1566–1703

ABOU-EL-HAJ, R.A. The narcissism of Mustafa II (1695-1703): a psychohistorical study. *SI* 40(1974), pp. 115-131.

ABOU-EL-HAJ, Rifa'at Ali. Ottoman attitudes toward peace making: the Karlowitz case. *Islam* 51(1974), pp. 131-137.

ABOU-EL-HAJ, Rifaat Ali. The Ottoman vezir and paşa households 1683-1703: a preliminary report. *JAOS* 94(1974), pp. 438-447.

XXIX TURKEY: HISTORY. CYPRUS

ABRAHAMOWICZ, Z. Die türkische Herrschaft in Podolien (1672-1699). *Actes I. Cong. int. et. balkan. et sud-est europ.* III (1969), pp. 777-780.

ALEXANDRESCU-DERSCA, M.M. La condition des captifs turcs dans l'empire des Habsbourgs (1688-1689) d'après les mémoires de'Osman Aga. *Studia et acta or.* 8(1971), pp. 125-144.

BARBAGALLO, F. Discussioni e progetti sul commercio tra Napoli e Constantinopoli nel '700. *Riv.stor.ital.* 83(1971), pp. 264-296.

BARNETT, R.D. The European merchants in Angora. *Anatolian stud.* 24(1974), pp. 135-141.

BARTL, P. Der Kosakenstaat und das Osmanische Reich im 17. und in der ersten Hälfte des 18. Jahrhunderts. *Südost-Forsch.* 33(1974), pp. 166-194.

BERGHAUS, P. Numismatische Erinnerungen an die Türkenkriege aus Westfalen. *Num. Z.* 87-88(1972), pp. 119-122.

BERINDEI, M., BERTHIER, A., MARTIN, M., VEINSTEIN, G. Code de lois de Murād III concernant le province de Smeredevo. *Südostforschungen* 31(1972), pp. 140-163.

BIEGMAN, N.H. Some peculiarities of firmans issued by the Ottoman treasury in the sixteenth century. *Archivum Ottomanicum* 1(1969), pp. 9-13.

BLAŠKOVIČ, J. Türkische historische Urkunden aus Gemer. *Asian and African studies* [Bratislava] 8(1972), pp. 71-89.

BOYER, P. La chiourme turque des galères de France de 1665 à 1687. *ROMM* 6(1969), pp. 53-74.

CVETKOVA, B. Novye dokumenty o sipakhiyskom zemlevladenii v osmanskoy imperii v kontze XVI v. (Nouveaux documents sur la propriété foncière sipahie de la fin du XVIe s.) *Fontes orientales* ... curavit A.S. Tveritinova, I, 1964, pp. 199-221.

FAROGHI, S. Social mobility among the Ottoman ʻulemā in the late sixteenth century. *IJMES* 4(1973), pp. 204-218.

FAROQHI, Suraiya Ein Günstling des osmanischen Sultans Murād III: David Passi. *Der Islam* 47(1971), pp. 290-297.

FAROGHI, S. Social mobility among the Ottoman *'ulemā* in the late sixteenth century. *IJMES* 4(1973), pp. 204-218.

GEMIL, Tahsin. La Moldavie dans les traités de paix turco-polonais du XVIIe siècle (1621-1672). *Rev. roumaine d'hist.* 12 (1973), pp. 687-714.

GIURESCU, C.C. La politique des grandes puissances dans le sud-est européen aux XVIIe et XVIIIe siècles. *Rev. roumaine d' hist.* 9(1970), pp. 945-951.

GÖKBILGIN, Tayyib. L'étendue du pouvoir de Soliman le Magnifique au XVIe siècle. *Recueils Soc. Jean Bodin* 20(1970), pp. 627-637.

GRANSTREM, E.E. Zametka sovremennika o nabegakh kazakhov na turetzkie vladeniya v nachale XVII v. *Vost sbornik 3*, 1972, pp. 37-40.

GRIGORYAN, V.R. Ob aktovykh knigakh armyanskogo suda g. Kamenetz-Podol'ska (XVI-XVII vv.) (Des livres des actes du tribunal Arménien de Kamenec-Podolsk (XVI-XVIIe siècles.) *Fontes orientales* ... curavit A.S. Tveritinova, I, 1964, pp. 276-296.

HEINISCH, R.R. Habsburg, die Pforte und der Böhmische Aufstand (1618-1620). *Südost-Forsch.* 33(1974), pp. 125-165.

HEYWOOD, C.J. Sir Paul Rycaut, a seventeenth-century observer of the Ottoman state: notes for a study. *English and continental views of the Ottoman Empire, 1500-1800,* 1972, pp. 31-59.

JENNINGS, R.C. Loans and credit in early 17th century Ottoman judicial records. The Sharia court of Anatolian Kayseri. *JESHO* 16(1973), pp. 168-216.

KÁLDY-NAGY, Gy. Macht und Immobiliarvermögen eines türkischen Beglerbegs im 16. Jahrhundert. *Acta Or. Hung.* 25(1972), pp. 441-450.

KISSLING, H.J. Die Köprülü - Restauration. *Int. Kulturhist. Symposium Mogersdorf* I: *Osterreich und die Türken* (Eisenstadt, 1972), pp. 75-83.

KOPČAN, Vojtech. Eine Quelle der Geschichte Silihdārs. *Asian and African studs.* 9(1973), pp. 129-139.

KOZAKIEWICZ, I. Legacja Numan-beja w Polsce. *Przegl. or.* 1(93, 1975), pp. 77-79.

KUNT, Metin Ibrahim. Ethnic-regional (*Cins*) solidarity in the seventeenth-century Ottoman establishment. *IJMES* 5(1974), pp. 233-239.

KÜTÜKOĞLU, Bekir. Les relations entre l'empire ottoman et l'Iran dans la seconde moitié du XVIe siècle. *Turcica* 6(1975), pp. 128-145.

LESURE, M. Notes et documents sur les relations vénéto-ottomanes, 1570-1573. *Turcica* 4(1972), pp. 134-164.

MANTRAN, R. La bataille de Lépante vue par un chroniqueur ottoman. *Cah.de ling.d'orientalisme et de slavistique* 1-2(1973), pp. 183-189.

MANTRAN, R. L'echo de la bataille de Lépante à Constantinople. *Annales ESC* 28 (1973), pp. 396-405.

MARTIN, B.G. Maî Idrîs of Bornu and the Ottoman Turks, 1576-78. *IJMES* 3(1972), pp. 470-490.

MEYER, M.S. Vliyanie "revolyutzii tzen" v Evrope na osmanskuyu imperiyu. *NAA* 1975(1), pp. 96-107.

MUTAFATCHIEVA, V. Opis' khassov velikogo vezira Sinan-Pashi. (Registre des "Hass" du Grand Vésir Sinan-Pacha.) *Fontes orientales* ... curavit A.S. Tveritinova, I, 1964, pp. 236-252.

PIPPIDI, A. Quelques drogmans de Constantinople au XVIIe siècle. *Rev. et. sud-est eur.* 10(1972), pp. 227-255.

RÖHRBORN, K. Die Emanzipation der Finanzbürokratie im Osmanischen Reich (Ende 16. Jahrhundert). *ZDMG* 122(1972), pp. 118-139.

SCHMUCKER, W. Die maltesischen Gefangenschaftserinnerungen eines türkischen Kadi von 1599. *Archivum Ottomanicum* 2(1970), pp. 191-251.

SHINDER, J. Career line formation in the Ottoman bureaucracy, 1648-1750: a new perspective. *JESHO* 16(1973), pp. 217-237.

SKILLITER, S.A. Catherine de' Medici's Turkish ladies-in-waiting; a dilemma in Franco-Ottoman diplomatic relations. *Turcica* 7(1975), pp. 188-204.

SKILLITER, S.A. The Hispano-Ottoman armistice of 1581. *Iran and Islam, in memory of V. Minorsky*, 1971, pp. 491-515

SPULER, B. La diplomatie européenne à la Sublime Porte aux XVIIe et XVIIIe siècles. *REI* 39(1971), pp. 3-28.

SUGAR, P.F. The Ottoman "Professional Prisoner" on the Western Borders of the Empire in the sixteenth and seventeenth centuries. *Études balkaniques* 7ii(1971), pp. 82-91.

TARDY, L. Les problèmes intérieurs de la Géorgie du XVIe siècle dans le repport envoyé de Stamboul par un diplomate impérial. *Bedi Kartlisa* 33(1975), pp. 191-203.

TEPLY, K. Eine Freilassungserklärung fur einen türkischen Gefangenen aus dem Türkenkrieg 1683-1699. *ZDMG* 121(1972), pp. 242-253.

TEPLY, K. Vom Los osmanischer Gefangener aus dem Grossen Türkenkrieg 1683-1699. *Südostforschungen* 32(1973), pp. 33-72.

TLILI, Béchir. Auz origines de la pensée réformiste ottomane moderne: un important document du šayḫ al-Aqḥiṣârî (XVIIe siècle). *ROMM* 18(1974), pp. 131-148.

TVERITINOVA, A.S. Darstvennaya gramota (Myul'k-name) Sultana Selima II na imya vezira i kapudana Piyale-Pashi (1587 g.) *Pis'mennye pamyatniki Vostoka* 1971, pp. 109-126.

See also III. a. 4. Jennings.

See also VIII. d. *Turkey*. Kissling.

See also VIII. f. Meinecke.

See also XV. e. Veronne.

See also XXIX. d. *Yugoslavia*. Majer.

See also XXIX. f. Alexandrescu
Carter
Tardy

See also XXIX. f. Bron.

See also XXIX. f. Berindei

See also XXIX. f. Erder.

See also XXIX. f. Fisher.

See also XXIX. f. Göyünç.

See also XXIX. f. Hütteroth.

See also XXIX. f. Laqueur.

See also XXIX. f. Mehmed.

See also XXXIV. g. Bennigsen, Lemercier-Quelquejay.

h 1703–1839

ANGHELOU, A. Private journal of a voyage from Smyrna to Venice, by J.O. Hanson. *Annual Brit. School Athens* 66(1971), pp. 13-48.

ARSH, G.L. O russkoy sisteme "pokrovitel'stva" i o nekotorykh ee sotzialno-ekonomicheskikh politichnskikh posledstviyakh dlya naseleniya Balkan (konetz XVIII nachalo XIX vv.). *Etudes balkaniques* 1975(2), pp. 108-113.

BERINDEI, D. et COJOCARU, E. La crise orientale et le problème des Principautés roumaines en été 1821. Information tirées des archives de Vienne. *Rev.ét.sud-est eur.* 9(1971), pp. 203-224.

BEŠEVLIEV, B. Wirtschaftskarte des europäischen Teils vom Osmanischen Imperium im 18. Jahrhundert. *Études balkaniques* 7ii(1971), pp. 92-103.

BOEV, R. Voenno-politicheskoe sotrudnichestvo mezhdu balkanskimi narodami i Rossiey v khode russko-turetzkoy voyny 1768-1774 godov. *Etudes balkaniques* 1975(2), pp. 118-127.

BOSKOV, V. Ein osmanischer Ketzer-Prozess im 18. Jahrhundert. *Südost-Forsch.* 33(1974), pp. 296-306.

CERNOVODEANU, P. Interese economice la Dunărea de Jos şi în Marea Neagră între 1803-1829. *Revista de istorie* 28(1975), pp. 1695-1709.

CIECIERSKA-CHŁAPOWA, T. Échanges commerciaux entre la Pologne et la Turquie au XVIIIe siècle. *Folia or.* 14(1972-73), pp. 261-287.

CLOGG, R. A further note on the French newspapers of Istanbul during the revolutionary period (1795-97). *Belleten T.T.K.* 39,no.155(1975), pp. 483-490.

DENIS-COMBET, M.Th. La collection Saint-Priest au Ministère des affaires étrangères. *Turcica* 7(1975), pp. 250-263.

DOSTYAN, I.S. Znachenie Kyuchuk-Kaynardzhiyskogo dogovora 1774 g. v politike Rossii na Balkanakh kontza XVIII i XIX vv. *Etudes balkaniques* 1975(2), pp. 97-107.

DRUZHININA, E.I. 22-letie Kyuchuk-Kaynardzhiyskogo mira. *Etudes balkaniques* 1975(2), pp. 83-96.

DZHIKIYA, S.S. Turetzkiy sudebnyy dokument XVIII v. *Pismennye pamyatniki vostoka,* 1969, pp. 142-144.

FINDLEY, C.V. The foundation of the Ottoman foreign ministry. *IJMES* 3(1972), pp. 388-416.

GENOV, Tz. Voennye deystviya russkikh voĭsk na Bolgarskoy zemle vo vremya russko-turetzkoy voyny 1768-1774 gg. *Etudes balkaniques* 1975(2), pp. 114-117.

HOPE, T.J. George Frederick Koehler, James Bland Burges et les relations anglo-turques de 1791 à 1793. *Rev. roumaine d'hist.* 13 (1974), pp. 95-114

HOPE, T.J. John Sibthorp's last expedition to the Balkans: the accounts of Sibthorp and Dallaway about their travels in 1794. *RESEE* 12(1974), pp. 87-102.

KIRKETERP-MØLLER, H. Fra København til Konstantinopel 1761 pa grundlag af F.C. von Havens dagbog. *Fund og forskning* 17(1970), pp. 79-94.

KRZEMIRSKI, A. Relacja Sejida Mehmeda Emina Wahida Effendiego z podróży do Polski w 1807 r. *Przeglad Or.* 77(1971), pp. 23-37.

LALOR, B. Promotion patterns of Ottoman bureaucratic statesmen from the Lâle devri until the Tanzimat. *Güney-Doğu Avrupa araştırmaları dergisi* 1(1972), pp. 77-92.

LEONE, E. de. L'apport des patriotes italiens dans la formation de la Turquie moderne. *Turcica* 3(1971), pp. 181-192.

LEVY, Avigdor. The Officer Corps in Sultan Mahmud II's New Ottoman Army, 1826-39. *IJMES* 2 (1971), pp. 21-39.

LEVY, Avigdor. The Ottoman Ulema and the military reforms of Sultan Mahmud II. *Asian & Afr.Studs.* 7(1971), pp. 13-39.

LISOWSKI, J. À propos d'un échange des prisonniers entre le Sultan Ahmed III et Charles XII, roi de Suède. *Folia or.* 14 (1972-73), pp. 289-292.

LISOWSKI, J. Zur Frage der Türkischen Polenpolitik der Jahre 1704-1714. *Folia Or.* 12(1970), pp. 135-139

MUTAFCHIEVA, V. "Kyrdjaliyskoe vremya". Opyt periodatzii kyrdzhaliystva. *Et. balkaniques* 1973(1), pp. 100-120.

MUTAFCHIEVA, V.P. Proverochnye spiski (yoklama defterleri) 1014-1016 gg. Kh. kak istochnik obshchestvenno-ekonomicheskoy istorii osmanskoy imperii XVII v. (Les "Yoklama defterleri" des années 1014-1016 (de l'Hégire) domme un source sur l'histoire sociale-économique de l'Empire Ottoman au XVIIIe siècle.) *Fontes orientales...curavit A.S. Tveritinova* II, 1969, pp. 212-217.

NEDKOV, B. Neskol'ko dokumentov o voennykh korablyakh, prodannykh russkimi turkam posle prutskogo pokhoda. (Quelques documents concernant les navires de guerre vendus par les Russes aux Turcs après l'expedition sur la rivière Pruth.) *Fontes orientales* ... curavit A.S. Tveritinova, I, 1964, pp. 186-198.

NOVICHEV, A.D. Gyul'khaneyskiy khatt-i sherif 1839 g. i ego vneshnepoliticheskiy aspekt. *Tyurkologicheskiy sbornik* 1972 *(Pamyati P.M. Melioranskogo),* pp. 382-395.

NOVIČEV, A.D. Die letzte Etappe der orientalischen Krise 1831-1841. *Zeits. f. Geschichtswissenschaft* 22(1974), pp. 1233-1242.

NOVICHEV, A.D. Turetzkiy istochnik o vnutrennem polozhenii osmanskoy imperii i prichinakh ee porazheniya v voyne s Rossiey v 1768-1774 gg. *Vestnik Leningradskogo Univ. ist., yazyk. lit.* 1975 (2), pp. 80-88.

OLSON, R.W. The esnaf and the Patrona Halil rebellion of 1730: a realignment in Ottoman politics? *JESHO* 17(1974), pp. 329-344

PANZAC, D. La peste à Smyrne au XVIIIe siècle. *Annales ESC* 28(1973), pp. 1071-1091.

PAPACOSTEA-DANIELOPOLU, C. La compagnie "grecque" de Braşov; la lutte pour la conservation des privilèges (1777-1850). *RESEE* 12(1974), pp. 59-78.

SADAT, Deena R. Âyân and Ağa: the transformation of the Bektashi corps in the eighteenth century. *MW* 63(1973), pp. 206-219.

SADAT, D.R. Rumeli ayanlari: the eighteenth century. *J. mod. hist.* 44(1972), pp. 346-363.

SHAMIR, Shimon. Belligerency in a disintegrating society. Factional warfare in Ottoman Syria on the eve of the period of modernization. *Abr-nahrain* 12(1971-2), pp. 75-84

SIRUNI, H.Dj. Ramiz Pacha et son activité. *Studia et acta or.* 8(1971), pp. 103-124.

SÜHEYL ÜNVER, A. Les épidémies de choléra dans les terres balkaniques aux XVIIIe et XIXe siècles. *Etudes balkaniques* 1973(4), pp. 89-97.

TAIROVA, N.V. Novye dokumenty o russko-turetzkikh otnosheniyakh v 1801-1815 gg. *Strany Blizhnego i Srednego Vostoka: istoriya, ekonomica,* 1972, pp. 177-186.

THIBAULT, G. Un rapport français inédit sur l'Empire ottoman en 1756. *JA* 258 (1970), pp. 319-370.

TODOROV, N. Kyuchuk-Kaynardzhiyskiy mirnyy dogovor. *Etudes balkaniques* 1975 (2), pp. 77-82.

TVERITINOVA, A.S. Ukaz sultana Abdulkhamida I po sluchayu pribytiya v Turtziyu russkogo kuptza. (L'edit du Sultan Abdulkhamed I à l'occasion de l'arrivée en Turquie d'un négociant russe.) *Fontes orientales ...* curavit A.S. Tveritinova, I, 1964, pp. 297-303.

VESELÁ-PŘENOSILOVÁ, Z. Turetzkiy traktat ob osmanskikh krepostyakh severnogo Prichernomor'ya v nachale XVIII v. (Un traite turc concernant les forteresses ottomanes au Nord de la Mer Noire au commencement du XVIIIe siecle.) *Fontes orientales...curavit A.S. Tveritinova* II, 1969, pp. 98-139.

See also XXIX. g. Giurescu.

See also XXIX. g. Spuler

i 1839-1922

ABU-MANNEH, Butrus. Sultan Abdülhamid II and the Sharifs of Mecca (1880-1900). *Asian and African studies* [Jerusalem] 9 (1973), pp. 1-21.

AGERON, C.R. Abd el-Kader souverain d'un royaume arabe d'Orient. *II.Cong.int.ét. nord-afr.* 1970, pp. 15-30.

ALI, Patria R. Enver Pasha. His status in modern Turkish history. *Egypt.hist.R.* 22(1975), pp. 3-36.

ALLAIN, J.C. Les débuts du conflit italo-turc: Octobre 1911-Janvier 1912. *Rev. hist. mod. contemp.* 18 (1971), pp. 106-115.

BAHA, Lal. Activities of Turkish agents in Khyber during World War I. *J. Asiatic Soc. Pakistan* 14(1969), pp. 185-192.

BEYLERIAN, A. Les origines de la question arménienne du traité de San Stéfano au congrès de Berlin (1878). *Rev. hist. dipl.* 87(1973), pp. 139-171.

BOISSEL, J. Un diplomate du XIXe siècle défenseur de l'Empire ottoman: Prosper Bourée. *Rev. hist. dipl.* 87(1973), pp. 115-138.

BRYSON, T.A. Admiral Mark L. Bristol, an open-door diplomat in Turkey. *IJMES* 5 (1974), pp. 450-467.

CALLAHAN, R. What about the Dardanelles? A review article. *Amer. hist. R.* 78 (1973), pp. 641-648.

CHAMBERS, R.L. The education of a nineteenth-century Ottoman *ālim*, Ahmed Cevdet Pasha. *IJMES* 4(1973), pp. 440-464.

CHAPKEVICH, E.I. Otzenka bol'shevikami mladoturetzkoy revolyutzii. *NAA* 1975(6), pp. 50-61.

DAMIANOV, S. La diplomatie française et le réformes en Turquie d'Europe. *Etudes balkaniques* 10ii-iii(1974), pp. 130-153.

DOSTYAN, I.S. Dokumenty o russkoy politike v otnoshenii Turtzii i balkanskikh narodov perioda napoleonovskikh voyn i venskogo kongressa v izdanii "vneshnyaya politika Rossii XIX i nachala XX vv". *Etudes balkaniques* 1973(4), pp. 98-108.

DUGUID, S. The politics of unity: Hamidian policy in Eastern Anatolia. *ME stud.* 9 (1973), pp. 139-155.

DUMONT, P. Une organisation socialiste ottomane: la Fédération ouvrière de Salonique (1908-1912). *Etudes balkaniques* 1975(1), pp. 76-88

DUMONT, P. La pacification du sud-est anatolien en 1865. *Turcica* 5(1975), pp. 108-130

DYER, G. The origins of the 'Nationalist' group of officers in Turkey, 1908-18. *J. contemp. hist.* 8(1973), pp. 121-164.

DYER, G. The Turkish armistice of 1918: 2, A lost opportunity: the armistice negotiations of Moudros. *M.E.Stud.* 8(1972), pp. 313-348.

DZHAFAROVA, A.A. Turetzkie zhenshchiny v natzional'no-osvoboditel'noy bor'be 1918-1923 gg. *Strany Blizhnego i Srednego Vostoka: istoriya, ekonomica,* 1972, pp. 66-78.

EMERIT, M. Les saint-simoniens en Grèce et en Turquie. *Rev. ét. sud-est europ.* 13(1975), pp. 241-251.

ERGIL, Dogu. A reassessment: the young Turks, their politics and anti-colonial struggle. *IC* 49(1975), pp. 75-97

ERGIL, Dogu. A reassessment: the Young Turks, their politics and anti-colonial struggle. *IC* 49(1975), pp. 133-149.

FADEEVA, I.E. K kharakteristike obshchestvenno-politicheskikh vzglyadov Akhmeda Midkhat-Pashi. *Arabskie strany, Turtziya, Iran, Afganistan,* 1973, pp. 147-157.

FARAH, C.E. Necip Pasha and the British in Syria, 1841-1842. *Archivum Ottomanicum* 2(1970), pp. 115-153.

FARHI, G. The Şeriat as a political slogan - or the 'Incident of the 31st Mart'. *ME stud.* 7(1971), pp. 275-300.

FINDIKOĞLU, Ziyaeddin Fahri. The westernization of economic thought in Turkey. *Proc.27th Int.Cong.Or.1967* (1971), pp. 294-295.

HAMILTON, K.A. An attempt to form an Anglo-French 'industrial entente'. *M.E. stud.* 11(1975), pp. 47-73.

HIRSZOWICZ, L. The Sultan and the Khedive, 1892-1908. *M.E.Stud.* 8(1972), pp. 287-311.

HOVANNISIAN, R.G. Armenia and the Caucasus in the genesis of the Soviet-Turkish entente. *IJMES* 4(1973), pp. 129-147.

ISSAWI, Charles. British consular views on Syria's economy in the 1850's-1860's. *American University of Beirut Festival book*, 1967, pp. 103-120.

ITZKOWITZ, N. 'Kimsiniz Bey Efendi', or a look at Tanzimat through Namier-colored glasses. *Near Eastern round table* 1967-68, ed. by R. Bayly Winder, pp. 41-52.

ITZKOWITZ, N. and SHINDER, J. The office of Şeyh ül-Islâm and the Tanzimat - a prosopographic enquiry. *ME stud.* 8(1972), pp. 93-101

JÄSCHKE, G. Die Grundung der türkischen Republik. Anfang der Reformen Kemal Atatürks. *Belleten T T K* 37(1973), pp. 471-473.

JÄSCHKE, G. Mustafa Kemal und England in neuer Sicht. *WI* N.S.16(1975), pp. 166-228.

JÄSCHKE, G. Zwei Streitfragen aus der Frühgeschichte der türkischen Revolution. *WI N.S.* 13(1971), pp. 162-167.

JELAVICH, B. Austria-Hungary, Rumania and the Eastern Crisis, 1876-1878. *Südostforschungen* 30(1971), pp. 111-141.

KÁLDY-NAGY, Gy. Turetzkie reestrovye knigi mukāṭaʿa kak istoricheskie istochniki. (Les livres de compte turc "Muqāṭaʿa" - source de documentation historique.) *Fontes orientales* ... curavit A.S. Tveritinova, I, 1964, pp. 76-90.

KARPAT, K.H. The memoirs of N. Batzaria: the Young Turks and nationalism. *IJMES* 6(1975), pp. 276-299.

KARPAT, Kemal. The Ottoman parliament of 1877 and its social significance. *Actes I. Cong. int. ét. balkan. et sud-est europ.* IV (1969), pp. 247-257.

KAYALOFF, J. From the Transcaucasian past: two documents about Turkish resistance in 1918. *J. Asian hist.* 6(1972), pp. 123-132.

KEDOURIE, Elie Young Turks, Freemasons and Jews. *ME studies* 7 (1971), pp. 89-104.

KENT, M. Agent of empire? The National Bank of Turkey and British foreign policy. *Hist.J.* 18(1975), pp. 367-389.

KORNRUMPF, H.J. Das dänische Konsulat in Smyrna. Eine osmanische Urkunde aus dem Jahre 1889. *Acta Or.* 34(1972), pp. 1-12.

KÖYMEN, O. The advent and consequences of free trade in the Ottoman Empire (19th century). *Études balkaniques* 7ii(1971), pp. 47-72.

LANDAU, J.M. A new manuscript on the Muslim pilgrimage. *Ve Congrès International d'Arabisants et d'Islamisants. Actes.*, [1970?], pp. 307-316.

MACFIE, A.L. The British decision regarding the future of Constantinople, November 1918-January 1920. *Hist.J.* 18 (1975), pp. 391-400.

MACIU, Vasile. Les relations Roumano-Turques pendant la Révolution de 1848. *Belleten (Türk Tarih Kurumu)* 35 (no.139, 1971), pp. 383-402.

MAKEDOWSKI, S. La révolution jeune-turque et les premières élections parlementaires de 1908 en Macédoine et Thrace orientale. *Et. balk.* 10iv(1974), pp. 133-146.

MANGO, A. The young Turks. *ME stud.* 8 (1972), pp. 107-117

MARDİN, Şerif. Super Westernization in urban life in the Ottoman empire in the last quarter of the nineteenth century. *Turkey; geographic and social perspectives*, ed. by P. Benedict [et al.], 1974, pp. 403-446.

MARINESCU, B.; WAGNER, G. The union of the Roumanian principalities in the concerns of Stratford Canning as ambassador in Constantinople, 1853-1858. *Rev. roumaine d'hist.* 9(1970), pp. 261-269.

MEDLICOTT, W.N. The Near Eastern crisis of 1875-78 reconsidered. *ME studies* 7 (1971), pp. 105-109.

MILLER, A.F. Revolyutziya 1908 g. v Turtzii i Mustafa Kemal'. *NAA* 1975(3), pp. 53-66.

MONTGOMERY, A.E. The making of the treaty of Sèvres of 10 August 1920. *Hist. J.* 15 (1972), pp. 775-787.

OBERLING, P. The Istanbul *Tünel*. *Archiv Ott.* 4(1972), pp. 217-263.

ORHONLU, Cengiz. Some thoughts on the results of the migrations and deportations during the Greek invasion of Anatolia. *J. Regional Cult.Inst.* 7(1974), pp. 113-119.

PETROSYAN, Yu.A. Iz istorii nelegal'noy propagandy mladoturok vo flote. *NAA* 1973 (5), pp. 151-152.

PINSON, M. Ottoman colonization of the Circassians in Rumili after the Crimean War. *Et. balkaniques* 1972(3), pp. 71-85.

PINSON, M. Russian policy and the emigration of the Crimean Tatars to the Ottoman Empire, 1854-1862. *Güney-Doğu Avrupa araştırmaları dergisi* 1(1972), pp. 37-56.

PINSON, M. Russian policy and the emigration of the Crimean Tatars to the Ottoman Empire, 1854-1862. *Güney-Doğu Avrupa araştırmaları dergisi* 2-3(1973-74), pp. 101-114.

PISAREV, Yu.A. Antivoennoe dvizhenie v russkikh voyskakh na salonikskom fronte v 1916-1918 gg. *Actes I. Cong. int. ét. balkan. et sud-est europ.* IV (1969), pp. 861-869.

QUATAERT, D. Dilemma of development: the Agricultural Bank and agricultural reform in Ottoman Turkey, 1888-1908. *IJMES* 6 (1975), pp. 210-227.

SAMARDŽIEV, B. Traits dominants de la politique d'Abdülhamid II relative au problèmè des nationalités (1876-1885). *Et. balkaniques* 8 iv (1972), pp. 57-79

SAMŠUTDINOV, A.M. Lénine et la Turquie. *Études balkaniques* 6i(1970), pp. 25-43.

SARKISYAN, E.K. K voprosu o vstuplenii osmanskoy imperii v pervuyu mirovuyu voynu na storone tzentral'nykh derzhav. *Sprache, Geschichte und Kultur der altaischen Völker,* hrsg. G. Hazai und P. Zieme (XII. PIAC, 1974), pp. 511-520.

SEMENOV, L.S., SHEREMET, V.I. Vneshneekonomicheskie svyazi Turtzii epokhi Krymskoy voyny. *VLU ist., yaz., lit.* 1973(3), pp. 44-49.

SHAW, S.J. The origins of representative government in the Ottoman Empire: an introduction to the Provincial Councils, 1839-1876. *Near Eastern round table* 1967-68, ed. by R. Bayly Winder, pp. 53-142.

SHAW, S.J. A promise of reform: two complementary documents. *IJMES* 4(1973), pp. 359-365.

SHAW, S.J. The *Yıldız* palace archives of *Abdülhamit II. Arch. ott.* 3(1971), pp. 211-237.

SHPIL'KOVA, V.I. Antipravitel'stvennye vystupleniya v vostochnoy Anatolii nakanune mladoturetskoy revolyutzii. (The anti-government movement in Eastern Anatolia, 1908.) *NAA* 1971(3), pp. 72-85.

SHPIL'KOVA, V.I. Pervyy proekt politicheskoy programmy mladoturok. *NAA* 1973(4), pp. 61-68.

SHUKLA, Ram Lakhan. The Pan-Islamic policy of the Young Turks and India. *Proc.32 Ind. hist.cong.* 1970, vol. 2, pp. 302-307.

SILIN, A.S. Germano-turetzkie otnosheniya nakanune pervoy mirovoy voyny. *Actes I. Cong. int. ét. balkan. et sud-est europ.* IV (1969), pp. 871-884.

SPECTOR, I. General Ali Fuat Cebesoy and the Kronstadt revolt (1921): a footnote to history. *IJMES* 3(1972), pp. 491-3.

STEPPAT, F. Kalifat, *Dār al-Islām* und die Loyalität der Araber zum osmanischen Reich bei Ḥanafitischen Juristen des 19. Jahrhunderts. *Ve Congrès International d'Arabisants et d'Islamisants. Actes.,* [1970?], pp. 443-462.

SUBAEV, N.A. Organ turetzkikh internatzionalistov "Eni dun'ya" kak istoricheskiy istochnik (1918-1919). *NAA* 1975 (2), pp. 62-71.

SUCIU, D. Aspects de la question d'orient reflétés dans les articles de Karl Marx et de Frédéric Engels des années 1853-1855. *Rev. Roumaine d'hist.* 12(1973), pp. 515-531.

SWANSON, G.W. The Ottoman police. *J. contemp. hist.* 7(1972), pp. 243-260.

SWANSON, G.W. War, technology, and society in the Ottoman Empire from the reign of Abdülhamid II to 1913: Mahmud Şevket and the German military mission. *War, technology and society in the Middle East,* ed. V.J. Parry and M.E. Yapp, 1975, pp. 367-385.

SWEETMAN, J. Military transport in the Crimean War, 1854-1856. *Engl. hist. R.* 88(1973), pp. 81-91.

THOBIE, J. Les puissances et Constantinople, 1911-1914. *Et.balk.* 10iv(1974), pp. 42-48.

TIBAWI, A.L. The last knight of the last caliphs. *IQ* 15(1971), pp. 159-163.

TORALDO-SERRA, N. Origini e sviluppi della questione vicino-orientale (a proposito di un recente libro di E. Kedourie). *OM* 53 (1973), pp. 509-521.

VELIKOV, S. Georges Dimitrov et quelques questions du mouvement ouvrier en Turquie. *Ét. balkaniques* 8(1972), pp. 115-122.

VELIKOV, S. Mouvement antimilitariste dans les rangs de l'armée turque pendant la Première Guerre mondiale. *Études balkaniques* 7iv(1971), pp. 14-27.

VELIKOV, St. Participation d'internationalistes turcs à la défense de la République soviétique hongroise.(1919). *Etudes balkaniques* 1974(1), pp. 86-91.

WALKER, C.J., DYER, G. Correspondence (on the Armenian question 1915). *M.E.stud.* 9 (1973), pp. 376-385.

WERNER, E. Die Türkeipolitik Österreich-Ungarns 1915-1918. *Etudes balkaniques* 1975(2), pp. 54-59.

ZEINE, Zeine N. Unpublished documents concerning independence movements in the Arab provinces of the Ottoman Empire. *Actes I. Cong. int. ét. balkan. et sud-est europ.* IV (1969), pp. 693-697.

ZHELTYAKOV, A.D. Iz istorii turetzkoy vol'noy pressy XIX veka. (From the history of the Turkish press.) *VLU* 1971(3), pp. 91-100.

ZÜRRER, W. Der Friedensvertrag von Sèvres. Ein kritischer Beitrag zur Problematik der Neuordnung des nahöstlichen Raumes nach dem Ersten Weltkrieg. *Saeculum* 25(1974), pp. 88-114.

Note Mustafa Kemals an Earl Curzon vom 30. April 1920. *WI* N.S.16(1975), pp. 231-233.

See also IX. m. Tlili.

See also XIX. j. Novichev

See also XXII. c. Landau.

See also XXIX. h. Novičev.

See also XXIX. h. Süheyl Ünver.

See also XXXI. i. Göyüne.

See also XXXI. i. Hornus.

See also XLIII. g. Spuler.

j 1922–

ABADAN, Nermin. Politics of students and young workers in Turkey. *Ankara Üniv. Siyasal bilgiler Fakültesi dergisi* 26i(1971) pp. 89-111.

AHMAD, Feroz. The role of Ali Fuat Cebesoy in the Turkish resolution. *IJMES* 4(1973), pp. 365-366.

AKBIL, Semih. L'association entre la Turquie et la Communauté économique européenne. *La Communauté et les pays méditerranéens* 1970, pp. 95-100.

ALASYA, Fikret. Die Türkische Republik und ihre Zypernpolitik. *Cultura Turcica* 8-10 (1971-73), pp. 110-131.

ALEXANDROV, E. Turkey's foreign policy and the problems of our time. *Etudes Balkaniques* 9(1973) (1), pp. 5-17.

ALTUĞ, Yılmaz. The creation of Turkish resident diplomacy. *Dış politika* 2ii(1972), pp. 81-100.

ALVAREZ, D.J. The *Missouri* visit to Turkey: an alternative perspective on Cold War diplomacy. *Balkan studies* 15(1974), pp. 225-236.

ANCIAUX, R. Religion et politique dans la Turquie contemporaine (1945-1971), *Corresp. d'Orient. Etudes* 17-18(1970), pp. 115-162.

ARMAOĞLU, Fahir H. Recent developments in Turkish foreign policy. *Dış politika* 1i (1971), pp. 85-94.

ARMAOĞLU, Fahir H. Turkey and the People's Republic of China. *Dış politika* 1iii(1971), pp. 109-127.

BAYKAL, B.S. Zur Geschichte der türkischen Republik. *Actes I. Cong. int. ét. balkan. et sud-est europ.* III (1969), pp. 169-178.

BAYÜLKEN, Ü. Haluk. Reform in the Ministry of Foreign Affairs. *Dış politika* 3ii(1973), pp. 51-58.

BAYÜLKEN, Ü. Halûk. Turkey and the United Nations. *Dış politika* 1iii(1971), pp. 95-108.

BAYÜLKEN, Ü. Haluk. Turkey's foreign policy. *Dış politika* 3i(1973), pp. 67-82.

BERKES, Niyazi. The two facets of the Kemalist revolution. *MW* 64(1974), pp. 292-306.

BIRGI, Muharrem Nuri. Developments within the Atlantic community and Turkey. *Dış politika* 3iv(1973), pp. 71-79.

BOZBAG, Ali F. Kemalismus als liberaler Entwicklungsweg für den gesellschaftlichen Transformationsprozess in der Türkei. *Vierteljahresberichte (Friedrich-Ebert-Stiftung* 55(1974), pp. 37-50.

BURNOUF, D. Les élections présidentielles en Turquie. Interactions entre le Haut-Commandement et le Parlement. *Politique étrangère* 38(1973), pp. 365-377.

BURNOUF, D. La situation en Turquie. *Politique étrangère* 36(1971), pp. 53-67.

BURNOUF, D. La situation en Turquie après les interventions du Haut-Commandement dans les affaires publiques. *Politique étrangère* 37(1972), pp. 101-113.

CARRETTO, G.E. La crisi di governo in Turchia e la formazione del governo Ecevit. *OM* 54 (1974), pp. 33-43.

CARRETTO, G.E. Cronaca della Turchia (gennaio-giugno 1975). *OM* 55(1975).

CARRETTO, G.E. Le elezioni politiche del 14 ottobre 1973 in Turchia. *OM* 53(1973), pp. 783-792.

CONETTI, G. Monsignor Roncalli, later Pope John XXII, and Turkish neutrality in the first period of the Second World War (September 1939-June 1941). *Turkish yearbook of int. relations* 9(1968), pp. 64-74.

DANILOV, V.I. Turtziya i problemy stran "tret'ego mira" v organizatzii ob-'edinennykh natziy. (Turkey and problems of the "Third World" in the UNO.). *NAA* 1972(4), pp. 121-127.

DUBIŃSKI, A. Przemiany społeczne i kulturalne w Republice Tureckiej. *Przegl.or.* 91 (1974), pp. 203-208.

ECEVIT, Bülent. Labor in Turkey as a new social and political force. *Social change and politics in Turkey,* by K.H. Karpat, 1973, pp. 151-181.

EKIN, Nusret. Strikes and lockouts in Turkey. *Iktisat Fak. Macmuası* 26 (1966-7), pp. 131-154.

EREN, Ahmet Cevat. Atatürk et les problèmes de l'émigration. *Cultura Turcica* 8-10(1971-73), pp. 153-156.

ERGIL, D. Class conflict and Turkish transformation (1950-1975). *SI* 41(1975), pp. 137-161.

ERGIL, Dogu. Turkish reform movement and beyond (1923-1938). *Islamic studies* 14 (1975), pp. 249-260.

ERIM, Nihat. The Turkish experience in the light of recent developments. *MEJ* 26(1972), pp. 245-252

FATIMI, S.Q. The Kemalist revolution and the Pakistan Freedom Movement. A study in historical parallelism. *J.Reg.Cult.Inst.* 7i (1974), pp. 15-29.

FRANZ, Erhard. Die Legislaturwahlen in der Türkei. *Orient* [Germany] 14(1973), pp. 185-187.

GERAY, Cevat. Problems of local administration at regional level in Turkey. *Ankara Univ. Siyasal bilgler Fakültesi dergisi* 25i (1970), pp. 1-11.

GERAY, Cevat. Turkish experience in community development. *Ankara Univ. Siyasal bilgler Fakültesi dergisi* 25i(1970), pp. 13-18.

GIL BENUMEYA, R. Un doble momento internacional en la actualidad de Turquia. *Rev. de politica int.* 115(1971), pp. 173-181

GLASNECK, J. Kemal Atatürk in der Historiographie. *Z.f.G.* 9(1971), pp. 1154-1166.

GÖKMEN, Oğuz. Turkish-German relations. *Dış politika* 1i(1971), pp. 101-111.

GÖNLÜBOL, Mehmet. NATO and Turkey: an overall appraisal. *Turkish yb.int.relations* 11(1971), pp. 1-38.

GÖNLÜBOL, Mehmet. Turkish-American relations: a general appraisal. *Dış politika* 1iv(1971), pp. 67-80.

GROTE, M., TIMM, Kl. Der Kemalismus und seine aktuelle Bedeutung; Bericht über eine wissenschaftliche Tagung an der Sektion Asienwissenschaft der Humboldt-Universität Berlin am 15. November 1973 in Berlin. *Asien, Afrika, Latein-Amerika* 2(1974), pp. 468-470.

GROTE, M. Sozialreformerische Gesellschaftstheorien innerhalb der Republikanischen Volkspartei der Türkei -- Bülent Ecevit und die Richtung "ortanin solu". *Asien. Afrika. Latein-Amerika* 3 (1975), pp. 837-840.

GUSEYNOV, A.A. O konfederatzii revolyutzionnykh rabochikh profsoyuzov Turtzii ("DISK") *Strany Blizhnego i Srednego Vostoka: istoriya, ekonomica,* 1972, pp. 56-66.

HALE, W.M. Aspects of the Turkish General Election of 1969. *M.E. Stud.* 8(1972), pp. 393-404

HARRIS, G.S. The Soviet Union and Turkey. *The Soviet Union and the Middle East,* ed. I.J. Lederer and W.S. Vucinich, 1974, pp. 25-54.

ILERI, M. Türkei: Bilanz funfzehnjähriger Arbeitskräfteabwanderung. Rückblick und Vorschau. *Orient* [Hamburg] 16ii(1975), pp. 132-146.

INALCIK, Halil. Foreign historians on Atatürk and the Atatürk revolution. *Cultura Turcica* 8-10(1971-73), pp. 15-31.

JÄSCHKE, G. VI. Mehmed'in Ingiltere'ye ikinci anlaşma teklifi. Zweites Vertragsangebot Mehmeds VI. an England. *Belleten T.T.K.* 38(1974), pp. 493-497

JEFFRIES-BRITTEN, P. Le programme du Parti des travailleurs de Turquie. *Orient* 49-50 (1969), pp. 75-121

KARPAT, Kemal H. Ideology in Turkey after the revolution of 1960. Nationalism and socialism. *Social change and politics in Turkey,* by K.H. Karpat, 1973, pp. 317-366.

KARPAT, Kemal H. The impact of the people's houses on the development of communication in Turkey - 1931-1951. *WI* 15(1974), pp. 69-84.

KARPAT, Kemal H. Ömer Seyfeddin and the transformation of Turkish thought. *Rev. ét. sud-est europ.* 10(1972), pp. 677-691.

KARPAT, Kemal H. Political developments in Turkey, 1950-70. *M.E.Stud.* 8(1972), pp. 349-375.

KARPAT, Kemal H. Social groups and the political system after 1960. *Social change and politics in Turkey,* by K.H. Karpat, 1973, pp. 227-281.

KARPAT, Kemal H. Structural change, historical stages of modernization, and the role of social groups in Turkish politics. *Social change and politics in Turkey,* by K.H. Karpat, 1973, pp. 11-92.

KAZANCIGIL, Ali. La participation et les élites dans un système politique en crise: le cas de la Turquie. *Rev. Fr. de Sci. pol.* 23(1973), pp. 5-32.

KHALID, D.H. Atatürk's concepts of Islamic reformism and Muslim unity. *J.Reg.Cult. Inst.* 7i(1974), pp. 39-52.

KHALID, Detlev H. The Kemalist attitude towards Muslim unity. *Islam and the modern age* 6ii(1975), pp. 23-40.

KHALID, Detlev H. A study of Ataturk's laicism in the light of Muslim history. *Islam and the modern age* 5iii(1974), pp. 43-73.

KHALID, D.H. 'Ubayd-Allah Sindhi in Turkey: first contacts between Pakistani and Turkish nationalism. *J. Reg. Cult. Inst.* 6i-ii(1973), pp. 29-42.

KILIÇ, Altemur. A visit and its implications: Professor Nihat Erim's visit to the United States. *Dış politika* 2i(1972), pp. 55-60.

KNIGHT, J. American statecraft and the 1946 Black Sea Straits controversy. *Pol. sci. Q.* 90(1975), pp. 451-475.

KOLARS, J. The integration of the villager into the national life of Turkey. *Social change and politics in Turkey,* by K.H. Karpat, 1973, pp. 182-202.

KONYAKHINA, T.V. "Pomoshch'" Turtzii po doktrine Trumena (po poslednim publikatziyam dokumentov gosudarstvennogo departmenta CShA). *NAA* 1975(3), pp. 135-143.

KORKHMAZYAN, R.S. K istorii germano-turetzkogo dogovora 18 yunya 1941 g. *Arabskie strany, Turtziya, Iran, Afganistan,* 1973, pp. 98-105.

KÖYMEN, Mehmet Altay. Einige Bemerkungen zur Geburt der neuen Türkei. *Cultura Turcica* 8-10(1971-73), pp. 10-14.

KUNISCH, Johannes. Das Nürnberger Reichsregiment und die Türkengefahr. *Historisches Jahrbuch* 93(1973), pp. 57-72.

KÜRKÇÜOĞLU, Ömer. An analysis of Turkish-Arab relations. *Ankara Univ. Siyasal Bilgiler Fak. Dergisi* 27i(1972), pp. 116-134.

KÜRKÇÜOĞLU, Ömer E. Recent developments in Turkey's Middle East policy. *Dış politika* 1ii(1971), pp. 93-99.

LOĞOĞLU, O. Faruk. Turkey's style of statecraft. *Dış politika* 2i(1972), pp. 61-77.

MACFIE, A.L. The Straits question: the Conference of Montreux (1936). *Balkan studies* 13(1972), pp. 203-219.

MANISALI, Erol. Turkey's defense policy and national defense industry. *Dış politika* 4iv(1974), pp. 129-143.

MARDIN, Şerif A. Ideology and religion in the Turkish revolution. *IJMES* 2 (1971), pp. 197-211.

MARDIN, Serif. Opposition and control in Turkey. *Government and opposition* 1 (1965-6), pp. 375-387.

MARTIN DE LA ESCALERA, C. Turquia, en una encrucijada. *Rev. de politica int.* 114(1971), pp. 111-131.

MARZARI, F. Western-Soviet rivalry in Turkey, 1939. *ME studies* 7 (1971), pp. 63-79; 201-220.

MIHÇIOĞLU, Cemal. The application of information processing in the Turkish public administration. *Ankara Üniv. Siyasal bilgiler Fakültesi dergisi* 26ii(1971), pp. 79-92.

MILLER, A.F. Premières pages de la biographie d'Atatürk. *Études balkaniques* 7i(1971), pp. 27-56

MILLER, A.F. Stanovlenie turetzkoy respubliki. *NAA* 1973(6), pp. 45-54.

MILLER, A.F. Sur la biographie de Kemal Atatürk. *Etudes balkaniques* 10ii-iii(1974), pp. 117-129.

NEYZİ, Nezih. The middle classes in Turkey. *Social change and politics in Turkey,* by K.H. Karpat, 1973, pp. 123-150.

NIKOLOV, M. Développement et problèmes de la presse turque subséquemment au 27 mai 1960. *Etudes Balkaniques* 9(1973) (3), pp. 59-71.

ÖGEL, Ali Şükrü. Some memories of Atatürk during the Turkish national war of liberation. *Cultura Turcica* 8-10(1971-73), pp. 45-49.

OKANDAN, R.G. La Révolution nationale et la proclamation de la République en Turquie. *Ann.Fac.Droit Istanbul* 19(1969), pp. 81-90.

OLCAY, Osman. Turkey's foreign policy. *Dış politika* 1ii(1971), pp. 79-84.

OLSON, R.W. Al-Fatah in Turkey: its influence on the March 12 coup. *ME stud.* 9 (1973), pp. 197-205.

ÖNDER, Mehmet. Das Atatürk-Haus in Saloniki. Kurzgefasste Geschichte des Hauses. *Cultura Turcica* 8-10(1971-73), pp. 39-44.

ORHONLU, Cengiz. Observations on reforms on Turkey. *J.Reg.Cult.Inst.* 7i(1974), pp. 5-14.

ORHONLY, Cengiz. Ataturk's view of history. *J. Reg. Cult. Inst.* 6i-ii(1973), pp. 43-50.

OSETROV, N. Sovetsko-turetzkoe soglashenie ob ekonomicheskom sotrudnichestve i turetzkaya pressa. *Strany Blizhnego i Srednego Vostoka: istoriya, ekonomica,* 1972, pp. 126-134.

PAPADIMITRIU, G. Die Präsidentenwahl vom März-April 1973 in der Türkei. *Verfassung und Recht* 1(1974), pp. 45-53.

RAHMETI ARAT, Reşid. Du Gazi Mustafa Kemal au premier ministre Ismet Paşa. *Cultura Turcica* 8-10(1971-73), pp. 50-58

REGANCHAR, N. Turquie: la démocratie en sursis. *Projet* 64(1972), pp. 500-503.

REYCHMAN, J. 50-lecie republiki Tureckiej. *Przegl. or.* 3(87,1973), pp. 189-191.

ROGUSHIN, A.A. Demokraticheskoe dvizhenie v Turtzii i proiski maoistskikh grupp. *NAA* 1975(2), pp. 118-128.

RUSTOW, D.A. Ataturk's political leadership. *Near Eastern round table* 1967-68, ed. by R. Bayly Winder, pp. 143-155.

RUSTOW, D.A. The modernization of Turkey in historical and comparative perspective. *Social change and politics in Turkey,* by K.H. Karpat, 1973, pp. 93-120.

SATTERTHWAITE, J.C. The Truman doctrine: Turkey. *America and the Middle East.* ed. P.T. Hart, 1972, pp. 74-84.

SERTEL, Yildiz. Le socialisme de l'Islam et la Turquie d'aujourd'hui. *Orient* 51-2 (1969), pp. 27-40

SHIRALIEV, V. Progressivnye sily Turtzii v bor'be za mir. *Arabskie strany, Turtziya, Iran, Afganistan,* 1973, pp. 166-169.

SILIER, Oya. The place of Anglo-Turkish relations in the foreign policy of the Turkish Republic (1923-1939). *Turkish yb.int.relations* 11(1971), pp. 86-101.

SIRKOV, D. La déclaration bulgaro-turque de non-agression du 17 février 1941. *Études balkaniques* 1972(2), pp. 73-83.

SOFIEV, M.M. Uchastie zakavkazskoy federatzii v sovetsko-turetzkikh kul'turnykh svyazyakh. *NAA* 1975(5), pp. 149-166.

SONYEL, Salâhi R. The Anglo-Turkish conflict fifty years ago. *Belleten TTK* 37(no. 145, 1973), pp. 113-122.

SONYEL, Salahi Ramadan. Fifty years ago: the Chanak crisis. *Balkan studies* 13 (1972), pp. 41-48.

SÖYLEMEZ, Yüksel. The question of narcotic drugs and Turkey. *Diş politika* 4iv(1974), pp. 144-155.

SPAIN, J.W. The United States, Turkey and the poppy. *MEJ* 29(1975), pp. 295-309.

SPECTOR, I. More on the role of Ali Fuat Cebesoy as Turkish military expert and diplomat. *IJMES* 6(1975), pp. 238-241.

SPULER, U. Nurculuk. Die Bewegung des "Bediüzzaman" Said Nursi in der modernen Türkei. *Studien zum Minderheitenproblem im Islam* I, 1973, pp. 100-182.

STARCHENKOV, G.I. Nauchno-tekhnicheskiy progress v Turtzii. *NAA* 1974(3), pp. 36-43.

SUNAR, Ilkay. A preliminary note on the politics of civil society formation in Turkey. *Ankara Univ. Siyasal Bilgiler Fak. dergisi* 28iii-iv, pp. 57-81.

SZYLIOWICZ, J.S. Elite recruitment in Turkey: the role of the Mülkiye. *World politics* 23 (1970-71), pp. 371-398.

TACHAU, F., GOOD, M-J.D. The anatomy of political and social change. Turkish parties, parliaments, and elections. *Contemporary politics* 5(1972-73), pp. 551-573.

TACHAU, F. Turkish provincial party politics. *Social change and politics in Turkey,* by K.H. Karpat, 1973, pp. 282-316.

TAMKOC, Metin. Stable instability of the Turkish polity. *MEJ* 27(1973), pp. 319-341.

TAMKOÇ, Metin. Traditional diplomacy of modern Turkish diplomats. *Dış politika* liv (1971), pp. 81-100.

TAMKOÇ, Metin. The warrior diplomat: Ismet Inönü. *Dış politika* 3iv(1973), pp. 80-92.

TAŞHAN, Seyfi. Foreign policy issues in the 1973 Turkish general election. *Dış politika* 3iii(1973), pp. 49-66.

TEZİÇ, Erdoğan. L'évolution du système électoral turc sous la seconde République. *Ann. Fac.Droit Istanbul* 18(1968), pp. 170-187.

TURKMEN, Ilter. Turkish-Greek relations. *Dış politika* liii(1971), pp. 85-94.

TZOUNIS, I. Turkish-Greek relations. *Dış politika* lii(1971), pp. 85-92.

ÜLKÜTAŞIR, M. Şakir. Wie wurde Atatürk dieser Familienname gegeben und wer hat ihn gefunden? *Cultura Turcica* 8-10(1971-73), pp. 32-38

ÜNAL, Tahsin. Die Geschichte der Kriegsschule und Mustafa Kemal. *Cultura Turcica* 8-10(1971-73), pp. 59-69.

VATIKIOTIS, P.J. Greece and the crisis in the Mediterranean. *J. internat. stud.* 4(1975), pp. 75-81.

VELIKOV, S. A l'occasion du cinquantenaire de la proclamation de la République turque. *Et. balkaniques* 9(1973), pp. 5-16.

VELIKOV, S. Le parti communiste bulgare sur le problème des Détroits à la Conférence de Lausanne. *Etudes balkaniques* 1973 (4), pp. 72-79.

WEIKER, W.F. "I have enough problems" - dilemmas of American relations with Turkey. *Continuing issues in international politics,* ed. Y.H. Ferguson and W.F. Weiker, 1973, pp. 243-262.

WEIKER, W.F. Social sciences in contemporary Turkey. *MESA Bull.* 5ii (1971), pp. 72-82.

WEISBAND, E. The Sanjak of Alexandretta 1920-1939. A case study. *Near Eastern round table* 1967-68, ed. by R. Bayly Winder, pp. 156-224.

YALÇINTAS, Nevzat. Planned development in Turkey. *Iktisat Fak. Mecmuası* 27 (1968), pp. 163-182.

YALMAN, Nur, On land disputes in Eastern Turkey. *Islam and its cultural divergence. Studies in honor of Gustave E. von Grunebaum,* 1971, pp. 180-217

YALMAN, Nur. Some observations on secularism in Islam: the cultural revolution in Turkey. *Daedalus* 102i(1973), pp. 139-168.

YILDIZ, Hakki Dursun. Die geistigen und psychischen Grundlagen des Unabhängigkeitskrieges. *Cultura Turcica* 8-10(1971-73), pp. 70-85.

YODFAT, Aryeh Y. The USSR and Turkey. *International problems* 14(1975), pp. 32-47.

YÜCEKOK, Ahmet Naki. The process of political development in Turkey. *Turkish yearbook of int. relations* 9(1968), pp. 96-111.

YÜCERÜRK, Alper. L'accroissement de la population dans la région d'Istanbul et les problèmes principaux qui en resultent. *Rev. Fac. Sci. Econ. Univ. Istanbul (Iktisat Fakültesi mecmuası)* 28(1968-69), pp. 123-144.

ZHIVKOVA, L. The Anglo-Turkish relations (1934-1935). *Études balkaniques* 7iv (1971), pp. 82-98.

ŽIVKOVA, L. The question of revising the regime of the Straits agreed upon in the Lausanne Convention (in the light of English archive documents of 1933). *Études balkaniques* 7ii(1971), pp. 73-81.

The rule of law in Turkey and the European Convention on Human Rights. *Rev. Int. Commis. Jurists* 11(1973), pp. 37-56.

See also XXIX. i. Bryson.

See also XXXI. j. Kheyfetz.

jj ECONOMICS

ABADAN-UNAT, Nermin. La récession de 1966/67 en Allemagne fédérale et ses répercussions sur les ouvriers turcs. *Turkish yb.int.relations* 11(1971), pp. 39-61.

AKTAN, Reşat. Analysis and assessment of land reform activities in Turkey. *Ankara Univ. Siyasal bilgler Fakültesi dergisi* 26i(1971), pp. 85-136.

AKTAN, Reşat. Basic characteristics of Turkish agriculture and problems of productivity. *Turkish yb.int.relations* 10(1969-70), pp. 50-98.

ALACAKAPTAN, Aydın. The objectives and strategy of tourism development in Turkey. *Dış politika* 2i(1972), pp. 78-87.

ALBAUM, M., DAVIES, C.S. The spatial structure of socio-economic attributes of Turkish provinces. *IJMES* 4(1973), pp. 288-310.

ALIEVA, A.A. Kratkaya kharakteristika deyatel'nosti gosudarstvennykh sel'skokhozyaystvennykh pokazatel'nykh ferm v Turtzii. *Strany Blizhnego i Srednego Vostoka: istoriya, ekonomica,* 1972, pp. 235-245.

ALIEVA, A. Sel'skokhozyaystvennaya kooperatziya v Turtzii na sovremennom etape. *Arabskie strany, Turtziya, Iran, Afganistan,* 1973, pp. 179-186.

AYSAN, Mustafa. Management education in Turkey. *South Africa international* 6 (1975-6), pp. 124-134.

BAHADIR, Sefik Alp. Das Genossenschaftswesen in der Türkei. *Vierteljahresberichte* 61(1975), pp. 249-268.

BALABAN, Ali. Land and water resource development for crop production in Turkey. *Annales Univ. Ankara* 13(1974), pp. 221-235.

BENEDICT, P. Change in the economic functions of a small Anatolian town: 1947-1967. *Rev. Geog. Inst., Univ. Istanbul* 14(1972-3), pp. 43-96.

BIRTEK, Faruk, KEYDER, Caglar. Agriculture and the state: an inquiry into agricultural differentiation and political alliances: the case of Turkey. *J.peasant stud.* 2(1975), pp. 446-467.

ÇAĞATAY, Neşet. Riba and interest concept and banking in the Ottoman Empire. *Vakıflar dergisi* 9(1971), pp. 57-66.

CAREY, J.P.C. and CAREY, A.G. Turkish agriculture and five-year development plans. *IJMES* 3(1972), pp. 45-58.

CAREY, J.P.C. & CAREY, A.G. Turkish industry and the five year plans. *MEJ* 25(1971), pp. 337-354.

CLARK, E.C. The Ottoman industrial revolution. *IJMES* 5(1974), pp. 65-76.

CLARK, J. The growth of Ankara 1961-1969. *Rev.Geog.Inst., Univ.Istanbul* 13(1970-71), pp. 119-139

CLARK, J.R. Residential patterns and social integration of Turks in Cologne. *Manpower Mobility across Cultural Boundaries,* ed. by R.E. Krane, 1975, pp. 61-76.

DESTREE, A. L'opium en Iran. *Correspondance d'Orient: Etudes* 15-16(1969), pp. 81-103.

EASTWOOD, T. Co-operation in Turkey. *Yearbook of agricultural co-operation* 1972, pp. 131-139.

ERGIL, Godu, RHODES, R.I. The impact of the world capitalist system on Ottoman society. *IC* 48(1974), pp. 77-91.

FARFUTDINOV, N.M. Problema podgotovki natzional'nykh tekhnicheskikh kadrov intelligentzii v Turtzii v 20-30-kh godakh XX v. *Arabskie strany, Turtziya, Iran, Afganistan,* 1973, pp. 235-244.

FRENCH, D. A sixteenth century English merchant in Ankara? *Anatol. stud.* 22(1972), pp. 241-247.

FRY, M.J. An application of the Stone model to the Turkish financial accounts. *J. dev. stud.* 7(1970-71), pp. 271-283.

FRY, M.J., ILKIN, Selim. Devaluation of the Turkish lira. *Turkish yearbook of int. relations* 9(1968), pp. 82-95.

FRY, M.J. Turkey's first 5-year development plan: an assessment. *Economic J.* 81(1971), pp. 306-326.

HERSHALG, Z.Y. Turning points in the economic history of the Middle East - the Turkish case. *Proc. 27th Int.Cong.Or. 1967* (1971), pp. 205-206

KAMINSKAYA, I.I. Nekotorye voprosy vzaimootnosheniy SENTO i Turtzii. *Strany Blizhnego i Srednego Vostoka: istoriya, ekonomica,* 1972, pp. 314-320.

KIRAY, Mübeccel. Business organizations and development. *Turkish yb.int.relations* 10 (1969-70), pp. 1-23.

KIRAY, Mübeccel B. Some notes on social planning objectives and strategies in third five-year plan of Turkey. *Turkish yb.int. relations* 11(1971), pp. 62-85.

KOLAN, Tufan. International labor migration and Turkish economic development. *Manpower Mobility across Cultural Boundaries*, ed. by R.E. Krane, 1975, pp. 138-160.

KRANE, R.E. Effects of international migration upon occupational mobility, acculturation and the labor market in Turkey. *Manpower Mobility across Cultural Boundaries*, ed. by R.E. Krane, 1975, pp. 161-204.

KUDAT, Ayşe. Structural change in the migrant Turkish family. *Manpower Mobility across Cultural Boundaries*, ed. by R.E. Krane, 1975, pp. 77-94.

KULIEV, R. Rol' gosudarstva v razvitii energeticheskoy promyshlennosti Turtzii. *Arabskie strany, Turtziya, Iran, Afganistan*, 1973, pp. 203-210.

LEVINE, N. Value orientation among migrants in Ankara, Turkey: a case study. *J. Asian and African studies* [York Univ.] 8(1973), pp. 50-68.

LEVY, A. The Eskenci project. *Abr-Nahrain* 14(1973-4), pp. 32-39.

MILLER, D.R. and ÇETİN, İhsan. Migrant workers, wages and labor markets: an economic model. *Manpower Mobility across Cultural Boundaries*, ed. by R.E. Krane, 1975, pp. 124-137.

MOISEYEV, P.P. Torgovo-ekonomicheskie otnosheniya mezhdu SSSR i Turtziey. (Trade and economic relations between the USSR and Turkey.) *NAA* 1972(6), pp. 117-124,

MONSON, T.D. Differences in industrial learning behavior of Turkish workers at home and abroad; causes and consequences. *Manpower Mobility across Cultural Boundaries*, ed. by R.E. Krane, 1975, pp. 95-123.

MONSON, T.D. Industrial learning patterns of Turkish workers at home and abroad. *J. developing areas* 9(1974), pp. 221-236.

MUNRO, J.M. Migration in Turkey. *Econ.development and cultural change* 22(1974), pp. 634-653.

NOEL, E. The expansion of the E.E.C. and its implications for Turkey. *Dış politika* 2iii (1972), pp. 95-102.

OĞUZKAN, Turhan. The Turkish brain-drain: migration tendencies among doctoral level manpower. *Manpower Mobility across Cultural Boundaries*, ed. by R.E. Krane, 1975, pp. 205-220.

OKYAR, Osman. Recent developments and the slow down in the economy. *Dış politika* liii(1971), pp. 151-164.

OKYAR, Osman. Turkish industrialization policies (1923-1970). *Dış politika* 3iv (1973), pp. 93-115.

OKYAR, Osman. The world monetary system and Turkey's monetary system. *Dış politika* lii (1971), pp. 119-134.

ORÇAN, Güler. Turkey's foreign trade in 1972 and her objectives for 1973. *Dış politika* 2iv(1972), pp. 182-195.

POROY, Ibrahim I. Planning with a large public sector: Turkey (1963-1967). *IJMES* 3(1972), pp. 348-360.

POSADA, A.J. Different systems of land reform relevant to the Turkish experience. *Land reform* 1971, (2), pp. 9-20.

ROY, D.A. The Zonguldak strike: a case study of industrial conflict in a developing society. *ME stud.* 10(1974), pp. 142-185.

SARAÇOGLU, Tevfik. The association between Turkey and the E.E.C.: the traditional phase. *Dış politika* lii(1971), pp. 100-109.

ŞENGÜN, Ismail. Macro-economic principles and the performance of the Turkish economy. *Dış politika* 2ii(1972), pp. 101-110.

SHIRINOV, A. O nekotorykh chertakh agrarnoy politiki turetzkogo pravitel'stva v 30-kh godakh. *Strany Blizhnego i Srednego Vostoka: istoriya, ekonomica*, 1972, pp. 453-462.

STARCHENKOV, G.I. Problemy rabochey sily v Turtzii. (Problems of labour in Turkey.) *NAA* 1971(1), pp. 29-37.

STARCHENKOV, G.I. Struktyrnye izmeneniya v ekonomike Turtzii. *Narody Azii i Afriki* 1973(3), pp. 17-29.

STEWIG, R. Die Industrialisierung in der Türkei. (Industrialization in Turkey.) *Die Erde* 103(1972), pp. 21-47

TOLUN, Bedriye. Die Bevölkerungsdichte-und Verteilung der Stadt Balikesir. *Rev.Geog. Inst., Univ.Istanbul* 13(1970-71), pp. 85-95

TROFIMOV, A.Z. Problemy finansirovaniya v pyatiletiem plane razvitiya ekonomiki Turtzii na 1963 - 1967 gg. *Strany Blizhnego i Srednego Vostoka: istoriya, ekonomica*, 1972, pp. 417-426.

TÜMERTEKİN, Erol Manufacturing and suburbanization in Istanbul. *Rev.Geog.Inst., Univ.Istanbul* 13(1970-71), pp. 1-40

TUNCER, Baran. Private and public savings in a high population growth economy. *Ankara Univ. Siyasal bilgler Fakültesi dergisi* 25ii(1970), pp. 251-269.

TÜRK, İsmail. The 1970 devaluation. *Dış politika* li(1971), pp. 146-155.

VÖLKER, G.E. Labor migration: aid to the West German economy? *Manpower Mobility across Cultural Boundaries*, ed. by R.E. Krane, 1975, pp. 7-45.

YALMAN, Nur. On land disputes in eastern Turkey. *Islam and its cultural divergence. Studies in honor of G.E. von Grunebaum*, 1971, pp. 180-218.

YASA, İbrahim. L'urbanisation aux communautés des bidonvilles d'Ankara. *Ankara Üniv. Siyasal bilgiler Fakültesi dergisi* 26i(1971), pp. 1-12.

YAZICIOĞLU, Turgut. Über die Herstellung und Zusammensetzung von türkischen Ankara-Whisky. *Annales Univ. Ankara* 13 (1974), pp. 187-204.

Eleventh co-operative management training course, Ankara, Turkey - 1971. *Year-book of agricultural co-operation* 1972, pp. 140-144.

See also III. a. 11. Çağatay.

See also III. c. *Turkey.* Elbir.

See also III. c. *Turkey.* İmre.

See also III. c. *Turkey.* Oğuzman.

See also III. c. *Turkey.* Postacioğlu.

See also IX. m. Steinbach.

See also XXVIII. a. Tümertekin

See also XXIX. i. Quataert.

See also XLIII. g. Ozelli.

See also XLIII. g. Spuler.

k CYPRUS

ADAMS, T.W. The American concern in Cyprus. *America and the Middle East,* ed. P.T. Hart, 1972, pp. 95-105.

BURNOUF, D. L'armée turque et Chypre. *Politique étrangère* 39(1974), pp. 567-583.

COUFOUDAKIS, V. The United Nations force in Cyprus: an end to a peace-keeping era? *Balkan studies* 15(1974), pp. 107-118.

DENKTAŞ, Rauf. Cyprus: on the threshold of new talks. *Dış politika* 2ii(1972), pp. 59-67.

DENKTAŞ, Rauf. The Cyprus problem. *Dış politika* 1i(1971), pp. 95-100.

KYRRIS, C. L'importance sociale de la conversion à l'Islam (volontaire ou non) d'une section des classes dirigeantes de Chypre à l'Islam pendant les premiers siècles de l'occupation turque (1570 - fin du XVIIe s.). *Actes I. Cong. int. ét. balkan. et sud-est europ.* III (1969), pp. 437-462.

LOIZOS, P. The progress of Greek nationalism in Cyprus, 1878-1970. *Choice and change; essays in honour of Lucy Mair,* 1974, pp. 114-133.

LUMSDEN, M. The Cyprus conflict as a prisoner's dilemma game. *J. conflict resolution* 17(1973), pp. 7-31.

MANERA, E. Chipre, víctima de la geopolítica. *Rev.polit.int.* 135(1974), pp. 61-81.

MARKIDES, K.C. Social change and the rise and decline of social movements: the case of Cyprus. *Amer.ethnologist* 1(1974), pp. 309-330.

POLLIS, A. Intergroup conflict and British colonial policy. The case of Cyprus. *Contemporary politics* 5(1972-73), pp. 575-599.

SHMAROV, V.A. Kiprskaya problema i NATO na sovremennom etape. *Strany Blizhnego i Srednego Vostoka: istoriya, ekonomica,* 1972, pp. 216-225.

THEODOULOU, Chr. A. Quelques aspects de la crise chypriote actuelle. *Politique étrangère* 37(1972), pp. 221-233.

See also I. c. 3. Landau

See also IX. m. Steinbach.

See also XXIX. j. Alasya.

See also XXXVI. 1. Tsapiera.

XXX IRAN. IRANIAN PEOPLES

a GEOGRAPHY

AHRENS, P.G. Die städtebauliche Entwicklung von Teheran. *Proc.27th Int. Cong.Or.1967* (1971), pp. 179-181.

BEAUMONT, P. Water resource development in Iran. *Geog. J.* 140(1975), pp. 418-431.

CLARK, B.D., COSTELLO, V. The urban system and social patterns in Iranian cities. *Trans. Inst. British Geog.* 59(1973), pp. 99-128.

DRESCH, J. Bassins arides iraniens. *Bull. Assoc.Géog.Franç.* 429-30(1975), pp. 337-351.

EHLERS, E. Die Stadt Bam und ihr Oasen-Umland/Zentraliran. Ein Beitrag zu Theorie und Praxis der Beziehungen ländlicher Räume zu ihren kleinstädtischen Zentren im Orient. *Erdkunde* 29(1975), pp. 38-52.

EHLERS, E. Die südkaspische Stadt - Typus oder Individuum? *Die Erde* 103(1972), pp. 186-190.

EILERS, W. Mongolische Ortsnamen in Iran. *La Persia nel medievo*, 1971, pp. 449-464

EISELT, J. Forschungsarbeit des Naturhistorischer Museums Wien im und für den Iran. *Bustan* 11iv-12i(1970-1), pp. 29-33.

FALCON, N.L. From Musandam to the Iranian Makran. *Geog. J.* 141(1975), pp. 55-58.

FALCON, N.L. An outline of the geology of the Iranian Makran. *Geog.J.* 140(1974), pp. 284-291.

FARHOUDI, G. Luftbild Schiras, Iran. Gefährdung moderner Stadtplanung durch tektonische Aktivitäten. *Erde* 106 (1975), pp. 1-9.

FECHARAKI, P. Les oasis des montagnes de la région de Bam et du Narmâšir. *Studia Iranica* 4(1975), pp. 219-236.

GODARD, A. D'Alep à Baghdad en caravane, 1908. *Persica* 6(1972-74), pp. 94-113.

HEMMASI, M. Tehran in transition: a study in comparative factorial ecology. *J.Reg.Cult. Inst.* 6(1973), pp. 159-176.

HOLZER, H.F. Die geologische Forschung im Iran. *Bustan* 11iv-12i(1970-1), pp. 34-37.

IPŞIROGLU, M.S. Die Entstehung des iranischen Landschaftsbildes. *Persica* 5(1970-1), pp. 15-26.

KORTUM, G. Siedlungsgenetische Untersuchungen in Fars. Ein Beitrag zum Wüstungsproblem im Orient. *Erdkunde* 29(1975), pp. 10-20.

MARTHELOT, P. Téhéran métropole. *Stud. iranica* 1(1972), pp. 299-310.

MARSACK, P. Bird life in the Alamut valley. *Asian affairs* 61(N.S.5, 1974), pp. 183-187.

MELAMID, A. Petroleum product distribution and the evolution of economic regions in Iran. *Geog. R.* 65(1975), pp. 510-525.

MELAMID, A. Satellization in Iranian crude-oil production. *Geog. rev.* 63(1973), pp. 27-43.

PLANCK, U. Dei Reintegrationsphase der iranischen Agrar-reform. *Erdkunde* 29 (1975), pp. 1-9.

POZDENA, H. Makran--das rückständigste Gebiet Irans. *Erdkunde* 29(1975), pp. 52-59.

REYCHMAN, J. Podróznicy polscy w Iranie. *Przegl. or.* 3(95,1975), pp. 235-242.

SCHWEIZER, G. Tabriz (Nordwest Iran) und der Tabrizer Bazar. *Erdkunde* 26(1972), pp. 32-46

SEGER, M. Strukturelelemente der Stadt Teheran und das Modell der modernen orientalischen Stadt. *Erdkunde* 29(1975), pp. 21-38.

SPOONER, B. City and river in Iran: urbanization and irrigation of the Iranian plateau. *Iranian stud.* 7iii-iv(1974), pp. 681-713.

SPOONER, B. Notes on the toponymy of the Persian Makran. *Iran and Islam, in memory of V. Minorsky*, 1971, pp. 517-533

VITA-FINZI, C. Quaternary deposits in the Iranian Makran. *Geog.J.* 141(1975), pp. 415-420.

WIRTH, E. Zum Problem des Bazars und der Umlandbeziehungen iranischer Städte. *Die Erde* 103(1972), pp. 184-186.

See also XXXI. a. Adle.

See also XXXI. e. Aubin.

b ETHNOLOGY. SOCIOLOGY. IRANIAN PEOPLES: GENERAL

AMANI, Mehdi. La population de l'Iran. *Population* [Paris] 27(1972), pp. 411-418.

ARBERRY, A.J. Fifty Persian folksongs. Translated. *Poure Davoud Memorial Vol.*, II, 1951, pp. 78-89.

BARTSCH, W.H. Attitudes of Irānian high school graduates towards vocational training and industrial work. *Tahqiqāt e eqtesādi* 8(no.22, 1971), pp. 26-39.

BASGÖZ, İlhan. Turkish *hikaye* - telling tradition in Azerbaijan, Iran. *J.Amer. folklore* 83(no. 330, 1970), pp. 391-405

BATTESTI, T. Iran "hommes du vent, gens de terre". *Objets et mondes* 11 (1971), pp. 5-24.

BAYĀNI, Shirin. A study of social structure in Iran during the Mongol period. *J. Regional Cult.Inst.* 7(1974), pp. 139-152.

BEHNAM, Djamchid. Note sur les tendances de la recherche ethnologique en Iran. *Objets et mondes* 11 (1971), pp. 25-26.

BEHNAM, Djamchid. Nuclear families and kinship groups in Iran. *Diogenes* 76(1971), pp. 115-131.

BEHNAM, Issa. La région méridionale de la Mer Caspienne. *Objets et mondes* 11 (1971), pp. 27-48.

BLACK-MICHAUD, J. An ethnographic and ecological survey of Luristan, Western Persia: modernization in a nomadic pastoral society. *ME stud.* 10(1974), pp. 210-228.

BOYCE, M. An old village *dakhma* of Iran. *Mémorial J. de Menasce*, 1974, pp. 3-9.

BOYCE, M. The Zoroastrian houses of Yazd. *Iran and Islam, in memory of V. Minorsky*, 1971, pp. 125-147

BROMBERGER, Chr. et DIGARD, J.P. Pourquoi, comment des cartes ethnographiques de l'Iran? *Objets et mondes* 15(1975), pp. 7-24.

CLOSS, I. Iranistik und Völkerkunde. *Acta Iranica*, 2. sér. *Monumentum H.S. Nyberg*, I (1975), pp. 157-177.

DAVIDIAN, H. The application of some basic psychological theories in the Iranian cultural context. *Int. Soc. Sci. J.* 25(1973), pp. 532-546.

DIGARD, J.P. Campements baxtyari. Observations d'un ethnologue sur des matériaux intéressant l'archéologue. *Studia Iranica* 4(1975), pp. 117-127.

DIGARD, J.P. Histoire et anthropologie des sociétés nomades: le cas d'un tribu d'Iran. *Annales ESC* 28(1973), pp. 1423-1435.

EHMANN, D. Migrationsformen im Nomadenrandgebiet von Südwest-Iran. *Erdkunde* 28(1974), pp. 141-145.

EHMANN, D. Verkehrsentwicklung und Kulturlandschaftswandel in Bekhtiyari (Mittlerer Zagros). *Sociologus* 24(1974), pp. 137-147.

EILERS, W. Ergänzung zu Persica 5, pp. 35-37. *Persica* 6(1972-74), p. 179.

ENAYAT, Hamid. The state of social sciences in Iran. *MESA bull.* 8iii(1974), pp. 1-12.

FORBES, A.P., RONAGHY, Hossein A. and MAJD, Massoud. Skeletal maturation of children in Shiraz, Iran. *Amer. J. phys. anthrop.* 35(1971), pp. 449-454.

FRYE, R.N. Historical evidence for the movement of people in Iran. *The Middle East; studies in honour of J. Germanus*, 1974, pp. 221-225.

GREUSSING, K. Politische Ökonomie des Dorfes im Iran. *Mardom nameh* 1(1975), pp. 26-65.

GRYUNBERG, A.L. Nuristan. Etnograficheskie i lingvisticheskie zametki. *Strany i narody Vostoka pod obshchey red. D.A. Ol'derogge*, X, 1971, pp. 264-287.

HONARI, Morteza. Importance du palmier-dattier dans la vie des habitants de Xor. *Objets et mondes* 11 (1971), pp. 49-58.

HOOGLUND, E.J. The khwushnishin population of Iran. *Iranian studies* 6(1973), pp. 229-245.

KEDDIE, N.R. Stratification, social control, and capitalism in Iranian villages: before and after land reform. *Rural politics and social change in the Middle East*, ed. by R. Antoun and I. Harik, 1972, pp. 364-401.

KOROGLY, Kh. Alper Tonga i Afrasyab po Yusufu Balasaguni, Makhmudu Kashgari i drugim avtoram (K voprosu o vzaimosvyazyakh iranskogo i tyurkskogo fol'klora). *Sov. Tyurkologiya* 1970(4), pp. 108-115.

KOZENKO, A.V., MONOGAROVA, L.F. Statisticheskoe izuchenie pokazateley odnonatzional'noy i smeshannoy brachnosti v Dushanbe. *Sov.etn.* 1971vi, pp. 112-118

LIEBERMAN, S.S., GILLESPIE, R., LOGHMANI, M. The Isfahan communications project. *Studies in family planning* 4iv(1973), pp. 73-100.

LOEB, L.D. The Jewish wedding in modern Shiraz. *Folklore Res. Center studies* 4 (1974), pp. 167-176.

LÖFFLER, R., *et al.* Die materielle Kultur von Boir Ahmad, Südiran. *Arch.f.Völkerkunde* 28(1975), pp. 61-142.

MACHALSKI, F. Notes on the folklore of Iran. *Folia Or.* 12(1970), pp. 141-154

MACHALSKI, F. Die Personennamen der Schuljugend von Iran. *Folia Or.* 12(1970), pp. 155-163

MAHDJOUB, Mohammad Ja'far. Le conteur en Iran. *Objets et mondes* 11 (1971), pp. 159-170.

MAHDJOUB, M. Dj. Les traditions des bardes. Les assauts poétiques. *Studia Iranica* 3(1974), pp. 115-122

MILLWARD, W.G. Traditional values and social change in Iran. *Iranian studs.* 4(1971), pp. 2-35.

MOORE, R., *et al.* Population and family planning in Iran. *MEJ* 28(1974), pp. 396-408.

NARAGHI, Ehsan. Meaning and scope of sociological research in Iran. *Proc. 27th Int.Cong.Or.1967* (1971), pp. 165-166.

ROUHOLAMINI, Mahmoud. Systèmes d'irrigation traditionnels dans la région de Kermân. *Objets et mondes* 11 (1971), pp. 59-66.

ROTBLAT, H.J. Social organization and development in an Iranian provincial bazaar. *Econ. dev. and cult. change* 23 (1975), pp. 292-305.

SALZMAN, P.C. Adaptation and political organization in Iranian Baluchistan. *Ethnology* 10(1971), pp. 433-444.

SALZMAN, P.C. Islam and authority in tribal Iran; a comparative comment. *MW* 65(1975), pp. 186-195.

SALZMAN, P.C. Multi-resource nomadism in Iranian Baluchistan. *J. Asian and African studies* [York Univ.] 7(1972), pp. 60-68.

SALZMAN, P.C. National integration of the tribes in modern Iran. *MEJ* 25(1971), pp. 325-336.

SALZMAN, P.C. The tribes of Iran: reflections on their past and future. *Iranian civilization and culture*, ed. C.J. Adams, 1972, pp. 71-75.

SEMSAR, Hassan. L'apparition du narghileh et de la chibouque. *Objets et mondes* 11 (1971), pp. 83-94.

SHOKURZADE, Ibrahim. Souvenirs de l'Iran ancien dans le folk-lore du Xorasan. *Acta Iranica*, sér. 1, III, 1974, pp. 361-378.

SHROFF, Phiroze J. Exalted status of women in ancient and modern Iran. *J. K.R. Cama Or. Inst.* 44(1973), pp. 63-70.

SINGER, A. The Jamshīdī of Khurasan: an historical note. *Iran* 10(1972), pp. 151-154

SPOONER, B. Continuity and change in rural Iran: the Eastern desserts. *Iran: continuity and variety, ed. by P.J. Chelkowski,* 1971, pp. 1-19

SPOONER, B. The Iranian plateau: an anthropological view. *Proc.27th Int. Cong.Or.1967* (1971), pp. 230-231.

SPOONER, B. Politics, kinship, and ecology in Southeast Persia. *Ethnology [Pittsburg]* 8(1969), pp. 139-152.

TAMRAZIAN, Seza Some factors affecting differential fertility in Iran. *Int population conf.* London, 1969, I, p. 470.

TOUBA, J.R. The relationship between urbanization and the changing status of women in Iran, 1956-1966. *Iranian stud.* 5(1972), pp. 25-36.

TUAL, A. Variations et usages du voile dans deux villes d'Iran. *Objets et mondes* 11 (1971), pp. 95-116.

VEILLE, P. La société rurale et le développement agricole du Khouzistan. *Année sociologique* 16(1965), pp. 85-112.

ZAGARELL, A. Nomad and settled in the Bakhtiari mountains. *Sociologus* N.S.25 (1975), pp. 127-138.

Attitudes vis-à-vis du plan familial en Iran. *Population* [Paris] 28(1973), pp. 1213-1215.

The population of Iran. *Ind.population bull.* 4(1967), pp. 135-151.

See also II. c. 4. Bouloukbachi.
V. m. l. Kalantari.
XXXI. i. Floor.
XXXI. k. Bémont.

See also V. u. l. Blum.

See also V. u. l. Kuckertz.

See also V. u. l. Massoudieh

See also V. v. l. Bromberger

See also XXVIII. b. Erdentuǧ.

See also XXXI. i. Floor.

See also XXXVIII. b. Bateni.

c KURDS

BOIS, T. L'impact national du problème kurde en Irak. *Bibl. Or.* 30(1973), pp. 16-18.

CHASSAGNOUX, J. et A. Atesh-kadeh dans un village kurde près de Robat-Qarehbil. *Studia Iranica* 9(1975), pp. 261-265.

EDMONDS, C.J. Kurdish nationalism. *J. contemp. hist.* 6 (1971), pp. 87-107.

GARCIA-BLANCO PEINADOR, E. El Kurdistan: la Polonia del Oriente Medio. *Rev.de política int.* 118(1971), pp. 61-99.

KAMAL', M. Kurdy v irakskom osvoboditel'nom dvizhenii 1920 goda. *NAA* 1973(5), pp. 147-150.

LABH, Kapileshwar. Settlement of the Kurdish problem in Iraq. *J. Afr. Asian stud.* 3(1970), pp. 216-218.

LANDAU, J.M. The Kurds in some Soviet works. *M.E. stud.* 11(1975), pp. 195-198.

RAVDONIKAS, T.D. Kurdskiy muzhskoy kostyum. Pervaya polovina XIX v. *SMAE* 28(1972). pp. 237-256.

RONDOT, P. Vêture masculine et artisanat du vêtement chez les Kurdes de la haute Djézireh syrienne (à la veille de la deuxième guerre mondiale). *BEO* 25(1972), pp. 257-264.

SABAR, Yona. First names, nicknames and family names among the Jews of Kurdistan. *JQR* 65(1974-75), pp. 43-51.

SANTUCCI, R. Irak: une solution a-t-elle été trouvée au problème kurde? *Asie et Afrique modernes* 104(1975), pp. 3-21.

SHAI, D. Wedding customs among Kurdish Jews in (Zakho) Kurdistan and in (Jerusalem) Israel. *Folklore Res. Center studies* 4(1974), pp. 253-266.

ZAZA, Moureddine. Les Kurdes et l'accord d'Alger. *Travaux et jours* 56-7(1975), pp. 43-54.

See also II. c. 4. Singer.

See also V. u. l. Christensen.

See also XXVII. c. Edmonds

d OSSETES

KALOEV, B.A. Osetino-balkarskie etnograficheskie paralleli. (Osset-Balkar ethnographic parallels). *Sov. etn.* 1972(3), pp. 20-30.

e TAJIKS

CHVYR', L.A. Yuveliry-remeslenniki i mestnaya khudozhestvennaya traditziya v Tadzhikistane. (Les joailliers-artisans et la tradition artistique au Tadjikistan.) *Sov.etn.* 1972(1), pp. 39-51.

ERSHOV, N.N. Sobranie etnograficheskikh kollektziy Instituta istorii im. A. Donisha Akademii nauk Tadzhikskoy SSR. *Sov. etn.* 1975(4), pp. 89-102.

XXX IRAN. IRANIAN PEOPLES

MONOGAROVA, L.F. Kompleksnaya tipologiya gorodov Tadzhikskoy SSR v svete problem etnicheskoy mozaichnosti ikh naseleniya. (A complex typology of urban places of the Tajik Soviet Socialist Republic in the light of problems arising from the mozaic structure of their populations.) *Sov. etn.* 1972(6), pp. 52-63.

MUKHIDDINOV, I. Obryady i obychai, svyazannye s zemledeliem, u pamirskikh tadzhikov Vakhana i Ishkashima v XIX-nachale XXv. *Sov. etn.* 1973(3), pp. 99-109.

MUKHIDDINOV, I. Traditzionnaya irrigatziya pamirskikh tadzhikov v XIX--nachale XX veka. *Sov. etn.* 1975(4), pp. 77-88.

MURODOV, O. Predstavleniya o devakh u tadzhikov sredney chasti doliny Zeravshana (La notion des "dev" chez les Tadjik de la vallée du Zarafchan.) *Sov. etn.* 1973(1), pp. 148-155.

MURODOV, O. Traditzionnye predstavleniya tadzhikov ob Adzhina. *Sov. etn.* 1975(5), pp. 96-105.

PESTRYAKOV, A.P. Antropologicheskoe issledovanie nekotorykh grupp naseleniya Tadzhikistana i Uzbekistana. *Sov. etn.* 1975(1), pp. 102-112.

ROZENFEL'D, A.Z. Darvazskiy fol'klor. *Strany i narody Vostoka pod obshchey red. D.A. Ol'derogge,* X, 1971, pp. 208-217.

SHIROKOVA, Z.A. Tunikoobraznye platya tadzhichek gornogo Tadzhikistana. (Les robes en tunique des femmes tadjiques du Tadjikstan de montagnes.) *Sov. etn.* 1973(5), pp. 88-98.

TILAVOV, B. Leksiko-grammaticheskiy i stilisticheskiy analiz poslovoennogo poslovichnogo repertuara tadzhikov. *Proverbium* 24(1974), pp. 947-952.

f OTHERS

DIGARD, J.P. La parure chez les Baxtyâri. *Objets et mondes* 11 (1971), pp. 117-132.

LYUSHKEVICH, F.D. Termin "Tat" kak etnonim v Sredney Azii, Irane i Zakavkaz'e. (The term "Tat" as an ethnonym in Middle Asia, Iran and Transcaucasia.) *Sov.Etn.* 1971(3), pp. 25-32.

NERAZIK, E.E. Iz istorii khorezmskogo sel'skogo zhilishcha. (Contribution à l'histoire de l'habitat rural de Khwarizm.) *Sov. etn.* 1972(3),

PASTNER, S.L. Co-operation in crisis among Baluch nomads. *Asian affairs* 62 (N.S.6, 1975), pp. 165-176.

SALZMAN, P.C. Adaptation and political organization in Iranian Baluchistan. *Ethnology [Pittsburg]* 10(1971), pp. 433-444.

SALZMAN, P.C. Continuity and change in Baluchi tribal leadership. *IJMES* 4(1973), pp. 428-439.

SALZMAN, P.C. Multi-resource nomadism in Iranian Baluchistan. *Iran-shināsi* 2ii (serial no.3, 1971), pp. 69-83.

TAPPER, R. Shāhsevan in Ṣafavid Persia. *BSOAS* 37(1974), pp. 321-354.

XXXI IRAN: HISTORY

a GENERAL

ADLE, Chahyâr. Contribution à la géographie historique du Damghan. *Le monde iranien et l'Islam,* 1971, pp. 69-104.

AHMAD, Sadruddin Bhagalpur's contribution to Persian studies. *Indo-Iranica* 23i-ii (1970), pp. 97-101.

AMIRANASHVILI, G. Sh. Nekotorye voprosy obshchestvennogo stroya Irana po dannym sasanidskikh epigraficheskikh pamyatnikov III. v. *Strany Blizhnego i Srednego Vostoka: istoriya, ekonomica,* 1972, pp. 9-20.

AUBIN, J. Elements pour l'étude des agglomerations urbaines dans l'Iran mediéval. *The Islamic city,* 1970, pp. 65-75.

BAQIR, Muhammad. The earliest progress, development and influence of Persian in the Pakistan-Hind sub-continent. *Yād-nāme-ye Irāni-ye Minorsky,* 1969, pp. 149-158.

BAUSANI, A. Iran, Islam e Italia nel medioevo. *Commémoration Cyrus. Hommage universel,* II, 1974, pp. 309-320.

BAUSANI, A. Iran, Islam e Italia nel Medioevo. *Veltro* 14i-ii(1970), pp. 29-37.

BAUSANI, A. Muhammad or Darius? The elements and basis of Iranian culture. *Islam and cultural change in the Middle Ages,* ed. Sp. Vryonis, Jr., 1975, pp. 43-57.

BOSWORTH, C.E. The heritage of rulership in early Islamic Iran and the search for dynastic connections with the past. *Iran* 11(1973), pp. 51-62.

BOYLE, J.A. The evolution of Iran as a national state. *Belleten T.T.K.* 39(1975), pp. 633-644.

BUSHEV, P.P. Russko-iranskie kontakty (do kontza XVI v.). *Vopr. ist.* 1973(4), pp. 130-140.

CAHEN, C. L'émigration persane des origines de l'Islam aux Mongols. *La Persia nel medievo,* 1971, pp. 181-194

CARACI, G. Viaggiatori italiani in Persia nel Medioevo. *Veltro* 14i-ii(1970), pp. 39-60.

CERULLI, E. Persia en los tres milenios de su historia. *And.* 35(1970), pp. 401-422.

DUTT, Chinmoy. Indo-Iranian relations. *Indo-Iranica* 23i-ii(1970), pp. 91-96.

FIEY, J.M. Les communautés syriaques en Iran des premiers siècles à 1552. *Acta Iranica,* sér. 1, III, 1974, pp. 279-297.

FISCHEL, W.J. The contribution of the Persian Jews to Iranian culture and literature. *Acta Iranica,* sér. 1, III, 1974, pp. 299-315.

FLOOR, W.M. The guilds in Iran - an overview from the earliest beginnings till 1972. *ZDMG* 125(1975), pp. 99-116.

FRAGNER, B. Der Schah im Schriftverkehr mit dem Abendland. *XVIII. Deutscher Orientalistentag 1972: Vorträge,* pp. 132-141.

GIL BENUMEYA, R. El Imperio del Irán, corazón del Oriente. *Rev.de política int.* 117(1971), pp. 123-130.

GOLOMBEK, L. Urban patterns in pre-Safavid Isfahan. *Iranian stud.* 7iii-iv(1974), pp. 18-44.

GRIGNASCHI, M. Les règles d'Ardaşîr b. Bâbak pour le gouvernement du Royaume. *Islam Tetkikleri Enst. dergisi* 5(1973), pp. 95-112.

GROUSSET, Rene. Celebration of the 2500th anniversary of the monarchy. *J. Reg. Cult. Inst.* 4(1971), pp. 19-22.

HANSMAN, J. Three topographical problems in the Southern Zagros. *BSOAS* 36(1973), pp. 43-54.

HASAN, Mumtaz. Pakistan and Iran: a historical outline. *J. Reg. Cult. Inst.* 4(1971), pp. 27-33.

HERRMANN, G. Urkunden-Funde in Āzarbāygān. *Archäol. Mitt. aus Iran* N.F.4(1971), pp. 249-262.

HOLOD, R. Comments on urban patterns. *Iranian stud.* 7iii-iv(1974), pp. 45-48.

HUSAIN, Agha Mahdi. Cultural aspect of contacts between Iran and the Indo-Pakistan sub-continent. *J. Reg. Cult. Inst.* 1 iii(1968), pp. 65-75.

JAHN, K. Täbris, ein mittelalterlicher Kulturzentrum zwischen Ost und West. *Anzeiger Österr.Akad.Wis.,Phil.-hist.Kl.* 105(1968), pp. 201-212.

KEDDIE, N.R. An assessment of American, British, and French works since 1940 on modern Iranian history. *Iranian stud.* 6 (1973), pp. 152-165.

KERVRAN, M. et RENIMEL, S. Suse islamique: remarques préliminaires perspectives. *Studia Iranica* 3(1974), pp. 253-266.

KHAN, M.A. Saleem. Religion and the State in Iran. A unique Muslim country. *Islam and the modern age* 2iii(1971), pp. 67-88.

KIPPENBERG, H.G. Anmerkungen zu einer sozialwissenschaftlichen Iranistik. *Mardom nameh* 1(1975), pp. 2-14.

KUROS, Mahmud. Die Bedeutung Irans aus dem Blickfeld der europäischen Kultur. *Festgabe deutscher Iranisten zur 2500 Jahrfeier Irans,* 1971, pp. 94-105.

LUTHER, K.A. The site of Karaj-i Abī Dulaf. *AARP* 1(1972), pp. 34-40.

MATOS, L.de. Les relations entre le Portugal et la Perse. *Acta Iranica,* sér. 1, III, 1974, pp. 411-417.

MUHAMMAD RIZA SHAH PAHLAVI. Principles of Iranian monarchy. *J. Reg. Cult. Inst.* 4(1971), pp. 10-18.

MUKHTAROV, A. Concerning the development of the social category of "Dihqans" in the middle ages. *Afghanistan* 25 i(1972), pp. 17-22.

NADVI, Syed Habibul Haq. Al-'Iqṭā' - or theory of land ownership in Islam. *Islamic stud.* 10(1971), pp. 257-276.

NOMANI, Farhad. The origin and development of feudalism in Iran: 300-1600 A.D. *Tahqiqāt-e eqtesādi* 9(nos. 27-8, 1972), pp. 5-61.

PARIZI, Mohammed Ebrahim Bastani. La "route de la soie" dans l'histoire de l'Iran. *Studia et acta or.* 8(1971), pp. 1-17.

PERRY, J. The Banū Ka'b: an amphibious brigand state in Khūzistān. *Le monde iranien et l'Islam,* 1971, pp. 131-152.

PISTOSO, M. Il Māzandarān e un passo di al-Hamadānī. *Ann.Fac.Ling.Lett.stran.Ca' Foscari* 5(1974), pp. 199-203.

POPE, A.U. Art as an essential of Iranian history. *Commémoration Cyrus. Hommage universel,* I, 1974, pp. 153-162.

REYCHMAN, J. Stosunki polsko-irańskie do końca XVIII wieku. *Przegl.or.* 4(80), 1971, pp. 325-331.

RICKS, T.M. Towards a social and economic history of eighteenth century Iran. *Iranian stud.* 6(1973), pp. 110-126.

ROEMER, H.R. Some suggestions for a comprehensive history of Iran. *Yād-nāme-ye Irāniye Minorsky,* 1969, pp. 159-168.

SADIQ, Isā. Le rôle de l'Iran dans la Renaissance. *Acta Iranica,* sér. 1, III, 1974, pp. 381-395.

SAVORY, R.M. Iran, a 2,500-year historical and cultural tradition. *Iranian civilization and culture*, ed. C.J. Adams. 1972, pp. 77-89.

SHAFA, Shojaeddin. L'Iran et l'Italie de l'Empire romain à nos jours. *Commémoration Cyrus. Hommage universel,* I, 1974, pp. 307-315.

SHAFA, Shojaeddin. Italia e Iran dall'Impero Romano ad oggi. *Veltro* 14i-ii(1970), pp. 17-24

SHIRAZI, Bagher. Isfahan, the old: Isfahan the new. *Iranian stud.* 7iii-iv(1974), pp. 586-592.

SHVILI, Giuna. A further note on the Ta'rikh-i Sistan manuscripts. *Afghanistan* 25 iv(1973), pp. 73-74.

SKŁADANEK, B. The structure of the Persian state. *Acta Iranica* 1(1974), pp. 117-123.

SPULER, B. Le rôle des Turcs dans l'histoire de l'Iran (XIème-XIIIème siècles). *La Persia nel medievo,* 1971, pp. 585-594

SPULER, B. Zoroasters Zeit nach einer islamischen Überlieferung des 12. Jh. n. Chr. *Archäol. Mitt. aus Iran* N.F.4 (1971), pp. 113-115.

THAISS, G. Unity and discord: the symbol of Husayn in Iran. *Iranian civilization and culture,* ed. C.J. Adams, 1972, pp. 111-119.

TUCCI, G. Iran et Tibet. *Commémoration Cyrus. Hommage universel,* I, 1974, pp. 299-306

TUCCI, G. Iran e Tibet. *La Persia nel medievo,* 1971, pp. 355-360

TUCCI, G. Le relazioni italo-iraniane. *Veltro* 14i-ii(1970), pp. 5-8.

VAISMAN, A. Anciennes relations roumano-iraniennes. *Studia et acta or.* 8(1971), pp. 21-24.

ZENAISHVILI, E.S. Iz istorii shkol'noy i religiozno-prosvetitel'skoy deyatel'nosti inostrannykh gosudarstv v Severnom Irane. *Arabskie strany, Turtziya, Iran, Afganistan,* 1973, pp. 69-78.

See also II. c. 8. Stroeva.

See also XXX. a. Fouchécour.

See also XXX. b. Battesti.

See also XXXII. c. Dehkan.

See also XXXII. c. Sarkar.

See also XXXII. c. Sherwani.

See also XXXII. i. Sherwani.

See also XXXII. j. Gorekar

b ARAB CONQUEST

BOSWORTH, C.E. The Ṭāhirids and Arabic culture. *Actas IV congresso de estudos árabes e islâmicos* 1968(1971), pp. 177-179.

FARAVASHI, Bahram. Les causes de la chute des Sassanides. *Iran-shināsi* 2ii(serial no.3, 1971), pp. 107-120.

REKAYA, M. Māzyār: résistance ou intégration d'une province iranienne au monde musulman au milieu du IXe siècle ap. J.C. *Studia Iranica* 2(1973), pp. 143-192.

REKAYA, M. La place des provinces sud-caspiennes dans l'histoire de l'Iran de la conquête arabe à l'avènement des Zaydites (16-250 H/637-864 J.C.): particularisme régional ou rôle "national"? *RSO* 48(1973-4), pp. 117-152.

SHABAN, M.A. Khurāsān at the time of the Arab conquest. *Iran and Islam, in memory of V. Minorsky,* 1971, pp. 479-490

STERN, S.M. Ya'qūb the Coppersmith and Persian national sentiment. *Iran and Islam, in memory of V. Minorsky,* 1971, pp. 535-555

See also X. f. Forstner.

c SAFFARIDS

BERADZE, G.G. K voprosu ob institute "gorodskikh raisov" v Irane X-XII vv. (Imushchestvennoe i sotzial'noe polozhenie "gorodskikh raisov".) *Iran (Pamyati B.N. Zakhodera)* 1971, pp. 62-71.

HOSSAIN, M.M. A brief survey of the sources for the Saffarid dynasty of Sistan. *JAS Pak.* 15(1970), pp. 139-150.

KAMPMAN, A.A. Nederlands-Perzische betrekkingen in de Gouden Eeuw. Nederlandse kooplieden en kunstenaars te Isfahan. *Persica* 5(1970-1), pp. 4-14.

PAZHWAK, Abdur-Rahman. A letter to the Caliph. (English translation of a Dari poem ... versifying the contents of a letter sent by Yaqoob Lais Saffarid in answer to the Caliph of Baghdad.) *Afghanistan* 26i (1973), pp. 46-51.

SKLADANEK, B. External policy and inter-dynastic relations under the Ṣaffārids. *RO* 36(1974), pp. 133-150.

d BUWAYHIDS

AZIZ, G.R. The Khwarazmshahs. *J.Pak.Hist. Soc.* 23(1975), pp. 104-139, 152-187.

BOSWORTH, C.E. The Banū Ilyās of Kirmān (320-57/932-68). *Iran and Islam, in memory of V. Minorsky,* 1971, pp. 107-124

XXXI IRAN. HISTORY

BULLIET, R.W. The political-religious history of Nishapur in the eleventh century. *Islamic civilization,* 1973, pp. 71-91.

BUSSE, H. The revival of Persian kingship under the Būyids. *Islamic civilization,* 1973, pp. 47-69.

HALM, H. Der Wesir Al-Kundurī und die Fitna von Nīšāpūr. *WO* 6(1971), pp. 205-233.

HEINZ, W. Die Rolle der Būjiden in der Geschichte Irans. *Festgabe deutscher Iranisten zur 2500 Jahrfeier Irans,* 1971, pp. 47-54.

MOTTAHEDEH, R. Administration in Būyid Qazwīn. *Islamic civilization,* 1973, pp. 33-45.

VAN DAMME, M. Les quarante-deux premières lettres du secrétaire Būyide Abū Isḥāq al-Ṣābī (m.en 384/994), et leur répartition dans quelques autres Ms. *Arabica* 21(1974), pp. 184-186.

e MONGOLS

AUBIN, J. La fin de l'état sarbadār du Khorassan. *JA* 262(1974), pp. 95-118.

AUBIN, J. Réseau pastoral et réseau caravanier. Les grand'routes du Khurassan à l'epoque mongole. *Le monde iranien et l'Islam,* 1971, pp. 105-130.

BOYLE, J.A. The capture of Isfahan by the Mongols. *La Persia nel medievo,* 1971, pp. 331-336

BOYLE, John Andrew. Some thoughts on the sources for the Il-Khanid period of Persian history. *Iran* 12(1974), pp. 185-188.

DAVIDOVICH, E.A. Svidetel'stvo Daulatshakha o razmerakh zemel'noy renty pri Ulugbeke. *Pis'mennye pamyatniki Vostoka* 1971, pp. 19-37.

FRAGNER, B. Zu einem Autograph des Mongolenwesirs Rašīd ad-Dīn Fazlallāh, der Stiftungsurkunde für das Tabrīzer Gelehrtenviertel Rab'i Rašīdī. *Festgabe deutscher Iranisten zur 2500 Jahrfeier Irans,* 1971, pp. 35-46.

HERRMANN, G. und DOERFER, G. Ein persisch-mongolischer Erlass aus dem Jahr 725/1325. *ZDMG* 125(1975), pp. 317-346.

HERRMANN, G. and DOERFER, G. Ein persisch-mongolischer Erlass des Ğalāyeriden Šeyh Oveys. *Central Asiatic J.* 19(1975), pp. 1-84.

HERRMANN, G. Zur Intitulatio timuridischer Urkunden. *XVIII. Deutscher Orientalistentag 1972: Vorträge,* pp. 498-521.

JAHN, K. Italy in Ilkhanid historiography. *La Persia nel medievo,* 1971, pp. 443-448

JAHN, K. Wissenschaftliche Kontakte zwischen Iran und China in der Mongolenzeit. *Anzeiger Osterr.Akad.Wis.,Phil.-hist.Kl.* 106(1969), pp. 199-211.

SALIM, Gholamreza. Rashid ed-Din Fazlollah's contribution to the advancement of education in his time with particular reference to his interest in medical training. *J.Reg.Cult. Inst.* 6(1973), pp. 137-142.

SOTUDEH, Hosseinqoli. The income and expenditure of Xājeh Rashid-ed-Din Fazl-ol-lāh. *Tahqiqat-e eqtesadi* 8(no.21, 1971), pp. 86-102.

ZAHMA, A.M. A social and geo-political study of Khurasan and Herat. *Adab* (Kabul) 17vi (1969), pp. 1-6; 18i-ii (1970), pp. 1-8.

ZARYAB, Abbas. The struggle of religious sects in the court of Ilkhanids and the fate of Shi'ism in that time. *Iranshināsi* 2ii(serial no.3, 1971), pp. 103-106.

ZARYAB, A. Struggle of religious sects in the Ilkhanid Court. *La Persia nel medievo,* 1971, pp. 465-466

Moghul-Dokhter and Arab-Bacha. From the collection of Hafizullah Baghban. *Adab* (Kabul) 17vi(1969), pp. 7-13.

f AQ-QOYUNLU. QARA-QOYUNLU

AUBIN, J. Les relations diplomatiques entre les Aq-qoyunlu et les Bahmanides. *Iran and Islam, in memory of V. Minorsky,* 1971, pp. 11-15

BACQUÉ-GRAMMONT, J.L. Un "fetiḥnâme" zû-l-Ḳadiride dans les archives ottomanes. *Turcica* 2(1970), pp. 138-150.

FORAND, P.G. Accounts of Western travelers concerning the role of Armenians and Georgians in 16th-century Iran. *MW* 65 (1975), pp. 264-278.

LIMBERT, J. A fourteenth-century guide to Shiraz. *Bull. Asia Inst. Pahlavi Univ.* 2(1971), pp. 16-18.

SCARCIA, G. Annotazioni Muša'ša'. *La Persia nel medievo,* 1971, pp. 633-637

SCARCIA AMORETTI, B. L'Islam in Persia fra Tīmūr e Nādir. *Ann.Fac.Ling.Lett.stran.Ca' Foscari* 5(1974), pp. 63-97.

SMITH, J.M. Mongol manpower and Persian population. *JESHO* 18(1975), pp. 271-299.

g SAFAVIDS

ADLE, Chahryar. La bataille de Mehmândust (1142/1729). *Studia Iranica* 2(1973), pp. 235-241.

ALGAR, Hamid. Some observations on religion in Safavid Persia. *Iranian stud.* 7iii-iv (1974), pp. 287-293.

BABAEV, K. Voennaya reforma Shakha Abbasa I (1587-1629). *Vestn. Mosk. Univ. Vostokovedenie* 1973(1), pp. 21-29.

BACQUÉ-GRAMMONT, J.L. Études turco-safavides, I Notes sur le blocus du commerce iranien par Selîm Ier. *Turcica* 6(1975), pp. 68-88.

BASTIAENSEN, M. La Persia safavide vista da un lessicografo. Presentazione del "Gazophylacium". *RSO* 48(1973-4), pp. 175-203.

BRAUN, H. Ein iranischer Grosswesir des 17. Jahrhunderts: Mīrzā Muḥammad-Taqī. *Festgabe deutscher Iranisten zur 2500 Jahrfeier I Irans*, 1971, pp. 1-7.

BRULEZ, W. Venetiaanse handelsbetrekkingen met Perzië en Indië omstreeks 1600. *Orientalia Gandensia* 1(1964), pp. 1-27.

DANEGYAN, L.G. Politika sefevidov po otnosheniyu k armyanskim koloniyam v Irane v pervoy polovine XVII v. *Arabskie strany, Turtziya, Iran, Afganistan*, 1973, pp. 43-49.

ECHRAQI, Ehsan. Le Kholâsat al-tawârikh de Qâzi Ahmad connu sous le nom de Mir Monshi. *Studia Iranica* 4(1975), pp. 73-89.

EFENDIEV, Oktaj. Le rôle des tribus de langue turque dans la création de l'état safavide. *Turcica* 6(1975), pp. 24-33.

FERRIER, R.W. The Armenians and the East India Company in the seventeenth and early eighteenth centuries. *Econ. hist. rev.* 2nd ser. 26(1973), pp. 38-62.

FERRIER, R.W. The European diplomacy of Shāh 'Abbās I and the first Persian embassy to England. *Iran* 11(1973), pp. 75-92.

FRAGNER, B. Ardabīl zwischen Sultan und Schah. Zehn Urkunden Schah Ṭahmāsps II. *Turcica* 6(1975), pp. 177-225.

FRAGNER, B. Das Ardabīler Heiligtum in den Urkunden. *WZKM* 67(1975), pp. 169-215.

FRAGNER, B. Der Schah im Schriftverkehr mit dem Abendland. *XVIII. Deutscher Orientalistentag* 1972, pp. 132-141.

GANDJEĪ, Tourkhan. Notes on the life and work of Ṣādiqī: a poet and painter of Ṣafavid times. *Der Islam* 52(1975), pp. 112-118.

GLASSEN, E. Schah Ismā'īl, ein Mahdī der anatolischen Turkmenen? *ZDMG* 121(1971), pp. 61-69

GLASSEN, E. Schah Ismā'īl I. und die Theologen seiner Zeit. *Der Islam* 48(1971-2), pp. 254-268

GREGORIAN, V. Minorities of Isfahan: the Armenian community of Isfahan 1587-1722. *Iranian stud.* 7iii-iv(1974), pp. 652-680.

GÜRSOY, Emine. An analysis of Nadir Shah's religious policy. *Boğazici Univ. J.* 2(1974), pp. 13-18.

HUSAIN, Agha Mahdi. Cultural influence of Safavid Iran over the Indo-Pakistan subcontinent under the great Mughals. *J. Reg Cult. Inst.* 1 ii(1967), pp. 58-65; 1 iv(1968), pp. 24-34.

KISLYAKOV, N.A. Nekotorye iranskie pover'ya i prazdniki v opisaniyakh zapadnoevropeyskikh puteshestvennikov XVII v. *Mifologiya i verovaniya narodov Vostochnoy i Yuzhnoy Azii*, 1973, pp. 179-194.

KISSLING, H.J. Šâh Ismâ'îl Ier, la nouvelle route des Indes et les Ottomans. *Turcica* 6(1975), pp. 89-102.

KOCHWASSER, F.H. Persien im Spiegel der Reisebeschreibung von Heinrich von Poser (1620/25). *Festgabe deutscher Iranisten zur 2500 Jahrfeier Irans*, 1971, pp. 80-93.

MAZZAOUI, M.M. The Ghāzī backgrounds of the Ṣafavid State. *Iqbal rev.* 12iii(1971), pp. 79-90

MEILINK-ROELOFSZ, M.A.P. The earliest relations between Persia and the Netherlands. *Persica* 6(1972-74), pp. 1-50.

MELIKOFF, I. Le problème ḳizilbaş. *Turcica* 6(1975), pp. 49-67.

MUSAWI, Mustafa Murtada al-. Persian trade under the Safavids (1514-1722). *Sumer* 25(1969), pp. 99-102.

NAQVI, Syed Muhammad Raza. Shah Abbas and the conflict between Jahangir and the Deccan states. *Medieval India* 1(1969), pp. 272-279.

NASR, Hossein. Religion in Safavid Persia. *Iranian stud.* 7iii-iv(1974), pp. 271-286.

PERRY, J.R. The last Ṣafavids, 1722-1773. *Iran* 9 (1971), pp. 59-69.

RAKHMANI, A.A. Iz istorii monetnogo obrashcheniya v sefevidskom gosudarstve (XVII v.). *Gruzinskoe istochnikovedenie* III, 1971, pp. 256-262.

ROBINSON, B. Comments [on Painting and patronage under Shah ʿAbbas I]. *Iranian stud.* 7iii-iv(1974), pp. 508-510.

ROEMER, H. Comments [on The Safavid state and polity]. *Iranian stud.* 7iii-iv(1974), pp. 213-216.

ROEMER, H. Das fruhsafawidische Isfahan: als historische Forschungsaufgabe. *Iranian stud.* 7iii-iv(1974), pp. 138-163.

ROEMER, H.R. Das frühsafawidische Isfahan als historische Forschungsaufgabe. *ZDMG* 124(1974), pp. 306-331.

ROEMER, H.R. Problèmes de l'histoire safavide avant la stabilisation de la dynastie sous Šāh ʿAbbās. *Ve Congrès International d'Arabisants et d'Islamisants. Actes.*, [1970?], pp. 399-409.

ROUX, J.-P. Une survivance des traditions turco-mongoles chez les Séfévides. *RHR* 183 (1973), pp. 11-18.

SAVORY, R.M. A curious episode of Ṣafavid history. *Iran and Islam, in memory of V. Minorsky*, 1971, pp. 461-473

SAVORY, R.M. The emergence of the modern Persian state under the Ṣafavids. *Iran-shināsī* 2ii(serial no.3, 1971), pp. 1-44.

SAVORY, R.M. The *qizilbāsh*, education and the arts. *Turcica* 6(1975), pp. 168-176.

SAVORY, R. The Safavid state and polity. *Iranian stud.* 7iii-iv(1974), pp. 179-212.

SAVORY, R.M. A 15th century Ṣafavid propagandist at Harāt. *Amer. Or. Soc., Middle West Branch. Semi-centennial volume*, ed. by D. Sinor, 1969, pp. 189-197.

SCARCIA, G. Venezia e la Persia tra Uzun Hasan e Tahmasp (1454-1572). *Acta Iranica*, sér. 1, III, 1974, pp. 419-438.

SCARCIA, G. Venezia e la Persia tra Uzun Hasan e Tahmasp (1454-1572). *Veltro* 14i-ii (1970), pp. 61-76.

SIROUX, M. Les caravanserais routiers safavids. *Iranian stud.* 7iii-iv(1974), pp. 348-379.

STEVENS, R. European visitors to the Safavid court. *Iranian stud.* 7iii-iv(1974), pp. 421-457.

SUKHAREVA, N.M. Sovetskie istoriki o sotzial'no-ekonomicheskikh prichinakh krizisa sefevidskogo Irana. *Iran (Pamyati B.N. Zakhodera)* 1971, pp. 41-56.

VERCELLIN, G. Il busto di Vincenzo degli Alessandri. *RSO* 49(1975), pp. 67-70.

WEAVER, M. Comments [on Aspects of the Safavid ensemble at Isfahan]. *Iranian stud.* 7iii-iv(1974), pp. 416-420.

WELCH, A. Painting and patronage under Shah ʿAbbas I. *Iranian stud.* 7iii-iv(1974), pp. 458-507.

WILBER, D. Aspects of the Safavid ensemble at Isfahan. *Iranian stud.* 7iii-iv(1974), pp. 406-415.

See also V. g. Aslanapa.

See also XXIX. c. Beldiceanu-Steinherr.

See also XXIX. f. Bacqué-Grammont.

See also XXIX. f. Niewöhner-Eberhard

See also XXX. f. Tapper.

See also XXXII. i. Ahmad

See also XXXII. j. Sarkar.

See also XXXIV. d. Abrahamowicz

h AFSHARIDS

BARBAROSSA, C., BARTOLOMEI, G. di. Notizie sulla medicina in Persia alla fine del 1700. *Pag.storia med.* 13(1969), pp. 38-48. [CWHM 64]

KROELL, A. Billon de Canceville et les relations franco-persanes au début du XVIIIe siècle. *Le monde iranien et l'Islam* II, 1974, pp. 127-156.

KUKANOVA, N.G. K voprosu o torgovle Rossii s Iranom v 50-80-e gody XVIII v. *Iran (Pamyati B.N. Zakhodera)* 1971, pp. 72-83.

NASIM, K.B. Nadir Shah Afshar in the North-West Frontier Province. *Peshawar Univ.rev.* 1i(1973), pp. 84-89.

SAIDMURADOV, D. Maloizvestnuiy istochnik po istorii vostochnogo Irana vtoroy poloviny XVIII v. *Iran (Pamyati B.N. Zakhodera)* 1971, pp. 57-61.

STROEVA, L.V. Russkie istochniki po istorii Irana vtoroy poloviny XVIII veka. *Vestnik Leningr. Univ., ser. ist., yaz. i lit.* 1974(4), pp. 67-75.

i QAJARS

ABANESOV, A.Kh. "Shukr-name-ye shahrinshakhri" Bakhman-Mirzy. *Gruzinskoe istochnikovedenie* III, 1971, pp. 316-322.

ABDULLAEV, Z.Z. Metodologicheskie i istochnikovedcheskie problemy issledovaniya "perevorota 3 khuta" 1921 goda v Irane. (Methodologic and source-research problems in the study of the coup d'etat of February 21st, 1921, in Iran). *NAA* 1971(5), pp. 76-84.

ABRAHAMIAN, E. Oriental despotism: the case of Qajar Iran. *IJMES* 5(1974), pp. 3-31.

AVERY, P.W. An enquiry into the outbreak of the second Russo-Persian War, 1826-28. *Iran and Islam, in memory of V. Minorsky*, 1971, pp. 17-45

BAKHASH, Shaul. The evolution of Qajar bureaucracy: 1779-1879. *ME studies* 7 (1971), pp. 139-168.

BUSHEV, P.P. Iranskiy kupchina Kazim-Bek v Rossii, 1706-1709 gg. *Iran: sbornik statey*, 1973, pp. 166-180.

DESTRÉE, A. Assistance technique en Perse 1898-1914. *Ve Congrès International d'Arabisants et d'Islamisants. Actes.*, [1970?], pp. 159-170.

XXXI IRAN. HISTORY

ERME, G. d'. Romualdo Tecco (1802-1867), diplomatico sardo "orientalista". *Annali Fac. Ling. Lett. stran. di Ca' Foscari (serie orientale)* 1(1970), pp. 107-122.

FARMAYAN, Hafez F. Observations on sources for the study of nineteenth- and twentieth-century Iranian historv. *IJMES* 5(1974), pp. 32-49.

FLOOR, W.M. The lūṭīs - a social phenomenon in Qājār Persia: a reappraisal. *WI* 13 (1971), pp. 103-120.

FLOOR, W.M. The office of Kalāntar in Qājār Persia. *JESHO* 14(1971), pp. 253-268

FLOOR, W.M. The police in Qājār Persia. *ZDMG* 123(1973), pp. 293-315.

FLOOR, W.M. Two communications. A. Note to Mahjūb's *Wer ist Naqīb ul-Mamālik* (ZDMG 114(1964), pp. 319-324). B. Note on *jarīd bāzī*. *ZDMG* 123(1973), pp. 79-82.

GARTHWAITE, G.R. The Bakhtiyâri Khans, the government of Iran, and the British, 1846-1915. *IJMES* 3(1972), pp. 24-44.

GÖYÜNE, Nejat. Displays of friendship between Persia and Turkey during the time of Mozaffaroddin Shah and Abdulhamit II. *J. Reg. Cult. Inst.* 4(1971), pp. 57-66.

HORNUS, J.M. Un rapport du consul de France à Erzéroum sur la situation des chrétiens en Perse au milieu du XIXe siècle. Texte du Comte de Challaye publié avec introduction et notes. *Proche-Orient chrétien* 21(1971), pp. 3-29, 127-151.

HORNUS, J.M. Un rapport du consul de France à Erzéroum sur la situation des chrétiens en Perse au milieu du XIXe siècle. Texte du Comte de Challaye. *Proche orient chrétien* 22(1972), pp. 288-304.

INGRAM, E. An aspiring buffer state: Anglo-Persian relations in the third coalition, 1804-1807. *Hist. J.* 16(1973), pp. 509-533.

KARNY, Azriel. The premierships of Mirzā Hosein Khān and his reforms in Iran. *Asian and African stud.* (Israel Or.Soc.) 10(1974-5), pp. 127-156.

KEDDIE, Nikki R. The assassination of the Amīn as-Sultān (Atābak-i A'zam) 31 August 1907. *Iran and Islam, in memory of V. Minorsky,* 1971, pp. 315-329

KLEIN, I. British intervention in the Persian revolution, 1905-1909. *Hist. J.* 15(1972), pp. 731-752.

KOMISSAROV, D.S. Zarozhdenie prosvetitel'stva v Irane (k kharakteristike vzglyadov Aga-Khana Kermani). *NAA* 1974(6), pp. 82-94.

KUKANOVA, N.G. Osveshchenie russko-iranskikh ekonomicheskikh svyazey kontza XVIII - nachala XIX v. v maloizvestnykh arkhivnykh dokumentakh. *Iran: sbornik statey,* 1973, pp. 181-194.

LAMBTON, A.K.S. The case of Ḥājjī ʿAbd al-Karīm. A study on the role of the merchant in mid-nineteenth century Persia. *Iran and Islam, in memory of V. Minorsky,* 1971, pp. 331-360

LORENTZ, J.H. Iran's great reformer of the nineteenth century: an analysis of Amīr Kabīr's reforms. *Iranian stud.* 4(1971), pp. 85-103.

McDANIEL, R.A. Economic change and economic resiliency in 19th century Persia. *Iranian studs.* 4(1971), pp. 36-49.

MATVEEV, A.M. Iz istorii vykhodtzev iz Irana v Sredney Azii vo vtoroy polovine XIX - nachale XX v. *Iran: sbornik statey,* 1973, pp. 195.214.

MEREDITH, C. Early Qajar administration: an analysis of its development and functions. *Iranian stud.* 4(1971), pp. 59-84.

NAGORNAYA, A. Russko-iranskie dogovory 1732 i 1735 gg. *Arabskie strany, Turtziya, Iran, Afganistan,* 1973, pp. 116-121.

PAKDAMAN, Homa; ROYCE, W. ʿAbbās Mīrzā's will. *Iranian stud.* 6(1973), pp. 136-151.

PHILIPP, Mangol Bayat. Mīrzā Āqā Khān Kirmānī: a nineteenth century Persian nationalist. *Middle East Stud.* 10(1974), pp. 36-59.

PIEMONTESE, A.M. L'esercito persiano nel 1874-75. Organizzazione e riforma secondo E. Andreini. *RSO* 49(1975), pp. 71-117.

PIEMONTESE, A.M. Profilo delle relazioni italo-persiane nel XIX secolo. *Veltro* 14i-ii(1970), pp. 77-85.

SAVORY, R.M. British and French diplomacy in Persia. 1800-1810. *Iran* 10(1972), pp. 31-44

SHEIKHOLESLAMI, A. Reza. The sale of offices in Qajar Iran, 1858-1896. *Iranian stud.* 4(1971), pp. 104-118.

SHEKHOYAN, L.G. Otrazhenie iranskoy revolyutzii 1905-1911 godov v armyanskom satiricheskom zhurnale "Khatabala". (The Iranian revolution of 1905-1911 as reflected in the Armenian satirical magazine Khatabala.) *NAA* 1971(4), pp. 128-131.

SIVAN, R. La rivalité des puissances en Perse au début du XIXe siècle (1801-1833). *Rev. hist. dipl.* 88(1974), pp. 312-331.

See also V. c. *Iran.* Piemontese.

j MODERN IRAN

ABDOH, Jalal. Impact of science and technology on the political, legal, economic and social developments in the society in Iran. *India and contemporary Islam*, ed. S.T. Lokhandwalla, 1971, pp. 299-310.

ABRAHEMIAN, Ervand. Kasravi: the integrative nationalist of Iran. *Middle Eastern stud.* 9(1973), pp. 271-295.

AGAEV, S.L. Imperskiy vozdushnyy put' i anglo-iranskie otnosheniya v 20-kh nachale 30-kh godov XX v. *Iran (Pamyati B.N. Zakhodera)* 1971, pp. 104-117

AGAEV, S.L. Iranskaya revolyutziya 1905-1911 gg. (K. tipologii revolyutziy epokhi "probuzhdeniya Azii"). *NAA* 1975 (4), pp. 55-68.

AMOUZEGAR, P. The influence of Kemalism on Rezā Shāh's reforms. *J.Reg.Cult.Inst.* 7i (1974), pp. 31-38.

BAGLEY, F.R.C. Religion and the state in Iran. *Islamic stud.* 10(1971), pp. 1-22.

BAGLEY, F.R.C. Religion and the State in modern Iran. *Ve Congrès International d' Arabisants et d'Islamisants. Actes.*, [1970?], pp. 75-88.

BAYNE, E.A. Intellectuals and Kingship. *Persica* 5(1970-1), pp. 119-132.

BEHRUZ, Jahangir. Le relazioni internazionali dell'Iran. *Veltro* 14i-ii(1970), pp. 109-114.

BELOVA, N.K., PLASTUN, V.N. Proklamatzii i ottiski pechatey iranskikh revolutzionerov (1906-1908 gg.) *NAA* 1973(1), pp. 156-167.

BHARIER, J. The growth of towns and villages in Iran, 1900-66. *ME stud.* 8 (1972), pp. 51-61

BILL, J.A. Elites and classes: confrontation or integration. *Iranian stud.* 8(1975), pp. 150-163.

BILL, J.A. The plasticity of informal politics: the case of Iran. *MEJ* 27(1973), pp. 131-151.

BINDER, L. Iran's potential as a regional power. *Political dynamics in the Middle East*, ed. P.Y. Hammond and S.S. Alexander, 1972, pp. 355-394.

BOYLE, J.A. The evolution of Iran as a national state. *Acta Iranica*, sér. 1, III, 1974, pp. 327-338.

BURRELL, R.M. Iranian foreign policy during the last decade. *Asian affairs* 61(N.S.5, 1974), pp. 7-15.

CAREY, J.P.C. Iran and control of its oil resources. *Pol. sci. Q.* 89(1974), pp. 147-174.

CHOPRA, Hira Lall. The white revolution of Iran. *Proc.All-India Or.Conf.* 1969, pp. 415-419.

COTTRELL, A.J. Iran, the Arabs and the Persian Gulf. *Orbis* [Tufts] 17(1973), pp. 978-988.

DEMIN, A.I. Rabochiy vopros i sotzial'no-ekonomicheskie reformy v Irane. *NAA* 1974 (3), pp. 20-35.

D'ERME, G. I Partiti politici in Persia dal 1941 al 1944. *OM* 51(1971), pp. 213-235.

DESTRÉE, A. La révolution Persane de 1905-06. *Ann. Inst. Phil. Hist. Or.* 20(1968-72), pp. 197-208.

DJALILI, M.R. Le rapprochement irano-irakien et ses conséquences. *Politique étrangère* 40(1975), pp. 273-291.

DOENECKE, J.D. Iran's role in cold war revisionism. *Iran. stud.* 5(1972), pp. 96-111.

DOROSHENKO, E.A. O nekotorykh kontzeptziyakh sovremennogo iranskogo dukhovenstva po voprosu religii i gosudarstva. *Iran (Pamyati B.N. Zakhodera)* 1971, pp. 118-134.

DOROSHENKO, E.A. O nekotorykh religionznykh institutakh i deyatel'nosti shiitskogo dukhovenstva v sovremennom Irane. *Religiya i obshchestvennaya mysl' narodov vostoka*, 1971, pp. 175-195.

DZHAFAROVA, A.A. Problemy obshchego i professional'nogo zhenskogo obrazovaniya v Irane. *Arabskie strany, Turtziya, Iran, Afganistan*, 1973, pp. 50-58.

EILERS, W. Iran zwischen Ost und West. *Festgabe deutscher Iranisten zur 2500 Jahrfeier Irans*, 1971, pp. 22-34.

ERDENTUĞ, Nermin. The basic points to be taken into consideration in relation to education in the efforts to modernize. *Ann. Univ. Ankara* 12(1966 - Publ. 1972), pp. 59-62.

FIROOZI, Ferydoon. Teheran - a demographic and economic analysis. *Middle East Stud.* 10(1974), pp. 60-76.

GIL BENUMEYA, R. El Irán, encrucijada política mundial. *Rev. de política int.* 127 (1973), pp. 113-122.

GIL BENUMEYA, R. Un nuevo eje internacional en el golfo Pérsico. *Rev. de política int.* 128(1973), pp. 117-124.

GIL BENUMEYA, R. El Shahinshah Reza Pahlavi en la actualidad mundial. *Rev.de política int.* 138(1975), pp. 137-146.

HAIRI, Abdul-Hadi. European and Asian influences on the Persian Revolution of 1906. *Asian affairs* 62(N.S.6, 1975), pp. 155-164.

HASSAN, Nader. Die Strategie der "Weissen Revolution": einige Aspekte der sozialökonomischen Entwicklung Irans. *Asien. Afrika. Latein-Amerika* 3(1975), pp. 833-836.

HESS, G.R. The Iranian crisis of 1945-46 and the Cold War. *Pol. sci. Q.* 89(1974), pp. 117-146.

HORNUS, J.M. Un rapport du consul de France à Erzéroum sur la situation des chrétiens en Perse au milieu du XIXe siècle. Texte du Comte de Challaye publié avec introduction et notes. *Proche Orient chrétien* 21 (1971), pp. 3-29; 127-151.

HOVEYDA, Amir Abbas. L'Iran sulla via del progresso. *Veltro* 14i-ii(1970), pp. 9-15.

HUSAIN, Mahdi. Contest for legal sovereignty between the last three Mughul emperors and the East India Company. *JAS Bangladesh* 17iii(1972), pp. 35-63.

ISMAILOV, D. Sozdanie i deyatel'nost' "Korpusa prosveshcheniya" v Irane. *Iran (Pamyati B.N. Zakhodera)* 1971, pp. 152-157.

KANUS-CREDE, H. Mohammad Mossadegh in memoriam. *Iranistische Mitt.* 1(1969), pp. 19-25.

KANUS-CREDE, H. Mossadegh's Sturz. *Iranistische Mitt.* 4(1970), pp. 62-103.

KANUS-CREDE, H. Die persische Presse der Ära Mossadegh. *Iranistische Mitt.* 2 (1968), pp. 2-85.

KAZEMI, Farhad. Economic indicators and political violence in Iran: 1946-1968. *Iranian studies* 8i-ii(1975), pp. 70-85.

KAZEMZADEH, Firuz. Soviet-Iranian relations: a quarter-century of freeze and thaw. *The Soviet Union and the Middle East*, ed. I.J. Lederer and W.S. Vucinich, 1974, pp. 55-77.

KEDDIE, Nikki R. The economic history of Iran, 1800-1914, and its political impact an overview. *Iran. stud.* 5(1972), pp. 58-78.

KEDDIE, N.R. The Iranian constitutional revolution of 1905-1911: a brief assessment. *Iran Society silver jubilee souvenir* 1944-1969, pp. 201-210.

KEDDIE, N.R. The Iranian power structure and social change 1800-1969: an overview. *IJMES* 2 (1971), pp. 3-20.

KHEYFETZ, A.N. Pyatidesyatiletie pervykh dogovorov sovetskoy strany s Iranom, Afganistanom i Turtzii (1921 g.) (Fifty years of the first agreements between the Soviet country and Iran, Afganistan and Turkey (1921)) *NAA* 1971(1), pp. 50-62.

KOTOBI, Mortéza et VILLETTE, M. Problèmes méthodologiques de l'enquête dans les pays en voie de développement, le cas de l'Iran. *Rev. franç. de sociologie* 15 (1974), pp. 293-404.

KUBRYATOVA, I.N. Pis'ma sotzial - demokratov Irana i Yaponii G.V. Plekhanovu. *Vost. sbornik 3*, 1972, pp. 7-36.

KULAGINA, L.M. Angliyskaya kontzessiya na sudokhodstvo po r. Karun (konetz XIX v.). *Iran (Pamyati B.N. Zakhodera)* 1971, pp. 92-103.

LAMBTON, A.K.S. The Persian constitutional revolution of 1905-6. *Revolution in the Middle East*, ed. P.J. Vatikiotis, 1972, pp. 173-182.

LANDFRIED, Klaus. The Shah's revolution: the dilemma of modernization in Iran. *Orient* [Germany] 14(1973), pp. 164-170.

LENCZOWSKI, G. United States' support for Iran's independence and integrity, 1945-1959. *America and the Middle East*, ed. P.T. Hart, 1972, pp. 45-55.

LÖFFLER, R. The national integration of Boir Aḥmad. *Iranian stud.* 6(1973), pp. 127-135.

MACHALSKI, F. Notes of the intellectual movement in Iran, 1921-1941. *Yádnáme-ye Jan Rypka* 1967, pp. 179-185.

MALEK, R. L'Iran per i giovani. *Veltro* 14 i-ii(1970), pp. 115-118.

MAMEDOVA, N.M. Kooperativnoe dvizhenie v sovremennom Irane. *Iran (Pamyati B.N. Zakhodera)* 1971, pp. 135-151.

MARTIROSOV, A.U. Novye materialy o sotzial-demokraticheskom dvishenii v Irane v 1905-1911 godakh. *NAA* 1973(2), pp. 116-122.

MIRAKHMEDOV, A. Neizvestnaya rukopis' K.N. Smirnova ob iranskoy revolyutzii (An unknown MS by K.N. Smirnov on the Iranian revolution). *NAA* 1972(4), pp. 127-130.

MOZAFARI, Mehdi. Les nouvelles dimensions de la politique étrangère de l'Iran. *Politique étrangère* 40(1975), pp. 141-159.

ORLOV, E.A. Vneshnyaya politika Irana posle vtoroy mirovoy voyny. *Mezhdunarodnye otnosheniya na Blizhnem i Srednem Vostoke*, 1974, pp. 74-105.

PFAU, R. The legal status of American forces in Iran. *MEJ* 29(1974), pp. 141-153

PLASTUN, V.N. Uchastie iranskikh trudyashehikhsya v grazhdanskoy voyne v Rossii. (Iranian workers in Soviet Russia, 1917-1920.) *NAA* 1972(2), pp. 55-63

RAMAZANI, Rouhollah K. Iran's 'white revolution': a study in political development. *IJMES* 5(1974), pp. 124-139.

RONDELI, A. O giperurbanizatzii stolichnykh gorodov razvivayushchikhsya stran (na primere Tegerana). *Arabskie strany, Turtziya, Iran, Afganistan*, 1973, pp. 141-146

SALZMAN, P.C. Persian land reform and the Shah: A critical comment on Lambton's view. *MW* 62(1972), pp. 241-246.

SAVORY, R.M. The principle of homeostasis considered in relation to political events in Iran in the 1960's. *IJMES* 3(1972), pp. 282-302.

SAYEED, Khalid B. Policy making process in the government of Iran. *Iranian civilization and culture*, ed. C.J. Adams, 1972, pp. 91-110.

SCARCE, J. Travels with telegraph and tiles in Persia: from the private papers of Major-General Sir Robert Murdoch Smith. *AARP* 3 (1973), pp. 70-81.

SEDEHI, Abolghassem, TABRIZTCHI, Sirousse. A theory of economic growth and political development: the case of Iran. *Internat.stud.* 13(1974), pp. 424-440.

SHEIKHOLESLAMI, A. Reza; WILSON, D. The memoirs of Ḥaydar Khān ʿAmū Ughlū. *Iranian stud.* 6(1973), pp. 21-51.

SHEKHOYAN, L.G. Otrazhenie iranskoy revolyutzii 1905-1911 godov v armyanskom satiricheskom zhurnale "Khatabala". *NAA* 1971(4), pp. 128-131.

SKLADANEK, B. Struktura państwa persów. *Przegl.or.* 4(80), 1971, pp. 343-348.

SKLADANEK, B. Uwagi o Polonii w Iranie w latach 1918-1945. *Przegl.or.* 4(80), 1971 pp. 378-380.

TRIPET, F. Les bouleversements de l'univers rural en Iran. *Afrique et Asie* 95-96(1971) pp. 27-40.

WEINBAUM, M.G. Iran finds a party system: the institutionalization of *Iran Novin*. *MEJ* 27(1973), pp. 439-455.

YOUSOFI, Gholam Hoseyn. Dekhodā's place in the Iranian constitutional movement. *ZDMG* 125(1975), pp. 117-132.

ZABIH, Sepehr. Change and continuity in Iran's foreign policy in modern times. *World politics* 23 (1970-71), pp. 522-543.

ZAGREBELNYY, V. Stanovlenie sovremennogo sporta v Irane i sovetsko-iranskie sportivnye kontakty. *Strany Blizhnego i Srednego Vostoka: istoriya, ekonomica*, 1972, pp. 78-85.

ZONIS, M. Classes, elites and Iranian politics: an exchange. *Iranian stud.* 8 (1975), pp. 134-149.

See also XXII. c. Yurov.

See also XXVII. c. Edmonds.

See also XXX. b. Salzman

See also XXXI. i. Farmayan.

k ECONOMICS

AVERY, P.W., SIMMONS, J.B. Persia on a cross of silver, 1880-1890. *ME stud.* 10(1974), pp. 259-286.

AZIMI, Hossein. Bibliography of economic publications on Iran. *Tahqiqat-e eqtesadi* 8(no.21, 1971), pp. 124-136.

BAHER, G.H. A planning model for the educational requirements of economic development: the case of Iran. *Tahqiqat-e-eqtesadi* 10(29&30,1973), pp. 170-205.

BARTSCH, W.H. The industrial labor force of Iran: problems of recruitment, training and productivity. *MEJ* 25 (1971), pp. 15-30.

BAZIN, M. Quelques données sur l'alimentation dans la région de Qom. *Studia Iranica* 2(1973), pp. 243-253.

BECK, P.J. The Anglo-Persian oil dispute 1932-33. *J.contemp.hist.* 9iv(1974), pp. 123-151.

BÊMONT, F. Bazars et caravansérails. *Objets et mondes* 11 (1971), pp. 67-82.

CANINO, R. L'ENI in Iran. *Veltro* 14i-ii (1970), pp. 175-176.

CAREY, J.P.C., CAREY, A.G. Industrial growth and development planning in Iran. *MEJ* 29 (1975), pp. 1-15.

DAFTARY, Farhad. The balance of payments deficit and the problem of inflation in Iran, 1955-1962. *Iranian stud.* 5(1972), pp. 2-24.

DAFTARY, Farhad. Development planning in Iran: a historical survey. *Iranian studies* 6(1973), pp. 176-228.

ESHAG, Eprime. Study on the excess cost of tied aid given to Iran in 1966/67. *Tahqiqāt e eqtesādi* 8(no.22, 1971), pp. 3-25.

ESLAMI, M. The world energy crisis and Iranian strategy. *Tahqiqat-e-eqtesadi* 10(29&30,1973), pp. 17-49.

FAMILI, A. Gidrotekhnicheskiy kompleks "Amir Kabir" i ego znachenie dlya ekonomicheskogo razvitiya rayona g. Tegerana. *Strany Blizhnego i Srednego Vostoka: istoriya, ekonomica*, 1972, pp. 426-432.

FINZI, A. L'impianto idroelettrico del Dez. *Veltro* 14i-ii(1970), pp. 177-181.

FIROOZI, Ferydoon. The Iranian budgets: 1964-1970. *IJMES* 5(1974), pp. 328-343.

FITZ, P. Der Iran als Wirtschafts- und Handelspartner. *Bustan* 11iv-12i(1970-1), pp. 14-17.

FREIVALDS, J. Farm corporations in Iran: an alternative to traditional agriculture. *MEJ* 26(1972), pp. 185-193.

GHADIRI, B. Income tax in Iran. *Tahqiqāt-e eqtesādi* 9(nos. 27-8, 1972), pp. 124-149.

GHADIRI-ASLI, B. The experience of rural co-operatives and co-operative unions in Iran. *Tahqiqat-e-eqtesadi* 10(29&30, 1973), pp. 80-81

GHADIRI-ASLI, B. Expérience des sociétés et unions coopératives rurales en Iran. *Tahqiqat-e-eqtesadi* 10(29&30,1973), pp. 82-107.

GHAFFARI, R. Saving and investment and the effects of financial intermediaries on the rate of change of G.N.P. in Iran 1936-71. *Tahqiqat-e-eqtesadi* 10(29&30, 1973), pp. 50-79.

HAGHIGHI, M. Index of economic articles in Tahqiqat-e-eqtesadi(nos.1-30). *Tahqiqat-e-eqtesadi* 10(29&30,1973), pp. 206-228.

HAMMEED, Kamal A., BENNETT, M.N. Iran's future economy. *MEJ* 29(1975), pp. 418-432

HOEPPNER, R.R. Bemerkungen zu entwicklungspolitischen Engpässen eines "take-off-Landes". Das Beispiel Irans. *Orient* [Hamburg] 16iii(1975), pp. 91-95.

HOEPPNER, Rolf-Roger. Gesellschafts-und steuerrechtliche Behandlung ausländischer Investitionen in Iran. *Orient* [Germany] 15 (1974), pp. 28-34.

IL'IN, G.N. Dobycha i ispol'zovanie gaza v Irane (1960-1965 gg.). *Arabskie strany, Turtziya, Iran, Afganistan,* 1973, pp. 196-202.

KARABADZHAN, A.Z. Perspektivy razvitiya gosudarstvennogo sektora v ekonomike Irana. *Iran: sbornik statey,* 1973, pp. 3-34.

KATOUZIAN, Mohammad Ali. Ahmad Kasravi's labour, occupation and money. *Tahqiqat-e eqtesadi* 8(no. 21, 1971), pp. 107-123.

KATOUZIAN, M.A. Land reform in Iran. A case study in the political economy of social engineering. *J. peasant studies* 1(1973-4), pp. 220-239.

KATOUZIAN, M.A. Some observations on the Iranian economy and its recent growth. *Tahqiqāt-e eqtesādi* 9(nos.27-8, 1972), pp. 62-87.

KEDDIE, W.H. Fish and futility in Iranian development. *J.devel. areas* 6 (1971), pp. 9-28.

KHATIBI, Nosratollah. Land reform in Iran and its role in rural development. *Land reform* 1972(2), pp. 61-68.

KOBIDZÉ, D. Saīd Naficy et la Géorgie. *Mélange d'iranologie en mémoir de feu Said Naficy,* 1972, pp. 110-112.

KOCH, Josef, SCHWEIZER, Günther, TAYEBI, Kejumars. Neue Bewässerungs-und Entwicklungsprojekte in Iran. Das Beispiel der Provinz West-Azerbaidschan. *Orient* [Germany] 15 (1974), pp. 8-16.

LAUDOR, C.R. and TABRIZTCHI, Sirousse. Predicting urban growth in Iran: a dynamic model. *Iranian stud.* 8(1975), pp. 124-133.

MAMEDOVA, N.M. Kooperatziya v sel'skom khozyaystve Irana. *Strany Blizhnego i Srednego Vostoka: istoriya, ekonomica,* 1972, pp. 347-358.

MARDUKHI, Bāyazid, A bibliography of economic publications on Irān. *Tahqiqāt e eqtesādi* 8(Nos. 23-4, 1971), pp. 214-218.

MAUROY, H. de. La lutte contre la lèpre en Iran. *Studia Iranica* 2(1973), pp. 267-279.

MICHEL, A. Expansion urbaine et spéculation foncière en Iran. *Rev. franc. sociol.* 12(1971), pp. 586-588.

NAINI, Ahmad. Entwicklungsplanung in Iran. *Orient* [Germany] 16iv(1975), pp. 105-130.

NIKOUKHAH, Farhad. L'Iran si apre agli stranieri. *Veltro* 14i-ii(1970), pp. 25-27.

NOWSHIRVANI, Vahid F.; BILDNER, R. Direct foreign investment in the non-oil sectors of the Iranian economy. *Iranian stud.* 6 (1973), pp. 66-109.

PAZEL'SKIY, S. Otnoshenie pravyashchikh krugov Irana k inostrannym chastnym investitziyam. *Strany Blizhnego i Srednego Vostoka: istoriya, ekonomica,* 1972, pp. 379-396.

PICKETT, L.E. Iran: rural co-operation on the move. *Year-book of agricultural co-operation* 1972, pp. 23-36.

RABBĀNI, Mehdi, A cost-benefit analysis of the Dez Multi-Purpose Project. *Tahqiqāt e eqtesādi* 8(Nos. 23-4, 1971), pp. 132-165.

ROZHDESTVENSKAYA, D.S. Rol' mezhdunarodnogo banka rekonstruktzii i razvitiya v finansirovanii planov ekonomicheskogo razvitiya Irana. *Strany Blizhnego i Srednego Vostoka: istoriya, ekonomica,* 1972, pp. 396-407.

SABA, Mohsen. A note on Lebās ol-Taqvā. *Tahqiqat-e eqtesadi* 8(no. 21, 1971), pp. 103—106.

SABĀ, Mohsen. A note on the Siāhat-Nameh of Ebrāhim Baik. *Tahqiqāt e eqtesādi* 8(no.22, 1971), pp. 123-127.

SADROLACHRAFI, M. Les nouvelles méthodes d'exploitation agricole dans les villages iraniens. *Tiers monde* 15(1974), pp. 397-406.

SCHULZ, A. The politics of municipal administration in Iran: a case-study of Isfahan. *J. admin. overseas* 14 (1975), pp. 228-239.

SHARIPOV, U.Z. Ekonomicheskoe sotrudnichestvo Irana s sotzialisticheskimi stranami vostochnoy Evropy. *Iran: sbornik statey,* 1973, pp. 35-73.

SHESTOPALOV, V.Ya. Iran i problema kontinental'nogo shel'fa v Persidskom zalive. *Iran: sbornik statey,* 1973, pp. 99-132.

SKORCIC, J. Iran - einer der interssantesten Wirtschaftspartner Österreiche. *Bustan* 11iv-12i(1970-1), pp. 42-43.

STICKLEY, S.T., HOSSEINI-NASAB, S. Ebrahim. Agricultural credit in Kermān. *Tahqiqat e eqtesādi* 9(25-26, 1972), pp. 81-90.

XXXI IRAN. HISTORY

STICKLEY, S.T. & NAJAFI, Bahaoldin. The effectiveness of farm corporations in Iran. *Tahqiqat-e eqtesadi* 8(no.21, 1971), pp. 18-28.

TONEKĀBONI, Zibā Farid, The consumption and distribution of oil products in Irān. *Tahqiqāt e eqtesādi* 8(Nos. 23-4, 1971), pp. 166-213.

TOS, E. Prospettive di sviluppo economico dell'Iran. *Veltro* 14i-ii(1970), pp. 169-174.

TZUKANOV, V.P. Problema regional'nogo razvitiya v Irane (k postanovke voprosa). *Iran: sbornik statey,* 1973, pp. 74-98.

VEILLE, P. et HAGCHENO, M. Le bazar et le tournant économique des années 1954-1960. *Stud. iranica* 1(1972), pp. 55-88.

VEILLE, P. Les paysans, la petite bourgeoisie rurale et l'État après la réforme agraire en Iran. *Annales ESC* 27(1972), pp. 347-372

See also I. c. 4. Azimi

See also XXX. b. Honari.

See also XXXI. j. Firoozi.

XXXII INDIA. PAKISTAN

a GEOGRAPHY

KARIMI, S.M. Changing capitals of late medieval Bengal. *JBRS* 54(1968), pp. 278-293.

MUKERJI, A.B. The Muslim population of Uttar Pradesh, India: a spatial interpretation. *IC* 47(1973), pp. 213-230.

See also VI. b. Madan.

See also VI. c. Maqbul Ahmad.

b ETHNOLOGY

AGGARWAL, Partap C. Widening integration and Islamization of a North Indian Muslim caste. *Themes in culture (essays in honor of Morris E. Opler),* 1971, pp. 165-172.

AHMAD, Saghir. Islam and Pakistani peasants. *Contributions to Asian studies* 2(1971), pp. 93-104.

AITKEN, A., STOECKEL, J. Muslim-Hindu differentials in family planning knowledge and attitude in rural East Pakistan. *J.compar.family stud.* 2(1971), pp. 75-87.

ANSARI, Hasan Nishat. Origin and appellation of the Momins. *JBRS* 57(1971), pp. 133-148.

ASCHENBRENNER, J. Politics and Islamic marriage practices in the Indian subcontinent. *Anthrop. Q.* 42(1969), pp. 305-315.

BHATTACHARYA, D.K. A note on authority and leadership in a matrilineal society. [Laccadive Islands.] *Eastern anthropologist* 26 (1973), pp. 95-99.

BHATTACHERJEE, Binoy. The Patuas - a study on Islamization. *Folklore[Calcutta]* 13 (1972), pp. 361-368.

DONINI, P.G. Notazioni di geografia antropica per un'analisi della disgregazione del Pakistan. *OM* 53(1973), pp. 377-381.

ELLICKSON, J. Islamic institutions: perception and practice in a village in Bangladesh. *Contrib. to Ind. sociol.* 6(1972), pp. 53-65

GABORIEAU, M. Muslims in the Hindu kingdom of Nepal. *Contrib. to Ind. sociol.* 6(1972), pp. 84-105.

GOUGH, K. Kinship and marriage in Southwest India. *Contribs.to Indian soc.* N.S.7(1973), pp. 104-134.

HABIB, Kamal Muhammad. Review article: *The Indian Muslims* by M. Mujeeb, London, 1967 . *J. Pakistan Hist. Soc.* 16(1968), pp. 242-276.

JAIN, S.P. Caste stratification among the Muslims. *Eastern anthropologist* 28(1975), pp. 255-270.

KABIRAJ, Shibnarayan. Women in the domestic rites and beliefs of the Hindus and the Muslims. *Folklore[Calcutta]* 10(1969), pp. 38-54.

KORSON, J.H. Endogamous marriage in a traditional Muslim society, West Pakistan: a study in intergenerational change. *J. compar.family stud.* 2(1971), pp. 145-155.

KORSON, J.H. Some aspects of social change in the Muslim family in West Pakistan. *Contributions to Asian studies* 3(1973), pp. 138-155.

KRISHNA, Gopal. Piety and politics in Indian Islam. *Contrib. to Ind. sociol.* 6 (1972), pp. 142-171.

LOKHANDWALLA, S.T., SABERWAL, Satish. Caste among the Muslims. *Eastern anthrop.* 27 (1974), pp. 251-261.

MADAN, T.N. Religious ideology in a plural society: the Muslims and Hindus of Kashmir. *Contrib. to Ind. sociol.* 6(1972), pp. 106-141.

MADAN, T.N. Two faces of Bengali ethnicity: Muslim Bengali or Bengali Muslim. *Developing economies* 10(1972), pp. 74-85.

MAUROOF, Mohamed. Aspects of religion, economy and society among the Muslims of Ceylon. *Contrib. to Ind. sociol.* 6(1972), pp. 66-83.

MINES, M. Islamisation and Muslim ethnicity in South India. *Man* 10(1975), pp. 404-419.

MINES, M. Muslim social stratification in India: the oasis for variation. *SWJ anthrop.* 28(1972), pp. 333-349.

MUKERJI, A.B. Salient features of the distributional patterns of the Muslim population of Uttar Pradesh, India. *J.Indian anthrop.Soc.* 8(1973), pp. 13-33.

MUSI RAZA, S. Changing purdah-system in Muslim society. (A survey study in Patna.) *Islam and the modern age* 6iv (1975), pp. 40-56.

NAIR, P. Thankappan Silver Jubilee of Anthropological Survey of India. *Ethnos [Stockholm]* 36(1971), pp. 131-151.

RIZVI, B.R. Resistance to innovation: a case study from a North Indian village. *Folklore* [Calcutta] 14(1973), pp. 77-82.

PASTNER, S. and PASTNER, C. McC. Agriculture, kinship and politics in Southern Baluchistan. *Man* N.S. 7(1972), pp. 128-136

SCHOLTZ, F. Der moderne Wandel in den nomadischen Belutschen- und Brahui-Stämmen der Gebirgsprovinz Belutschistan. *Sociologus* 24 (1974), pp. 117-137.

SEN, D.K. and GUPTA, P. Physical characteristics of the rural Kashmiri Muslims. *J. Ind. Anthrop. Soc.* 1(1966), pp. 81-88.

SHARMA, S.L. and SRIVASTAVA, R.N. Institutional resistance to induced Islamization in a convert community--an empiric study in sociology of religion. *Sociol. bull.* 16i(1967), pp. 69-80.

WOLSKI, K. La décoration des animaux par découpage des toisons dans la région du désert de Thar en Inde et au Pakistan. *Folia Or.* 12(1970), pp. 303-326

Some Mohammadan customs. *Folklore[Calcutta]* 10(1969), pp. 309-312.

See also II. a. 2. *India.* Hansen.

See also XXVIII. b. Erdentug.

c HISTORY : GENERAL

ABBOTT, F. The historical background of Islamic India and Pakistan. *Contributions to Asian studies* 2(1971), pp. 6-21.

AHLUWALLA, M.S. Early phase of Muslim expansion in Rajasthan - a study based on epigraphic evidence. *J.Ind.hist.*, Golden jubilee vol. 1973, pp. 369-385.

AHMAD, Aziz. The British Museum Mīrzānāma and the seventeenth century Mīrzā in India. *Iran* 13(1975), pp. 99-110.

AHMAD, Qeyamuddin. An eighteenth-century Indian historian on early British administration. *J.Ind.hist.*, Golden jubilee vol. 1973, pp. 893-907.

AHMAD, Safi. Darshan Singh - a refractory Talukdar of Awadh. *Quart. rev. hist. studs.* 10 (1970-71), pp. 101-103.

ALI, A.K.M. Yaqub. Barind in the history of Muslim Bengal. *J. Pakistan Hist. Soc.* 16(1968), pp. 81-87.

BALOCH, N.A. The *Tarikh "Ṭabaqāt-i-Bahādur-Shāhī". J. Pak. Hist. Soc.* 13(1965), pp. 306-309.

DATTA, K.K. Periodisation of history. *Indo Asian culture* 20i(1971), pp. 12-17.

DEHKAN, Abul Hassan. The influence of Persian culture in the sub-continent of India and vice versa, after the advent of Islam. *Proc.32 Ind.hist.cong.* 1970, vol. 2, pp. 269-280.

DOBBIN, C. Competing elites in Bombay city politics in the mid-nineteenth century. *Elites in South Asia,* 1970, pp. 79-94.

FATIMI, S. Qudratullah. Glimpses of the maritime history of Pakistan. *J. Pakistan Hist. Soc.* 16(1968), pp. 190-197.

GÁTHY, V. Islamic culture -- Indian culture. *The Middle East; studies in honour of J. Germanus,* 1974, pp. 227-251.

GHARAVI, S.M. The impact of Sasanian culture in medieval India. *J. K.R. Cama Or. Inst.* 44(1973), pp. 152-160.

GOKHALE, B.G. Burhanpur. Notes on the history of an Indian city in the XVIIth century. *JESHO* 15(1972), pp. 316-323.

GURU, S.D. History of Gwalior fort as a royal prison. *J. Madhya Pradesh Itihasa Parishad* 7(1969), pp. 63-70

HARDY, P. The 'Ulama in British India. *J. Ind.hist.*, Golden jubilee vol. 1973, pp. 821-845.

KAIL, O. C. Dutch commercial and territorial influence in India. *JAS Bombay* 43-44(1968-9), pp. 155-226

KARIMI, S.M. Late medieval towns of Bihar plain (12th century A.D. to mid 18th century). *J. Bihar Res. Soc.* 56(1970), pp. 172-190.

KHALID, M.B. The caravan of Islam on the Indo-Pakistan sub-continent. *J.Reg.Cult. Inst.* 6(1973), pp. 177-187.

KHAN, Ahmad Nabi. Debalpur through the ages. *J.Research Soc.Pakistan* 7i(1970), pp. 69-77.

KHAN, Munawwar. Swat in history. *Peshawar Univ.rev.* 1i(1973), pp. 51-63.

KURUP, K.K.N. Ali Rajas of Cannanore, English East India Company and Laccadive Islands. *Proc.32 Ind.hist.cong.* 1970, vol. 2, pp. 44-53.

MALIK, Zahiruddin. The rise of Tegh Beg Khān - first Nawab of Surat, 1733-1746. *IC* 46(1972), pp. 153-162.

MARTIN, B.G. Migrations from the Hadramawt to East Africa and Indonesia, c. 1200 to 1900. *Res. bull. CAD Ibadan* 7(1971), pp. 1-21.

MUKHERJEE, S.N. Class, caste and politics in Calcutta, 1815-1838. *Elites in South Asia,* 1970, pp. 33-78

MUSHIRUL HAQ. The Shaikh al-Islam in Indian history. *Stud. in Islam* 6(1969), pp. 231-236.

NAQVI, Hameeda K. Urbanisation and Muslim rulers of India. *Islam and the modern age* 2iii(1971), pp. 52-66.

OHRI, V.K. Agriculture and economic expansion during the Middle Ages; a comparative study of India and Britain. *J.Afr.Asiat.stud.* 3i(1969), pp. 61-78.

RAHIM, M.A. History of the *Shiqqdār*. *J. Pak. Hist. Soc.* 13(1965), pp. 328-341.

RASHID, A. Industry and industrial workers in medieval India (1206-1526). *JBRS* 54(1968), pp. 245-254.

RASHID, A. Merchants and artisans in medieval North Indian economy (1206-1526). *Dr. Satkari Mookerji felicitation volume,* 1969, pp. 313-321.

ROY, Atul Chandra. Navy in medieval India (in the light of Persian sources). *Indo-Iranica* 26i(1973), pp. 3-13.

SARKAR, Jagadish Narayan. Guerrilla warfare in medieval India. *Q.rev.hist.stud.* 13 (1973-74), pp. 29-36.

SARKAR, Jagadish Narayan. India and Iran in the medieval period: a bird's eye view. *Indo Iranica* 26ii-iii(1973), pp. 1-61.

SARKAR, Jagadish Narayan. Islam in Bengal (thirteenth to eighteenth centuries). *J. Ind.hist.* 48(1970), pp. 469-512.

SARKAR, Jagadish Narayan. Men and beasts in medieval warfare. *J.Ind.hist.,* Golden jubilee vol. 1973, pp. 463-494.

SARKAR, Jagadish Narayan. Some aspects of military administration in medieval India. *J.Ind.hist.* 51(1973), pp. 559-593.

SHERWANI, H.K. Indo-Persian chronicles as connecting links between North and South during the Indian Middle Ages. *Indo-Iranica* 25iii-iv(1972), pp. 8-19.

SIDDIQI, Iqtidar Hussain, AHMAD, Qazi Mohammad An Arab account of India in the fourteenth century: an analysis of the chapters on India from Shihāb al-Dīn al-'Umarī's *Masālik al-abṣār fī-mamālik al-amṣār*. *Studies in Islam* 7(1970), pp. 205-227.

SIDDIQI, Mahmudul Hasan. The Balūch migration in Sind and their clash with the Arghūns. *J. Pak. Hist. Soc.* 13(1965), pp. 350-355.

SINGH, Mahendra Pal. The custom and the custom house at Surat in the seventeenth century. *Quart. rev. hist. studs.* 10 (1970-71), pp. 80-90.

SINGH, Mahendra Pal. The custom house at the port of Surat during the seventeenth century. *Studs. in Islam* 8(1971), pp. 132-164.

SINGH AGRE, Jagat Vir. Use of intoxicants in medieval Rajasthan. *Medieval India* 1(1969), pp. 263-271.

SRIVASTAVA, A.L. Agra and Fatehpur Sikri in the 16th century. *JIH* 48i(1970), pp. 43-49.

TROLL, C.W. A note on an early topographical work of Sayyid Aḥmad Khān: *Āṣār al-Ṣanādīd*. *JRAS* (1972), pp. 135-146.

YUSUF, K.M. Sir Jadunath's *Military history of India*. *Indo-Iranica* 24i-ii (1971), pp. 29-33.

See also III. a. 4. Yaduvansh.

See also IX. d. Mohibbul Hasan

See also XXXI. a. Dutt.

See also XXXI. a. Hasan.

d EARLY MUSLIM PERIOD

AWASTHI, A.B.L. Garuḍa Purāṇa on the Turkish conquest of India. *JUPHS* N.S.10 (1962), pp. 139-142

BUDDHA PRAKASH. Some aspects of Indian culture on the eve of Muslim invasions. *Research bull. (arts) U. Panjab* 39 (1962), 117 pp.

FRIEDMANN, Y. Minor problems in al-Balādhuri's account of the conquest of Sind. *RSO* 45(1970), pp. 253-260.

KHAN, Hussain. The motive behind the Arab invasion of Sind as gleaned from the *Fatuh al-Buldan*. *J. Asiatic Soc. Pakistan* 14 (1969), pp. 60-64.

KHAN, Hussain. The role of the people of Sind in the struggle between Muḥammad ibn Qāsim and Rāja Dāhir. *J. Asiatic Soc. Pakistan.* 14 (1969), pp. 325-341.

SRIVASTAVA, Ashirbadi Lal. A survey of India's resistance to medieval invaders from the North-West: causes of eventual Hindu defeat. *Itihāsa-Chayanikā (Dr. Sampurnanand Felicitation vol.* = JUPHS 11-13), Part 1(1965), pp. 21-40

See also II. c. 8. Khan.

e GHAZNAVIDS

ARENDS, A.K. K istorii zakhvata Khorezma Makhmudom Gaznevi. *Vostochnaya filologiya. Philologia Orientalis.* II(Pamyati V.S. Puturidze, 1972, pp. 127-134.

DIKSHIT, R.K. The Chandellas and the Yaminis. *Itihāsa-Chayanikā (Dr. Sampurnanand Felicitation vol.* = JUPHS 11-13), Part II (1965), pp. 47-65

SHARMA, Dasharatha. Some new light on the route of Mahmūd Ghaznavī's raid on Somanātha; Multān to Somanātha and Somanātha to Multān. *Dr. Satkari Mookerji felicitation volume,* 1969, pp. 165-168.

g KINGS OF DELHI

ANSARI, Hasan Nishat. Political history of Bihar under the Khaljīs (A.D. 1290-1320/A.H. 690-720). *JBRS* 54(1968), pp. 255-277.

ASKARI, S.H. Material of historical interest in I'jaz-i-Khusravi. *Medieval India* 1(1969), pp. 1-20.

HABIBI, A.H. Khaljis are Afghan Tarak or Turk. *Afghanistan* 24ii-iii(1971), pp. 76-88

HAMBLY, G. Who were the *Chihilgānī*, the forty slaves of Sulṭān Shams al-Dīn Iltutmish of Delhi?. *Iran* 10(1972), pp. 57-62

HAQUE, M.A. Route of Firuz Shah's invasion of Orissa in 1360 A.D. *Orissa Inst.res.J.* 15iii-iv(1967), pp. 62-68.

HUDA, M.Z. Sultān Sikandar Lūdī - a poet and patron of letters. *J. Asiatic Soc. Pakistan* 14 (1969), pp. 289-304.

NIZAMI, K.A. Attitude of Muslim mystic toward society and state during the Sultanate period. *Dr. Adilya Nath Jha felicitation volume,* III, 1969, pp. 539-558.

NIZAMI, K.A. Some documents of Sultan Muhammad bin Tughluq. *Medieval India* 1(1969), pp. 301-313.

SCHIMMEL, A. Turk and Hindu: a poetical image and its application to historical fact. *Islam and cultural change in the Middle Ages,* ed. Sp. Vryonis, Jr., 1975, pp. 107-126.

SHARMA, Sri Ram. Punjab during the Sultanate (economic condition). *J. Madhya Pradesh Itihasa Parishad, Bhopal* 6(1968), pp. 93-132.

SIDDIQI, Iqtidar Husain. Diplomatic relations between the rulers of Delhi and Gujarat during the sixteenth century. *Medieval India* 3(1975), pp. 113-126.

SIDDIQI, Iqtidar Husain. Sher Khān Sūr's relations with the Sultans of Bengal. *Stud. in Islam* 6(1969), pp. 172-87.

SIDDIQI, Iqtidar Hussain. Wajh'-i-Ma'ash grants under the Afghan kings (1451-1555). *Medieval India* 2(1972), pp. 19-44.

SIDDIQI, Mohd. Yasin Mazhar. Arzdasht of Badr Hajib. *Medieval India* 2(1972), pp. 291-297.

See also II. c. 4. Das.

See also XXXIV. d. Jackson.

h PROVINCIAL DYNASTIES

ACHARYA, P. The relation of Ilyas Shah and Fịroz Shah with the Ganga Kings Narasimha Dēva III and Bhanu Dēva III. *Orissa Inst. res.J.* 13iii(1965), pp. 1-15.

BURKE, Ata Karim Tárīkh-i-Bangála (an unpublished Persian work). *Indo-Iranica* 23iv(1970), pp. 3-10.

DAS, Sunilkumar. A note on Husain Shah's Assam expedition. *J.Indian hist.* 51(1973), pp. 337-343.

GOKHALE, B.G. Broach and Baroda. Notes on the economic history of two Gujarat cities in the XVIIth century. *JAS Bombay* 43-44(1968-9), pp. 142-154.

NIZAMI, K.A. Shaikh Ahmad Maghribi as a great historical personality of medieval Gujarat. *Medieval India* 3(1975), pp. 234-259.

SIDDIQI, Iqtidar Hussain. Rise and fall of the Nuhani Afghans in Bihar. *IC* 45(1971), pp. 255-262

See also VIII. c. *India.* Digby.

See also XXXI. f. Aubin

See also XXXII. g. Siddiqi.

i SULTANATES OF THE DECCAN

AHMAD, Nazir. Letters of the rulers of the Deccan to Shah Abbas of Iran. *Medieval India* 1(1969), pp. 280-300.

AHMAD, Nazir. A portrait of Ibrahim 'Adil Shah II by Farrukh Beg. *Iran Society silver jubilee souvenir* 1944-1969, pp. 3-19.

EATON, R.M. The court and the dargah in the seventeenth century Deccan. *Ind. econ. soc. hist. R.* 10i(1973), pp. 50-63.

GHAURI, Iftikhar Ahmad. Duelling in the Deccan. *J. Pakistan Hist. Soc.* 19(1971), pp. 110-112.

GHAURI, Iftikhar Ahmad. Kingship in the Sultanates of Bijapur and Golconda. *IC* 46(1972), pp. 39-52, 137-151.

GHAURI, Iftikhar Ahmad. Origin of the Qutb Shahs of Golconda. *J. Pakistan Hist. Soc.* 17(1969), pp. 228-230.

GHAURI, Iftikhar Ahmad. Origins of the Adil Shahs of Bijapur. *J. Pakistan Hist. Soc.* 17(1969), pp. 84-88.

GUPTA, Satya Prakash. Jhain of the Delhi Sultanate. *Medieval India* 3(1975), pp. 209-215.

HUDA, M.Z. Tā'rikh i-Nāsir Shāhī. *JAS Pak.* 15(1970), pp. 151-166.

KANBARGIMATH, S.S. A study of the battle of Talikote. *QJMS* 60(1969), pp. 47-55.

KULKARNI, A.R., DESHPANDE, P.B. Nilanga farmans. *Bull. Deccan Coll. R.I.* 31-32(1970-72), pp. 228-238.

KULKARNI, G.T. Some observations on the medieval history of the Deccan. *BDCRI* 34(1974), pp. 91-102.

MALIK, Zahiruddin. Documents relating to pargana administration in the Deccan under Asaf Jah I. *Medieval India* 3 (1975), pp. 152-183.

RAY, A. An aspect of Indo-French history: Mausalipatam, 1670. *Proc.32 Ind.hist.cong.* 1970, vol. 1, pp. 320-335.

RICHARDS, J.F. The seventeenth century concentration of state power at Hyderabad. *J. Pak. Hist. Soc.* 23(1975), pp. 1-35.

RITTI, Shrinivas. A Sanskrit document relating to the Adil Shahis of Bijapur. *Studies in Indian history and culture* ... presented to P.D. Desai, 1971, pp. 110-120.

SHERWANI, H.K. Cultural picture of the Deccan in the 15th century. *Medieval India* 3(1975), pp. 216-233.

SHERWANI, H.K. The Qutb Shahis and Iran. *J.Ind.hist.,* Golden jubilee vol. 1973, pp. 387-402.

SHERWANI, H.K. Some cultural aspects of the Qutb Shahi kingdom on the eve of its dissolution. *Iran Society silver jubilee souvenir* 1944-1969, pp. 301-323.

SRIVASTAVA, K.L. Ikhtiyaruddin Muhammad Ibn Bakhtiyar Khalji - his career and conquests. *J.Ind.hist.,* Golden jubilee vol. 1973, pp. 525-534.

SWAMINATHAN, K.D. Two nawabs of the Carnatic and the Sri Rangam temple. *Medieval India* 3(1975), pp. 184-187.

TAMASKAR, B.G. Historical geography of Malik Ambar's territory (1600-1626 A.D.). *J.Ind.hist.* 53(1975), pp. 255-268.

j MOGHUL EMPERORS

ABDUL KARIM. *Tawārīkh-i-Bangalah* on Shujā'al-Dīn Muhammad Khān's succession to the Ṣūbahdārī of Bengal. *J. Pak. Hist. Soc.* 13(1965), pp. 342-349.

AHMAD, Rafiq. Land taxation in the Punjab under the Mughuls. *J.res.(humanities)* 5i(1970), pp. 23-49.

AHMAD, Tasneem. Ishwardas: a Hindu chronicler of Aurangzeb's reign. *IC* 49(1975), pp. 223-231.

AHMED, Qeyamuddin. Meaning and usage of some terms of land revenue administration. *Medieval India* 2(1972), pp. 275-281.

AHUJA, N.D. Babur and polity - a reappraisal (with particular reference to the social and political background.) *Research bull. (arts) U. Panjab* 63 (1968), 12 pp.

ALAM, Muzaffar. The zamindars and Mughal power in the Deccan, 1685-1712. *Ind.econ. soc.hist.R.* 11(1974), pp. 74-91.

ALAVI, Rafi Ahmad. Mughal geographical accounts of Khandesh. *Medieval India* 3(1975), pp. 127-151.

ALAVI, Rafi Ahmad. New light on Mughal cavalry. *Medieval India* 2(1972), pp. 70-98.

AMAR, V.B. Shah Jahan's rebellion and Abdur Rahim Khan Khanan. *J.Ind.hist.,* Golden jubilee vol. 1973, pp. 438-455.

ANAND, Mulk Raj. The treatment of environment by the Mughals. *Marg* 26i(1972), pp. 3-8.

ASKARI, Syed Hasan. Mughal naval weakness and Aurangzib's attitude towards the traders and pirates on the Western coast as revealed from Persian documents. *Indo-Iranica* 25 iii-iv(1972), pp. 102-117.

ATHAR ALI, M. The passing of empire: the Mughal case. *Modern Asian stud.* 9(1975), pp. 385-396.

ATHAR ALI, M. Provincial governors under Aurangzeb - an analysis. *Medieval India* 1(1969), pp. 96-133.

ATHAR ALI, M. Provincial governors under Shah Jahan. An analysis. *Medieval India* 3(1975), pp. 80-112.

ATHAR ALI, M. Provincial governors under Shah Jahan - an analysis. *Proc.32 Ind. hist.cong.* 1970, vol. 1, pp. 288-319.

ATHAR ALI, M. Sidelights into ideological and religious attitudes in the Punjab during the 17th century. *Medieval India* 2(1972), pp. 187-194.

AZMI, Arshad Ali. The decay of the city of Lucknow, 1840-1870. *Proc.32 Ind.hist.cong.* 1970, vol. 2, pp. 168-172.

BEG, Azmat Ali. Aurangzeb's second viceroyalty of the Deccan and his relations with Bijapur. *IC* 48(1974), pp. 39-47.

BEG, Azmat Ali. Murshid Quli Khan Khurasani (with special reference to his Deccan deeds). *Q.rev.hist.stud.* 13(1973-74), pp. 212-216.

BHATT, S.K. A farman of Jalaluddin Muhammad Akbar Badshah Ghazi, 978 H. *Proc.32 Ind. hist.cong.* 1970, vol. 1, pp. 374-375.

BILGRAMI, Rafat. Akbar's Maḥḍar of 1579. *IC* 47(1973), pp. 231-240.

BILGIRAMI, Rafat. Some Mughal revenue grants to the family and khanqah of Saiyid Ashraf Jahangir. *Medieval India* 2(1972), pp. 298-335.

BUKHARI, Y.K. Unknown historical letters of Shayasta Khan. *J. Madhya Pradesh Itihasa Parishad* 7(1969), pp. 71-83.

CHAGHATAI, M. Abdulla. A rare scroll of Shahjahan's reign. *JAS Pakistan* 16(1971) pp. 63-77.

CHANDRA, Satish. Some religious grants of Aurangzeb to *maths* in the state of Marwar. *Proc.32 Ind.hist.cong.* 1970, vol. 1, pp. 405-407.

CHATTERJEE, Ashok Kumar. Battle of Burhanpur and the role of Husain Ali Khan. *J.Ind. hist.*, Golden jubilee vol. 1973, pp. 501-510.

DAS GUPTA, Ashin. The merchants of Surat, c.1700-50. *Elites in South Asia,* 1970, pp. 201-222.

DATTA, Kali Kinkar. India in the eighteenth century. *J.Ind.hist.*, Golden jubilee vol. 1973, pp. 687-702.

DESAI, Ashok V. Population and standards of living in Akbar's time. *Ind. econ. soc. hist. rev.* 9(1972), pp. 43-62.

DWIVEDI, Radhey Dhar. Powers and functions of the Kotwal in Mughal India from 1526 to 1605 A.D. *J. Ind. hist.* 53(1975), pp. 57-62.

FAROOQI, Anis. The establishment of Akbar's atelier. *Indica* 11i(1974), pp. 33-41.

GOPAL, Surendra. Social set-up of science and technology in Mughal India. *Ind. J. hist. sci.* 4(1969), pp. 52-58.

GOPAL, Surendra. Gujarati shipping in the seventeenth century. *Ind. econ. soc. hist. rev.* 8 (1971), pp. 31-39.

GOREKAR, N.S. Indo-Iranian relations during the Mughal period. *Indica* 12(1975), pp. 11-21.

GOSWAMY, B.N., MALHOTRA, R.I. An early eighteenth century document from Kangra. *JAOS* 93(1973), pp. 203-206.

GUPTA, S.P. Ijara system in Eastern Rajasthan (c.1650-1750). *Medieval India* 2(1972), pp. 263-274.

HABIB, Irfan. The family of Nur Jahan during Jahangir's reign. *Medieval India* 1(1969), pp. 74-95.

HABIB, Irfan. Potentialities of capitalistic development in the economy of Mughal India. *J.econ.hist.* 29(1969), pp. 32-78.

HAMBLY, G. A note on the trade in eunuchs in Mughul Bengal. *JAOS* 94(1974), pp. 125-130.

HAMBYE, E.R. The Mogul court, the Portuguese and the Jesuits 1614-1617. *J.Ind.hist.*, Golden jubilee vol. 1973, pp. 457-462.

HUSAIN, Afzal. The family of Shaikh Salim Chishti during the reign of Jagangir. *Medieval India* 2(1972), pp. 61-69.

HUSAIN, Afzal. Provincial governors under Akbar (1580-1605). *Proc.32 Ind.hist.cong.* 1970, vol. 1, pp. 269-277.

JALALUDDIN. Sultān Salīm (Jahāngīr) as a rebel king. *IC* 47(1973), pp. 121-125.

JAN QAISAR, A. Shahbaz Khan Kambu. *Medieval India* 1(1969), pp. 48-73.

JHA, Hetukar. The Oinwaras in the Mughal period. *JBRS* 55(1969), pp. 144-150.

JOSHI, P.S. The escape of Chhatrapati Rajaram from Panhala to Jinji. *Quart. rev. hist. studs.* 10 (1970-71), pp. 91-100.

KANWAR, H.I.S. ʿAlī Mardan Khaān. *IC* 47 (1973), pp. 105-119.

KARIM, K.M. Mughal Nawwara in Bengal. *J. Asiatic Soc. Pakistan* 14 (1969), pp. 51-57.

KHAN, Ansar Zahid. The *arbābs* of Sind. *J. Pak.Hist.Soc.* 22(1974), pp. 18-31.

KHAN, Bazlur Rahman. Royal dishes and drinks under Akbar and Jahangir. *J. Pakistan Hist. Soc.* 17(1969), pp. 145-160.

KHAN, Iqtidar Alam. The Mughal court politics during Bairam Khan's regency. *Medieval India* 1(1969), pp. 21-38.

KHAN, Mubarak Ali. The Mughul encampment. *J.Pak.Hist.Soc.* 23(1975), pp. 225-232.

KHAN, Yar Muhammad. ʿĀlamgīr and Golconda. *J. Pak. Hist. Soc.* 13(1965), pp. 322-327.

KOFFSKY, P.L. Postal systems of India, 1600-1785. *BPP* 90i(1971), pp. 47-74.

MALIK, Zahiruddin Chauth-collection in the Subah of Hyderabad 1726-1748. *Ind.econ. soc.hist.rev.* 8(1971), pp. 395-414

MALIK, Zahiruddin. Documents of Madad-i-Maʿāsh grants during the reign of Muḥammad Shāh, 1719-1748. *Indo Iranica* 26ii-iii (1973), pp. 97-123.

MALIK, Zahiruddin. Khan-i-Dauran, the Mir Bakshi of Muhammad Shah. *Medieval India* 1(1969), pp. 134-232.

MALIK, Z. The subah of Kashmir under the later Mughals 1708-1748. *Medieval India* 2(1972), pp. 249-262.

MAYANK, Mangi Lal Vyas. Mughal Marwar relations. *QJMS* 62(1971), pp. 23-42.

MISHRA, N.K. Some aspects of piracy in early eighteenth century Western India. *Proc. 32 Ind. hist. cong.* 1970, vol. 1, pp. 398-404; vol. 2, pp. 131-137.

MOHIBBUL HASAN. An Indian prince and the French Revolution. *Iran Society silver jubilee souvenir* 1944-1969, pp. 137-140.

MOINUL HAQ, S. 'Ālamgīr's character and policy, with special reference to the Deccan. *J.Pak.Hist.Soc.* 21(1973), pp. 164-170.

MOINUL HAQ, S. Khafi Khan's history of Alamgir. *J. Pakistan Hist. Soc.* 17(1969), pp. 41-64, 109-140, 251-290; 19(1971), pp. 113-144, 175-222

MOINUL HAQ, S. Khāfi Khān's History of 'Ālamgīr (English translation). *J.Pak. Hist.Soc.* 20(1972), pp. 97-144, 176-223, 279-302.

MOINUL HAQ, S. Khāfī' Khān's History of Ālamgīr (English translation). *J. Pak. Hist. Soc.* 21(1973), pp. 33-63.

MOOSVI, Shireen. Production, consumption and population in Akbar's time. *Ind. econ. soc. hist. R.* 10(1973), pp. 181-195.

NAQVI, Hamida Khatoon. Incidents of rebellions during the reign of Emperor Akbar. *Medieval India* 2(1972), pp. 152-186.

NATH, R. Mughal concept of sovereignty in the inscriptions of Fatehpur Sikri, Agra and Delhi (1570-1654). *Indica* 11 (1974), pp. 90-100.

NATH, R. The personality of Akbar as revealed in the inscriptions at Fatehpur Sikri and Agra. *Indo-Iranica* 25iii-iv (1972), pp. 144-157.

NIJJAR, Bakhshish Singh. The north-west Frontier under the later Mughals (1707-1759). *Q.rev.hist.stud.* 11(1971-2), pp. 41-45

PAL SINGH, Mahendra. Merchants and the local administration and civic life in Gujarat during the 17th century. *Medieval India* 2 (1972), pp. 221-226.

PAWAR, Jaising B. The Mughal-Maratha struggle in 1689. *J.Ind.hist.*, Golden jubilee vol. 1973, pp. 511-523.

PEARSON, M.N. Political participation in Mughal India. *Ind. econ. soc. hist. rev.* 9(1972), pp. 113-131.

QAISAR, A.J. Merchant shipping in India during the seventeenth century. *Medieval India* 2(1972), pp. 195-220.

QUAMARUDDIN, M. A study of the character and personality of Murād Bakhsh (1624-1661). *Indo-Iranica* 24i-ii(1971), pp. 64-76.

RAHIM, M.A. Emperor Aurangzeb's annexation of Jodhpur and the Rajput rebellion. *J. Asiatic Soc. Pakistan* 14(1969), pp. 65-90.

RAHIM, M.A. Emperor Aurangzeb Alamgir's ideal as ruler. *J.Research Soc.Pakistan* 7i(1970), pp. 51-68.

RAJAYYAN, K. Moghal conquest of Trichinoply. *J. Ind. hist.* 49(1971), pp. 113-123.

RAMZAN, M. 'Īsa Khan *Masnad-i-A'la*, the leader of Barah Bhuyas. *J. Pakistan Hist. Soc.* 17(1969), pp. 161-168.

RIZVI, S.A.A. The Maktab Khāna. *Dr. Adilya Nath Jha felicitation volume*, III, 1969, pp. 166-185.

RIZVI, S.A.A. The Mughal elite in the sixteenth and seventeenth century. *Abr-Nahrain* 11(1971), pp. 69-104.

ROOMAN, M. Anwar. The thirty years Rind-Lashar war. *J. Pakistan Hist. Soc.* 17(1969), pp. 191-210.

SACHDEVA, Krishan Lal. Some industries of Delhi territory, 1803-1857. *Proc. 32 Ind. hist. cong.* 1970, vol. 2, pp. 160-167.

SAKSENA, B.P. Two firmans of Aurangzib. *Ind. archives* 17(1967-1968), pp. 31-37.

SARKAR, Ashok Kumar. Itimad-ud-Daulah - a sketch of his life and career. *Quart. rev. hist. studs.* 10 (1970-71), pp. 154-164.

SARKAR, Jagadish Narayan. A little known chapter in Indo-Iranian diplomacy in mid-seventeenth century. *Indo-Iranica* 25iii-iv (1972), pp. 51-56.

SARKAR, J.N. New light on Mughal-Portuguese relations, 1965-67. *J.Madhya Pradesh Itihasa Parishad, Bhopal* 6(1968), pp. 78-92.

SARKAR, Jagadish Narayan. Shivaji, the Mughals and the Europeans (1664-67) - a study in diplomacy. *J.Ind.hist.* 53(1975), pp. 269-281.

SAXENA, A.N. Early relations of Raja Rai Singh of Bikaner with the Mughals. *Quart. rev. hist. stud.* 12(1972-3), pp. 63-66.

SCHACHT, J. On the title of the *Fatāwā al-'Ālamgiriyya*. *Iran and Islam, in memory of V. Minorsky*, 1971, pp. 475-478

SERAJUDDIN, A.M. The origin of the Rajas of the Chittagong Hill tracts and their relations with the Mughuls and the East India Company in the eighteenth century. *J. Pakistan Hist. Soc.* 19(1971), pp. 51-60.

SERAJUDDIN, A.M. The revenue accounts of Chittagong in the Ā'in-i-Akbarī. *JAS Bangladesh* 16(1971), pp. 243-248.

SHAN, Harnam Singh. Introducing the Zafarnameh (an epistle of victory by Guru Gobind Singh). *Proc. 27th Int. Cong. Or. 1967* (1971), pp. 399-400.

SHARMA, B.D. Shivaji's escape from Agra. *Q. rev.hist.stud.* 11(1971-2), pp. 51-52

SHARMA, G.D. Role of Durgadas Rathor in the politics of Marwar, 1693 - 1697. *BPP* 91(1972), pp. 176-181.

SHARMA, Ramesh Chandra. Bahadur Shah's petition for non-intervention during the second siege of Chittaud. *Indica* 11 (1974), pp. 87-89.

SHYAM, Radhey. Honours, ranks and titles under the Great Mughals (Babur and Humayun). *IC* 46(1972), pp. 101-117.

SHYAM, Radhey. Honours, ranks and titles under the great Mughals (Akbar). *IC* 47 (1973), pp. 335-353.

SHYAM, Radhey. Mirza Hindal (a biographical study). *IC* 45 (1971), pp. 115-136.

SIDDIQI, Iqtidar Husain. Nuhani rule in Bihar. *Proc.32 Ind.hist.cong.* 1970, vol. 1, pp. 282-287.

SIDDIQI, Muhammad Zameeruddin. The intelligence services under the Mughals. *Medieval India* 2(1972), pp. 53-60.

SIDDIQI, Zameeruddin. The institution of the qazi under the Mughals. *Medieval India* 1(1969), pp. 240-259.

SMITH, W.C. The crystallization of religious communities in Mughal India. *Yād-nāme-ye Irāni-ye Minorsky,* 1969, pp. 197-220.

SPEAR, P. The Mughal 'mansabdari' system. *Elites in South Asia,* 1970, pp. 1-15.

SRIVASTAVA, K.P. Jahandar Shah and his successors in Banaras. *J.Ind.hist.,* Golden jubilee vol. 1973, pp. 495-500.

TIRMIZI, S.A.I. Inayat Jang collection [of Mughal archives]. *Ind. archives* 18i(1969), pp. 37-45.

UMAR, Muhammad. Causes of the decline of North Indian industries. *Stud. in Islam* 9(1972), pp. 38-55.

UMAR, Muhammed. Foreign trade of India during the eighteenth century. *Medieval India* 2(1972), pp. 227-248.

VARADARAJAN, L. Jahangir the diarist - an interpretation based on the "Tuzuk-i-Jahangiri". *J.Ind.hist.,* Golden jubilee vol. 1973, pp. 403-418.

VARADARAJAN, L. The Marathas and the changing history of the Deccan. *Indica* 9(1972), pp. 101-113.

VERMA, Birendra. Indian solicitations for Afghan military intervention, 1793-1800. *Proc.32 Ind.hist.cong.* 1970, vol. 2, pp. 38-43.

VERMA, Birendra. Shah Alam's negotiations with the Durrani Afghans (1757-1800). *JBRS* 57(1971), pp. 102-117.

VERMA, Som Prakash. Wine-pots at the Mughal court. *Medieval India* 3(1975), pp. 67-79.

VERMA, S.R. Some (unpublished) Mughal farmans of the year 1068 H. *Proc.32 Ind.hist. cong.* 1970, vol. 1, pp. 278-281.

ZILLI, I.A. Two administrative documents of Akbar's reign. *Proc.32 Ind.hist.cong.* 1970, vol. 1, pp. 367-373.

See also II. a. 7. Sangar

See also II. a. 8. Ahmad.

See also IV. c. 8. Sangar

See also V. c. *India* Nath

See also V. g. Ivanov.

See also V. m. 1. Grek.

See also V. m. 1. Krishna.

See also XXXI. g. Naqvi

See also XXXIX. c. Bausani.

See also XXXIX. d. Rizvi.

k NAWABS OF OUDH

AHMAD, Safi. The Awadh treaty of 1837. *Medieval India* 2(1972), pp. 282-290.

BHATNAGAR, G.D. A Muslim king's dilemma: Hindu-Muslim clash at Hanumangarhi. *Itihāsa-Chayanikā (Dr. Sampurnanand Felicitation vol.* = JUPHS 11-13), Part 1(1965), pp. 71-90

MALIK, Zahiruddin. The rise of Tegh Beg Khan - first Nawab of Surat, 1733-1746. *IC* 46(1972), pp. 53-62

MUKHERJEE, Anshuman. Muhammad Ali Shah and the administration of Oudh. *Q.rev.hist. stud.* 12(1972-73), pp. 104-110.

SHARMA, Madhu. Costume and costume-craft in Nawabi Awadh. *Proc.32 Ind.hist.cong.* 1970, vol. 2, pp. 177-181.

l NAWABS OF ARCOT

DALE, S.F. Communal relations in pre-modern India. 16th century Kerala. *JESHO* 16 (1973), pp. 319-327.

GUPTA, Maya. The Vellore Mutiny, July 1806. *J. Ind. hist.* 49(1971), pp. 91-112.

RAJAYYAN, K. British annexation of the Carnatic, 1801. *Proc.32 Ind.hist.cong.* 1970, vol. 2, pp. 54-62.

RAMANUJAM, Chidambaram S. The Madras revolution. *K.A. Nilakanta Sastri felicitation volume,* Madras, 1971, pp. 131-158.

m NAWABS OF BENGAL

CHAUDHURI, Sushil. Prices of provisions in Bengal in the second half of the seventeenth century - Moreland refuted. *Proc.32 Ind. hist.cong.* 1970, vol. 1, pp. 387-397.

DE, Amalendu, A note on the black hole tragedy (Part II). *Q'ly rev.hist.stud.* 10(1970-1), pp. 187-192.

HUSAIN, Iqbal. The role of Ghulam Husain in the formation of Anglo-Rohilla relations between 1766-71. *Medieval India* 3(1975), pp. 188-197.

KULKARNI, G.T. Diary of political affairs of North India from May to July 1757 A.D. *Bull. Deccan Coll. R.I.* 31-32(1970-72), pp. 215-220.

MAJUMDAR, R.C. The cultivators of Bengal in the nineteenth century. *J.Ind.hist.*, Golden jubilee vol. 1973, pp. 703-722.

NATH, R. Three studies of Zamindari system. *Medieval India* 1(1969), pp. 233-239.

RAY, Jayati. Ostend East India Company in Bengal during the reign of Nawab Shuja-ud-Din Khan (1727-1739 A.D.) - a short history. *Q.R.hist.stud.* 15(1975-6), pp. 90-94.

SARKAR, Jagadish Narayan. Mir Jumla's peace with the Ahoms: a rejoinder. *Q.R. hist.stud.* 15(1975-6), pp. 102-105.

SRIVASTAVA, A.L. Shah Walli-Ullah and the Maratha-Afghan contest for supremacy. *J. Ind. hist.* 49(1971), pp. 217-228.

SUBHAN, Abdus. Early career of Nawab Ali Vardi Khan of Bengal. *J.Ind.hist.* 48 (1970), pp. 535-547.

n NIZAMS OF HYDERABAD

ACHARYA, A.M. Medical care of the Nazim's army. *Bull. Ind. Inst. Hist. Med.* 4(1974), pp. 176-191.

LEONARD, K. The Deccani synthesis in old Hyderabad; an historiographic essay. *J. Pak.Hist.Soc.* 21(1973), pp. 205-218.

MALIK, Zaheeruddin. Documents relating to Chauth collection in the subah of Hyderabad, 1726-1748. *Proc.32 Ind.hist.cong.* 1970, vol. 1, pp. 336-352.

PAGADI, Setu Madhavarao, Maratha-Nizam relations: Nizam-ul-Mulk's letters. *ABORI* 51 (1970), pp. 93-121.

PATWARDHAN, Dileep. Nizam-Portuguese negotiations, 1947-48. *J.Ind.hist.* 53(1975), pp. 303-322.

SAJUNLAL, K. Mīr Lāiq ʿAlī Khān Sālār Jung II, Prime Minister of Hyderabad, and his relations with His Highness Nawab Mīr Maḥboob ʿAlī Khān, ʿĀṣaf Jāh Nizām IV. *IC* 48(1974), pp. 221-235.

o HAIDAR ALI

D'COSTA, A. The life of Haidar ʿAlī according to Eustachio Delfini. *Indica* 8(1971), pp. 91-106.

HUSAIN, Syed Hamza. Waqae-i-Hydari. Ed. Syed Hamza Husain. *Bull. Govt. Or. Mss. Lib., Madras* 19i(1969), Persian sect. pp. 1-36; 19ii(1972), Persian sect. pp. 1-38.

SHASTRY, B.S. Portuguese relations with Hyder Ali (1763-1769). *Q.rev.hist.stud.* 14(1974-5), pp. 75-81.

q THE MUTINY. THE POST-MUTINY PERIOD

ADAS, M. Twentieth century approaches to the Indian mutiny of 1857-58. *J. Asian history* 5 (1971), pp. 1-19.

AHMAD, Aziz. L'Islam et la démocratie dans le sous-continent indo-pakistanais. *Orient* 51-2(1969), pp. 9-26

AHMAD, Imtiaz. The Muslim electorate and election alternatives in U.P. *Religion and society* 21ii(1974), pp. 55-77.

AHMAD, Imtiaz. Muslim politics in India: a revaluation. *Islam and the modern age* 2iv(1971), pp. 71-95.

AHMAD, Jamil-ud-Din. Evolution of the concept of Pakistan. *J. Pakistan Hist. Soc.* 16(1968), pp. 19-34.

AHMAD, Jamil-ud-Din. Origin of the two-nation concept. *J.Research Soc.Pakistan* 7i(1970), pp. 29-50.

AHMAD, Waheed. Choudhary Rahmat Ali and the concept of Pakistan. *J.Research Soc.Pakistan* 7i(1970), pp. 11-28.

AHMED, Ashrafuddin. The political career of Abdur Rasul. *Dacca Univ. studies* 19A(1971), pp. 101-108.

BAHA, Lal. Politics in the North-West Frontier Province, 1901-1919. *Peshawar Univ. rev.* 1i(1973), pp. 109-117.

BAHADUR, Kalim. The Jama'at-i-Islami of Pakistan: ideology and political action. *Internat. studies* 14(1975), pp. 69-84.

BRODKIN, E.I. The struggle for succession: rebels and loyalists in the Indian Mutiny of 1857. *Modern Asian stud.* 6(1972), pp. 277-290.

BURKI, R.J. The idea of Pakistan and Iqbal's universalism. *J. Reg. Cult. Inst.* 2 iv(1969), pp. 245-251.

CHUGHTAI, Munir ud-Din. Post-1857 economic and administrative policies of the British in India and the Muslims. *Pak. econ. soc. R.* 12(1974), pp. 243-254.

DE, Amalendu. Fazlul Huq and his reaction to the two-nation theory (1940-47). *BPP* 93 (1974), pp. 23-38.

DE, Amalendu. A new light on the Lahore resolution. *Q.rev.hist.stud.* 12(1972-73), pp. 86-98.

DE, Amalendu. A separate homeland for the Muslims of India. *Qly. rev. hist stud.* 11(1972-2), pp. 127-139.

DE, Amalendu. Two-nation theory challenged by A.K. Fazlul Huq. *Q.rev.hist.stud.* 14 (1974-5), pp. 129-137.

DIVEKAR, V.D. Hostile attitude of the Muslim League towards national planning (1944-1947). *J. Ind. hist.* 49(1971), pp. 281-287.

DOUGLAS, I.H. *Abul Kalam Azad and Pakistan.* A post-Bangladesh reconsideration of an Indian Muslim's opposition to partition. *J.Amer.Acad.Religion* 40(1972), pp. 458-479.

FRIEDMANN, Yohannan. The attitude of the *Jam'iyyat-i 'Ulamā'-i Hind* to the Indian national movement and the establishment of Pakistan. *Asian & Afr.Studs.* 7(1971), pp. 157-180.

GHOSH, Shyamali. Fazlul Haq and Muslim politics in pre-partition Bengal. *Internat. stud.* 13(1974), pp. 441-464.

GOBIND SINGH. A survey of English novels dealing with the Indian Mutiny of 1857. *Research bull. (arts) U. Panjab* 42 (1963), 27 pp.

HALDAR, Sisir Kumar. How London reacted to the 'Sepoy Mutiny'. *Bengal past and present* 92i(1973), pp. 84-88.

KARUNAKARAN, K.P. The Mopla rebellion 1921. *India and contemporary Islam,* ed. S.T. Lokhandwalla, 1971, pp. 158-167.

KHAN, Husain. Why was the Congress founded in 1885? *J. Pakistan Hist. Soc.* 17(1969), pp. 169-176.

KORESHI, S.M. The ideology of Pakistan: a historical interpretation of Muslim nationalism in the subcontinent. *Papers 3rd annual conf. Nigerian Soc. Int. Law,* 1971, pp. 51-85.

KRISHNASWAMIENGAR, B.S. The spirit of 1857. *Studies in Indian history and culture ...* presented to P.D. Desai, 1971, pp. 255-257.

LAVAN, S. The Kanpur mosque incident of 1913: the North Indian Muslim press and its reaction to community crisis. *J.Amer. Acad.Religion* 42(1974), pp. 263-279.

LELYVELD, D. Three Aligarh students: Aftab Ahmad Khan, Ziauddin Ahmad and Muhammad Ali. *Modern Asian stud.* 9 (1975), pp. 227-240.

MALIK, Hafeez. The spirit of capitalism and Pakistani Islam. *Islam and the modern age* 2ii(1971), pp. 19-48.

MALIK, Salahuddin. Nineteenth century approaches to the Indian "Mutiny". *J.Asian hist.* 7(1973), pp. 95-127.

MALIK, Salahuddin. Religious and economic factors in 19th century India: a case study of the Indian "mutiny". *IC* 46(1972), pp. 187-207.

MATHUR, R.M. Indian Mutiny and the states of Jodhpur, Bikaner and Jaisalmer. *J. Ind.hist.* 48(1970), pp. 357-376.

MATHUR, Y.B. Religious disturbances in India. *Studs. in Islam* 8(1971), pp. 81-131.

MATI-UR-RAHMAN. The first Hindu-Muslim unity conference. *J.Research Soc.Pakistan* 7i(1970), pp. 1-10.

MOHAR ALI, Md. The Bengal Muslims' repudiation of the concept of British India as *Darul Harb,* 1870. *Dacca Univ. studies* 19A (1971), pp. 47-68.

MUSHIRUL HASAN. The role of Ansari in Muslim politics. *Islam and the modern age* 3iii(1972), pp. 36-53.

NARAIN, Prem. Political views of Sayyid Ahmad Khan: evolution and impact. *J. Ind. hist.* 53(1975), pp. 105-153.

NEOGY, Ajit. British role in the selection of the Nizam's Dewan in the 19th century. *Qly. rev. hist.stud.* 11(1972-2), pp. 145-153.

ODDIE, G.A. Bengali reactions to western impact (1800-1857). *JOS Australia* 4ii (1966), pp. 2-11.

PAPANEK, H. Pakistan's big businessmen: Muslim separatism, entrepreneurship, and partial modernization. *Econ. devel. and cultural change* 21(1972), pp. 1-32.

PRASAD SINGH, Raj Kishore. Khudi Ram Bose and his times (1889-1908). *JBRS* 57(1971), pp. 154-164.

RAHIM, M.A. Syed Ameer Ali and Muslim politics in the Subcontinent. *Univ. studies* [Karachi] 5i(1968), pp. 49-72.

RAHMAN, F. Islam and the constitutional problem of Pakistan. *SI* 32(1970), pp. 275-287.

RAZI WASTI, S. British policy towards the Indian Muslims immediately after 1857. *J. hist. and pol. sci.* 1i(1971-72), pp. 78-97.

ROBINSON, F. Municipal government and Muslim separatism in the United Provinces, 1883 to 1916. *Modern Asia stud.* 7(1973), pp. 389-441.

SAIYIDAIN, Mirza S. Communal conflict in India with special reference to July 1973 riots in Ahmedabad. *Islam and the modern age* 5iv(1974), pp. 65-80.

SAREEN, T.R. The Simla Deputation, 1906. *Q. rev. hist. stud.* 11(1971-2), pp. 67-70.

SARKAR, Sumit. Hindu-Muslim relations in Swadeshi Bengal, 1903-1908. *Ind. econ. soc. rev.* 9(1972), pp. 161-216.

XXXII INDIA. PAKISTAN

SCHALLER, E. Zu einigen Aspekten der politischen und ideologischen Orientierung des islamischen Flügels der indischen Bourgeoisie. *Asien, Afrika, Lateinamerika* 3(1975), pp. 965-970.

SEN, S.P. Jinnah, Mohammed Ali (Quaid-i-Azam) (1875-1948). *Q.rev.hist.stud.* 13 (1973-4), pp. 187-193.

SHIBLY, A.H. The composition of the Indian regiments after the Mutiny. *JAS Bangladesh* 18(1973), pp. 195-206.

SIDDIQI, M.H. El surgimiento del nacionalismo musulmán en India. *Estudios orientales* 4(1969), no. 10, pp. 137-153.

SINHA, N.K. The mutiny and revolt of 1857 -- A survey in retrospection. *BPP* 91(1972), pp. 122-128.

SUR, Nikhil. The sepoy Mutiny and the Porahat chief of Singbhum. *Q.rev.hist.stud.* 12(1972-73), pp. 117-122.

TEWARI, J.P. A class analysis of the prominent rebels of 1857 in Meerut district. *Proc.32 Ind.hist.cong.* 1970, vol. 2, pp. 69-72.

UMAR, Muhammad. Some non-textile industries of Northern India during the 18th century and their decline. *Studies in Islam* 7(1970), pp. 228-249.

VARMA, Birendra. Ahmad Shah Abdali's ninth invasion and its repercussions on East India Company. *Dr. Satkari Mookerji felicitation volume,* 1969, pp. 322-326.

VERMA, N.P. Echoes of 1857 in the Russian press. *J.Ind.hist.*, Golden jubilee vol. 1973, pp. 623-633.

WAHEED-UZ-ZAMAN. Qa'id-e-Azam and the making of Pakistan. *Peshawar Univ.rev.* 1i(1973), pp. 104-108.

WALKER, D. The birth of a mass-protest movement: the Bengali language "agitation" in post-partition East Pakistan. *Islam and the modern age* 5iv(1974), pp. 24-45.

WALKER, D. The birth of a mass-protest movement. *Islam and the modern age* 6i (1975), pp. 5-31.

WRIGHT, T.P. Indian Muslim refugees in the politics of Pakistan. *J. Cmw. comp. politics* 12(1974), pp. 189-205.

YANUCK, M. The Kanpur mosque affair of 1913. *MW* 64(1974), pp. 307-321.

ZABAR SINGH. Mutiny of the Jodhpur legion (1857). *Proc.32 Ind.hist.cong.* 1970, vol. 2, pp. 73-78.

ZAHEER, Sajjad. Recent Muslim politics in India and the problems of national unity. *India and contemporary Islam,* ed. S.T. Lokhandwalla, 1971, pp. 202-213.

Letters of Iqbal to Jinnah. *Iqbal: poet-philosopher of Pakistan,* ed. Hafeez Malik, 1971, pp. 383-388.

The proclamations of the leaders of the struggle of 1857. *Dr. Adilya Nath Jha felicitation volume,* III, 1969, pp. 21-28.

See also IX. g. Jawed.

See also XXIX. j. Fatimi.

XXXIII AFGHANISTAN

a GEOGRAPHY

BALSAN, F. Exploring the Registan desert. *Asian aff.* 59(N.S. 3, 1972), pp. 153-156.

BARRAT, J. Quelques traits caractéristiques de l'Afghanistan. *Annales de géog.* 81(no. 444, 1972), pp. 206-229

BREND, B. Afghan sketches. *Asian aff.* 59(N.S. 3,1972), pp. 157-163.

BRUGGEY, J. Grabdenkmäler als Zeugen "angewandter Geologie" in der Provinz Paktia (SE. Afghanistan). *Cent.Asiatic J.* 15(1971), pp. 211-213.

DESIO, A. Esplorazioni geologiche e geofisiche. *Veltro* 16v-vi(1972), pp. 531-539.

DONINI, G. L'orografia del Ǧūzǧānī (sec. XIII). *Annali Fac. Ling. Lett. stran. di Ca' Foscari (serie orientale)* 3(1972), pp. 191-195.

GANDY, C. Afghanistan: the Society's 1972 tour. *Asian aff.* N.S.4(1973), pp. 27-35.

GILLME, C. Note sur les scos d'araire d'Afghanistan. *Afghanistan* 27ii(1974), pp. 34-45.

HAHN, H. Wachstumsabläufe in einer orientalischen Stadt, am Beispiel von Kabul/ Afghanistan. *Erdkunde* 26(1972), pp. 16-32

KIEFFER, Ch. *Wardak,* toponyme et ethnique d'Afghanistan. *Acta Iranica,* 2. sér. *Monumentum H.S. Nyberg,* I (1975), pp. 475-483.

MOUCHET, J. et BLANC, J.-C. Khandud, village de la Vallée du Wakhan. *Afghanistan* 25ii(1972), pp. 57-70.

PINELLI, C.A. Esploratori e alpinisti itali-ani. *Veltro* 16v-vi(1972), pp. 541-548.

RATHJENS, C. Witterungsbedingte Schwankungen der Ernährungsbasis in Afghanistan. *Erdkunde* 29(1975), pp. 182-188.

SIDKY, Moh. O. A short historical and geographical description of the cities of Aryana. *Afghanistan* 28i(1975), pp. 94-96.

VERCELLIN, G. Il monte-santuario di Qal'e-kah nel Sistān afghano. *Annali Fac. Ling. Lett. stran. di Ca' Foscari (serie orientale)* 3(1972), pp. 75-117.

VERCELLIN, G. Šindanḍ. Le vicende di un toponimo afghano. *Ann.Fac.Ling.Lett.stran. Ca' Foscari* 5(1974), pp. 99-107.

b ETHNOLOGY

ANDERSON, J. Tribe and community among the Ghilzai Pashtun. Preliminary notes on ethnographic distribution and variation in Eastern Afghanistan. *Anthropos* 70(1975), pp. 575-601.

BAUER, W.P., JANATA, A. Kosmetik, Schmuck und Symbolik in Afghanistan. *Arch.f.Völkerkunde* 28(1975). pp. 1-43.

BAUSANI, A. Ossarvazioni sul sistema calendariale degli Hazara di Afghanistan. *OM* 54(1974), pp. 341-354.

BRESHNA, A.G. Haji Mirwais Khan A historical play, *Afghanistan* 23 ii(1970), pp. 59-81.

CENTLIVRES, P. La contribution française et suisse à l'ethnographie de l'Afghanistan depuis la seconde guerre mondiale. *Cent. Asiatic J.* 16(1972), pp. 181-193.

CENTLIVRES, M. & P. and SLOBIN, M. A Muslim Shaman of Afghan Turkestan. *Ethnology [Pittsburg]* 10(1971), pp. 160-173.

CENTLIVRES, P. Noms, surnoms et termes d'adresse dans le Nord Afghan. *Stud. iranica* 1(1972), pp. 89-102.

CHARPENTIER, C.J. The use of haschish and opium in Afghanistan. *Anthropos* 68(1973), pp. 482-490.

CHARPENTIER, C.J. Water-pipes, tobacco and snuff in Afghanistan. *Anthropos* 69(1974), pp. 939-944.

DUPREE, L. Settlement and migration patterns in Afghanistan: a tentative statement. *Modern Asian stud.* 9(1975), pp. 397-413.

FARHĀDI, Abd-ul-Ghafour Ravan. Les quatraines populaires de la région de Kaboul. *Adab* (Kabul) 22iii(1974), pp. 1-14.

FARHADI, Rawan. A comparison of folklore and letters. *Afghanistan* 28ii(1975), pp. 14-19.

FERDINAND, K. Ost-afghanischer Nomadismus - ein Beitrag zur Anpassungsfähigkeit der Nomaden. *Nomadismus als Entwicklungsproblem* 1969, pp. 107-128.

FRANZ, E. Zur gegenwärtigen Vernreitung und Gruppierung der Turkmenen in Afghanistan. *Baessler-Archiv* N.F.20(45, 1972), pp. 191-238.

GRATZL, K., SENARCLENS DE GRANCY, R. Materielle und geistige Struktur einer Siedlung am Oberlauf des Amu Darya. Dokumentation der Ortschaft Wark im Wakhan (NO-Afghanistan). *EZZ* 1973(1), pp. 54-105.

GREVEMEYER, J.H., HOLZWARTH, W., KIPPENBERG, H.G. Jurm: Bericht aus einer afghanischen Stadt. *Mardom nameh* 1(1975), pp. 14-25.

HABIBI, A.H. Afghan nationality and its factors on the basis of history. *Afghanistan* 23i(1970), pp. 29-35.

HALLAJI, Ja'far. Hypnotherapeutic techniques in a Central Asian community. *Int. J. clinical and experimental hypnosis* 10 (1926), pp. 271-274.

KEISER, R. Lincoln. Social structure in the Southeastern Hindu-Kush: some implications for Pashai ethno-history. *Anthropos* 69 (1974), pp. 445-456.

KIEFER, C.M. Über das Volk der Paṣ̌tunen und seinen *Paṣ̌tunwali*. Beitrag zur afghanischen Ethnologie. *Mitt. Inst. Orientforschung* 17(1972), pp. 614-624.

KISLYAKOV, V.N. Khazareytzy, Aymaki, Mogoly (k voprosu ob ikh proiskhozhdenii i rasselenii). (Les Khazara, Aïmak et Moghol - sur le problème de leurs origines.) *Sov. etn.* 1973(4), pp. 130-139.

KRAUS, R. Siedlungsprojekte in der Provinz Helmand (Afghanistan) unter besonderer Berücksichtigung gesiedelter Nomaden. *Vierteljahresberichte* 46(1971), pp. 419-432.

MAJRUH, Sayd B. Aktuelle Fragen des Nomadismus in Afghanistan. *Nomadismus als Entwicklungsproblem* 1969, pp. 155-160.

RAVAN FARHADI, A.G. Les quatrains populaires de la région de Kaboul. *Adab* [Kabul] 22iv(1975), pp. 19-27.

RENESSE, E.-A. von and SPONECK, H.C. Graf. Nomadism in Afghanistan. *Nomadismus als Entwicklungsproblem* 1969, pp. 173-182.

RENESSE, E.-A. von und SPONECK, H.C. Graf. Nomadismus in Afghanistan als sozioökonomisches Problem. *Nomadismus als Entwicklungsproblem* 1969, pp. 161-170.

SUKH DEV SINGH CHARAK. The ethnic problem of the Hindu-Sahis of Kabul. *Panjab Univ. research bull. (arts)* 1 (1970), pp. 1-8.

TAPPER, N. The advent of Pashtūn *Māldārs* in north-western Afghanistan. *BSOAS* 36(1973), pp. 55-79.

WALD, H.-J. "Tawa-Khana" (Fussboden-heizung) in Afghanistan. *Z. f. Ethnol.* 98(1973), pp. 287-290.

WEIERS, M. Bericht über weitere Arbeiten bei den Moghol von Afghanistan, 1971. *Zentralasiat. Studien* 6(1972), pp. 575-584.

WEIERS, M. Das Moghol-Vokabular von W.R.H. Merk. *Zentralasiat.Studien* 5(1971), pp. 157-189

Population of Afghanistan and how it is estimated. *Ind.population bull.* 4(1967), pp. 1-4.

See also XXXIII. a. Kieffer.

See also XXXVIII. c. Kieffer.

See also XL. y. Laude-Cirtautas.

c HISTORY

AHANG, Mohammad Kazem. The background and the beginning of the Afghan press system. *Afghanistan* 23i(1970), pp. 6-11, 57-61; 23iii(1970), pp. 50-54; 23iv(1970), pp. 14-19; 25iii(1972), pp. 53-55.

ALDER, G.J. The key to India? Britain and the Herat problem, 1830-1863. *ME stud.* 10 (1974), pp. 186-209, 287-311.

ANTOINE, G. Aux sources de l'Afghanistan moderne: l'oeuvre intérieure de l'émir Abdur Rahman Khan (1880-1901). *Afghanistan* 26i(1973), pp. 90-105.

AYBEK, Zafer Hasan. Ubayd-Allah Sindhi in Afghanistan. *J.Reg.Cult.Inst.* 6(1973), pp. 129-136.

BABAKHODJAYEV, M.A. Afghanistan's armed forces and Amir Abdul Rahman's military reform. *Afghanistan* 23ii(1970), pp. 8-20; 23iii(1970), pp. 9-23.

BABA KHODJAYEV, M.A. To question for the formation of an all-Afghan market and the trade and industrial policy pursued by Amir Abdur Rahman. Part II. *Afghanistan* 25ii(1972), pp. 42-48.

CRANGLE, J.V. Liberal opposition to the Afghan War of 1878. *Afghanistan* 25 iii (1972), pp. 56-67.

DESAI, Z.A. Cultural relations between Afghanistan and India during the medieval period. *Afghanistan* 28iii(1975), pp. 9-17.

DUPREE, N.H. Jalalabad during the first Anglo-Afghan War. *Asian affairs* 62(N.S. 6, 1975), pp. 177-189.

DUPREE, N.H. The question of Jalalabad during the first Anglo-Afghan War. *Asian affairs* 62(N.S.6, 1975), pp. 45-60.

FARHADI, Ravan. L'Afghanistan: una politica di equilibrio e di pace. *Veltro* 16v-vi (1972), pp. 427-432.

GIL BENUMEYA, R. Actualidad del Afganistán en la encrucijada asiática mundial. *Rev. de política int.* 119(1972), pp. 177-185

GOBEDZHISHVILI. Svedenie Sekhnia Chkheidze o Kandakhare. *Gruzinskoe istochnikovedenie* III, 1971, pp. 273-277.

GUL'DZHANOV, M. Nekotorye aspekty modernizatzii Islama v sovremennom Afganistane. *Religiya i obshchestvennaya mysl' narodov vostoka,* 1971, pp. 196-206.

GUL'DZHANOV, M. Politika Abdurrakhman-Khana v otnoshenii dukhovenstva (1880-1901 gg.) *Strany Blizhnego i srednego Vostoka: istoriya, ekonomica,* 1972, pp. 49-56.

HABIBI, A.H. Afghanistan at the end of the Koshan period. *Afghanistan* 23iv (1971), pp. 51-56.

HABIBI, A.H. Nazuko. (A true story related to the Independence War). *Afghanistan* 25 iii (1972), pp. 78-80.

HABIBI, A.H. New points in the history of Afghanistan. *Afghanistan* 25 iii (1972), pp. 1-10.

HASRAT, B.J. Anglo-Sikh relations during the first Anglo-Afghan War. *Research bull. (arts) U. Panjab* 27 (1959), 34 pp.

HAYE, Kh.A. The British commercial mission to Kabul. *J. Pakistan Hist. Soc.* 16(1968), pp. 35-45.

HERAWE, Nayer. An historical edict from Amir Shair Ali Khan. *Afghanistan* 25 iv(1973), pp. 69-72.

HOKOKI, Walid. L'organisation juridictionnelle en Afghanistan. *BIIAP* 21(1972), pp. 63-81.

INGRAM, E. A preview of the Great Game in Asia - II: the proposal of an alliance with Afghanistan, 1798-1800. *ME stud.* 9 (1973), pp. 157-174.

JANATA, A. On the origin of the Firuzkuhis in western Afghanistan. *Arch. f. Völkerkunde* 25(1971), pp. 57-65.

KAKAR, Hasan. Afghanistan from disintegration to reunification: 1880-1884. *Afghanistan* 23i(1970), pp. 12-23.

KHAN, Hussain. The genesis of Roh (the medieval homeland of the Afghans). *JAS Pakistan* 15(1970), pp. 191-197.

KLEIN, I. Who made the Second Afghan War? *J.Asian hist.* 8(1974), pp. 97-121.

KORGUN, V.G. K voprosu o roli kochevnikov v Afganistane noveyshego vremeni. *Arabskie strany, Turtziya, Iran. Afganistan,* 1973, pp. 89-97.

MUSTAFA, Zubeida. Afghanistan and the Asian power balance. *Pacific community* 6(1975), pp. 283-299.

OREN, Stephen. Bedrohliche Polarisierung im Mittleren Osten. Aussenpolitische Auswirkungen des afghanischen Umsturzes. *Europa-Archiv* 29ii(1974), pp. 55-62.

PALWAL, A.R. The history of former Kafiristan. *Afghanistan* 23ii(1970), pp. 21-52; 24ii-iii(1971), pp. 10-17.

PAZHWAK, A.R. The wanderer. *Afghanistan* 23i(1970), pp. 36-42.

QUARONI, P. Ricordi e considerazioni politiche. *Veltro* 16v-vi(1972), pp. 441-445.

RASTOGI, Ram Sagar. Abdur Rahman Amir of Afghanistan. *JUPHS* N.S.9(1961), pp. 23-31

RIDOUT, C. Authority patterns and the Afghan coup of 1973. *MEJ* 29(1975), pp. 165-178.

ROMODIN, V.A. Poslednie gody domusul'manskoy istorii kafirov Gindukusha i politika Abdur-rakhman-Khana (po *Siradzh at-tavarikh*). *Strany i narody Vostoka pod obshchey red. D.A. Ol'derogge*, X, 1971, pp. 249-263.

RUBIO GARCIA, L. Los componentes del Afganistan contemporaneo. *Rev.de política int.* 138(1975), pp. 73-98; 139 (1975), pp. 93-124; 140(1975), pp. 81-118; 141(1975), pp. 149-176.

SCHINASI, M. Sirâdj al-Akhbâr: l'opinion afghane et la Russie. *Afghanistan* 25ii(1972), pp. 29-41.

SEIDOV, T.M. K voprosu o demokratizatzii afganskogo prosveshcheniya. *Strany Blizhnego i Srednego Vostoka: istoriya, ekonomica*, 1972, pp. 171-177.

SIDIQI, Mohammed O. A short historical and geographical description of the cities of Aryana. *Afghanistan* 27iii (1974), pp. 1-19; 27iv(1975), pp. 36-39.

SINGER, A. Tribal migrations on the Irano-Afghan border. *Asian aff.* N.S.4(1973), pp. 160-165.

SKŁADANEK, Bogdan. Settlements in Gharchistān during the early Islamic period. (up to the 11th century A.D.) *RO* 34ii(1971), pp. 57-71.

SPULER, B. Afghanistan in the Middle Ages. *Yádnáme-ye Jan Rypka* 1967, pp. 141-146.

SVETOZAROV, V.B. Istoricheskoe obshchestvo Afghanistana. *Strany Blizhnego i Srednego Vostoka: istoriya, ekonomica*, 1972, pp. 163-170.

TABIBI, Abdul Hakim. Afghanistan and India: historical ties. *Afghanistan* 26i(1973), pp. 86-89.

TARZI, Mohammad Seddiq and AHANG, Mohammad Kazem. Is it Pand Nama-i-Donya Wa Din or Taj-ot-Tawarikh. *Afghanistan* 23iii (1970), pp. 73-81.

UNGARO, M. Ricordi afghani. *Veltro* 16v-vi (1972), pp. 433-440.

VERCELLIN, G. Afghanistan 1919-1971. Cronologia degli avvenimenti. *OM* 53(1973), pp. 382-428.

VERCELLIN, G. La proclamazione della Repubblica Afghana. *OM* 53(1973), pp. 765-782.

WEINBAUM, M.G. Afghanistan: nonparty parliamentary democracy. *J. devel. areas* 7(1972), pp. 57-74.

WHITTERIDGE, G. Afghanistan: background for the visitor. *Asian aff.* 59(N.S. 3,1972), pp. 147-152.

ZÜRRER, Werner. Die sowjetisch-afghanischen Beziehungen und Grossbritannien 1918-1926. *Jb. f. Gesch. Osteuropas* N.F. 21(1973), pp. 196-249.

See also I. b. 2. Franz.

See also I. c. 3. Miller.

See also I. d. 1. Arunova

See also IX. f. Schinasi

See also XXXI. j. Kheyfetz.

See also XXXII. j. Verma.

See also XXXII. q. Varma

d ECONOMICS

ASHRAFI, Mohammad Naim. Neue Tendenzen der Wirtschaftsordnung und des Wirtschaftsrechts in der Republik Afghanistan seit dem Umsturz vom 17.7.1973. *Orient* [Germany] 16iv(1975), pp. 131-141.

DUCLOS, D.J. Un deuxième accord de désengagement entre l'Égypte et Israel. *Maghreb Machrek* 70(1975), pp. 55-62.

GENTELLE, P. Le blé en Afghanistan. *Stud. iranica* 1(1972), pp. 103-114.

HANSEN, B. Simulation of fiscal, monetary and exchange policy in a primitive economy: Afghanistan. *Economic structure and development, essays in honour of Jan Tinbergen*, ed. H.C. Bos, H. Linnemann and P. de Wolff, 1973, pp. 215-237.

JANATA, A. Zur landwirtschaftlichen Entwicklung in Afghanistan. *WVM* 16-17 (1969-1970), pp. 91-106.

KHODJAYEV, M.A.B. To question for the formation of an all-Afghan market and the trade and industrial policy pursued by Amir Abdur Rahman. *Afghanistan* 25 i(1972), pp. 88-95.

KRAUS, R.W.H. Land settlement in Afghanistan: Nad-i-Ali and Marja - two land settlement projects in the Helmand province. *Land reform* 1971, (2), pp. 29-35.

LOBASHEV, A.I. Problemy statistiki sel'skogo naseleniya i sel'skogo khozyaystva Afghanistana. *Strany Blizhnego i Srednego Vostoka: istoriya, ekonomica*, 1972, pp. 334-347.

XXXIII AFGHANISTAN

TOEPFER, H. Ökonomische Verhaltensweisen von Familien mit landwirtschaftlichen Vollerwerbsbetrieben in Afghanistan (mit einem Simultationsmodell). *Orient* [Hamburg] 16ii(1975), pp. 147-163.

XXXIV CENTRAL ASIA. CAUCASUS. CRIMEA. THE MONGOLS. S.E. ASIA AND THE FAR EAST

a GEOGRAPHY

ITINA, M.A. Srednyaya Aziya na karte Stralenberga. *Sov.Etn.* 1974(1), pp. 70-83.

KARCZMARCZUK, R. Badania i prace geograficzne Karola Bohdanowicza odnoszące się do Azji Środkowej. (Les recherches et les travaux géographiques de Karol Bohdanowicz se rapportant à l'Asie Centrale.) *Studia i materiały z dziejów nauki polskiej,* ser.C, 16(1972), pp. 79-111.

LASCELLES, D. Siberia: its wealth and world impact. *Asian affairs* 62(N.S.6, 1975), pp. 190-195.

MINORSKY, V.F. Grecheskaya pereprava na Amudar'e. *Philologia orientalis* II, 1972, pp. 118-126.

STADELBAUER, J. Die wirtschaftliche Regionalentwicklung zwischen dem Amu-Darja-Delta und Westkazachstan unter dem Einfluss des Eisenbahnbaus. *Erdkunde* 28(1974), pp. 282-295.

SYMONS, L. Tadzhikistan: a developing country in the Soviet Union. *Asian affairs* 61(N.S.5, 1974), pp. 249-256.

VÁSÁRY, I. *Käm,* an early Samoyed name of Yenisey. *Studia Turcica, ed. L. Ligeti,* 1971, pp. 469-482

YAMADA, Nobuo. Japanese travellers to Central Asia. *Proc.27th Int.Cong.Or.1967* (1971), pp. 609-610.

ZEYMAL', T.I. Drevnie i srednevekovye kanaly Vakhskoy doliny. *Strany i narody Vostoka pod obshchey red. D.A. Ol'derogge,* X, 1971, pp. 37-57.

See also I. c. 3. Manzi.

b ETHNOLOGY. SOCIOLOGY. (CENTRAL ASIA)

AALTO, P. The horse in Central Asian nomadic cultures. *SO* 46(1975), pp. 1-9.

BAKHTOVARSHOEVA, L. Tkani kustarnogo proizvodstva v Pripamir'e v XIX - nachale XX veka. *Sov. etn.* 1973(3), pp. 110-118.

BOROZNA, N.G. Vidy zhenskikh yubilirnykh ukrasheniy u narodov Sredney Azii i Kazakhstana. *Sov. Etn.* 1974(1), pp. 32-44.

BOYLE, J.A. Turkish and Mongol Shamanism in the Middle Ages. *Folklore* 83(1972), pp. 177-193.

CHEN CHING-LUNG. Aksakals in the Moslem region of Eastern Turkistan. *UAJ* 47(1975), pp. 41-46.

FLYNN, J.T. Magnitskii's purge of Kazan University: a case study in the uses of reaction in nineteenth-century Russia. *J. mod.hist.* 43(1971), pp. 598-614.

LANE, D. Ethnic and class stratification in Soviet Kazakhstan, 1917-39. *Comp. stud. soc. hist.* 17(1975), pp. 165-189.

MUKHITDINOV, I. Zhatva i svyazannye s neyu obryady v Vakhane i Ishkashime (XIX - nachalo XX veka). Materialy k istoriko-etnograficheskomu atlasu narodov Sredney Azii. (La moisson et les rites en rapport avec celle-ci au Vakhan et Ichkachim.) *Sov.Etn.* 1971 (5), pp. 118-127.

NEUBERT, H. Die Bedeutung des Yaks (Bos grunniens) und seiner Kreuzungen für die Bevölkerung in den Hochgebirgszonen Zentralasiens. *Jhb.Mus.Völkerk.Leipzig* 30(1975), pp. 93-100.

ORANSKIY, I.M. O termine "mazang" v Sredney Azii. *Strany i narody Vostoka pod obshchey red. D.A. Ol'derogge,* X, 1971, pp. 202-207.

POLEVOY, B.P. K trekhsotletiyu sozdaniya etnograficheskogo chertezha Sibiri 1673 g. (Pour le 300e anniversaire de la rédaction du Plan ethnographique de la Sibérie de 1673.) *Sov. etn.* 1973(4), pp. 96-105.

POTAPOV, L.P. Über den Pferdekult bei den turksprachigen Völkern des Sajan-Altai-Gebirges. *Abh. Ber. Staatl. Mus. Völkerk., Dresden* 34(1975), pp. 473-487.

RASSUDOVA, R.Ya. Znachenie termina *kosh* v nekotorykh zemledel'cheskikh rayonakh Sredney Azii v XIX - nachale XX veka. *Sov. etn.* 1974(6), pp. 78-86.

SERDOBOV, N.A. O nekotorykh voprosakh etnicheskoy istorii narodov Yuzhnoy Sibiri. (Some notes on the ethnic history of South Siberian peoples.) *Sov.Etn.* 1971(3), pp. 53-58.

SERGEEVA, G.A., SMIRNOVA, Ya.S. K voprosu o natzional'nom samosoznanii gorodskoy molodezhi (po dannym pasportnykh stolov otdeleniy militzii gorodov Makhachkaly, Ordzhonikidze, Cherkesska). *Sov.Etn.* 1971(3), pp. 86-92.

TOGAN, Z.V. The ethnography of Inner Asia during the 10th-12th centuries according chiefly to Islamic sources. (Synopsis of 14 lectures.) *Islâm Tetkikleri Enstitüsü dergisi* 4(1964), pp. 85-88.

TURSUNOV, N. Iz istorii remeslennykh tzekhov Sredney Azii (na materialakh tkatzkikh promyslov Khodzhenta kontza XIX - nachala XX v.) (De l'histoire des corporations artisanales de l'Asie Centrale (d'après les matériaux en rapport avec les industries de tissage à Khodjent à la fin du XIXe et au début du XXe siècles.) *Sov.etn.* 1972(1), pp. 110-118.

URAY-KÖHALMI. Die Bedeutung der Kulturgeschichte des Karpatenbeckens für die Erforschung der Kultur der zentralasiatischen Reiternomaden. *Sprache, Geschichte und Kultur der altaischen Völker,* hrsg. G. Hazai und P. Zieme (XII. PIAC, 1974), pp. 637-644.

ZHDANKO, T.A. Istoriko-etnograficheskiy atlas Sredney Azii i Kazakhstana. (The atlas of historical ethnography for Middle Asia and Kazakhstan: principles and methods of compilation.) *Sov.Etn.* 1971(3), pp. 31-42.

ZHDANKO, T.A. Die nationale Abgrenzung in Mittelasien unter dem Aspekt der ethnographischen Wissenschaft. *Jhb. Mus. Völkerk. Leipzig* 28(1972), pp. 164-175.

ZHDANKO, T.A. Natzional' no-gosudarstvennoe razmezhevanie i protzessy etnicheskogo razvitiya u narodov Sredney Azii. (The delimitation of nationalities and states and processes of ethnic development among the peoples of Middle Asia). *Sov. etn.* 1972(5), pp. 13-29.

See also V. b. *Central Asia.* Brentjes.

See also XXVIII. b. Mukhamed'yarov.

See also XL. c. Klyashtornyy.

c ETHNOLOGY. SOCIOLOGY. (CAUCASUS)

BOMBACI, A. Qui était Ǯebu Xak'an? *Turcica* 2(1970), pp. 7-24.

HOUSSEINOV, R. Superpositions ethniques en Transcaucasie aux XIe et XIIe siècles. *Turcica* 2(1970), pp. 71-80.

DIBIROV, M. O kanatokhodstve v Dagestane. (Sur l'art des danseurs de corde au Daghestan.) *Sov.etn.* 1972(1), pp. 122-127.

NAGRODZKA, T. Rzemioslo artystyczne Dagestanu. *Przegl.or.* 4(80), 1971, pp. 390-392.

d HISTORY. (CENTRAL ASIA)

ABRAHAMOWICZ, Z. The unrealized legation of Kasper Szymański to the Kalmuks and Persia in 1653. *Folia Or.* 12(1970), pp. 9-23

ANTONENKO, B.A., ISKANDAROV, B.I. Razvitie istoricheskoy nauki v Sovetskom Tadzhikistane. *Vopr.ist.* 1974(7), pp. 3-19.

ARENDS, A.K. K istorii zakhvata Khorezma Makhmudom Gaznevi. *Philologia orientalis* II, 1972, pp. 127-134.

AYTMAMBETOV, D.O. Vliyanie Rossii na khozyaystvennoe i kul'turnoe razvitie Kirgizii. (The influence exerted by Russia on Kirghizia's economic and cultural development.) *Vopr. ist.* 1971(4), pp. 55-67.

BACQUÉ-GRAMMONT, J.L. Les événements d'Asie Centrale en 1510 d'après un document ottoman. *Cah.du monde russe et sov.* 12(1971), pp. 189-207.

BACQUÉ-GRAMMONT, J.-L. Tûrân, une description du khanat de Khokand vers 1832 d'après un document ottoman. *Cah. du monde russe et sov.* 13(1972), pp. 192-231.

BAISHEV, S.B., DAKHSHLEYGER, G.F. Sotzial'no-ekonomicheskie itogi osvoeniya zemel' v Kazakhskoy SSR. *Vopr. ist.* 1975(3), pp. 21-40.

BEČKA, J. Traditional schools in the works of Sadriddin Aynī and other writers of Central Asia II. *Archiv or.* 40(1972), pp. 130-163.

BEKMAKHANOVA, N.E. Istoriya dorevolyutzionnogo Kazakhstana v noveyshey sovetskoy literature (1968-1971 gg.). *Vopr. ist.* 1972(10), pp. 127-134.

BENNIGSEN, A. et LEMERCIER-QUELQUEJAY, C. Musulmans et missions orthodoxes en Russie Orientale avant 1917. Essai de bibliographie critique. *Cah. monde russe et sov.* 13(1972), pp. 57-113

BENSIDOUN, S. L'Asie centrale et la Russie au milieu du XIXe siècle. *Rev. hist.* 254(1975), pp. 135-148.

BOSWORTH, C.E. An alleged embassy from the Emperor of China to the Amir Naṣr B. Aḥmad: a contribution to Sâmânid military history. *Yād-nāme-ye Irāni-ye Minorsky,* 1969, pp. 17-29.

BOYLE, J.A. Minorsky's marginal commentary on Houdas's translation of Nasavi's life of Sultan Jalâl-ad-Dīn Khwarâzm-Shâh. *Yād-nāme-ye Irāni-ye Minorsky,* 1969, pp. 30-36.

BREGEL', Yu.E. K izucheniyu zemel'nykh otnosheniy v khivinskom khanstve (istochniki i ikh ispol'zovanie). *Pismennye pamyatniki vostoka,* 1969, pp. 28-103.

BREGEL', Yu. Termin *vilayet* v khivinskikh dokumentakh. *Pis'mennye pamyatniki Vostoka* 1968, pp. 32-34.

XXXIV CENTRAL ASIA

CAHEN, C. 'Abdallaṭīf al-Baghdādī et les Khwārizmiens. *Iran and Islam, in memory of V. Minorsky,* 1971, pp. 149-166

CHATTERJI, Suniti Kumar. Hindus and Turks: India-Central Asia relations: Buddhism, Chinese culture and Islam. *J.Ganganatha Jha Kendriya Sanskrit Vidyapeetha* 29(1973), pp. 173-201

CHEKHOVICH, O.D. Novye nakhodki dokumentov Khodzha Akhrara XV-XVI vv. *Vostochnaya filologiya. Philologia Orientalis.* II(Pamyati V.S. Puturidze), 1972, pp. 135-146.

CHEKHOVICH, O.D. Skazanie o Tashkente. *Pis'mennye pamyatniki Vostoka* 1968, pp. 172-195.

CONOLLY, V. "The second trans-Siberian railway". *Asian affairs* 62(N.S.6, 1975), pp. 23-29.

CZEGLÉDY, K. Gardizi on the history of Central Asia (746-780 A.D.). *Acta Or. Acad. Sci. Hung.* 27(1973), pp. 257-267.

DANILOV, V.P. Agrarnye reformy 20-kh godov v respublikath sovetskogo Vostoka. (Agrarian reforms of the twentieth century in the republics of the Soviet East.) *NAA* 1972(6), pp. 47-59.

DRIKKER, Kh. N. Preodolenie mnogoukladnosti v protzesse stroitel'stva sotzializma v Tadzhikistane. (Basic features in the process of socialist development in Tadjikistan.) *NAA* 1972(6), pp. 60-71.

DUMONT, P. La revue *Türk yurdu* et les musulmans de l'empire russe 1911-1914. *Cah. monde russe soviétique* 15(1974), pp. 315-331.

EGOROV, V.L. O vremeni vozniknoveniya Kazani. (Sur l'époque de la fondation de Kazan.) *Sov. arkheol.* 1975(4), pp. 80-87.

ESIN, Emel. Ṭabarī's report on the warfare with the Türgiš and the testimony of eighth century Central Asian art. *Central Asiatic J.* 17(1973), pp. 130-149.

FEDOROV, M.N. K voprosu ob istoricheskikh sud'bakh dikhkhanstva pri Karakhanidakh (po dannym karakhanidskoy numizmatiki). Du problème des destinées historiques des "dikhkans" sous les Karakhanides. *Sov. arkheol.* 1975(1), pp. 109-117.

GAFUROVA, K.A. Ideologicheskaya bor'ba v Sredney Azii i Kazakhstane v pervye gody sovetskoy vlasti. *Vopr. ist.* 1973(7), pp. 17-28.

GOPAL, Surendra. Reaching for the Oxus. (A study of Central Asian politics in the first half of the 19th century.) *J.Ind.hist.*, Golden jubilee vol. 1973, pp. 745-760.

GRIGNASCHI, M. La monarchie karakhanide de Kachgar et les relations de dépendance personnelle dans le "Kutadǧubilig" (la science qui donne le bonheur) de Yūsuf Haṣṣ Ḥâcib. *Recueils Soc. Jean Bodin* 20(1970), pp. 515-626.

GUREVICH, B.P. Velikokhan'skiy shovinizm i nekotorye voprosy istorii narodov Tzentral'-noy Azii v XVIII-XIX vekakh. *Vopr.ist.* 1974 (9), pp. 45-63.

GURVICH, I.S. Russkie na Severo-Vostoke Sibiri v XVII v. *Sibirskiy etnog.sbornik* 5(1963), pp. 71-91.

GUSEV, D.I. Razvitie kul'tury narodov Povolzh'ya i Prikam'ya v period stroitel'stva kommunizma. (Cultural development of the peoples inhabiting the Volga and the Kama country in the period of communist construction.) *Vopr. ist.* 1971(4), pp. 41-54.

HAARMANN, U. Staat und Religion in Transoxanien im frühen 16. Jahrhundert. *ZDMG* 124(1974), pp. 332-369.

HAIDER, Mansura. Agrarian system in the Uzbek khanates of Central Asia, 16th-17th centuries. *Turcica* 7(1975), pp. 157-178.

HASAN, S.A. A survey of the expansion of Islam into Central Asia during the Umayyad Caliphate. *IC* 45(1971), pp. 95-113; 47(1973), pp. 1-13; 48(1974), pp. 177-186.

HOLDSWORTH, M. An introduction to the study of General K.P. Kaufman, first Governor-General of Turkestan, 1867-82. *Proc.27th Int.Cong.Or.1967* (1971), pp. 614-615.

HUMAYUN, Ghulam Sarwar. On Ay Khanom. *Afghanistan* 25 iv(1973), pp. 96-103.

JACKSON, P. The Mongols and the Delhi Sultanate in the reign of Muhammad Tughluq (1325-1351). *Central Asiatic J.* 19(1975), pp. 118-157.

JARRING, G. Swedish relations with Central Asia and Swedish Central Asian research. *Asian affairs* 61(N.S.5, 1974), pp. 257-266.

JENKINS, G. A note on climatic cycles and the rise of Chinggis Khan. *Central Asiatic J.* 18(1974), pp. 217-226.

KHALFIN, N.A. Obshchestvo dlya sodeystva russkoy promyshlennosti i torgovle i Srednyaya Aziya. *Vopr. ist.* 1975(8), pp. 45-63.

KINYAPINA, N.S. Srednyaya Aziya vo vneshnepoliticheskikh planakh tzarizma (50-80-e gody XIX v.). *Vopr. ist.* 1974(2), pp. 36-51.

KLYASHTORNYY, S.G. Epokha "Kutadgu bilig". *Sov.Tyurkologiya* 1970(4), pp. 82-86.

KLYCHMURADOV, K.K. Ashkhabadskaya epopeya. *Vopr.ist.* 1975(1), pp. 94-104.

KUZNETZOV, V.S. Iz istorii osvoboditel'noy bor'by uygurskogo naroda. Vosstanie v Uch-Turfane (1765 g.). *NAA* 1974(1), pp. 134-137.

XXXIV CENTRAL ASIA

KUZNETZOV, V.S. K voprosu o vladychestve Dzhungarskogo khanstva nad Vostochnym Turkestanom. *Materialy po istorii i filologii Tzentral'noy Azii* 5(1970), pp. 21-28.

KWANTEN, L. Chingis Khan's conquest of Tibet. Myth or reality? *J.Asian hist.* 8(1974), pp. 1-20.

LANDA, L.M. Pervye tzentry marksistskoy istoricheskoy nauki v Sredney Azii. (The earliest centres of Marxist historical science in Central Asia.) *NAA* 1972(2), pp. 44-54

MELIKHOV, G.V. Ekspansiya tzinskogo Kitaya v Priamurye i Tzentral'noy Azii v XVII-XVIII vekakh. *Vopr.ist.* 1974(7), pp. 55-73.

MINORSKY, V.F. Grecheskaya pereprava na Amudar'e. (Transl. from the English article published in BSOAS, 30, 1967, pp. 45-53.) *Vostochnaya filologiya. Philologia Orientalis.* II(Pamyati V.S. Puturidze), 1972, pp. 119-126.

MINORSKY, V.F. Kuda ezdili drevnie rusy? ("Ou se rendaient les anciens Rus?") *Fontes orientales* ... curavit A.S. Tveritinova, I, 1964, pp. 19-28.

MIRKASYMOV, Surat M. The Central Asian republics in the USSSR today. *Indo-Iranica* 26i(1973), pp. 14-19.

MIROSHNIKOV, L. Les civilisations d'Asie centrale et leur étude. *Afghanistan* 27i (1974), pp. 55-62.

MIROSHNIKOV, Lev. Les civilisations d'Asie central et leur étude. *J.world hist.* 13(1971), pp. 631-646.

MORRIS, P. The Russians in Central Asia 1870-1887. *Slav. and E. Eur. R.* 53 (1975), pp. 521-538.

MOUCHET, J. La vallee du Wakhan. *Afghanistan* 25 i(1972), pp. 78-87.

MUKHAMED'YAROV, Sh.F. Izuchenie v SSSR etapov voenno-politicheskoy istorii tyurkskikh narodov Povolzh'ya i Priural'ya. *Central Asiatic J.* 17(1973), pp. 200-211.

PIEMONTESE, A.M. La questione centroasiatica in E. Andreini (1872-'86). *Veltro* 16v-vi(1972), pp. 475-530.

POGOREL'SKIY, I.V. V.I. Lenin i Khorezmskaya Narodnaya Sovetskaya Respublika. (V. I. Lenin and the Khorezm People's Soviet Republic (1920-1924). *VLU* 1971(4), pp. 14-24.

POLEVOJ, L.P. Die nationalstaatliche Gliederung Mittelasiens nach der Errichtung der Sowjetmacht. *Z. f. Geschichtswiss.* 23(1975), pp. 516-527.

POLUBOYARINOVA, M.D. Russkie veshchi na territorii Zolotoy Ordy. (Les objets d'origine russe dans la Horde d'or.) *Sov. arkheologiya* 1972(3), pp. 164-187.

POPPE, N. On some proper names in the Secret history. *UAJ* 47(1975), pp. 160-167.

RABBANI, G.A. The Khwārazm Shāhs (III). *J.Pak.Hist.Soc.* 23(1975), pp. 185-224.

RAHUL, Ram. Major problems of modern Central Asia: report of a seminar. *Int. studies* 12 (1973), pp. 251-255.

RAHUL, R. The role of Mullahs in Central Asian politics. *Central Asiatic J.* 15 (1971), pp. 118-130.

RASPOPOVA, V.I. Odin iz bazarov Pendzhikenta VII-VIII vv. *Strany i narody Vostoka pod obshchey red. D.A. Ol'derogge,* X, 1971, pp. 67-75.

SARKISYANZ, M. Russian conquest in Central Asia: transformation and acculturation. *Russia and Asia,* ed. W.S. Vucinich, 1972, pp. 248-288.

SAZONOVA, M.V. Novoe v izuchenii sotzial'no-ekonomicheskikh otnosheniy v Kokandskom khanstve XIX v. *Sov. etn.* 1975(2), pp. 108-111.

SERRUYS, H. Jünggen, a title of Mongol princesses. *UAJ,* 47(1975), pp. 177-185.

SERRUYS, H. Sino-Mongol trade during the Ming. *J. Asian hist.* 9(1975), pp. 34-56.

SHUKUROV, M.R. Opyt likvidatzii negramotnosti v sovetskikh respublikakh Sredney Azii. (The experience of liquidation of illiteracy in the Soviet Republics of Central Asia.) *NAA* 1972(6), pp. 129-133.

SKRŽINSKAJA, E.Č. Un ambasciatore veneziano all'Orda d'oro (analisi dell'epitafio di Jacopo Cornaro-Tana, 1362). *Studi veneziani* 16(1974), pp. 67-96.

SKRCHINSKAYA, E.Ch. Venetzianskiy posol v Zolotoy Orde (po nadgrobiyu Yakopo Kornaro, 1362 g.). *Viz. vrem.* 35(1973), pp. 103-118.

SMIRNOVA, O.I. Mesta domusul'manskikh kul'tov v Sredney Azii (po materialam toponimiki). Sogdiyskiy βυρ 'khram' i βυ 'bog' v sredneaziatskoy toponimike. *Strany i narody Vostoka pod obshchey red. D.A. Ol'derogge,* X, 1971, pp. 90-108.

SUBAJEW, Nijaz A. Les internationalistes polonais en Tatarie (1917-1921). *Z pola walki* 12(1969), pp. 165-172 [*Polish sci. per.* 10(70), 1969 .]

TARDY, L., VÁSÁRY, I. Andrzej Taranowskis Bericht über seine Gesandtschaftsreise in der Tartarei (1569). *Acta Or.Hung.* 28(1974), pp. 213-252.

TROITZKAYA, A.L. Neskol'ko dokumentov po voennomu delu iz arkhiva kokandskikh khanov XIX veka. *Vost. sbornik 3,* 1972, pp. 138-148.

TZKITISHVILI, O.V. K voprosu o kharaktere vnutrenney zastroyki nekotorykh shakhristanov Sredney Azii i Madiny al-Mansura. *Gruzinskoe istochnikovedenie* III, 1971, pp. 52-58.

TZULAYA, G.V. Gruzinskaya knizhnaya legenda o Chingiskhane. (Une légende géorgienne sur Tchêngiz-Khan.) *Sov. etn.* 1973(5), pp. 114-122.

VIL'DANOVA, A.B. Podlinnik bukharskogo traktata o chinakh i zvaniyakh. *Pis'mennye pamyatniki Vostoka* 1968, pp. 40-67.

VIL'DANOVA, A.B. Rukovodstvo po gosudarstvennomu deloproizvodstvu Bukhary XVIII v. *Pismennye pamyatniki vostoka,* 1969, pp. 104-109.

WALKER, D. Muslim responses to Russian conquests. *IC* 47(1973), pp. 85-104.

WILLIAMS, D.S.M. Fiscal reform in Turkestan. *Slav. East Eur. R.* 52(1974), pp. 382-392.

WILLIAMS, D.S.M. Imperial Russian rule in Turkestan: the Pahlen investigation, 1908-09. *Asian aff.* 58(N.S.2, 1971), pp. 173-179.

WILLIAMS, D.S.M. Land reform in Turkestan. *Slav. East Eur. R.* 51(1973), pp. 428-438.

ZHIGALINA, O. Angliyskaya istoriografiya mezhdunarodnykh otnosheniy na Srednem Vostoke v XIX v. *Arabskie strany, Turtziya, Iran, Afganistan,* 1973, pp. 59-68.

See also V. c. *Central Asia.* Palimpsestova.

See also V. o. Bulatov.

See also V. o. Mikhal'chenko.

See also XXXI. i. Matveev.

See also XXXII. e. Arends.

dd ECONOMICS

CONOLLY, V. Die Industrialisierung Sibiriens. *Osteuropa* 25(1975), pp. 916-926; 1008-1019

IVANOV, Yu.M., TKACHENKO, A.I. Opyt agrarnykh preobrazovaniy v sovetskoy Sredney Azii i Kazakhstane i nekotorye problemy resheniya agrarnogo voprosa v stranakh Vostoka. *NAA* 1974(6), pp. 57-67.

e THE KHAZARS

CZEGLÉDY, K. Pseudo-Zacharias Rhetor on the Nomads. *Studia Turcica, ed. L. Ligeti,* 1971, pp. 133-148

MAGOMEDOV, M.G. Drevnie politicheskie tzentry Khazarii. (Les anciens centres politiques de la Khazarie.) *Sov. arkheol.* 1975(3), pp. 63-74.

MAGOMEDOV, M.G. Khazarskie poseleniya v Dagestane. (Les établissements khazars au Daghestan.) *Sov. arkheol.* 1975(2), pp. 200-216.

NAGRODZKA, T. Zarys historii badań nad Chazarami. *Przeglad or.* 3(79, 1971), pp. 245-255.

SZYSZMAN, S. Où la conversion du roi khazar Bulan a-t-elle eu lieu? *Hommages à A. Dupont-Sommer,* 1971, pp. 523-538.

f HISTORY (CAUCASUS)

BUNIYATOV, Z.M. Svedeniya Shikhab an-Nasavi o Gruzii. *Gruzinskoe istochnikovedenie* III, 1971, pp. 159-171.

SCHÜTZ, E. Tatarenstürme in Gebirgsgelände (Transkaukasien, 1220, 1236). *Central Asiatic J.* 17(1973), pp. 253-273.

SHARAFUTDINOVA, R.Sh. Arabskiy dokument iz arkhiva Akademika B.A. Dorna. (Materialy k istorii osvoboditel'nogo dvizheniya gortzev na Severnom Kavkaze v 20-50-kh godakh XIX v.) *Pis'mennye pamyatniki Vostoka* 1971, pp. 162-170.

SUMBATZADE, A.S. Istoricheskaya nauka Azerbaydzhana na sovremennom etape. *Vopr. ist.* 1972(12), pp. 53-61.

SUNY, R.G. Labor and liquidators: revolutionaries and the "reaction" in Baku, May 1908-April 1912. *Slav.R.* 34(1975), pp. 319-340.

See also X. e. Biró.

See also XXIX. h. Dzhikiya.

g HISTORY (CRIMEA)

BENNIGSEN, A. et LEMERCIER-QUELQUEJAY, C. Le khanat de Crimée au début du xvie siècle. De la tradition Mongole à la suzeraineté Ottomane, d'après un document inédit des Archives Ottomanes. *Cah. du monde russe et sov.* 13(1972), pp. 321-337.

BENNIGSEN, A., LEMERCIER-QUELQUEJAY, Ch. La Moscovie, l'empire ottoman et la crise successorale de 1577-1588 dans le khanat de Crimée. La tradition nomade contre le modèle des monarchies sédentaires. *Cahiers monde russe soviétique* 14(1973), pp. 453-487.

COLLINS, L.J.D. The military organization and tactics of the Crimean Tatars, 16th-17th centuries. *War, technology and society in the Middle East,* ed. V.J. Parry and M.E. Yapp, 1975, pp. 257-276.

DESAIVE, Dilek. Le khanat de Crimée dans les Archives ottomanes. Correspondance entre khans de Crimée et padichahs ottomans dans les registres des *nâme-i hümâyûn. Cah. du monde russe et sov.* 13 (1972), pp. 560-583.

FISHER, Alan W. Azov in the sixteenth and seventeenth centuries. *Jb. f. Gesch. Osteuropas* N.F. 21(1973), pp. 161-174.

GRIGOR'EV, A.P. Zhalovannaya gramota Ulug-Mukhammeda. *Voprosy filologii stran Azii i Afriki, 1. Sbornik I.N. Vinnikova* 1971, pp. 170-177.

HERKLESS, J.L. Stratford, the Cabinet and the outbreak of the Crimean War. *Hist.J.* 18(1975), pp. 497-523.

JONES, M.V The sad and curious story of Karass 1802-35. *Oxford Slav. papers* N.S.8(1975), pp. 53-81.

KOEHLER, P. Le khanat de Crimée en mai 1607 vu par un voyageur français. *Cah. du monde russe et sov.* 12(1971), pp. 316-326.

LEMERCIER-QUELQUEJAY, C. Les expéditions de Devlet Girây contre Moscou en 1571 et 1572 d'après les documents des Archives ottomanes. *Cah. du monde russe et sov.* 13(1972), pp. 555-559.

LEMERCIER-QUELQUEJAY, C. Les khanats de Kazan et de Crimée face à la Moscovie en 1521, d'après un document inédit des Archives du Musée du Palais de Topkapı. *Cah.monde russe et sov.* 12(1971), pp. 480-490

MATUZ, J. Qalğa. *Turcica* 2(1970), pp. 101-129.

SCHÜTZ, E. Eine armenische Chronik von Kaffa aus des ersten Halfte des 17. Jahrhunderts. *Acta Or. Hung.* 29(1975), pp. 133-186.

SHARAFUTDINOVA, R.Sh. Arabskie pis'ma Shamilya iz arkhiva B.A. Dorna. *Pis'mennye pamuatniki Vostoka* 1970, pp. 204-225.

SHEPHERD, J.A. The surgeons in the Crimea 1854-1856. *J.Roy.Coll.Surgeons Edinburgh* 17(1972), pp. 269-286.

VEINSTEIN, G. La révolte des *mirza* tatars contre le khan, 1724-1725. *Cah. du monde russe et sov.* 12(1971), pp. 327-328.

ZAJĄCZKOWSKI, A. "Letopis' kipchakskoy stepi" *(tevarikh-i desht-i kipchak)* kak istochnik po istorii Kryma. ("La chronique des steppes Kiptchak" (Tevarih-i dešt-i Qipčaq) comme la source de l'histoire de Crimée.) *Fontes orientales... curavit A.S. Tveritinova II*, 1969, pp. 1o-28.

See also XXIX. f. Mehmed.

See also XXIX. i. Pinson.

See also XL. i. Ivanics.

h THE MONGOLS

ALI-ZADE, A.A. Upotreblenie tyurko-mongol'skikh terminov v proizvedeniyakh Rashid ad-Dina i Vassafa. *Gruzinskoe istochnikovedenie,* III, 1971, pp. 177-190.

AYALON, D. The great Yāsa of Chingiz Khān. A reexamination. *SI* 33(1971), pp. 97-140; 34(1971), pp. 151-180; 38(1973), pp. 107-156.

BOYLE, J.A. Ghazan's letter to Boniface VIII: where was it written? *Proc.27th Int.Cong.Or.1967* (1971), pp. 601-602.

BOYLE, J.A. The seasonal residences of the Great Khan Ögedei. *Sprache, Geschichte und Kultur der altaischen Völker,* hrsg. G.Hazai und P. Zieme, 1974, pp. 145-151.

BOYLE, J.A. Some additional notes on the Mongolian names in the history of the nation of the archers. *Researches in Altaic languages,* ed. L. Ligeti, 1975, pp. 33-42.

BOYLE, J.A. The summer and winter camping grounds of the Kereit. *Central Asiatic J.* 17(1973), pp. 108-110.

BRYER, A.A.M. The fate of George Komnenos, ruler of Trebizond (1266-1280). *Byz. Z.* 66(1973), pp. 332-350.

CHAGDARSUREN, Ts. A propos des enveloppes des "lettres urgentes" mongoles. *RO* 35(1972), pp. 111-116.

CHERNYSHEV, E.I. Seleniya kazanskogo khanstva (po pistzovym knigam). *Voprosy etnogeneza tyurkoyazychnykh narodov Srednego Povolzh'ya* 1971, pp. 272-292

CLARK, L.V. On a Mongol decree of Yisün Temür (1339). *CAJ* 19(1975), pp. 194-198.

DECEI, A. L'invasion des Tatars de 1241/1242 dans nos régions selon la *Djāmi' ot-Tevārīkh* de Fäzl Ol-Lāh Räšīd od-Dīn. *Rev. Roumaine d'hist.* 12(1973), pp. 101-121.

DE RACHEWILTZ, I. The Secret History of the Mongols. Translated. *Papers on Far Eastern history* 4(1971), pp. 115-163; 5(1972), pp. 149-175; 10(1974), pp. 55-82.

EGOROV, V.L. Razvitie tzentrobezhnykh ustremleniy v Zolotoy Orde. *Vopr.ist.* 1974 (8), pp. 36-50.

GUZMAN, G.G. The encyclopedist Vincent of Beauvais and his Mongol extracts from John of Piano Carpini and Simon of Saint-Quentin. *Speculum* 49(1974), pp. 287-307.

GUZMAN, G.G. Simon of Saint-Quentin as historian of the Mongols and Seljuk Turks. *Medievalia et humanistica* N.S.3 (1972), pp. 155-178.

HAARMANN, U. Alṭun Hān und Čingiz Hān bei den ägyptischen Mamluken. *Islam* 51(1974), pp. 1-36.

HERRMANN, G. Zur Intitulatio timuridischer Urkunden. *XVIII. Deutscher Orientalistentag* 1972, pp. 498-521.

JAHN, K. Timur und die Frauen. *Anzeiger Osterr.Akad.Wis.,Phil.-hist.Kl.* 111(1974), pp. 515-529.

KHAN, Iqtidar Alam. The Turko-Mongol theory of kingship. *Medieval India* 2(1972), pp. 8-18.

KIKNADZE, R.K. Nekotorye svedeniya gruzinskikh istochnikov o Timure. *Gruzinskoe istochnikovedenie* III, 1971, pp. 196-205.

LORENZ, M. Die Leninsche Nationalitätenpolitik und die Sprachenpolitik in Sowjet-Mittelasien. *Asien, Afrika, Latein-Amerika* 1(3, 1973), pp. 5-15.

LORINCZ, L. Ein historisches Lied in der Geheimen Geschichte der Mongolen. *Researches in Altaic languages*, ed. L. Ligeti, 1975, pp. 117-126.

MANALJAW, L. Two translations of the Secret history of the Mongols in the Ulanbator State Library. *Researches in Altaic languages*, ed. L. Ligeti, 1975, pp. 147-150.

NOONAN, T.S. Medieval Russia, the Mongols and the West: Novgorod's relations with the Baltic, 1100-1350. *Medieval studies* 37(1975), pp. 316-339.

NOVOSEL'TZEV, A.P. Ob istoricheskoy otzenke. (Concerning the historical appraisal of Tamerlane.) *Vopr. ist.* 1973(2), pp. 3-20.

OKADA, Hidehiro. The Secret History of the Mongols, a pseudo-historical novel. *J. Asian and African studies* [Tokyo] 5 (1972), pp. 61-68.

RATCHNEVSKY, P. Die Yasa (J̌asaq) činggis-khans und ihre Problematik. *Sprache, Geschichte und Kultur der altaischen Völker*, hrsg. G. Hazai und P. Zieme (XII. PIAC, 1974), pp. 471-487.

RICHARD, J. Ultimatums mongols et lettres apocryphes: l'Occident et les motifs de guerre des Tartares. *Central Asiatic J.* 17(1973), pp. 212-222.

ROEMER, H.R. Die Nachfolger Timurs. Abriss der Geschichte Zentral- und Vorderasiens im 15. Jahrhundert. *Islamwissenschaftliche Abhandlungen F. Meier*, 1974, pp. 226-262.

SAGASTER, K. Herrschaftsideologie und Friedensgedanke bei den Mongolen. *Central Asiatic J.* 17(1973), pp. 223-242.

TAUBE, M. Eine unbekannte Handschrift der Geheimen Geschichte der Mongolen. *Asien in Vergangenheit und Gegenwart*, 1974, pp. 459-471.

TEREKHOVA, N.N. Tekhnologiya chuguno-liteynogo proizvodstva u drevnykh mongolov. (Tekhnologie de la fonderie de fonte chez les mongols moyenageux.) *Sov. arkh.* 1974(1), pp. 69-78.

ZUEV, Yu.A. "Dzhami' at-tavarikh" Rashid ad-Dina kak istochnik po ranney istorii Dzhalairov. *Pismennye pamyatniki vostoka*, 1969, pp. 178-185.

See also V. o. Grazhdankina.

See also XIX. g. Rogers.

See also XXVIII. b. Shastina.

See also XXXI. f. Smith.

i SOUTH EAST ASIA AND THE FAR EAST

ABUBAKAR, Asiri. Muslim Philippines: with reference to the Sulus, Muslim-Christian contradictions, and the Mindanao crisis. *Asian studies* 11(1973), pp. 112-128.

ATTAS, Said M. Nagib al-. Islam v malayskoy istorii i kul'ture. *NAA* 1974(5), pp. 88-99.

DOBBIN, C. Islamic revivalism in Minangkabau at the turn of the nineteenth century. *Modern Asian stud.* 8(1974), pp. 319-356.

DONNI, G. Distribuzione geografica dei Musulmani nell'arcipelago delle Filippine. *OM* 53(1973), pp. 1-111.

FEDERSPIEL, H.M. The military and Islam in Sukarno's Indonesia. *Pacific aff.* 46(1973), pp. 407-420.

HAGLUND, A. Some remarks about Muslims in China. *Ex orbe religionum. Studia Geo. Widengren oblata*, II, 1972, pp. 120-125.

HOOKER, M.B. Law, religion and bureaucracy in a Malay state: a study in conflicting power centers. *Amer.J.comp.law* 19(1971), pp. 264-286.

ISRAELI, R. The Muslim minority in traditional China. *Asian and African stud.* (Israel Or.Soc.) 10(1974-5), pp. 101-126.

MAEJIMA, Shinji The character of the Persian Rebellion in Fuchien province in the 14th century. *Proc.27th Int.Cong.Or. 1967* (1971), pp. 286-287.

MAEJIMA, Shinji. The Muslims in Ch'üan-chou at the end of the Yüan dynasty. *Memoirs Res. Dept. Toyo Bunko* 32(1974), pp. 47-71.

MATHESON, V. The Tuhfat al-Nafis; structure and sources. *BTLV* 127(1971), pp. 375-392.

PETROV, V.P. Minority problems of North-west China. *Proc.27th Int.Cong.Or.1967* (1971), pp. 602-603.

SAMSON, A.A. Army and Islam in Indonesia. *Pacific aff.* 44(1971), pp. 545-565

SANTOSO, Soewito. The Islamization of Indonesian/Malay literature in its earlier period. *JOS Aust.* 8(1971), pp. 9-27.

SEAH, Chee-Meow. The Muslim issue and implications for ASEAN. *Pacific community* 6(1975), pp. 139-160.

STINNER, W.F., MADER, P.D. Government policy and personal family planning approval in conflict settings: the case of the Muslim minority in the Southern Philippines. *Population stud.* 29(1975), pp. 53-59.

XXXIV CENTRAL ASIA

SUHRKE, A. Irredentism contained. The Thai-Muslim case. *Comp. politics* 7 (1975), pp. 187-203.

WALKER, D. Conflict between the Thai and Islamic cultures in Southern Thailand 1948-1970. *Studies in Islam* 9(1972), pp. 135-153.

WANG, Shu-Hwai Origins and consequences of the Mohammedan uprising in Yunnan, 1856-1873. *Proc.27th Int.Cong.Or.1967* (1971), pp. 517-518.

See also IX. e. Menges.

XXXV MUSLIMS IN EUROPE

a GENERAL

ARCAS CAMPOY, M. El *Iqlīm* de Lorca. Contribución al estudio de la división administrativa y a los itinerarios de al-Andalus. *Cuadernos de historia del Islam, ser. misc.: Islamica occidentalia* 1(1971), pp. 83-95.

ARIÉ, R. Remarques sur quelques aspects de la civilisation hispano-musulmane. *BAEO* 9(1973), pp. 131-150.

BARBOUR, N. L'influence de la géographie et de la puissance navale sur le destin de l'Espagne musulmane et du Maroc. *II. Cong.int.ét.nord-afr.* 1970, pp. 45-54.

BARBOUR, N. The significance of the word *Maurus* with its derivatives *Moro* and *Moor,* and of other terms used by medieval writers in Latin to describe the inhabitants of Muslim Spain. *Actas IV congresso de estudos árabes e islâmicos* 1968(1971), pp. 253-266.

BENALI, M., EPALZA, M. de, GAFSI, A. Producción tunecina y argelina sobre historia de España desde la independencia (1956 y 1962). *Indice hist.esp.* 15, 1969(1975), pp. XI-LXIII.

BOYKO, K.A. Vozniknovenie arabskoy istoriografii v Ispanii (711-929 gg.). *Narody Azii i Afriki* 1973(3), pp. 168-177.

BRAHIMI, D. Quelques jugements sur les Maures andalous dans les régences turques au XVIIIe siècle. *Rev. d'hist. et de civ. du Maghreb* 9(1970), pp. 39-51.

BURNS, R.I. Spanish Islam in transition: acculturative survival and its price in the Christian kingdom of Valencia, 1240-1280. *Islam and cultural change in the Middle Ages,* ed. Sp. Vryonis, Jr., 1975, pp. 87-105.

CABRILLANA, N. Almería en el siglo XVI: moriscos encomendados. *RABM* 78(1975), pp. 31-68.

CABRILLANA, N. Esclavos moriscos en la Almería del siglo XVI. *And.* 40(1975), pp. 53-128.

CASEY, J. Moriscos and the depopulation of Valencia. *Past and present* 50 (1971), pp. 19-40.

CASTRILLO MÁRQUEZ, R. A propósito de una descripción de al-Andalus. *And.* 40(1975), pp. 221-224.

CASTRILLO MÁRQUEZ, R. Descripción de al-Andalus según un MS. de la Biblioteca de Palacio. *And* 34(1969), pp. 83-103.

CASTRO GARCÍA, L. de. Situación geográfica de Palencia musulmana y altomedieval. *BAEO* 9(1973), pp. 207-216.

CHALMETA GENDRÓN, P. Feudalismo en al-Andalus? *Orientalia Hispanica* I, 1974, pp. 168-194.

CHALMETA GENDRÓN, P. Historiográfia medieval hispana: arabica. *And.* 37(1972), pp. 353-404.

CHALMETA, P. Le problème de la féodalite hors de l'Europe chrétienne: le cas de l'Espagne musulmane. *Actas II Col. hisp.-tunec. estud. hist.,* 1973, pp. 91-115.

CHEJNE, Anwar G. Islamization and arabization in al-Andalus: a general view. *Islam and cultural change in the Middle Ages,* ed. Sp. Vryonis, Jr., 1975, pp. 59-86.

DUFOURCQ, C.E. et GAUTIER-DALCHÉ, J. Les royaumes chrétiens d'Espagne au temps de la "reconquista" d'après les recherches récentes (1948-1969). *Rev. hist.* 248 (1972), pp. 367-402.

EPALZA, M. de. L'histoire d'al-Andalus dans les livres de texte de l'enseignement secondaire. *Actas II Coloquio hispano-tunecino,* 1972, pp. 116-129.

EPALZA, M. de. Recherches récentes sur les émigrations des "Moriscos" en Tunisie. *CT* 18(nos. 69-70, 1970), pp. 139-147.

FERNÁNDEZ-CAPEL BAÑOS, B. Un fragmento del *Kitab al-Ǧu'rāfiyya* de al-Zuhrī sobre Granada. *Cuadernos de historia del Islam, ser. misc.: Islamica occidentalia* 1(1971), pp. 109-124.

GAIS, N.E. Aperçu sur la population musulmane de Majorque au XIVe siècle. *Rev. d'hist. et de civ. du Maghreb* 9(1970) pp. 19-30.

XXXV MUSLIMS IN EUROPE

GARCIA DOMINGUES, J.D. Aspectos da cultura luso-árabe. *Actas IV congresso de estudos árabes e islâmicos* 1968 (1971), pp. 235-252.

GARCÍA GÓMEZ, E. Sobre la diferencia en el castigo de plebeyos y nobles. *And.* 36(1971), pp. 71-79.

GIBERT DE VALLVE, S. La ville d'Alméria à l'époque musulmane. *CT* 18(nos. 69-70, 1970), pp. 61-72.

GÓMEZ MORENO, M. La dominación árabe en España. *Bol. Real Acad. Hist.* 169(1972), pp. 227-246.

GOMEZ NOGALES, S. Ideological influence of Spain on the Muslim culture. *Peshawar Univ. rev.* 1i(1973), pp. 22-35.

GUASTAVINO, G. A propos du sens et des dimensions sociales, artistiques et littéraires du concept "Mudéjar" hispano-arabe. *Rev.d'hist.maghrebine* 3(1975), pp. 19-26.

GUICHARD, P. Les Arabes ont bien envahi l'Espagne. Les structures sociales de l'Espagne musulmane. *Annales ESC* 29(1974), pp. 1483-1513.

HERNÁNDEZ GIMÉNEZ, F. La travesía de la sierra de Guadarrama en el acceso a la raya musulmana del Duero. *And.* 38(1973), pp. 69-185, 415-454.

HITCHCOCK, R. El rito hispánico, las ordalías y los mozárabes en el reinado de Alfonso VI. *Estudios orientales* 8(1973), pp. 19-41.

ʿIMRĀNI, ʿAbd Allāh al- El "Manual Biografico" de Aḥmad b. ʿAlī al-Balawī al-Wādī Āšī. *BAEO* 8(1972), pp. 119-145.

LA GRANJA, F. de. Fiestas cristianas en al-Andalus. (Materiales para su estudio). I: "Al-Durr al-munaẓẓam" de al-ʿAzafī. *And* 34(1969), pp. 1-53.

LA GRANJA, F. de Fiestas christianas en al-Andalus: II. Textos de Ṭurṭūšī, el cadí ʿIyāḍ y Wanšarīsī. *And.* 35(1970), pp. 119-142.

LATHAM, J.D. Contribution à l'étude des immigrations andalouses et leur place dans l'histoire de la Tunisie. *Recueil d'études sur les moriscos andalous en Tunisie*, préparé par M. de Epalza et R. Petit, 1973, pp. 21-63.

MOLINA LÓPEZ, E. *Iyyu(h):* otra ciudad yerma hispanomusulmana. *Cuadernos de historia del Islam, ser. misc.: Islamica occidentalia* 1(1971), pp. 67-81.

OLIVER ASÍN, J. En torno a los orígenes de Castilla: su toponimia en relación con los árabes y los beréberes. *And.* 38(1973), pp. 319-391.

PETIT, O. Les relations intellectuelles entre l'Espagne et l'Ifriqiya aux XIIIe et XIVe siècles. *IBLA* 127 (1971), pp. 93-121.

PIKE, R. An urban minority: the Moriscos of Seville. *IJMES* 2(1971), pp. 368-377.

PONCET, J. La chanson de Roland à la lumière de l'histoire: Vérité de Baligant. *ROMM* 8(1970), pp. 125-139.

PONSOT, P. Les Morisques, la culture irriguée du blé, et le problème de la décadence de l'agriculture espagnole au XVIIe siècle. Un témoignage sur la Vega de Tarazona. *Mélanges de la Casa de Velazquez* 7(1971), pp. 237-262.

ROSSELLO-BORDOY, G. Algunas anotaciones sobre la vida económica de las Baleares durante la dominación musulmana. *Bol. Camara oficial de comercio, industria y navegación de Palma de Mallorca* 58, no. 621(1958), pp. 139-145. [Offprint in SOAS]

ROSSELLO-BORDOY, G. La evolución urbana de Palma en la Antigüedad. I: Palma Romana, II: Palma musulmana. *Bol. Camara oficial de comercio, industria y navegación de Palma de Mallorca* 61, nos. 632-633(1961),pp. 121-139, 182-197

SANCHEZ MARTINEZ, M. Rāzī, fuente de al-ʿUḏrī para la España pre-islámica. *Cuadernos de historia del Islam, ser. misc.: Islamica occidentalia* 1(1971), pp. 7-49.

SANTIAGO SIMÓN, E. de. Unas notas en torno a la "Bāb al-Ṣūra" de Córdoba. *MEAH* 18-19i (1969-70), pp. 129-136.

SCHIPPERGES, H. Zur Wirkungsgeschichte des Arabismus in Spanien. *Sudhoffs Archiv* 56(1972), pp. 225-254.

SECO DE LUCENA PAREDES, L. Escrituras árabes de la Universidad de Granada. *And.* 35(1970), pp. 315-353.

SPIVAKOVSKY, I. Un episodio de la guerra contra los moriscos. La perdida del gobierno de la Alhambra por el quinto conde de Tendilla (1569). *Hispania* 31 (no.118,1971), pp. 399-431.

TEMIMI, A. Une lettre des Morisques de Grenade au Sultan Suleimān Al-Ḳānūnī en 1541. *Rev.d'hist.maghrebine* 3(1975), pp. 100-106.

TERES, E. Le développement de la civilisation arabe à Tolède. *CT* 18 (nos. 69-70, 1970), pp. 73-86.

TERÊS, E. Dos familias Marwāníes de al-Andalus. *And.* 35(1970), pp. 93-117.

TERÉS, E. "An-Nāẓūr", "al-Manẓar" y "an-Naẓra" en la toponimia hispanoárabe. *And.* 37(1972), pp. 325-335.

TERRASSE, M. Talavera hispano-musulmane (notes historico-archéologiques). *Mélanges de la Casa de Velazquez* 6(1970), pp. 79-112.

URVOY, D. Sur l'évolution de la notion de ǧihād dans l'Espagne musulmane. *Mélanges de la Casa de Velazquez* 9(1973), pp. 335-371.

URVOY, D. La vie intellectuelle et spirituelle dans les Baléares musulmanes. *And.* 37(1972), pp. 87-132.

VALLVÉ BERMEJO, J. La división territorial en la España musulmana. La Cora de Jaén. *And* 34(1969), pp. 55-82.

VALLVE BERMEJO, J. La división territorial en la Espana musulmana (II): La cora de "Tudmir" (Murcia). *And.* 37(1972), pp. 145-189.

VALLVÉ BERMEJO, J. Sobre el repartimiento de Comares. *al-Andalus* 39(1974), pp. 256-272.

VINCENT, B. L'Albaicin de Grenade au XVIe siècle (1527-1587). *Mélanges de la Casa de Velazquez* 7(1971), pp. 189-222.

VINCENT, B. Les bandits morisques en Andalousie au XVIe siècle. *Rev. hist. mod. contemp.* 21(1974), pp. 389-400.

VINCENT, B. Combien de Morisques ont été expulsés du Royaume de Grenade? *Mélanges de la Casa de Velazquez* 7(1971), pp. 397-398.

VINCENT, B. L'expulsion des Morisques du Royaume de Grenade et leur répartition en Castille (1570-1571). *Mélanges de la Casa de Velazquez* 6(1970), pp. 211-246.

WAGNER, K. Un padrón desconocido de los mudéjares de Sevilla y la expulsión de 1502. *And.* 36(1971), pp. 373-382.

See also I. a. 1. Gabrieli.

See also I. d. 1. Udina Martorell.

See also IV. c. 1. Hourani.

See also IV. c. 6. Samsó.

See also XII. b. Barbour.

See also XIII. a. Vallve

See also XXXVI. j. Oliver Asin

See also XLIII. a. Epalza.

b OMAYYADS OF CORDOVA

BRUNSCHVIG, R. Ibn 'Abd al-Hakam et la conquête de l'Afrique du Nord par les Arabes. *And.* 40(1975), pp. 129-179.

CERULLI, E. Le Calife ʿAbd Ar-Raḥmān III de Cordoue et le martyr Pélage dans un poème de Hrotsvitha. *SI* 32(1970), pp. 69-76.

HOENERBACH, W. Notas para una caracterización de Wallāda. *And.* 36(1971), pp. 467-473.

HORRENT, J. La bataille des Pyrénées de 778. *Le Moyen age* 4.sér.,27(1972), pp. 197-227.

LA GRANJA, F. de. A propósito de una embajada cristiana en la corte de ʿAbd al-Raḥmān III. *al-Andalus* 39(1974), pp. 391-406.

LA GRANJA, F. de Un cuento oriental en la historia de al-Andalus. *And.* 35(1970), pp. 211-222.

SANTIAGO SIMÓN, E.de. Los itinerarios de la conquista musulmana de al-Andalus a la luz de una nueva fuente: Ibn al-Šabbāṭ. *Cuadernos de historia del Islam, ser. misc.: Islamica occidentalia* 1(1971), pp. 51-65.

TERÉS, E. Anecdotario de "al-Qalfāṭ", poeta cordobés. *And.* 35(1970), pp. 227-240.

VALLVÉ, J. Carthage et Carthagène au VIIIe siècle. *Actas II Col. hisp.-tunec. estud. hist.*, 1973, pp. 7-12.

VERMEULEN, U. Een bevelschrift van 'Al-Manṣūr tot het herstel van de islam in de boor het christendom beinvloede gebieden van Spanje. *Orientalia Gandensia* 2(1965), pp. 91-110.

See also XIV. d. Yalaoui.

c KINGS OF THE TAIFAS

BOSCH VILÁ, J. De nuevo sobre Barbastro 1064-1065. Nuevos aspectos y precisiones sobre la conquista cristiana y la reconquista musulmana. *Actas IV congresso de estudos árabes e islâmicos* 1968(1971), pp. 225-233.

GUICHARD, P. Un seigneur musulman dans l'Espagne chrétienne: le "ra'is" de Crevillente (1243-1318). *Mélanges de la Casa de Velazques* 9(1973), pp. 283-334.

URVOY, D. Une étude sociologique des mouvements religieux dans l'Espagne musulmane de la chute du califat au milieu du XIIIe siècle. *Mélanges de la Casa de Velazquez* 8(1972), pp. 223-293.

See also XXI. a. Burns.

d ALMORAVIDS

TURK, Afif. El reino de Zaragoza en el siglo XI de Cristo (V de la hégira). *RIEEI* 17(1972-3), pp. 7-122.

See also XIV. g. Rubiera.

e ALMOHADES

BARBOUR, N. The relations of King Sancho VII (the Strong) of Navarre with the Almohad rulers of Spain. *Proc.27th Int. Cong.Or.1967* (1971), pp. 285-286.

GOITEIN, S.D. Judaeo-Arabic letters from Spain (early twelfth century). *Orientalia Hispanica* I, 1974, pp. 331-350.

HORRENT, J. Le récit des batailles dans le Cantar de mío Cid. *Acad. roy. Belgique, Bull. cl. lettres* 5e sér., 60(1974), pp. 73-89.

See also XIV. g. Rubiera.

See also XIV. h. Le Tourneau.

f NASRIDS OF GRANADA

ARIÉ, R. Les relations entre Grenade et la Berbérie au XIVe siècle. *Orientalia Hispanica* I, 1974, pp. 33-44.

CABANELAS, D. Arias Montano y los libros plúmbeos de Granada. *MEAH* 18-19i(1969-70) pp. 7-41.

CHABANA, Mohamed Kamal. Historia política del reinado del sultán nasrí Yūsuf I. *MEAH* 16-17 (1967-8), pp. 165-190.

IRVING, T.B. Intellectual figures in fourteenth century Granada. *Stud. in Islam* 6(1969), pp. 188-192.

LADERO QUESADA, M.A. Algunas consideraciones sobre Granada en el siglo XIV. *Anuario estud.med.* 7(1970-71), pp. 279-284.

LADERO QUESADA, M.A. La defensa de Granada a raíz de la conquista. Comienzos de un problema. *MEAH* 16-17 (1967-8), pp. 7-46.

LAFAYE, J. Reconquest, djihad, diaspora: three visions of Spain at the discovery of America. *Diogenes* 87(1974), pp. 50-60.

LA GRANJA, F. de. Condena de Boabdil por los alfaquíes de Granada. *And.* 36(1971), pp. 145-176.

LÓPEZ ELUM, P. Apresamiento y venta de moros cautivos en 1441 por "acaptar" sin licencia. *And* 34(1969), pp. 329-379

RUBIERA MATA, M.J. El arraez Abū Sa'īd Faraŷ b. Ismā'īl de Malaga y eponimo de la segunda dinastia naṣrī de Granada. *Bol. Asoc. Esp. Orientàlistas* 11(1975), pp. 127-133.

RUBIERA MATA, J. Datos sobre una "Madrasa" en Málaga anterior a la Naṣrī de Granada. *And.* 35(1970), pp. 223-226.

RUBIERA MATA, M.J. El Dū l-wizāratayn Ibn al-Ḥakīm de Ronda. *And* 34(1969), pp. 105-121.

SANTIAGO SIMÓN, E. de. Algunas datos sobre la posesión de bienes raices moriscos en el lugar de Cenes de Granada (1572). *MEAH* 22 (1973), pp. 153-161.

SECO DE LUCENA PAREDES, L. Un aspecto del orientalismo literario en Granada. *MEAH* 18-19i(1969-70), pp. 107-115.

TORRES FONTES, J. La regencia de don Fernando el de Antequera y las relaciones castellanogranadinas (1407-1416) (Conclusión). *MEAH* 16-17 (1967-8), pp. 89-145.

TORRES FONTES, J. [La regencia de Don Fernando.] IV. Treguas. *MEAH* 22(1973), pp. 7-59.

See also VIII. f. Pavón Maldonado.

See also XIV. i. Talbi.

g ITALIAN MAINLAND AND ISLANDS. MALTA. CRETE

BARNARD, J.B. The Arab conquest. *J. Fac. Arts Malta* 6(1975), pp. 161-171.

BRESC, H. Pantelleria entre l'Islam et la Chrétienté. *CT* 19, nos. 75-76(1971), pp. 105-127.

COLLESS, B.E. The traders of the pearl. *Abr-Nahrain* 11(1971), pp. 1-21; 13(1972-73), pp. 115-135.

FILESI, T. Il programma di recerca, selezione e pubblicazione dei documenti esisteni negli archivi della Campania e relativi ai rapporti con i Paesi dell'Africa del Nord nei secoli XVIIIe XIX. *Africa [Rome]* 27(1972), pp. 421-427.

GABRIELI, F. Federico II e la cultura musulmana. *Ann.Fac.Arts Ain Shams* 1(1951), pp. 125-141.

GOLB, N. A Judaeo-Arabic court document of Syracuse, A.D. 1020. *JNES* 32(1973), pp. 105-123.

GUIFFRIDA, A., ROCCO, B. Una bilingue arabo-sicula. *AION* 34(n.s.24, 1974), pp. 109-122.

HENRIET, M.-O. Habitat et communauté villageoise à Gozo. *Actes I. Cong. et. cult. mediterr. d'infl. arabo-berb.*, 1973, pp. 528-532.

OMAN, G. Vestiges arabes en Sardaigne. *II. Cong.int.ét.nord-afr.* 1970, pp. 175-184.

OMAN, G. Vestigia arabe in Italia. *Studi sul Vicino Oriente in Italia,* II, 1971, pp. 277-290.

REDJALA, Mbarek. L'archipel maltais dans la littérature historico-géographique d'expression arabe à l'époque médiévale. *Actes I. Cong. et. cult. mediterr. d'infl. arabo-berb.*, 1973, pp. 203-208.

RIZZITANO, U. La Sicilia musulmana hija espiritual de al-Andalus. *Orientalia Hispanica* I, 1974, pp. 551-565.

SCANDURA, A. Influence ethnologique et linguistique de la civilisation arabo-berbère en Sicile au cours des IXème, Xème et XIème siècles. *Actes I. Cong. et. cult. mediterr. d'infl. arabo-berb.*, 1973, pp. 478-484.

See also I. b. 3. Rizzitano.

See also XXXVII. f. Bouyahia.

XXXVI LANGUAGE: GENERAL. ARABIC

a LANGUAGE: GENERAL

ABOU, S. Langues et culture au Liban. *Travaux et jours* 50(1974), pp. 105-128.

ABOU, Selim. Le problème de la diglossie. *Cah. d'hist. mondiale* 14(1972), pp. 833-843.

ARVEILLER, R. Addenda au FEW XIX/1 (abar-qubba). *Z. f. roman. Philol.* 85(1969), pp. 108-109; 86(1970), pp. 340-341; 87 (1971), pp. 520-545; 88(1972), pp. 403-434; 90(1974), pp. 449-482.

AZIZ, Yowell Y. Journalistic English in Iraq: is it correct English? *Adab al-rafidain* 1(1971), pp. 16-39.

CHARNAY, J.P. Communication et société (variations sur parole, armour et cuisine dans la culture arabe). *L'ambivalence dans la culture arabe,* 1967, pp. 172-190.

EDEL'MAN, D.I. Voprosi periodizatzii indoiranskikh yazyikov, ne imeyushikh drevney pismennosti. (Questions of periodization in Indo-Iranian languages, where ancient writings are non-existent). *NAA* 1972(3), pp. 113-119.

FELLMAN, J. Language and national identity: the case of the Middle East. *Anthrop. ling.* 15(1973), pp. 244-249.

FRONZAROLI, P. Réflexions sur la paléontologie linguistique. *Actes 1. Cong. int. ling. sém. cham.-sém.,* 1969 (1974), pp. 173-180.

HADDAD, Fuad S. Alfarabi's theory of language. *American University of Beirut Festival book,* 1967, pp. 327-351.

HAMZAOUI, Rachad. Interférences stylistiques: Français-Arabe. *CT* 22(85-86, 1974), pp. 163-173.

HARVEY, L.P. Textes de littérature religieuse des moriscos tunisiens. *Recueil d'études sur les moriscos andalous en Tunisie,* préparé par M. de Epalza et R. Petit, 1973, pp. 199-204.

HUNWICK, J.O. African language material in Arabic sources - the case of Songhay (Sonrai). *African lang. R.* 9(1970-71), pp. 51-73.

LOUCEL, H. La langue Arabe et les langues occidentales. *Cah. d'hist. mondiale* 14(1972), pp. 844-857.

MAZRUI, Alī A. Islam and the English language in East and West Africa. *Wort und Religion, Kalima na dini, E. Dammann zum 65. Geburtstag,* 1969, pp. 179-197.

MOGHADAM, Mohamad The origin of the alphabet. *Proc.27th Int.Cong.Or.1967* (1971), pp. 247-248.

MOHANTY, Bansidhar and TRIPATHI, B.K. Perso-Arabic influence on Oriya. *Orissa Inst.res.J.* 15i-ii(1967), pp. 65-112.

RIZZITANO, U. L'Algérie et son problème linguistique. *Ve Congrès International d'Arabisants et d'Islamisants. Actes.,* [1970?], pp. 377-387.

SKIK, Hichem. Une enquête statistique sur le vocabulaire de l'enfant tunisien. *Linguistique* 8ii(1972), pp. 151-152.

TAFAZZOLI, Ahmad. Some Middle-Persian quotations in classical Arabic and Persian texts. *Mémorial J. de Menasce,* 1974, pp. 337-349.

WEIERS, M. Eine fünfsprachige Wörtersammlung aus dem Gebiet der Moghul von Herat in Afghanistan. *Zentralasiat. Studien* 7(1973), pp. 503-523.

L'état actuel des recherches linguistiques en Tunisie. *Actes 1. Cong. int. ling. sém. cham.-sém.,* 1969 (1974), pp. 338-346.

See also XXXV. g. Guiffrida.

b SEMITIC LANGUAGES: COMPARATIVE STUDY

BLAU, J. Marginalia Semitica I. *Israel Oriental studies* 1(1971), pp. 1-35.

BLAU, J. Marginalia Semitica II. *In memoriam S.M. Stern* (Israel Or. studies, II, 1972), pp. 57-82.

BREYDY, Michael. Der melodische Rhythmus in der Kultdichtung des syro-aramäischen Sprachraumes (von Phönizien bis Chaldäa und Malabar). *Oriens Christianus* 57(1973), pp. 121-141.

CLAUSON, G. Nostratic. *JRAS* 1973(1), pp. 46-55.

COHEN, D. Phrase nominale et verbalisation en sémitique. *Mél. ling. E. Benveniste,* 1975, pp. 87-98.

XXXVI LANGUAGE: GENERAL ARABIC

CORRÉ, A.D. A suprasegmental feature of length in Semitic. *Afroasiatic linguistics* 2ix(1975), pp. 9-14.

CORRÉ, A.D. Wāw and digamma. *Afroasiatic linguistics* 2ix(1975), pp. 1-7.

CORRIENTE, F. Again on the functional yield of some synthetic devices in Arabic and semitic morphology. (A reply to J.Blau). *JQR* 64(1973-74), pp. 154-163.

CORRIENTE, F.C. On the functional yield of some synthetic devices in Arabic and Semitic morphology. *JQR* (1971-2), pp. 20-50.

DANKOFF, R. Baraq and Burāq. *Central Asiatic J.* 15 (1971), pp. 102-117.

DIAKONOFF, I.M. On root structure in proto-Semitic. *Hamito-Semitica,* ed. J and Th. Bynon, 1975, pp. 133-153.

DIEM, W. Gedanken zur Frage der Mimation und Nunation in den semitischen Sprachen. *ZDMG* 125(1975), pp. 239-258.

DREYER, H.J. The roots qr, 'r, gr and ṣ/ṭr = "stone, wall, city" etc. *De fructu oris sui: essays in honour of Adrianus van Selms,* ed. by I.H. Eybers *et al.,* 1971, pp. 17-25.

FLEISCH, H. Le verbe du sémitique commun. Les discussions à son sujet. *Semitica* 25 (1975), pp. 5-18.

FRONZAROLI, P. On the common Semitic lexicon and its evological and cultural background. *Hamito-Semitica,* ed. J. and Th. Bynon, 1975, pp. 43-53.

FRONZAROLI, P. Problemi della lessicografia comparativa semitica. *Oriens antiquus* 11 (1972), pp. 241-262.

FRONZAROLI, P. La semitistica. *Studi sul Vicino Oriente in Italia,* I, 1971, pp. 11-31.

FRONZAROLI, P. Studi sul lessico comune semitico. VII. - L'alimentazione. *Rend. Accad. Lincei* 26(1971), pp. 603-642.

GARBINI, G. Linguistica semitica 1969-1971. *AION* 33(N.S.23, 1973), pp. 81-92.

GARBINI, G. La position du sémitique dans le chamito-sémitique. *Actes 1. Cong. int. ling. sém. cham.-sém.,* 1969 (1974), pp. 21-29.

GAZOV-KINZBERG, A.M. Dvuznachnost' imperfektnoy formy t.P'L i sledy ee korrektzii v Biblii. (Ambiguity of Semitic T.P'L form and its correctives in the Bible.) *Palestinskiy sbornik* 25(88, 1974), pp. 77-80.

GOLDENBERG, G. Tautological infinitive. *Israel Oriental studies* 1(1971), pp. 36-85.

GREENFIELD, J.C. and SHAKED, Shaul. Three Iranian words in the Targum of Job from Qumran. *ZDMG* 122(1972), pp. 37-45.

HAMORI, A. A note on *yaqtulu* in East and West Semitic. *Archiv or.* 41(1973), pp. 319-324.

HETZRON, R. La division des langues sémitiques. *Actes 1. Cong. int. ling. sém. cham.-sém.,* 1969 (1974), pp. 181-193.

HODGE, C.T. The nominal sentence in Semitic. *Afroasiatic linguistics* 2 (1975), pp. 69-75.

JANSSENS, G. The feminine ending -(a)t in Semitic. *Orientalia Lovanensia periodica* 6/7(1975-6), pp. 277-284.

JANSSENS, G. The Semitic verbal tense system. *Afroasiatic linguistics* 2(1975), pp. 77-82.

JUCQUOIS, G. Trois questions de linguistique sémitique. *Muséon,* 86(1973), pp. 475-497.

KURILOWICZ, J. Verbal aspect in Semitic. *Orientalia* NS 42(1973), pp. 114-120.

LAMBDIN, T.O. The junctural origin of the West Semitic definite article. *Near Eastern studies in honor of W.F. Albright,* 1971, pp. 315-333.

LEK'IAŠVILI, A. Über die Kasusflexion in den semitischen Sprachen. *Zeits.f. Phonetik* 24(1971), pp. 76-90.

LEVIN, S. The Indo-European and Semitic languages: a reply to Oswald Szemerényi. *Gen.linguistics* 15(1975), pp. 197-205.

MACKENZIE, D.N. The vocabulary of the Lahore *Tafsīr*. *Iran and Islam, in memory of V. Minorsky,* 1971, pp. 407-419

MACLAURIN, E.C.B. The Semitic background of use of 'en splanchnois'. *PEQ* 103 (1971), pp. 42-45.

MAGNANINI, P. Sulla corrispondenza consonantica arabe /š/ - ebraico /š/. *AION* 34 (N.S.24, 1974), pp. 401-408.

MARRASSINI, P. A proposito del duale nelle lingue semitiche. *RSO* 49(1975), pp. 35-47.

MILITAREV, A.Yu. Issledovanie S.S. Mayzelya v oblasti korneobrazovaniya semasiologii semitskikh yazykov. (S.S. Maizel's work on the Semitic root-formation and semasiology.) *NAA* 1973(1), pp. 114-121.

OELSNER, J. Zur Problematik der Klassifikation der semitischen Sprachen. *Philologia orientalis* II, 1972, pp. 241-247.

PENNACCHIETTI, F.A. Appunti per una storia comparata dei sistemi preposizionali semitici. *AION* N.S.24(34, 1974), pp. 161-208.

PENNACCHIETTI, F.A. La classe degli aggettivi denotativi nelle lingue semitiche e nelle lingue berbere. *Actes 1. Cong. int. ling. sém. cham.-sém.,* 1969 (1974), pp. 30-39.

PETRÁČEK, K. Le dynamisme du système phonologique protosémitique et les problèmes de la phonologie chamito-sémitique. *Hamito-Semitica,* ed. J. and Th. Bynon, 1975, pp. 161-168.

RABIN, Chaim. La correspondance *d* hébreu - *d* arabe. *Mélanges Marcel Cohen,* 1970, pp. 290-297.

RUNDGREN, F. Der Fisch im Semitischen. *Ex orbe religionum. Studia Geo Widengren oblata,* I, 1972, pp. 72-80.

RUNDGREN, Fr. Réflexions sur le participe actif du sémitique. *Actes I Cong.int. ling.sém.et chamito-sém.,* 1969(1974), pp. 194-202.

SCHUHMACHER, W.W. Khoisan traces in Iranian (or Semitic traces in Khoisan)? *African stud.* 34(1975), pp. 57-58.

SELMS, A. van. Some reflections on the formation of the feminine in Semitic languages. *Near Eastern studies in honor of W.F. Albright,* 1971, pp. 421-431.

SODEN, W. von. Ein semitisches Wurzelwörterbuch: Probleme und Möglichkeiten. *Orientalia* NS 42(1973), pp. 142-148.

SZEMERÉNYI, O. The Indo-European and the Semitic languages: a rejoinder to Saul Levin's reply. *Gen.linguistics* 15(1975), pp. 206-213.

TYLOCH, W. The evidence of the proto-lexicon for the cultural background of the Semitic peoples. *Hamito-Semitica,* ed. J. and Th. Bynon, 1975, pp. 55-61.

See also IV. c. 10. Schmucker.

See also XXXVI. c. Garbini

See also XLII. Castellino.

c HAMITIC-SEMITIC CONNECTIONS

ADAMS, G.B. Hamito-Semitic and the pre-Celtic substratum in Ireland and Britain. *Hamito-Semitica,* ed. J. and Th. Bynon, 1975, pp. 233-247.

ANDRZEJEWSKI, B.W. Verbs with vocalic mutation in Somali and their significance for Hamitic-Semitic comparative studies. *Hamito-Semitica,* ed. J. and Th. Bynon, 1975, pp. 361-376.

COHEN, D. Alternances vocaliques dans le système verbal couchitique et chamito-sémitique. *Actes 1. Cong. int. ling. sém. cham.-sém.,* 1969 (1974), pp. 40-48.

COHEN, D. Problèmes de linguistique Chamito-Sémitique. *REI* 40(1972), pp. 43-68.

COHEN, M. Quelques mots sur comparaison et restitution. *Hamito-Semitica,* ed. J. and Th. Bynon, 1975, pp. 21-24.

COHEN, D. La situation aspectivo-temporelle dans quelques langues couchitiques et le système verbal chamito-sémitique. *Langues et techniques, nature et société. Hommage à A.G. Haudricourt,* I, 1972, pp. 57-63.

DAVID, M.V. L'histoire de l'écriture et les textes du domaine linguistique chamito-sémitique. *Actes 1. Cong. int. ling. sém. cham.-sém.,* 1969 (1974), pp. 76-84.

DIAKONOFF, I.M. Opening address. *Hamito-Semitica,* ed. J. and Th. Bynon, 1975, pp. 25-39.

DOLGOPOL'SKIY, A.B. Struktura semito-khamitskogo kornya v sravnitel'no-istoricheskom osveshchenii. *Actes X.Cong. int.linguistes* 1967, vol. IV, p. 673.

GARBINI, G. Il corpo umano nella comparazione lessicale egitto-semitica. *RSO* 46(1971), pp. 129-141.

GARBINI, G. La position du sémitique dans le chamito-sémitique. *Actes I Cong.int. ling.sém.et chamito-sém.,* 1969(1974), pp. 21-26.

ISSERLIN, B.J. Some aspects of the present state of Hamito-Semitic studies. *Hamito-Semitica,* ed. J. and Th. Bynon, 1975, pp. 479-492.

KNAPPERT, J. Origin and development of the concept of Hamitic: the first sixty years: 1851-1911. *Orientalia Lovanensia periodica* 6/7(1975-6), pp. 303-320.

MÜLLER, W.W. Beiträge zur hamito-semitischen Wortvergleichung. *Hamito-Semitica,* ed. J. and Th. Bynon, 1975, pp. 63-74.

NEWBY, G.D. The dependent pronoun in Semitic and Egyptian. *JQR* 62(1971-2), pp. 193-198

PETRÁČEK, K. A propos des limites du chamito-sémitique: les systèmes phonologiques des langues chamito-sémitiques et des langues du Sahara central. *Actes I Cong.int.ling.sém.et chamito-sém.,* 1969 (1974), pp. 27-29.

PETRÁČEK, Karel. Die Grenzen des Semitohamitischen. Zentralsaharanische und semitohamitische Sprachen in phonologischer Hinsicht. *Arch.or.* 40(1972), pp. 6-50

TUCKER, A.N. What's in a name? *Hamito-Semitica,* ed. J. and Th. Bynon, 1975, pp. 471-477.

VERGOTE, J. La position intermédiare de l'ancien égyptien entre l'hébreu et l'arabe. *Hamito-Semitica,* ed. J. and Th. Bynon, 1975, pp. 193-199.

VERGOTE, J. Le rapport de l'égyptien avec les langues sémitiques: quelques aspects du problème. *Actes 1. cong. int. ling. sém. cham.-sém.,* 1969 (1974), pp. 49-54.

VYCICHL, W. Egyptian and the other Hamito-Semitic languages. *Hamito-Semitica,* ed. J. and Th. Bynon, 1975.

VYCICHL, W. Les études chamito-semitiques. *Actes I. Cong. et. cult. mediterr. d'infl. arabo-berb.,* 1973, pp. 128-135.

VYCICHL, W. Les études chamito-sémitiques à l'Université de Fribourg et le 'Laméкhitique'. *Actes 1. Cong. int. ling. sém. cham.-sém.,* 1969 (1974), pp. 60-67.

See also XXV. c. Novikov.

See also XXXVI. b. Garbini.

See also XLII. Pennacchietti.

See also XLII. Zavadovskij

d ARABIC: GRAMMAR

ABBOUD, P.F. Arabic language instruction. *MESA Bull.* 5ii(1971), pp. 1-23.

ABBOUD, P. The Arabic teachers' workshops of 1965, 66 and 67. *Proc.27th Int.Cong.Or.1967* (1971), pp. 219-220.

AHLBERG, H. Esquisse d'une théorie sur la formation de *qitl* en arabe. *Orientalia Suecana* 21(1972), pp. 26-33.

AHMAD, Muhammad Khalafallah. The role and future of classical Arabic in the life and thought of the modern Arab people. *Proc.27th Int.Cong.Or.1967* (1971), pp. 197-199.

ALWAYE, Mohiaddin. The importance of Arabic language. *Majallat al-Azhar* 46i(1974), pp. 1-4.

AMBROS, A.A. Funktionalität und Redundanz in der arabischen Kasusdeklination. *WZKM* 63-64(1972), pp. 105-127.

AMBROS, A.A. Die morphologische Funktion des Systems der Vokalqualitäten im Althocharabischen. *WZKM* 65/66(1973-74), pp. 77-150; 67(1975), pp. 93-164.

ANGHELESCU, N. Sur le sens de la flexion désinentielle dans la grammaire arabe traditionelle. *Folia Or.* 16(1975), pp. 7-12.

ANGHELESCU, N. Sur le système de l'article en arabe. *Rev.roum.ling.* 19(1974), pp. 45-52.

ANI, Salman H. al- An acoustical and physiological investigation of the Arabic ع . *Actes X.Cong.int.linguistes* 1967, vol. IV, pp. 155-160.

BABAKHANOV, Sh.Z. Dvoystvennoe chislo v arabskom yazyke (klassicheskom i v dialektakh) kak odin iz sposobov vyrazheniya mnozhestvennosti. *Vost.yazyki,* 1971, pp. 26-37

BABAKHANOV, Sh.Z. Mnozhestvennoe chislo vnutrennego obrazovaniya v arabskom yazyke. *Narody Azii i Afriki* 1973(3), pp. 151-156.

BACCOUCHE, Taieb. Esquisse d'une étude comparative des schèmes des verbes en arabe classique et en arabe tunisien. *CT* 22(nos.87-88,1974), pp. 167-176.

BALL, M. Prestige languages and word borrowing: the changing status of Arabic and English in Kenya. *Studies in African ling.,* suppl. 2(1971), pp. 131-137.

BAUSANI, A. Osservazioni sugli *Aḍdād* Arabi. *Ve Congrès International d'Arabisants et d'Islamisants. Actes.,* [1970?], pp. 97-106.

BECKER-MAKKAI, V. Problems in the computational parsing of the Arabic verb. *Actes Xe Cong.int.linguistes,* 1967, IV, pp. 927-931.

BERQUE, J. L'expression de l'ambiguïté en arabe. *L'ambivalence dans la culture arabe,* 1967, pp. 347-355.

BERQUE, J. La langue arabe, de l'être à l'histoire. *L'ambivalence dans la culture arabe,* 1967, pp. 404-406.

BLAU, J. Middle and old Arabic material for the history of stress in Arabic. *BSOAS* 35(1972), pp. 476-484.

BLAU, J. On the problem of the synthetic character of classical Arabic as against Judaeo-Arabic (middle Arabic). *JQR* 63(1972), pp. 29-38.

BLOHM, D., REUSCHEL, W. Das arabische Aktiv-Partizip als Prädikat. *Asien, Afrika, Latein-Amerika* 1(Sonderheft, 1973), pp. 111-149.

BRAVMANN, M.M. The Aramaic *nomen agentis qātōl* and some similar phenomena of Arabic. *BSOAS* 34 (1971), pp. 1-4.

BRAVMANN, M.M. The expression of instantaneousness in Arabic. *Muséon* 84 (1971), pp. 499-523.

BRAVMANN, M.M. The origin of the Arabic object pronouns formed with "*īyā-*". *JSS* 16 (1971), pp. 50-52.

BRAVMANN, M.M. The 3d pers.sing.fem. of the perfect of roots III *y/w* in Arabic. *Arabica* 18(1971), pp. 213-215.

CARTER, M.G. An Arab grammarian of the eighth century A.D.: a contribution to the history of linguistics. *JAOS* 93(1973), pp. 146-157.

CARTER, M.G. Les origines de la grammaire arabe. *REI* 40(1972), pp. 69-97.

CARTER, M.G. *Sarf* et *hilāf,* contribution à l'histoire de la grammaire arabe. *Arabica* 20(1973), pp. 292-304.

CARTER, M.G. "Twenty dirhams" in the *Kitāb* of Sībawaihi. *BSOAS* 35(1972), pp. 485-496.

COHEN, D. *Ad'dād* et ambiguïté linguistique en arabe. *L'ambivalence dans la culture arabe,* 1967, pp. 25-50.

COHEN, D. Ambivalence, indifférence et neutralisation de sèmes. *L'ambivalence dans la culture arabe,* 1967, pp. 291-295.

COHEN, D. Les études linguistiques arabes. A propos de quelques ouvrages récents. *REI* 39(1971), pp. 177-183.

COHEN, D. Les formes du prédicat en arabe et la théorie de la phrase chez les anciens grammairiens. *Mélanges Marcel Cohen*, 1970, pp. 224-228.

COHEN, D. Pour un atlas linguistique et sociolinguistique de l'arabe. *Actes I. Cong. et. cult. mediterr. d'infl. arabo-berb.*, 1973, pp. 63-69.

COHEN, D. Variantes, variétés dialectales et contacts linguistiques en domaine arabe. *BSLP* 68(1973), pp. 215-248.

CORRIENTE, F. Marginalia on Arabic diglossia and evidence thereof in the Kitab al-Agani. *J. Semitic stud.* 20(1975), pp. 38-61.

DEZSO, L. A word order typology of three-member sentences (S,V,O). *Actes du Xe Congrès International des Linguistes, 1967* vol. III, (1970), pp. 551-555.

DIEM, W. Nomen, Substantativ und Adjektiv bei den arabischen Grammatikern. *Oriens* 23-24(1974), pp. 312-332.

DIEM, W. Über eine Einführung in die europäische Sprachwissenschaft auf Arabisch. *WI* 13 (1971), pp. 11-19.

DREWES, G.W.J. The study of Arabic grammar in Indonesia. *Acta Orientalia Neerlandica* ed. P.W. Pestman, 1971, pp. 61-70.

DROZDÍK, L. Collective and unit nouns as sex-gender pairs in Arabic. *Asian and African studies* [Bratislava] 10(1974), pp. 41-48.

DROZDÍK, L. Definiteness patterning in Arabic. *Asian and African studies* [Bratislava] 6(1970), pp. 9-49.

DROZDÍK, L. The dual number in Arabic nouns. *Graecolatina et Orientalia* 4(1972), pp. 123-159.

DROZDÍK, L. An early grammar of colloquial Arabic. *Medieval and Middle Eastern studies ... A.S. Atiya* 1972, pp. 122-132.

DROZDÍK, L. Grammatical gender in Arabic nouns. *Graecolatina et Orientalia* 5(1973), pp. 217-248.

DROZDÍK, L. Hypothesis of a transition value of definiteness in Arabic. *Asian and African studies* [Bratislava] 5(1969), pp. 39-48.

DROZDÍK, L. Inflectional background of the Arabic nisba derivation. *Asian and African studies* [Bratislava] 11(1975), pp. 119-138.

DROZDÍK, L. Near-far distinction in the Arabic demonstration. *Asian and African studies* [Bratislava] 7(1971), pp. 11-15.

DROZDÍK, L. Recent trends in expressing potentiality in Arabic. *Graecolatina et Orientalia* 6(1974), pp. 191-199.

FAUBLÉE, J. L'influence arabe dans le sud-est de Madagascar. *Actes 1. Cong. int. ling. sém. cham.-sém.*, 1969 (1974), pp. 399-411.

FLEISCH, H. Les démonstratifs arabes *'ulā, 'ulī, 'ulā'ika*. *MUSJ* 46(1970-1), pp. 467-478

FLEISCH, H. Note sur al-Astarābādhī. *Historiographia linguistica* 1(1974), pp. 165-168.

FLEISCH, H. Sur l'aspect dans le verbe en arabe classique. *Arabica* 21(1974), pp. 11-19.

FLEISCH, H. Le *taṣrīf* selon les grammairiens arabes. *Actes 1. Cong. int. ling. sém. cham.-sém.*, 1969 (1974), pp. 292-304.

GABRIELI, Fr. Quelques remarques sur la diglossie arabe. *Actas IV congresso de estudos árabes e islâmicos* 1968(1971), pp. 9-13.

GARDET, L. La dialectique en morphologie et logique arabes. *L'ambivalence dans la culture arabe*, 1967, pp. 116-132.

GREIMAS, J. Le problème des *ad'dād* et les niveaux de signification. *L'ambivalence dans la culture arabe*, 1967, pp. 283-290.

HAARMANN, U. Religiöses Recht und Grammatik im klassischen Islam. *XVIII. Deutscher Orientalistentag* 1972, pp. 149-169.

HAMZAOUI, Rached. Idéologie et langue ou l'emprunt linguistique d'après les exegètes du Coran et les théologiens: interprétation socio-linguistique. *CT* 22 nos.87-88(1974), pp. 177-195.

HANNA, Sami A. Intensive versus non intensive Arabic. *Al-Lisaniyyat* 1ii(1971), pp. 63-67.

JABBOUR, S. Classification et explication des *ad'dād* d'après le *Kitāb al-ad'dād* d'al-Anbârî. *L'ambivalence dans la culture arabe*, 1967, pp. 65-80.

JABBOUR, S. L'interprétation psychanalytique des *ad'dād*. *L'ambivalence dans la culture arabe*, 1967, pp. 296-302.

JANSSENS, G. Het woordeinde in het Nabatees Arabisch. *Orientalia Gandensia* 2(1965), pp. 67-90.

KAMAL, Ribhi. Le *tad'ādd*. *L'ambivalence dans la culture arabe*, 1967, pp. 51-64.

KAYE, A.S. Review article: More on diglossia in Arabic. *IJMES* 6(1975), pp. 325-340.

KHRAKOVSKIY, V.S. Formal'naya kharakteristika i upotreblenie passivnykh konstruktziy v literaturnom arabskom yazyke. *Folia Or.* 16(1975), pp. 13-36.

KLOPTER, H. Arabisch als Fremdsprache. Gedanken über ein arabisches Sprachzentrum. *Z.f.Kulturaustausch* 24ii(1974), pp. 26-28.

XXXVI LANGUAGE: GENERAL ARABIC

KOLESNIKOVA, G.F. Sravnitel'naya kharakteristika vysokochastotnykh leksem avtorskoy rechi i rechi personazhey v pod'yazyke sovremennoy arabskoy khudozhestvennoy prozy. *Vostokovedenie, yazykovedenie* 1973, pp. 120-134.

KRAHL, G. Die hybriden Bildungen im Arabischen. *Asien, Afrika, Latein-Amerika* 1(Sonderheft, 1973), pp. 151-162.

KRAPIVA, G.P. Sinonimicheskiy ryad i obshchaya klassifikatziya sinonimov v arabskom yazyke. *Vost.yazyki,* 1971, pp. 104-115

LEEMHUIS, F. Sibawaih's treatment of the D stem. *JSS* 18(1973), pp. 238-256.

LEK'IAŠVILI, A. Das diptotische System in klassischen Arabisch. *Arch. or.* 39 (1971), pp. 57-69.

LEVY, M. & FIDELHOLTZ, J.L. Arabic broken plurals, rule features, and lexical features. *Glossa* 5(1971), pp. 57-70.

LOUCEL, H. Signification du nombre et de la fréquence des racines verbales quadriconsonantiques dans «Anā Aḥyā» de Laylā Ba'albakī. *SI* 35(1972), pp. 121-167.

MACHRAFI, M. El-. Réflexions sur quelques problèmes posés par l'utilisation de la langue arabe. *Bull. Soc. hist. Maroc* 2 (1969), pp. 47-58.

MAHDI, Muhsin. Language and logic in classical Islam. *Logic in classical Islamic culture,* ed. by G.E. von Grunebaum, 1970, pp. 51-83.

MAHSUD, Mir Wali Khan. The Arabic language as a vital vehicle for conveying the message of Islam. *J. Univ. Peshawar* 13(1970), pp. 10-13.

MATTAR, A.C. The Arabic language and the present conditions and prospects for the future of the Arabic-speaking world. *Diogenes* 83(1973), pp. 64-76.

MEL'YANTZEV, A.N. Arabskiy masdar i voprosy teorii chastey rechi. *Vestnik Moskovskogo Univ., Vostokovedenie* 1975 (1), pp. 83-91.

MEYNET, R. Vers une nouvelle pédagogie de l'arabe. *Travaux et jours* 56-7(1975), pp. 33-41.

MINEDZHAN, G.Z. K voprosu o periodizatzii stanovleniya nauchno-tekhnicheskoy terminologii v arabskom yazyke. *Issledovaniya po vostochnym yazykam,* 1973, pp. 133-144.

MORSI, Mahmoud A. und KOS, A. Die Funktionen des Personalpronomens im Arabischen. *Z. f. Phonetik* 28(1975), pp. 378-386.

MORSI, Mahmoud A., KOS, A. Die Witterungsverben. Konfrontation Deutsch/Arabisch. *Zeits. f. Phonetik* 26(1973), pp. 36-46.

NAKAMURA, Kōjirō. Ibn Maḍā's criticism of Arabic grammarians. *Orient* [Japan] 10 (1974), pp. 89-113.

PETIT, O. Le *Kitāb al-ad'dād* d'Abû'l-T'ayyîb al-Lughawî. *L'ambivalence dans la culture arabe,* 1967, pp. 81-84.

PETRÁČEK, K. La fonction phatique dans la communication en Arabe. *Arch. or.* 39 (1971), pp. 70-75.

PETRÁČEK, K. Pedagogical problems of Arabic and their linguistic background. *Archiv or.* 41(1973), pp. 350-354.

PIOLLE, J., ROMAN, A. Pour un traitement automatique de textes arabes. *Cah.de ling. d'orientalisme et de slavistique* 1-2(1973), pp. 209-251.

POIRIER, J. Le concept d'hétéronymie. La notion de *d'idd* et la signification ethnologique de certains *ad'dād. L'ambivalence dans la culture arabe,* 1967, pp. 303-321.

RAUFOVA, A.G. Vydelenie narechiya kak osoboy kategorii chastey rechi v arabskom rechi v arabskom yazyke. *Vostokovedenie, yazykovedenie* 1973, pp. 109-120.

RAYYAH, Muhammad Ali al-. Sibawaihi and Al-Kitab. (The reliability of the printed text). *Adab: J. Fac. Arts, Khartoum* 2-3 (1975), pp. 134-143.

REIG, D. Antonymie des semblables et corrélation des opposés en arabe. *BEO* 24(1971), pp. 135-155.

SAADA, L. Les structures du purisme grammatical arabe à travers les termes essentiels de son lexique technique. *Actes 1. Cong. int. ling. sém. cham.-sém.,* 1969 (1974), pp. 329-337.

SCHABERT, P. Eine automatisches Verfahren zur morphologischen Analyse und zur Herstellungen von Indices für arabische Texte. *ZDMG* 123(1973), pp. 238-251.

SEMAAN, Khalil I.H. Arabic: classical or vulgar. *Proc.27th Int.Cong.Or.1967* (1971), pp. 195-197.

SPITALER, A. Zwei sekundäre arabische Nominaltypen aus der Affektsprache. *Islamwissenschaftliche Abhandlungen F. Meier,* 1974, pp. 292-305.

TOMICHE, Nada. Sur la genèse des "contradictoires". *L'ambivalence dans la culture arabe,* 1967, pp. 85-88.

VECCIA VAGLIERI, L. Gli studi di lingua e grammatica araba. *Studi sul Vicino Oriente in Italia,* II, 1971, pp. 109-129.

VYCICHL, W. Arabisch *'Aqrab-u* und *al-'aqrab-u. Muséon* 85(1972), pp. 531-2.

WEXLER, P. The cartography of unspoken languages of culture and liturgy. (Reflexions on the diffusion of Arabic and Hebrew). *Orbis* 23(1974), pp. 30-51.

ZABIROV, F.S. Uslovnye konstruktzii v "Knige o skupykh" al'-Dzhakhiza. *Vost. yazyki*, 1971, pp. 77-85

See also III. a. 1. Haarmann.

See also XXXVII. 1. Schub.

See also XLIII. k. Drewes.

e SYNTAX

BEESTON, A.F.L. Embedding of the theme-predicate structure in Arabic. *Language* 50 (1974), pp. 474-477.

BELGUEDJ, M.S. La démarche des premiers grammariens arabes dans le domaine de la syntaxe. *Arabica* 20(1973), pp. 168-185.

BLOHM, D., MUTLAK, I. Zur Wiedergabe der deutschen adverbialen Modalbestimmung im Arabischen mittels Akkusativ. *Asien in Vergangenheit und Gegenwart*, 1974, pp. 383-425.

BRAVMANN, M.M. An arabic construction implying the concept of "suddenly". *Muséon* 85(1972), pp. 527-529.

BRAVMANN, M.M. Arabic parallels to the English phrase *I am friends with him*. *Muséon* 87(1974), pp. 223-236.

BRAVMANN, M.M. The syntactic background of Arabic nouns with prefix *ma* and related syntactic phenomena. *In memoriam S.M. Stern* (Israel Or. studies, II, 1972), pp. 92-116.

CARTER, M.G. A note on classical Arabic exceptive sentences. *J. Semitic stud.* 20(1975), pp. 69-72.

COWAN, W. The historical syntax of the Arabic numbers. *Glossa* 6(1972), pp. 131-146.

DENZ, A. Zur Noetik des arabischen *ʾin*-Satz - Hauptsatzgefüges. *ZDMG* 121(1971), pp. 37-45.

FISCHER, W. Die Perioden des Klassischen Arabisch. *Abr-nahrain* 12(1971-2), pp. 15-18

HETZRON, R. Extrinsic ordering in classical Arabic. *Afroasiatic linguistics* liii(1974), 20 pp.

JAMME, A. The grammatical usage of the Safaitic verb *rʿy, to pasture*. *AION N.S.* 21 (1971), pp. 21-40.

KHRAKOVSKIY, V.S. Nekotorye problemy sintaksicheskoy derivatzii (na materiale konstruktziy s passivno-kauzativnymi glagolami v arabskom literaturnom yazyke). (Some problems of syntactic derivation, on material concerning constructions with passive-causative verbs in literary Arabic) *NAA* 1971(6), pp. 88-100.

KRAHL, G. Verbale Neubildungen im Arabischen. *Asien in Vergangenheit und Gegenwart*, 1974, pp. 371-382.

LEWIN, B. Non-conditional '*if*'-clauses in Arabic. *ZDMG* 120 (1970), pp. 264-270.

LEWKOWICZ, N.K. Topic-comment and relative clause in Arabic. *Language* 47 (1971), pp. 810-825.

PELLAT, C. Note sur un contresens de Ǧāḥiẓ. *Arabica* 21(1974), pp. 183-1ß'

REUSCHEL, W. Darstellung und Gebrauch der Form yakūnu (qad) fa'ala im Arabischen. *Asien in Vergangenheit und Gegenwart*, 1974, pp. 355-370.

SCHEN, I. Usama ibn Munqidh's memoirs: some further light on Muslim Middle Arabic. *JSS* 18(1973), pp. 64-97.

VITESTAM, G. *As-sidra(t?) al-muntahā*. Quelques commentaires linguistiques sur des textes existants. *Actes I Cong.int. ling.sém.et chamito-sém.*, 1969(1974), pp. 305-308.

f WRITING. TRANSLITERATION

BAUSANI, A. Um caso extremo de difusão da escrita árabe: o árabe-chinês. *Actas IV congresso de estudos árabes e islâmicos* 1968(1971), pp. 3-7.

BOSWORTH, C.E. A Mamlūk text on the orthographic distinction of *ḍād* and *ẓā*. *Orientalia Hispanica* I, 1974, pp. 135-149.

BOSWORTH, C.E. A Mamlūk text on the orthographical distinction of *ḍād* and *ẓā*'. *Parole de l'Orient* 3i(1972), pp. 153-169.

D'ERME, G.M. Proposta di un sistema simultaneo di trascrizione-traslitterazione de alcune lingue scritte in alfabeto di tipo arabo. *RSO* 48(1973-4), pp. 243-249.

DIEM, W. Die nabatäischen Inschriften und die Frage der Kasusflexion im Altarabischen *ZDMG* 123(1973), pp. 227-237.

EGUCHI, P.K. Notes on the Arabic-Fulfulde translational reading in Northern Cameroun. *Kyoto Univ. Afr. stud.* 9 (1975), pp. 177-250.

HUSHYAR, M.B. A new way to teach the Persian-Arabic script. *Poure Davoud Memorial Vol.*, II, 1951, pp. 100-102.

ISHAQUE, M. The Persian alphabet. *Indo-Iranica* 23i-ii(1970), pp. 51-69

KALEŠI, Hasan. Albanska Aljamijado književnost. (Die Albanische Aljamiado Literatur.) *Prilozi Or.Fil.Ist.* 16-17 (1966-7), pp. 49-76

MANZANARES de CIRRE, M. Textos aljamiados. Poesia religiosa morisca. *Bull.Hispanique* 72(1970), pp. 311-315

MUFTIC, Teufik. O arebici i njenom pravopisu. (On orthography of Arabic script used for Serbo-Croatian). *Prilozi Or.Fil.Ist.* 14-15(1964-5), pp. 101-121

NAIM, C. Mohammed. Arabic orthography and some non-Semitic languages. *Islam and its cultural divergence. Studies in honor of Gustave E. von Grunebaum*, 1971, pp. 113-144

NEYSÂRI, Salim. Transliteration of oriental words into latin characters. *J. Reg. Cult. Inst.* 1 ii(1968), pp. 5-11; 1 iv(1968), pp. 37-39(comment).

PREISBERG, R.D. Zur Transliteration orientalischer Sprachen für maschinelle Dokumentation. *Mitt. Dokumentationsdienst moderner Orient* 1iii(1972), pp. 57-61.

REVELL, E.J. The diacritical dots and the development of the Arabic alphabet. *JSS* 20(1975), pp. 178-190.

THEODORIDIS, D. Birgiwī's Katechismus in griechisch-aljamiadischer Übersetzung. *Südost-Forsch.* 33(1974), pp. 307-310.

WHEELER, G. The transliteration of Arabic script. *Asian aff.* 58(N.S.2, 1971), pp. 317-320.

See also VIII. e. Isserlin.

See also XXXVI. d. Zabirov

See also XXXVII. 1. Grotzfeld.

g PROSODY. PHONETICS

ALWAHAB, Abbas S. A generative phonological analysis of "One thousand and one nights". *Al-Mustansiriya Univ.R.* 4(1973-4), pp. 7-25.

AMBROS, A.A. Einige phonologische und morphologische Aspekte der arabischen Diglossie. *Ve Congrès International d'Arabisants et d'Islamisants. Actes.*, [1970?], pp. 35-40.

ANI, Salman H. al-. An accoustical and physiological investigation of the Arabic ع. *Actes Xe Cong.int.linguistes*, 1967, IV, pp. 155-160.

ANI, Salman al-, MAY, D.R. The phonological structure of the syllable in Arabic. *AJAS* 1(1973), pp. 37-49.

AVRAM, A. Sur la classification des phonèmes notés *'alif* et *ʻayn* en arabe classique. *Rev.Roumaine de Ling.* 16 (1971), pp. 459-468.

BOHAS, G. Le métrique arabe classique. *Linguistics* 140(1974), pp. 59-68.

BRAME, M.K. On the abstractness of phonology: Maltese ʕ. *Contributions to generative phonology*, 1972, pp. 22-61.

BRAME, M.K. Stress in Arabic and generative phonology. *Found. lang.* 7(1971), pp. 556-591.

COHEN, D. Sur le statut phonologique de l'*emphase* en arabe. *Word* 25(1969), pp. 59-69.

COWAN, W. The vowels of Egyptian Arabic. *Word* 26(1970), pp. 94-100.

DELATTRE, P. Pharyngeal features in the consonants of Arabic, German, Spanish, French, and American English. *Phonetica* 23(1971), pp. 129-155.

FLEISCH, H. Réflexions sur l'état des études philologiques en arabe classique. *Ve Congrès International d'Arabisants et d'Islamisants. Actes.*, [1970?], pp. 209-217.

GERRESCH, Cl. Le livre "Mubayyin al-Iškâl" du Cadi Madiakhâté Kala: introduction historique, texte arabe, traduction et glossaire. *Bull. IFAN* 36 (1974), pp. 714-832.

HADJ-SALAH, A. La notion de syllabe et la théorie cinético-impulsionnelle des phonéticiens arabes. *Al-Lisaniyyat* 1i(1971), pp. 63-83.

KAHN, M. Arabic emphatics: the evidence for cultural determinants of phonetic sex-typing. *Phonetica* 31(1975), pp. 38-50.

KAYE, A.S. Towards a generative phonology of Arabic: a review article. *IJMES* 5 (1974), pp. 93-113.

LECERF, J. L'accent de mot en arabe d'Orient. *Actes 1. Cong. int. ling. sém. cham.-sém.*, 1969 (1974), pp. 322-328.

McDONALD, M.V. The order and phonetic value of Arabic sibilants in the "abjad". *JSS* 19(1974), pp. 36-46.

OBRECHT, D.H. Factors in the perception of some unvoiced stops in Arabic. *Word* 26 (1970), pp. 230-243.

RODINSON, M. Sur la prononciation ancienne du *qāf* arabe. *Mélanges Marcel Cohen*, 1970, pp. 298-319.

ROMAN, A. Remarques générales sur la phonologie de l'arabe classique. *ROMM* 15-16 (1973), pp. 291-300.

ROMAN, A. Le système phonologique de l'arabe "classique" contemporain. *ROMM* 18(1974), pp. 125-130.

VIAL, C. Les idées de Yahʻyâ Hʼaqqî sur la langue. *ROMM* 15-16(1973), pp. 403-414.

ZACCAGNINI, C. Il fonema ẓ in arabo classico. *AION* 33(N.S.23, 1973), pp. 531-549.

See also XXXVI. 1. Brame.

See also XXXVI. 1. Ingham

See also XXXVI. 1. Satzinger.

h LEXICOGRAPHY. ETYMOLOGY

ALLARD, M. Note sur l'informatique au service de la langue arabe. *Ve Congrès International d'Arabisants et d'Islamisants. Actes.*, [1970?], pp. 31-33.

ATTALLAH, W. Sur un vers de Ğarīr. Etymologie de *zūn* et de *hirbid̲*. *Arabica* 18 (1971), pp. 49-56.

BLACHÈRE, R. Réflexions sur le développement de la lexicographie arabe. *ROMM* 13-14 (1973), pp. 125-129.

BLAU, J. Arabic lexicographical miscellanies. *J. Semitic stud.* 17(1972), pp. 173-190.

BORISOV, V.M. O printzipakh sostavleniya polnogo slovarya chastotnosti (na materiale russko-arabskogo slovarya). (The principles of compilation of a complete dictionary of frequencies, based on the Russo-Arabic dictionary.) *NAA* 1971(2), pp. 113-121.

BOUDOT-LAMOTTE, A. Notes sur les emplois métaphoriques des noms de quelques parties du corps humain. *Arabica* 18(1971), pp. 152-160

BRAVMANN, M.M. Notes on Ḫalil b. Ahmad's *Kitāb al-ʿAin.* *Der Islam* 47(1971), pp. 238-244.

BURTON, J. The meaning of "ihsan". *JSS* 19 (1974), pp. 47-75.

DEMEERSEMAN, A. Recherche sémantique sur cinq mots-clefs de la Tunisie contemporaine. *IBLA* 38,no.135(1975), pp. 113-167.

GHALI, Wagdy Rizk. Arabic dictionaries: an annotated comprehensive bibliography. Supplement. *MIDEO* 12(1974), pp. 243-287.

HAMZAOUI, R. Importance du "Muḫaṣṣas" d'Ibn Sida dans la lexicographie arabe moderne. *Actas II Col. hisp.-tunec. estud. hist.*, 1973, pp. 215-233.

JUYNBOLL, G.H.A. The Qurrā' in early Islamic history. *JESHO* 16(1973), pp. 113-129.

KARIEV, U.Z. Nekotorye zamechaniya o slovare Makhmuda Zamakhshari "Al-fā'ik fī garīb al-khadīs". *Vostokovedenie, yazykovedenie* 1973, pp. 103-108.

KELLY, J.M. On defining *Dhū ath-Thalāthah* and *Dhū al-Arbaʿah.* *JAOS* 91 (1971), pp. 132-136.

KISELEVA, L.N. Terminologiya arabsko-persidskogo aruza i slovar'. *Ind. i iran. filol.*, 1971, pp. 24-42.

LECOMTE, G. Nouvelles réflexions sur un vocabulaire technique en formation, suivi d'un Nouveau lexique français-arabe de l'automobile. *Arabica* 20(1973), pp. 113-141.

MADKOUR, I. Le grand dictionnaire "Al Muʿgam Al Kabīr". *Abr-nahrain* 12(1971-2), pp. 40-43

MARCOS-MARÍN, F. Arabismos en Azorín. (Contribución al estudio del léxico de "Las confesiones de un pequeño filósofo".) *And* 34(1969), pp. 143-158

MIQUEL, A. La particule *ḥattā* dans le Coran. *BEO* 21 (1968), pp. 411-436.

OMAN, G. L'ittionimia araba delle acque interne. *OM* 54(1974), pp. 355-383.

OMAN, G. L'ittionimia araba delle acque interne. I. Addenda. *OM* 54(1974), pp. 635-641.

OMAN, G. Sui nomi generici di "pesce" nell' arabo. *Orientalia Hispanica* I, 1974, pp. 531-536.

PARET, Rudi. Die Bedeutungsentwicklung von arabisch *fatḥ*. *Orientalia Hispanica* I, 1974, pp. 537-541.

PELLAT, C. Sur l'expression arabe *ašʿār m.n.ṣ.fa/āt.* *Mélanges Marcel Cohen*, 1970, pp. 277-285.

PIEMONTESE, A.M. Note morfologiche ed etimologiche su al-Burāq. *Ann.Fac.Ling.Lett. stran.Ca' Foscari* 5(1974), pp. 109-133.

RITCHIE, J.M. Some thoughts on the word *tawaffā* as used in the Qur'an. *Glasgow Univ. Or. Soc. Trans.* 24(1974), pp. 66-75.

SAADA, L. Les structures du purisme grammatical arabe à travers les termes essentiels de son lexique technique. *Actes I Cong.int.ling.sém.et chamito-sém.*, 1969(1974), pp. 329-337.

ULLMANN, M. *sāraqanī n-nazara ilaihā.* *Der Islam* 49(1972), pp. 120-121.

USHAKOV, V.D. O dvukh opisaniya idiomatichnosti (na materiale arabskogo i russkogo yazykov). *NAA* 1974(6), pp. 95-104.

VITESTAM, G. *As-sidra(-t?) al-muntahā.* Quelques commentaires linguistiques sur des textes existants. *Actes 1. Cong. int. ling. sém. cham.-sém.*, 1969 (1974), pp. 305-308.

VOLKOVA, Z.N. O nekotorykh strukturnykh osobennostyakh semanticheskogo polya "doblest'" v srednevekovom arabskom yazyke v sravnenii so starofrantzuzskim yazykom. *Issledovaniya po vostochnym yazykam*, 1973, pp. 19-31.

WEIERS, M. Ein arabisch-mongolischer Wörterspiegel aus der Biblioteca Corsini in Rom. *Zentralasiat. Studien* 6(1972), pp. 7-61.

See also V. c. *General.* Diem.

See also VI. a. Schliephake.

See also VI. d. Grosset-Grange

See also VII. a. Atallah

See also IX. g. Lewis.

See also XII. f. Teyssier

See also XXXVI. k. Dobrisan.

See also XXXVI. k. Hamzaoui.

See also XXXVII. l. Barbat.

See also XXXVII. l. Boudot-Lamotte.

XXXVI LANGUAGE: GENERAL ARABIC

i LOAN WORDS

BA, Oumar. L'expression du temps en *poulâr* et en *hassaniyya*. *Bull. IFAN* 36 (1974), pp. 853-875.

BRZUSKI, W.K. Arabic loanwords in Amharic connected with textiles, leather products and jewelry. *Africana bull.* 20 (1974), pp. 63-89.

EILERS, W. Iranisches Lehngut im Arabischen. *Actas IV congresso de estudos árabes e islâmicos* 1968(1971), pp. 581-660.

FAUBLÉE, J. L'influence arabe dans le sud-est de Madagascar. *Actes I Cong.int. ling.sém.et chamito-sém.,* 1969(1974), pp. 399-411.

LA GRANJA, F. de. Un arabismo inédito: al-mayar/almayal. *And.* 38(1973), pp. 483-490.

LATHAM, J.D. Arabic into medieval Latin. *J. Semitic stud.* 17(1972), pp. 30-67.

MARCOS MARÍN, F. Doce nuevos arabismos para el Diccionario Histórico. *And* 34(1969), pp. 441-450

MUFTIĆ, T. Prilog semantičkom izučavanju arabizama u srpskohrvatskom jeziku. *Prilozi za or. filol.* 18-19(1968-9), pp. 59-87.

SCHELLER, Meinrad, DIEM, W. Spanisch *almena* "Mauerzinne": Abkömmling von lat. *minae* oder arabischen Ursprungs? *Sprache* 17 (1971), pp. 34-41.

SPIES, O. Sechs tunesische Arbeitslieder aus Gabes. *Islamwissenschaftliche Abhandlungen F. Meier,* 1974, pp. 285-291.

STERN, S.M. Arabico-Persica. *W.B. Henning memorial vol.,* 1970, pp. 409-416.

TERÉS, E. Ǧinān Dāwūd > Gerindote. *And* 35(1970), pp. 203-209.

See also XXXVIII. c. Khashimbekov

j NAMES
Place names. Personal names

ALLYARI, Husain. Research on variations of the word "Munkberti". *Afghanistan* 25 iv(1973), pp. 19-21.

ANTOUN, R.T. On the significance of names in an Arab village. *Ethnology [Pittsburg]* 7(1968), pp. 158-170.

CORCOS, D. Réflexions sur l'onomastique judéo-nord-africaine. *Folklore Research Centre Studies* 1,1970, pp. 1-27.

GOZALBES BUSTO, G. El nombre de Xauen. *Cuadernos de la Bibl.Esp.de Tetuan* 7(1973), pp. 37-55.

GRAF, H.J. Zum Ortsnamen 'Arba' (Arboga). *Beitr.z.Namenforschung* 8(1973), pp. 345-346.

KOLVENBACH, P.H. L'agressivité génératrice. *Travaux et jours* 51(1974), pp. 93-111.

McCARTHY, K.M. Street names in Beirut, Lebanon. *Names* 23(1975), pp. 74-88.

OLIVER ASIN, J. Les Tunisiens en Espagne, à travers la toponymie. *CT* 18 (nos. 69-70, 1970), pp. 15-20.

PAXTON, E. Arabic names. *Asian aff.* 59(N.S. 3,1972), pp. 198-200.

PLANCKE, M. The Onomasticon Arabicum project. *Onoma* 18(1974), pp. 426-432.

SCARCIA AMORETTI, B. L'Onomasticon arabicum: un esempio di collaborazione internazionale. *Studi sul Vicino Oriente in Italia,* II, 1971, pp. 291-306.

SCHEIBER, A. War der Name Balaam gebräuchlich bei den Juden? *The Middle East; studies in honour of J. Germanus,* 1974, pp. 35-37.

See VI. b. Ayoubi.

See also VI. c. Graf

k MODERN ARABIC

ABDEL-MALEK, Z.N. The design of a textbook lesson for teaching colloquial Egyptian Arabic as a foreign language. *IRAL* 10(1972), pp. 47-60.

ABEL, A. Hedendaagse richtingen in de modernisering van de Arabische taal. *Orientalia Gandensia* 3(1966), pp. 119-133.

ALTOMA, S.J. Observations on the use of broken plurals in modern Arabic prose. *Amer. Or. Soc., Middle West Branch. Semicentennial volume,* ed. by D. Sinor, 1969, pp. 3-19.

BEESTON, A.F.L. Some features of modern standard Arabic. *J. Semitic stud.* 20 (1975), pp. 62-68.

BLANC, Haim. Style variations in spoken Arabic: a sample of interdialectal educated conversation. *Contributions to Arabic linguistics,* C.A. Ferguson, editor, 1960, pp. 79-161.

BOCHEŃSKI, F. Niektóre problemy językowe w trzech krajach północnej Afryki: Algierii, Maroku i Tunezji. *Przegląd socjologiczy* 24(1971), pp. 253-283. (*English summary*: Language problems in three countries of North Africa - Algeria, Morocco and Tunesia [*sic*], pp. 447-449.)

CHAHINE, Abdel-Sabbour. Concerning the article by Antoine C. Mattar (in *Diogenes* 83, 1973, pp. 64-76). *Diogenes* 91(1975), pp.

CZAPKIEWICZ, A. The accumulation of functions in the categorial morphemes of the verb in modern spoken Arabic. *Folia Or* 13(1971), pp. 15-32.

DOBRISAN, N. Technical terminology of a building site. *Romano-Arabica,* ed. M. Anghelescu, 1974, pp. 93-113.

DOHAISH, A.A. and YOUNG, M.J.L. Modes of address and epistolary forms in Saudi Arabia. *Ann. Leeds Univ. Or. Soc.* 7 (1969-73), pp. 110-117.

DROZDÍK, L. Generic definiteness in arabic. *Zborník Filos. Fak. Univ. Komenského: Graecolatina et orientalia* 2(1970), pp. 177-190.

FELLMAN, J. Sociolinguistic problems in the Middle Eastern Arab World: an overview. *Anthrop. ling.* 15(1973), pp. 24-32.

HAMZAOUI, R. Importance du "Muḫaṣṣaṣ" d'ibn Sīda dans la lexicographie arabe moderne. *Actas II Coloquio hispano-tunecino*, 1972, pp. 215-233.

KAHTAN, Nour el Sabah. The teaching of "standard Arabic" to university students whose mother tongue is not Arabic. *Actas IV congresso de estudos árabes e islâmicos* 1968(1971), pp. 33-39.

KAYE, A.S. Modern standard Arabic and the colloquials. *Proc.27th Int.Cong.Or. 1967* (1971), pp. 194-195.

LOVELL, E.K. A native speaker learns modern standard Arabic. *Milla wa-milla* 15(1975), pp. 47-50.

McLOUGHLIN, L.J. Towards a definition of modern standard Arabic. *Archivum ling.* N.S. 3(1972), pp. 57-73

MITCHELL, T.F. Forthcoming research on the Arabic *koine:* a pilot project at Leeds. *BSMES bull.* 2(1975), pp. 19-20.

MITCHELL, T.F. Some preliminary observations on the Arabic *koine*. *BSMES bull.* 2 (1975), pp. 70-86.

MONTEIL, V. The problem of modernization of Arabic. *Modernization of languages in Asia, ed. by S. Takdir Alisjahbana*, pp. 344-349

PALVA, H. Notes on classicization in modern colloquial Arabic. *SO* 40(1971) iii, pp. 41.

POPOVIC, A. L'arabe comme langue d'expression littéraire dans les territoires yougoslaves. *Actes I. Cong. et. cult. mediterr. d'infl. arabo-berb.*, 1973, pp. 251-255.

RAUFOVA, A.G. Sposoby obrazovaniya narechiy v sovremennom arabskom literaturnom yazyke. *Vost.yazyki*, 1971, pp. 129-139

SIENY, M.I. Diglossia and foreign language teaching. *Bull.Fac.Arts U.Riyad* 3(1973-74), pp. 66-83.

TEUFEL, J.K. Anpassungen an die indogermanische Grammatik in den arabischen Fassungen von Staatsverträgen. *Proc. 27th Int.Cong.Or.1967* (1971), pp. 159-161.

See also XXXVI. 1. Anghelescu.

1 DIALECTS. MALTESE. MODERN SOUTH ARABIC

ABBOUD, P. Some features of the verbal system of Najdi Arabic. *Proc.27th Int. Cong.Or.1967* (1971), pp. 157-158.

ABDEL-MALEK, Zaki N. On defining colloquial Egyptian Arabic stems. *AJAS* 1(1973), pp. 30-36.

AGIUS, D. Il-pellegrinaġġ (Al Hajj). *J. Maltese stud.* 10(1975), pp. 128-133.

ALI, Latif H. Observations on the preverb negative particle *ma* in Baghdad Arabic. *Studia linguistica* 26(1972), pp. 48-60.

ANGHELESCU, N. Arabic diglossia and its methodological implications. *Romano-Arabica*, ed. M. Anghelescu, 1974, pp. 81-92.

ANTONOV, N.M. Morfologicheskaya i semanticheskaya evolyutziya klassicheskoy arabskoy sistemy glagol'nykh porod v irakskom dialekte. *Vost.yazyki*, 1971, pp. 3-13

ANTONOV, N.M. O sisteme vremen v irakskom dialekte arabskogo yazyka. *Vost.yazyki*, 1971, pp. 14-25

AQUILINA, J. The Berber element in Maltese. *Hamito-Semitica*, ed. J. and Th. Bynon, 1975, pp. 297-313.

AQUILINA, G. Due epoche linguistiche nella lingua maltese. *J.Fac.Arts Malta* 7(1971), pp. 1-36.

AQUILINA, J. L-Inkwiet tas-Sur Martin [One-act comedy in Maltese and English]. *J. Maltese studies* 6 (1971), pp. 47-93.

AQUILINA, J. Maltese Christian words of Arabic origin. *Actes I. Cong. et. cult. mediterr. d'infl. arabo-berb.*, 1973, pp. 70-74.

AQUILINA, J. Maltese etymological glossary. *J. Maltese Stud.* 8(1973), pp. 1-62.

AQUILINA, J. Maltese plant names. *J. Maltese Stud.* 8(1973), pp. 63-92.

AQUILINA, J. Popular witty retorts. *J. Maltese stud.* 10(1975), pp. 65-79.

AQUILINA, J. Prepositional verbs in Maltese. *Actes 1. Cong. int. ling. sém. cham.-sém.*, 1969 (1974), pp. 309-321.

AQUILINA, J. The role of Maltese and English in Malta. *J.Fac.Arts Malta* 4 (1971), pp. 171-182.

AQUILINA, J. A study in violent language. *J.Maltese stud.* 10(1975), pp. 29-54.

AQUILINA, J. Verbs. *J. Maltese Stud.* 8(1973), pp. 93-98.

ATTAL, R. Les missions protestantes anglicanes en Afrique du nord et leurs publications en judéo-arabe à l'intention des juifs. *REJ* 132(1973), pp. 95-118.

BELGUEDJ, Mohammed Salah. Les mots turcs dans le parler algérien. *Turcica* 3(1971), pp. 133-142.

BELGUEDJ, M.S. Les verbes quadrilitères de types *faw'al* et *fay'al* dans l'arabe dialectal algérien. *Études philos. et litt.* 6 (1973), pp. 3-20.

BELYAEV, V.I. Arabskaya istoricheskaya dialektologiya i arabskie rukopisi v Leningrade. *Voprosy filol. stran Azii i Afriki* II(1973), pp. 3-9.

BELYAEV, V.I. Dialektizmy v "Tuisyacha odnoy nochi". *Voprosy filologii stran Azii i Afriki, 1. Sbornik I.N. Vinnikova* 1971, pp. 19-27.

BEN-SHAMMAI, H. Some Judaeo-Arabic Karaite fragments in the British Museum collection. *BSOAS* 38(1975), pp. 126-132.

BLANC, Haim. The Arabic dialect of the Negev Bedouins. *Proc.Israel Acad.* 4 (1969-70), pp. 112-150.

BLOCH, A.A. The distribution of the cardinal numerals from three to ten in the modern Arabic dialects. *Proc.27th Int.Cong.Or.1967* (1971), pp. 193-194.

BLOCH, A.A. Morphological doublets in Arabic dialects. *JSS* 16 (1971), pp. 53-73.

BORG, A. Maltese morphophonemics. *J. Maltese stud.* 10(1975), pp. 11-28.

BORG, A. Maltese numerals. *ZDMG* 124(1974), pp. 291-305.

BORG, A. The segmental phonemes of Maltese. *Linguistics* 109(1973), pp. 5-11.

BOUDOT-LAMOTTE, A. L'expression de la malédiction et de l'insulte dans les dialectes arabes maghrébins. Recherches lexicographiques et phraséologiques. *Arabica* 21 (1974), pp. 53-71.

BRAME, M.K. The cycle in phonology: stress in Palestinian, Maltese, and Spanish. *Ling. inquiry* 5(1974), pp. 39-60.

BRAME, M.K. On stress assignment in the Arabic dialects. *Fest.M.Halle,* 1973, pp. 14-25.

BRAME, M.K. On the abstractness of phonology, Maltese. *Contributions to generative phonology,* ed. M.K. Brame, 1972, pp. 22-61.

BRETEAU, Cl.H. et GALLEY, M. Réflexions sur deux versions algériennes de Dyâb le Hilâlien. *Actes I. Cong. et. cult. mediterr. d'infl. arabo-berb.,* 1973, pp. 358-364.

BRINCAT, J.M. Alcuni esempi di omonia risultante dalla convergenza fonetica di voci italiane nel maltese. *J.Maltese stud.* 10(1975), pp. 80-88.

BUTROS, A. Turkish, Italian, and French loanwords in the colloquial Arabic of Palestine and Jordan. *Studies in linguistics* 23(1973), pp. 87-104.

BUTTIGIEG, J.A. Edmund F. Sutcliffe S.J. - a postscript. *J. Maltese stud.* 9(1973), pp. 45-58.

CHIAUZZI, G. Intervista nel Nefûsa. *OM* 51(1971), pp. 834-853.

CIFOLETTI, G. Il dialetto arabo parlato dalla "Zingana" del Giancarli. *AION* 34 (N.S.24, 1974), pp. 457-464.

COLIN, G.S. Emprunts grecs et turcs dans le dialecte arabe de Malte. *Mélanges Marcel Cohen,* 1970, pp. 229-231.

CORRELL, C. Die selbständigen Personalpronomina der 3. Personen als proniminale Vertreter direkter (zweiter) Objekte in syrisch- und libanesisch-arabischen Dialekten. *ZDMG* 124(1974), pp. 286-290.

CORRELL, C. Textproben im arabischen Dialekt von Ǧubb ʿAdīn. *ZDMG* 122(1972), pp. 49-87.

COWAN, W. Caxaro's Cantilena: a checkpoint for change in Maltese. *J.Maltese stud.* 10 (1975), pp. 4-10.

COWAN, W. Rules for segholization in Maltese. *Actes I. Cong. et. cult. mediterr. d'infl. arabo-berb.,* 1973, pp. 75-82.

COWAN, W. An underground rule in Maltese. *J.linguistics* 7(1971), pp. 245-251.

CREMONA, A. The ransom of the peasants. (A dramatic poem in five acts and a tableau.) (Translated by May Butcher from the Maltese original.) *J.Fac.Arts Malta* 4(1971), pp. 244-260, 334-349.

DASH, Linda el- and TUCKER, G.R. Subjective reactions to various speech styles in Egypt. *Linguistics* 166(1975), pp. 33-54.

DIEM, W. A historical interpretation of Iraqi Arabic 'aku "there is". *Orbis* 23 (1974), pp. 448-453.

DIEM, W. Noch einmal zum Problem der unregelmässigen Formen der 3. fem. Sing. Perf. in arabischen Dialekten: Der Befund der Jemenitischen Dialekte. *Orbis* 21 (1972), pp. 312-314.

DIEM, W. Zum Problem der Personalpronomina hənne (3.Pl.), -kon (2.Pl.) und -hon (3.Pl.) in den syrisch-libanesischen Dialekten. *ZDMG* 121(1972), pp. 223-230.

DROZDÍK, L. The vowel system of Egyptian colloquial Arabic. *Asian and African studs.* 9(1973), pp. 121-127.

ERICKSON, J.L. Some observations on Cowan's Maltese 'underground' rule. *J. ling.* 9 (1973), pp. 307-311.

FERGUSON, C.A. The /g/ in Syrian Arabic: filling a gap in a phonological pattern. *Word* 25(1969), pp. 114-119.

FLEISCH, H. Un texte arabe, dialectal, de Zgharta (Liban Nord). *Mélanges Marcel Cohen,* 1970, pp. 240-244.

FLEISCH, H. La IIIe f. du verbe dans un parler arabe du Liban-sud (Khirbet Salem). *Orientalia Hispanica* I, 1974, pp. 273-289.

FRYE, R.N. The Arabic language in Khurasan. *Iran Society silver jubilee souvenir* 1944-1969, pp. 131-134.

GARCÍA GÓMEZ, E. Una nota de Levi della Vida sobre el uso de "Āllăh" por "Allāh". *And.* 36(1971), pp. 239-240.

GAYNULLIN, N.A. O leksike egipetskogo dialekta XVI v. *Issledovaniya po vostochnym yazykam,* 1973, pp. 32-40.

GOLDENBERG, Y. A distributional analysis of negative morphemes in Egyptian colloquial Arabic. *Rev.roumaine ling.* 19(1974), pp. 385-397.

GOLDENBERG, Y. Some observations on the syntax of Egyptian colloquial Arabic. *Studia et acta or.* 8(1971), pp. 229-244.

GRAND'HENRY, J. Observations sur la phonétique des parlers arabes de Ténès (Algérie occidentale). *Orbis* 20(1971), pp. 99-101.

GRAND'HENRY, J. Le verbe réfléchi-passif à *t*-préfixé de la forme simple dans les dialectes arabes. *Muséon* 88(1975), pp. 441-447.

GREIS, Naguib. Notes on some functional distinctions in cultivated Cairene Arabic. *AJAS* 2(1974), pp. 1-6.

GROTZFELD, H. L'expérience de Saʿīd Aql. L'arabe libanais employé comme langue littéraire. *Orientalia suecana* 22(1973), pp. 37-51.

HALASI-KUN, T. The Ottoman elements in the Syrian dialects. *Archivum Ottomanicum* 1 (1969), pp. 14-91.

HANNA, Sami, GREIS, Naguib. Dialect variations and the teaching of Arabic as a living language. *Asian and African studies* [Bratislava] 7(1971), pp. 17-31.

HARRELL, R.S. A linguistic analysis of Egyptian radio Arabic. *Contributions to Arabic linguistics,* C.A. Ferguson, editor, 1960, pp. 3-77.

HARVEY, L.P. The Arabic dialect of Valencia in 1595. *And* 36(1971), pp. 81-115.

HILTY, G. Celoso - Raqīb. *And.* 36(1971), pp. 127-144.

INGHAM, B. Some characteristics of Meccan speech. *BSOAS* 34 (1971), pp. 273-297.

INGHAM, B. Urban and rural Arabic in Khūzistān. *BSOAS* 36(1973), pp. 523-553.

JOHNSTONE, T.M. Contrasting articulations in the modern South Arabian languages. *Hamito-Semitica,* ed. J. and Th. Bynon, 1975, pp. 155-159.

JOHNSTONE, T.M. Diminutive patterns in the modern South Arabian languages. *JSS* 18 (1973), pp. 98-107.

JOHNSTONE, T.M. The modern South Arabian languages. *Afroasiatic linguistics* 1v (1975), pp. 93-121.

JOHNSTONE, T.M. The spoken Arabic of Tikrīt. *Ann. Leeds Univ. Or. Soc.* 7 (1969-73), pp. 89-109.

JOUIN, J. Du langage imagé des citadines marocaines. *Actes I. Cong. et. cult. mediterr. d'infl. arabo-berb.,* 1973, pp. 365-370.

KARIMOV, A.U. O prostykh vremennykh formakh glagola v yemenskom dialekte. *Vost.yazyki,* 1971, pp. 93-103

KARIMOV, A.U. Tipy prostykh predlozheniy v iemenskom dialekte arabskogo yazyka. *Issledovaniya po vostochnym yazykam,* 1973, pp. 99-108.

KARIMOV, A.U. Udvoennye glagoly v iemenskom dialekte arabskogo yazyka. *Issledovaniya po vostochnym yazykam,* 1973, pp. 109-114.

KAYE, A.S. Arabic/Žiim/ A synchronic and diachronic study. *Linguistics* 79(1972), pp. 31-72

KAYE, A.S. Remarks on diglossia in Arabic: well-defined vs. ill-defined. *Linguistics* 81(1972), pp. 32-48.

KILLEAN, C.G. Linguistic models and Arabic dialectology. *JAOS* 92(1972), pp. 65-69

KOLVENBACH, P.-H. Pistes sociolinguistiques. *Travaux et jours* 55(1975), pp. 81-102.

KRIER, F. Analyse phonologique du maltais. *Phonetica* 32(1975), pp. 103-129.

KRIER, F. Analyse syntaxique de la phrase nominale en maltais. *Linguistique* 1lii (1975), pp. 93-116.

KROTKOFF, G. Bagdader Studien. *ZDMG* 122(1972), pp. 93-101.

LECERF, J. L'accent de mot en arabe d'Orient. *Actes I Cong.int.ling.sém.et chamito-sém.,* 1969(1974), pp. 322-328.

LECERF, J.J. Une forme anormale de participe actif à Bagdad (Mākil). *GLECS* 14(1969-70), pp. 88-92.

LECERF, J. Structure syllabique en arabe de Bagdad et accent de mot en arabe oriental. *Word* 25(1969), pp. 160-179.

LEEMHUIS, F. Palestijnse notities. *Babbels. Toespraken over en uit het Egyptologisch Inst. en het Inst. voor Semitistiek en Archeologie van het Nabije Oosten der Rijksuniv. te Groningen.* 1971, pp. 31-36.

LOMBARD, A. Un rapprochement nouveau - l'histoire du maltais peut-elle nous aider à mieux comprendre celle du roumain? *Rev. roum.ling.* 19(1974), pp. 3-22.

MAAMOURI, Mohamed. The linguistic situation in independent Tunisia. *AJAS* 1(1973), pp. 50-65.

XXXVI LANGUAGE: GENERAL ARABIC

MANGION, G. A bibliography of Maltese (1953-1973). *Melita historica* 6(1974), pp. 279-306.

MANSOUR, J. Anaptyxis in final clusters in the Judaeo-Arabic dialect of Baghdad. *Abr-Nahrain* 15(1974-1975), pp. 20-26.

MARSHALL, D.R. A comparative study of some semantic differences between Maltese and Koranic Arabic. *J.Maltese stud.* 9(1973), pp. 1-44.

MARSHALL, D.R., VELLA BONAVITA, R. Four anonymous old Maltese poems. Edited and with an introduction. *J.Maltese stud.* 10 (1975), pp. 89-127.

MARSHALL, D.R. Two old Maltese poems. *J.Fac.Arts Malta* 7(1971), pp. 37-51.

MIFSUD, E. The demonstrative in Maltese. *J.Fac.Arts Malta* 7(1971), pp. 77-91.

MISHKUROV, E.N. Pronominalizuetsya li leksema ši(šay) > ŠAY' v alzhirskom dialekte arabskogo yazyka? *Issledovaniya po vostochnym yazykam*, 1973, pp. 145-155.

MITCHELL, T.F. Aspects of concord revisited, with special reference to Sindhi and Cairene arabic. *Archivum Linguisticum* N.S. 4(1973), pp. 27-50.

MOĪNFAR, Mohammad Djafar. L'accentuation dans les parlers arabes du Tchad. *Mél. ling. É. Benveniste*, 1975, pp. 427-430.

MUJIĆ, M.A. Neke morfološko semantičke specifičnosti u savremenom jeziku u Tunisu. (Some morfological-semantic features in modern Arabic of Tunisia.) *POF* 20-21(1970-71), pp. 7-50.

MÜLLER, W.W. Zum Plan für ein Wörterbuch der neusüdarabischen Mehrī-Sprache. *Proc. 27th Int.Cong.Or.1967* (1971), pp. 158-159.

NADWI, A.A. Notes on the Arabic dialects of the Bilād Ghāmid and Zahrān region of Saudi Arabia. *Ann. Leeds Univ. Or. Soc.* 7(1969-73), pp. 75-88.

NASYROV, K. Lichnye mestoimeniya v chadskom dialekte arabskogo yazyka. *Vostokovedenie, yazykovedenie* 1973, pp. 135-142.

NEWBY, G. Observations about an early Judaeo-Arabic. *JQR* 61 (1970-71), pp. 212-221.

PALVA, H. Balgāwi Arabic. 1. Texts from Mādabā; 2. Texts in the dialect of the Yigūl-group. *SO* 40i(1969), pp. 1-13; 40ii (1969), pp. 1-15.

PALVA, H. Balgāwi Arabic 3. Texts from Ṣāfūt. *SO* 43(1974), 1, p. 26.

PALVA, H. Notes on classicization in modern colloquial Arabic. *SO* 40iii(1969), pp. 1-41.

PELED, M. Yāsīn the gate-crasher. *Middle Eastern stud.* 9(1973), pp. 341-346.

POPOVKIN, A.V. Vyrazhenie passiva v arabskikh dialektakh Magriba. *VLU* 1974, (3), pp. 150-151.

PROCHAZKA, Th. The perfect tense ending *k*(-) in the spoken Arabic of Ta'izz. *BSOAS* 37(1974), pp. 439-445.

REDJALA, Mbarek. Remarques sur les problèmes linguistiques en Algérie. *GLECS* 14(1969-70), pp. 109-124.

ROMANOV, B.V. Mestoimeniya v sudanskom dialekte arabskogo yazyka. *Issledovaniya po vostochnym yazykam*, 1973, pp. 165-178.

SAADA, L. Le langage de femmes tunisiennes. *Mélanges Marcel Cohen*, 1970, pp. 320-325.

SARNELLI CERQUA, Cl. Il contributo italiano agli studi di dialettologia araba. *Studi sul Vicino Oriente in Italia*, II, 1971, pp. 131-139.

SASI, Omar al- Zum arabischen Dialekt von Mekka. *ZDMG* 122(1972), pp. 88-92.

SATZINGER, H. Zur Phonetik des Bohairischen und des Ägyptisch-Arabischen im Mittelalter. *WZKM* 63-64(1972), pp. 40-65.

SCHEN, I. Usama ibn Munqidh's memoirs: some further light on Muslim Middle Arabic. pt. 1. *J. Semitic stud.* 17(1972), pp. 218-236.

SCHUB, M.B. A note on the dialect of Abī Tamīm and Barth's law. *Arabica* 20(1973), pp. 307-308.

SERRACINO-INGLOTT, P. Maltese poetry, 1960-1970 (Abstract in Maltese text). *J. Fac.Arts, Royal Univ.Malta* 5i(1972), pp. 3-24

SINGER, H.-R. Spirantendissimilation im Maghrebinischen. *ZDMG* 123(1973), pp. 262-268.

SĪRAT, Abdul-Sattār. Notes on the Arabic dialect spoken in the Balkh region of Afghanistan. Annotated by E.E. Knudsen. *Acta Or.* 35(1973), pp. 89-101.

SLEIMAN, Najah. La chute du témoin. *Travaux et jours* 40(1971), pp. 3-16.

TALAAT, A. Comparative study of Maltese and Egyptian proverbs. *J.Maltese stud.* 10 (1975), pp. 55-64.

TAYIB, Abdalla Al-. Commentary on the names of Red Sea fishes. *SNR* 53(1972), pp. 182-186.

THELWALL, R.E.W. A linguistic survey in El Fasher secondary school. *SNR* 52(1971), pp. 46-55.

TORRES PALOMO, M.P. Sobre la carta de Abenaboo en árabe granadino. *MEAH* 18-19i(1969-70), pp. 125-128.

TRIMBLE, L.P. Phonemic change and the growth of homophones in Maltese. *J.Fac. Arts Malta* 7(1971), pp. 92-98.

TRIMBLE, L.P. Some linguistic comments on religious terms in Maltese. *J. Maltese stud.* 9(1973), pp. 59-67.

TROUPEAU, G. Un vocabulaire arabe dialectal-éthiopien. *Mélanges Marcel Cohen,* 1970, pp. 333-342.

TSAPIERA, M. The Maronite Arabs in Cyprus: a linguistic discussion. *Actes I. Cong. et. cult. mediterr. d'infl. arabo-berb.,* 1973, pp. 136-139.

TSERETELI, K. The Aramaic dialects of Iraq. *AION* 32(N.S. 22, 1972), pp. 245-250.

TSERETELI, G. The verbal particle m/mi in Bukhara Arabic. *Folia Or.* 12(1970), pp. 291-295

USHAKOV, V.D. Nekotorye voprosy leksikografii arabskikh narodno-razgovornykh yazykov. *NAA* 1972(5), pp. 128-132.

VOCKE, H. Die Beschwerde der 'Addil-Moschee. Eine Satire des jemenitischen Dichters 'Alī Ḥasan al-Ḥafanǧī. *ZDMG* 123(1973), pp. 56-73.

WANSBROUGH, J. A Judeo-Arabic document from Sicily. *BSOAS* 30(1967), pp. 305-313.

WETTINGER, C. Arabo-Berber influences in Malta: onomastic evidence. *Actes I. Cong. et. cult. mediterr. d'infl. arabo-berb.,* 1973, pp. 484-495.

WETTINGER, G. Late medieval Maltese nicknames. *J. Maltese studies* 6 (1971), pp. 34-46.

WISE, H. Concord in spoken Egyptian Arabic. *Archivum ling.* N.S. 3(1972), pp. 7-17

WOIDISCH, M. Zur Funktion des aktiven Partizips im Kairenisch-Arabischen. *ZDMG* 125(1975), pp. 273-293.

See also I. b. 3. Cerqua.

See also V. u. 3. Roth-Laly.

See also VII. d. Aquilina.

See also IX. f. Brouwers

See also XII. f. Teyssier

See also XXVI. c. Goitein.

See also XXXVI. d. Babakhanov

See also XXXVI. d. Cohen.

See also XXXVI. k. Dohaish and Young.

See also XXXVI. l. Correll.

See also XXXVII. l. Boudot-Lamotte.

See also XXXVIII. b. Sadeghi.

XXXVII LITERATURE. ARABIC LITERATURE

a LITERATURE: GENERAL AND COMPARATIVE

ABDEL-HAI, M. Shelley and the Arabs. *J. Arabic lit.* 3(1972), pp. 72-89.

ABDEL-HAMID, Mohammed Samir Oriental influences in English literature from the Middle Ages to the middle of the eighteenth century. *Ann.Fac.Arts Ain Shams* 8 (1963), pp. 1-12.

ANGHELESCU, M. Une vision de la spiritualité arabe à travers les contes roumains d'origine orientale. *Romano-Arabica,* ed. M. Anghelescu, 1974, pp. 55-68.

ARTEMEL, Süheylâ. 'Turkish' imagery in Elisabethan drama. *Rev.nat.lit.* 4i(1973), pp. 82-98.

BABAN, Naman. English writers on the Arab world. *Bull.Fac.Arts Libya* 4(1972), pp. 23-34.

BAUSANI, A. Elementi epici nelle letterature islamiche. *La poesia epica e la sua formazione,* 1970, pp. 759-769.

BONN, C. L'image de la littérature algérienne de langue française auprès de ses lecteurs potentiels, et ce qu'ils attendent. *Annuaire Afrique du Nord* 12 (1973), pp. 233-247.

BOUSQUET, G.H. Goethe et l'Islâm. *SI* 33 (1971), pp. 151-164.

BOYLE, J.A. The Alexander romance in Central Asia. *Zentralasiat. Studien* 9 (1975), pp. 267-273.

BRAGINSKIY, I.S. Leninskiy printzip internatzionalizma v sovetskikh literaturakh narodov Sredney Azii. *NAA* 1973(2), pp. 67-78.

BROMS, H. How does the Middle Eastern literary taste differ from the European? *SO* 44(1972), pp. 94.

CELNAROVÁ, X. Typologische Auswertung einiger europäischer und westasiatischer Rebellengestalten auf Grund der Volksdichtung und deren Bearbeitung in der Kunstliteratur. *Asian and African studies* [Bratislava] 8(1972), pp. 95-162.

CERULLI, E. Conclusiones históricas sobre el "Libro de la escala" y el cococimiento del Islam en Occidente. *And.* 37(1972), pp. 77-86.

DÉJEUX, J. Bibliographie méthodique et critique de la littérature algérienne d'expression française, 1945-1970. *ROMM* 10 (1971), pp. 111-307.

DÉJEUX, J. Littérature maghrébine d'expression française. *Etudes philos. et litt. (Actes du Coll. de Mohammédia)* 5(1971), pp. 119-127.

DÉJEUX, J. Les structures de l'imaginaire dans l'oeuvre de Kateb Yacine. *ROMM* 13-14 (1973), pp. 267-292.

DEKHTYAR, A. Problema ramki teksta v dastanakh urdu. *Voprosy vostochnogo literaturovedeniya i tekstologii,* 1975, pp. 134-143.

DEMIREL, Hamide. The love story of Laylā va Majnūn. *Doğu dilleri* 2ii(1975), pp. 191-202.

DOUTRELANT, J.L. L'orient tragique au XVIIIe siècle. *Rev. des sci. hum.* 146(1972), pp. 283-300.

FÄHNDRICH, H. Literaturwissenschaft und Arabistik. Einzelfall oder Symptom einer "Altertumswissenschaft". *WO* 7(1974), pp. 259-266.

FRANCIS, R.A. À l'écoute d'Andrée Chédid, romancière. *ROMM* 13-14(1973), pp. 343-356.

GABRIELI, F. Ḥasan 'Osmān, dantista egiziano. *Levante* 20iii-iv(1973), pp. 26-28.

GOODY, J. The impact of Islamic writing on the oral cultures of West Africa. *Cah. ét. afr.* 11(no. 43, 1971), pp. 455-466.

HAWARI, Rida. On some oriental sources of English literature in 18th and 19th century England. *Bull. Fac. Arts, Univ. Riyad* 2 (1971-2), pp. 31-59.

HAWARI, Rida. Thackeray's Oriental reading. *Rev. lit. comp.* 48(1974), pp. 114-127.

HINZ, W. Dantes persische Voläufer. *Archäol. Mitt. aus Iran* N.F.4(1971), pp. 117-126.

HORALEK, K. Zur Frage der türkischen Einflüsse in den griechischen Volksmärchen. *Serta Slavica in memoriam A. Schmaus,* 1971, pp. 270-277.

JASIŃSKA, J. Tradycje prozy w literaturze arabskiej. *Przegl.or.* 91(1974), pp. 219-224.

JAVADI, Hasan. James Morier and his Hajji Baba of Ispahan. *Iran Society silver jubilee souvenir* 1944-1969, pp. 163-177.

JAVADI, Hasan. Matthew Arnold's "Sohrab and Rustum" and its Persian original. *Rev.nat.lit.* 2i(1971), pp. 61-73.

JOHNSTONE, T.M. Nasīb and the mansöngur. *J. Arabic lit.* 3(1972), pp. 90-95.

KALESHI, Hasan. Orientalische Einflüsse in den albanischen Volkserzählungen. *Südostforschungen* 31(1972), pp. 267-301.

KATARSKIY, I.M. Vostochnye motivy v angliyskoy literature XIX veka. *NAA* 1974(3), pp. 95-107.

KHAZRADZHI, S.L. al-. Ob odnom paremiologicheskom eksperimente (sopostavlenie russkikh poslovitz i pogovorok s arabskimi, tadzhiksko-persidskimi i angliyskimi). *NAA* 1974 (1), pp. 147-151.

KOKAN, Md. Yousuf. India's contribution to Arabic literature. *Dr. V. Raghavan Shashtyabdapurti felicitation vol.,* 1971, pp. 296-303.

KOLVENBACH, P.H. Analyse de récits. *Travaux et jours* 49(1973), pp. 105-121.

KUNITZSCH, P. *Dodekin* und andere türkisch-arabische Namen in den Chansons de geste. *Z. f. roman. Philol.* 88(1972), pp. 34-44.

LA GRANJA, F. de. Cuentos árabes en "El Sobremesa" de Timoneda. *And* 34(1969), pp. 381-394

LŐRINCZ, L. Epos in Innerasien? *Central Asiatic J.* 17(1973), pp. 176-179.

MIKHAIL, M.N. Images of women in North African literature myth or reality? *AJAS* 3(1975), pp. 37-47.

MOHANDESSI, Manoutchehr. Hedayat and Rilke. *Comparative lit.* 23(1971), pp. 209-219.

MORTIMER, M.P. Algerian poetry of French expression. *African literature today* 6 [1973], pp. 68-78.

NOTERMANS, J. Muhammedaanse elementen in twee abele spelen: Esmoreit en Gloriant. *Rev. belge philol.* 51(1973), pp. 624-642.

OLIVER ASIN, J. Un morisco de Tunis, admirateur de Lope. Étude du MS.S.2 de la collection Gayangos. *Recueil d'études sur les moriscos andalous en Tunisie,* préparé par M. de Epalza et R. Petit, 1973, pp. 205-239.

OLIVER ASIN, J. Le "Quichotte" de 1604. *Recueil d'études sur les moriscos andalous en Tunisie,* préparé par M. de Epalza et R. Petit, 1973, pp. 240-247.

PENELLA, J. Introduction au manuscrit D.565 de la Bibliothèque universitaire de Bologne. *Recueil d'études sur les moriscos andalous en Tunisie,* préparé par M. de Epalza et R. Petit, 1973, pp. 258-263.

PENELLA, J. Littérature morisque en espagnol en Tunisie. *Recueil d'études sur les moriscos andalous en Tunisie,* préparé par M. de Epalza et R. Petit, 1973, pp. 187-198.

PETROVA, L.A. "Arabskaya" gipoteza proiskhozhdeniya provansal'skoy poezii v trudakh ispanskikh arabistov (1930-1960). *Voprosy filol. stran Azii i Afriki* II(1973), pp. 124-131.

POLAK, L. *Tristan* and *Vis and Ramin*. *Romania* 95(1974), pp. 216-234.

ROSE, E. Persian mysticism in Goethe's "West-Östlicher Divan". *Rev.nat.lit.* 2i (1971), pp. 92-111.

RUBIERA MATA, M.J. De nuevo sobre las tres morillas. *And.* 37(1972), pp. 133-143.

RUNDGREN, F. Arabische literatur und orientalische Antike. *Orientalia Suecana* 19-20(1970-71), pp. 81-124

SAMOYLOVICH, A.N. Obshchiy vzglyad na vozniknovenie i razvitie musul'mansko-turetzkikh literaturnykh yazykov v svyazi s razgovornymi narechiyami. *ST* 1973(5), pp. 105-110.

SARNELLI, Cl. L'écrivain hispano-marocain al-Hagari et son "Kitāb Nāṣir al-Dīn". *Recueil d'études sur les moriscos andalous en Tunisie,* préparé par M. de Epalza et R. Petit, 1973, pp. 248-257.

SEFRIOUI, Ahmed. Le romain marocain d'expression française. *Etudes philos. et litt. (Actes du Coll. de Mohammédia)* 5(1971), pp. 107-117.

SELLIN, E. Algerian poetry; poetic values, Mohammed Dib and Kateb Yacine. *J. new Afr. lit. and the arts* 9-10(1971), pp. 451-468.

SEMAAN, Khalil I.H. T.S. Eliot's influence on Arabic poetry and theater. *Comp.lit. studies* 6(1969), pp. 472-489.

SOUTHERN, R.W. Dante and Islam. *Relations between East and West in the Middle Ages,* ed. D. Baker, 1973, pp. 133-145.

STETKEVYCH, J. The Arabic lyrical phenomenon in context. *J. Arabic lit.* 6 (1975), pp. 57-77.

STETKEVYCH, J. The confluence of Arabic and Hebrew literature. *JNES* 32(1973), pp. 216-222.

STRIKA, Vincenzo. Un poeta musulmano Bosniaco: Musa Ćazim Catić. *OM* 52(1972), pp. 594-611.

THOMSON, J. The "Divan" of Goethe. *Rev. nat.lit.* 2i(1971), pp. 112-120.

TYLOCH, W. II Międzynarodowe Sympozjum na temat "Teoretyczne problemy literatur Wschodu". (IIe Symposium International sur "Les Problèmes Théoriques des Littératures Orientales"). *Przeglad Or.* 4(84) (1972), pp. 363-367.

VOLKOVA, Z.N. Znachenie arabskikh kronik dlya opredeleniya genezisa "Pesni o Rolande" (The importance of Arabic chronicles in determining the genesis in the "Chanson de Roland"). *NAA* 1972(4), pp. 140-145.

WALKER, D.H. L'inspiration orientale des *Nourritures terrestres*. *Comparative lit.* 26(1974), pp. 203-219.

WALTERS, J.R. Michel Butor and *The thousand and one nights*. *Neophilologus* 59(1975), pp. 213-222.

YOHANAN, J.D. The fin de siècle cult of Fitzgerald's "Rubaiyat" of Omar Khayyam. *Rev.nat.lit.* 2i(1971), pp. 74-91.

Istoriko-revolyutzionnaya tema v sovetskikh literaturakh narodov Sredney Azii i Kazakhstana. *NAA* 1974(6), pp. 68-81.

See also XII. b. Arnaud.

See also XXXIX. b. Hadidi.

b ARABIC LITERATURE: GENERAL. RHETORIC

ABDEL-RAHMAN, Ibrahim, Islam and poetry. *Ann.Fac.Arts Ain Shams* 10(1967), pp. 223-241.

ABDUL-HAI, M. Translations and the emergence of the language of Arabic romantic poetry (1830-1920); an essay in comparative literature. *Adab: J. Fac. Arts, Khartoum* 2-3(1975), pp. 99-118.

ABU-HAIDAR, Jareer. Maqāmāt literature and the picaresque novel. *J. Arab. lit.* 5 (1974), pp. 1-10.

ABOUL-MAGUID, Mohamed Bahr The Maqāmāt in Arabic and Hebrew literature. *Annals Fac.Arts Ain Shams Univ.* 12(1969), pp 49-53.

ACHÉCHE, Taïeb El-. La Kifāyat al-tālib attribuée à Ḍiyā al-dīn Ibn al-Atīr. *Arabica* 19(1972), pp. 177-189.

BAILEY, C. The narrative context of the Bedouin Qaṣīdah-poem. *Folklore Re earch Center studies* 3(1972), pp. 67-105.

BEESTON, A.F.L. Parallelism in Arabic prose. *J. Arab. lit.* 5(1974), pp. 134-146.

BEN-AMI, Issachar. La qṣida chez les juifs marocains. *Scripta hierososlymitana* 22(1971), pp. 1-17.

BÜRGEL, J.C. "Die beste Dichtung ist die lügenreichste". Wesen und Bedeutung eines literarischen Streites des arabischen Mittelalters im Lichte komparatistischer Betrachtung. *Oriens* 23-24(1974), pp. 7-102.

BÜRGEL, J.C. Klamstwo i prawda w klasycznej poezji muzulmanskiej. *Przegl.or.* 90(1974), pp. 113-129.

BÜRGEL, J. Ch. Lüge und Wahrheit in der klassischen islamischen Dichtung. Ein Beitrag zur Wesensbestimmung der arabischen und persischen Poesie. *Folia Or.* 15(1974), pp. 259-262.

BÜRGEL, J.C. Remarques sur une relation entre la logique aristotélienne et la poésie arabo-persane. *Ve Congrès International d'Arabisants et d'Islamisants. Actes.*, [1970?], pp. 131-143.

FAHNDRICH, H.E. The *Wafayāt al-a'yān* of Ibn Khallikān: a new approach. *JAOS* 93(1973), pp. 432-445.

FANJUL, S. Aspectos técnicos en el mawwāl popular egipcio. *MEAH* 23(1974), pp. 85-112.

FIL'SHTINSKIY, I.M. Tipologicheskie osobennosti arabskoy literatury VII-XII vekov. (Typological limits in Arab literature.) *NAA* 1971(2), pp. 78-88.

FONTAINE, J. Le IX Congrès des écrivains arabes (Tunis, 18-25 mars 1973). *OM* 55 (1975), pp. 49-53.

GABRIELI, F. Religious poetry in early Islam. *Arabic poetry; theory and development*, ed. G.E. von Grunebaum, 1973, pp. 1-17.

GIFFEN, L.A. Love poetry and love theory in medieval Arabic literature. *Arabic poetry; theory and development*, ed. G.E. von Grunebaum, 1973, pp. 107-124.

GORTON, T.J. Arabic influence on the troubadours: documents and directions. *J. Arab. lit.* 5(1974), pp. 11-16.

HEINRICHS, W. Literary theory; the problem of its efficiency. *Arabic poetry; theory and development*, ed. G.E. von Grunebaum, 1973, pp. 18-69.

HEINRICHS, W. Ta'lab's treatise on the foundations of poetry (*Qawā'id aš-ši'r*) reconsidered. *Proc.27th Int.Cong.Or. 1967* (1971), pp. 211-212.

JACOBI, R. Dichtung und Lüge in der arabischen Literaturtheorie. *Der Islam* 49(1972), pp. 85-99.

JOHNSTONE, T.M. The language of poetry in Dhofar. *BSOAS* 35(1972), pp. 1-17

KANAZI, G. Abu Hilal al-'Askari's attitude towards poetry and poets. *J. Semitic stud.* 20(1975), pp. 73-81.

KANAZI, G.J. Organic unity in the Kitāb aṣ-Ṣinā'atayn of Abū Hilāl al-'Askarī. *Semitics* 3(1973), pp. 1-17.

KHOURY, R.G. L'importance de l'Iṣāba d'Ibn Ḥağar al-Asqalānī pour l'étude de la littérature arabe des premiers siècles islamiques vue à travers l'exemple des oeuvres de 'Abdallāh ibn al-Mubārak (118/736-181/797). *SI* 42(1975), pp. 115-145.

LOYA, Arieh. The detribalization of Arabic poetry. *IJMES* 5(1974), pp. 202-215.

LOYA, Arieh. The detribalization of Arab society and its effects on Arabic poetry. *Modern Near East: literature and society*, ed. by C.M. Kortepeter, 1971, pp. 1-17.

LYONS, M.C. The two companions convention. *Islamic philosophy and the classical tradition*, 1972, pp. 225-233.

MACHWE, Prabhakar. Literary movements in India. *India and the Arab World, ed. by S. Maqbul Ahmed*, 1969, pp. 29-31.

NALLINO, M. Gli studi di letteratura araba (età classica e decadenza). *Studi sul Vicino Oriente in Italia*, II, 1971, pp. 141-157.

PELED, Mattityahu. The controversy over concepts of Arabic literary history. *Asian and African stud.* (Israel Or.Soc.) 10(1974-5), pp. 1-23.

PETRAČEK, K. Synchronie a diachronie v systému arabské literatury. (Die Synchronie und die Diachronie im System der arabischen Literatur). *Slovo a Slovesnost* 30(1969), pp. 258-261.

REINERT, B. Probleme der vormongolischen arabisch-persischen Poesiegemeinschaft und ihr Reflex in der Poetik. *Arabic poetry; theory and development*, ed. G.E. von Grunebaum, 1973, pp. 71-105.

RINGGREN, H. The root ṣdq in poetry and the Koran. *Ex orbe religionum. Studia Geo Widengren oblata*, II, 1972, pp. 134-142.

SCHOELER, G. Die Einteilung der Dichtung bei den Arabern. *ZDMG* 123(1973), pp. 9-55.

SIVAN, E. The beginnings of the "Faḍā'il al Quds" literature. *Der Islam* 48 (1971), pp. 100-110.

SIVAN, E. The beginnings of the Fada'il al-Quds literature. *Israel Oriental studies* 1(1971), pp. 263-271.

TAYIB, Abdullah el-. Themes of hospitality in Arabic poetry. *Kano studies* 2(1966), pp. 16-32.

WANSBROUGH, J. A note on Arabic rhetoric. *Lebende Antike: Symposion für Rudolf Sühnel*, edd. H. Meller and H.J. Zimmermann. Berlin, 1967, pp. 55-63.

See also I. b. 3. Gabrieli.

See also XXXIX. a. Reinert.

c PRE-ISLAMIC POETRY

ABU-DEEB, Kamal. Towards a structural analysis of pre-Islamic poetry. *IJMES* 6(1975), pp. 148-184.

ALWAN, Mohammed Bakir. Is Hammad the collector of the Mu'allaqat? *IC* 45(1971), pp. 263-265

BEESTON, A.F.L. The heart of Shanfara. *JSS* 18(1973), pp. 257-258.

DALGLEISH, K. Some aspects of the treatment of emotion in the *Dīwān* of al-A'shā. *J. Arab. lit.* 4(1973), pp. 97-111.

GABRIELI, F. 'Alqama al-Faḥl. *RSO* 47(1972), pp. 59-75.

GABRIELI, F. Elementi epici nell'antica poesia araba. *La poesia epica e la sua formazione,* 1970, pp. 751-758.

GABRIELI, F. La poèsie religieuse de l'ancien Islam. *REI* 41(1973), pp. 7-50.

HEINRICHS, W. Die altarabische Qaṣīde als Dichtkunst. Bemerkungen und Gedanken zu einem neuen Buch. *Islam* 51(1974), pp. 118-124.

KHATIB, Issam al-. The Moallakat in English literature. *Adab al-rafidain* 3(1971), pp. 1-25.

MATTOCK, J.N. Repetition in the poetry of Imru' al-Qays. *Glasgow Univ. Or. Soc. Trans.* 24(1974), pp. 34-50.

MIQUEL, A. Le désert dans la poèsie préislamique: la Mu'allaqa de Labid. *CT* 23 (nos.89-90,1975), pp. 191-211.

MONROE, J.T. Oral composition in pre-Islamic poetry. *J. Arabic lit.* 3(1972), pp. 1-53.

PIOTROVSKIY, M. Tema sud'by v yuzhno-arabskom predanii ob As'ade al-Kamile. *Pal. sb.* 25(88), 1974, pp. 119-128.

PURTZELADZE, N.N. K ponimaniyu odnoy osobennosti semantiki doislamskoy poezii arabov. *Problemy literatur orientalnykh,* 1974, pp. 131-141.

ROMAN, A. A propos des vers des yeux et du regard dans l'oeuvre du poète aveugle Baššār b. Burd. *MUSJ* 46(1970-1), pp. 479-514

TARTLER, G. Versuch einer Interpretation der Qasida von Imru-l-Qais. *Romano-Arabica,* ed. M. Anghelescu, 1974, pp. 69-76.

TREADGOLD, W.T. A verse translation of the *Lāmīyah* of Shanfarā. *J. Arabic lit.* 6(1975), pp. 30-34.

d POETS OF THE TIME OF MUHAMMAD

See also XXXVII. c. Gabrieli.

e UMAYYAD POETRY AND PROSE

PARET, Rudi Die legendare Futūh-Literatur, ein arabisches Volksepos? *La poesia epica e la sua formazione,* 1970, pp. 735-749.

PASTUKHOVA, L.E. Poeticheskaya polemika mezhdu omeyyadskimi panergiristami (po knige pesen al-Isfakhani). *NAA* 1974(4), pp. 103-111.

See also XXXVI. h. Attallah.

f ABBASID LITERATURE

ABU DEEB, Kamal. Al-Jurjānī's classification of *isti'āra* with special reference to Aristotle's classification of Metaphor. *J.Arabic lit.* 2(1971), pp. 48-75.

BEESTON, A.F.L. The genesis of the *Maqāmāt* genre. *J.Arabic lit.* 2(1971), pp. 1-12.

BENCHEIKH, Jamel E. Les secrétaires poètes et animateurs de cénacles aux IIe et IIIe siècles de l'Hégire. Contribution à l'analyse d'une production poétique. *JA* 263(1975), pp. 264-315.

BERGÉ, M. Genèse et fortune du *Kitāb al-Imtā' wa l-mu'anasa* d'Abū Ḥayyān al-Tawḥīdī (m.en 414/1023). *BEO* 25(1972), pp. 97-104.

BERGÉ, M. Justification d'un autodafé de livres. Lettre d'Abū Ḥayyān al-Tawḥīdī au Qāḍī Abū Sahl 'Alī ibn Muḥammad. Introduction et traduction [et texte]. *Ann. Islamologiques* 9(1970), pp. 65-85.

BERGÉ, M. Une profession de foi politico-religieuse sous les apparences d'une pièce d'archive: la Riwāyat al-Saqīfa d'Abū Ḥayyān al-Tawḥīdī. *Ann.Islamologiques* 9 (1970), pp. 87-95.

BERGÉ, M. Structure et signification du *Kitāb al-Baṣā'ir wa l-dahā'ir* d'Abū Ḥayyān al-Tawhīdī (m.414/1023). *Ann. Islamologiques* 10(1972), pp. 53-62.

BONEBAKKER, S.A. Ibn Abi'l-Isba''s text of the kitāb al-badī' of Ibn al-Mu'tazz. *In memoriam S.M. Stern* (Israel Or. studies, II, 1972), pp. 83-91.

BONEBAKKER, S.A. Poets and critics in the third century A.H. *Logic in classical Islamic culture,* ed. by G.E. von Grunebaum, 1970, pp. 85-111.

BORISOV, V.M., DOLININA, A.A. *Makamy* al-Khariri i prinzipy ikh Khudozhestvennogo perevoda. (The Makamas of al-Khariri: principles of poetic translation. *NAA* 1972(2), pp. 113-122

BOULLATA, Issa J. The beleaguered unicorn: a study of Tawfīq Ṣāyigh. *J. Arab. lit.* 4 (1973), pp. 69-93.

BOUYAHIA, Chedly. Le patriotisme militant d'un poète arabo-sicilien des XIème-XIIème siècles, Ibn Ḥamdîs (1055-1132/447-527). *Actes I. Cong. et. cult. mediterr. d'infl. arabo-berb.,* 1973, pp. 199-202.

DAGORN, R. L'histoire d'al-Kindî, extraite du Kitāb al-Buhalā' d'al-Ǧāḥiẓ. [With Arabic text.] *IBLA* 38(no.136, 1975), pp. 281-298.

DUTT, Chinmoy. Contribution of Bengal to Arabic and Persian literature in the Turko-Afghan period (A.D. 1203-1538). *Iran Society silver jubilee souvenir* 1944-1969, pp. 81-104.

EBIED, R.Y. and YOUNG, M.J.L. Shams al-Dīn al-Jazarī and his *al-Maqāmāt al-zayniyyah. Ann. Leeds Univ. Or. Soc.* 7(1969-73), pp. 54-60.

EBIED, R.Y., YOUNG, M.J.L. Some verses in praise of al-Hariri. *JSS* 19(1974), pp. 76-81.

FLEISCHER, E. An overlooked fragment of the translation by Yehudah al-Ḥarizi of the Maqāmas of al-Ḥariri. *J. Jewish studies* 24(1973), pp. 179-184.

FOUCHÉCOUR, C.H. de, Ḥadāyeq al-Siyar, un miroir des princes de la cour de Qonya au VIIe-XIIIe siècle. *Stud. iranica* 1(1972), pp. 219-228.

FRIEDMANN, Y. Some notes on the *Luzumiyyat* of al-Ma'arri. *Israel Oriental studies* 1 (1971), pp. 257-262.

GARCÍA GÓMEZ, E. Sobre un verso de Mutanabbi con dos refranos, uno de ellos pasado al español. *And.* 38(1973), pp. 187-194.

ISSAWI, C. Al-Mutanabbi in Egypt (957-962). *Medieval and Middle Eastern studies ... A. S. Atiya* 1972, pp. 236-239.

JACOBI, R. Ibn al-Mu'tazz: Dair 'Abdūn. A structural analysis. *J. Arabic lit.* 6 (1975), pp. 35-56.

KAFRAWY, M.A.A. el and LATHAM, J.D. Perspective of Abū al-'Atāhiya. *IQ* 17 (1973), pp. 160-176.

KLEIN-FRANKE, F. The Ḥamāsa of Abū Tammām. *J.Arabic lit.* 2(1971), pp. 13-36.

KLEIN-FRANKE, F. The Ḥamāsa of Abū Tammām II. *J. Arabic lit.* 3(1972), pp. 142-178.

MARSHALL, D.R. An Arab humorist - Al-Jāhiz and 'The Book of Misers'. *J. Fac. Arts Malta* 4 (1970), pp. 77-97.

MUSAEV, O. Antologiya al-Bakharzi "Dumyat al-kasr" kak pamyatnik araboyazychnoy literatury Sredney Azii. *Voprosy vostochnogo literaturovedeniya i tekstologii*, 1975, pp. 17-31.

NOURI, Moufid. Abū Tammām: biography and works. *Adab al-rafidain* 3(1971), pp. 26-37.

PAULINY, J. Literarischer Charakter des Werkes Kisā'īs *Kitāb qisas al-anbiyā. Zborník filoz Fak. Univ. Komenského: Graecolatina et orientalia* 3(1971), pp. 107-124.

PELLAT, Ch. Al-Ǧāḥiẓ et les peuples du sous-continent. *Orientalia Hispanica* I, 1974, pp. 542-550.

PELLAT, Ch. Encore deux vers de Ma'dān al-Šumayṭī. *Arabica* 22(1975), pp. 300-302.

POONAWALA, Ismail K. The church of Saint George at Urfa (Edessa). *BSOAS* 36(1973), pp. 109-115.

RĀĠIB, Yūsuf. L'auteur de *L'Egypte de Murtadi fils du Gaphiphe. Arabica* 21(1974), pp. 203-209.

RAHMANI, Aftab Ahmad. The life and works of Ibn Hajar al-ʿAsqalani. *IC* 46(1972), pp. 75-81

REIG, D. Le *Ṣayd al-Ḫāṭir* d'Abū l-Faraǧ ibn al-Ǧawzī. *SI* 34(1971), pp. 89-123

ROMAN, A. Les thèmes de l'oeuvre de Baššār inspirée par ʿAbda. *BEO* 24(1971), pp. 157-226.

RUIZ FIGUEROA, M. Dos narraciones de Al Yahiz, prosista clásico del siglo IX. *Estudios orientales* 23(8iii, 1973), pp. 278-285.

SAMARRAI, Qasim al-. Some biographical notes on al-Tha'â-libî. *Bibl.Or.* 32(1975), pp. 175-186.

SHUYSKIY, S. Abu Nuvas v svode zhizneopisaniy Ibn Khallikana. *Voprosy vostochnogo literaturovedeniya i tekstologii*, 1975, pp. 39-60.

SKARZYNSKA-BOCHENSKA, K. Les ornements du style selon la conception d'al-Ǧāḥiẓ. *RO* 36(1973), pp. 5-46.

TROUPEAU, G. Les couvents chrétiens dans la littérature arabe. *Nouvelle Rev. du Caire* 1(1975), pp. 265-279.

VAN ESS, J. Neue Verse des Maʿdān aš-Šumaitī. *Der Islam* 47(1971), pp. 245-251.

VERITY, A.C.F. Two poems of Abū'l-ʿAlā al-Maʿarrī. *J.Arabic lit.* 2(1971), pp. 37-47.

WEIL, J.W. Epigramme auf Musikerinnen in der Gedichtsammlung. *Alf ǧāriya wa-ǧāriya* (Teil I). *RO* 37ii(1975), pp. 7-12.

Al-Ma'arrī: "peace on earth?". *J. Arab. lit.* 4(1973), pp. 57-68.

See also I. c. 5. Saleh

See also I. c. 6. Maʿarri.

See also IV. c. 10. Bachmann

See also X. f. Strika.

See also XIV. e. Belfiore.

See also XXXVI. d. Corriente.

See also XXXVI. h. Pellat.

g POST-CLASSICAL LITERATURE

DELANQUE, G. "L'Epître des huit mots" du cheikh Husayn al-Marṣafī (Analyse). *Annales Islamologiques* 5(1963), pp. 1-30.

HEINRICHS, W. "Manierismus" in der arabischen Literatur. *Islamwissenschaftliche Abhandlungen F. Meier*, 1974, pp. 118-128.

HILA, Muhammad al-Habib al-. L'élément andalou en Tunisie, selon le "Hulal al-sundusiyya" d'al-Sarrāg al-Andalusī. *Recueil d'études sur les moriscos andalous en Tunisie*, préparé par M. de Epalza et R. Petit, 1973, pp. 264-266.

HUDA, M.Z. Jamālī. The poet of Lūdīs and Mughals. *J. Asiatic Soc. Pakistan* 14(1969), pp. 21-49.

QAMAR UDDIN. Amir Khusrau and his *Pandnama:* lessons in socio-political morality. *Ind. econ. soc. hist. rev.* 9(1972), pp. 349-366.

See also II. c. 7. Pellat

See also XLI. a. Demirel.

h ARABIC LITERATURE IN SPAIN

ARMISTEAD, S.G. A Mozarabic *ḫarǧa* and a Provencal refrain. *Hispanic R.* 41(1973), pp. 416-417.

BOUROUIBA, Rachid. La poésie à l'époque de Abd al-Mu'min. *Rev. hist. civ. Maghreb* 11(1974), pp. 7-15.

CABANELAS, D. A propósito de "Todo Ben Quzman". *MEAH* 22(1973), pp. 163-171.

CONTINENTE, J.M. Abū Marwān al-Ŷazīrī, poeta ʿāmirí. *And* 34(1969), pp. 123-141.

CONTINENTE FERRER, J.M. Datos bibliográficos sobre algunos poetas cordobeses emigrados de al-Andalus durante la dominación Almohade. *al-Andalus* 39 (1974), pp. 455-464.

CONTINENTE FERRER, J.M. El "Kitāb al-sihr wa-l-šiʿr" de Ibn al-Jatīb (libro de la magia y de la poesía). *And.* 38(1973), pp. 393-414.

CONTINENTE, J.M. Notas sobre la poesía amorosa de Ibn ʿAbd Rabbihi. *And.* 35(1970), pp. 355-380.

COROMINAS, J. El nuevo Abencuzmán. *And.* 36 (1971), pp. 241-254.

COWELL, D.C. Ibn 'Abd Rabbihi and his *ghazal* verse. *J. Arab. lit.* 5(1974), pp. 72-82.

DANECKI, J. Twórczość poetycka Ibn Chafadzy. *Przeglad Or.* 1973(1, no.85), pp. 19-27.

FORNEAS, J.M. el "Barnāmaŷ" de Muhammad Ibn Ŷabir al- Wādī Āšī. *al-Andalus* 37 (1973), pp. 1-67; 39(1974), pp. 301-361.

FORNÉAS, J.M. Dos rectificaciones. I. Un inexistente Muḥammad ibn Aḥmad ibn Ḥarb. II. El *Fihrist* del MS. Escurialense 1160/2 no es obra de Ibn Sayyid al-Nās. *MEAH* 24(1975), pp. 99-105.

GALMÉS DE FUENTES, A. Epica árabe y epica castellana. (Problema critico de sus posibles relaciones) *La poesia epica e la sua formazione,* 1970, pp. 195-261.

GARCÍA GOMEZ, E. Hacia un "refranero" arábigoandaluz. I. Los refranes de Ibn Hišām Lajmī. *And.* 35(1970), pp. 1-68.

GARCÍA GÓMEZ, E. Hacia un "Refranero" arábigoandaluz. II: el refranero de Ibn ʿĀsim en el MS. londinense. *And.* 35(1970), pp. 241-314.

GARCÍA GÓMEZ, E. Hacia un "refranero" arábigoandaluz. III: los refranes poéticos de Ben Šaraf (texto inédito). *And.* 36 (1971), pp. 255-328.

GARCÍA GÓMEZ, E. Introducción a una métrica de Ben Quzmān. *And.* 33 (1968), pp. 241-290.

GARCIA GOMEZ, E. Métrica de la moaxaja y metrica española. *al-Andalus* 39 (1974), pp. 1-256.

GARCÍA GÓMEZ, E.; GRANJA, F. de la. Muḥammad ben Mas'ūd, poeta herbolario de comienzos del s. XI, vago predecesor de Ben Quzmān. *And.* 37(1972), pp. 405-443.

GARCÍA GÓMEZ, E. Un poema paremiológico de Hilli (s. XIV) en "kān wa-kān" con unas observaciones sobre esta forma poética. *And.* 36(1971), pp. 329-372.

GARCÍA GÓMEZ, E. Romancismos interesantes en una Moaxaja sobre Málaga. *And.* 36(1971), pp. 63-70.

GARCÍA GÓMEZ, E. Sobre algunos pasajes difíciles de Ben Quzmān. *And.* 38(1973), pp. 249-318.

GARCÍA GÓMEZ, E. Sobre una edición oriental de "Ŷayš al-tawšīḥ" de Ibn al-Jatīb. *And* 34(1969), pp. 205-216.

GIBERT, S. Algunas curiosidades de la poesía arábigoandaluza. (Versos correlativos, versos con eco, versos concatenados en el dīwān de un poeta de siglo XIV). *And.* 33 (1968), pp. 95-122.

GIBERT, S. Sobre el "Todo Ben Quzmān" de García Gómez. *And.* 37(1972), pp. 233-248.

GORTON, T.J. The metre of Ibn Quzmān: a 'classical' approach. *J. Arabic lit.* 6 (1975), pp. 1-29.

GRANJA, F. de la. Del perro de Olías y otros perros. *And.* 37(1972), pp. 463-482.

GRANJA, F. de la. Milagros españoles en una obra polémica musulmana (El "Kitāb Maqāmīʿ al-ṣulbān" del Jazraŷī). *And.* 33 (1968), pp. 311-365.

GRANJA, F. de la. Tres cuentos españoles de origen árabe. *And.* 33 (1968), pp. 123-141.

HARVEY, L.P. The *alfaquí* in *La dança general de la muerte*. *Hispanic R.* 41 (1973), pp. 498-510.

HATHAWAY, R.L. The art of the epic epithets in the "Cantar de mio Cid". *Hispanic R.* 42(1974), pp. 311-321.

HOENERBACH, W. La metáfora astral en las literaturas árabe y española. *MEAH* 16-17 (1967-8), pp. 147-163.

HOENERBACH, W. Zur Charakteristik Wallādas, der Geliebten Ibn Zaidūns. *WI* 13 (1971), pp. 20-25.

JIMÉNEZ MATA, C. A propósito del *'ayā'ib* del Olivo Maravilloso y su versión cristiana en el milagro de San Torcuato. *Cuadernos de historia del Islam, ser. misc.: Islamica occidentalia* 1(1971), pp. 97-108.

KROTKOFF, G. The Arabic line in the *Canzoniero de Baena*. *Hispanic R.* 42 (1974), pp. 427-429.

MAJED, Jaafar. Abū-l-Baqā' al-Rundī (601-684/1204-1285). *Actas II Col. hisp.-tunec. estud. hist.*, 1973, pp. 261-286.

MAKKI, Mahmud A. La poesía árabe en América Latina. *Estudios orientales* 5 (1970), no. 12, pp. 22-36.

MANZANARES DE CIRRE, M. Nota sobre la aljamía. *Anuario estud.med.* 5(1968), pp. 479-481.

MANZANARES DE CIRRE, M. El otro mundo en la literatura aljamiado-morisca. *Hispanic R.* 41(1973), pp. 599-608.

MONROE, J.T. The historical *Arjūza* of ibn 'Abd Rabbihi, a tenth century Hispano-Arabic epic poem. *JAOS* 91(1971), pp. 67-95.

MONROE, J.T. Hispano-Arabic poetry during the Caliphate of Cordoba: theory and practice. *Arabic poetry; theory and development*, ed. G.E. von Grunebaum, 1973, pp. 125-154.

MONROE, J.T. La poesía hispanoárabe durante el califato de Córdoba: teoría y práctica. *Estudios orientales* 6ii(no. 16, 1971), pp. 113-151.

MONROE, J.T. Two new bilingual "ḫarǧas" (Arabic and Romance in Arabic "Muwaššaḥs"). *Hispanic R.* 42(1974), pp. 243-264.

NEMAH, H. Andalusian *maqāmāt*. *J. Arab lit.* 5(1974), pp. 83-92.

RAMIREZ CALVENTE, A. Jarchas, moaxajas, zejeles. *al-Andalus* 39(1974), pp. 273-299.

RIZZITANO, Umberto. Abū'l-Ḥasan 'Ali B. Abd Ar-Raḥmān Aṣ-Ṣiqilli detto "Al-Ballānūbī" (Sec. V/XI). *Ann.Fac.Arts Ain Shams* 5(1959), pp. 45-51.

RUBIERA MATA, M.J. La poesia cinegética árabe. *Orientalia Hispanica* I, 1974, pp. 566-573.

SANTIAGO SIMÓN, E. de. Unos versos satíricos de al-Sumaysir contra Bādis b. Ḥabūs de Granada. *MEAH* 24(1975), pp. 115-118.

SCHEINDLIN, R.P. Poetic structure in Arabic: three poems by al-Mu'tamid Ibn 'Abbād. *Humaniora Islamica* 1(1973), pp. 173-186.

SINGER, H.R. Morisken als Übersetzer. *FAS. Univ.Mainz in Germersheim, Reihe A, Band 1 (Fest.R.Brummer)*, pp. 37-49.

SOBḤ, Maḥmūd. La poesía amorosa arábigo-andaluza. *RIEI Madrid* 16(1971), pp. 71-109.

SOLA-SOLE, J.M. Una composición bilingüe hispano-árabe en un cancionero catalán del siglo XV. *Hispanic R.* 40(1972), pp. 386-389.

TERÉS, E. La epístola sobre el canto con música instrumental, de Ibn Ḥazm de Córdoba. *And.* 36(1971), pp. 203-214.

WALSH, J.K. Notes on the Arabisms in Corominas' "DCELC". *Hispanic R.* 42 (1974), pp. 323-331.

See also V. c. *Spain*. Rubiera Mata.

See also VII. d. García Gómez.

See also XXXVII. 1. Barbot.

i LEGENDS AND STORIES

ABEL, A. Formation et constitution du Roman d'Antar. *La poesia epica e la sua formazione*, 1970, pp. 717-733.

AMBROS, A.A., WEIL, J.W. 22 Rätsel-Epigramme aus der Gedichtsammlung Alf ǧariya wa-ǧariya. *Orientalia Hispanica* I, 1974, pp. 20-32.

BACHMANN, P. Muḥammad 'Azīz al-Ḥababī: al-'Aḍḍ 'alā l-ḥadīd -- sechs neue marokkanische Erzählungen. *XVIII. Deutscher Orientalistentag 1972: Vorträge*, pp. 115-123.

BROCKWAY, D. The MacDonald collection of Arabian nights: a bibliography. *MW* 61 (1971), pp. 256-266; 63(1973), pp. 185-205; 64(1974), pp. 16-32.

CERULLI, E. La regina di Sicilia e la regina Saba in una tradizione dell'Egitto medievale. *Athenaeum* 47(1969), pp. 84-92.

CHAPOUTOT-REMADI, Mounira. L'image de la femme dans Kalilah wa Dimnah. *CT* 23(nos. 91-92, 1975), pp. 17-39.

COLETTI, A. Quesito e implorazione di Mokbel Al Issa. Traduzione. *Levante* 19iv(1972).

CONNELLY, B. The structure of four Banī Hilāl tales: prolegomena to the study of *sira* literature. *J. Arab. lit.* 4(1973), pp. 18-47.

DANKOFF, R. The Alexander romance in the Dīwān lughāt at-Turk. *Humaniora Islamica* 1(1973), pp. 233-244.

DESTRÉE, A. Quelques réflexions sur le héros des récits apocalyptiques persans et sur le mythe de la ville de cuivre. *La Persia nel medievo*, 1971, pp. 639-654

EBIED, R.Y. and YOUNG, M.J.L. An unknown Arabic poem on Joseph and his brethren. *JRAS* 1974, pp. 2-7.

GAÁL, E. Aladdin and the wonderful lamp. *Acta Or. Acad. Sci. Hung.* 27(1973), pp. 291-300.

GERRESCH, Cl. Un récit des Mille et une nuits: Tawaddud. Petite encyclopédie de l'Islam médiéval. *Bull. IFAN* 35(1973), pp. 57-175.

GIL, R. Notas sobre la personalidad del héroe y del antihéroe en la narración maravillosa del Occidente árabe. *Orientalia Hispanica* I, 1974, pp. 320-330.

HAMORI, A. An allegory from the 'Arabian nights': the city of brass. *BSOAS* 34 (1971), pp. 9-19.

HEMMERDINGER, B. Saint Jean Damascène, Barlaam et Joasaph: l'intermédiaire arabe. *Byz. Zeits.* 64 (1971), pp. 35-36.

KNIPP, C. The *Arabian nights* in England: Galland's translation and its successors. *J. Arab. lit.* 5(1974), pp. 44-54.

KOVAL'SKA, M. Zamechaniya o strukture "Puteshestviy Sindbada". *Problemy literatur orientalnykh,* 1974, pp. 109-113.

KRSTIĆ, N. Zajednički motivi u *Hiljadu i jednoj noći* i u Vukovoj zbirci narodnih pripovedaka i pesama. *Prilozi za or. filol.* 18-19(1968-9), pp. 121-204.

LA GRANJA, F. de. El castigo del galán. (Origen árabe de un cuento de Luis Zapata). *And* 34(1969), pp. 229-243.

LANG, D.M. Oriental materials on the Georgian "Balavariani". *Bedi Kartlisa* 28 (1971), pp. 106-121.

LEBEDEV, V.V. Sbornik arabskikh izrecheniy VIII - X vv. v karaimskoy rukopisi. *Pal. sb.* 25(88), 1974, pp. 157-161.

LEBEDEV, V.V. Sredy yuzhnoarabskoy fol'klornoy traditzii v skazkakh "1001 nochi". (Traces of Southern Arabian folklore tradition in the 1001 nights.) *NAA* 1973(1), pp. 102-113.

NEGRYA, L.V. Dva predaniya iz sbornika "Ayyam al-arab". *NAA* 1975(4), pp. 149-155.

OLIVERIUS, J. Themen und Motiven im arabischen Volksbuch von Zir Sālim. *Arch. or.* 39 (1971), pp. 129-145.

ONAEVA, D. K kharakteristike struktury "Sirat Bani Khilal...". *Voprosy vostochnogo literaturovedeniya i tekstologii,* 1975, pp. 3-16.

PAULINY, J. Buḫtnaṣṣars Feldzug gegen die Araber. *Asian and African studies* [Bratislava] 8(1972), pp. 91-94.

PAULINY, J. Islamische Legende über Buḫtnaṣṣar (Nebukadnezar). *Graecolatina et Orientalia* 4(1972), pp. 161-183.

PAULINY, J. Islamische Legende über ǧirǧīs (St. Georg). *Asian and African studies* [Bratislava] 7(1971), pp. 79-88.

PAULINY, J. Kisā'ī und sein Werk Kitāb 'Aǧā'ib al-malakūt. Untersuchungen zur arabischen religiösen Volksliteratur. *Graecolatina et Orientalia* 6(1974), pp. 157-189.

PAULINY, J. 'Ūǧ ibn 'Anāq, ein sagenhafter Riese. Untersuchungen zu den islamischen Riesengeschichten. *Graecolatina et Orientalia* 5(1973), pp. 249-268.

PAULINY, J. Ein unbekanntes Autograph "Qiṣaṣ al-anbiyā'" von Aḥmad ibn Abī 'Udhayba. *Asian and African studies* [Bratislava] 5(1969), pp. 71-76; 6(1970), pp. 87-91.

PETRÁČEK, K. Die Poesie als Kriterium des arabischen "Volksromans". *Oriens* 23-24 (1974), pp. 301-305.

PIOTROVSKIY, M. Tema sudby v yuzhnoarabskom predanii ob As'ade al-Kamile. (The theme of fate in the South Arabian legend of As'd al-Kāmil.) *Palestinskiy sbornik* 25(88, 1974), pp. 119-128.

SCHÜTZINGER, H. Die Schelmengeschichten in Tausenundeiner Nacht als Ausdruck der ägyptischen Volksmeinung. *Rhein. Jhb. Volkskunde* 21(1973?), pp. 200-215.

SOUKA, F. Les précurseurs de La Fontaine dans la littérature arabe. *Ann.Fac.Arts Ain Shams* 10(1967), pp. 257-262.

STROHMAIER, G. Diogenesanekdoten auf Papyrus und in arabischen Gnomologien. *Archiv f. Papyrusforsch.* 22-23(1974), pp. 285-288.

TERÉS, E. Poetas hispanoárabes en la obra "Al-Muḥammadūn min al-šu'arā'" de al-Qifṭī. *And* 34(1969), pp. 217-228.

TRAINI, R. Una storia d'amore "yemenica". *OM* 54(1974), pp. 312-327.

See also V. u. 3. Bencheneb.

See also XXXVII. a. Boyle.

See also XXXVII. a. Walters.

j TRANSLATIONS

AZIZ, Yowell Y. Some pitfalls in translation. *Adab al-rafidain* 2(1971), pp. 15-41.

BACHMANN, P. ʿAbd al-Ġaffār Mikkāwī traducteur et prosateur égyptien contemporain. *Ve Congrès International d'Arabisants et d'Islamisants. Actes.,* [1970?], pp. 63-73.

BADAWI, M.M. Modern Arabic poetry [translations by M.M. Badawi] *J.Arabic lit.* 2(1971), pp. 98-103.

BENCHENEB, Rachid. Une adaptation algérienne de l'Avare. *ROMM* 13-14(1973), pp. 87-95.

DARWICHE, Mahmoud, Poèmes, traduits par Najah Sleiman. *Travaux et jours* 40 (1971), pp. 17-29.

DOLININA, A.A. Arabskiy perevod "Kreytzerovoy sonaty" L.N. Tolstogo (Kair, 1904). *Voprosy filol. stran Azii i Afriki* II(1973), pp. 116-123.

EBIED, R.Y. and YOUNG, M.J.L. Two decades of translation into Arabic. *BSMES bull.* 1(1974-5), pp. 40-46.

GHANEM, G. Poèmes, traduits par André Roman. *Travaux et jours* 40(1971), pp. 31-37.

GIFFEN, L. Islamic literature in translation. *MESA Bull.* 6ii(1972), pp. 37-43

KANE, T.L. Arabic translations into Amharic. *BSOAS* 37(1974), pp. 608-627.

MOCK, C.C. Readability tests for Arabic. *Technical papers for the Bible translator* 25i(1974), pp. 117-131.

PULLICINO, G.C. Due recensioni su un poemetto di Dun Karm nel 1920. *J.Fac.Arts, Royal Univ.Malta* 5i(1972), pp. 25-33

VAN RIET, S. Traductions arabo-latines et informatique. *Ve Congrès International d'Arabisants et d'Islamisants. Actes.*, [1970?], pp. 473-487.

See also VI. b. Takács.

See also XXXVII. h. Singer.

See also XXXVII. l. Khoury.

See also XXXIX. e. Sahsarami.

l MODERN ARABIC LITERATURE

'ABD AL-HALIM, M.A.S. Al-Sayyāb - a study of his poetry. *Studies in Arabic literature*, ed. R.C. Ostle, 1975, pp. 69-85.

ABDEL-HAI, M. Night and silence. Experience and language in romanticism and mysticism. *J. Arabic lit.* 6(1975), pp. 107-124.

ABDUL JABBAR, Ahmed. "Smarrimento". Traduzione di A. Coletti. *Levante* 20ii(1973), pp. 35-36.

ABDEL-MALEK, Zaki N. The influence of diglossia on the novels of Yuusif al-Sibaa'i. *J. Arabic lit.* 3(1972), pp. 132-141.

ABD as-SABUR, Salah. Wiersze (z arabskiego przełożyła Krystyna Skarżyńska-Bocheńska) (les Poèmes, traduit de l'arabe par Krystyna Skarżyńska-Bocheńska). *Przeglad or.* 1(81, 1972), pp. 43-52

ABOU-SAIF, L. Najīb al-Rīḥānī: from buffoonery to social comedy. *J.Arab. lit.* 4(1973), pp. 1-17.

AGREDA, F. de. Muhammad Ibrāhīm Bū 'Allū y la narrativa contemporanea en Marruecos. *Orientalia Hispanica* I, 1974, pp. 1-10.

ALLEN, R.M.A. "Mirrors" by Najīb Maḥfūẓ. *MW* 62(1972), pp. 115-125; 63(1973), pp. 15-27.

ALLEN, R. Poetry and poetic criticism at the turn of the century. *Studies in Arabic literature*, ed. R.C. Ostle, 1975, pp. 1-17.

ALLEN, R. Some new al-Muwailiḥī materials or the unpublished *Ḥadīth 'Isā ibn Hishām*. *Humaniora Islamica* 2(1974), pp. 139-180.

ALOUCHE, R. L'image de la femme à travers le roman libanais. *Travaux et jours* 47 (1973), pp. 73-90.

ALWAN, Mohammed Bakir. A bibliography of modern Arabic fiction in English. *MEJ* 26(1972), pp. 195-200.

ALWAN, M. Bakir, STRUNK, W.T. Ta'rīh ḥiṣār al-ifranǧ li-'akka l-maḥrūsa wa-ḥuṣūl al-naṣr 'alayhim by Muḥammad Budayr Effendi translated and edited. *Arabica* 20(1973), pp. 246-260.

AMALDI, D. Nagib Mahfuz e il realismo. *OM* 55(1975), pp. 196-199.

AMALDI, D. *Zuqāq al-midaqq* di Nagīb Maḥfūẓ *OM* 54(1974), pp. 164-167.

'AWAḌ, L. Problems of the Egyptian theatre. *Studies in Arabic literature*, ed. R.C. Ostle, 1975, pp. 179-193.

AWIT, H. Un poète et son langage. *Travaux et jours* 55(1975), pp. 69-79.

BACHMANN, P. Muhammad 'Azīz al-Ḥabābī: al'Aḍḍ 'alā l-ḥadīd -- sechs neue marokkanische Erzählungen. *XVIII. Deutscher Orientalistentag* 1972, pp. 115-123.

BADAWI, M.M. Commitment in contemporary Arabic literature. *Cah. d'hist. mondiale* 14(1972), pp. 858-879.

BADAWI, M.M. Convention and revolt in modern Arabic poetry. *Arabic poetry; theory and development*, ed. G.E. von Grunebaum, 1973, pp. 181-208.

BADAWI, M.M. Al-hilāl [of Shawqī, with a translation and critical appreciation by M.M. Badawi, and three first impressions of the poem by other readers]. *J.Arabic lit.* 2(1971), pp. 127-142.

BADAWI, M.M. Islam in modern Egyptian literature. *J.Arabic lit.* 2(1971), pp. 154-177.

BADAWI, M.M. Al-Māzinī the novelist. *J. Arab. lit.* 4(1973), pp. 112-145.

BADAWI, M.M. On al-Tijani the Sudanese poet. *J. Arabic lit.* 6(1975), pp. 125-129.

BADAWI, M.N. Shukrī the poet - a reconsideration. *Studies in Arabic literature*, ed. R.C. Ostle, 1975, pp. 18-33.

BADAWI, M.M. Ten modern Arabic poems. Tr. *J. Arabic lit.* 6(1975), pp. 130-139.

BALDISSERA, E. Cantori siriani della guerra di *Tishrin*. *OM* 54(1974), pp. 180-186

BALDISERRA, E. Poesia d'occasione in Soleimān al-'Isā. *OM* 55(1975), pp. 200-207.

BAMIEH, Aida. Literature and ideology: early Arabic short fiction in Algeria. *Ufahamu* 4i(1973), pp. 93-103.

BARAKAT, Halīm. Arabic novels and social transformation. *Studies in Arabic literature*, ed. R.C. Ostle, 1975, pp. 126-139.

BARBOT, M. Notes lexicographiques sur les orfèvres et bijoutiers de Damas. *ROMM* 13-14(1973), pp. 67-74.

BARBOT, M. Notes lexicographiques sur les orfèvres et bijoutiers de Damas (texte révisé). *Arabica* 21(1974), pp. 72-83.

BEN ALHOUSSEINI. Aperçu sur la poésie maure de l'Azaouad (région de Tombouctou). *Etudes maliennes* 9(1974), pp. 19-43.

BENNANI, Badreddine. Two Palestinian poems. Mu'ine Bessissou, Palestine. *J. Arab. lit.* 5(1974), pp. 129-133.

BENNENI, B.M. My beloved rises from her sleep. Mahmoud Darweesh: 1942- . Tr. *J. Arabic lit.* 6(1975), pp. 101-106.

BOUDOT-LAMOTTE, A. Des šawqiyyāt en arabe dialectal. *Arabica* 20(1973), pp. 225-245.

BOULLATA, Issa J. The poetic technique of Badr Shākir al-Sayyāb (1926-1964). *J.Arabic lit.* 2(1971), pp. 104-115.

BRETEAU, C.H. et GALLEY, M. Littérature populaire et société. *Annuaire Afrique du Nord* 12(1973), pp. 265-271.

CACHIA, P. 'Antar and Juliette. A short story by Yahyā Haqqī. Translated. *J. Arab. lit.* 4(1973), pp. 146-156.

CACHIA, P. A god in spite of himself [by Fathī Raḍwān]. Translated. *J. Arab. lit.* 5(1974), pp. 108-126.

CACHIA, P. In the Ladies' compartment. A short story by Rashād Rushdī, translated. *J.Arabic lit.* 2(1971), pp. 92-97.

CACHIA, P.J. Social values reflected in Egyptian popular ballads. *Studies in Arabic literature*, ed. R.C. Ostle, 1975, pp. 86-98.

CACHIA, P. Themes related to Christianity and Judaism in modern Egyptian drama and fiction. *J.Arabic lit.* 2(1971), pp. 178-194.

CAMERA D'AFFLITTO, I. Una novella di Fu'ad Tekerli. *OM* 54(1974), pp. 197-203.

CANOVA, G. Due poetesse: Fadwà Ṭūqān e Salmà 'l-Khaḍrā' al-Ǧayyūsi. *OM* 53(1973), pp. 876-893.

CANOVA, G. Nizār Qabbānī: "la mia storia con la poesia". *OM* 54(1974), pp. 204-213.

CANOVA, G. Nizār Qabbānī: poesie d'amore e di lotta. *OM* 52(1972), pp. 451-466.

CANOVA, G. La poesia della Resistenza palestinese. *OM* 51(1971), pp. 583-630

CECCATO, R.D. Una casa libanese. [Extract from a work by Mikha'il Nu'aymah.] *Annali Fac. Ling. Lett. stran. di Ca' Foscari (serie orientale)* 3(1972), pp. 155-161.

CERBELLA, G. La vita beduina nella poesia dell'emiro 'Abd el-Qāder. *OM* 54(1974), pp. 28-32.

CHARTIER, M. 'Abd al-Rahmân al-Sharqâwî interprète de la révolte des opprimés. *IBLA* 38,no.135(1975), pp. 1-31.

CHEHATA, Abdel Moneim. Les influences étrangères sur la trilogie de Maḥfūẓ. *Arabica* 22(1975), pp. 280-291.

CHIAUZZI, G. La Tâgza di ʿIsà. *Levante* 20ii(1973), pp. 29-34.

CHUKOV, B.V. Irakskaya khudozhestvennaya proza i russkaya literatura. *NAA* 1975 (6), pp. 101-109.

CHUKOV, B.V. Sotzialisticheskie idei v irakskoy proze (na primere tvorchestva M.A. As-Seyida, Zu-n-Nuna Ayyuba i G.T. Farmana). *NAA* 1974(1), pp. 96-103.

COBHAM, C. Sex and society in Yūsuf Idrīs: 'Qā' al-madīna'. *J. Arabic lit.* 6(1975), pp. 78-88.

DE SIMONE, A. Notizie bio-bibliografiche su ʿIsà an-Na'ūrī. *OM* 50 (1970), 589-592.

DE SIMONE, A. Notizie bio-bibliografiche su Ḥasan 'Utmān. *OM* 54(1974), pp. 23-27.

DOLININA, A.A. Arabskiy prosvetitel'skiy roman. *Problemy literatur orientalnych*, 1974, pp. 59-66.

DOLININA, A.A. K voprosu o poeticheskikh perevodakh s arabskogo (na primere "Kasidy o Lenine" Ridvana ash-Shakhkhalya). *NAA* 1973(2), pp. 128-134.

DOLININA, A.A. Na puti k romanu (traditziya makamy v prosvetitel'skoy literature Egipta). *Vestnik Leningradskogo Univ., ist., yazyk. lit.* 1975(2), pp. 108-114.

DOLININA, A.A. Nazidatel'nyy roman Farakha Antuna "Zver'! Zver'! Zver'!". *Voprosy filologii stran Azii i Afriki, 1. Sbornik I.N. Vinnikova* 1971, pp. 106-113.

ENDE, Werner. Zu einer Einführung in die moderne arabische Literatur. *Der Islam* 50 (1973), pp. 325-330.

ERPENBECK, D. Über die realistische Gestaltungsweise in der modernen ägyptischen Kurzgeschichte. *Asien in Vergangenheit und Gegenwart*, 1974, pp. 259-277.

FADL, Kadreya Zaki. Un autor y un cuento egipcio. "¿No es así?" de Yusuf Idris. *Estudios de Asia y Africa* 10(1975), pp. 198-210.

FAURE, G. Un écrivain entre deux cultures: biographie de Kateb Yacine. *ROMM* 18(1974), pp. 65-92.

FONTAINE, J. Amīn Rayḥānī: chrétien ou musulman? *Travaux et jours* 38 (1971), pp. 103-114.

FONTAINE, J. Aspects de la littérature tunisienne contemporaine. (Mohamed Marzouqi, Najia Thameur, Hind Azouz.) *IBLA* 36(no.131, 1973), pp. 119-139.

FONTAINE, J. and RENAUD, E. Aspects de la littérature tunisienne contemporaine: Rachid GHALI, Zohra JLASI, Mahmoud TOUNSI. *IBLA* 35(no.129, 1972), pp. 149-171.

FONTAINE, J. Aspects de la littérature tunisienne contemporaine: Tahar Guiga. *IBLA* 37(no.133, 1974), pp. 163-177.

FONTAINE, J., MAURY, R., LELONG, M. Aspects de la littérature tunisienne contemporaine: Samir Ayadi, Abdelkader Bencheikh. *IBLA* 127 (1971), pp. 149-165.

FONTAINE, J. La conversion de Mīḫā'īl Mašāqa et de Buṭrus Bustānī. *Travaux et jours* 40(1971), pp. 57-65.

FONTAINE, J. Le courant formaliste tunisien. *Annuaire Afrique du Nord* 12(1973), pp. 193-209.

FONTAINE, J. Mohieddine Benkhelifa. [Incl. trans. from *Aš-Šaǧara*]. *IBLA* 35(no.130, 1972), pp. 345-352.

FONTAINE, J. Mohsen Bendhiaf. [Incl. trans. from *At-Taḥaddī*]. *IBLA* 35(no.130, 1972), pp. 353-361.

FONTAINE, J. Les "scientistes" libanais de la Nahḍa devant leur foi. *IBLA* 34 (no. 128, 1971), pp. 225-258.

FONTAINE, J. Situation de la femme écrivain en Tunisie. *CT* 20(nos.79-80, 1972), pp. 285-307.

FONTAINE, J. Le IX Congrès des écrivains arabes (Tunis, 18-25 mars 1973). *OM* 55 (1975), pp. 49-53.

FRANCIS, R. Les extrêmes sociaux dans l'oeuvre du dramatuge égyptien No'man 'Achour. *ROMM* 6(1969), pp. 75-87.

FRANCIS, R. Itinéraire de Taha Hussein. *Nouvelle Rev. du Caire* 1(1975), pp. 31-47.

FRIGGIERI, J. Poems. (Translations by P. Serracino-Inglott.) *J.Fac.Arts Malta* 5 (1974), pp. 339-347.

FROLOVA, O.B. Pesni egipetskogo poeta Ibragima Suleymana ash-Sheykha, ispolnyaemye Mukhammedom Takha. *Voprosy filol. stran Azii i Afriki* II(1973), pp. 132-140.

FROLOVA, O.B. Sbornik egiptskikh narodnykh pesen. *Voprosy filologii stran Azii i Afriki, 1. Sbornik I.N. Vinnikova* 1971, pp. 125-132.

FROLOVA, O.B. Tema natzional'no-osvoboditel'noy bor'by v tvorchestve egipetskikh narodnykh poetov. *NAA* 1972(5), pp. 121-127.

FROLOVA, O.B. Tema truda v proizvedeniyakh egipetskikh narodnykh poetov. *NAA* 1975(2), pp. 133-138.

GABAY, Z. Nizār Qabbānī, the poet and his poetry. *ME stud.* 9(1973), pp. 207-222.

GABRIELI, F. The autobiography of Mikhail Nu[c]aima. *Islam and its cultural divergence. Studies in honor of Gustave E. von Grunebaum,* 1971, pp. 52-62

GELLA, J. Quelques remarques sur le style de la nouvelle "al-aǧniḥa al-mutakassira" (les ailes cassées) par Ǧ.H. Ǧubran. *Graecolatina et Orientalia* 4(1972), pp. 185-191.

GERMANUS, A.K. Julius. Modern poetry of Yemen. *Orientalia Hispanica* I, 1974, pp. 305-319.

GERMANUS, A.K.J. The new Palestinian poetry from beneath the crossfire. *IC* 47(1973), pp. 127-158.

GRZESKOWIAK, M. Gesellschaftliche Entwicklung und Islam in der neueren Ägyptischen Literatur. *Asien in Vergangenheit und Gegenwart,* 1974, pp. 225-237.

HABIBI, A.H. The jewelry chest. *Afghanistan* 25ii(1972), pp. 71-74.

HADJ SADOK, Mohammed. La guerre 1939-40 selon un soldat poète algérien. *ROMM* 15-16(1973), pp. 21-34.

HĀFEẒ, Sabry. Innovation in the Egyptian short story. *Studies in Arabic literature,* ed. R.C. Ostle, 1975, pp. 99-113.

HAIKAL, Abdel Fattah. Rifā'a at-Ṭahṭāwī; Leben und Werk eines ägyptischen Aufklärers (1801-1873). *Asien, Afrika, Latein-Amerika* 2(1974), pp. 287-298.

HAKIM, Tewfik el-. L'homme riche. *Nouvelle Rev. du Caire* 1(1975), pp. 11-30.

HAKIM, Tewfik el-. Le prestidigateur. *Nouvelle Rev. du Caire* 1(1975), pp. 1-10.

HAMARNEH, Saleh K. Aš-Šabībī - poet and scholar. *Folia or.* 14(1972-73), pp. 293-297.

HAMZAWI, Rachad. The realities of contemporary Tunisian literature; a documentary survey. *AJAS* 2(1974), pp. 53-74.

HANNA, Sami, SALTI, R. Ahmad Shauqi: a pioneer of modern Arabic drama. *AJAS* 1 (1973), pp. 81-117.

HANNA, Sami A. The Arabic renaissance or Al-Nahda and the development of the novel. *IC* 45(1971), pp. 221-253

HANNA, Sami A. Some aspects of the modern literary history of Tunisia. *IC* 45(1971), pp. 181-192.

HANNA, Suhail Ibn-Salim. L'autobiographie chez Ṭaha Ḥusain et Salāma Mūsā. *IBLA* 35(no. 129, 1972), pp. 59-71.

IDRIS, Yusuf. The journey. *J. Arabic lit.* 3(1972), pp. 127-131.

ISMAIL, Sidky. New trends in the commitment of Arab writers. *Lotus* 1973ii(no.16), pp. 47-63.

JABRA, Jabra I. Modern Arabic literature and the West. *J.Arabic lit.* 2(1971), pp. 76-91.

JASIŃSKA, J. Współczesna proza w Sudanie. *Przegl. or.* 4(88,1973), pp. 305-314.

JAYYŪSĪ, Salmā Khaḍrā. Contemporary poetry - vision and attitudes. *Studies in Arabic literature,* ed. R.C. Ostle, 1975, pp. 46-68.

JOMIER, J. "Les tristesses d'une ville". *MIDEO* 12(1974), pp. 237-242.

JUYNBOLL, G.H.A. Ismā'īl Ahmad Adham (1911-1940), the Atheist. *J. Arabic lit.* 3(1972), pp. 54-71.

KACEM, Abdelaziz. Situation de la poésie tunisienne dans *al-Fikr* de 1955 à 1965. *Arabica* 18(1971), pp. 57-98, 113-151

KHATEEB, H. al- A modern Syrian short story. [*Wajh al-qamar* by Z. Tāmir]. *J. Arabic lit.* 3(1972), pp. 96-105.

KHAUVAL', Kh.A. al-. Sheykh Mukhammed Ayyad Tantavi po rabotam Akademika I.Yu. Krachdovskogo. *Voprosy filologii stran Azii i Afriki, 1. Sbornik I.N. Vinnikova* 1971, pp. 132-135.

KHOURI, Mouna A. Revolution and renaissance in al-Bārūdī's poetry. *Islam and its cultural divergence. Studies in honor of Gustave E. von Grunebaum,* 1971, pp. 76-95

KHOURY, R.G. Die Rolle der Übersetzungen in der modernen Renaissance des arabischen Schrifttums, dargestellt am Beispiel Ägyptens. *WI* 13 (1971), pp. 1-10.

KHOURY, R.G. Ṭāhā Ḥusayn (1889-1973) et la France. Notes bibliographiques commentées. *Arabica* 22(1975), pp. 225-266.

KILPATRICK, H. The Arabic novel - a single tradition? *J. Arab. lit.* 5(1974), pp. 93-107.

KILPATRICK, H. *Ḥawwā' bilā Adam:* an Egyptian novel of the 1930's. *J. Arab. lit.* 4(1973), pp. 48-56.

LANDAU, J.M. A note on the language problems of the Jews in modern Egypt. *Orientalia Hispanica* I, 1974, pp. 438-444.

LECERF, J. 'Anī 'ummak y Šāker: pièce en deux actes de Yūsuf al-'Ānī. *Arabica* 18(1971), pp. 225-261.

LE GASSICK, T. An analysis of al-Ḥubb taḥt al-Maṭar (Love in the rain) - a novel by Najīb Maḥfūz. *Studies in Arabic literature,* ed. R.C. Ostle, 1975, pp. 140-151.

LE GASSICK, T.J. Literature in translation - modern Arabic. *MESA Bull.* 5i (1971), pp. 26-38.

LEGASSICK, T.J. Some recent war-related Arabic fiction. *MEJ* 25(1971), pp. 491-505.

LOUCA, Anouar. Taha Hussein and the West. *Cultures* 2ii(1975), pp. 115-139.

LOYA, Arieh. Poetry as a social document: the social position of the Arab woman as reflected in the poetry of Nizār Qabbānī. *MW* 63(1973), pp. 39-52.

LOYA, Arieh. Al-Sayyāb and the influence of T.S. Eliot. *MW* 61 (1971), pp. 187-201.

LYONS, M.C. The *Sīrat Baybars.* *Orientalia Hispanica* I, 1974, pp. 490-504.

MARTÍNEZ MONTÁVEZ, P. Un poeta "morisco" contemporaneo: 'Abd al-Razzāq Karābaka (1901-1945). *Actas II Col. hisp.-tunec. estud. hist.,* 1973, pp. 235-259.

MARTÍNEZ MONTÁVEZ, P. Presencia de Federico Garcia Lorca en la literatura árabe actual. *Actas IV congresso de estudos árabes e islâmicos* 1968(1971), pp. 41-62.

MASHIAH, Yaakov. In search of an insane universe. A study of Dār al-Majānīn, the Lunatic Asylum, by Sayyid Muḥammad 'Alī Jamāl-Zādeh. *Muséon* 86(1973), pp. 147-174.

MASLIYAH, Sadok. Monorhyme, stanzaic poetry and blank verse in the poetry of the Iraqi poet Jamīl S. Az-Zahāwī (1863-1936). *AJAS* 3(1975), pp. 14-36.

MASON, H. Arab Algerian literature revisited. *Humaniora Islamica* 1(1973), pp. 77-87.

MAZMI, M.I. al-. 'Ali Aḥmad Bā Kathīr and the historical novel. *Bull. Fac. Arts, Univ. Riyad* 2(1971-2), pp. 61-75.

MIKHAIL, M.N. Broken idols. The death of religion as reflected in two short stories by Idris and Maḥfūẓ. *J. Arab. lit.* 5 (1974), pp. 147-157.

MILSON, Menahem. An allegory on the social and cultural crisis in Egypt: "Walîd al-'anâ'" by Najîb Maḥfûẓ. *IJMES* 3(1972), pp. 324-347.

MIQUEL, A. Réflexions sur la structure poétique à propos d'Eliās Abū Šabaka. *BEO* 25 (1972), pp. 265-274.

MOKTÂR OULD BAH, Mohamd el. Introduction à la poésie mauritanienne (1650-1900). *Arabica* 18 (1971), pp. 1-48.

MONTAINA, G. Tawfīq al-Hakīm e il problema della "terza lingua". *OM* 53(1973), pp. 742-755.

MOOSA, Matti. Ya'qûb Ṣanû' and the rise of Arab drama in Egypt. *IJMES* 5(1974), pp. 401-433.

MOREH, S. Five writers of Shi'r manthūr in modern Arabic. *ME stud.* 10(1974), pp. 229-233.

MOREH, S. The neoclassical Qaṣīda; modern poets and critics. *Arabic poetry; theory and development,* ed. G.E. von Grunebaum, 1973, pp. 155-179.

MOREH, Shmuel. An outline of the development of modern Arabic literature. *OM* 55 (1975), pp. 8-28.

NAIMY, N. The mind and thought of Khalīl Gibrān. *J. Arab. lit.* 5(1974), pp. 55-71.

OGUNBIYI, I.A. Twentieth-century Tunisian Arabic creative writing as a study in the social, cultural and political history of the country. *Odu* N.S.11(1975), pp. 61-74.

O'KANE, J.P. "The Mosque in the Alley" by Najīb Maḥfūẓ. A translation, with notes. *MW* 63(1973), pp. 28-38.

OLIVERIUS, J. Le monde des idées et des significations dans les pièces de théâtre de Tawfīq al-Ḥakīm. *Archiv or.* 41(1973), pp. 355-374.

OLIVERIUS, J. The reaction of some Egyptian writers and critics to the influence of European literature. *The East under Western impact* (Dissertationes Orientales 17, 1969), pp. 101-106.

OSTLE, R.C. Īlyā Abū Māḍī and Arabic poetry in the inter-war period. *Studies in Arabic literature,* ed. R.C. Ostle, 1975, pp. 34-45.

OSTLE, R.C. Khalīl Muṭrān: the precursor of lyrical poetry in modern Arabic. *J. Arabic lit.* 2(1971), pp. 116-126.

PAXTON, E. Taha Husain and Mahmud Taimur: an appreciation. *Asian affairs* 61(N.S.5, 1974), pp. 176-178.

PAZ, Fr. X. Women and sexual morality in the novels of Najīb Mahfūz. *Actas IV congresso de estudos árabes e islâmicos* 1968(1971), pp. 15-26.

PERLMANN, M. The Memoirs of Taha Husayn. *Bibl. Or.* 30(1973), pp. 13-15.

PHILIPP, T.D. Approaches to history in the work of Jurji Zaydan. *Asian and African studies* [Jerusalem] 9(1973), pp. 63-85.

PHILIPP, T. Language, history, and Arab national consciousness in the thought of Jurjī Zaidān (1861-1914). *IJMES* 4(1973), pp. 3-22.

PLANCKE, M. De plaats van Mahmud Taymur in de moderne Arabische letterkunde. *Orientalia Gandensia* 3(1966), pp. 135-145.

PROZHOZINA, S.V. Alzhirskie pisateli v usloviyakh bilingvisma. (Algerian writers in conditions of bilingualism.) *NAA* 1971(5), pp. 99-106.

RĀ'I, 'Alī al-. Some aspects of modern Arabic drama. *Studies in Arabic literature,* ed. R.C. Ostle, 1975, pp. 167-178.

RIAHI, Zohra. Le roman tunisien des dix dernières années. *Actes I. Cong. et. cult. mediterr. d'infl. arabo-berb.,* 1973, pp. 292-304.

SAKKOUT, Hamdī. Najīb Maḥfūz's short stories. *Studies in Arabic literature,* ed. R.C. Ostle, 1975, pp. 114-125.

SALAMA, Adel. Two Kuwaiti poems. From the Arabic of Ahmad Adwani. Translated. *J. Arab. lit.* 5(1974), pp. 127-128.

SAMSÓ MOYA, J. Problemas lingüisticos de la *nahda* vistos a traves de algunos textos autobiograficos de Muḥammad 'Abduh, Aḥmad Amīn y Ṭāhā Ḥusayn. *Orientalia Hispanica* I, 1974, pp. 601-621.

SANTINI, F. Giubran Khalil Giubran. *Levante* 18iv(1971), pp. 36-44

SANTINI, F. Khalil Giubràn: "Jesus the son of Man". *Levante* 21iii(1974), pp. 5-18.

SATTI, Nur al-Din. Mustafa Sa'id: Le migrateur sans baggages. *Adab: J. Fac. Arts, Khartoum* 2-3(1975), pp. 144-154.

SCHUB, M.B. An instance of colloquial influence in Tawfīq al-Ḥakīm: a problem of diglossia in Arabic. *ZDMG* 125(1975), pp. 270-272.

SEMAH, D. Muḥammad Mandūr and the "new poetry". *J.Arabic lit.* 2(1971), pp. 143-153.

SHĀMĪ, Aḥmad Muhammad al-. Yemeni literature in Ḥajjah prisons 1367/1948-1374/1955. *Arabian studies* 2(1975), pp. 43-60.

SHĀRŪNĪ, Yūsuf al-. Glimpses from the life of Mawjūd 'Abd al-Mawjūd. *Humaniora Islamica* 2(1974), pp. 181-194.

SHIDFAR, B.Ya. Ot skazki k romanu (nekotorye cherty arabskogo "narodnogo" romana). *NAA* 1975(1), pp. 130-138.

SHOUKR, Samir et WITKOWSKA, A. Mahmud Darwisz. Wiersze. (Les poèmes. Traduit de l'arabe par Samir Shoukr et Aleksandra Wsitkowska.) *Przegląd or.* 82(1972), pp. 143-146.

SILAGADZE, A.A. K probleme inostrannykh vliyaniy na obrazovanie novykh arabskikh versifikatzionnykh form. *Soobshch.AN Gruz. SSR* 80(1975), pp. 221-224.

SIMONE, A. de. *Fez in sette racconti* di Aḥmad Bannānī. *Orientalia Hispanica* I, 1974, pp. 622-639.

SKARZYŃSKA-BOCHEŃSKA, Kr. Rozwój nowelistyki Mahmuda Tajmura. *Przegl. Or.* 1 (93, 1975), pp. 31-42.

SOMEKH, S. Language and theme in the short stories of Yūsuf Idrīs. *J. Arabic lit.* 6(1975), pp. 89-100.

SOMEKH, S. The sad millenarian: an examination of Awlād Ḥāratinā. *ME studies* 7 (1971), pp. 49-61.

SOUKA, F. Partie de chasse, pièce de Tewfik El-Hakim. Traduite. *Ann.Fac.Arts Ain Shams* 9(1964), pp. 145-168.

SPEIGHT, R. A modern Tunisian poet: Abû al-Qâsim al-Shâbbî (1909-1934). *IJMES* 4(1973), pp. 178-189.

SPLETT, O. Literaturbrief aus Tunesien. *Z.f.Kulturaustausch* 24ii(1974), pp. 115-116.

STETKEVYCH, J. Classical Arabic on stage. *Studies in Arabic literature,* ed. R.C. Ostle, 1975, pp. 152-166.

STRIKA, V. Due raccolte di poesie di Taufīq Ṣāyigh. *Levante* 20ii(1973), pp. 20-28.

STRIKA, V. Filosofia a religione in ʿAbbās Maḥmūd al ʿAqqād. *OM* 52(1972), pp. 329-339.

STRIKA, V. Un narratore egiziano moderno: Yūsuf as-Sibāʿī. *Annali Fac. Ling. Lett. stran. di Ca' Foscari (serie orientale)* 1 (1970), pp. 23-37.

SULTANOVA, L.F. Pisatel' i boretz za mir Zhorzh Khanna. (George Hanna, writer and fighter for peace.) *NAA* 1972(2), pp. 136-140

TADIÉ, A. Le troisième *Livre des Jours. Nouvelle Rev. du Caire* 1(1975), pp. 49-58.

TAHA-HUSSEIN, Moenis. Pierres d'Egypte. *Nouvelle Rev. du Caire* 1(1975), pp. 173-179.

TOMICHE, N. Un dramaturge égyptien, Tawfiq al-Hakim et l'"avant-garde". *Rev. lit. comp.* 45(1971), pp. 541-553.

TOMICHE, Nada. Najib Mahʿfûzʿ et l'éclatement du roman arabe après 1967. *ROMM* 15-16 (1973), pp. 345-357.

VACCA, V. Gli studi di letteratura araba contemporanea. *Studi sul Vicino Oriente in Italia,* II, 1971, pp. 159-181.

VATIKIOTIS, P.J. The corruption of Futuwwa: a consideration of despair in Nagib Maḥfūẓ's Awlād Ḥāritnā. *ME studies* 7 (1971), pp. 169-184.

VATIN, J.C. Littérature et société en algérie: Rachid Boudjedra ou le jeu des confrontations. *Ann.Afr.nord* 12(1973), pp. 211-231.

VATIN, J.C. Structure romanesque et système social: sur quatre romans parus en 1973. *Ann.Afr.nord* 12(1973), pp. 273-294.

VIAL, C. A propos des deux derniers livres de Yaḥyā Ḥaqqī, *Le parfum des amis* et *Les obscurs. Cah.de ling.d'orientalisme et de slavistique* 1-2(1973), pp. 279-289.

VIAL, C. La femme dans la trilogie de Nağīb Maḥfūẓ. *BEO* 25(1972), pp. 275-289.

VIAL, C. Yaḥyā Ḥaqqī humoriste. *Annales islamol.* 11(1972), pp. 351-365.

WALTHER, W. Das Bild der ägyptischen Gesellschaft in einigen Werken von Nağīb Maḥfūẓ aus den sechziger Jahren. *Asien in Vergangenheit und Gegenwart,* 1974, pp. 239-258.

WALTHER, W. Mittel der Darstellungskunst und des Stils in einigen Romanen von Nağīb Maḥfūẓ aus den sechziger Jahren. *Problemy literatur orientalnykh,* 1974, pp. 199-213.

WESSELS, A. Nagīb Maḥfūẓ and secular man. *Humaniora Islamica* 2(1974), pp. 105-119.

WILD, S. Friedrich Nietzsche and Gibran Kahlil Gibran. *Al-Abhath* 22iii-iv (1969), pp. 47-57.

WITKAM, J.J. Tewfik al-Hakim: Bewustzijn herwonnen. Inleiding en naschrift. *De Gids* 139(1976), pp. 239-258.

YASIN'SKA, Y. Nekotorye elementy struktury sotzial'no-bytovogo romana Nagiba Makhfuza. *Problemy literatur orientalnych,* 1974, pp. 87-91.

YETIV, Isaac. L'aliénation dans le roman maghrébin contemporain. *ROMM* 18(1974), pp. 149-158.

YUNUSOV, K.O. Elementy irratzionalizma v sovremennoy egiptskoy dramaturgii (po p'ese Taufika al-Khakima "Vzbirayushchiysys na derevo"). *Voprosy filologii stran Azii i Afriki, 1. Sbornik I.N. Vinnikova* 1971, pp. 136-143.

ZAYYAT, Mohamed H. El-. Taha Hussein and the Arab world. *Cultures* 2ii(1975), pp. 101-114.

ZUBAIDI, A.M.K. The Apollo school's early experiments in "free verse". *J. Arab. lit.* 5(1974), pp. 17-43.

Modern Arabic poetry [Translations]. *J. Arabic lit.* 3(1972), pp. 118-126.

See also I. b. 3. Borruso, Rizzitano.

See also II. a. 5. Bachmann.

See also II. a. 5. Husaini.

See also V. u. 1. Ghānim

See also VII. c. Grand'Henry.

See also XIX. j. Allen

See also XXXVI. k. Altoma

See also XXXVI. l. Vocke.

XXXVIII IRANIAN LANGUAGES. PERSIAN

a GENERAL

BAILEY, H.W. A range of Iranica. *W.B. Henning memorial vol.*, 1970, pp. 20-36.

BHUIYA, Sultan Ahmed. The influence of Persian on Bengali language and literature. *J. Reg. Cult. Inst.* 4(1971), pp. 81-90.

BOGDANOVIĆ, D. Les étymologies iraniennes des orientalismes dans la langue serbo-croate. *Balcanica* 4(1973), pp. 631-637.

EDEL'MAN, D.I. K voprosu o slovoobrazovanii mestoimeniy v indoiranskikh yazykakh. *Ind. i iran. filol.*, 1971, pp. 151-160.

EDEL'MAN, D.I. O konstruktziyakh predlozheniya v iranskikh yazykakh. *Vopr.yaz.* 1974(1), pp. 23-33.

EDEL'MAN, D.I. Les verbes "être" et "avoir" dans les langues iraniennes. *Mél. ling. É. Benveniste*, 1975, pp. 151-158.

EILERS, W. Le caviar. *Commémoration Cyrus. Hommage universel*, II, 1974, pp. 381-390.

EILERS, W. Verbreitung und Fortleben alter Epenthese. *Commémoration Cyrus. Hommage universel*, I, 1974, pp. 280-291.

ELWELL-SUTTON, L.P. The foundations of Persian prosody and metrics. *Iran* 13(1975), pp. 75-97.

FRYE, R.N. Continuing Iranian influences on Armenian. *Yād-nāme-ye Irāni-ye Minorsky*, 1969, pp. 80-89.

GERSHEVITCH, Ilya. Iranian words containing -ān-. *Iran and Islam, in memory of V. Minorsky*, 1971, pp. 267-291

HABIBI, A.H. The mother of the Dari language. *Afghanistan* 23i(1970), pp. 1-5; 23ii(1970), pp. 1-70; 23iii(1970), pp. 1-8; 23iv(1971), pp. 1-8; 24i(1971), pp. 1-10; 24ii-iii(1971), pp. 1-9; 24iv(1972), pp. 1-10; 25i(1972), pp. 1-8; 25ii(1972), pp. 1-3.

HEMMERDINGER, B. 173 noms communs grecs d'origine iranienne. *Byzantinoslavica* 32 (1971), pp. 52-55

JAZAYERY, Mohammad Ali. On the nature of a cultural history of the languages of Iranian culture. *Commémoration Cyrus. Hommage universel*, II, 1974, pp. 323-335.

LAZARD, G. *Pahlavi, Pârsi, Dari:* les langues de l'Iran d'après Ibn al-Muqaffa'. *Iran and Islam, in memory of V. Minorsky*, 1971, pp. 361-391

LYTKIN, V.I. Permsko-iranskie yazykovye kontakty. *Vopr. yaz.* 1975(3), pp. 84-97.

MALAMOUD, Ch. Remarques sur les dérivés indo-iraniens en-*man*. *Mél. ling. É. Benveniste*, 1975, pp. 397-406.

MORGENSTIERNE, G. Ancient contacts between N.E. Iranian and Indo-Aryan? *Mél. ling. É. Benveniste*, 1975, pp. 431-434.

OSTROVSKIY, B.Ya. Morfonologicheskie skhemy gipermorfem persidskogo, dari i tadzhikskogo yazykov. *NAA* 1973(2), pp. 135-140.

PAKHALINA, T.N. Éléments indo-aryens dans les langues iraniennes orientales. *Mél. ling. É. Benveniste*, 1975, pp. 441-445.

POGHIRC, C. Irano-Daco-Romanica. *Studia et acta or.* 8(1971), pp. 25-28.

RIZA, A. Concordances lexicales entre éléments roumains anciens et éléments relevant des aires iranienne et caucasienne. *Studia et acta or.* 8(1971), pp. 29-44.

ŠTOLBOVÁ, E. Some characteristic features of older Persian linguistic literature. *Yād-nāme-ye Jan Rypka* 1967, pp. 149-154.

WINDEKENS, A.J. van. Sur quelques éléments indo-iraniens dans le vocabulaire tokharien. *Orbis* 23(1974), pp. 224-228.

WINDEKENS, A.J. van. Sur quelques termes Indo-Iraniens empruntés par le Tokharien. *JQR* 63(1972), pp. 46-51.

WINDFUHR, G.L. Isoglosses: a sketch on Persians and Parthians, Kurds and Medes. *Acta Iranica*, 2. sér. *Monumentum H.S. Nyberg*, II (1975), pp. 457-472.

See also XXXVI. i. Eilers.

b MODERN PERSIAN

ACHENA, Mohammad. Signification et portée de l'anecdote dans la poésie mystique persane. *Yād-nāme-ye Irāni-ye Minorsky*, 1969, pp. 1-6.

ÁPOR, É. Some problems of word-formation in modern Persian. *Actes Xe Cong.int.linguistes*, 1967, IV, pp. 617-621.

BAEVSKIY, S.I. Neizdannyy slovar' XV veka "Shamil al-lugat" v rukopisnoy kollektzii persidsko-turetzkikh slovarey LO IV. *Istoriya, kul'tura, yazyki narodov Vostoka* 1970, pp. 39-41.

BAQIR, Muhammad. The earliest progress, development and influence of Persian in the Indo-Pakistan sub-continent. *Proc. 27th Int.Cong.Or.1967* (1971), pp. 168-169.

BASTIAENSEN, M. Le morphème d'indétermination en persan. *Correspondance d'Orient: Etudes* 19-20(1971-2), pp. 77-109.

BATENI, M.R. Kinship terms in Persian. *Anthropol. linguistics* 15(1973), pp. 324-327.

BAUSANI, A. Notes sur les mots persans en malayo-indonésien. *Commémoration Cyrus. Hommage universel,* II, 1974, pp. 347-379.

BELITZIN, A.P. Osnovnye strukturno-semanticheskie tipy bezlichnykh predlozheniy v persidskom yazyke. *Vost.yazyki,* 1971, pp. 38-51

BUDDRUSS, G. Neuiranische Wortstudien. *Münchener Stud.z.Sprachwissenschaft* 32(1974), pp. 9-40.

CHAVCHAVADZE, T.A. Yu.N. Marr i voprosy sostavleniya persidskorusskogo slovarya. *Vostochnaya filologiya. Philologia Orientalis.* II(Pamyati V.S. Puturidze), 1972, pp. 104-113.

CHOWDHURY, A.M. Faiz Ahmad. The influence of Persian on Bengali and Urdu. *J. Reg. Cult. Inst.* 1 iv(1968), pp. 5-11.

DEHGHAN, Iraf. *Dāstan* as an auxiliary in contemporary Persian. *Arch. or.* 40(1972), pp. 198-205.

EILERS, W. Kult und Sprachform in Iran. *XVIII. Deutscher Orientalistentag 1972: Vorträge,* pp. 471-497.

EILERS, W. The new Persian type *kirdar* 'work, action'--a semasiological problem. *Iran Society silver jubilee souvenir* 1944-1969, pp. 107-112.

ERME, G. d'. In margine al Dizionario persiano-italiano: I. Il "Paese dell'Ischia di Mezzo". II. Per una definizione dell' eẓāfè persiana. *Annali Fac. Ling. Lett. stran. di Ca' Foscari (serie orientale)* 3 (1972), pp. 173-189.

ERME, G.M. d'.Sintemi e locuzioni verbali in neopersiano. *OM* 54(1974), pp. 226-235.

EREMINA, K.N. Nekotorye voprosy foneticheskoy peredachi evropeyskikh leksicheskikh zaimstvovaniy v sovremennom persidskom literaturnom yazyke. *Issledovaniya po vostochnym yazykam,* 1973, pp. 55-68.

EREMINA, K.N. O peredache na russkiy yazyk nekotorykh toponimov Irana. *Issledovaniya po vostochnym yazykam,* 1973, pp. 49-54.

FRYE, R.N. The rise of the new Persian language. *J. K.R. Cama Or. Inst.* 44(1973), pp. 76-80.

GIUNASHVILI, Dzh.Sh. K tolkovaniyu termina "bīstgānī". *Gruzinskoe istochnikovedenie* III, 1971, pp. 106-114.

GVENTZADZE, G.S. K voprosu o glagol'nom frazeologizme v persidskom yazyke. *NAA* 1975(2), pp. 151-156.

HAKHAMANESHI, Kaikhusroo. The role of Persian language in international relations. *J. K.R. Cama Or. Inst.* 44(1973), pp. 161-171.

HENNING, W.B. Pages servant de spécimen du projété Dictionnaire étymologique de la langue persane. *Iran-shināsi* 2ii(serial no.3, 1971), pp. 61-68.

INAYATULLAH, Shaikh. The Persian language in its international aspects. *Indo-Iranica* 23iii(197), pp. 1-13.

ISKHAKOVA, F.S. Osnovnye sposoby slovoobrazovaniya persidskikh imen prilagatel'nykh. *Ind. i iran. filol.,* 1971, pp. 3-14.

ISLAM, Muhammad Ziaul. The rise and development of the Persian language in the Indo-Pakistan sub-continent. *J. Reg. Cult. Inst.* 1 iii(1968), pp. 44-50.

ISMAILOV, A.K. Voprosy formirovaniya leksicheskogo sostava persidskogo yazyka i deyatel'nost' Akademii yazyka i literatury. *Issledovaniya po vostochnym yazykam,* 1973, pp. 69-82.

ISMAILOV, A.K. Znachenie yazykogo formirovaniya dlya sovremennogo literaturnogo persidskogo yazyka. *Issledovaniya po vostochnym yazykam,* 1973, pp. 83-93.

JAZAYERY, Mohammad Ali. The Arabic element in Persian grammar. *Proc.27th Int.Cong. Or.1967* (1971), pp. 243-244.

JAZAYERY, M.A. Observations on stylistic variation in Persian. *Actes Xe Cong.int. linguistes,* 1967, III, pp. 447-457.

JAZAYERY, Mohammad Ali. Persian verbs derivable from other parts of speech. *Amer. Or. Soc., Middle West Branch. Semi-centennial volume,* ed. by D. Sinor, 1969, pp. 111-126.

JUNGE, F. Zum "Yā der Erzählung" und seiner Funktion bei Neẓāmo'l-Molk. *ZDMG* 123(1973), pp. 74-78.

KARIEV, Sh.Z. O sposobakh obrazovaniya mnozhestvennogo chisla imen sushchestvitel'nykh v romane "Samak-e ayyar". *Vost.yazyki,* 1971, pp. 86-92

KARIEV, Sh. Z. Ob upotreblenii formy proshedshego dlitel'nogo vremeni v materialakh pamyatnika XII-XIII vv. "Samak-e Ayar". *Vostokovedenie, yazykovedenie* 1973, pp. 71-75.

KHRISANOV, N.V. Adverbializatziya predlozhno-imennykh sochetaniy v sovremennom persidskom yazyke. *Ind. i iran. filol.,* 1971, pp. 127-145.

KOSMINA, E.M. Predvaritel'nye rezul'taty statisticheskogo issledovaniya leksiki sovremennogo persidskogo yazyka. *Vostokovedenie, yazykovedenie* 1973, pp. 31-48.

KURYLOWICZ, J. Les éléments persans dans le fonds lexical européen. *Commemoration Cyrus. Hommage universel*, II, 1974, pp. 391-397.

LAZARD, G. Etude quantitative de l'évolution d'un morphème: La postposition *râ* en persan. *Mélanges Marcel Cohen*, 1970, pp. 381-388.

LAZARD, G. Une neutralisation en phonologie persane. *Langues et techniques, nature et société. Hommage à A.G. Haudricourt*, I, 1972, pp. 145-148.

MAHMOUDIAN, Mortēza. Du role de la position dans l'indication des rapports syntaxiques: l'exemple du persan. *Linguistique* 9(1973), pp. 17-40.

MARASHI, Mehdi. Modals and auxiliaries in Persian. *Orbis* 21(1972), pp. 417-428.

MATINI, Jalāl. Persian characters during the fifth century of Hegira. *Proc.27th Int.Cong.Or.1967* (1971), pp. 244-246.

MEYER-INGWERSEN, J. The common use of some idiomatic expressions in different Oriental languages. *Proc.27th Int.Cong. Or.1967* (1971), pp. 246-247.

MILANIAN, Hormoz. Les Monèmes et les procédés de passage en persan. De la catégorie verbale à la catégorie nominale et vice versa. *Word* 25(1969), pp. 214-227.

MOINFAR, Djafar. "Défini" et "non-défini" en persan. Essai de formalisation. *Langues et techniques, nature et société. Hommage à A.G. Haudricourt*, I, 1972, pp. 175-177.

MOTAMEDI, Ahmad Ali. A Mongol-Persian versified glossary from Afghanistan. *Adab* [Kabul] 23iii(1975), pp. 8-21.

MOYNE, J.A. The so-called passive in Persian. *Foundations of language* 12(1974), pp. 249-267.

MOYNE, J., CARDEN, G. Subject reduplication in Persian. *Linguistic inquiry* 5(1974), pp. 205-249.

MUKHAMEDOVA, N. K voprosu ob otgranichenim slozhnykh slov ot slovosochetaniy v persidskom yazyke. *Vostokovedenie, yazykovedenie* 1973, pp. 21-30.

NAVABI, Y. Mahyar -*ang* in Persian. *Bull.Iranian Culture Found.* Ii(1969), pp. 139-150.

NILSEN, D.L.F. and KAMAL, Sajida The influence of Dari phonetic laws on words borrowed from English. *Adab* (Kabul) 18iii-iv(1970), pp. 1-20.

NILSEN, D.L.F. Syntactic and semantic categories of echo words in Persian. *Iran. stud.* 5(1972), pp. 88-95.

OSMANOV, M. -N.O. K kharakteristike nekotorykh semanticheskikh poley v yazyke persidskoy poezii X v. *Ind. i iran. filol.*, 1971, pp. 161-169.

OSTROVSKIY, B.Ya. K kharakteristike distributzii persidskogo vokalizma. *Vestnik Moskovsk. Univ.*, XIV: *Vostokoved.* 1975(2), pp. 87-95.

OSVALD, J. Alliteration in colloquial Persian. *Arch. or.* 39 (1971), pp. 346-351.

OVCHINNIKOVA, I.K. K voprosu ob udel'nom vese inoyazychnykh zaimstvovaniy v leksike sovremennogo literaturnogo persidskogo yazyka. *Ind. i iran. filol.*, 1971, pp. 43-60.

PIEMONTESE, A.M. Cinquant'anni di persianologia. *Studi sul Vicino Oriente in Italia*, II, 1971, pp. 307-408.

PISTOSO, M. L'ausiliare *daštan* in neopersiano: un costrutto linguistico nord-iranico? *OM* 54(1974), pp. 298-303.

RADOVIL'SKIY, M.E. Ispol'zovanie leksikofrazeologicheskikh sinonimov kak stilisticheskogo sredstva v sovremennoy persidskoy proze. *Ind. i iran. filol.*, 1971, pp. 61-84.

RADOVIL'SKIY, M.E. Issledovanie problem persidskoy stilistiki iranskimi filologami. (Iranian philologists' researches in problems of Persian stylistics). *NAA* 1972(3), pp. 174-183.

RUBINCHIK, Yu.A. Frazeologizmy-predlozheniya i ikh mesto v sostave frazeologii persidskogo yazyka. *NAA* 1974(5), pp. 144-150.

RUBINCHIK, Yu. A. Persidskiy slozhnyy glagol kak raznovidnost' glagol'nykh frazeologizmov. *Ind. i iran. filol.*, 1972, pp. 170-183.

SADEGHI, Ali-Ashraf. L'influence de l'arabe sur le système du persan. *Linguistique* 11ii(1975), pp. 145-152.

SCARCIA, G., VERCELLIN, G. Leucippidi e Dioscuri in Iran: I.- Samand e Hing. - II.- Zur e Arzur. *Annali Fac. Ling. Lett. stran. di Ca' Foscari (serie orientale)* 1(1970), pp. 39-62.

SUNDERMANN, W. Einige Bemerkungen zum syrisch-neupersischen Psalmenbruchstück aus Chinesisch-Turkistan. *Mémorial J. de Menasce*, 1974, pp. 441-452.

TELEGDI, Zs. Remarques sur les emprunts arabes en persan. *Acta linguistica Acad. Sci. Hung.* 23(1973), pp. 51-58.

TELEGDI, Z. Remarques sur les emprunts arabes en persan. *Commémoration Cyrus. Hommage universel*, II, 1974, pp. 337-343.

TZABOLOV, R.L. Osnovy proshedshego vremeni na -*t*- v kurdskom yazyke. *Ind. i iran. filol.*, 1971, pp. 146-150.

USMANOVA, O.R. K voprosu ob izuchennosti omonimii v persidskom yazyke. *Vostokovedenie, yazykovedenie* 1973, pp. 57-70.

VON GRUNEBAUM, G.E. Arabic and Persian literature: problems of aesthetic analysis. *La Persia nel medievo,* 1971, pp. 337-349

WERYHO, J.W. Syriac influence on Islamic Iran. (The evidence of loanwords.) *Folia Or.* 13(1971), pp. 299-321.

WINDFUHR, L. Particle *ke* in modern Persian. *Proc.27th Int.Cong.Or.1967* (1971), p. 244.

L'opera di redazione del Dizionario persiano-italiano. *RSO* 48(1973-4), pp. 205-242.

See also IV. b. *Iqbāl.* Burki.

See also V. u. l. Reinhard

See also XXXVI. h. Kiseleva

See also XL. aa. Abrahamowicz

c MODERN PERSIAN DIALECTS

APOR, É. Gilanica: Langerudi. *Acta Or. Acad. Sci. Hung.* 27(1973), pp. 351-372.

ENTEZAR, M. Ehsan. "If" clauses in Dari. *Adab* 20i-ii(1972), pp. 1-7.

GERSHEVITCH, Ilya. The crushing of the third singular present. *W.B. Henning memorial vol.,* 1970, pp. 161-174.

HENDERSON, M.M.T. Diglossia in Kabul Persian phonology. *JAOS* 95(1975), pp. 651-654.

KANUS-CREDE, H. Notizen zum Dialekt von Anārak. *Iranistische Mitt.* 5(1971), pp. 10-22.

KARIEV, Sh.Z. K voprosu ob upotreblenii glagol'nogo prefiksa *bi-* v yazyke dari. (Nablyudeniya po materialam pamyatnika XII v. "Samak-e Ayyar".) *Issledovaniya po vostochnym yazykam,* 1973, pp. 94-98.

KHASHIMBEKOV, Kh. Arabskie zaimstvovaniya v yazyke dari. *Vost.yazyki,* 1971, pp. 178-184

KHASHIMBEKOV, Kh. Pashtonizmy v yazyke dari. *Vost.yazyki,* 1971, pp. 185-190

KHASHIMBEKOV, Kh. Problema evropeizmov v terminologii afganskogo dari. *Ind. i iran. filol.,* 1971, pp. 116-126.

KIEFFER, Ch.M. Les formules de lamentation funèbre des femmes à Caboul: *awaz andaxtan-e zana.* Note de dialectologie et d'ethnographie afghane. *Mél. ling. É. Benveniste,* 1975, pp. 313-323.

KIEFFER, C.M. Le multilinguisme des Ormuṛs de Baraki-Barak (Afghanistan) *Stud. iranica* 1(1972), pp. 115-126.

LAZARD, G. La catégorie de l'éventuel. *Mél. ling. É. Benveniste,* 1975, pp. 347-358.

LAZARD, G. Morphologie du verbe dans le parler persan du Sistan. *Studia Iranica* 3(1974), pp. 65-85.

LECOQ, P. Le dialecte d'Abu Zeyd Ābād. *Acta Iranica,* 2. sér. *Monumentum H.S. Nyberg,* II (1975), pp. 15-38.

LECOQ, P. Le dialecte d'Abyāne. *Studia Iranica* 3(1974), pp. 51-63.

ORANSKIY, I.M. O formakh 2-go litza mnozhestvennogo chisla na *-en/-in* v persidsko-tadzhikskikh govorakh. *Istoriya, kul tura. yazyki narodov Vostoka* 1970, pp. 201-206.

SHAHRANI, Enayatullah. The "Falaks" of the mountains. [Dari couplets from Badakhshan.] *Afghanistan* 26i(1973), pp. 68-75.

SKJAERVØ, P.O. Notes on the dialects of Minab and Hormoz. *Norwegian J. linguistics* 29(1975), pp. 113-128.

URALOV, Kh.U. Sopostavitel'nyy analiz modeley terminoobrazovaniya v dari i tadzhikskom yazyke. *NAA* 1974(2), pp. 145-149.

YAR-SHATER, E. The Jewish communities of Persia and their dialects. *Mémorial J. de Menasce,* 1974, pp. 453-466.

ZOMORRODIAN, Réza. Le système verbal du persan parlé à Qâyen. *Studia Iranica* 3 (1974), pp. 87-112.

Opyt lingvisticheskoy karty Nuristana. *Strany i narody Vostoka pod obshchey red. D.A. Ol'derogge,* X, 1971, pp. 288-289.

d OTHER IRANIAN LANGUAGES

Bactrian

HUMBACH, H. Die baktrische Āra der Tochi-Inschriften. *Festgabe deutscher Iranisten zur 2500 Jahrfeier Irans,* 1971, pp. 74-79.

MĘKARSKA, Barbara. An attempt at the reconstruction of the Bactrian language system. *Folia Or.* 15(1974), pp. 149-165.

SIMS-WILLIAMS, N. A note on Bactrian syntax. *Indog. Forschungen* 78(1973), pp. 95-99.

Balochi

BAUSANI, A. Recenti notizie dal Pakistan sulle letterature brahui e beluci. *OM* 54 (1974), pp. 187-196.

KAMIL AL-QADR, S.M. Mast Tawakkuli, a Baluchi poet. *J.Pak.Hist.Soc.* 20(1972), pp. 87-91.

QADRI, S.M. Kamil al-. Jām Durrak, a Baluch poet. *J. Pakistan Hist. Soc.* 19(1971), pp. 101-109.

ROOMAN, M. Anwar. A brief survey of Baluchi literature and language. *J. Pakistan Hist. Soc.* 16(1968), pp. 62-80.

Caspian dialects

AKHMEDOV, T.M. Nekotorye drevnetyurkskie slova v tatskom yazyke. (Some ancient Turkic words in the Tat language). *Sov. Tyurkologiya* 1971(6), pp. 69-79.

YAR-SHATER, E. Distinction of the feminine gender in Southern Tāti. *Studia classica et orientalia A. Pagliaro oblata,* III, 1969, pp. 281-301

YARSHATER, Ehsan. The Tati dialects of Ṭārom. *W.B. Henning memorial vol.,* 1970, pp. 451-467.

YAR-SHATER, Ehsan. The use of postpositions in Southern Tati. *Yād-nāme-ye Irāni-ye Minorsky,* 1969, pp. 221-255.

Judaeo-Persian

ASMUSSEN, J.P. A Jewish-Persian Munazare. *Iran Society silver jubilee souvenir* 1944-1969, pp. 23-30.

ASMUSSEN, J.P. Jüdisch-persische Hosea-stücke. *Acta Iranica,* 2. sér. *Monumentum H.S. Nyberg,* I (1975), pp. 15-29.

ASMUSSEN, J.P. Eine jüdisch-persische Übersetzung des Ben Sira-Alphabets. *Ex orbe religionum. Studia Geo Widengren oblata,* I, 1972, pp. 144-155.

ASMUSSEN, J.P. Šihab, a Judeo-Persian poet from Yazd. *Mémorial J. de Menasce,* 1974, pp. 415-418.

MAINZ, E. L'Ecclésiaste en judéo-persan. *Studia Iranica* 3(1974), pp. 211-228.

MAINZ, E. Esther en judéo-persan. *JA* 258(1970), pp. 95-106.

MAINZ, E. Les Lamentations en judéo-persan. *Studia Iranica* 2(1973), pp. 193-202.

NETZER, Amnon. Dāniyāl-Nāme: an exposition of Judeo-Persian. *Islam and its cultural divergence. Studies in honor of Gustave E. von Grunebaum,* 1971, pp. 145-164

NETZER, A. Dāniyāl-nāma and its linguistic features. *In memoriam S.M. Stern* (Israel Or. studies, II, 1972), pp. 305-314.

NETZER, Amnon. Some notes on the characterization of Cyrus the Great in Jewish and Judeo-Persian writings. *Commémoration Cyrus. Hommage universel,* II, 1974, pp. 35-52.

PAPER, H.H. Another Judeo-Persian Pentateuch translation: MS HUC 2193. *HUCA* 43(1972), pp. 207-251.

PAPER, H.H. Ecclesiastes in Judeo-Persian. *Orientalia* NS 42(1973), pp. 328-337.

PAPER, H.H. Isaiah in Judeo-Persian. *Acta Iranica,* 2. sér. *Monumentum H.S. Nyberg,* II (1975), pp. 145-161.

PAPER, H.H. Notes to a Judeo-Persian Bible manuscript: Ben-Zvi Institute, Jerusalem, MS 1028. *Indo-Iranian J.* 17(1975), pp. 217-243.

SHAKED, S. Judaeo-Persian notes. *Israel Oriental studies* 1(1971), pp. 178-182.

Khorezmian

HUMBACH, H. Neue chwaresmologische Arbeiten. *ZDMG* 123(1973), pp. 83-97.

LIVSHITZ, V.A. Khorezmskiy kalendar' i ery drevnego Khorezma. *Istoriya, kul'tura, yazyki narodov Vostoka* 1970, pp. 5-16.

MacKENZIE, D.N. The Khwarezmian glossary - II, III, IV. *BSOAS* 34(1971), pp. 74-90, 314-330, 521-537

MACKENZIE, D.N. Khwarezmian imperfect stems. *Mél. ling. É. Benveniste*, 1975, pp. 389-395.

SCHWARTZ, Martin. Miscellanea Iranica. *W. B. Henning memorial vol.,* 1970, pp. 385-394.

SCHWARTZ, M. On the vocabulary of the Khwarezmian *Muqaddimatu l-Adab,* as edited by J. Benzing. *ZDMG* 120 (1970), pp. 288-304.

Kurdish

KURDOEV, K.K. Izuchenie kurdskoy literatury v Irake. *NAA* 1975(2), pp. 171-179.

MACKENZIE, D.N. Malâ-ê Jizrî and Faqî Ṭayrân. *Yād-nāme-ye Irāni-ye Minorsky,* 1969, pp. 125-130.

MOKRI, Mohammad. Le *kalām* gourani sur le cavalier au coursier gris, le dompteur du vent. (Étude d'hérésiologie islamique et de thèmes mythiques iraniens). *JA* 262 (1974), pp. 47-93.

MUSAELYAN, Zh.S. Novye varianty kurdskogo narodnogo skazaniya "Zambil'frosh". *Istoriya, kul'tura, yazyki narodov Vostoka* 1970, pp. 103-108.

NEBEZ, Jemal. Die Schriftsprache der Kurden. *Acta Iranica,* 2. sér. *Monumentum H.S. Nyberg,* II (1975), pp. 97-122.

RITTER, H. Kurmānci-Texte aus dem Ṭūrabdîn. I. Kärboran. *Oriens* 21-22(1968-69), pp. 1-135.

RUDENKO, M.B. Kurdskaya literatura XVII veka. (Kurdi literature in the seventeenth century.) *NAA* 1971(3), pp. 93-105.

RUDENKO, M.B. Neopublikovannye stikhi kurdskikh poetov. *Vost. sbornik 3,* 1972, pp. 111-137.

TZABOLOV, R.L. K istorii kurdskikh plavnykh. *Issledovaniya po vostochnym yazykam,* 1973, pp. 230-241.

YUSUPOVA, Z.A. Upotreblenie pervichnykh predlogov s mestoimennoy enklitikoy -ê v yuzhnom dialekte kurdskogo yazyka. *Istoriya, kul'tura, yazyki narodov Vostoka* 1970, pp. 207-209.

Ossetic

ABAYEV, V.I. The names of the months in Ossetic. *W.B. Henning memorial vol.,* 1970, pp. 1-7.

BAILEY, H.W. Excursus iranocaucasicus. *Acta Iranica,* 2. sér. *Monumentum H.S. Nyberg,* I (1975), pp. 31-35.

BAILEY, H.W. North-Iranian traditions. *Commémoration Cyrus. Hommage universel,* I, 1974, pp. 292-296.

JOKI, A.J. Ossetisch und die Finnougristik. (Eine Übersicht.). *Acta ling. Hung.* 24(1974), pp. 191-196.

RICHTER, E. Die ossetische Bibliographie. Ein kurzer Überblick über die von der S.-M.-Kirov-Bibliothek in Ordschonikidse herausgegebene laufende Bibliographie. *Biblos* 23(1974), pp. 37-45.

THORDARSON, F. Ossetic and Caucasian - stray notes. *Norwegian J. ling.* 27(1973), pp. 85-92.

THORDARSON, F. Some notes on Anatolian Ossetic. *Acta Or.* 33(1971), pp. 145-167.

ZGUSTA, L. De Osseticae praesertim et Rossicae bilinguitatis modis variis nec non de bilinguarum enuntiationum transformatione Chomskiana. *Studia classica et orientalia A. Pagliaro oblata,* III, 1969, pp. 303-309

Pamir dialects

ALEKSEEV, M.E. Imennye slovosochetaniya v shunganskom yazyke. *NAA* 1973(6), pp. 131-136.

DODYCHUDOJEV, Rahim. Die Pamir-Sprachen. (Zum Problem der Konvergenz.) *Mitt.Inst. Orientforschung* 17(1971-72), pp. 463-470.

KHROMOV, A.L. Die Präposition *par* und Postposition *-yow* im Yaghnobi. *W.B. Henning memorial vol.,* 1970, pp. 228-230.

MORGENSTIERNE, G. The development of Iranian *r* + consonant in the Shughni group. *W.B. Henning memorial vol.,* 1970, pp. 334-342.

Pashto

ELFENBEIN, J. The Waneci dialect of Paxto *Afghanistan* 25 i(1972), pp. 28-72.

ELHAM, Mohammed Rahim. On the genealogy of Pashto. *Adab* [Kabul] 23iii(1975), pp. 1-7.

ENEVOLDSEN, Jens. Five specimens of Rahman Baba's poems. *Afghanistan* 24ii-iii(1971), pp. 18-25

GANIEV, A. Glagolnye frazeologicheskie edinitzy sovremennogo afganskogo yazyka. Opyt klassifikatzii strukturno-semanticheskikh tipov. *Vostokovedenie, yazykovedenie* 1973, pp. 3-20.

GANIEV, A. Nekotorye voprosy leksikograficheskogo opisaniya glagol'nykh frazeologicheskikh edinitz sovremennogo afganskogo yazyka. *Vostokovedenie, yazykovedenie* 1973, pp. 76-102.

GERASIMOVA, A.S. Sud'by afganskogo rasskaza 60-kh godov. *NAA* 1974(1), pp. 104-110.

KALININA, Z.M. Bezaffiksnoe slovoobrazovanie v sovremennom literaturnom pushtu. *Ind. i iran. filol.,* 1971, pp. 15-23.

KUSHEV, V.V. Grammatiko-leksikograficheskoe sochinenie "Riyāz al-makhabbat" i ego mesto y afganovedenii. *Pis'mennye pamyatniki Vostoka* 1970, pp. 73-82.

LEBEDEVA, G.D. Rukopisi *Divana* afganskogo poeta XVII v. Rakhmana-Baba v sobranii Leningradskogo otdeleniya Instituta vostokovedeniya AN SSSR. *Pismennye pamyatniki vostoka,* 1969, pp. 186-207.

MAJROUH, Sayd B. La femme contestaire. Un certain visage de la femme Pashtoune dans la poésie populaire de la langue Pashtô. *Adab* [Kabul] 23iii(1975), pp. 1-20.

MOHMAND, D.M. Kamil. Energism in Khushhal's didactics. *Pakistan philos. J.* 10i(1971), pp. 73-86.

MORGENSTIERNE, G. Traces of Indo-European accentuation in Pashto? *Norwegian J. ling.* 27(1973), pp. 61-65.

NILSEN, D.L.F., NUR, Fazel and KAMAL, Sajida. A partially annotated bibliography of Afghan linguistics. *Afghanistan* 23 ii(1970), pp. 82-101; 24 i(1971), pp. 55-63.

PSTRUSIŃSKA, Jadwiga. About the origin of comparison of adjectives in Pashto. *Folia Or.* 15(1974), pp. 167-180.

PSTRUSIŃSKA, J. On Afghan classification of poetic figures. *Folia or.* 14(1972-73), pp. 161-188.

PSTRUSIŃSKA, J. Poetic Forms in Afghan Poetry. *Folia Or.* 13(1971), pp. 233-256.

SCARCIA, R. Liriche di Khushhal Khan. *Veltro* 16v-vi(1972), pp. 465-473.

SIKOEV, R.R. Imennoe slovoslozhenie v sovremennom literaturnom pushtu. *Ind. iran. filol.,* 1971, pp. 85-102.

SKALMOWSKI, W. Two stories in Afridi dialect from F.C. Andreas' notes. *Acta Iranica,* 2. sér. *Monumentum H.S. Nyberg,* II (1975), pp. 243-249.

XXXVIII IRANIAN LANGUAGES. PERSIAN

TEGEY, Habibullah. The interaction of phonological and syntactic processes: examples from Pashto. *Papers from the 11th regional meeting, Chicago ling. soc.*, 1975, pp. 571-582.

VERCELLIN, G. Quartine di Khushhal Khān Khattak. *OM* 54(1974), pp. 336-340.

See also XXXVIII. c. Khashimbekov

Tajik

ABDULLAEV, R. K voprosu o slovoobrazovanii glagolov dvizheniya v tadzhikskom yazyke. *VLU* 1974, (2), pp. 137-139.

BEČKA, J. The historical veracity and topicality of the novel *Margi sudkhūr* by Sadriddin Aynī. *Yādnāme-ye Jan Rypka* 1967, pp. 197-207.

BEČKA, J. Traditional schools in the works of Sadriddin Aynī and other writers of Central Asia. *Arch. or.* 39 (1971), pp. 284-321.

BELAN, V.G. Sadriddin Ayni's works in the socialist countries. *OLZ* 67(1972). cols. 439-442.

IBRAGIMOVA, M.S. K probleme vydeleniya kategorii modal'nykh slov v sovremennom tadzhikskom yazyke. *Uchenye zapiski, Tadzh. Gos. Univ., seriya filol.* 4(1971), pp. 53-71.

KHASKASHEV, T.N. Slovesnoe udarenie i dlitel'nost' glasnykh v tadzhikskom Yazyke. (Word stress and vowel duration in Tagik.) *VLU* 1972(2), pp. 111-118.

LORENZ, M. Sadriddin Aini zur Entwicklung der modernen Tağikischen National sprache. *Z. f. Phonetik* 28(1975), pp. 271-280.

MA'SUMI, N. Poem on the transformation of life. *Yādnāme-ye Jan Rypka* 1967, pp. 209-217.

MIRZOEV, A.M., NIKOLAEV, I.L. Razvitie yazykoznaniya v Tadzhikistane v 1965-1970 gg. *Vop. Yaz.* 5(1971), pp. 146-150.

NAZIROVA, Kh. Peredacha persidsko-tadzhikskoy bezekvivalentoy leksiki v angliyskom perevode. *Voprosy vostochnogo literaturovedeniya i tekstologii*, 1975, pp. 92-99.

ORANSKIJ, I.M. Indo-Iranica IV: Tadjik (régional) *buruj* "bouleau". *Mél. ling. É. Benveniste*, 1975, pp. 435-440.

ROZENFEL'D, A.Z. Vyrazhenie budushchego vremeni s pomoshch'yu dvukh nesoglasovannykh glagolov v yugo-vostochnykh govorakh tadzhikskogo yazyka. *Voprosy filol. stran Azii i Afriki* II(1973), pp. 18-22.

SADYKOVA, K.N. Leksicheskie i grammaticheskie sredstva vyrazheniya kolichestvennykh otntsheniy v russkom i tadzhikskom yazykakh. *Uchenye zapiski, Tadzh. Gos. Univ., seriya filol.* 4(1971), pp. 72-81.

SHUKUROV, M. Elements of rhyming prose in the *Ëddoshtho* of S. Aynī. *Yādnāme-ye Jan Rypka* 1967, pp. 219-224.

TELEGDI, Zs. La construction *abrūi muhoyaš daroz* en Tadjik. *W.B. Henning memorial vol.*, 1970, pp. 427-446.

TRETIAKOFF, A. Comparaison des lois de succession des voyelles en Uzbek et en Tadjik. *Zeits. f. Phonetik* 25(1972), pp. 85-94.

See also XXXVIII. c. Oranskiy.

See also XXXVIII. c. Uralov.

Others

MAMEDOV, M.A. Zametki o leksike yazyka Khaladzhey. (Notes on the vocabulary of the Khaladji language.) *NAA* 1973(1), pp. 153-155.

XXXIX PERSIAN LITERATURE

a GENERAL

ABDUR RAHMAN, Maulana Syed Sabahuddin. Gifts of Indian scholars to Iranian purists. *Indo-Iranica* 23i-ii(1970), pp. 70-73.

ABDUR RAHMAN, Syed Sabahuddin. Persian poets of Indian origin. *Iran Society silver jubilee souvenir* 1944-1969, pp. 261-285.

ABDUR RAHMAN, Syed Sabahuddin. Sentiments of love and adoration for India in Indo-Persian literature with special reference to Bengal. *Indo-Iranica* 25iii-iv(1972), pp. 62-101.

AHMAD, Aziz. The formation of *Sabk-i Hindi*. *Iran and Islam, in memory of V. Minorsky*, 1971, pp. 1-9

AKIMUSHKIN, O.F. K voprosu o traditzii zhanra iskusstvennoy kasuidy v persidskoy poezii. *Iran (Pamyati B.N. Zakhodera)* (1971), pp. 158-168.

XXXIX PERSIAN LITERATURE

APOR, E. Local poets in Qajar-*tazkeres* -- a study on the *Safinat ul-Mahmud* of the Hungarian Academy Library in Budapest. *The Middle East; studies in honour of J. Germanus*, 1974, pp. 213-220.

BAUSANI, A. Considerazioni sull'origine del ghazal. *La Persia nel medievo*, 1971, pp. 195-208

BAUSANI, A. Note sui prestiti arabi nella più antica poesia neopersiana. *Studia Classica et Orientalia Antonino Pagliaro oblata* 1(1969), pp. 173-188

BERTHELS, A. Some remarks on Persian textology. *Yádnáme-ye Jan Rypka* 1967, pp. 57-64.

BOISSEL, J. Pour une esthétique de la poésie persane. *Rev.litt.comp.* 49(1975), pp. 531-546.

BURRILL, K.R.F. The Fārhād and Shīrīn story and its further development from Persian into Turkish literature. *Studies in art and literature of the Near East in honor of R. Ettinghausen*, 1974, pp. 53-78.

CHELKOWSKI, P. Dramatic and literary aspects of Ta'zieh-Khani - Iranian passion play. *Review of national literatures*, 2i (1971), pp. 121-138.

CHELKOWSKI, P. Dramatic aspects of *ta'zieh-khani*, Iranian Passion play. *Proc.27th Int.Cong.Or.1967* (1971), pp. 200-202.

CHELKOWSKI, P. Literature in pre-Safavid Isfahan. *Iranian stud.* 7iii-iv(1974), pp. 112-131.

CHELKOWSKI, P. Society and literature in Iran. *Modern Near East: literature and society*, ed. by C.M. Kortepeter, 1971, pp. 19-34.

CLARK, R.C. Review article: Perspectives from London and Prague. [On Arberry, *Classical Persian literature* and Rypka, *History of Iranian literature.*] *Review of national literatures*, 2i(1971), pp. 182-191.

DE BRUIJN, J.T.P. The religious use of Persian poetry. *Studies on Islam*, 1974, pp. 63-74.

EBADIAN, M. Der Fatalismus in der persischen Epik und sein Wesenszug. *XVIII. Deutscher Orientalistentag 1972: Vorträge*, pp. 465-470.

FOUCHÉCOUR, C.H. de. Le testament moral de Chosroes dans la littérature persane. *Mémorial J. de Menasce*, 1974, pp. 419-431.

GANDJEI, T. The genesis and definition of a literary composition: the Dah-nāma ('Ten love-letters'). *Der Islam* 47(1971), pp. 59-66.

GVAKHARIYA, A.A. Iz istorii gruzino-persidskikh literaturnykh vzaimo-otnosheniy. *Problemy literatur oriental-nych*, 1974, pp. 77-80.

HANAWAY, W. Comments on literature before the Safavid period. *Iranian stud.* 7iii-iv (1974), pp. 132-137.

HANAWAY, W.L., Jr. Formal elements in the Persian popular romances. *Review of national literatures*, 2i(1971), pp. 139-161.

HANAWAY, W.L. Popular literature in Iran. *Iran: continuity and variety, ed. by P.J. Chelkowski*, 1971, pp. 59-75

HASAN, Syed. Sí-Námehs in Persian. *Indo Iranica* 26ii-iii(1973), pp. 62-71.

HAUG, Walter. Die Tristansage und das persische Epos Wîs und Râmîn. *Germanisch-romanische Monatsschrift* N.F. 23(1973), pp. 404-423.

IMAMNAZAROV, M.S. Opyt statisticheskogo sravneniya raznozhanrovykh tekstov persidskoy poezii. *NAA* 1974(5), pp. 150-153.

INAYATULLAH, Shaikh. Persian literature and its extension in the Indo-Pakistan sub-continent. *J. Reg. Cult. Inst.* 4(1971), pp. 131-137.

JAVADI, Hasan. Matthew Arnold's "Sohrab and Rustum" and its Persian original. *Review of national literatures* 2i(1971), pp. 61-73.

JAVADI, H. Persian literary influence in English literature. I - The early image: classical and Biblical sources. *Indo-Iranica* 25(1972), pp. 1-25, 52-100; 26(1973), pp. 20-59.

JAZAYERY, Mohammad Ali. Aḥmad Kasravî and the controversy over Persian poetry. 1. Kasravî's analysis of Persian poetry. *IJMES* 4(1973), pp. 190-203.

JAZAYERY, M.A. Observations on stylistic variation in Persian. *Actes du Xe Congrès International des Linguistes, 1967* vol. III, (1970), pp. 447-457.

KOBIDZE, D. On the antecedents of Vis-u-Ramin. *Yádnáme-ye Jan Rypka* 1967, pp. 89-93.

LAZARD, G. *Āhu-ye kuhi*, le chamois d'Abu Hafs de Sogdiane, et les origines du *robāi*. *W.B. Henning memorial vol.*, 1970, pp. 238-244.

MONCHI-ZADEH, D. Iranische Miszellen. *Acta Iranica*, 2. sér. *Monumentum H.S. Nyberg*, II (1975), pp. 59-75.

NAIMUDDIN, Sayyid. Evil and freewill in Rumi and Iqbal. *IC* 46(1972), pp. 227-234.

QAZI, Nabibakhsh. Life-values in Persian literature. *J. Reg. Cult. Inst.* 2 iv(1969), pp. 226-232.

RAHMAN, M. Influence of legendary kings and heroes on Persian literature. *Indo-Iranica* 24i-ii(1971), pp. 50-63.

REINERT, B. Die prosodische Unterschiedlichkeit von persischem und arabischem Ruba'ī. *Islamwissenschaftliche Abhandlungen F. Meier,* 1974, pp. 205-225.

ROSE, E. Persian mysticism in Goethe's "West Östlicher Divan". *Review of national literatures* 2i(1971), pp. 92-111.

SAFA, Z. Un aperçu sur l'évolution de la pensée à travers la poésie persane. *Yādnāme-ye Irāni-ye Minorsky,* 1969, pp. 169-189.

SCHIMMEL, A. The eternal charm of classical Persian poetry. *Islam and the modern age* 1 i (1970), pp. 65-69.

SCHIMMEL, A. Turk and Hindu; a literary symbol. *Acta Iranica,* sér. 1, III, 1974, pp. 243-248.

SEMENOV, A.A. Persian literature of Central Asia (1500-1900 A.D.) *Indo-Iranica* 25(1972), pp. 26-35.

SLOMP, J. The triangle: Hafiz, Goethe and Iqbal. *al-Mushir* 16(1974), pp. 199-214.

SOUCEK, P.P. Farhād and Ṭāq-i Būstān: the growth of a legend. *Studies in art and literature of the Near East in honor of R. Ettinghausen,* 1974, pp. 27-52.

SULTANOV, R.S. O printzipakh perevoda klassicheskoy persoyazychnoy khudozhestvennoy literatury. *Problemy literatur orientalnykh,* 1974, pp. 151-165.

SULTANOV, M. On the problem of "Literary School" in Orientology. *Yádnáme-ye Jan Rypka* 1967, pp. 147-148.

ṢURATGAR, Loṭf'alī. Grundzüge der persischen Literatur. *Iranistische Mitteilungen* 3i (1969), pp. 2-29.

THOMSON, J. The "Divan" of Goethe. *Review of national literatures,* 2i(1971), pp. 112-120.

WICKENS, G.M. Persian literature as an affirmation of national identity. *Review of national literatures* 2i(1971), pp. 29-60.

WILBER, D.N. Iran: bibliographical spectrum. *Review of national literatures,* 2i(1971), pp. 161-181.

WINDFUHR, G.L. and WORKMAN, J.R. Literature in translation -- Iranian into English. (Teaching Materials III). *MESA Bull.* 7i(1973), pp. 9-41.

ZAND, M. Some light on bilingualism in literature of Transoxania, Khurasan and Western Iran in the 10th century A.D. *Yádnáme-ye Jan Rypka* 1967, pp. 161-164.

See also II. a. 7. Melikian-Chirvani.

See also II. c. 2. Baig.

See also IX. g. Lambton

See also XXXI. a. Fischel.

See also XXXVII. b. Reinert.

See also XXXVII. b. Von Grunebaum

See also XLI. a. Borolina.

b FROM THE BEGINNINGS TO 1290 A. D.

AHSAN, A. Shakoor The home town of Rabi'ah Bint-i Ka'b. *Iqbal* 18iii(1971), pp. 83-91

AKIMUSHKIN, O.F. Stikhotvoreniya Nizami v antologii Mukhammada 'Ali Sa'iba. *Pismennye pamyatniki vostoka,* 1969, pp. 7-27.

AZIZ, Ghulam Rabbani. Literary and cultural activity in Khwarazm (11th-12th century). *J.Pak.Hist.Soc.* 22(1974), pp. 83-112.

BAEVSKIY, S.I. Pervoe neizvestnoe izdanie slovarya Shams-i Fakhri "Mi'yar-i Dzhamali". *Pis'mennye pamyatniki Vostoka* 1971, pp. 5-8.

BANANI, Amin. Ferdowsi and the art of tragic epic. *Islam and its cultural divergence. Studies in honor of Gustave E. von Grunebaum,* 1971, pp. 3-9

BASSIM, Tamara Omar. Les Rubayats d'Omar Khayyam. *Ann.Fac.Arts Ain Shams* 8 (1963), pp. 237-239.

BAUSANI, A. Nizāmī di Gangia e la "Pluralità dei Mondi". *RSO* 46(1971), pp. 197-215.

BAYBURDI, CR. G. Predvaritel'noe sopostavlenie dvukh rukopisey kulliyata Nizari. *Vost. sbornik 3,* 1972, pp. 101-110.

BERTELS, E.E. Zur russischen Schahname-Ausgabe. *Iranistische Mitt.* 6(1972), pp. 3-41.

BOWEN, J.C.E. The Rubā'iyāt of Omar Khayyam. A critical assessment of Robert Graves' and Omar Ali Shah's translation *Iran* 11(1973), pp. 63-73.

BÜRGEL, J.C. Lautsymbolik und funktionales Wortspiel bei Rumi. *Islam* 51(1974), pp. 261-281.

BUSSE, H. Thron, Kosmos und Lebensbaum im Schāhnāme. *Festgabe deutscher Iranisten zur 2500 Jahrfeier Irans,* 1971, pp. 8-21.

DUDA, H.W. Nâsir-e Khosrou: Der Adler. *Bustan* 11iv-12i(1970-1), pp. 18-19.

EBADIAN, M. Der Fatalismus in der persischen Epik und sein Wesenszug. *XVIII. Deutscher Orientalistentag* 1972, pp. 465-470.

EILERS, W. Erinnerung an Schiras. *Islamwissenschaftliche Abhandlungen F. Meier,* 1974, pp. 33-48.

FRYE, R.N. Development of Persian literature under the Samanids and Qarakhanids. *Yádnáme-ye Jan Rypka* 1967, pp. 69-74.

GABRIELI, F. L'epopea firdusiana e la letteratura araba. *La Persia nel medievo*, 1971, pp. 209-213

GRAMLICH, R. Die achtzehn Eingangsverse aus Maulanas Masnawi übersetzt. *Asiat. Studien* 28(1974), pp. 65-66.

GRIGOR'EV, A.P. Khudozhestvennye obrazy i sredstva "Shakhname" v "Knige puteshestviya" Evlii Chelebi . *Voprosy filol. stran Azii i Afriki* II(1973), pp. 105-115.

GUSEYNOV, R. O chetverostishiyakh Baba Takhira. *Voprosy vostochnogo literaturovedeniya i tekstologii*, 1975, pp. 84-91.

GÜVEN, Rasih. Mawlānā Djalāl al-Dīn al-Rūmī and Shams-i Tabrīzī. *Doğu dilleri* lii(1966), pp. 223-239.

HADIDI, Djavad. Firdowsy dans la littérature française. *Rev. lit. comp.* 49(1975), pp. 365-372.

HANSEN, K.H. Die Krone im Schahname. *Iranistische Mitteilungen* lii(1967), pp. 26-44.

HERMAN, A.L. Ṣūfīsm, fatalism and evil in the *Mathnawī* of Jalāl al-Din Rūmi. *Iqbal rev.* 12iii(1971), pp. 1-15

ISHAQUE, M. Abu'l-Hasan of Laukar. *Indo-Iranica* 23iv(1970), pp. 1-2.

ISHAQUE, M. Qamari of Gurgan. *Indo-Iranica* 25iii-iv(1972), pp. 57-61.

ISHAQUE, M. Rudaki, the father of neo-Persian poetry. *Iran Society silver jubilee souvenir* 1944-1969, pp. 143-160.

JAMALPUR, B. The mystical religion of Mowlavi. *J.Reg.Cult.Inst.* 7(1974), pp. 217-231.

KAAK, Othman. Mevlana Celal ed Dine--miroir de son siècle. *Doğu dilleri* liii(1969), pp. 165-172.

KANUS-CREDÉ, H. Did Firdousi know Middle-Persian? *Iranistische Mitteilungen* 5(1971), pp. 2-10.

KANUS-CREDE, H. Firdousi, Schahname, V. Der Dahhāk. Deutsch. *Iranistische Mitt.* 9(1975), pp. 45-75.

KANUS-CREDE, H. Das Königsbuch des Firdousi. *Iranistische Mitt.* 6(1972), pp. 54-74.

KLIMENKO, A.A. "Rubayat" Omara Khayyama na Ukraine. (Omar Khayyam's "Rubaiyat" in the Ukraine.) *NAA* 1971(6), pp. 116-122.

KONIECZNA, A. Dakiki, poeta perski X w. *Przegl.or.* 4(80), 1971, pp. 385-390.

KOZMOYAN, A.K. Razvitie uslozhnennogo stilya v lyubovnykh chetverosttishiyakh Unsuri. *NAA* 1975(1), pp. 172-176.

LANG, David M. Parable and precept in the Marzubān-Nāme. *W.B. Henning memorial vol.*, 1970, pp. 231-237.

LAZARD, G. Abu l-Mu'ayyad Balxī. *Yádnáme-ye Jan Rypka* 1967, pp. 95-101.

LAZARD, G. Deux poèmes persans de tradition pehlevie. *Mémorial J. de Menasce*, 1974, pp. 433-440.

LAZARD, G. Les origines de la poésie persane. *Cahiers de civ. méd.* 14(1971), pp. 305-317.

LAZARD, G. Le poète Manteqi de Rey. *Mélange d'iranologie en mémoir de feu Said Naficy*, 1972, pp. 56-82.

MAGUIRE, M.E. The *Haft Khvān* of Rustam and Isfandiyār. *Studies in art and literature of the Near East in honor of R. Ettinghausen*, 1974, pp. 137-147.

MAJID, M.A. Firdausī's influence on Indian literature. *Indo-Iranica* 23iv (1970), pp. 11-14.

MAJID, M.A. Muḥammad bin Waṣīf of Sīstán, an early neo-Persian poet. *Indo-Iranica* 25ii(1972), pp. 101-104.

MASSÉ, H. The poetess Rābi'a Qozdāri. *Yádnáme-ye Jan Rypka* 1967, pp. 103-106.

MEIER, F. Zum 700. Todestag Mawlānās, des Vater der tanzenden Derwische. *Asiat. Studien* 28(1974), pp. 54-64.

MELIKIAN-CHIRVANI, Asadullah Souren. Le roman de Varqe et Golšāh: essai sur les rapports de l'esthétique littéraire et de l'esthétique plastique dans l'Iran prémongol, suivi de la traduction du poème. *Arts asiatiques* 22 (1970), 262 pp.

MEREDITH-OWENS, G.M. An early Persian miscellany. *Iran and Islam, in memory of V. Minorsky*, 1971, pp. 435-441

MINORSKY, V. The earliest collections of O. Khayyam. *Yádnáme-ye Jan Rypka* 1967, pp. 107-118.

MINORSKY, V. Ibn-Farighun and the Hudud Al-'Alam. *Afghanistan* 25ii(1972), pp. 4-10

MIRZOEV, Abdul-Ghani. One more spurious manuscript of Rudaki's verses. *Iran Society silver jubilee souvenir* 1944-1969, pp. 247-260.

MOAYYAD, Heshmat. Some remarks on the Nasirean ethics by Naṣīr ad-Dīn Ṭūsī. *JNES* 31 (1972), pp. 179-186.

MOIN, Mohd. The number 'seven' and Nizami's Haft paykar (The seven images). *Poure Davoud Memorial Vol.*, II, 1951, pp. 50-61.

MOIN, Moh. The prologue and the epilogue of the Mathnavi. *Doğu dilleri* liii (1969), pp. 79-81.

MORRISON, G. Flowers and witchcraft in the 'Vīs o Rāmīn' of Fakhr ud-Dīn Gurgānī. *Acta Iranica*, sér. 1, III, 1974, pp. 249-259.

NAIMUDDIN, Sayyid. The ideal man in Rumi and Iqbal. *IC* 45 (1971), pp. 81-94.

OSMANOV, M-N.O. Raznochteniya i opiski v spiskakh Shakh-name i ikh fiksatiya v kriticheskom tekste. *Pis'mennye pamyatniki Vostoka* 1968, pp. 135-141.

PASHAEV, S. Nizami i azerbaydzhanskie narodnye predaniya. *Voprosy vostochnogo literaturovedeniya i tekstologii,* 1975, pp. 120-126.

REHDER, R.M. The text of Ḥāfiẓ. *JAOS* 94 (1974), pp. 145-156.

REHDER, R.M. The unity of the ghazals of Ḥāfiẓ. *Islam* 51(1974), pp. 55-96.

REMPIS, C. Kurzfassung der Grundsätze für eine kritische Standardtextausgabe des Schāhnāmé. *Proc.27th Int.Cong.Or.1967* (1971), pp. 167-168.

RICHTER-BERNBURG, L. Linguistic Shu'ūbīya and early neo-Persian prose. *JAOS* 94(1974), pp. 55-64.

SOUTHGATE, M.S. Fate in Firdawsīs "Rustam va Suhrāb". *Studies in art and literature of the Near East in honor of R. Ettinghausen,* 1974, pp. 149-159.

VOROZHEYKINA, Z.N. Neizdannye stroki Anvari. *Pis'mennye pamyatniki Vostoka* 1968, pp. 68-72.

VOROZHEYKINA, Z.N.; NIYAZOV, Kh.N. Persidskaya literatura domongol skogo perioda v rukipisnom sobranii IV AN SSSR. *Istoriya, Kul'tura, yazyki narodov Vostoka* 1970, pp. 32-38.

VOROZHEYKINA, Z.N. Primechanie k Divanu Ustada Abū-l-Faradzha Rūnī. *Pis'mennye pamyatniki Vostoka* 1970, pp. 69-72.

WICKENS, G.M. The imperial epic of Iran: a literary approach. *Iranian civilization and culture,* ed. C.J. Adams, 1972, pp. 133-144; *Acta Iranica,* sér. 1, III, 1974, pp. 261-275.

WIŚNIEWSKA-PISOWICZOWA, J. Quelques remarques sur l'art de Nizāmi dans son poème *Haft paikar. Folia or.* 14(1972-73), pp. 189-206.

YOHANNAN, J.D. The fin de siècle cult of FitzGerald's "Rubaiyat" of Omar Khayyam. *Review of national literatures* 2i(1971), pp. 74-91.

ZAIDI, Nazir Hasan. Mas'ud Sa'd Salman. *J.Reg.Cult.Inst.* 3(nos. 11-12, 1970), pp. 125-134.

ZAJĄCZKOWSKI, A. La composition et la formation historique de l'épopée iranienne (Le Šāh-nāme de Firdausi). *La poesia epica e la sua formazione,* 1970, pp. 679-695.

Das Königsbuch des Firdousi. *Iranistische Mitteilungen* 6(1972), pp. 54-74.

Das Vorwort des Baysonghor. *Iranistische Mitteilungen* 6(1972), pp. 42-53.

See also II. c. 3. Soliman.

See also IV. c. 10 Brandenburg

See also V. m. 1. Kalantari.

See also V. m. 1. Maguire.

See also V. m. 1. Soucek.

See also XXIX. a. Seljuque.

See also XXXIX. e. Bowen.

c FROM 1265 TO 1502

ABDUR RAHMAN, Syed Sabahuddin. A glance on Amír Khusrau's *Wastu'l-Hayát. Indo-Iranica* 24iii.iv (1971), pp. 37-66.

ABIDI, S.A.H. The supplement of Tughlaqnama. *Afghanistan* 27iv(1975), pp. 40-46.

AHMAD, Ayaz. Amír Khusrau - The *Ṭūṭī-i-Hind. Indo-Iranica* 24iii-iv (1971), pp. 82-95.

AHMAD, Nazir. Badi-ud-Din Turku Sistani. *Afghanistan* 24i(1971), pp. 28-43

AHMAD, Nazir. A critical examination of Baihaqi's narration of the Indian expeditions during the reign of Masud of Ghazna. *Afghanistan* 24iv(1972), pp. 68-92

ANAND, Mulk Raj. Homage to Amir Khusrau. *Marg* 28iii(1974-5), pp. 3-12.

ARBERRY, A.J. Plato's 'testament to Aristotle'. *BSOAS* 34(1971), pp. 475-490.

BALDICK, J. The authenticity of 'Irāqī's 'Ushshāq-nāma. *Studia Iranica* 2(1973), pp. 67-78.

BARAKAEVA, G.B., DEMIDCHIK, V.P. Zametki k perevodam Khafiza na angliyskiy yazyk. *Uchenye zapiski, Tadzh. Gos. Univ., seriya filol.* 4(1971), pp. 82-87.

BAUSANI, A. Bēdil as a narrator. *Yádnáme-ye Jan Rypka* 1967, pp. 227-235.

BEGUM, Iqbal Jehan. Historical romances of Amír Khusrau. *Indo-Iranica* 24iii-iv (1971), pp. 96-101.

BOLDYREV, A.N. Literary-critical opinions of Jāmī and his contemporaries. *Yádnáme-ye Jan Rypka* 1967, pp. 65-67.

BOYLE, J.A. The chronology of Sa'di's years of travel. *Islamwissenschaftliche Abhandlungen F. Meier,* 1974, pp. 1-8.

BROMS, H. Euphony and the Weltanschauung in Ḥāfiẓ's poetry. *SO* 46(1975), pp. 31-37.

BÜRGEL, J.Ch. Nizami über Sprache und Dichtung. Ein Abschnitt aus der "Schatzkammer der Geheimnisse" eingeleitet, übertragen und erläutert. *Islamwissenschaftkuche Abhandlungen F. Meier,* 1974, pp. 9-28.

CALASSO, G. Il Xāvar-nāmè di Ibn Ḥosām: note introduttive. *RSO* 48(1973-4), pp. 153-173.

CHAUHAN, D.V. Sanskrit influence on Amīr Khusrau. *ABORI* 51 (1970), pp. 51-58.

DEHGHAN, Iraj. Jāmī's *Salāmān and Absāl*. *JNES* 30 (1971), pp. 118-126.

FARHĀDĪ, Abd-ul-Ghafour Ravan. L'amour dans les récits de Jāmī. *Adab* (Kabul) 22ii(1974), pp. 1-11.

HAMER, A.C.M. An unknown Mawlawî-poet: Aḥmad-i Rûmî. *Studia Iranica* 3(1974), pp. 229-249.

HILLMANN, M.C. Ḥāfeẓ and poetic unity through verse rhythms. *JNES* 31(1972), pp. 1-10

HILLMANN, M.C. Hafez's "Turk of Shiraz" again. *Iranian stud.* 8(1975), pp. 164-182.

HILLMANN, M.C. Sound and sense in a *ghazal* of Ḥāfiẓ. *MW* 61 (1971), pp. 111-121.

HILLMANN, M.C. The text of Ḥāfiẓ: addenda. *JAOS* 95(1975), pp. 719-720.

KARAMANLIOĞLU, A.F. Über die Ausgabe der "Gulistān - Übersetzung" von Sayf-i Sarāyī. *OLZ* 67(1972), col. 325-333.

KASUR, Muhammad Inamul Haq. Hilālī. *J.Pak. Hist. Soc.* 21(1973), pp. 20-36.

KAUSAR, Inamul Haq. Jami. *J. Pakistan Hist. Soc.* 17(1969), pp. 93-108; 231-250.

KAUSAR, M. Inamul Haq. Some less known Persian poets of 9th century H. *J.Pak. Hist.Soc.* 21(1973), pp. 227-232; 22(1974), pp. 32-38, 113-124.

KAUSAR, M. Inamul Haq. Some less known Persian poets of the 9th century H. *J. Pak. Hist. Soc.* 23(1975), pp. 58-70.

MASON, H. The parrot and the merchant. Adapted from the Persian poem 'Hekayat tuti va bazargan', by Rumi. *Humaniora Islamica* 2(1974), pp. 89-102.

MASSÉ, H. Le Divan de la princesse Djehane. *Mélange d'iranologie en mémoir de feu Said Naficy,* 1972, pp. 1-55.

MIRZA, Mohammad Wahid. The secret of Khusrau's greatness. *Indo-Iranica* 24iii-iv (1971), pp. 1-5.

MIRZOYEV, Abdulghanḳ. Rauzat al-ʿuššāḳ and its author. *Yádnáme-ye Jan Rypka* 1967, pp. 119-123.

NASR, Seyyed Hossein. Rūmī and the Sufi tradition. *Studies in comparative religion* 8(1974), pp. 74-89.

NIGAM, S.B.P. Amír Khusrau and India. *Indo-Iranica* 24iii-iv (1971), pp. 67-73.

PIEMONTESE, A.M. 'Omar Khayyām in Italia. *OM* 54(1974), pp. 275-297.

RAHMAN, M. Amír Khusrau (652-725 A.H.). A harbinger of Hindo-Muslim culture. *Indo-Iranica* 24iii-iv (1971), pp. 74-81.

RAVAN FARHĀDI, Abd-ol-Ghafour. L'amour dans les récits de Djâmi. *Studia Iranica* 4(1975), pp. 207-218.

RAVAN FARHADI, A.G. Chronological tables on the life and works of Amīr Khusraw. *Adab* [Kabul] 22iv(1975), pp. 1-18.

SAMOKHVALOVA, V.I. Literaturno-esteticheskie vzglady Dzhami i ikh znachenie dlya razvitiya poezii. *NAA* 1974(4), pp. 139-146.

SARKAR, Jagadish Narayan. Amír Khusrau and the art of war in medieval India. *Indo-Iranica* 24iii-iv (1971), pp. 6-36.

SCARCIA, G. Dieci *ghazal* di Ṣā'eb per Francesco Gabrieli. *OM* 54(1974), pp. 304-308.

SCHIMMEL, A. Feiern zum Gedenken an Maulānā Galāluddīn Balhī-Rūmī. *WI* N.S.16(1975), pp. 229-231.

SERĪKOVA, L.N. Ideyno-tematicheskaya osnova malykh form *(kit'a, rubai, fard)* liriki Navoi. *NAA* 1975(3), pp. 146-153.

SHOMUHAMEDOV, Sh. M. Hafiz and his humanism. *Yádnáme-ye Jan Rypka* 1967, pp. 133-140.

SLOMP, J. The triangle: Hafiz, Goethe and Iqbal. *Main currents of contemporary thought in Pakistan,* ed. Hakim Mohammed Said, Karachi, 1973, vol. II, pp. 388-414.

TAGIRDZHANOV, A.T. Amir Khosrov Dikhlevi. *Vestn. Leningrad. Univ., Ist., Yaz., lit.* 1975(4), pp. 95-102.

URUNBAYEV, A.; EPIFANOVA, L. The letters of Abdarrahman Jami as a source of the characteristics of the poet's personality. *Yádnáme-ye Jan Rypka* 1967, pp. 155-159.

URUNBAYEV, A., EPIFANOVA, L. The letters of Abdarrahman Jami as a source of the characteristics of the poet's personality. *Afghanistan* 27ii(1974), pp. 79-85.

UTAS, B. Tariq ut-tahqiq. II. *Afghanistan* 28ii(1975), pp. 56-92.

YAR-SHATER, Ehsan. Safavid literature: progress or decline. *Iranian stud.* 7iii-iv (1974), pp. 217-270.

See also II. c. 2. Chittick.

See also II. c. 2. Nasr.

See also IV. b. *Iqbal.* Farooqi.

See also XXXVII. f. Dutt.

d MODERN LITERATURE

ABIDI, S.A.H. Ṣā'ib Tabrīzī Iṣfahānī: life and poetry. *Yadname-ye Jan Rypka* 1967, pp. 49-55.

XXXIX PERSIAN LITERATURE

ALAMI, Schahnas. Die iranische Dichterin Parwin E'tesami. *Mitt Inst. Orientforschung* 17(1971), pp. 49-62.

ALAVI, B. From modern Iranian literature. *Yádnáme-ye Jan Rypka* 1967, pp. 167-172.

BAŇÁK, Kamil. Moḥammad Mas'ūd "Tafrīḥāt-e shab" - analytical approach to the composition of the novel. *Asian and African studs.* 9(1973), pp. 81-96.

BAUSANI, A. Ghalib's Persian poetry. *Ghalib: the poet and his age,* 1972, pp. 70-104.

BAUSANI, A. Indian elements in the Indo-Persian poetry: the style of Ganīmat Kunǧāhī. *Orientalia Hispanica* I, 1974, pp. 105-119.

BAUSANI, A. The life and work of Iqbal. *Iqbal R.* 14iii(1973), pp. 45-60.

BAUSANI, A. Note sui prestiti arabi nella più antica poesia neopersiana. *Studia Classica et Orientalia Antonino Pagliaro oblata,* 1969, Vol. I, pp. 173-188.

BAUSANI, A. L'opera di Mirza Abdul Qadir Bedil. *Veltro* 16v-vi(1972), pp. 447-463.

BURKI, R.J. Iqbal's legacy to the world. *J.Reg.Cult.Inst.* 3(nos. 11-12, 1970), pp. 119-124.

CELNAROVÁ, X. Das dramatische Werk Mīrzā Feth-'Alī Ahundzāde's. *Asian and African studies* [Bratislava] 10(1974), pp. 169-176.

CLAVEL, Leothiny S. Islamic allusions in the poetry of Iqbal. *Asian studs.* 8(1970), pp. 378-385.

CLINTON, J.W. The wedding. Gholamhusayn Sa'edi. Translated. *Iranian studies* 8i-ii(1975), pp. 2-48.

CORTIANA, R. Riscontri di Nerval in Ṣadeq Hedāyat. *Annali Fac. Ling. Lett. stran. di Ca' Foscari (serie orientale)* 1(1970), pp. 123-130.

DAR, B.A. Address to Javid. *Iqbal rev.* 12i(1971), pp. 12-38.

DESAI, Z.A. Ganj-i-ma'ani of Muti'i. *Iran Society silver jubilee souvenir* 1944-1969, pp. 59-78.

DJAMALZADEH, M.A. "Chauhare Ahou Khanom" (The husband of Ahou Khanom): a recent Persian novel of outstanding quality. *Yádnáme-ye Jan Rypka* 1967, pp. 173-178.

DORRI, Dzh. Satira Sadeka Chubaka. *NAA* 1975(5), pp. 106-114.

DORRI, Dzh. Stareyshina iranskikh pisateley. *Iran (Pamyati B.N. Zakhodera)* 1971, pp. 169-184.

DORRI, Dzh. Yumor i satira v persidskom narodnom tvorchestve. *Problemy literatur orientalnych,* 1974, pp. 67-75.

ELWELL-SUTTON, L.P. The influence of folktale and legend on modern Persian literature. *Iran and Islam, in memory of V. Minorsky,* 1971, pp. 247-254

FAROOQUI, M.A.H. Muhammad 'Arif Shaida. *Iran Society silver jubilee souvenir* 1944-1969, pp. 115-127.

FARROKHZAD, Forough. Two poems by Forough Farrokhzad, translated by Massud Farzan. *Iranian stud.* 6(1973), pp. 52-57.

GIUNASHVILI, L.S. O rasskaze M. Dzhamalzade "Shurabad". *Vostochnaya filologiya. Philologia Orientalis.* II(Pamyati V.S. Puturidze), 1972, pp. 98-103.

HABIB, Kamal M. Iqbal: towards an ethical theory of poetry. *Iqbal R.* 16i(1975), pp. 49-65.

HADI HUSSAIN. Conseption of poetry and the poet. *Iqbal: poet-philosopher of Pakistan,* ed. Hafeez Malik, 1971, pp. 327-346.

HADI HUSSAIN, M. Prologue to Iqbal's *Asrar-i-khudi.* Translated. *Iqbal R.* 14iii(1973), pp. 1-8.

HADI HUSSAIN, M. "Who is" Ghalib. *Iqbal R.* 14i(1973), pp. 9-23.

HASAN, Syed. Tarqīmu's-Sa'ādat - A unique collection of Persian epistles. *Indo-Iranica* 25(1972), pp. 36-50.

HEINZ, W. Der indo-persische Dichter Bīdil, sein Leben und Werk. *Ex orbe religionum. Studia Geo Widengren oblata,* II, 1972, pp. 32-41.

HUSSAIN, Rizwan. Ghalib and the school of Bedel: style as an aspect of sensibility. *Afghanistan* 28iii(1975), pp. 1-8.

INAL, Saime. The life and works of 'Abd-al Latif b. 'Abd-Allâh al-'Abbâsi of Gujarat. *J.Reg.Cult.Inst.* 5i(1972), pp. 45-49

JAZAYERY, Mohammad Ali. Recent Persian literature. Observations on themes and tendencies. *Review of national literatures* 2i(1971), pp. 11-28.

JHAVERI, K.M. A few observations on the development of the language and literature of Iran. *Poure Davoud Memorial Vol.,* II, 1951, pp. 103-106.

KANUS-CREDE, H. Die Bildersprache Suratgars. *Iranistische Mitt.* 5(1971), pp. 23-78.

KANUS-CREDE, H. In memoriam Lotf'ali Suratgar (d. 27.10.1969). *Iranistische Mitt.* 4(1970), pp. 48-59.

KANUS-CREDE, H. Lotf'ali Suratgar, ein Dichter und Denker des modernen Persien. *Iranistische Mitt.* 3ii(1969), pp. 1-106.

KARIM, K.M. Kh̲ān-i-Kh̲ānān 'Abd al-Raḥīm - A great literary genius. *J. Pakistan Hist. Soc.* 19(1971), pp. 79-84.

KAUSAR, M. Inamul Haq. Some less known Persian poets of the 9th century H. *J. Pak.Hist.Soc.* 23(1975), pp. 246-279.

KAUSAR, Inamul Haq. Two less known poets of Iran: Anlī Khurāsānī and Āṣafī. *J.Pakistan Hist.Soc.* 19(1971), pp. 159-174

KHABIB, Asadulla. K voprosu ob autentichnosti proizvedeniy Bedilya "Nukat" i "Isharat-o-khekayat". *NAA* 1973(4), pp. 100-111.

KHAN, Hyder Ali. Ali Husain Khan Mājid, the poet prince. *Ann. Or. Res. Univ. Madras* 24(1972), pp. 1-50. Arabic section.

KLYASHTORINA, V.B. K voprosu o razvitii literaturnoy kritiki v Irane na rubezhe 50-60-kh godov. *Iran (Pamyati B.N. Zakhodera)* 1971, pp. 185-197.

KLYASHTORINA, V.B. Literaturno-obshchestvennaya mysl' i "novaya poeziya" v Irane. *NAA* 1975(6), pp. 88-100.

KLYASHTORINA, V.B. Mayakovskiy i "novaya poeziya" Irana (na primere tvorchestva Akhmada Shamlu). *NAA* 1975(2), pp. 84-95.

KLYASHTORINA, V. "Novaya poeziya" ("she're nou") v Irane na rubezhe 60-kh -- nachale 70-kh gg. XX v. *Problemy literatur orientalnych,* 1974, pp. 93-98.

KOMISSAROV, D.S. O sblizhenii natzional'nogo i internatzional'nogo v noveyshey persidskoy literature. (Connections between the national and international in modern Persian literature.) *NAA* 1971(4), pp. 88-94.

KOMISSAROV, D. O sovremennom iranskom literaturovedenenii. *Problemy literatur orientalnych,* 1974, pp. 99-108.

KOMISSAROV, D.S. Realisticheskie cherty persidskogo romana i povesti 60-kh godov. *NAA* 1974(3), pp. 88-94.

KOMISSAROV, D.S. Sadek Khedayat (k semidesyatiletiuy so dnya rozhdeniya). *Narody Azii i Afriki* 1973(3), pp. 138-144.

KRÜGER, E. Die Reisetagebücher Nāṣir ad-Dins -- ein autobiographisches Zeugnis? *WI* N.S.14(1973), pp. 171-191.

LESCOT, R. Deux contes S. Naficy. Traduits par R. Lescot. *Mélange d'iranologie on mémoir de feu Said Naficy,* 1972, pp. 83-92.

LORAINE, M.B. Bahār in the context of Persian constitutional revolution. *Iran. stud.* 5(1972), pp. 79-87.

LORAINE, M.B. A memoir on the life and poetical works of Maliku'l-Shu'arâ' Bahâr. *IJMES* 3(1972), pp. 140-168

MACHALSKI, F. Iranian magazine "Kāveh". (A contribution to the history of Iranian press abroad). *Folia Or.* 13(1971), pp. 343-348.

MACHALSKI, Fr. Literatura perska XX w. *Przegl.or.* 4(80), 1971, pp. 333-341.

MACHALSKI, Fr. Muhammad Taqi Bahar as a painter of nature. *Iran Society silver jubilee souvenir* 1944-1969, pp. 233-237.

MAJID, M.A. Shurida of Shiraz. *Indo-Iranica* 23i-ii(1970), pp. 74-90.

MAREK, J. Notes of some social ideas contained in Iqbāl's *Book of eternity. Yádnáme-ye Jan Rypka* 1967, pp. 237-244.

MASHIAH, Yaakov. Once upon a time. A study of *Yeki Bud, Yeki Nabud,* the first collection of short stories by Sayyid Muhammad Ali Jamal-Zadeh. *Acta Or.* 33 (1971), pp. 109-143.

MASSÉ, H. Le chant funebre de Mohtacham-e Kachani en mémoire de son frère Khadjè Abd al-Ghani. *Yād-nāme-ye Irāni-ye Minorsky,* 1969, pp. 131-138.

MOAYYAD, Heshmat. Parvin's poems, a cry in the wilderness. *Islamwissenschaftliche Abhandlungen F. Meier,* 1974, pp. 164-190.

OSIPOV, Yu.I. Didakticheskaya traditziya na nachal'nom etape razvitiya sovremennogo persidskogo romana. *NAA* 1974(1), pp. 142-147.

PIEMONTESE, A.M. Il poeta Meskin e l'onorificenza di Pio IX all' Emāmjom'è d'Esfahān. *RSO* 47(1972), pp. 81-95.

QASMI, Sharif Hussain. A psychological study of 'Urfi and his works: Qaṣīdas and ghazals. *Indo-Iranica* 25ii(1972), pp. 105-121.

RAHMATULLAH, S. Imagery in Iqbal. *Iqbal R.* 16i(1975), pp. 6-13.

REYAZUL HASAN. Iqbal's *Tulip of Sinai:* Prof. A.J. Arberry's translation. *Iqbal R.* 16i(1975), pp. 43-48.

RIAZ, Muhammad. Influence of Baba *Faghani's* style on *Iqbal. J. Pakistan Hist. Soc.* 16(1968), pp. 220-241.

RIZVI, S.N.H. Literary extracts from *Kitab Subh Sadiq. JAS Pakistan* 16(1971), pp. 1-61.

SABRI-TABRIZI, G.R. Human values in the works of two persian writers. *Ve Congrès International d'Arabisants et d'Islamisants. Actes.,* [1970?], pp. 411-418.

SAFA, Zabihollah. La letteratura persiana contemporanea. *Veltro* 14i-ii(1970), pp. 87-98.

SAKSENA, B.P. Chār Chaman of Chandra Bhān. *Dr. Adilya Nath Jha felicitation volume,* III, 1969, pp. 455-463.

SHAH, A.A. English rendering of ghazal in Bal-i-Jibril. *Iqbal R.* 16i(1975), pp. 14-20.

SHAKI, Mansour. Modern Persian poetry. *Yádnáme-ye Jan Rypka* 1967, pp. 187-194.

SOHRWEIDE, H. Der Verfasser der als *Sulaymān-nāma* bekannten Istanbûler Prachthandschrift. *Der Islam* 47(1971), pp. 286-289.

SOROUDI, Sorour. The dispute of 'the old and the new' in Persian poetry. *Asian and African stud.* (Israel Or.Soc.) 10(1974-5), pp. 25-38.

ṢŪRATGAR, Loṭf'alī. Aus den Memoiren eines Esels. *Iranistische Mitteilungen* 3i(1969), pp. 30-36.

ṢŪRATGAR, Loṭf'alī. Der erste Tag, an den ich mich erinnere. *Iranistische Mitteilungen* 3i(1969), pp. 37-42.

SURATGAR, Lotf'ali. Grundzüge der persischen Literatur. *Iranistische Mitt.* 3i(1969), pp. 2-29.

TAUER, F. Two additional chapters to my outline of the Persian learned literature, from its beginnings to the end of the 18th century. *Arch. or.* 39 (1971), pp. 268-283.

TIKKU, Girdhari L. Some socio-religious themes in modern Persian fiction. *Islam and its cultural divergence. Studies in honor of Gustave E. von Grunebaum,* 1971, pp. 165-179

VAHID, S.A. Iqbal - a survey of his work. *Iqbal R.* 14i(1973), pp. 61-68.

VAHID, S.A. Iqbal and Western poets. *Iqbal: poet-philosopher of Pakistan,* ed. Hafeez Malik, 1971, pp. 347-379.

WICKENS, G.M. Persian literature as an affirmation of national identity. *Rev.nat. lit.* 2i(1971), pp. 29-60.

YAR-SHATER, Ehsan. Development of Persian drama in the context of cultural confrontation. *Iran: continuity and variety.* Ed. P.J. Chelkowski, New York, 1971. pp. 21-38.

ZOROUFI, Mohammad. Forûg Farrohzâd, Persiens Dichterin der sinnlichen Liebe. *Islamkundliche Abhandlungen H.J. Kissling,* 1974, pp. 190-194.

In memoriam Loṭf'alī Ṣūratgar. *Iranistische Mitteilungen* 4(1970), pp. 48-59.

See also V. v. l. Iqbal's poetry.

See also XXXI. j. Machalski.

See also XXXVII. a. Mohandessi.

See also XXXVIII. b. Kariev

See also XXXIX. b. Naimuddin.

See also XXXIX. c. Slomp.

See also XLI. a. Borolina.

e TRANSLATIONS

JEWETT, Iran B. FitzGerald and Jami's *Salāmān and Absāl.* *Orientalia Suecana* 19-20(1970-71), pp. 179-185

KUROS, Mahmud. Übertragung von Goethes Faust in persische Dichtung. *XVIII. Deutscher Orientalistentag* 1972, pp. 522-526.

RAWAN FARHADI, A.G. Rabindranath Tagore, Gitanjali. Sorud-e-Neyayesh (song offerings). Versified translation into Dari. *Adab* [Kabul] 23ii(1975).

SAHSARAMI, M. Kalim. On the translation of Amrit Kunda, a Sanskrit work on yoga, into Persian and Arabic. *JAS Bangladesh* 18(1973), pp. 75-81.

XL TURKISH LANGUAGES

a GENERAL. TURKISH STUDIES

AALTO, P. G.J. Ramstedt and Altaic linguistics. *CAJ* 19(1975), pp. 161-193.

ABDULLAEV, A.Z. Bessoyuznye slozhnopodchinennye predlozheniya. *ST* 1971(4), pp. 30-42.

ABDULLAEV, A.Z. Puti vozniknoveniya slozhnopodchinennykh predlozheniy v tyurkskikh yazykakh. *Sov.Tyurkologiya* 1970(3), pp. 53-59.

ABDULLAEV, A.Z. Razvitie napravitel'nogo padezha v tyurkskikh yazykakh. *Sprache, Geschichte und Kultur der altaischen Völker,* hrsg. G. Hazai und P. Zieme, 1974, pp. 59-63.

ABDURAKHMANOV, G.A. Izuchenie sintaksisa tyurkskikh yazykov. *Sov.Tyurkologiya* 1970(1), pp. 42-48.

ABDURAKHMANOV, G. Sintaksis oslozhnennogo predlozheniya. (K nekotorym spornym voprosam sintaksisa tyurkskikh yazykov.) *Struktura i istoriya tyurkskikh yazykov,* 1971, pp. 138-147.

ALEKPEROV, A.K. Iz istorii razrabotki problemy glagol'nogo slovoslozheniya. *ST* 1971 (5), pp. 101-113.

ALEKPEROV, A.K. O sistemno-strukturnom podkhode k leksicheskoy semantike. *ST* 1974(2), pp. 13-25.

XL TURKISH LANGUAGES

AMANZHOLOV, A.S. "Shumero"-tyurkskie sootvetstviya i izobrazitel'nye logogrammy. *Sprache, Geschichte und Kultur der altaischen Völker*, hrsg. G. Hazai und P. Zieme, 1974, pp. 65-71.

AMIROV, R.S. Priem diafragmirovaniya v tyurkskikh yazykakh (na primere kazakhskogo yazyka). (The diaphragm method in the Turkic languages (exemplifying the Kazakh language.)). *NAA* 1972(2), pp. 144-146

ANNANUROV, A. Funktzional'noe razvitie grammaticheskikh kategoriy, svyazannykh s deeprichastiem na -p. (Functional development of grammar categories connected with -p form of adverbial participle.) *Sov. Tyurkologiya* 1972(2), pp. 32-39.

ASLANOV, V.I. K probleme genezisa odnogo iz tipov slozhnopodchinennogo predlozheniya s pridatochnym dopolnitel'nym. *ST* 1971(4), pp. 43-49.

ATAMIRZAEVA, S. K voprosu o proiskhozhdenii umlauta v tyurkskikh yazykakh. *Sprache, Geschichte und Kultur der altaischen Völker*, hrsg. G. Hazai und P. Zieme, 1974, pp. 73-76.

ATENOV, Sh. Obosoblenie kak grammaticheskaya kategoriya v tyurkskikh yazykakh. *ST* 1971 (3), pp. 82-86.

AZNABAEV, A., PSYANCHIN, V. K probleme istoricheskogo razvitiya affiksa mnozhestvennogo chisla *-lar* v tyurkskikh yazykakh. *ST* 1971(5), pp. 11-20.

BABAEV, K.R. Semanticheskie izmeneniya tyurkismov pri ikh zaimstvovanii. (Semantic changes of Turkisms by their borrowing.) *Sov. Tyurkologiya* 1972(2), pp. 47-53.

BAITCHURA, Uzbek. The sound structure of the Turkic languages in connection with that of the Fenno-Ugric ones. (An instrumental-phonetic and phonological investigation.) *Central Asiatic J.* 19(1975), pp. 85-104, 241-263.

BAJRAKTAREVIĆ, Fehim. The influence of Oriental languages on Serbo-Croat. *Actes du VIIIe Congrès International des Linguistes* (1958), pp. 128-130.

BAKAEVA, Kh.D. O zolotom shit'e Bukhary i svyazannykh s nim terminakh. *Sov.Tyurkologiya* 1970(3), pp. 94-98

BALAKAEV, M.B. Dialektnye yavleniya v yazyke khudozhestvennoy literatury. *ST* 1973(6), pp. 79-82.

BANCZEROWSKI, J. Über ein hypothetisches Modell der uralischen Apophonie. *Lingua Posnaniensis* 18(1975), pp. 67-77.

BASKAKOV, N.A. Areal'naya konsolidatziya drevneyshikh narechiy i geneticheskoe rodstvo altayskikh yazykov. *Sprache, Geschichte und Kultur der altaischen Völker*, hrsg. G. Hazai und P. Zieme, 1974, pp. 89-96.

BASKAKOV, N.A. Binarnye oppozitzii v strukture sintaksisa tyurkskikh yazykov. *ST* 1970(6), pp. 17-27.

BASKAKOV, N.A. K voprosu o strukture skazuemogo v tyurkskikh yazykakh. (On the problem of predicate structure in Turkic languages.) *Sov. Tyurkologiya* 1972(2), pp. 68-79.

BASKAKOV, N.A. Nekotorye affiksy slovoobrazovaniya funktzional'nykh form glagola obshchie dlya altayskikh yazykov. *Central Asiatic J.* 17(1973), pp. 87-98.

BASKAKOV, N.A. O kategoriyakh nakloneniya i vremeni v tyurkskikh yazykakh. *Struktura i istoriya tyurkskikh yazykov*, 1971, pp. 72-80.

BASKAKOV, N.A. O proekte programmy kandidatskogo minimuma po tyurkskomu yazykoznaniyu dlya aspirantov. (Towards the problem of post-graduate examinations on turkic languages.) *Sov. Tyurkologiya* 1972(4), pp. 78-93.

BASKAKOV, N.A. On the common origin of the categories of person and personal possession in the Altaic languages. *Researches in Altaic languages*, ed. L. Ligeti, 1975, pp. 7-13.

BASKAKOV, N.A. Osnovnye teoreticheskie napravleniya v izuchenii altayskoy sem'i yazykov. *Sov.Tyurkologiya* 1970(1), pp. 24-41.

BASKAKOV, A.N. Otrazhenie nauchno-tekhnicheskoy revolyutzii v rosstvennykh yazykakh, obsluzhivayushchikh razlichnye obshchestvennye formatzii. *ST* 1975(1), pp. 3-9.

BASKAKOV, N.A. Perezhitki tabu i totemizma v yazykakh narodov Altaya. *ST* 1975(2), pp. 3-8.

BASKAKOV, N.A. Printzipy vybora priznakov dlya naimenovaniya gor u Altaytzev (k probleme oronimii Gornogo Altaya). *Issledovaniya po vostochnoy filologii. K. semidesyatiletiyu G.D.Sanzheeva*, 1974, pp. 22-27.

BASKAKOV, N.A. Priroda i funktzional'noe znachenie svyazki v sostave predlozheniya v tyurkskikh yazykakh. *Studia Turcica, ed. L. Ligeti*, 1971, pp. 47-54

BASKAKOV, N.A. Priroda prityazhatelnykh opredelitel'nykh slovosochetaniy i ikh rol' v evolyutzii slozhnykh sintaksicheskikh konstruktziy v tyurkskikh yazykakh. *ST* 1971(4), pp. 15-23.

BASKAKOV, N.A. Proiskhozhdenie form povelitel'no-zhelatel'nogo nakloneniya v tyurkskikh yazykakh. *Vopr. yaz.* 1975 (1), pp. 91-103.

BASKAKOV, N.A. Razlichnye struktury dialektnykh sistem tyurkskikh yazykov i kharakter izogloss obshchetyurkskogo atlasa. (Different structures of Turkic dialect systems and the character of isoglottic lines of common-Turkic atlas. *Sov. Tyurkologiya* 1972(5), pp. 3-9.

XL TURKISH LANGUAGES

BASKAKOV, N.A. Razvitie grammaticheskoy struktury yazykov v svyazi s rasshireniem ikh obshchestvennykh funktziy (na materiale tyurkskikh yazykov). *Actes X. Cong.int.linguistes* 1967, vol. I, pp. 589-590.

BAYCHURA, U.Sh. O slogovoy strukture slova v altayskikh yazykakh sravnitel'no s ural'skimi i indoevropeyskimi po statistticheskim i instrumental'nym dannym. *Sprache, Geschichte und Kultur der altaischen Völker*, hrsg. G. Hazai und P. Zieme, 1974, pp. 77-87.

BAZIN, L. Les interdits de vocabulaire et la comparaison turco-mongole. *Sprache, Geschichte und Kultur der altaischen Völker*, hrsg. G. Hazai und P. Zieme, 1974, pp. 97-103.

BAZIN, L. Les noms turcs de l'aigle. *Turcica* 3(1971), pp. 128-132.

BAZIN, L. Les noms turcs de l'or. *Langues et techniques, nature et société. Hommage à A.G. Haudricourt*, I, 1972, pp. 327-336.

BAZIN, L. Note sur **angyïrt*, nom turco-mongol d'une variété de "canard". *Studia Turcica, ed. L. Ligeti*, 1971, pp. 55-59

BEKTAEV, K.B., ERMOLENKO, G.V. Vsesoyuznyy seminar po voprosam statisticheskogo i informatzionnogo izucheniya tyurkskikh yazykov. *Sov.Tyurkologiya* 1970(3), pp. 135-137

BERTAGAEV, T.A. Kultovye znacheniya kornevogo slova *ut* i ego proizvodnye. *Sprache, Geschichte und Kultur der altaischen Völker*, hrsg. G. Hazai und P. Zieme, 1974, pp. 105-113.

BERTAGAEV, T.A. O sootnositel'nosti nekotorykh kornevykh glagolov v tyurksko-mongol'skikh yazykakh. *Central Asiatic J.* 17 (1973), pp. 99-107.

BERTAGAEV, T.A. Ob anlaute i nekotorykh etimologicheskikh nablyudeniyakh v altayskikh yazykakh. *Struktura i istoriya tyurkskikh yazykov*, 1971, pp. 301-307.

BERTAGAEV, T.A. On some common semantic indices of root elements in the Altaic languages. *Researches in Altaic languages*, ed. L. Ligeti, 1975, pp. 29-31.

BIISHEV, A. Sootvestvie -r//-z v altayskikh yazykakh. *Issledovaniya po uygurskomu yazyku* I, 1965, pp. 192-205.

BLAGOVA, G.F. Analiticheskiy sposob funktzional'noy transpozitzii i glagol'nye slovosochetaniya. *Struktura i istoriya tyurkskikh yazykov*, 1971, pp. 81-94.

BLAGOVA, G.F. K istorii razvitiya mestoimennogo i imennogo padezhnykh skloneniy v tyurkskikh yazykakh. *ST* 1971(2), pp. 39-49.

BLAGOVA, G.F. K metodike istoriko-areal'nykh sopostavleniy v tyurkologii. *Vop. yaz.* 1972 (5), pp. 97-112.

BLAGOVA, G.F. O prieme tipologicheskoy verifikatzii pri sravnitel'no-istoricheskom izuchenii tyurkskoy grammatiki. *ST* 1971 (3), pp. 25-32.

BLAGOVA, G.F. O russkom naimenovanii tyurkov i tyurkskikh yazykov. *ST* 1973(4), pp. 11-23.

BLAGOVA, G.F. O tipakh i strukturnykh raznovidnostyakh padezhnogo skloneniya v tyurkskikh yazykakh. *Vopr. yaz.* 1975 (1), pp. 65-80.

BLAGOVA, G.F. Razvitie sravnitel'no-istoricheskogo izucheniya tyurkskikh yazykov i uroven' kandidatskikh dissertatziy. *ST* 1973(6), pp. 102-110.

BLAGOVA, G.F. Stroenie form zhelatel'nogo nakloneniya v tyurkskikh yazykakh i tendentziya k sverkhnormal'nomu ikh uslozheniyu. *ST* 1973(1), pp. 10-25.

BLAGOVA, G.F. Über vergleichende sprachtypologische Methode und ihre Verwendung auf dem Gebiet der Turkologie. *Ar. Or.* 43(1975), pp. 172-177.

BLAGOVA, G.F. Variantnye zaimstvovaniya *turok ~ tyurk* i ikh leksicheskoe obosloblenie v russkom yazyke. (K stanovleniyu obobshchayushchego imeni tyurkoyazychnykh harodov.). *Tyurkologicheskiy sbornik* 1972 *(Pamyati P.M. Melioranskogo)*, pp. 93-140.

BLANAR, V. Über strukturelle Übereinstimmungen im Wortschatz der Balkansprachen. *Actes du Xe Congrès International des Linguistes, 1967* vol. III, (1970), pp. 661-665.

BLAŠKOVICŚ, J. Some toponyms of Turkic origin in Slovakia. *Acta Or. Acad. Sci. Hung.* 27(1973), pp. 191-199.

BLAŠKOVIĆ, J. Toponimy starotyurkskogo proiskhozhdeniya na territorii Slovakii. (Toponyms of Old Turkic origin on the territory of Slovakia). *Vopr. yaz.* 1972(6), pp. 62-75.

BLAŠKOVIĆŚ, J. Türkische Quellen, das Wort *kuruc* betreffend. *Studia Turcica, ed. L. Ligeti*, 1971, pp. 73-88

BONNERJEA, R. Is there any relationship between Eskimo-Aleut and Uralo-Altaic? *Acta Ling.Acad.Sci.Hung.* 21(1971), pp. 401-407.

BORGOYAKOV, M.I. K voprosu ob etimologii gidronima "Molochnyy". *Sov.Tyurkologiya* 1970(5), pp. 85-87.

BORGOYAKOV, M.I. Slovnik G. F. Millera po tyurkskim yazykam Sibiri. *Tyurk.leksikologiya i leksikografiya*, 1971, pp. 122-130

BOUDA, K. Berichtigungen und Ergänzungen zu M. Räsänen, *Versuch eines etymologischen Wörterbuchs der Türksprachen. CAJ* 18(1974), pp. 74-76.

BRANDS, H.W. Zum metaphorischen Gebrauch türkischer Tierbezeichnungen. *CAJ* 17 (1974), pp. 129-134; 19(1975), pp. 264-273.

XL TURKISH LANGUAGES

CAFEROĞLU, A. Die charakteristischen Züge der in der Toponymik gebrauchten "epitheta ornantia" im Osmanischen Reiche. *Proc.8th Int.Cong.Onomastic Sciences* 1966, pp. 82-84.

CHARIEV, A. K izucheniyu sintaksicheskoy soyuzi v prityazhatel'no-opreddelitel'noy konstruktzii v tyurkskikh yazykakh. *ST* 1974(2), pp. 26-33.

CLARK, L.V. The Turkic and Mongol words in William of Rubruck's *Journey* (1253-1255). *JAOS* 93(1973), pp. 181-189.

CLAUSON, Sir G. On the idea of Sumerian-Ural-Altaic affinities. *Current anthropology* 14(1973), pp. 493-495.

CLAUSON, Sir G. Turkish philology in Hungary. (Review article on Ligeti, *Studia Turcica.*) *Asia Major* 18(1973), pp. 209-219.

CSILLAGHY, A. I prestiti iranici nelle lingue ugrofinniche e il problema dell'appartenenza uralo-altaica. (Lo stato di una questione linguistica.) *Ann.Fac.Ling.Lett.stran.Ca' Foscari* 5(1974), pp. 35-62.

DAHER, Y. Agricultura Anatolica I. *SO* 43 (1974), 2, pp.12.

DÉCSY, Gy. Zur Transliteration/Transkription der Kyrilliza in der Uralistik und Altaistik. *UAJ* 47(1975), pp. 47-50.

DEMIRCHIZADE, A.M. Sravnitel'nyy metod Makhmuda Kashgari. *Sov.tyurkologiya* 1972 (1), pp. 31-42

DMITRIEVA, L.V. K etimologii nekotorykh nazvaniy rasteniy v tyurkskikh yazykakh (nazvaniya s kornem *boŋ- - *bok-). *ST* 1973 (6), pp. 40-43.

DMITRIEVA, L.V. Nekotorye itogi izucheniya nazvaniy rasteniy v tyurkskikh yazykakh sopostavitel'no s drugimi yazykami altayskoy sem'i (odnoleksemye nazvaniya). *ST* 1975(2), pp. 13-24.

DMITRIEVA, L.V. Nekotorye semanticheskie modeli nazvaniy rasteniy v altayskikh yazykakh. (Modeli nazvaniy vetvey.) *Sprache, Geschichte und Kultur der altaischen Völker*, hrsg. G. Hazai und P. Zieme, 1974, pp. 187-192.

DMITRIEVA, L.V. Obshchealtayskie nazvaniya i osnovy v tyurkskoy fitonimike. *ST* 1975(6), pp. 49-54.

DOBRODOMOV, I.G. K istorii kul'turnykh terminov tyurkskogo proiskhozhdeniya. *Sov. Tyurkologiya* 1970(3), pp. 67-70

DOBRODOMOV, I.G. Tyurkizmy slavyanskikh yazykov kak istochnik svedeniy po istoricheskoy fonetiki tyurkskikh yazykov. *ST* 1971 (2), pp. 81-92.

DOBRODOMOV, I.G. Tyurkskie leksicheskie elementy v vostochnykh i zapadnykh slavyanskikh yazykakh. *Sov.Tyurkologiya* 1970 (3), pp. 131-134

DOERFER, G. Bemerkungen zur Methodik der türkischen Lautlehre. *OLZ* 66(1971), col. 325-344.

DOERFER, G. Gedanken zur Gestaltung eines idealen Türkischen Etymologischen Wörterbuchs. *OLZ* 66(1971), pp. 437-454.

DOERFER, G. Mozhno li problemu rodstva altayskikh yazykov razreshit s pozitziy indoevropefistiki? *Vopr. yaz.* 1972(3), pp. 50-66.

DUL'ZON, A.P. Etnolingvisticheskaya differentziatziya tyurkov Sibiri. *Struktura i istoriya tyurkskikh yazykov*, 1971, pp. 198-208.

DUL'ZON, A.P. Ketsko-tyurkskie paralleli v oblasti skloneniya. *ST* 1971(1), pp. 20-26.

DUL'ZON, A.P. Nekotorye voprosy metodiki rekonstruktzii obshchetyurkskoy sistemy zvukov. *ST* 1971(2), pp. 17-20.

DUL'ZON, A.P. Otrazhenie dnevnikh glagol' nuikh form sastoyanii v uralo-altaiskikh yazuikakh. (The reflection of ancient verbal forms denoting state in the Uralic-Altaic languages.) *Vopr. yaz.* 1971(1), pp. 76-83.

DUL'ZON, A.P. Proiskhozhdenie altayskikh pokazateley mnozhestvennogo chisla. (The origin of the Altaic markers of plural number.) *Sov. Tyurkologiya* 1972(2), pp. 3-15.

DUL'ZON, A.P. Ustanovlenie arkhetipa fonemy po mezh'yazykovym ryadam al'ternatziy. *ST* 1973(5), pp. 93-104.

DZHIDALAEV, N.S. O diakhronii tyurko-dagestanskikh yazykovykh kontaktov. *Sov.Tyurkologiya* 1970(3), pp. 99-108

DZHURABAEVA, M. Ob affiksal'noy omonimii v tyurkskikh yazykakh (na materiale uzbekskogo yazyka). (On affixal homonymy in Turkic languages). *Sov. Tyurkologiya* 1971(6), pp. 17-25.

EGOROV, V.G. Slovoslozhenie v tyurkskikh yazykakh. *Struktura i istoriya tyurkskikh yazykov*, 1971, pp. 95-107.

EREN, Hasan. Le terme "altaïque" sauya "cadeau". *Acta Or. Hung.* 25(1972), pp. 237-243.

ERÖZ, Mehmet The influence of Middle-Asia toponyms on the toponyms of Turkey. *Proc.8th Int.Cong.Onomastic Sciences* 1966, pp. 134-137.

FAZYLOV, E.I. Ob izdaniyakh i izdatelyakh "Divana" Makhmuda Kashgari. *Sov.tyurkologiya* 1972(1), pp. 140-149

FAZYLOV, E.I. S.E. Malov - issledovatel' istorii tyurkskikh yazykov SSSR. *ST* 1975 (5), pp. 60-68.

FAZYLOV, E.J. Turkic languages in the works of Oriental philologists (11th-18th cc.). *Researches in Altaic languages*, ed. L. Ligeti, 1975, pp. 51-58.

XL TURKISH LANGUAGES

FESER, R.E. Probleme der etymologischen Erforschung der altajischen Sprachen, dargestellt an einigen gleichklingenden Wurzeln. *Islamkundliche Abhandlungen H.J. Kissling,* 1974, pp. 84-91.

FINDIKOĞLU, Z.F. L'influence des changements sociaux sur l'emploi des patronymes en Turquie. *Proc.8th Int.Cong.Onomastic Sciences* 1966, pp. 174-177.

GADZHIEV, T.I. O proiskhozhdenii geminat v tyurkskikh yazykakh. (On the origin of geminates in Turkic languages). *Sov. Tyurkologiya* 1971(6), pp. 26-31.

GADZHIEVA, N.Z. Agglyutinatziya kak opredelyayushchiy faktor razvitiya sintaksicheskoy struktury tyurkskikh yazykov. *Actes X.Cong.int.linguistes* 1967, vol. II, pp. 919-921.

GADZHIEVA, N.Z. Dva istochnika proiskhozhdeniya uslovnogo perioda v tyurkskikh yazykakh. *Sprache, Geschichte und Kultur der altaischen Völker,* hrsg. G. Hazai und P. Zieme, 1974, pp. 251-256.

GADZHIEVA, N.Z. Glukhoe nachalo slova v tyurkskom prayazyke. *ST* 1973(4), pp. 3-9.

GADZHIEVA, N.Z. Metody postroeniya sravnitel'no-istoricheskogo sintaksisa tyurkskikh yazykov. *ST* 1971(2), pp. 26-38.

GADZHIEVA, N.Z. O dvukh istochnikakh razvitiya soyuznykh slozhnykh predlozheniy v tyurkskikh yazykakh. *ST* 1973(2), pp. 30-39.

GADZHIEVA, N.Z. O roli nekotorykh vnutrennikh i vneshnikh faktorov v izmeneniyakh struktury tyurkskikh yazykov. *Sov. Tyurkologiya* 1972 (3), pp. 3-15.

GADZHIEVA, N.Z. Ponyatie sintaksicheskogo arkhetipa (na materiale tyurkskikh yazykov). *Proc.11 Int.Cong.Ling.,* 1972, vol. 1, 1974, pp. 963-966.

GADZHIEVA, N.Z. Priroda izafeta v tyurkskikh yazykakh. *Sov.Tyurkologiya* 1970(2), pp. 18-26.

GADZHIEVA, N.Z., SEREBRENNIKOV, B.A. Proiskhozhdenie affiksov s modal'nym znacheniem v tyurkskikh yazykov. *ST* 1974 (1), pp. 3-12.

GADZHIEVA, N.Z. The role of the Altaic languages in the reconstruction of the Turkic syntactic archetype. *Researches in Altaic languages,* ed. L. Ligeti, 1975, pp. 59-65.

GADZHIEVA, N.Z. Slovosochetanie kak ob'ekt sravnitel'no-istoricheskoy grammatiki tyurkskikh yazykov. *Struktura i istoriya tyurkskikh yazykov,* 1971, pp. 209-222.

GADZHIEVA, N.Z. Sushchestvoval li glagol-svyazka nastoyashchego vremeni v tyurkskikh yazykakh? *ST* 1971(5), pp. 3-10.

GADZHIEVA, N.Z. Zadachi i metody tyurkskoy areal'noy lingvistiki. *Vopr. yaz.* 1975(1), pp. 13-26.

GANIEV, F.A. Slozhnye glagoly v tyurkskikh yazykakh. *Sov. Tyurkologiya* 1972 (3), pp. 63-66.

GEORGACAS, D.J. Historical and language contacts and a place-name on Samos and in Macedonia (Greece): *Karlovasi. Names* 22 (1974), pp. 1-33.

GERTZENBERG, L.G. Ob issledovanii rodstva altayskikh yazykov. *Vopr.yaz.* 1974(2), pp. 46-55.

GUSEYNZADE, A. K etimologii toponima *Biläšäri.* (Towards etymology of toponym *Biläšäri.*) *Sov. Tyurkologiya* 1972(5), pp. 58-63.

GUSEYNZADE, A. Ob etimologii toponima *Kuba. ST* 1971(2), pp. 119-125.

GUSEYNZADE, A. Ob etnotoponimakh Apsheronskogo poluostrova: *Dzhorat, Saray, Sumgayt. ST* 1973(3), pp. 38-46.

GUSEYNZADE, A. O proiskhozhdenii toponima *Baku. Sov.Tyurkologiya* 1970(3), pp. 82-85

GUZEV, B.G., NASILOV, D.M. Konkretno-predmetnye znacheniya tyurkskogo imeni sushchestvitel'nogo kak zona relevantnosti kategoriy chisla i opredelennosti - neopredelennosti. *ST* 1971(5), pp. 21-25.

GUZEV, V.G., NASILOV, D.M. K interpretatzii kategorii chisla imen sushchestvitel'nykh v tyurkskikh yazykakh. *Vopr. yaz.* 1975(3), pp. 98-111.

HAMBIS, L. Le nom turc des "Mille Sources" à l'époque des Ming. *JA* 258(1970), pp. 315-317.

HAMP, E.P. The Altaic non-obstruents. *BSOAS* 37(1974), pp. 672-674.

HAMP, E.P. The Altaic non-obstruents. *Researches in Altaic languages,* ed. L. Ligeti, 1975, pp. 67-70.

HAMP, E.P. Turkic 5, 6, 7, 60, and 70. *BSOAS* 37(1974), pp. 675-677.

HANSER, O. Türkische Nebensätze in der Form direkter Rede. *Turcica* 7(1975), pp. 20-31.

HATTORI, Shirô. The studies of the Turkic languages in Japan after World War II. *Türk dili araştırmaları* 1973-74, pp. 25-39.

HOVDHAUGEN, E. Izuchenie tyurkskikh yazykov v Norvegii. *ST* 1973(1), p. 117.

HOVDHAUGEN, E. The Mongolian suffix *lig* and its Turkic origin. *Researches in Altaic languages,* ed. L. Ligeti, 1975, pp. 71-77.

HŘEBÍČEK, L. The phonemic structure of the first syllable in several Turkic languages. *Researches in Altaic languages,* ed. L. Ligeti, 1975, pp. 79-82.

HŘEBÍČEK, L. The Turkic first syllable and its correlation analysis. *Archiv or.* 41 (1973), pp. 340-349.

XL TURKISH LANGUAGES

IBRAGIMOV, S., ASAMUDDINOVA, M. Otrazhenie professional'noy terminologii v "Divanu lugat-it-tyurk" i "Kutadgu Bilig". *Sov. tyurkologiya* 1972(1), pp. 114-122

ISENGALIEVA, V.A. Internatzional'nye osnovy v tyurkskikh yazykakh. *Sov. Tyurkologiya* 1970(5), pp. 36-50.

ISKHAKOVA, Kh. F. K voprosu o formal'nom opisanii morfologii tyurkskikh yazykov. (Towards the formal description of Turkic languages morphology). *Sov. Tyurkologiya* 1971(6), pp. 32-44.

IVANOV, S.N. K istolkovaniyu mnogoznachnosti grammaticheskikh form (Na materiale tyurkskikh yazykov.) *Voprosy yazykoznaniya* 1973, (6), pp. 101-109.

JOHANSON, L. Some remarks on Turkic "hypotaxis". *UAJ* 47(1975), pp. 104-118.

JOHANSON, L. Sprachbau und Inhaltssyntax am Beispiel des Türkischen. *Orientalia suecana* 22(1973), pp. 82-106.

JUNKER, H.F.J. 20 Jahre Altaistik in der DDR. *Sprache, Geschichte und Kultur des altaischen Völker,* hrsg. G. Hazai und P. Zieme, 1974, pp. 25-33.

KARAEV, O. Istoriko-geograficheskie dannye, soobshchaemye Makhmudom Kashgari (po Tyan'-Shanyu i Semirech'yu). *Sov.tyurkologiya* 1972(1), pp. 111-113

KAYDAROV, A.T. Razlichnye sposoby vyrazheniya odnikh i tekh zhe grammaticheskikh otnosheniy v blizkorodstvennykh yazykakh. (Different means expressing the identical grammar relations in cognate languages.) *Sov. Tyurkologiya* 1972(2), pp. 16-22.

KENESBAEV, S.K., PIOTROVSKIY, R.G., BEKTAEV, K.B. Inzhenernaya lingvistika i tyurkologiya. *ST* 1970(6), pp. 3-16.

KENESBAEV, S.K. K voprosu o tyurko-mongolskoy yazykovoy obshchnosti (na materiale nekotorykh grammaticheskikh yavleniy kazakhskogo yazyka). *Sprache, Geschichte und Kultur der altaischen Völker,* hrsg. G. Hazai und P. Zieme (XII. PIAC, 1974), pp.

KHABICHEV, M.A. Ob etnonimakh alan, buzuneulu, malkarlu, karacajlu, tegejli. *ST* 1971 (2), pp. 126-129.

KHYDYROV, M.N. K istorii izucheniya formy nastoyashchego vremeni glagola v yugo-zapadnoy gruppe tyurkskikh yazykakh. (Towards history of study of verb's present tense form in south-west group of Turkic languages.) *Sov. Tyurkologiya* 1971(6), pp. 45-49.

KIBIROV, Sh. K voprosu o vidakh glagola b tyurkskikh yazykakh (na materiale uygurskogo yazyka). *Issledovaniya po uygurskomu yazyku* I, 1965, pp. 117-136.

KLYASHTORNYY, S.G. Epokha Makhmuda Kashgarskogo. *Sov.tyurkologiya* 1972(1), pp. 18-23

KOBESHAVIDZE, I.N. K kharakteristike grafiki i fonemnogo sostava yazyka orkhono-eniseyskikh nadpisey. (Towards characteristics of graphics and phoneme system of Orkhon-Enisei inscriptions.) *Sov. Tyurkologiya* 1972(2), pp. 40-46.

KOLESNIKOVA, V.D. O nazvaniyakh chastey tela v altayskikh yazykakh. *Sprache, Geschichte und Kultur der altaischen Völker,* hrsg. G. Hazai und P. Zieme (XII. PIAC, 1974), pp. 327-332.

KONONOV, A.N. Aktual'nye tyurkologicheskie zametki. *ST* 1975(2), pp. 77-86.

KONONOV. A.N. Makhmud Kashgarskiy i ego 'Divanu lugat it-türk'. *Sov.tyurkologiya* 1972(1), pp. 1-17

KONONOV, A.N. O fuzii v tyurkskikh yazykakh. *Struktura i istoriya tyurkskikh yazykov,* 1971, pp. 108-120.

KONONOV, A.N. Türkische Philologie in der UdSSR 1917-1967. *Mitt.Inst.Orientforschung* 17(1971-72), pp. 293-317.

KONONOV, A.N. Tyurkskoe yazykoznanie v Akademii nauk. *Vopr.yaz.* 1974(3), pp. 38-51

KONSTANTINOVA, O.A. K kharakteristike leksicheskogo kompleksa ochag-zhilishche-narod v osnovnykh altayskikh yazykakh. *Sprache, Geschichte und Kultur der altaischen Völker,* hrsg. G. Hazai und P. Zieme (XII. PIAC, 1974), pp. 333-339.

KORMUSHIN, I.V. Leksiko-semanticheskoe razvitie kornya **qa* v altayskikh yazykakh. *Tyurk. leksikologiya i leksikografiya,* 1971, pp. 9-28

KORMUSHIN, I.V. Yavlenie fuzii v istorii altayskikh yazykov i ego znachenie dlya resheniya problemy obshchnosti altayskikh yazykov. *Sprache, Geschichte und Kultur der altaischen Völker,* hrsg. G. Hazai und P. Zieme (XII. PIAC, 1974), pp. 353-356.

KORNILOV, G.E. K etimologii toponima *Čeboksary.* (Towards etimology of toponym *Čeboksary.*) *Sov. Tyurkologiya* 1972(2), pp. 54-62.

KURBATOV, Kh. Strukturno-lineynyy analiz yazyka poezii. *ST* 1975(6), pp. 91-96.

KURTKAN, Amirau. The relationship between toponyms and the changing character of the social and economic life in Istanbul. *Proc.8th Int.Cong.Onomastic Sciences* 1966, pp. 266-269.

KUZNETZOV, P.I. Statisticheskiy analiz modeley "N+G^3" i "N+G^0" v tyurkskikh yazykakh. *ST* 1975(6), pp. 42-48.

LATYPOV, Ch.Yu. O sub'ektno-predikativnykh svyazyakh mezhdu chlenami sintaksicheskikh struktur s nelichnymi formami glagola v angliyskom i tyurkskikh yazykakh. (On subject-predicate relations between members of syntactical structures with verbals in English and Turkic languages.) *Sov. Tyurkologiya* 1972(5), pp. 69-77.

XL TURKISH LANGUAGES

LIGETI, L. Altayskaya teoriya i leksikostatistika. *Vopr. yaz.* 1971(3), pp. 21-33.

LIGETI, L. La théorie altäique et la lexico-statistique. *Researches in Altaic languages,* ed. L. Ligeti, 1975, pp. 99-115.

LYUBIMOV, K.M. O chislovom znachenii nulevoy formy tyurkskikh sushchestvitel'nykh. (On numerative meaning of zero form of Turkic nouns.) *Sov. Tyurkologiya* 1972(5), pp. 78-83.

MAKAEV, E.A. Voprosy postroeniya sravnitel'noy grammatiki tyurkskikh yazykov. *ST* 1971(2), pp. 21-25.

MAMEDOV, A.M. Assimiliyatziya v svete vzaimootnosheniya fonetiki i grammatiki. (Assimilation in the light of phonetics and grammar.) *Sov. Tyurkologiya* 1972(4), pp. 12-16.

MAMEDOV, A.M. Drevnetyurkskaya aktzentzuatziya i nekotorye voprosy razvitiya fonologicheskikh sistem tyurkskikh yazykov (istoriko-tipologichesko issledovanie). *Sov.Tyurkologiya* 1970(5), pp. 58-69.

MAMEDOV, M.B. Ob ispol'zovanii fol'klornykh materialov frazeologicheskogo kharaktera v publitzisticheskom stile. *ST* 1975(2), pp. 91-101.

MEL'NIKOV, G.P. K etimologii otritzaniya *tegül* (po materialam "drevnetyurkskogo slovarya"). *Sov.Tyurkologiya* 1970(4), pp. 57-66.

MEL'NIKOV, G.P. Printzipy sistemnoy lingvistiki v primenenii k problemam tyurkologii. *Struktura i istoriya tyurkskikh yazykov,* 1971, pp. 121-137.

MEL'NIKOV, G.P. Semantika i problemy tyurkologii. (Semantics and problems of Turkology). *Sov. Tyurkologiya* 1971(6), pp. 3-16.

MEL'NIKOV, G.P. Stroy altayskikh yazykov kak sistema. *Sprache, Geschichte und Kultur der altaischen Völker,* hrsg. G. Hazai und P. Zieme (XII. PIAC, 1974), pp. 397-403.

MENGES, K.H. Altajische Wörter im Russischen und ihre Etymologien. Nachträge und Zusätze zu Vasmers Russischem etymologischen Wörterbuch. *Z. für slav. Philol.* 37(1973-4), pp. 1-35.

MENGES, K.H. Dravidian and Altaic. *CAJ* 19(1975), pp. 202-205.

MENGES, K.H. Einige Bemerkungen zu türk. SAΓDAQ, Qur und Keš. *CAJ* 18(1974), pp. 55-69.

MENGES, Karl H. Etymologika. *W.B. Henning memorial vol.,* 1970, pp. 307-325.

MENGES, K.H. Ein wertvolles Kompendium zu aktuellen Forschungesfragen der Turkologie. (Ligeti, L., *ed., Studia Turcica,* 1971.) *OLZ* 69(1974), pp. 325-338.

MENGES, K. Zur Etymologie von türkisch avurt etc. "mundvoll', avuč, avut/aďut "handvoll". *Zentralasiat.Studien* 5(1971), pp. 139-143

MENGES, K.H. Zum Nachdruck der Übersetzungsbände von Radloffs "Probens". *UAJ* 43(1971), pp. 130-131.

MIJATEV, P. Der heutige Stand der Altaistik in Bulgarien. *Sprache, Geschichte und Kultur der altaischen Völker,* hrsg. G. Hazai und P. Zieme (XII. PIAC, 1974), pp. 413-418.

MILLER, R.A. Japanese-Altaic lexical evidence and the proto-Turkic "zetacism-sigmatism". *Researches in Altaic languages,* ed. L. Ligeti, 1975, pp. 157-172.

MINISSI, N. Genuskategorie im Ural Altaischen. *Acta ling. Hung.* 24(1974), pp. 261-266.

MOLCHANOVA, O.T. K voprosu o geograficheskoy terminologii i toponimii territorii. (Towards the question on geographica terminology and toponymy of the territory.) *Sov. Tyurkologiya* 1972(6), pp. 68-73.

MOLLOVA, M. Coïncidence des zones linguistiques bulgares et turques dans les Balkans. *Actes du Xe Congrès International des Linguistes, 1967* vol. II, (1970), pp. 217-221.

MUKMINOVA, R.G. K izucheniyu sredneaziatskikh terminov *tagdzha, sukniyat, ichki. Pis'mennye pamyatniki Vostoka* 1968, pp. 127-134.

MURATALIEVA, D.M. O podache i raskrytii znacheniy slov v tolkovykh slovaryakh. *Sov. Tyurkologiya* 1972 (3), pp. 70-76.

MURATOV, S.N. Some regular changes of the phonetic structure of root in the Altaic languages. *Researches in Altaic languages,* ed. L. Ligeti, 1975, pp. 173-179.

MURAYAMA, Shichiro. Altaische Komponente der japanischen Sprache. *Researches in Altaic languages,* ed. L. Ligeti, 1975, pp. 181-188.

MUSAFV, K.M. On some plant names in the Altaic languages. *Researches in Altaic languages,* ed. L. Ligeti, 1975, pp. 189-194.

MUSAEV, K.M. Znachenie dialektnoy leksiki v sravnitel'noy leksikologii tyurkskikh yazykov. *ST* 1973(6), pp. 45-50.

NADZHIP, E.N. O nekotorykh nedostatkakh v izuchenii istorii tyurkskikh yazykakh. *ST* 1970(6), pp. 48-55.

NARTYEV, N. Slozhnopodchinennoe predlozhenie v tyurkskikh yazykakh. *ST* 1975 (5), pp. 12-20.

NASILOV, D.M., KHRAKOVSKIY, V.S. Primenenie printzipa derivatzii k opisaniyu sintaksicheskikh struktur predlozheniya v tyurkskikh yazykakh. *Sov.Tyurkologiya* 1970(5), pp. 25-35

NASILOV, D.M. Tipologicheskie sopostavleniya v ramkakh sravnitel'nogo-istoricheskogo izucheniya otdel'nykh grammaticheskikh kategoriy v tyurkskikh yazykakh. *ST* 1971 (2), pp. 59-66.

NÉMETH, J. Zoltán Gombocz, ein ungarischer Sprachforscher (1877-1935). *Acta ling. (Hung.)* 22(1972), pp. 1-40.

NIGMATOV, Kh.G. Nekotorye osobennosti tyurkskikh avtorskikh primerov v "Divane" Makhmuda Kashgari. *Sov.tyurkologiya* 1972 (1), pp. 100-101

NIKOLAEV, R.V. Obshchie elementy v ketskikh i khakasskikh epicheskikh skazaniyakh. *Sov.etn.* 1974(1), pp. 145-150.

NIKONOV, V.A. Razmezhevanie lichnykh imen po polu u turkoyazychnykh narodov. (Delimitation of Turkic personal names according to sex.) *Sov. Tyurkologiya* 1972(2), pp. 63-67.

ORUZBAEVA, B.O. O kirgizskikh i mongol'skikh leksicheskikh parallelyakh po toponimike. *Sprache, Geschichte und Kultur der altaischen Völker*, hrsg. G. Hazai und P. Zieme (XII. PIAC, 1974), pp. 459-463.

PAIS, D. A propos de l'étymologie de l'ethnique *oγur*. *Studia Turcica, ed. L. Ligeti,* 1971, pp. 361-373

PALLÓ, Margit K. Ung. *gyúl* "sich entzünden" und *gyújt* "anzünden" und ihr türkischer Hintergrund. *Studia Turcica, ed. L. Ligeti,* 1971, pp. 375-383

PANFILOV, V.Z. Nivkhsko-altayskie yazykovye svyazi. *Voprosy yazykoznaniya* 1973, (5), pp. 3-12.

PETROV, N.E. O.N. Bëtlingk i nekotorye voprosy izucheniya sluzhebnykh slov v tyurkskikh yazykakh. (O.N. Bötlingk and some problems of syntactic words in Turkic languages.) *Sov. Tyurkologiya* 1972(4), pp. 62-71.

PINES, V.Ya. O modelirovanii struktury glagol'nykh form v tyurkskikh yazykakh. *ST* 1971(3), pp. 68-81.

POKROVSKAYA, L.A. Ob ustoychivosti semanticheskoy gruppy slov, oboznachayushchikh rodstvennye otnosheniya v tyurkskikh yazykakh. *Sprache, Geschichte und Kultur der altaischen Völker*, hrsg. G. Hazai und P. Zieme (XII. PIAC, 1974), pp. 465-470.

POPPE, N. A new symposium on the Altaic theory. *Central Asiatic J.* 16(1972), pp. 37-58.

POPPE, N. On some cases of fusion and vowel alternation in the Altaic languages. *CAJ* 19(1975), pp. 307-322.

POPPE, N. Remarks on comparative study of the vocabulary of the Altaic languages. *UAJ* 46(1974), pp. 120-134.

POPPE, N. Über einige Verbalstammbildungssuffixe in den altaischen Sprachen. *Orientalia Suecana* 21(1972), pp. 119-141.

POTAPOV, L.P. K semantike nazvaniy shamanskikh bubnov u narodnostey Altaya. *Sov Tyurkologiya* 1970(3), pp. 86-93

PSYANCHIN, V.Sh. Istoriya razvitiya form poryadkovykh, razdelitelnykh i sobiratel'nykh chislitelnykh v tyurkskikh yazykakh. *ST* 1973(3), pp. 49-58.

RAGIMOV, M. Sh., ASLANOV, V.I. Sravnitel'no-istoricheskoe izuchenie tyurkskikh yazykov. *Sov.Tyurkologiya* 1970(5), pp. 130-134.

RAKHMATOV, T. Etimologiya toponima "Samarkand". *ST* 1973(4), pp. 43-50.

RAKHMATOV, T. Odonimy Samarkanda. (Odonyms of Samarkand) *Sov. Tyurkologiya* 1972(4), pp. 54-61.

RAMAZANOV, K.T. Parnye slova v tyurkskikh yazykakh yugo-zapadnoy gruppy (nazvaniya zhivotnykh, ptitz i nasekomykh). (Double words in Turkic languages of southwest group.) *Sov. Tyurkologiya* 1971(6), pp. 101-112.

RONA-TAS, A. The Altaic theory and the history of a middle Mongolian loan word in Chuvash. *Researches in Altaic languages*, ed. L. Ligeti, 1975, pp. 201-211.

RÓNA-TAS, A. Some comments on the Altaic theory. *Proc.27th Int.Cong.Or.1967* (1971), pp. 599-600.

RÓNA-TAS, A. Tocharische Elemente in den altaischen Sprachen? *Sprache, Geschichte und Kultur der altaischen Völker*, hrsg. G. Hazai und P. Zieme (XII. PIAC, 1974), pp. 499-504.

RUNDGREN, Fr. Über einige Verba für "kaufen" und "verkaufen". *UAJ* 47(1975), pp. 168-171.

RUSTAMOV, A. O perevode "Divanu lugat-it-tyurk" Makhmuda Kashgari na russkiy yazyk. *Sov.tyurkologiya* 1972(1), pp. 129-139

SANZHEEV, G.D. O tyurksko-mongol'skikh lingvisticheskikh parallelyakh. *ST* 1973 (6), pp. 73-78.

SANŽHEEV, G.D. Zur Frage des sogenannten Rhotazismus und Lambdazismus in den altaischen Sprachen. *Sprache, Geschichte und Kultur der altaischen Völker*, hrsg. G. Hazai und P. Zieme (XII. PIAC, 1974), pp. 505-509.

SARYBAEV, Sh.Sh. Nekotorye voprosy tyurkskoy regional'noy leksikografii. *ST* 1973(6), pp. 111-116.

SCHMITT, G. Der früheste Beleg für türkisch yoġ «Totenfest». *AION* 32(N.S. 22, 1972), pp. 251-252.

SCHÜTZ, E. Remarks on Altaic personal pronouns. *Acta Or. Hung.* 28(1974), pp. 139-145.

ŞEHSUVAROĞLU, V.N. Des transformations et des formes adoptées, à cause du respect religieux, par les noms islamiques, chez les Turcs. *Proc.8th Int.Cong.Onomastic Sciences* 1966, pp. 486-487.

XL TURKISH LANGUAGES

SEREBRENNIKOV, B.A. Chto bylo pervichnym r^2 ili z? *ST* 1971(1), pp. 13-19.

SEREBRENNIKOV, B.A. K istorii suffiksa denominativnykh glagolov *-la* v tyurkskikh yazykakh. (Towards history of the suffix *-la* of denominative verbs in Turkic languages.) *Sov. Tyurkologiya* 1972(5), pp. 64-68.

SEREBRENNIKOV, B.A. Metody izucheniya istorii yazykov, primenyaemye v indoevropeistike i v tyurkologii. *Voprosy metodov izucheniya istorii tyurkskikh yazykov*, 1961, pp. 42-64.

SEREBRENNIKOV, B.A. O logitzizme v tyurkologicheskikh issledovaniyakh. *ST* 1971(5), pp. 73-85.

SEREBRENNIKOV, B.A. O nekotorykh chastnykh detalyakh protzessa obrazovaniya affiksa mnozhestvennogo chisla *-lar* v tyurkskikh yazykakh. *Sov.Tyurkologiya* 1970(1), pp. 49-53.

SEREBRENNIKOV, B.A. O nekotorykh problemakh istoricheskoy morfologii tyurkskikh yazykakh. *Struktura i istoriya tyurkskikh yazykov*, 1971, pp. 276-288.

SEREBRENNIKOV, B.A. Prichiny rezkogo umen'sheniya chisla affiksov mnogokratnogo deystviya i sokrashcheniya sfery ikh upotrebleniya v tyurkskikh yazykakh. *ST* 1975(6), pp. 3-10.

SEVORTYAN, E.V. K istochnikam i metodam pratyurkskikh rekonstruktzii. *Voprosy yazykoznaniya* 1973, (2), pp. 35-45.

SEVORTYAN, E.V. K semasiologicheskim voprosam slozhnogo predlozheniya v tyurkskikh yazykakh. *ST* 1971(4), pp. 24-29.

SEVORTYAN, E.V. Morfologicheskoe stroenie slova v svyazi s drugimi ego kharakteristikami (po dannym tyurkskikh yazykov). *Tyurkolog. sbornik (Pamyati V.V. Radlova,* 1972), pp. 132-144.

SEVORTYAN, E.V. Neskol'ko zamechaniy k tyurkologicheskim issledovaniyam po grammatike. *Sov.Tyurkologiya* 1970(3), pp. 3-16.

SEVORTYAN, E.V. Ob "etimologicheskom slovare tyurkskikh yazuikov". On "The etymological dictionary of the Turkic languages". *Vop.Yaz.* 6(1971), pp. 74-87.

SEVORTYAN, E.V. O soderzhanii termina "obshchetyurkskiy". *ST* 1971(2), pp. 3-12.

SEVORTYAN, E.V. Posleoktyabrskaya tyurkologiya v Akademii nauk SSSR. *Vopr.yaz.* 1974 (5), pp. 17-33.

SEVORTYAN, E.V. Sovremennoe sostoyanie i nekotorye voprosy istoricheskogo izucheniya tyurkskikh yazykakh v SSSR. *Voprosy metodov izucheniya istorii tyurkskikh yazykov*, 1961, pp. 11-41.

SEYIDOV, M.A. Ob etimologii slova *ozan / uzan*. *ST* 1971(1), pp. 38-48.

SHCHERBAK, A.M. K kharakteristike sistemy tyurkskikh padezhey v plane soderzhaniya. (Towards characteristics of Turkic case system on the level of content.) *Sov. Tyurkologiya* 1972(4), pp. 3-11.

SHCHERBAK, A.M. K voprosu o formakh na *-ra, -ru, -ry* v tyurkskikh yazykakh. *ST* 1970 (6), pp. 28-33.

SHCHERBAK, A.M. K voprosu o proiskhozhdenii glagola v tyurkskikh yazykakh. *Vopr. yaz.* 1975(5), pp. 18-29.

SHCHERBAK, A.M. Metody i zadachi etimologicheskogo issledovaniya affiksal'nykh morfem v tyurkskikh yazykakh. *ST* 1974(1), pp. 31-40.

SHCHERBAK, A.M. O morfologicheskom sostave obraznykh glagolov tipa *bakyr-, čakyr-, hajkyr-*. *ST* 1971(3), pp. 8-12.

SHCHERBAK, A.M. O nekotoruikh osobennostyakh obrazovaniya padezhnuikh form v tyurkskikh yazuikakh. (Some features in the formation of case-forms in the Turkic languages.) *Vopr. yaz.* 1971(1), pp. 84-88.

SHCHERBAK, A.M. O prichinakh strukturnofoneticheskikh raskhozh- v tyurko-mongol'skikh leksicheskikh parallelakh. *Issledovaniya po vostochnoy filologii. K semidesyatiletiyu G.D.Sanzheeva,* 1974, pp. 340-350.

SHCHERBAK, A.M. Sostoyanie raboty i zadachi sostavleniya etimologicheskikh slovarey tyurkskikh yazykoy. *ST* 1975(4), pp. 3-10.

SHCHERBAK, A.M. Sushchestvoval li v tyurkskom prayazyke datel'no-napravitel'nyy padezh na -k? *ST* 1973(3), pp. 59-62.

SHIRALIEV, M.Sh. Makhmūd Kashgari kak dialektolog. *Sov.tyurkologiya* 1972(1), pp. 24-30

SHIRALIEV, M. Sh. O nesostoyatel'nykh etimologiyakh nekotorykh slov i affiksov tyurkskikh yazykov. *ST* 1975(1), pp. 87-89.

SHIRALIEV, M.Sh. O sintaksicheskoy funktzii chastey rechi. *Struktura i istoriya tyurkskikh yazykov*, 1971, pp. 178-178.

SHIRALIEV, M.Sh. Sostoyanie i zadachi dal'neyshego razvitiya tyurkskoy dialektologii v SSSR. *ST* 1973(2), pp. 3-9.

SHIRALIEV, M. Sh., ASADULLAEV, S.G. Sovetskaya tyurkskaya filogiya i zadachi zhurnala "Sovetskaya tyurkologiya". *Sov. Tyurkologiya* 1970(1), pp. 3-15.

SHIRVANI, Yusif-Ziya. Nekotorye zamechaniya otnositel'no Ibn-Mukhanny i ego sochineniya. *Struktura i istoriya tyurkskikh yazykov*, 1971, pp. 296-300.

SHUKYUROV, A.D. O kategorii narechiya v tyurkskikh yazykakh. *Istoriya, kul'tura, yazyki narodov Vostoka* 1970, pp. 197-200.

XL TURKISH LANGUAGES

SINOR, D. Stand und Aufgaben der internationalen altaistischen Forschung. *Sprache, Geschichte und Kultur der altaischen Völker*, hrsg. G. Hazai und P. Zieme, 1974, pp. 35-43.

SINOR, D. Uralo-Tunguz lexical correspondences. *Researches in Altaic languages*, ed. L. Ligeti, 1975, pp. 245-265.

SJOBERG, A.F. Negative verb roots in Davidian and Ural-Altaic. *Actes X. Cong.int.linguistes* 1967, vol. II, pp. 777-778.

STEBLEVA, I.V. Proiskhozhdenie i razvitie tyurkskoy alliteratzionnoy sistemy v svyazi s istoricheskim rodstvom tyurkskikh i mongol'skikh yazykov. (Origin and development of Turkic alliterational system in connection with historical relationship of Turkic and Mongolian languages). *Sov. Tyurkologiya* 1971(6), pp. 80-84.

SÜHEYL ÜNVER. Au sujet des noms des arrondissements et des quartiers d'Istanbul. *Proc. 8th Int.Cong.Onomastic Sciences* 1966, pp. 557-560.

SULAYMANOV, K. K voprosu o kategorii kharaktera protekaniya deystviya glagolov v tyurkskikh yazykakh. *Töid orientalistika alalt* 2(1973), pp. 104-115.

SUNIK, O.P. K voprosu o vozvratnykh mestoimeniyakh v altayskikh yazykakh. *Sprache, Geschichte und Kultur der altaischen Völker*, hrsg. G. Hazai und P. Zieme (XII. PIAC, 1974), pp. 553-567.

SYROMYATNIKOV, N.A. Kak otlichit' zaimstvovaniya ot iskonnykh obshchnostey v altayskikh yazykakh. *Vopr. yaz.* 1975 (3), pp. 50-61.

TARASENKO, R.F. Kategoriya prinadlezhnosti v tyurkskikh yazykakh. *Issledovaniya po vostochnoy filologii. K semidesyatiletiyu G.D.Sanzheeva*, 1974, pp. 235-249.

TEKIN, T. Further evidence for "zetacism" and "sigmatism". *Researches in Altaic languages*, ed. L. Ligeti, 1975, pp. 275-284.

TEKIN, T. On the alternation *l* ~ *s* in Turkic and Mongolian. *Sprache, Geschichte und Kultur der altaischen Völker*, hrsg. G. Hazai und P. Zieme (XII. PIAC, 1974), pp. 609-612.

TENISHEV, E. K istorii tyurkskogo uslovnogo nakloneniya. *Studia Turcica, ed. L. Ligeti*, 1971, pp. 441-449

TENISHEV, E.R. K ponyatiyu "obshchetyurkskoe sostoyanie". *ST* 1971(2), pp. 13-16.

TENISHEV, E.R. O metodakh istochnikakh sravnitel'no-istoricheskikh issledovaniy tyurkskikh yazykov. *ST* 1973(5), pp. 119-124.

TENISHEV, E.R. Tyurkskaya istoricheskaya dialektologiya i Makhmud Kashgarskiy. *ST* 1973(6), pp. 54-61.

TEPLYASHINA, T.I. Ob odnom volzhsko-kamskom areal'nom yavlenii. *Sov. Tyurkologiya* 1972 (3), pp. 35-40.

TOGAN, Z.V. Die Bedeutung der türkischen Ortsnamen in Ostiran für die vorislamische Geschichte der Türken. *Proc.8th Int. Cong.Onomastic Sciences* 1966, pp. 542-543.

TROIKE, R.C. The Glottochronology of six Turkic languages. *Inst. J. Amer. ling.* 35 (1969), pp. 183-191.

TSINTSIUS, V.I. On the pre-Altaic system of consonants. *Researches in Altaic languages*, ed. L. Ligeti, 1975, pp. 299-306.

TZINTZIUS, V.I. Altayskie terminy rodstva i problema ikh etimologii. *Sprache, Geschichte und Kultur der altaischen Völker*, hrsg. G. Hazai und P. Zieme, 1974, pp. 169-174.

TUMASHEVA, D.G. K voprosu o tipakh dialektnykh leksicheskikh razlichiy. *ST* 1973(6), pp. 67-72.

UMAROV, E.A. Frazeologicheskie slovari tyurkskikh yazykov. *Sov.Tyurkologiya* 1970(5), pp. 121-124.

UMAROV, E.A. K istorii odnogo frazeologizma iz slovarya V.V. Radlova. *Sov. Tyurkologiya* 1970(1), pp. 84-86.

UMAROV, E.A. O dvukh omonimakh v "Divane" Makhmuda Kashgari. *Sov.tyurkologiya* 1972 (1), pp. 103-105

VAGO, R.M. Abstract vowel harmony systems in Uralic and Altaic languages. *Language* 49(1973), pp. 579-605.

VASIL'EV, A.I. Imeyutsya li v tyurkskikh yazykakh fonemy, zaimstvovannye iz russkogo? (Do phonemes borrowed from Russian exist in Turkic languages ?) *Sov. Tyurkologiya* 1971(6), pp. 96-100.

VIETZE, H.P. Rückläufige Wörterbücher und ihre Bedeutung für die altaistische Forschung. *Researches in Altaic languages*, ed. L. Ligeti, 1975, pp. 315-321.

WHEELER, G. Language problems in multinational Asian communities. Discussion group with a paper. *Asian affairs* 60(N.S. 4,1973), pp. 287-294.

WIKANDER, S. Chichentiza - an Altaic name. *Studia linguistica* 25(1971), pp. 129-130.

WIKANDER, S. Maya and Altaic III. *Orientalia Suecana* 19-20(1970-71), pp. 186-204

WU, Shun-Chi. Altaistik in Taiwan. *UAJ* 47 (1975), pp. 229-230.

YAMPOL'SKIY, Z.I. Ob etnonime "Sevordii". *ST* 1973(1), pp. 83-86.

YÜCE, Nuri. Über das Gerundium *-araq/-erek*. *Central Asiatic J.* 17(1973), pp. 276-281.

YULDASHEV, A.A. Konversiya v tyurkskikh yazykakh i ee otrazhenie v slovaryakh. *Sov.Tyurkologiya* 1970(1), pp. 70-81.

YULDASHEV, A.A. Printzipy vydeleniya i razmeshcheniya v slovaryakh tyurkskikh yazykov zvukopodrazhatel'nykh i obrazopodrazhatel'nykh slov. *Tyurk. leksikologiya i leksikografiya,* 1971, pp. 153-172

YUND, Kerim. The origin and the meaning of some toponyms in İçel (İchel). *Proc. 8th Int.Cong.Onomastic Sciences* 1966, pp. 578-580.

ZAKIEV, M.Z. Klassifikatziya chastey rechi i affiksov v tyurkskikh yazykakh. *ST* 1973(6), pp. 3-8.

ZAKIEV, M.Z. Nekotorye voprosy formirovaniya slozhnopodchinennykh predlozheniy. (Some problems of complex sentences formation.) *Sov. Tyurkologiya* 1972(2), pp. 23-31.

ZAKIEV, M.S. Voraltaische syntaktische Modelle. *Sprache, Geschichte und Kultur der altaischen Völker,* hrsg. G. Hazai und P. Zieme (XII. PIAC, 1974), pp. 645-649.

ZAKIEV, M.Z. O periodizatzii istorii tyurkskikh pis'mennykh literaturykh yazykov. *ST* 1975(5), pp. 3-11.

ZEINALOV, Farhad. La catégorie de l'aspect et sa manifestation dans les langues turques. *Acta Or. Hung.* 29 (1975), pp. 301-312.

ZEYLANOVA, K. Neizvestnaya rukopis' M. Shakhtakhtinskogo o reforme alfabita. *ST* 1971(5), pp. 91-94.

ZEYNALOV, F.R. Kategoriya modal'nosti i sposoby ee vyrazheniya v tyurkskikh yazykakh. *Sov.Tyurkologiya* 1970(2), pp. 95-101.

ZEYNALOV, F.R. Kategoriya modal'nosti i sposoby ee vyrazheniya v tyurkskikh yazykakh. *Sprache, Geschichte und Kultur der altaischen Völker,* hrsg. G. Hazai und P. Zieme (XII. PIAC, 1974), pp. 651-659.

ZEYNALOV, F.R. O neobkhodimosti sozdaniya sravnitel'nogo slovarya lingvisticheskikh terminov tyurkskikh yazykov. *ST* 1973(4), pp. 68-70.

ZHIRMUNSKIY, V.M. Zametki o podgotovke "Dialektologicheskogo atlasa tyurkshikh yazykov SSSR". *Vopr.yaz.* 4(1971), pp. 15-16.

ZHURAVSKIY, A.I. Leksikograficheskaya obrabotka tyurkizmov starobelorusskogo yazyka. *Sov.Tyurkologiya* 1970(5), pp. 70-76.

Tyurkskoe yazykoznanie v SSSR za pyat'desyat let. (Turkic linguistics in the USSR for 50 years.) *Sov. Tyurkologiya* 1972(6), pp. 3-19.

See also I. b. 2. Vietze.

See also I. b. 3. Blagova.

See also I. b. 3. Guseynov.

See also I. b. 3. Kononov

See also I. b. 3. Musaev.

See also I. b. 3. Nasilov.

See also I. d. 1. Dmitrieva.

See also XXVIII. b. Blagova.

See also XXVIII. b. Daher.

See also XXVIII. b. Shastina.

See also XXXVII. a. Samoylovich.

See also XL. h. Nauta.

b LOAN WORDS

ARAKIN, V.D. Tyurkskie leksicheskie elementy v russkikh povestyakh i skazaniyakh XIII-XV vv. *ST* 1973(3), pp. 28-37.

AUSTIN, P.M. Russian loan words in the proposed reform of Soviet Turkic alphabets. *Gen.linguistics* 13(1973), pp. 16-25.

BAKHTIEV, Sh.Z. K etimologii nazvaniya "zhiguli" i nyekotorykh terminov sudokhodstva tyurkoyazychnogo proiskhozhdeniya. *ST* 1974(2), pp. 62-65.

BÁRCZI, G. Quelques conclusions tirées de l'étude des plus anciens mots d'emprunt turcs du hongrois. *Acta Or. Hung.* 25(1972), pp. 383-390.

BÁRCZI, G. Le traitement de š et de č turcs dans les mots d'emprunt turcs du protohongrois. *Studia Turcica, ed. L. Ligeti,* 1971, pp. 39-46

BLAGOVA, G.F. Opyt areal'nogo izucheniya tyurkizmov (*ordu/orda, saray, koshk/kiosk* v tyurkskikh yazykakh, v russkom i ukrainskom). *ST* 1975(4), pp. 37-45.

BORETZKY, N. Ein semantischer Turzismus in den Balkansprachen. *Z.Balkanologie* 7 (1969-70), pp. 16-21.

CHUMBALOVA, G.M. Tyurkskie leksicheskie elementy v yazyke romana Ivana Vazova "Pod igom". *ST* 1975(2), pp. 48-54.

CLAUSON, Sir G. The foreign elements in early Turkish. *Researches in Altaic languages,* ed. L. Ligeti, 1975, pp. 43-49.

DARASZ, Zd. The word-formation of Serbo-Croatian substantives of Turkish origin. *Folia Or.* 15(1974), pp. 119-139; 16(1975), pp. 193-213.

DOBRODOMOV, I.G. Tyurkizmy slavyanskikh yazykov kak istochnik svedeniy po istoricheskoy fonetike tyurkskikh yazykov. *ST* 1974(2), pp. 34-43.

GARIPOV, T.M. "Turco-slavica" in Baschkirien. *Sprache, Geschichte und Kultur der altaischen Völker,* hrsg. G. Hazai und P. Zieme, (XII. PIAC, 1974), pp. 257-262.

GRANNES, A. Les turcismes dans un parler bulgare de la Bulgarie de l'Est. *Acta Or. Hung.* 28(1974), pp. 269-285.

XL TURKISH LANGUAGES

HAMP, E.P. Greek τέλι, Albanian *tel. Sprache, Geschichte und Kultur der altaischen Völker*, hrsg. G. Hazai und P. Zieme (XII. PIAC, 1974), p. 263.

HOVDHAUGEN, Even. Turkish words in Khotanese texts. A linguistic analysis. *NTS* 24 (1971), pp. 163-209.

JASHAR-NASTEVA, O. Za fonetskata adaptacija na turcizmite vo makedonskiot jazik. *Serta Slavica in memoriam A. Schmaus*, 1971, pp. 316-322.

KALESHI, H. Der Einfluss des Türkischen auf die Wortbildung des Albanischen. *Sprache, Geschichte und Kultur der altaischen Völker*, hrsg. G. Hazai und P. Zieme (XII. PIAC, 1974), pp. 279-286.

KALESHI, H. Einige Beispiele fur den Einfluss der türkischen Sprache bei zusammengesetzten Wörtern im Albanischen. *Serta Slavica in memoriam A. Schmaus*, 1971, pp. 330-337.

KALESHI, Hasan. The importance of Turkish influence upon word formation in Albanian. *Balcanica* 2(1971), pp. 271-293.

KAZAZIS, K. Ταχυδρομος's 'Turkish lessons'. *Essays in linguistics ... in honor of Henry and Renée Kahane*, 1973, pp. 394-407.

KHABICHEV, M.A. *Bagr, bagor. ST* 1975(4), pp. 46-48.

KISSLING, H.-J. Türkisch-slavische Sprachprobleme. *Anzeiger slav. philol.* 6(1972), pp. 49-59.

KOSTOV, K. Lehnwörter zigeunerischen Ursprungs im türkischen Argot. *Sprache, Geschichte und Kultur der altaischen Völker*, hrsg. G. Hazai und P. Zieme (XII. PIAC, 1974), pp. 357-361.

LIGETI, L. Quelques problèmes étymologiques des anciens mots d'emprunt turcs de la langue hongroise. *Acta Or. Hung.* 29(1975), pp. 279-288.

MAL'KOV, F.V. Tyurkskie elementy v leksike koreyskogo yazyka. *Sprache, Geschichte und Kultur der altaischen Völker*, hrsg. G. Haza und P. Zieme (XII. PIAC, 1974), pp. 383-390

MANDOKY, E. Etymologie de deux mots hongrois provenant de l'ancien turc. *Acta Or. Hung.* 25(1972), pp. 391-403.

MENGES, K.H. Zum neuen *B'lgarski etimoligichen rechnik* und den türkischen Elementen im Bulgarischen. *Z.Balkanologie* 7(1969-70), pp. 55-83.

MOLLOVA, M. Quelques lexèmes turks septentrionaux en *ǧ~č~j*... dans les langues slaves méridionales. *Z.Balkanologie* 9 (1973), pp. 89-127.

NAMETAK, Alija. Turcizmi u pripovjestima Nike H.P. Besarevića. (Turzismen in den Erzählungen Niko Besarevics.) *Prilozi Or. Fil.Ist.* 16-17 (1966-7), pp. 183-212

NÉMETH, J. Türkische und ungarische Ethnonyme. *UAJ* 47(1975), pp. 154-160.

PALLÓ, M.K. Zur Etymologie des ungarischen Verbs üdül-. *Acta Or. Hung.* 25(1972), pp. 405-412.

POPPE, N., jr. On some Turkic loan words attested in Old Russian sources. *UAJ* 45 (1973), pp. 251-254.

RÁSONYI, L. L'origine du hongrois igen «oui». *Acta Or. Hung.* 25(1972), pp. 413-414.

RASSADIN, V.I. Tyurkizmy v khalkhamongol'skom yazyke. *Materialy po istorii i filologii Tzentral'noy Azii* 5(1970), pp. 52-58.

RUSKOVA, M.P. Turetzkie zaimstvovaniya v bolgarskikh pis'mennykh pamyatnikakh XVIII veka. *ST* 1973(2), pp. 60-70.

SANZHEYEV, G.D. A Mongolistic reconstruction of Turkisms. *Researches in Altaic languages*, ed. L. Ligeti, 1975, pp. 213-218.

SCHALLER, H.W. Die türkischen Lehnwörter in der bulgarischen Sprache. Eine Betrachtung nach sprachlichen Merkmalen und Bedeutungsgruppen. *Z.Balkanologie* 9(1973), pp. 174-186.

SETAROV, D.S. Tyurkizmy v russkikh nazvaniyakh ptitz. *Sov.Tyurkologiya* 1970(2), pp. 86-94.

SIKIRIĆ, Saćir. Prilog proučavanju turcizama. Povoda knjige Abdulaha Škaljića. *Turcizmi u srpskohrvatskom jeziku*, Sarajevo 1965. *Prilozi Or.Fil.Ist.* 16-17 (1966-7), pp. 343-368

SYMEONIDIS, Ch. Griechische Lehnwörter im Türkischen. *Balkan studies* 14(1973), pp. 167-200.

TEUBNER, J.K. Altaisches, fernöstliches und malaiisches Wortgut im Suaheli. *XVIII. Deutscher Orientalistentag 1972: Vorträge*, pp. 629-636.

THEODORIDIS, D. Καφτουργάς: eine türkische Entlehnung im Mittelgriechischen. *Z.Balkanologie* 7(1969-70), pp. 166-169.

TIETZE, A. Ein slavisches Lehnwort in den früh-osmanischen Chroniken. *WZKM* 65/66 (1973-74), pp. 219-222.

UMAROV, E.A. O nekotorykh frazeologizmakh, sozdannykh Alisherom Navoi. *ST* 1975(5), pp. 90-95.

UNBEGAUN, B. Russian *razgil'djaj. UAJ* 47 (1975), pp. 201-228

YUSIFOV, Yu.B. O nekotorykh yazykovykh elementakh tyurkskogo proiskhozhdeniya v sochinenii albanskogo istorika. *ST* 1974(2), pp. 71-79.

See also I. b. 3. Popov.

See also I. b. 3. Shcherbak.

See also XL. aa. Stachowski.

c ORKHON INSCRIPTIONS. OLD TURKISH

AALTO, Pentti and TRYJARSKI, E. A Runic tombstone inscription presumedly from Minusinsk. *RO* 34 i(1971), pp. 35-38.

AKYLBEKOVA, Z., ASHIRALIEV, K., OSMONALIEVA, B., SYDYKOV, S. Glossariy. Transliteratziya kornevykh slov pamyatnikov. Russko-drevnetyurkskiy glossariy. *Drevnie tyurkskie dialekty ... pod. red. I.A. Batmanova,* 1971, pp. 32-169.

AMANZHOLOV, A.S. Forefather Goat or the Ancient Turkic inscription in early Greek alphabet. *Ar.Or.* 42(1974), pp. 33-36.

ARLOTTO, A. Old Turkic oracle books. *Monumenta Serica* 29(1970-71), pp. 685-696.

ARSLANOVA, F.Kh., KLYASHTORNYY, S.G. Runicheskaya nadpis' na zerkale iz Verkhnego Priirtysh'ya. *Tyurkologicheskiy sbornik* 1972 *(Pamyati P.M. Melioranskogo),* pp. 306-315.

ASANALIEV, U. Affiksy, vstretivshiesya v eniseyskikh i orkhonskikh pamyatnikakh. *Drevnie tyurkskie dialekty ... pod. red. I.A. Batmanova,* 1971, pp. 170-195.

BATMANOV, I.A. Drevnie tyurkskie dialekty i ikh otrazhenie v sovremennykh yazykakh. *Drevnie tyurkskie dialekty ... pod. red. I.A. Batmanova,* 1971, pp. 3-30.

BAZAROVA, D.Kh. K etimologii nekotorykh drevnetyurkskikh nazvaniy ptitz. *ST* 1975 (4), pp. 11-22.

CLAUSON, Sir G. and TRYJARSKI, E. The inscription at Ikhe Khushotu. *RO* 34 i(1971), pp. 7-33.

CLAUSON, G. Some Notes on the Inscription of Toñuquq. *Studia Turcica, ed. L. Ligeti,* 1971, pp. 125-132

DOERFER, G. Eine seltsame alttürkisch-chaladsch Parallele. *Türk dili araştırmaları* 1973-74, pp. 13-24.

HAMILTON, J. Le colophon de l'Irq bitig. *Turcica* 7(1975), pp. 7-19.

HAMILTON, J., BAZIN, L. Un manuscrit chinois et turc runiforme de Touen-Houang, British Museum Or. 8212 (78) et (79). *Turcica* 4 (1972), pp. 25-42.

HAMILTON, J. Le nom de lieu *K.č.n* dans les inscriptions turques runiformes. *T'oung Pao* 60(1974), pp. 294-303.

HAMILTON, J. Opla-/yopla-, uf-/yuf- et autres formes semblables en turc ancien. *Acta Or. Hung.* 28(1974), pp. 111-117.

HAZAI, G. Zu einer Stelle der Tonyukuk-Inschrift. *Sprache, Geschichte und Kultur der altaischen Völker,* hrsg. G. Hazai und P. Zieme (XII. PIAC, 1974), pp. 265-269.

HOVDHAUGEN, E. The relationship between the two Orkhon inscriptions. *Acta Or.* 36(1974), pp. 55-82.

JOHANSON, L. Zur Syntax der alttürkischen Kausativa. *XVIII. Deutscher Orientalistentag 1972: Vorträge,* pp. 529-540.

KHABICHEV, M.A. O drevnetyurkskikh runicheskikh nadpisyakh v Alanskikh katakombakh. *Sov.Tyurkologiya* 1970(2), pp. 64-69.

KLYASHTORNYY, S.G. Drevnetyurkskaya pismennost' i kul'tura narodov Tzentral'noy Azii. (Po materialam polevykh issledovaniy v Mongolii, 1968-1969 gg.) *Tyurkologicheskiy sbornik* 1972 *(Pamyati P.M. Melioranskogo),* pp. 254-264.

KLYASHTORNYY, S.G. Moneta s runicheskoy nadpis'yu iz Mongolii. *Tyurkologicheskiy sbornik* 1972 *(Pamyati P.M. Melioranskogo),* pp. 334-338.

KLYASHTORNYY, S.G. Runicheskaya nadpis' iz Vostochnoy Gobi. *Studia Turcica, ed. L. Ligeti,* 1971, pp. 249-258

KLYASHTORNYY, S.G., LIVSHITZ, V.A. Sevreyskiy kamen'. *ST* 1971(3), pp. 106-112.

KONDRAT'EV, V.G. K vos'midesyatiletiyu deshirovki tyurkskoy runicheskoy pis'mennosti. *ST* 1974(1), pp. 58-62.

KONDRAT'EV, V.G. Ob otnoshenii yazyka pamyatnikov Orkhono-Eniseyskoy pis'mennosti k yazyku drevneuygurskikh pamyatnikov. *ST* 1973(3), pp. 23-27.

KORMUSHIN, I.V. K osnovnym ponyatiyam tyurkskoy runicheskoy paleografii. *ST* 1975(2), pp. 25-47.

KOROGLY, Kh. Stilisticheskie osobennosti "Knigi moego deda Korkuta". *ST* 1975(2), pp. 55-68.

KUZNETZOV, P.I. Bessoyuznye pridatochnye predlozheniya s formoy na -duk v pamyatnikakh orkhono-eniseyskoy pis'mennosti. *ST* 1971(4), pp. 62-67.

LIGETI, L. Autour du *Säkiz yükmäk yaruq. Studia Turcica, ed. L. Ligeti,* 1971, pp. 291-319

MATUZ, J. Trois fragments inconnus de l'Orkhon. *Turcica* 4(1972), pp. 15-24.

MOLLOVA, Mefküre. Sur la valeur de ǵ dans les monuments turcs. *Folia Or.* 12(1970), pp. 171-174

NASILOV, D.M. Nekotorye zamechaniya k prochteniyu eniseyskikh pamyatnikov. *Pis'mennye pamyatniki Vostoka* 1971, pp. 204-214.

NASILOV, D.M. O lingvisticheskom izuchenii pamyatnikov tyurkskoy pis'mennosti. *Tyurkologicheskiy sbornik* 1972 *(Pamyati P.M. Melioranskogo),* pp. 62-68.

PALLÓ, K.M. Ung. *tor* 'Gastmahl, Bewirtung' zu alttürk. *tod-* 'sich sättigen'. *UAJ* 46(1974), pp. 109-119.

RADZHABOV, A.A. Ob onginskom pamyatnike. *Sov.Tyurkologiya* 1970(2), pp. 33-43.

SEYIDOV, M.A. K voprosu o traktovke ponyatiy *jer sub* v drevnetyurkskikh pamyatnikakh. *ST* 1973(3), pp. 63-69.

SHCHERBAK, A.M. Ob odnom sochetanii v runicheskikh nadpisakh. *ST* 1975(6), pp. 88-90.

SHCHERBAK, A.M. S.E. Malov - issledovatel' drevnetyurkskikh i drevneuygurskikh pamyatnikov. *ST* 1975(5), pp. 69-73.

STEBLEVA, I.V. Drevnetyurkskaya kniga gadaniy kak proizvedeniye poezii. *Istoriya, kul'tura, yazyki narodov Vostoka* 1970, pp. 150-177.

TENISHEV, E. Pereboy *s/š* v tyurkskikh runicheskikh pamyatnikakh. *Struktura i istoriya tyurkskikh yazykov,* 1971, pp. 289-295.

TENISHEV, E.R. Smychnye soglasnye v yazyke tyurkskikh runicheskikh pamyatnikov. *ST* 1973(2), pp. 40-45.

THOMSEN, V. Zur Deutung der Talas-Inschriften. *Acta ling. Acad. sci. hung.* 22(1972), pp. 245-250.

TRYJARSKI, E. et HAMILTON, J. L'inscription turque runiforme de Khutuk-Ula. *JA* 263(1975), pp. 171-182.

TRYJARSKI, E., AALTO, P. Two old Turkic monuments of Mongolia. *Commentationes Fenno-Ugricae in honorem E. Itkonen* (Mém. Soc. Finno-ougrienne 150), 1973, pp. 413-420.

TRYJARSKI, E. Zur neueren Geschichte des Ongin-Denkmals. *Sprache, Geschichte und Kultur der altaischen Völker,* hrsg. G. Hazai und P. Zieme (XII. PIAC, 1974), pp. 629-630.

TUGUSHEVA, L.Yu. Uygurskaya versiya biografii Syuan'-Tzzana (fragmenty iz gl. X). *Pis'mennye pamyatniki Vostoka* 1971, -p. 253-296.

UNGVITZKAYA, M.A. Pamyatniki eniseyskoy pis'mennosti i pesennyy fol'klor Khakasov. *ST* 1971(5), pp. 61-72.

VASIL'EV, D.D., KLYASHTORNYY, S.G. Runicheskaya nadpis' Yir-Sayyr. *ST* 1973(2), pp. 105-110.

See also V. g. Klyashtornyy.

See also XXXVIII. d. Akhmedov.

See also XL. o. Ungvitzkaya.

d MIDDLE TURKISH

ALI-ZADE, A.A. Upotreblenie tyurko-mongol'skikh terminov v proizvedeniyakh Rashid ad-Dina i Vassafa. *Gruzinskoe istochnikovedenie* III, 1971, pp. 176-190.

CHIRVANI, Y.Z. Muhammed Ibn-Keys et son glossaire turc. *Turcica* 2(1970), pp. 81-100.

CHAYKOVSKAYA, A.I. Ob araboyazychnykh grammatikakh starotyurkskogo yazyka. *ST* 1975(6), pp. 77-84.

CLAUSON, Sir G. The Turkish-Khotanese vocabulary re-edited. *Islam Tetkikleri Enst. dergisi* 5(1973), pp. 37-45.

FAZYLOV, E., CHAYKOVSKAYA. K istorii publikatzii tyurkskikh turfanskikh pamyatnikov. *ST* 1973(3), pp. 88-91.

GARIPOV, T.M. Starotyurkskie pis'mennye pamyatniki Bashkirii. (Old Turkic relics of Bashkiria.) *Sov. Tyurkologiya* 1972(4), pp. 39-45.

GRUNINA, E.A. K voprosu o pis'mennoy traditzii v anatoliyskikh pamyatnikakh XIII-XIV vv. *ST* 1971(4), pp. 98-104.

GUKASYAN, V. Tyurkizmy v "Istorii alban" Moiseya Utiyskogo. *Struktura i istoriya tyurkskikh yazykov,* 1971, pp. 238-250.

GUZEV, V.G. Kratkiy obzor issledovaniy po yazyku tyurkov Maloy Azii XIII-XVI vv. *Tyurkologicheskiy sbornik* 1972 *(Pamyati P.M. Melioranskogo),* pp. 69-92.

HAZAI, G. Sur un passage de l'inscription de Tonyuquq. *Turcica* 2(1970), pp. 25-31.

KARAHAN, A. Les caractéristiques essentiels de la littérature de l'époque des Karahanides et "Kutadgu Bilig". *Sprache, Geschichte und Kultur der altaischen Völker,* hrsg. G. Hazai und P. Zieme (XII. PIAC, 1974), pp. 291-296.

KELLY, J.M. Remarks on Kāšgharī's phonology. *UAJ* 42(1972), pp. 178-193.

KHADZHIOLOVA, K.A. Glagol'naya forma na -P v turetzkikh literaturnykh pamyatnikakh XIII - XVI vekov. (-P- form of verbs in Turkish literary manuscripts of the 13th - 16th centuries.) *Sov. Tyurkologiya* 1972(6), pp. 83-90.

KOBESHAVIDZE, I.N. Lichnye glagol'nye pokazateli v yazyke orkhono-eniseyskikh nadpisey. *Strany Blizhnego i Srednego Vostoka: istoriya, ekonomica,* 1972, pp. 467-477.

KOBESHAVIDZE, I.N. Razgranichenie sfer glagol'nogo slovoobrazovaniya slovoizmeneniya v yazyke orkhono-eniseyskikh nadpisey. (Delimitation of derivational and inflexional spheres of verb in the language of orkhono-enisry inscriptions.) *Sov. Tyurkologiya* 1972(5), pp. 91-95.

KOROGLY, Kh. Shaman, polkovodetz, ozan. (Evolyutziya obraza Dede-Korkuta.) *Sov. Tyurkologiya* 1972 (3), pp. 48-62.

KULIEV, G.K. O forme vinitel'nogo podezha tipa *sözin, tewesin* v tekste *"Divanü lûgat-it-türk"* Makhmuda Kashgari. *Sov. Tyurkologiya* 1970(4), pp. 67-70.

NIGMATOV, Kh. G. O glagol'nykh kornyakh tipa SGS i SG po materialam slovarya Makhmuda Kashgarskogo. *Sov.Tyurkologiya* 1970(3), pp. 39-44.

NIGMATOV, Kh. G. Sootnoshenie kategoriy vremeni i nakloneniya v tyurkskom glagole (po materialam slovarya Makhmuda Kashgarskogo). *Sov.Tyurkologiya* 1970(5), pp. 51-57.

POTAPOV, L.P. Tyul'bery eniseyskikh runicheskikh nadpisey. *Tyurkolog. sbornik (Pamyati V.V. Radlova,* 1972), pp. 145-166.

SHCHERBAK, A.M. O runicheskoy pis'mennosti v yugo-vostochnoy Evrope. *ST* 1971(4), pp. 76-82.

SIKALIEV, A. Drevnetyurkskie pis'mennye pamyatniki i nogaytzy. *Sov.Tyurkologiya* 1970(4), pp. 131-135.

STEBLEVA, I.V. K rekonstruktzii drevnetyurkskoy religiozno-mifologicheskoy sistemy. *Tyurkolog. sbornik (Pamyati V.V. Radlova,* 1972), pp. 213-226.

STEBLEVA, I.V. Sinkopirovanie slov v poeticheskikh tekstakh "Divan lugat at-turk" Makhmuda al-Kashgari. *Tyurkolog. sbornik (Pamyati V.V. Radlova,* 1972), pp. 206-212.

ZEYNALOV, F.R. Ob odnom "drevnem tyurkskom yazyke" v srednem Irane. (on one ancient Turkish language in Middle Iran) *Sov. Tyurkologiya* 1972(6), pp. 76-79.

See also I. b. 3. Fazylov.

See also XXXVII. i. Dankoff.

See also XLI. b. Stebleva

e EASTERN TURKISH. CHAGHATAI

BLAGOVA, G.F. Nekotorye voprosy razvitiya srednevekogo sredneaziatskogo tyurkskogo literaturnogo yazyka. *ST* 1971(4), pp. 68-75.

BLAGOVA, G.F. Smena dialektnoy orientatzii sredneaziatsko-tyurkskogo literaturno-pis'mennogo yazyka XV - nachala XVI v. *ST* 1975(6), pp. 21-32.

BLAGOVA, G.F. Tyurksk. *Chaghataj-/dzhagatay-* (Opyt sravnitel'nogo izucheniya starogo zaimstvovaniya). *Tyurkolog. sbornik (Pamyati V.V. Radlova,* 1972), pp. 167-205.

BODROLIGETI, A. Ahmad's Baraq-nāma: a Central Asian Islamic work in Eastern Middle Turkic. *CAJ* 17(1974), pp. 83-128.

BODROGLIGETI, A. Islamic terms in eastern middle Turkic. *Acta Or. Hung.* 25(1972), pp. 355-367.

DANKOFF, R. A note on *khutu* and *chatuq*. *JAOS* 93(1973), pp. 542-543.

ECKMANN, J. Chagataica. *Acta Or. Hung.* 25(1972), pp. 349-353.

ECKMANN, J. Eastern Turkic translations of the Koran. *Studia Turcica, ed. L. Ligeti,* 1971, pp. 149-159

FAZYLOV, E.I. Un texte inédit en protoçagatay. *Turcica* 4(1972), pp. 43-77.

GANDJEÏ, T. The prosodic structure of an Old Turkish poem. *W.B. Henning memorial vol.,* 1970, pp. 157-160.

KHAFIZOVA, A. "Kelurname" Mukhammeda Yakuba Chingi. *Sov. Tyurkologiya* 1972 (3), pp. 97-102.

KILICHEV, E.R. Materialy vostochnotyurkskogo yazyka XI veka i drevniy plast leksiki bukharskogo dvuyazychnogo govora. *ST* 1975(6), pp. 85-87.

MUKHAMEDOVA, Z.B. Predvaritel'nye zamechaniya o slovare "Hell-i luɣat-i čaɣatai". *Tyurk.leksikologiya i leksikografiya,* 1971, pp. 111-121

NIGMATOV, Kh.G. Otymennoe osnoobrazovanie tyurkskogo glagola v XI veke. *ST* 1971(3), pp. 33-42.

NIGMATOV, Kh.G. Printzipy opisaniya morfologii vostochno-tyurkskogo yazyka XI-XII vv. *ST* 1973(6), pp. 27-35.

NIGMATOV, Kh.G. Semanticheskaya i sintaksicheskaya funktzii padezhey v yazyke vostochno-tyurkskikh pamyatnikov XI-XII vekov. *ST* 1975(4), pp. 23-36.

NIGMATOV, Kh.G. Sintaksicheskaya suchchnost' form prinadlezhnosti v yazyke vostochno-tyurkskikh pamyatnikov XI-XII vv. *ST* 1975(5), pp. 21-26.

NIGMATOV, Kh.G. Zalogi glagola v vostochnotyurkskom yazyke XI-XII vekov. *ST* 1973(1), pp. 46-61.

SERIKOVA, L. Poeticheskaya rech' Alishera Navoi. (O yazyke kyt'a iz "Khazoyin ul-Maoniy".) *ST* 1971(3), pp. 97-105.

TENISHEV, E.R. Novyy istochnik chagatayskogo yazyka rannego perioda. *Sov. Tyurkologiya* 1970(1), pp. 82-83.

TOGAN, Zeki Velidi. The earliest translation of the Qur'an into Turkish. *Islâm Tetkikleri Enstitüsü dergisi* 4 (1964), pp. 1-19.

UMAROV, E.A. Inoyazychnye frazeologizmy v yazyke Navoi. (Foreign phraseologizms in the language of Navai.) *Sov. Tyurkologiya* 1972(4), pp. 46-53.

ZIEME, P. Zu den nestorianisch-türkischen Turfantexten. *Sprache, Geschichte und Kultur der altaischen Völker,* hrsg. G. Hazai und P. Zieme (XII. PIAC, 1974), pp. 661-668.

f AZERBAIJANI

ABDULLAEV, A.Z. O transformatzii komponentov slozhnopodchinennykh predlozheniy. (On transformation of components of complex sentences.) *Sov. Tyurkologiya* 1972(6), pp. 20-29.

ABDULLAEV, A.Z. Slozhnye predlozheniya us lozhnennogo tipa v azerbaydzhanskom yazyke. *ST* 1971(3), pp. 13-24.

ADILOV, M., SADYKOV, Z. Ob azerbaydzhanskoy antroponimii. *ST* 1971(3), pp. 113-117.

AKHMEDOV, Dzh. S. Vyrazhenie otritzaniya predikativami s konstatiruyushchey funktziey v sovremennom azerbaydzhanskom yazyke. *Sov.Tyurkologiya* 1970(2), pp. 82-85.

ALIEVA, R. Nekotorye zamechaniya po tvorchestvu B. Sakhanda (po materialam tzikla poem "Pesni moego saza"). *Voprosy vostochnogo literaturovedeniya i tekstologii,* 1975, pp. 127-133.

ASLANOV, V.I. 'Divanu lugat-it-tyurk' Makhmuda Kashgari i azerbaydzhanskiy yazyk. *Sov.tyurkologiya* 1972(1), pp. 61-74

ASLANOV, V.I. K probleme rekonstruktzii kornevykh morfem (na materiale istoricheskoy leksikologii azerbaydzhanskogo yazyka). *ST* 1971(2), pp. 67-75.

ASLANOV, V.I. K voprosu ob izuchenii tvorcheskogo naslediya Imadeddina Nasimi. *ST* 1973(5), pp. 15-21.

BRANDS, H.W. Aserbaidschanische satirische Dichtung im 19. Jahrhundert. *Der Islam* 48(1971-2), pp. 280-297

BUDAGOVA, Z.I. Ellipticheskie predlozheniya v sovremennom azerbaydzhanskom yazyke. (Elyptical sentences in modern Azerbaijani.) *Sov. Tyurkologiya* 1972(5), pp. 10-16.

BUDAGOVA, Z.I. O khudozhestvenno-izobrazitel'nykh sredstvakh yazyka (na materiale azerbaydzhanskoy sovetskoy poezii). *ST* 1975(5), pp. 101-106.

BUDAGOVA, Z.I. Ritoricheskoe voprositel'noe predlozhenie kak odna iz stilisticheskikh figur v sovremennom azerbaydzhanskom yazyke. *ST* 1973(6), pp. 17-26.

DEMIRCHIZADE, A.M. O periodizatzii istorii azerbaydzhanskogo literaturnogo yazyka. *Struktura i istoriya tyurkskikh yazykov,* 1971, pp. 251-260.

DOERFER, G. O sostoyanii issledovaniya khaladzhskoy gruppy yazykov. *Vop.Yaz.* 1972(1), pp. 89-96.

DOERFER, G. Yavlyaetsya li khaladzhskiy yazyk dialektom azerbaydzhanskogo yazyka? *ST* 1974(1), pp. 45-51.

DZHANASHIYA, N.N. Zalogi v sovremennom azerbaydzhanskom yazyke. *ST* 1974(1), pp. 41-44.

GASANOV, A.G. Ob etimologii slova hejvərə. *Tyurk.leksikologiya i leksikografiya,* 1971, pp. 29-36

GASYMOV, M. Sh. Iz istorii obrazovaniya i razvitiya terminologii v Azerbaydzhane. *Tyurk.leksikologiya i leksikografiya,* 1971, pp. 194-208

GASYMOV, M.Sh. Osnovnye sposoby obrazovaniya terminov v sovremennom azerbaydzhanskom literaturnom yazyke. (The main method of terms-formation in modern literary Azerbaijani.) *Sov. Tyurkologiya* 1972(4), pp. 23-31.

GULIZADE, M.Yu. Azerbaydzhanskoe sovetskoe literaturovedenie. *Sov.Tyurkologiya* 1970 (5), pp. 13-19

GULIZADE, M.Yu. Imadeddin Nasimi - velikiy poet i mysitel'. *ST* 1973(5), pp. 1-14.

GULI-ZADÉ, Mirza Aga et DADACH-ZADÉ, Araz. Histoire de la littérature azerbaïdjanaise. (Essai sommaire.) *Bedi Kartlisa* 28 (1971), pp. 71-91.

HOUSEHOLDER, F. Vowel overlap in Azerbaijani. *Papers in linguistics and phonetics to the memory of P. Delattre,* 1972, pp. 229-230.

ISLAMOV, M.I. Drevnie formy lichnykh mestoimeniy v dialektakh i govorakh azerbaydzhanskogo yazyka. *Sov. Tyurkologiya* 1972 (3), pp. 16-28.

ISLAMOV, M.I. Proiskhozhdenie i struktura nekotorykh slozhnykh form ukazatel'nykh mestoimeniy (po materialam dialektov i govorov azerbaydzkanskogo yazyka). *ST* 1973 (1), pp. 37-45.

IVANOV, S.N. Lirika Nasimi i voprosy ee perevodcheskogo istolkovaniya. *ST* 1973 (5), pp. 22-30.

KAGRAMANOV, Dzh.V. O rukopisyakh proizvedeniy Imadeddina Nasimi. *ST* 1973(5), pp. 31-36.

KHIDIROV, V.S. K probleme tipologicheskikh tozhdestv v raznosistemykh yazykakh (na materiale analiticheskikh form glagola v azerbaydzhanskom yazyke i v yazykakh lezginskoy gruppy). *ST* 1971(5), pp. 33-45.

PINES, V.Ya. O foneme /k/ v azerbaydzhanskom yazyke. *ST* 1973(4), pp. 64-70.

RAGIMOV, M.Sh. 'Divanu lugat-it-tyurk' Makhmuda Kashgari i drevnetyrukskie elementy v dialektakh i govorakh azerbaydzhanskogo yazyka. *Sov.tyurkologiya* 1972(1), pp. 75-82

RAGIMOV, M.Sh., ALEKPEROV, A.K. Sovremennoe sostoyanie i perspektivy razvitiya azerbaydzhanskogo yazykoznaniya. *Sov.Tyurkologiya* 1970(5), pp. 3-12

RICHTER, E. Die aserbaidschanische Bibliographie. Ein kurzer Überblick über die von der Bücherkammer der Aserbaidschanischen SSR in Baku herausgegebende laufende Bibliographie. *Biblos* 22(1973), pp. 329-342.

SADYGOV, A.Sh. Ob odnom neizuchennom pamyatnike azerbaydzhanskogo yazyka XVI veka. (On one unexplored Azerbaijanian manuscript of the 16th century.) *Sov. Tyurkologiya* 1972(4), pp. 125-133.

SADYKHOV, A.Sh. Znachenie dialektnykh faktov v izuchenii istoricheskogo sintaksisa azerbaydzhanskogo yazyka. *ST* 1975 (6), pp. 68-73.

SEVORTYAN, E.V. Tyurkizmy u rannikh armyanskikh pisateley. *Struktura i istoriya tyurkskikh yazykov,* 1971, pp. 261-275.

SHARIF, Aziz. Velikiy eretik (k 600-letiyu so dnya rozhdeniya Seid-Imadeddina Nasimi). *NAA* 1974(1), pp. 137-142.

SHIRALIEV, M.Sh. N.I. Ashmarin i razvitie azerbaydzhanskoy dialektologii (K 100-letiyu so dnya rozhdeniya). *ST* 1970(6), pp. 70-76.

SHIRALIEV, M.Sh. Nekotorye voprosy formirovaniya azerbaydzhanskogo literaturnogo yazyka v gody sovetskoy vlasti. *Vopr.yaz.* 1972(4), pp. 125-129.

SHIRALIEV, M.Sh. Novye dialektnye dannye dlya istorii tyurkskikh yazykov (po materialam azerbaydzhanskikh dialektov). *Sov.Tyurkologiya* 1970(5), pp. 20-24

SHIRALIEV, M.Sh. Ob etimologii imperativnoy formy vtorogo litza edinstvennogo chisla *-gynan, g'inän* (na materiale dialektov i govorov azerbaydzhanskogo yazyka). *ST* 1973 (3), pp. 47-48.

SHIRALIEV, M.Sh. Razvitie azerbaydzhanskogo yazykoznaniya za poslednie gody. *Vop. yaz* 1972(5), pp. 113-118.

SHIRALIEV, M.Sh. Zametki o slozhnopodchinennom bessoyuznom predlozhenii. (Na materiale azerbaydzhanskogo yazyka.) *ST* 1971(4), pp. 13-14.

TAGI-ZADE, Z.Kh., POTAPOVA, P.K. Akusticheskiy analiz glasnykh sovremennogo azerbaydzhanskogo literaturnogo yazyka. *ST* 1971 (1), pp. 60-69.

TAGI-ZADE, Z. Kh., POTAPOVA, R.K. Akusticheskiy analiz soglasnykh sovremennogo azerbaydzhanskogo literaturnogo yazyka. (Accoustic analysis of consonants in literary Azerbaijani.) *Sov. Tyurkologiya* 1972(6), pp. 50-54.

URAKSIN, Z.G. Razvitie bashkirskogo yazykoznaniya za gody sovetskoy vlasti. (Development of Bashkir linguistics for the years of Soviet power.) *Sov. Tyurkologiya* 1972(2), pp. 95-102.

ZEYNALOV, F.R. "Dastan ob Akhmede Kherami" - drevneshiy pamyatnik azerbaydzhanskogo yazyka. *ST* 1975(5), pp. 82-89.

See also XXXVIII. b. Pashaev

See also XL. t. Yusupov.

See also XL. x. Aslanov

g BASHKIR

CSIKAI, V. Eine unveröffentlichte baschkirische Volksmärchen-Variante. *Acta Or. Hung.* 28(1974), pp. 37-61.

FATYKHOV, A.Kh. O perspektivakh upotrebleniya soyuzov i nekotorykh osobennostyakh bessoyuznykh slozhnopodchinennykh predlozheniy (na materiale bashkirskogo i tatarskogo yazykakh). *ST* 1971(5), pp. 26-32.

FEDOTOV, M.R. K voprosu o drevnechuvashskoy pis'mennosti. (Toward the problem of ancient Chuvash writing.) *Sov. Tyurkologiya* 1972(5), pp. 108-114.

GALIN, S.A. Ob odnom bashkirskom epicheskom skazanii ("Kyzbatyr i Kyrbatyr"). *ST* 1975(4), pp. 49-55.

MIRZHANOVA, S.F. Terminologiya rodstva v dialektakh bashkirskogo yazyka. *ST* 1973 (4), pp. 99-109.

MURATOV, S.N. Bashkirskaya skazka v zapisi A.G. Bessonova iz rukopisnogo sobraniya Instituta Vostokovedeniya AN SSSR. *Istoriya, kul'tura, yazyki narodov Vostoka* 1970, pp. 178-189.

SEREBRENNIKOV, B.A. O prichinakh prevrashcheniya nachal'nogo *s* v *h* v bashkirskom yazyke. *ST* 1973(2), pp. 10-15.

ZAYNULLIN, M.V. Moladnost' dolzhenstvovaniya v bashkirskom yazyke. *ST* 1973(2), pp. 53-59.

See also XL. b. Garipov.

See also XL. n. Laude-Cirtautas.

See also XL. t. Lisowski.

h CHUVASH

ALEKSEEV, A.A. Imennye opredelitel'nye slovosochetaniya v sovremennom chuvashskom yazyke. *Chuvashskiy yazyk, literatura i fol'klor,* I, 1972, pp. 261-280.

BASIN, K.K. Tvorcheskie vzaimosvyazi chuvashskoy i mariyskoy literatur. *Chuvashskiy yazyk, literatura i fol'klor,* I, 1972, pp. 281-295.

DOERFER, G. Tschuwaschisch *-m* < urtürkisch **-m* (> gemeintürkisch *-n*). *UAJ* 45(1973), pp. 174-212.

FEDOTOV, M.R. O chuvashkom karitivnom affikse -sǎr - sěr i ego reflekse v nekotorykh finno-ugorskikh yazykakh. *Sov. Tyurkologiya* 1970(3), pp. 60-66.

FEDOTOV, M.R. V.V. Radlov i N.I. Ashmarin o proiskhozhdenii chuvashskogo yazyka. *ST* 1971(5), pp. 114-120.

HOVDHAUGEN, E. The Chuvash dialect of Martinka. Phonological analysis and texts with translation and commentary. *UAJ* 45 (1973), pp. 163-173.

HOVDHAUGEN, E. The phonemic system of early 18th century Chuvash. *CAJ* 19 (1975), pp. 274-286.

HOVDHAUGEN, E. A phonological problem in Chuvash. *Norwegian J. ling.* 27(1973), pp. 53-56.

HOVDHAUGEN, E. Some remarks on the development of nasal phonemes in Chuvash. *UAJ* 42(1972), pp. 208-211.

IVANOV, A.I. Chuvashskiy yazyk v uralo-altayskoy sem'e yazykov. *Chuvashskiy yazyk, literatura i fol'klor*, I, 1972, pp. 3-53.

KORNILOV, G.E. K opredeleniyu ob'ema i kharaktera bulgaro-chuvashsko-kartvel'skikh leksicheskikh paralleley. *Chuvashskiy yazyk, literatura i fol'klor*, I, 1972, pp. 54-93.

LEVITZSKAYA, L.S. Chuvashskie etimologii. *ST* 1974(2), pp. 80-84.

LEVITSKAYA, L.S. Novyy vklad v chuvashskuyu istoricheskuyu leksikografiyu. *Tyurk. leksikologiya i leksikografiya*, 1971, pp. 301-304

LISOWSKI, J. Zusammengesetzte Verba der Bewegung im Tschuwaschischen. *Folia or.* 14(1972-73), pp. 155-159.

L'VOV, A.S. Mladopis'mennyy li chuvashskiy yazyk? *ST* 1971(5), pp. 86-90.

NAUTA, A. Rhotazismus, Zetazismus und Betonung im Türkischen. *Central Asiatic J* 16(1972), pp. 1-13.

PALLO, M.K. Die mittlere Stufe des tschuwaschischen Lautwandels $\underline{d} > \delta > \underline{r}$ *UAJ* 43(1971), pp. 79-88.

PETROV, N.P. Terminologicheskaya rabota v Chuvashii v 30-kh godakh. *Chuvashskiy yazyk, literatura i fol'klor*, I, 1972, pp. 207-260.

PETROV, N.P. 100-letie novoy chuvashskoy pis'mennosti. *Sov. Tyurkologiya* 1972 (3), pp. 103-107.

PETROVA, A.P. Foneticheskie varianty glagolov, obrazovannykh ot podrazhatel-'nykh slov v chuvashskom yazyke. *Chuvashskiy yazyk, literatura i fol'klor*, I, 1972, pp. 371-392.

POPPE, N. Zur Stellung des Tschuwaschischen. *CAJ* 17(1974), pp. 135-147.

REYCHMAN, J. Tschuwassisch *salygaj* = Nachtigall (luscinia luscinia)? *Studia Turcica, ed. L. Ligeti*, 1971, pp. 385-387

RÓNA-TAS, A. On the Chuvash guttural stops in the final position. *Studia Turcica, ed. L. Ligeti*, 1971, pp. 389-391

SERGEEV, V.I. Genezis i semantika formanta mnozhestvennosti *-sem* v chuvashskom yazyke. *Sov. Tyurkologiya* 1972 (3), pp. 29-34

SERGEEV, V.I. Leksicheskiy sposob vyrazheniya mnozhestvennosti v chuvashskom yazyke. *ST* 1973(3), pp. 3-8.

SERGEEV, L.A. O dialektologicheskom atlase chuvashskogo yazyka. *Sov.Tyurkologiya* 1970(5), pp. 105-120.

SERGEEV, L.P. Vokalizm verkhogo dialekta chuvashskogo yazyka. *Chuvashskiy yazyk, literatura i fol'klor*, I, 1972, pp. 137-206.

SKVORTZOV, M.I. O nekotorykh osobennostyakh chuvashskikh narodnykh nazvaniy rasteniy. *Tyurk.leksikologiya i leksikografiya*, 1971, pp. 264-275

SKVORTZOV, M.I. Otrazhenie starogo obshchestvenno-yuridicheskogo byta v chuvashskoy leksike. *Chuvashskiy yazyk, literatura i fol'klor*, I, 1972, pp. 392-406.

See also XL. a. Rona-Tas.

i CRIMEAN TATAR

FILONENKO, V.I. Krymchakskie etyudy. *RO* 35(1972), pp. 5-35.

HESCHE, W. und SCHEINHARDT, H. Eine krimtatarische Wörterliste. *Central Asiatic J.* 18(1974), pp. 227-250.

IVANICS, M. Formal and linguistic peculiarities of 17th century Crimean Tatar letters addressed to princes of Transylvania. *Acta Or. Hung.* 29(1975), pp. 213-224.

LEBEDEV, V.V. Karaimskiy dokument 1743 g. iz Kaira. *Pis'mennye pamyatniki Vostoka* 1971, pp. 38-49.

MEMETOV, A. Nekotorye foneticheskie izmeneniya glasnykh zvukov v persidskikh leksicheskikh zaimstvovaniyakh v krymsko-tatarskom yazyke. *ST* 1973(5), pp. 111-114.

SULIMOWICZ, J. Material leksykalny krymskokaraimskiego zabytku jezykowego (druk z 1734 r.). *RO* 36(1973), pp. 47-107.

SULIMOWICZ, J. Material leksykalny krymskokaraimskiego zabytku językowego (druk z 1734 r.) *RO* 35(1972), pp. 38-64; 36(1973), pp. 47-107.

ZAJACZKOWSKI, W. Karaimische kultische Lieder. *Folia Or.* 16(1975), pp. 131-143.

j CUMAN

KHABICHEV, M.A. Pamyatnik kumanskikh yazykov. *ST* 1974(2), pp. 66-70.

MÁNDOKY, I. Der Wandel zweier Konsonanten in der ungarländischen komanischen Sprache *Sprache, Geschichte und Kultur der altaischen Völker*, hrsg. G. Hazai und P. Zieme (XII. PIAC, 1974), pp. 391-395.

k GAGAUZI

BASKAKOV, N.A., POKROVSKAYA, L.A., TUKAN, B. P. Osnovnye printzipy sostavleniya trekh'-yazychnykh slovarey (na materiale "Gagauzko-russko-moldavskogo slovarya"). *Tyurk.leksikologiya i leksikografiya*, 1971, pp. 172-186

GAYDARZHI, G.A. Slozhnye predlozheniya s pridatochnymi otnositel'nogo podchineniya v gagauzskom yazyke. *ST* 1971(4), pp. 50-56.

GAYDARZHI, G.A. Sposoby podchineniya i tipy pridatochnykh predlozheniy v gagauzskom yazyke. *ST* 1971(3), pp. 43-59.

GUBOGLO, M.N. Gagauzskaya antroponimiya kak etnogeneticheskiy istochnik. *ST* 1973(2), pp. 84-92.

GUBOGLO, M. Gagauzskaya terminologiya po skotovodstvu. *Tyurk. leksikologiya i leksikografiya,* 1971, pp. 217-236

POKROVSKAYA, L.A. Gagauzsko-turetzkie foneticheskie paralleli. *Struktura i istoriya tyurkskikh yazykov,* 1971, pp. 62-71.

POKROVSKAYA, L.A. O sostoyanii izucheniya i razvitii gagauzskogo yazyka. *Sov. Tyurkologiya* 1970(2), pp. 27-32.

POKROVSKAYA, L.A. Ob odnom "balkanizme" v gagauzskom yazyko i v balkano-turetzkikh dialektakh. *Vopr. yaz.* 1972(3), pp. 67-75.

SYCHEVA, V.A. Arabskie i persidskie zaimstvovaniya v leksicheskom sostave gagauzskogo yazyka. *ST* 1973(4), pp. 24-30.

TUKAN, B.P., UDLER, R. Ya. Moldavsko-gagauzskie yazykovye vzaimootnosheniya. (Interrelations of Moldavian and Gagauz languages.) *Sov. Tyurkologiya* 1972(6), pp. 55-67.

l KARACHAY

BRANDS, H.W. Eine kaukasustürkische Novelle als Zeitdokument. *WI* 13 (1971), pp. 99-102.

FILONENKO, V.I. Balkarskiy yazyk i ego dialekty. *RO* 37(1974), pp. 29-45.

GRANNES, A. *Zajčiki-majčiki; turki-murki* - an example of linguistic interference between the Turkic language Karachai (Northern Caucasus) and Russian, in the spoken Russian of a Karachi woman. *Orbis* 22(1973), pp. 526-534.

GUZEEV, Zh. M. O pravopisanii uzkikh glasnykh *(u,i,y)* v karachaevo- balkarskom yazyke. *ST* 1975(2), pp. 87-90.

GUZEEV, Zh.M. O sostave fonem sovremennogo karachaevo-balkarskogo yazyka. *ST* 1973(4), pp. 59-63.

See also XL. t. Arslanov.

m KARAKALPAK

BASKAKOV, N.A. S.E. Malov i izuchenie karakalpakskogo yazyka. *ST* 1975(5), pp. 53-59.

BERDIMURATOV, E. O terminologii karakalpakskogo yazyka. *Tyurk. leksikologiya i leksikografiya,* 1971, pp. 208-217

BEGZHANOV, T., ABDIMURATOV, K. Struktura karakalpakskikh toponimov. (Structure of Karakalpak toponyms). *Sov. Tyurkologiya* 1971(6), pp. 85-88.

DAULETOV, A. Fonematicheskaya priroda nekotorykh foneticheskikh diftongov v sovremennom karakalpakskom literaturnom yazyke. *ST* 1973(4), pp. 93-98.

DAULETOV, A. Kachestvennaya kharakteristika karakalpakskikh glasnykh pod udareniem. *ST* 1971(3), pp. 60-67.

DOSPANOV, U. O leksicheskikh dubletakh v yuzhnom dialekte karakalpakskogo yazyka. *Tyurk. leksikologiya i leksikografiya,* 1971, pp. 290-292

DOSPANOV, U. Tzennyy vklad v karakalpakskoe yazykoznanie. *ST* 1975(5), pp. 74-77.

NASYROV, D.S. Razvitie karakalpakskogo yazykosnaniya za gody sovetskoy vlasti. *ST* 1973(3), pp. 104-112.

NASYROV, D.S. Sostoyanie i zadachi izucheniya dialektov karakalpakskogo yazyka. (State and problems of study of Karakalpak language dialects.) *Sov. Tyurkologiya* 1972(4), pp. 94-101.

n KAZAKH

AKHMETOV, Z.A. K voprosu izucheniya teorii tyurkskogo stikha (na materiale kazakhskoy poezii). (Towards the theory of Turkic verse.) *Sov. Tyurkologiya* 1972(2), pp. 80-87.

AMIROV, R.S. O kazakhskoy razgovornoy rechi. (On Kazakh colloquial speech.) *Sov. Tyurkologiya* 1972(5), pp. 102-107.

AMIROV, R.S. Sposoby aktual'nogo chleneniya v kazakhskom yazyke. *ST* 1970(6), pp. 34-38.

ATENOV, Sh. Intonatziya prilozheniya v sovremennom kazakhskom yazyke. (Intonation of the apposition in the modern Kazakh language.) *Sov. Tyurkologiya* 1972(4), pp. 102-111.

DEMESINOVA, N. Kh. Izuchenie bessoyuznogo slozhnopodchinennogo predlozheniya v kazakhskom yazyke. *Sov. Tyurkologiya* 1972 (3), pp. 93-96.

EMEL'CHENKO, I.R. A.I. Levshin kak issledovatel' kazakhskogo yazyka. *ST* 1975 (4), pp. 56-65.

ESENOV, Kh.M. Osnovnye sredstva svyazi komponentov slozhnopodchinennykh predlozheniy. (The main means of complex sentence components' bond.) *Sov. Tyurkologiya* 1972(4), pp. 17-22.

ESENOV, Kh. M. Prichastnyy oborot v kazakhskom yazyke (v sravnenii s tem zhe oborotom v nekotorykh drugikh tyurkskikh yazykakh). *ST* 1975(1), pp. 26-32.

GRIGOR'EV, A.P. K tolkovaniyu etnotoponimov "Saraykamysh" i "Butkaly". *ST* 1974(1), pp. 28-30.

ISENGEL'DINA, A.A. Otnositel'naya chastotnost' fonem i artikulyatzionnaya baza kazakhskom yazyka. *ST* 1973(1), pp. 97-104.

KASKABASOV, S. Geroi kazakhskoy volshebnoy skazki. *Sov.Tyurkologiya* 1970(3), pp. 109-118

KENESBAEW, S., SARYBAEW, Sch. Kasachisch-mongolische lexikalische Vergleiche in der Verwandtschaftsterminologie und in den Namen der Körperteile. *Researches in Altaic languages*, ed. L. Ligeti, 1975, pp. 83-90.

KENESBAEV, S.K., KAYDAROV, A.T. Kazakhskoe yazykoznanie za 50 let. (the Kazakh linguistics during 50 years.) *Vop. yaz.* 1973(1), pp. 99-108.

KENESBAEV, S.K. Ob ispol'zovanii sobstvennykh imen v kazakhskom yazyke v naritzatel'nom znachenii. *ST* 1973(1), pp. 87-91.

KOSHKAROV, A.B. Spektral'nyy analiz frikativnykh soglasnykh kazakhskogo yazyka v strukturakh tipa SGS, GSG. *ST* 1974 (1), pp. 63-73.

KUMISBAEV, U. Ob odnom kazakhskom perevode-perelozhenii skazaniya o Rustame i Sukhrabe. *Voprosy vostochnogo literaturovedeniya i tekstologii*, 1975, pp. 110-119.

LAUDE-CIRTAUTAS, I. Blessings and curses in Kazakh and in Kirghiz. *CAJ* 18(1974), pp. 9-22.

LAUDE-CIRTAUTAS, I. On some lexical and morphological particularities of literary Kazakh, Kirghiz, and Uzbek. *CAJ* 19 (1975), pp. 287-306.

LAUDE-CIRTAUTAS, I. The past tense in Kazakh and Uzbek as a means of emphasising present and future actions. *CAJ* 18(1974), pp. 149-158.

ORALBAEVA, N. Kategoriya kharaktera protekaniya deystviya v sovremennom kazakhskom yazyke. *ST* 1971(5), pp. 95-100.

PANKRAC, G. Ja., ŽARMAKIN, O.K. Funktionen der Wortfolge im Aufforderungssatz (am Beispiel der gegenwärtigen kazachischen Sprache). *UAJ* 43(1971), pp. 116-121.

RABINOVICH, A.I. K voprosu o fonologicheskom statuse kazakhskikh soglasnykh /k, k, g, g, kh/. *Sov. Tyurkologiya* 1972(3), pp. 67-69.

RABINOVICH, A.I. Sochetaemost' soglasnykh v kazakhskom yazyke. *Sov.Tyurkologiya* 1970(5), pp. 77-84.

SARYBAEV, Sh. Dialektologicheskiy atlas kazakhskogo yazyka. *Sov. Tyurkologiya* 1972 (3), pp. 85-92.

SMIRNOVA, N.S. Kazakhskie poslovitzy, zapisannye i opublikovannye P.M. Melioranskim. *Tyurkologicheskiy sbornik* 1972 *(Pamyati P.M. Melioranskogo)*, pp. 231-234.

SULEYMENOVA, B.A. O sostoyanii issledovaniya yazyka drevnetyurkskikh i srednevekovykh pis'mennykh pamyatnikov v Kazakhstane. *ST* 1970(6), pp. 96-101.

TATUBAEV, S.S. Ob udarenii v dvuslozhnykh slovakh kazakhskogo yazyka. *ST* 1973(3), pp. 81-87.

ZUBOV, A.A. Materialy po odontologii kazakhov. (The dentition of the Kazakhs). *Sov. etn.* 1972(4), pp. 51-63.

See also XL. a. Amirov

See also XL. a. Kenesbaev.

See also XL. w. Nasilov

See also XL. cc. Smirnova.

o KHAKASS

ANZHIGANOVA, O.P. Slovosochetaniya s numerativnymi slovami v khakasskom yazyke. *ST* 1973(4), pp. 87-92.

BORGOYAKOV, M.I. O perekhode *s* v *č* v kachinskom dialekte khakasskogo yazyka. *ST* 1973(3), pp. 79-80.

OGLOBLIN, I.A. Artikulyatzionnye i akusticheskie kharakteristiki khakassikh kratkikh glasnykh [i] i [ı]. *ST* 1970(6), pp. 39-47.

UNGVITZKAYA, M.A. Khakasskie geroicheskie skazaniya - "semeynye khroniki" i pamyatniki eniseyskoy pis'mennosti. *ST* 1973(2), pp. 71-83.

p KIPCHAK

ABDULLIN, I.A. "Pamyatnaya zapiska" Agopa na armyano-kypchakskom yazyke. *ST* 1971(3), pp. 118-129.

ABRAHAMOWICZ, Z. Drei Veröffentlichungen der armenisch-kiptschakischen Denkmäler aus Kamieniec Podolski. *Asian and African studies* [Bratislava] 8(1972), pp. 165-177.

BODROGLIGETI, A. A Grammar of Mameluke-Kipchak. *Studia Turcica, ed. L. Ligeti,* 1971, pp. 89-102

CLAUSON, Sir G. Armeno-Qïpčaq. *RO* 34 ii(1971), pp. 7-13.

DASHKEVICH, Ya.R. -- TRYYARSKI, E. Armyano-kypchakskie dolgovye obyazatel'stva iz Edirne (1609 g.) i L'vova (1615 g.). *RO* 37(1974), pp. 47-59.

DASHKEVICH, Ya.R., TRYJARSKI, E. Armyano-kypchakskoe zaveshchanie iz L'vova 1617 g. i sovremennyy emu pol'skiy perevod. *RO* 36(1974), pp. 119-131.

DASHKEVICH, Ya., TRYYARSKI, E. Drevneyshiy armyano-kypchakskiy dokument iz l'vovskikh kollektziy (1583 g.) i izuchenie bilingv predbrachnykh dogovorov l'vovskikh armyan. *Jhb.Mus.Völkerk.Leipzig* 30(1975), pp. 33-46.

DOBOS, E. A Qïpčaq-Uzbeg tale from Qarabau. *Acta Or. Acad. Sci. Hung.* 27(1973), pp. 163-189.

FAYZULLAEVA, Sh.A. Ob arabsko-kypchakskom slovare Dzhamal ad-Dina Abu-Mukhammada Abd Allakha at-Turki. *ST* 1973(1), pp. 109-111.

GARIPOV, T.M. Makhmud Kashgari i kypchakskie yazyki Uralo-Povolzh'ya. *Sov. tyurkologiya* 1972(1), pp. 47-51

GARIPOV, T.M. Ponyatie obshchetyurkskogo yazykovogo sostoyaniya i voprosy istoricheskogo razvitiya kypchakskikh yazykov Uralo-Povol'zhya. *ST* 1971(2), pp. 76-80.

KECSKEMÉTI, I. Rückläufiges Verzeichnis der tatarischen Suffixe und Suffixkombinationen. *SO* 43(1974), 3, pp.19.

KURYSHZHANOV, A.K. Makhmud Kashgari o kypchakskom yazyke. *Sov.tyurkologiya* 1972(1), pp. 52-60

MENGES, K.H. Zur Etymologie des Armeno-Qypčaqischen. Slavo-Türko-Armenische Kontakte und Kontamination. *Der Islam* 48 (1971-2), pp. 298-332

MUSAEV, K.M. Nazvaniya dney nedeli v zapadnokypchakskikh tyurkskikh yazykakh. (Names of week-days in west-kypchak Turkic languages.) *Sov. Tyurkologiya* 1972(4), pp. 32-38.

MUSAEV, K.M. Terminy rodstva v sovremennykh zapadno-kypchakskikh tyurkskikh yazykakh. *Sprache, Geschichte und Kultur der altaischen Völker,* hrsg. G. Hazai und P. Zieme (XII. PIAC, 1974), pp. 451-457.

SCHÜTZ, E. Armeno-Kiptschakische Ehekontrakte und Testamente. *Acta or. Hung.* 24 (1971), pp. 265-300.

SCHÜTZ, E. Remarks on initial d- in Kipchak languages. *Acta Or. Hung.* 25(1972), pp. 369-381.

TANSEL, F.A. Cümcüme Sulṭān, Ottoman translations of the fourteenth century Kipchak Turkic story. *Archivum Ottomanicum* 2(1970), pp. 252-269.

TRYJARSKI, E. Une liste arméno-kiptchak des signes du zodiaque. *XI. Türk Dil Kurultayında okunan bilimsel bildiriler* 1966, pp. 139-152.

See also IV. c. 10. Bodroligeti.

q KIRGHIZ

BAZHINA, I. K voprosu o kirgizskikh zaimstvovaniyakh v russkom yazyke. (Towards the problem of Kirghiz borrowings in Russian.) *Sov. Tyurkologiya* 1972(5), pp. 32-45.

CONSTANTIN, Gh. I. The first mention of the Yenesei Old-Kirghiz inscriptions: the diary of the Rumanian traveller to China - Nicolaie Milescu (Spathary) - 1675. *Turcica* 2(1970), pp. 151-158.

HATTO, A.T. The Kirgiz original of *Kukotay* found. *BSOAS* 34 (1971), pp. 379-386.

HATTO, A.T. Köz-Kaman. *Central Asiatic J.* 15 (1971), pp. 81-101.

HATTO, A.T. Semetey. [Son of Manas in the Kirgiz epic.] *Asia Major* 18(1973), pp. 154-180.

KASACK, W. Tschingis Aitmatow. *Ost-Europa* 24(1974), pp. 254-256.

MEHNEN, Kl. Aitmatows "Weisser Dampfer". *Ost-Europa* 24(1974), pp. 257-258.

MEIER, G.F. Zur kirgissischen, altaischen und tuvinischen nationalen Literatursprache. *Z. f. Phonetik* 28(1975), pp. 288-297.

MEL'NIKOV, G.P. Prichiny narusheniy simmetrii v sisteme kirgizskikh glasnykh. *Sov.Tyurkologiya* 1970(1), pp. 54-69.

MURATALIEV, M. Slozhnosochinennoe i slozhnopodchinennoe predlozhenie v kirgizskom yazyke. *ST* 1975(1), pp. 20-26.

ORUSBAEV, A.K. Iz materialov eksperimental'nogo issledovaniya kirgizskogo udareniya. (From the materials of experimental research of Kirgiz stress.) *Sov. Tyurkologiya* 1972(4), pp. 112-124.

ORUZBAEVA, B.O. O strukturno-morfologicheskikh osobennostyakh kornevykh morfem tipa GS v kirgizskom yazyke. *ST* 1975(5), pp. 78-81.

ORUZBAEVA. B.O. Slovar' Makhmuda Kashgari kak istochnik dlya izucheniya leksiki kirgizskogo yazyka v istoricheskom plane. *Sov.tyurkologiya* 1972(1), pp. 43-46

ORUZBAEVA, B.O. Sovremennaya kirgizskaya terminologiya. (Modern Kirghiz terminology.) *Sov. Tyurkologiya* 1972(4), pp. 72-77.

OSMONALIEVA, B. Ob otrazhenii leksiki kirgizskogo yazyka v slovare Makhmuda Kashgari "Divanu lugat-it-tyurk". *Sov. tyurkologiya* 1972(1), pp. 97-99

SAMOYLOVICH, A.N. Variant skazaniya o Edigee i Tokhtamyshe, zapisannyy N, Khakimovym. *Tyurkologicheskiy sbornik* 1972 *(Pamyati P.M. Melioranskogo),* pp. 186-211.

SUPRUNENKO, G.P. Iz drevnekyrgyskoy onomastiki. *Sov.Tyurkologiya* 1970(3), pp. 79-81

SYDYKOV, Zh.K. Eksperimental'no-foneticheskoe issledovanie bezudarnykh glasnykh kirgizskogo yazyka. (Experimental-phonetic research of unstressed vowels of the Kirghiz language.) *Sov. Tyurkologiya* 1972(5), pp. 84-90.

TRETIAKOFF, A. Recherche quantitative sur l'harmonie vocalique. Application au Kirgiz. *Turcica* 5(1975), pp. 19-31.

YULDASHEV, A.A. O "Kirgizsko-russkom Slovare" K.K. Yudakhina. *Tyurk. leksikologiya i leksikografiya,* 1971, pp. 293-301

ZHIRMUNSKIY, V.M. P.M. Melioranskiy i izuchenie eposa "Edigey". *Tyurkologicheskiy sbornik* 1972 *(Pamyati P.M. Melioranskogo),* pp. 141-185.

See also XL. n. Laude-Cirtautas.

XL TURKISH LANGUAGES

r KUMYK

ASTEMIROVA, F.B. Foneticheskoe osvoenie russkikh zaimstvovaniy v kumykskom yazyke. *ST* 1974(2), pp. 44-50.

LEVITSKAYA, L.S. K istorii kumykskoy leksiki. *ST* 1973(3), pp. 74-78.

SCHERNER, B. Arabische und neupersische Lehnwörter im Kumükischen. *Central Asiatic J.* 17(1973), pp. 243-252.

s OIROT

BASKAKOV, N.A. Protzessy interferentzii v razvitii severnykh i yuzhykh dialektov altayskogo (oyrotskogo) yazyka. *ST* 1973 (6), pp. 51-53.

KECSKEMÊTI, I. Die Frauensprache als Tabu im Oirotischen. *SO* 43(1974), 8, pp. 9.

KRUEGER, J.R. The Ch'ien-Lung inscriptions of 1755 and 1758 in Oirat-Mongolian. *Central Asiatic J.* 16(1972), pp. 59-69.

LUVSANBALDAN, Ch. Deux syllabaires oïrates. *Acta Or. Hung.* 25(1972), pp. 209-219.

LUVSANBALDAN, Ch. Le Subhāṣitaratnanidhi oïrate du Zaya Paṇḍita. *Acta Or. Acad. Sci. Hung.* 26(1972), pp. 195-225.

t TATAR

AKHMETGALEEVA, Ya. S. Neskol'ko slov o yazyke "Kisekbash Kitaby". *Sov.Tyurkologiya* 1970(4), pp. 127-130.

AKHMET'YANOV, R.G. Nekotorye nazvaniya loshadey v tatarskom yazyke. *ST* 1975 (2), pp. 69-76.

AKHUNZYANOV, G.Kh. Frazeologiya kakrazdel tatarskogo yazykoznaniya. *Voprosy tatarskogo yazykoznaniya* 1971, pp. 76-86.

AMIROV, G.S. Sinonimy v proizvedeniyakh G. Tukaya. *Tyurk.leksikologiya i leksikografiya,* 1971, pp. 47-61

AMIROV, G.S. Slovar' yazyka Tukaya. *Tyurk.leksikologiya i leksikografiya,* 1971, pp. 186-193

AMIROV, G.S. Sostsyanie i zadachi izucheniya yazyka tatarskikh pisateley. *Voprosy tatarskogo yazykoznaniya* 1971, pp. 130-141.

ARSLANOV, J. Sh. O vliyanii nogayskogo yazyka na tatarskie govory Stavropol'skogo kraya. (On the influence of the Nogay language on Tatar dialects of the Stavropol area.) *Sov. Tyurkologiya* 1972(5), pp. 25-31.

ASYLGARAEV, Sh.N., SAFIULLINA, F.S. Nekotorye itogi izucheniya foneticheskogo stroya tatarskogo yazyka. *Voprosy tatarskogo yazykoznaniya* 1971, pp. 19-31.

ASYLGARAEVA, R.A. Bibliografiya avtoreferatov kandidatskikh i doktorskikh dissertatziy, zashchishchennykh za gody sovetskoy vlasti po tatarskoy lingvistike. *Voprosy tatarskogo yazykoznaniya* 1971, pp. 180-185.

BAYRAMOVA, L.K., KHALITOVA, N.A. Izuchenie tatarskogo yazyka metodami prikladnoy lingvistiki. *Voprosy tatarskogo yazykoznaniya* 1971, pp. 164-170.

CĂLIN, C. A Tatar idiom from Dobrudja (Roumania). *RO* 37ii(1975), pp. 13-31.

CIOPINSKI, J. *Kêsik Bâš Kitābÿ,* Variante de Kazan. *Folia Or.* 12(1970), pp. 61-68; 13(1971), pp. 9-13.

DUBINSKIY, A.I. Zametki o yazyke litovskikh tatar. *Vop.Yaz.* 1972(1), pp. 82-88.

FASEEV, F.S. Novyy tip dialektologicheskogo slovarya. *ST* 1970(6), pp. 102-109.

GANIEV, F.A. Nekotorye itogi issledovaniya slovoobrazovaniya v sovremennom tatarskom yazyke i zadachi ego dal'neyshego izucheniya. *Voprosy tatarskogo yazykoznaniya* 1971, pp. 87-100.

GANIEV, F.A. Nekotorye voprosy foneticheskogo sposoba slovoobrazovaniya v tatarskom yazyke v istoricheskom osvashchenii. *ST* 1971(2), pp. 93-97.

GUSEYNZADE, A. K etimologii toponima *Kuščču.* (Towards etymology of toponym Kuščču). *Sov. Tyurkologiya* 1971(6), pp. 89-95.

HATTORI, Shirô. Phonological interpretation of Tatar high vowels. *UAJ* 47(1975), pp. 89-94.

IBRAGIMOV, S.M. Izuchenie sintaksicheskogo stroya tatarskogo yazyka. *Voprosy tatarskogo yazykoznaniya* 1971, pp. 108-119.

ISKHAKOVA, S.M. Drevnetyurkskie elementy v narodnorazgovornom yazyke zapadnosibirskikh tatar. *ST* 1973(6), pp. 36-39.

ISKHAKOVA, S. Yazykovye kontakty zapadnosibirskikh tatar s altayskimi plemenyami. *ST* 1975(5), pp. 33-38.

KHAKOV, V.Kh. Nekotorye voprosy i zadachi izucheniya istorii tatarskogo literaturnogo yazyka. *Voprosy tatarskogo yazykoznaniya* 1971, pp. 120-129.

KURBATOV, Kh.R. Metrika "aruz" v tatarskom stikhoslozhenii. *ST* 1973(6), pp. 83-90.

LISOWSKI, Jerzy. Zur Klassifizierung der Zusammensetzungen von Zeitwörtern der Bewegung im Tatarischen und im Baschkirischen. *Folia Or.* 15(1974), pp. 141-147.

MAKHMUTOV, Kh. Tatarskie paralleli kumanskikh zagadok. *ST* 1971(3), pp. 87-96

MAKHMUTOVA, L.T. Sovremennoe sostoyanie i perspektivy razvitiya tatarskogo yazykoznaniya. *ST* 1970(6), pp. 90-95.

MÁNDOKY, E. Trois contes populaires tatares du Dobroudja. *Acta Or. Hung.* 28(1974), pp. 127-137.

RÓNA-TAS, A. Towards a new edition of the Volga Bulgarian inscriptions. *Turcica* 5 (1975), pp. 14-18.

RORLICH, Azade-Ayse. *Which way will Tatar culture go?* A controversial essay by Galimdzhan Ibragimov. *Cah. monde russe soviétique* 15(1974), pp. 363-371.

SAGITOV, M.A. Razvitie tatarskoy terminologii. *Voprosy tatarskogo yazykoznaniya* 1971, pp. 67-75.

SATTAROV, G.F. Otchestva i kategoriya vezhlivosti-pochtitel'nosti v sovremennoy tatarskoy antroponimii. *ST* 1975(1), pp. 80-86.

SATTAROV, G.F. Tatarskaya onomastika za 50 let. *Voprosy tatarskogo yazykoznaniya* 1971, pp. 52-66.

SCHERNER, B. Probleme arabischer und neupersischer Lehnworter im Tatarischen. *Researches in Altaic languages,* ed. L. Ligeti, 1975, pp. 219-229.

SCHERNER, B. Probleme arabischer und neupersischer Lehnwörter im Tatarischen. *UAJ* 42(1972), pp. 200-207.

SCHERNER, B. Zur Geschichte der arabischen und neupersischen Lehnwörter im Tatarischen. *XVIII. Deutscher Orientalistentag 1972: Vorträge,* pp. 541-553.

SUBAEVA, R. Kh. O nesovpadenii ob'ema znacheniy slov v russkom i tatarskom yazykakh. *Tyurk. leksikologiya i leksikografiya,* 1971, pp. 276-281

TEPLYASHINA, T.I. Iz patronimii karinskikh tatar. (Patronymics of Karin Tatars.) *Sov. Tyurkologiya* 1972(5), pp. 53-57.

YUSUPOV, G.B. Bulgaro-tatarskaya epigrafika i toponimika kak istochnik issledovaniya etnogeneza Kazanskikh tatar. *Voprosui etnogeneza tyurkoyazuichnuikh narodov Srednego Povolzh'ya* 1971, pp. 217-231.

VALEEVA, F.S. Razvitie i zadachi metodiki tatarskogo yazyka. *Voprosy tatarskogo yazykoznaniya* 1971, pp. 171-180.

VALIULLINA, Z.M. K istorii sopostavitel'nogo izucheniya tatarskogo i russkogo yazykov. *Voprosy tatarskogo yazykoznaniya* 1971, pp. 142-149.

YULDASHEV, A.A. Dostizheniya tatarskogo yazykoznaniya v oblasti leksikografii. *Voprosy tatarskogo yazykoznaniya* 1971, pp. 44-51.

YUSUPOV, R.A. Razvitie tatarskogo perevoda. *Voprosy tatarskogo yazykoznaniya* 1971, pp. 150-163.

ZAKIEV, M.Z. O dostizheniyakh i zadachakh tatarskoy leksikologii. *Voprosy tatarskogo yazykoznaniya* 1971, pp. 32-43.

ZAKIEV, M.Z. Torzhestvo leninskoy natzional'noy politiki i razvitie tatarskogo natzional'nogo yazyka. *Voprosy tatarskogo yazykoznaniya* 1971, pp. 3-18.

ZINNATULLINA, K.Z. Uspekhi izucheniya morfologicheskogo stroya tatarskogo yazyka. *Voprosy tatarskogo yazykoznaniya* 1971, pp. 101-107.

See also XL. g. Fatykhov.

u TURCO-BOLGAR

ABILOV, Sh. "Kutadgu bilig" v bulgarotatarskoy literature. *ST* 1970(6), pp. 77-89.

BEŠEVLIEV, V. Les inscriptions protobulgares et leur portée culturelle et historique. *Byzantinoslavica* 32(1971), pp. 35-51

BEŠEVLIEV, V. Eine neue protobulgarische Gedenkschrift. *Byz. Z.* 65(1972), pp. 394-399.

GALYAUTDINOV, I.G. Padezhnye formy i ikh fonktzional'nogo-semanticheskoe soderzhanie v yazyke pamyatnika "Tarikh-name bulgar" T. Yaslygulova. *ST* 1975(4), pp. 66-71.

NEMETH, J. Das Wolga-bulgarische Wort baqšī 'gelehrter Herr' in Ungarn. *Islam Tetkikleri Enst. dergisi* 5(1973), pp. 165-170.

SIMONOV, R.A. Vizantiyskaya numeratziya v epigrafike pervogo bolgarskogo tzarstva i nachalo slavyanskoy pismennosti. (La numération byzantine dans les inscriptions du premier royaume bulgare et le début de l'écriture slave.) *Sov. arkheologiya* 1973(1), pp. 71-82.

v TURKOMAN

AZIMOV, P., ERSHOVA, E. Nekotorye formy proyavleniya turkmensko-russkogo dvuyazychiya na sovremennom etape. *ST* 1971(3), pp. 3-7.

CHARYYAROV, B. O razvitii turkmenskogo yazykoznaniya. (On development of the Turkmen linguistics.) *Sov. Tyurkologiya* 1972(6), pp. 93-100.

KHYDYROV, M.N. Voprosy postroeniya kursa istorii turkmenskogo yazyka. *Voprosy metodov izucheniya istorii tyurkskikh yazykov,* 1961, pp. 70-78.

MUKHAMEDOVA, Z.B. O nekotorykh gidronimakh zapadnoy Turkmenii. *Struktura i istoriya tyurkskikh yazykov,* 1971, pp. 179-186.

MUKHAMEDOVA, Z.B. Ob odnom iz tipov slozhnopodchinennogo bessoyuznogo predlozheniya v proizvedeniyakh turkmenskikh poetov XVIII-XIX vv. *ST* 1971(4), pp. 57-61.

MUKHAMEDOVA, Z.B. Opyt sozdaniya ocherkov po istorii turkmenskogo yazyka. *Voprosy metodov izucheniya istorii tyurkskikh yazykov,* 1961, pp. 65-69.

MURADOVA, S. O terminologii turkmenskogo kovrotkachestva. *Tyurk. leksikologiya i leksikografiya,* 1971, pp. 243-255

PENZHIEV, M. Ob irrigatzionnoy terminologii turkmenskogo yazyka. *Tyurk. leksikologiya i leksikografiya,* 1971, pp. 255-264

ZAJACZKOWSKI, W. Die türkmenischen Personennamen. *Folia Or.* 13(1971), pp. 323-342

See also I. b. 3. Nuraliev.

See also XXVIII. o. Mukhamedova.

See also XL. cc. Mukhamedova.

w TUVAN

LETYAGINA, N.I., NASILOV, D.M. Passiv v tuvinskom yazyke. *ST* 1974(1), pp. 13-24.

NASILOV, V.M. Onomastika okhotnich'ego byta tuvintzev, uygurov i kazakhov. *Sov. Tyurkologiya* 1970(3), pp. 71-78

TATARINTZEV, V.I. Russkie leksicheskie zaimstvovaniya v tuvinskom literaturnom yazyke (1930 g. - pervaya polovina 40-kh godov). *Tyurk. leksikologiya i leksikografiya,* 1971, pp. 61-81

TAUBE, E. Zum Problem der Ersatzwörter im Tuwinischen des Cengel-sum. *Sprache, Geschichte und Kultur der altaischen Völker,* hrsg. G. Hazai und P. Zieme (XII. PIAC, 1974), pp. 589-607.

VERNER, G.K. Problema proiskhozhdeniya faringalizatzii v tuvinskom i tofalarskom yazykakh. (The origin of pharyngalization in Touvinian and Tophalar languages.) *Sov. Tyurkologiya* 1972(5), pp. 17-24.

See also XL. q. Meier.

x UIGHUR

ABDURAKHMANOV, G.A. K perevodu "Kutadgu bilig" na russkiy yazyk. *Sov. Tyurkologiya* 1970(4), pp. 120-126.

AGLAMOVA, M. O znacheniyakh form uslovnogo nakloneniya v uygurskom yazyke. *Issledovaniya po uygurskomu yazyku* II, 1970, pp. 106-112.

AMANZHOLOV, A.S. K voprosu o sootvetstvii s//sh v drevetyurkskikh dialektakh. *Issledovaniya po uygurskomu yazyku* II, 1970, pp. 167-169.

ASLANOV, V.I. O leksicheskikh parallelyakh v "Kutadgu bilig" i v azerbaydzhanskom yazyke. *Sov. Tyurkologiya* 1970(4), pp. 43-47.

AYDAROV, G. Morfologicheskiy ukazatel' k uygurskomu pamyatniku Moyun-Ghuru (VIII v.) *Issledovaniya po uygurskomu yazyku* I, 1965, pp. 206-208.

BASKAKOV, N.A. Nekotorye zadachi izucheniya sovremennogo uygurskogo yazyka. *Issledovaniya po uygurskomu yazyku* II, 1970, pp. 7-16.

BASKAKOV, N.A. Rol' uyguro-karlukskogo literaturnogo yazyka karakhanidskogo gosudarstva v razvitii literaturnykh tyurkskikh yazykov srednevekov'ya. *Sov. Tyurkologiya* 1970(4), pp. 13-19.

BAYCHURA, U.Sh. Nekotorye eksperimental'nye dannye o melodike rechi i slovesnom udarenii v uygurskom yazyke. *Struktura i istoriya tyurkskikh yazykov,* 1971, pp. 42-61.

BLAGOVA, G.F. "Kutadgu bilig", "Baburname" i metodika istoriko-lingvisticheskogo sopostavleniya. *Sov. Tyurkologiya* 1970(4), pp. 32-39.

CLAUSON, Sir G. A late uy̆gur family archive. *Iran and Islam, in memory of V. Minorsky,* 1971, pp. 167-196

CLAUSON, Sir G. O nazvanii "Uygur". *Issledovaniya po uygurskomu yazyku* I, 1965, pp. 209-220.

CLAUSON, Sir G. Two Uygur administrative orders. *UAJ* 45(1973), pp. 213-222.

EMILOGLU, Abudullah T. Changes in the Uighur script during the past 50 years. *Central Asiatic J.* 17(1973), pp. 128-129.

FAZYLOV, E.I. Leksika "Kutadgu bilig" v drevnetyurkskom slovare. *Sov. Tyurkologiya* 1970(4), pp. 48-56.

GEISSLER, F. und ZIEME, P. Uigurische Pañcatantra-Fragmente. *Turcica* 2(1970), pp. 32-70.

ISMAILOV, I.A. Zametki o russkikh leksicheskikh zaimstvovaniyakh v sovremennom uygurskom yazyke. *Issledovaniya po uygurskomu yazyku* I, 1965, pp. 104-109.

JARRING, G. Uygurovedenie v Shvetzii. *Issledovaniya po uygurskomu yazyku* II, 1970, pp. 17-20.

KAKUK, S. Chants ouigours de Chine. *Acta Or. Hung.* 25(1972), pp. 415-429.

KARA, G. On a lost Mongol book and its Uigur version. *Sprache, Geschichte und Kultur der altaischen Völker,* hrsg. G. Hazai und P. Zieme (XII. PIAC, 1974), pp. 287-289.

KARIMOV, K. Nekotorye voprosy kompozitzii, metra i zhanra "Kutadgu bilig". *ST* 1973 (2), pp. 100-104.

KAYDAROV, A.T. O frazeologicheskikh variantakh v uygurskom yazyke. *Sov. Tyurkologiya* 1970(2), pp. 70-81.

XL TURKISH LANGUAGES

KAYDAROV, A.T. Sluchai vypadeniya soglasnykh v ustnoy rechi uygurov i ikh otrazhenie v pis'menno-literaturnom yazyke. *ST* 1973(6), pp. 62-66.

KAYDAROV, A.T. Uygurovedenie v Kazakhstane. *Issledovaniya po uygurskomu yazyku* II, 1970, pp. 21-30.

KAYDAROV, A. Uygurskiy literaturnyy yazyk i voprosy razrabotki nauchnykh printzipov terminotvorchestva. *Issledovaniya po uygurskomu yazyku* I, 1965, pp. 5-59.

KAYDAROV, A. Uygursko-mongol'skie yazykovye svyazi v oblasti fonetiki. *Issledovaniya po uygurskomu yazyku* II, 1970, pp. 57-67.

KELLY, J.M. Remarks on Kāšgarī's phonology. II. Orthography. *UAJ* 45(1973), pp. 144-162.

KHYDYROV, M.N. Otnoshenie turkmenskogo yazyka k yazyku "Kutadgu bilig". *Sov. Tyurkologiya* 1970(4), pp. 40-42.

KLJAŠTORNYJ, S.G. et LIVŠIC, V.A. Une inscription inédite turque et sogdienne: la stèle de Sevrey (Gobi méridional). *JA* 259 (1971), pp. 11-20

KLYASHTORNYY, S.G. Ob izuchenii drevneuygurskikh pamyatnikov v SSSR. *Issledovaniya po uygurskomu yazyku* II, 1970, pp. 54-56.

KONDRAT'EV, V.G. Ob otnoshenii yazyka drevneuygurskikh pamyatnikov k sovremennym tyurkskim yazykam. *Vestnik Leningr. Univ., ser. ist., yaz. i lit.* 1974(4), pp. 147-150.

KONONOV, A.N. Izuchenie "Divanü lüghat ittürk" Makhmuda Kashgarskogo v Sovetskom Soyuze. *ST* 1973(1), pp. 3-9.

KONONOV, A.N. Slovo o Yusufe iz Balasaguna i ego poeme "Kutadgu Bilig". *Sov. Tyurkologiya* 1970(4), pp. 3-12.

MARAZZI, U. I prestiti cinesi in uyɣur: aspetti politici di una penetrazione linguistica. *AION* 35(NS 25, 1975), pp. 81-109.

MELIEV, K.M. O reduktzii shirokikh glasnykh v uygurskom yazyke. (On reduction of broad vowels in the Uighur language.) *Sov. Tyurkologiya* 1972(6), pp. 91-92.

MUKHLISOV, Yu. Ob uygurskom perevode "Divanu lugat-it-tyurk". *Sov. tyurkologiya* 1972(1), p. 150

NADZHIP, E.N. O pamyatnike XIV veka "nakhdzh al-faradis" i ego yazyke. (Manuscript of the 14th century "Nakhj al-Faradis" and its language). *Sov. Tyurkologiya* 1971(6), pp. 56-68.

NASILOV, V.M. Yazuik snednevekovuikh tyurkskikh pamyatnikov uigurskogo pis'ma. (The language of the medieval monuments of Uigur writing.) *Vopr. yaz.* 1971(1), pp. 104-110.

RÖHRBORN, K. Kausativ und Passiv im Uigurischen. *Central Asiatic J.* 16(1972), pp. 70-77.

ROZBAKIEV, S.K. Sud'by uygurskoy literatury v Sin'tzzyane. *NAA* 1973(5), pp. 153-157.

RUSTAMOVA, A. O nekotorykh parallelyakh v "Kutadgu bilig" Yusufa Balasaguni i srednevekovoy azerbaydzhanskoy poezii. *Sov. Tyurkologiya* 1970(4), pp. 116-119.

SADVAKASOV, G. Imeetsya li v sovremennom uygurskom yazyke foneticheskiy sposob slovoobrazovaniya? (Is there a phonetic manner of word-building in modern Uygur language?) *Sov. Tyurkologiya* 1972(6), pp. 80-82.

SADVAKASOV, G. O nekotorykh svoystvakh sonornogo r v sovremennom uygurskom yazyke. *Issledovaniya po uygurskomu yazyku* II, 1970, pp. 68-77.

SADVAKASOV, G. Ob izuchenii dialektov yazyka sovetskikh uygurov. *Issledovaniya po uygurskomu yazyku* II, 1970, pp. 31-38.

SHCHERBAK, A.M. O foneticheskikh osobennostyakh yazyka "Kutadgu bilig" i drevneuygurskom konsonantizme. *Sov. Tyurkologiya* 1970(4), pp. 20-23.

SERTKAYA, Osman F. Some new documents written in the Uigur script in Anatolia. *CAJ* 18(1974), pp. 179-192.

SKVORTZOV, M.I. Vstrecha uygurovedov. *Sov. Tyurkologiya* 1970(5), p. 135.

STEBLEVA, I.V. Poetika "Kutadgu bilig". *Sov. Tyurkologiya* 1970(4), pp. 94-100.

TALIPOV, T. K voprosu ob indifferentnykh i i *ye(e)* i svyazannykh k nimi zvukovykh izmeneniyakh v sovremennom uygurskom yazyke. *Issledovaniya po uygurskomu yazyku* II, 1970, pp. 39-48.

TENISHEV, E.R. Dolany i ikh yazyk. *Issledovaniya po uygurskomu yazyku* I, 1965, pp. 94-103.

TENISHEV, E.R. "Kutadgu bilig" i "Altyn yaruk". *Sov. Tyurkologiya* 1970(4), pp. 24-31.

TENISHEV, E.R. Mesto salarskogo i saryg uygurskogo yazykov v sisteme tyurkskikh yazykov. *Issledovaniya po uygurskomu yazyku* II, 1970, pp. 49-53.

TENISHEV, E.R. Printzipy vydeleniya dialektov uygurskogo yazyka. *Vopr. yaz.* 1974(5), pp. 124-129.

TENISHEV, E.R. Zametka o uigurskikh yazuikakh. (A note on the Uigur languages.) *Vopr. yaz.* 1971(1), pp. 89-90.

TEZCAN, S., ZIEME, P. Uigurische Brieffragmente. *Studia Turcica, ed. L. Ligeti,* 1971, pp. 451-460

TROFIMOV, M.I. O rasshirenii glasnykh v sovremennom uygurskom yazyke. *ST* 1973(1), pp. 105-108.

TROFIMOV, M.I. O vliyanii dlitel'nykh soglasnykh na slogodelenie v uygurskom yazyke. *Sov. Tyurkologiya* 1970(3), pp. 33-38.

TROFIMOV, M.N. Ob oformlenii vokalizatzii rusizmov v sovremennom uygurskom yazyke. *ST* 1975(1), pp. 57-66.

TUGUSHEVA, L. Yu. Drevneuygurskaya poeziya. *Sov.Tyurkologiya* 1970(4), pp. 101-107.

TUGUSHEVA, L. Yu. Drevnie uygurskie stikhi (rukopis' iz sobraniya Leningradskogo otdeleniya Instituta vostokovedeniya AN SSSR). *Sov.Tyurkologiya* 1970(2), pp. 102-106.

TUGUSHEVA, L.Yu. Dva uygurskikh dokumenta iz Rukopisnogo sobraniya Leningradskogo otdeleniya Instituta vostokovedeniya Akademiya nauk SSSR. *ST* 1975(4), pp. 92-101.

TUGUSHEVA, L.Yu. Poeticheskie pamyatniki drevnikh uygurov. *Tyurkologicheskiy sbornik* 1972 *(Pamyati P.M. Melioranskogo)*, pp. 235-253.

TUGUŠEVA, L. Ju. Three letters of Uighur Princes from the MS. collection of the Leningrad section of the Institute of Oriental Studies. *Acta or. Hung.* 24 (1971), pp. 173-187.

TUGUSHEVA, L.Yu. Uygurskaya rukopis' iz sobraniya LO IVAN SSSR. *Pismennye pamyatniki vostoka*, 1969, pp. 315-339.

TUGUSHEVA, L.Yu. Yarlyki uygurskikh knyazey iz rukopisnogo sobraniya LO IVAN SSSR. *Tyurkolog. sbornik (Pamyati V.V. Radlova*, 1972), pp. 244-260.

TUGUSHEVA, L.Yu. Yazykovye i vneyazykovye znacheniya v deshirovke drevneuygurskoy pis'mennosti. *ST* 1975(5), pp. 27-32.

VALITOVA, A. Osnovnye printzipy publikatzii poemy Yusufa Balasagunskogo "Kutadgu Bilig". *Issledovaniya po uygurskomu yazyku* II, 1970, pp. 144-166.

YAMADA, N. Four notes on several names for weights and measures in Uighur Documents. *Studia Turcica, ed. L. Ligeti*, 1971, pp. 491-498

ZIEME, P. Ein uigurischer Text über die Wirtschaft manichäischer Klöster im uigurischen Reich. *Researches in Altaic languages*, ed. L. Ligeti, 1975, pp. 331-338.

ZIEME, P. Ein uigurisches Turfanfragment der Erzählung vom guten und vom bösen Prinzen. *Acta Or.Hung.* 28(1974), pp. 263-268.

See also XL. a. Kibirov

See also XL. c. Kondrat'ev.

See also XL. w. Nasilov

y UZBEK

ABDUGAFUROV, A. Kh. O "Risolai Khusayn Boykaro". *Sov. Tyurkologiya* 1972(5), pp. 46-52.

AKABIROV, S.F. O granitzakh i istochnikakh tolkovogo slovarya uzbekskogo yazyka. *Tyurk.leksikologiya i leksikografiya*, 1971, pp. 130-152

ASKAROVA, M.A. K kriteriyam pridatochnykh predlozheniy v sovremennom uzbekskom yazyke. *Struktura i istoriya tyurkskikh yazykov*, 1971, pp. 148-155.

BATTERSBY, H.R. Asqad Mukhtor: an Uzbek writer and his works. *Central Asiatic J.* 15 (1971), pp. 55-74.

BAZAROVA, D.Kh. O narodno-etimologicheskom osmyslenii nekotorykh zvukopodrazhatel'nykh nazvaniy ptitz v uzbekskom yazyke. *ST* 1975(5), pp. 96-100.

BENZING, J. Ein islamischer Rechtsfall in einem usbekischen historischen Roman. *WI* 15(1974), pp. 39-44.

BOROVKOV, A.K. Nazvaniya rasteniy po bukharskomu spisku "Mukaddimat al-adab". (K izucheniyu uzbekskoy botanicheskoy terminologii.) *Tyurk.Leksikologiya i leksikografiya*, 1971, pp. 96-111

BRANDS, H.W. "Askiya", ein wenig bekanntes Genre de usbekischen Volksdichtung. *UAJ* 43(1971), pp. 100-106.

CHARIEV, A. Strukturno-morfologicheskaya i leksiko-grammaticheskaya kharakteristika prityazhatel'noy konstruktzii s voditel'nym padezhom v uzbekskom yazyke. *ST* 1975(6), pp. 11-20.

DOBOS, E. An Oghuz dialect of Uzbek spoken in Urgench. *Acta Or. Hung.* 28(1974), pp. 75-97.

FAZYLOV, E. Starouzbekskiy yazyk. (Ranniy period.) *Sprache, Geschichte und Kultur der altaischen Völker*, hrsg. G. Hazai und P. Zieme, 1974, pp. 227-232.

FAZYLOV, E.I., RASULOVA, N. Yazykoznanie v Uzbekistane za poslednie gody. *ST* 1971(1), pp. 82-89.

FINKEL'SHTEYN, M.B. Strukturnye osobennosti nekotorykh uzbekskikh sintaksicheskikh konstruktziy (uzbekskie sootvestviya russkikh sochetaniy sushchestvitel'nogo s drugim sushchestvitel'nym v tvoritel'nom padezhe s predlogom S). *Sov.Tyurkologiya* 1970(3), pp. 45-52.

KHAYITMETOV, A.Kh. Ob otnoshenii Alishera Navoi k Sarbadaram. (The relations of Alisher Navoi with the Sarbadars.) *NAA* 1972(2), pp. 102-112

KUCHKARTAEV, I. Leksika "Divanu lugat-it-tyurk" Makhmuda Kashgari i sovremennyy uzbekskiy literaturnyy yazyk. *Sov.tyurkologiya* 1972(1), pp. 83-90

LAUDE-CIRTAUTAS, I. A glimpse at the Uzbeks in Afghanistan: an Uzbek radio programme in Kabul. *UAJ* 45(1973), pp. 265-267.

LAUDE-CIRTAUTAS, Ilse. Uzbek matrimonial forms of address. *Studia Turcica, ed. L. Ligeti*, 1971, pp. 281-289

XL TURKISH LANGUAGES

MATGAZIEV, A. K istorii foneticheskogo izmeneniya slov v uzbekskom yazyke. *Sov. tyurkologiya* 1972(1), pp. 106-110

NAMAZOV, K., KHODZHAEV, T. O vidakh kosvennoy rechi v sovremennom uzbekskom yazyke. *ST* 1975(1), pp. 33-40.

NASILOV, D.M., KHRAKOVSKIY, V.S. O passivnoy derivatzii v uzbekskom yazyke. (On passive derivation in the Uzbek language.) *Sov. Tyurkologiya* 1972(6), pp. 40-49.

NAUTA, A.H. Der Lautwandel von a>o und von a>ä in der özbekischen Schriftsprache. *Cent. Asiatic J.* 16(1972), pp. 104-118.

NIGMATOV, Kh. G. Sootnoshenie chastey rechi v vostochnotyurkskom yazyke XI-XII vv. *ST* 1975(1), pp. 41-56.

SADYKOVA, M.S. Grammaticheskie i stilisticheskie osobennosti aspekta otritzaniya uzbekskogo glagola. *ST* 1973(2), pp. 46-52.

SAIDOV, Yu. Formy glagola, vyrazhayushchie nereal'nost' v sovremennom uzbekskom yazyke. *ST* 1971(1), pp. 49-59.

SHUKUROV, Sh. Starouzbekskiy i sovremennyy uzbekskiy literaturnye yazyki. *Sov. tyurkologiya* 1972(1), pp. 91-96

TRETIAKOFF, A. Remarques sur l'oeuvre de Qhamza Qhakimzade Nijazi. *Mitt.Inst.Orientforschung* 17(1971-72), pp. 180-205.

TURSUNOV, U.T.; RADZHABOV, N.R. Iz istorii izucheniya omonimov v uzbekskom literaturnom yazyke. *Tyurk.leksikologiya i leksikografiya,* 1971, pp. 37-47

UMAROV, Z.A. Grammatika starouzbekskogo yazyka "Mabāni al-lugat" persidskogo tyurkologa Mirzy Mekhdikhana. *Vostokovedenie, yazykovedenie* 1973, pp. 49-56.

UMAROV, E.A. Variantes lexicales des parties constituantes de la phrase en Uzbek d'après le *Khazojin-ul-maonij* d'-Ališer Navoī. *Turcica* 5(1975), pp. 9-13.

USMANOV, S. O morfologicheskom analize slova i ego grammaticheskoy forme v sovremennom uzbekskom yazyke. *Struktura i istoriya tyurkskikh yazykov,* 1971, pp. 165-175.

See also XXXVIII. d. *Tajik.* Tretiakoff.

See also XL. a. Dzhurabaeva.

See also XL. n. Laude-Cirtautas.

See also XL. p. Dobos.

See also XL. aa. Tretiakoff

z YAKUT

ANISIMOV, V.M. Udvoenie soglasnykh v yakutskom yazyke. *ST* 1975(2), pp. 9-12.

ANTONOV, N.K. Zametki ob epose yakutov. *ST* 1974(1), pp. 25-27.

KARA, G. Le glossaire yakoute de Witsen. *Acta Or. Hung.* 25(1972), pp. 431-439.

KORKINA, E.I. Rabota O.N. Bëtlingka "O yazyke yakutov". *ST* 1971(4), pp. 124-131.

PUKHOV, I.V. Iz poetiki olonkho. *ST* 1975 (5), pp. 39-43.

RICHTER, E. Die jakutische Bibliographie. Ein kurzer Überblick über die von der A.-S.-Puschkin-Bibliothek in Jakutsk herausgegebene laufende Bibliographie. *Biblos* 23(1974), pp. 151-158.

aa OTTOMAN

ABRAHAMOWICZ, Z. The expressions "Fish-Tooth" and "Lion-Fish" in Turkish and Persian. *Folia Or.* 12(1970), pp. 25-32

ADAMOVIĆ, M. Ein italienisch-türkisches Sprachbuch aus den Jahren 1525-1530. *WZKM* 67(1975), pp. 217-247.

BASKAKOV, A.N. Nekotorye spornye voprosy sintaksisa bessoyuznykh slozhnopodchinennykh predlozeniy v turetzkom yazyke. *Sov. Tyurkologiya* 1972 (3), pp. 77-80.

BASKAKOV, A.N. Slozhnosochinennye soyuznye predlozheniya v sovremennom turetzkom yazyke. *Sov.Tyurkologiya* 1970 (3), pp. 17-32.

BASKAKOV, A.N. Sovremennaya turetzkaya yuridicheskaya terminologiya i ee leksikograficheskoe oformlenie. *Tyurk. leksikologiya i leksikografiya,* 1971, pp. 236-243

BLAŠKOVIČ, J. Das Osmanisch-Türkische im 17. Jahrhundert im Donauraum. *Sprache, Geschichte und Kultur der altaischen Völker,* hrsg. G. Hazai und P. Zieme, 1974, pp. 125-138.

BODROGLIGETI, A. On modern Turkish *üstünkörü* and *yüzükoyun. Acta or. Hung.* 26(1972), pp. 145-150.

BROCKI, Z. Z wędrówek tureckiego wyrazu *köşk. Przegl. Or.* 1(93, 1975), pp. 73-75.

BURRILL, K.R.F. Turkish language instruction. *MESA Bull.* 6ii(1972), pp. 1-26

BUSCH, R.C. Over the bounding domains--the limits of kinship and kinship terms in Turkish. *Anthropol. ling.* 16(1974), pp. 415-419.

CHOCHIEV, V.G. K tolkovaniyu termina "arnavut". (po povodu odnoy oshibki Khammera.) *Vostochnaya filologiya. Philologia Orientalis.* II(Pamyati V.S. Puturidze), 1972, pp. 217-219.

EILERS, W. Toponymische Satznamen der Türken. *WI* 15(1974), pp. 45-68.

FAZYLOV, E. O slovare "Khosrov i Shirin" Kutba. *Tyurk. leksikologiya i leksikografiya,* 1971, pp. 304-310

XL TURKISH LANGUAGES

GOLUBEVA, N.P. Kharakteristika znacheniy polisemichnogo glagola po stepeni semanticheskoy svyazannosti (na primere turetzkogo glagola *yarmak)*. *Tyurk. leksikologiya i leksikografiya*, 1971, pp. 82-95

GOLUBEVA, N.P. Sintagmaticheskie svyazi glagola kak sredstvo snyatiya polisemii (na primere perekhodnykh turetzkikh glagolov). *Issledovaniya po vostochnym yazykam*, 1973, pp. 41-48.

GOLUBEVA, N.P. Slovoobrazovatelnaya funktziya affiksa *-dan -den -tan/ -ten* v sovremennom turetzkom yazyke. *Sov. Tyurkologiya* 1972 (3), pp. 81-84.

GRUNINA, E.A. K istorii ukazatel'nykh mestoimeniy v turetzkom yazyke. *Struktura i istoriya tyurkskikh yazykov*, 1971, pp. 223-237.

GRUNINA, E.A. Ob izuchenii semanticheskoy struktury vremennykh form indikativa. *ST* 1975(4), pp. 82-91.

GUZEV, V.G. Nekotorye problemy istoricheskoy fonetiki turetzkogo yazyka. *Istorika, kul'tura, yazyki narodov Vostoka* 1970, pp. 193-196

GUZEV, V.G. O yarlyke Mekhmeda II. *Tyurkolog. sbornik (Pamyati V.V. Radlova*, 1972), pp. 227-243.

GUZEV, V.G. Strukturnye tipy slovosochetaniy i predlozheniy v sovremennom turetzkom yazyke. *ST* 1973(1), p. 138.

HANSER, O. Türkischer Satzbau. Die Nebensatzgrammatik des Türkischen, untersucht an ausgewählten Beispielen. *WZKM* 65/66(1973-74), pp. 155-218.

HAZAI, G. Linguistics and language issues in Turkey. *Advances in language planning*, ed. J.A. Fishman, 1974, pp. 127-161.

HAZAI, G. On some questions of the Turkish historical grammar. *Proc. 27th Int. Cong. Or. 1967* (1971), pp. 596-597.

HAZAI, G. Zur Frage der historischen Entwicklung der Personalendungen im Osmanisch-Türkischen. *Studia Turcica, ed. L. Ligeti*, 1971, pp. 231-234

HAZAI, G., MEYER, I. Zur historischen Morphonologie des Osmanisch-Türkischen. *Archivum Ottomanicum* 1(1969), pp. 92-104.

HŘEBÍČEK, L. A method of semantic analysis of the Turkish text, with an application to a newspaper text. *Asian and African languages in social context*, 1974, pp. 187-209.

HŘEBÍČEK, L. Several Turkish homonymous constructions and their generative description. *Arch. or.* 39 (1971), pp. 146-154.

HŘEBÍČEK, L. The Turkish language reform and contemporary texts. A contribution to the stylistic evaluation of borrowings. *Ar. Or.* 43(1975), pp. 223-231.

IVANOV, S.N. K istolkovaniyu kategorii prinadlezhnosti (na materiale turetzkogo yazyka). *ST* 1973(1), pp. 26-36.

IVANOV, S.N. O sokhranenii v stroe yazyka sledov ego prezhnikh sostoyaniy (po materialam turetzkogo yazyka). *ST* 1973(6), pp. 9-16.

KAKUK, Zs. Anthroponymes turcs mahométans. *The Middle East; studies in honour of J. Germanus*, 1974, pp. 161-173.

KAKUK, S. Die osmanisch-türkischen Elemente der ungarischen Sprache als Denkmäler der Osmanisch-türkischen Sprache. *Sprache, Geschichte und Kultur der altaischen Völker*, hrsg. G. Hazai und P. Zieme (XII. PIAC, 1974), pp. 273-277.

KAKUK, S. Quelques catégories de noms de personne turcs. *Acta Or. Hung.* 28(1974), pp. 1-35.

KEMPF, Zdz. Semantic scope of the locative (in Turkish and Indo-European perspective). *Linguistics* 100(1973), pp. 47-62.

KENESSEY, M. A Turkish grammar from the 17th century. *Acta Or. Hung.* 28(1974), pp. 119-125.

KHUSAINOV, M.M. O prirode slovoobrazovatel'nykh modeley (na materiale affiksal'nogo obrazovaniya neologizmov v turetzkom yazyke). *ST* 1975(1), pp. 10-19.

KLEINMICHEL, S. Beitrag zur Geschichte der Nomenverbindungen im Osmanisch-Türkischen (Izafet). *Sprache, Geschichte und Kultur der altaischen Völker*, hrsg. G. Hazai und P. Zieme (XII. PIAC, 1974), pp. 307-316.

KLEINMICHEL, S. Verbalnomina und Partizipien im Altosmanischen. *Central Asiatic J.* 17 (1973), pp. 164-175.

KONONOV, A.N. O nekotorykh tipakh bessoyuznogo slozhnopodchinennogo predlozheniya v turetzkom yazyke. *ST* 1971(4), pp. 3-12.

KORKUT, Dervišu. Tursko-srpskohrvatski rječnik nepoznatog autora iz XVII stoljeća. *Prilozi Or. Fil. Ist.* 16-17 (1966-7), pp. 135-182

KUZNETZOV, P.I. Chastnost' upotrebleniya funktzional'nych form turetzkogo glagola. *ST* 1974(3), pp. 87-89.

KUZNETZOV, P.I. Izdaniya i publikatzii "Turetzkogo lingvisticheskogo obshchestva" (1971 god). (Publications of "Turkish linguistic society 1971") *Sov. Tyurkologiya* pp. 101-107.

KUZNETZOV, P.I. Ob odnom sluchae "nepravil'nogo" upotrebleniya vinitel'nogo padezha v turetzkom yazyke. (A case of "wrong" usage of the accusative in the Turk language.) *Sov. Tyurkologiya* 1972 (5), pp. 96-97.

LEES, R.B. Turkish voice. *Essays in linguistics ... in honor of Henry and Renée Kahane*, 1973, pp. 504-514.

XL TURKISH LANGUAGES

LEHFELDT, W. Zur serbokroatischen Übersetzung arabisch-islamischer Termini in einem Text des 15./16. Jahrhunderts. *Z. Balkanologie* 7(1969-70), pp. 23-54.

LOTZ, J. The Turkish vowel system and phonological theory. *Researches in Altaic languages*, ed. L. Ligeti, 1975, pp. 137-145.

LYUBIMOV, K.M. Abstraktnoe naklonenie v turetzkom yazyke. *ST* 1973(3), pp. 9-22.

LYUBIMOV, K.M. Predikativnoe prilagatel'-noe var/bar v tyurkskikh yazykakh. (Na materiale turetzkogo yazyka.) *ST* 1974(4), pp. 85-88.

LYUBIMOV, K.M. Sem' znacheniy turetzkoy slovoformy *yazmiş*. (Seven meanings of Turkish wordform *yazmiş*). *Sov. Tyurkologiya* 1971(6), pp. 50-55.

LYUBIMOV, K.M. Sistema grammaticheskikh vremen v sovremennom turetzkom yazyke. *Sov.Tyurkologiya* 1970(2), pp. 44-63.

LYUBIMOV, K.M. Sistema prichastiy v sovremennom turetzkom yazyke. *Issledovaniya po vostochnoy filologii. K semidesyatiletiyu G.D.Sanzheeva*, 1974, pp. 133-148.

MATUZ, J. Die Emanzipation der türkischen Sprache in der osmanischen Staatsverwaltung. *Ethnogenese und Staatsbildung in Südosteuropa*, 1974, pp. 62-71.

MATUZ, J. Zur Sprache der Urkunden Süleymāns des Prächtigen. *Acta Or. Acad. Sci. Hung.* 26(1972), pp. 285-297.

MÉNAGE, V.L. On the Ottoman word ahriyān/ahiryān. *Archivum Ottomanicum* 1(1969), pp. 197-212.

MOLLOVA, M. Etude phonétique sur les mots transcrits dans le Dictionnaire turc-français de Samy-Bey. *Z.Balkanologie* 9 (1973), pp. 128-173.

NURMEKUND, P. Ob odnom rukopisnom turetzkom slovare. *ST* 1973(1), pp. 112-116.

SCHÜTZ, E. Jeremia Čelebis türkische Werke (Zur Phonetik des Mittelosmanischen). *Studia Turcica, ed. L. Ligeti*, 1971, pp. 401-430

SEBÜKTEKIN, I. Hikmet. Morphotactics of Turkish verb suffixation. *Boğazici Univ. J.* 2(1974), pp. 87-116.

SOKOLOV, S.A. Dvukhkomponentnye sverkhfrazovye edinstva, odnotipnye so slozhnosochinennymi predlozheniyami i slozhnopodchinennymi predlozheniyami n turetzkom yazyke. *ST* 1973(4), pp. 51-58.

SOKOLOV, S.A. Funktzional' no-semanticheskiy analiz slova *bir* i ego proizvodnykh v turetzkom yazyke. *Tyurk. leksikologiya i leksikografiya*, 1971, pp. 282-289

SOKOLOV, S.A. K voprosu o klassifikatzii slozhnykh predlozheniy v sovremennom literaturnom turetzkom yazyke. *Struktura i istoriya tyurkskikh yazykov*, 1971, pp. 156-164.

SOKOLOV, S.A. Kategoriya chisla v turetzkom literaturnom yazyke i ee vzaimosvyaz' so smezhnymi leksiko-grammaticheskimi kategoriyami. *Sov.Tyurkologiya* 1970(4), pp. 71-81.

SOKOLOV, S.A. Sintaksicheskaya parenteza v slozhnom predlozhenii. (Syntactic parenthesis in composite sentence.) *Sov. Tyurkologiya* 1972(6), pp. 30-39.

STACHOWSKI, S. Beiträge zur Geschichte der griechischen Lehnwörter im Osmanisch-türkischen. *Folia Or.* 13(1971), pp. 267-298.

STACHOWSKI, S. Studien über die neupersischen Lehnwörter im Osmanisch-türkischen. *Folia or.* 14(1972-73), pp. 77-118; 15 (1974), pp. 87-118; 16(1975), pp. 145-192.

SUCIU, E. L'origine et les valeurs du suffixe - *v* en turc de Turquie. *Rev.roum. ling.* 19(1974), pp. 156-171.

THEODORIDIS, D. Aus dem griechischen Lehngut im Osmanischen. *Turcica* 7(1975), pp. 32-49.

THEODORIDIS, D. Türkeitürkisch piliç. *Münchener Studien zur Sprachwis.* 33 (1975), pp. 85-88.

THEODORIDIS, D. Türkeitürkisch tarator. *Folia Or.* 15(1974), pp. 69-76.

THEODORIDIS, D. Türkeitürkisch torik. *Islamkundliche Abhandlungen H.J. Kissling*, 1974, pp. 172-177.

TRETIAKOFF, A. Comparaison des lois de succession des voyelles en turc et en mongol. *Researches in Altaic languages*, ed. L. Ligeti, 1975, pp. 285-297.

TRETIAKOFF, A. Recherche quantitative sur l'harmonie vocalique. Application au turc et à l'uzbec. *BSLP* 65(1970), pp. 29-43.

TRETIAKOFF, A. Transcription automatique des textes turcs écrits en caractères arabes. *BSLP* 69(1974), pp. 247-253.

TZALKAMANIDZE, A.A. Ob odnoy osobennosti obstoyatel'stva mesta v yazyke "Atebat-ul-khakayyk". *ST* 1975(6), pp. 74-76.

UNDERHILL, R. Turkish participles. *Linguistic inquiry* 3(1972), pp. 87-99.

YUSIPOVA, R.R. K leksiko-semanticheskoy kharakteristike imennykh frazeologizmov turetzkogo yazyka. *Sov. Tyurkologiya* 1972 (3), pp. 41-47.

YUSIPOVA, R.R. Struktura imennykh frazeologizmov turetzkogo yazyka. *Issledovaniya po vostochnoy filologii. K semidesyatiletiyu G.D.Sanzheeva*, 1974, pp. 351-364.

See also I. b. 3. Adamocić.

See also V. v. 3. Soucek

See also XXXVIII. b. Baevskiy.

See also XXIX. c. Tveritinova.

XL TURKISH LANGUAGES

bb OTTOMAN DIALECTS

ALPARSLAN, O. Le parler besney de Zennun Köyü IV. *JA* 259(1971), pp. 163-213

BEYTULLOV, M., GECHGEL'DIEV, Kh. Umen'-shitel'nye formy lichnykh imen v turetzkikh dialektakh Bolgarii. *ST* 1973(2), pp. 93-99.

BULUÇ, S. Über einige Konjugationsformen in den anatolischen Mundarten. *Sprache, Geschichte und Kultur der altaischen Völker*, hrsg. G. Hazai und P. Zieme, 1974, pp. 161-164.

KORKMAZ, Zeynep. Die Frage des Verhältnisses der anatolischen Mundarten zu ihrer etnischen Struktur. *Türk dili araştırmaları yıllığı. Belleten* (1971), pp. 33-46

KORKMAZ, Z. Die Frage des Verhältnisses der anatolischen Mundarten zu ihrer ethnischen Struktur. *Sprache, Geschichte und Kultur der altaischen Völker*, hrsg. G. Hazai und P. Zieme (XII. PIAC, 1974), pp. 341-353.

MEYER, I. Der mittelanatolische Dialekt von Sivas. *Sprache, Geschichte und Kultur der altaischen Völker*, hrsg. G. Hazai und P. Zieme (XII. PIAC, 1974), pp. 405-411.

MIJATEV, P. Gegenseitige Beziehungen und fremde Einflüsse auf die Sprache der Türken in Bulgarien. *Researches in Altaic languages*, ed. L. Ligeti, 1975, pp. 151-156.

MOLLOV, Riza. Quelques mots sur deux acrostiches- abecedarius turques. *Folia Or.* 12 (1970), pp. 165-169

MOLLOVA, M. Coïncidence des zones linguistiques bulgares et turques dans les Balkans. *Actes X. Cong.int.linguistes* 1967, vol. II, pp. 217-221.

NEMETH, J. Die türkische Sprache in Ungarn im siebzehnten Jahrhundert. *ST* 1971(1), pp. 90-107.

TENISHEV, E.R. Govor urumov sela Praskoveevki. *ST* 1973(1), pp. 92-96.

VEKILOV, A.P. O nekotorykh osobennostyakh sintaksicheskikh funktziy padezhey v turetzkikh dialektakh Maloy Azii. *Voprosy filol. stran Azii i Afriki* II(1973), pp. 9-15.

YÜCE, Nuri. Einige auffällige Gerundialformen im Türkischen. *Researches in Altaic languages*, ed. L. Ligeti, 1975, pp. 323-329.

YÜCE, Nuri. Einige auffällige Gerundialformen im Türkischen. *UAJ* 42(1972), pp. 194-199.

cc OTHER TURKISH LANGUAGES

ABBASOV, A.M. Nekotorye zametki ob afsharakh Afganistana. *ST* 1975(4), pp. 72-81.

AKBAEV, Sh.Kh. Sravnitel'no-istoricheskiy metod v tyurkologii i genezis balkarskogo tzokan'ya. *ST* 1971(2), pp. 98-101

BIRYUKOVICH, R.M. O pervichnykh dolgikh glasnykh v chulymsko-tyurkskom yazyke. *ST* 1975(6), pp. 55-67.

BODROGLIGETI, A. The fragments of the Cavāhiru'l-Asrār. *Cent. Asiatic. J.* 16(1972), pp. 290-303.

DOERFER, G. Bericht über eine linguistische Forschungsreise in Iran. *Türk dili araştırmaları* 1973-74, pp. 199-202.

DRIMBA, V. Sur la classification de la langue salare. *Proc.27th Int.Cong.Or. 1967* (1971), p. 597.

DUL'ZON, A.P. Dialekty i govory tyurkov Chulyma. *ST* 1973(2), pp. 16-29.

DZHIDALAEV, N.S. K voprosu o yazyke drevnikh tyurkov vostochnogo Kavkaza. *ST* 1971(5), pp. 46-60.

DZUMANAZAROV, Yu. Ob izuchenii sintaksisa oguzskikh govorov Sredney Azii. (Study of syntac of Middle Asia Oguz dialects.) *Sov. Tyurkologiya* 1972(5), pp. 98-101.

FAZYLOV, E.I. Oguzskie yazyki v trudakh vostochnykh filologov XI-XVIII vv. *ST* 1971 (4), pp. 83-97.

GEYBULLAEV, G.A. O proiskhozhdenii nazvaniya goroda "Chol" v kavkazskoy Albanii. *ST* 1975(6), pp. 38-41.

JAŠAR-NASTEVA, O. Bilinguität bei der türkischen Bevölkerung in der Gegend von Gostivar und dadurch bedingte phonologische Veränderungen in ihrem Dialekt. *Z. Balkanologie* 8(1972), pp. 57-83.

KAKUK, S. Le dialecte turc d'Ohrid en Macédoine. *Acta Or. Acad. Sci. Hung.* 26(1972), pp. 228-283.

KAKUK, S. Quelques catégories de noms de personne turcs. *Acta Or.Hung.* 28(1974), pp. 1-35.

KORKMAZ, Z. Das Oghusische im XII und XIII, Jahrhundert als Schriftsprache. *Central Asiatic J.* 17(1973), pp. 294-303.

MOLLOVA, M. Coïncidence des zones linguistiques bulgares et turques dans les Balkans. *Actes Xe Cong.int.linguistes*, 1967, II, pp. 217-221.

MOLLOVA, Mefkür. Sur la création, la poétique, le reflet des formations religieuses, le langage des šiñ chez les Tatares des Balkans. *Ar.Or.* 42(1974), pp. 120-138, 225-231.

MUKHAMEDOVA, Z.B. Oguzsko-turkmenskie etnonimy. *ST* 1971(1), pp. 27-37.

RAGIMOV, M.Sh. Znachenie nerodstvennykh yazykov na territorii Azerbaydzhana v sravnitel'no-istoricheskom izuchenii tyurkskikh yazykov oguzskoy gruppy. *ST* 1971(2), pp. 50-58.

RASSADIN, V.I. Mongol'skie zaimstvovaniya v altayskom yazyke. *ST* 1973(1), pp. 62-72.

XL TURKISH LANGUAGES

SMIRNOVA, N.S. Altayskie i kazakhskie versii eposa "Kozy-Korpesh". (Opyt sopostavitel'nogo rassmotreniya.) *Sprache, Geschichte und Kultur der altaischen Völker*, hrsg. G. Hazai und P. Zieme (XII. PIAC, 1974), pp. 537-544.

TEPLYASHINA, T.I. O besermyanskikh familiyakh. *Struktura i istoriya tyurkskikh yazykov*, 1971, pp. 187-197.

TEZCAN, S. Zum Stand der Chaladsch-Forschung. *Sprache, Geschichte und Kultur der altaischen Völker*, hrsg. G. Hazai und P. Zieme (XII. PIAC, 1974), pp. 613-619.

WEIERS, M. Grundzüge der Sprache der Moghol von Afghanistan. *XVIII. Deutscher Orientalistentag 1972: Vorträge*, pp. 567-571.

See also XL. c. Doerfer.

See also XL. f. Doerfer.

See also XL. q. Meier.

See also XL. w. Verner.

XLI TURKISH LITERATURE

a GENERAL. OTTOMAN LITERATURE

ANCIAUX, R. Le "réalisme social" dans la littérature turque contemporaine. *Correspondance d'Orient: Etudes* 19-20 (1971-2), pp. 111-175.

ANDREWS, W.G. A critical-interpretive approach to the Ottoman Turkish Ġazel. *IJMES* 4(1973), pp. 97-111.

APAYDIN, Talip. Sprzedawcy syropu winogronowego. (Les marchands du suc des raisins. Traduit du turc par Tadeusz Majda.) *Przeglad or.* 82(1972), pp. 137-141.

AYZENSHTEYN, N. Prosvetitel'skaya kontzeptziya cheloveka v turetzkoy literature (na materiale romana Namyka Kemalya *Dzhezmi*). *Problemy literatur orientalnych*, 1974, pp. 41-49.

BAŞGÖZ, İlhan. Love themes in Turkish folk poetry. *Rev.nat.lit.* 4i(1973), pp. 99-114.

BICARI, H. Fuzulinin allegorik eserleri. *Studia Turcica, ed. L. Ligeti*, 1971, pp. 61-72

BOMBACI, A. The place and date of birth of Fużūlī. *Iran and Islam, in memory of V. Minorsky*, 1971, pp. 91-105

BORATAV, P.N. Sur Nasreddin Hoca et son pays d'origine, Sivrihisar. *Sprache, Geschichte und Kultur der altaischen Völker*, hrsg. G. Hazai und P. Zieme, 1974, pp. 139-143.

BOROLINA, I. K tipologicheskoy kharakteristike srednevekovoy turetzkoy literatury. *Problemy literatur orientalnych*, 1974, pp. 49-57.

BOROLINA, I.V., NIKITINA, V.B., PAEVSKAYA, E.V. K voprosu o natzional'nykh kornyakh literatury prosveshcheniya (na materiale literatur Turtzii, Irana, Indii.) *Vestnik Moskovsk. Univ.*, XIV: *Vostokoved.* 1975(2), pp. 51-67.

BOROLINA, I.V., NIKITINA, V.B., PAEVSKAYA, E.V. Osnovnye tendentzii v razvitii literatur Vostoka novogo vremeni. (K kharakteristike epokhi Prosveshcheniya v Turtzii, Irane, Indii.) *Problemy literatur orientalnych*, 1974, pp. 17-23.

BOŠKOV, V. Zum Problem des Objekts der Liebe in der osmanischen Divan-Poesie. *XVIII. Deutscher Orientalistentag 1972: Vorträge*, pp. 124-130.

BRANDS, H.W. Zum Stand der Theaterdichtung in der Türkei (Anmerkung zu einer Monographie). *WI* 13 (1971), pp. 79-98.

BROSNAHAN, T. Orhan Veli Kanik and the beginnings of modern Turkish poetry. *Humaniora Islamica* 1(1973), pp. 219-231.

BURRILL, K. Modern Turkish literature. *Rev.nat.lit.* 4i(1973), pp. 13-26.

BURRILL, K.R.F. The *Nasreddin Hoca Stories* I, An early Ottoman manuscript at the University of Groningen. *Archivum Ottomanicum* 2(1970), pp. 7-114.

CARRETTO, G.E. Di Ümit Yaşar o di "certa" poesia. *Ann.Fac.Ling.Lett.stran.Ca' Foscari* 5(1974), pp. 165-178.

CARRETTO, G.E. Sulla poesia di Hasan Hüseyin. *OM* 54(1974), pp. 214-221.

CARRETTO, G.E. Yakup Kadri (1887-1974). *OM* 55(1975), pp. 193-195.

ČEHAJIĆ, Dž. Pjesme Fevzije Mostarca na turskom jeziku. *Prilozi za or. filol.* 18-19(1968-9), pp. 285-314.

CELNAROVÁ, X. Die thematischen und kompositionellen Merkmale der letzten Erzählungen Orhan Kemals. *Asian and African studies* [Bratislava] 11(1975), pp. 73-86.

CLARK, R.C. Is Ottoman literature Turkish literature? *Rev.nat.lit.* 4i(1973), pp. 133-142.

XLI TURKISH LITERATURE

DEMIREL, Hamide. A Ph.D. thesis on Fuzūlī. *Ankara Üniv. Dil ve tarih-coğrafya Fak. dergisi* 27iii-iv(1969), pp. 9-31.

DEMIREL, Hamide. Fuzuli as an adviser. *Doğu dilleri* 2i(1971), pp. 127-142.

DEMİREL, Hamide. Fuzūlī's Arabic dīvān. *Ankara Üniversitesi. Dil ve Tarih-Coğrafya Fakültesi Dergisi* 28i-ii(1970), pp. 75-85.

DINESCU, V. La littérature turque en Roumanie. *Studia et acta or.* 8(1971), pp. 199-207.

DIRIOZ, Haydar Ali. Tevfik Fikret. *J. Reg. Cult. Inst.* 1 iv(1968), pp. 12-15.

DUCHEMIN, A. Un grand mystique turc, Yunus Emre, 1248-1320, petit livre de conseils (1307). *Turcica* 7(1975), pp. 73-104.

DUMONT, P. Littérature et sous-developpement: les "romans paysans" en Turquie. *Annales ESC* 28(1973), pp. 745-764.

ELÇIN, Şükrü. Gündeşlioğlu, poète populaire turkmène d'Anatolie. *Turcica* 4(1972), pp. 165-167.

FISH, R. Neskolko mysley o poezii Nazyma Khikmeta. *Sprache, Geschichte und Kultur der altaischen Völker*, hrsg. G. Hazai und P. Zieme, 1974, pp. 233-240.

FLEMMING, B. Bemerkungen zur türkischen Prosa vor der Tanẓīmāt-Zeit. *Der Islam* 50(1973), pp. 157-167.

GANJEĪ, T. Pseudo-Khaṭā'ī. *Iran and Islam, in memory of V. Minorsky*, 1971, pp. 263-266

GARBUZOVA, V.S. O lirike turetzkogo poeta Yakh'ya Kemal'ya Beyatly (1885-1958). *Voprosy filol. stran Azii i Afriki* II(1973), pp. 97-105.

GAZIĆ, L. Autobiografija u stihu mostarskog pjesnika Hurremija. (The autobiography in verse of Mustafa Hurremi al-Mostari.) *POF* 20-21(1970-71), pp. 205-211.

HALMAN, Talat Sait. The ancient and Ottoman legacy. *Rev.nat.lit.* 4i(1973), pp. 27-52.

HALMAN, Talât Sait. Poetry and society: the Turkish experience. *Modern Near East: literature and society*, ed. by C.M. Kortepeter, 1971, pp. 35-72.

HÜSEYIN, H. Fiumerosso. Con una nota di G. Scarcia sull'arte poetica del turanismo impegnato. *Annali Fac. Ling. Lett. stran. di Ca' Foscari (serie orientale)* 3(1972), pp. 13-54

KALESHI, Hasan. Le rôle de Chemseddin Sami Frachery dans la formation de deux langues littéraires: turc et albanais. *Balcanica* 1(1970), pp. 197-216.

KARAHAN, Abdülkadir. The Golden Age of the classical Turkish poetry and Sultan Süleyman the Magnificent as a poet and protector of arts. *Proc. 27th Int. Cong. Or. 1967* (1971), pp. 253-254.

KOCAGÖZ, Samim. Król szoferów (z tureckiego przełożył Wojciech Hensel). (Le roi des chauffeurs, traduit du turc par Wojciech Hensel). *Przeglad or.* 1(81, 1972), pp. 35-41

KÖSEMIHAL, Nurettin Şazi. Quelques recherches sur la sociologie de la littérature en Turquie. *Sosyoloji dergisi* 21-22(1967-8), pp. 193-197.

KORKMAZ, Zeynep. Wer ist der Übersetzer des *Qābūs-nāme* und des *Marzubān-nāme*? *Studia Turcica, ed. L. Ligeti*, 1971, pp. 259-266

KURBATOV, Kh. Svobodnyy stikh. *ST* 1975 (1), pp. 67-79.

LABECKA-KOECHEROWA, M. La plus ancienne comédie turque dans les collections polonaises. *RO* 36(1974), pp. 5-119.

ŁABĘCKA-KOECHEROWA, Małgorzata. Typy stab w dawnym teatrze tureckim i włoskiej komedii dell'Arte. (Les personnages fixes dans l'ancien théâtre turc et dans la comédie dell-arte italienne.) *Przegląd or.* 1(81, 1972), pp. 17-23

MAJDA, T. Slowo o Meliku Daniszmendzie. *Przegl. or.* 3(87,1973), pp. 203-222.

MAMEDOV, Azizaga. Le plus ancien manuscrit du *Dīvān* de Shah Ismail Khatayi. *Turcica* 6(1975), pp. 11-23.

MARTYNTZEV, A.E. Priblizitel'naya rifma v gazelyakh Yunusa Emre. *ST* 1973(5), pp. 115-118.

MASHTAKOVA, E.I. Iz sobraniya satir Nef'i "Strely sud'by". *Pis'mennye pamyatniki Vostoka* 1971, pp. 50-60.

MASHTAKOVA, E.I. O turetzkikh sefaret-name. (Iz istorii literatury XVIII v.) *Problemy literatur orientalnykh*, 1974, pp. 115-121

MASHTAKOVA, E.I. Ob odnoy rukopisi stikhov Mikhri-Khatun. *Pismennye pamyatniki vostoka* 1969, pp. 208-219.

MASHTAKOVA, E.I. V.D. Smirnov - issledovatel turetzkoy literatury. *ST* 1971(4), pp. 115-123.

MATUZ, J. Der Ausdruck *gazdag pasa* "reicher Pascha" in einem angeblichen Petőfi-Gedicht. *UAJ* 47(1975), pp. 140-144.

MELIKOV, T.D. "Vtoroe novoe" i problemy modernizma v turetzkoy poezii 50-60-kh gg. *Problemy literatur orientalnykh*, 1974, pp. 123-129.

MELIKOV, T.D. "Vtoroe novoe" v turetzkoy poezii. *NAA* 1973(2), pp. 79-87

MOLLOV, R. Utopies sociales dans la littérature turque moyenâgeuse. *Sprache, Geschich und Kultur der altaischen Völker*, hrsg. G. Hazai und P. Zieme (XII. PIAC, 1974), pp. 419-425.

MUŠIĆ, O. Hadži Mustafa Bošnjak-Muhlisi. *Prilozi za or. filol.* 18-19(1968-9), pp. 89-119.

MUŠIĆ, Omer. Mostar u turskoj pjesmi iz XVII vijeka. (Mostar in Turkish poetry of XVII ct.) *Prilozi Or.Fil.Ist.* 14-15(1964-5), pp. 73-100

NADZHIP, E.N. O srednevekovykh literaturnykh traditziyakh i smeshannykh pis'mennykh tyurkskikh yazykakh. *Sov.Tyurkologiya* 1970(1), pp. 87-92.

NEKLYUDOV, S. Yu. Cherty obshchnosti i svoeobraziya v tzentral'noaziatskom epose. (Problemy istoricheskoy tipologii i zhanrovoy evolyutzii). (Common and distinctive features in Central-Asian folk epics). *NAA* 1972(3), pp. 96-105.

ÖZTELLI, Cahit. Les oeuvres de Hatâyî. *Turcica* 6(1975), pp. 7-10.

PŁASKOWICKA-RYMKIEWICZ, St. Une étude sur la stylistique turque: quelques motifs poétiques dans les oeuvres des poètes du XIIIe siècle: Sultan Veled, Ahmed Fakih et Şeyyad Hamza. *RO* 35(1973), pp. 137-154.

POPOVIC, A. La littérature ottomane des musulmans yougoslaves. Essai de bibliographie raisonée. *JA* 259(1971), pp. 309-376.

SHCHERBAK, A. Zamechaniya o tekste i yazyke Ta'ashshuq-name. *Studia Turcica, ed. L. Ligeti,* 1971, pp. 431-440

SIL'CHENKO, M.S. O tipologicheskom izuchenii tvorchestva poetov-prosvetiteley tyurkoyazychnykh narodov. *Sprache, Geschichte und Kultur der altaischen Völker,* hrsg. G. Hazai und P. Zieme (XII. PIAC, 1974), pp. 529-536.

SÖNMEZ, Emel. The novelist Halide Edib Adivar and Turkish feminism. *WI* N.S.14 (1973), pp. 81-115.

SOROKOUMOVSKAYA, G.M. Novye dannye o turetzkoy pisatel'nitze Suad Dervish. *NAA* 1974 (5), pp. 133-138.

SPIES, O. Beiträge zur türkischen Literaturgeschichte. *WI* 15(1974), pp. 183-232.

STACHOWSKI, S. Studien über die neupersischen Lehnwörter im Osmanisch-türkischen. *Folia or.* 14(1972-73), pp. 77-118; 15 (1974), pp. 87-118; 16(1975), pp. 145-192.

STEBLEVA, I.V. De quelques particularités du vers turc. *Turcica* 3(1971), pp. 117-127.

STEBLEVA, I.V. Nekotorye osobennosti tyurkskogo stikha. *Sov.Tyurkologiya* 1970(5), pp. 98-104.

STEWART-ROBINSON, J. 'Ahdī and his biography of poets. *Iran and Islam, in memory of V. Minorsky,* 1971, pp. 557-564

SVERCHEVSKAYA, A. Obzor sovetskikh issledovaniy v oblasti turetzkoy literatury (1950-1972 gg.) *Problemy literatur orientalnykh,* 1974, pp. 167-174.

TARTAKOVSKIY, P.I. Poeziya Bunina i arabskiy Vostok. (Bunin's poetry and the Arab East.) *NAA* 1971(1), pp. 106-121.

TATARLY, I. Preodolenie religioznykh vzglyadov v novoy i sovremennoy turetzkoy literature. *Problemy literatur orientalnykh,* 1974, pp. 175-182.

TATARLY, Ibragim. Sabakhattin Ali i A.S. Pushkin. (Sabattin Ali and A.S. Pushkin.) *NAA* 1971(3), pp. 86-92.

TATARLY, I. Sabakhattin Ali i F.M. Dostoevskiy. *ST* 1973(1), pp. 73-82.

TATARLY, I.T. Sabakhattin Ali i zapadnaya literatura. *Sprache, Geschichte und Kultur der altaischen Völker,* hrsg. G. Hazai und P. Zieme (XII. PIAC, 1974), pp. 573-588.

TIETZE, A. The generation rhythm in the literature of Republican Turkey. *Boğazici Univ. J.* 2(1974), pp.117-121.

UMAROV, E.A. Novonaydennyy slovar' k proizvedeniyam Navoi. *ST* 1974(1), pp. 74-78.

UNGVITZKAYA, M.A. Problema fol'klorizma v tyurkskikh literaturakh (k istorii voprosa). *Sov.Tyurkologiya* 1970(5), pp. 88-97.

UTURGAURI, S.N. O problemakh modernizma v sovremennoy turetzkoy proze (na primere tvorchestva N. Tosunera i I.L. Erbil'). *NAA* 1973(5), pp. 101-111.

UTURGAURI, S. Problemy modernizma v sovremennoy turetzkoy literature. *Problemy literatur orientalnykh,* 1974, pp. 193-198.

UTURGAURI, S.N. Vostokotzentristskie tendentzii v sovremennoy turetzkoy proze (na primere romana K. Takhira "Rodina-Mat'"). *NAA* 1975(1), pp. 122-129.

UZUNOĞLU-OCHERBAUER, A. Ein türkischer Schriftsteller zwischen gestern und heute: Abdülhak Şinasi Hisar. *WZKM* 63-64(1972), pp. 187-223.

VAJURI, G. Due racconti di Hasan Hüseyin. *OM* 54(1974), pp. 327-335.

VALITOVA, A.A. Tipologiya vostochnoy poemy. (Problemy razvitiya zhanra v protzesse vzaimosvyazey tyurkoyazychnykh literatur) *ST* 1973(4), pp. 31-42.

WALSH, J.R. The Esālibü'l-mekātib (Münşe'āt) of Meḥmed Nergisi Efendi. *Archivum Ottomanicum* 1(1969), pp. 213-302.

WALSH, J.R. Turkey: bibliographical spectrum. *Rev.nat.lit.* 4i(1973), pp. 115-132.

YAKOVLEVA, N.S. Aziz Nesin - vydayushiysya predstavitel' progressivnoy literatury sovremennoy Turtzii. (Aziz Necin - an outstanding representative of the progressive literature of contemporary Turkey). *VLU* 14 ist., yaz., lit. 1972(3), pp. 87-95.

YÜCEL, Tahsin. Serenada (La sérénade (traduit du turc par Tadeusz Majda)). *Przeglad Or.* 4(84) (1972), pp. 355-358.

XLI TURKISH LITERATURE

ZHELTYAKOV, A.D. Iz istorii turetzkoy zhurnalistki (gazeta Ali Suari "Mukhbir"). (Extracts from the history of Turkish journalism). *NAA* 1972(3), pp. 134-139.

Turecka liryka miłosna. *Przeglad Or.* 1973(1, no.85), pp. 33-36.

See also II. c. 3. Mehinagić.

See also V. b. *Turkey.* Burrill.

See also XXVIII. b. Boratav

See also XXXIX. a. Burrill.

See also XXXIX. a. Gandjei

b OTHER TURKISH LITERATURE

ADZHIEV, A.M. Kumykskiy "yyr" o dzhavate i skazanie o Deli Domrule iz "Kitabi Dedem Korkut". *ST* 1975(6), pp. 33-37.

KHAYITMETOV, A. O drevney poezii tyurkov (po materialam "Divanu lugat-it-tyurk" Makhmuda Kashgari). *Sov.tyurkologiya* 1972 (1), pp. 123-128

KOROGLY, Kh. Pesni Korkuta. *ST* 1971(2), pp. 108-118.

KOROGLY, Kh. Proza ili poeziya? ("O Knige moego Deda Korkuta".) *ST* 1974(2), pp. 51-61.

NADZHIP, E.N. O novonaydennykh arabopis'-mennykh spiskakh "Mukhabbat-name" Khorezmi. *ST* 1973(3), pp. 92-103.

NADZHIP, E.N. Ozherel'ye mudrostey. *Issledovaniya po vostochnoy filologii. K semidesyatiletiyu G.D.Sanzheeva*, 1974, pp. 159-179.

NEKLYUDOV, S. The common and the specific in the Central Asian epic. *Social sciences* [Moscow] 4(2), 1973, pp. 94-104.

OSMANOVA, Z. The aesthetic conception of man in the literatures of the Soviet East. *Social sciences* [Moscow] 4(2), 1973, pp. 78-93.

PEDERIN, I. Murad Efendi -- Franz Werner. *Südostforschungen* 32(1973), pp. 106-122.

SERIKOVA, L.N. Nekotorye tipy organizatzii rubai Alishera Navoi. *ST* 1973(6), pp. 91-101.

STEBLEVA, I.V. Izvlecheniya iz traktata Babura po stikhoslozheniyu (aruzu). *Pis'-mennye pamyatniki Vostoka* 1968, pp. 166-171.

STEBLEVA, I.V. K voprosu o razvitii tyurk-skikh poeticheskikh form v XI veke. *Sprache, Geschichte und Kultur der altaischen Völker*, hrsg. G. Hazai und P. Zieme (XII. PIAC, 1974), pp. 545-551.

STEBLEVA, I.V. O stabil'nosti nekotorykh ritmicheskikh struktur v tyurkoyazychnoy poezii. *Tyurkologicheskiy sbornik* 1972 *(Pamyati P.M. Melioranskogo)*, pp. 218-230.

STEBLEVA, I.V. Poeticheskaya struktura "Oguz-name". *Pismennye pamyatniki vostoka*, 1969, pp. 289-309.

STEBLEVA, I.V. Rifma v tyurkoyazychnoy poezii XI veka. *Sov.Tyurkologiya* 1970(1), pp. 93-99.

UMAROV, E.A. Priem *iykhom* v proizvedeniyakh Alishera Navoi. *ST* 1971(1), pp. 76-81.

ZIEME, P. Äsop in Zentralasien. *Das Altertum* 17(1971), pp. 40-42.

See also V. m. 1. Akimushkin

See also XL. cc. Smirnova.

See also XL. e. Bodroligeti.

XLII BERBER LANGUAGE AND LITERATURE

APPLEGATE, J.R. Semantic correlates of Berber syntactic patterns. *Hamito-Semitica*, ed. J. and Th. Bynon, 1975, pp. 291-296.

BROGAN, O. Inscriptions in the Libyan alphabet from Tripolitania, and some notes on the tribes of the region. *Hamito-Semitica*, ed. J. and Th. Bynon, 1975, pp. 267-289.

BROWN, K. Violence and justice in the Sus: a nineteenth century Berber (Tashelhit) poem. *Actes I. Cong. et. cult. mediterr. d'infl. arabo-berb.*, 1973, pp. 341-357.

CASTELLINO, G.R. Berber-Semitic contacts in the verbal system. *Actes I. Cong. et. cult. mediterr. d'infl. arabo-berb.*, 1973, pp. 121-127.

CHAKER, Salem. La langue berbère au Sahara. *ROMM* 11(1972), pp. 163-167.

COHEN, D. L'inaccompli en -n- du bédja et le système verbal chamito-sémitique. (Observation par P. Galand-Pernet.) *GLECS* 14 (1969-70), pp. 69-75.

DANIELS, C.M. An ancient people of the Libyan Sahara. *Hamito-Semitica*, ed. J. and Th. Bynon, 1975, pp. 249-265.

GABRINI, G. Note libiche - II. *Studi magrebini II*,1968, pp. 113-122.

GALAND, L. L'alphabet libyque de Dougga. *ROMM* 13-14(1973), pp. 361-368.

GALAND, L. Défini, indéfini, non-défini: les supports de détermination en touareg. *BSLP* 69(1974), pp. 205-224.

GALAND, L. Les études de linguistique berbère (IX). *Annuaire Afrique du Nord* 12(1973), pp. 1045-1061

GALAND, L. Latin *Stāmen*, français *étaim*, berbère *idd* 'Fil de chaîne'. *Mélanges Marcel Cohen*, 1970, pp. 245-253.

GALAND, L. Notes de vocabulaire Touareg. *Folia Or.* 12(1970), pp. 69-78

GALAND, L. Observations sur l'enchaînement du récit en berbère. *Actes I. Cong. et. cult. mediterr. d'infl. arabo-berb.*, 1973, pp. 91-97.

GALAND, L. "Représentation syntaxique" et redondance en berbère. *Mél. ling. É. Benveniste*, 1975, pp. 171-177.

GALAND, L. "Signe arbitraire et signe motivé" en berbère. *Actes 1. Cong. int. ling. sém. cham.-sém.*, 1969 (1974), pp. 90-101.

GALAND-PERNET, P. "Genou" et "force" en berbère. *Mélanges Marcel Cohen*, 1970, pp. 254-262.

GALAND-PERNET, P. Notes sur les manuscrits à poèmes chleuhs de la Bibliothèque général de Rabat. *JA* 260(1972), pp. 300-316.

GALAND-PERNET, P. Notes sur les manuscrits à poèmes chleuhs du fonds berbère de la bibliothèque nationale de Paris. *REI* 41(1973), pp. 283-296.

GALAND-PERNET, P. Poèsies berbères. *Annuaire Afrique du Nord* 12(1973), pp. 259-264.

GALAND-PERNET, P. Un "Schème-grille" de la poésie berbère: Étude du motif des métamorphoses dans les poèmes chleuhs. *Word* 25(1969), pp. 120-130.

GALAND-PERNET, P. Sidi'bdrrah'man u Ms'ud des Mtougga (Maroc), thaumaturge et poète. *ROMM* 13-14(1973), pp. 369-380.

GALAND-PERNET, P. et ZAFRANI, H. Sur la transcription en caractères hébraîques d'une version berbère de la *Haggadah* de *Pesaḥ*. *Actes 1. Cong. int. ling. sém. cham.-sém.*, 1969 (1974), pp. 113-146.

GALAND-PERNET, P. Tradition et modernisme dans les littératures berbères. *Actes I. Cong. et. cult. mediterr. d'infl. arabo-berb.*, 1973, pp. 312-325.

GALAND-PERNET, P. Trois notes de lexicographie berbère: (I) yahu, (II) uq miyṭ, (III) aẓiẓn. *GLECS* 14(1969-70), pp. 127-136

GALAND-PERNET, P. and ZAFRANI, Haïm. Une version berbère de la Haggadah de Pesah. *Comptes rendus du G.L.E.C.S.* Suppl. I. vol. 1-2 (1970), 373 pp.

GOUFFÉ, Cl. Contacts de vocabulaire entre le haoussa et le touareg. *Actes 1. Cong. int. ling. sém. cham.-sém.*, 1969 (1974), pp. 357-380.

HARRIES, J. Locatives and prepositions in some Berber dialects. *Actes I. Cong. et. cult. mediterr. d'infl. arabo-berb.*, 1973, pp. 98-110.

LACOSTE-DUJARDIN, C. À propos d'une version kabyle du cyclope. *Actes I. Cong. et. cult. mediterr. d'infl. arabo-berb.*, 1973, pp. 326-334.

LACOSTE-DUJARDIN, C. Littérature orale populaire maghrébine. Le conte en berbère: l'exemple du conte kabyle. *Annuaire Afrique du Nord* 12(1973), pp. 249-257.

LEWICKI, T. Les noms propres berbères employés chez les Nafūsa médiévaux (VIIIe-XVIe siècle). Observations d'un arabisant. *Folia or.* 14(1972-73), pp. 5-35; 15(1974), pp. 7-21.

LEWICKI, T. Quelques observations sur la production poétique des Berbères médiévaux. *Problemy literatur orientalnykh*, 1974, pp. 317-325.

MASSON, O. Libyca. *Semitica* 25(1975), pp. 75-85.

NAKANO, Aki'o. Texts of folktales in Berber. *J. Asian and African stud.* [Tokyo] 7(1974), pp. 183-224; 8(1974), pp. 161-205.

PANETTA, E. Gli studi di berberistica e di etnologia islamica in Italia. *Studi sul Vicino Oriente in Italia*, II, 1971, pp. 183-219.

PRASSE, K.G. Éléments de phonologie touarègue (instructions d'enquête). *GLECS* 14(1969-70), pp. 93-105.

PRASSE, K.G. Établissement d'un nouveau phonème vocalique en berbère oriental ou saharien (touareg etc.) ǎ voyelle centrale distinct de ə. *Actes 1. Cong. int. ling. sém. cham.-sém.*, 1969 (1974), pp. 87-89.

PRASSE, K.-G. The reconstruction of proto-Berber short vowels. *Hamito-Semitica*, ed. J. and Th. Bynon, 1975, pp. 215-231.

PROVASI, E. Testi berberi di Žâdo (Tripolitania). *AION* 33(N.S.23, 1973), pp. 501-530.

SERRA, L. Due racconti in dialetto berbero di Zuara (Tripolitania). *Studi magrebini II*,1968, pp. 123-128.

SERRA, L. Le vocabulaire berbère de la mer. *Actes I. Cong. et. cult. mediterr. d'infl. arabo-berb.*, 1973, pp. 111-120.

XLII BERBER LANGUAGE AND LITERATURE

VYCICHL, W. À propos du lexique français-touareg. *Libyca* 17(1969), pp. 377-381.

VYCICHL, W. Begadkefat im Berberischen. *Hamito-Semitica,* ed. J. and Th. Bynon, 1975, pp. 315-317.

VYCICHL, W. Berberisch *Taramt n Baba Rebbi* "Mantis religiosa". *Muséon* 84 (1971), pp. 525-527.

VYCICHL, W. Berberisch *TINĚLLI* "Faden, Schnur" und seine semitische Etymologie. *Muséon* 85(1972), pp. 275-279.

VYCICHL, W. Berberische *Nomina actoris* im Dialekt des Djebel Nefusa (Tripolitanien). *OLZ* 77(1972), pp. 533-535.

VYCICHL, W. L'origine du nom du Nil. *Aegyptus* 52(1972), pp. 8-18.

VYCICHL, W. Vier hebräische Lehnwörter im Berberischen. *AION* 32(N.S. 22, 1972), pp. 242-244.

ZAVADOVSKIJ, Ju.N. Les noms de nombre berbères à la lumière des études comparées chamito-sémitiques. *Actes 1. Cong. int. ling. sém. cham.-sém.,* 1969 (1974), pp. 102-111.

See also XXXVI. b. Pennacchietti

See also XXXVI. c. Adams.

See also XXXVII. 1. Aquilina.

XLIII EDUCATION

a GENERAL

ABBOUD, P.F. Arabic language instruction. *MESA Bull.* 5ii (1971), pp. 1-24.

ALTOMA, Salih J. Language education in Arab countries and the role of ˋ academies. *Advances in language* ˉ ˀ, ed. J.A. Fishman, 1974, pp. 2ˀ

'ALWAYE, Mohiaddin. Tʰ towards the upbrin' *al-Azhar* 47vi(1ᵒʳ

BOULLATA, Iˢ Ahmad Amˀ (1975⁾

Bʹʹ

MAKDISI, G. The Madrasa as a charitable trust and the university as a corporation in the middle ages. *Ve Congrès International d'Arabisants et d'Islamisants. Actes.,* [1970?], pp. 329-337.

MAKDISI, G. The scholastic method in medieval education: an inquiry into its origins in law and theology. *Speculum* 49(1974), pp. 640-661.

MEYER, M.S. K voprosu o provedenii proseminarskikh zanyatiy so studentami, spetzializiruyushchimisya po istorii stran Azii i Afriki (na primere proseminarov po srednevekovoy istorii Turtzii). ˀstnik *Moskovsk. Univ.,* XIV: *Vostokoved.* ˀ(2). pp. 96-99.

ˀ. Treatment of the Middle East in high school textbooks. *J.* *stud.* 4iii(1975), pp. 46-58.

ˀelques Fatwās de Muḥammad ˀ5-1935) relatives à l'éduca- ˀgnement. *Ann. Inst. Phil.* 72), pp. 339-344.

Arbeit des Deutschen ˀienstes. Stipendien- ˀierende. *Z.f.* , pp. 83-85.

ˀkawayh on *ˀeg. Cult.*

WAARDENBURG, J. Enseignement supérieur et culture arabe. *Renaissance du monde arabe. Colloque interarabe de Louvain*, 1972, pp. 533-551.

ZAHLAN, A.B. The Arab brain drain. *MESA Bull.* 6iii(1972), pp. 1-16.

The care of Islam for bringing up the youth. *Maj.al-Azhar* 45viii(1973), pp. 14-16; 45ix(1973), pp. 7-11.

See also II. a. 5. Gisr, Labban

See also IX. e. Ahmad

See also XXIII. d. Lazarus-Yafeh.

b NORTH AFRICA

ARON, H. Au Maroc: des coopérants enseignants pour quoi faire? *Tiers monde* 13(no. 51, 1972), pp. 559-573.

BERTRAND, O. *et al.* Prévisions de main d'oeuvre et planification de l'éducation. Le cas de l'Algérie. *Tiers monde* 15 (1974), pp. 511-548.

BONO, S. L'istruzione pubblica in Algeria. *Levante* 18iii(1971), pp. 15-24.

BORRMANS, M. L'enseignement originel en Algérie. *Travaux et jours* 43(1972), pp. 67-73.

BREWER, E.F. Some considerations on foreign language teaching in the Faculty of Arts, including uses of the language laboratory and the question of a period of residence abroad. *Bull.Fac.Arts Libya* 4(1972), pp. 35-46.

BURESI, M. Graphie et prononciation du français chez les élèves tunisiens. *IBLA* 37(no.133, 1974), pp. 139-162; 37(no.134, 1974), pp. 279-314.

CHENOUFI, Ali. Note sur le Collège Sadiki (1875-1975). *CT* 23(nos. 91-92, 1975), pp. 371-394.

COLONNA, F. Le système d'enseignement de l'Algérie coloniale. *Arch. eur. sociol.* 13(1972), pp. 195-220.

DAMIS, J. The free-school phenomenon: the cases of Tunisia and Algeria. *IJMES* 5 (1974), pp. 434-449.

DERO, A.C. Notes sur l'assistance culturelle et l'arabisation. *Correspondance d'Orient: Etudes* 19-20(1971-2), pp. 67-76.

FLORY, M. Kulturelle Identität und Interdependenz der Hochschulmodelle. *Z. f. Kulturaustausch* 25iv(1975), pp. 70-74.

KOMOROWSKI, Z. Le système scolaire et les orientations des transformations culturelles en Afrique occidentale et dans le Maghreb. *Africana bull.* 17(1972), pp. 29-41.

LELONG, M. Les évolutions récentes de l'enseignement islamique en Tunisie. *IBLA* 37 (no.133, 1974), pp. 179-189.

LUCAS, P. Une génération de technophiles? Les étudiants de l'Instit d'Etudes Politiques d'Alger. *Rev. alg. des sci. jur., econ. et pol.* 10(1973), pp. 451-464.

MACKEN, R.A. Louis Machuel and educational reform in Tunisia during the early years of the French Protectorate. *Rev.d'hist. maghrebine* 3(1975), pp. 45-55.

MIGNOT-LEFEBVRE, Y. Bilinguisme et système scolaire en Algérie. *Tiers monde* 15(1974), pp. 671-693.

MOATASSIME, Ahmed. Le "bilingualisme sauvage": blocage linguistique, sous-développement et coopération hypothéquée. L'exemple maghrebin. Cas du Maroc. *Tiers monde* 15(1974), pp. 619-670.

PERONCEL-HUGOZ, J.P. L'enseignement en Algérie. *Rev. fr. ét. pol. africaines* 52 (1970), pp. 21-34.

PLANCKE, M. Education in Tunisia during the Ottoman period (1574-1881). *Ve Congrès International d'Arabisants et d'Islamisants. Actes.*, [1970?], pp. 355-366.

PLANCKE, M. Islamic education in Tunisia (ca. 800-1574). *Humaniora Islamica* 1 (1973), pp. 5-14.

R, A. Les expériences des Instituts de technologie en Algérie. *Maghreb-Machrek* 58(1973), pp. 27-36.

TARIFA, C. L'enseignement du 1er et du 2e degré en Tunisie. *Population (Paris)* 26, num. spéc. (mars 1971), pp. 149-180.

TOUMI, Mohsen. La scolarisation et le tissu social en Tunisie. *Rev.fr.d'ét.pol.afr.* 10 (109, 1975), pp. 32-61.

TOUSCOZ, J. Problematik der interuniversitären Kooperation zwischen Frankreich und dem Maghreb. *Z. f. Kulturaustausch* 25iv(1975), pp. 65-69.

TURIN, Y. La culture dans "l'authenticité et l'ouverture" au Ministère de l'Enseignement originel et des Affaires religieuses. *Ann.Afr.nord* 12(1973), pp. 97-105.

TURIN, Y. L'instruction sans l'école? Les débuts du Mobacher, d'après une correspondance inédite d'Ismail Urbain. *ROMM* 15-16 (1973), pp. 367-374.

ZWOBADA, J. Les difficultés d'ordre phonétique dans l'apprentissage de la lecture et de l'écriture en milieu scolaire algérien. *al-Lisāniyyat* 2i(1972), pp. 100-152.

See also XII. e. Etienne, Leca.

See also XII. f. Kacem.

See also XXXVI. a. Skik.

c EGYPT. SUDAN. EAST AND WEST AFRICA

ALBAN, K. Die Deutsche Evangelische Oberschule in Kairo heute: Versuch einer Begründung und Zielsetzung. *Z.f.Kulturaustausch* 24ii(1974), pp. 57-61.

ALKALI, Hamidu. A note on Arabic teaching in Northern Nigeria. *Kano studies* 3(1967), pp. 10-11.

BESHIR, M.O. The foundations of extramural work in Ghana, Nigeria and the Sudan. *Sudan notes and records* 54(1973), pp. 94-103.

BOUCHE, D. L'école française et les musulmans au Sénégal de 1850 à 1920. *RHOM* 62(1974), pp. 218-235

BRAIMAH, B.A.R. Islamic education in Ghana. *Ghana bull.theology* 4v(1973), pp. 1-16.

CANNON, B.D. Social tensions and the teaching of European law in Egypt before 1900. *History of Education Q.* 15(1975), pp. 299-315.

DOI, A. Rahman I. Islamic education in Nigeria (11th century to 20th century). *IC* 46(1972), pp. 1-16

FAFUNWA, A. Babs. Islamic concept of education with particular reference to modern Nigeria. *Nigerian J. Islam* 1i (1970), pp. 15-20.

GALADANCI, Alhaji S.A. Education of women in Islam with reference to Nigeria. *Nigerian J. Islam* 1ii(1971), pp. 5-10.

GARDNER, G.H. Modernization and role redefinition pressures: a study of some social correlates of modernization among Egyptian secondary school and college youth. *Medieval and Middle Eastern studies ... A. S. Atiya* 1972, pp. 158-174.

JASIŃSKA, Jolanta Tysiąclecie Uniwersytetu al-Azhar w Kairze. (Le millénaire de l'Université al-Azhar de Caire.) *Przegląd or.* 1(81, 1972), pp. 53-59

JIMOH, S.A. A critical appraisal of Islamic education with particular reference to relevant happenings on the Nigerian scene. *Nigerian J. Islam* 2i (1971-2), pp. 31-50.

OMAR, Ibrahim., HEGAZY, Abdel Rahman. Teaching of local government in the Arab Republic of Egypt. *African affairs* 74 (1975), pp. 193-201.

SAAD, Mahasin. Notes on higher education for women in the Sudan. *SNR* 53(1972), pp. 174-181.

TAWFIQ, Muhammad Amin. A glance at the foundation history of al-Azhar. *Maj.al-Azhar* 46v(1974), pp. 9-15.

TAYIB, Abdullah el-. The teaching of Arabic in Nigeria. *Kano studies* 2(1966), pp. 11-14.

TAYIB, Griselda el-. Women's education in the Sudan. *Kano studies* 1(1965), pp. 43-46.

WEIGHTMAN, G.H. Children of the ancient regime in a changing society: study of the Egyptian students at American University in Cairo. *Asian studs.* 8 (1970), pp. 307-317.

See also XIX. j. Sharipova.

See also XIX. l. Young.

d ARABIA

DOHAISH, A.A., YOUNG, M.J.L. An unpublished educational document from the Ḥijāz (A.H. 1299). *AION* 35(NS 25, 1975), pp. 133-137.

STRIKA, V. Istruzione e ideologia islamica nell'Arabia Saudiana. *AION* 34(N.S.24, 1974), pp. 437-456.

e PALESTINE. JORDAN. SYRIA. LEBANON

ABU-HILAL, Ahmad. The adaptive function of education in the Jordanian society. *Fac. Arts J. Univ. Jordan* 3i(1972), pp. 46-56.

ALLARD, M. Arabisation. *Travaux et jours* 39 (1971), pp. 5-22.

ATIYEH, Naim N. Schools of Beirut. *Beirut, crossroads of cultures,* 1970, pp. 133-166.

AUCAGNE, J. Aspects de l'enseignement technique. *Travaux et jours* 39 (1971), pp. 39-48.

AUPÈCLE, M. L'enseignement du français au Liban. *Travaux et jours* 38(1971), pp. 7-20

BILLEH, V., SALAH, Munthir, TAKI, Ahmad. The prediction of academic achievement at the University of Jordan from the scholastic background through the stepwise multiple regression techniques. *Dirasat* 1(1974), pp. 87-117.

CHAMUSSY, R. Les enseignants en grève. *Travaux et jours* 54(1975), pp. 81-104.

CHAMUSSY, R. Des enseignants parlent. *Travaux et jours* 54(1975), pp. 11-70.

CHAMUSSY, R. Pour les analphabètes: une éducation libératrice avec une interview de Mademoiselle Nada Sikias. *Travaux et jours* 39 (1971), pp. 57-70.

DONOHUE, J.J. Ghassan Tuéni et les étudiants des écoles secondaires. *Travaux et jours* 38 (1971), pp. 65-80.

DZHALALOV, A. Bor'ba za likvidatziyu negramotnosti v Sirii. *NAA* 1974(6), pp. 113-120.

ISKANDAR, Adnan. Evaluation of civil service training programs: the experience of the Lebanese national institute of administration and development. *al-Abhath* 24(1971), pp. 133-146.

MÁLEK, Z. Contemporary Islamic education in the secondary schools of the Syrian Arab Republic. *Ar.Or.* 42(1974), pp. 1-15.

MARIÉ, J. Éducation et cinéma. *Travaux et jours* 47(1973), pp. 49-57.

MÉGARBANÉ, Chr. L'enseignement en Syrie. *Travaux et jours* 51(1974), pp. 69-84.

MESSARRA, A. Déclarations ministérielles et éducation (1943-1970). *Travaux et jours* 38 (1971), pp. 57-63.

TIBAWI, A.L. The genesis and early history of the Syrian Protestant College. *American University of Beirut Festival book*, 1967, pp. 257-294.

Culture française et réalité proche-orient: enseigner à l'École Supérieure des lettres de Beyrouth. *Travaux et jours* 39(1971), pp. 25-37

Pour une communauté éducative. *Travaux et jours* 54(1975), pp. 71-79.

See also XXIII. d. Abu Lughod.

See also XXIII. d. Dickerson.

See also XXIII. d. Hadamard.

See also XXVI. b. Geahchan.

See also XXVI. b. Nasr.

f IRAQ

ISHOW, Habîb. L'enseignement technique en Irak. *Afrique et Asie* 95-96(1971), pp. 3-26.

SAWAF, H.B.M.AL-. An approach to English conversation with Iraqi university students. *Adāb al rāfidayn* 5(1974), pp. 13-17.

SAWAF, H.B.M. al-. A blackboard composition technique for Iraqi university students. *Adab al-Rafidain* 4(1972), pp. 11-19.

SAWAF, H.B.M. al-. Teaching scientific or technical English to Iraqi university students. *Adab al-Rafidain* 4(1972), pp. 25-31.

g TURKEY

BAŞGÖZ, Ilhan. The free boarding (leyli meccani) schools. *Social change and politics in Turkey*, by K.H. Karpat, 1973, pp. 203-223.

BAŞRAN, Fatma. A psycho-social study on the students of the Faculty of Letters. *Annales Univ. Ankara* 13(1974), pp. 111-129.

OZELLI, M.T. The evolution of the formal educational system and its relation to economic growth policies in the first Turkish republic. *IJMES* 5(1974), pp. 77-92.

SAYILI, Aydin. Turkish contributions to and reform in higher education, and Hüseyin Rifki and his work in geometry. *Ann. Univ. Ankara* 12(1966 - Publ. 1972), pp. 89-98.

SPULER, B. Das türkische Unterrichtswesen zur Zeit der Tanzimat sowie unter Atatürk. *Festschrift E. Klingmüller*, 1974, pp. 465-475.

STONE, F.A. The evolution of contemporary Turkish educational thought. *History of Education Q.* 13(1973), pp. 145-161.

TEMELKURAN, Tevfik. The first teacher training college for girls in Turkey. *J. Reg.Cult.Inst.* 5i(1972), pp. 37-44

See also II. a. 2. Scott

See also XXIX. i. Chambers.

h IRAN

ENGELHART, C. Persische Studenten in Wien. *Bustan* 11iv-12i(1970-1), pp. 38-41.

KLITZ, B. and CHERLIN, N. Musical acculturation in Iran. *Iranian stud.* 4(1971), pp. 157-166.

KOMISSAROV, D.S. Iranskiy prosvetitel' Fazyl-Khan Garrusi. *NAA* 1975(6), pp. 139-144.

MIRZOBADALOV, N. K voprosu o razvitii vysshego obrazovaniya v sobremennom Irane. *Arabskie strany, Turtziya, Iran, Afganistan*, 1973, pp. 106-115.

RAHMĀNI, Mohammad, The application of a systems analysis approach to educational planning in Irān. *Tahqiqāt e eqtesādi* 8(Nos. 23-4, 1971), pp. 5-32.

RIAZ, Muhammad. Iranian monarchs as patrons of learning. *J.Pakistan Hist.Soc.* 19 (1971), pp. 147-158

SHEIKHAI, Mehdi Education under the Pahlavi dynasty. *Indo-Iranica* 23i-ii (1970), pp. 119-122.

STREET, B. The mullah, the Shahname and the madrasseh. *Asian affairs* 62(N.S.6, 1975), pp. 290-306.

VARASTEH, M. The necessity and advantages of foreign language teaching for Iran. *J.Reg.Cult.Inst.* 3(nos. 11-12, 1970), pp. 116-118.

YARMOHAMMADI, Lotfollah. Problems of Iranians learning English reported speech. *IRAL* 11 (1973), pp. 357-368.

See also II. c. 8. Vahdati.

See also V. 1. Neysari.

See also XXX. b. Bartsch.

See also XXXI. e. Salim.

XLIII EDUCATION

i INDIA. PAKISTAN

ABDIN HUSSEIN, S.Z. El-. The teaching of Indian history in our schools. *India and the Arab World, ed. by S. Maqbul Ahmed,* 1969, pp. 131-135.

ABDUL HAKIM, M. The University of Dacca. *J. Pakistan Hist. Soc.* 16(1968), pp. 46-61.

ALI, Syed Murtaza. Muslim education in Bengal, 1837-1937. *Islamic stud.* 10 (1971), pp. 181-199.

FRIEDMANN, Yohanan. The beginnings of Islamic learning in Sind - a reconsideration. *BSOAS* 37(1974), pp. 659-664.

JAIN, M.S. 'The Muhammadan Educational Conference' (1886-1906). A study of its nature and objects. *JUPHS* N.S.9(1961), pp. 111-118

KAZIMI, Asadullah. Arabic Madrassas in India. *Islam and the modern age* 2iii (1971), pp. 45-51.

KAZIMI, Asadullah. Mektab education in India. *Islam and the modern age* 2ii (1971), pp. 57-73.

KRUSE, H. The Islamic educational system and the diffusion of innovations. *India and contemporary Islam,* ed. S.T. Lokhandwalla, 1971, pp. 322-332.

MAHROOF, M.M.M. Muslim education in Ceylon 1780-1880. *IC* 46(1972), pp. 119-136.

MAHROOF, M.M.M. Muslim education in Ceylon (Sri Lanka) 1881-1901. *IC* 47(1973), pp. 301-325.

MAQBUL AHMAD, S. Madrasa system of education and Indian Muslim society. *India and contemporary Islam,* ed. S.T. Lokhandwalla, 1971, pp. 25-36.

MINAULT, G. and LELYVELD, D. The campaign for a Muslim university, 1898-1920. *Modern Asian stud.* 8(1974), pp. 145-189.

NARAIN, V.A. The Bhagalpur madarsa. *Proc. 32 Ind.hist.cong.* 1970, vol. 2, pp. 173-176.

PATHAK, S.M. Attitudes of the British and American missionaries towards the growth of English education in India in the first three quarters of the 19th century. *JIH* 48i(1970), pp. 103-115.

PRASAD, S. Muslim education in Bihar (1854-1882). *JIH* 48i(1970), pp. 135-140.

SESHAGIRO RAO, K.L. Religious studies in Indian Universities. *Islam and the modern age* 2i(1971), pp. 63-74.

SIDDIQI, Iqtidar Husain. Writings on Muslim educational movements in modern India. *Stud. in Islam* 9(1972), pp. 86-131.

SINHA, B.K. Syed Imdad Ali Khan: the eminent educationist of Bihar. *J. Bihar Res. Soc.* 56(1970), pp. 241-244.

ZIAUL HAQUE. Muslim religious education in Indo-Pakistan. *Islamic studies* 14 (1975), pp. 271-292.

j AFGHANISTAN. CENTRAL ASIA

ANSARY, Amanuddin Mir. Planning for university development in Afghānistān. *Tahqiqat e eqtesādi* 9(25-26, 1972), pp. 91-100.

BERTRAND, O. L'éducation en Afghanistan. Évolution récente et problèmes actuels. *Stud. iranica* 1(1972), pp. 335-342.

ZIGANSHINA, N.A. Pervye shagi sovetskoy knigi v Uzbekistane. *NAA* 1974(6), pp. 120-125.

l ELSEWHERE

BALIC, Ismail. The Islamic educational system in the West. *Maj.al-Azhar* 44vii(1972), pp. 13-16.

MAKDISI, G. The Madrasa in Spain; some remarks. *ROMM* 15-16(1973), pp. 153-158.

See also XXXI. j. Erdentuğ

AUTHOR INDEX

Names in brackets (not underlined) refer to the first author in a combined work.
Names in brackets (underlined) refer to obituaries and festschriften.

Sudan, joy of peace, 213
Survey of excavations in Iran, 91

Tables décennales des cahiers de Tunisie, 15
Tavola rotonda italo-araba, 152
Textes fondamentaux des organisations de résistance, 231
Turecka liryka miłosna, 394
Tyurkskoe yazykoznanie v SSSR, 371

United Nations: report of the Secretary General on the Middle East, 136

The virtues of the true servants of God, 31
Das Vorwort des Baysonghor, 357

What kind of nation Muslims must be, 31
Work in progress in British universities, 14

The year in review for 1971, 83
La XXX fiera del Mediterraneo, 152